CADOGANguides

THE GREEK ISLANDS

'It's as fine a place as any to do nothing; a dreaminess surrounds all activities, and the visitor who neglects to wind his or her watch is in danger of losing all track of time.'

About the Guide

The **full-colour introduction** gives the author's overview of the country, together with a suggested **itinerary** and a regional **'where to go' map** and **feature** to help you plan your trip.

Illuminating and entertaining **cultural chapters** on local history, art, architecture, food, wine and everyday life give you a rich flavour of the country.

Planning Your Trip starts with the basics of when to go, getting there and getting around, coupled with other useful information, including a section for disabled travellers. The **Practical A–Z** deals with all the **essential information** and contact details that you may need while you are away.

The **regional chapters** are arranged in a loose touring order, with ferry, island transport and driving information. The author's top **'Don't Miss'** ⭐ sights are highlighted at the start of each chapter and there are also **short-tour itineraries**.

A **language and pronunciation guide**, a **glossary** of cultural terms, ideas for **further reading** and a comprehensive **index** can be found at the end of the book.

Although everything we list in this guide is **personally recommended**, our author inevitably has her own favourite places to eat and stay. Whenever you see this **Author's Choice** ⭐ icon beside a listing, you will know that it is a little bit out of the ordinary.

Hotel Price Guide

Luxury	€€€€€	€150 and above
Very Expensive	€€€€	€120–150
Expensive	€€€	€80–120
Moderate	€€	€50–80
Inexpensive	€	€50 and under

Restaurant Price Guide

The majority of tavernas will charge €15–20 a head for a meal with wine. Unless otherwise stated, taverna and restaurant prices in this guide fall within this range; if a particular place is more expensive or cheaper, we state the average cost per person for a two-course meal with wine.

About the Author

Dana Facaros, whose father is from the Greek island of Ikaría, started her travel-writing career with the first edition of Cadogan's *Greek Islands* in 1977. With her husband and fellow writer Michael Pauls, she has lived all over Europe, and is currently happily installed in a farmhouse in southwest France. She recently celebrated getting Greek citizenship by breaking every plate in the house.

9th Edition Published 2007

01 INTRODUCING THE GREEK ISLANDS

Above: Dusk, Mýkonos, pp.269–75

O n a map of the world they look like tiny freckles in a corner of the Mediterranean, but up close the Greek islands are among the most engaging and potent pieces of land on the planet. Microcosms of clarity and focus, they are defined by a crystal-clear sea in a hundred shimmering shades of blue and turquoise, with none of the messiness of tides to blur their edges. Their mountains and cypresses, their church domes and colourful caiques bobbing in port stand out sharp and crisp against the bluest of skies. Their villages are abstract, Cubist works of art, so white that they reflect starlight – but here, of course, the stars blaze with the fury of the crown jewels.

Islands by nature tend to have unique personalities, and it is fascinating how even a relatively homogenous group of islands such as the Cyclades, many within sight of one other and sharing a history, culture and the typical sugar-cube architecture, can be so different. The islanders themselves tend to have strong, quirky characters yet display an easygoing, tolerant nature; they have bright eyes and are quick to laugh or cry, or shamelessly enquire into your personal life ('Just how much *do* you weigh?') or offer unsolicited lectures on politics, marriage or how to brush your teeth. 'Greece,' as the country's late president Konstantínos Karamanlís said, 'reminds me of an enormous madhouse.' But it's a casual, kick-off-your-shoes madhouse; most visitors feel at home in about ten minutes, and, before they know it, find themselves indulging in the Greek national pastime: sitting around in a café under an olive or plane tree, daydreaming.

Since the 1960s, when the first backpackers hopped on to rusty old ferries and slept on the beaches, tourism has become a major

Above: Whitewashed villa

Opposite: Terraced coastline, Ithaca, pp.470–77

source of income for the Greek islands. Along with a national facelift for the 2004 summer Olympics, new marinas, better roads, fast ferries and catamarans have been added, and hotels have been spruced up across the board. These improvements come on top of each island's own adjustment over the past few decades to the new economy. Some have become venues for art, theatre and music, while others, in a movement often led by young Greeks returning from Athens or even America and Australia to make a go of it in their grandparents' villages, have taken to organic farming, wine and cuisine and the revival of old traditions. A few out-of-the-way islands offer the simplicity of the 'Old Greece' beloved by the first tourists; others have gone swanky and boast top boutique hotels and 'fusion' restaurants. Some – especially those with the winning combination of airports and beautiful beaches – are in thrall to the tour operators who control charter flights (the reason there are almost no low-cost flights to Greece) and who pay peanuts to the owners of the accommodation they block-book; some outside operators have even built their own all-inclusive hotels and give nothing back to the islands. On the other hand, many islands and hotels now have websites where you can book directly; organizing flights, ferries and accommodation independently has never been easier.

For some people the tickets have been one-way. Níkos Kazantzákis said, 'Happy is the man who, before dying, has the good fortune to travel the Aegean seas. Nowhere else can one pass so easily from reality to dream.' But 'You have two birth-places,' wrote Lawrence Durrell. 'You have the place where you were really born and then you have a place of predilection where you really wake up to reality.' And for many the Greek islands have been that place. Reality here is just more fun – as good, in fact, as a dream.

Where to Go

The 3,000 Greek islands (of which a mere 170 or so are inhabited) are divided into seven groups: the **Argo-Saronic islands** (AS), between Piraeus and the coast of the Peloponnese; the **Cyclades** (C) in the mid-Aegean; the **Dodecanese** (D), off the southwest coast of Asia Minor; the **Ionian islands** (I) off the west coast of Greece; the **Northeastern Aegean islands** (NA), stretching from Thássos to Ikaría; the **Sporades** (S), off the coast of Thessaly and Évia; and **Crete**. If you've never been to the islands, the following thumbnail sketches offer an idea of what to expect, starting with the most popular.

Crete is the biggest and has everything for everyone: the glories of Minoan civilization, Byzantine masterpieces, the Venetian charms of Chaniá and Réthymnon, the ritzy riviera around Ag. Nikólaos and Eloúnda (which now rivals Mýkonos in designer chic) beautiful beaches, four mountain ranges, gorges for treks, traditional villages, and a strong sense of island identity.

Corfu (I) and **Rhodes** (D) come next, both endowed with unique historical towns, big beaches, great restaurants, and plenty to see, although many of their resorts are as packaged as Christmas. Glamorous, design-crazy **Mýkonos** (C) has beautiful sands and stellar nightlife (both gay and straight) and is only a short boat ride from **Délos** (C), one of Greece's great archaeological sites. Neighbouring **Páros** (C), with its golden beaches and excellent windsurfing, has become the alternative Mýkonos for a younger, sportier and less posey crowd, while **Náxos** (C), the biggest and greenest of the Cyclades, is another degree calmer and attracts a mix of families, walkers and beach-lovers. Spectacular **Santoríni** (C), with its towns hanging over the black cliffs of a volcanic caldera, is the number one spot for cruise ships and honeymooners. Green, lush **Skiáthos** (S) has some of the best beaches and nightlife in the Med. **Kos** (D) also has fine beaches and an attractive town but has package holidaymakers *en masse*; **Zákynthos** (I), too, gets too many packagers but, like the other Ionian islands of **Kefaloniá** (I), **Ithaca** (I), **Paxí** (I) and **Lefkáda** (I), it also has a number of villas and boutique hotels, to go with enchanting scenery, cypresses and olive groves.

The islands closest to Athens, **Aegina** (AS), with its superb Temple of Aphaia, and friendly **Póros** (AS), **Salamína** (AS) and **Spétses** (AS), are easy targets for daytrippers and weekend crowds.

Hýdra (AS) and **Sými** (D) are small, dry islands boasting stunning neoclassical towns on steps over their ports, built by shipowners, that are now arty and fashionable; **Chálki** (D) and **Kastellórizo** (D), halfway to Cyprus, are similar but without the swank. **Sýros** (C), once Greece's main port, is also stylish, although it has a much larger town that doesn't merely rely on tourism. Other rather trendy islands these days are: **Pátmos** (D), the island of the *Apocalypse*, with

a famous Byzantine monastery and otherworldly air, that draws its share of celebrities (and scores of cruise ships); **Skópelos** (S), next door to noisy Skiáthos but pine-wooded, pebble-coved and serene, scattered with villas; tiny **Koufoníssi** (C), one of the 'Back islands', with lovely sandy beaches behind Náxos; **Folégandros** (C), for its stunning Cycladic town sprawled over the cliffs and sea; and **Chíos** (NA), mountainous and wild and home to unique mastic villages, Byzantine mosaics and lovely Genoese mansions, many now converted into charming hotels. Greece's third-largest island, **Lésvos** (NA), like Chíos, has more than tourism on its plate, as well as authentic villages, magnificent scenery, good beaches, art and birdwatching. Migrating birds also call on **Límnos** (NA), an island with a prehistoric culture related to Troy and long , scarcely developed beaches that have begun to attract Greek urbanites yearning for space.

Lovely **Sámos** (NA), a powerhouse in archaic Greece, has vines, beaches and mountains and archaeological treasures, and is a firm favourite of the middle-class and middle-aged. At the opposite extreme, on **Íos** (C) you'll feel old at 25. Wooded **Thássos** (NA), ringed with sandy beaches, is a perennial family favourite, but its lack of an airport has spared it the worst ravages of tourism. **Kárpathos** (D) has

Above: Fríkes Bay, Ithaca, p.477

Opposite, top to bottom: Líndos, Rhodes, pp.423–5; Parliament guards, Athens, p.76; Shops, Póros Town, p.120

01

Introduction | Where to Go

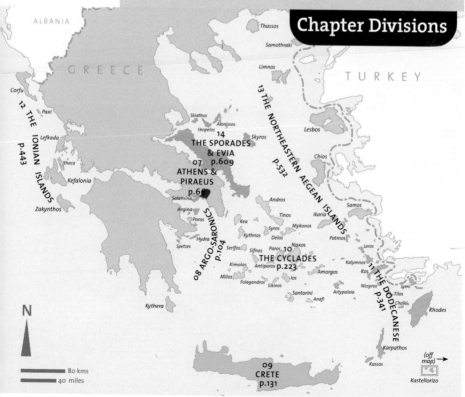

Chapter Divisions

wild, rugged scenery, beaches (with excellent windsurfing) and a vibrant folk tradition.

Évia is Greece's second-largest island and perhaps its best-kept secret, with lovely scenery and yet an elusive, hard-to-pin-down identity that keeps it under most foreign tourists' radars.

The lack of an airport (or having a dinky small-plane airport) has kept mass tourism off some very attractive islands, including all the Western Cyclades: **Kýthnos** (C), **Sérifos** (C), **Sífnos** (C) and **Mílos** (C), the latter full of colourful geological marvels. Then there's **Alónissos** (S), at the centre of a programme to save the monk seal; **Skýros** (S), with its traditional houses and the renowned Skýros Centre; **Ándros** (C) and **Kéa** (C), both beautiful and very Greek, yet close to Attica; laid-back **Ikaría** (NA); and overlooked gems such as **Astypálaia** (D), **Amorgós** (C), **Léros** (D), **Tilos** (D) and **Kýthera** (I), isolated south of the Peloponnese and near **Elafónissos** (I), a tiny island with some of the best beaches in Greece. Others on this list are **Kálymnos** (D), famous for sponge-divers, now a mecca for rock-climbers; holy **Tínos** (C), sprinkled with white dovecotes, the Lourdes of Greece; **Samothráki** (NA), a mountain in the sea once sacred to gods of the underworld, and **Níssyros** (D), where you can walk on a still-warm volcano.

If you really long to get away from English newspapers and have a genuine (and peaceful) Greek experience, and don't mind a limited choice of tavernas, head for **Síkinos** (C), **Kímolos** (C), **Kássos** (D), **Anáfi** (C), **Lipsí** (D) or the smaller islets of **Meganísi** (I), **Schinoússa** (C), **Heráklia** (C), **Foúrni** (NA), **Donoússa** (C), **Psará** (NA) **Inoússes** (NA), **Ag. Efstrátios** (NA), **Agathónissi** (D), **Arkí** (D), **Gávdos** (off Crete), **Mathráki** (I) **Othoní** (I), **Eríkousa** (I), or **Antikýthera** (I).

Above: House with bougainvillaea, Kéa

Below: Fishing boat

ΚΑΠΤΑΒΑΣΙΛΗΣ Λ.ΜΥ.3ί5

Above: Mýrtos Beach, Kefaloniá, p.491

Feeling Just Beachy

Whoever manufactures the Blue Flags for the European Union must love Greece, because it buys more than any other country – over 400 beaches qualify to plant that standard of high cleanliness in their sands, and a high percentage of those are on the islands. Decorated with cliffs, boulders, baby islets, tamarisks, olives, pines or palms, they come in all styles and sizes, from great sand dunes to manicured strands with sunbeds and cocktail bars; some are holiday playgrounds equipped with everything from pedalos to jet-skis; others get the breezes that make them the joy of wind- and kite-surfers. Then there are intimate pebbly coves under the pines, with space just enough for two where you can hear the *flísvos* – the sound of the sea kissing the shore – a word that exists only in Greek.

See p.16 for where to find some of the best beaches.

Old Stones with Stories

The Greek islands were world-class hot-shots in Archaic times, but some 2,000 years of wars, earthquakes and local builders have decimated much of what they built in their glory days; temples, ports, even entire cities survive only in the descriptions of ancient writers. Some of the monuments that have remained are stunning (*see* list, p.16). But also keep an eye out for bits and bobs woven over the centuries into the fabric of everyday life: a Hellenistic wall in a back garden, a Corinthian capital used as baptismal font, an elaborate architrave embedded in a Venetian wall, a Roman sarcophagus converted into fountain or trough, or a marble relief over the door of a house, stuck there centuries ago.

Clockwise from top: Pyramid at Exogi, Ithaca, p.476; Temple of Aphaia, Aegina, p.109; Dolphin mural, church wall

Sacred Ground

As igloos say Arctic, whitewashed churches say Greek islands, and there is certainly are no lack of them. Even dinky islands insist that they have 365 – one for every day of the year. Usually small, and usually domed or barrel-vaulted, they appear in the most startling places, at least by Catholic or Protestant standards: in the port smack by the fishing caiques, deep in caves, clinging to cliffs, and perched on nearly every mountaintop, no matter how inaccessible. *See* p.16 for a selection of the most interesting. The older ones often christianized ancient pagan places (Crete's Panagía Arkoudiótissa, 'Our Lady of the Bear', in a cave formerly dedicated to Artemis, p.159). Many others were built by individuals who vowed to build a church in return for a favour granted, often the survival of storms and shipwrecks. And, where churches in the rest of Europe are being converted into bars and restaurants, the Greeks are still building new ones, even though these, like ninety nine per cent of the rest, will only have a service one day a year.

01 Introduction | Sacred Ground

Island Rhythms

If Greeks have retained a remarkable sense of community, it's partly because the climate allows them to be outside in each other's company much of the day, much of year. Nine-tenths of the day's activities – shopping, cleaning, cooking, banking, sightseeing and so on – are concentrated in the cool of the morning. By 3pm everyone has legged it for a lazy lunch in a taverna followed by a siesta; at 5pm, villages look completely deserted.

Above, from top: Blue-topped dome, Íos, p.245; Kafeneíon culture, Crete, pp.131–222

The Day, Part II begins a couple of hours later, but at a more mellow pace: shops re-open, children play, ice cream is licked, backgammon boards and worry beads click. At 10pm on a summer night, even a small seaside town can seem like downtown Athens with all the people heading off to the tavernas. By 2am or so, things begin to wind down – after all, in a few hours it'll all begin again.

Above: Evening dining, Réthymnon, Crete, pp.165–71

Right: Colourful restaurant, Fiskárdo, Kefaloniá, p.492

Gaia in her Glad Rags

The Greeks gave the Earth goddess a lovely name, Gaia, and in return she has left them a generous helping of natural charm. But some of the islands were given the works – starter, main course and dessert: Santoríni rimming an indigo caldera or western Crete with its famous Gorge of Samariá. Yet even the smallest, humblest island is endowed with its drum-roll moments – even if it's only the colour of the rocks washed by the waves, an ancient plane tree, or a fertile little valley tucked in an arid tumble of hills.

Above, from top: Melissáni Cave, Kefaloniá, p.490; Paleokastrítsa, Corfu, p.465

Above: Sunset, Santorini,
pp.303–15

Twilight of the Gods

Homer sang of 'rosy-fingered dawn', but it's the light at the close of day that casts an enthralling spell. As the sun begins to set, the sea, no matter how breezy it was during the day, grows respectfully still into a calm liquid sheet, absorbing the pinks and oranges of the sky, shimmering with the fire trail of the sun. As the last round edge of the solar disc slips away, islands on the horizon slowly appear to rise a little and float above the water, hovering dream-like as the sky turns crimson and violet and the first star appears. Then even the patrons in a noisy cocktail bar by the sea fall silent, understanding why, in Greek myth, the gods so often came to earth.

Itinerary
A First Timer's Best of the Greek Islands

Day 1 Arrive in **Athens** and visit the Acropolis – it's got to be done! In the late afternoon, stroll along the beautiful new pedestrian walk for a overview of the ancient city, ending up with the sunset views from the Philopáppos Monument.

Day 2 See the glory that was Greece at the National Archaeological Museum in the morning, then have a long lunch and stroll around Sýntagma Square and Pláka. At 6pm or so, start making your way to Piraeus to take the overnight ferry to **Chaniá, Crete**.

Day 3 The ferry arrives early, so take a taxi to the Venetian harbour and watch Chaniá come alive. Visit the town, and in the late afternoon flop on a beach; then have dinner by the sea.

Days 4–6 Hire a car for day to explore Chaniá's hinterland – the Venetian estates, beaches and Byzantine monasteries around **Akrotíri** and **Drápanon**. Book a day's excursion through the **Samariá Gorge**, then spend a quiet beach day recovering.

Day 7 Take the bus to **Heráklion** and see the exquisite Minoan treasures in the Archaeology Museum. Visit the outdoor market, the Venetian walls, Ag. Títos and the port.

Day 8 Hire a car for the day to visit **Knossós**, then head south to visit Crete's lovely wine country around **Archánes** and **Myrtiá**. Return to the coast for a swim.

Days 9–11 Take the morning catamaran to **Santoríni**. Drink in the marvellous views over the caldera, visit Akrotíri, the 'Bronze Age Pompeii', swim off black beaches, and watch the sunset from Oía.

Days 12–14 Sail to **Náxos**. Wander through Náxos Town and visit the Cycladic art in the Archaeology Museum; go for a long walk in the hinterland, seeking out old Byzantine churches; laze on the beach, or go windsurfing.

Days 15–16 Take the ferry to **Mýkonos**. Take a morning excursion to ancient Délos, then, back in Chóra, stock up on jewellery, go to the beach, have cocktails in Little Venice and stay up all night at the town-wide party.

Days 17–19 Hop over to **Sýros**. Explore its fascinating neoclassical town on two peaks, go to the beach, eat *mezédes* and listen to *rembetiká*, and try your luck at the casino. Be lazy.

Days 20–21 Return to **Athens**, and on your final night in Greece splurge on a rooftop restaurant with views of the Parthenon.

Above: Theatre of Dionysos, Acropolis, Athens, p.80; Cruise liners docking, Firá, Santoríni, p.307

Below: Private beach, western Corfu, pp.465–8

Islands Best For...

(NB Crete is best for almost everything!)

Castles Évia, Tínos, Límnos, Léros, Corfu, Rhodes, Kos, Astypálaía.

Couples Santoríni, Hýdra, Mýkonos, Páxos, Skopélos, Pátmos, Ithaca.

Small children Náxos, Sífos, Thássos, Zákynthos, Corfu, Kefaloniá.

Teenagers Páros, Rhodes, Corfu, Spétses, Skíathos, Zákynthos.

Nightlife Mýkonos, Skiáthos, Páros, Spétses, Rhodes, Corfu, Kos.

Restaurants Mýkonos, Rhodes, Santorini, Sými, Páros, Sífnos, Pátmos, Sýros, Kefaloniá, Corfu.

Spas Évia (Edipsóu), Lésvos, Ikaría, Kýthnos.

Traditional festivals Lésvos, Skýros, Spétses, Kárpathos, Ikaría.

Scenery Santoríni, Kefaloniá, Corfu, Crete, Folégandros, Sérifos, Mílos, Zákynthos, Póros, all the Ionians, northern Évia, Sámos, Thássos, Samothráki, Lésvos, Ikaría, Ándros, Skópelos, Skíathos.

Walks Náxos, Alónissos, Crete, Corfu, Sámos, Chíos, Évia, Ándros, Skópelos, Kéa, Lésvos.

Beaches Skiáthos, Thássos, Corfu, Mýkonos, Crete, Elafónissos, Zákynthos, Rhodes, Kos, Páros, Sífnos, Mílos, Íos, Koufoníssi.

Archaeological sites Aegina, Délos, Crete, Rhodes, Kos, Sámos, Thássos, Santoríni, Samothráki, Náxos, southern Évia.

Archaeological museums Heráklion, Sámos, Náxos, Kos, Corfu, Lésvos, Évia (Erétria), Límnos, Mílos, Kéa, Mýkonos.

Beautiful towns and cities Rhodes, Corfu, Ermoúpolis (Sýros), Chaniá and Réthymnon (Crete), Mýkonos, Hýdra, Sými, Náxos, Páros, Líndos (Rhodes), Kéa, Oía (Santoríni), Skópelos, Skýros, Spétses, Pátmos, Folégrandros, Mólyvos (Lésvos), Límni (Évia), Ag. Nikólaos and Sitía (Crete), Gaíos (Páxos), Póros, Váthi (Ithaca).

Charming villages Mastikochória (Chíos), Ólympos (Kárpathos), Fískardo (Kefaloniá), Paleokastrítsa (Corfu), Panagía (Thássos), Agiássos (Lésvos), plus lots on Níssyros, Sífnos, Sérifos, Antíparos, Astypálaia, Amorgós, Chálki.

Early Christian churches Ag. Paraskevi, (Chalki, Évia), Ag. Títos, (Górtyn, Crete), Ekatontopyliani (Páros).

Byzantine churches and monasteries Néa Móni (Chíos), St John the Theologian (Pátmos); Kándanos, Krísta, Thrónos, Fódele (all Crete); Chozoviótissa (Amorgós); Thárri and Kímisis Theotókou, at Asklipío (Rhodes); Panachrándou (Ándros); around Chálki (Náxos).

Post-Byzantine churches and monasteries Préveli, Akrotíri's Ag. Tríada and Gouvernétou, Toploú (all Crete); Panagía Paraportianí (Mýkonos); Moní Faneroméni (Salamína).

Above, from top: Byzantine church, Stavrós, Ithaca, p.476;

Below: Church bells; Bay, northeast Corfu, pp.462–3

CONTENTS

Maps and Plans

Reference

History, Art and Architecture

O2

An Outline of Greek History

Greece has been undergoing a political crisis for the past 3,000 years.
A politician, during a recent election campaign

Aristotle declared man to be a political animal, and to this day no animal is as political as a Greek. If there are two *kafeneíons* in a village, one will be for the rightist sympathizers, the other for the left. Over 50 parties crowd the typical ballot, including five different flavours of Communists and exotica like the Self-respect Party and the popular Fatalist Party. If you visit during an election, all transport to the islands will be swamped with Athenians returning to their villages to vote.

To begin to understand current Greek attitudes, a bit of history is essential.

8000–1200 BC: The Beginnings of Greece

c. **8000–7000 BC** *First inhabitants arrive on Crete*
c. **7500–6000** *Oldest known settlement on Cyclades (Kýthnos)*
c. **4000** *Precocious civilization at Poliochní, Limnos*
c. **3000** *Mílos exports obsidian*
c. **3000** *'Early Cycladic' civilization*
c. **2500** *'Middle Cycladic' civilization*
c. **2600–1900** *Early Minoan civilization in Crete*
c. **2000** *'Late Cycladic' civilization*
c. **1900–1700** *'Old Palace' period on Crete: Cretan thalassocracy rules the Aegean*
c. **1700–1450** *'New Palace' period on Crete*
c. **1600** *Mycenaeans invade the Peloponnese*
c. **1600** *Great volcanic eruption of Santorini*
c. **1450–1100** *'Post-palace' period; Mycenaeans occupy Crete and other islands*
c. **1250 or 1180** *Traditional dates given for the fall of Troy*

Human habitation in Greece goes back some 700,000 years at least, but nobody knows which humans first figured out canoes and paddled out to the islands. Finds for the period 8000–4000 BC are tantalizing and scarce, though plenty of evidence has been uncovered for a Neolithic farming culture between 6000 and 4000 in the Cyclades. These early arrivals were probably immigrants from Anatolia.

The first big story here is the **Cycladic civilization**. While the Egyptians were building their pyramids, and the Mesopotamians their ziggurats, these precociously talented islanders were mining and exporting obsidian, the hard, black, glassy status stone of the Stone Age. They are best known for their ceramics and wonderful marble 'idols', betraying a hyper-modern artistic sensibility that inspires sculptors in our own day.

The Cycladic culture was already in decline when its neighbours on Crete were beginning their astonishing career as Europe's first great civilization. The **Minoans** built their wealth on trade and sea power as early as 2000 BC; their commercial outposts spread from Kýthera to Rhodes, and as far as Sicily and Cyprus. The Minoans had it all – great art, writing (in the apparently non-Greek 'Linear A' script), three-storey townhouses, excellent plumbing – and they left behind enough mysteries to puzzle scholars for centuries to come. We still have no clear idea of

Minoan political arrangements or religious practices, and the contrast of the cool, joyous sophistication suggested in their art with the increasing evidence of human sacrifice is just too strange to fathom (for more on the Minoans, *see* pp.134–8).

You have probably read that a great volcanic eruption blew up the island of Santoríni in about 1450 BC and wrecked Minoan civilization. This makes a good introduction to the uncertainty and constant revision that bedevils the dating of Greek early history. According to the most recent tests, that event really occurred *c.* 1627–1600 BC, and it's still an open question how much of an effect it had on Crete's decline. Other dates will undoubtedly be pushed back too, and for now we can only say that at some time during these centuries the Minoans faded and were replaced by the **Mycenaeans**. These Greek-speakers occupied the mainland around 1600 BC, dividing it into city-states dominated by the impressive palace-citadels of Mycenae, Tiryns, Pýlos, Athens and the rest, with colonies or trade counters on the islands. After a few centuries of startling opulence, things started to go very wrong for the Mycenaeans. Homer's sack of Troy provides a dark mirror for a time of dislocations, invasions and constant war that began about 1200 BC. We know little for sure about the events or the protagonists, but the Mycenaean palaces were gradually abandoned, and after so many centuries of brilliant life and activity the Greek world was about to take a very long nap.

1200–500 BC: The First 'Dark Age', and a Strong Recovery

c. 1200 BC *Dorian invasions; Ionians begin to settle Asia Minor and islands*
c. 1000 *Délos becomes religious capital of the Ionians*
1100–700 *'Geometric Period' in art*
c. 900 *Founding of Rhodes' three cities by Dorians*
776 *Traditional date of first Olympic games*
c. 750 *Chalkís begins its colonization programme*
734 *Corinth founds its trading colony on Corfu*
c. 720–650 *'Lelantine Wars' between Chalkís and Erétria*
c. 710 *Birth of Terpander, of Lésvos, father of Greek music*
c. 700 *Kos and the three cities of Rhodes join Doric Hexapolis*
700–500 *'Archaic Period' in art*
660 *Rebuilding of the Temple of Hera on Sámos, one of the 'Seven Wonders'*
c. 650 *Birth of Sappho, on Lésvos*
650 *Aegina is first in Greece to mint coins*
598–79 *Rule of Pittakos on Lésvos, one of the Seven Sages of Greece*
570–480 *Pythagoras of Sámos*
546 *Ionia comes under Persian control*
540–22 *Polycrates, tyrant of Sámos*

Ancient traditions have it that this was the age of the **Dorian** invasions, though who exactly the Dorians were, and whether they invaded at all, are still matters of scholarly dispute. It does seem likely that new tribes of Greeks had been moving in from the north; the other side of the old tradition mentions the **Ionian Greeks**, fleeing the Dorians (except in Athens) and settling most of the Cyclades, Sporades and North Aegean islands and the coasts of Anatolia (Asia Minor). The Dorians settled Corfu, Lefkáda, Aegina, Crete, Mílos, Santoríni and the Dodecanese, while much of Évia and Lésvos were left to the third division of the Greeks, the **Aeolians**.

Trade, building and art came to a virtual standstill for four centuries. But when Greece decided to blossom again, in the 8th century, the change was dramatic. In the Dark Age, Greeks had forgotten how to read and write; now they started over with a new alphabet, borrowed from the **Phoenicians**, who had installed themselves on many of the islands as traders. New city-states appeared everywhere, and the **Olympic Games** began. This is also the time of Homer (most likely), and the rebirth of art in what has come to be called the 'Archaic' style.

Things were going so well, in fact, that quite suddenly there were too many Greeks to fit the country; the great age of colonization, to Italy, France, Libya and the Black Sea, starts in the mid-8th century BC. Here the islanders played a prominent role, especially the rivals Chalkís and Erétria on Évia. Chalkís led the colonization of Magna Graecia, founding no fewer than three important southern Italian cities (Messina, Reggio Calabria and Cumae). Corcyra (Corfu), founded by Corinth, became a wealthy trading centre and eventually an enemy to its mother city. Besides these, important island city-states appeared on Sámos, Rhodes, Náxos and Lésvos.

Islanders made great contributions to Greek culture: the philosopher and mathematician Pythagoras of Sámos, or the poet Sappho of Lésvos. You can see the beginnings of Greek monumental sculpture in the *kouroi* left in the marble quarries of Náxos (7th century), and one of the greatest early sculptors, Daedalus (not to be confused with the legendary inventor), came from Crete.

500–323 BC: The Classical Age, Where the Brilliant Athenians Push Everyone Around

506 *Athens defeats Chalkís and Erétria, and gains control of Évia*

490–79 *Persian Wars*

490 *Destruction of Erétria and Náxos by the Persians*

480 *Battle of Salamis, and birth of Euripides there, traditionally both on 23 Sept*

479 *Defeat of Persian army and fleet*

478 *Athens and its allies form the Delian League*

476 *Kimon of Athens grabs the Sporades*

465 *Rebellion and siege of Thássos*

460–377 *Hippocrates of Kos*

458 *Athenians finally gain control of Aegina*

454 *Athenians loot the Treasury at Délos*

440 *Athenians crush revolt on Sámos*

431–404 *Peloponnesian War*

412 *Athenians sack Chíos after revolt*

378 *Second Delian League*

365 *Athenians seize Sámos and deport its entire population*

338 *Battle of Chaeronea: Philip of Macedon owns Athens and the rest of Greece*

334–323 *Conquests of Alexander the Great*

In previous centuries, we see island-states building, creating, colonizing and fighting on their own; now, in Greece's golden age, whenever they appear in the chronicles they are usually getting clobbered by larger powers. This is the political background to the brilliant age of Pericles and Sophocles and Plato. First, a burgeoning Persian Empire grows weary of impudent resistance from the pesky Greek statelets on its western frontier. The full-scale Persian invasion leads to a successful national defence led by Athens and Sparta. Famous battles at Marathon, Salamis, Plataea – the **Persian Wars** are over; Greeks win.

Next, the victorious Athenians find themselves with more money and more ships than anyone in the Mediterranean. They corral their allies, including most of the islands, into the new **Delian League**. But only 13 years later, in 465, one member, the island of Thássos, tries to pull out and is crushed by Athens; it is clear that the League is no alliance of equals but an Athenian empire. Conservative, unartistic Sparta, the great land power, becomes the defender of Greek liberties, and a show-down is inevitable. It comes with another dispute over an island, Corfu, and the long, dreadful **Peloponnesian War**, in which many islands are chewed up and spat out by the contenders. Athens' hubris was rewarded with a great plague (430), the destruction of the army and fleet she sent against Syracuse in Sicily (415) and finally total defeat in 404. But Athens wasn't completely sunk; she survived as a smaller player on the Greek chessboard, along with Sparta, Thebes and others, through a busy 4th century full of ever-changing alliances and pointless, inconclusive wars. In the end, all would be swallowed up by a bigger fish, the northern kingdom of **Macedon**, which had found new gold mines to finance its ambitions, and irresistibly clever leaders in **King Philip** and his son, **Alexander the Great**.

323 BC–AD 527: Hellenistic and Roman Greece – Maybe Foreign Rule's not so Bad after All

310–230 BC *Aristarchus, astronomer and mathematician of Sámos*
305–304 *Siege of Rhodes by Dimitrios Poliorketes*
290 *Colossus of Rhodes built, collapses in 225 BC*
164 *Rhodians ally with Rome*
146 *Roman rule established through most of Greece*
88 *Mithridates VI of Pontus, enemy of Rome, invades the Aegean*
86 *Romans under Sulla destroy Athens and other rebels who supported Mithridates*
69–67 *Quintus Caecelius Metellus conquers Crete for Rome in bloody campaign*
43 *Sack of Rhodes during Roman civil wars*
32 *Antony and Cleopatra dally on Sámos; Corfu wasted by Augustus*
31 BC *Battle of Actium, final triumph of Augustus*
AD 58 *St Paul visits Rhodes*
AD 67 *Emperor Nero holidays on Corfu*
AD 95 *St John the Divine writes the* Apocalypse *on Pátmos*
AD 330 *Founding of Constantinople*

Alexander the Great conquered the world and promptly died; the passing of this fizzy little comet left his winnings, and Greece, in the hands of his generals, who divvied up the empire and almost immediately began fighting each other. Their successors, in the new dynasties of Macedon, Syria and Egypt, continued the same game for over a century and a half. We call it the **Hellenistic Era**, a time of brilliant advances in science and technology, big egos and big armies, and virtuoso art that often crosses the line into mannerism.

One island, at least, had the brains and luck to make a brilliant career for itself through all the sound and fury. **Rhodes**' talent was for usually guessing right in its choice of allies. Favoured lavishly by Alexander the Great, the island built itself a strong navy and trade connections that extended across the Mediterranean. And as early as 200, Rhodes was seeking protection from the new big kid on the block, **Rome**. Fresh from destroying Carthage in the Punic Wars, Rome was assuming an ever-greater role in Greek affairs. The legions trashed Macedon in 197, and by 164 the Romans had tired of the traditional Greek in-fighting and backstabbing and simply annexed the entire peninsula. Islands were gobbled up gradually, like cherries. Crete, one of the last to fall, kept its independence until 69 BC. Like the Macedonians, the Romans allowed the Greeks a pretence of freedom: nominal self-government, all the civic trappings of the old city-states, and for some, even the right to mint coins. The only troubles came when a city or island got caught up in Rome's civil wars; proud Rhodes got a looting the year after the assassination of Julius Caesar. Twelve years later, Augustus cemented his victory at the naval **battle of Actium**, off the island of Lefkáda. Life was pretty quiet after that, though, as the centuries passed and the Roman Empire morphed into the Byzantine, the islands, like the rest of Greece, were looking increasingly poor and shabby.

527–1204: Byzantines: The Greeks Keep the Flag Flying in a World Full of Troubles

c. 550 *Goths pillage the Ionians*
654 *First Arab raid in the Aegean, against Rhodes*
727–843 *Iconoclasm in the Eastern Church*
823 *Saracen/Arab occupation of Crete*
902 *Arabs sack Límnos*
961 *Emperor Nikephóros Phókas reconquers Crete from the Saracens*
1054 *Pope excommunicates Patriarch of Constantinople over differences in the creed*
1071 *Battle of Manzikert*
1081 *Robert Guiscard and the Normans capture Corfu*
1088 *Foundation of the Monastery on Pátmos*
1187 *Venetians take the Ionian islands*

Despite that one Gothic escapade in the Ionians, the Greek islands were well positioned to avoid the worst of the imperial decline. On many, you'll see ruins of impressive church buildings near their shores from the 4th–6th centuries, a sign that peace and security were being maintained.

The real disaster came in the 7th, with the sudden explosion of the **Arabs** across the Mediterranean world. **Heraclius**, a great emperor (610–41), knew some dramatic days. He reorganized the country, made Greek the sole official language and beat the Sassanid Persians, but lost all his gains again to the Arabs. These were learning to sail too, and their disruption of sea lanes that had been peaceful for centuries brought a rapid decline in the Greek economy. For the islands, the experience was traumatic; the Byzantines and the Greeks fought over Crete for over a century.

The victories of **Basil II** (976–1025) finally made the Aegean a Byzantine lake once more, but this empire just couldn't get a break. Soon after, the people destined to be the Greek nemesis for almost a millennium make their appearance: the **Turks**. Specifically it was the Selçuk Turks who first found their way into Asia Minor, smashing the Byzantine army in 1071 at Manzikert and leaving the empire little more than an empty shell. The 11th century also marks a return of the Westerners to the Greek world. Venetians, Pisans and Genoese ships and merchants resuscitated commerce. Norman freebooters, already masters of southern Italy, flexed their muscle in the Ionians. In 1095, Emperor Alexios I's appeal for help against the Turks led to the **First Crusade**. The Crusaders used the Dodecanese as stepping-stones, recapturing Chíos and Rhodes as well as much of Asia Minor. Altogether, the century that followed would be a good time for the Greeks and for the islands, with a Renaissance of Byzantine art and the founding of many new monasteries.

The replacement of the solid Comnenos dynasty with the decadent, feckless Angelos in 1180 meant another change in course: revolts, palace intrigues and fiscal troubles brought a weakness that the omnipresent Italians were quick to exploit. In 1204, the **Venetians** under the blind, bitter Doge **Enrico Dandolo** diverted the Fourth Crusade on a quest for booty. After a long siege, he and the Crusaders took Constantinople for the first time in its 900-year history.

1204–1453: Anarchy: Venetians, Franks and Turks Prowl the Aegean

1204 *Venetians lead Fourth Crusade conquest of Constantinople*
1210 *Marco Sanudo declares himself 'Duke of the Archipelago' (Cyclades)*
1254 *Angevin rule begins in Corfu*
1261 *Greeks retake Constantinople from Latins; Chíos given to Giustiniani of Genoa*
1306 *Knights of St John established on Rhodes*
1346 *Palace of the Grand Masters built at Rhodes*
1386 *Corfu invites the Venetians in to rule*

Not long after the sacking, a committee of Crusader bosses and Venetian officials met to carve up the empire they had just assassinated. According to the terms of their 'Deed of Partition', Venice was to receive three-eighths of it, including most of the islands – ideal bases for protecting their trade routes to the east. New '**Latin Emperor**' Baldwin I kept those around the coasts of Asia Minor for himself.

Greeks still ruled Byzantine lands in Anatolia and Épirus, and a reviving Byzantine government at Nicaea took control of the coastal islands from Lésvos to Kos in the 1220s. In 1261 the Greeks battered their way back into Constantinople and re-established the empire, but for the next two centuries the Aegean and most of the lands around it would be up for grabs. The power vacuum Enrico Dandolo had created would attract the Angevins (who had taken over as rulers of southern Italy), the Genoese (Venice's most bitter enemy), the Catalans of Barcelona (at Aegina, from 1317 to 1541), various Greek and Italian adventurers, and even a wealthy Crusading order, the **Knights of St John** (or Hospitallers), who made a comfortable home for themselves on Rhodes and the Dodecanese after they were chased out of the Holy Land in 1291. One of the most durable island-states was set up by Enrico Dandolo's nephew, **Marco Sanudo**, the '**Duchy of the Archipelago**' based at Náxos.

Above all, it was a strapping, romantic age for **pirates**: state-sponsored or protected, or simply privateers. Among them were Greeks, Turks, Basques, Italians, Spaniards, even Corsicans. Hollywood should make more films about it.

1453–1821: The Four Gloomy Centuries of the *Turkokratía*

1453 *Ottomans take Constantinople and the Byzantine Empire is no more*
1522 *Ottomans capture Rhodes*
1537 *Barbarossa's Turks besiege Corfu, and sack Kýthera and Mýkonos*
1541 *El Greco born on Crete*
1571 *Battle of Lepanto, in the Gulf of Corinth*
1669 *Venetians lose Heráklion and all of Crete to the Turks after a 20-year siege*
1771–4 *Catherine the Great sends Russian fleet into the Aegean to harry the Sultan*
1783 *Russo-Turkish treaty allows Greek ships to trade under the Russian flag*
1796 *Napoleon captures Venice and her Ionian islands*
1813 *Thássos ruled by Egyptians, until 1902*
1815–64 *British rule the 'Septinsular Republic' of the Ionian islands*

It was just what the Greeks needed in tough times – a fresh supply of Turks, galloping in from the empty spaces of central Asia. Even worse, these were specially gifted, world-beating Turks: the **Ottomans**, named for their matchless founder Osman I (1299–1326), who conquered much of Asia Minor. The Turks saluted each new sultan with the toast, 'May he be as good as Osman!', and for a while, the successors measured up. **Mehmet II the Conqueror** took Constantinople once and for all in 1453. **Suleiman the Magnificent** (1520–66) presided over the brilliant Ottoman noonday. The Turks spread their rule over the Aegean gradually, mostly through the use of more pirates, such as Greek-born **Barbarossa**, who terrorized the Mediterranean. It was a terrible age for Greeks on the Aegean shores; such tactics could depopulate islands, but never build a happy, prosperous state. The Turks reached their high-water mark with a defeat at the hands of European powers at **Lepanto** in 1571 – yet another crucial sea battle fought in Greek waters.

The Venetians held on to their last possessions tenaciously. They kept **Crete** until 1669; under their 465 years of rule Crete had developed a substantial literature, including the poetry of Vitsentzos Kornaros, and an artistic tradition that includes Doménikos Theotokópoulos, better known as El Greco.

The Ottoman trajectory would be straight up, slowly but inevitably down. After Suleiman bequeathed his sultanate to his favourite's pervert son, there would never again be a sultan 'as good as Osman'. By 1700 the empire was already the 'Sick Man of Europe', with Russia trying to push it out of the Balkans and the Black Sea. For the Greeks, like the other captive nations, the Ottomans generally collected their taxes and left people alone, but their decadence meant centuries of economic and cultural stagnation. When westerners returned to the Aegean, during the Napoleonic Wars, it was clear that this new power vacuum wouldn't last.

1821–1900: Greek Independence, and its Discontents

1821–7 *Greek War of Independence*
1822 *Miraculous icon of Virgin discovered, Tínos; 30,000 Greeks slaughtered on Chios*

1823 *Founding of Ermoúpolis, Sýros*
1823 *Aegina made the capital of free Greece*
1824 *Massacres by the Turks at Kássos*
1827 *Annihilation of Turkish fleet by British, French and Russians at Battle of Navarino*
1827 *Count John Capodistria of Corfu becomes first president of Greece*
1833 *Otho of Bavaria becomes the first king of the Greeks*
1856 *Greek Steamship Company founded in Ermoúpolis*
1864 *Ionians ceded to Greece by Britain*
1866 *Cretan revolt*
1863 *Winged Victory uncovered on Samothráki, and hustled off to the Louvre*
1898 *Great Powers' occupation of Crete*
1898–9 *Archaeologist Chrístos Tsoúntas discovers Cycladic civilization*

The revolutionary fires that swept through Europe at the end of the 18th century found plenty of kindling among Greeks. The **War of Independence** began in the Peloponnese in 1821, and continued for over six years. In the end, Britain, Russia and France assisted the Greek cause, and, in the decisive **Battle of Navarino** in 1827, gave the new Greek state the Peloponnese and the mainland peninsula. They also bestowed a king: **Otho**, son of Ludwig I of Bavaria. The islands played an important role in everything that happened, even if many of them remained under Turkish rule. The 1783 Russo-Turkish treaty that allowed Greeks to sail and trade under Russian protection was the start of a booming shipping industry, a mainstay of the national economy even today. In the 1820s, it provided Greece with ships and money for the cause. The new city of Ermoúpolis on Sýros became Greece's biggest port, while Hýdra, Sými and other islands grew important shipbuilding firms.

Recovery from centuries of *turkokratía* could not occur overnight, and the new Greece would remain a poor and backward country. Times were even rougher for places that remained under Ottoman rule. On Crete, where nearly half the population was Greek converts to Islam, the War of Independence meant vicious intercommunal fighting, which was followed by a plague and famine. After the war **Crete** was prevented from joining the new Greece by Britain, and became a miserable backwater under the rule of Egypt (autonomous, and very influential in late Ottoman times). Cretans liked the Egyptians so much that they revolted in 1840, 1866, 1878, 1889, 1895 and 1897; the last fracas saw the Muslim population besieged in the towns. After that, the Great Powers intervened, forcing the creation of an independent Crete in 1898.

1900–1945: Colourful Banners, Cheering Crowds, Starving Children

1905 *Venizélos' 'Revolution of Therissio' on Crete*
1908 *Reconstruction of palace at Knóssos*
1909 *Venizélos becomes Prime Minister of Greece*
1883–1957 *Cretan writer Níkos Kazantzákis*
1912 *Italians occupy Dodecanese*
1912–13 *Balkan Wars give Greece Macedonia, Crete and the Northeastern Aegean islands; the Italians pick up the Dodecanese*
1912 *Ikaría becomes an independent state, for five months*

1913 *Anti-Turkish revolt on Kastellorízo put down by the French*

1922–3 *Disastrous attempt to conquer Asia Minor; burning of Izmir; 'Exchange of Populations'*

1923 *Mussolini briefly occupies Corfu over diplomatic dispute*

1924 *Greece becomes a republic*

1935 *Restoration of the monarchy*

1936–41 *Ioánnis Metaxás becomes dictator of Greece*

1940–41 *Winter famine kills 100,000 Greeks*

1941 *Nazi paratroopers complete first-ever invasion by air on Crete*

1943 *Nazi massacre of Italian troops on Kefaloniá*

1945 *Treaty signed returning Dodecanese islands to Greece*

Greece's story in the early 20th century is largely the story of **Elefthérios Venizélos**, the intense, charismatic, doll-faced, warmongering politician from Crete who became prime minister in 1909. The Balkans were always in the headlines then; a decaying Ottoman state could no longer hold its lands there, and its neighbours were ready to grab what they could. Venizélos struck it big in the 1912–13 **Balkan Wars**, finally bringing his home island into the nation, along with other islands and Thessaloníki.

Venizélos led Greece into the **First World War** on the side of the Allies, and after the final Ottoman collapse it seemed for a brief shining moment that all the Greeks might finally be brought under the national flag. Since independence, Greek politics had been poisoned by the *Megáli Idéa* (Great Idea) of taking back Constantinople and the Greek parts of Asia Minor, creating a kind of reconstituted Byzantium. Venizélos fostered such fantasies more than anyone, though he was not in power in 1921 when the Greek government, egged on by Britain, got greedy and sent their army marching towards Ankara. **Kemal Atatürk** and his new Nationalist army defeated them halfway and chased them all the way back to Smyrna (Izmir), where Turks burned down the Greek parts of the city while thousands of desperate refugees scrambled for boats. The Great Idea became the Great Disaster, and it ended in a great crime. The '**Exchange of Populations**' agreed by the two nations was a ghoulish, state-sponsored ethnic cleansing. Greece had to absorb over a million refugees from Asia Minor, ending a community and a cultural presence that was 3,000 years old. Some 300,000 Muslims, mostly from Crete, got shipped the other way, allowed to keep only what they could carry.

Greece became a republic in 1924 – a banana republic, thanks largely to the endless plots and intrigues of Venizélos. After he died, it became a banana monarchy again, and power soon fell into the hands of another islander, General **Ioánnis Metaxás** of Kefaloniá, whose rule emulated the Fascist trappings of Italy and Germany. Metaxás is a hero to Greeks today, though, for his curt (if probably apocryphal) reply to a Mussolini ultimatum in 1940. 'ΟΞΙ!', the general said, and 'No' Day (28 October) has become a proud national holiday. At first, the Greek army pushed the invading Italians back into Albania. Hitler was alarmed, and sent his own boys to finish the job. The terrible famine of the winter of 1940, the fall of Crete, built up as an impregnable fortress by the British, and the tenacity of a fierce resistance made Greece as tragic and miserable as any country occupied in the **Second World War**.

1945–Present: More Political Fun – and Finally, a Spark of Goodwill

1946 *Civil war breaks out across Greece*
1948 *Dodecanese islands reunite with Greece*
1949 *End of civil war between Communists and US-backed government*
1953 *Earthquake shatters the Ionian islands*
1967 *Colonels' coup establishes a dictatorship under George Papadópoulos*
1974 *Failure of the Junta's Cyprus adventure leads to the restoration of democracy*
1981 *First-ever socialist government (PASOK) elected*
1983 *Greece joins the EU*
1996 *Greece and Turkey quarrel over uninhabited islets in the Dodecanese*
2004 *Olympic Games in Athens*
2006 *Discovery of Ajax's Mycenaean Palace on Salamína*

That fierce resistance was divided between **Communists (ELAS)** and **monarchists**, and they were ready to bite each other's throats as soon as Greece was free of Nazis. The Communists had been building strength since the 1920s; they had done the lion's share of the fighting, and in a fair fight or a free election they would have won Greece. Winston Churchill wasn't about to let it happen, and Joseph Stalin proved surprisingly *complaisant*. He kissed off the Greek Communists while the British and Americans poured guns and butter into the rightists' camp, and the bitter three-year **Civil War** became a rout; leftists who were not shot or imprisoned went into exile. Greece and Turkey were both dragooned into **NATO** in 1951, and ordered to behave themselves. Beginning in 1955, a useful conservative government under **Konstantínos Karamanlís** brought in the beginnings of reconciliation and recovery. He lasted eight years, but after that Greece's old banana republic tendencies asserted themselves once more. By 1967, as the political situation seemed utterly hopeless, a cabal of cheap thug **colonels** (most of them CIA assets) made a coup that caught everyone by surprise. Leftist prime minister Papandréou went to jail, while the rightist King Constantine fled to Rome. The colonels, backed by the USA, proposed a 'moral cleansing' for Greece, which in practice meant martial law, censorship and torture. They met their come-uppance in a last shabby echo of the *Megáli Idéa*, when their attempt to force Cyprus into union with Greece ended in a Turkish invasion of the island and a revolt in the Greek army.

In the November 1974 elections, old Konstantínos Karamanlís and his **Néa Demokratía (ND)** party came back to lead Greece towards civil peace and sanity. Greeks voted to become a republic again, and eventually decided they wanted more economic and social reforms, replacing Karamanlís in 1981 with **Andréas Papandréou**, son of the last, pre-coup leftist leader, and his new **Pan-Hellenic Socialist Movement (PASOK)**. Papandréou (yet another islander, born on Chíos), who had once been head of the economics department at the University of California at Berkeley and a campaign advisor to Adlai Stevenson, had a fair idea who Greece's real enemy was; in the end he was able to end the pervasive American influence without actually pulling Greece out of NATO.

Papandréou did much to bring Greece closer to modern Europe, though economic mismanagement, corruption and a senile, very public dalliance with a pneumatic ex-airline hostess finally did him in. The country has been growing up fast. Today, politics can seem almost normal, and the leaders of both left and right would be a credit to any nation. Billions in EU subsidies pouring in for infrastructure, education and new business have certainly helped. After a thousand years of animosity, Greeks and Turks are suddenly doing their damnedest to get along.

The new Greece got a chance to show itself off to the world with the 2004 Olympic Games. In the nation's arrogant old nemesis, Britain, the press and public scoffed nearly every day that the Greeks would never get anything done on time or done right. The result, even if cobbled together at the last minute, was flawless and delightful. Now the Greeks sit back and watch the Brits try to finish Wembley Stadium or build a Eurostar train station, and they just laugh.

Greek Art and Architecture

Art begins on the Greek islands in the 7th millennium BC with their oldest settlements – Knossós and Phaistós on **Crete**, Phylokopí on **Mílos**, Poliochní on **Límnos** and Ag. Iríni on **Kéa**. Their art is typical of the age: dark burnished pottery, decorated with spirals and wavy lines and statuettes of the fertility goddess in stone or terracotta.

3000–1100 BC: Bronze Age: Cycladic and Minoan Styles

Early contacts with Anatolia and the Near East put Crete and the **Cyclades** on the cutting edge of European civilization. By 2600 BC, Cycladic dead were being buried with flat, abstract marble statues (*see* collections in Náxos and Athens) and the people of **Crete**, dubbed the '**Minoans**' by Sir Arthur Evans, were demonstrating a rare talent in polychrome pottery and gold jewellery. Over the next period (Middle Minoan, traditionally dated 2000–1700 BC), when Crete's fleet ruled the seas, the Minoans built themselves complex unfortified palaces. They constructed canals and roads, and kept accounts of the oil, wine and grain stored in huge *pithoi*.

Crete's civilization reached its apogee between 1700 and 1450 BC when Minoan colonies stretched across the Aegean. Minoan palaces at **Knossós**, **Phaistós**, **Zákros**, **Mália** and at their outpost of **Akrotíri** on Santoríni and **Phylokopí** on Mílos were adorned with elegant frescoes (in the archaeology museums of Heráklion and Athens). Built of wood and unbaked brick, the palaces collapsed in the earthquakes that marked the end of Minoan civilization. The **Mycenaeans**, based on the mainland, filled the power vacuum, taking over the Minoan colonies and artistic traditions. Little of this reached the islands, although many have Mycenaean stone walls, known as **cyclopean** after their gigantic blocks, **Kefaloniá** has a royal *tholos* tomb and, in a recent discovery, **Salamína** can now claim **Ajax's Mycenaean Palace**.

1000–500 BC: Geometric (1000–700 BC) and Archaic (700–500 BC)

The splintering of the Mycenaean world ushered in a Dark Age, although the discovery in 1981 of the huge Proto-Geometric sanctuary at **Lefkandí** on **Évia**, from *c.* 950 BC, has made it slightly less dark (finds are in the nearby museum at Erétria). Lefkándi traded with Athens, where in *c.* 900 BC, a new style of pottery appears known as **Geometric** for the simple, abstract designs. The 8th century was marked by the evolution of the *pólis*, or city-state, the egg from which the Greek miracle would hatch. **Emborió**, on **Chíos**, offers an example of a town founded by Ionian refugees in the 8th century. The first peristyle stone **Temple of Hera** on **Sámos** was up by 718 BC. **Corfu**'s Doric **Temple of Artemis** (580 BC) was a more advanced prototype with its pediments decorated with a formidable 3.6m (12ft) relief of Medusa. The Doric **Temple of Aphaia** on **Aegina** was begun in the same period and decorated with a pediment showing scenes from the Trojan War. The 6th-century **Efpalinion tunnel** on **Sámos** was the engineering feat of the age.

The **Archaic era** also saw the beginning of life-size figure sculpture, inspired by the Egyptians. The male version is a *kouros* (see the giants of **Sámos** and **Náxos**); the female is a *kore*. As they evolved, their formal poses relaxed and reveal a new interest in anatomy. The 7th century witnessed the development of regional schools of pottery, influenced by the black-figured techniques of Corinth: **Rhodes** and the **Cyclades** produced some of the best.

500–380 BC: Classical

Dominating the Aegean, **Athens** sucked up the artistic talent in Greece, culminating with the mathematical perfection of the **Parthenon**, the greatest of all Doric temples, built without a single straight line. Nothing on the islands comes close, but there are a few Classical sites to visit, starting with holy **Délos**. **Liménas** on **Thássos** and **Erétria** on **Évia**, and **Líndos**, **Kámiros** and **Ialysós** on **Rhodes**.

380–30 BC: Hellenistic

This era brought stylistic influences from the eastern lands conquered by Alexander the Great and his successors. Compared to aloof Classical perfection, Hellenistic sculpture adopts a more emotional, Baroque approach, all windswept drapery, violence and passion, such as the Louvre's *Winged Victory* from **Samothráki**'s **Sanctuary of the Great Gods**. Powerful **Rhodes** produced its long-gone **Colossus** and the writhing *Laocoön* (in the Vatican museum) and Aphrodites (including Durrell's *Marine Venus*) in the Rhodes museum. Houses became plush, many decorated with mosaics and frescoes as in the commercial town of **Délos** and in the suburbs of **Kos**.

30 BC–AD 529: Roman

The Pax Romana ended the rivalries between the Greek city-states and dried up their sources of inspiration, although sculptors and architects found a ready market in Rome, cranking out copies of Classic and Hellenistic masterpieces. The Romans built little in Greece: the **Stoa** and **Theatre of Herodes Atticus** (AD 160) were the last large monuments erected in ancient Athens. On the islands, the most important site is **Górtyna**, on **Crete**, the Roman capital of the island and Libya.

527–1460: Byzantine

The Byzantines revealed their stylistic distinction under the reign of Justinian (527–65), while the post-Justinian period saw a golden age in the splendour of Ag. Sofia in Istanbul and the churches of Ravenna, Italy. On the islands you'll find only the remains of simple three-naved basilicas – with two exceptions: the

6th-century **Ekatontapylianí** of **Páros** and 7th-century **Ag. Títos** at Górtyna, **Crete**. After the austere, puritanical Iconoclasm (726–843) the Macedonian painting style infiltrated the Greek provinces. The Roman basilica plan was replaced with a central Greek cross crowned by a dome, elongated in front by a vestibule (narthex) and outer porch (exonarthex) and at the back by a choir and three apses. Two of these churches, **Dafní** near Athens and **Néa Moní** on **Chíos**, are decorated with superb mosaics from the second golden age of Byzantine art, under the Comnenes (12th–14th centuries). This period marked a renewed interest in antique models: the stiff figures are given more naturalistic proportions. It also produced fine paintings: the 12th-century frescoes and manuscripts at the **Monastery of St John** on **Pátmos**, culminating in the early 13th-century church of **Kerá Panagía** at Kritsá, near Ag. Nikólaos, **Crete**. Crete's occupation by Venice after 1204 heralded an artistic cross-fertilization that developed into the Cretan school that in the 16th century produced Michail Damaskinos and El Greco.

What never changed was the intent of Byzantine art. Choreographed to a strict iconography, a Byzantine Christ and the Virgin *Panagía* reside on a purely spiritual and intellectual plane, miles away from Western art invented in the Renaissance 'based on horror, physical charm, infant-worship and easy weeping' as Patrick Leigh Fermor put it. Byzantine art never asks the viewer to relive the passion of Christ or coo over Baby Jesus; the holy figures never stray from their remote otherworldliness. And yet, in the last gasp of Byzantine art under the Paleologos emperors (14th–early 15th centuries), humanist and naturalistic influences produced the Byzantine equivalent of the late Gothic/early Renaissance painting in Italy, in Mistrás in the Peloponnese. After the Turkish conquest, painters fled to Mount Áthos, Zákynthos and Corfu, but none of their work radiates the same charm or confidence in the temporal world.

Turkish Occupation to the Present

The Turks left few important monuments in Greece. **Rhodes town**, followed by **Kos**, has the best surviving mosques and hammams. **Crete** and **Corfu** remained Venetian longer than most places, recalled by impressive fortifications and public buildings. Islands that had their own fleets, especially **Hýdra**, **Spétses** and **Sými**, have proud sea captains' mansions, while other islands continued traditional architectural styles, such as the whitewashed asymmetry of the **Cyclades**. Folk art thrived in this period and the collections in the island museums (especially **Skýros** and the Historical Museum of Heráklion, **Crete**) are worth a look.

In the 19th century, Athens and **Ermoúpolis**, **Sýros** (briefly Greece's chief port) were built in a simple but elegant neoclassical style. Grandiose neo-Byzantine churches appeared, while older ones were tarted up. The 1930s Rationalist/Art Deco public buildings left by the Italians in the **Dodecanese** are stylish (and are finally being restored). The islands did produce one painter of note: the delightful Theóphilos Hadzimichaíl (1873–1934) of **Lésvos** which has a museum of his works, that he exchanged for ouzo and lodging. Other islands such as **Rhodes**, **Crete** (Réthymnon) and **Ándros** boast excellent collections of modern art, and **Aegina** has something unique to see: a newfangled Camera Obscura.

Topics

O3

The Bull in the Calendar

...there too is Knossós, a mighty city, where Minos was king for nine years.
Homer, *The Odyssey*, book XIX

The so-called 'Toreador Fresco', found in the palace at Knossós, is a compelling icon of the lost world of ancient Crete. The sensual bare-breasted maidens who seem to be controlling the action are painted in white, the moon's colour, as in all Cretan frescoes, while the athlete vaulting through the bull's horns appears like all males in red, the colour of the sun. Mythology and archaeology begin to agree, and the roots of the story of Theseus, Ariadne and the Minotaur seem tantalizingly close at hand. When you see this fresco in Heráklion's Archaeology Museum, study the decorative border – four striped bands and a row of multicoloured lunettes. Neither Arthur Evans nor any archaeologist since noticed anything unusual about it. It was Charles F. Herberger, a professor in Maine (*The Thread of Ariadne*, Philosophical Library, New York, 1972), who discovered that this border is a complex ritual calendar, including the key to the myth of Theseus in the Labyrinth. The pairs of stripes on the tracks, alternately dark and light, for day and night, count on average 29 through each cycle of the five-coloured lunettes, representing the phases of the moon – this is the number of days in a lunar month. By counting all the stripes on the four tracks, Herberger found that each track gives roughly the number of days in a year; the whole, when doubled, totals exactly the number of days in an eight-year cycle of 99 lunar months, a period in which the solar and lunar years coincide – the marriage of the sun and moon.

To decipher the calendar, you can't simply count in circuits around the border; there are regular diagonal jumps to each new row, giving the course of the eight-year cycle the form of a rectangle with an 'x' in it. The box with the 'x' is intriguing, a motif in the art of the Minoans and other ancient peoples as far afield as the Urartians of eastern Anatolia. A Cretan seal shows a bull apparently diving into a crossed rectangle of this sort, while a human figure vaults through his horns. It also

recalls the most common and enigmatic of all Minoan symbols, the double axe or *labrys*, echoed in signet-rings that show the 'x' between the horns of a bull, or between what appears to be a pair of crescent moons.

The home of the *labrys*, the axe that cuts two ways, is the labyrinth. Arthur Evans believed the enormous palace of Knossós itself to be the labyrinth, a pile so confusing that even a Greek hero would have needed Ariadne's golden thread to find his way through it. In the childhood of archaeology, men could read myths so literally as to think there was a tangible labyrinth, and perhaps even a Minotaur. Now, it seems more likely that the labyrinth was the calendar itself, the twisting path that a Minos (generic name for Cretan priest-kings, representing the sun) followed in his eight-year reign before his rendezvous with the great goddess. This meeting may originally have meant his death and replacement by another Theseus. Later it would have been simply a ceremony of remarriage to the priestess that stood in the transcendent goddess' place, celebrated by the bull-vaulting ritual. It has been claimed that the occasion was also accompanied by popular dancing, following the shape of the labyrinth, where the dancers proceeded in a line holding a cord – Ariadne's thread. Homer said 'nine years', and other sources give nine years as the period after which the Athenians had to send their captives to Crete to be devoured by the Minotaur – it's a common ancient confusion, really meaning 'until the ninth', in the way the French still call the interval of a week *huit jours*. Whatever this climax of the Minoan cycle was, it occurred with astronomical precision according to the calendar, and followed a rich, layered symbolism difficult for us scoffing moderns to comprehend.

That the Minoans had such a complex calendar should be no surprise – these people managed modern plumbing and three-storey apartment blocks, while still finding time to rule the seas of the eastern Mediterranean. The real attraction lies not in the intricacies of the calendar (many other peoples had equally interesting ones) but in the scene in the middle, where the diagonals cross and where the ancient science translates into celebration, into dance. No other art of antiquity displays such an irresistible grace and joy, qualities which must have come from a profound appreciation of the beauties and rhythms of nature – the rhythms captured and framed in the ancient calendar.

Endangered Animals and Plain Old Pests

In spite of living in one of the most stunningly beautiful countries in the world, the Greeks as a whole have only recently taken any interest in nature. When Western Europe was busy discovering the great outdoors in the Romantic era, Greece was fighting for survival; when the rest of the West was promoting environmental awareness in the 1970s, most Greeks, still pulling themselves out of poverty, only saw the land as something to exploit. Even when well-meaning laws were passed forbidding building on forested land, Greek property-owners were not deterred – they just burned the forest. Laws limiting industrial fishing and dynamiting are still constantly flouted – demand for fish has drained the Aegean's key resource by nearly 60 per cent in recent years.

The quest for tourism's fast bucks has been responsible for much of the damage, the sprawl and ugliness on many a Greek coast, but tourism's concerns have also led to a much cleaner Greece, which now proudly claims the most Blue Flag beaches in Europe. Nor are beaches the be-all and end-all they used to be. Solar and wind power provide a hefty portion of the islands' electricity. Litter has declined a thousandfold in the past thirty years. Eco-tourism is growing on islands such as Lésvos, which is a major stepping stone on migratory paths – swallows, storks, pelicans, herons, egrets and a wide variety of indigenous birds – and even on small, forward-looking islands such as Tílos. Old mule paths and *kalderími* are being restored and waymarked (including a new cross-island path on Corfu) to allow visitors to explore Greece's mountains and gorges, and its wild flowers (6,000 native species) and butterflies.

Attempts to save the most endangered animals on Greek shores have resulted in two National Marine Parks – for the rarest mammal on earth, the monk seal on the islets around Alónissos (*see* p.613) and for the loggerhead turtle on Zákynthos (*see* p.526). Yet in spite of the hoopla, government planning and funding have been disappointing, and for the most part successes have been thanks to dedicated volunteers.

As for creatures unfortunately not on the endangered list, the mosquito tops the list for pure incivility. Pick up an inexpensive electric mosquito repellent. Greek mosquitoes don't spread malaria, but their sand-fly cousins can occasionally cause a nasty parasite infection. Wasps, especially on the lusher islands, will appear out of nowhere to nibble your baklava. Pests also lurk in the sea: harmless pale brown jellyfish (*méduses*) drift everywhere depending on winds and currents, but the oval transparent *tsoúchtres* are stinging devils; pharmacies sell soothing unguents. Sea urchins live by rocky beaches, and if you step on one, it hurts like hell (swimming shoes do offer some protection). The spines may break and embed themselves deeper if you try to force them out; the Greeks recommend olive oil, a big pin and a lot of patience. Less common but more dangerous, the *drákena*, dragon (or weever) fish, with a poisonous spine, hides in the sand. If you step on one, you'll feel a mix of pain and numbness and should go the doctor for an injection. Greece's shy scorpions hide in between the rocks in rural areas, but their sting is no more painful than a bee's. The really lethal creatures are rare: several species of small shy viper live in old stone walls, but only come out occasionally to sun themselves.

On *Kéfi*, Music and Dancing

As a general rule, the far corners of Europe are the most fun – the Irish, Spaniards and Greeks are among the last who still make their own music and dance to it spontaneously without feeling the least bit self-conscious or *folklorique*. All have words to describe the mood, the high spirit that comes over you: the *craic* in Ireland, the ecstatic *duende* of Spain, and the *kéfi* in Greece. For a Greek to give his all, he must have *kéfi*; to dance without it could be considered dishonest. The dancers performing at a 'Greek Night' taverna for tourists don't have it. Two craggy fishermen in a smoky *kafeneíon*, who hear an old song on the radio and dance for their own pleasure, do. So does an entire village at Easter, when everyone joins hands to dance a *kalamatianó*.

Greek music has been influenced by Italy (notably on the Ionian islands), Turkey, the Middle East and the Balkans, all of whom were once influenced by the Byzantines, who heard it from ancient Greeks, who heard it from the Phrygians – and so on. Traditional island songs, *nisiótika*, often heard at saint's days or weddings, are played on bagpipes (*tsamboúna*), clarinet (*klaríno*), but mostly on stringed instruments – the *laoúto* (a large mandolin, used for backing, traditionally picked with an eagle's quill), the three-string *lýra*, held upright on the knee, played on Crete and Kárpathos, the *violí* (violin), the *kítara* (guitar) and the double-stringed hammer dulcimer (*sandoúri*).

Greece's most famous composer, Míkis Theodorákis, often sets modern Greek poetry to music, but even current Greek pop has surprisingly poetic moments. It owes much of its origins to *rembétika*, the 'Greek blues', brought over and developed by the more 'sophisticated' Asia Minor Greeks after 1922, who in their longing and homesickness haunted the hashish dens of Athens and Piraeus. *Rembétika* introduced the *bouzoúki*, the long-necked metallic string instrument that dominates Greek music today, to the extent that nightclubs are called *bouzoúkia*, where singers croon throbbing, passionate music that offers Greeks (or at least those who can afford to go) some of the catharsis that ancient tragedies brought their ancestors.

Summer festivals and weddings are the places to see traditional dancing. Cretan dances are among the most ancient and vigorous, fuelled by massive intakes of *raki*; the *pedektó* demands furious steps, which resound under tall Cretan boots. Novice dancers would do better starting with a *syrtó*, with a slow shuffling pace throughout, or perhaps the *kalamatianó*, a 12-step *syrtó*, the national dance for many people; everyone joins in, holding hands at shoulder-level, while men and women take turns improvising steps. Nearly as common is the dignified *tsamikó*, where the leader and the next dancer in line hold the ends of a handkerchief. Women often shine in the *tsíphte téli*, a free-spirited belly dance – but as often as not men steal the show. Other dances are also normally performed by men. The *zeybékiko* is a serious, deliberate, highly charged solo dance with outstretched arms, evoking the swooping flight of the eagle; a companion will go down on one knee to encourage the dancer, hiss like a snake and clap out the rhythm. An introspective dance from the soul, the performer will always keep his eyes lowered; because it's private, you must never applaud. Another intense dance, the *hasápiko*, or butchers' dance, is better known as the Zorba dance in the West. The *syrtáki* is more exuberant, traditionally performed by two or three men, often to the *rembétika* tune; the leader signals the steps and it requires some practice but is well worth learning – as Alan Bates discovered, when he finally began to fathom *kéfi* from Anthony Quinn at the end of the film *Zorba the Greek*.

An Orthodox Life

A vast majority of Greeks belong to the Orthodox church. In fact, Orthodoxy is so fundamental to Greek identity that only the greatest sceptics can conceive of marrying outside the church, or neglecting to baptize their children, even though civil marriages were made valid by the Socialists in the 1980s.

One reason for this deep-seated national feeling is that, unlike everything else in Greece, Orthodoxy has scarcely changed since the founding of the Church by Emperor Constantine in the 4th century. As Constantinople took the place of Rome as the political and religious capital of the empire, the Greeks believe their church to be the only true successor to the church of Rome. Therefore, a true Greek is called a *Romiós* or Roman, and the Greek language is sometimes called *Roméika*. The Orthodox Church is considered perfect and eternal; if it weren't, its adherents could not expect to be saved. The Greeks have been spared the changes that have rocked the West, from Vatican II and discussions over female clergy and married priests to political questions of abortion and birth control.

This determination to never change explains the violence of Iconoclasm, the one time someone tried to tinker with the rules. Back in the early 8th century, Byzantine Emperor Leo III, shamed by what his Muslim neighbours labelled idolatry, deemed the images of divine beings to be sacrilegious. This opened up the first major rift with Rome, and it worsened in 800 when the Patriarch of Rome (aka the Pope) crowned Charlemagne as emperor, usurping the position of the Emperor of Constantinople. Further divisions arose over the celibacy of the clergy (Orthodox priests may marry before they are ordained) and the use of the phrase *filioque* ('and the son'), in the Holy Creed. This phrase caused the final, fatal schism in 1054 when the Papal legate Cardinal Humbert excommunicated the Patriarch of Constantinople and the Patriarch excommunicated the Pope. Ever since then, the Orthodox hierarchy has kept a patriarchal throne vacant, ready for the day when the Pope returns to his senses. The Turks tolerated the Orthodox Church (Christians had to pay more taxes), and had the political astuteness to impart considerable powers to the Patriarch. The church preserved Greek tradition, education and identity during Ottoman rule, but it also left Greece a deeply conservative country and often abused its power. According to an old saying, priests, headmen and Turks were the three curses of Greece.

The fantastic number of churches on the islands (many claim to have 365) has little to do with the priests, however. Nearly all were built by individuals, to keep a vow or to thank a saint for service rendered. Most are locked up thanks to light-fingered tourists and have only one service a year, on the saint's day. This could also be cause for a celebration or *panegýri*, with a feast, market, music and dancing the night before or after the church service. Apart from Easter, the Assumption of the Virgin (15 August) is the biggest holiday in Greece. The faithful sail to Tínos and other centres connected with Mary, making mid-August a very busy time to travel.

Orthodox weddings are a lovely if long-winded ritual. White crowns, bound together by ribbon, are placed over the heads of bride and groom by the *koumbáros*, or best man, as they are led around the altar three times, in the 'Dance of Isaiah' as guests enthusiastically lambast them with rice and flower petals. Often on islands, the whole village is invited to the feast; in the old days, they could last up to five days.

Baptisms are cause for similar celebration. The priest immerses the baby in the Holy Water three times (unlike Achilles, there are no vulnerable spots on modern Greeks). Although the custom is fading, you can still see babies wearing a *filaktó*, or amulet, the omnipresent blue glass eye bead. Compliments to the parents should be kept to a minimum: the gods do get jealous, so much so that many babies are given pet names until they're christened, to fool supernatural ill-wishers.

Funerals in Greece are carried out within 24 hours of death. The dead are buried for three to seven years, after which time the bones are often exhumed and placed in an ossuary; *aforismós*, or excommunication, is believed to prevent the body decaying after death. Memorials take place three, nine, 40 days and a year after death, when sweet buns and *koúliva* (sugared grains) are given out. But for all the trappings of Christianity, the spirit of Charon, the ferryman of death and personification of inexorable nature, is never far away, as expressed in a famous dirge:

Why are the mountains dark and why so woe-begone?
Is the wind at war there, or does the rain storm scourge them?
It is not the wind at war there, it is not the rain that scourges,
It is only Charos passing across them with the dead;
He drives the youths before him, the old folk drag behind,
And he bears the tender little ones in a line at his saddle-bow.
The old men beg a grace, the young kneel to impore him,
'Good Charos, halt in the village, or halt by some cool fountain,
That the old men may drink water, the young men play at the stone-throwing,
And that the little children may go and gather flowers.'
'In never a village will I halt, nor yet by a cool fountain,
The mothers would come for water, and recognize their children,
The married folk would know each other, and I should never part them.'

The *Períptero* and the Plane Tree

In Greece you'll see it everywhere, the greatest of modern Greek inventions, the indispensable *períptero*. It is the best-equipped kiosk in the world, a substitute bar, selling everything from water to cold beer; an emergency pharmacy stocked with aspirin, mosquito-killers and condoms; a convenient newsagent for publications, from *Ta Néa* to *Die Zeit*; a tourist shop offering maps, postcards and stamps; a toy shop and general store for shoelaces, cigarettes, batteries and film. In Athens they're at most traffic lights. On the islands they are a more common sight than a donkey. You'll wonder how you ever survived before *perípteros* and the treasures they contain.

The other great meeting centre of Greek life is the mighty plane tree, or *plátanos*. The Greeks believe that plane shade is wholesome and beneficial: one of the most extraordinary sights in the islands is 'Hippocrates' plane tree' on Kos, propped up on scaffolding and protected as a national monument. In Greek the expression '*cheréte mou ton plátano*' loosely translates as 'go tell it to the marines', presumably because the tree has heard all that nonsense before. The *plátanos* represents the village's identity; the tree is a source of life, and only grows near abundant fresh water, its deep roots a symbol of stability and continuity – a huge, majestic umbrella, as even the rain cannot penetrate its sturdy leaves. Sit under its spreading branches and sip coffee as the morning unfolds; the temptation to linger for the day is irresistible.

Lamp Chops and Sweat Coffee

Greeks often speak excellent English. It's not only mandatory in school, but many students take private lessons as well. Older islanders have spent time in America or Australia. Their dislike of, and incompetence at, dubbing means television shows are usually in English with Greek subtitles.

Which makes the devoted observer of Greek ways suspect that English mistakes on taverna menus are no accident, but rather part of a plot to keep tourists amused and coming back for more Lamp Chops, Sandwitches, Stuffed Vine Lives, and Beet Poots. Some offer Harmbougger, but perhaps it's best to stick with dishes the Greeks do well: Staffed Tomatoes, Souvlaki Privates, Grumps Salad, T-Buogne Rum Stake and Veal Gogglets, or vegetable dishes such as Zucchini Bulls, Cheek Pees, or perhaps Grass Hill (a small mound of boiled greens). On Skópelos, you can smack your lips over a Rude Sausage; on Páros, you can ponder where your parents went wrong over a Freud Juice; cannibals can find solace at a place on Kos where 'We Serve Hot Tasty Friendly Family!' Then it's off to the Snake Bar for a Sweat Coffee, before driving off in your Fully Incurable Rent-a-Care from the Vague Travel Agency of Piraeus.

A Traditional Greek Island Calendar

If the Greek islands were on the cutting edge of European culture from 3000 BC to 500 BC, the past thousand years have shoved them into such obscurity that they were until recently goldmines for students of old customs and beliefs, which are now quickly dying out in the face of rural depopulation, tourism and television. Some customs linger – St Basil (Ag. Vassiléos), the Greek Santa Claus, still comes from Caesarea on New Year's Eve with gifts (rather than on Christmas Day); coins are still baked in pies called *vassilopíta*.

Since ancient times **January** has also been associated with the Fates; everyone gambles on New Year's Day to see what the year will bring. In Crete, water would be brought from a spring where the Fates have bathed; pomegranates, symbols of abundance, were smashed on thresholds. On 6 January, Epiphany (*Theofánia*, or *Ta Fóta*, the feast of lights, Christ's baptism), houses are sprinkled with holy water, and ashes from the hearth, kept ablaze since Christmas to ward off goblins (the *kallikántzaroi*), are scattered for good luck; the priest tosses a crucifix in the sea, and young men dive after it, hoping to be the lucky finder.

One of **February**'s names, Flevarius, suggests opening of veins (*fleva*) of water; a dry February means Greece is in for a drought. Olive groves are ploughed in **March**, a variable month with strange nicknames – the Five-Minded, the Grumbler, the Flayer and *Paloukokáftis*, 'the Burning Pale'. The first swallows come back on Annunciation Day; in Chálki they were greeted with 2,000-year-old Swallow Songs.

On Rhodes, **April** was called the Goggler; food supplies would run low, leaving everyone 'goggle-eyed' – hungry. Conveniently, most people are fasting anyway, for Lent. Wild flowers are gathered to decorate the Good Friday *Epitáphios*, or bier of Christ; the flowers or candles used in the service were in demand for their power against the evil eye. Easter eggs are dyed red, and just after midnight, when the priest announces the Resurrection (*Christós Anésti!* 'Christ has risen!'), general pandemonium breaks out as bells ring, fireworks explode and people embrace. On Corfu women smash old crockery, symbolizing the shattering of death; on Kálymnos and Sými men throw dynamite. Families return home with lighted candles and tuck into *magirítsa*, a soup made of lamb's tripe that soothes the stomach after the Lenten fast. On Easter Day everyone feasts on spit-roast lamb, drinking, singing and dancing into the night.

May is the month of flowers, when the dead are granted a brief return to earth between Easter and Whitsun. In ancient times temples would be purified and it's bad luck to lend anything or be married. On 1 May it's important to get up early and eat garlic before the first donkey brays or the first cuckoo sings to avoid being made asinine or a cuckold. Everyone goes to the countryside to 'fetch the May' and make garlands to bring spring's blessing to the house. On Ándros a pig's tongue is cooked to ward off backbiting. In **June** bonfires are lit for St John's Eve and the young people leap over the flames. As the year changes with the summer solstice, so does luck. A once widespread custom is the *kledónas* 'prophecy': water is drawn by girls named Maria to fill an urn, into which everyone deposits a personal item and makes a wish. The water is left open to the stars and on St John's Day, as the wishes are recited, a Maria pulls the items out; the owner of each item as it is drawn gets the wish being sung at the moment, usually leading to great hilarity.

Hot **July** is the month for threshing. On 17 July, songs summon Ag. Marína to cure the bites and stings of snakes, scorpions and insects; on 20 July it's the turn of Elijah (Profítis Ilías), the saint of mountaintop chapels, who inherited Zeus' meteorological tasks, controlling the rain, winds and sun. Cretans say anyone who sees a headless shadow at noon will not survive the year. **August** is known as the Vintner, or the Fig-gatherer and is sacred to the Virgin, who has feast days on the 15, 23 and 31 (her birthday) and it's the best month to eat mackerel, fruit and vegetables. However, the first six days, the *Drymes*, are unlucky, associated with nymphs who make hair fall out if it's washed or combed. The Assumption of the Virgin on 15 August is celebrated everywhere but especially on Tínos, Lésvos (Agiássos), Astypália, Sámos and Kefaloniá (Markópoulo).

September is the month of wine-making. In Byzantine times (and on the Orthodox ecclesiastical calendar) 1 September was New Year's Day, when St Michael gets out his book and notes all the souls he will take during the coming year. On Kos children made New Year's garlands of garlic, grapes, pomegranates and a leaf from Hippocrates' plane tree; on Crete people would put a walnut on their roof at midnight and judge their chances for survival for the next year by the kernel. **October** usually has the first rains but generally fine weather; a Greek Indian summer is the 'little summer of Ag. Dimítros'. Cranes fly south to Africa, priests bless and open the first wine barrel.

November, 'the showery', signals the beginning of the olive harvests. Flocks are brought down from the mountain pastures, and pancakes are made on the 30th for St Andrew, who is known as *Trypanoteganitís*, the 'frying pan piercer'; a good housewife would use all her frying pans that day to keep them from getting holes. **December** is called 'good morning, good evening' for its short days. Eating sweet things on 4 December, St Barbara's Day, was believed to ward off smallpox, and women hide their brooms and refrain from cooking beans. Her holiday elides with that of St Nikólaos on the 6th, the protector of sailors, when boats are decorated and blessed. Christmas Eve marks the beginning of the twelve-days when the demonic *kallikántzaroi* are afoot, but they can be kept at bay by not letting the hearth fire go out. Pigs are slaughtered for the Christmas meal. Among the many cakes are sweets made with flaky filo to represent Christ's swaddling clothes.

A Quick Guide to the Gods

Like all good polytheists, the ancient Greeks filled their pantheon with a colourful assortment of divinities, full of contradictions, subtleties and regional nuances. Every island has stories about their doings, myths that have become part of the baggage of western civilization; others read like strange collective dreams. But by Classical times the gods were rounded up and made to live on the sanitized heights of Mount Olympos as idols of patriarchal state religion. The meatier matters of birth, sex, death and a possible afterlife – the real religion – went underground in the mystery cults of Eleusis (near Athens) and the Great Gods on Samothráki.

The big cheese on Olympos was **Zeus** (Jupiter, to the Romans), a native of Crete, the great Indo-European sky god, lord of the thunderbolt with a libido to match. He was married to his sister **Hera** (Juno), a once-great goddess whose role in myth was reduced to that of the wronged, jealous wife, who periodically returned to Sámos to renew her virginity. Zeus' two younger brothers had their own realms: **Poseidon** (Neptune) ruled the sea (he had special sanctuaries on Póros, Tínos and Sýros), while **Hades** (Pluto) ruled the underworld and rarely left his dismal realm. Their sister was **Demeter** (Ceres), goddess of corn and growing things, who was worshipped in the mysteries of Eleusis. **Aphrodite** (Venus), the goddess of love, was born when Zeus overthrew their father **Cronus** (Saturn) by castrating him and tossing the bloody member in the sea foam. She landed at Kýthera but later preferred Cyprus.

The second generation of Olympians were the offspring of Zeus: **Athena**, the urbane virgin goddess of wisdom, born full-grown straight out of Zeus' brain and always associated with Athens; **Ares** (Mars), the whining bully god of war, disliked by the Greeks and associated with barbarian Thrace; **Hermes** (Mercury), the messenger, occasional trickster, and god of commerce; **Hephaistos** (Vulcan), the god of fire and the forge and metalworking, married to Aphrodite and worshipped on Límnos; **Apollo**, the god of light, music, reason, poetry and prophecy, worshipped on his birth island Délos, along with his twin sister **Artemis** (Diana), the often cruel virgin moon goddess of the hunt, who was also worshipped on Léros. Their half-brother **Dionysos** (Bacchus), the god of wine, orgies and theatre, was the favourite on Náxos. In addition to the canonical twelve, the Greeks had an array of other gods such as **Helios** (Sol), the sun god, whose special island has always been Rhodes, as well as nymphs, satyrs, and heroes, the greatest of which was, of course, **Herakles** (Hercules).

Food and Drink

04

*Life's fundamental principle is the satisfaction of the needs and wants of the
stomach. All important and trivial matters depend on this principle and cannot
be differentiated from it.*
Epicurus, 3rd century BC

Epicurus may have lent his name to gourmets, but in reality his philosophy
advocated maximizing simple pleasures: rather than continually seeking novelty,
Epicurus suggests making bread and olives taste sublime by fasting for a couple of
days. In that way Greeks have long been epicureans: centuries of poverty taught
them to relish food more than 'cuisine'. What has changed, especially on the
islands, is that cuisine has arrived. Tourist demand is partly responsible, but so is
the rise of a well-travelled generation of Greeks. Fusion and 'Mediterranean
creative' are the rage, with a broad Italian slant: the popular islands also have
Chinese, Tex-Mex, Thai, Indian, Japanese and even Turkish restaurants to keep
food fatigue at bay.

Of course most restaurants are still Greek, serving fish from the seas, lamb, fresh
herbs and honey from the mountains, wild young greens from the hills, olives, fruits
and vegetables from the family patch. Many dishes are prepared early in the day,
then allowed to sit to enhance their natural flavours. One criticism levelled at Greek
food is that it's served tepid; on hot days, Greeks believe, it's better for the digestion.

It used to be that the hardest foods to find were native island dishes, many of
which make ingenious use of meagre resources – recipes often tainted in Greek
minds with poverty. Under the leadership of a few inquisitive chefs, this, however,
is changing; traditional dishes are undergoing a delightful revival on many islands.

Greek Dishes

Many Greek dishes need no introduction – *tárama*, moussaka, *gýros*, feta, retsina,
Greek yoghurt and baklava have achieved the universality of lasagne and chicken
tikka. A typical meal begins with bread (usually excellent) and starters (*mezédes*) to
be communally shared: olives, tzatziki (cucumbers and yoghurt), prawns, *tíro saláta*
(feta cheese dip), *koponistá* (pungent smoked or salted fish), roasted sweet peppers,
cheese or spinach pies, meatballs, or *saganáki* (fried cheese sprinkled with lemon).
These are followed (often within minutes) by a shared salad and potatoes, and your
own main course. This could be a gorgeously fresh omelette, or an oven dish or
stew (called 'ready dishes') such as moussaka, *pastítsio* (cooked macaroni, layered
with ground meat, cheese, cream and topped with béchamel sauce), roast lamb or
chicken, *makaroniá* (spaghetti with meat sauce), *yemistá* (stuffed tomatoes or
peppers), *stifádo* (spiced beef stew with baby onions), *lagostifádo* (rabbit stew,
similar but flavoured with orange), *kokinistó* (beef cooked with tomatoes and a hint
of cinnamon), lamb or veal *youvétsi* (baked with tomatoes and with teardrop
pasta), *chirinó me sélino* (pork with wild celery, in egg and lemon sauce), or *kréas
stin stámna* (lamb or beef baked in a clay dish). Meats grilled to order are *tis óras*
('the On-Times') – pork chops (*brizóles*), lamb cutlets (*paidákia*), kebabs (*souvláki*),
minced steak (*biftéki*), meatballs (*keftédes* or *sousoukákia*), sausage (*lukániko*), or
grilled chicken (*koutópoulo skára*).

Vegetarian Dishes

Of all the people in the EU, the Greeks now eat the most meat per capita, but they also eat the most cheese, more than even the French, and follow only the Italians in eating pasta. Vegetarians (*chortofágos*) won't go hungry either. Because of the demands of Orthodox fasts (which forbid animal and dairy products), Greece has many traditional dishes: *gigántes* (butter beans in tomato sauce), bean soups (*fasoláda*), ratatouille-like *laderá* (vegetables cooked in olive oil), salads, sometimes enlivened with *kápari* (pickled caper plant), *patzária* (beetroot drizzled with olive oil and vinegar), *yemistá* (peppers or tomatoes stuffed with rice), *briáms* (potato and aubergine/courgette, baked with olive oil), *imams* (aubergine stuffed with tomato and onion), *keftédes* (vegetable fritters of carrot, tomato, chickpeas to courgette, which are the most popular but also the hardest-to-pronounce *kolokythiakeftédes*), *dolmádes* (rice and dill-filled vine leaves), or potatoes roasted with lemon, olive oil and garlic; tavernas offer endless chips, although of late many use frozen. *Skordaliá*, the classic garlic dip, is made with puréed potatoes and olive oil.

Seafood is relatively expensive (blame overfishing) but you can usually find reasonably priced whitebait (*marídes*), fresh sardines (*sardínas*) and squid rings (*kalamári*). Baked or fried *bakaliáros* (cod) is always a treat and shouldn't break the bank. Some places serve soups – *psarósoupa* (with potatoes and carrots) or spicy tomato-based *kakávia*, a meal in themselves with hunks of bread and a bottle of wine. Prawns (*garídes*) are lightly fried or baked with garlic, tomatoes and feta as *garídes saganáki*, a dish invented in the 1960s; spaghetti with lobster (*astakomakaronáda*) is another recent addition to many Greek menus. Note that fish is usually priced by the kilo, so negotiate for the portion you want.

Desserts are rare; Greeks make lovely sweets, puddings, cakes and ice creams but tend to eat them in the late afternoon, after the siesta.

Greek Restaurants

On the popular islands, there are plenty of places offering breakfasts, lunches and dinners at familiar hours for visitors, but you may find getting into the Greek pace of life more enjoyable. This means a light **breakfast**, supplemented **mid-morning** with a cheese pie (*tirópita*). At 2 or 3pm, indulge in a long al fresco **lunch** with wine, followed by a siesta or *mesiméri* to avoid the scorching afternoon heat. Get up at 6 or 7pm for a swim and an ice cream. Around 8pm, it's time for a *vólta*, or stroll and a sunset drink, while deciding where to go. Greeks rarely eat before 10pm and meals can go on into the small hours. Children are welcome in restaurants (they too nap in the afternoon).

The sociable Greeks eat out more than most Europeans, and it's only recently that they've paid much attention to the food (witness all the cookery shows and celebrity chefs on Greek television). *Estiatória* (restaurants) are formal; *tavernas* are more casual and numerous, and can range from beach shacks to barn-like affairs with live music; waiters will reel off what's available and, if there's a written menu, home-made translations may leave you baffled and amused (*see* **Topics**, p.40). *Mezedopoleíons* specialize in tapas-like *mezédes*, served with ouzo, *rakí*, beer or wine. Of late, there's been a revival of the old-fashioned cookshop or *mageireftá* (μαγειρευτά) with pots simmering on the stove and casseroles such as moussaka.

At the seaside fish tavernas, *psarotavérnes*, specialize in all kinds of seafood – some of the best of these are owned by fishermen. Most carry a meat dish or two for fish-haters who get dragged along. *Psistariá* on the other hand specialize in charcoal-grilled meats. A *hasapotavérna* is a restaurant attached to a butcher's shop, often with carcasses strung up and waiters in bloodstained aprons for added carnivorous effect.

Bakeries (*artopoleíon*) sell sweet and savoury hot pies. For pastries, cakes, baklava and desserts, look in any *zacharoplasteío*.

Kafeneíons and Cafés

Every village has a *kafeneíon*: a coffee house but, more importantly, a gathering place to discuss the latest news, read the papers, play cards and incidentally drink coffee. Some men seem to live in them. They are so essential that some villages have municipal *kafeneíon*. The bill of fare features thick Greek **coffee** (*café ellinikó*), prepared in 40 different ways, although *glykó* (sweet), *métrio* (medium) and *skéto* (no sugar) are the basic orders. It is always served with a cold glass of water. Thanks to the influx of Italians, you can often get a good espresso. 'Nes' (aka instant Nescafé) has become a Greek word, and comes either hot or whipped and iced as a frappé. Soft drinks, brandy, beer and ouzo round out the old-style *kafeneíon* fare. Newer cafés often serve full English breakfasts, sandwiches, crêpes, yoghurt and honey – just about anything.

Bars (*Barákia*) and Ouzeries

Even the smallest island has at least one summer music bar, coming to life at cocktail hour and again at midnight; closing times vary but dawn isn't unusual in the summer. In general, bars are not cheap and drinks are sometimes outrageously dear by Greek standards, although measures are often triples by British standards. If in doubt stick to **beer** (Amstel or Heineken, although Greece has its own brand, the slightly sweet Mýthos), ouzo, *soúma* (like ouzo, but sweeter), wine and Metaxá.

A grand old Greek institution, the ouzerie, features the national *apéritif*, **ouzo** (the *rakí* drunk by the Byzantines and Venetians, renamed ouzo in the 18th century from the Latin *usere*, 'usable'). Clear and anise-flavoured, it is served in tall glasses or a *karafáki* holding three or four doses which habitués dilute and cloud with water or ice. If you dislike aniseed, the Greeks also make an unflavoured **grappa** – *tsikoúdia* or *rakí*). Ouzo is traditionally served with *mezédes*; for an assortment, ask for a *pikilía*.

Wine

Greece has 300 different indigenous vines, and there could well be something to the myths that wine was invented here. Despite this big head start, the average Greek wine was long that – average, if not wretched. This has changed dramatically in the past few decades: better education, foreign expertise and modern techniques have improved many wines dramatically; even humble Deméstica bears little resemblance to the rough stuff that earned it unflattering nicknames. Besides the island wines (*see* box, opposite), don't miss some of the country's noble reds – Náoussa, Nemea, or Limnio – a variety mentioned by Aristotle. A good *káva*, or wine shop, will stock them. In a typical taverna, the wine list will probably be very short (most people just opt for the house wine). It's even getting hard to find that Greek classic, **retsína**, with its distinctive piney taste so suited to Greek food. The ancient Greeks stored their wine in amphorae sealed with resin; the disintegration of the resin helped prevent oxidation and lent the wine its unique flavour (now supplied by pieces of resin). Order draught retsina (*retsína varelísio*) if it's on offer; Kourtaki is a reliable bottled variety.

Traditionally, retsína or any house wine (or loose wine, *krasí chíma*) comes in chilled copper-anodized cans, by the kilo (about a litre), or *misó kiló* (half) or *tetárto* (250ml) and is served in tumblers. If you're in doubt, start with a *tetárto* – you can always order more (or not). In summer, the reds often come as chilled as the whites. When eating with Greeks, keep topping up your companions' glasses, while drinking toasts – *Stín yámass*, good health to us, or, in Crete, *Avíva* or *Áspro páto* – bottoms up.

Wines of the Greek Islands

Some island wines are quite unusual: Santoríni's Gaia, for instance, offers a wine called Thalassitis, inspired by an ancient Greek wine that was mixed with a dollop of sea water. The most common varietals on the islands are:

Aidani: Somewhat rarified white grape found on the Aegean islands, especially Santoríni and known for its flowery bouquet.

Assyrtiko: One of Greece's best white grapes, the base for AO Santoríni (*see* p.310). Because the grapes adopt the character of the soil, the wines come in a surprising variety of styles – fruity, crispy or even slightly smoky.

Athiri: An Aegean grape often blended with Assyrtiko; makes fragrant, lemony white wines, the base of AO Rhodes.

Kotsifali: Sweet and spicy red grape unique to Archánes and Péza on Crete; it's blended with the Mandelaria for colour.

Liatiko: Red grape grown on the Aegean islands and on Crete, where it yields AO Daphnes and Sitía. The name comes from 'July', when these grapes ripen.

Malvazia: Grown on Páros and Sýros, this white grape from Monemvasía in the Peloponnese was used to make the popular sweet wine, malvasia or 'malmsey' imported by the Venetians to Europe. Modern wines have a peachy, aromatic tone.

Mandelaria: Ancient almost black grape, used for blending with grapes low in tannins. On Rhodes, where it's sometimes known as Amorgiano, it is used by itself.

Mavrodaphne: Named after the grape, Mavro, and a beautiful grape picker named Daphne, who died before the wine maker who employed her could tell her he loved her. Grown Kefaloniá, it yields delicious rich, velvet wines like port.

Muscat: Like Assyrtiko, a white grape produced in a vast range of styles from dry to dessert wines. Grown on Kefaloniá, Rhodes and Sámos, for both a dry white and a lovely dessert wine with ripe apricot nuances named after the island.

Robola: A grape of extremely low yields, unique to the mountain sides of Kefaloniá (*see* p.486), producing an excellent fragrant, bone-dry white wine.

Savatiano: The most common variety grown in Attica and Évia, yielding the light white wines made into retsina. Also a soft fruity white wine.

Villana: Indigenous to Péza on Crete; produces that area's crisp white AO wines.

The Greek Menu (Katálogos)

Ορεκτικά (Μεζέδες)	Orektiká (Mezédes)	Appetisers
τζατζίκι	tzatziki	yoghurt and cucumbers
ελιές	eliés	olives
κοπανιστί (τυροσαλάτα)	kopanisti (tirosaláta)	cheese purée, often spicy
ντολμάδες	dolmáthes	stuffed vine leaves
μελιτζανοσαλατα	melitzanosaláta	eggplant (aubergine) dip
σαγανάκη	saganáki	fried cheese with lemon
ποικιλία	pikilía	mixed hors d'œuvres
μπουρεκι	bouréki	cheese and vegetable pie
τυροπιττα	tirópitta	cheese pie
αχινοί	achini	sea urchin roe (quite salty)

Σούπες	Soópes	Soups
αυγολέμονο	avgolémono	egg and lemon soup
χορτόσουπα	chortósoupa	vegetable soup
ψαρόσουπα	psarósoupa	fish soup
φασολάδα	fasoláda	bean soup
μαγειρίτσα	magiritsa	giblets in egg and lemon
πατσάς	patsás	tripe and pig's foot soup (for late nights and hangovers)

Λάδερα	Ládera	'Cooked in Oil'
μπάμιες	bámies	okra, ladies' fingers
γίγαντες	yigantes	butter beans in tomato sauce
μπριαμ	briám	aubergines and mixed veg
φακής	fakés	lentils

Ζυμαρικά	Zimariká	Pasta and Rice
πιλάφι / ρύζι	piláfi/rízi	pilaf/rice
σπαγκέτι	spagéti	spaghetti
μακαρόνια	macarónia	macaroni
πλιγγούρι	plingoúri	bulgar wheat

Ψάρια	Psária	Fish
αστακός	astakós	lobster
αθερίνα	atherína	smelt
γάυρος	gávros	mock anchovy
καλαμάρια	kalamária	squid
κέφαλος	kéfalos	grey mullet
χταπόδι	chtapóthi	octopus
χριστόψαρο	christópsaro	John Dory
μπαρμπούνι	barboúni	red mullet
γαρίδες	garíthes	prawns (shrimps)
γοπα	gópa	bogue (boops boops)
ξιφίας	ksifías	swordfish
μαρίδες	maríthes	whitebait
συναγρίδα	sinagrítha	sea bream
σουπιές	soupiés	cuttlefish
φάγγρι	fángri	bream
κιδόνια	kidónia	cherrystone clams
σαρδέλλα	sardélla	sardines
μπακαλιάρος (σκορδαλιά)	bakaliáros (skorthaliá)	cod (with garlic sauce)
σαργός	sargós	white bream
σκαθάρι	skathári	black bream
στρείδια	strithia	oysters
λιθρίνια	lithrínia	bass
μίδια	mídia	mussels

Εντραδες	Entrádes	Main Courses
κουνέλι	kounéli	rabbit
στιφάδο	stifádo	casserole with onions
γιουβέτσι	yiouvétsi	meat baked with pasta
συκώτι	seekóti	liver
μουσκάρι	moskári	veal
αρνί	arní	lamb
κατσικι	katsíki	kid
κοτόπουλο	kotópoulo	chicken
χοιρινό	chirinó	pork

Κυμάδες	Kymádes	Minced Meat
παστίτσιο	pastítsio	mince and macaroni pie
μουσακά	moussaká	meat and aubergine baked with white sauce
μακαρόνια με κυμά	makarónia me kymá	spaghetti Bolognese
μπιφτέκι	biftéki	hamburger, usually bunless
σουτζουκάκια	soutzoukákia	meatballs in sauce
μελιτζάνες γεμιστές	melitzánes yemistés	stuffed aubergine/eggplant
πιπεριές γεμιστές	piperies yemistés	stuffed peppers

Της Ωρας	Tis Óras	Grills to Order
μπριζόλες χοιρινές	brizólas chirinés	pork chops
σουβλάκι	souvláki	meat on a skewer
κοκορέτσι	kokorétsi	offal kebabs
κοτολέτες	kotolétes	veal chops
παιδάκια	paidákia	lamb chops
κεφτέδες	keftéthes (th as in 'th')	meatballs

Σαλάτες	Salátes	Salads and Vegetables
ντομάτες	domátes	tomatoes
αγγούρι	angoúri	cucumber
ρώσσικη σαλάτα	róssiki saláta	Russian salad
σπανάκι	spanáki	spinach
χωριάτικη	choriátiki	tomato and cucumber salad with feta cheese and olives
κολοκυθάκια	kolokithákia	courgettes/zucchini
πιπεριεσ	piperiés	peppers
κρεμιδι	kremídi	onions
πατάτες	patátes	potatoes
παντσάρια	pantsária	beetroot
μαρούλι	maroúli	lettuce
χόρτα	chórta	wild greens
αγκινάρες	anginátes	artichokes
κουκιά	koukiá	fava beans

Τυρια	Tiriá	Cheeses
φέτα	féta	sheep's milk cheese
κασέρι	kasséri	hard buttery cheese
γραβιέρα	graviéra	Greek 'Gruyère'
μυζήθρα	mizíthra	soft white cheese

Γλυκά	Glyká	Sweets
παγωτό	pagotó	ice cream
κουραμπιέδες	kourabiéthes	sugared biscuits
λουκουμάδες	loukoumáthes	hot honey fritters
χαλβά	halvá	sesame seed sweet
μπακλαβά	baklavá	nuts and honey in filo pastry

γιαούρτι (με μελι)	yiaoúrti (me méli)	yoghurt (with honey)
καριδοπιτα	karidópita	walnut cake
μήλο	mílo	apple
μπουγάτσα	bougátsa	custard tart

Miscellaneous

ψωμί	psomí	bread
βούτυρο	voútiro	butter
μέλι	méli	honey
μαρμελάδα	marmelátha	jam
λάδι	láthi	oil
πιάτο	piáto	plate
λογαριασμό	logariasmó	the bill/check

Drinks

κρασί	krasí	wine
άσπρο/κόκκινο/κοκκινέλι	áspro/kókkino/kokkinéli	white/red/rosé
ρετσίνα	retsina	wine (resinated)/retsina
νερό (βραστο/μεταλικο)	neró (vrastó/metalikó)	water (boiled/mineral)
μπύρα	bíra	beer
χυμός πορτοκάλι	chimós portokáli	orange juice
γάλα	gála	milk
τσάί	tsái	tea
σοκολάτα	sokoláta	chocolate
καφέ	kafé	coffee
φραππέ	frappé	iced coffee
πάγος	págos	ice
ποτίρι	potíri	glass
μπουκάλι	boukáli	bottle
καράφα	karáfa	carafe
στήν γειά σας!	stín yiásas (formal, pl)	To your health! Cheers!
στήν γειά σου!	stín yiásou (sing)	

Planning Your Trip

05

Average Daily Temperatures in °C/°F

	Athens	Crete (Herákl'n)	Cyclades (Mýkonos)	Dodecs (Rhodes)	Ionian (Corfu)	N.E. Aeg (Mytilíni)	Saronic (Hýdra)	Sporades (Skýros)
Jan	11/48	12/54	12/54	12/54	10/50	10/50	12/53	10/51
April	16/60	17/62	17/60	17/60	15/60	16/60	16/61	15/58
July	28/82	26/78	25/76	27/78	27/78	27/80	28/82	25/77
Aug	28/82	26/78	25/76	27/79	27/78	27/80	28/82	25/77
Sept	25/76	25/76	23/74	25/78	23/74	23/74	25/76	22/71
Nov	15/58	18/64	17/62	17/66	15/58	15/58	17/62	15/58

When to Go

Climate

Greece enjoys hot, dry, clear and bright Mediterranean **summers**, cooled by winds, of which the *meltémi* from the northeast is the most likely to upset Aegean sailing schedules. In general the **wet season** begins in mid-October when it can rain 'tables and chairs' as the Greeks say. It begins to feel **springlike** in February, especially in Crete and Rhodes.

Festivals

Every village has its *panegýri*, or patron saint's festival, some celebrated merely with a special service, others with events culminating in a feast and music and dancing till dawn. Other events celebrate victories, liberation from the Turks, wine, music, theatre, sailing, sardines, sultanas – main ones are in the box below, and you'll find others listed in the text. For **national holidays**, *see p.64*.

Tourist Information

Greek National Tourist Offices

UK and Ireland: 4 Conduit Street, London W1S 2DJ, **t** (020) 7495 9300, *www.gnto.co.uk*.

USA: Olympic Tower, 645 Fifth Avenue, Suite 903, New York, NY 10022, **t** (212) 421 5777, *www.greektourism.com*.

Canada: 1500 Don Mills Road, Suite 102, Toronto, Ontario, M3B 3K4, **t** (416) 968 2220.

Australia and New Zealand: 37–49 Pitt Street, Sydney, NSW 2000, **t** (02) 9241 1663.

In Greece

The multilingual tourist information number in Athens, **t** 171, is good for all Greece (outside Athens, **t** 210 171). Many islands have local tourist offices or at least tourist police.

Calendar of Events

Feb Carnival, big celebrations in Réthymnon, Chíos, Lésvos (Agiássos), Zákynthos and Skýros.

Mar/April Easter; celebrations everywhere.

Late May Chaniá Festival, celebrating Crete's liberation.

June The *Miaoúlia*: Hýdra honours its great Admiral Miaoúlis.

June Eco-film Festival, Rhodes.

June–Sept Athens Festival: concerts, ballet, opera by international companies.

July Crete Wine Festival, Réthymnon.

Late July Pelákas Streetbeat Music, Corfu.

July–Aug Sými Festival: music, dance and film.

July–Sept *Hippocratia* culture festival, Kos.

Late July–Aug Ermoúpoleia Arts Festival, Sýros.

July–mid-Sept Heráklion Festival, Crete: music, theatre, dance.

First week Aug *Dionýsia*, wine, food and dance, Náxos.

Early Aug Wine festival, Sámos.

First 10 days Aug *Alindeia*, rowing and sea regattas, Léros.

Aug *Simonidia* cultural festival, Kéa.

First two weeks Aug *Elymnia* cultural festival, Límni (Évia).

Aug International Folklore Festival, Lefkáda.

Late Aug–Sept Réthymnon Renaissance Festival, Crete.

Early Sept International Festival of Sacred Music, Pátmos.

Sept Corfu Festival, classical music and ballet; chamber music is in late Sept/early Oct.

8 Sept (nearest weekend) The *Armáta*, Spétses – War of Independence re-enactment.

Late Oct Rock-climbing festival, Kálymnos.

Embassies and Consulates

Foreign Embassies in Athens

UK: 1 Ploutárchou St, **t** 210 727 2600. Also *see* Corfu Town, Rhodes and Heráklion (Crete).

USA: 91 Vassilías Sofías, **t** 210 721 2951.

Canada: 4 Ioan. Gennadíou, **t** 210 727 3400.

Ireland: 7 Vass. Konstantínou, **t** 210 723 2771. Also *see* Corfu Town.

Greek Embassies Abroad

UK: 1A Holland Park, London W11 3TP, **t** (020) 7229 3850, *www.greekembassy.org.uk.*

USA: 2217 Massachusetts Ave N.W., Washington DC 20008, **t** (202) 667 3169/ **t** (202) 939 1300, *www.greekembassy.org.*

Canada: 76–80 Maclaren Street, Ottawa, Ontario, K2P oK6, **t** (613) 238 6271, *www.greekembassy.ca.*

Ireland: 1 Upper Pembroke St, Dublin 2, **t** (01) 676 7254.

Entry Formalities

Passports and Visas

All **European Union** members can stay indefinitely. Most **non-EU tourists** entering Greece don't need a visa (including American, Australian, New Zealand and Canadian citizens) for stays of up to 90 days in Greece on presentation of a valid passport. Anyone staying in the Schengen zone beyond the 90-day period may be subject to a fine at the time of departure and will be barred from entry into any other Schengen country for 90 days. In Greece, fines for overstaying the three months run from €587 to a whopping €1,174. To stay longer, get a visa before you leave home or take your passport, photos and bank statements (or other proof that you can support yourself) and lots of money – €464 at the time of writing – 20 days before your time in Greece expires to the **Aliens Bureau**, 173 Leof. Alexándras, 11522 Athens, **t** 210 770 5711, or your local police station.

Customs

EU nationals can now import a limitless amount of goods for their personal use. For travellers entering the EU from outside, the

Advice for Disabled Travellers

In the UK

RADAR, 12 City Forum, 250 City Rd, London EC1V 8AF, **t** (020) 7250 3222, *www.radar.org.uk.*

Holiday Care Service, t 0845 124 9971, *www. holidaycare.org.uk.*

Disability Now, 6 Markets Road, London N7, **t** (020) 7619 7323, *www.disabilitynow.org.uk..*

In the USA and Canada.

Mobility International USA, t (541) 343 1284, *www.miusa.org.*

SATH (Society for Accessible Travel and Hospitality), t (212) 447 7284, *www.sath.org.*

Emerging Horizons, *www.emerginghorizons.com.*

duty-free limits are 1 litre of spirits or 2 litres of liquors (port, sherry or champagne), plus 2 litres of wine, 200 cigarettes and 50 grams of perfume. Much larger quantities – up to 10 litres of spirits, 90 litres of wine, 110 litres of beer and 3,200 cigarettes – bought locally and provided you are travelling between EU countries, can be taken through customs if you can prove that they are for private consumption only and taxes have been paid in the country of purchase.

Disabled Travellers

Many of the Greek islands, with their ubiquitous steps and absence of suitable transport, would put severe constraints on visitors in chairs, and ferry and hydrofoil access is difficult. Major islands such as Corfu and Rhodes and many smaller ones that receive lots of visitors (such as Skiáthos, Zákynthos and Kos) have hotels with disabled facilities. Post-Olympics Athens is well equipped: there's even a lift to the Acropolis.

Insurance and EHIC Cards

EU citizens are entitled to free medical care at the basic **IKA** (Greek NHS) **hospitals** with their **European Health Insurance Card (EHIC)**; apply at post offices, online at *www.ehic.org. uk,* or by calling **t** 0845 606 2030. Unlike the old E111 forms, you'll need to apply for a card for every member of the family .

Consultations with Greek dentists and doctors are free, but you will have to pay part of the cost of X-rays, etc. If you have a prescription, expect to pay a small standard charge plus 25 per cent of the actual cost of the medicine, which is non-refundable. If you are charged in full, obtain a receipt and keep the prescriptions as well as the self-adhesive labels from the medicines. (If you obtain any medicine or treatment privately, you pay the full cost.) Take the original receipts and your EHIC to the nearest IKA office within one month, and they will reimburse you. If you are staying where there is no IKA office, you must pay the full costs and apply for a refund on return to the UK. Keep all original prescriptions, self-adhesive labels and receipts.

In any case, consider a **travel insurance** policy with adequate repatriation cover.

Non-European nationals should check their health insurance schemes to see if they are covered in Greece.

Money and Banks

The official currency in Greece is the **euro**, pronounced *evró*. Cents are *leptá*.

The word for **bank** in Greek is *trápeza*. **Banking hours** are Mon–Thurs 8.20–2, Fri 8.20–1.30. If there's no bank, then travel agents, tourist offices or post offices will change money. The number of **ATMs** grows every year and now most islands have at least one (if in doubt, bring sufficient cash).

Major hotels, luxury shops and resort restaurants take **credit cards** (look for the little signs), but smaller hotels and tavernas certainly won't, and many petrol stations don't either. Visa is the most widely accepted.

Traveller's cheques are always useful as a back-up. The major brands (Thomas Cook and American Express) are accepted in all banks; take your passport as ID, and shop around for the best rates (which are usually in banks).

You can have money sent to Greek post offices via the **Girobank Eurogiro system**.

Getting There

By Air

From the UK and Ireland

Scheduled flights direct to **Athens** operate from the UK on British Airways, easyJet, KLM, Globespan and Greece's national carrier, Olympic (which may be renamed Pantheon when it's partially privatized). There are scheduled flights from Dublin to Athens on Malev Hungarian Airlines.

Airline Carriers

UK and Ireland
British Airways, UK t 0870 850 9850; Ireland t 1 890 626747, www.ba.com.
easyJet, t 0905 821 0905, www.easyjet.com.
Globespan, t 0870 556 1522, www.flyglobespan.com.
KLM, t 08705 074074, www.klm.com.
Olympic Airlines, UK t 0870 6060 460, www.olympicairlines.com.
Malev Hungarian Airlines, Ireland t (01) 844 4303, www.malev.hu.

USA and Canada
Air Canada, Canada t 1 888 247 2262, www.aircanada.com.
British Airways, USA t 800 AIRWAYS, www.ba.com.
Delta, t 800 221 1212, www.delta.com.
KLM (Northwest), USA t 800 225 2525, www.nwa.com.
Lufthansa, t 800 609 9976, www.weflyhome.com.
Olympic Airways, www.olympicairlines.com.

Charters and Discounts

UK and Ireland
Avro, t 0870 458 2841, www.avro.co.uk. Cheap flights to the islands.
Budget, t (01) 631 1111, www.budgettravel.ie. Last-minute bargains/charters from Ireland.
Charter Flight Centre, t (020) 7854 8434, www.charterflightcentre.co.uk.
Fly Thomas Cook, www.flythomascook.co.uk.
Just the Flight, t 0870 758 9589, www.justthe-flight.co.uk. Charters to the islands.
STA Travel, t 08701 630 026, www.statravel.co.uk. Student discounts.

UK Websites
www.cheapflights.co.uk
www.expedia.co.uk
http://travel.kelkoo.co.uk
www.lastminute.com
www.opodo.co.uk
www.skyscanner.net
www.travelocity.co.uk
www.travelrepublic.co.uk

USA and Canada

Air Brokers International, USA **t** 800 883 3273, *www.airbrokers.com*. Discount agency.

Homeric Tours, USA **t** 800 223 5570, *www.homerictours.com*. Charter flights and tours.

Last Minute Travel Club, USA **t** 877 970 5400, *www.lastminuteclub.com*. Annual membership fee gets you cheap stand-by deals.

Travel Cuts, Canada **t** 1866 246 9762, *www.travelcuts.ca*; USA **t** 800 592 2887, *www.travelcuts.com*.

STA Travel, **t** 800 781 4040, *www.statravel.com*. Student travel discounts.

US/Canadian Websites

http://greeceflights.com (specializes in Greece)
www.cheapflights.com
www.cheapflights.ca
www.ebookers.com
www.expedia.com
www.orbitz.com
www.travelocity.com

For the northern Aegean islands, find flights to **Thessaloníki**. BA fly direct to **Rhodes** from London, and to Heráklion, **Crete**, from Manchester and London, and Globespan also fly from Glasgow to Heráklion.

Charter flights fly direct from many UK and Irish airports to many islands, often at ridiculous hours. If you don't want a package you can book just the flight. *See* box, below left. Most run from May to mid-October but there are also early specials, in March and April, depending on when Greek Easter falls.

Make sure to **confirm your return flight** prior to departure.

From the USA and Canada

Olympic, Delta and Lufthansa have daily flights from the USA to Athens in summer; Olympic also flies direct from Toronto and Montreal, but check the Internet for deals.

Getting from the Airport

For connections from Athens airport to the city centre, Piraeus, bus stations and the ports of Lávrio and Ráfina, *see* p.71.

Airlines in Athens

Aegean Airlines, t 210 353 0101.
Air France, t 210 353 0380.
Alitalia, t 210 353 4284.
British Airways, t 210 353 0453.
Cyprus Airways, t 210 353 4312.
Delta, t 210 353 0116.
Easyjet, t 210 356 8120.
KLM, t 210 356 8120.
Lufthansa, t 210 353 0155.
Malev, t 210 324 1116.
Olympic, t 210 936 8424.
Singapore Airlines, t 210 353 1259.
Thai Airways, t 210 353 1237.

By Train

The best route by train from the UK to Greece is through Italy. Starting with the **Eurostar** from London to Paris, the furthest port, Brindisi, is about 24 hours away, but it also has the shortest ferry journey to Greece – it sails to Corfu and Pátras.

For information on trains from the UK to Greece, and the various **rail passes** available for the British (e.g. Inter-Rail) or for North Americans (e.g. Eurail), contact Rail Europe.

Rail Europe (UK): 178 Piccadilly, London W1, **t** 08708 371 371, *www.raileurope.co.uk*.

Rail Europe (USA and Canada): **t** 877 257 2887 (USA), or **t** 800 361 RAIL (Canada), *www.raileurope.com*.

Eurostar, t 08705 186 186, *www.eurostar.com*.

By Sea

The most common route to Greece by sea is from Italy; routes are well established, with daily overnight ferry services from various east coast ports (*see* box, overleaf). Prices vary, so shop around. Check timetables, compare prices and book tickets on all the lines on these general websites:

Greek Ferries Club, *www.greekferries.gr*.
Hellas Ferries Center, *www.hellasferries.gr*.
Paleologos, *www.ferries.gr*.

You can also book ferries through:

UK: Viamare Travel, t 0800 0681 676.
Canada: Omega Travel, t 604 738 3433.
USA: Amphitrion Holidays, t 800 424 2471.

In high summer, reserve – you'll also save money by booking at least 45 days in advance. There are special rates for families, children under 12 and seniors over 60, and sometimes for holders of Eurail/Inter-Rail cards. Many offer camping on board.

Italy–Greece Ferries

ANEK, t 210 419 7430, *www.anek.gr*. Venice and Ancona to Igoumenítsa and Pátras; also Venice to Corfu.

Superfast, t 210 891 9130, *www.superfast.com*. Ancona and Bari to Igoumenítsa and Pátras.

Minoan, t 210 414 5700, *www.minoan.gr*. Venice and Ancona to Igoumenítsa and Pátras; also Venice to Corfu.

Ventouris, t 210 482 8001, *www.ventouris.gr*. Bari to Corfu, Igoumenítsa and Kefaloniá.

Maritime Way, t (00 39) 040 676 0411 (Italy), *www.maritimeway.com*. Brindisi to Pátras, Kefaloniá and Igoumenítsa.

Fragline, t 210 821 4171, *www.fragline.gr*. Brindisi to Corfu and Igoumenítsa.

Agoudimos, t 210 412 6680, *www.agoudimos-lines.com*. Brindisi to Corfu and Igoumenítsa; Bari to Kefaloniá.

Blue Star, t 210 891 9800, *www.bluestarferries.com*. Bari to Pátras and Igoumenítsa.

By Car

Driving from London to Athens (and taking the ferry from Italy to Greece) at a normal pace takes around 3½ days.

An **International Driving Licence** is not required for EU citizens. Other nationals can obtain one at home, or at an Automobile Club (ELPA) office in Greece by presenting a national driving licence, passport and photo.

The **Motor Insurance Bureau, t** 210 322 3324, *www.mib-hellas.gr*, can tell you which Greek insurance company represents your own, or provide additional cover for Greece.

The **Greek Automobile Club** (**ELPA**), in Athens, **t** 210 606 8800, gives advice.

Customs formalities for bringing in a car are easy. You're allowed six months' free use of a car in Greece (or 15 months by paying a fee) before it must leave the country. To avoid difficulties when you leave, make sure your car is stamped in your passport on arrival.

Getting Around

By Air

Domestic flights to the islands are on **Olympic Airlines** (*www.olympicairlines.com*), **Aegean Airlines** (*www.aegean-airlines.gr*), and the Heráklion (Crete)-based **Sky Express** (*www.skyexpress.gr*), with a growing number of island-to-island flights that avoid the need to go via Athens. As many planes are small, book as far in advance as possible. Note that some can't take off or land in high winds, and you could end up back where you started. Baggage allowances tend to be enforced – check when you buy your ticket.

AirSea Lines, t 210 940 2880, *www.airsealines.com*, Europe's first regular seaplane service, linking Corfu, Páxos, Ioánnina, Pátras, Lefkáda and Itháki, with more destinations promised soon.

Interjet, *www.interjet.gr*. Hire a helicopter or private jet to an island with this Athens-based company.

By Train

Domestic trains are slow, with the exception of intercity trains, which by other European standards are still found wanting. However, train **fares** are cheaper than buses by up to 40 per cent. The **Greek Railways** website is *www.ose.gr*, and the **national information** number is **t** 1110.

In Athens, the station for northern Greece is Lárissa, on Deligiánni St. The station for the Peloponnese is behind it, reached by a pedestrian bridge. In Piraeus, the station for the Peloponnese is near the metro on Aktí Kalimassióti; the station for northern Greece is further down the road on Aktí Kondýli.

Train Routes for the Islands

Athens–Thessaloníki (for N.E. Aegean Islands): 10 per day.

Thessaloníki–Alexandroúpolis (for Samothráki): 5 per day.

Athens–Chalkída (on Évia): 17 per day.

Athens–Pátras (for Ionian Islands): 8 per day.

Athens–Kalamáta (for Kýthera): 4 per day.

Athens–Vólos (for Sporades): 2 per day.

By Bus

Domestic buses (**KTEL**, *www.ktel.org*) are useful for reaching mainland ports other than Piraeus (*see* box). In August, reserve seats in advance on the long-distance buses.

To get to the **terminal** at 100 Kifissoú Street (**t** 210 512 4910), take bus E93 from the airport or bus 051 from Omónia Square (Zínonos and Menandroú Sts). For the terminal at 260

Domestic Bus Routes from Athens

Athens to	No. daily	Terminal	t (210–)	Duration
Ag. Konstantínos (Sporades)	13	Lióssion	831 7147	2.30hrs
Chalkída (Évia)	33	Lióssion	831 7153	1.30hrs
Edipsoú (Évia)	3–4	Lióssion	831 7153	3.15hrs
Gýthion (for Kýthera)	4	Kifissoú	512 4913	4.30hrs
Ithaca	1	Kifissoú	515 0785	7 hrs
Kefaloniá	4	Kifissoú	515 0785	8hrs
Kérkyra (Corfu)	2	Kifissoú	512 9443	11hrs
Lefkáda	3	Kifissoú	515 0108	5.30hrs
Lávrio (for Cyclades, Límnos)	12	Mavromatéon	823 0179	2 hrs
Pátras (for Ionians, Italy)	16	Kifissoú	514 7310	3hrs
Rafína (for Cyclades and Évia)	18	Mavromatéon	821 0872	1.30hrs
Thessaloníki (for NE Aegean Is.)	10	Kifissoú	514 8856	7.30hrs
Vólos (for Sporades)	10	Lióssion	832 9585	5.15hrs
Zákynthos	4	Kifissoú	512 9432	6hrs

Liossíon Street (t 210 831 7163), take the same bus E93 from the airport or bus 024 from Leofóros Amalías by Sýntagma Square (tell the driver you want the terminal). For the Mavromatéon terminal (t 210 821 0872), go to the Victoria metro stop.

There are never enough buses on the islands in the summer, nor is it customary to queue. However, you will not be left behind if it is humanly possible for you to squeeze on. Different timetables apply at weekends.

By Sea

As the seas have been opened to competition, Greek ferry companies have invested massively in new ships, and ferries as a general rule are more reliable, faster and more comfortable than ever. Most offer first (or business) class tickets, which give access to a plush lounge and private cabin; cheaper shared cabins; and economy or deck class. On summer nights the deck can be the most pleasant alternative, especially if you have a sleeping bag. All ferries sell water, beer, coffee and soft drinks, while the larger ones offer sandwiches, self-service food or meals.

If you're travelling to the islands during Greek Easter or July and August, reserve a return ticket in advance or you may well get stuck. Check schedules on the *Greek Travel Pages* (*www.gtp.gr*) and see which companies serve your island(s). Some of the larger firms, such as **Hellenic Seaways** (*www.hellenic seaways.gr*) allow you to book online. Or try a general provider such as **Danae Online Tickets** (*www.danae.gr*).

Athens' port, **Piraeus**, is the main launchpad for Crete, the Cyclades, the Dodecanese, the Saronic islands and most of the Northeastern Aegean Islands; *see* the map on p.100 for points of departure. Because Piraeus gets so busy there's a trend to use smaller mainland ports, especially **Rafína** and **Lávrio**; both are linked by bus to Athens (*see* above), but most tourists see them as a bother, which means that islands served by these outlying ports tend be quieter and more 'Greek'. The main port for the Ionian islands is **Pátras** in western Greece, linked by bus and train from Athens, while Évia, the Sporades and the more northerly Aegean islands have their own mainland links that involve overland travel from Athens; nearly all have airports.

Weather, health emergencies and unforeseen repairs can throw **timetables** out of the window, so if you have to catch a flight home, leave a day early to be safe. For the latest on departures and arrivals, ring the relevant **port authorities** (*limenarchíon*). Numbers are listed for islands in the text. All daily departures from Piraeus and Rafína are also listed in English at *www.yen.gr/en*.

Before buying a ticket, check timetables in competing agencies – some ferries are faster

Mainland Port Authorities

Piraeus, t 210 422 6000.
Rafína, t 229 402 8888.
Lávrio, t 229 202 5249.
Pátras, t 261 034 1024.
Thessaloníki, t 231 053 1504.

than others, and others can take half a day stopping at other ports.

In 2006, **fares** were deregulated for the busiest island routes, although for the time being the least profitable routes are still protected by government subsidies. The expectation is that pricing will follow that of low-cost airlines – that you'll save money by booking early on the Internet, or by travelling at non-peak periods. In most cases kids under 4 travel free, and between 4 and 10 for half-fare. In the summer, buy tickets well in advance if you have a car or want a cabin. If you miss your ship, you forfeit your ticket; if you cancel in advance, you will generally receive a 50 per cent refund, or 100 per cent in the case of major delays or cancellations, except those caused by *force majeure*.

Hydrofoils and Catamarans

Hydrofoils, catamarans and extra-fast ferries thump over the Greek seas. Most services (especially to the Saronic Islands) run throughout the year but are less frequent between November and May. As a rule they travel at least twice as fast as slow ferries and are twice as expensive. On most hydrofoils you can sit outside in the back, but on the catamarans and fast ferries you have to stay indoors. In the peak season they're often fully booked, so buy tickets early. Beware: if the weather is very bad, they won't leave.

Tourist Excursion Boats

These are generally more expensive than the regular ferries. But they often have schedules that allow visitors to make day trips to nearby islands and faraway beaches. Hydrofoils may allow for day trips to neighbouring islands too, but all water transport is at the mercy of fickle Greek gales.

Ferries to Turkey and Albania

Ferries run daily year-round between Rhodes and Marmaris; Kos and Bodrum; Chíos and Çeşme; Sámos and Kuşadasi near Ephesus; and from Lésbos to Ayvalik; in season excursion boats sail from most of the smaller Dodecanese. On the other side of Greece, there are regular ferries from Corfu to Saranda, Albania. Expect to pay €15 for a Turkish visa as you enter (Canadians €45) and €10 for an Albanian visa.

By Car

There are countless rent-a-car firms on the islands; most are family-run and reliable. If an island has a lot of unpaved roads and not a lot of competition, prices tend to be higher; at the time of writing, hiring a small car averages around €20–30 a day, and open-air Jeeps at least a third more. Most require that you be at least 21, some 25. In the off season, negiotiate. **Fuel** at the time of writing is around €1.10 per litre.

While driving in the centre of Athens may be a hair-raising experience, the rest of Greece is fairly pleasant. There are few cars on most roads, and most signs, when you're lucky enough to find one, have their Latin equivalents. Traffic regulations and signalling comply with standard practice on the European continent (i.e. driving on the right). Where there are no right-of-way signs at a crossroads, give priority to traffic coming from the right, and always beep your horn on blind corners. You may want to take a spare container of petrol along, as stations can be scarce and only open shop hours.

ELPA (the Greek automobile club) have a free tourist helpline in English, **t** 174 (*open 8–3*). They also operate a **breakdown service** (**t** 10400); if you belong to an affiliated automobile club at home, it's free anywhere.

By Motorbike

Motorbikes and scooters (and increasingly quads) are popular summer modes of transport. Rental **rates** vary (€12–20 a day for a scooter, anything over 250cc will be similar to a car), and include third party **insurance** coverage. You will need a valid driving licence and for anything over 125cc a full motorcycle licence. The downsides: many of the bikes are poorly maintained, many of the roads are poorly maintained, and everyone takes too many risks: hospital beds in Greece fill up each summer with foreign and Greek casualties. Most islands have laws about operating motorbikes after midnight but they are as enforced as often as the helmet requirement.

By Bicycle

Cycling has not caught on in mountainous Greece, either as a sport or as a means of transport, though you can usually hire a bike in major resorts to pedal to the beach. Trains and planes carry bicycles for free or a small fee, and Greek boats generally take them along for nothing. That said, several firms offer cycling holidays (see p.60).

Yachting, Sailing and Flotilla Holidays

Greece was made for sailing, with 100,000 miles of coastline and 3,000 islands. Facilities are being improved and new marinas have been added everywhere. The only real problem is the strong winds in parts of the country, notably April to October. The Ionian Sea and the west coast of the Peloponnese are affected by the *maistros*, an afternoon-only light-to-moderate northwest wind. South of Attica and east of the Peloponnese, the sea is largely sheltered by land masses and it's not until summer that the menacing *meltémi* blows. The Aegean Sea is affected by a northwest wind in the south, and a north-easterly in the north, and when the *meltémi* blows in August and September it can reach force eight. The Turkish coast has light, variable breezes, which are rudely interrupted by the forceful *meltémi*.

Yacht charter can be cheaper than staying in a hotel (if you have enough friends to share expenses). Between the various firms there are over 4,000 vessels available in all sizes, with or without a crew.

For wannabe sailors who want to float among the islands, a **flotilla holiday** may be the answer. A number of companies offer holidays (see p.60). The yachts have 4–8 berths (shared boats available for couples and singles) and sail in flotillas of 6–12 yachts, with experienced skipper, engineer and hostess.

Yacht Charter Companies

Anemos Yachting, *www.anemos-yachting.gr*.
Cosmos Yachting, *www.cosmosyachting.com*.
Ghiolman Yachts, *www.ghiolman.com*.
Interpac Yachts, *www.interpacyachts.com*.
Odyssey Sailing, *www.odysseysailing.gr*.
Odysseus Yachting Holidays, *www.odysseus.co.uk*.
Tenrag, *www.tenrag.com*.
Valef, *http://valefyachts.com*.
Yacht Agency, *www.yachtagency.com*.

Hotel Price Ranges

Price ranges in this guide are for a double room in July and August.

luxury	€€€€€	€150 to astronomical
very expensive	€€€€	€120–150
expensive	€€€	€80–120
moderate	€€	€50–80
inexpensive	€	less than €50

Where to Stay

Hotels

All hotels in Greece are classed into six categories: Luxury, A, B, C, D and E, depending on how the building is constructed, size of bedrooms, lifts and so on; i.e. if the hotel has a marble bathroom it gets a higher rating.

Prices are posted in every room. Off season (i.e. mid-September–July) these are often very negotiable, which is why prices are not always posted on websites. Check for online discounts. In season there may be a 10 per cent surcharge for stays of only one or two days, an air-conditioning surcharge, as well as a 20 per cent surcharge for an extra bed. If you have any reason to believe all is not on the level, complain to the tourist police.

Rooms and Studios

Privately run rooms (ΔOMATIA, *domátia*) are generally cheaper than hotels and sometimes more pleasant. Many have basic kitchen facilities, which may turn a room into a 'studio'. Until June and after August, prices are always negotiable; owners will nearly always drop the price per day the longer you stay. On some islands you will be courted with all kinds of proposals as you come off the ferry. On others, room and hotel owners have co-operated to organize accommodation booths at the port; if the room is not within walking distance, they'll collect you in a car or minivan.

Camping

Greece's summer climate is perfect for camping, especially close to the sea, where breezes keep the mosquitoes at bay. Unauthorized camping is illegal, although each village enforces the ban as it sees fit. Ask around. Islands with no campsites usually have a beach for freelance camping.

Specialist Tour Operators

In the UK

Explore Worldwide, t 0870 333 4001, *www.exploreworldwide.com*. Active Kefaloniá, rambles in Crete; caique cruises; Aegean hikes.

Headwater, t 08700 662 650, *www.headwater.com*. Walking holidays.

Inntravel, t (01653) 617949, *www.inntravel.co.uk*. Walking holidays on Sámos; plus villas and boutique hotels on Kefaloniá and Crete.

Island Wandering, t 0870 777 99 44, *www.islandwandering.com*. Island-hopping holidays.

Mark Warner, t 0870 770 4227, *www.markwarner.co.uk*. Family holidays: Límnos and Kos.

Neilson, t 0870 333 3336, *www.neilson.co.uk*. Sailing and flotilla holidays.

Ramblers, t (01707) 331133, *www.ramblersholidays.co.uk*. Walking tours in Crete.

Skýros Holidays, t (020) 7267 4424, *www.skyros.co.uk*. Creative writing, watersports, spiritual development, art and music, yoga, dance.

Sunsail, *www.sunsail.com*. Flotillas, bareboats, tuitional sailing and water sports.

Swan Hellenic Cruises, t 0845 3 555 111, *www.swanhellenic.com*. Cultural, archaeological and art history cruises.

Waymark, t 0870 950 9800, *www.waymarkholidays.com*. Guided hiking: Crete and Lésvos.

2Wheel Treks, t 0845 612 6106, *www.2wheeltreks.co.uk*. Island cruising and cycling.

In the USA and Canada

Aegean Arts Circle, *www.aegeanartscircle.com*. Writing workshops and retreats on Ándros.

Classic Adventures, t 800 777 8090, *www.classicadventures.com*. Crete cycling/walking.

Cloud Tours, t 800 223 7880, *www.cloudtours.com*. Island-hopping and luxury hotels and bungalows with pools.

Crete's Culinary Sanctuaries, *www.cookingincrete.com*. Mediterranean diet wanderings with Greek-American Nikki Rose.

Cuisine International, t (214) 373 1161, *www.cuisineinternational.com*. Learn to cook Greek style with Diane Kochilas on Ikaría.

Friends Travel, t (310) 652 9600, *www.friendstravel.net*. Gay tours.

Greek Island Photography, t (415) 459 2001, *www.greekislandphotography.com*. Santoríni.

Into Adventure, t 808 280 3341, *www.intoadventure.com*. Cycling in the Cyclades.

Meander Adventures, t 888 616 7272, *www.greece-travel-turkey-travel.com*. Honeymoons, hiking and sailing holidays.

Mind and Body Travels, t 800 874 1996, *www.mindbodytravel.com*. Aegean island hikes, trails of Minoan Crete, and cruises.

In Greece (t + 30)

Aegean Center, t 228 402 3287, *www.aegeancenter.org*. Arts on Páros.

Athens Centre, t 210 701 2268, *www.athenscentre.gr*. Learn Greek or take an art course in the summer on Spétses.

Candili, t 097 406 2100, UK t 07887 991931, *www.candili.co.uk*. Creative courses in Évia.

Omilo, t 210 612 2896, *www.angelfire.com/la/omilo*. Modern Greek culture.

Thalpos Holidays, on the waterfront, Skópelos Town, Skópelos, t 242 402 9036, *www.holidayislands.com*. Villas on Skópelos, Alónissos and Skíathos, and special interest holidays (walking, sailing, diving, dancing, painting, pottery).

Self-catering Operators

Telephone numbers are for the UK, unless specified otherwise.

Abercrombie & Kent, t 0845 0700 615, *www.villa-rentals.com*. Crete and Mýkonos.

Catherine Secker, t (020) 8460 8022, *www.catherine-secker-crete.co.uk*. Villas with pools on the Akrotíri Peninsula near Chaniá.

CV Travel, t 0870 603 9018, *www.cvtravel.net*. Upmarket villas on many islands.

Direct Greece, t 0870 191 9244, *www.directgreece.co.uk*. Wide choice of villas and flats.

Elysian Holidays, t (01580) 766 599, *www.elysianholidays.co.uk*. Upmarket villas.

Five Star Greece, t (020) 8422 4885, *www.fivestargreece.com*. Select island villas.

Greek Islands Club, t (020) 8232 9780, *www.greekislandsclub.co.uk*.

Greek Sun Holidays, t (01732) 740317, *www.greeksun.co.uk*. Unusual islands – Síkinos, Anáfi, Foúrni and Kárpathos.

Hidden Greece, t (020) 8758 4707, *www.hidden-greece.co.uk*. Small, lesser-known islands.

Kosmar, t 0871 7000 747, *www.kosmar.co.uk*. Self-catering on the most popular islands.

Manos, t 08707 530 530, *www.manos.co.uk*. Self-catering holidays to the major resorts.

Meon Villas, t 0870 909 755, *www.meonvillas.co.uk*. Luxury villas.

Pure Crete, t (020) 8760 0879, *www.purecrete.com*. Traditional village accommodation.

Sunvil, t (020) 8568 4499, *www.sunvil.co.uk*. Villas on some of the more unusual islands.

Travel à la Carte, t (01635) 201250, *www.travelalacarte.co.uk*. Skíathos, Corfu, Páxos, Sými.

Practical A–Z

06

Imperial–Metric Conversions

Length (multiply by)
Inches to centimetres: 2.54
Centimetres to inches: 0.39
Feet to metres: 0.3
Metres to feet: 3.28
Yards to metres: 0.91
Metres to yards: 1.1
Miles to kilometres: 1.61
Kilometres to miles: 0.62

Area (multiply by)
Inches square to centimetres square: 6.45
Centimetres square to inches square: 0.15
Feet square to metres square: 0.09
Metres square to feet square: 10.76
Miles square to kilometres square: 2.59
Kilometres square to miles square: 0.39
Acres to hectares: 0.40
Hectares to acres: 2.47

Weight (multiply by)
Ounces to grams: 28.35
Grammes to ounces: 0.035
Pounds to kilograms: 0.45
Kilograms to pounds: 2.2
Stones to kilograms: 6.35
Kilograms to stones: 0.16
Tons (UK) to kilograms: 1,016
Kilograms to tons (UK): 0.0009
1 UK ton (2,240lbs) = 1.12 US tonnes (2,000lbs)

Volume (multiply by)
Pints (UK) to litres: 0.57
Litres to pints (UK): 1.76
Quarts (UK) to litres: 1.13
Litres to quarts (UK): 0.88
Gallons (UK) to litres: 4.55
Litres to gallons (UK): 0.22
1 UK pint/quart/gallon =
1.2 US pints/quarts/
gallons

Temperature
Celsius to Fahrenheit:
multiply by 1.8 then
add 32

Fahrenheit to Celsius:
subtract 32 then multiply
by 0.55

°C	°F
40	104
35	95
30	86
25	77
20	68
15	59
10	50
5	41
-0	32
-5	23
-10	14
-15	5

Greece Information

Time Differences
Country: + 2hrs GMT; + 7hrs EST

Dialling Codes
Greece country code 30

To Greece from: UK, Ireland, New Zealand 00 /
USA, Canada 011 / Australia 0011 then dial 30
and the full 10-digit number

From Greece to: UK 00 44; Ireland 00 353; USA,
Canada 001; Australia 00 61; New Zealand 00
64 then the number without the initial zero

Operator: 132
International operator: 139

Emergency Numbers
European emergency number in English 112
Police: 100
Ambulance: 166
Fire: 199
Car breakdown (ELPA) 10400; tourist helpline
in English 174

Embassy Numbers in Greece
UK: 210 727 2699; **Ireland** 210 723 2771;
USA: 210 721 2851; **Canada** 210 727 3400

Greek Measurements
Two uniquely Greek measurements you may
come across (especially if you are looking at
property) are the *strémma*, a Greek land
measurement (1 *strémma* = ¼ acre); and the
oká, an old-fashioned weight standard, divided
into 400 *drams* (1 *oká* = 3lb; 140 *drams* = 1lb)

Shoe Sizes

Europe	UK	USA
35	2½ / 3	4
36	3 / 3½	4½ / 5
37	4	5½ / 6
38	5	6½
39	5½ / 6	7 / 7½
40	6 / 6½	8 / 8½
41	7	9 / 9½
42	8	9½ / 10
43	9	10½
44	9½ / 10	11
45	10½	12
46	11	12½ / 13

Women's Clothing Sizes

UK	6	8	10	12	14	16	18	20
USA	2	4	6	8	10	12	14	16

Children

Greeks love children, and children usually love Greece. Depending on their age, they go free or receive discounts on ships and buses. However, don't count on island pharmacies stocking your brand of milk powder or baby foods – it's safest to bring your own supply. Disposable nappies are widely available.

Greek children usually have an afternoon nap (as do their parents), so it's quite normal for Greeks to eat *en famille* until the small hours. Even so, finding a babysitter is rarely a problem: just ask at your hotel.

Crime and Safety

Police t 100/**t** 112
Fire t 199/**t** 112

With one of the lowest crime rates in Europe, Greece is a safe country for travellers, although you should be cautious in busy tourist hotspots. As you would anywhere, lock your car and don't leave valuables on show inside, and don't leave personal possessions unattended. If you have a theft and you intend to make an insurance claim, report it to the police in order to get paperwork to show. Unscrupulous taxi drivers overcharging tourists, however, is rife; if it happens, write down the licence number and threaten to complain and the issue is usually resolved.

Women travelling alone will not usually be harassed, but should be prepared for a fusillade of questions. Greeks tend to do everything in groups or pairs and can't understand people who want to go solo.

It is advisable, as events in recent years have proved, to avoid taking photographs anywhere near airports or military sites.

Eating Out

Eating out in Greece gets better all the time, as the Greeks themselves are becoming more demanding. If you join them for dinner, there's no Western nit-picking over who's had what. You share the food, drink, company and the bill, *to logariasmó*, although hosts will seldom let guests part with a cent.

Waiters are often paid a cut of the profits (which is why some obnoxiously tout for custom in busy resorts); tipping is discre-

Restaurant and Taverna Prices

A meal at the huge majority of tavernas – if you don't order a major fish – usually runs at around €15–20 a head with generous carafes of wine. Prices at sophisticated restaurants can be much higher.

In this guide, if the prices for tavernas and restaurants fall within this usual range, no price is mentioned, but for higher-priced or much cheaper places we state the average cost for a two-course meal for one with wine.

tionary but much appreciated. By law, there's a book for registering any complaints.

For more about eating and drinking in the Greek islands, including local specialities, wines and a menu decoder, *see* the **Food and Drink** chapter, pp.43–50.

Electricity

Note that the electric current in Greece is 220 volts, 50Hz; plugs are continental two-pin. Bring an adaptor/transformer from home, as they are rare in Greece.

Health and Emergencies

Ambulance t 166/**t** 112

For **first aid**, go to the nearest Local Health Centre (**ESY** or 'kentro eEas'), which are well equipped to deal with snake bites, jelly fish stings, grippe, etc., and treat foreigners for free. Where there are no ESYs, **rural doctors** (*iatrós* – there is at least one on every island) do the same work, also free..

For more serious illnesses or accidents, you'll need the **hospital** (*nosokomío*); the larger islands have them, and helicopters act as ambulances when necessary.

Most doctors pride themselves on their English, as do the **pharmacists** (found in the *farmakeío*), whose advice on minor ailments is good, although their medicine is not particularly cheap. Pharmacies also sell condoms (*kapótes*), seasickness remedies, sunscreen, tampons, insect repellent, etc., and you can get the morning-after pill and the Pill without a prescription – show your old packet. However, bring extras of any prescription drug you need, and stock up before heading off to remote islands.

National Holidays

1 Jan New Year's Day
6 Jan Epiphany, *Ta Fóta/Theofánia*
Feb–Mar 'Clean Monday'
25 Mar Greek Independence Day
Late Mar–April Good Friday and Easter Monday
1 May Labour Day
40 days after Easter Pentecost (Whit Monday)
15 Aug Assumption of the Virgin
28 Oct 'Ochí' Day (in celebration of Metaxás' 'No' to Mussolini, *see* p.28)
25 Dec Christmas
26 Dec Gathering of the Virgin

The strong sun is the most likely cause of grief, so be careful, hatted and sunscreened. *See* pp.35–6 for possibly unkind wildlife. If anything else goes wrong, do what the islanders have done for centuries: pee on it. Greek **tap water** is perfectly safe to drink, and inexpensive plastic bottles of spring water are widely available (and responsible for untold pollution in landfill sites).

National Holidays

Museums, archaeological sites, offices and shops close down on these holiday dates (*see* box, above); many businesses and shops also close down for the afternoon before and the morning after a religious holiday. If a national holiday falls on a Sunday, the following Monday is observed.

In Greece, Orthodox Easter is the equivalent in significance of Christmas and New Year in northern climes – the time when far-flung relatives return to see their families back home. It's a good time of year to visit for the atmosphere, feasts and fireworks – but beware that the ferries and roads are packed.

After Easter and 1 May, spring (*ánixi* – the opening) has officially come, and the tourist season begins. It's also worth remembering when planning your visit that the main partying often happens the night *before* the saint's day.

Opening Hours

For **banks**, see p.54. For **post offices** and **shops**, *see* the relevant sections below.

Museums and Sites

In Greece, **archaeological sites** and **museums** are generally closed on Monday, and hours are shorter in the winter. **Admission fees** are usually between €1.50 and €7; if they cost more, this guide will say '*adm exp*' instead of '*adm*'. **Students** with valid ID get a discount, and in state museums EU visitors under 18 or over 65 with ID get in cheaper or often free.

Churches and Monasteries

Because of a surge in thefts, **churches** only open when there is someone around, often in the late afternoon (6–7pm); at other times you may have to hunt down the key (*kleethEE*). **Monasteries** close for a couple of hours at midday. Note that visitors are expected to dress respectfully – long trousers for men, knees covered for women. Many provide long skirts or robes for the scantily clad.

Post Offices

Offices of the **Hellenic Post/ELTA**, which is also useful for changing money, are **open** Mon–Fri 7.30am–2pm, although in large towns they may be open till 7.30–8pm and on Saturday morning as well. Signs for **post offices** (*tachidromío*) as well as **postboxes** (*grammatokivótio*) are bright yellow and easy to find. On two-slot boxes, *Esorekó* is for domestic mail, and *Exorekó* is for overseas.

Stamps (*grammatósima*) can also be bought at kiosks and in some tourist shops. **Postcards** cost the same as letters and are given the same priority (about three days to the UK, unless posted from a remote island).

If you do not have an address, mail can be sent to you *poste restante* to any post office in Greece, and picked up with proof of identity (you'll find the postal codes in the text, which will get your letters there faster). After one month all unretrieved letters are returned to sender.

Shopping

Official **shopping hours** are Mon and Wed 9–5, Tues, Thurs and Fri 10–7, Sat 8.30–3.30 and Sun closed; in practice, tourist shops stay open as late as 1am in season.

Leather goods, gold and jewellery, traditional handicrafts, embroideries and weavings, ceramics, alabaster, herbs and spices are favourite purchases.

Non-EU citizens tempted by big ticket items can justify their indulgences by having the sales tax (VAT) reimbursed – this is 18% of the purchase price. Make sure the shop has a TAX FREE FOR TOURISTS sticker in the window, and pick up a tax-free shopping cheque for your purchases, along with instructions for reimbursement at the airport as you depart (allow an extra hour – it's a bit complicated).

Sports and Activities

Water Sports

Greece was made for water sports, and by law, all the **beaches** are public. Hundreds fly the European Blue Flag. Resort beaches have parasols and sunbed concessions and snack bars, and if there's a breeze you'll probably find a **windsurfer** to rent (favourite spots are Páros, Lefkáda, Rhodes and Kárpathos). Bigger beaches have **paragliding, kite surfing** and **jet skis. Waterskiing** is available on most islands and **sea kayaking** is a growing sport, especially in the Ionian sea and on Mílos.

Naturism is tolerated in designated or out-of-the-way areas. On the other hand, topless sunbathing is legal on the majority of popular beaches as long as they're not smack in the middle of a village; exercise discretion.

Scuba-diving, once controlled to protect Greece's shipwrecks and marine life, is as of 2006 open everywhere, which should soon translate into more diving centres on the islands. Contact the **Owners of Diving Centres**, 67 Zéas, Piraeus, t 210 922 9532. Also see the *Hellenic Underwater Times*, *www.huts.gr*.

Land Sports

Walking is the favourite activity on every island, but especially on Crete, with its superb natural scenery, gorges, wild flowers and wide open spaces. Increasingly locals are arranging treks, and their maps and guides are a great help for finding the best paths. Never set out without a hat and water. If you like altitudes, Crete has four mountain shelters, and there's one on Évia, too. For daredevil **rock climbing**, try Kálymnos.

Tennis is popular at major resorts (many are lit up at night so you can beat the heat). Crete, Rhodes and Corfu have **golf** courses.

Telephones and the Internet

Operator t 132 (Greek), t 139 (international)

The **Organismós Tilefikinonía Elládos**, or OTE, operates public card phones. **Phone cards** (*télekartas*), sold in kiosks, come in denominations from €4 to €12. OTE also offers a *Xronocarta*, which is cheaper for long-distance calls, but involves dialling more numbers. Some **kiosks** (*periptera; see* p.39) have a telephone with a meter. These are getting rare, as all Greeks own mobiles.

British and Irish **mobile phones** work in Greece if they have a roaming facility; check with your service provider. Frequencies on the country's four networks are 900 and 1800 MHz. If you're going to be in Greece a while and using your mobile a lot, and as long as your mobile is not locked to a UK network, avoid the astronomical roaming charges (both outgoing and incoming) by temporarily replacing your UK SIM card with a local or international one (see *www.0044.co.uk*), or buy a pay-as-you-go phone locally. You can also rent a mobile phone in Greece: try **Cellular Abroad**, *www.cellularabroad.com*, or **Planet Omni**, *www.planetomni.com*.

To **phone Greece from abroad**, the country code is 30. To **call home from Greece**, dial the international prefix (UK 00 44, Ireland 00 353, USA and Canada 00 1, Australia 00 61, New Zealand 00 64).

All Greek **phone numbers** are 10-digit and you must dial all 10 digits wherever you are, and when phoning from abroad. Numbers

Average Sea Temperatures in °C/°F

Jan	April	May	July	Aug	Sept	Oct	Nov	Dec
15/59	16/61	18/64	24/75	25/77	24/75	22/72	18/64	17/63

that begin with 2 are landlines; numbers that begin with 6 are for mobiles.

Any popular tourist destination will have at least one **cybercafé**, charging between €4–6 an hour; many hotels and even some tavernas offer Internet access as well. Just ask. If you have a web-based email account, you will be able to check mail on the move.

Time

'God gave watches to the Europeans and time to the Greeks,' they say, but if you need more precision, Greek time is Eastern European, 2hrs ahead of Greenwich Mean Time, 7hrs ahead of Eastern Standard Time in North America.

Tipping

This is discretionary in restaurants and bars but, if the service has been good, a tip is appreciated. In taxis, one generally just rounds up, or adds an extra euro or two depending on the fare. During certain holidays such as Greek Easter, an extra euro is built into the price.

Toilets

Greek plumbing has improved dramatically in the past few years. Tavernas, *kafeneíons*, museums, bus stations and sweet shops almost always have facilities (it's good manners to buy something), and occasionally you'll find public toilets (usually pretty grotty) in the towns. 'Women' is ΓΥΝΑΙΚΑ (*gynéka*), 'men' ΑΝΔΡΟΣ (*ándros*), though there's usually a picture on the doors.

In older *pensions* and tavernas, do not tempt fate by disobeying the little notices 'the papers they please to throw in the basket', or it's bound to lead to trouble.

If you stay in a private room or *pension* you may have to have the electric water-heater turned on for about 20 minutes before you take a shower. In most smaller *pensions*, water is heated by a solar panel on the roof, so the best time to take a shower is in the late afternoon or the early evening. In larger hotels there is often hot water in the mornings and evenings, but not in the afternoons.

Transliteration and Pronunciation

There is no general agreement on a standard method of transliterating the Greek alphabet into Roman letters, which means that you will constantly come across variations in the spellings of place names and words, on maps, in books and on road signs.

When transcribing, in this guide we have used D for the Greek *delta* (Δ), which you may see elsewhere as DH or TH; CH for *chi* (Χ), which is pronounced like the 'ch' in 'loch' and which you may see written as H, e.g. in Chaniá or Chóra; F for *fi* (Φ), which you may see elsewhere as PH; and G for the Greek *gamma* (Γ), which sounds more like a guttural GH verging on a Y when followed by *i* or *e*, as in *agios* (saint), pronounced 'ayios'. Exceptions are made where there is a common ancient name or accepted modern English spelling such as Phaistos or Rhodes.

Stressing the right syllable is vital to pronunciation, so the stressed letter of each word or name is accented with an acute (´) accent.

See also **Language**, pp.653–6.

Athens
and Piraeus

Athens is rarely love at first sight. Under the sublime Acropolis, the modern city pales into an urban crazy quilt. At second glance, you realize that it may not be pretty, but it can be an awful lot of fun; Athens' redeeming features were always its innumerable oases tucked away amidst the bustle, its feverish nightlife, summer festivals and the Athenians themselves, whose friendliness belies the reputation of most urbanites.

07

Don't miss

⭐ **The most famous building in the world**
The Parthenon **p.78**

⭐ **Ancient beauty**
National Archaeological Museum **p.89**

⭐ **Ouzo and *mezédes***
Psirrí **pp.88 and 97**

⭐ **Where Socrates walked**
Ancient Agora **p.84**

⭐ **The view from the top**
Lykavitós Hill **p.92**

See map overleaf

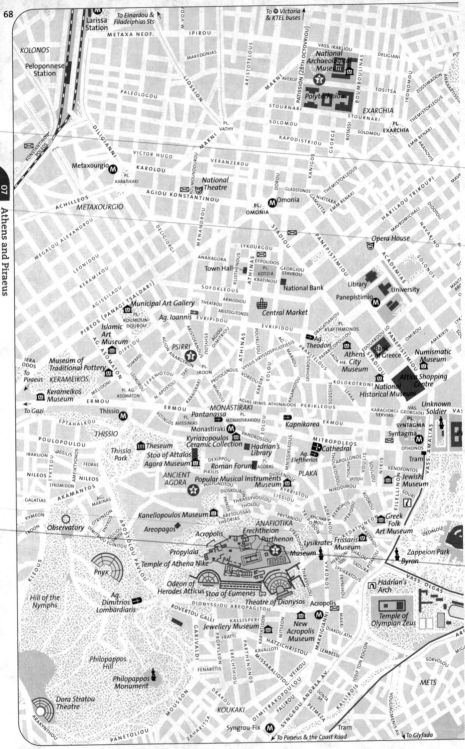

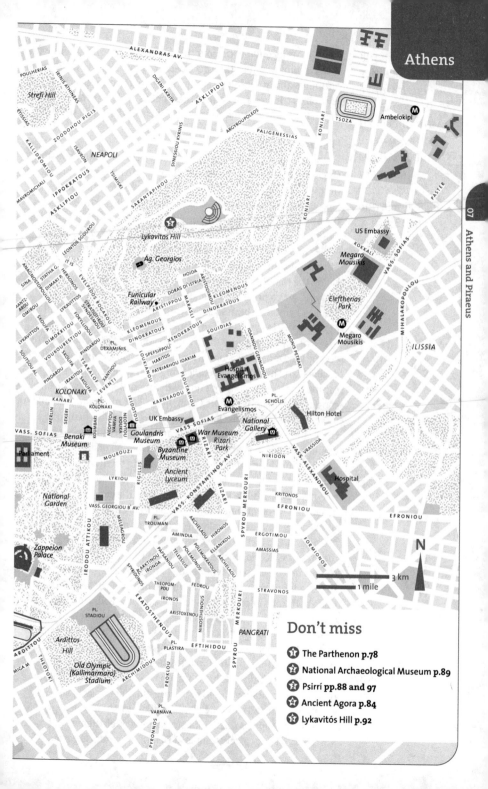

Don't miss

⭐ **The Parthenon p.78**

⭐ **National Archaeological Museum p.89**

⭐ **Psirrí pp.88 and 97**

⭐ **Ancient Agora p.84**

⭐ **Lykavitós Hill p.92**

> *Who doesn't desire to see Athens is stupid; who sees it without liking it is even more stupid; but the height of stupidity is to see it, like it, and then leave it.*
>
> Lysippus
> (4th century BC)

As well as its original charms, the 2004 Olympics left Athens with vastly improved public transport, pedestrianized streets, overhauled museums and archaeological sites, renovated neoclassical buildings revitalized squares and gardens, new hotels and restaurants – and the changes are continuing apace: Athens gets better all the time.

History

Athens was inhabited by c. 3500 BC, but her real debut on history's stage began in the second millennium BC, when invaders, probably from Asia Minor, entered Attica and established fortified enclaves. Snake from the waist down, **King Erechtheos**, 'the earth-born', was the official founder of Athens; he introduced the worship of Athena. The snake and the owl, her symbols, became the city's as well.

The city's Mycenaean rulers had a walled palace on the Acropolis; Athens' hero **Theseus** dates from this era. Although best known for killing the Minotaur in Crete, Theseus was also credited with unifying Attica under Athenian leadership. The city's politicians would scramble to be associated with his exploits; at the height of Athens' glory in 475 BC, Kimon brought his bones back from the island of Skýros and gave them a hero's burial. Athens managed to escape the Dorian invasions after 1200 BC and, although her culture declined and many of her people emigrated to Asia Minor, the escape was a great point of pride with Athenians, who as a result considered themselves more Greek, more legitimate and certainly more refined than their Dorian neighbours. All of this helped to create the amazing self-confidence and sense of difference that would lead to, among other things, the invention of democracy.

Some time during the 8th century BC all the towns of Attica were indeed peaceably united under Athens. This city-state was jointly ruled by a *basileus*, the king who doubled as the chief priest, a *polemarch* (general) and an *archon* (civil ruler), positions that by the 6th century BC were annually elected by the aristocracy on the Areopagus. Conflict arose between the aristocrats and rising commercial classes, and reached such a point that **Solon**, an aristocrat elected *archon* in 594 BC, was asked to re-establish 'good order'. He complied, writing new laws in exquisite poetry. Debts were forgiven, trade and crafts encouraged, and the **Council of Four Hundred** established to include a broader base of citizens in government.

But Solon's good start didn't stop his kinsman **Pisistratos** from making himself a 'popular' dictator or *tyrannos* in 560 BC. He began the naval build-up that first made Athens a threat to other Greek city-states. He reformed the Panathenaic Games in an attempt to rival the Olympics, instituted grandiose building projects and encouraged the arts and the planting of olives. His increasingly despotic son **Hippias** ruled until 510 BC, when **Kleisthenes**, an aristocrat, paid for a new temple at Delphi, and then 'suggested'

Getting to Athens

For details of flights to Athens from the UK and USA/Canada, *see* **Planning Your Trip**, pp.54–5.

Elefthérios Venizélos airport is 25km northeast of the centre of Athens. **Airport information**, t (+ 30) 210 353 0000, *www.aia.gr*, 24hrs a day in English and Greek. The airport has up-to-date facilities for the disabled, and a five-star Sofitel Hotel outside the main terminal. English is spoken in the **information booths**, which also have a complimentary phone service to every airport facility and airline, plus brochures about public transport in Athens.

Most of the action is on **level 0** (Arrivals): a **post office** (*open daily 7am–9pm*); an **Internet-fax** office (*open 8am–10pm*); **Pacific Baggage Storage and Courier**, t 210 353 0352 (*open 24hrs*), a **pharmacy** (*open daily 6am–midnight*); **exchange bureaux** (*open 24hrs*) and several **banks**, all bristling with automatic tellers; plus an office of the **EOT** (the Greek National Tourist Office), t 210 353 0448, with brochures and maps (*open Mon–Fri 9–6, Sat, Sun and hols 10–3*).

Getting to and from the Airport

By metro: Line 3 goes to Sýntagma and Monastiráki, where you can make connections to Piraeus (1hr from the airport). Tickets are €6.

By airport bus: Buses depart from the airport's main terminal. A good safe time-estimate from the terminal to the end of their lines might be an hour, slightly more in peak traffic periods. Every stop has a sign showing exact timetables. One-way tickets cost €3.20. Validate your ticket on the machine in the airport bus to mark the time and date. Children under six travel free.

E93, to the Kifissós bus station (via the Liossíon bus station) 24hrs a day (*every 45mins, 5am to midnight, every hour from midnight to 5am*).

E94, to the Ethnikí Ámyna metro station (on a direct line to Sýntagma), every 7mins from 5.30am until 8.10pm and then every 15–30mins.

E95, to Athens' central Sýntagma Square, every 10–30mins.

E96, to Karaïskaki Square, by Piraeus' main harbour, every 15–30mins.

KTEL buses from the airport also go directly to the ports of Rafína and Lávrio from Door 3. For schedules call t 1440.

By car: a toll road, the Attikí Ódos (€3) links the airport to the centre of Athens and on west to Kifissós and the Lamia–Piraeus highway, and to Elefsína and the Peloponnese.

By taxi: *See* 'Getting around Athens', overleaf. Taxis to Athens centre cost around €25, to Piraeus port €30, and the fare is doubled between midnight and 5am (so if you arrive near to 5am, it's best to wait until 5).

that the Oracle command the Spartans to liberate Athens from the tyrant. In the aftermath, as the aristocrats squabbled, Kleisthenes proposed reforms to check their power. They responded by trying to dissolve the Council of Four Hundred, and before they knew it they were cornered on the Acropolis by a spontaneous uprising; after 50 years of tyranny, the people were ripe for a new order.

Kleisthenes' reforms were revolutionary. For the first time, government would base itself on the concept of *isonomia*, or equal rights (at least for all male citizens). The population of Attica was divided into ten political *phylae* (tribes); each would draw lots to select 50 members to serve in the new **Council of Five Hundred**, which would vote on new laws and proposals sent by the old aristocratic assembly on the Areopagos – the Greek House of Lords. Kleisthenes also introduced ostracism – if any man was deemed too powerful, the citizens could vote him into exile for a decade.

Meanwhile, Ionian Greeks in Asia Minor (whom the Athenians regarded as cousins) urged Athens to come to their aid against the Persian Empire, which was forcing them to pay tribute. Recklessly, Athens agreed, and sent an army that burned the Persian city of

Athens Metro

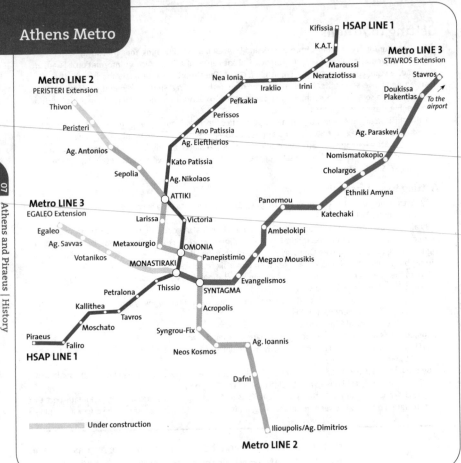

Metro LINE 1
HSAP LINE 1
Kifissia
K.A.T.
Maroussi
Neratziotissa
Nea Ionia
Iraklio
Irini
Pefkakia
Perissos

Metro LINE 3
STAVROS Extension
Stavros
To the airport
Doukissa Plakentias

Metro LINE 2
PERISTERI Extension
Thivon
Peristeri
Ag. Antonios
Sepolia

Ag. Paraskevi
Nomismatokopio
Cholargos
Ethniki Amyna
Ano Patissia
Ag. Eleftherios
Kato Patissia
Ag. Nikolaos
ATTIKI
Panormou
Katechaki

Metro LINE 3
EGALEO Extension
Larissa
Victoria
Egaleo
Ag. Savvas
Metaxourgio
Votanikos
OMONIA
MONASTIRAKI
Panepistimio
Megaro Mousikis
Ambelokipi

Petralona
Thissio
SYNTAGMA
Evangelismos
Kallithea
Tavros
Acropolis
Moschato
Syngrou-Fix
Piraeus
Faliro
Neos Kosmos
Ag. Ioannis
HSAP LINE 1

Dafni

Under construction

Ilioupolis/Ag. Dimitriou

Metro LINE 2

Sardis and returned home. It was provocation enough to land the city in the soup with **Darius**, the Persian king of kings, who in 490 BC sent an expeditionary force to **Marathon**, where it was defeated by the Athenians under **Miltiades**. Although Sparta and the other Greek states recognized the Persian threat, Athens was the only one seriously to prepare for it, thanks to **Themistocles**, a 'new man' (his father was a greengrocer), who persuaded the Athenians to invest in a much bigger navy. Perhaps even more astonishingly, in 480, when Darius' son **Xerxes** duly returned with the greatest army and navy yet seen, Themistocles convinced the Athenians to abandon their city altogether and trust in their fleet. Xerxes occupied Athens and razed it, just before he snatched defeat from the jaws of victory at **Sálamis**.

After the allied Greeks defeated the Persian army at **Plataea**, Themistocles engaged in a diplomatic war of nerves with Athens' powerful ally **Sparta**, hastily building city walls in 478 BC. The Spartans strongly believed that Athens should have no such thing,

Getting around Athens

By Metro, Tram and Bus

The **metro** is an important means of getting across Athens, especially from Piraeus. Tickets are 80¢. Purchase bus and trolley tickets (50¢) at the kiosks before boarding, and punch in the machine; if you're caught without a ticket the fine is €20 and up. There are no transfers allowed between surface routes, or between the metro and surface routes. It is possible to buy a day ticket for just under €4, good on all city transport, even to the airport (one-way), for 24hrs. Note that all city transport, except the airport buses and the Piraeus–Athens bus, begins at 5am and stops at midnight, so do plan to *arrive* at your destination *before* midnight. For metro or bus info within the city, call **t** 185 Mon–Fri 7am–9pm, Sat–Sun 9–5.

The air-conditioned Athens Tram System links the city to its seaside suburbs. The terminal is on Leofóros Amalía a couple of streets south of Sýntagma, with spurs along the coast to Piraeus/Falíro, and from Glyfáda to Voúla, putting Athens' beaches within 20 minutes or so of the centre.

By Taxi

There are stands in some squares, at the airport, train station and bus stations, but most taxis cruise the streets. Sharing is common (*see* below). The minimum charge (Tariff One) is €2.50; the almost double Tariff Two is for the period between midnight and 5am. If you travel on the Attikí Ódos, you'll be charged for the road tolls. Each bag over 10kg is 30¢. The charge for being picked up at the airport is €3. On major holidays, such as Easter, the driver gets a mandatory 'present' of €1. Taxis are regulated by the Athens Traffic Department, 24–6 Deligiánni St, Metaxoúrgio, **t** 210 523 0111. Not all drivers are honest, but merely showing this address to a driver usually solves disputes.

Radio taxis charge €2.50 from the moment you call, and slightly more if you book in advance. In many cases, especially if you're going to the airport, it's worth it. Try:

Athens 1, t 210 921 7942.
Parthenon, t 210 532 3300.
Enotita, t 210 645 9000.
Ikaros, t 210 515 2800 and **t** 801 112 4000.

Because fares are so low and demand so great, Athenians often **share cabs**. Usually, the cabbie leaves his flag lit, even if he has passengers, to indicate that he is willing to take more. Hailing a cab this way is not for the faint-hearted; the usual procedure is to stand by the street, flag down any passing cab, and if they slow down and cock an ear, shout out your general destination. If the taxi is going that way, the driver will stop; if not, he won't. Check the meter when you board, and pay from there, adding €2.50 (the minimum fare), plus any baggage charges. If the cabbie asks for the full fare, start writing down his licence number and ask for a receipt; that usually settles the issue on the spot.

By Car

Not fun. Besides the traffic jams, the one-way system is confusing and parking is almost impossible. If you need assistance, call **ELPA** (the Greek Automobile Club), **t** 104.

but Themistocles kept Sparta distracted until the walls were a *fait accompli*. The following year, Themistocles made the Athenian fleet – the only one in Greece capable of resisting the still constant Persian threat – the foundation of a web of alliances modern historians call the **Delian League**. Headquartered on the holy island of Délos, its membership eventually reached 200 city-states (but significantly, not Sparta), who contributed money, men or ships in return for protection. Athenian triremes challenged the Persians in Egypt and elsewhere, not always with success. Trade followed the flag, and one thing led to another; to keep the navy in fighting shape and justify its existence (and expense), the Athenians were soon sticking their fingers in every pie around, and what began as a league became a *de facto* empire.

The Athenians were sailing in some uncharted social and political waters, and **theatre** played a role in helping them cope with it all psychologically. The oldest tragedy to come down to us is Aeschylus' *The Persians*, from 479 BC. Sculptors may have achieved the calm Classical ideal in art, but political change in Classical Athens continued at a breakneck pace: in 470 or so Themistocles was ostracized, much to his surprise, and the popular, easygoing **Kimon**, son of Miltiades, became the leading politico. In 465 BC, wealthy Thássos, objecting to Athenian meddling in northern Greece, became the first major state to defect from the Delian League. Kimon took it after a two-year siege, and settled Athenians there in a *cleruchy*, or self-supporting garrison.

In 463–462 BC, while Kimon was away on Thássos, a younger generation, led by **Ephialtes**, pushed through a motion that abolished nearly all the powers of the aristocratic Areopagos and established annually elected council in its place. Now the people were in control from top to bottom; even the courts, until then run by officials, adopted a jury system. Other Greek states viewed the Athenian experiment in radical democracy with the same fascinated horror as Europe would the French Revolution. Now it was Kimon's turn to be ostracized; Ephialtes was assassinated and **Pericles** emerged as the popular leader when he proposed the final demo-cractic touch: pay for jurors and members of the Council of Five Hundred, making it possible for even the poorest *thetes*, the lowest class who rowed the triremes, to participate.

'Born into the world to take no rest themselves and to give none to others,' was Thucydides' description of his fellow Athenians. Their wealth, their feeling of unlimited potential and their addiction to novelty attracted artists and intellectuals to the city such as Phidias, Sophocles, Euripides, Aristophanes, Herodotus, Anaximander and Socrates. And the Athenians agreed with Pericles, that they could only keep going forward, wherever their momentum might take them. They would use the dues of the Delian League to do it, with enough left over to rebuild the temples destroyed by the Persians, beginning with the Parthenon, completed in 438 BC.

While she was busy creating the fundamentals of Western culture, Athens never passed a year without a war somewhere. The day of the independent *polis* was over: Athens signed a 30-year peace treaty with Sparta in 446 BC, each recognizing the other's sphere of influence in Greece. But Pericles always suspected a showdown between the two was inevitable. He linked Athens to Piraeus with long walls, ensuring the city's lifeline in a siege, and then followed policies designed to provoke the Spartans. War-weary Athenians would later come to blame him for everything.

In 431 BC, the uneasy *détente* in Greece unravelled into the **Peloponnesian War**. Although fighting Sparta and Sparta's allies as well as rebellious members of the Delian League (eager to slip away from the 300 per cent increase in dues Athens demanded), it was still Athens' war to lose, and she lost it. The first year saw a Spartan army occupy Attica. Everyone took refuge in Athens, only to suffer the **Great Plague** of 430 BC, which carried off thousands, Pericles among them. The city's new leader, the demagogue **Kleon**, refused every chance for peace, leaving the Spartans, especially their young and just general **Brasidas**, to pose as the liberators of Greece; when both Kleon and Brasidas were killed in battle, both sides signed the **Peace of Nicias** (421 BC). It wasn't worth the stone it was carved on. Egged on by irresponsible politicians, especially **Alcibiades**, student of Socrates, the Athenians overreached themselves by attempting to conquer **Syracuse** in Magna Graecia, where they suffered their gravest defeat (413 BC). Yet Athens battled on for another seven years. Revolts of allies and a Spartan alliance with Persia sealed her doom; Lysander and the Spartans brought the city to her knees with a crushing naval defeat at **Aegospotami** in 405 BC.

The Spartans resisted calls from other cities to destroy Athens, content merely to raze the long walls and the fortifications of Piraeus. The brutal regime they installed, the **Thirty Tyrants**, killed over 1,500, before they themselves were executed in a revolt. Democracy made a quick recovery. By 378 BC the city had set up a **second Delian League**, but the Peloponnesian War had struck a blow from which Athens would never recover; though still the most important city in Greece, it would never again be a political force. Although Socrates was put to death (399 BC), Athens' intellectual traditions held true in the 4th century, the age of Praxiteles, Menander and Plato.

When **Philip II** made a power of **Macedonia**, Athenian patriotism was kept alive by the orator Demosthenes even as Philip subdued all of Greece (338 BC). Losing control of its own destiny, the city would become a prize fought over by Alexander's generals, beginning with **Demetrios Poliorketes**, who captured it in 294 BC. In the new Hellenistic world, Alexandria, **Rhodes** and **Pergamon** gradually displaced Athens as cultural centres. In 168 BC **Rome** captured Athens, but in honour of past glory left her with many privileges; 80 years later, though, Sulla punished the city for supporting Mithridates of Pontus by destroying Piraeus, the Agora and the walls. Later Romans would remember their cultural debt; while the city dwindled, they attended the academies and endowed the city with monuments. **St Paul** started the Athenians on the road to Christianity in AD 44. In the 3rd century **Goths** sacked the city; in 529, **Justinian** closed the philosophy schools and made the Parthenon a cathedral.

Athens re-enters history as the plaything of the **Franks** after they seized Constantinople in 1204. **Guy de la Roche** was made the Duke of Athens, a title held at various times by the Catalans, Neapolitans and Venetians. In 1456 it was the turn of the **Ottomans**, who converted the Parthenon into a mosque and the Erechtheion into a harem. The **Venetians** made several attempts to wrench Athens away; in **Morosini**'s siege of 1687, a shell struck the Parthenon, igniting the Turkish gunpowder stores.

In 1834, after the **War of Independence**, Athens – population 200, living in a clutch of houses under the Acropolis – was declared the capital of the state for the old glory of its name. **Otto of Bavaria**, the first king of the Greeks, brought his own architects with him to lay out a new city, based on a grid running northeast of Stadíou and Panepistimíou (El. Venizélou) Streets. Neoclassical public buildings, evoking ancestral glory, went up everywhere, many of the more elaborate ones financed by wealthy Greeks of the diaspora, keen to show off their Hellenic credentials. By 1860 the population had risen to 30,000. Yet even the best laid plans could not cope with the flood of people from the countyside who came looking for jobs and the thousands of Greek refugees who arrived after the population exchange in 1922.

Today Athens resembles a dense domino game stacked over the dry hills of Attica. The metropolis squeezes in four million lively, opinionated inhabitants – over a third of the population of Greece – who are now more prosperous than they have been since the age of Pericles, and enjoying all the post-2004 Olympic improvements that have made their home, after 2,000 years, a world-class city again.

Sýntagma Square and Pláka

Athens' very new and very ancient personalities begin to unfold at their classic intersection at **Sýntagma** or 'Constitution' **Square**, where bus, trolley, tram and metro lines converge, *períptera* sell newspapers from around the world, and Greeks who don't give a hang about cultural pollution pack the great big McDonald's. The square was designed to set off the neoclassical royal palace, now the **Parliament Building** (Voulí), fronted by the **Monument to the Unknown Soldier**, whose guards in *evzone* uniform astonish passers-by every hour with some of the strangest steps ever invented by the military mind. Stretching beyond the Parliament are the **National Gardens**, a cool haven of shade to escape the summer heat.

South of Sýntagma, a short walk up Filellínon Street leads to Kydathinéon Street, the main artery into **Pláka**, the old neighbourhood gathered under the skirts of the Acropolis. The atmosphere changes abruptly: the narrow streets of Pláka follow the city's ancient and medieval plan. Pláka is the Athens that became Greece's capital in 1834; now it is the capital of tourist Athens, a favourite for serious souvenir shopping.

Jewish Museum
39 Nikis St, t 210 322 5582, www. jewish museum.gr; open Mon–Fri 9–2.30 and Sun 10–2; adm

Amid the hubbub lie a smattering of museums. A handsome neoclassical building houses the **Jewish Museum**, with one of the most important collections in Europe, arranged by theme. Although Jews lived in Greece since Hellenistic times (and became assimilated as Romiótes), the Sephardic majority arrived from Spain after 1492; only a fraction survived the Holocaust. Opposite the Byzantine church of the **Metamorphósis**, the **Greek Folk Art Museum** offers several floors of needlework, carvings, silver, weapons, jewellery, shadow puppets, bridal costumes and a delightful room painted by Theóphilos Hatzimicháil (*see* pp.561–2). For something completely different, the **Frissíras Museum**, around the corner, offers an important private collection of 20th-century art and special exhibits.

Greek Folk Art Museum
17 Kydathinéon St, t 210 322 9031; open summer Mon 12–7, Tues–Sun 8–7; winter Tues–Sun 8.30–3; adm

Frissíras Museum
3–7 Monis Asteríou St, t 210 323 4678, www. frissirasmuseum.com; open Wed–Fri 11–7, Sat and Sun 10–3; adm exp

Further east, Kydathinéon runs into Adrianoú, the oldest street in Athens still in use. Kydathinéon next meets Tripodón Street, once an important intersection for theatre-lovers. On the fifth day of the Great Dionysia, a panel would choose best actor, best playwright and best producer/sponsor (*choregós*). Every winner was allowed to put up a monument – usually a tripod – to his victory in this area; Tripodón Street, as its name suggests, was lined with them. One of the more elaborate is just along Séllei Street: the **Monument of Lysikrátes**, put up by a winning *choregós* of 334 BC. Its Corinthian columns stood under a frieze depicting Dionysos and the Tyrrhenian pirates. Later, the monument was incorporated into a Capuchin friary as a **library**, where Byron used to sit and read by lamplight.

Just south of here you can pick up the new 4km **pedestrian walk** that has transformed the ancient city centre into a lovely archaeological park, allowing visitors to take in the highlights of classical Athens along the way. But start with the Acropolis.

The Acropolis

The Acropolis
site (t 210 321 0219) and museum (t 210 323 6665); open summer 8–7.30; Oct–April 8–5; ticket for both costs €12 and includes adm to the ancient Agora, Temple of Zeus (Olympeion), Roman Agora, Theatre of Dionysos and Kerameikós – all the sights on the pedestrian walkway – so visit the Acropolis first; there's a lift to the top for the disabled (ring ahead)

Acropolis means 'top of the town' and, although many Greek cities grew up around natural citadels, Athens has *the* Acropolis, a limestone rock standing a proud 90m (300ft) over the city which goes straight to the core of its very being. Inhabited by the end of the Neolithic era, it later supported a Mycenaean palace with a Temple of Athena inside it, surrounded by Cyclopean walls. Before democracy, the tyrants lived here as well, sharing the rock with a Temple of Poseidon and Athena, built after their famous contest to become patron of the city. Poseidon struck the Acropolis with his trident to create the salt spring Klepsydra; Athena invented the olive tree, and won. In 480 BC her wooden cult statue was hurriedly bundled off to Sálamis, just before the Persians burnt everything. This allowed for renovations and the creation of the Acropolis as we see it today, a showcase dedicated to the wealth and glory of Athens.

The processional ramp, rebuilt by Themistocles, rises to the **Propylaia**. Architects consider this majestic Pentelic marble entrance gate, ingeniously built over an uneven slope by Pericles' architect Mnesikles, the equal of the Parthenon, its five gates with wood and bronze doors big enough to admit horsemen and chariots for the annual Panathenaic procession. On either side of its entrance are wings; the one to the north held a picture gallery (*pinakothéke*) which also served as a VIP lounge, while the smaller one to the south is a *trompe l'œil* work that appears to have the same dimensions as the *pinakothéke*, although in fact it is little more than a façade because the priests of Athena Nike refused to have a wing in their precinct.

To the right of the Propylaia, on a bastion of the Mycenaean wall, stands the pretty little Ionic **Temple of Athena Nike**, built of Pentelic marble by Kallikrates in 478 BC. In 1687 the Turks dismantled it to build a nearby wall, making it easy to rebuild it in 1835, 1936, and recently again, over a titanium skeleton. From the temple platform, King Aegeus watched for the return of his son Theseus from Minos' Crete. Theseus was to have signalled his safe return with a white sail but forgot; at the sight of the black sail Aegeus swooned, fell off the precipice and gave his name to the Aegean sea.

The Parthenon

🔟 The Parthenon

The Parthenon, probably the most famous building in the world, is a Doric temple constructed between 447 and 432 BC by Iktinos and Kallikrates, and supervised by Phidias, the Michelangelo of the Periclean age. Originally called the Great Temple, brightly painted and shimmering with gold, it took the name Parthenon (Chamber of the Virgin) a hundred years after its completion. An estimated 13,400 blocks of Pentelic marble went into its construction, each cut to precise mathematical calculations; the largest weighed 10 tons and no two were alike. Its architects wrote the book on *entasis* or 'tension' to imitate nature, shaping the columns so that they swelled slightly in the centre, as if they were live things supporting the weight. As there are no straight lines in nature, there is none in the whole building: the foundation is slightly curved to prevent the illusion of drooping caused by straight horizontals. The columns bend a few centimetres inward, and those on the corners are wider. These minute details give the Parthenon its incomparable life, harmony and bounce.

The Doric order, symbolic of strength, was used in the outer colonnade of 46 columns. It was decorated with 92 *metopes*, carved with scenes of conquests over 'barbarians' that echoed the recent triumph over the Persians: the east side portrayed the Battle of Giants and Gods, the south that of the Lapiths and Centaurs, on the west were the Athenians and the Amazons, and on the north the

Battle of Troy. Only fragments (mostly in the British Museum) survive of the pediment sculptures of the birth of Athena and her contest with Poseidon – after shelling the Parthenon, Morosini then tried to remove the pediment as a souvenir for Venice but the ropes broke and the whole thing shattered. The inner colonnade was Ionic, symbolic of Athens' culture, and had a more peaceful and spiritual decoration: a sublime 160m (524ft) continuous frieze of 400 human figures and 200 animals in low relief designed by Phidias, depicting the Panathenaic Procession. Here, too, subtle calculations (the lower bits are sculpted to a depth of 3cm, the upper to 5.5cm) and a slight downward tilt gave the figures added life.

The Parthenon was designed to hold Phidias' chryselephantine (ivory- and gold-covered) **statue of Athena**, which stood over 11m (36ft) high; small surviving copies give an inkling of its majestic appearance. Altogether, the Parthenon, with its masterful perfection and elaborate decoration, all paid for by diverted Delian League dues, was built not to the gods (it lacked even the most basic cult necessity, a permanent stone altar outside) but to the glory and wealth of Athens. The statue of Athena was clad with 44 talents of gold, a big part of the state treasury – the goddess's robes as Fort Knox, there for all to see. And it was visible thanks to a unique roof, tiled with white marble slabs sliced so thin that light could filter through.

The Parthenon later found a religious role as a church and mosque, remaining intact until 1687, when Morosini's bomb hit the Turks' powder stores and blew off the roof. The scaffolding removed for the Olympics has returned: since 1983, the temple has been the subject of an intense rehabilitation programme. While discovering how to clean it, engineers have learned a good deal about ancient building techniques and will reconstruct as much as possible, using rust-free titanium rods.

Acropolis Museum

Acropolis Museum
in late 2007, this museum should reopen in its new quarters (see p.81), along with artefacts that have never before been displayed because of lack of space

In ancient times the Acropolis was thronged with exquisite Attic sculptures, including Phidias' 12m (40ft) statue of Athena Promachos, whose golden spear-tip could be seen miles out at sea. Although this has vanished without trace, smaller works were buried over the centuries (the rule was that anything dedicated to the gods could never be taken away, but could be buried in their sacred precinct). The Archaic works in particular stand out: painted pediments from the 6th-century BC Hecatompedon (or 'Old' Parthenon) and from the Temple of Athena Polias; the *Calf-Bearer* (Moschoforos) from 570 BC; lovely painted *kore* statues; the famous *Rampin Horseman*, and several panels of the Parthenon frieze, and the pollution-scarred *caryatids* from the Erechtheion, in a case filled with nitrogen.

The Greek flag flying on the nearby belvedere has a special meaning. The first thing the Nazis did in their occupation was add their swastika. On the night of 30 May 1941, two teenagers crept up the secret Mycenaean stair and stole it from under the guards' noses, in what became the opening salvo of the Greek resistance.

The Erechtheion

The second great temple of the Acropolis, the Erechtheion, was completed only in 395 BC, after the Peloponnesian War. This complex Ionic temple with three porches owes its idiosyncrasies to the much older holies of holies it encompassed – the sanctuaries of Athena Polias, Poseidon Erechtheus, and the olive tree planted by the goddess – yet such is the genius of its structure that it appears harmonious. The southern porch is supported by six **caryatids** (now casts), to complement the Parthenon opposite. Behind the **east portico**, with its six Ionic columns, the **cella** was divided to serve both Athena Polias and Poseidon Erechtheos, and held the biggest juju of them all: the primitive cult **statue of Athena Polias**, wearer of the sacred *peplos*. Down the steps is the Erechtheion's **north porch**, defined by six tall and elegant Ionic columns. Part of the floor and roof were cut away to reveal the marks left by Poseidon's trident; when the Turks made the temple a harem, they used the sacred place as a toilet. This porch was the tomb of the city's founder Erechtheos. A small **olive tree** replaces the Athena-created original in the western court of the temple.

Theatre of Dionysos and Odeon of Herodes Atticus

Theatre of Dionysos
and Odeon of
Herodes Atticus
*t 210 322 4625;
open May–Sept daily
8–7; Oct–April daily
8–5; adm*

Built into the side of the Acropolis, the **Theatre of Dionysos** is the oldest playhouse in the world. But its stone seats never saw a first night performance of the great tragedies of the Classical period; Aeschylus, Sophocles and Euripides made do with seats dug into the hill or wooden bleachers. The existing theatre was begun from 342 to 326 BC and reached its present form by the time of Nero when it seated 17,000.

It was Pisistratos who inaugurated the annual **Great Dionysia**, a contest in which playwrights presented plays to honour the god and to be judged by their peers. For each of three days the Athenians attended three tragedies and a satyr play, followed by a fourth day of comedies. All were paid for by *choregoi*, or producers, selected by the state, who were also expected to fork out for a banquet for their amateur troupe after the performance. Well over a thousand men and boys would be rehearsing each year. From this festival emerged comedy that even the Marx brothers could only approach, and dramas whose lyric power and brilliance has seldom been equalled.

Such was the reputation of Athens after its heyday that it had a slew of wealthy benefactors, all keen to enjoy a bit of reflected glory. One was Eumenes II of Pergamon (d. 159 BC) who built the long **Stoa of Eumenes** next to the theatre, where the audience could relax and buy drinks and snacks; its roof supported a road, the *peripatos*, that encircled the Acropolis. Off this was an **Asklepeion**, dedicated to the healing god Asklepios, founded after Athens was decimated by plague in 429 BC. Next to the Stoa of Eumenes is the **Odeon** (AD 161), another gift, this time from the Rockefeller of his day, the Roman Herodes Atticus. Famous in its time for having no interior columns to support its long-gone cedar roof, the 6,000-seat odeon now hosts the excellent **Festival of Athens**, where modern European and ancient Greek cultures meet in theatre, ballet and classical concerts performed by companies from all over the world.

South and East of the Acropolis

The neighbourhood south of the Acropolis, looking towards the theatre, is named **Markrigiánni**, after the likeable general of the Greek War of Independence, whose statue is on Dionysíou Areopagítou Street, part of the new pedestrian walkway. At the corner of Makrigiánni Street, behind the Acropolis metro station, stands the €129 million **New Acropolis Museum**, designed by Bernard Tschumi and dogged by controversy but now slated to open in late 2007. Bigger than the Parthenon, it stands on pillars to protect the excavations of Neolithic Athens. *See* the old Acropolis Museum (p. 79) for a description of some of the contents, although expect new marvels: this has ten times more exhibition space, and thousands of items in storage for decades will be put on display. A vast upper glass hall with a view of the Parthenon will be ready to house the famous marbles by Phidias, taken by Lord Elgin just before the Greek War of Independence – if Britain ever sends them back.

Ilías Lalaoúnis Jewellery Museum
4a Karyátidon St, t 210 922 1044; open Mon, Thurs, Fri and Sat 9–4, Wed 9–9, closed Tues and Sun; adm free on Wed after 3

Another museum here: the **Ilías Lalaoúnis Jewellery Museum**, is where Lalaoúnis, the only jeweller admitted into the Académie des Beaux Arts, displays his work based on ancient designs.

The Temple of Olympian Zeus

Temple of Olympian Zeus
t 210 922 6330; open May–Aug 8–7.30; Sept–April 8–5; adm

Just to the east, the pedestrian walkway leads to busy Leofóros Amalías and the **Temple of Olympian Zeus**. Fifteen enormous columns and one prone and broken like spilled breath mints recall what Livy called 'the only temple on earth of a size adequate to the greatness of the god'. The spot was long sacred: not far away stood a very ancient temple to the Earth, with a cleft in the floor that drained the deluge sent by Zeus to punish humanity, killing all but Deucalion and his wife. The ambitious foundations were laid by Pisistratos, only to be continued centuries later in 175 BC by a Roman architect, Cossutius. It was half finished when Cossutius' patron, Antiochos IV of Syria, died, leaving Hadrian to complete it in AD 131. Nearby are the ruins of a well-appointed Roman bath. The view to the east is tranquil, closed by the violet-tinted slopes of Mount

Hymettos, while just to the west, where the traffic hums down Amalías, stands **Hadrian's Arch**, in Pentelic marble, erected by the Athenians to thank him for his benevolence. The complimentary inscription reads, on the Acropolis side, 'This is Athens, the ancient city of Theseus,' while the other side reads, 'This is the city of Hadrian, not of Theseus.'

Záppeion Park just north, an extension of the National Gardens, surrounds the handsome horseshoe-shaped **Záppeion Palace** (1888), now used for summit meetings and other events. On the corner by Leof. Amalías, don't miss the statue of Hellas to Lord Byron, in which a maiden representing Greece hugs the poet while sticking her hand in his pocket – a fairly accurate allegory of what occurred during the War of Independence, which Byron was the first Western celebrity to support.

West and North of the Acropolis

Philopáppos Hill, the Pnyx and the Areopagos

The pedestrian walkway west of the Acropolis leads around to the stepped lane up **Philopáppos Hill**, past the lovely Byzantine church of **Ag. Dimítrios Lombardiáris**. Various paths, paved with stone and ancient marbles, wind up to the lofty **Philopáppos Monument** (AD 114) built in honour of Caius Julius Antiochos Philopappos, a Syrian Prince and friend of Athens. The views of the Acropolis, almost level with the monument, are among the best, and the sunsets are famous – but after dark it's very isolated, so take care. The **Dora Stratou Theatre**, where the city's professional folk dance troupe (*see* p.99) performs nightly in summer, is tucked behind.

To the right of Ag. Dimítrios, another path leads to the shallow bowl of the **Pnyx**, where the democractic assembly, the Ekklesia, met 30 to 40 times a year and heard Pericles and Demosthenes, or any citizen (i.e. any free Athenian male over the age of 20 who had performed military service) who donned a wreath and mounted the rostrum. Sometimes it was necessary to summon the police (Scythian slaves, who were excused from the taboo of laying hands on a citizen) to lasso the Athenians – literally, with a rope dipped in red paint as a mark of shame – to fill the minimum attendance quota of 5,000. What you see dates from the 4th century BC; in Roman times the assembly moved to the Theatre of Dionysos. Beyond this is the **Hill of the Nymphs**, where the magical maidens were replaced in 1842 by the **Observatory**.

Slightly to the north, across the walkway, is the bald **Areopagos**, or hill of Ares, the seat of the original aristocratic assembly. Here the High Council heard murder trials, in the open, so that the councillors could avoid the pollution of being under the same roof as a murderer. Even in the days of radical democracy, the council continued to advise on the Athenian constitution. One of its tasks was to judge foreign religions, including Christianity and its Unknown God as expounded by St Paul in AD 52 (verdict: not impressed, although a certain Dionysos converted and became Athens' first bishop and saint, Dionysos the Areopagite).

Anafiótika and the Roman Forum

Below the Areopagos, pedestrian-only Theorías Street descends into Pláka, by way of the back entrance to the ancient Agora (*see* below) and through **Anafiótika**, a residential enclave left by the builders of Otto's palaces, who came from Anáfi and, homesick, tried to recreate their island village here. One neoclassical mansion holds the Kanellópoulos Museum, a sampler of Greek civilization, from Neolithic times to the 19th century, with choice *objets d'art* from every period.

Kanellópoulos Museum
corner of Theorías and Panós Sts, t 210 321 2313; closed for restoration at the time of writing

Below, on Pelopída and Aiólou lies the Romaïkí Agorá, or **Roman Forum**. Feeling uncomfortable in the ancient Agora after Sulla wasted it, the Romans built their own marketplace, which remained a market into Ottoman times. They knew the time, thanks to a *klepsydra* (hydraulic clock) in the lovely octagonal 1st-century BC **Tower of the Winds**, built by Andronicus of Cyrrhus to prove there were eight winds rather than four, but lacking its bronze weathervane. At its west end, the forum's **Gate of Athena Archegetis** was paid for by Julius and Augustus Caesar; one of its posts displays the market-pricing rules of Hadrian. There is also a court and ruined *stoa*, and the **Fethiyé Tzamí**, the Victory or Corn Market Mosque.

Roman Forum
t 210 324 5220; open May–Sept 8–7.30; Oct–April 8–5; adm

Plateía Agorás, just north of the forum, is a pleasant place to sip a drink while contemplating **Hadrian's Library**, an enormous building (120 by 82m/400 by 269ft) donated by that most philhellene of emperors, equipped with an inner peristyle courtyard and garden with a long pool. At the top of nearby Diogénous Street, the **Popular Musical Instruments Museum** offers a fascinating collection of Greek folk instruments with headphones to listen to what they sound like.

Hadrian's Library
open Mon–Fri 8.30–3

Popular Musical Instruments Museum
t 210 325 0198; open Tues and Thurs–Sun 10–2, Wed 12–6

Below Hadrian's Library, Monastiráki metro station shares its square with the charming little 10th-century Byzantine basilica of the **Pantánassa** (the Queen of Heaven) and the **Tsizdaráki Mosque**, built by the governor of Athens in 1759. It now houses the Kyriazópoulos Ceramic Collection, with a display of traditional and contemporary works. West of the square, **Monastiráki** is Athens' souk, where bulging shops sell antiques, clothes, trinkets and souvenirs; **Plateía Avissinías**, at the centre, is chock-full of old furniture, and on Sunday comes to life with a bustling outdoor antiques and flea market. But this part of Athens has always been a market: the Agora is adjacent.

Kyriazópoulos Ceramic Collection
t 210 324 2066; open Wed–Mon 9–2.30; adm

The Ancient Agora, Kerameikós and Around

The Agora

⭐ The Agora
entrance on Adrianoú St, Theorías St or Apostoloú Pávlou St, t 210 321 0185; open May–Sept 8–7.30; Oct–April 8–5; adm

The Agora was the heart of ancient Athens: not just a market, but a stage for public life, for elections, meetings, festivals and court proceedings. It had many of the characteristics of a *temenos* (sacred precinct), marked with boundary stones, and was strictly off limits to draft-dodgers, murderers, traitors and other political outcasts. For citizens, the news, political manoeuvrings and social contacts available in the shade of its *stoas* were life itself. By citizens, of course, we mean men. Only flute girls (prostitutes) and poor women selling fish or other goods were regulars in the Agora. Men even did the shopping. Aristophanes satirized the way they looked as they sashayed about during the Peloponnesian War, parcels dangling from their spears. Here a man could get lucky, and be buttonholed by the likes of Socrates or Demosthenes. The conversations in this public arena changed the course of Western civilization.

The Agora started out as a large open space, with *stoas* and buildings around its perimeter. After the Persians razed it in 480 BC, it was rebuilt on a much grander scale. Once again, after suffering desecration at the hand of Sulla's Romans, most of the structures were rebuilt, and then more added to create a clutter a 5th-century Athenian would scarcely have recognized. Athenians in need of cut stone pillaged the ruins for centuries to build walls, churches and houses. What remains covers every era of ancient history. Only the foundations remain of the council house or **Bouleuterion**, built in the late 6th century BC after its establishment by Kleisthenes, and the neighbouring Temple of the Mother of the Gods, the **Metroön**, built by the Athenians as reparation for the slaying of a priest from her cult. Rooms on either side served as the public records archive and citizens' registry (to this day *mitroön* in Greek means 'register'). The annually elected *prytanes* governed from the round **Tholos** or **Prytaneon**. Since some had to be on call day and night, it had kitchens and sleeping quarters. Official guests were fêted here, and honoured citizens, such as Olympic winners and their descendants, were given dining rights in perpetuity. When Socrates was on trial, he was asked to choose a just sentence for himself. He replied that he should be given the right to eat free at the Prytaneon, meaning that he regarded himself as a valuable member of the state. He got to drink hemlock instead, in a building further south that has been tentatively identified as **Socrates' Prison**.

Near the Tholos is a **Horos**, one of the Agora's boundary stones still in situ. Opposite the Metroön, a stone fence and statue bases mark the **Sanctuary of the Eponymous Heroes of Athens**, which once

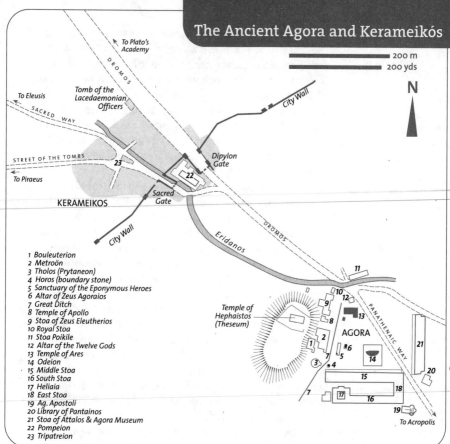

200 m
200 yds

N

To Plato's Academy

DROMOS

Tomb of the Lacedaemonian Officers

To Eleusis

SACRED WAY

City Wall

Dipylon Gate

STREET OF THE TOMBS

To Piraeus

23

22

Sacred Gate

KERAMEIKOS

City Wall

DROMOS

Eridanos

1 Bouleuterion
2 Metroön
3 Tholos (Prytaneon)
4 Horos (boundary stone)
5 Sanctuary of the Eponymous Heroes
6 Altar of Zeus Agoraios
7 Great Ditch
8 Temple of Apollo
9 Stoa of Zeus Eleutherios
10 Royal Stoa
11 Stoa Poikile
12 Altar of the Twelve Gods
13 Temple of Ares
14 Odeion
15 Middle Stoa
16 South Stoa
17 Heliaia
18 East Stoa
19 Ag. Apostoli
20 Library of Pantainos
21 Stoa of Áttalos & Agora Museum
22 Pompeion
23 Tripatreion

Temple of Hephaistos (Theseum)

AGORA

PANATHENAIC WAY

To Acropolis

contained the statues of the ten heroes instituted by Kleisthenes to give their names to the ten tribes of Athens. Since each tribal ward was spread all over Attica to avoid one large geographical area taking precedence, members came here to read announcements concerning their tribe. The nearby **Altar of Zeus Agoraios** received the oaths of the new *archons*, leaders of the tribes, a practice initiated by Solon. Running between the enclosure to the ten heroes and the Metroön is the **Great Ditch**; it still dutifully drains rainwater from the Acropolis through the Agora to the Eridanos river that flows through the Kerameikós cemetery.

The small 4th-century BC **Temple of Apollo** by the Metroön was dedicated to the forebear of the Ionians, who believed themselves descended from Apollo's son Ion. Almost nothing remains of the **Stoa of Zeus Eleutherios**, one of the haunts of Socrates. It was partly built into the rock in 430 BC in honour of Zeus the Saviour for his role in saving the city from the Persians. Some of it disappears into the metro tracks. A bridge crosses to the pathetic little strip of ruins by the tracks that was once the small **Royal Stoa** (*stoa basileios*) where

Athenian laws were written in stone for all to see; Socrates faced them when the indictment was read out against him. A massive slab built into the *stoa*'s step, believed to be a lintel from a *tholos* tomb, was the traditional **oath stone** where the Athenians swore their most sacred vows. If walking through the embankment north at this point were possible, you would come to the once-famed **Stoa Poikile**, decorated with paintings of the Battle of Marathon, where Zeno of Kition taught in the late 4th century; hence 'Stoic' philosophy. Now it and a temple share a dismal hole on the other side of Adrianoú St.

Back over the bridge, in front and beyond the Stoa of Zeus, stands the **Altar of the Twelve Gods**, from which all distances in Attica were measured, although this too was partially obliterated with the laying of the Piraeus–Thissío train tracks in 1868, when no one knew exactly where the Agora was. Beside the Altar of the Twelve Gods, right at the Agora's main entrance, is part of the **Panathenaic Way**, the ceremonial path from the Dipylon Gate (*see* overleaf) to the Acropolis, laid out by Pisistratos at the consecration of the Panathenaic Festival in 566 BC. In Athens' heyday, it was a gravel path.

South of the Altar of Twelve Gods stood a 5th-century BC Doric **Temple to Ares**. But it wasn't always here: it was dismantled stone by stone and brought to town from the suburbs by the Romans. The Roman also filled in other blanks to the south. The three giants standing sentinel nearby were originally part of the **Odeon of Agrippa**, built in 15 BC; parts of the orchestra remain intact, but the massive roof collapsed in AD 190. Both the site and giants were reused in the façade of a 5th-century gymnasium. Near the 2nd-century BC **Middle Stoa** are the ruins of a Roman temple and ancient shops. On the other side of the Middle Stoa was the **South Stoa**, where the rooms used for symposia can still be made out. These were for intimate stag parties, with wine, women and song. Beside it, to the west, is the large square people's court, or **Heliaia**, organized by Solon in the 6th century BC to hear political questions. It has been identified as one of the possible sites of the jury trials; since the jurors could number in the hundreds, a big space was required.

Between the South and **East Stoa** (2nd century BC) is the 11th-century church of **Ag. Apóstoli**, built on the site where St Paul addressed the Athenians; it has fine frescoes, and sports a tall, elegant octagonal dome held up by four Roman columns. Across the Panathenaic Way runs **Valerian's Wall**, thrown up in AD 257 against the barbarians, made of stone from buildings wrecked by the Romans. Between Valerian's Wall and the Stoa of Attalos are higgledy-piggledy ruins of the **Library of Pantainos**, built by Flavius Pantainos in AD 100 and destroyed 167 years later. Beside it, the **Stoa of Attalos** was built as a kind of luxury shopping mall in the 2nd century BC by one of Athens' benefactors, King Attalos II of

Pergamon, and carefully reconstructed in 1953–5 with funds from the Rockefellers. It contains the **Agora Museum**, a great introduction to everyday life in ancient times. Among its delights are a complex balloting mechanism for choosing jurors, a Spartan shield hauled home as a trophy and a 4th-century BC child's training potty. Also on display are the *óstraka* (potsherds) used to ostracize anyone whom the Athenians thought was getting too uppity.

On the east edge of the Agora, the mid-5th-century BC **Theseum** is nothing less than the best-preserved Greek temple in existence. It was given this name by archaeologists who thought it was the tomb built by Kimon for Theseus, but they were wrong. This Doric temple was dedicated to Hephaistos, the god of metals and smiths. It is constructed almost entirely of Pentelic marble and decorated with *metopes* depicting the lives of Heracles and Theseus. Converted into a church in the 5th century, it was used as a burial place for Protestants until 1834 and gave its name to **Thissío**, the now mostly pedestrianized neighbourhood filled with cafés west of the temple.

Kerameikós: the Graveyard Shift

Kerameikós
148 Ermoú St, *t* 210 346
3552; open May–Sept
daily 8–7.30; Oct–April
daily 8–5; adm.

Extending from the Agora was the Athenian West End, a large quarter known as Kerameikós, or 'pottery district', where Athenian potters lived near the superb clay they used to create their masterpieces. The Germans excavated the quarter, then delightfully filled it up again to look as much as possible as it did in late 5th century BC, when travellers would arrive in Athens through the recessed 'two towered' or **Dipylon Gate**, the city's front door and the largest gate in ancient Greece. The marble floor of the **fountain house**, where they abluted before entering the city, survives just inside its double doors. South of the gate stretches a section of Themistocles' **city walls**, thrown up on the double in 478 BC, and the smaller but more imposing **Sacred Gate**, where the Sacred Way to Eleusis made its exit. In the Pompeion, located just inside the walls, officials organized the parade (*pompe*) for the Panathenaea Festival and lolled about on one of the 60 dining couches.

Kerameikós' residents were used to living cheek by jowl with the dead, who as ancient custom dictated were buried along the road outside of the city precinct; burials in Kerameikós go back to Mycenaean times. Merchants and sailors would have gone down the Sacred Way to the **Tripatreion**, an easy-to-spot triangular enclosure honouring all of the dead, and then left on the **Street of Tombs**, to Piraeus. Plato must have strolled on the **Dromos**, the wide street leading through the Dipylon Gate to his academy to the north. And punctuating all this: funerals and burials, over 2,000 years' worth. Many of the tombs (or copies) have been re-erected in situ.

The **museum** by the entrance is a treasure house of pottery, with Proto-Geometric pieces with Mycenaean designs, Geometric ware and a little *caryatid* with an Archaic smile. Look for the *katára*, a lead box containing a manacled lead doll, scratched with the names of people to be cursed – a message sent to Hades with the corpse.

Around Kerameikós: Gázi

West of Kerameikós, **Gázi**, the former gasworks (1857) with its neon-lit smokestacks, is finding a new life as the fashionable location for galleries, clubs and designer restaurants. Along Piréos Street there's **Technópolis**, a multi-function cultural space in the old foundry, with a **Maria Callas Museum**. Just south on Piréos Street, the spanking new **Pireos Street Annexe**, part of the Benáki art empire (*see* below) has become a top venue for temporary art and photography exhibitions in Athens.

Maria Callas Museum
t 210 346 0981;
open Mon–Fri 10–3

Pireos Street Annexe
t 210 345 3111, open
Wed, Thurs, Sun 10–6, Fri
and Sat 10–10

Heading Back East: Ermoú Street, Psirrí and Athens Cathedral

Hermes was the conductor of dead souls at Kerameikós, but he was also the patron of commerce, and the east end of his street, Ermoú, is dedicated to shopping. Just off this to the north, on the corner of Ag. Asomáton and Dipylou Sts, is the new **Islamic Art Museum**, spread out in two neoclassical buildings, incorporating an ancient wall and a tomb. This houses the Benáki family's fabulous collection of 8th–19th-century Islamic art, one of the ten most important in the world, acquired during their residence in Egypt.

Islamic Art Museum
t 210 325 1311,
www.benaki.gr;
open Thurs–Sun and
Tues 9–3, Wed 9–9; adm

 Psirrí

The very trendy nest of lanes just to the east is **Psirrí**. Its name comes from slang for 'shaved' or 'fleeced', from its days as a tough district famous for gangs. Now one of the trendiest spots to eat and play, the city is fixing up the streets radiating from Psirrí's central **Plateía Iróon**. They are almost perfect, like stage sets, an effect heightened by the squalor of the ungentrified edges and sparks from body shops whose elderly owner-welders have stayed put.

Further along Ermoú, the Byzantine church sunken in the middle of the street is the late 11th-century **Kapnikaréa**; it has a charming central cupola supported by four Roman columns, fine frescoes, and old bas reliefs and inscriptions embedded on the outer walls. The next parallel street south of Ermoú, Mitropóleos, leads to the **Metrópolis**, Athens' cathedral. Look first at the adjacent 'little cathedral', the 12th-century **Ag. Eleuthérios**, or Panagía Gorgoepíkoös, 'Our Lady who Grants Requests Quickly', the loveliest church in Athens, built almost entirely of ancient marbles, one carved with a calendar of state festivals and another with the zodiac. The 'big' cathedral was built in 1840–55 with the same collage technique, using bits and pieces from 72 destroyed churches around Athens. The Kings of Greece were crowned here between 1863 and 1964, and it contains the tomb of the Patriarch of Constantinople, Gregory V, hanged by the Sultan in 1821 for failing to prevent the uprising.

North of Sýntagma to Omónia Square

From Sýntagma Square, King Otto's planners laid out two parallel streets, Stadíou and Panepistimíou, to link up to Omónia Square. If you take the latter, you'll soon find the **Numismatic Museum**, in Heinrich Schliemann's neoclassical mansion, the Ilion Megaron (1881). Inside and out, motifs recall Schliemann's discoveries at Troy and Mycenae – don't miss the delightful salon frieze of baby archaeologists, merrily digging up pots. English explanations relate the history of money, from the bronze weights used back in the 16th century BC, to the first silver and gold coins minted in the 7th century BC, in Lydia and Ionia in Asia Minor, to the beautiful examples minted in Classical and Hellenistic times.

Numismatic Museum
12 Panepistimíou St,
t 210 364 3774; open
Tues–Sun 8.30–3; adm

Cross from here to Stadíou via Amerikís St for the Old Parliament building (1875–1935), guarded by a flamboyant equestrian statue of Independence hero Kolokotrónis. Now the **National Historical Museum**, this covers the last two centuries of Greek history: folk costumes; ships' figureheads; the Zográfos paintings (25 colourful scenes narrating Greek history from the fall of Constantinople to the War of Independence, commissioned by General Makrigiánnis); and memorabilia of heroes of the War of Independence and of Byron, along with items used to rouse the world to the Greek cause.

National Historical Museum
t 210 323 7617; open
Tues–Sun 9–2; adm

Two streets up Stadíou, flanking Plateía Klafthmónos, a former residence of King Otto and Queen Amalia now houses the **Athens City Museum**, with models, memorabilia and romantic paintings of Athens as it was, and furnishings from Otto's bumpy reign. Among the paintings, don't miss the portrait of Byron, Turner's *Allegory of Enslaved Greece* (1822) or Nikólaos Gýzis' charming *Carnival in Athens*.

Athens City Museum
7 Paparigópoulou,
t 210 324 6164; open
Mon and Wed–Fri 9–4,
Sat and Sun 10–3; adm

At the north end of Stadíou, at the top of the central Athenian triangle, is **Omónia** ('Concord') **Square**, or 'ammonia' as Henry Miller called it in *The Colossus of Maroussi*. This was Athens' Times Square, revamped in 2003 in pricey minimalist grey marble that looked like cement, causing such a huge outcry that it has since been re-re-vamped. Take Athinás Street south to the palatial **Dimarchíon** or City Hall and the city's colourful **Central Market**.

Central Market
open Mon–Sat
until 3pm

National Archaeological Museum

This is the big one, all refurbished after the Olympics and containing some of the most sublime works of the ancient Greek world. The oldest artefacts are **Neolithic**, including finds from Troy and its close cultural cousin, Poliochní on Límnos. The **Cycladic** civilization that blossomed in the 3rd millennium BC was famous for its sleek marble idols; the museum has the famous *Harpist*, mysterious 'frying pans' found in Early Cycladic graves and a unique silver diadem from Sýros. The longest-lasting Cycladic settlement

National Archaeological Museum
Patission (28 Oktovríou) and Tossitsa Sts, t 210 821 7717 (a 10min walk north from Omónia); open April–mid-Oct Mon 1–7, Tues–Fri 8–7.30; adm

was Phylokopi on Mílos; under the influence of the Minoans it produced the delightful frescoes of flying fish and lyrical vases shaped like birds.

In the main hall the museum displays the most important **Mycenaean** collection anywhere, with fabulous gold masks and jewellery, bronze niello-work and cloisonné daggers, a magnificent bull's head rhyton, lovely ivories and charming frescoes from Tiryns and Pýlos, Linear B tablets, and the two exquisite gold cups found at Vapheío, of Minoan manufacture, with vivid *repoussée* scenes of capturing a bull.

After the collapse of the Mycenaeans (*c.* 1150 BC), Greek art began its revival with ceramics: don't miss the monumental **Late Geometric** grave amphorae (760 BC), and the flat linear 'Daedalic' figures with their triangular heads. These are a prelude to the **Archaic** figures of the *kouros* and *kore* with their haunting smiles, as if they had 'known Divinity', as John Fowles put it. The collection spans the oldest extant *kouros* (610 BC), to the perfect *Phrasikleia Kore* by Aristion of Páros, holding a mushroom, to the *Aristodikos Kouros* (510 BC) whose vigour, muscles and relaxed pose points directly to the Classical age. Other key Archaic works include the earliest known *Nike* or *Victory* (550 BC) from Délos, a *krater* of 640 BC showing Apollo's return to Délos from the Hyperboreans, and the bases of *kouros* statues with reliefs of wrestlers, long jumpers, hockey players and two punters egging on a cat and dog.

After the Persian Wars, the Archaic smiles are replaced by the **early Classical** 'severe style', epitomized in the relief of a serious-looking boy crowning himself. The museum has an unsurpassed collection of Classical funerary art, including the *Stele of Hegeso*, an Athenian beauty; its discovery at Kerameikós inspired a poem by Palamas. Another highlight is a pair of exquisite votive reliefs: of *Hermes and Nymphs* and *Dionysos and the Actors*, both *c.* 410 BC. Roman copies of works by the great sculptors of the age offer hints of what's been lost; one is a lifeless copy of Phidias' *Athena* that stood in the Parthenon, another, the marble *Diadoumenos*, is a copy of a bronze by Polykleitos, author of the 'canon' on the proportions of Classical beauty. Surviving Greek originals have mostly been found on shipwrecks: one is the splendidly virile bronze *Poseidon* (*c.* 460 BC) about to launch his trident, found off Cape Artemísion.

The same wreck yielded the bronze *Jockey* (*c.* 140 BC), one of the most dramatic works of the **Hellenistic** era, the horse straining and the boy's face distorted by the speed; other bronze originals are the *Marathon Boy*, attributed to Praxiteles, and *Antikythera Youth*. Also note the beautiful and melancholy *Ilissos stele* and a relief of a young Ethiopian groom, trying to calm a horse, a bust of Plato (a Roman copy) and a bizarre double herm head of an elderly Aristotle; the *Wounded Gaul*, the base of a statue by Praxiteles, showing the music

contest between Apollo and Marsyas; and a charming group of
Aphrodite, raising her slipper to whack a pesky Pan.

From the 500 years of **Roman** rule, there's a bronze Augustus from
an equestrian statue, and a group of 2nd- and 3rd-century AD
portrait *herms* from the Diogeneion gymnasium, offering a rare look
at the upper-class Athenians of the day. Roman busts include ones of
Hadrian, Antinous and Marcus Aurelius, whose portrait shows a last
attempt at psychological analysis. A peculiar one is the bust of Julia
Mamaea, mother of emperor Alexander Severus (AD 232–235), who
was sentenced to death, which required that all her portraits be
hammered. The most fascinating item from the age is the
Antikýthera Mechanism from the 1st century BC, thought to be the
oldest surviving 'computer' and currently undergoing extensive
research (*see* p.501).

The long-closed upper floor has a sumptuous display of Greek
vases and small bronzes going back to 1000 BC. Another section has
lovely finds from Akrotíri on Santoríni, although many have now
been returned to the island (*see* p.307): vases and frescoes of *Boxing
Children*, the *Antelopes* and *Spring* from the 18th–17th century BC.

Around the Museum

South of the museum is the **Polytechnion** (1880), the school where
students began the uprising against the military junta in 1973, and
met tanks in response. The neighbourhood behind this is **Exárchia**,
Athens' Latin Quarter, home of trendies, students and literati. *Terra
incognita* for tourists, its leafy heart, **Plateía Exárchia**, is lively after
dark. Above the square, there are lovely views of the Acropolis from
the top of **Stréfi Hill**.

East of Sýntagma Square

Benáki Museum

Benáki Museum
Koumbári St, t 210 367
1000; open Mon, Wed,
Fri and Sat 9–5,
Thurs 9–midnight,
Sun 9–3; adm; book
ahead for lunch or the
Thurs night buffet

Another main artery, Leofóros Vass. Sofías, begins next to the
Parliament and heads east, passing ministries, embassies and the
excellent Benáki Museum at the corner of Koumbári St. This is the
museum the Athenians themselves love the most. Antónios Benáki,
born in 1873 in Alexandria, spent 35 years amassing treasures, and in
1930 was the first individual in Greece to open a museum, here in his
beautiful neoclassical mansion. Hundreds of donors since have
made this an ideal place for a complete overview of Greek civilization, beginning with Cycladic and Minoan works, through some
exceptional Hellenistic and Roman artefacts, 3rd-century El Fayyum
portraits, 6th-century Coptic textiles, frescoes, illuminated manuscripts and a superb collection of icons, including two painted by
El Greco before he left Crete for Venice and Spain. A Florentine
Madonna attributed to Nicoló di Pietro Gerini keeps them company;

some icons show how close the Greeks came to adopting the Renaissance before the Turkish conquest.

The first floor offers an overview of what the Greeks were up to under the Ottomans – their costumes, jewellery, painted wooden chests, ceramics and embroideries. There's a reconstructed traditional room from the plate-collecting island of Skýros (*see* p.631), and two exquisite 18th-century rooms from a wealthy merchant's mansion in Kozáni. Rooms 22 and 23 contain items made by visitors to Greece, including two watercolours by Edward Lear. The second floor has a large room for special exhibits, folk pieces and items from the pre-War of Independence period. The third floor covers modern Greece, from 1821 to the present: here you'll find Alí Pasha's silver and gold rifle (a gift from Britain's George IV); Byron's portable desk (the size of a laptop computer); the original score to Dionýssios Solomós' *Hymn to Freedom*, the Greek national anthem; the swords, flags and portraits of the Greek heroes; and 32 lithographs by Peter von Hess on the *Liberation of Greece*, all that survives of the murals commissioned by Ludwig I in the (now destroyed) Royal Palace in Munich. Other exhibits include the court dress of his son King Otto, memorabilia and photos of Venizélos and Cavafy's notebook.

Kolonáki and Lykavitós

Koumbári Street, next to the Benáki Museum, leads up to **Kolonáki Square**, Athens' Knightsbridge in miniature, complete with boutiques, upmarket restaurants and cafés, the British Council office and plenty of gilded 'Kolonáki Greeks'. Take a taxi (or a steep walk) up to the **funicular** at the corner of Aristippoú and Ploutarchoúis, which ascends the city's highest hill, **Lykavitós** (Lycabettos), illuminated like a fairytale tower at night. The summit offers a 360° view over Athens; here too is the white 19th-century chapel of **Ag. Geórgios**, a restaurant/bar, and a lovely outdoor theatre.

⭐ Lykavitós Hill

Kolonáki's sleek **Goulandrís Museum of Cycladic and Ancient Greek Art** is just east of the Benáki. The Cycladic art (3200–2000 BC) is a beautiful display of some 300 white marble statuettes as they evolved from the earliest abstract violin-shapes. Although most are female, the *Toastmaster* who has been raising his glass now for around 4,500 years steals the show. The second and fourth floors have a choice collection of art from Mycenaean to early Christian times. A glass corridor leads to the lovely **Stathátos Mansion**.

Goulandrís
Museum of
Cycladic and
Ancient Greek Art
4 Neofýtou Doúka St,
t 210 722 8321; open
Mon, Thurs, Fri 10–4,
Wed 10–8, Sat 10–3,
closed Sun and
Tues; adm

Near here, a French philhellene, the Duchesse de Plaisance, had her beautiful **Villa Ilissia** (1848) on the idyllic banks of the Ilissos. The river is now underground, but the villa contains the **Byzantine Museum**, the most important collection in the country – not only icons but marble sculptures, mosaics, woodcarvings, frescoes, manuscripts, ecclesiastical robes, the 7th-century Mytilíni treasure, and exquisite pieces from Constantinople. Outside, you can visit the

Byzantine Museum
22 Vass. Sofias, t 210
721 1027; open Tues–Sun
8.30–3; adm

excavations of the **Lyceum**, where Aristotle, angry after failing to become Plato's successor at the Academy, set up his own school.

Just down Vass. Sofías, fighter planes mark the **War Museum of Greece**, containing weapons and battle relics from earliest times to Greece's expeditionary force in the Korean War; there's a display on the ancient beacons that just may have informed Mycenae that Troy had fallen. Further east on Vass. Sofías, **Rizári Park** is unmissable for its huge statue of *The Runner* by Kóstas Varotsós; turn right here for the National Gallery on Vass. Konstantínou.

National Gallery (Ethnikí Pinakothéki)

The National Gallery offers a enjoyable journey through five centuries of secular Greek art, even if El Greco is the only Greek artist you've ever heard of when you walk through the door. Nor is it exclusively Greek. On the ground floor, highlights include the likes of Lorenzo Veneziano's *Crucifixion*, Luca Giordano (*The Healing of the Lame* and *Esther and Ahasuerus*) that show his vast range, a 16th-century *Self-sacrifice of Marcus Curtius* attributed to Lambert van Noort, showing the brave Roman plummeting into the Forum's abyss, with nonchalant beetles in the foreground, and the only known *Rest during the Flight into Egypt* that stars guinea pigs, painted in the 17th century by Jan Breugel II and Hendrich van Balen.

But the focus is on Greek art. The oldest works are by El Greco from his Toledo days (the shimmering *Concert of Angels*, *St Peter*, and the *Burial of Christ*), and by Greeks living on Venetian Crete and the Ionian islands during Turkish rule. After independence, many Greek painters went to Bavaria for training and, in the polished academic style, supplied the portraits, genre scenes, landscapes and romantic views demanded by the bourgeoisie: especially the delightful works of Nikólaos Gýzis and Geórgios Iakovídis. The upper floor is dedicated to the 20th century, with works by the versatile Konstantínos Parthénis (Athanássios Diákos), Nikifóros Lýstras, Iánnis Tsaroúchis, Theóphilos Hatzimicháil and the 'Phototropic Cubist' Níkos Hadzikyriákos-Ghíkas.

From the museum, Leofóros Vass. Konstantínos runs south to the landmark that is the big white horseshoe of the **Kallimármaro Stadium**. Good old Herodes Atticus, Athens' big benefactor, built a marble stadium for the Panathenaea Festival in AD 140; it was restored for the first modern Olympics in 1896 by another benefactor, Georgíos Averoff, and used again in 2004 for the end of the marathon. In the other direction, in the northern district of Maroúsi, the 80,000-seat **Olympic Stadium** (Ⓜ Iríni) was built in 1982, in anticipation of the 1996 games that ended up in Atlanta. For the 2004 games, it was given its striking roof of sweeping steel arches designed by Santiago Calatrava. It's now home to two Athenian football squads, AEK Athens FC and Panathinaikos.

Useful Information in Athens

The **tourist police** have a 24hr magic number: **t** 171. A voice in English will answer any question you may have, including lost property queries.

At the **National Tourist Organization office**, pick up their free booklet *Athens/Attica* with excellent maps and all museums and sites. The helpful weekly *Athens News* comes out on Fridays and is on sale at most kiosks.

Save money at Athens' ancient sites with an all-inclusive ticket (*see* p.77).

(i) Athens >

*EOT: 26 Amalías, near Sýntagma Square, **t** 210 331 0392, www.gnto.gr; open Mon–Fri 9–6 and Sat, Sun and hols 11–4*

Emergencies

First aid (ambulance): t 166.
Police: t 100.
Fire: t 199.
Hospital: t 108.
Pharmacies on duty: t 107.
European emergency number (all cases, in English): **t** 112.

Useful Addresses

Main post office (ELTA): Sýntagma Square, **t** 210 323 7573. *Open Mon–Fri 7.30am–8pm, Sat 7.30–2, and Sun 9–1.*
Aliens Bureau (for non-EU passport holders who need visa extensions): 173 Alexándras, **t** 210 770 5711.
Left luggage: Besides the airport's 24hr left-luggage facility, you can leave your bags in central Athens at **Pacific Limited**, 26 Níkis St, **t** 210 353 0352.

Shopping in Athens

A new law has decreed that shopping hours in Greece are Mon–Fri 9–9, and Sat 9–6.

Ermoú Street is the centre of mid-range fashion shopping; for designer fashions, prowl the boutiques of **Kolonáki** and **Kifissía**. **Pláka** and **Monastiráki** are the place to go for light-up Parthenons, but are also not bad for casual clothes, accessories, leather, ceramics, rugs, some real antiques and genuine junk. The **Central Market** on Athinás St (*open 8am–3pm exc Sun*) is fun, even if you don't need any food. **Evripídou St**, west of Athinás St, is the spice street of Athens.

Attica on Panepistimíou Street near Sýntagama is Greece's biggest and new state-of-the-art shopping heaven, with 8 floors of mostly designer goods.

For books in English: try **Eleftheroudákis**, 17 Panepistimíou St, **t** 210 325 8440, or 20 Níkis St, **t** 210 322 9388, the latter with a good selection of guide books. **Compendium**, 28 Níkis St, **t** 210 322 1248, is a cosy English-only shop, with an eclectic selection of used paperbacks to buy or swap.

Where to Stay in Athens

Athens is a big, noisy city, especially so at night when you want to sleep – unless you do as the Greeks do and take a long afternoon siesta.

Luxury (€€€€€)

Athenian Callirhoe, 32 Kalliroís and Petmezá, **t** 210 921 5353, *www.tac.gr*. Friendly soundproofed boutique hotel near the Temple of Zeus, with a delightful modern look and a rooftop restaurant with a view of the Acropolis. **Ⓜ** Acropolis.

AVA, 9–11 Lyssikrátous, Pláka, **t** 210 325 9000, *www.avahotel.gr*. Very comfortable central apartments and suites with balconies and broadband. **Ⓜ** Acropolis.

Eridanus, 78 Piréos, **t** 210 520 5360, *www.eridanus.gr*. Hip hotel near Technopolis that opened for the Olympics, with French (**Jerome Serres**) and Greek (**Varoulka**) gourmet restaurants.

Grande Bretagne, 1 Vass. Georgíou, on Sýntagma Square, **t** 210 333 0000, *www.grandebretagne.gr*. Built in 1862 to house members of the Greek royal family who couldn't squeeze into the palace (the current Parliament building). It was used as a Nazi headquarters, then by Winston Churchill, who had a lucky escape from a bomb while spending Christmas here in 1944. Totally renovated, it offers style and service that the newer hotels may never achieve. It now has a spa as well. **Ⓜ** Sýntagma.

Life Gallery, 103 Thisséos, in the northern suburb of Ekáli, **t** 210 626 0400, *www.bluegr.com*. New design hotel of glass, out near Kifissiá with two pools, gym and spa, plasma TV, broadband and more, plus a gourmet restaurant.

Ochre & Brown, Leokouríou 7 , t 210 331 2950, *www.ochreandbrown.com*. Small (11 rooms) and very, very hip urban hotel, with a lounge/restaurant to match. Thissío.

St George Lycabettus, 2 Kleoménous (Plateía Dexaménis, Kolonáki), t 210 729 0711, *www.sglycabettus.gr*. An intimate atmosphere and wonderful views of the Parthenon or out to sea, and a pool, too. Evangelismós.

Titania, 52 Panepistimíou, t 210 330 0111, *www.titania.gr*. Practically on top of lively Omónia Square. Pleasant rooms with broadband and a rooftop restaurant, the **Olive Garden**, planted with old olives, and gorgeous views. Omónia.

Very Expensive (€€€€)
Achilleas, 21 Lekka, t 210 321 6777, *www.achilleashotel.gr*. Small, cosy, renovated, central and has suites for families. Sýntagma.

Astor, 16 Karagiórgi Servías (just off Sýntagma Square), t 210 335 1000, *www.astorhotel.gr*. Standard A class hotel in a great location, with a view of the Acropolis with breakfast. At the lower end of this price category. Sýntagma.

Austria, 7 Moussón-Filopáppou, t 210 923 5151, *www.austriahotel.com*. In a great location facing the Philopáppos Hill close to the Acropolis entrance. Makes the complicated navigation required to reach it by car worth it. Book online for discounts. Acropolis.

Magna Grecia, 54 Mitrópolis, t 210 324 0314, *www.magnagreciahotel.com*. Small boutique hotel in a neoclassical building with wooden floors and high ceilings next to the Pláka, with lovely views. Sýntagma.

Parthenon, 6 Makrí (Makrigiánni), t 210 923 4594, *www.airotel.gr*. Great location and a pretty outdoor breakfast area. Ask for the rooms with balconies. Acropolis.

Pláka, 7 Kapnikaréas and Metropóleos (Ermoú–Pláka area), t 210 322 2096, *www.plakahotel.gr*. Homey, small, totally renovated, right in the shopping district, with a roof garden view of the Acropolis. Sýntagma.

Expensive (€€€)
Acropolis House, 6–8 Kódrou (off Kydathinéon St in Pláka), t 210 322 2344. A neoclassical house with modernized rooms but in a traditional style, with antique furnishings, frescoes and a family welcome. Sýntagma/Acropolis.

Acropolis Select, 37–39 Fálirou St, Koukáki, t 210 921 1610, *www.acropolis elect.gr*. Tucked away on a quiet street, an easy walk to the Acropolis, this is a charming boutique hotel (renovated in 2000) that offers a lot that higher-category hotels offer, including family rooms, babysitting service and private parking. Syngroú-Fix.

Art Gallery Pension, 5 Eréchthiou and Veíkou Sts, t 210 923 8376, *ecotec@otenet.gr*. A quiet, well-run, old-style hotel which has raised its rates into the stratosphere for what it offers. Each room has its own bathroom, it is quaint, and Pláka is a 15min walk away. Syngroú-Fix.

Carolina, 55 Kolokotróni (Sýntagma–Pláka), t 210 324 3551, *www.hotel carolina.gr*. A classic since 1934, but old hands won't recognize anything but the old-fashioned 'cage elevator' and its friendly owner: it was all spruced up for the Olympics. At the bottom of this price category. Sýntagma.

Jason Inn, 12 Asómaton, by Asómaton Square in Psirrí, t 210 325 1106, *www.douros-hotels.com*. This modest hotel has been renovated and is perfect for excusions to Monastiráki, Psirrí, the Acropolis and Kerameikós. Thissío.

Nefeli, 16 Iperídou, Pláka, t 210 322 8044. A perfectly adequate, charming little hotel, at the bottom of this price category. Sýntagma.

Moderate (€€)
Adonis, 3 Kódrou, Pláka, t 210 324 9737. Central and noisy; all rooms have balconies, and there's a breakfast roof garden and bar with views. Sýntagma.

Arethousa, 6–8 Mitrópolis, t 210 322 9431, *www.arethusahotel.gr*. Typical hotel in a great location, just around the corner from Sýntagma Square, and a roof garden with Acropolis views. Sýntagma.

Byron, 19 Býronis, Pláka, t 210 323 0327. Small, on a quiet street. Acropolis.

Dryades, Emm. Benáki (Exárchia, by the Stréfi Hill), t 210 330 2387. All rooms en suite and the top three and roof

★ **Magna Grecia** >

★ **Acropolis House** >

garden have lovely views; the adjacent **Orion** (same owners) has smaller, cheaper rooms.

Metropolis, 46 Mitropólis, t 210 321 7871, *www.hotelmetropolis.gr*. Cute, homey and old-style air-conditioned rooms with TV, right opposite Athens cathedral. Ⓜ Sýntagma.

Oscar, 25 Filadelphías and Samoú, by Lárissa station, t 210 883 4215, *www.oscar.gr*. A standard hotel good for train connections and with a small pool and roof garden. At the higher end of this price category. Ⓜ Lárissa.

Phaedra, 16 Herefóndos (Pláka, near the Lysikrátes Monument), t 210 323 8461, *www.hotelphaedra.com*. Renovated with air-conditioning and TV, but still 'old-style', quiet on a lovely pedestrian square with a Byzantine church. Some balconies and rooms overlook the Acropolis. An old standby. Ⓜ Acropolis.

Inexpensive (€)
Adam's, 6 Herefóndos (Pláka), t 210 322 5381, *adams@otenet.gr*. Quiet, central, just 3mins from Hadrian's Arch; the rooms are comfortable and the location's great. Ⓜ Acropolis.

Dióskouri, 6 Pitákou (near Hadrian's Arch, Pláka), t 210 324 8165. Delightful, old-fashioned place with high-ceilinged rooms in a neoclassical building in a fairly quiet spot. Ⓜ Sýntagma/Acropolis.

John's Place, 5 Patróu (behind the large Metropólis church), t 210 322 9719. Simple, with bathrooms down the hall. No towels, though. Ⓜ Syntagma.

Kouros, 11 Kódrou (off Kydathinéou St, Pláka), t 210 322 7431. In an attractive old house near the Greek Folk Art Museum. Prices may be up for discussion if not full. Ⓜ Sýntagma.

Marble House, 35 A. Zínni (Koukáki), t 210 922 8294, *www.marblehouse.gr*. A comfortable Greek-French-run hotel, a bit of a hike south of the Syngroú-Fix metro; air-conditioning extra. Ⓜ Syngroú-Fix.

Pella Inn, Ermoú and Karaskáki, t 210 321 2229, *www.pellainn.gr*. En suites and non en-suites, clean and in a good spot. Ⓜ Monastiráki.

Tembi, 29 Eólou, t 210 321 3175, *www.travelling.gr/tempihotel*. Nothing special, but it has pleasant

management and a terrific central location. Prices plummet out of season. Ⓜ Monastiráki.

Hostel Aphrodite, 12 Einhárdou and Micháil Vóda, t 210 881 0589, *www.hostelaphrodite.com*. Private rooms sleeping up to four and a dorm, a bar, laundry service and Internet café. Ⓜ Lárissa/Victoria.

The Student and Travellers' Inn, 16 Kydathinéon (Pláka), t 210 324 4808, *www.studenttravellersinn.com*. Hostel with air-conditioned private rooms sleeping up to four, some en suite, and Internet facilities. Ⓜ Sýntagma/Acropolis.

Victor Hugo Hostel, 16 Victor Hugo, t 210 523 2540, *www.aiyh-victorhugo.com*. Under new management and renovated in 2006. En-suite double rooms and quads and Internet facilities. Ⓜ Metaxourgeío.

Eating Out in Athens

Athenians rarely dine out before 10 or 11pm, although most places are open by 8pm. Also note that many restaurants close in August.

As elsewhere in this guide, assume a cost of €15–20 per head with wine unless otherwise stated.

Sýntagma and Around

Aigli, Záppeion Park, t 210 336 9363 (€50). Far from the traffic, near Záppeion Palace, in the restored Aigli complex, which also includes a music bar and outdoor cinema. A lovely place to feast on taste-packed delicate Mediterranean dishes while contemplating the Acropolis. *Book*.

Cellier Le Bistrot, 10 Panepistimíou (in the *stoa*), t 210 363 8525 (€30). Old restaurant revamped into a stylish bistro, with an Italian chandelier and the biggest mirror in Greece; Greek and international classics and a good wine list.

Delphi, 13 Níkis, t 323 4869. Reasonably priced traditional Greek food served in air-conditioned surroundings all year round. It has been a standby for more than 30 years. No smoking policy.

Pláka

Pláka, the traditional tourist ghetto, is still fun, and it caters to the non-

⭐ Dining in Psirrí

★ Bakaliarakiá ›

Greek urge to dine before 10pm. Touts, however, can be real pests; a blank stare tends to discourage them.

Bakaliarakiá, 41 Kydathinéon, t 210 322 5084. Great old-fashioned Greek atmosphere in a cellar supported by an ancient column; good snacks, fried cod and barrel wine since the 1900s. *Open eves only; closed summer.*

Byzantino, 18 Kydathinéon, t 210 322 7368 (€20–22). In the heart of Pláka, serving big portions (the fish soup and lamb fricassée are excellent) under the trees. It's also one of the few decent places open for Sunday lunch.

Daphne's, 4 Lysikrátous (by the Lysikrátes monument), t 210 322 7971 (€40). In a neoclassical mansion with Pompeiian frescoes and beautiful courtyard – a rarity in Athens – serving generous, refined Greek and international dishes. *Closed lunchtimes.*

Eden, 12 Lissíou, t 210 324 8858. Athens' oldest vegetarian restaurant and very popular, even with carnivores, with vegetarian quiches and soya moussakas. *Closed Tues and Aug.*

Platanos, 4 Diogénis, t 210 322 0666. The oldest taverna in Pláka, near the Tower of the Four Winds, serves good wholesome food in the shade of an enormous plane tree. *Closed Sun.*

To Kafeneío, 1 Epicharmoú, t 210 324 6916. Excellent *mezédes* (famous meatballs in sauce), snacks and sweets till 1am in a building from 1836. *Closed Aug.*

Monastiráki and Thissío

Abyssínia Café, Plateía Avissínia, Monastiráki, t 210 321 7047 (€20–22). An institution – an old Greek taverna with traditional fare and live music, attracting a local and trendy crowd. *Closed Sat, Sun eve, Mon.*

Brachera, Plateía Avissínia, Monastiráki, t 210 321 1720 (€35). Art Deco design and roof garden with superb Acropolis views, with Mediterranean cuisine that attracts ship-owners, web designers and fashionistas. *Closed Mon and Sun eves.*

Pil-Poul, 51 Apostólou Pávlou, t 210 342 3665 (€55). Luxurious, romantic setting with lovely Acropolis views from the terrace, to go with some of the finest French cuisine in Greece, with wine list to match. *Closed lunch and Sun.*

Psirrí

Atelier Agrotikon, 48 Sarri St, t 210 324 0121 (€35). Classy, chef-owned, featuring simple modern cuisine, only using the finest ingredients. *Closed lunch plus all day Sun and Mon, and June–Aug.*

Gelato Mania, 21 Aísopou. The best ice cream in Athens.

Hýtra, 7 N. Apostóli, t 210 331 6767 (€45). The 'Stewpot' is one of Athens' finest, where a new head chef from France takes a refined look at Greek tradition. *Closed lunch and Sun in Oct–May.*

Pak, 13 Menandroú, t 210 321 9412 (€15). Indian classics for a change of pace.

Taki 13, 13 Táki St, t 210 325 4707 (€25). The first, and still fun. It has a superb atmosphere and, although the food is simple, it's a great party bar, featuring live music and sing-songs till 1.30am.

Taverna tou Psirrí (Yurriv), 12 Aischýlou, t 210 321 4923 (€14). The last workaday taverna that has somehow so far resisted gentrification; it's small, plain, but homey, and good.

Zeidoron, 10 Táki and Ag. Anárgyro, t 210 321 5368. Always crowded for their changing selection of *mezédes*. Good if you arrive on the right day; try the *kolokythiakeftédes* – courgette rissoles. *Closed Mon, Aug.*

Gázi and Rouf

Some of the best restaurants in Athens have parked themselves in this former industrial area and gasworks, a short walk west of Kekrameikós.

Aristerá-Dexiá, 3 Androníkou (just off the map in Rouf near Gázi, a 5min taxi hop from Plateía Omónia), t 210 342 2380 (€50). Former garage, now one of Athens' trendiest spots for a special evening out, thanks to its elegantly simple décor, arty and imaginative Mediterranean dishes and subdued snob appeal. *Reservations required. Closed lunch and Sun.*

Dirty Fish, 12 Tripotopolemoú, t 210 347 4763 (€40). Popular restaurant with nice décor, a pretty garden, friendly service and innovative Greek delights from both sea and land. *Closed lunch except Sun.*

Interni, 152 Ermoú, t 210 346 8900 (€55). The ultimate in Athenian

⭐ **Díporto >>**

designer restaurants – worth a visit for the décor alone – and serving exquisite Italian-Asian fusion dishes. *Closed lunch, all day Sun and May–Sept.*

Kítrino Podílato, 116 Keramikoú and Iéra Ódos, **t** 210 346 5830 (€45). The 'yellow bicycle' may serve the most inventive nouvelle Greek cuisine in the country and a great Greek wine list, too. *Closed lunch, all day Sun and June–Sept.*

Jerome Serres, 78 Piréos, **t** 210 520 0360 (€60). Named for its chef, former head at Spondi, with an emphasis on French and Mediterranean cuisine. *Closed lunch and Sun.*

Mamacas, 41 Persephónis, **t** 210 346 4984 (€30). Greek classics in an updated setting; great views of the Acropolis from the top level.

Varoulko, 78 Piréos, **t** 210 522 8400 (€60). One of Greece's most imaginative seafood restaurants, long in Piraeus, is now linked to the Eridanus Hotel, where Michelin-starred chef Leftéris Lazaroú has added kid, rabbit and tripe to his repertoire. *Open eves only; closed Sun.*

South of the Acropolis and Makrigiánni

MániMáni, 10 Falírou, **t** 210 921 8180 (€20). Taverna serving delicious courgette fritters and other 'cooked dishes'. *Closed Aug.*

Symposio, 46 Erecthioú (close to the Odeion of Herodes Atticus), **t** 210 922 5321 (€45). Upscale Mediterranean cuisine served in the garden in summer or in the conservatory of an old neoclassical house; the chef is famous for preparing just the right sauce for every dish. *Closed lunch and Sun; book.*

Koukáki (south of Makrigiánni)

Claudios, 38 Veíkou, **t** 210 923 5128 (€20–25). New, small and casual, specializing in good, filling Italian dishes. No garden, but air-conditioned.

Edodi, 80 Veíkou, **t** 210 921 3013 (€45). The restaurant that put Koukáki on the map. Superb *haute* Mediterranean *cuisine*, down to the desserts – just let your waiter guide you through the day's delights. Rated one of the five best in the city. *Closed lunch and Sun, plus Aug.*

⭐ **Spondí >>**

Omónia

Díporto, Central Market, **t** 210 321 1463, opposite the parking garage (€12). An institution that needs no sign; it's down some steps and has remained unchanged for at least 50 years, serving Hellenic soul food. *Patsás* (tripe soup), the traditional hangover cure, is served on paper-covered tables set on a bare cement floor. If not the tripe, try whatever soup is on offer (the chickpea soup is delicious); portions are huge. *Closed after 6pm and all day Sun.*

Ideal, 46 Panepistimíou, **t** 210 330 3000 (€25). Historic restaurant, making diners happy with well-prepared Greek classics for over 40 years. *Closed Sun.*

Exárchia

Bárba Iánnis, 94 Em. Benáki (corner of Derveníou, close to Exárchia Square), **t** 210 382 4138 (€10). This cheap, popular old relic of Old Athens (point to what you want) in a neoclassical house – with the original toilet too. *Closed Aug.*

Alexándra, Leof. Alexándros & Zonará, Panathénaia Park, **t** 210 642 0874 (€20). A classic restaurant with classic Greek dishes, served al fresco.

Kolonáki and Around

L'Abreuvoir, 51 Xenokrátous, **t** 210 722 9106 (€60). Athens' oldest French restaurant, and still going strong with all the Gallic classics.

Boschetto, Evangelismós Park off Vass. Sofias, **t** 210 721 0893 (€60). Lovely Italian delicacies in a bosky setting, outside in the summer or in a winter garden. *Closed lunch and Sun.*

Orizontes Lykavitou, Lykavitós Hill, **t** 210 722 7605 (€50). Under St Georges Chapel, with tables spread across the terrace and views over all of Athens. Excellent modern Greek cuisine.

Sale e Pepe, 34 Aristippoú, **t** 210 723 4102 (€60). One of the best wine cellars in Greece to go with exquisite Mediterranean cuisine – try the oysters with sabayon sauce. *Closed lunch and all day Sun.*

Pangráti (east of the Kallimármaro Stadium)

Spondí, 5 Pýrronos (off Plateía Varnava), **t** 210 752 0658, *www.spondi.gr* (€60). By common acclaim, Athens' best restaurant. True *haute cuisine* with imagination and flair in a lovely old mansion with a garden courtyard. Extraordinary desserts, and huge wine list. *Book. Closed Sun in summer.*

Taverna Kavarítis, 35 Arktinoú and 4 Pausanioú, **t** 210 721 5155 (€15). Friendly and authentic neighbourhood favourite for al fresco dining under the vines.

Vlássis, 8 Pastér , **t** 210 646 3060 (around €20). Out towards the US embassy, a superb family-run taverna, the place to find true Greek cuisine and one of the rare ones with excellent wines and desserts, too. *Book. Closed Sun eve and mid-July–Sept.*

Entertainment and Nightlife in Athens

The summer is filled with festivals, headlined by the eclectic **Athens Festival**, **t** 210 928 2900, *www. greekfestival.gr*, which attracts big names from around the world.

At other times, **classical music** fans should try to take in a performance at the **Mégaron Musikís**, on Vass. Sofías and Kokkáli, **t** 210 728 2333, Athens' acoustically wonderful concert hall. Maria Callas got her start at the **Greek National Opera House**, 59–61 Akademías St, **t** 210 361 2461, which is shared with the national ballet.

From May to Sept there are nightly **folk dance** performances at the **Dora Stratou Theatre** on Philopáppos Hill, **t** 210 921 4650, not far from the **Sound and Light Show** on the Pnyx (April–Oct).

Rembétika, the Greek blues, is in full revival in Athens; the real thing may be heard live (in winter) upstairs in the Athens' meat market at **Stoa Athanaton**, 19 Sofokléous St, **t** 210 321 4362 (*closed Sun*) and a score of other places.

For **jazz**, try **Half Note**, 17 Trivonianoú in Mets, **t** 210 921 3310 and **Upstairs at the Bar Guru**, Plateia Theátrou, Omónia, **t** 210 324 6530, *www.bargurubar.gr/ jazzupstairs.htm*; **Cafe Alavastron**, 78 Damaréos, Pangráti, **t** 210 756 0102, has jazz and ethnic sounds by local musicians but closes in summer; **Paraphono**, 130 Asklipíou St, **t** 210 644 6512, in Exárchia, plays mostly jazz.

For **salsa** try **Cubanita**, 28 Karaïskáki, in Psirrí, **t** 210 331 4605. **Discokafeneio** and **Rebeka**, both on Miaoúlis St in Psirrí, are lively way into the night; nearby, **Soul**, 65 Evripidoú, **t** 210 331 0907, has tasty international cuisine and a very hip music bar upstairs.

In summer, **clubs** in Glyfáda and Voúla are favourites as others in the city close down. Some of the best live rock happens at the **Gagarin Live Music Space**, 205 Liosíon near Ⓜ Attikís, **t** 210 854 7600. **Toy Café Bar**, near Sýntagma at 10 Karýtsi, just off Stadioú, is a favourite informal hangout of media types. In Gázi, a former kindergarten, **Nipiagogeio**, 8 Kleanthoús, **t** 210 345 8534, is one of the city's hottest freestyle dance bars.

Gay Athens gathers from 11pm at **Blue Train**, a hot new spot at 84 Konstantinoupoléos, in Gázi, and at **Lámda** and **Granázi** along Lembéssi St, off Syngroú.

In summer, **outdoor cinemas** are a treat and all the films are in their original language. Two of the nicest are in Kolonáki: **Dexamení**, in Dexamení Square halfway up Lykavitós, **t** 210 360 2363; **Athinaía**, 50 Harítos St, **t** 210 721 5717. Also try **Ciné Paris** on Kydathinéon in Pláka, **t** 210 322 2071 (next to wonderful old-fashioned **Brettos Bar and Distillery**, which distills its own ouzo); **Thission**, 7 Apostólou Pávlou St, **t** 210 342 0864 (with an Acropolis view); and **Aigli** in the Záppeion Gardens, **t** 210 336 9369, which has the best sound system.

Piraeus (ΠΕΙΡΑΙΑΣ / Πειραιας)

A visit to the islands often means a visit to Piraeus – pronounced pi-ray-A, immortalized in *Never on a Sunday*. While it may not win you over at first glance, in a country that derives most of its livelihood from the sea, Piraeus is the true capital (and the third city in

Greece), while Athens is a sprawling suburb where the bureaucrats live. It has a buzz, excellent seafood, and two good museums.

History

In 479 BC, when Fáliron could no longer meet Athens' needs, Themistocles made Piraeus the city's chief port. Security was foremost in his mind: he surrounded its three harbours with walls and left plans for the famous Long Walls – a 7km corridor to Athens. These were completed by Pericles, who, being Pericles, also wanted to make the port a showcase, and hired the geometer Hippodamos of Miletus, a proto-hippie with long hair and outlandish dress, to lay out the city. The grid plan Hippodamos chose (and which still exists) was not designed like modern grids, to make land easy to parcel out

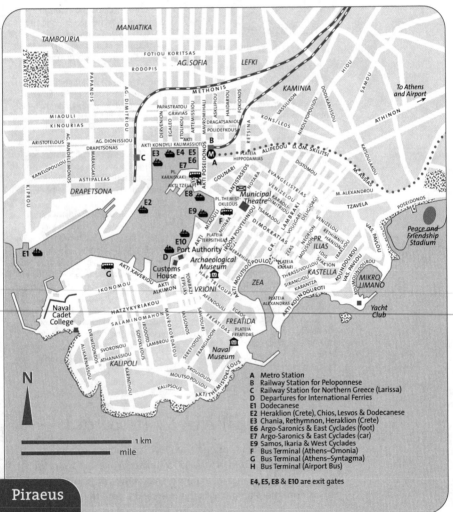

A	Metro Station
B	Railway Station for Peloponnese
C	Railway Station for Northern Greece (Larissa)
D	Departures for International Ferries
E1	Dodecanese
E2	Heraklion (Crete), Chios, Lesvos & Dodecanese
E3	Chania, Rethymnon, Heraklion (Crete)
E6	Argo-Saronics & East Cyclades (foot)
E7	Argo-Saronics & East Cyclades (car)
E9	Samos, Ikaria & West Cyclades
F	Bus Terminal (Athens–Omonia)
G	Bus Terminal (Athens–Syntagma)
H	Bus Terminal (Airport Bus)

E4, E5, E8 & E10 are exit gates

Getting to and from Piraeus

By sea: Piraeus is the launchpad for the islands and ports in the Argive and Saronic Gulfs, as well as for most of Greece's Aegean islands; *see* the map, left, for points of departure. For schedules call the Piraeus **port authority, t** 210 422 6000, or **tourist information, t** 171.

By train: The station for the Peloponnese (SPAP) is near the metro on Aktí Kalimassióti and has a left-luggage service. The station for northern Greece (OSE) lies further on Aktí Kondíli.

By metro and bus: The metro is the quickest way into Athens, or take bus 40 from Plateía Karaiskáki, by the main harbour, which runs 24hrs to Filellínon St. The E96 to the airport leaves from the same square.

and sell, but to promote equality among citizens, and for a while at least he succeeded. Piraeus quickly became the business district of Athens. All religions were tolerated, and women were allowed for the first time to work outside the home. Hippodamos also designed a huge *agora*, for the world's first commercial fairs and international trade exhibitions. Ship sheds lined the harbours, each capable of sheltering two triremes in winter, and near Zéa Marína stood the huge Skeuotheke, an arsenal capable of holding the riggings and weapons for a thousand triremes, considered the architectural equal of the Parthenon in ancient times.

In 404 BC, at the end of the Peloponnesian War, the Spartans destroyed all Piraeus' fortifications. Admiral Konon rebuilt them, but they weren't good enough to keep out Sulla, who decimated the city in 88 BC, nor Alaric, who sacked it in 396. For 1,900 years Piraeus dwindled away, with a population as low as 20, even losing its name to become Porto Leone (after an ancient lion statue, carved in 1040 with runes by Harald Hardrada and his Vikings, that was later carted off by Morosini to embellish Venice's Arsenale). As port to the capital, Piraeus has regained its former glory, although much of it dates from after 1941, when German bombers blew it to bits.

Three Harbours, Two Museums and the Acropolis

The **main harbour** of Piraeus was known in ancient times as the Kantharos or 'goblet' for its shape, and most visitors never get beyond this busy sheet of water, the metro and the ticket agencies, missing the excellent **Archaeological Museum of Piraeus**, by the ruins of a Hellenistic theatre. This is a museum full of surprises, including the 7m (24ft) **Monument of Nikeratos** (325 BC), the largest funerary monument ever found in Greece. Nikeratos was a *metic* (foreign resident), many of whom were merchants and formed the bulk of Piraeus' population. It was *nouveau riche* piles like this, however, that led to a law banning big, showy tombs. Look for the marble engraved with a foot, arm and finger, used as standard measures, a Mycenaean pig's head rhyton, Minoan finds from Kýthera, the bronze beak and 'eye' from a trireme, an ancient harp from the Tomb of the Poet, and marble plaques manufactured for the Roman market in the 2nd century AD, pandering to the Roman vision of ancient Greece. The stars of the museum are upstairs: five

Archaeological Museum of Piraeus
31 Char. Trikoúpi Street,
***t** 210 452 1598; open
Tues–Sun 8.30–3; adm*

large bronzes found by Piraeus' cathedral in 1959, including two statues of Artemis, a majestic Athena, a tragic mask and an exquisite *kouros*, the Apollo of Piraeus, the oldest known Greek hollow-cast bronze statue (*c.* 500 BC).

Naval Museum of Greece
Plateía Freatída, t 210 451 6264; open Tues–Fri 9–2, Sat 9–1; adm

A submarine marks the **Naval Museum of Greece**, built around a section of Themistocles' walls. It has plans of anicent naval battles, a model of the triremes used at Sálamis, maritime mementoes, and tiny ships made of bone by French prisoners in England during the Napoleonic Wars, which Aristotle Onassis used to keep on his yacht.

One of the best things to do, especially towards evening, is take a taxi up to **Kastélla**, Piraeus' ancient acropolis, with gorgeous views over the city and the Saronic Gulf. Snug in a pretty amphitheatre below, **Mikrolímano** is an almost perfectly round harbour filled with fish restaurants. The landmark on the reclaimed land east of Piraeus at **Paléo Fáliro** is the dramatic ship-shaped **Peace and Friendship Stadium** (1985), visible from the metro line and used for volleyball in the 2004 Olympics.

Where to Stay in Piraeus

Savoy, 93 Iróon Polytechnioú, t 210 428 4580, *www.savoyhotel.gr* (€€€). A few minutes from the port, renovated, smart, well-run hotel with broadband in the rooms.

Triton, 8 Tsamadoú, t 210 417 3457, *users.otenet.gr/~htriton* (€€€). Standard hotel within walking distance of the docks.

Glaros, 4 Chariláou Trikoúpi, t 210 451 5421, *www.glaros-hotel.gr* (€€). Near the Ideal, same friendly owners.

Ideal, 142 Notára (in from Gate E10), t 210 429 4050, *www.ideal-hotel.gr* (€€). Pleasant air-conditioned rooms, recently renovated, plus Internet service.

Pireaus Dream, 78 Notára, t 210 411 0555, *www.piraeusdream.gr* (€€). Just in from Gate E9, a contemporary and comfortable haven.

Ionion, 10 Kapodistrioú, t 210 417 7537, *www.ionionhotel.com* (€€–€). The classic One Onion, only 2mins' walk from the Metro; recently renovated rooms with air-conditioning.

Achillion, 63 Notára, t 210 412 4029 (€). The cheapest in Piraeus but not bad at all – air-conditioned rooms 5mins from the quay.

Eating Out in Piraeus

Chryssopsaro, 61 Al. Papanastasíou Street, Kastélla, t 210 412 0333 (€40). Tasty, trendy seafood.

H ΦΩΛΙΑ, 30 Aktí Poseidónos, t 210 412 0781 (€10). Family-run restaurant in business since 1968: pick what you want from the pans of home-cooked 'ready' dishes and sit down at one of the Formica tables. *Closed eves.*

Jimmy the Fish, 46 Aktí Koumoundoúrou in Mikrolímano, t 210 412 4417 (€35). Great salads, octopus, spaghetti with lobster, or the fish of your choice, perfectly prepared.

Margaró, 126 Chatzikyriákou, t 210 451 4226 (€14–17). Unpretentious but wonderful fish taverna near the naval academy, that attracts both locals and the élite.

Nine Brothers (Énnea Adélfi), 48 Sotiros (behind Plateía Kanári at Zéa Marina), t 210 411 5273 (€9–12). A popular taverna with lots of locals, and a big choice of dishes.

Pireaus Yacht Club, Aktí Mikrolímanou, t 210 413 4084 (€36). Pretty setting, and *numero uno* in Piraeus for innovative Mediterranean cuisine – starring an exquisite cuttlefish risotto.

Tony Bonanno, 63 Panapastasíou, t 210 411 1901 (€28). Art Deco atmosphere, superb Italian food. *Open eves only.*

The Argo-Saronic Islands

The Argo-Saronics were the first Greek holiday islands. In the early 1900s, fashionable Athenian families hired villas for the summer while father commuted to and fro at weekends. These days, thanks to frequent hydrofoils and catamarans, the closer islands – Aegina, Angístri and Póros – lend themselves to visitors who only have a little time, or want the joys of being on an island while dipping into Athens on day trips.

Aegina is the most visited island in Greece; beautiful, arty, posy Hýdra has earned itself the nickname 'the St-Tropez of Greece', and Spétses is knocking on fashion's door as well.

08

⭐ **Car-free glamour**
Hýdra pp.114–18

⭐ **Early Classical perfection**
Temple of Aphaia, Aegina p.109

⭐ **Pines, beaches and seafood**
Spétses p.129

⭐ **The Greek Grand Canal**
Póros sailing passage p.118

⭐ **Walls of frescoes**
Moní Faneroméni, Salamína p.124

See map overleaf

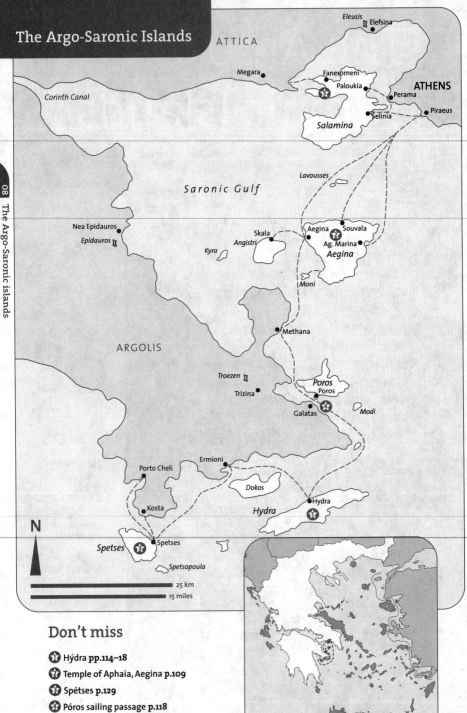

The Argo-Saronic Islands

ATTICA

Eleusis Elefsina

Megara

Faneromeni
Paloukia

ATHENS

Corinth Canal

Perama

Salamina

Selinia

Piraeus

S a r o n i c   G u l f

Lavousses

Nea Epidauros

Epidauros

Skala

Angistri

Aegina Souvala

Ag. Marina

Aegina

Kyra

Moni

Methana

A R G O L I S

Troezen

Poros
Poros

Trizina

Galatas

Modi

Ermioni

Porto Cheli

Dokos

Hydra

Kosta

Hydra

N

Spetses

Spetses

Spetsopoula

25 km

15 miles

Don't miss

⭐ Hýdra **pp.114–18**

⭐ Temple of Aphaia, Aegina **p.109**

⭐ Spétses **p.129**

⭐ Póros sailing passage **p.118**

⭐ Moní Faneroméni, Salamína **p.124**

Getting to the Argo-Saronic Islands

Except for Salamína, all **ferries**, **hydrofoils** and **catamarans** to the Argo-Saronics depart from Gate E8 or E9 in Piraeus. Contact **Hellenic Seaways**, t 210 411 7341, *www.hellenicseaways.gr*, or **Euroseas**, t 210 413 2105, *www.euroseas.com*.

Scattered in the fast lane of Greek history, between Attica and the Peloponnese, the six Argo-Saronic islands have often played starring roles on the national stage. In a way they are a microcosm of Greece, whose fate has always been inextricably bound up with the sea: ancient **Aegina** was one of the most powerful maritime states in Greece, a rival to Athens itself; **Póros** was the holy island of Poseidon; **Salamína**, the island of the Homeric hero Ajax, witnessed a sea battle that saved Greek civilization, and **Hýdra** and **Spétses** led the Greek fleets in the War of Independence.

Avoid coming at weekends if you can, when it seems half of Athens escapes to the islands.

Aegina (ΑΙΓΙΝΑ)

Connections between Aegina ('EGG-ee-na') and Piraeus are so frequent that many islanders commute to work. Yet Aegina has a distinctly villagey, laid-back atmosphere. It has a traditional fishing fleet, a handful of beaches and good tavernas; it has the best-preserved ancient temple on any Greek island, and the basilica and tomb of one of the most popular Greek saints – in fact, many who come here are pilgrims. It is also the only island with a Camera Obscura, the legacy of the Aegina Academy, a European forum for art and science that showcases the island in odd-numbered years.

Aegina is also the supreme island of pistachios. Introduced in ancient times from Persia, perhaps by Alexander the Great, what the Greeks call 'Aegina nuts' grow better here than anywhere else in Greece. In late August, harvesters using long sticks dislodge the nuts into canvas sheets; they are then sun-dried on flat terraces. The nuts

The Ant People

Aegina was one of Zeus' many loves, with whom he fathered Aeacus, the first king of the island, then called Oenone. When Aeacus renamed the island after his mother, Zeus' jealous wife Hera punished him by sending a plague of serpents, who killed all the inhabitants. Aeacus begged Zeus for help, wishing for as many people to repopulate Aegina as there were ants on a nearby oak; hence the Aeginetians were known as the ant folk, or Myrmidons.

In gratitude Aeacus founded the Sanctuary of Zeus Hellanion on Aegina's highest mountain. He had three sons – Peleus, Telemon and Phocos. When Telemon and Peleus in a fit of jealousy killed Phocos, their father's favourite, they fled, Telemon going to nearby Salamína and Peleus to Thessaly. The two then went on to father two heroes of the Trojan War, Ajax and Achilles respectively. When Aeacus died, Zeus made him a judge of the dead in Hades along with two of his own sons by Europa – Rhadamanthys and Minos, the arch enemy of Aeacus.

08

The Argo-Saronic Islands | Aegina

Getting to and around Aegina

By sea: From Piraeus there is an hourly **hydrofoil** (35mins) until late afternoon, or **ferry** (one hour); also frequent connections with Méthana and other Argo-Saronic islands. The ferries go to Aegina Town or to Ag. Marína on the east coast; some call at Souvála. **Port authority**: t 229 702 2328.

By bus: Buses from Aegina Town (t 229 702 2787) depart from Plateía Ethnegersías and run to most villages, including Ag. Marína via the Temple of Aphaia and Nektários Monastery.

Taxi: t 229 702 2635.

---

are on sale in all the shops; they're no bargain, but avoid the cheaper ones – they're artificially dried and lose their natural oils.

History

Why need we say that Ægina is one of the most celebrated of islands...which once enjoyed the dominion of the seas, and contended with Athens itself for the prize of superior glory in the battle with the Persian fleet at Sálamis?

Strabo, 1st century BC

Midway between Athens and the Peloponnese, Aegina was a precocious place: after 800 BC it joined one of the first confederations in Greece, the Amphictyony of Calauria, a league of seven cities in the Saronic and Argive Gulfs. Unlike most Greek city-states, it never had a tyrant, but became an oligarchy early on. In c. 600 BC it minted Europe's first coins, silver ones with turtles, and developed its first system of weights and measures. Trade, thanks to its powerful fleet, made Aegina fat, and its coins have been found throughout the ancient world.

But Aegina was far too close to Athens to wax fat comfortably; the pressures were such in the early 490s BC that Aegina's oligarchs slaughtered 700 would-be democrats on the island. They also sided with Persia, one of their main trading partners, against Athens; Athens held several prominent citizens hostage in return for Aegina's neutrality in 490 BC when the Persians landed at Marathon. By 480 BC, however, Aegina had had a change of heart and sent 30 ships to the Battle of Sálamis, where her fearless sailors won the hightest honours among the Greeks. Even so, Athens never trusted Aegina nor forgave it for its prosperity; Pericles sneeringly referred to it as 'a speck that blocked the view from Piraeus'. In 458 BC Athens attacked, and three years later Aegina was forced to surrender, destroy its fortifications and hand over its fleet. When the Peloponnesian War broke out, the Athenians, knowing they had few friends on Aegina, deported all the islanders, who were welcomed by the Spartans and later returned to their homes by Lysander. But it was too late: ancient Aegina never recovered its former importance.

In 896, a Saracen raid convinced the islanders to move inland to the safey of Paleochóra, and they only returned to the seaside during the War of Independence, when Aegina was liberated early and flooded with Greek refugees. In 1828 Aegina Town became the capital of Greece under its first president, Iánnis Capodístria. Fittingly for the place that minted the first coins in Europe, Aegina minted the first modern drachma, bearing a phoenix. But its day in the sun was short: the capital was soon relocated to Naúplio, before its final move to Athens.

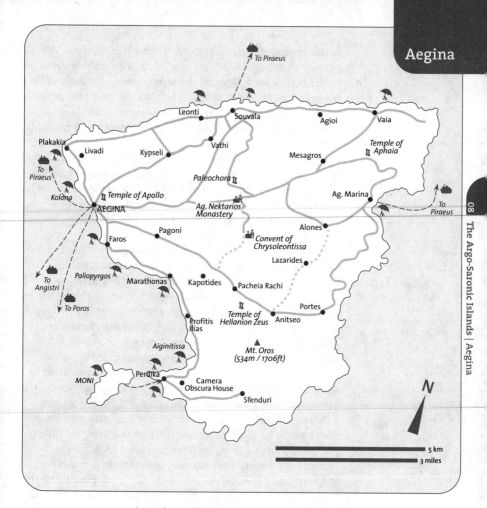

Aegina Town

Aegina Town, island capital and chief port, is the kind of place where octopi hang on the line in poky little ouzerie, and locals in their slippers buy fruit and vegetables off the back of a boat. It retains a whiff of grandeur and neoclassical elegance from its days as the first capital of Greece, even if many of the 19th-century buildings are hidden behind shops touting pistachios; the horse-drawn carriages add a nice touch amid the cars and general hustle and bustle of the port.

The large crescent **harbour** and mole, almost too grand for an island, was financed in 1826 by Dr Samuel Greenly Howe, an American surgeon and husband of Julia, the author of *The Battle Hymn of the Republic*. Inspired by Byron's example, the philhellene Dr Howe had fought in the Greek War of Independence, and was so appalled by the postwar suffering that he led a massive American relief campaign on Aegina, employing locals in public works. The harbour's landmark, the white chapel of **Ag. Nikólaos**, celebrated its completion. Near Ag. Nikólaos, the austere rose-tinted **Tower of Markellos**, built by the Venetians under Morosini, was used as the first Greek government building and now serves as the Capodistrian Intellectual Centre. In the equally spartan **Residence** (now the public library) on Kyvernéou Street, President Capodístria, the dapper count from Corfu and foreign minister to the Tsar, slept in his office on the upper floor, while downstairs the first Greek mint churned out the first drachmas. The *de rigueur* evening stroll along the waterfront is often accompanied by spectacular sunsets (the smog or *néfos* emanating from Athens is good for something), that bathe the town in a gentle light.

Ancient writers often referred to the '**secret port**' just north of the city – only the islanders knew its entrance. It has a little sandy beach, and overlooking it, on the hill of **Kolóna**, stood the **ancient city of Aegina**. This dates back to the Early Helladic Period (2400 BC): there's a jumbly walled settlement, a mosaic from a 7th-century synagogue and a lonely Doric column from an early 5th-century **Temple of Apollo**; the rest of it, with Capodistria's permission, went into building Aegina's quay. The nearby **necropolis** yielded the British Museum's 'Aegina Treasure' of Minoan gold jewellery, plundered by ancient tomb-robbers from Crete. Admission to the site includes the nearby **Archaeological Museum**, the oldest in Greece (1829), with a good collection of prehistoric pottery, some decorated with rare Early Helladic naval scenes, Archaic ceramics (including the superb 7th-century 'ram jug' showing Odysseus hiding to escape the Cyclops Polyphemus), 6th-century BC pediments from two temples at Kolóna, and a Classical marble sphinx. At the museum, ask for the key to the **Ómorfi Eklisía** (beautiful church') at Asómati just outside town, a chapel beautifully frescoed in 1282.

Ancient Aegina
t 229 702 2248; open Tues–Sun 8.30–3; adm includes site and archaeological museum

Near Aegina Town

From Kolóna, a 15-minute walk takes you along the coast to **Livádi**, which had a lively artists' and writers' colony after the Second World War. A plaque marks the **House of Kazantzákis**, where the writer penned *Zorba the Greek* in 1946. The **Museum Chrístos Caprálos** occupies the workshop used by the sculptor from 1963–93, and contains his most important work: the Archaic-style *Battle of Pindus*, a monumental 45m (150ft)-long limestone relief on 20th-century Greek history.

Carrying on east from Livádi, the road skirting the north coast is a good cycling route, with swimming possibilities at the rocky beaches of **Leónti**, and further east at **Souvála**, a modest if dullish resort, which lured the island's first visitors decades ago with radioactive baths for rheumatism and arthritis.

Museum Chrístos Caprálos
t 229 702 2001; open June–Oct Tues–Sun 10–2 and 6–8; Nov–May Fri, Sat and Sun 10–2

Around the Island

Ag. Nektários and Paleochóra

The bus from Aegina Town to Ag. Marína passes by the Temple of Aphaia (*see* below), but most Greeks on board will pile out earlier, at the **Moní Ag. Nektários**. Nektários (d. 1920) was a teacher and founder of the local convent. After assorted miracles (right after his death in an Athens hospital, his sweater was laid on the bed of a paraplegic, who was instantly cured), he was canonized in 1967 – the latest saint to join Orthodoxy's inner circle. His church is the largest in Greece. Even so, it's not big enough on 9 November, when hordes of pilgrims come for the last great outdoor festival of the Greek calendar, queueing for hours the night before to kiss his tomb; the next morning, his crowned skull reliquary is carried in a grand but festive procession through Aegina Town, accompanied by a brass band and national politicians.

If you're not in need of Nektários' services, consider climbing up to the Byzantine ghost town of **Paleochóra**, behind the monastery (*the caretaker is usually around with the church keys in the morning; wear good walking shoes*). Founded in what seemed to be a safe location in the 9th century, Paleochóra nonetheless twice proved vulnerable: Barbarossa slaughtered the men and carried off the women and children in 1538, and Morosini pummelled it in his siege of 1654. Some 28 churches – out of the original legendary 365 – still stand, sheltering 13th-century frescoes and stone iconostases; among the best are the **Basilica of Ag. Anárgyroi**, the **Chapel of Taxiárchis** and the **Episkopí**. Looming over all of them is Morosini's dilapidated Venetian **castle**.

A road from in front of Ag. Nektários leads to the **Convent of Chrysoleóntissa** (1600), with a fine wooden iconostasis and a famous rain-making icon of the Virgin (a job once held on Aegina by Zeus). The nuns are known for their garden produce.

The Temple of Aphaia and Ag. Marína

East of Ag. Nektários, the road passes by the pretty village of **Mesagrós**, surrounded by vines and pines, the origins of Aegina's excellent retsina. Above stands Aegina's pride and joy, the beautiful Doric **Temple of Aphaia**, built in *c.* 500 BC and forming an equilateral triangle with the Parthenon and the Temple of Poseidon at Soúnion (it's not the only one in the Aegean that does that, either: *see* p.298). Aphaia, the local version of the Mediterranean Great Goddess, was worshipped here from *c.* 2000 BC; the archaeologists found several older sanctuaries and temples, with inscriptions to Artemis Aphaia (the 'not dark'). In Crete her name was Britomartis or Diktynna – Artemis again, the Minoan mistress of mountains and animals, and

 Temple of Aphaia
t 229 703 2398; open summer daily 8.30–7.15; winter daily 9–4.30; adm

protectress of shipping. Later mythographers made Aphaia a child of Zeus and Leto, who hunted with her sister Artemis. When King Minos of Crete fell in love with her, she fled and, on reaching Aegina, threw herself in despair into the sea, hence the other meaning of her name, 'the disappeared one'. She suffered a final transformation, becoming Aphaia-Athena, in a desire to please the goddess who helped the Greeks in the Trojan War.

The temple, built at the height of Aegina's power, is of local limestone and was originally covered with brightly painted stucco. Of the original 32 columns, 25 still stand; an unusual internal colonnade and a metal grille surrounded the *cella*, where the cult statue of Aphaia stood (note the 19th-century graffiti) – locked up, because the Aegitans feared the Athenians would try to steal it. The superb pediment sculptures of Parian marble, depicting scenes of the Trojan war, are among the finest works of Archaic art, but you have to go to Munich to see them; in 1812 an agent of Ludwig I of Bavaria (father of Greece's first king, Otto), purchased them from Haller (German) and Cockernell (English), a pair of cat and fox antiquarians who were inspired by Lord Elgin to strip Greece of every frieze they could get their hands on. A little **museum** on site has casts of the temple and its predecessor that burned down in 510 BC.

The café opposite the temple offers a splendid view of the east coast of Aegina, including **Ag. Marína**, the island's busiest resort, with its glossiest nightlife and a long, sandy beach – Aegina's best, but don't expect much in the way of elbow-room. If you want to foot it from Aphaia, it's a half-hour walk downhill.

Marathónas and Mount Óros

Water Park
t 229 702 2540

Heading south of Aegina Town, past **Fáros** and its **Water Park**, is **Marathónas**, a pretty village with a pair of beaches, not far from the prettier sandy cove and eucalyptuses of **Aiginitíssa**, further south.

Up from Marathónas (a longish walk, or get there directly by bus from Aegina Town), outside the traditional village of **Pacheiá Ráchi**

Wildlife Sanctuary
t 697 723 1983

is Aegina's **wildlife sanctuary**. Probably the most effective animal protection and rehabilitation centre in Greece, it accepts wounded and sick birds, wolves and other mammals from all over the country. Visitors are welcome.

Dominant here is **Mount Óros** (520m/1,706ft), an extinct volcano and the highest peak in the Saronic Gulf; its name simply means 'mountain'. On its north slope, about a mile from Marathónas, the church of the Taxiárchis was built over a monumental Hellenistic-era **Sanctuary of Hellanion Zeus**, excavated in the early 20th century and explored again since 1995. There are two terraces, one with the foundations of a large peristyle enclosed on three sides by *stoas*, as well as a polygonal wall and a monumental stepped road, probably added in the 2nd century BC when the island was under the kings of

Pergamon. From here it's an hour's walk up to the summit, site of the original Mycenean-era temple, dedicated by Aeacus to Zeus, father of the Hellenes. This Zeus was notable for his rain-making skills, and you can enjoy magnificent views all across the Saronic Gulf when he's having a day off.

Pérdika and Moní Islet

The scenery grows increasingly barren south towards **Pérdika** ('partridge'), a charming village, with a small beach, hotels and excellent fish tavernas, as well as Aegina's newest attraction: the cylindrical **Camera Obscura House**, a unique combination of camera obscura and 19th-century panorama, with twelve slit openings, commissioned by the Aegina Academy in their 2003 *Light Image Reality* project and designed by two Viennese, architect Franz Berzi and film-maker Gustav Deutsch.

Camera Obscura House open Easter–Oct daily 10–7

Boat taxis from Pérdika go out in 15 minutes to the steep islet of **Moní**, a wildlife sanctuary for shy *kri-kri* mountain goats from Crete, brazen peacocks, miniature horses and hares. It once belonged to the Convent of Chrysoleóntissa and has the junky ruins of a failed resort complex and a small beach. Moní is popular for picnics and has a summer snack bar. A path leads up to a Second World War German look-out post for a wonderful view of the gulf.

Useful Information on Aegina

ⓘ **Aegina >**
www.aeginagreece.com

Tourist police, t 229 702 7777.

Aegina has lovely walks: pick up Gerald Thompson's *A Walking Guide to Aegina*, at Kalezis bookshop in Aegina Town, 35 Dimokratías.

Aegina Festivals

Odd-numbered years, months vary: Aegina Academy project, *see www.light-image.net*.

17 July: Ag. Marína, with a fair.

Aug: The Aegina Festival, with various events and exhibitions.

9 Nov: Ag. Nektários, with processions.

Where to Stay and Eat on Aegina

Aegina Town ✉ 18010

Danae, 1km from the centre, **t** 229 702 2424, *www.danaehotel.gr* (€€€–€€). Up-to-date 54-room hotel, with a lush veranda, restaurant and a pool.

Aeginitiko Archontiko, t 229 702 4968, Ag. Nikólaou/1 Thomaídos, *www. aeginitikoarchontiko.gr* (€€). A stylish converted 18th-century mansion; Ag. Nektários and Kazantzákis stayed here. *Open all year*.

Brown, by the sea, **t** 229 702 2271, *www. hotelbrown.gr* (€€). Originally a Greek-English sponge factory, with recently renovated garden bungalows and rooms.

Nafsika, N. Kazantzáki Av, 10mins' walk north from the centre, **t** 229 702 2333 (€€). Run by a scholar, this is where Nobel-prize winners George Seferis and Odysseas Elytis spent several summers; verandas overlook the sea.

Pavlou, 21 P. Aeginítou, **t** 229 702 2795 (€€). Comfortable places, a street from the waterfront. *Open all year*.

Marmarinos, 24 Leon. Ladá St, **t** 229 702 3510 (€). In a quiet back street, with a garden opposite.

Pension Rena, by the sea, **t** 229 702 2970 (€). Pleasant and intimate and prettily furnished, all rooms with air-conditioning, plus delicious home-made breakfasts prepared by Rena.

⊛ **Unnamed
tavernas >**

Walk through the little fish market to a pair of excellent little tavernas that serve delicious grilled octopus and fish from the stands next door and good home-produced wines.

Avli, Irióti St, one block in from the waterfront, **t** 229 702 6438. Popular with locals and tourists for meals, pizza, snacks and drinks, including draught Guinness.

Flisvos, next to Plaza Hotel, **t** 229 702 6459. Taverna with a big choice of excellent *mezédes* (don't miss the 'pumpkin fritters') and reasonably priced fish.

Ippokambos, 9 Faneroménis, **t** 229 702 6540. Specializes in *mezédes*, presented on a tray for you to pick and choose.

Maridaki, **t** 229 702 5869, near the hydrofoils. Has a name for excellent fish dishes.

Skotadis, on the waterfront, **t** 229 702 4014. Probably the best taverna in town, with delicious salads and more.

Vatzoulia's, **t** 229 702 2711. The local favourite, a few minutes from town on the road to the Temple of Aphaia, is very lively. Great Greek food and music. *Open eves only, but ring ahead.*

Souvála ✉ 18010

Villa Iviski, 300m from the sea, **t** 229 705 2700, *www.iviski.gr* (€€–€). Apartment hotel in a pretty garden with a pool and bar.

Chryssi Akti, **t** 229 705 2786 (€). Rooms and studios with a pool.

Giannaros, **t** 229 705 3061. Long-time favourite, serving *kleftikó* and *kokorétsi* all year.

Ag. Marína ✉ 18010

There are plenty of hotels (too many) on Ag. Marína beach.

Helios, **t** 229 703 2098, *www.helios hotel.net* (€€€). The nicest accommodation here – apartments set back

from the brouhaha, with a garden, Jacuzzi and pool.

Galini, in a garden 3mins from the centre, **t** 229 703 2203 (€€). Panoramic pool and decent restaurant.

Karyatides, **t** 670 383 0776 (€). Comfortable, many rooms with sea views. *Open May–Oct.*

Kostas, on the road to Alones, **t** 229 703 2424. Good grilled meats and the usuals in a garden setting.

Tholos, **t** 229 703 2129. Classic family taverna.

Marathónas ✉ 18010

Crown View Suites, **t** 229 702 8470, *www.crownviewsuites.com* (€€). Opened in 2004, pristine and well-equipped studios if a bit stark and angular for Aegina, but they are by the sea.

Sissy, Marathónas, **t** 229 702 6222 (€). Pleasant; tough *hombres* welcome.

O Kyriakos, Marathónas, **t** 229 702 4025. A wide range of fish and baked dishes.

Pérdika ✉ 18010

Moondy Bay Bungalows, at Profitis Ilías, north of Pérdika, **t** 229 706 1146 (€€€). The cushiest place to stay on Aegina, right on the sea in a well-tended garden, with pool, tennis, canoes and cycling, massage, etc. and a restaurant on the beach; book well in advance. *Open April–Oct.*

Hippocampus, Pérdika, **t** 229 706 1363, *www.hippocampus-hotel-greece.com* (€). Simple air-conditioned rooms with TV and a shady courtyard.

Nontas, Pérdika, **t** 229 706 1233. Large selection of delicious seafood, but the prices a bit over the odds.

To Proraion, Pérdika, **t** 229 706 1577. One of Aegina's best fish restaurants. *Open all year.*

Angístri (ΑΓΚΙΣΤΡΙ)

The baby sister of the Saronics, pine-clad Angístri ('hook') has given up its best-kept secret status; its sandy beaches and sparkling sea for snorkellers now draw crowds of Athenians at weekends, as well as a band of (mostly British) philhellenes in search of the basic pleasures of Greece without the glitz. Visitors tend to return often.

Getting to and around Angístri

Several **ferries** and **catamarans** from Piraeus to Aegina carry on to Angístri in another 30 minutes or so. A local boat, the *Agistri Express*, travels between Aegina and the two ports, Skála and Mílos.

A **water taxi** from Aegina to Angístri is about €30.

Port authority: t 229 709 1541.

A small **bus** links the villages.

Places in Skála hire out **bicycles** and **scooters**.

Most of the 1,000 or so inhabitants are descendants from Albanian refugees (Arvanites), although even they often spent long centuries elsewhere, because of pirates and the lack of water (today it comes in on tankers); in the 1920s the island was almost uninhabited. There are two 'ports': **Mýlo** (aka **Megalochóri**), with two beaches, and the modernish resort of **Skála** with its big white church, new apartment blocks, and long sandy beach under the older hamlet of **Metóchi**.

In **Sklirí**, a 20-minute walk from Skála, a track descends steeply to the white pebble **Chalikáda Beach**, Greece's first naturist beach, where the famous Adam and Eve Conference took place in 1983; it still attracts skinny-dippers, but not exclusively.

Angístri's 10km of road links the two ports with pebble and shady **Dragonéra Beach** and **Limenária**, with a lake and a gold-domed church; the road ends at a little taverna near beautiful **Apónissos** and a sandy lagoon. The walking is good too – there are plenty of tracks in the pines, passing coves and lovely views of the other Saronics and the mainland.

08 The Argo-Saronic Islands | Angístri

Useful Information on Angístri

Agistri Tours, t 229 709 1307, *www. agistri-tours.com*. Organize around-the-island cruises and excursions to Athens, the Argolis and special trips to Epidaúros during the theatre festival.

Where to Stay on Angístri

Angístri ✉ 18010

 Angístri Club >

Angístri Club, 5mins from town on the beach at Sklirí, **t** 229 709 1242, *www. agistri.com* (€€). Fun, casual, relaxing hotel restaurant, a favourite of old Greek hands. Bryan, its Welsh owner, has lived here for over two decades. *Open April–Oct.*

Rosy's Little Village, 400m from Skála in the pines, **t** 229 709 1610, *www. rosyslittlevillage.com* (€€). Built like a

tiny village, a laid-back hotel by the sea (you can swim off the rocks); rooms have air-conditioning and TVs. Sailing lessons available; in summer it hosts getaways for writers and editors (see *www.liberato.co.uk*). *Open all year.*

Abatis, 6mins walk south of the port, **t** 229 709 1254 (€€–€). Apartments with TVs and air-conditioning. The friendly owner speaks English. *Open May–Oct.*

Agristi, Skála, **t** 229 709 1356, *www. holidaysinagistri.com* (€€–€). Air-conditioned studios and family rooms. The same family (same details) runs the **Yianna Hotel**, by the **Alterego Bar**.

Andreas, Skála, **t** 229 709 1346 (€€–€). 700m from the sea in town. *Open May–Oct.*

Scala Beach, Skála, **t** 299 709 1085, *www.agistrihotels.com* (€). New, with a pool, pool bar and a variety of rooms, including quads and maisonettes. *Open all year.*

Hýdra (ΥΔΡΑ)

 Hýdra

Hýdra is a long, grey, very fashionable rock with an outrageously picturesque town of stone and pastel mansions rising steeply over the harbour. As the last sea captains and merchants moved out, artists, writers and their camp followers moved in, inspired by the scenes of Hýdra in *A Boy on a Dolphin* (1957) starring Sophia Loren, and *Phaedra* (1962), Jules Dassin's remake of *Hippolytus*, with Melina Mercouri. Known as the Greek St-Tropez, Hýdra is wonderfully free of cars and motorbikes (except for two rubbish trucks), functioning on donkey power; it has a hopping night scene, but was snoozing when God was handing out beaches.

History

The first permanent population on Hýdra didn't arrive until the 15th century, when it was settled by Greeks and Albanians from Épirus, fleeing the growing ambitions of Serbia under Stephen Dusan. By necessity, they turned to the sea to survive: building up a fleet of 150 merchant ships, nearly monopolizing the corn market from the Black Sea to Europe, with a bit of smuggling and piracy on the side. By the late 18th century, Hýdra was for all purposes an autonomous state, to which the Turks turned a blind eye as long as it paid its taxes. It boasted a wealthy population of 25,000, and the sailors Hýdra sent as a tribute to the Sultan were prized – especially the Albanians, who made fortunes running the British blockade in the Napoleonic Wars.

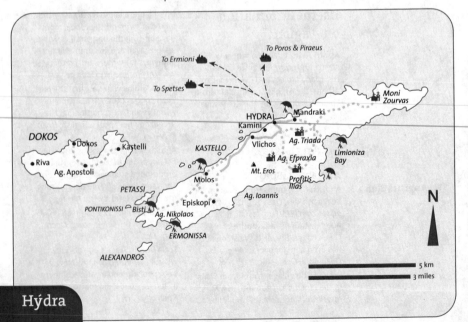

Getting to and around Hýdra

Up to 20 **hydrofoils**, **catamarans** and **ferries** sail daily from Piraeus, some going 'express' to Hýdra in about 1½ hours; also frequent connections to Póros and Spétses, and Ermióni.

Port authority: t 229 805 2279.

Donkeys wait by the quay to transport you and your luggage to your hotel (always work out the price before setting off).

Water taxis by the quay ferry up to 10 people at a time to the swimming holes at Kamíni, Mandráki and Vlíchos, and the islet of Dokós; they have fixed fares and are fairly cheap if you join the crowd.

Hýdra did so well under the Ottomans that the outbreak of the War of Independence in 1821 left its captains lukewarm, until their rivals on Spétses had chalked up a few victories and the people of Hýdra threatened to revolt. Once the decision to fight was made, however, they threw themselves wholeheartedly into the fray. Merchants (notably the Koundouriótis family) converted their fleets into warships and, under such leaders as Tombázis and Miaoúlis, commander-in-chief of the Greek navy, the Hydriots terrorized the Turks. Fire ships were their secret weapon: at night, some 20 daredevils would sail a decrepit vessel full of explosives alongside Turkish ships, light it and row for their lives in an escape boat. Hýdra's arch-enemy, Ibrahim Pasha, grudgingly nicknamed the bold island 'Little England'.

Ironically, the independence Hýdra fought so hard to win brought an end to its prosperity. By the 1950s Hýdra was almost abandoned, when fortune's wheel was oiled once again by the arrival of Greek painter Hadjikyriákos Ghíkas, the pioneer of the artists' colony that paved the way for today's glitterati; in 1960 Leonard Cohen bought a house, and still returns periodically.

The Man who Captivated Nelson

Before becoming commander-in-chief of the Greek navy, Miaoúlis (Andréas Vókos, 1769–1835) was elected admiral by the fleet, in recognition not only of his seamanship, but of his exceptional integrity – a rare trait in 1821, when many Greek leaders had no qualms about jeopardizing the entire enterprise for their own profit; Miaoúlis (who took his *nom de guerre* from the Turkish word for a felucca, *miaoul*) instead devoted his fortune to the war. The Greeks tell the story that Nelson once captured Miaoúlis on one of his more piratical adventures, but Miaoúlis in turn captured Nelson with his charm, and was released with a pat on the back.

He needed all the charm he could muster to deal with the difficult, independent-minded sailors of Hýdra and Spétses, who were accustomed to the medieval system that gave each crew member a right to the profits and a say in all matters; if the majority disagreed with a captain's decision, even if they were about to do battle, they would go on strike. The fact that Miaoúlis avoided mutiny, kept his ships together and harried the massive, well-organized Egyptian invasion fleet of Ibrahim Pasha for four months was an accomplishment in itself, even if it ultimately failed. Afterwards, while all but a handful of Greek admirals refused to sail without being paid in advance, Miaoúlis struggled to relieve the besieged city of Messolóngi, and always outfoxed the enemy when he had a fighting chance. After handing over his command to Lord Dundonald in 1827, when the real power in Greece had shifted to Britain, France and Russia, he bowed out of the entangled politics after the war with a bang (*see* 'Póros', p.121) and is fondly remembered on his native island in the Miaoúlia (20 June).

Hýdra Town

Just arriving is an extraordinary experience. The island looks like an arid rock pile until your vessel makes a sharp turn, and – *voilà*, the sublime port, the pearl in the oyster shell, the scene that launched a thousand cruise ships. The typically three-storey grey and white mansions, built in the late 18th century by Venetian and Genoese architects, attest to the loot amassed by Hydriot privateers and blockade runners; nearly all have terraces atop cisterns, where the owners used to hide their treasures. Some of the mansions are now hotels, while others have found assorted uses: the **Athens School of Fine Arts** has a branch in the old Tombáazi mansion, and the **Skolí Eborikís Naftilías**, Greece's oldest school for merchant marine captains, is housed in the Tsámados house.

The loveliest mansions – and the largest – belonged to the Koundouriótis family, Albanians who could barely speak a word of Greek but who contributed two leaders to the cause: the fat, jovial Geórgios, who was elected president of the executive for 1823–6, and Lázaros, who converted his merchant fleet into warships at his own expense. In 2001, after decades of restoration, the big yellow **Lázaros Koundouriótis Historical Mansion** was opened to the public as an annexe of the National Historical Museum in Athens, preserving its original walls and ceilings; it holds costumes, antiques and a gallery with paintings by Constantínos Byzántios. On the left side of the harbour, the **Museum and Archives of Hýdra** contains a rich collection of portraits of Hydriot captains and heroes, folk paintings, ships' models, and weapons.

The churches in Hýdra also reflect the island's former wealth and influence. The most beautiful is the 18th-century **Panagía tis Theotókou**, next to the port, with a lovely marble iconostasis and silver chandelier; the cells of its **convent**, now used as town offices, encompass a serene marble courtyard (quarried from Póros' Temple of Poseidon); there's also a little **museum** of ecclesiastical items. From the church, climb up Miaoúlis Street to the lovely square of **Kaló Pigádi**, site of two 18th-century mansions and two deep wells that supplied the town with fresh water.

The one real beach on Hýdra is a good 20-minute walk away at **Mandráki**, by the old docks; alternatively, dive off the lovely rocks at **Kamíni**. On Good Friday, Kamíni is packed with Hydriots and visitors who come to watch the moving candlelit procession of Christ's bier, the *epitafiós*, which culminates here by the sea.

Lázaros Koundouriótis Historical Mansion
*t 229 805 2421;
open Mar–Oct Tues–Sun
10–4.30; adm*

Museum and Archives of Hýdra
*t 229 805 2355;
open daily 9–4.30
and 7–9; adm*

Around the Island

Other excursions require more walking or a donkey ride, a guaranteed way to escape the idle throng. At **Kastéllo**, behind Hýdra, are the ruins of a thick-walled castle near the shore. **Vlíchos**, a 6km walk west of town, is a pretty hamlet with a rocky beach, a picturesque little bridge and a good taverna; water taxis from the port also make the trip. Pines and coves for swimming make **Mólos** a popular place for outings and for spotting Joan Collins, who often spends the summer here.

Hýdra was a pious place, and has a disportionate number of religious houses per capita. Mule tracks lead south from Hýdra Town in about an hour to the **Profítis Ilías Monastery** (1813) and the nearby **Convent of Ag. Efpráxia** (1863), where the nuns make embroideries. Start early in the day, and take a bottle of water to reach the **Monastery of Ag. Triáda** (1704; men only) and the **Convent of Ag. Nikoláos** (1724), both above **Mandráki** – the latter has a frescoed church and superb views. Furthest of all is the **Monastery of Zourvas** (1814) near the lighthouse, with great views, a two-hour walk from Ag. Triáda. There's also a clutch of hunters' lodges at **Episkopí**, in Hýdra's fire-scarred pine forest.

Dokós

From Hýdra it's an hour by caique to Dokós, an islet named after the family of Hydriot captains who once owned it. It has been inhabited off and on since the late Neolithic period, and two families live on the island today; there's a **beach** and excellent snorkelling in a pretty bay, often used by passing yachties. In 1975, a shipwreck dated to 2200 BC (Early Helladic II) – the oldest ever found in Greece – was discovered, with its cargo of ceramics made just before the introduction of the potter's wheel.

Inland are ruins of the walls and towers of the **Kástro**, built in the 7th century and last used by Morosini. Quarries yield *marmarópita*, a hard grey and red marble, often used in building.

Useful Information on Hýdra

Tourist police: Vótsi Street, **t** 229 805 2205. *Open summer only.*

Hýdra Festivals

20 June: The Miaoúlia.
July: Festival of Marionettes.

Where to Stay on Hýdra

Hýdra ✉ 18040

Be warned: it is sheer madness to arrive in Hýdra in the summer without a booking. Most of the hotels are small, and have better rates if you stay at least three days.

Bratsera, t 229 805 3971, *www.greek hotel.com* (€€€€). Combines traditional design with glamour in a beautifully converted sponge factory. Most rooms overlook the colonnaded pool and lantern-lit restaurant. *Closed Nov.*

Angelica, 42 Miaoúli, **t** 229 805 3202, *www.angelica.gr* (€€€). Calm, a 5min walk from the port. Lovely shady terrace. *Open all year.*

Ippokampos, 100m from the port, **t** 229 805 3453, *www.ippokampos.com* (€€€). Restored mansion, with a pretty courtyard.

Leto, t 229 805 3385, *www.letohydra.gr* (€€€). Two minutes from the port, a traditional mansion with antique-furnished rooms, including some sleeping four. *Open Mar–Dec.*

Miramare, at Mandráki, **t** 229 805 2300, *www.miramare.gr* (€€€). Stone

★ **Miranda** ›

★ **Kondylenia** ››

bungalow complex, linked to the port by boat; overlooking the island's sole bit of sand. *Open April–Oct.*

Miranda, t 229 805 2230, *www. mirandahotel.gr* (€€€). Another elegant 19th-century sea captain's town house, with stunning Venetian painted ceilings. *Open May–Oct.*

Mistral, t 229 805 2509, *www. mistralhydra.gr* (€€€). An old stone tower mansion, with simple but attractive rooms in mint condition.

Orloff, near the port, t 229 805 2564, *www.orloff.gr* (€€€). Beautifully restored 19th-century mansion, its nine rooms individually designed and set around a courtyard; excellent breakfast. *Open Mar–Oct.*

Phaedra, a few minutes from the port on level streets, t 229 805 3330, *www.phaedrahotel.com* (€€€). A former carpet factory converted into lovely spacious doubles and suites.

Delfini, by the hydrofoils, t 229 805 2082, 11 rooms. *Open April–Oct.*

Hýdra, 2 steep mins from the clock tower, *hydrahotel@aig.forthnet.gr*, t 229 805 2102 (€€). You'll need your mountain goat skills to stay here; you'll receive a warm welcome and have fine views from this historic mansion.

Erofili, 2mins from the port, t 229 805 4049, *www.pensionerofili.gr* (€). A young couple run this child friendly *pension* with a vine-shaded courtyard.

Eating Out on Hýdra

Geitoniko (aka **Christina**), t 229 805 3615. Courtyard setting in an old stone building; excellent traditional cuisine – good stewed dishes – at fair prices.

Iliovassilema (or **Marina's**), Vlíchos Beach, t 229 805 2496. Delicious food (try the sea urchin spaghetti) and

superb sunsets; take a water taxi (c. €10).

Paradosiakó, near the Alpha Bank, t 229 805 4155. Recommended especially for its *mezédes*.

Porfyra, t 229 805 3660. For reasonably priced stuffed vegetables, lamb and home-made desserts.

Sto Steki, by the clock tower, t 229 805 3517. Serves home-cooked favourites from moussaka to lobster; try the famous fish soup. *Open all year.*

Vigla, t 229 805 4154. Verandas with lovely views; serves excellent seafood. From €32.

Kondylenia, 15mins' walk from town on Kamíni Beach, t 229 805 3520. Outstanding, with views over the quaint harbour; try the squid in tomato sauce or the sea urchin dip. Around €35.

Nightlife on Hýdra

Hýdra comes into its own at night, but bring a wad of euros if you want to join the party.

Ydronetta, t 229 805 4160, *www. ydronetta.gr*. Cool bar on the west end of town with lovely views and swimming platforms in beach-poor Hýdra, with romantic music and cocktails at sunset – and dance music late at night.

Amalour, Tombázi, t 229 805 3125. With a mix of jazz and Greek music.

Pirate, south end of the harbour, t 229 805 2711. The classic, playing old and new hits till it's time for breakfast in July and August.

Nautilus, west of the harbour, t 229 805 3563. Where the Athenians head for trendy Greek music, often live.

Disco Heaven, t 229 805 2716. Perched high on the west side of the harbour; the evergreen favourite.

Póros (ΠΟΡΟΣ)

Sailing passage

A mere 400 metres separates Póros ('the passage') from Galatás and the mountains of the Peloponnese, lending the island a uniquely intimate charm; if you sail through on a large ferry you can see what people on the second floors are watching on TV. This **Greek Grand Canal** is as busy as Venice's, with ships of every size to-ing and fro-ing, all for the diversion of Póros café society. Besides the beauty

Getting to and around Póros

By sea: Car ferry (about 2hrs), catamarans and hydrofoil (less than an hour) run from Piraeus, Aegina, Hýdra and Spétses several times a day. Car ferries go every 30mins to Galatás on the mainland and water taxis make the short trip as well when they fill up. **Port authority**: t 229 802 2274.

By road: Buses go as far as Russian Bay and the monastery, passing most of the beach hotels. If you want to go exploring on the Peloponnese, **hire a car** in Galatáas at Pops, t 229 802 4910.

If there is one dream which I like above all others it is that of sailing on land. Coming into Póros gives the illusion of that deep dream.

Henry Miller,
The Colossus of Maroussi

of its location, its beaches and Póros Town, the island is only an hour from Piraeus by hydrofoil, and within easy driving distance of Epidauros, Naúplio, Mycenae and Troezen for mainland exploring.

History

The Minoan presence on Póros is remembered in the myth of Skylla, whose father the king had a lock of hair that made him immortal. When Minos of Crete besieged Póros, Skylla caught sight of him and fell in love with him, then cut off her father's magic lock while he slept and brought it to Minos. Minos killed the king and easily took Póros, but he was revolted by Skylla's betrayal and left for Crete without her. Desperate, Skylla swam after him, but she was attacked by her father's avenging spirit in the form of an eagle, and drowned in the bay which bears her name (Askéli).

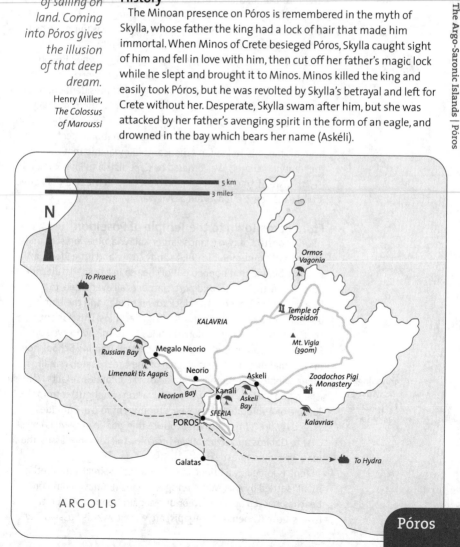

In antiquity Póros was named Kalavria (Calauria), 'gentle breeze', and served as the headquarters of a 7th-century BC maritime amphictyony that operated under the protection of Poseidon, who had a famous sanctuary here. Little remains of it today beyond the memory of the orator, Demosthenes, who, unlike today's Greeks, didn't think Macedonia was quite Greek and roused his native Athens against the expanding influence of Philip II. Briefly silenced by Athens' defeat by Philip at Chairóneia (338 BC), Demosthenes continued his defiance of Philip's successor, Alexander, and, after Alexander's death in 322, led another revolt against the Macedonians. This time Alexander's general Antipater lost all patience and went after him. Demosthenes fled to Póros and sought sanctuary at the Temple of Poseidon, only the Macedonians impiously burst in, swords raised. But Demosthenes died proving his pen was mightier; he had bitten off the poison he had concealed in the nib.

Póros' Russian Bay recalls the events of 1828–31, when British, French and Russian emissaries gathered on Póros for a conference on Greece. The Russians were close to the first president Capodístria, one-time foreign minister to the Tsar – too close, thought many revolutionaries from Hýdra and Póros. Tensions rose significantly in 1831, when Admiral Miaoúlis, overseeing the national fleet at Póros from his flagship *Hellas* (an American-built warship that cost twice the national budget), was ordered by Capodístria to loan Russia the *Hellas*. Instead, the honest admiral blew it up in the Strait of Póros; it broke his heart, but averted a civil war.

From Póros Town to the Temple of Poseidon

Póros consists of two islands: larger **Kalávria**, pine-forested and blessed with innumerable quiet sandy coves, and little **Sferiá**, a volcanic bubble that popped out of the sea in 273 BC. Picturesque **Póros Town**, the capital and port, clambers all over Sferiá, topped by a pair of landmarks – the **clock tower** of 1927 and the blue-domed campanile of the cathedral, **Ag. Geórgios**. This has 20th-century wall paintings by Konstantínos Parthénis, who lived on Póros from 1909–11. Cadets attend the **Naval Training School**, housed in the buildings of the first arsenal of the Greek state. A small **Archaeological Museum** in Plateía Koryzí contains artefacts from the island and ancient Troezen, including a lion spout gutter from the Temple of Aphrodite that played a prominent role in Euripides' tragedy *Hippolytus*. Another favourite thing to do in town is cross over to **Galatás** and swim at the beach by the **Lemonódassos**, the massive lemon forest 2km southeast.

Archaeological
Museum
*t 229 802 3276;
open Tues–Sun 9–3*

Sferiá is joined by a bridge to Kalávria at the **Sinikismós** ('settlement', settled by Asia Minor refugees in 1923). Kalávria has Póros' **beaches**, backed by pines: **Neórion**, **Megálo Neórion** and pretty Lovers' Cove (**Limenáki tis Agápis**) are west, towards Russian Bay.

The latter was named for warehouses and a ships' biscuit bakery (now partly ruined) built by the Russian navy in 1831, which they used into the 1900s.

Other beaches, **Askéli** and **Kanáli**, are to the east of Sinikismós. From Kanáli the road continues into the trees to the 18th-century **Monastery of Zoodóchos Pigí**, with a miraculous spring, a lofty 17th-century gilt iconostasis made in Cappadocia and the tomb of Admiral Miaoúlis; below is a charming pebble beach, **Kalávrias**. From the monastery you can drive up to the plateau of Palatia and the scant remains – the locals call it 'the five stones' – of the once celebrated Doric **Temple of Poseidon**. First built in brick by the Mycenaeans, it was rebuilt in marble c. 500 BC; when Pausanias visited it, he saw the tomb of Demosthenes in the precinct. All this is dust in the wind (and most of the marble is now in Hýdra), but the view across the Saronic Gulf is spectacular. A narrow roads descends to the northern beach of **Vagonia**.

Although it's out of print, keep an eye peeled for *In Argolis*, a delightful book about Póros written by George Horton, editor of the *Philadelphia Enquirer* who became US consul in Greece and helped organize the first modern Olympics in 1896. In 1922 he was in Smyrna, and helped to save the lives of thousands of Greeks; he wrote *Blight of Asia* about the experience, a book that influenced US foreign policy of the day.

08

The Argo-Saronic Islands | Póros

Useful Information on Póros

Tourist police, on the waterfront, **t** 229 802 2462.

Where to Stay on Póros

For a complete list of apartments and rooms, call **t** 229 802 5577, *www.poros.com.gr*.

Póros Town ⊠ 18020

 Sto Roloï >

Sto Roloï, 13 Chartzopoúlou-Karrá, **t** 229 802 5808, *www.storoloi-poros.gr* (€€€€–€€). Under the clock tower, romantic hotel-apartments in a 200-year-old stone house with a pool.

Diónysos, near the ferry, **t** 229 802 3511, *www.hoteldionysos.com* (€€€). Attractive old building with cool, stone wall rooms, air-conditioning and satellite TV. Low off-season rates.

Manessis, **t** 229 802 2273, *www.manessis.com* (€€). Tidy rooms by the port in a neoclassical-style building.

Seven Brothers, just back from the waterfront, **t** 229 802 3412, *www.7brothers.gr* (€€). Convenient and comfortable rooms, that come with air-conditioning and TV.

Nikolaos Douros, 9 Dimósthenous (first road right after the high school), **t** 229 802 2633 (€). Pleasant rooms with air-conditioning and TV and a view.

Caravella, on the waterfront, **t** 229 802 3666. Greek and international dishes made from organic produce.

Karavolos, behind the cinema, **t** 229 802 6158. The 'Snail' is popular for its good Greek fare. Get there early to find a table.

Kathestos, by the post office, **t** 229 802 4770. Simple taverna that serves some of the best food on Póros.

Neórion ⊠ 18020

Pavlou, **t** 229 802 2734, *www.poros.com.gr/pavlou* (€€€). The best choice here, and at the lower end of the price scale; it has a lovely pool and tennis courts.

Mortzoukos, **t** 229 802 3924. Very good food; try the stuffed pork or the mouthwatering soufflé.

Askéli ✉ 18020

Christina Studios, **t** 229 802 4900, *www.poros.com.gr/christina* (€€€). Close to the beach, with lovely sea views from the big balconies.

New Aegli, **t** 229 802 2372, *www. newaegli.com* (€€€). Resort hotel with

a real Greek flavour, pool, beach and water sports; all rooms have sea views.

Sirene, near the monastery, **t** 229 802 2741, *www.hotelsirene.gr* (€€€). The most luxurious on Póros, with two salt-water pools, and its own beach. *Open April–Oct.*

Panorama, **t** 229 802 4563. One of the island's best tavernas, serving very reliable Greek staples.

Salamína/Sálamis (ΣΑΛΑΜΙΝΑ)

Bathing in the same bathwater as Piraeus, only 3km across the Strait which saw the dramatic victory over the Persians in 480 BC, Salamína (pop. 34,000) is the most suburban of islands, gritty and busy with shipyards but also a time-warp, its complete lack of pretensions, cheap tavernas and ouzeries a reminder of the Greece of yesteryear. The pine-forested southeast is the prettiest part of the island, and the villages of Moúlki (or Eádio) and Selínia with their

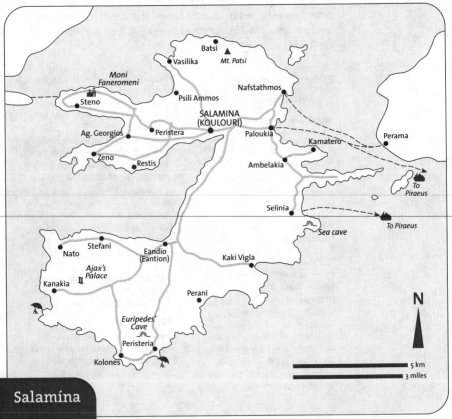

Salamína

Getting to and around Salamína

There is a **ferry** every 15 mins from Pérama to Paloúkia and at least 5 a day from Piraeus, some stopping also at Selínia, Porto Fino, Doulápi and Peristéria. **Port authority: t** 210 467 7277.

Villages are connected by an efficient **bus** system, t 210 467 1333.

For a **taxi**, call **t** 210 467 1575.

Drivers beware: the confusing geography and dearth of signposting means you may get to see every inch of the island, whether you want to or not.

---

beaches are popular weekend retreats for working-class families. Some time in the future, visitors may be flooding over to visit Ajax's recently discovered palace once the excavations are finished.

History

When Telemon and Peleus slew their brother Phocos (*see* 'Aegina'), Telemon took refuge on Salamína, then the island of serpents: a particularly destructive one had been killed by its first king, Kychreus, a shadowy character who himself began his career as the snake in Eleusis, on the mainland opposite. Telemon became king by marrying Kychreus' daughter, and fathered the great Ajax of Trojan War fame. For his part, snaky Kychreus never abandoned the island; during the Battle of Sálamis, the Athenians saw him in the form of a sea serpent, spurring them on to victory.

Salamína wasn't entirely unprepared in the September of 480 BC, when a massive Persian invasion fleet under Xerxes (the ancient Greeks put it at 1,200 ships; modern historians suggest 650) came to conquer Greece once and for all: Athens had fortified the island's weak places, and had sent her older men and hurriedly recalled exiles to defend them. After inconclusively challenging the Persians at Artemissíon, Athens and her allies fell back to Sálamis to join the reserves at the three ports facing Pérama; their ships totalled 378. They could see the smoke rising from the Acropolis, put to the sack by the Persian army as their fleet sailed into Fáliron Bay. When news came that the Persians would soon be advancing to the Isthmus of Corinth, the Corinthians and Spartans were keen to abandon Athens to defend their own homes, and Themistocles, the Athenian commander, had to resort to threats to keep them at Sálamis. But he was tricky too, and sent a secret letter to Xerxes saying that the Greeks were in disarray, half were about to sail home, and that the Persians, if they acted fast, could capture the entire Greek fleet if they blocked the narrow straits to the east and west of Sálamis. Xerxes fell for it hook, line and sinker. He ordered his fleet to divide and block the straits that very night, and had his silver throne carried to the summit of Mount Egáleo, for a ringside seat over his victory.

But the Greeks had other plans: at dawn half of their fleet in the east pretended to flee north. The Persian commander at once gave the order to advance and, as the Persian fleet lumbered forward, the

Greeks quickly spun their more agile triremes around and rammed the leading Persian ships, killing the Persian commander. No one was in charge, and no one could stop the momentum of Persian ships advancing into the narrow strait where they couldn't manoeuvre, creating a log-jam at the mercy of the crack fleet from Aegina, who attacked their flank. 'Crushed hulls lay upturned on the sea, so thick you could not see the water, choked with wrecks and slaughtered men,' Aeschylus (who fought in the battle) wrote in *The Persians*. Xerxes watched in agony; the Persians managed to create a diversion to escape with their last 300 ships.

Kouloúri (Salamína) and Moní Faneroméni

Salamína Town, the island capital, is known as Kouloúri ('crescent') for its leisurely curl around its harbour, with cafés and tavernas and a pair of windmills on the ridge making up for the town's general lack of distinction. The harbour hosts Japanese pearl oysters – stowaways from the freighters that have stopped there There's a small, unattractive beach and a **Museum of Folk Art** in the town hall (*dimarchíon*), with traditional costumes and dolls, ships' models and sea paintings by Aristídis Glýkas. Above Kouloúri, **Mount Profítis Ilías** offers views across the island.

Museum of Folk Art
1 Konstantínou Karamanlí, t *210 465 4180; open summer Mon–Fri 8–2.30 and 6–9, Sun 10.30–1; winter Mon–Fri 8–2.30 and 4–7, Sun 10.30–1*

From Kouloúri a bus leaves every hour for **Moní Faneroméni**, built in 1661, reusing the foundation of an ancient temple. The church has fine frescoes (in need of a clean), including an extraordinary *Last Judgement* containing over 3,000 figures painted in 1735 by Argítis Márkos. To the east is **Psilí Ámmos Beach**, which unfortunately often smells of petrol. Above, on **Mount Pátsi** are the remains of ancient fire towers – perhaps the same that helped to relay the news across the Aegean that the Persians were on their way.

🛑 **Moní Faneroméni**
t *210 468 1861; church open 7–12 and 3–7.30; dress appropriately*

South Salamína

Six km south of Kouloúri is the pleasant village of **Eádio**, set in the pines and with a nice pebble beach. Ruins found at **Kolonés**, or 'the columns', are believed to belong to the town from the time of Ajax. From Eádio a bus goes to the pleasant cove of **Kakí Vígla** and a rough road leads south to **Ag. Nikólaos Lemonión**, a monastery with a 15th-century chapel, decorated with 12th-century marble reliefs and plates from Rhodes. Between Ag. Nikólaos and Kakí Vígla there are sandy beaches, such as **Peristéria**, where in 1996 a cave was identified by archaeologist Yánnos Lólos as **Euripides' Cave** (*see box, right; to find it, keep your eyes peeled for the signpost in Peristéria, follow the dirt road up as far as you can, then continue on foot*).

Yánnos Lólos had spent his childhood summers on Salamína, and as his interest in archaeology grew he made walking surveys of the island. At age 15 he read in Strabo that 'Old Salamis' towards the south predated the Classical-era city on the east coast. It stuck in his

Euripides' Cave: a Poet's Hideaway

Euripides had an estate on Sálamis and wrote his tragedies in a cave facing the sea. In the 5th century BC this retreat from society was highly unusual, but Euripides was by all accounts an unusual man. Born into the landed middle class during the triumph over the Persians, Euripides served in the Peloponnesian War and lost his fortune through expensive political posts and contributions to the war effort, and spent the rest of his money on books – he was the first Greek to accumulate a private library. He was considered the greatest poet of his age (some 18 plays have survived), yet he won only four first prizes. No one was quite sure what to think of his work. Where Aeschylus and Sophocles maintained a level of restraint and dignity in their characters, Euripides' are full of passion; he broke sexual taboos, and refused to idealize anyone. He loved women (at a time when most men wanted to lock them up at home) and made them his special study, most famously in his *Medea*.

Idealistic, but deeply troubled by his times, Euripides wrote truths that disturbed his contemporaries' basic assumptions about society, the state, their gods and themselves. He loathed their wars; both the wealthy élite and the great rabble of Athenian democracy infuriated him, and he, in turn, infuriated them, even while they hung on his every word. They took out their frustrations by mocking him and even beating him up, until he took refuge in the court of Macedonia, where he died the next year, in 406 BC. Yet a century later, the playwright Philemon wrote: 'If I were certain that the dead had consciousness, I would hang myself to see Euripides.'

After Euripides' death, his writer's retreat became a tourist attraction that was visited well into Roman times. In 1994, Yánnos Lólos, finding that the cave at Peristéria matched the ancient descriptions, began investigations that yielded artefacts going back to the Neolithic times, including votive offerings that suggested that the cave was identified as the lair of Kychreus, the man-snake. Then, in 1996, Lólos proved that it was also the retreat of the great tragedian, when he came across an archaeologist's dream: a wine cup with Euripides' name on it, left behind in the 2nd century BC by admirers of the poet.

---

mind, and in 1999, while walking around a wooded hill by sandy Kanákia Beach, Lólos noticed Mycenaean-era potsherds scattered on the ground – leading to excavations and another remarkable find, which he announced in 2006 was the remains of the **Palace of Ajax**, in a 5ha (12½ acre) complex, including a large Mycenaean palace that had two royal halls (*megara*) and 33 rooms on four levels. The settlement dates from 3000 BC, and flourished and was then abandoned at the same time as ancient Mycenae, *c.* 1180 BC, during the period of upheavals and unrest following the traditional date of the Trojan War. In this case, the ruling class escaped to Cyprus, where their descendants under Ajax's half-brother Teucrus founded a new city of Salamina in 1100 BC. Lólos found no sign of enemy attacks at Kanákia, but he also found little art or jewellery – evidence that the inhabitants packed their valuables and went. One item he did find was a fragment of a copper mail shirt stamped with the name of Pharaoh Ramses II, who ruled from 1279–1213 BC, which suggests either the presence of an Egyptian mercenary, or the possibility that Salamína's Mycenaeans had themselves fought as mercenaries in Egypt. Unlike other Mycenaean palaces, Ajax's is unique in that it was never again built on. If you come in September while the team is excavating and Lólos is not too busy, he'll give you a tour.

On the east coast of Salamína, **Paloúkia** is a ferry-boat landing stage from Pérama. The sea here sheltered beds of purple-dye-

Where to Stay and Eat on Salamína

Salamína ✉ 18900

Hotels on Salamína are simple and few. Because Salamína gets few tourists, its tavernas are pure Greek, and the food inexpensive.

Gabriel Apartments, Eádio, **t** 210 466 2275 (€€). The best on the island, with a restaurant. *Open April–Sept.*

Akroyali, 92 Themistokléous, Kouloúri, **t** 210 467 3263. (€). *Open all year.*

Votsalakia, 64 Themistokléous, Kouloúri, **t** 210 467 1432 (€).

Ali, just outside Kouloúri at 301 Leof. Aianteíou, **t** 210 465 3586. Plain and simple, serving excellent Arabic specialities, besides the usual Greek fare. Phone a day ahead for *kibe*, a Syrian speciality.

O Christos, at Restí, **t** 210 468 2536. Above the tiny but clean beach, with a lovely view, excellent food and low prices.

Vassiliou, in Selínia, **t** 210 467 1625. An island institution: a family-run taverna.

Notis, in Kaki Vígla, **t** 210 466 2247. Good old-fashioned Greek food and hearty retsina.

yielding murex shells, which sustained a local industry until the Second World War and the advent of chemicals.

South of Paloúkia, woebegone **Ambelákia** was the harbour of Classical and Hellenistic Salamína. The mole is visible in the shallows, but little else – it's now a ships' rubbish dump. It has never been excavated, and probably never will be.

Spétses (ΣΠΕΤΣΕΣ)

Spétses is a beautiful low-lying, pine-scented island in the Argive Gulf, the furthest from Athens, a factor that long kept it more relaxed than its more accessible sisters. For all that, it's an old hand at tourism: since the First World War Athenian families have come every summer for its safe beaches and climate. The island still attracts visitors lured by the luscious descriptions of John Fowles' *The Magus*, as well as a merry mix of British and Athenians, nearly all on motorbikes – it's a lot noisier than Hýdra and considerably less posey, although the opening of new boutique hotels seems set to make it a more upmarket place.

History

Although discoveries at Ag. Marína indicate that Pityoussa, as Spétses was called, has been inhabited since 2500 BC, it stayed out of the spotlight for the next 4,000 years. No one is even sure how the island got its current name; the best guess is that the Venetians called it 'Spice,' or *spezie*. Like the other Saronics, Spétses was eventually repopulated with refugees from Albania and Épiros; the first shipyards date from the early 17th century. By the 19th century Spétses was renowned for its seamanship and, like Hýdra, prospered from the derring-do of its merchants and sea captains.

'Old Spice' made the history books by helping to ignite the War of Independence. During the years of Napoleonic blockade-running, the

Getting to and around Spétses

By sea: Several **hydrofoils**, **catamarans** (2hrs) and **ferries** (4hrs) connect daily with Piraeus and other Argo-Saronic islands year-round; there are also frequent boats to the nearby port of Kósta.

Port authority: t 229 807 2245.

Note: **cars** aren't allowed on the island. **Bicycles** and **scooters**, however, are for hire everywhere. There are four **taxis** on the island and two **buses** run from the Dápia to Anárgyri, and from Hotel Possidonion to Ligonéri. **Sea taxis** (at the Dápia) and caiques can take you to the beaches along the coast; book one at **t** 229 807 2072. **Horse-drawn carriages** for hire along the waterfront add a touch of elegance, but don't go any further than Ligonéri or Ag. Marína and agree on a price before setting out.

Spetsiots established a small fleet ready to take on the Turks, and the island raised the flag of war on 13 March 1821, under the influence of Laskarína Bouboulína, the wealthy, twice-widowed mother of seven, and the only female member of the revolutionary Friendly Society, the Philikí Etairía. Her flagship, the *Agamemnon*, was the finest in the country, and on 4 April the indomitable lady admiral, leading her 'brave lads', won Greece's first naval victory, capturing three Turkish ships as she led her fleet of eight vessels over to Naúplio to help blockade the port. She personally led the attack against the seaside fortifications; if the hottest fighting was happening on shore, Bouboulína would abandon ship for a horse and sabre. She stayed there until Naúplio fell in 1822, then participated in the blockade of Monemvasía; later she personally intervened to save the women and children of the Pasha's harem during one of the worst Greek atrocities of a war filled with atrocities: the massacre at Trípolis in the Peloponnese.

Spétses Town

Spétses, the capital and port, is not your typical Greek island town: where most are very dense, it spreads out leisurely amid orchards and gardens, into a score of neighbourhoods. Some of the oldest houses – proud neoclassical captains' mansions – are inland, safely invisible from the waterfront. Another distinctive feature is a love for black and white pebble mosaic pavements (*choklakía*). One commemorates the revolt of 1821 on the **Dápia**, the elegant square that sweeps down to the new quay. Bristling with cannon, the Dápia was once the town's frontline defence, but now it plays a more peaceful role as the vortex of Spétses' café society. On the esplanade there's a she-means-business statue of Bouboulína, who was assassinated in 1825 in her mansion nearby – over a dispute over her son's elopement with a local girl. The mansion was restored and is run by her great-great-great-grandson as the delightful **Bouboulína Museum**; here are her weapons and headscarf, a model of the *Agamemnon* and a portrait of Bouboulína looking improbably dainty. Apparently she is still the only woman admiral, ever.

Behind Bouboulína's statue stretches the Edwardian façade of one of the first tourist hotels on any Greek island, the **Hotel Possidonion**,

Bouboulína Museum
t 229 807 2416; www. bouboulinamuseum-spetses.gr; open mid-Mar–Oct; 45min tours daily 9.45–8; adm

Spétses

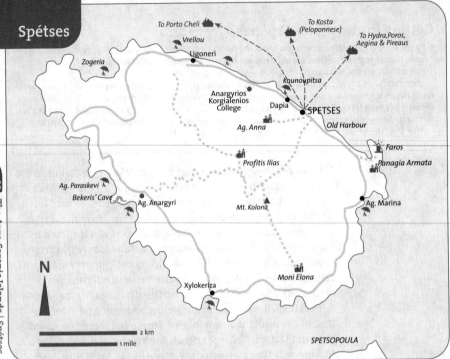

Zogeria

Vrellou

Ligoneri

To Porto Cheli

Anargyrios
Korgialenios
College

Kounoupitsa

To Kosta
(Peloponnese)

To Hydra, Poros,
Aegina & Pireaus

Dapia

SPETSES

Ag. Anna

Old Harbour

Faros

Profitis Ilias

Panagia Armata

Ag. Paraskevi
Bekeris' Cave

Ag. Anargyri

Mt. Kolona

Ag. Marina

N

Moni Elona

Xylokeriza

2 km
1 mile

SPETSOPOULA

built in 1914 by philanthropist Sotíris Anárgyro who, after making his fortune in the tobacco trade in New York, decided to make that of Spétses; when it was built it was considered the most luxurious hotel in the Balkans, and may soon undergo renovation. A dedicated Anglophile, he also founded the **Anárgyrios Korgialénios College** in 1927, on the English public school model. John Fowles taught here, a not altogether happy experience, and made it his model for the Lord Byron School in *The Magus*. Closed in 1983, it's now used as a centre for seminars. Anárgyro's other contribution to the island, Spétses' **pine forests**, were sadly much damaged in fires in 2000 and 2005. Anárgyro's **mansion**, built in 1903 (behind the Roumani Hotel), is a turn-of-the-century bombast modelled on an Egyptian temple.

Spétses Museum
t 229 807 2994; open Tues–Sun 8.30–3; adm

Spétses' **museum** is housed in the handsome mansion (1795) of Hadziyiánnis Méxis, another shipowner and revolutionary; it has many of its original furnishings, archaeological finds, a box holding Bouboulína's bones, the 'Freedom or Death' flag of the War of Independence, and ships' models, paintings and figureheads.

The picturesque **Paléo Limáni**, or Old Harbour, is shared by fishermen, yachts, caique-builders and the oldest church, **Ag. Nikólaos**. On its pretty white bell tower the Spetsiots raised their defiant flag in 1821 – a bronze cast is displayed opposite and a pebble *choklakia* in the courtyard tells the tale. When they heard the Turks were sailing over to crush their revolt, the inhabitants created mannequins out of barrels and flowerpots, dressing them in red fezes and Turkish-appearing uniforms, and set them up along the quay. Seeing them from a distance, the Turkish commander thought that the island had already been taken, and sailed by.

Further east, near the **Fáros** (lighthouse), the church of **Panagía Armáta** was built after a Spétses fireboat sent the invading Turks fleeing on 8 September 1822, an event celebrated annually with gusto during the Armata; inside, a painting by Koútzis commemorates the triumph. Just beyond is **Ag. Marína Beach**, looking across to **Spetsopoúla**, owned the Niárchos family, whose late paterfamilias Stávros was one of the 'Super-Greeks' of the 1960s and '70s, and whose financial and romantic doings in the tabloids were only overshadowed by those of arch-rival Aristotle Onassis – in fact, one of Niárchos' six wives was an Onassis ex. Many believe he was the original for Fowles' enigmatic Colchis. Sometimes the 325ft Niárchos yacht is moored here, nearly as big as Spetsopoúla itself. Two other fine churches are up the hill at **Kastélli**, where the houses are mostly ruined: the 17th-century **Koimistís Theotókou** has frescoes, and **Ag. Triáda** a superb carved iconostasis (*ask the tourist police for keys*).

Around the Island

🔆 Pines, beaches and seafood of Spétses

It's 26km around Spétses' pretty coast, embellished with pebbly beaches and rocky swimming coves. Heading clockwise, the first likely place for a swim is **Xylokeríza**, with a pleasant shingle beach that rarely gets crowded. The opposite holds true of **Ag. Anárgyri**, the only other settlement on the island, on an irresistible bay, rimmed with trees, bars and tavernas. From the beach it's a short swim or walk to **Bekeris' Cave**. You can enter from the sea or there is a low entrance by land; go in the afternoon, when the sun illuminates the stalactites inside.

Continuing clockwise, some caiques continue to **Ag. Paraskeví**, a delightful pebbly cove, watched over by the **Villa Jasemia**, the house Fowles used as the residence of his endlessly tricky Magus. A hop over the rocks at the west end is Spétses' official naturist beach. **Zogeriá**, further west, is a pretty, double-coved bay, a hardish slog from the road. On the north, the beaches **Vréllou** (aka Paradise) and shady **Ligonéri** are nicest.

08 The Argo-Saronic Islands | Spétses

Useful Information on Spétses

Tourist police: on the far side of the Dápia, above OTE (telephone office), t 229 807 3100 or 229 807 3744.
Athens Centre, t 210 701 2268, *www. athenscentre.gr*. Runs summer cultural programmes on Spétses.

Spétses Festivals

1 July: Ag. Anárgyri.
26 July: Ag. Paraskeví at Zogeriá.
8 Sept (nearest weekend): the Armáta, when the Spetsiots commemorate their victory in the Straits of Spétses, in 1822. The attacking Turks were held at bay by the island's fleet and had to

withdraw when confronted with a drifting fireboat. The battle is re-enacted in the harbour, with fireworks and dancing.

Where to Stay on Spétses

Spétses Town ✉ 18050

Unless you arrive for Easter, August or the Armáta, you can generally find a room; ask at one of the tourist offices on the Dápia.

Economou, near the town hall, **t** 229 807 3400, *www.spetsesyc.gr* (€€€€€). Large studios in a traditional, renovated mansion with a pool.

Nissia, on the seafront, 500m from the Dápia, **t** 229 807 5000, *www.nissia.gr* (€€€€€). 'Traditional residences' in a 1920s industrial building, with a magnificent pool, excellent restaurant and fully equipped studios and maisonettes.

Orloff Resort, a mile from town, **t** 229 807 5444, *www.orloffresort.com* (€€€€€). Bright white apartments around a pool, with marble baths, Internet, the works.

Villa Christina, in town, **t** 229 807 2218, *www.villachristinahotel.com* (€€). A central, charming and deservedly popular little place.

Villa Kriezi, 5mins' walk from town, **t** 229 807 4086, *adlogothetis@yahoo.gr* (€€). En suites with TV and air-conditioning; many have sea views.

Mimosa, close to the Old Harbour and Ag. Marína beach, **t** 229 807 4087, *www.spetsesdirect.com* (€€–€, including breakfast). Good-value studios.

Klimis, on the east end of the waterfront, **t** 229 807 2334 (€). Pleasant seafront rooms over a pastry shop. *Open all year.*

Ag. Anárgyri ✉ 18050

Acrogiali, **t** 229 807 3695, *www.acrogiali.com* (€€€). Has beautifully designed suites with plasma TVs, Persian rugs and Korres beauty products in a lush Mediterranean garden, overlooking a pool. *Open April–Oct.*

⭐ **Tarsanas >>**

Eating Out on Spétses

Spétses Town

Exedra, in the old harbour, **t** 229 807 3497. Renowned for its seafood, including pasta with lobster.

Kipos. Well-priced, with barrelled wine and a delightful garden setting, off the main square.

Lazaros, uphill from the Dápia, **t** 229 807 2600. Full of character; good for vegetarians and meat-eaters, but they also have fish. *Closed lunch.*

Patralis, 10min walk along the front to the right of the main harbour, **t** 229 807 2134. Very popular. Try fish *à la spetsiota*, baked with tomato, olive oil, garlic and pepper.

Stelios, **t** 229 807 3748. In addition to fish fresh from the nearby market, come for excellent vegetarian dishes and a wide choice of set-price menus.

Tarsanas, in the old harbour, **t** 229 807 4490. A big favourite (*book in summer*). Owned by a fishing family and serving *mezédes* and fresh seafood, including a superb fish soup. *Closed Mon–Fri in low season.*

Ag. Anárgyri ✉ 18050

Tassos. An example of how wonderful Greek food can taste; try the house speciality, 'lamb in a bag'.

Nightlife on Spétses

There are two outdoor cinemas in summer; otherwise Spétses Town starts to swing at around 1am.

Figaro. With its seaside patio in the Old Harbour, this is the hot spot for dancing. In the early hours, the Greek music comes on and everyone changes their steps to dance along. *Open every night in high season; Fri and Sat only in low season.*

Halcyon, town centre. Greek music bar.

Spetsa Bar, Plateía Ag. Mámmas. Popular rock bar.

Bracciera, by the marina. Wood décor; shimmy to American and Europop.

Veranda, upstairs. For something quieter, have a drink here, listening to soft Greek music.

Crete

On the map a horned, wasp-waisted creature scooting along the 35th parallel, Crete is Greece's largest island (260km by 50km), and its most extraordinary. Endowed with every earthly delight, Crete nurtured the first civilization on European soil, the Minoan, which, judging by its art and architecture, was so graceful and inventive that Europe has yet to see the like. It is a terribly old place, older than the rest of Greece, the birthplace (and tomb) of the great sky god Zeus, the cradle of the earliest myths.

09

1 Minoan art and a Labyrinth
Archaeology Museum, Heráklion, and nearby Knossós **pp.181 and 188**

2 Hiking Europe's longest canyon
Gorge of Samariá **p.156**

3 Lively Venetian and Turkish charm
Chaniá **p.141**

4 A pink sand lagoon
Elafonísi **p.152**

5 Frescoes and antiquities
Kéra Panagía and Lato **pp.214 and 215**

See map overleaf

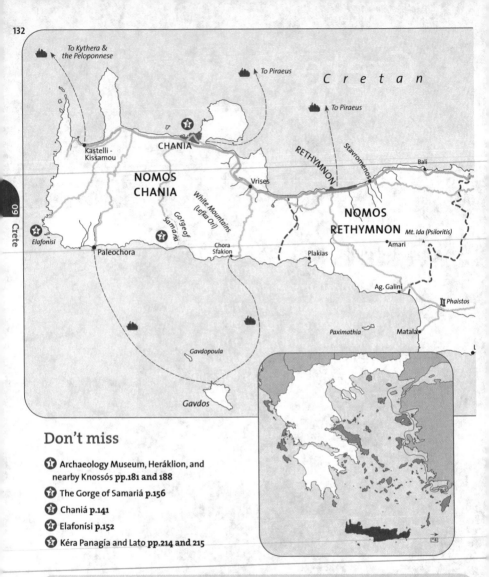

Don't miss

⭐ Archaeology Museum, Heráklion, and nearby Knossós **pp.181 and 188**

⭐ The Gorge of Samariá **p.156**

⭐ Chaniá **p.141**

⭐ Elafonísi **p.152**

⭐ Kéra Panagía and Lato **pp.214 and 215**

How Crete Is Divided

Mountain ranges neatly divide the island into four sections that have become modern Crete's political divisions. West of the White Mountains is the *nomós* (province) of **Chaniá**; between the White Mountains and Psilorítis (Mount Ida) is the *nomós* of **Réthymnon**; between Psilorítis and the Lassíthi Mountains lies the *nomós* of **Heráklion**; and east of the Lassíthi Mountains is the *nomós* of **Lassíthi**, of which Ag. Nikólaos is the capital. The description in the text covers Crete from west to east.

When to Go

Crete is a year-round destination, but April and May are especially lovely: the Libyan Sea is warm enough for bathing, the flowers are glorious and the higher mountains are still capped with snow. Note that the Gorge of Samariá rarely opens until May, when its torrent recedes sufficiently for safe passage. September and October are also good, with many perfect days and a lingering warm sea.

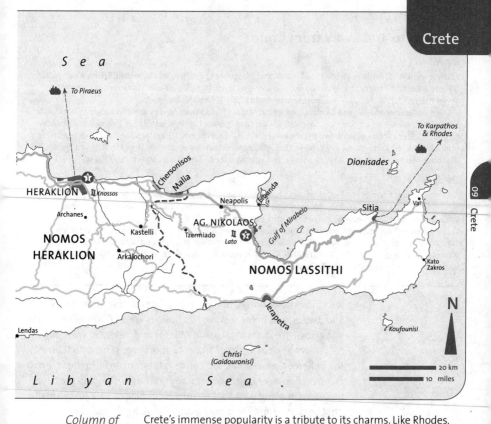

*Column of
the Levant,*

*My Crete,
beautiful island,*

*Your soil is made
of gold,*

*Your each stone
a diamond.*

traditional Cretan
matináda

Crete's immense popularity is a tribute to its charms. Like Rhodes, the season is long here – and charters from all across Europe arrive from early spring until the end of October. If you have fantasies of tripping alone through the labyrinth of Knossós, come in winter: after the Acropolis, it's the most visited site in Greece. But Crete remains lively all winter – and mild, especially along the south coast.

But there is also a lot of Crete to go around, even in summer. Four mighty mountain ranges, one sliced with the Gorge of Samariá, the longest canyon in Europe, lend the island a grandeur that is out of proportion to its size. Some 1,500 species of wild flowers brighten spring landscapes with the intensity of 1950s Technicolor. No place in Greece can approach Crete's agricultural diversity: vineyards, olive and citrus groves cover the coastal plains and hills; cereals, potatoes, apples and walnuts grow on the mountain plateaux; and acres of plastic greenhouses blanket the south coast, providing bushels of winter vegetables and fruit for the rest of Greece.

Cretan art and architecture afford an equally rich feast: the fabled Minoan sites and artefacts in Heráklion's superb Archaeology Museum; Byzantine monasteries glowing with frescoes and icons; the Venetian and Turkish quarters of Chaniá and Réthymnon. Of all the islands, Crete has the sharpest sense of a separate identity and a

Getting to and away from Crete

By Air

There are direct flights from London Stansted and Glasgow to Heráklion on **Globespan**; **British Airways** flies 5 times a week in summer to Heráklion from London and twice from Manchester; both Heráklion and to a lesser extent Chaniá are linked by direct **charter flights** from UK and Irish airports.

Olympic Airlines and **Aegean Airways** have frequent daily flights from Athens to Heráklion and Chaniá, and several times a week from Thessaloníki. Both airlines also operate flights several times a week from Heráklion to Rhodes. Olympic has at least two flights a week from Sitía from Athens, Thessaloníki and Alexandroúpolis.

In addition, the Crete-based **Sky Express** runs Jetstream turboprops in summer from Heráklion to Rhodes, Mýkonos and Santoríni several times a week, and at least once to Sámos, Kos, Mytilíni and Ikaría.

By Sea

Large **overnight ferries** link Heráklion and Chaniá to Piraeus daily; and others go at least weekly to Ag. Nikólaos, Sitía and Réthymnon. **Minoan** high-speed boats can do it in six hours, and in summer the catamarans of **Hellenic Seaways** make the trip in 4hrs 45mins.

Daily 'Flying Dolphins' and ferries in summer link Heráklion and Réthymnon to Santoríni, Mýkonos, Íos, Náxos, Páros, Tínos, Sýros and Mílos; others, sometimes calling at Ag. Nikólaos and Sitía, sail to Kárpathos, Kássos, Chálki, and Rhodes. Another line links Kastélli-Kíssamou on the west coast with Kýthera, Antikýthera, and Gýthion and Kalamáta in the Peloponnese.

---

ferocious love of liberty, manifest in its own culture, dialect, music and dances, and in the works of its famous sons, El Greco, Elefthérios Venizélos, Níkos Kazantzákis and Míkis Theodorákis. On feast days, *matinádes* or *rizítika* ('songs from the roots') are sung with themes full of fierce Cretan pride. Such pride is far from dead. In the face of a creeping homogenized Europe, many Cretans are helping preserve traditions, moving back to their ancestral villages. Paradoxes are rife, but the island can take some credit for making paradox an art form, when the Cretan sage Epimenides declared, 'All Cretans are liars.'

History

The first Cretans were Neolithic sailors, probably from Asia Minor, who arrived on the island *c.* 8000 BC. They built small houses in Knossós and other future **Minoan** sites, with rooms clustered around a central open area, presaging the floor-plans of the famous palaces. They worshipped fertility goddesses, especially in caves on top of mountains. These shrines evolved into peak sanctuaries.

Homer was the first to describe Europe's first literate civilization:

One of the great islands of the world in midsea, in the winedark sea, is Krete: spacious and rich and populous, with 90 cities and a mingling of tongues. Akhaians there are found, along with Kretan hillmen of the old stock, and Kydonians, Dorians[...], Pelasgians – and one among their 90 towns is Knossós. Here lived King Minos whom great Zeus received every 9th year in private council.

(translated by Robert Fitzgerald)

Yet the 'Kretan hillmen of the old stock' only left the realm of myth in 1900, when Arthur Evans discovered a new pre-Greek civilization at Knossós that he called 'Minoan'. Since then, discoveries have

Everything We Knew is Wrong!

And so, unfortunately, are many of the dates in this chapter for the ancient Minoans. Recently (2006), scientists found an olive tree buried in ash from the volcanic explosion that destroyed Santoríni and took much of Minoan civilization with it. They dated it to 1627–1600 BC, not 1450 or 1550 as everyone had expected. The result: many of the dates for sites on Crete will have to be changed, and classifications such as the 'New Palace' and 'Post-Palace' periods will need adjusting. Worse, some are starting to question just how much of an effect the eruption really had on Crete. It will take the experts many years and many arguments to get this mess straightened out; in the meantime take the dates with a grain of salt.

continued apace, including finds that have altered Evans' vision of the Minoans as a non-violent society of artsy flower children. Trade with Egypt, the Cyclades and the Middle East at the end of the Neolithic era introduced bronze to Crete and brought about the changes that distinguish the first Minoan period, the **Pre-Palatial** (2600–1900 BC), according to Níkos Pláton's revision of Evans' chronology. Characteristic of the Pre-Palatial era are the first monumental *tholos* tombs (as at Archánes), the building of high sanctuaries and the beginning of a ruling priestly class, who dwelt in palaces with red-plastered walls. The Minoan taste for refinement shines through in exquisite work in gold, semi-precious stones and sealstones, some bearing the first signs of writing in ideograms.

Pláton's **Old Palace period** (Evans' Middle Minoan; 1900–1700 BC) saw a hitherto unheard-of wealth on Crete. Power was concentrated in the 'palaces' of Knossós, Mália, Phaistós and Zákros, which were kitted out with the first-known plumbing and lavishly decorated with frescoes and sacred 'horns of consecration'. Bulls played an important role in religion, which was dominated by the Goddess, pictured in Minoan imagery in three aspects: as the mistress of the wild animals and earth; as the snake goddess, mistress of the underworld; and as the dove goddess, mistress of the sky. Towns and palaces were unfortified, suggesting political unity and giving substance to the myth of Minos' thalassocracy, or sea reign; and a fleet precluded the need for walls. Cretan ships, laden with olive oil, honey, wine, precious balsams and art, traded extensively. The palaces all had important stores, acting either as warehouses or distribution points. Writing was in ideograms, as on the Phaistós Disc. Roads paved with flagstones linked settlements, and the first large irrigation projects were begun. Art reached new heights, in gold and in ceramics. Then, about 1700 BC, a huge earthquake ripped across the Eastern Mediterranean and devastated the buildings.

Forced to start afresh, the Minoans built better than ever in the **New Palace period** (1700–1450 BC). The palaces were rebuilt in the same style: warrens of rooms illuminated by light wells, overlooking a central and a western court, where religious ceremonies and the famous bull-leaping may have occurred. To make them more resistant to earthquakes, wooden beams and columns were combined with stone. Workshops and vast store-rooms were clustered nearby, their contents recorded on clay tablets in a system known as Linear A. Villas were built outside the palaces, and scattered throughout the countryside were centralized farms. Densely populated towns existed at Gourniá, Móchlos, Palaíkastro, Zákros and Pseíra island. Burials became more elaborate; many were in painted clay sarcophagi, or *larnaxes*. Impressive port facilities were built and new trade colonies established on Santoríni, Rhodes, Skópelos, and Greece and Asia Minor. Shields, daggers, swords and helmets have been found, although land defences were still non-existent.

The Heráklion Museum is full of testimonials to the exuberant art of the New Palace period. The Minoans delighted in natural designs, especially floral and marine motifs. They portrayed themselves with wasp waists and long black curls, the men clad in codpieces and

The Birth of Zeus, and Europe's Bullish Origins

As Cronos (the Roman Saturn), the ruler of the world, had been warned that he would be usurped by his own child, he swallowed every baby his wife Rhea, daughter of the Earth, presented to him. After this had happened five times, Rhea determined on a different fate for her sixth child, Zeus. When he was born she smuggled him to Crete and gave Cronos a swaddled stone to swallow instead. Mother Earth hid the baby in the Diktean Cave and set Cretan warriors called Kouretes to guard him. As prophesied, Zeus grew up and dethroned his father by castrating him with a sickle.

When a Phoenician princess, Europa, caught Zeus' fancy, the god disguised himself as a beautiful bull and carried her off to Crete, where she bore him three sons: Minos, Rhadamanthys and Sarpedon, and gave her name to an entire continent. When Minos became the King of Crete at Knossós, he was asked to prove that his claim to the throne had divine sanction. Minos remembered the form his father had taken and asked Poseidon to send him a bull from the sea to sacrifice. But the bull was so magnificent that Minos didn't kill it, but sent it to service his herds. The kingdom of Minos prospered, but Poseidon, weary of waiting for the promised sacrifice, caused Minos' wife Pasiphaë to fall in love with the bull. The unfortunate Pasiphaë confided her problem to the inventor Daedalus, who constructed a hollow wooden cow covered with hide for her to enter. Their unnatural union resulted in the Minotaur, born with the head of a bull and the body of a man. Minos hid the monster in another invention of Daedalus, the Labyrinth (an impossible maze of corridors under his palace) and fed it with the blood of his enemies. Among these were seven maidens and seven youths from Athens, sent to Crete every nine years, the tribute extorted by Minos when his son was slain in an Athenian game.

Two tributes had been paid when Theseus, the handsome son of Aegeus, King of Athens, demanded to be sent as one of the victims. Minos' daughter Ariadne fell in love with him at first sight and asked Daedalus to save his life, and the inventor supplied a ball of thread. Unwinding the thread as he went, Theseus made his way into the labyrinth, slew the Minotaur, retraced his way out with the thread and escaped, taking Ariadne and the other Athenians with him. Minos was furious when he discovered the part Daedalus had played in the escape, and threw the inventor and his young son Icarus into the Labyrinth. Although they found their way out, escape from Crete was impossible, as Minos controlled the seas. But Daedalus, never at a loss, fashioned wings of feathers and wax for himself and Icarus, and they flew off. All went well until an exhilarated Icarus disobeyed his father's command not to fly too close to the sun. The wax in his wings melted, and he plunged and drowned off the island that took his name.

Minos then pursued Daedalus all over the Mediterranean, hoping to trap the inventor by offering a reward to whoever could pass a thread through a nautilus shell. Finally, in Sicily, Minos met a king who took the shell away and brought it back threaded – it was Daedalus who had performed the task, by tying the thread to an ant. Minos demanded the inventor be handed over. The king promised to, then invited Minos to stay at his palace. While Minos was in his bath, Daedalus put a pipe through the ceiling and poured boiling water through it, scalding him to death.

loincloths, the women with eyes blackened with kohl and lips red, clad in their famous bodices that exposed the breast, flounced skirts and exotic hats. All move with a natural, sensuous grace, completely unlike the stiffly stylized figures in Egyptian and Near Eastern art. The strong feminine quality of the art suggests that Minoan society was matriarchal, and that women were the equals of men, participating in the same sports and ceremonies. Vases and rhytons (libation vessels) of basalt, marble and porphyry are unsurpassed in beauty and technique. Culturally Minoan influence spread north to mainland Greece, recently invaded by northerners known as Achaeans or Mycenaeans; the Minoans communicated with them in the *lingua franca* of the day, Linear B – proto-ancient Greek.

But some time around 1450 BC (according to the old, discredited dating system – *see* box, p.135) disaster struck again. The tremendous volcanic eruption of Santoríni, and subsequent tsunami and earthquakes, left Crete in ruins; in some places along the north coast a 20cm layer of tephra (volcanic ash) has been found – *under* structures belonging to the Late Minoan or **Post-Palace period** (1450–1180 BC). The old theory that mainland Mycenaeans invaded Crete, taking advantage of its disarray, has lost favour before the idea that their infiltration was gradual, and that for a long period the Mycenaeans co-existed peacefully with the Minoans. Of the great palaces, Knossós alone was rebuilt, only to burn down once and for all in *c.* 1380 BC; in other places, such as Ag. Triáda, typical Mycenaean palaces (*megarons*) have been found. Linear B became the dominant script, and the natural, graceful motifs of the New Palace period grew ever more stylized. Clay figurines of the goddess lose not only their sex appeal but any pretensions to realism, resembling bells. But the island still maintained its great fleet, and according to Homer it contributed 90 ships to the Trojan War.

After the Minoans: The Dorians

By 1180 BC, Minoan-Mycenaean civilization had ground to a halt, probably caused by drought. Trade disintegrated as Crete entered a cultural dark age (the **Proto-Geometric period**, 1100–900 BC). Traditionally the decline is blamed on the **Dorians**, a new wave of Greek-speakers who invaded, armed with the latest technology – iron weapons. Whatever happened, the last Minoans took to the hills, especially south of Sitía, surviving in memory as the **Eteocretans**, or true Cretans, Homer's 'hillmen of the old stock'. The art of these last Minoans grew weird, and in Praisós they left mysterious inscriptions in the Greek alphabet, still waiting to be translated. Other Cretans – the **Mycenaeans** – were treated according to the amount of resistance they had offered; those who fought the most were enslaved.

By the **Geometric period** (900–650 BC) Crete was divided, like the mainland, into autonomous city-states. The Minoan goddess was adopted into the Greek pantheon – Britomartis became Artemis; Atana became Athena; her son and consort Welchanos became Zeus, father of the gods. Art from the period shows Eastern influences. Towards the end, bronze statuettes attributed to 'Daedalos' (not to be confused with the inventor) appear, with their characteristic wide eyes, thick hair and parted legs. The style reached its peak in the **Archaic period** (700–500 BC), when Doric Crete was one of the art centres of Greece. Like the Spartans, the Cretans were an austere lot, not caring to join in the Ionian commercial and cultural influence in the Mediterranean that created Greece's Classical Age. By the 2nd century BC Crete's coasts were little more than pirates' bases. When these pirates niggled Rome by kidnapping the families of nobles at Ostia, right under Rome's nose, the Senate sent **Quintus Caecilius Metellus** to subdue the anarchic island once and for all (69–67 BC).

Roman and Byzantine Crete

With the Romans, the centre of power on the island moved south to Górtyn, on the fertile Mesará plain, especially once it was made the capital of the Roman province of Crete and Cyrene (Libya) in West Africa. With peace, the population soared to some 300,000. **Christianity** came early when St Paul appointed his Greek disciple, Titus, to found the first church at Górtyn in AD 58. Richly decorated basilicas were constructed at Knossós, Chersónisos, Górtyn, Lissós, Sýia, Itanos and Kainoúrios. In 823, the **Saracens** from North Africa conquered Crete, plunging much of it into misery and decimating Górtyn. They built the first castle at Heráklion, called Kandak ('deep moat') or Candia, a name which grew to encompass all of Crete in the Middle Ages. In 961 the future Byzantine emperor **Nikephóros Phokás** reconquered Crete and sent the fabulous treasure of the Saracens back to Constantinople. The victorious Greek soldiers were among the first new colonists given tracts of land; Emperor **Aléxis Comnénus** later sent his son and other young Byzantine aristocrats, establishing a ruling class that would dominate Crete for centuries.

Venetian and Ottoman Crete

With the conquest of Constantinople in 1204 and the division of spoils, Crete was awarded to Boniface of Montferrat, who in 1210 sold it to the **Venetians**. The first two centuries of rule by the Most Serene Republic were neither serene nor republican; the Venetians imposed an unpopular feudal system with a doge in Heráklion, and tried to replace the Orthodox hierarchy with a Catholic one. Uprisings occurred, often led by the *árchons*, or Byzantine nobles. They won concessions from Venice, until, by the 15th century, the Orthodox and Catholics (some 10,000) lived together harmoniously. Happiness was for the few, however – the majority of Cretans were compelled to build immense walls around the port cities, but

Food and Wine: The Old/New Cretan Diet

In 1947, researchers for the Rockefeller Foundation noted how healthy elderly Cretans were compared to their American counterparts, in spite of the privations of the war and their 'primitive' way of life. In 1956, the foundation began a 15-year study in Japan, Finland, Yugoslavia, the USA, Holland, Italy, Corfu and Crete comparing diet, lifestyle and the incidence of cardiovascular disease and cancer. If health were a race, Crete lapped the competition; the difference in death rates, even compared with Corfu, was striking. And this in spite of the fact that Cretans consume as much fat as the Finns, who did the worst in coronary disease; in fact, the only Cretan who died of coronary failure during the study was a butcher.

Olive oil (the main source of fat), lots of legumes, greens and fresh vegetables, and little meat, proved to be the secret and the basis of the Cretan diet that nutritionists, and now the Cretans, like to promote. The island grows vegetables, nuts, olives and every kind of fruit from apples to bananas and citrus; market counters heave with herbs. Cretan honey and cheeses have had a high reputation since antiquity: the best is *myzíthra*, a white soft cheese similar to fresh ricotta, often served on rusks with tomatoes (*dákos*), as a starter; another is *stáka*, a rich white cheese, often baked in a cheese pie or served fried as a hot creamy dip. When Cretans do eat meat, they do delicious things to it, as in lamb *kriotópita* (baked in pastry with cheese), or kid stewed in fruit juice; and they eat more snails (*saligária*) than most Greeks.

No milk, but wine in moderation is definitely part of the diet. Crete itself produces two AO wines of distinction: fresh white Péza and spicy Archánes. *Tsikoudiá*, an *eau-de-vie* distilled in a hundred mountain stills, is Crete's firewater, its moonshine, its pure hot-blooded soul, its cure-all; try it hot, with honey.

were not allowed to live inside them. Relations with Venice were cemented with the **fall of Constantinople** in 1453, when the Venetians were keen to keep the Cretans on their side against the Turks. In Greece's age-old tradition of absorbing the invader, many Venetians became Hellenized. As a refuge for scholars and painters from Constantinople and mainland Greece, Crete became the key point of contact between the East and the Italian Renaissance in the 15th and 16th centuries, producing, most famously, Doménicos Theotokópoulos, who moved to Venice and Spain and became known as El Greco. Cretan-Venetian academies, architecture, literature, song and romantic poetry blossomed, culminating in the dialect epic poem *Erotókritos* by Vicénzo Kornáros.

Although they had raided Crete periodically, the **Ottomans** finally caught the island by surprise. In 1645, **Sultan Ibrahim** declared war on the Knights of Malta and sent a huge fleet after them. They stopped in Kýthera for coffee and sugar, and the Venetian comman-der there sent word to his counterpart in Chaniá to allow the fleet safe passage; but, as the Sultan's ships began to sail past, they turned their guns on the city. Chaniá and the rest of Crete soon fell, but Heráklion, with its massive walls and port, resisted for 21 years, until 1669. Crete proved to be a mixed blessing for the Ottomans. The fertile lands were given to Turkish colonists, causing resentment, and, although their religion was tolerated, many Orthodox Cretans converted to Islam to avoid punishing taxes. Some emigrated to the Venetian-held Ionian islands; those who couldn't rose up in revolt.

In 1898, Greece declared war on Turkey and asked the Great Powers for aid. **Britain** did little until the Turks made the mistake of killing the British consul and 14 soldiers in Heráklion. As British, French,

Useful Information on Crete

Crete has its own English language monthly, called the *Crete Gazette* (*www.cretegazette.com*), with news and features.

There are innumerable websites – their own *www.explorecrete.com* is one of the most useful.

Russian and Italian troops subdued the island, **Prince George** was appointed high commissioner of an independent Crete. His high-handed ways and imposition of a foreign (i.e. Greek, non-Cretan) administration led in 1905 to the **Revolution of Therisso**, led by **Elefthérios Venizélos**. In 1909 Venizélos was appointed prime minister of Greece, a position that enabled him to secure Crete's union with Greece in 1913; this legendary Cretan statesman would remain the most influential national figure for the next 20 years.

The Battle of Crete

But Crete was to suffer one last invasion. As the Germans overran Greece in the Second World War, the Greek government took refuge on Crete (23 April 1943), defended by 30,000 British, New Zealand and Australian troops hastily transferred from the mainland. Crete's own battalions were trapped on the Albanian frontier; the only Greek soldiers on the island were cadets. But then again, no one suspected what Goering and General Student, second-in-command of the Luftwaffe, had in store. After a week of bombing raids, Nazi paratroopers launched the world's first successful invasion by air (20 May 1941). The Allied and Greek forces, along with hundreds of poorly armed men, women and children, put up such resistance that the Germans were forced to expend the cream of their forces to subdue the island over the next 10 days – at the cost of 170 aircraft, 4,000 specially trained paratroopers, and their 7th airborne division. As Churchill wrote, 'In Crete Goering won a Pyrrhic victory, because with the forces he wasted there he could easily have conquered Cyprus, Syria, Iraq or even Persia...' In spite of brutal German reprisals, resistance to the occupation, aided by British agents, was legendary, especially the daring abduction in 1943 of German commander General Kreipe by Major Patrick Leigh Fermor and Captain Billy Moss. As a massive manhunt combed the island, the British and Cretan Resistance spirited Kreipe away to Egypt.

Nomós Chaniá

Crete's western province (for map, *see* pp.148–9) is its most beautiful, the land of orange groves, olives, vineyards and cypresses, dotted with old Venetian farming estates. The White Mountains in the centre hit the sky at Mount Pachnés (2,451m/8,041ft) and plunge into stunning gorges, most famously the Gorge of Samariá, the classic day-walk that emerges by the Libyan Sea. Crete's best beaches line the west coast, from Falassarná to the tropical lagoon of Elafonísi. And the icing on the cake is beautiful Chaniá.

Chaniá (XANIA)

⭐ Chaniá

Chaniá, Crete's second city (pop. 73,000), is the most elegant and seductive of the island's four provincial capitals, with the ghostly forms of the snow-capped White Mountains hovering over its palm trees. The old streets are lined with Venetian, Turkish and neo-classical monuments. Although many were lost in bombing raids during the Battle of Crete, the war-scarred ruins stood neglected for so many decades that they've now been incorporated into garden settings for bars and restaurants, boutiques and galleries. The lovely inner and outer Venetian harbours are evening magnets.

The ancient historian Diodorus Siculus wrote that Chaniá, one of the three great cities of Crete, was founded by Minos. Buildings excavated in the Kastélli quarter go back to 2200 BC, and archaeologists are sure that the Minoan palace and town, KY-DO-NI-JA, referred to on a Linear B tablet, lie hidden under the modern town. *Kydóni* means quince, a fruit loved by the Minoans, and for a time the city was so important that 'Kydonia' referred to all of Crete. Quince Town survived the rest of Cretan history to get a mention in Homer, to know glory days in the Hellenistic and Roman periods, then to decline so far between the 10th and 13th centuries that it was better known as 'Rubbish City'. Revived under the Venetians, who renamed it La Canea, it was so splendid by the 1500s that it was called the 'Venice of the East'. Crete's capital from 1850–1971, Chaniá was the island's window on the outside world, with consulates and embassies, and it prospered as the fief of statesman Elefthérios Venizélos.

Into Old Chaniá

The vortex of daily life in Chaniá is its covered market, or **Agora** (1911) at the entrance to the old town. Down the back stairs and turn left and you're in **Skrídlof Street**, a narrow lane jam-packed for as long as anyone can remember with leather shops. Skrídlof gives on to **Chalídon Street**, Chaniá's jewellery-shop-lined funnel to the sea. Midway down, at No.21, the 14th-century Gothic church of San Francesco is now Chaniá's excellent **Archaeology Museum**. Its prize is a clay seal (*c.* 1450 BC) showing the commanding figure of a Minoan mortal or god holding a staff, standing over the sea as it breaks against the gates of a city where the roofs are crowned with horns of consecration. Other exhibits include mosaic floors on the legend of Dionysos from a 3rd-century AD house, the beautiful gold necklaces of Sossima, who perished in childbirth around the 3rd century BC, and cases of Linear A and Linear B tablets, the latter

Archaeology Museum
t 282 109 0334; open Tues–Sun 8.30–3; adm

09
Crete | Chaniá

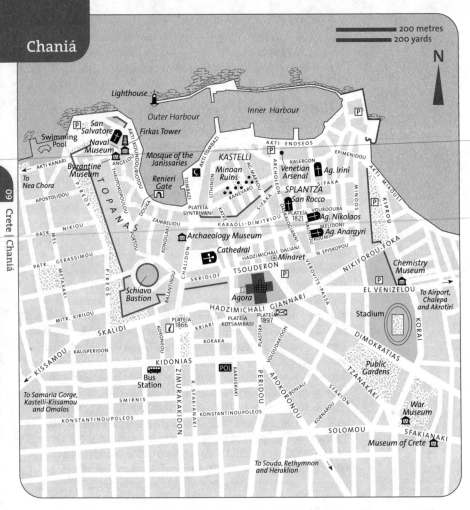

200 metres
200 yards

N

Lighthouse

Outer Harbour

Inner Harbour

P

P

San Salvatore

Firkas Tower

AKTI ENOSEOS

Swimming Pool

Naval Museum

P

KASTELLI

Mosque of the Janissaries

Minoan Ruins

KALERGON

EPIMENIDOU

Venetian Arsenal

Ag. Irini

To Nea Chora

Byzantine Museum

Renieri Gate

SPLANTZA

San Rocco

SIFAKA

APOSTOLIDOU

PLATEÍA SYNTRIVANI

KARAOLI-DIMITRIOU

PLATEÍA 1821

Ag. Nikolaos

Ag. Anargyri

PATR. NIKIOU

Archaeology Museum

NIKIFOROU-FOKA

Chemistry Museum

PATR. GERASSIMOU

Cathedral

HADZIMICHALI DALIANI

Minaret

TSOUDERON

P

EL VENIZELOU

To Airport, Chalepa and Akrotiri

Schiavo Bastion

SKRIDLOF

Agora

HADZIMICHALI GIANNARI

Stadium

KORAI

MITR. KIRILOU

PLATEÍA 1866

KRIARI

PLATEÍA KOTSAMBASI

PLATEÍA 1897

DIMOKRATIAS

SKALIDI

KORAKA

KISSAMOU

KALISPERIDON

KIDONIAS

POL

Public Gardens

Bus Station

TZANAKAKI

To Samaria Gorge, Kastelli-Kissamou and Omalos

SMIRNIS

KONSTANTINOUPOLEOS

War Museum

KONSTANTINOUPOLEOS

SOLOMOU

SFAKIANAKI

Museum of Crete

To Souda, Rethymnon and Heraklion

proved on a hunch by Michael Ventris in 1952 to be an ancient form of Greek. Disappointingly, the tablets are mostly inventories.

Across the street, baby domes top a **Turkish bath**. This is next to the large square holding the **Trimartyr Cathedral**, which should be more interesting than it is. In the 1850s a soap factory belonging to Mustafa Nily Pasha stood here; as a gesture of reconciliation he donated it to the Christians, along with funds to build a church.

Around the Old Port and Venetian Harbour

Chalídon Street flows into the crescent of the outer port, lined with handsome Venetian buildings. The neighbourhood on the west side of the port, **Topanás**, has landmark status, although the interiors have nearly all been converted into bars and restaurants. The **Fírkas Tower** at the far west end of the port saw the first official raising of the Greek flag over Crete in November 1913, in the presence of King

Getting to Chaniá

Chaniá **airport** is on the Akrotíri Peninsula, t 282 108 3800; there are 5 buses a day to the centre, and a taxi costs around €15. The **Olympic Airways** office is located at 88 Stratigoú Tzanakáki, t 282 105 7700. **Aegean** is at the airport, t 282 106 3366.

Two ferries travel from Piraeus–Chaniá daily, one overnight, pulling in around 5.30am and met by local buses. Ferry tickets from Soúda to Piraeus are available from **ANEK** (departs daily at 8pm), on Venizélou, in the market square, and from **Minoan Lines** (three times a week), also in the market square. **Port authority**: t 282 109 8888.

Getting around Chaniá

KTEL **buses**, t 282 109 3306. travel from the station at Kidonías hourly to Heráklion and Réthymnon, at least hourly along the Stálos/Ag. Marína/Plataniás/Geráni route and almost as often to Kolimbári; the other larger villages of the *nomós* are serviced at least daily. For transport to the Gorge of Samariá, *see* p.157.

Radio taxi: t 282 109 8700 or t 282 109 8288. **Car hire** agencies line Chalídon St.

Naval Museum
t 282 109 1875; open Tues–Sun 9–3; adm

Byzantine Museum
78 Theotokopoúlou; open Tues–Sun 8.30–2.30; combined ticket with Archaeology Museum

Constantine and Prime Minister Venizélos. Long used as a prison, the tower is now a **Naval Museum**, containing photos, models of Venetian galleys, and mock-ups of key Greek naval victories. The first floor has photos and memorabilia from the Battle of Crete.

Behind the tower, the simple little church of **San Salvatore** belonged to a Franciscan monastery and was converted by the Turks into a mosque. Near here begins picturesque **Theotokopoúlou Street**, lined with Venetian houses remodelled by the Turks. The **Byzantine Museum** has a collection of Cretan icons, pottery coins and mosaics. On Theofánou Street (off Zambéliou) the Renieri Gate bears a Venetian coat-of-arms dated 1608. Further south stood the Jewish ghetto, or **Ovraiki**, with a dilapidated synagogue on **Kondiláki Street**; the owner of Synagogi Bar next door can tell you its story. At the top of Kondiláki, along Portoú Lane, are the last of the **Venetian walls**. In 1538, just after Barbarossa devastated Réthymnon, the Venetians hired fortifications wizard Michele Sammichele to surround Chaniá with walls and a moat over 45m (147ft) wide and 8.5m (28ft) deep. Unlike Heráklion's, however, they weren't up to the job; in 1645, the Ottomans captured Chaniá in two months.

The entrance of the **outer** (or Venetian) **port** is framed with two great landmarks: a graceful Venetian **lighthouse** in golden stone, restored by the Egyptians, and the **Mosque of the Janissaries** (1645), crowned with distinctive ostrich- and chicken-egg domes. Here the Christian-born slave troops of the Ottoman Empire worshipped, although it did little to improve their character; not only did they terrorize the Greeks, but in 1690 they murdered the Pasha of Chaniá and fed his body to the dogs. By 1812, even the Sublime Porte had had enough and sent Hadji Osman Pasha, 'the Throttler', into Crete to hang the lot of them, an act that so impressed the Greeks that rumours flew that 'the Throttler' must be a crypto-Christian.

Behind the mosque lies the **Kastélli** quarter, spread across a low hill above the inner harbour. This was the acropolis of **ancient**

Kydonia, and excavations along Kaneváro Street revealed a complex of Middle Minoan buildings. The discovery of nearly 100 Linear B tablets and a large deposit of Linear A tablets unearthed in nearby Katre Street suggests the proximity of a palace. Kastélli took the brunt of the Luftwaffe, but you can still pick out the odd Venetian detail, especially along Kaneváro and Lithínon streets. On the top of Ag. Markoú stand the ruins of the Venetian cathedral, **Santa Maria degli Miracoli**. Below, overlooking the inner harbour, rise seven of the original 17 vaulted shipyards of the **Venetian Arsenal** (1600), now serving as the **Centre for the Study of Mediterranean Architecture**.

East of Kastélli, **Splántza**, the Turkish quarter, has intriguing churches, such as the underground **Ag. Iríni** from the 1400s, in Roúgia Square. South, in Vourdoúba Street, the early 14th-century Dominican church of **Ag. Nikólaos** was converted by the Turks into an imperial mosque to shelter a magical healing sword which the imam held up while leading the Friday prayers. Note the *tughra*, the Sultan's stylized thumbprint that was the emblem of the Ottoman state, on the entrance and minaret. The little **Mosque of Ahmet Aga** still stands in Hadzimicháli Daliáni Street, while to the east in Koúmi Street the 16th-century **Ag. Anargýri** was the only church in Chaniá allowed to hold Orthodox services during the Venetian and Turkish occupations.

Chaniá's Newer Quarters and Beaches

War Museum
t 282 104 4156; open Tues–Sat 9–1

Museum of Crete
t 282 102 3082; open Mon–Sat 9.30–4; adm

From the Agora, Tzanakáki Street leads to the shady **public gardens**, with a small zoo, café and outdoor cinema, often showing films in English. On the corner of Tzanakáki and Sfakianáki, the **War Museum** chronicles Crete's remarkable 20th-century battle history, while a villa just south, at 20 Sfakianáki Street, houses the **Museum of Crete**. This new museum, dedicated to the island's history and traditions, incorporates Greece's second largest archive, dating from the Venetian occupation to the liberation of Crete in 1944. **Plateía Venizélos** to the east has the house of Venizélos, the government palace built for Prince George (now the court-house), and a **Russian Orthodox church**. Further east, by the sea, is the fancy **Chalépa** residential quarter, dotted with neoclassical mansions and ex-consulates from Crete's years of autonomy. The town beach, **Néa Chorá**, is a 15-minute walk west, beyond the Fírkas tower. Although sandy and safe for children, it's not very attractive. The beaches improve further west; city buses from Plateía 1866 go as far as lovely sandy **Oasis** beach and **Kalamáki**. The strip is well developed.

Useful Information in Chaniá

ⓘ **Chaniá >**
EOT: 40 Kriári St, t 282 109 2943

Tourist police: 23 Iráklion St, t 282 105 3333.

Chaniá Festivals

Mid–end May: Chaniá Festival, commemorating the anniversary of the Battle of Crete.

24 June: St John's Day.

15 Aug: Chaniá hosts the lively Pan-Cretan Festival.

Shopping in Chaniá

Chaniá is one of the best places in Crete to spend money.

Apogio, 80 Hadzimicháli Giannári. Books, new and old, tapes and CDs.

Apostolos Pachtikos, 14 Sífaka. Among several traditional knife-makers here, this one also deals in mountain-goat horns and battered Nazi helmets.

Eolos, 7 Chalídon. Beautiful creations in lapis lazuli.

International Shop, Plateía Sýntrivani. The best choice of books and news-papers in English.

Lefteris Kildaras Herb Centre, in the Agora. A wide range of spices, Cretan wines and other local products.

Monastiáki, 121 Kissamoú. Cretan antiques and bric and brac.

Neféli, 20 Kondiláki. Jewellery based on traditional and ancient Greek designs.

Top Hanas, 3 Angélou, in the Old Town. A red lair of traditional Cretan weavings and blankets.

Where to Stay in Chaniá

Chaniá ✉ 73100

Beware that some of the picturesque places around the Venetian port can be very noisy.

Casa Delfino, 9 Theofánous, **t** 282 108 7400, *www.casadelfino.com* (€€€€€) Classy conversion of a 17th-century town house; some suites have Internet access as well as Jacuzzis.

Metochi Kindelis, 3km south in Perivólia, **t** 282 104 1321, *www.metohi-kindelis.gr* (€€€€€). Two guesthouses, with period furnishing and private pools, each sleeping four, in a Venetian farmhouse.

Villa Andromeda, 150 El. Venizélou, **t** 282 102 8300, *www.villandromeda.gr* (€€€€€). Out east in the Chalépa quarter. Former German consulate, now divided into eight air-conditioned suites; a lush garden, Turkish bath and pool are some of the amenities.

Ammos, 4km west of the city on Gláros Beach, **t** 282 103 3003, *www.ammoshotel.com* (€€€€).

(★) **Porto del Colombo** ›

Colourful designer rooms and suites with a beautiful pool, Korres toiletries, broadband and more.

Minoa, 23 Tsanakáki (near the market), **t** 282 102 7970, *www.minoa-hotel.gr* (€€€€). Stylishly restored Art Deco villa, with 15 rooms and five suites and views over the gardens.

Belmondo, 10 Zabelíou, **t** 282 103 6216, *www.belmondohotel.com* (€€€). In the old port, 17th-century Venetian palace converted into a charming hotel.

Contessa, 15 Theofános, **t** 282 109 8566 (€€€). Has the intimate air of an old-fashioned guesthouse, furnished in traditional style.

Doma, 124 El. Venizélou, **t** 282 105 1772, *www.hotel-doma.gr* (€€€). Comfortable rooms in a neoclassical mansion, decked out in antiques and Cretan rusticana. The owner has an unusual collection of hats (of all things) from around the world.

El Greco, 49 Theotokopoúlou, **t** 282 109 0432, *www.elgreco.gr* (€€€). Modern rooms in an old building on Chaniá's prettiest street. Has wi-fi connection.

Halepa, 164 El. Venizélou, **t** 282 102 8440, *www.halepa.com* (€€€). Once the British consulate; rooms of character in a quiet palm garden.

Nostos, 46 Zambelíou, **t** 282 109 4740, *www.nostos-hotel.com* (€€€). A small refurbished Venetian house on a busy lane.

Palazzo, 54 Theotokopoúlou, **t** 282 109 3227 (€€). For those seeking divine inspiration, this is the place, with each room named after a god.

Porto del Colombo, Theofánous and Móshon, **t** 282 107 0945 (€€). Beautiful traditional hotel in a Venetian *palazzo* that once served as Venizélos' offices; they also have family apartments.

Thereza, 8 Angélou, **t** 282 109 2798 (€€). Charming rooms and studios oozing with character, and a tempting roof terrace in another restored Venetian house.

Chaniá's vast selection of cheaper rooms are mostly located within a few blocks of the Venetian or inner harbour. The pick of the bunch are:

Konaki, 43 Kondiláki, **t** 282 107 8859 (€). Eight rooms in a quirky house – the two ground-floor ones have private bathrooms and open on to the banana palm garden. Good taverna, too, sometimes with traditional music,

Kydonia, 20 Chalídon, **t** 282 107 4650 (€). Well-designed doubles, triples and quads in a quiet courtyard next to the archaeological museum.

Meltémi, 2 Angélou, **t** 282 109 2802 (€). Above the mellow Meltémi café, with space to swing several cats in the bigger rooms, some of which have lovely views across the port to the White Mountains. *Open all year.*

(★) Nikterida >>

Monastiri, 18 Ag. Markoú, **t** 282 105 4776 (€). In the ruined cloister of a Venetian church.

Stella, 10 Angélou, **t** 282 107 3756 (€). Airy, traditional rooms (cheaper at the back) that share a fridge, and perch above the eponymous boutique selling psychedelic hand-blown glass.

(★) To Pigadi tou Tourkou >>

Camping Ag. Marína, **t** 282 106 8596 (€). 8km west near the beaches, and open throughout the season (buses from the bus station).

Camping Chaniá, Ag. Apóstoli, **t** 282 103 1138 (€). 1.5km west of town (city bus from Plateía 1866). More basic. *Open Mar–Oct.*

Eating Out in Chaniá

It's difficult not to find a restaurant in Chaniá – the harbour area is one great crescent of traditional tavernas and pizzerias touting for business.

Antigoni, **t** 282 104 5236 (€20). One of several excellent tavernas along Aktí Énoseos.

Apovrado, Isódon Street, **t** 282 105 8151 (€10–12). Chaniot specialities, local wine (try the Nobeli, which isn't imported) and country sausages.

Dino's, 3 Aktí Enóseos and Sarpidóna, **t** 282 104 1865 (€20–25). A long-time reliable favourite overlooking the inner harbour, specializing in fish, but also has a good selection of meat.

Ela, 47 Kondiláki, **t** 282 107 4128 (€12–15). Good Cretan specialities in the creatively recycled ruins of an old building.

Kariatis, 1 Plateía Katecháki, **t** 282 105 5600 (€35, less for pizza). Elegant restaurant serving authentic Italian dishes by the old port. *Closed Sun–Tues in winter.*

Karnágio, 8 Plateía Katecháki, **t** 282 105 3366. Fish but also excellent Cretan dishes and a good wine list.

Mirovolos, 19 Zambelíou, **t** 282 109 1960 (€18–22). In the lovely courtyard of a Venetian building dating from 1290, featuring ample well-prepared dishes and Cretan music and dancing.

Monastiri, behind the Mosque of the Janissaries, **t** 282 105 5527 (€20). Serves fresh fish, traditional Cretan dishes and barrelled wine, frequented by ex-prime ministers and the like.

Nikterida, 7km east at Korakiés on the Akrotíri peninsula, **t** 282 106 4215. In the evening Chaniots like to head up here to one of the best tavernas in Crete, open since 1938, with music and traditional dancing on Saturday nights; book well in advance. *Closed Sun.*

To Pigadi tou Tourkou ('The Well of the Turk'), 1 Kalliníkou Sarpáki, **t** 282 105 4547 (€18–22). In the old Turkish quarter, this establishment has been delighting tastebuds for years with specialities from Egypt, Lebanon and Tunisia. Dishes include Arabian pies (try the spinach pie with walnuts and raisins), and lamb with lemon.

To Thalassinó Agéri, 35 Viviláki, **t** 282 105 6672. In a magical setting in an ex-tannery by the sea, delicious seafood specialities. *Book or arrive early.*

Entertainment and Nightlife in Chaniá

Cinema

The municipal cinema shows open-air films in the public gardens each summer. Plataniás, along the west coast, has a summer cinema.

Bars and Cafés

Chaniá is a delightful place after dark, for its vibrant tavernas and bars.

Dio Lux, on the Venetian port. Chaniá's most desperately arty café.

Four Seasons, by the port police. Very popular bar.

Monastíri tou Károlou, 22 Hadzimicháli Daliáni, behind the market. A restored 16th-century monastery with a café, theatre, galleries and a hairdresser.

Synagogi. An atmospheric bar housed in the old Jewish baths.

Street, 51 Aktí Koundouriotí, on the west end of the outer harbour. Another very popular music bar, playing a wide range of styles.

Tsikoudadiko, 31 Zambelioú. A good choice for a more distinctly Cretan experience, try the particularly good *tsikoudiá* and *mezédes* dishes.

Music and Clubs

Chaniá definitely loves its music. Plataniás, along the west coast, has built up a reputation for its big, trendy clubs.

Kriti, 22 Kallergón. This hole-in-the-wall is something of an institution, where from 9pm into the early hours of the morning, you can hear traditional Cretan music for the price of a drink.

Aktí Miaoúlis, in Kuóm Kapí area. Beautiful Chaniots decorate the cafés in this area. The Kuóm Kapí seafront venues are the place to be for a late-night drink, and to watch the world pass by into the early hours.

Fedra, 7 Isóderon, t 282 104 0789. Hosts very similar acts to Plateía, but also partial to a bit of jazz.

Fortezza, by the lighthouse. This bar (and restaurant) has its own shuttle boat to ferry about lively guests. Live Greek music.

Plateía, in the old harbour. This club frequently offers blues nights, and other live music acts feature.

Owl and **Nimfes**, in Akrotíri. These are also very popular local nightspots.

South of Chaniá: Venizélos and Citrus Villages

South of Chaniá, the rugged 18km (11-mile) **Thérisson Gorge** is famous in Cretan history for the Revolutionary Assembly convened here in 1905 by Venizélos, beginning the revolt against Prince George. Venizélos knew the territory; the future prime minister was born near the gorge entrance, in the sleepy village of **Mourniés**; his mother had dreamt that her son would liberate Crete so she named him Elefthérios ('Freedom'). The best oranges in Crete grow in the lush **Keríti Valley** south of Chaniá. During the Battle of Crete, however, it was known as 'Prison Valley' after the big calaboose near **Alikianós**, just off the main Chaniá–Omalós road. A memorial honours the Cretans who kept on fighting here, unaware that the Allies elsewhere were in retreat; their ignorance enabled the majority of British and ANZAC troops to be evacuated from the Libyan coast. During the Occupation, prisoners were executed at the crossroads. But this is a place of trouble: the wedding massacre of Kantanoléo's Cretans (*see* p.151) took place at Alikianós' ruined Venetian tower; next to the tower, the church of **Ag. Geórgios** (1243) has exceptional frescoes, painted in 1430 by Pávlos Provatás.

Chaniá to the Rodópou Peninsula

Not a single hotel stood along this coast on 20 May 1941 when suddenly 'out of the sky the winged devils of Hitler were falling everywhere', as George Psychoundákis wrote in *The Cretan Runner*, his fascinating memoire of the Cretan-Anglo resistance. They were met with locals armed antique guns, knives, shovels and mad

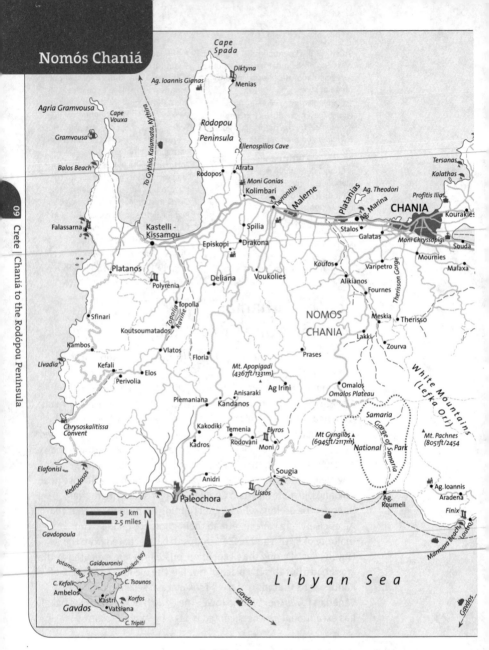

courage, who killed 2,000 on the first day alone. A German memorial to the 2nd Parachute Regiment – a diving eagle, known as the Kakó Poulí, or 'Bad Bird' – stands 2km west of Chaniá.

The beach strip of **Káto Stálos** merges with **Ag. Marína**, an old town with Venetian and Turkish houses and a vast tourist sprawl below. It looks out over the islet of **Ag. Theódori**, a refuge for the rare Cretan ibex, the *kri-kri*. The gaping mouth of its cave once belonged

to a sea monster just about to take a bite out of Crete when Zeus petrified it with a thunderbolt. Just west, **Plataniás** has two faces: an old village above, and a resort by the beach and a forest, planted to protect the orange groves from the wind. The Battle of Crete began west at **Máleme**, site of an airfield and German war cemetery.

At the foot of rugged **Cape Spáda**, just before the road to Kastélli splits into old and new, **Kolimbári** has a beach of large smooth

Getting to the Rodópou Peninsula

There's a **bus** at least every half-hour from Chaniá to all the resorts as far as Máleme; roughly every hour they continue to Kastélli-Kíssamou.

---

pebbles and, a short walk north, the most important monastery in western Crete. **Moní Gonías** was founded in 1618, high over a sandy cove at the corner (*gonías*, in Greek) of the Rodópou Peninsula. The monks were often besieged by the Turks; a cannonball fired in 1866 is still embedded in the seaward wall. The church contains a fine gilt iconostasis, a venerable *Last Judgement* painted on wood and a beautifully drawn *St Nicholas*, although the juju is concentrated in an icon of the *Virgin*, covered with votive *tamáta* and jewellery.

The road veers dizzyingly up the peninsula to **Afráta** and **Rodópos**, from where you can make the 3hr trek north to **Diktyna**, site of an unexcavated shrine to Artemis (Britomartis) dating back to the Minoans, once the holiest shrine in western Crete. Its little port, **Meniás**, is rocky, but the sea is transparent and caves offer shade.

South of Kolimbári, villages and Byzantine churches lie amid the orange groves, many of the churches boasting fine medieval frescoes: **Spiliá**, **Drakóna**, **Delianá** and best of all, the domed, golden stone-built church at Epískopi called the 'Rotunda'.

Where to Stay and Eat West of Chaniá and on the Rodópou Peninsula

 Mylos tou Kerata >>

Káto Stalós ✉ 73100

Cretan Dream Royal, t 282 103 6800, *www.cretandreamroyal.gr* (€€€€). New swish complex of studios and apartments, set around swimming pools across the road from the beach.

Leventis, Áno Stalós, **t** 282 106 8155. A temple of exquisite Cretan cuisine – and it's not expensive, either.

Ag. Marína ✉ 73100

Santa Marina Plaza, on the beach, **t** 282 103 6860, *www.santamarina-plaza.gr* (€€€€€). Somewhat bland but has all the amenities; set in a garden with a pool, gym, Jacuzzi and a beach.

Alexia Beach, near the beach at the west end of town, **t** 282 106 8110 (€). Small and attractive, with a pool.

Plataniás ✉ 73014

Geraniotis Beach, **t** 282 106 8681 (€€€). One of the more attractive of Plataniás' many hotels, set in lush

green lawns on the edge of town. *Open April–Oct.*

Kronos Apartments, t 282 106 8630 (€€€). Well-kept complex with a pool near the sea. *Open April–Oct.*

Mylos tou Kerata, t 282 106 8578 (€25). A 15th-century water mill; a lovely place with superb Cretan and Greek food and spit-roast meats. *Book.*

Haroupia, up in Áno Plataniás, **t** 282 106 8603 (€15). Enjoys lovely sunset views and delicious Cretan food from its creeper-covered terrace.

See p.147 for clubs in Plataniás.

Máleme ✉ 73014

Creta Paradise Beach, in nearby Geráni, **t** 282 106 1315, *www.cretaparadise.gr* (€€€€€). Big resort complex on the beach; orientated towards sports, and families. *Open April–Oct.*

Máleme Mare, t 282 106 2121 (€€€). Typical apartments by the beach, with a pool.

Kolimbári and Around ✉ 73014

Elia Traditional Hotel, 8km south in Áno Voúves, **t** 282 408 3056, *www.elia-crete.com.gr* (€€€€). A 19th-century

Elia Traditional Hotel >>

farmhouse converted into a stunning guest house with a pool and well-equipped spa, in walking distance of one of the oldest olive trees in the world. *Open all year.*

Diktyna, t 282 402 2611. Fresh fish from the owner's caique, fresh vegetables and excellent olive oil.

Spiliá ✉ 73014

Spilia Village, t 282 408 3300, *www.spiliavillage.gr* (€€€€€). Luxurious rooms with whirlpool baths in stone houses

from the 13th–17th centuries, a pool in the orange grove, and a restaurant in a Venetian country house.

Ravdoúcha ✉ 73014

Don Rosario, Ravdoúcha (up the Rodópou), **t** 282 402 3781 (€35). An intimate restaurant serving refined carpaccio, roast vegetables with balsamic vinegar, etc., but also Greek favourites like lobster spaghetti. Cretan and Italian wine list. *Open April–Oct; winter weekends only.*

Kastélli-Kíssamou and the West Coast

West of the Rodópou Peninsula, the coastal plain and knobbly hills are densely planted with olives and vines: the often wild and unruly west coast offers some of the island's biggest beaches. The capital is Kastélli-Kíssamou, a working wine town charmingly devoid of any tourist attraction whatsoever.

Kastélli-Kíssamou, Gramvoúsa and Polyrénia

Set at the bottom of a deep, rectangular gulf, **Kastélli-Kíssamou**'s double-barrelled name recalls its predecessor, Kissamos, the port of Dorian city of Polyrenia. An ancient temple and theatre were dismantled by the Venetians in 1550 and refashioned as a castle: when the Cretan Kaptános Kantanoléo captured it, the Venetians pretended to recognize Kantanoléo's authority and offered a high-born Venetian girl as his son's bride. At the wedding the Cretans were given drugged wine, and the Venetians slit their throats and took Kastélli back. Today its quiet beach attracts visitors who shun the fleshpots. Behind the health centre there's a mosaic floor from a 2nd-century AD villa; after a decade of promises, an **Archaeology Museum** just may open soon in the Venetian commandery.

From Kastélli, excursion boats sail around wild Cape Voúxa to the triangular islet of **Ágria**, better known by the name of its Venetian fortress, **Gramvoúsa**. Like Néa Soúda and Spinalónga to the east, the fort held out against the Turks until the 18th century, when the Venetians gave up hope of ever reconquering Crete. The Renaissance church is fairly intact and the reservoirs, long unused, are full to the brim. Opposite, **Bálos Beach** is a gorgeous sweep of white sand.

A scenic 8km south of Kastélli, **Polyrénia** is an old-fashioned village on a natural balcony, guarded by Roman tower (itself a collage of older ruins). Founded in the 8th century BC by Dorians, Polyrenia survived the Romans with the attitude that if you can't lick them, join them, but fell to the Saracens in the 9th century. Up on the **acropolis**, the massive base of a 4th-century BC temple and altar of dressed stone now supports the **Church of the 99 Holy Fathers**.

Getting to and around the West Coast

Kastélli's port (2km from the centre) is linked by **ferry** to Gýthion (for Kýthera and Antikýthera) (ANEN, **t** 282 102 4148, *www.anen.gr*). There are **buses** from Kastélli 3 times a week (Mon, Wed, Fri) to Polyrénia, 3 a day to Falassarná, 5 to Chóra Sfakíon, 6 to Paleochóra, 3 to Omalós and one morning bus to Chrysoskalítissa and Elafonísi. A direct **bus** to Elafonísi leaves Chaniá at 7.30am.

Way Out West

Crete's west coast is dramatic, where mountains plunge straight into the sea around wide, sandy beaches. A coastal plain coated in plastic tomato tunnels and a clutch of hotels and tavernas heralds the beautiful sandy beaches at **Falassarná**, 15km from Kastélli-Kíssamou. North of the beach at Koutrí stood ancient Falassarna, once Polyrenia's bitter rival and dramatic proof that western Crete has been slowly rising over the centuries – Falassarná's port is now 200m (650ft) from the sea. Bits of the ancient city lie scattered while, further up, archaeologists found a bathhouse. Most curious of all is a Hellenistic **stone throne**, possibly dedicated to Poseidon.

South of Falassarná, the coastal road takes in spectacular scenery; try to travel in the morning to avoid the sea glare. In sprawling **Plátanos** a Proto-geometric tomb was unearthed during the road construction, while down in **Sfinári** there's a pebble beach. The road then rides a high corniche to **Kámbos**, where a 3km track leads down to the wild sandy beach of **Livádia**. The main road becomes increasingly rough as it winds south to the Libyan Sea and the sheer rock pedestal of the bleached **Convent of Chrysoskalítissa**, 'of the Golden Stair'. The story goes that only persons without sin, or non-liars, can see which of the 90 steps is made of gold; a more prosaic version claims the Patriarch in Constantinople ordered the convent to sell off the golden step in the 15th century to pay off his debts. Tour buses besiege the last nun and monk.

⭐ Elafonísi

The five-star attraction in this corner, however, lies another 5km southwest: the sandy islet of **Elafonísi**, joined to Crete by a shallow reef. It's a dreamy *Paradise Lost* in a sea ranging from turquoise to violet, rimmed by pink sand; the water is only 60cm (2ft) deep so you can wade. Children love it. A little less virgin every year, it has so far managed to hold off the advances of the big resort hotel ventures.

Inland from here is chestnut country, where the lush mountains are reminiscent of Corsica. Its nine villages, the **Enneachória**, are famous for throwing some of the best weddings in Crete. On the road up from Elafonísi, **Kefáli** has magnificent sea views and fine frescoes in its church, **Metamórphosis tou Sotírou** (1320); note the English graffiti from 1553. Nearby **Perivólia** is a charming green oasis, home of a private **Ethnographic Museum**. **Élos**, the largest of the villages, is beautifully set in plane and chestnut trees. Six km beyond, the road forks for Paleochóra (*see* next section).

West Coast Festivals

Early Aug: Kastélli wine festival.

14–15 Aug: A huge festival at Monastery Chrysoskalítissa in Elafonísi.

First Sun after 20 Oct: Chestnut Festival in Élos.

Where to Stay and Eat on the West Coast

Kastélli ✉ 73400

Kissimos Windmills, t 282 203 1752, *www.anemomyloi.gr* (€€). Sleep (up to six) in a renovated windmill, with pool.

Galini Beach, at the far end of the beach, t 282 202 3288, *www. galinibeach.com* (€). Quiet rooms.

Nopigia Camping, t 282 203 1111. With a large swimming pool. *Open April–Oct.*

Stimadóris, at the west end of town, t 282 202 2057. Fresh fish caught by the owners. *In winter, closed lunch.*

Papadakis, on the main seafront. Serves up the day's catch.

Falassarná ✉ 73400

Plakures, t 282 204 1581, *www.plakures. de* (€€€). Immaculate little hotel in a garden setting with a pool, owned by a German family; it has an excellent restaurant serving Cretan and continental dishes, using oil from the family groves.

Aqua Marine, t 282 204 1414, www. *aqua-marine.ws* (€€–€). New and spotless rooms.

SunSet, on the beach, t 282 204 1204, in winter t 282 202 2155 (€€–€). Modest rooms with a popular fish taverna.

Panorama, next to the Ipanema Club, t 282 204 1336. Good, reliable taverna.

Elafonísi

Innachório, 2km before the beach, t 282 206 1111. Home-made bread and cheese and delicious vegetable dishes.

Vlátos (near Élos)

Mília, t 282 104 6774, *www.milia.gr* (€€). Experience the rural Crete of centuries past in a serene, eco-friendly environment. Rooms in this restored medieval hamlet are furnished with antiques, heated by wood stoves and lit by candles. One house serves as a refectory, with delicious organic food, mostly produced on site. Cooking lessons available. *Open all year.*

 ⭐ Milia »

The Southwest: Paleochóra and the Sélino

The White Mountains only permit a few north–south roads to breach their rocky fastness. Those to the southwest run into the Eparchy of Sélino, where the seaside town of Paleochóra is the main attraction, along with a score of medieval churches near Kándanos. Most are locked, but ask in the nearest *kafeneíon* for the key.

Along the Road from Tavronítis to Paleochóra

Of the three roads from the north that wriggle down to the Sélino, the main one from **Tavronítis** gets the most takers. En route lies lush **Kándanos**, with the highest rainfall in Crete. Its nickname is 'the city of victory'. Although inhabited since Roman times, nothing is over 50 years old; in the Battle of Crete the townspeople resisted the Nazi advance with such stubborn ferocity that the Germans were forced to retreat. They returned with reinforcements the next day, shooting everyone and burning the town to the ground.

From Kándanos, take the left turn on the Soúgia road into an area famed for its frescoed Byzantine churches. **Anisaráki** has three from

Getting to and around the Southwest

Paleochóra is served by 5 **buses** a day from Chaniá. Two buses run daily between Chaniá and Soúgia. Small **boats** leave Paleochóra 3 times a week for Gávdos (see p.164); a **car ferry** sails daily to Soúgia, Ag. Roúmeli, Chóra Sfakíon, Loutró and Elafónisi. **Passenger boats** sail daily to Elafónisi. **Port authority: t** 282 304 1214. Soúgia is linked daily by boat to Ag. Roúmeli when the Gorge of Samariá is open.

the 14th century, and a fourth, **Ag. Anna**, from the 1460s, with beautiful scenes of St Anne nursing the baby Mary and St George on horseback. Another church, **Taxiárchos Michaíl** near **Koufalotó**, was frescoed in 1327 by Ioánnis Pagoménos, one of western Crete's finest artists.

South of Kándanos, **Plemanianá** has two more frescoed 15th-century churches: **Ag. Geórgios** with vigorous scenes of the saint's life, and the **Panagía Myrtiótissa**. Others are in **Kakodíki** to the southwest, where springs flow with mineral waters; the church of the **Panagía** in nearby **Kádros** has very well-preserved frescoes, too.

Paleochóra, and Inland to Ánidri and Azogyrés

One of Crete's hippy enclaves in the 1960s and '70s, **Paleochóra**, the 'Old Town', still has a friendly, laid-back air. As a resort it has the advantage of straddling two beaches, one stony, the other sandy, with superb windsurfing. The Venetians built the landmark **Castello Selino** in 1279, to police the ornery Greeks, but it was easily destroyed in 1539 by the passing Barbarossa. There are quieter beaches to the west of Paleochóra, although greenhouses keep them off the postcards. But the water around pebbly **Ag. Kyriáki** at the end of the track is exceptionally crystal-clear.

Paleochóra lies below pretty mountain villages. In **Ánidri** to the northeast, the church of **Ag. Geórgios** was frescoed by Ioánnis Pagoménos in 1323. On the winding road through cypress forests towards Soúgia (see below), **Azogyrés** offers the pleasures of its deep green surroundings and gurgling stream, a fascinating one-room

Historical museum
open Sat and Sun 9–2

historical museum and one of Crete's rare evergreen plane trees, an enormous specimen growing next to the 19th-century cliffside chapel of **Ag. Páteres**. The museum guardian has the key to the chapel with its charming iconostasis. Two km above Azogyrés, the **Cave of Souré** is said to have been the temporary home for the 99 *Ágii Páteres*, or Holy Fathers, who came out of Egypt with St John the Hermit after the Byzantine reconquest of Crete. An iron stair leads steeply down to the little chapel, now home to 99 pigeons.

Along the Road from Chaniá to Soúgia

A ferry sails between Paleochóra and Soúgia, but if you're coming from Chaniá there's a road branching off at Alikianós (see p.147). It ascends the west edge of the Omalós plateau to **Ag. Iríni**, at the top of beautiful walkable 8km **Ag. Iríni gorge**; the path continues down to Soúgia (Chaniá tourist office has a map). Ag. Iríni's predecessor, **ancient Elyros**, is just south: a pugnacious Dorian city, Elyros had risen to the level of a bishopric before the Saracens destroyed it in the 9th century. Walls and the acropolis lie unexcavated. The church of the **Panagía** has a pretty 6th-century mosaic floor from an earlier church. Four km west, muscat-producing **Teménia** has a photogenic old stone church, the **Sotír**, and the double Cyclopean walls of **ancient Irtakina**, which once minted coins with bees, deer, dolphins and eight-pointed stars. Further along, **Moní**'s church, **Ag. Nikólaos**, was frescoed by the indefatigable Ioánnis Pagómeno.

The paved road ends at **Soúgia** (ΣΟΥΓΙΑ), a higgledy-piggledy wannabe resort with a long pebbly beach and a resident pelican. The port of Elyros, its ancient name was Syia or 'pig town' for the porkers it raised; the nude beach is still known unflatteringly as the 'Bay of Pigs'. The ruins that stand are a modest blast from Syia's Roman past, as is the fine 6th-century mosaic floor in the church of **Ag. Pantaleímonos**. Another, **Ag. Antónios** (1382), has frescoes, and a nearby cave, **Spýliara**, is one of a multitude in the Mediterranean that claims to have belonged to the Cyclops Polyphemos.

From Soúgia you can sail in 20 minutes or take a pretty 1½hr walk to **Lissós**. Renowned for its medicinal springs, it attracted enough trade at its 3rd-century BC Doric **Asklepeion** to afford to mint gold coins. The sanctuary has a pebble mosaic floor and a pit for sacred snakes. The population of Lissós is precisely one: the caretaker, who watches over the theatre, baths, and two old Christian basilicas.

Southwest Festivals

1–10 Aug: Paleochóra Musical.

Where to Stay and Eat in the Southwest

Paleochóra ✉ 73001

Anthea, t 282 304 1594, *www.anthea-paleochora.gr* (€€€). Classy studios and apartments; see website for offers.

On the Rocks, 3mins from town, t 282 304 1735, *www.crete-hotels-rooms.com* (€€€). Charming rooms and apartments with sea views and Internet access; boats and jet-skis available.

Glaros, on the beach, t 282 304 1635, *www.hotelglaros.gr* (€€). Friendly family-run hotel with a beautiful terrace covered with bougainvillaea.

Ánidri ✉ 73001

Anidri Eco-Cottages, 3.5km north of Paleochóra, t 282 304 2188, *www.*

ferienhaus-anidri.de (€). A German couple in love with the area have created a little eco-friendly oasis in a pair of three-bedroom cottages, which you can rent as a B&B; wi-fi available.

Ostria, on the sandy beach, t 282 304 1055 (€). Rooms and a taverna.

Campsite Paleochóra, by the pebble beach, t 282 304 1120.

Caravella, on the waterfront, t 282 304 1248. Friendly service; Greek classics.

Niki, in the centre, t 282 304 1532. Good inexpensive pizzeria.

The Third Eye, near the beach, t 282 304 1234. Vegetarian place, offering spicy Asian and Mexican specialities.

Soúgia ✉ 73011

Santa Irene, t 282 305 1181 (€€). A small and friendly complex of apartments and rooms, with a breakfast bar.

Lissos, t 282 304 1266 (€). *Open all year.*

Koumakakis, t 282 305 1298 (€).

Maria Marináki, t 282 305 1338 (€).

⭐ Anidri Eco-Cottages >

The Gorge of Samariá
(ΦΑΡΑΓΓΙ ΣΑΜΑΡΙΑΣ)

🏛 **The Gorge of Samariá**

The single most spectacular stretch of Crete is squeezed into the 18km Gorge of Samariá, the longest in Europe and a national park, the last refuge of much of the island's unique fauna and flora, especially rare chasm-loving plants known as *chasmophytes*. The walk takes most people between five and eight hours going down from Omalós south to Ag. Roúmeli on the Libyan Sea.

Some people return from the Gorge of Samariá having only seen their own feet and the back of the person in front of them. Staying in Ag. Roúmeli may be the answer; it will allow you more leisure to enjoy the gorge and the rare flowers and herbs that infuse the gorge. Although Samariá is a refuge of the *kri-kri*, they are shy and seldom seen. Lammergeiers, buzzards and eagles are bolder, and often circle high overhead.

Walking the Gorge

Just getting there is part of the fun. If you're on an early bus, dawn breaks in time for you to look over the most vertiginous section of the road, as it climbs 1,200m (3,937ft) to the pass before descending to the Omalós Plateau, 25 sq km (almost 10 sq miles) and itself no shorty at 1,080m (3,543ft). In winter, snows from the fairy circle of peaks flood this uncanny plateau so often that the one village, **Omalós** ①, is uninhabitable.

The gorge **tourist pavilion** ② is a few kilometres south of Omalós. Some of the most spectacular views are from the pavilion, hanging over the edge of the chasm, overlooking the sheer limestone face of mighty 2,117m (6,945ft) **Mount Gýngilos**, a favourite resort of Zeus when the shenanigans at Mount Olympus got on his nerves. If you come prepared, you can go up from here rather than down: a 90-minute trail from the pavilion leads up to the Greek Mountain Club's **Kallergi Hut** ③.

Kallergi Hut
t 282 103 3199; open April–Oct; book ahead

Just after dawn, the first people begin to trickle down the **Xylóskalo**, a zigzag stone path with a wooden railing and lookouts

Getting to the Gorge of Samariá

Buses leave for Omalós from Chaniá at 6.15, 7.30 and 8.30am and at 4.30pm; from Kastélli-Kíssamou at 5, 6 and 7am; and Réthymnon at 6.15 and 7am. Others leave early from Plataniás, Ag. Marína, Tavronítis, Chandrís and Kolimbári. Organized tour buses leave almost as early (you can, however, get a slight jump on the crowds by staying in Omalós or the Kallergi Hut, *see* opposite).

Once through the gorge to Ag. Roúmeli, **boats** run all afternoon to Chóra Sfakíon, Soúgia and Paleochóra, where you can pick up a bus to the north coast (at 3.45 and 6 for Chaniá and 5.30, 6 and 7pm for Réthymnon). Consider paying the bit extra for a tour bus to make sure you have a seat on the return journey.

along the way. The name Samariá derives from **Ossa Maria** ④, a chapel (1379) and abandoned village halfway down the gorge, now used as the guardians' station and picnic ground. There are several other abandoned chapels along the way, traditional stone *mitáto* huts (used by shepherds for cheese-making) and, near the end, the famous **Sideróportes** ('iron gates') ⑤, where the sheer walls rise almost 300m (1,000ft) on either side of a passage only 3m (9ft) wide.

At the southern end of the gorge stands **old Ag. Roúmeli** ⑥, abandoned after a torrent swept through in 1954. Some of the empty houses have been recycled as stalls selling Greece's most expensive cold drinks. When tourists began to appear in the 1960s, a new Ag. Roúmeli rose out of the cement mixer like a phoenix (toadstool is more apt), a blistering 2km away, on the coast – which can make it as enticing as a desert oasis to the footsore. This **new Ag. Roúmeli** is built over ancient Tarra, where Apollo hid from the wrath of Zeus after slaying Python at Delphi. Here he fell so in love with a nymph that he forgot to make the sun rise and got into an even bigger jam with his dad. A sanctuary of Tarranean Apollo marked the spot, and on top of its foundations the Venetians built a church, **Panagías**.

From Ag. Roúmeli, caiques sail to Paleochóra, Chóra Sfakíon (*see* pp.162–3) and Soúgia. But if you stay, the beach to aim for is **Ag. Pávlos** ⑦, a 90-minute walk away, with fresh springs and a lyrical 10th-century stone church.

Gorge Practicalities

The gorge is **open** from 6am to 4pm when weather permits, usually from May to mid-October, during which time the water is low enough to ensure safe fording of the streams. **Admission** is by dated ticket. Although the **last admission** to the gorge is at 3pm, almost everyone starts earlier, to avoid the midday heat and to make the excursion a single day's round-trip outing.

It is absolutely essential to **wear** good walking shoes and socks; a hat and food are only slightly less vital, and binoculars are a decided bonus. Most importantly, watch out for falling rocks. The tourist offices don't mention it, but one or two visitors get beaned every year; they're considering making helmets mandatory. Dressing appropriately is difficult: it's usually chilly at Omalós and sizzling at Ag. Roúmeli. It's a good idea to remove rings in case your hands swell. Fresh streams along the gorge provide **drinking water** at regular intervals. Mules and a helicopter landing pad are on hand for **emergency exits**; tickets are date-stamped and must be turned in at the lower gate, to make sure no one is lost.

If you haven't the energy to make the whole trek, you can at least sample Samariá by descending a mile or so into the gorge down the big wooden stair (the rub is, you have to walk back up again). For up-to-date information and walking conditions, call **t** 282 106 7140/7179.

Where to Stay and Eat in the Gorge of Samariá

Omalós ✉ 73005

Neos Omalós, t 282 106 7269, *www. neos-omalos.gr* (€). Recently built, with centrally heated rooms, bar and restaurant. *Open all year.*

To Exari, t 282 106 7180 (€). A bit larger and almost as nice.

Ag. Roúmeli ✉ 73011
  Ag. Roúmeli has plenty of rooms, but prices are over the odds. There are several restaurants with rooms: try **Ag. Roúmeli**, t 282 509 1432 (€) (*open Mar–Oct*), or **Tara**, t 282 509 1231.

East of Chaniá: Akrotíri (ΑΚΡΩΤΗΡΙ)

Akrotíri, the bulbous headland east of Chaniá, shelters the island's safest port, Soúda, from northerly winds. Its strategic position has assured it plenty of history, and, now that Crete is safe from imminent invasion, the steep access road, Eleftheríou Venizélou, is often chock-a-block with locals heading out to Akrotíri's beaches, nightclubs and villas. Outside these suburban tentacles, Akrotíri is a moody place, junky with military zones by the airport, lonely and wild around its famous monasteries. First stop should be little **Profítis Ilías** church (4.5km from Chaniá), Crete's chief memorial to Venizélos. Elefthérios Venizélos (1864–1936) and his son Sophoklís (1896–1964) asked to be buried here so they could posthumously enjoy the superb views over Chaniá, but they had patriotic reasons as well: in the rebellion of 1897, Profítis Ilías was briefly the Revolutionary Military Camp of Akrotíri, located just within the Great Powers' 6km exclusion zone around Chaniá. To rout out the Greeks, the British, French, Italian and Russian navies bombarded it. In response, the Cretans raised the Greek flag, holding it up with their bare hands even after it was shot off its pole, which so impressed the admirals that they stopped bombing and applauded. Afterwards a Russian shell destroyed the monastery, but the Prophet Elijah (Ilías) got his revenge when the Russian ship itself was blown up the next day. When the news reached Europe that the Great Powers had bombed heroic Christian Greeks, it caused such a stir that it led the Allies to offer Crete its autonomy.

Akrotíri's first seaside playgrounds are **Kalathás** and its quieter beach of **Tersanás**. Further north, **Stavrós** is the end of the trail for buses from Chaniá and owes its popularity to a lovely circular bay with shallow water; it was used for the beach scenes in the film *Zorba the Greek*. Above Stavrós, the mountain is said to be the body of one of Zeus' lovers, petrified by jealous Hera, lying head-first in the sea. East of Stavrós, **Moní Ag. Triáda**, or Tzagaróliou, has a grand cruciform church with a colonnaded Venetian façade, and in the narthex an inscription in Greek and Latin telling how Ag. Triáda was re-founded in 1634 by Jeremiah Zangarola, a Venetian who became an Orthodox monk. A museum contains icons, codices and a *Last Judgement* (17th-century); a shop sells the monks' olive oil and wine.

Tzagaróliou
t 282 106 3310; open daily 6–2 and 5–7

Where to Stay and Eat on Akrotíri

Stavrós ✉ 73100

Perle Spa, between Stavrós and Tarsanás, **t** 282 103 9400, *www.perle-spa.com* (€€€€). Plush spa and fitness hotel with thalassotherapy and children's play pools.

Rea, back from the sea, **t** 282 103 9001 (€€€). Air-conditioned complex offering everything from basketball and tennis to babysitting. *Open April–Oct.*

Zorba's Studio Flats, by the beach, **t** 282 105 2525, *www.hotel-zorbas.gr* (€€€–€€).

Good for families, with a swimming pool, tennis courts, garden, seaside taverna and a playground.

Blue Beach, adjacent to Zorba's, **t** 282 103 9404 (€€). Villa and apartment complex and oh, so blue, with a pool, restaurant, bar and sea sports. *Open April–Oct.*

Kavos Beach, **t** 282 103 9155, *www.kavosbeach.gr* (€€–€). Some of the nicest rooms to rent, a lovely setting with a pool and bar.

Taverna Thanasis, between Zorba's and Blue Beach, **t** 282 103 9110. Varied food and wine selection; free sunbeds for customers.

Moní Gouvernétou
t 284 306 3319; open Mon, Tues, Thurs 9–12 and 5–7, Sat and Sun 5–11 and 5–8; closed Wed and Fri

An even older monastery, fortified **Moní Gouvernétou**, stands on a remote plateau, 5km above Ag. Triáda along a narrow road that just squeezes through the rocky terrain. Gouvernétou played a major role in reconciling the Cretans and Venetians at the end of the 16th century; the grotesque sandstone heads on the portal are Venetian fancies far from home, while a small chapel has some of the oldest frescoes in Crete. The monastery supplanted two holy places – a path (*bring water*) leads in 10 minutes to the cave **Arkoudiótissa** ('Bear') named after its bear-shaped stalagmite, worshipped since earliest Minoan times in the cult of Artemis, the Mistress of the Wild Animals. The low ceiling is blackened with candle-smoke. A corner contains a 16th-century chapel dedicated to Panagía Arkoudiótissa, who shares the feast day with Artemis: 2 February (Candlemas).

The path continues down, 20 minutes or so, past hermits' huts and a sea rock shaped like a boat (naturally a pirate ship petrified by the Panagía) to the **Cave of St John the Hermit** (or the Stranger), who sailed from Egypt to Crete, founded a score of monasteries and retired here, becoming so stooped from his diet of roots and vegetables that a hunter shot him, mistaking him for an animal (7 October 1042 – the anniversary still brings pilgrims here). St John's followers founded the **Katholikón monastery** here, with a church gouged into the living rock of the precipice, straddled by a stone bridge. A path descends to a rocky but delightful swimming nook.

Soúda and Ancient Aptera

Greater Chaniá trickles scrubbily along the road to its port, **Soúda** (ΣΟΥΔΑ), tucked into the magnificent sheltered bay, dominated by a Greek naval base and former NATO base. The Venetians fortified the bay's islet, **Néa Soúda**, and only surrendered it to the Turks in 1715, after frequent attacks and a gruesome pyramid of 5,000 Christian heads piled around the walls. Signs in Soúda point the way to the immaculate lawns of the seaside **Commonwealth War Cemetery**, where lie 1,497 young British and ANZAC troops who perished in the Battle of Crete. Two km west of Soúda, a road forks south for the 16th-century **Moní Chryssopigí**; the church and museum house an exceptional collection of icons from the 15th century on.

Moní Chryssopigí
open daily 3.30–6

The Turks had an excellent, if frustrating, view of Néa Soúda from **Idzeddin fortress**, east of Soúda on Cape Kalámi. Now Chaniá's prison, Idzeddin was built of stone from **Aptera**, an ancient city high on a plateau above Megála Choráfia. Known in Linear B tablets as A-pa-ta-wa, this was one of western Crete's chief cities, reaching its apogee in Hellenistic times, and surviving until it was destroyed by an earthquake in AD 700. Its mighty 4km walls have been compared to the famous defences of Mycenaean Tiryns. There are the foundations of a Classical-era bipartate shrine, an impressive Roman cistern, and Byzantine buildings. In 2006, two large underground funerary monuments were discovered. The city's name (*aptera*, or 'featherless') came from a singing contest between the Muses and the Sirens. The Sirens, sore losers, tore out their feathers and plunged into the sea, where they turned into the islets in Soúda Bay.

Aptera
open Tues–Sun 8.30–3

Cape Drápanon

East of Aptera, the highway dives inland to avoid rugged Cape Drápanon, leaving the vineyards, olive groves and cypresses draped on rolling hills in relative peace. There are a pair of small resorts on the somewhat exposed north coast of Drápanon: **Kalýves**, with a long beach under the Apokoróna, a fortress built by the Genoese when they tried to pinch Crete from the Venetians, and **Almirída**, smaller and more attractive and full of Brits, with a sandy beach and good windsurfing. From here, it's 4km to **Gavalochóri**, with an excellent **Historical and Folklore Museum**; in the main square a women's agrotourism co-operative sells their beautiful laces and embroideries, some inspired by the exhibits in the museum.

Historical and Folklore Museum
t 282 502 3222; open Mon–Sat 9–7, Sun 10–1.30 and 5–8; adm

East of Almirída, the road swings in from the rocky coast and continues up to picturesque **Pláka** and straggly **Kókkini Chório**, the latter used for most of the village scenes in *Zorba the Greek*. **Drápanos** and **Kefalás** are sleepy villages reeking of past grandeur, but now attracting retirees; **Vámos**, the local capital, seems quite urban in comparison and stands out as one of the pioneers of alternative tourism in Crete. In **Karýdi**, 4km south of Vámos, the **Metóchi Ag. Georgioú** is both a working monastery and a Venetian farm, including a huge olive press. If you're heading south, stop in **Exópoli**, where the tavernas enjoy breathtaking sea views.

Metóchi Ag. Georgioú
open Mon, Tues, Thurs–Sat 7–3 and 4–7, Wed 3–7, Sun 4–7

Where to Stay and Eat on Cape Drápanon

Kalýves/Almirída ✉ 73003

Dimitra Hotel, t 282 503 1956 (€€€). Stylish, with pool bar and tennis.

Kalives Beach, in Kalýves, **t** 282 503 1285 (€€€). By the sea, the best here.

Almyrida Beach, t 282 503 1881, *www. almyridabeach.com* (€€€–€€). With an indoor pool.

The Enchanted Owl, t 282 503 2494. The English owners serve dishes not offered by their Greek neighbours and even English roast dinners on Sundays.

Vámos ✉ 73008

Vámos Village, t 282 502 3100, *www. vamossa.gr* (€€€). A local co-operative that has converted old stone olive presses and stables into traditional accommodation with a kitchen. They organize walks to nearby caves and monasteries, and offer lessons in Greek dancing, cooking, language, ceramics and icon-painting. *Open all year.*

I Sterna tou Bloumosofi (around €20–25). Taverna run by the above, serving Cretan specialities baked in the wood oven and wine from its own barrels in the cellar.

Macherí (south of Aptera) ✉ 73100

Kamares, t 282 504 1111, *www.kamares-houses.gr* (€€€) Apartments around a courtyard in a restored Venetian complex in the middle of a little mountain village; there's a pool in the garden, sea views, and guests can pick their own fruit from the organic orchards.

Vríses, Georgioúpolis and Lake Kournás

South of the highway from Vámos, **Vríses** (ΒΡΥΣΕΣ) is an important crossroads, with lofty plane trees and cafés along the Almirós river, and a dozen busts of heroic, moustachioed Cretans. The road follows the Amirós as it flows down to **Georgioúpolis** (ΓΕΩΡΓΙΟΥΠΟΛΗ), set in a eucalyptus grove in the crook of Cape Drápanon. Named in honour of Prince George, it has a long, sandy (if sometimes windy) beach. Companies offer boat trips up the river, home to turtles and an impressive array of birds. Inland from Georgioúpolis, barren hills form a striking amphitheatre around Crete's only lake, **Kournás**, deep and eerie and full of eels. A place on the shore hires out boats for a closer look; there is a story of a lost city dedicated to Athena in its environs, but not a trace has ever been found. To the south (turn at Episkopí), the attractive hill town of **Argiroúpolis** was the ancient Doric city of Lappa, destroyed by the Romans in 67 BC. In the later war Lappa supported Octavian over Mark Antony, and was rewarded with money to rebuild when he became Augustus. The ruins of the baths and aqueduct are southeast of the centre; a canopy protects a geometric mosaic in town.

Just down the Asi Goniá road are the **Mýli** or watermills, where Réthymnon's drinking water comes spilling through the little troglodyte chapel of Ag. Dínami and down a stepped waterfall. A grove of plane trees and outdoor tavernas make this a favourite oasis on hot summer days. From here the road rises through a narrow gorge to a famous nest of Cretan daredevilry, **Ási Goniá**, an old village and a slightly introspective one now that there isn't an enemy for its brave *pallikári* to fight.

Where to Stay and Eat around Georgioúpolis

Georgioúpolis ✉ 73007

Come prepared: it's not unusual to see hotels in Georgioúpolis advertising their mosquito nets.

Mare Monte, t 282 506 1390, *www. mare-monte-beach.com* (€€€€€). On an excellent stretch of beach, the area's most luxurious hotel, with plenty of sports and enterrtainment.

Pilot Beach, t 282 506 1002, *www.pilot-beach.gr* (€€€). Stylish complex with a pool, good for families.

Mina, at Kourvrá, next beach east, **t** 282 506 1257 (€€). A pleasant, medium-sized hotel.

Almyros, 100m from the sea, **t** 282 506 1349 (€).

Voula, t 282 506 1358 (€). Cheaper.

Apolithos, just up from the beach, **t** 282 506 1406. Wide choice of Greek and international dishes.

Fanis, on the port, **t** 282 506 1374. FIne fish, grilled meats and barrelled wine.

Poseidon, off the main road, **t** 282 506 1026. Good for fish.

Lake Kournás ✉ 73007

Omorphi Limni, on Lake Kournás, **t** 282 509 1665 (€). Rooms on the lake; serves delicious *gýros*.

Korisia, just before the village of Kournás, **t** 282 506 1753. Come here for home-made *kaltsounákia* filled with spinach and cheese.

South to Sfakiá and Chóra Sfakíon

Cut off by the White Mountains, the remote eparchy of Sfakiá was the cradle of the island's most daring desperados, who clobbered each other in blood feuds but in times of need united to become Crete's bravest freedom fighters. Now linked to civilization by a beautiful road, it still harbours dark tales of vendettas and honour killings.

South from Vríses to Chóra Sfakíon (ΧΩΡΑ ΣΦΑΚΙΩΝ)

From Vríses the road ascends the Krapí valley (prettier than it sounds) to the **Lággos tou Katré**, a 2km ravine known as the Thermopylae of Sfakiá. This was a favourite spot for a Cretan ambush, and spelt doom to 400 Turkish soldiers after the capture of Frangokástello, and again in 1866 to a Turkish army fleeing south after the explosion of Arkádi. Next comes the plateau of **Askýfou**, where the ruins of the fortress of Koulés cast a long shadow over the fields. Further south, the Libyan sea sparkles into view, as the road noodles above the steep, wooded **Ímbros Gorge**. It has a well-marked path at the bottom, and is just as beautiful as Samariá.

Legendary viper's nest of feuds and hot-blooded revolutionaries, **Chóra Sfakíon** is now, like any coastal village, given over to the needs of tourists. At one time, however, it was the capital of a province, one that, with few resources of its own, survived by taking everyone else's: smuggling, sheep-rustling and piracy brought home the bacon for centuries. To police the locals, the Venetians constructed the fortress at Frangokástello just to the east in 1317, then, after the revolt of 1570, added the castle over Chóra. After the Battle of Crete, locals helped ANZAC soldiers flee to North Africa; commemorated by a monument by the sea, while a memorial above the town honours

Getting to and from Chóra Sfakíon

Chóra Sfakíon is linked by **bus** to Chaniá 3–4 times a day, and 4 times a day to Omalós, Georgioúpolis, Réthymnon, twice a day to Plakiás, and 2–3 times a day from Chaniá to Anópolis, Frangokástello and Skalotí. **Ferries** sail four times a day in summer between Chóra Sfakíon and Ag. Roúmeli (the Samariá Gorge) and 3–4 times a day to Soúgia and Paleochóra. Morning **excursion boats** link Chóra Sfakíon to Sweetwater Beach; 4 ferries a week (most at weekends) sail to the island of Gávdos. Check with the **port authority**: **t** 282 509 1292.

locals executed by the Germans for their role. The big war, however, was only an intermission in a deadly private war between two Sfakiot families known as the 'Omalós feud' or the 'Vendetta of the Century', which took 90 lives before ending in 1960.

Buses leave at 11am and 6pm for **Anópolis**, a pleasant, rustic village on a plateau offering a few rooms and places to eat. A statue honours Daskaloyánnis, the native son who organized the first revolt against the Turks in 1770. It went all terribly wrong; promised aid from Russia never arrived, and in March 1771, when Daskaloyánnis gave himself up, hoping to spare Sfakiá from reprisals, the pasha ordered him to be flayed alive. From Anópolis, it's 4km west to the new bridge that spans the dizzying gorge, making the once arduous journey up and down the steep rockface to **Arádena** a snap. The bridge arrived too late for Arádena, now a near-ghost town after a particularly bloody feud. It has a famous Byzantine church, the **Astratigos**, dedicated to Archangel Michael and sporting a dome that looks like a tiled toupée. Of all the saints, Michael, weigher of souls, is the most remorseless; a Sfakiot suspected of sheep-rustling would be brought here to be questioned before the stern-eyed saint.

Loutró (ΛΟΥΤΡΟ)

Linked to the rest of the world only by foot or by boat (several daily from Chóra Sfakíon), Loutró has attained cult status as a quiet get-away. Although Loutró's little bay is sheltered and perfectly transparent, it doesn't have much of a beach, but there are coves nearby. Boats sail to **Mármara Beach** (from where you can walk up the gorge to Arádena) and white pebble **Glyká Nerá (Sweetwater) Beach**, under sheer cliffs. True to its name, springs provide fresh water, and there's a taverna for more substantial needs.

The Ghosts of Frangokástello (ΦΡΑΓΚΟΚΑΣΤΕΛΛΟ)

The Venetians built it, but, as medieval Greeks called all Westerners 'Franks', the austere, crenellated 14th-century fortress of Ag. Nikítas is known as Frangokástello. On a sandy beach 14km east of Chóra Sfakíon, it was boldly captured in 1828 during the Greek War of Independence, by an Epirot insurgent, Hatzimichális Daliánis, and 650 Cretans. Soon 8,000 Turkish troops arrived and killed all the Greeks. But bands of Cretans who'd remained outside the Frangokástello captured the mountain passes and wreaked a terrible vengence on the Turks when they marched north.

Where to Stay and Eat near Chóra Sfakíon

⭐ Marmara Cottages >>

⭐ Oasis >>

Chóra Sfakíon ✉ 73001

Livikon, on the quay next to the Samaria Hotel, **t** 282 509 1211, *www.sfakia-livikon.com* (€). New, stylish and comfortable, with a taverna.

Limani, by the port, **t** 282 509 1082. Fish-fry (from their own fishing boat) or mixed grill and salad. Bakery has Sfakiá's famous *myzithrópittes*. They also have rooms (€) to let.

Loutró ✉ 73001

For a list of rooms, see *www.loutro.com* or *www.loutro.net*.

Porto Loutró I and II, Loutró, **t** 282 509 1433, *www.hotelportoloutro.com* (€€€). Two hotels, same owners, English Alison and Greek Stavros. Newish, comfortable, with water sports. *Open mid-Mar–Oct.*

Blue House, **t** 282 509 1127 (€€–€). Rooms and an excellent restaurant, with plenty of vegetarian specialities.

Marmára Cottages, by Marmára Beach, **t** 694 220 1456 (€). A romantic hideyhole – three simple cabins in a village without electricity – but they have gas lanterns.

The Old Phoenix, **t** 282 509 1257, *www.old-phoenix.com* (€). A peaceful, isolated nook.

Frangokástello ✉ 73001

Fata Morgana, **t** 282 509 2077, *www.fatamorgana-kreta.com* (€€). Basic studios in an olive grove, close to the beach.

Oasis, above the beach road, **t** 282 508 3562. A bit hard to find but well worth it, for some of the tastiest traditional food on this coast – good meat and Sfakian pies, the day's catch and good local wine. *Closed Nov–Mar.*

The Massacre of Frangokástello has given rise to one of the most authenticated of all Greek ghost stories. At the end of May, the anniversary of the massacre, phantoms of the Cretan dead, the *Drosoulités* (the 'dew shades') rise up at dawn from Ag. Charalámbos cemetery, mounted and fully armed, and proceed silently towards the shell of the fortress, before disappearing into the sea. Thousands have seen them, but many more haven't; the morning must be perfectly clear. Meteorologists pooh-pooh the ghosts – mere heat mirages from the Libyan desert, they say.

Europe at its Southernmost: Gávdos

If you suffer from *mal de civilisation*, catch one of the small ferries from Chóra Sfakíon or Paleochóra that sail 24 nautical miles to the triangular maquis-matted islet of Gávdos, at 35°10' the southernmost point in Europe. The year-round population is around 40 – down from 8,000 in the 1200s. Known in ancient times as Clauda, it is said to be the Homeric Ogygia, the isle of Calypso; today it's seductive for anyone seeking the peaceful Greek island of yore. Beware that although cedars provide some shade, it can get hot, and that the unpredictable sea can make your stay longer than you intended. Out-of-season ferries are so irregular that you'll have to stick around Chóra Sfakíon and wait for one to appear. There are pristine beaches, especially sandy **Sarakinikós**, **Aï Iánnis**, and **Kórfos**, to the south, with a taverna and rooms. A pierced rock, **Tripití** or 'Three Holes', marks the southernmost end of Europe.

Where to Stay and Eat on Gávdos

Sarakinikós ✉ 73001
Vailakakis Studios, t 282 304 1103 (€€).
Rooms, with a restaurant, bike and
quad hire.

Aï Iánnis ✉ 73001
Has shady camping (€) under the
cedar trees.

Kórfos ✉ 73001
Here there is a taverna and some
rooms (€).

Nomós Réthymnon

Crete's smallest province, Réthymnon, is also the most mountainous, wedged between the White Mountains to the west and Mount
Ida, or Psilorítis (2,456m/8,057ft), to the east. The north coast, fringed
by a 12km sandy beach on either side of lively Réthymnon town, is a
popular base for exploring Crete; the Minoan sites to the east and
beaches to the west are all within striking distance. Ag. Galíni, one of
Crete's most picturesque resorts, and the unique Moní Préveli are
the stars of the south coast, while inland, the lovely Amári valley is
Crete at its most traditional. A string of mountain villages en route
to Heráklion also offer a good day's exploration. For a map, *see* p.172.

Réthymnon (ΡΕΘΥΜΝΟ)

Delightful Réthymnon, Crete's third city (pop. 26,000), has for
centuries paid a price for its beach and lack of a proper harbour. The
Venetians dug a cute round one, but it keeps silting up. This may
have proved a blessing, inhibiting the economy enough to spare
Réthymnon much of what passes for progress. Like Chaniá, its
Venetian and Turkish buildings are listed; but unlike Chaniá
Réthymnon escaped the Luftwaffe's attentions. The fortress and its
minarets lend the skyline an exotic touch; wooden Turkish balconies
project overhead. Its relative isolation attracted scholars who fled
Constantinople, giving Réthymnon the reputation of the brain of
Crete, confirmed by the University of Crete's Arts faculty here.

The Old Town

Although Réthymnon has been inhabited since Minoan times (the
name, *Rithymna*, is pre-Greek), the oldest monuments in town are
Venetian, beginning with the **Guóra Gate**, just below the **Square of
the Four Martyrs**. Built in 1566 by the Venetian governor, it's the sole
survivor of the walls erected after the sackings by Barbarossa in 1538,
and by Uluch Ali in 1562 and 1571. Outside the gate, note the 17th-
century **Porta Grande** or **Valide Sultana Mosque** dedicated to the
Sultan's mother; the Sultana's cemetery was converted after 1923
into the municipal garden.

From the Guóra Gate, **Ethnikís Antistáseos Street** passes **San
Francesco**, the friary where Crete's contribution to the papacy,

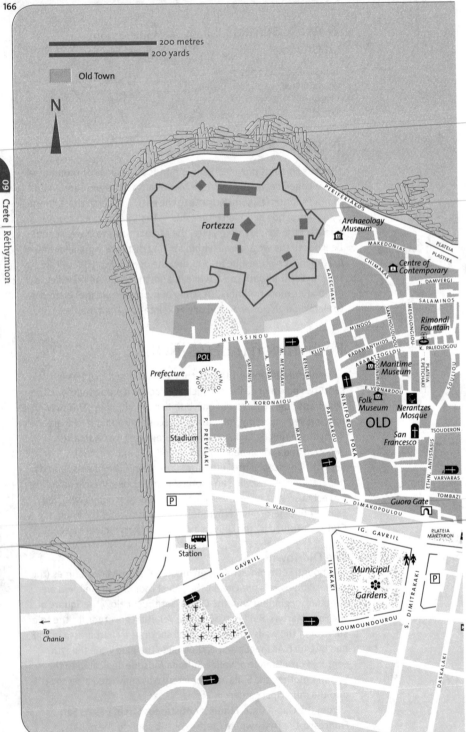

200 metres
200 yards

Old Town

N

Fortezza

Archaeology Museum

PERIFERIAKOS

MAKEDONIAS

PLATEIA PLASTIRA

CHIMARAS

Centre of Contemporary

J. DAMVERGI

SALAMINOS

Rimondi Fountain

KATECHAKI

MINOOS

XANTHOUDIDOU

MESOLONGIOU

K. PALEOLOGOU

MELISSINOU

RADAMANTHIOS

ARABATZOGLOU

DIOUNISIOU

PLATEIA T. PETICHAKI

SOULIOU

POL

Prefecture

IROON POLITECHNIOU

SMILENIS

A. KORAI

M. METAXAKI

M. RENIERI

KLIDI

Maritime Museum

E. VERNARDOU

NIKIFOROU FOKA

Folk Museum

OLD

Nerantzes Mosque

TSOUDERON

P. KORONAIOU

MAVILI

PATELAROU

San Francesco

ETHN. ANTISTASIS

VARVARAS

Stadium

P. PREVELAKI

TOMBAZI

S. VLASTOU

I. DIMAKOPOULOU

Guora Gate

P

PLATEIA MARTYRON

IG. GAVRIIL

Bus Station

IG. GAVRIIL

ILIAKAKI

KRIARI

Municipal Gardens

S. DIMITRAKAKI

P

To Chania

KOUMOUNDOUROU

DASKALAKI

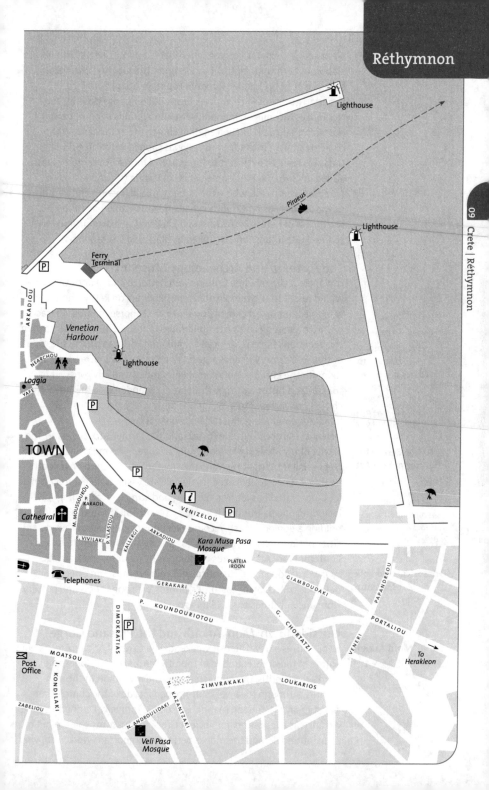

Lighthouse

Piraeus

Lighthouse

Lighthouse

Ferry Terminal

P

ARKADIOU

Venetian Harbour

NEARCHOU

Loggia

YAFE

TOWN

P

Cathedral

M. MOUSSOUROU

P. KARAOLI

E. VIVILAKI

P. VLASTOU

KALLERGI

ARKADIOU

E. VENIZELOU

P

P

i

Kara Musa Pasa Mosque

PLATEIA IROON

Telephones

GERAKARI

GIAMBOUDAKI

DIMOKRATIAS

P. KOUNDOURIOTOU

P

G. CHORTATZI

VENERI

PAPANDREOU

PORTALIOU

To Herakleon

Post Office

MOATSOU

I. KONDILAKI

ZABELIOU

N. ANDROULIDAKI

KAZANTZAKI

ZIMVRAKAKI

LOUKARIOS

Veli Pasa Mosque

Alexander V, began his career; when elected pontiff, he paid for its elaborate Corinthian portal. Further up, at the junction of several streets is the lion-headed **Rimondi Fountain** (1629) built by a Venetian governor. Réthymnon's finest buildings are close by. The **Nerandzes Mosque** on Manoúli Vernárdou retains a monumental portal from its days as the Venetian church of Santa Maria. When converted into a mosque in 1657, it was capped with three domes; today it's used as a concert hall. A graceful rocket of a minaret was added in 1890. The handsome Venetian **Loggia** (1550s), nearby on Arkadíou, was a club where the nobility would hobnob and gamble; it now does duty as an exhibition hall and museum replica shop. Northeast of here is Réthymnon's bijou Venetian **harbour**, lined with seafood restaurants and patrolled by black and white swans.

The Fortezza and Archaeology Museum

Fortezza
open 9–sunset; adm

Archaeology Museum
t 283 105 4668; open April–Oct Tues–Fri 9–1 and 7–10, Sat–Sun 11–3; Nov–Mar Tues, Thurs and Fri 9–2, Sat 9–3, Wed 9–2 and 5–9; adm

In ancient times, when Cretans were bitten by rabid dogs they would resort to the temple of Artemis Roccaea on Réthymnon's acropolis, and take a cure of dog's liver or seahorse innards. All traces of this interesting cult were obliterated in the late 16th century, when the Venetians forced the locals to build the **Fortezza** on the site. One of the best-preserved and largest Venetian castles in Greece, it had room for the entire population of Réthymnon and environs; yet in 1645, after a bitter two-month siege, it surrendered to the Turks. The church, converted into a mosque, is fairly well preserved; other buildings are undergoing reclamation work.

Centre for Contemporary Art
t 283 105 5847, www. rca.gr; open April–Oct Tues–Fri 9–1 and 7–10, Sat and Sun 11–3; Nov–Mar Tues and Thurs 9–2, Wed and Fri 9–2 and 6–9, Sat–Sun 10–3

Near the entrance to the Fortezza, in the former Turkish prison, the **Archaeology Museum** is beautifully arranged. The most dazzling pieces hail from the Late Minoan cemetery at Arméni: a boar-tooth helmet, bronze double axes, lovely delicate vases, fragile remains of a loop-decorated basket from 1200 BC, and *larnaxes* (sarcophagi), including one painted with a wild goat and bull chase and a hunter holding a dog on a leash. A coin collection covers most of the ancient cities of Crete. Nearby, on Chimáras, the **Réthymnon Centre for Contemporary Art** features exhibitions by modern Greek artists.

Historical and Folk Art Museum
t 283 102 3998; open Mon–Sat 10–2; adm

On Vernadoú St, the **Historical and Folk Art Museum** offers a delicious collection of costumes, photos, weavings, tools and pottery from ancient times to 50 years ago.

Outside Town: Moní Arkádi and the Prasanó Gorge

Moní Arkádi
t 283 108 3076; open Tues–Sun 8.30–3; adm to Historical Museum

Four buses a day (three at weekends) go to **Moní Arkádi**, Crete's holy shrine of freedom. Founded in the 11th century on the lonesome flanks of Psilorítis, the monastery was mostly rebuilt in the 17th century, although the lovely sun-ripened façade of the church, Crete's finest essay in Venetian Mannerism, dates from 1587. During this time Arkádi was a repository for ancient Greek manuscripts spirited out of Constantinople, and the monks performed important work in copying

Getting to and from Réthymnon

ANEK **ferries** sail from and to Piraeus at least three times a week, daily in summer (ANEK Lines, 250 Arkadíou, **t** 283 102 9874, *www.anek.gr*). **Port authority: t** 283 102 2276.

The **bus station** is by the sea in the west end, between Igoúm Gavríl and the Periferiákos, **t** 283 102 2212; those labelled 'El Greco/Skaleta' depart every 20mins for the stretch of hotels along the eastern beaches.

the texts and disseminating them in Europe. Arkádi resembles a small fort, which is one reason why Koronéos, head of the Revolutionary Committee of 1866, chose it for a base and a store for his powder magazine. When the Turks demanded that the abbot hand over the rebels, he refused; in response, a Turkish expeditionary force attacked on 7 November 1866. After a two-day siege they breached the monastery walls. Rather than surrender, Abbot Gabriel set fire to the powder magazines, blowing up 829 Turks and Greeks. The suicidal explosion caused a furore in Europe, as Swinburne and Victor Hugo took up the cause of Cretan independence. There's the **Gunpowder Room**, where the blast left a gaping hole in the roof, and a **Historical Museum** containing the holey, holy banner and portraits of the heroes of 1866, monkish embroideries and icons. An old windmill was made into an **ossuary**, displaying a stack of skulls blasted with holes.

Just east of Réthymnon, the **Prasanó Gorge** was formed by the Plataniás river, which dries up between mid-June and mid-October so you can walk down the gorge (*4–5hrs*). Take the early Amári bus as far as the first bend in the road after **Prasiés**, where the track begins; walk past the sheepfold and bear left. Lined with plane trees, dates, olives and cypresses, the gorge has three narrow 'gates' where the walls climb up to 146m (480ft). The track ends near **Misiriá**, where you can swim and catch a bus back the last 5km to Réthymnon.

09 Crete | Réthymnon

Useful Information in Réthymnon

(i) Réthymnon >
EOT: along the town beach at E. Venizélou, **t** 283 102 9148; open Mon–Fri 8–2.30

Tourist police: next door to the EOT, **t** 283 102 8156. Get the free monthly English-language paper *Cretasummer*.

Réthymnon Festivals

Carnival: A three-day street party with music and dancing everywhere, and a treasure hunt, one of the best carnivals in Greece. Have a look at *http://carnival-in-rethymnon-crete-greece.com*.

Midsummer's Day: Klidónas Festival; dancing, singing and jumping over bonfires.

Last 10 days of July: The Cretan Wine Festival and Handicrafts Exhibition, in the municipal gardens.

July–Sept: Renaissance Festival, performances in the Venetian fortress.

Shopping in Réthymnon

On **Thursdays** Réthymnon hosts a big weekly **market** and fair off Odós Kanzantzáki. **Soúliou Street**, the city's narrow tourist bazaar, is crammed with desirable arty stuff and crafts. **Arkadíou Street** is full of gold and jewellery shops.

International Press, 81 El. Venizélou. Stocks a range of English-language papers, as well as a vast selection of guides and literature about Crete.

Traditional Cretan, 28 Soúliou. Just what the name implies: spices, herbs, *raki*, honey and more.

Vasilis Psycharakis, 41 Ethnikis Antistaséos. An institution: an old-fashioned barber shop that sells hand-made Cretan knives.

Sports and Activities in Réthymnon

The corny *Pirate Ship Barbarossa* and its sister *Captain Hook* make daily **excursions** from the Venetian harbour to Maráthi (a fishing village in eastern Akrotíri) and to Bali. Nearby there are also excursion cruises to Santoríni on offer, **dolphin cruises**, and **mini-motorboats** for hire.

Atlantis Diving Centre, t 283 107 1640, operates from the Grecotel Rithymna Beach Hotel.

The Happy Walker, 56 Tombázi St, **t** 283 105 2920, *www.happywalker.nl.* Organized treks in the most scenic areas of western Crete.

Hellas Bike Travel, 118 Máchis Krítis, **t** 283 105 3328, *www.hellasbike.com*. For those who'd love to cycle down Mt Ida or the White Mountains but not up.

Where to Stay in Réthymnon

Réthymnon ✉ 74100

Avli Lounge Apartments, 22 Xanthou-dídou, **t** 283 102 6213, *www.avli.gr* (€€€€€). Venetian *palazzo* made into seven superb suites in various shades, with a Jacuzzi and pool.

Mythos Suites, 12 Plateía Karaóli, **t** 283 105 3917, *www.mythos-crete.gr* (€€€€€–€€€€). Ten suites sleeping 2–5 and furnished in a traditional style, in a 16th-century manor house; there's a pool in the central patio.

Palazzo di Corina, 7–9 Damvérgi, **t** 283 102 1205, *www.corina.gr* (€€€€). Handsome rooms with stone walls and oak beams in one of the city's oldest buildings, with a pool and restaurant.

Palazzo Rimondi, 19 Xanthoudídou, **t** 283 105 1289, *www.palazzorimondi. com* (€€€€). 25 suites in a renovated 15th-century mansion, built around a courtyard with a small pool.

Veneto, 4 Epimenídou, **t** 283 105 6634, *www.veneto.gr* (€€€). Atmospheric, airy rooms in a 700-year-old Dominican

monastery with a garden courtyard and a good restaurant; Internet discounts available.

Fortezza, 16 Melissínou, **t** 283 105 5551, *www.fortezza.gr* (€€€–€€). Just under the castle walls; all rooms have balconies, and there's a garden courtyard and pool.

Brascos, at Ch. Daskaláki and Th. Moátsou, **t** 283 102 3721, *www. brascos.com* (€€). Slick, with a pool and roof garden. *Open all year*.

Ideon, Plateía Plastíra, **t** 283 102 8667, *www.hotelideon.gr* (€€). Enjoys a fine spot overlooking the dock and has a small pool.

Leon, 2 Váfe, **t** 283 102 6197 (€€). A centrally located charmer, done up in traditional Cretan style. *Open all year*.

Ralia Rooms, at Salamnós and Athan. Niákou, **t** 283 105 0163 (€). More atmospheric than most, with lots of wood.

Sea Front, 161 Arkadíou, **t** 283 105 1981 (€). Run by friendly Ellotia Tours next door; nice pine-clad rooms; the one at the top benefits from a terrace.

Zania, Pávlou Vlasátou, **t** 283 102 8169 (€). A handful of pleasant rooms in a traditional house.

Zorbas Beach, at the east end of the town beach, 2 A. Schweitzer, **t** 283 102 8540 (€). This is a good choice for peace and quiet and it's reasonable.

Youth hostel, 41 Tombázi, **t** 283 102 2848, *www.yhrethymno.com*. Friendly, clean and central; breakfast and cooking facilities available.

Elizabeth Campsite, a few km east of Réthymnon at Misiriá, **t** 283 102 8694.

Eating Out in Réthymnon

With its tiny fish restaurants, the Venetian harbour is the place to dine, but expect to pay at least €25–30. Scan the menus – some places offer lobster lunches for two for €35–55.

Alana, 11 Salamínas, just the other side of the fountain, **t** 283 102 7737 (€25 for two). In a pretty courtyard, a nice enough place to bring your parents; offers a good fish-based menu.

Antonias Zoumas, by the bus station next to the small church. Doesn't look

★ **Veneto >**

like much but on Sunday afternoons it's packed with locals jawing through a four-hour lunch.

⭐ Avli ›

Avli, in the hotel (€25). One of the prettiest places to eat on Crete, serving exquisite Cretan cuisine with a creative touch, using the finest raw materials; superb wine list, too.

Castelvecchio George, 29 Chimáras (just under the Fortezza), **t** 283 105 2886. Good Cretan atmosphere and plenty of fish dishes; also **rooms** (€).

Kyria Maria, 20 Moshovitou, **t** 283 102 9078. Traditional meals accompanied by the chirping songbirds.

Melina, Chimáras and Katecháki, **t** 283 102 1580 (€25). Excellent traditional Cretan cuisine and wine near the Fortezza, offering many dishes rarely seen elsewhere

Samaria, **t** 283 102 4681 (€15). An exception to the mediocre restaurants along the beach and El. Venizélou, with tasty Greek cooking.

Veneto, in the hotel (€30–35). High class Greek and Cretan specialities; big wine cellar.

Entertainment and Nightlife in Réthymnon

Cinema Asteria. Summer outdoor cinema, mostly in English.

La Conga, on Salamínas. A favourite, with mostly Greek pop. In summer they move to the beach at Mísiria.

Fortezza Disco, near the water. Big and noisy, Greek and Euro-pop.

Oinodeio, 9 Melissinoú. Live Cretan music and occasional *rembétiko*.

T. N. Gounakis, 6 Koronaíou St (near the church of the Mikrí Panagías). Simple but fun place summed up by its own sign: 'Every day folk Cretan music with Gounakis Sons and their father gratis/free/for nothing and Cretan meal/dish/food/dinner thank you'.

From Réthymnon to the Libyan Sea

The *nómos* of Réthymnon encompasses the narrow 'neck' of Crete, and there's a good road that cuts between the mountains for the south, where Plakiás and Ag. Galíni are major resorts, with Moní Préveli as the favourite day trip in between.

Arméni to Plakiás

Ten km south of Réthymnon, the village of **Arméni** was named after the Armenian soldiers granted land here by Nikephóros Phokás, following his reconquest of Crete from the Saracens in 961. They weren't the first here, though: an unusually large **Late Minoan III cemetery** was discovered near the crossroads with Somatás. Some 200 chamber tombs from 1350–1200 BC fill nearly three hectares (seven acres), including elaborate underground chambers.

Minoan cemetery
t 283 102 9975; open Mon–Sat 8.30–3

South of Arméni, the road cuts through the **Kourtaliótis Gorge** and emerges at **Asómatos**, the crossroads for Préveli and Plakiás, with magnificent sea views. **Plakiás**, a good centre for walks in the area, has grown into a big resort on its rather exposed grey sands, though there are nicer sandy coves east of the headland at **Damnóni**, where concrete pillboxes offer a reminder from the war when this coast was an important escape route to Egypt. Half an hour's walk west of Plakiás, **Soúda Beach** has a lovely taverna in a palm grove. Late in the day, head for **Mýrthios**, where the tavernas offer sunset sea views.

From Plakiás or Damnóni, the Posidonia Fast Boat makes daily excursions to Préveli (*see* below); there's also one bus a day to Préveli,

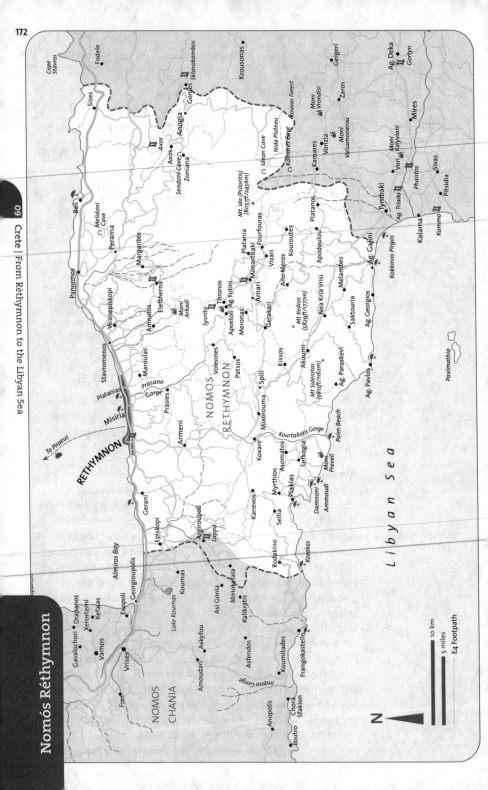

Nomós Réthymnon

Getting around South of Réthymnon

Plakiás has 7 **buses** a day to Réthymnon, and two a day west along the south coast as far as Chóra Sfakíon, by way of Frangokástello, and one bus a day to Préveli. Ag. Galíni has 5 buses a day from Réthymnon, as well as connections to Heráklion, Phaistós, and Mátala by way of Míres.

two to Ag. Galíni, and one to Chóra Sfakíon. The latter passes via **Séllia**, with beautiful views from its church, and **Rodákino** ('peach'), a village hanging over a ravine with a grey beach; it was from here that Patrick Leigh Fermor and the Resistance spirited General Kreipe off Crete to Egypt in a submarine.

Moní Préveli

Moní Préveli, 7km east of Lefkógia, is *the* beauty spot on the central Libyan coast. The road passes palm groves along the Megálo Pótamos river, just before the 19th-century bridge and abandoned lower monastery, **Káto Préveli**, where the monks' farming activities were centred. A few decades after Daskaloyánnis' aborted revolt in Sfakía, Abbot Melchisedek Tsouderos began to collect arms for a new uprising. The Turks got wind of it, and in 1821, shortly before the War of Independence on the mainland, they came to destroy the monastery. Rather than resist, the abbot welcomed the Turks and got them so drunk they fell asleep, so the monks were able to flee before the Turks woke up. The monks were nothing daunted, and continued resisting and fighting throughout the century.

Píso Préveli
t 283 203 1246,
www.preveli.org; open
8–1.30 and 3–7; adm

The 'Back' monastery, **Píso Préveli**, is 3km over the bridge, high on the coast. The original Byzantine church was demolished by the monks in the 1830s, after the Turks kept refusing them permission to make repairs. They did, however, preserve the furnishing in the rebuilt church and museum: the intricate gilt iconostasis, the icons, the miraculous silver cross the monks took into battle, and the beautiful *Making of the World* icon by Michael Prevelis, *c.* 1750. Note the Byzantine palindrome NIΨONANOMHMATA MHMONANOΨIN ('Cleanse your sins, not only your face') on the fountain. Throughout Crete's revolts in the 19th century, Píso Préveli took in refugees until boats could ferry them to independent Greece. In 1941, the monks sheltered hundreds of Allied troops until they could be picked up by submarine. On the edge of the cliff stands a new memorial: a statue of a British soldier and the abbot holding rifles. A long stairway descends to lovely **Palm Beach**, the sandy cove at mouth of the Megálo Pótamos, exotic with a lush palm forest (you can also take a boat from Plakiás or Ag. Galíni). The big, lonesome rock by the sea at **Límni** was used to tie up British submarines.

Spíli and Ag. Galíni

The main road south of Réthymnon continues past the Plakiás turn-off, passing by way of **Spíli**, a charming village immersed in greenery, with a long fountain in the centre, where water splashes from a row of 17 Venetian lion-heads. Further along are turn-offs for beaches: at **Akoúmia** a rough road leads down in 10km to pristine **Ag. Paraskeví**, while further east at **Néa Kría Vrísi** you can turn south for **Ag. Pávlos**, a sheltered sandy beach.

The roads end up at **Ag. Galíni**, an old fishing village under a backdrop of mountains, easily the most photogenic resort on Crete's south coast. The beach is puny for the number of bodies that try to squeeze on it, but boat excursions sail in search of others, at Moní Préveli, **Mátala**, **Ag. Geórgios** (shingly with three tavernas) and Ag. Pávlos (50mins) and to the pebble-beached islets of **Paximádia**.

Where to Stay and Eat South of Réthymnon

Plakiás and Around ✉ 74060

Damnoni Bay, t 283 203 1372, *www. damnonibay.net* (€€€). Cream-coloured complex with studios, pool, water sports, and a seafood restaurant.

Stefanos Village, Mýrthios, 3km above, **t** 283 203 2252, *www.stefanosvillage. com* (€€€–€€) New complex of studios, apartments and pool; stunning views.

Alianthos Beach, t 283 203 1851 (€€). Neo-Minoan family hotel, with green lawns and a pool near the beach.

Lamon, t 283 203 1425 (€€). Pretty blue and white place.

Youth Hostel Plakiás, t 283 203 2118, *www.yhplakias.com* (€). Among olives.

Apollonia Camping, t 283 203 1318. Has a pool, laundry and mini-market. *Open April–Oct.*

Christos, by the little port, **t** 283 203 1472. Does a roaring trade under the tamarisks, with the locals; **rooms** (€).

(★) **Iliomanolis** ›

Iliomanolis, north of Séllia in Kánevos, **t** 283 205 1053. Famous restaurant where Mrs Iliáki makes divine traditional stews and casseroles on Crete (8 choices every day, 15 on Sunday when people drive for miles to eat here), all served with the family's own wine and *rakí. Closed Mon in Nov–Mar.*

Plateía, in Mýrthios, **t** 283 203 1560. Delicious Greek standards.

Tassomanólis, on the road to Soúda Beach, **t** 283 203 1129. Excellent *psarotáverna*: he fishes, and his wife knows just how to prepare the ultra-fresh seafood he brings home.

Spíli ✉ 74200

Green Hotel, t 283 202 2225, *www. greenhotel.gr* (€€€). Bedecked with flowers, a delightful refuge when the coasts are unbearably hot and crowded; book in the summer. Offers a sauna, massage and aromatherapy.

Costas Inn, on the main road near the fountains, **t** 283 202 2040. Serves tasty Cretan mountain food and also has **rooms** (€) for rent.

Ag. Galíni ✉ 74056

Although it is stacked with all sorts of accommodation, don't arrive in Ag. Galíni without a reservation. Places generally not booked by package companies are:

Galíni Mare, t 283 209 1358 (€€). Good views and facilities.

Aktaeon, Kountouriótou, **t** 283 209 1208 (€). Private baths and good views over the town; good value.

Argiro's Studios and Rooms, t 283 209 1470, *www.argiro-crete.gr* (€).

Kostas, east of the beach, **t** 283 209 1323 (€).

Ariston, t 283 209 1122 (€12). Very good *stifádo*, moussaka, and an excellent aubergine salad. Also **rooms** (€) to let.

Nightlife South of Réthymnon

Zorbas Club, Ag. Galíni. For after midnight.

Jukebox Club, Ag. Galíni. An institution for over 20 years.

MilesTone, Ag. Galíni. An excellent jazz bar.

Amári: The Western Slopes of Mount Ida

Wedged under Mount Ida, the ancient province of Amári consists of two valleys, known for their spirited resistance in the last war, and for their lush charms, cherry orchards, olive groves and frescoed Byzantine churches. Both valleys are prime walking territory. Get there by way of Prasiés and **Apóstoli**, with grand views and a frescoed church, Ag. Nikólaos, from the 1300s; **Ag. Fotiní** just beyond marks the crossroads of the east and west valleys.

Many west valley villages were torched by the Nazis, but they have been rebuilt pretty much as they were. **Méronas** is worth a stop for its church of the **Panagía**, with the arms of the Byzantine Kallergis family over the Venetian Gothic doorway. Inside (*key across the road*), early 14th-century frescoes show the more naturalistic artistic trends from Constantinople. **Gerakári**, famous for cherries, is the starting point for a stunning drive over the Kédros Mountains to Spíli (*see* above). But if you have time for only one route, the east valley is lovelier. From Ag. Fotiní, turn left for **Thrónos**, the heir of **ancient Sybrito**, a city destroyed by the Saracens in 824. The setting, especially Sybrito's acropolis, is superb, and in the centre of Thrónos the mosaic carpet of a large basilica overflows from under the simple little church of the **Panagía**, containing exceptional frescoes.

Back on the main route, the University of Crete excavated a **Minoan Proto-Palatial villa or palace** (*visible through the fence*) at **Monastiráki**. One of the most important sites discovered in western Crete, it had big storage rooms, where the *pithoi* still contained grape pips. **Amári**, one-time capital of the province, is a lovely village, surrounded by views, especially from the Venetian tower. **Ag. Ánna**, outside the village, has the oldest dated frescoes in Crete (1225).

Réthymnon to Heráklion: The Coast

Between Réthymnon and Heráklion you can choose between the highway or the old roads winding over the northern slopes of Mount Ida. The highway passes Réthymnon's beach sprawl and **Pánormos**, a pretty place with a ruined 5th-century basilica and small beach, guarded by a Genoese fortress of 1206. Pánormos made its fortune in the 19th century as a port for carob beans – once an essential ingredient in the manufacture of film. A short drive above Pánormos, the **Melidóni Cave** (*signposted*) is enormous: the ceiling, ragged with stalactites, rises 300m (990ft) overhead. The Minoans worshipped in this gloomy place, and near the entrance is a 3rd-century BC inscription to Hermes Talaios, who shared offerings here with Zeus Talaios and Talos, the giant bronze robot that patrolled the Crete coasts until Medea pulled the pin out of his heel and drained away his life-giving ichor. In 1824, when the Turks were doing their best to

Where to Stay and Eat on the North Coast

Pánormos ✉ 74057

Villa Kynthia, t 283 405 1102, *www.villakynthia.gr* (€€€). Intimate luxury in an 1898 mansion, air-conditioned rooms with antiques and pool. *Open Mar–Oct.*

★ Villa Kynthia ›

Lucy's, t 283 405 1212, *www.lucy.gr*. Pleasant, cheap rooms.

To Steki. One of the best places to eat.

Balí ✉ 74057

Only worth trying in the off-season.

Bali Beach and Village, t 283 409 4210, *www.balibeach.gr* (€€€). This was one of the first hotels here and still nicest.

Sophia, t 283 409 4202 (€€–€). Good value for money, clean apartments, with pool and family-run taverna.

Ag. Pelagía ✉ 71500

Alexander House, t 281 281 1303, *www.alexanderhouse.gr* (€€€–€€). Comfortable air-conditioned rooms with satellite TV, mini-bars and balconies, and a good Chinese restaurant.

Scala, t 281 081 1333, *www.scala.gr* (€€). Modern, and posh for the price.

Le Gourmet. Pleasant waterfront taverna with a very good wine list.

Mouragio, by the sea. Delicious fish.

Valentino. Greek and Italian: lots of seafood either way, and pizzas.

cut short Crete's participation in the Greek War of Independence, 324 women and children and 30 revolutionaries took refuge in the cave. When the Turks found them, the Greeks refused to surrender; the Turks built a fire and asphyxiated them all. With its crumbling altar and broken ossuary the cave still seems haunted.

Further east, **Balí** has been transformed from a steeply sloping village of bee-keepers (the name means 'honey' in Turkish) to a jam-packed resort, overlooking a trio of sandy coves. A short drive above Balí, the lovely partially restored 17th-century **Monastery of Ag. Ioánnis** has frescoes, a Renaissance façade and fountain.

Monastery of Ag. Ioánnis
open daily 1–12 and 4–7

The Old Road between Pérama and Heráklion is pure rural Crete. **Fódele**, immersed in orange groves, is one of the best places to stop. According to tradition, Doménikos Theotokópoulos was born here in 1541; a plaque was put up by Spain's University of Toledo in 1934 and a '**House of El Greco**' has memorabilia, reproductions, and a café. Although he never returned after leaving in 1567 for Venice (where he studied with Titian and Tintoretto), Rome and Spain, he always signed his paintings in Greek. Nearby is the 11th-century church of the **Evangelismós**, with Middle Byzantine frescoes. East of Fódele is the upmarket resort of **Ag. Pelagía**, strewn over the headland and sandy beach that marks the outer gate of the Bay of Heráklion.

House of El Greco
open April–Oct Tues–Sun 9–5; adm

Evangelismós
open Tues–Sun 8.30–3

Réthymnon to Heráklion: Ancient Cities along the Inland Route

A choice of roads skirts the northern flanks of Psilorítis, and to see everything there is to see will involve backtracking. From Réthymnon, follow the coast as far as Stavroménos, then turn for **Viranepiskopí**, with a 10th-century basilica near a sanctuary of Artemis, and a 16th-century Venetian church. Higher up, colourful

Margarítes is home to a thriving pottery industry (they even make huge *pithoi*) and two Byzantine churches: the 14th-century **Ag. Demétrius** and 12th-century **Ag. Ioánnis**. Another 4km south, **Eléftherna** is just below the ancient city of the same name, founded by the Dorians in the 8th century BC. The setting, above two tributaries of the Milopótamos river, is spectacular: its mighty walls and a formidable tower, rebuilt in Hellenistic times, kept out most foes. Historian Dio Cassius wrote that the Romans under Metellus Creticus were only able to capture Eléftherna after the tower was soaked in vinegar (!). Near here is a section of the aqueduct carved into the stone, which leads to two massive Roman cisterns capable of holding 10,000 cubic metres (353,357 cubic feet) of water. At the bottom of the glade a bridge has Mycenaean-style corbelled arches.

Even higher and more precipitous, **Axós**, 30km east, was founded *c.* 1100 BC by Minoan refugees from the Dorians. Axós was the only town on Crete to have a king of its own into the 7th century BC, and it continued to thrive well into the Byzantine period, when it counted 46 churches; today 11 survive, of which **Ag. Iríni**, with fragmentary frescoes, is the most important. The scattered remains of **ancient Axos** reveal a huge town in its 8th-century BC walls, under an acropolis scattered on terraces. On the road to the east of Axós, a splendid panorama of all the hill towns of the Milopótamo opens up. Just below the first, **Zonianá**, the **Sendóni Cave** (aka Sfentoni's Hole) contains Crete's most striking collections of stalactites and stalagmites, cave draperies and petrified waves.

Sendóni Cave
*guided tours
in summer
8–sunset; adm*

Anógia and the Idean Cave

The next village east is **Anógia**, where the inhabitants of Axós moved in the Middle Ages. A stalwart resistance centre, it was burned by both the Turks and the Germans, the latter in reprisal for hiding the kidnapped General Kreipe, when all the men in the village were rounded up and shot (a long-time German resident of the village, Karen Raeck, assisted by local shepherds, has recently built a memorial in boulders on the upper plateau). Today rebuilt in an upper, modern town and lower, more traditional-looking town, Anógia is not without charm. Cradle of many of Crete's musicians, it is a centre of traditional music. Beyond that, Anógia lives off its weavings; brace yourself for a mugging by little old ladies.

East of Anógia 26km road rises south to the 1,540m (5,052ft) **Idean Cave**. In Archaic times, the Idean Cave took over the Diktean Cave's thunder, so to speak, as the birthplace of Zeus. Ancient even to the ancients, the Idean cult preserved remnants of Minoan religion into classical times, presided over by Idean Dactyls, or 'finger men'. According to his 5th-century BC biographer, Pythagoras was initiated by the Dactyls into the Orphic mysteries of midnight Zagreus (i.e. Zeus fused with the mystic role of Dionysos), a cult that may have

09

Crete | Réthymnon to Heráklion: Ancient Cities along the Inland Route influenced his mystical theories on numbers and vegetarianism. Ioánnis and Éfi Sakellarákis' excavations in the 1980s produced votive offerings from 3000 BC to the 5th century AD. A marked track from the cave to the summit of **Psilorítis**, Crete's highest peak at 2,456m (8,057ft), about seven hours' round trip if you're experienced. The Greek Mountaineering Federation operates two shelters: at 1,100m (3,609ft) Prinos (*t 281 022 7609*), and at 1,500m (4,921ft) Stoumbotos Prinos (*t 283 105 7766*).

East of Anógia, **Goniés** is a village in an amphitheatre at the entrance to the Malevízi region, which once produced Malmsey, a favourite sweet wine in medieval Venice and England. Nearby, at **Sklavokámbos**, a Minoan villa went up in flames so intense that its limestone walls were baked; its ruins are next to the road.

The Minoan Villas of Týlisos

Minoan Villas of Týlisos
t 281 022 6092; open Tues–Sun 8.30–3; adm

Much more remains to be seen east of Sklavokámbos at Týlisos, a village surrounded by mountains and swathed in olives and vineyards, where three large **Minoan villas** were unearthed between 1902 and 1913. Built in the prosperous New Palace period and destroyed *c*. 1450 BC, the villas stood two or even three storeys high and contained small apartments and extensive storage facilities; palatial elements such as light-wells, lustral basins, colonnaded courts and cult shrines are produced here in miniature.

The Minoan love of twisting little corridors is further complicated here by the fact that the Dorians founded a town re-using many of the walls. Rectangular **Villa B**, nearest the entrance, is the oldest and least intact; **Villas A** and **C** are extremely well built of finely dressed stone: door jambs, stairs, pillars and the drainage system survive. The presence of these elaborate villas in Týlisos and Sklavokámbos suggests that the Minoan nobility liked to take a few weeks off in the country, but the fact that they stand along the Knossós–Idean Cave road may be the true key to their purpose.

Northern Festivals

Anógia hosts two festivals of music and arts: the Yakintheía, in the first four days of July, and the Anogéia in early August. Any other time, it's a good place to chance upon an impromptu concert in one of the cafés.

Where to Stay and Eat in the North

Margarítes ✉ 74100
Kouriton House, t 283 105 5828, *www. kouritonhouse.gr* (€€€). Handsome old stone manor on a farm, built in 1750, with pretty, individually styled rooms sleeping up to four.

Axós ✉ 74100
Enagron, t 283 406 1611, *www. enagron. gr* (€€€). Traditionally built studios and apartments sleeping up to six on a farm, with a pool, restaurant and plenty of chances to meet and talk to the locals.

Nomós Heráklion

This province, between Psilorítis and the Diktean Mountain, was the core of Minoan Crete: not only Knossós, but Mália, Phaistós, Archánes and Ag. Triáda, along with countless smaller sites, are here. The magnificent works of art they yielded, now in the Heráklion Museum, are one of the glories of Greece. Besides the finest Cretan art and culture, the province also contains much of the dark side of what the last 40 years have wrought – the beach resorts along the lovely north coast, thrown up in the first flush of mass tourism in the 1960s; what the Venetians, Turks and Germans couldn't conquer, money has undone without a fight. Big, busy Heráklion is both the capital of the province and of Crete. For a province map, see pp.194–5.

Heráklion (ΗΡΑΚΛΕΙΟ)

Hustling, bustling Heráklion is Crete's capital and Greece's fourth city (pop. 150,000) – the kind of place that many people go on holiday to escape. But Heráklion boasts two unmissable attractions: a museum containing the world's greatest collection of Minoan art, and the grand palace of Knossós in its suburbs.

Heráklion has gone through more names than Elizabeth Taylor. It began as Katsamba, the smaller of Knossós' two ports, and took its current name in the Classical age. In the 800s the Saracens saw the potential of the site and built their chief town here, named Kandak ('moats') after the trench they dug around its walls. By the time Crete was reconquered by Nikephóros Phokás, Kandak was the main slave market in the Mediterranean. The Venetians made Kandak into Candia; the mighty walls they built around it so impressed the Cretans that they called it Megálo Kástro, the 'Big Castle'. The Turks kept it their seat of government until 1850, when they transferred it to Chaniá. When Crete became autonomous, the classical name, Heráklion, was revived, and it reclaimed its capital role in 1971.

Venetian Heráklion

When Crete won its autonomy in 1898, Arthur Evans, already a local hero for his news reports in Britain on Turkish atrocities, was instrumental in persuading the Cretans to safeguard their Venetian heritage, and it's a good thing he did because otherwise sprawling Heráklion would be a mess. The **Venetian Harbour**, west of the ferry docks, is an important landmark, guarded by the 16th-century fortress **Rocco al Mare**, still wearing its lion of St Mark. The harbour's **Arsenali**, or shipyards, recall the superiority of Venice at sea, that allowed it to suppy Heráklion during the great 21-year siege.

The street up from the Venetian Harbour, newly pedestrianized **Odós 25 Ávgoustou**, has always been lined with businesses it

Rocco al Mare
t 281 024 6211; open daily 9–3 (hours changeable); adm

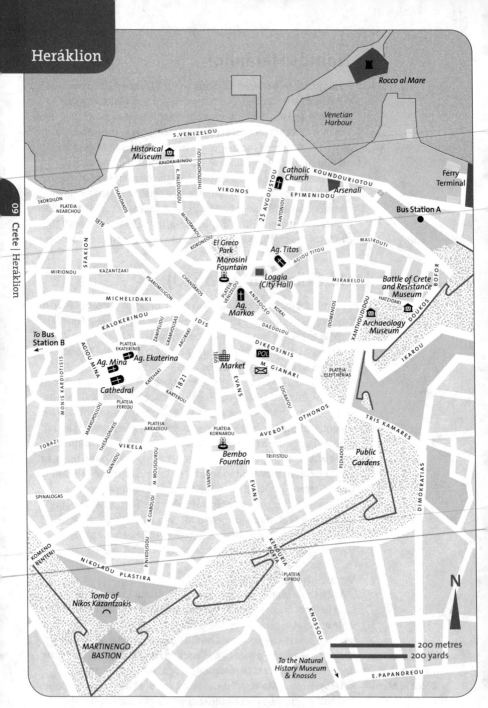

Rocco al Mare

Venetian Harbour

Ferry Terminal

S.VENIZELOU

Historical Museum
KALOKAIRINOU

K. PALEOLOGOU

THEOTOKOPOULOU

Catholic Church

KOUNDOURIOTOU

Arsenali

Bus Station A

SKORDILON

PLATEIA NEARCHOU

1878

CHANDAKOS

VIRONOS

25 AVGOUSTOU

P. ANTONIOU

EPIMENIDOU

MALIKOUTI

BOFOR

SFAKION

MINOTAVROU

KORONEOU

El Greco Park
Morosini Fountain

Ag. Títos

AGIOU TITOU

MIRABELOU

Battle of Crete and Resistance Museum

HATZIDAKI

DOUKOS

MIRIONOU

KAZANTZAKI

PSAROMILIGON

CHANDAKOS

PLATEIA VENIZELOU

Loggia (City Hall)

ANDROGEO

KORAI

MIRABELOU

XANTHOUDIDOU

Archaeology Museum

IKAROU

To Bus Station B

MICHELIDAKI

KALOKERINOU

ZAMPELIOU

GRAMMOUSAS

ARGIRAKI

IDIS

Ag. Markos

DAEDALOU

DIKEOSINIS

IDOMENEOS

PLATEIA ELEFTHERIAS

TRIS KAMARES

AGIOU MINA

MONIS KARDIOTISIS

PLATEIA EKATERINIS

Ag. Mina

Ag. Ekaterina

KATEHAKI

1821

1866

Market

POL

GIANARI

EVANS

ZOGRAFOU

Cathedral

PLATEIA FEREOU

KARTEROU

OTHONOS

MARKOPOULOU

THESSALONIKIS

PLATEIA ARKADIOU

PLATEIA KORNAROU

AVEROF

PEDIADOS

TOBAZI

VIKELA

GIANIKOU

M. MOUSOUROU

Bembo Fountain

TRIFISTOU

Public Gardens

DIMOKRATIAS

SPINALOGAS

K. GIABOUDI

VIANON

EVANS

KOMENO BENTENI

NIKOLAOU PLASTIRA

P. NIKOUSIOU

KENOURIA PORTA

PLATEIA KIPROU

Tomb of Nikos Kazantzakis

KNOSSOU

N

MARTINENGO BASTION

200 metres

200 yards

To the Natural History Museum & Knossós

E. PAPANDREOU

supports today: shipping agents and banks. Halfway up, the church of **Ag. Títos** owes its cubic form to the Turks, who used it as a mosque and rebuilt it after several earthquakes. The chapel to the

Getting to, away from and around Heráklion

By air: Heráklion **airport**, 4km east, **t** 281 039 7129, is linked to the city by public bus (no.1) from Plateía Eleftherías in the centre of town. A taxi costs €10. **Olympic** information, 27 Odós 25 Ávgoustou, **t** 281 024 4846. **Aegean**, 11 Dimokratías, **t** 281 034 4324. For **Sky Express**, and its flights to Rhodes, Santoríni, Mýkonos, Sámos and Kos, call **t** 281 022 3500.

By sea: Travel agents line Odós 25 Ávgoustou, at the Venetian harbour; try **Paleologos** at No.5, **t** 281 034 6185, who are agents for all lines including the summer **hydrofoils** to the Cyclades. **Ferries** sail daily to Piraeus on **Minoan Lines**, **t** 281 022 9602, *www.minoan.gr*, and ANEK, **t** 281 022 3067. **LANE** ships, **t** 281 034 6185, travel at least once a week to Rhodes and Kárpathos. **Port authority**: **t** 281 024 4912.

By bus: Almost all long-distance buses leave from **Bus Station A**, **t** 281 024 5019, outside the walls near the ferry port. City and suburban buses (including those for Knossós) use the adjacent **local station**, **t** 281 022 0755. If you're heading west or southwest (Ag. Galíni, Górtyn, Phaistós, Mátala, Týlisos, Anógia, Milapótamos), you'll need to get to **Bus Station B**, west of the centre, outside the walls at the Pórta Chaniá, **t** 281 025 5965.

By car: Besides stands in the airport, there are no end of **car hire** agencies around Odós 25 Ávgoustou and Doukós Bofór; the rates are reasonable, but be prepared to haggle. Try **Mike Tours**, 76 Ikaroú, **t** 281 024 1362, *www. miketours.gr*, or **Blue Sea**, 5 Kósma Zótou, **t** 281 024 1097, which also rents scooters and bikes.

By taxi: **t** 281 021 0102, **t** 281 021 0146, **t** 281 021 0124.

---

left of the narthex houses the island's most precious relic, the head of St Titus, a disciple of St Paul and the apostle of Crete. When forced to give up Crete, the Venetians made off with Titus' skull and only returned it when Pope Paul VI forced them to, in 1966.

It takes imagination to reconstruct, but the Venetians designed what is now **Plateía Venizélou**, at the top of 25 Ávgoustou, as a miniature Piazza San Marco. Heráklion's City Hall occupies the Venetian **Loggia** (1628), built as a meeting place for the nobility, and completely reconstructed after being hit in the Battle of Crete. San Marco (**Ag. Márkos**), the first Venetian church on Crete (1239), was twice rebuilt after earthquakes and converted into a mosque. Water dribbles from the lions of the **Morosini Fountain**, commissioned in 1626 by governor Francesco Morosini, who brought water in from Mount Júktas to replace the old wells. Although the fountain is minus its figure of Neptune, the remaining sea nymphs, dolphins and bulls are some of the finest Venetian works left on Crete.

South of Plateía Venizélou, the city's busy outdoor **market** runs along Odós 1866. Several stalls sell dried Cretan wedding cakes – golden wreaths decorated with scrolls and rosettes. Similar forays into the Baroque await at the south end of the market in **Plateía Kornárou**, in the carvings adorning the **Bembo Fountain** (1588), which was cobbled together by the Venetians from ancient fragments; the Turks added the charming kiosk-fountain, or **Koúbes**, now converted into a café, and the Cretans added the sculptures of Erotókritos and Arethoúsa, the heroes of their national epic poem.

 Archaeology Museum

t 281 022 6092; open summer Tues–Sun 8–5, Mon 12–7; winter daily 8.30–5 (Jan 8.30–3); adm; you may go out and return with your date-stamped ticket

The Archaeology Museum

A few blocks east of Plateía Venizélou, north of huge Plateía Eleftherías, Heráklion's Archaeology Museum is an ungainly coffer packed with a treasury of Minoan art. Thanks to local archaeologist Joseph Hadzidákis, a law was passed in the early days of Crete's autonomy stating that every important antiquity found on the island belongs to the museum. The result is dazzling and delightful.

The collection is arranged in chronological order. In **Room I**, containing Neolithic (from 5000 BC) and Pre-Palatial periods (2600–2000 BC), the craftsmanship that would characterize Minoan civilization is already apparent in the delicate golden leaf pendants and bold, irregularly fired red and black Vasiliki ware. Early Cycladic idols and Egyptian seals point to a precocious trade network. **Rooms II** and **III** are devoted to the Old Palace period (2000–1700 BC), when the Minoans made their first polychromatic Kamares ware, marrying form and decoration with stylized motifs from nature and virtuoso 'eggshell-ware' cups. One case displays the Knossós Town Mosaic: faïence plaques of miniature Minoan houses. The mysterious clay **Phaistós Disc** (c. 1700 BC) is the world's first example of moveable type: 45 different symbols, believed to be phonetic ideograms, are stamped on both sides in a spiral.

Items from the Minoans' Golden Age, the New Palace period (1700–1450 BC), are divided geographically in **Rooms IV–IX**. Potters and stone-carvers turned to even freer, more naturalistic designs and stone-carving became more rarefied as the Minoans used porphyries and semi-precious stones. **Room IV** contains some gems: a naturalistic bull's head rhyton carved in black steatite, the leopard axe from Mália, and bare-breasted snake goddess statuettes from Knossós; the draughtsboard in ivory, rock crystal and blue glass paste; and the ivory bull leaper, the first known statue of a freely moving human figure, with muscles and tendons exquisitely carved. **Room V** contains finds from Knossós, including a model of a palace c. 1600 BC. Artefacts from cemeteries fill **Room VI**, where sculptures hint of funerary practices, banquets and dances; an ivory *pyxis* shows a band of men hunting a bull. Goldwork reached its height; on the famous Isopata ring, four ladies dance ecstatically. The Mycenaeans are made to answer for the weapons – the boar-tusk helmets and 'gold-nailed swords' as described by Homer.

Room VII (central Crete) contains the superb gold pendant of two bees depositing a drop of honey in a comb from Mália, and the three steatite vessels from Ag. Triáda, decorated in low reliefs. The contents of **Room VIII** come from Zákros. The stone vases are superb, most notably a rock crystal amphora (it was in over 300 pieces when found) and a rhyton showing a Minoan peak sanctuary, with goats springing all around and birds appearing as an epiphany of the goddess. **Room IX** has items from ordinary Minoan houses. The seal-engravers achieved an astounding technique; the suspicion that they had to use lenses to execute such tiny detail was confirmed when one made of rock crystal was found in Knossós.

After the Golden Age, the Post-Palace period artefacts in **Room X** (1450–1100 BC) show a coarsening Mycenaean influence. Figures lose their *joie de vivre*; goddesses are stiff, their flouncy skirts reduced to smooth bells, their arms invariably lifted, supplicating the fickle heavens. One goddess wears an opium poppy hat; the Minoan use of opium and alcohol may possibly explain the lack of aggression typical of other 'cradles of civilization'.

The Dorians are held responsible for the artistic decline apparent in **Room XI** (1100–900 BC); the quality of the work is poor all round, whether made by pockets of unconquered Minoans or by the invaders. The pieces in **Room XII** show an improvement in the Mature Geometric and Orientalizing periods (900–650 BC), as familiar gods make an appearance: Zeus holding an eagle and thunderbolts on a pot lid, Hermes with sheep and goats on a bronze plaque. Orientalizing pottery shows the Eastern influences that dominated Greek civilization in the 8th–7th centuries BC. Griffons, lions and sphinxes are favourite motifs; one vase shows a pair of lovers, presumed to be Theseus and Ariadne. At the foot of the stairs, **Room XIII** contains Minoan *larnaxes*, or terracotta sarcophagi. Minoans were laid out in a foetal position, so they are quite small. In the Old Palace days they were made of wood; the changeover to clay suggests the Minoans were over-exploiting their forests.

The Frescoes and Ag. Triáda Sarcophagus

Upstairs, **Rooms XIV–XVI** are dedicated to Minoan **frescoes**. Almost as fascinating as the paintings themselves is their reconstruction, often from tiny fragments, by the Swiss father-and-son team hired by Evans. Cretan artists followed Egyptian conventions in colour – women are white, men are red, monkeys are blue – a revelation that led to the re-restoration of *The Saffron Gatherers*, one of the oldest frescoes. From the palace of Knossós, there's the nearly intact *Cup-Bearer* (one of around 350 figures from the Procession fresco), *The Dolphins*, *The Prince of the Lilies*, *The Shields*, and also *The Partridges* found in the 'Caravanserai'. The 'miniature frescoes' in the other two rooms include the *Parisienne*, as she was dubbed in 1903, with her eye-paint, lipstick and 'sacral knot' jauntily tied at the back. The most famous fresco, *The Bull Leapers*, doubled as a calendar (*see* pp.34–5).

Occupying pride of place, the **Ag. Triáda sarcophagus** is a Minoan one-off, made of stone and frescoed with a scenes of sacred rites: a bull is sacrificed while a woman makes an offering on an altar next to a sacred tree with a bird in its branches, the epiphany of the goddess. On the other side, two women bear buckets, perhaps of bull's blood, accompanied by a man in female dress, playing a lyre. On the right, three men are bearing animals and a model boat, which they offer to either a dead man, wrapped up like a mummy, or an idol (*xoanan*), as worshipped at Archánes.

The **Giamalakis collection** (**Room XVII**) contains unique items from all periods, while back downstairs, **Rooms XVIII** and **XIX** display ancient Crete's last breath of inspiration in the bold, severe and powerful 'Daedalic style' from the Archaic period (700–650 BC). There is a frieze of warriors from Priniás and bronze shields and cymbals from the Idean Cave. The bronze figures of Apollo, Artemis and Leto from Dreros are key works: the goddesses are reduced to anthropomorphic pillars, their arms glued to their sides, their hats, jewellery and flounced skirts as plain as a nun's habit. They could be a salt-and-pepper set. Yet the real anticlimax is reserved for **Room XX**, the classical Greek and Graeco-Roman periods (5th century BC –4th century AD), when Crete was reduced to a backwater.

The Cathedral and Byzantine Museum

West of Plateía Venizélou, and south of Kalokairinoú, the over-blown cathedral dedicated to Heráklion's patron, **Ag. Minás** (1895), dwarfs its predecessor. The interior is illuminated by an insanely overdecorated chandelier, the vaults frescoed with stern saints and a ferocious *Pantokrator*. Old Ag. Minás has a beautiful iconostasis and fine icons; that of Ag. Minás on his white horse has long been the protector of Heráklion (martyrologies claim that Minas was a 3rd-century Egyptian soldier, but his cult may also have something to do with a lingering memory of Minos).

Nearby, the sunbleached **Ag. Ekaterína** (1555) was a school linked to the Monastery of St Catherine in the Sinai. El Greco studied icon-painting here before leaving for Venice, and today the church holds a **Museum of Byzantine Icons**. The best are six by Mikális Damaskinós, a contemporary of El Greco who also went to Venice but returned; the use of a gold background and Greek letters are the only Byzantine elements in his *Adoration of the Magi*; in his *Last Supper*, Damaskinós placed a Byzantine Jesus in a setting from an Italian engraving – a bizarre effect heightened by the fact that Christ seems to be holding a hamburger.

Museum of Byzantine Icons
t 281 028 8825; open Mon–Fri 10–1; adm

Other Museums in Heráklion

Chronologically the Historical Museum of Crete picks up where the Archaeology Museum leaves off, with artefacts from Early Christian times. The basement contains delightful 18th-century Turkish frescoes of imaginary towns and a Venetian wall fountain made of tiny jutting ships' prows. On the ground floor are portraits of Cretan revolutionaries and their 'Freedom or Death' flag, and 14th-century murals in a chapel setting, from Kardoulianó Pediádos. Next door hangs the *Imaginary View of Mount Sinai and the Monastery of St Catherine* (c. 1576) by Doménikos Theotokópoulos (El Greco), his only known painting on Crete and one of his few landscapes. Upstairs are portraits of mustachioed Cretan *kapetános* and the reconstructed libraries of Níkos Kazantzákis and Emmanuél Tsouderós, once prime minister of Greece. Other rooms contain

Historical Museum of Crete
Lisimáchou Kalokairinoú, t 281 028 3219; open Mon–Fri 9–3, Sat 9–2; adm

Battle of Crete and Resistance Museum
cnr Doukós Bófor and Hatzidáki Sts, t 281 034 6554; open Mon–Fri 9–3

Natural History Museum of Crete
157 Knossós, t 281 032 4711; open Mon–Fri 9–3, Sun 10–6; adm

a sumptuous array of traditional arts, in particular red embroideries, a noteworthy artistic achievement by Ottoman Cretans.

Behind the Archaeology Museum, the **Battle of Crete and Resistance Museum** houses a fine collection of weapons, photos and uniforms from the war years. Outside the city walls, the **Natural History Museum of Crete** southeast of town is run by the University of Crete and takes a serious look at the flora and fauna of the island, with a botanical garden devoted to plants endemic to Crete.

The Venetian Walls and the Tomb of Kazantzákis

Michele Sammicheli, Venice's great military architect of the 16th century, designed Candia's walls so well that it took the Turks from 1648 to 1667 to breach them. The Venetians tried to rally Europe to the cause of defending Candia as the last Christian outpost in the East, but only received ineffectual aid from the French. Stalemate characterized the first 18 years of the siege; the Sultan found it so frustrating that he banned the mention of Candia in his presence. In 1667 both sides, wanting to end the issue, sent in their most brilliant generals, the Venetian Francesco Morosini (uncle of the Morosini who blew the top off the Parthenon) and the Turk Köprülü. The arrival of Köprülü with 40,000 troops finally triggered the Europeans, but their aid was too little, too late. Morosini negotiated the city's surrender, and, with 20 days of safe conduct, sailed away with most of the Christian inhabitants and the city's archives – an outcome that cost the lives of 30,000 Christians and 137,000 Turks.

Even today Sammicheli's massive walls are nearly as vexing to get on top of today as they were for the besieging Turks – 4km long, in places 13.4m (44ft) thick, punctuated with 12 fort-like bastions. Tunnels have been punched through the old gates, although the **Pórta Chaniá** at the end of Kalokairinoú preserves much of its original appearance. From Plastirá Street, a lane leads up to the **Martinengo Bastion** and the simple **tomb of Níkos Kazantzákis**, who died in 1957 and chose his own epitaph: 'I believe in nothing, I hope for nothing, I am free,' a sentiment repeated on a thousand T-shirts. In the distance note the profile of Zeus in Mount Júktas (*see* p.192).

Beaches around Heráklion

Heráklion is surrounded by sand, and you have a choice of back-drops for your beach idyll: a power plant and cement works at **Ammoudára**, just west, linked by bus 6 from Hotel Astoria in Plateía Elefthería; and, to the east, the airport – from the same Hotel Astoria, bus 7 crawls through the suburbs to the not exceptionally attractive city beach of **Karterós** (7km) and beyond to **Amnisós**, an ancient port of Knossós. It overlooks **Día**, an islet once sacred to Zeus and now a sanctuary for Crete's endangered ibexes, or *kri-kri*, who somehow have learned to cope with the air traffic.

Amnisós has been a busy place since Neolithic times. Idomeneus and his 90 ships sailed for Troy from here; here the north wind kept Odysseus's ship in port. The Minoans must have encountered the same problem, and got around it by loading their ships at a south-facing port on Día. Two other Minoan harbours were on either side of the hill; by the easterly one, a fenced-off villa of 1600 BC yielded the *Fresco of the Lilies*; on the northwest side is an Archaic sanctuary of Zeus Thenatas. In the 1930s, while excavating Amnisós' Minoan 'Harbour Master's Office', Spýridon Marinátos discovered a layer of pumice, the evidence he needed to support his theory that Minoan civilization had been devastated by ash from Santoríni (*see* pp.305–306).

Cave of Eileithyia
ask at the Archaeology Museum in Heráklion if you wish to visit

One km from Amnisós is the Cave of Eileithyia, goddess of fertility and childbirth, daughter of Zeus and Hera. Few divinities enjoyed Eileithyia's staying power; her cave, which was also mentioned by Homer, attracted women from the Neolithic era to the 5th century AD. Stalagmites resembling a mother and her children were the main focus; pregnant women would rub their bellies against a third one, resembling a pregnant belly.

Useful Information in Heráklion

(i) **Heráklion >**
Crete Regional Tourist Office: 1 Xantoulídou,
t 281 022 8203

Tourist police: 10 Dikeosínis St, **t** 281 028 3190. Also see the city website, *www.heraklion-city.gr.*

British Vice Consulate: 16 Papalandroú, **t** 281 022 4012.

Lexis, Evans St. A good bookshop for English titles.

Planet International, at the corner of Kydonías and Chándakos Sts. A wide choice of books in English.

Heráklion Festivals

2–6 June: Heráklion flower festival.
July–mid-Sept: The Heráklion Summer Festival brings in big-league theatre, ballet, opera and traditional music.
25 Aug: Ag. Títos, patron of Crete
11–19 Sept: Grape festival.
11 Nov: Huge *panegýri* for Ag. Minás.

Shopping in Heráklion

The city's **market**, along Odós 1866, is a good bet for edible and drinkable souvenirs, as well as tourist claptrap.

Aerákis, 34 Daedálou. Cretan music and honey and herbs too.

Cretaphone, 6–10 Odós 1821. A wide choice of Cretan music.

Kastrinogianni, Plateía Eleftherías. The best shop for traditional Cretan crafts.

Where to Stay in Heráklion

Heráklion ✉ 71202
Many of the moderate-range hotels are near the port and bus stations.

Atlantis, 2 Igeías (near the Archaeology Museum), **t** 281 022 9103, *www.theatlantishotel.gr* (€€€€€). Luxurious rooms, pool, satellite TV, roof garden and huge breakfast buffet.

Galaxy, 67 Demokratías (just outside the walls to the southeast), **t** 281 023 8812, *www.galaxy-hotel.com.gr* (€€€€€). Contemporary serenity and broadband connections in the rooms. Ask for a room overlooking the pool.

GDM Megaron, 9 Doukós Bofór, **t** 281 030 5300, *www.gdmmegaron.gr* (€€€€€). The latest in the centre of Heráklion, in a totally revamped building from 1925; very swish, with king-size beds and all mod cons.

⭐ **Kyriakos »**

⭐ **Merastri »**

Astoria Capsis, Plateía Eleftherías, t 281 034 3080, *www.astoriacapsis.gr* (€€€€). Smart hotel, with rooftop pool and bar.

Lato, 15 Epimenídou, t 281 022 8103, *www.lato.gr* (€€€€). The city centre's first boutique hotel, with lovely sea views, roof garden, gym, sauna and a Jacuzzi.

Atrion, 9 Chronáki, by the Historical Museum, t 281 024 6000, *www.atrion. gr* (€€€). Beautifully revamped in a cool contemporary style, with broadband.

Minoa Palace, east in Amnisós, t 281 038 0422, *www.akshotels.com* (€€€). A big, fancy beachside complex with a pool, floodlit tennis court, and activities and sports for all ages.

Daedalos, 15 Daedálou, t 281 024 4812 (€€). Plain and modern, convenient for the Archaeology Museum and centre, on a pedestrian-only street.

Ilaira, 1 Ariádnis, t 281 022 7103 (€€). Traditionally decorated rooms with balcony, and a cafeteria roof terrace.

Kris, 2 Doúkos Bófor, t 281 022 3211 (€€). Friendly, with cheerful blue and red colour scheme and well-positioned rooms with fridge/sink.

Lena, 10 Lachaná, t 281 022 3280 (€). Clean, simple rooms on a quiet street west of 25 Ávgoustou.

Rea, 1 Kalimeráki, t 281 022 3638 (€). A good, quiet choice near the sea.

Atlas, 6 Kandanoléontos, t 281 028 8989 (€). A touch of streamlined Art Deco on a pedestrian-only street, although rooms are basic. *Open April–Oct.*

Heraklion Youth Hostel, 5 Výronos, t 281 028 6281 (€). Well-run and convenient.

Camping Creta, at Kókkini Hani, near Gournés, t 281 041 400, and at Goúves, t 289 704 1400.

Eating Out in Heráklion

Head for the car-free haven between Daedálou St and Ag. Títou. The restaurants around the Morosini fountain tend to be rip-offs, but the tavernas along the narrow Fotíou ('Dirty') Lane, between the market and Evans Street, all offer Greek standards at moderate prices.

Elies, 19 Sófokli Venizélou, t 281 030 1448 (€28). Contemporary-styled restaurant with an open kitchen, specializing in refined Cretan recipes, using top ingredients. Great wine cellar.

Kyriakos, 53 Leof. Dimokratías, t 281 022 4649 (€17). A local institution – often packed out for its genuinely delicious Greek cuisine. *Closed Sun.*

Ionia, Evans St, t 281 028 3213. Claims to be the oldest taverna in town, serving some unusual mountain dishes, such as goat with chestnuts and liver with rosemary.

Loukoulous, 5 Korái, t 281 022 4435 (€30). Elegant Mediterranean and Greek restaurant in a beautifully restored mansion; famous for its exquisite *mezédes*.

Merastri, 17 Chrisostómou, t 281 022 1910 (€25). One of the best on Crete: simple but exquisite Cretan cuisine prepared on a wood-burning oven. Good wine list, too.

Odeon, Mirabélou and Adriádnis (behind the Atlantis Hotel), t 281 022 3393 (€25). The former hotel is now a restaurant with over 100 wines and seafood crêpes and tasty meat dishes to eat with them. *Closed Mon.*

Odos Aegaiou, Aegaíou and Spanáki, on the east end of the waterfront, t 281 024 1410 (€35). Fashionable place for a beautifully prepared seafood feast.

Pagopoieio, Plateía Ag. Títou, t 281 034 4028 (€25). Very pretty place, serving a mix of Greek and international dishes.

Entertainment and Nightlife in Heráklion

In summer, the clubs move out to Chersónisos and Ammoudára. Nightspots here that are especially popular include the **New York Bar**, **Camelot Club** and **Status Club**.

Doúkos Bófor Street, in town, above the main bus station, has a whole strip of clubs, including:

Privilege. Summer disco HQ.

Kastro. Cretan music played nightly after 10pm by the island's best *lýra* maestros.

Café Veneto, on Epimenídou. Elegant nightspot with an alluring roof terrace overlooking the port.

Ideion Andron, Korai at Perdikári. For quiet backgammon and drinks.

Knossós (ΚΝΩΣΟΣ)

⭐ **Knossós**
*t 281 023 1940; open
summer daily 8–5;
winter daily 8–3; adm; to
avoid the crowds, arrive
as the gate opens, or
come late in the day*

The weird dream image has come down through the ages: Knossós, the House of the Double Axe, the Labyrinth of Minos. The bull dances, mysteries and archetypes evoke a mythopœic resonance that few places can equal. Thanks to Arthur Evans' reconstructions, rising up against the hill-girded plain, Knossós is now the most visited place in Greece after the Acropolis. Evans' reconstructions are now themselves historical monuments; the work you'll see on the site is reconstructions of reconstructions.

History

The first Neolithic houses on the hill by the river Kairatos date from the 7th millennium BC, or earlier; few Neolithic sites in Europe lie so deeply embedded in the earth. In the 3rd millennium BC, a Minoan Pre-Palace settlement was built over the houses, and *c.* 1950 BC the first palace on Crete was erected on top. After collapsing in an earthquake of 1700 BC, a new, grander palace, the **Labyrinth**, was built on its ruins. 'Labyrinth' is from *labrys*, or 'double axe', a potent symbol that suggests the killing of both the victim and slayer; you'll see them etched in the pillars and walls throughout Knossós. In 1450 BC (but *see* box, p.135). Knossós was again destroyed, this time by fire but unlike the other Minoan palaces it was repaired once more, probably by Mycenaeans, and survived until at least 1380 BC. After a final destruction, the site of the Labyrinth was never built on again; it was considered cursed. Evans noted that the guardians he hired to watch the site heard ghosts moaning in the night.

In the Geometric era, a community near Knossós adopted the venerable name. By the 3rd century BC this new Knossós became Crete's second city after Górtyn and survived until the early Byzantine period. Meanwhile, the ruined palace was slowly buried, but not forgotten; unlike Troy and Mycenae, the site was always known. Cretans would go there to gather sealstones, which they called *galopetres* – 'milkstones' – prized by mothers as amulets to increase their milk. The Labyrinth lay undisturbed until Schliemann's excavations of Troy and Mycenae electrified the world. In 1878, a Heráklion merchant named Mínos Kalokairinós dug the first trenches into the palace of his namesake, at once finding walls, enormous *pithoi* and the first **Linear B tablet**. Schliemann heard the news, and in 1887 negotiated the purchase of the Knossós site. However, the Turkish owners were impossible to deal with and the German gave up in despair, dying in 1890.

The field thus cleared, Evans, then curator of the Ashmolean Museum in Oxford, arrived in Crete in 1894. A student of early forms of writing, he was fascinated by the sealstones and Linear B tablet shown him by Kalokairinós. With dogged persistence, he spent the

Getting to Knossós

Every 10mins a **city bus** (no.2) departs from Heráklion for Knossós, with a stop in Plateía Venizélou.

next five years buying the property with the help of Cretan archaeologist Joseph Hadzadákis, while sending reports of Turkish oppression to British newspapers. His purchase of Knossós coincided with Cretan independence, and in March 1900 he got permission to dig. Evans hired a half-Greek and half-Turkish workforce as a symbol of co-operation, and within the first three weeks they had found the throne room, fresco fragments and the first **Linear A tablets**, belonging to a new civilization that Evans labelled '**Minoan**' for ever after.

In 1908, Evans used his considerable inheritance to embark on his dream, to 'reconstitute' part of Minos' palace. Scholars have long disputed the wisdom (and accuracy) of his reconstructions, sniffing at them as if they were an archaeological theme park; they disagree even more on the purposes Evans assigned to the rooms, along with his interpretation of the Minoans as peaceful, flower-loving sophisticates. Evans' queen's bathroom, for instance, is another man's basin where dead bodies were pickled. No single conjecture seems to cover all the physical evidence, all the myths; the true meaning and use of Knossós may only lie in an epiphany of the imagination.

The Site

Evans' reconstructions result from guesses as good as anyone else's and do succeed in his goal of making Knossós come alive for visitors, evoking the grandeur of a 1,500-room Minoan palace of c.1700 BC that none of the unreconstructed sites can match; a visit here first will make Phaistós and Mália easier to understand. Tours go through so frequently that it's easy to overhear the explanations.

Unlike their contemporaries in the Near East, the Minoans orientated their palaces to the west, not the east, and the modern entrance is still by way of the **West Court**. The three large pits were grain silos, originally protected by domes. A porch on the right from the West Court leads to the **Corridor of the Procession**, named after the fresco in the Heráklion Museum, and to the **Propylon**, or south entrance, with reproductions of original frescoes. A staircase from the Propylon leads to an upper floor, which Evans, inspired by Venetian palaces, called the '**Piano Nobile**' (of all his reconstructions, this is considered the most fanciful). The **Tripartite Shrine**, with its three columns, is a typical feature of Minoan palaces, and may have been used to worship the Goddess in her three aspects as mistress of heaven, earth and the underworld.

A narrow staircase descends to the **Central Court**, measuring 58m (190ft) by 29m (95ft). Originally this was closed in by tall buildings, which may have provided safe seats to view the bull leaping,

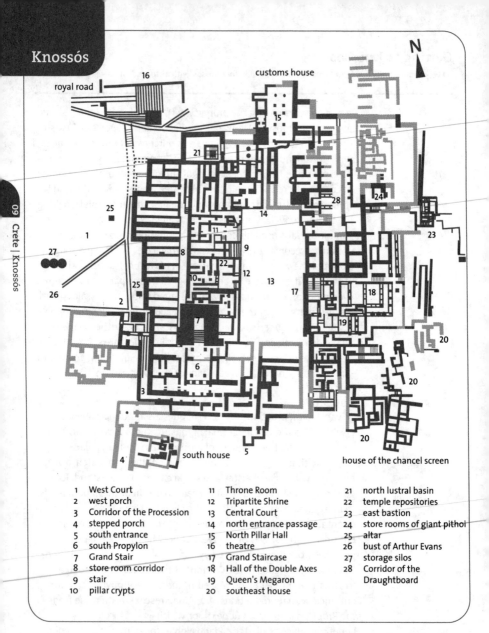

royal road

customs house

16

15

21

25

1

27

26

2

25

8

22

10

11

9

12

13

17

14

28

24

23

18

19

20

20

20

7

6

3

4   south house   5

house of the chancel screen

1	West Court	11	Throne Room	21	north lustral basin
2	west porch	12	Tripartite Shrine	22	temple repositories
3	Corridor of the Procession	13	Central Court	23	east bastion
4	stepped porch	14	north entrance passage	24	store rooms of giant pithoi
5	south entrance	15	North Pillar Hall	25	altar
6	south Propylon	16	theatre	26	bust of Arthur Evans
7	Grand Stair	17	Grand Staircase	27	storage silos
8	store room corridor	18	Hall of the Double Axes	28	Corridor of the
9	stair	19	Queen's Megaron		Draughtboard
10	pillar crypts	20	southeast house		

although, like much in Knossós, this is problematic: how did they lead bulls in through the Labyrinth? How could they squeeze in all the action? Or was the Central Court really Homer's 'Ariadne's dancing floor'? The sacral horns on cornices and altars (one pair, in fragments, stood about a metre (3ft) high) are a universal Minoan symbol; one famous picture even shows a bull with a double axe between its horns. From the Central Court, enter the lower levels of the **West Wing**, site of the tiny **Throne Room**, where Evans uncovered

a scallop-edged stone throne in the same place as it stood 3,800 years ago (judges at the Court of International Justice in The Hague sit on replicas). On either side are gypsum benches and frescoes of griffons, the heraldic escorts of the goddess. The **Lustral Basin** in the Throne Room, like others throughout Knossós, may have held water used in rituals, or reflected light from light wells, or perhaps both. Evans found evidence here of what appeared to be a last-ditch effort to placate the gods as disaster swept through Knossós.

The stair south of the antechamber of the Throne Room ascends to an upper floor, used partly for storage, as in the **Room of the Tall Pithos** and the **Temple Repositories**, where the Snake Goddess statuette was found. The pillars thicken near the top, unique to Minoan architecture and similar to the trunk of the 'horizontal' cypress native to the Gorge of Samariá. Back in the Central Court, note the relief fresco copy of *The Prince of the Lilies* to the south, at the end of the **Corridor of the Procession**.

Evans, who as an Edwardian took monarchies for granted, had no doubt that the more elaborate **East Wing** of the palace contained the **Royal Apartments**. Here the **Grand Staircase** and **Central Light Well** are a dazzling architectural *tour de force*; almost five flights of broad gypsum steps are preserved. However, descending to the two lower floors (which were found intact) it is hard to imagine that anyone of any class would choose to live buried so deep, with little light and air; the proximity of the 'Royal Workshops' would have made them noisy as well. The rooms did have something that modern royals couldn't live without: plumbing. The excellent water and sewer system is visible under the floor in the **Queen's Megaron** and its bathroom, complete with a flush toilet – an amenity that Versailles could scarcely manage. The **King's Megaron**, also known as the **Hall of the Double Axes** from the many carvings on the walls, opens on to the **Hall of the Royal Guard**, decorated with a copy of the fresco of cowhide figure-of-eight shields.

North of the Royal Apartments, the game-board in the Heráklion Museum was found in the **Corridor of the Draughtboard**; here you can see the clay pipes from the Mt Júktas aqueduct. The **Magazines of Giant Pithoi** bring to mind the strange old myth of Minos' young son Glaukos. While wandering in the Labyrinth, the boy climbed up into a *pithos* of honey to steal a taste, but fell in and drowned. The anxious father eventually located his body thanks to his prophet Polyidos. In grief, Minos locked Polyidos in a room with Glaukos' body and ordered him to bring the boy back to life. As Polyidos despaired, a snake came out of a hole in the wall. He killed it, and then watched in amazement as another snake appeared with a herb in its mouth, which it rubbed against its friend and brought it back to life. Polyidos tried the same on Glaukos and revived the boy, but Minos, rather than reward Polyidos, ordered him to teach Glaukos the art of prophecy. Polyidos obeyed, but as he sailed away from Crete, he told the boy to spit in his mouth, so that he forgot everything.

As you leave through the north, there's a relief copy of the bull fresco, and near this the so-called **Customs House**, supported by eight pillars, which may have been used for processing imports and exports. Below is the oldest paved road in Europe, the **Royal Road**, lined with various buildings and ending abruptly at the modern road; originally it continued to the Little Palace and beyond. It ends at the **Theatre** (it looks more like a large stairway), where 500 people could sit to view processions or dances, as pictured in the frescoes.

Around Knossós

Other Minoan buildings lie outside the palace. Nearest are the reconstructed three-storey **South House**, complete with a bathroom and latrine, the **Southeast House**, and the **House of the Chancel Screen**, both perhaps residences of VIPs – the latter has a dais for a throne or altar. Other sites require special permission to visit, such as the **Royal Villa**, with its throne and beautifully preserved **Pillar Crypt**. The **Little Palace**, just across the modern road, had three pillar crypts and was used after the Minoans as a shrine; the magnificent bull's head rhyton was found here.

To the south, a sign on the main road points the way to the **Caravanserai**, as Evans named it, believing travellers would pause here to wash their feet in the stone trough. The walls have a copy of the lovely partridge fresco. Further south are four pillars from the Minoan **aqueduct** that carried water over a stream, and south of that the unique **Royal Temple Tomb**, where the natural rock ceiling was painted blue and a stair leads up to a temple. One controversial find was Peter Warren's 1980 unearthing of the **House of the Sacrificed Children**, named after a cache of children's bones bearing the marks of knives, as if they'd been carved up for supper. The Minoans, having been found guilty of human sacrifice at Archánes (see below), now had cannibalism to answer for. But maybe the children had already died and their bones were stripped of flesh before re-burial – a Greek custom that survived into the 19th century.

South of Knossós: Archánes

One of the ancient proofs of Epimenides' paradox 'All Cretans are liars' was the fact that not only was immortal Zeus born on Crete, but buried here as well; the profile of his bearded face is easily discerned in Mount Júktas as you head south of Knossós. The modern road follows a Minoan highway, and has seen high drama: at the T-junction turn-off for Archánes, Cretan Resistance fighters, led by Major Patrick Leigh Fermor and Captain W. Stanley Moss, kidnapped General Kreipe on 26 April 1944. His car was abandoned on Pánormos Beach with a note saying that it was the work of English commandoes and that civilian reprisals would be against international law. But the Germans were (rightly) convinced that the General was still on Crete and launched a massive search for him.

Well-watered Archánes has often supplied the north; Minoan and Venetian aqueducts began here, the latter ending in Morosini's fountain in Heráklion. Archánes produces wine and table grapes called *rozáki*, and won a prize for its historical preservation. Its church of the **Panagía** has exceptional 16th–19th-century icons; another just south, the **Asómatos**, is decorated with frescoes dated 1315: *The Battle of Jericho, The Sacrifice of Abraham* and *The Punishment of the Damned* are especially good. The **Cretan Historical and Folklore Museum**, 3km from Archánes, has a vast collection of memorabilia from the Battle of Crete, including personal belongings of General Kreipe, and displays on his abduction.

Cretan Historical and Folklore Museum
t 281 075 1853; open Wed–Mon 9.30–5

From the 15th century on, visitors would come up to Archánes, intrigued by the story of Zeus' tomb, but the first hint of something more than stories here had to wait until the early 1900s, when an alabaster ladle inscribed with Linear A was found. In 1922 Evans surmised the existence of a 'summer palace' in Archánes.

Then, in 1964, Ioánnis and Éfi Sakellarákis began excavating what was to become, after Zákros, the biggest Minoan discovery since the war. They found the **palace** in the centre of town, on a site inhabited continuously since 2000 BC (the largest visible section lies between Mákri Sokáki and Ierolóchiton streets). Dating from the New Palace period (*c.* 1700–1450 BC), the walls are very thick, to support one or more storeys; only in Knossós and Phaistós were similar coloured marbles, gypsum and other luxury materials used. It had elaborate frescoes, a drainage system and a large cister. A 'theatrical area', with raised walkways forming the usual triangle, a small *exedra*, horns of consecration and an archive of Linear A tablets were also found. Finds are kept in a small but informative **Archaeological Museum** nearby.

Archaeological Museum
open Wed–Mon 8.30–3; closed Tues; adm

Necropolis of Phourní
t 281 075 1907; closed indefinitely

In Minoan times, a paved road from the palace led to the **necropolis of Phourní**, set on a ridge 1.5km to the southwest. In use for from 2500–1250 BC, this 2ha (five-acre) site is one of the most important in the Mediterranean. One tomb, Tholos A, had (behind a false wall), the remains of a priestess or princess from the 14th century BC, buried in a gold-trimmed garment and surrounded by gold and ivory and the remains of a sacrificed horse and bull, carved into bits. Tholos C, going back to 2500 BC, yielded Cycladic idols and jewellery in the same style as the Treasure of Priam at Troy. Phourní's Mycenaean grave enclosure with seven shaft tombs and three stelae is unique on Crete. Its libation pit (*bothros*), was so saturated with offerings from thousands of years ago that when the Sakellarákis team found it they were overwhelmed by 'the unbearable stench'.

To Piraeus, Thessaloníki, Cyclades

Cape Stavros

Panormos
Bali
Sises
Ag. Pelagia

Stavromenos
Melidoni Cave
Fodele

Viranepiskopi
Perama
Savvathiana Convent
Palaiokastro

Margarites
Ammoudara

Amnatos
Eleftherna
Skavidaras

Moni Arkadi
Axos
Tylisos
HERAKLION

Axos
Anogiá
Tylisos
Knossos

Thronos
Zoniana
Gonies
Sklavokambos

Apostoli
Ag. Fotini
Fourni

Platania
Anemospiliá
Archánes

Amari
Mt. Ida (Psiloritis)
(8057ft/2456m)
Ag. Myronas
Dafnes
Profitis Ilias

Gerakari
Vizari
Idean Cave
Krousonas
Venerato
Mt Juktas
Vathypetro

Mt Kedros
(5829ft/1777m)
Ano-Meros
Kouroutes
Nida Plateau
Ano Asites
Moni Paliani
Choudetsi

Rouvas Forest
Prinias

Nea Kria Vrisi
Apodoulou
Platanes
Kamares Cave
Ryzenia

Kamares
Vorizia
Moni Vrondisi
NOMOS
HERAKLION

Melambes
Moni Valsamonerou
Gergeri
Ag. Varvara
Metaxochori

Saktouria
Ag. Georgios
Ag. Galini
Kamilario
Zaros

Tymbaki
Moni Kalyviani

Kokkinos Pirgos
Ag. Triada
Vori
Ampelouzos
Ag. Deka
Loures

Kalamaki
Phaistos
Mires
Gortyn
Protoria

Kommo
Sivas
Platanos
Geropotamos
Vagonia
Charakas
Pyrgos

Paximathia
Pitsidia

Matala
Loukia

Moni Odgigitrias
Kapetania

Vathi
Moni Koudouma

Kali Limenes
Lendas

Cape Lithino
Gerokambos
Levin

Libyan Sea

Tripartite shrine
*t 281 075 1907;
closed indefinitely*

Five km southwest of Archánes, on the windswept promontory of **Anemospiliá**, the Sakellarákises discovered an isolated **tripartite shrine** in 1979. The middle room contained a pair of clay feet from a *xoanon*, or idol made from wood and other perishable materials; Pausanius wrote that the Greeks believed the first ones were made by Daedalos on Crete. The eastern room was apparently used for bloodless sacrifices. The western room, however, produced a startling find: the bodies of people caught in the sanctuary as a

massive earthquake struck c. 1700 BC. The skeleton of a 17-year-old boy was found bound on an altar, next to a dagger; examination showed that the blood had been drained from his upper body, and that he had probably had his throat cut. The other skeletons belonged to a man wearing an iron ring and a woman who carried sickle cell anaemia. By a fourth skeleton, a precious Kamáres-ware vase was found; it may have been full of the boy's blood, perhaps an offering to appease their god, possibly Poseidon, the Earth-shaker.

The Anemospiliá findings came as a shock. Evans' Minoans seemed too sophisticated for human sacrifices, despite hints in myth – for instance, the tribute of youths to the Minotaur. But perhaps such extreme acts were resorted to only in extraordinary circumstancs, where the sacrifice of one is made in the hope of saving many, in this case from violent earth tremors. Even then, the practice was so disagreeable that it was hidden behind the doors of the shrine.

Vathýpetro

Vathýpetro
open Tues–Sun 8.30–3; adm

Just south of Archánes, the Minoan villa of Vathýpetro is spectacularly set on a spur facing Mount Júktas. In plan it resembles a baby Knossós: it has a small west court and larger central court, a tripartite shrine, and a three-columned portico with a courtyard, closed off by a unique, fancy recessed structure, supported by symmetrical square plinths. Built c. 1580 BC, the villa was shattered by an earthquake only 30 years later. It seems to have been rebuilt as a craft centre; loom weights and potters' wheels were found, along with the oldest wine press in Greece. To this day, winemakers in the area repeat a ritual that may be just as old: a road just before Vathýpetro leads up to a church on Mount Júktas where every 6 August the first fruits of the harvest are offered to the deity. Coincidentally or not, the Minoan peak sanctuary of **Psilí Korfí** is just to the north. This yielded large quantities of votive gifts and bronze double axes. A young Poseidon was one of the gods worshipped here; the mountain was an important navigational landmark.

Around Vathýpetro

The road south of Vathýpetro continues to **Ag. Vasílios** and the **Moní Spiliótissa**, a convent with a frescoed church built into a dim cave; the spring water bubbling out of its foundations was known for its curative properties and was piped into Heráklion by the pashas. It's a pretty walk to the church of **Ag. Ioánnis**, with frescoes dated 1291. Just south, a white road to the west allows you to circle back behind Mount Júktas via **Profítis Ilías**, a village under twin peaks; the Turks called it Kanlí Kastélli, or the Bloody Fortress, after the Castle of Temenos built by Niképhoros Phokás in 961.

Alternatively, turn back east from Ag. Vasílios to Heráklion by way of **Pezá**, Crete's most prestigious wine region, and **Myrtiá**, a village high on a ridge over a majestic sweeping landscape (coming from Heráklion, the turn-off is just before the road to Archánes). Myrtiá's **Kazantzákis Museum** is in the house where the writer's father was born: a DVD documentary, photos, documents, dioramas and memorabilia evoke the life and travels of the father of *Zorba the Greek*. Kazantzákis was 74 when he was nominated one last time for the Nobel Prize (the Church lobbied against him, and he lost by one vote to Albert Camus) and he died shortly after, in October 1957.

Kazantzákis Museum
t 281 074 2451, www.kazantzakis-museum.gr; open Mar–Oct daily 9–7; Nov–Feb ring ahead; adm

Where to Stay and Eat South of Knossós

⭐ Villa Arhanes >>

Archánes ✉ 70100

Archánes has become a trendy place to stay – in the country, but only 15km from Heráklion.

Kalimera Archanes Village, t 281 075 2999, www.archanes-village.com (€€€€). Beautifully renovated village houses filled with antiques, for up to five; you can arrange for a Cretan chef to prepare meals in your kitchen.

Arhontikó, Áno Archánes, t 281 075 2985, www.arhontikoarhanes.gr (€€€). Four apartments in the old school of 1893, each with a fireplace, furnished with antiques, sleeping up to four.

Troullos, Áno Archánes, t 281 075 3153, www.troullos.gr (€€€). Ten stylishly traditional one- and two-bedroom apartments in the village centre, overlooking a courtyard.

Villa Arhanes, t 281 039 0770, www.maris.gr (€€€). Six traditional apartments in a restored farmhouse; pool.

Neraidospilios, t 697 272 0879, www.neraidospilios.gr (€€). The 'Fairy Grottoes' is a new building with three studios and three apartments with rustic furnishings and a small pool.

Orestes, t 281 075 1619 (€). Simple rooms just out of the centre.

Spitiko, in the main square, t 281 075 1591. Delicious hot *mezédes, laderá* and lamb on the spit. *Closed Tues–Sun lunch in winter.*

Lykastos, nearby, t 281 075 2433. Very popular for its excellent Cretan food. *Closed lunch in July and Aug.*

Southwest of Heráklion

The main road southwest of Heráklion to Górtyn, Phaistós and Mátala passes through dense vineyards. **Veneráto** offers the principal reason to stop, with a 2km detour to the serene convent of **Palianí**, home to 50 nuns. Besides early Christian capitals and 13th-century frescoes, Palianí boasts the venerable Holy Myrtle; the nuns claim there's an icon of the Virgin in the heart of the tree and use a pair of ancient capitals for the consecration of bread offerings every 23 September. To the south, the large, straggling village of **Ag. Varvára** stands amid orchards at the geographical centre of the island, and in June shopfronts are festooned with garlands of cherries; a chapel dedicated to the Prophet Elijah sits atop a large rock known as the '*omphalos*', or navel, of Crete. The weather in this area can be dramatic: at **Mégali Vríssi**, to the east, V-39 Vesta windmills, the biggest in Greece, harness the cross-island winds.

A lovely road west of Ag. Varvára skirts the southern flanks of Psilorítis. Nearly all the villages here were once Minoan farming communities, among them **Zarós**, a local beauty spot and source of bottled mineral water. The Romans built an aqueduct from here to Górtyn so they wouldn't have to drink anything else. The leafy **gorge of Zarós** is a good place to bring a picnic: the walk begins at the monastery of **Ag. Nikólaos**. Another monastery to the west, **Vrondísi**, was burned by the Turks in 1821, but still has a pretty gate and a charming 15th-century Venetian fountain and a massive plane tree blasted hollow by lightning and used to house a café kitchen. The 14th-century frescoes in the church are only a shadow of Vrondísi's treasures – in 1800, having had a premonition of its sacking, the abbot sent its finest works, by Michael Damáskinos, to Ag. Kateríni in Heráklion, where they remain. **Moní Valsamonérou**, 5km west, is reached by path from **Vorízia**, a village rebuilt after being obliterated in Nazi reprisals (*locate the guardian before setting off*). Once important, Valsamonérou is now reduced to an enchanting church dedicated to Ag. Fanoúrios, in charge of heaven's lost and found; the exceptional 14th-century frescoes are by Konstantínos Ríkos.

The road continues to **Kamáres**, base for the 3–4hr walk up Mount Ida to the **Kamáres Cave**, an important Minoan cave sanctuary. Its gaping mouth, 20m (66ft) high and 40m (130ft) wide, is visible from Phaistós; pilgrims brought their offerings in the colourful pottery first discovered here – hence the Minoan 'Kamáres ware'.

The Mesará Plain and Górtyn (ΓΟΡΤΥΣ)

Tucked under the southern flanks of Mount Ida, the long densely populated **Mesará Plain** is the breadbasket of Crete. Under the Dorians, **Górtyn** (or Górtys) gradually supplanted Phaistós and then Knossós to become the ruling city of Crete. Hannibal's brief sojourn here in 189 BC after his defeat by Rome may have given the inhabitants some insight into the Big Noise from Italy, because they helped the Romans capture Crete. In reward, Rome made Górtyn the capital of Crete and Cyrenaica, which included much of North Africa. In AD 828 the Saracens wiped it off the map.

In its prime, Górtyn counted 300,000 souls. Its ruins are scattered through a mile of olive groves – only the basilica and Odeon are fenced in. The apse is all that survives of the 6th-century **Basilica of Ag. Títos**, once one of the most important churches in Greece. Titus, originally buried here, was one of Paul's favourite disciples and first bishop of Górtyn. Nearby, built into the walls of the elegant Roman **Odeon** (reconstructed by Trajan in AD 100), is Górtyn's prize, the **Law Code of Górtyn** (*see* box, below), now under a shelter. Just behind the law code is the famous evergreen **Plane Tree of Górtyn**, by the Lethaios River. The story goes that it has kept its leaves for

Górtyn

t 289 203 1144; open daily 8.30–3; adm; if you're arriving by bus, get off at the Górtyn entrance and walk back towards the village of Ag. Déka

Human Rights, Dorian-style

The first block of limestone, discovered in a mill stream in 1857, was purchased by the Louvre. It attracted a good deal of attention. At the time no one had ever seen such an ancient inscription in Greek, and it wasn't until 1878 that this first bit, dealing with adoption, was translated, using the writing on ancient coins as a guide. No one suspected there was more until 1884, when the archaeologist Halbherr noticed a submerged building – the Odeon – while cooling his feet in the same mill stream. The rest of the inscription, over 600 lines on 12 blocks, was found nearby; only the tops of blocks X and XII and a piece of block IX are missing. The law code, written in *boustrophedon*, 'as the ox ploughs' – from left to right, then right to left – is in the Doric dialect of *c.* 500 BC. It is the longest such inscription to survive and, due to it, the civil laws of Archaic Crete are better known in their specific detail than Roman law. The code was made for public display, and significantly, in spite of the ancient Greek class system, which had different rules for citizens, serfs (the native Minoans) and slaves, the Górtyn Code allows women property rights. Slaves had recourse against cruel masters, and there was a presumption of innocence until proven guilty long before this became the core of Anglo-American law.

modesty's sake ever since Zeus in bull disguise brought the Phoenician princess Europa into its shade and had his evil way with her, resulting in the birth of Minos, Rhadamanthys and Sarpedon. An archaeology museum is planned for 2008.

If it's not too hot, consider climbing up the **Acropolis**, with the remains of an 8th-century BC temple and sacrificial altar, Roman walls and a well-preserved defensive building, perhaps built at the expense of the **Theatre**, chewed away in the hillside below. A few minutes' walk down to the **Mitrópolis** reveals an Early Byzantine **church** with a mosaic floor, cut in two by the modern road. The ground is littered with broken tiles. There's a small **Temple of Isis and Serapis**, the Egyptian gods popular in the late Empire, and the elaborate **Temple of Pythian Apollo**, the most important in Górtyn; the inscription is another segment of Górtyn's law code, written in an even older dialect. Most imposing of all is the 2nd-century AD **Praetorium**, seat of the Roman governor; the building continued in use as a monastery until Venetian times. Part of the complex includes the **Nymphaeum**, where the waters from the Zarós aqueduct flowed into the city. Further south are the ruins of the gate, amphitheatre, stadium and cemetery, while the main path leads into the village of **Ag. Déka**, named after ten martyrs of c. AD 250. The block on which they were beheaded is in the church, and their tombs in the chapel are the subject of much devotion.

Lively **Míres**, 9km to the west, is an agricultural town that has taken over Górtyn's role as the capital of the Mesará, and hosts a big farmers' market on Saturdays.

Phaistós (ΦΑΙΣΤΟΣ)

Phaistós
t 289 204 2315; open daily 8–3; adm; arrive early to avoid the crowds

Superbly sited, overlooking the Mesará Plain and Psiloritís, Phaistós was the fief of Minos' brother Rhadamanthys and birthplace of the sage Epimenides. The first palace was constructed here in the Old Palace period, c. 2000 BC, and destroyed in an earthquake in 1700 BC; the second one was destroyed in turn c. 1450 BC. Like Knossós but on a smaller scale, Phaistós was built of alabaster and gypsum. Its workshops produced exquisite art, and yet no frescoes were found. Below the palace, 50,000 people lived and worked, and Minoan villages dependent on the palace were scattered across the Mesará. Phaistós survived as a city-state, warring with Górtyn, until the latter crushed it in the 3rd century BC. Excavations by the Italians, led by Halbherr, began in 1900, just after Evans began digging at Knossós.

Purists dismayed by Evans' reconstructions will breathe a sigh of relief at Phaistós, where only your imagination will reconstruct the three-storey palace from the low, complicated walls and foundations; the fact that much of the second palace was built over the first means that, unless you have an especially good imagination, or opt for a guided tour, you may leave feeling unenlightened. Visits

09

Crete | Southwest of Heráklion

begin in the northwest, in the paved **Upper Court** with its raised **Processional Way**. This continues down the steps into the **West Court**, originally part of the Old Palace – the only section the New Palace architects re-used after the earthquake, when the lines of the building were otherwise completely reorientated; the lower façade of the Old Palace survives just before the Grand Stairway. The West Court has the eight straight tiers known as the **Theatre**, where people may have watched performances, and two circular granaries or silos, originally protected by domes.

The **Grand Stairway** was carved with special care, partly from stone and partly from the living rock; note how the steps are slightly convex, to allow rainwater to run off quickly. At the top, the **Great Propylon**, the main entrance to the **West Wing**, stands just before a light-well with three columns. Another stair descends to the **Antechamber of the Store Rooms**, where Halbherr found a huge cache of sealstones, while beyond are the **Store Rooms**; one, covered with a roof, still contains its giant *pithoi*, along with a stone stool for standing on to scoop out the contents, and a built-in vessel in the floor to collect wine or oil run-offs. An important corridor separated the storage areas from the main **Shrine**, lined with stone benches.

From the Antechamber of the Store Rooms opens the **Central Court**, its long sides originally sheltered by porticoes; buildings on all

to tourist
pavilion

N

Central
Court

1 Upper Court
2 stair (entrance)
3 West Court
4 theatre
5 Grand Stairway
6 shrine
7 entrance to old palace

8 Great Propylon
9 store rooms
10 corridors
11 entrance to north wing
12 court
13 royal apartments
14 east wing (prince's) apartments
15 lustral basin
16 metal furnace from old palace
17 south entrance
18 archives
19 Peristyle House
20 antechamber of the store room
21 Classical Temple
22 granaries

Phaistós

sides would have hidden the tremendous vistas it enjoys today. A stepped block in the northwest corner may have been the platform used by bull dancers as a springboard for 'diving leaps'. To the southwest is a series of rooms fenced off and mingled with bits of the Old Palace and a Classical-era temple. Landslides have swept away the **East Wing**, but the chamber just to the north, a bathroom and a gypsum-paved **lustral basin** with steps, earned it the name of '**Prince's Apartment**'. A horseshoe-shaped **Forge** from the Old Palace era is at the end of the corridor to the north.

North of the Central Court, a grand entrance with niches in the walls and another corridor leads to more **Royal Apartments**, paved with delicate alabaster and gypsum and now fenced off; you can barely make out the **Queen's Megaron**, furnished with alabaster benches. An open peristyle court tops the **King's Megaron**, which once must have offered a royal view to the Kamáres cave sanctuary (that dark patch between the twin summits). The famous Phaistós Disc was found east of here, with pottery from 1700 BC.

The 'Summer Villa' of Ag. Triáda (ΑΓ. ΤΡΙΑΔΑ)

Ag. Triáda
*t 289 209 1360;
open Tues–Sun
8.30–3; adm*

Just 3km west of Phaistós is this smaller Minoan palace, named after a Venetian church on the site. No one knows why such a lavish little estate was built so close to Phaistós. Perhaps a wealthy Minoan fell in love with the setting, or it may have been a summer palace; Phaistós can turn into a frying pan in the summer and Ag. Triáda usually has a sea breeze. It's certainly old; Neolithic tombs were discovered under the 'palace', built *c.* 1600 BC. It burned in the destruction of 1450 BC. The Minoans rebuilt it and the Mycenaeans added a *megaron* over the top and a village, dominated by a building that looks like a *stoa* – a row of shops under a porch – 1,000 years before they were invented. The site yielded the finest art, including frescoes, the Harvesters' Vase and the Sarcophagus of Ag. Triáda, all in the Heráklion museum. The intimate scale and setting – and lack of tour groups – make Ag. Tríada the most charming of the major Minoan sites. The villa had two wings. The north–south wing, overlooking the sea, was the most elaborate, with flagstone floors, and gypsum and alabaster walls and benches. One room had frescoes (the stalking cat), another had built-in closets. *Pithoi* still stand intact in the store rooms. At the entrance, **Ag. Geórgios Galatás** (1302) has good frescoes (*the guardian has the key*).

⭐ **Votomos >>**

Where to Stay and Eat Southwest of Heráklion

Zarós ✉ 70002

Idi, t 289 403 1302, *www.votomos.com* (€€). Pretty mountain hotel, with a verdant garden surrounding pools.

Votomos, **t** 289 403 1666. With lovely views of the valley. Fresh salmon and trout, served with delicious rice, hold pride of place on the menu.

Limni, t 289 403 1338. By Votomou Lake, serving all the classics of Cretan cuisine.

Around the Southwest Coast

This corner offers more than the exquisite fossils of long-lost civilizations. North of Phaistós, the old village of **Vóri** on the road to Ag. Galíni boasts the superb **Museum of Cretan Ethnology**, the best place to learn about traditional Cretan life – a civilization not yet lost, if in danger of extinction – with excellent detailed descriptions in English. Charmless **Tymbáki**, 3km west, combines tomatoes under plastic and dogged tourism, thanks to its long, ugly beach **Kókkinos Pírgos** ('red tower'), a name that predates its career as the Ketchup Coast. Elsewhere, this is a wild shore, which only here and there permits roads to descend to the sea. One south of Phaistós leads to **Mátala**, the lovely beach enclosed by sandstone cliffs riddled with tombs from the 1st and 2nd centuries AD. Over the centuries the locals enlarged the tombs into cosy little rooms, and in the early 1960s Americans bumming around Europe found that the caves made a perfect place to crash in the winter; before long Mátala was an international hippy colony. In the killjoy 1990s, the impecunious hippies were banished for the hard currency of package tourism. If the beach is a body jam, a 20-minute scramble over the rocks will take you to Mátala's second beach, **Kókkinos Ámmos**, 'red sand', with caves; excursion boats sail south to other small beaches at **Ag. Farágo** and **Vathí**. Avoid walking on the beaches on summer nights, when loggerhead turtles make their nests.

Mátala has been a midwife of tourism for **Pitsídia**, and more recently for **Kalamáki**, down by the long beach north of Mátala. **Kómmo**, at the south end of Kalamáki (most easily reached from Pitsídia), has the substantial remains of a large Minoan port – a massive building of dressed stone (probably a warehouse), dry docks with five slips and a paved road with worn ruts that led to Phaistós. Near the beach stood an important sanctuary, sacred long after the Minoans: the Dorians built a temple here in the 10th century BC, as did the Phoenicians, and the Classical and Hellenistic-era Greeks.

Phaistós' rival Górtyn had ports to the east, including **Kalí Liménes**, the 'Fair Havens', a steep, winding drive by way of Sívas. This is where the ship carrying St Paul put in on its way to be wrecked off Malta. Unlike its neighbours, Kalí Liménes has kept pace with the times; instead of saints, the 'Fair Havens' now host oil tankers. The ruins of another of Górtyn's harbours, **Levín** (or Lebena), lie near the ramshackle fishing village of **Léndas**, most easily reached from Górtyn. The natural hot springs east of the village (pumped elsewhere) led to the construction in the 4th century BC of an **Asklepeion**; there are mosaics, bits of a temple, and a pool where patients used to wallow. Nearly all the wallowing in Léndas these days happens 3km west at **Gerókambos**, a magnificent long beach where clothes are optional and a few tavernas rent rooms.

Museum of Cretan Ethnology
t 289 209 1392; open daily 10–6; adm

Where to Stay and Eat on the Southwest Coast

Mátala ✉ 70200

At Easter it's nearly impossible to find a room as many Greeks come down for their first swim of the year.

Valley Village, on the village edge, t 289 204 5776, *www.valleyvillage.gr* (€€–€; *7-day minimum stay in high season*). Family-run, with a pool, Greek dancing shows and barbecue nights.

Zafira, t 289 204 5112 (€€). Handy for town and beach, and reasonably priced, although completely booked by German tour operators in season.

Nikos, t 289 204 5375 (€). A pleasant choice with a little garden.

Mátala Camping, just behind the beach, t 289 204 5720. Offering plenty of shade and low prices.

Syrtaki. Has centre spot in the row of seaside tavernas and serves all the Greek favourites at reasonable prices.

Southeast of Heráklion to the Coast

Southeast of Heráklion, **Pediáda** is a pretty region of foothills under Mount Díkti. Hidden away just north of **Kastélli**, the largest village, signs for 'Paradise Tavern' point the way to lovely **Ag. Pandeleímonos**, under huge plane trees by a spring, built in AD 450 over a temple to Asklepeios. The church is said to have had 101 doors, but after being ravaged by the Saracens it was rebuilt on a more modest scale c. 1100. The bell is made out of a German shell and, inside, the nave is supported by marble columns from ancient Lyttos, including one made of nothing but Corinthian capitals.

Ag. Pandeleímonos
the taverna owners will summon the caretakers

A short detour west of Kastélli to **Sklaverochóri** has its reward in the 15th-century church **Eisódia tis Theotókou**, decorated with excellent frescoes. Four km east of Kastélli, **ancient Lyttos** (modern Xidás) was a fierce rival of Knossós after the Minoans and remained sufficiently wealthy to mint its own coins until 220 BC, when Knossós, allied with Górtyn, demolished it while Lyttos' army went to attack Ierapetra. The site is just beginning to be investigated: besides views, you can see walls, a theatre and a frescoed church.

Potters in **Thrapsanó**, 8km southwest, have made *pithoi* for centuries, using the same technique as the Minoans. **Arkalochóri**, just south, hosts a large Saturday farm fair. In 1932, Marinátos and Pláton excavated the village's **sacred cave** and found Minoan ritual weapons: the longest prehistoric Greek bronze sword and bronze axes, one engraved with Linear A, the other with symbols similar to those on the Phaistós Disc – proving that the disc was not a forgery.

Further south at **Mártha** you can turn west for Górtyn or continue south to **Áno Viánnos**, hanging on the flanks of Mount Díkti. Inhabited since early Minoan times, it founded a colony (Vienne) on the Rhône – the main route to the tin mines of Britain. Áno Viánnos was a citadel of resistance against the Turks and then against the Germans. On the acropolis are the ruins of a Venetian castle and Turkish tower; lower down, the 14th-century church of Ag. Geórgios stands near the incredible ancient, massive plane tree.

Two km west, near **Káto Viánnos**, a road to the coast descends by way of Chóndros to **Keratókambos**, an attractive fishing village that was especially well defended: this was the beachhead used by the Saracens to invade Crete in 823, and to make sure it wouldn't happen again the Venetians built a fort and another one to the east. A rough coastal road links Keratókambos to **Árvi**, but the road down from Amirás east of Áno Viánnos is easier; the landmark here is a monument to the 600 Cretans killed by the Nazis in September 1943. Set in the cliffs, Árvi is enclosed in its own little world, at the head of a valley of banana plantations. It has good pebble beaches and a monastery built on the foundations of a temple to Zeus.

The main road continues east, passing **Áno Sími**, base for a trek up the mountain to the ruins of three terraces and an altar dedicated to Aphrodite and Hermes which remained in use from 1600 BC and AD 300. Beyond, the road descends towards the oasis of Mýrtos.

Heráklion's East Coast: Chersónisos and Mália

East of Heráklion and Amnisós (*see* p.185), Europa, once raped on the island by Zeus, gets her revenge on Crete. Yet there are a couple of reasons to put on the brakes. At **Vathianó Kambó**, by the Hotel Demetrato, there's a well-preserved Minoan villa, **Nírou Cháni** or the **House of the High Priest**, where a trove of 40 tripods and double axes was found. It has two paved courts with stone benches, perhaps used in ceremonies. At **Goúves**, signs point the way to **Skotinó** and the path to the enormous cave of Skotinó. The cave has a 55m (180ft)-high ballroom lit by sun pouring through the cave mouth, with a stalagmite mass in the centre. A huge amount of Minoan cult activity took place in the low-ceilinged chambers at the back, around natural altars and formations like the 'head of Zeus'.

Nírou Cháni
t 289 707 6110; open Tues–Sun 8.30–3

Further east, **Chersónisos** (Liménas Chersonísou) is Crete's biggest package ghetto, complete with aquaparks, video game parlours, and a Cretan 'museum village', an unfathomable collision of theme-park kitsch and ethno-environmental high seriousness called the **Lychnostatis Museum**. Chersónisos was the port of ancient Lyttos and had a famous temple to Britomartis Artemis. Little remains of its ancient glories: a reconstructed Roman fountain by the beach, a Roman aqueduct (inland at Xerokámares) and, to the west, overlooking the harbour, the ruins of a 5th-century basilica.

Lychnostatis Museum
t 289 702 3660; open Sun–Fri 9–2; multilingual guided tour; adm

Mália (ΜΑΛΙΑ)

East of Chersónisos, in the centre of a wide sandy bay, Mália is the garish party centre of Crete, with bars and clubs all along the beach road. But there is an older, wiser village inland, and the

Minoan Palace of Mália

t 289 703 159; open Tues–Sun 8.30–3; adm

Minoan Palace of Mália, 3km east (*buses to Ag. Nikólaos will drop you nearby*). The legendary fief of Minos' brother Sarpedon, Mália controlled the fertile coastal plain under the Lassíthi mountains. Its history follows that of Knossós: inhabited in the Neolithic era, the first palace was built in 1900 BC. Devastated by the earthquake 200 years later, another palace was built on top, then ruined in the catastrophe traditionally dated 1450 BC. Compared to Knossós and Phaistós, Mália is 'provincial': built from local stone rather than alabaster, marble and gypsum, and without frescoes. However, the lack of later constructions makes it easy to understand.

Entrance is by way of the **West Court**, crossed by the usual raised flagstones of the **Processional Way**. Eight grain 'silos', originally covered with beehive domes (similar ones have been found in Egypt), are at the south end. The **Central Court**, re-used from the Old Palace, had galleries to the north and east; in the middle are the supports of a hollow altar, or sacrificial pit. A **Grand Stairway** led up into the **West Wing**, which may have had a ritual role: the raised **Loggia**, possibly used for ceremonies, is near a mysterious round stone stuck in the ground. The **Treasury**, behind it, yielded a sword with a rock crystal pommel and a stone axe shaped like a pouncing panther. The **Pillar Crypt** has a variety of symbols (double axes, stars and tridents) carved in its square pillars. The four broad steps here may have been 'theatre' tiers, while in the southwest corner is a limestone wheel of an altar with a hollow in the centre and 34 smaller hollows around the sides that looks exactly like the *kernos* used in Classical times; perhaps the Minoans originated the rite of *panspermia*, or offering of the first fruits to the deity.

A portico of square stone pillars and round wooden columns ran along the east side of the Central Court. The narrow **store rooms** of the **East Wing** (protected by a roof) are equipped with drainage channels from the first palace. North of the centre, the **Pillar Hall** is the largest room in the palace; the chamber above it, reached by the surviving stair, may have been for banquets. Behind it is another pillar room, and the **Oblique Room**, its orientation suggesting some kind of astronomical observation. A suite of **Royal Apartments**, with a sunken lustral basin, are in the northwest corner. Linear A tablets were found in the **Archive Room**. A paved road leads north to the **Hypostyle Crypt**; no one has any idea what went on here.

If Mália seems rather poor next to Knossós and Phaistós, the Minoan estates found in the outskirts were sumptuous, especially to the northeast, where Mália's only fresco was found. In the cemetery, the **Chrysolakkos tomb** may have been the family vault of Mália's rulers; although the 'gold pit' was looted, the French found the magnificent twin bee pendant inside. Stylistic similarities suggest the Aegina Treasure in the British Museum was pillaged from here in antiquity.

(i) **Chersónisos >**
Giaboúdaki St

Where to Stay and Eat on the East Coast

Chersónisos (Liménas Chersonísou) ✉ 70014

Huge all-inclusive package playgrounds rule the roost here; the **tourist office** will do its best to help if you want to stay in the real world.

Creta Maris, t 289 702 7000, *www. maris.gr* (€€€€€). One of a dozen similar – sports, six bars, kindergarten, open-air cinema, spa and thalassotherapy and even bowling alleys.

Katrin, t 289 703 2137 (€€). The pick of this category, with three pools.

Caravan Camping, t 289 702 2025. Plenty of shade.

Ta Petrina, Áno Chersónisos, **t** 289 702 1976 (€20). The best in the area: courtyard dining, with tasty meat and home-grown vegetarian dishes.

Artemis, t 289 703 2131, by the beach in Stalída. Greek and Cretan specialities.

Kavouri, Archéou Théatro, Chersónisos (€12). Jolly, and above-average cooking.

After dinner, everyone gathers in the bars and clubs around El. Venizélou St.

Mália ✉ 70007

Alexander Beach, t 289 703 2124, *aegeon1@otenet.gr* (€€€–€€). A recently built complex, a stone's throw from the beach, with a pool, tennis and sports.

Ermioni, in Mália proper, **t** 289 703 1093 (€). A blessing for budget travellers.

Ibiscus, just along the main road, **t** 289 703 1313 (€). Has a pool.

Kalesma, 8 Omírou, **t** 289 703 3125. A *mezedopoleío* in a stone house serving all kinds of titbits, one of several good, reasonably priced tavernas in the old village (Paliá Mália), far from the cacophony along the beach road.

Apolafsi and **Kalimera** are also good.

Nomós Lassíthi (ΛΑΣΙΘΙ)

Crete's easternmost province, Lassíthi (from the Greek mispronunciation of the Venetian La Sitía) doesn't have the towering peaks that dominate the rest of Crete (although Díkti isn't a peewee at 2148m/7,027ft), but it manages to be the big island's most varied province, framed in the west by a plateau hanging in the clouds, planted with apple orchards and wheat, while its east coast ends at Vaï's palm-lined beach. Ag. Nikólaos, set in the Gulf of Mirabélo, is the most cosmopolitan of Crete's four capitals, with the island's top luxury hotels. But traditional Crete awaits a few miles inland.

Lassíthi was densely populated in Minoan times: if the unplundered palace of Zákros is the most spectacular find, town sites such as Gourniá, Palaíkastro, Vasilikí, Fournoú Korifí and Móchlos have provided important clues about everyday Minoan life. Sitía is a delightful provincial town. Lassíthians tend to be gentler than other Cretans, and claim to be the best lovers; other Cretans grant them only superlative potatoes and pigs.

The Plateau of Lassíthi and the Birthplace of Zeus

A parade of tour buses makes the ascent to the spectacular Plateau of Lassíthi, one of the high points of Crete both in altitude and atmosphere; although accommodation is paltry, you may want

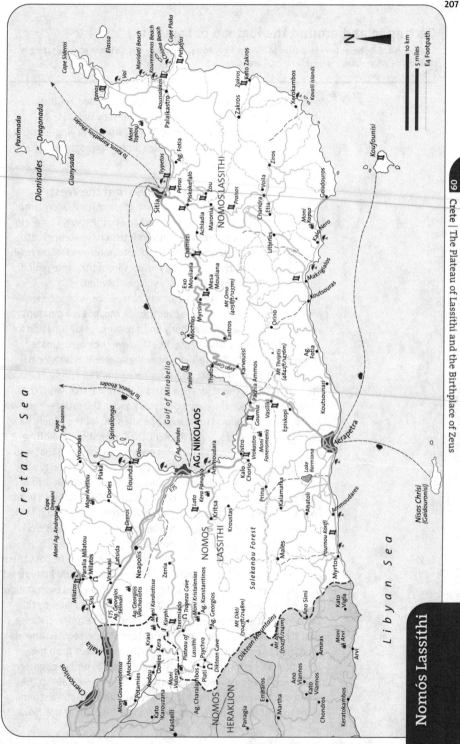

Nomós Lassíthi

Getting to and around the Plateau of Lassíthi

One or two daily **buses** from Heráklion, Mália and Ag. Nikólaos wind their way up to the plateau, taking in most of the villages and ending up at the Díktean Cave.

to spend more time there after the groups have gone. For it is unique: a green carpet hemmed in on all sides by the Díktean Mountains, snowcapped into April. The uncanny cave where Zeus was born is the chief attraction, while Karphí, a Minoan last refuge, is just as weird, but harder to reach.

The Lassíthi Plateau: Approaches from the West

There are two roads up from the coast. The one from Chersónisos passes a series of old villages; above **Potamiés**, the lovely cruciform church at the abandoned **Moní Gouverniótissa** has excellent 14th-century frescoes, including a powerful Pantocrator who stares holes into sinners (key at the *kafeneíon*). Frescoes from the same period decorate **Ag. Antónios** in the pretty village of **Avdoú**.

The other road from **Stalída**, east of Chersónisos, is far steeper. After 8.5km of bird's-eye views over the sea, **Mochós** is a pleasant antidote to the coastal cacophony and a pilgrimage destination for Swedish tourists, who know Mochós through their assassinated prime minister Olaf Palme; his summer residence is now a local shrine. Further south, **Krási** is famous for its curative spring. Perhaps the best advertisement for the waters is the plane tree, which has thrived on them for the past 2,000 years and in the 19th century had a café inside its hollow trunk; today people stop for the superb country Taverna Karés. In nearby **Kerá**, the **Convent of Kardiótissa** was founded in the 1100s and contains a miraculous icon that was twice carried off by the Turks to Constantinople but made its way home; the third time the Turks chained it to a column, but it flew back to Crete with column and chain attached. The column is in the courtyard, while the chain, hanging on the iconostasis, is said to relieve pain if wrapped around the body. During restoration work, beautiful 14th-century frescoes were discovered.

Beyond the stone windmills, the road finally reaches the pass then descends into the strange and dreamlike bowl of **Lassíthi Plateau** set in barren mountains. An emerald chequerboard divided by irrigation ditches, the plateau was farmed by the Minoans, and later by the Dorians of Lyttos. However, in 1293 it was such a nest of resistance that the Venetians demolished the villages and persecuted anyone who tried to return. Only in 1543 were Greek refugees from the Peloponnese permitted to resettle the plateau; Venetian engineers built 10,000 white-sailed irrigation windmills to re-establish the orchards and farms. In the 1970s the windmills were still a stunning sight to behold, filmed by Werner Herzog in his *Signs of Life*. Now sadly all but a few have become derelict in favour of the more reliable petrol pump.

Eighteen villages dot the plateau's circumference. The largest, **Tzermiádon**, is near a sacred Minoan cave and peak sanctuary. The cave, **Trápeza**, was used from 5000 BC; long before the first temples, Cretans left ivory votive offerings in the *penumbra* behind its narrow opening; the Middle Minoans used it for burials. The loftiest of all Minoan peak sanctuaries (1,158m/3,800ft) is an hour's walk up a strenuous path: **Karphí**, the 'nail', an accurate description of its mountain. Excavated by John Pendlebury between 1937 and 1939 – his last project before he was killed in the Battle of Crete – Karphí was the refuge of some 3,000 Minoans, or Eteocretans fleeing the Dorian invaders in 1100 BC. For a century they tried to keep the fires of their civilization burning, before the harsh winters got to them. In this mighty setting, Pendlebury found 150 small houses, a temple, a chieftain's house, a tower and barracks, and a shrine that contained five of the very last Minoan clay goddesses (*c.*1050 BC, now in the Heráklion Museum), distorted and a metre (3ft) tall, with cylinder skirts, detachable feet and long necks, resembling Alice in Wonderland when she was mistaken for a serpent.

Clockwise from Tzermiádon, **Ag. Konstantínos** has the most souvenir shops on the plateau, while just above it the 13th-century **Moní Kristalénias** enjoys a lovely panoramic spot. In **Ag. Geórgios**, the next village, a 200-year-old farmhouse contains a **Folk Museum**, including a wine-press that doubled as a bed; it also has a fascinating collection of photos of Níkos Kazantzákis.

Folk Museum
open June–Aug 10–4

Psychró and the Díktean Cave

Díktean Cave
t 284 403 1316; open daily 8–7; adm

Psychró, to the southwest, is the base for visiting the **Díktean Cave**, the birthplace of Zeus. From the car park it's a 1km ascent up a rocky path; sure-footed donkeys are available, while local guides at the entrance hire out lanterns. Rubber-soled shoes are important; the descent is slippery and a bit dangerous, especially for the elderly.

If you get there before or after the groups, the cave is an other-worldly place worthy of myth. Rediscovered in the 1880s, it contained cult items from Middle Minoan up to Archaic times; its role as the birthplace and hiding place of Zeus from his cannibal father Cronos was confirmed by the discovery in Paleókastro of an inscription of the *Hymn of the Kouretes* (the young men who banged their shields to drown out the baby's cries). Down in the cave's bowels the guides point out formations that, if you squint, resemble the baby god, his cradle and the place where the goat Amaltheia nursed him; to help conceal the birth, Rhea, his mother, spurted her own breast milk into the heavens, creating the Milky Way. Tradition has it that Minos came up here to receive the Law of Zeus every nine years, and that Epimenides the Sage lived in the cave as a hermit, having visions.

Lasinthos >>

Where to Stay and Eat on the Lassíthi Plateau

Avdoú ✉ 75005
Villa Avdoú, t 281 030 0540, *www.avdou.com* (€€€). Well-appointed studios and villas with Internet access on an organic farm, on the road up to the plateau. They organize paragliding and riding excursions.

Tzermiádon ✉ 72052
Argoylias, t 284 402 2754, *www.argoulias.gr* (€€). New stone guesthouse with views and a restaurant.

Kourites, t 284 402 2194 (€). A pleasant place to stay. *Open all year.*

Lassithi, t 284 402 2194 (€). Owned by the same family as the Kourites, with a restaurant. *Open all year.*

Ag. Geórgios ✉ 72052
Lasinthos, t 284 402 9101, *www.lasinthos.gr* (€€). Traditional guest house in an ecological park with an organic garden, source of the ingredients in the excellent restaurant.

Rhea, t 284 403 1209 (€).

Psychró
Dikteon Andron, t 284 403 1504 (€).

Zeus, t 284 403 1284 (€).

Sísi ✉ 72400
Hellenic Palace, west end of the village, **t** 284 107 1502, *www.hellenicpalace.gr* (€€€). Stylish, modern and comfortable, near the local riding centre.

Zygos Apartments, t 284 107 1279 (€€). Reasonable choice with kitchenettes.

Angela, t 284 107 1176 (€€). With pool and bar.

Between Mália and Ag. Nikólaos

After Mália, the New Road cuts inland, avoiding rugged Cape Ag. Ioánnis. This is good news for Sísi and Milátos, free of the heavy traffic that bedevils the coastal resorts to the west. Laid-back **Sísi** resembles a chunk of southern California, with its modern pastel architecture, sandy beaches and little port – a turquoise *crique* under the cliffs, lined with a palm garden and a cascade of tavernas.

Paralía Milátou is just the opposite: low-key and a bit dumpy. Yet ancient Milatos was one of the most important cities of Homeric Crete. In myth, Minos, Rhadamanthys and Sarpedon once competed for the favours of a beautiful boy. When the boy chose Sarpedon, his brothers were such poor losers that Sarpedon moved to Asia Minor, taking with him not only the boy but the inhabitants of Milatos, where they founded the great city of Miletus. The dusty old village still wears a forsaken air, but has another reason to look forlorn as well. In 1823, during the War of Independence, the large stalactite **Cave of Milátos** on the edge of a wild ravine served as a refuge for 3,600 people. The Turks forced the Greeks to surrender and, in spite of promising them safe conduct, all the men and children were massacred and the women enslaved. Inside the cave is a chapel containing a glass reliquary full of bones.

Cave of Milátos
6km drive from the beach then a 10-minute walk from the car park

Neápolis (ΝΕΑΠΟΛΙΣ) and Ancient Dreros

Immersed in almond groves, **Neápolis** is the largest town on the Heráklion–Ag. Nikólaos road. In its former incarnation as Karés, it was the birthplace of Pétros Fílagros in 1340. Raised by Catholics, he became a professor of theology and was elected Pope Alexander V in

Neápolis museum
temporarily closed,
t 284 202 8721

Dreros
cross under the New
Road and follow signs
for Kouroúnes; from
the parking area,
a rough path leads
up to a saddle
between two peaks

1409, one of several popes-for-a-year during the Great Schism. Karés predeceased him, when the Venetians destroyed it in 1347 after a revolt. The rebuilt village grew into the 'new town', Neápolis, the provincial capital before Ag. Nikólaos. It has a leafy central square and a small **museum** housing traditional crafts and finds from **Dreros**, a wild place a few miles north. There's an Archaic agora and a 7th-century BC Geometric Temple to Apollo Delphinios; the latter yielded the oldest hammered bronze statues ever found in Greece (now in the Heráklion Museum) and Eteocretan inscriptions – Minoan words in Greek letters.

Ag. Nikólaos (ΑΓ. ΝΙΚΟΛΑΟΣ)

When Ag. Nikólaos was selected capital of *nomós* Lassíthi in 1905, only 95 people lived in the village, beautifully set in an amphitheatre overlooking a round lake and the breathtaking Gulf of Mirabélo. It didn't have a proper port; ships had to call at Pachiá Ámmos to the east. A new port in 1965 attracted the first yachties, and what has happened since is not exactly hard to guess: the resident population of 'Agnik' has multiplied by 100. Today the little city and neighbouring Eloúnda host some of the swishest hotels and villas and best restaurants in all Greece.

Ag. Nikólaos was ancient Lato Pros Kamara, the port of ancient Lato. The busy seafront overlooks the islet of **Ag. Pándes** with a chapel and *kri-kri*, the only inhabitants. Just inland, **Lake Voulisméni**, the 'bottomless' (although it has been measured at 64m/210ft) was often stagnant until 1867, when the local pasha connected it to the sea. Fish fattened by bread from the surrounding restaurants appear later on their menus. Behind the tourist office, there's a small but choice **Folk Art Museum**, with icons, embroideries, instruments and stamps. Aktí S. Koundoúrou follows the waterfront past rocky swimming places to a beach and the little stone church that gave the town its name, **Ag. Nikólaos**, with rare 9th-century frescoes from the Iconoclastic period (*key at the Minos Palace Hotel*).

Folk Art Museum
t 284 102 5093; open
Sun–Fri 10–4; adm

Archaeology Museum
68 K. Paleológou,
t 284 102 2382; open
Tues–Sun 8.30–3; adm

Up the hill, the **Archaeology Museum** displays artefacts from eastern Crete: a Neolithic idol from Zákros, the Early Minoan pinhead chicken-like 'Goddess of Mýrtos', jewellery from Móchlos, a stone vase from Mália in the form of a triton shell, engraved with demons making a libation, a Daedalic bust from the 7th century BC that looks like Christopher Columbus. In the last room, a 1st-century AD skull has a fine set of teeth, a gold burial wreath embedded in the bone of its brow, a silver coin from Polyrenia (to pay Charon, the ferryman), and a plate of knucklebones, perhaps used for divination.

For all its fame, Agnik was asleep when God was handing out beaches: there's a little sand at shingly **Kitroplateía**, sheltered and safe for children, named after the cypress wood once exported from

Getting to and around Ag. Nikólaos

The **Olympic Airways** office is at Plastíra 20, **t** 284 102 2033 (but the airport is at Sitía; *see* below).

There are 2 **ferries** a week to Piraeus via Sitía, 2 to Santorini and Mílos, and at least one a week to Rhodes, Kássos and Kárpathos. In summer there are also **Flying Dolphins** to Santoríni and other Cyclades, and one-day **excursion cruises** to Santoríni. **Port authority: t** 284 102 2312.

The **bus station** (**t** 284 102 2234 or 8284) is near the beach of Ámmos at the end of Sof. Venizélou. Beaches within easy bus range are Eloúnda and Kaló Chorió (on the road to Sitía). For **taxis**, **t** 284 102 4102, 2281 or 8770.

here. The pocket-sized sand beach of **Ammoudára** is at the end of Aktí S. Koundoúrou, while at the other end of town, near the bus station, sandy **Ámmos** is clean, but not terribly atmospheric. To the south, on the other side of the stadium, is the crowded but clean **municipal beach** *(fee for use of facilities)*; from here, a path leads past little, sandy **Gargardóros Beach** and beyond that to **Almyrós**, the best beach within a reasonable distance of Ag. Nikólaos.

Useful Information in Ag. Nikólaos

ⓘ **Ag. Nikólaos >**
EOT: between the lake and the sea, 20 Aktí S. Koundoúrou,
t 284 102 2357.

Tourist police and lost property:
47 Erithoú Stavroú, **t** 284 102 6900.

Ag. Nikólaos Festivals

Easter: festivities including burning of an effigy of Judas in the harbour.
6 Dec: Ag. Nikólaos.

Shopping in Ag. Nikólaos

Try not to confuse the three streets named after the Koundoúrou family.
Anna Karteri, 5 R. Koundoúrou. Wide range of titles in English.
Kerazoza, 42 R. Koundoúrou. Puppets, toys and postcards from the 1950s.
Maria Patsaki, 2 K. Sfakianáki. Embroideries, clothes and antiques.
Natural Sea Sponge Workshop, 15 R. Koundoúrou. Sponges, herbs, spices, teas and oils.
Syllogi, Aktí S. Koundoúrou. Antiques, old paintings, silver and fine crafts.

Where to Stay in Ag. Nikólaos

Ag. Nikólaos ✉ 72100
Minos Beach Art Hotel, 1km from the centre, **t** 284 102 2345, *www.bluegr.com* (€€€€€). State-of-the-art luxury and

self-indulgence in a wide choice of rooms, bungalows and suites; **La Bouillabaisse,** its restaurant (€70), serves superb cuisine. *Open April–Oct.*
Pleiades Luxurious Villas, Plákes, **t** 284 109 0450, *www.pleiadesvillas.gr* (€€€€€). Nine luminous designer villas (sleeping up to six), all equipped with private patios, pools, Jacuzzis – the works.
St Nicholas Bay, spread over a narrow peninsula 2km from Ag. Nikólaos, **t** 284 102 5041, *www.stnicolasbay.gr* (€€€€€). Bungalow complex with a sandy beach, five pools, and private pools with some suites, a health club and an art gallery. *Open April–Oct.*
Coral, on the waterfront along Aktí Koundoúrou, **t** 284 102 8363 (€€€). A smart town option, with rooftop pool and terrace.
Melas, 26 Koundoúrou, **t** 284 102 8734 (€€€). Stylish apartments for 2–5.
Ormos, near the sea, **t** 284 102 4094, *www.ormos-crystal.gr* (€€€). Family-orientated, with air-conditioning, pool and playground; cheaper off-season.
Panorama, also on Aktí Koundoúrou, **t** 284 102 8890 (€€). Offers just that over the harbour, and all rooms come with their own bath.
Doxa, 7 Idomenéos, **t** 284 102 4214 (€). A good, year-round bet.
Green House, 15 Modátsou, **t** 284 102 2025 (€). A cheapie, with little rooms leading out to a small courtyard, overflowing with greenery, and patrolled by a small army of cats.

Synantysi >>

Perla, t 284 102 3379 (€). Pleasant, clean guesthouse in the centre.

Rea, on the corner of Marathónos and Milátou, t 284 108 2023 (€). A good value hotel with character and excellent sea views.

Eating Out in Ag. Nikólaos

Aouas, K. Paleológou, halfway up to the Archaeology Museum. Small, inexpensive and good, serving Cretan dishes in a green shady courtyard.

Grigoris, at Stavrós, 200m after the bridge to Almyrós. Exceptionally friendly and reasonable.

Itanos, next to the cathedral on Str. Kíprou, t 284 102 5340. Traditional fare (lamb and spinach in egg-lemon sauce is excellent), good barrelled wine.

Migomis, 20 N. Plastíra, t 284 102 4353 (€25). Pretty place with views; a good mix of Greek and international dishes.

Pefko (or 'The Pines'). On the lake, with delicious, reasonable taverna food.

Pelagos, on Str. Kóraka, just in from Aktí Koundoúrou, t 284 102 5737 (€25). Trendy seafood restaurant, with a long list of tasty *mezédes. Closed Dec–Feb.*

Synantysi, on the Old Road to Heráklion, t 284 102 5384 (€15). Popular with locals for its excellent array of *mezédes*, including mussels and squid. Good selection of wines and desserts.

La Strada, 5 N. Plastíra, t 284 102 5841 (€20) Ag. Nik's best Italian restaurant.

Nightlife in Ag. Nikólaos

After-dark action is not hard to find, concentrated around the lake and port.

Armida. Floating harbour café-bar.

Alexandros, K. Paleológou. Its popular roof terrace has background music.

Lipstick, overlooking the main port. One of the dancing disco bars churning out more pulsating sounds, or try one of the string along 25 Martíou.

Kri-Kri, opposite the Minos Beach Hotel. Live Greek music and dancing.

Eloúnda, Olous and Spinalónga

Tantalizing views across the Gulf of Mirabélo unfold along the 12km from Ag. Nikólaos north to **Eloúnda**, where the rocky coastline, interspersed with tiny coves, draped with Greece's most glamorous hotels. South of the town centre, a bridge crosses a channel dug by the French in 1897 to separate the promontory of Spinalónga from Crete. Along this channel lies the sunken harbour of **Olous**, the port of ancient Dreros (*see* p.211) and goal of the 'sunken city' excursions from Ag. Nikólaos. The moon goddess Britomartis/Artemis, inventor of the fishing net, was worshipped here, represented by a wooden cult statue (a *xoanon*) with a fishtail, made by Daedalos. Fish also figure in the mosaic floor of an early Byzantine basilica.

Spinalónga
visits June–Sept daily 8.30–7.30; April, May and Oct daily 8.30–6; adm

The tiny island of **Spinalónga**, not to be confused with the promontory, is a half-hour caique trip from Eloúnda, or an hour from Ag. Nikólaos. Venetian engineers detached it in 1579 when they dug a channel to defend their fortress, which held out against the Turks until 1715, when the Venetians surrendered it by treaty. When the Turks left in 1904, Spinalónga became a leper colony, nicknamed 'the Isle of Tears' until 1957 – one of the last in Europe. **Pláka**, opposite, was its supply centre and now has a laid-back colony of its own, dedicated to relaxation by the pebble beach and eating fish in the tavernas.

Where to Stay and Eat in Eloúnda

⭐ Elounda Island Villas >>

Eloúnda ✉ 72053

Elounda Beach, t 284 106 3000, *www.eloundabeach.gr* (€€€€€). One of the first here (in 1971) and constantly updated to match its rivals in luxury.

Eloúnda Gulf Villas, in a commanding position, **t** 284 109 0300, *www.eloundavillas.com* (€€€€€). Rated one of the 101 best hotels in the world – 14 villas with their own pool and Jacuzzi, 10 suites, infinity pools and waterfalls, with a spa and gym.

Eloúnda Mare, t 284 104 1102, *www.eloundamare.gr* (€€€€€). Relais & Châteaux complex, renovated in 2000, including bungalows with private pools, restaurants, boutiques, a nine-hole par 3 golf course and water sports.

Eloúnda Peninsula, t 284 106 8250, *www.eloundapeninsula.com* (€€€€€). Perhaps the most exclusive hotel in Greece; its restaurant, **Calypso** (€100) serving contemporary cuisine, is rated the best on Crete.

Akti Olous, near causeway, **t** 284 104 1270 (€€€). With pool and roof garden.

Eloúnda Blue Bay, t 284 104 1512, *www.eloundabluebay.gr* (€€€). Complex offering a pool, playground and tennis.

Elounda Island Villas, the only buildings on little Koloytha Island, **t** 284 104 1274, *www.eloundaisland.gr* (€€). A 10min walk from the centre, over the bridge. Ten simple self-catering apartments sleeping up to four with a taverna; tennis court. *Open April–Oct.*

Korfos Beach, t 284 104 1591 (€). Within spitting distance of the strand, with water sports.

All of the top hotels have superb restaurants but Eloúnda is also well endowed with tavernas.

Vritomartis, out on its little islet, **t** 284 104 1325 (€22). Well-prepared seafood and lobster.

Kalidon, t 284 104 1451 (€15–20). Out on a small pontoon, with a good selection of vegetarian dishes and *mezédes*.

Marilena, t 284 104 1322 (€20–25). Attractive garden; Cypriot and fish dishes.

Above Ag. Nikólaos

✪ Kéra Panagía
t 284 105 1525; open summer 8–5; adm

From Ag. Nikólaos, it's a short hop up to Kritsá and, 1km before the village, the church of **Kéra Panagía**. It looks like no other: the three naves, coated with centuries of whitewash, trail long triangular buttresses. Within, it's alive with the colours of Crete's best fresco cycle, aptly illustrating the evolution of Byzantine art. The central aisle, dedicated to the Virgin, dates from the 12th to mid-13th centuries: on the northwest pillar look for St Francis, with his tonsure. It's rare that a Western saint earns a place among the Orthodox, but Francis, introduced by the Venetians, became a popular favourite on Crete. The side aisles were later additions, painted in the more naturalistic style from Constantinople in the early 14th century. The south aisle is devoted to St Anne, while the north belongs to Christ Pantocrator and a *Last Judgement* covers most of the nearby vaults. Among the saints here, don't miss the donors with their small daughter, rare portraits of medieval Cretans.

In 1956, Jules Dassin chose lovely white **Kritsá** as the location for his film *He Who Must Die* starring Melina Mercouri, and ever since its role has been that of a film set – a traditional village swamped by Agnik tourists, who are in turn swamped by villagers selling tablecloths. Kritsá is famous for its roll-out-the-barrel Cretan weddings and in August, they are re-enacted for fee-paying 'guests'.

⊗ Ancient Lato
the path begins near
the crossroads; open
Tues–Sun 8.30–3

A scenic 3km walk or drive north of Kritsá leads to the remains of Dorian **Lato** or, more properly, Lato Etera. Named after the Minoan goddess Leto (or Lato), the city was founded in the 7th century BC; it flourished before being abandoned in favour of its port, Lato Kamara (Ag. Nikólaos). Lato displays unusual Minoan influences in the double gateway, the street of 80 steps lined with houses, and the architecture of the *agora*, with its columnless sanctuary and central cistern. The wide steps that continue up to a peristyle court and Prytaneion date from the 7th century BC and may have been inspired by Minoan 'theatres'; spectators could watch events in the *agora* below. Monumental towers stood on either side of a narrower stair leading up to the altar. On the second hill stands a columnless temple, an isolated altar and a primitive theatre.

The Gulf of Mirabélo

The coastline that lends Ag. Nikólaos its panache owes its name to the Genoese fortress of Mirabélo, 'Beautiful View', demolished by the Turks. The fertile land has been populated for 5,000 years. Frequent buses run the 12km out to the sandy beach of **Kaló Chório**; the road east continues past the up-and-coming resort of **Ístro** to the turn-off for the 12th-century **Moní Faneroménis**, built into the cliff, sheltering a frescoed cave church with a miraculous icon of the Virgin.

Gourniá
t 284 209 4604; open
Tues–Sun 8.30–3; adm

East of Ístro, the road passes below the striking hillside site of **Gourniá**, a Minoan excavated in 1901–1904 by American Harriet Boyd, the first woman to lead a major dig. Gourniá reached its peak at around 1550 BC, and was never rebuilt after a fire in *c.*1225 BC. At the highest point, a small 'palace' with store rooms surrounds a rectangular court; there's a mini theatrical area and Shrine of the Snake Goddess, with a shelf for long, tube-like snake vases.

Pachiá Ámmos, a woebegone seaside village that corners most of the garbage in the sea, stands at the start of the Ierápetra road bisecting the 12km 'isthmus of Crete' separating the Aegean and Libyan seas. This was settled by the Minoans by 2600 BC at **Vasilikí**, 5km south of Pachiá Ámmos and the source of the first examples of 'Vasilikí ware', the Minoans' first distinctive pottery style, mottled in red and black, an effect produced by uneven firing. Archaeologists have been combing the area ever since, and in 2006 in **Karvoússi** (east of Pachiá Ámmos), Léfteris Hatzopoúlos of the University of North Carolina uncovered a large Archaic settlement, with big communal buildings – an Andreion and Prytaneion for feasts, store rooms, houses filled with pottery and a sanctuary and altar.

East of Karvoússi, a corniche road slithers along the precipitous coast. A byway descends to **Móchlos**, a charming fishing village set between barren cliffs and a small islet; originally attached to the mainland, it gave Minoan Móchlos two harbours. The Minoans of

Where to Stay and Eat in the Gulf of Mirabélo

Móchlos ✉ 72057

Mochlos, t 284 104 1512 (€). Close to the beach. *Open all year.*

Sofia, t 283 409 4554 (€). Small, pleasant and well-run.

Ta Kochylia, t 284 309 4432. Fish taverna (also meat) on the waterfront.

Taverna Bogazi, t 284 309 4200. Good fish, and some vegetarian dishes.

Móchlos specialized in pots with lid handles shaped like reclining dogs; some were found in the chamber tombs cut into the cliffs. One building is called the 'House of the Theran Refugees' for its similarities to the timbered houses at Akrotíri; on Santoríni (*see* p.311) potsherds from Akrotíri littered the floor on top of a layer of volcanic ash. Life obviously went on after the Big Bang.

Another Minoan settlement existed from 3000 BC on the islet of **Pseíra**, 2km offshore, where the inhabitants used the pumice that floated ashore to build the floor of their shrine. Judging by the rich finds, it was prosperous. Pseíra's 'House of the Pillar Partitions', with a bathroom equipped with a sunken tub, plughole and drains, is the most elegant in eastern Crete. Further east towards Sítia, the *rakí*-distilling village of **Chamézi** has early Minoan ruins.

Sitía (ΣΗΤΕΙΑ)

Set in an amphitheatre, Sitía is a pleasant, unpretentious place, filled with provincial bustle (sultanas and wine are its main concerns), while those schmoozing along the waterfront and sandy beach enjoy the pranks of its pet pelicans. Its Byzantine, Genoese and Venetian walls fell to earthquakes and Barbarossa's bombardments, leaving only a restored Venetian **fortress** to close off the western end of the port. But *la dolce vita* is nothing new here; under the fortress are the ruins of a Roman fish tank, where denizens of the deep were kept alive and fresh for the table.

Archaeology Museum

Itanos St, t 284 302 3917; open Tues–Sun 8.30–3; adm

The **Archaeology Museum** has a collection of Minoan *larnaxes*, a wine press and Linear A tablets from Zákros, and offerings from the 7th century in the Daedalic style. Other finds are from Pétras, just south of Sitía, where a large structure from the New Palace period was found; it may well be the Se-to-i-ja of the Minoan tablets. If the town beach is too crowded, try the sandy cove of **Ag. Fotía**, 5km to the east, where a Pre-Palatial Minoan cemetery of 250 chamber tombs was discovered near the sea. The hill above had a large Old Palace building that was mysteriously but peacefully destroyed just after its construction and replaced by a round fortlike building.

Around Sitía

Along the main road south of Sitía, **ancient Praisos** was the last stronghold of the Eteocretans – the 'true Cretans', or Minoans – who took refuge here during the Dorian invasion and survived into the

Getting to and around Sitía

Sitía's little **airport**, 1km out of town, t 284 302 4424, is linked to Athens 3 times a week.

Sitía is a stop on Ag. Nikólaos-Dodecanese **ferry** lines, as well as the twice-weekly services to Piraeus and Santorini. **Port authority: t** 284 302 2310.

The **bus station** at the south end of the waterfront, t 284 302 2272, has connections 5 times a day to Ag. Nikólaos and Ierápetra, 4 to Vaï and 3 to Káto Zákro. **Taxis: t** 284 302 2317.

3rd century BC, running their shrine of Díktean Zeus at Palaíkastro and keeping other Minoan cults alive. When Praisos began to compete too openly with Dorian Ierapytna in 146 BC, it was decimated. Ironically, this last Minoan town was one of the first to be discovered, in 1884 by the Italian Halbherr, who was mystified by the inscriptions in Greek letters, now held to be in the native Minoan language of Linear A. The scenery is lovely, the ruins pretty sparse.

The slightly more substantial remains of another vanished civilization may be seen further south in pretty **Etiá**. In the Middle Ages, Etiá was the fief of the Venetian Di Mezzo family, who in the 15th century built themselves a beautiful fortified **villa** (*temporarily closed*). Destruction of it began when Turkish administrators were besieged here by angry locals in 1828, and a fire and earthquake finished the job. Now partially restored, the entrance, ground floor and fountain house hint of the villa's former grandeur.

Monastery of Toploú
monastery open daily 9–1 and 2–6; *museum* open Tues–Sun 8.30–3; adm

East of Sitía, one of Crete's wealthiest monasteries is properly called Panagía Akroterianí, but **Toploú** ('cannoned' in Turkish) more aptly evokes this fortress of the faith, isolated on a plateau 3.5km from the Sitía–Palaíkastro road. It started off with a chapel dating from the liberation of Crete (961), while the monastery itself was

ⓘ **Sitía ›**
Municipal tourist office: on the marina, t 284 302 8300.

Useful Information in Sitía

Tourist police: t 284 302 4200.

Sitía Festivals

24 June: Large local festival, Piskokéfalo.

Mid-July–mid-Aug: Kornaria cultural festival.

Mid-Aug: Three-day wine and sultana festival, Sitía.

Where to Stay in Sitía

Sitía ✉ 72300

Itanos, 4 Karamanlí, t 284 302 2900 (€€). Stylish hotel with roof garden and rooms for the disabled.

Archontikon, 16 Kondiláki, t 284 302 8172 (€). Small, clean, quiet and friendly.

Nora, 31 Rouseláki, near the new port, t 284 302 3017 (€).

Stars, 37 M. Kalyváki, t 284 302 2917 (€). Offers peace and quiet.

Sitía Youth Hostel, 4 Theríssou St, just east of town, t 284 302 2693. With kitchen, and camping in the garden.

Eating Out in Sitía

Balconi, just up Kazantzáki from the water, t 284 302 5084 (€25). Great seasonal menu, including delicious Asian dishes, pasta with seafood and roast meats with local veg.

Mixos Taverna Ouzerie, close to the port. Serves lamb baked or on the spit.

Zorba's, t 284 302 2689 (€18). Wonderful location on the waterfront; seafood.

Neromilos, 4km east of Sitía in Ag. Fotía. Local favourite, in a former watermill; good view.

founded in the 15th century by the Kornáros family and rebuilt after the earthquake of 1612. Square 9m (30ft) walls defend it; the gate is directly under a hole named the *foniás* ('killer'), through which the besieged monks used to pour rocks and boiling oil on their attackers. Much of Toploú's building stone came from ancient Itanos: note the inscription from the 2nd century BC embedded in the façade.

Toploú has a venerable history as a place of refuge, revolution and resistance. At the start of the War of Independence in 1821, the Turks hanged 12 monks over the gate as a warning, although by the end of the war Toploú was Cretan again. During the Second World War, the abbot was shot by the Germans for operating a radio transmitter for the Resistance. Icons and artefacts are on display in the **museum**.

Palaíkastro, Vaï and Itanos

All roads on the east coast converge at **Palaíkastro**, with a beach below that has become a hot spot for windsurfing. The first edition of the town, the **Archaeological Site of Palaíkastro** at Roussolákos, was a Late Minoan settlement similar to Gourniá. The site also includes a 4th-century BC Sanctuary of Díktean Zeus on the hill at Kastrí, in use until the 4th century AD. The *Hymn of the Kouretes* (*see* p.209) was found here, engraved on a stone. About that time, the inhabitants resettled on the site of the current Palaíkastro.

Palaíkastro
*open Tues–Sun
8.30–3; adm*

Just north is the stunningly beautiful beach at **Vaï**. Its silver sands are lined with Europe's only wild palm trees, a species unique to Crete called *Phoenix theophrastii*; a banana plantation completes the Caribbean ambience. The only way to avoid sharing this paradise with thousands is to arrive at the crack of dawn. Small surrounding beaches act as crowd-overflow tanks and free campsites. The three best lie north of Vaï, 1.5km up Cape Síderos near **ancient Itanos**. Inhabited from Early Minoan times, Itanos minted the first coins on Crete. After the razing of Praisos, the city was a rival of Ierápetra for control of Palaíkastro's Sanctuary of Díktean Zeus, leading to the Arbitration of the Magnesians of 132 BC – a decision in Itanos' favour, as we know from the inscription embedded in Toploú's wall.

Ancient Itanos
*open Tues–Sun
8.30–3; adm*

Where to Stay and Eat around Palaíkastro and Zákros

Palaíkastro ✉ 72300

Marina Village, 1km out of town, 500m from the sea, t 284 306 1284, *www.palaikastro.com* (€€). A little resort complex with snack bar, pool and tennis.

Thalia, t 284 306 1448, *www.palaikastro.com* (€). Smothered in bougainvillaea.

Vaï

Vaï, near the beach, t 284 306 1129. The best taverna here; authentic Greek and Cretan dishes. *Closed Nov–Mar*.

Zákros

In summer there are a few rooms on the road to Káto Zákros, and about 50 beds (€30–35) near the sea, very much in demand.

Athena, on the sea at the end of the beach road, t 284 302 6893 (€).

09

Crete | The Minoan Palace of Zákros

George, Káto Zákros, **t** 284 302 6883 (€).
Clean, tasteful rooms and a terrace.
Zákros, upper village, **t** 284 309 3379
(€). Small and a bit frayed at the edges.

Nikos Platanákis, near the archaeological site, **t** 284 302 6887. Delicious
specialities including rabbit *stifádo*,
meat casserole in tomato sauce and
grilled fish. *Closed Nov–Mar.*

The Minoan Palace of Zákros

Zákros
*with sensible shoes
it's an 8km walk down
from Zakros to Káto
Zákros; buses from
Sitía will take you
down as well;t 284
309 3323; open daily
8.30–3; adm*

From Palaíkastro, the road south cuts through olive groves and sleepy hamlets to **Zákros**. A rich Minoan villa of the New Palace era, with wall paintings, sewers and wine presses, was found near the head of a dramatic gorge, the 'Valley of Death', named after the Minoan cliff tombs from 2600 BC.

For decades farmers dug up seals at **Káto Zákros**, and it was there that English archaeologist David Hogarth, who excavated the villa at upper Zákros in 1901, uncovered 12 houses before a torrential downpour forced him to abandon the dig – literally a few feet from the prize. This, the **Palace of Zákros**, the fourth largest on Crete, waited patiently underground until 1961, when Níkos Pláton began digging where Hogarth left off. Built over an older site in the New Palace period (*c.* 1700 BC), the surrounding town was probably the Minoans' chief port for Egypt. The importance of trade for Zákros is highlighted by the fact that the valley could never have supplied such a large settlement with sufficient food. Pláton found quantities of unworked ivory, which suggests that sculpture may have been a local speciality. The palace collapsed in the catastrophe traditionally dated 1450 BC and was never rebuilt, never plundered; the discovery of cult items suggests that disaster overwhelmed the residents. The subsidence of the east coast has left the harbour under the sea.

The **palace entrance** is by way of the original harbour road, leading into the **Northeast Court**; the covered area is a foundry predating the palace. A corridor leads into the long **Central Court**, which preserves the base of an altar. As usual, there are sanctuaries and ritual chambers in the **West Wing**, entered by way of a monolithic portal near the altar base. The large **Hall of Ceremonies** extends to the west, with a paved light-well in front and two windows; traces of frescoes were found here. A quantity of wine vessels found in the large room to the south led the archaeologists to dub it the **Banquet Hall**. Behind this are a **Shrine** and **Lustral Basin**, probably used for purification, and the **Shrine Treasury**, where Pláton found the precious rock-crystal libation vase now in Heráklion's Archaeology Museum. Boxes of Linear A tablets came out of the shrine's **Archive**; unfortunately the wet dissolved the bulk of them into a clay mass. In the southeast corner, a **Well** with worn steps was used for sacrificial offerings. At the bottom, Pláton found a bowl of perfectly preserved Minoan olives, which apparenty tasted pretty good. The **East Wing** of the palace is tentatively identified as the **Royal Apartments**. Behind

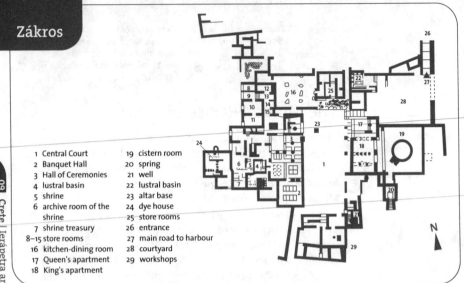

1 Central Court
2 Banquet Hall
3 Hall of Ceremonies
4 lustral basin
5 shrine
6 archive room of the shrine
7 shrine treasury
8–15 store rooms
16 kitchen-dining room
17 Queen's apartment
18 King's apartment
19 cistern room
20 spring
21 well
22 lustral basin
23 altar base
24 dye house
25 store rooms
26 entrance
27 main road to harbour
28 courtyard
29 workshops

them, the so-called **Cistern Room**, with a balustrade and steps leading down to the paved floor, is even more of an enigma: guesses are that it was a swimming pool, a fish pond, or a basin to float a Egyptian-style sacred ship. Steps lead down to a 'well-fashioned spring', as Pláton called it after Homer's description. At the north end is a large **Kitchen** – the only one ever found in a palace.

As a protected archaeological zone, the fishing hamlet of **Káto Zákros** is idyllic, with no new buildings or big hotels. The pebbly beach is fine for swimming, but for remote soft white sands make your way 10km south down the coastal road to **Xerókambos**.

Ierápetra and the Southeast

As the southernmost town in Europe, boasting the highest per capita income in Greece, **Ierápetra** (ΙΕΡΑΠΕΤΡΑ) should be a fascinating place instead of irritatingly dull. The myths say it was founded by the mysterious, mist-making Telchines who named it Kamiros. The Dorians, in turn, renamed the town Ierapytna. By Hellenistic times they had much of eastern Crete under their thumbs, and they held out against the Romans even after they'd conquered all the rest of Crete. Piqued, the Romans flattened it; then rebuilt it. The Byzantines made it a bishopric, but it was sacked by the Saracens and toppled by an earthquake in 1508. Its current fortunes are tied up with winter vegetables. A Dutch agriculturalist named Paul Coopers set up the first greenhouse in the early 1960s; local farmers have recently erected a statue of him on the site.

Dominating Ierápetra's seafront is the 13th-century Venetian **Kastélli** in the ancient harbour, once Roman Crete's chief port for

Getting to Ierápetra

The **bus station** on Lasthénou, **t** 284 202 8237 has several daily connections to Sitía (by way of Makrigialós), Gourniá and Ag. Nikólaos, Mýrtos, Koustounári, and Fermá.

Africa. Nearby is a house where Napoleon supposedly spent the night of 26 June 1798, before sailing off to Egypt. The most beautiful things in Ierápetra are a Late Minoan *larnax* painted with scenes of a hunt, and a charming Roman-era Demeter, both residents of the Archaeology Museum.

Archaeology Museum
Plateía Dimarchíou,
t 284 102 4943; open
Tues–Sat 8.30–3; adm

All in all, however, the best thing to do in Ierápetra is leave – take an excursion boat to the sands of **Nísos Chrisí** ('Golden Island', though the locals still call it by its real name, Gaidouronísi – 'Donkey Island'). This uninhabited islet is home to one of Crete's last natural cedar forests. The sea deposits seashells by the million on Chrisí's shores; there are sunbeds, and in season a taverna. In summer you can also find excursion boats to **Koufonísi**, a remote islet to the east, where prized murex seashells were collected, the source of royal purple dye. Ierápetra and Itanos fought over the island endlessly. Business was good; ruins include temples, a Roman-era bath complex, and a theatre with seats for a thousand people. Later on, Christians worshipped at Koufonísi's cave chapels, with images of saints painted as late as 1638 . East of Ierápetra, the once abandoned village of **Koutsounári** is now a popular place to stay, and **Ag. Fotiá** has an attractive beach and plenty of rooms. The best sandy beach is further east, at **Makrigialós**, with shallow waters.

09
Crete | Ierápetra and the Southeast

Ierápetra Festivals

July and Aug: Kyrvia cultural festival.

Where to Stay in and around Ierápetra

 Ierápetra ✉ 72200

Astron, 56 Kothrí, **t** 284 202 5114 (€€€–€€). Pristine and pleasant. All rooms have sea-view balconies. *Open all year.*

Petra Mare, 15mins' walk from the centre at 6 A. Filothéou, **t** 284 202 3341, *www.petramare.com* (€€€–€€). Resort hotel with a water park for the kids and plenty of activities.

Cretan Villa, 16 Oplarchygoú Lakérda, **t** 284 202 8522, *www.cretan-villa.com* (€€). Pretty rooms in old stone house.

Iris, 36 Kothrí, **t** 284 202 3136 (€€). By the water, with 12 pleasant rooms.

Coral, 12 Emm. Nikikatsanváki, **t** 284 202 2743 (€). Quiet area. *Open all year.*

Tavernas line the *parália* along Samonil and Kougoumoutzáki, on either side of the fort.

Lambrakis, 1km east, **t** 284 202 3393. Meat and fish grills, and delicious *myzithropitákia* (Cretan cheese pies).

Napoleon, on the waterfront (€18 for fish). Great favourite with authentic Greek and Cretan food. Fresh fish and snail dishes.

Siciliana, near town beach, **t** 284 202 4185. A real pizza oven and good honest pie.

Odeio, 18 Lasthénous, **t** 284 202 7429. Very popular for its tasty *mezédes*.

Koutsounári ✉ 72200

Koutsounari Traditional Cottages, **t** 284 206 1291, *www.traditionalcottages.gr* (€€). Restored cottages sleeping up to five with a pool, rented by the week only. The same people run the newly built **Nakou Village**, with self-catering apartments. *Open April–Oct.*

ⓘ **Ierápetra** ›
town hall,
t 284 202 8721

★ **Odeio** »

Nikos, t 284 206 1415. Beach taverna featuring home cooking by mamma.

Makrigialós ✉ 72200

White River Cottages, 1km north at Áspro Potamós, t 284 205 1120 (€€). Atmospheric minimalist little restored cottages, in a peaceful olive and carob grove, with a pool. Perfect for walkers but also for families. *Open April–Oct.*

Spiliá tou Drákou, Tráchylas, above the beach Kaló Neró, t 284 305 1494. One of the best places to eat on the south coast, with a wide choice of superbly prepared traditional dishes using ingredients from the family farm. *Open all year.*

Mýrtos ✉ 72200

Esperides, 200m from the sea, t 284 205 1207, *www.esperides-hotel.gr* (€€). New, large hotel with some family rooms.

Mýrtos, t 284 205 1227 (€€). Has a good restaurant. *Open all year.*

Mertiza, t 284 205 1208 (€€–€). Furnished apartments.

⭐ White River Cottages >

Along the Costa Plastica to Mýrtos

Spain has its *costas*, so it seems only fair that Crete should take the public relations bull by the horns and flaunt the greatest assets of its southeastern coast: sand and plastic, the latter to force endless tomatoes to redden before their time. West of Ierápetra, the Costa Plastica stretches on and on. In the coastal hills, however, pretty villages such as **Kalamáfka** have a sense of place; the hill just above it is the only spot on Crete where you can see both the Libyan and Cretan seas.

West of Gra Lygiá there's a beach with a plastic hinterland at **Ammoudáres**. Things were no doubt prettier back in the days when the early Minoans lived at Néa Mýrtos, a site better known as **Fournoú Korifí**. In 1968 the British School excavated this Minoan proto-town of close to 100 rooms, occupied in two periods between 2600 and 2100 BC, when it was destroyed by fire. Finds here proved vital in reconstructing life in the Pre-Palatial period. The small quantity of precious goods such as metal, obsidian from Mílos and stone vases from Mochlós suggest that such valuables were exchanged as dowries or gifts. Cereals, grape pips, olive stones and the bones of cattle, goats and sheep confirm that the essentials of the Cretan diet were already established; the oldest known potter's wheel in Greece was found here, from 2500 BC, with discs which were turned by hand, predating the later, spindle-turned wheels. From the find-places of the storage vessels and the cooking and dining areas, it has been estimated that the population ranged between 25 and 30 people in five families. The shrine is one of the oldest on Crete and yielded the Goddess of Mýrtos in the Ag. Nikólaos Museum.

Further west, **Mýrtos** is a great place to linger: although burned down by the Germans, it was rebuilt with a good deal of charm and atmosphere – the way a Cretan fishing village is supposed to be. The beach is clean but shingly.

The Cyclades

Say 'Greek island', and most people picture one of the Cyclades (the 'circling' islands, surrounding sacred Délos): barren rocks rising from the bluest of seas, where crags spill over with villages of asymmetrical white houses, with a pocket-sized church squeezed in at every corner. Few places are so irresistibly stark and clear, so visually pure and honest, so sharply defined in light and shadow. The Cyclades are relatively small and numerous, and as you sail or look out to sea you can always see several floating on the horizon, beckoning, framing a sunset or a rosy-fingered dawn.

10

⭐ Sunset over black cliffs
Oía, Santoríni p.314

⭐ Soft sands and windsurfing
Golden Beach, Páros p.299

⭐ Dancing till dawn
Mýkonos p.275

⭐ White Venetian dovecotes
Tínos p.335

⭐ Neoclassical urbanity
Ermoúpolis, Sýros p.329

See map overleaf

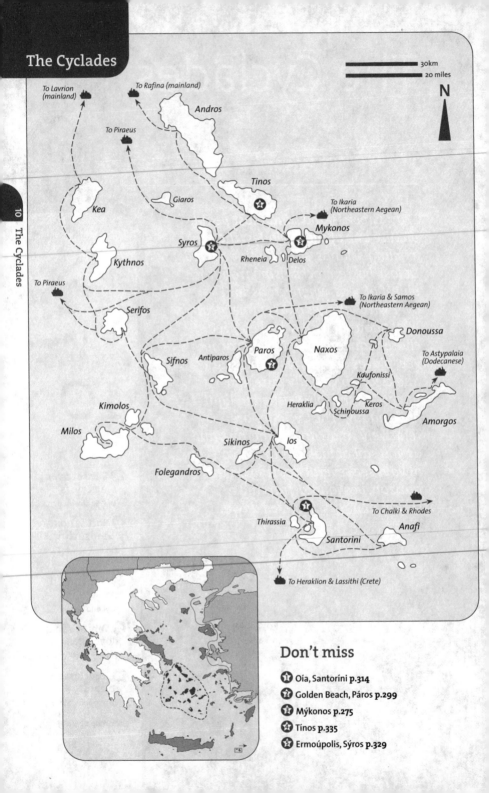

The Cyclades

30km
20 miles

N

To Lavrion (mainland)

To Rafina (mainland)

Andros

To Piraeus

Tinos

Giaros

Kea

To Ikaria (Northeastern Aegean)

Mykonos

Syros

Rheneia

Delos

Kythnos

To Piraeus

Serifos

To Ikaria & Samos (Northeastern Aegean)

Donoussa

Paros

Naxos

To Astypalaia (Dodecanese)

Sifnos

Antiparos

Kaufonissi

Kimolos

Heraklia

Keros

Schinoussa

Amorgos

Milos

Sikinos

Ios

Folegandros

To Chalki & Rhodes

Thirassia

Anafi

Santorini

To Heraklion & Lassithi (Crete)

Don't miss

⭐ Oía, Santoríni **p.314**

⭐ Golden Beach, Páros **p.299**

⭐ Mýkonos **p.275**

⭐ Tínos **p.335**

⭐ Ermoúpolis, Sýros **p.329**

Here lies harmony, here lies human scale.
Le Corbusier, on the islands, in 1936

The light in the Cyclades is so pure because the Aegean is a fairly arid place, knocked about by winds. In winter, when many islanders take refuge in Athens, the islands are plagued by the northerly *voreas* that turns ship schedules into fiction. After March the *sirocco* warms islands still green from winter rains. From July to September, when many of the Cyclades look parched, the *meltémi* from the Russian steppes huffs and puffs, providing natural air-conditioning.

By the end of the Second World War, the population of the islands had dropped to an all-time low; it was simply too hard to make a living from the dry, rocky soil. Tourism, of course, waved its golden wand over the Aegean and changed all that. **Mýkonos** is now the reigning queen of hip and cosmopolitan style in Greece. Spectacular **Santoríni** on its volcanic caldera lures cruise ships and romantics: **Páros** and **Náxos** are great all-rounders with lovely beaches. There are unique islands such as **Délos**, now a fabulous outdoor archaeological museum, **Sýros** with its stunning neoclassical city of Ermoúpolis, and **Tínos** with its dovecotes and pilgrims. The Cyclades closest to Athens, **Kéa**, **Kýthnos** and **Ándros**, have no airports, are harder to reach, and so have remained very Greek. Then a few islands come under the heading of 'almost away from it all': **Folégandros**, **Mílos**, **Amorgós**, **Sérifos**, **Sífnos** and the tiny, but fashionable 'Back islands' near **Náxos**: Koufoníssi, Schinoússa, Donoússa and Heráklia.

History

Geologists believe the Cyclades started off as an ancient land bridge, Aigeida, that over the millennia sank into the sea, leaving only the mountaintops above water. By 6000 BC, the first settlers arrived from Karia in Asia Minor. Three thousand years later, at the beginning of the Bronze Age, the islands' Early Cycladic culture was under way, producing elegant, iconic sculptures in pure white marble – the Cycladic idols, patiently, laboriously sanded into shape using nothing but emery.

In myth, King Minos of Crete conquered the islands in order to rid himself of his overly just brother Rhadamanthys, whom he sent to administer the new colonies. This corresponds to the Minoan influence that marks the prosperous Middle Cycladic period, when artists adopted a more natural style. The Late Cycladic period coincides with the fall of Crete and the rise of the Mycenaeans. When they in turn collapsed, the islands dropped out of history for hundreds of years. The luckier ones, especially Náxos and Páros, fell under the sway of the Ionians, and at the end of the 8th century BC were part of the great Ionian cultural rebirth.

The rise of the Persians forced the Ionians to flee to Attica, leaving the islands in Persian hands; several aided the Persians at Marathon and Salamis, and were punished by Athens. To prevent future break-aways, Athens obliged the islands to enter into the new maritime league at Délos in 478 BC. But what began as a league of allies turned into vassals paying tribute to the Athenians. Cycladic resentment often flared into revolt, and the Athenians had to work ever harder to extort the islands' annual contribution of money and ships.

During the Peloponnesian War the islands tended to side with the front-runner at any given time, and many jumped at the chance to support Sparta against Athens. But when Athens recovered from the war in 378 BC, it was only to form a second Delian League, again subjugating the Cyclades. Most of the islands turned to Philip of Macedon as a saviour, only to be fought over a generation later by the generals of Alexander the Great. The 2nd-century BC Roman conquest finally brought peace, except for the islands given to Rhodes, a less kindly ruler than distant Rome. The fall of Rome spelt centuries of hardship; although the Cyclades remained part of the Byzantine Empire, the islanders were left to fend for themselves against the pirates who plagued the seas, building villages in the most inaccessible places possible.

When Constantinople fell in 1204, the Archipelago, as the Byzantines called it, became the prey of grasping young Venetian noblemen and pirates (often one and the same). Marco Sanudo, nephew of Doge Enrico Dandolo, declared himself Duke of Náxos, and gave his faithful thugs the smaller Cyclades as fiefs. The Sanudos gave way to the Crispi Dynasty in 1383 but, threatened by pirates and the growing Ottoman Empire, Venice herself stepped in to police the Cyclades at the end of the 15th century. There was little even Venice could do against the fierce renegade admiral Khair-ed-din-Barbarossa, who decimated the islands in the name of the Sultan. By the mid-16th century they were under Turkish domination.

Venetian priests had converted many on the Cyclades, and during the Ottoman occupation both Orthodox and Catholic monasteries thrived. Turkish rule in the Archipelago was harsh only in economic terms, and most of the islands were spared the cruelties inflicted on Crete. From 1771–4, one of the more outlandish episodes in Greek history brought a brief interlude: Russia and Turkey were fighting over Poland, so Catherine the Great opened a second front in the war by capitalizing on Greek discontent. Her fleet in the Aegean led an insurrection against the Sultan and occupied some of the Cyclades. By the time the Russians went home, they had made themselves unpopular with all concerned.

When the Greek War of Independence broke out, the Cyclades offered naval support and a safe harbour for refugees; the islands with large Catholic populations were brought under French protection and remained neutral. The Cyclades were incorporated in the new Greek state, and Sýros became the country's leading port until Piraeus took over. Today Sýros' capital, Ermoúpolis, is still the largest town and administrative centre of the Cyclades.

Amorgós (ΑΜΟΡΓΟΣ)

Easternmost of the Cyclades, Amorgós is also one of the most dramatically rugged islands, with a south coast of cliffs plunging into the sea. For centuries it was virtually two islands, with the main port of Katápola almost a stranger to Aegiáli in the northeast, until a road built in 1995 brought them together. An island of political exile in the 1960s, Amorgós became a destination for the adventurous, then whoosh! – the first scenes in Luc Besson's 1988 cult movie *The Big Blue* were shot here, and travellers poured in, seeking the Cycladic idyll of their dreams.

History

Amorgós and its neighbouring islet of Kéros were inhabited by 3300 BC and remarkably prosperous; in 1885, 11 ancient cemeteries were uncovered, yielding ceramics and marbles now in Oxford and Copenhagen, and the largest Cycladic idol in the National Archaeological Museum in Athens. In later times a commonwealth of three cities shared Amorgós, each minting coins and worshipping Dionysos and Athena: Kástri (modern Arkesíni) was settled by Naxians, Minoa by Samians, and Aegiáli by Milians.

Ptolemy of Egypt made Amorgós a centre of worship of the Alexandrian gods Serapis and Isis. The Romans were the first to use the island as a place of exile, beginning a downhill trend which continued as Goths, Vandals and Slavs ravaged it during the Byzantine period. In 1209 the Duke of Náxos, Marco Sanudo, seized the island, and gave it to the Gizzi, who built the town castle. In spite of the Turkish occupation, Amorgós prospered in the 17th century, mostly from the export of exquisite embroideries, some of which are now in the Victoria and Albert Museum in London. Between the 17th and 19th centuries so many pieces were sold that War of Independence hero General Makriyiánnis threatened to declare war should the island send any more abroad. Rather than fight Makriyiánnis, the islanders just stopped making them.

Middle Amorgós: Katápola and Chóra

On a sheltered horseshoe bay looking out towards Kéros, **Katápola** is an attractive, workaday port with smallholders selling produce from their trucks and villagers sending parcels via the bus to families in Chóra. It runs into two other villages – **Rachídi** on the hillside and **Xylokeratídi**, the fishing port to the north, with two beaches. From Katápola you can walk up the Mudúlias Hill to **ancient Minoa**, with bits of the acropolis, a gymnasium and a Temple of Apollo; as the name suggests, it may have begun as a colony of Crete. Beyond Minoa is the little village of **Léfkes** and its frescoed church of Ag. Geórgios Balsamítis, built on the site of an ancient

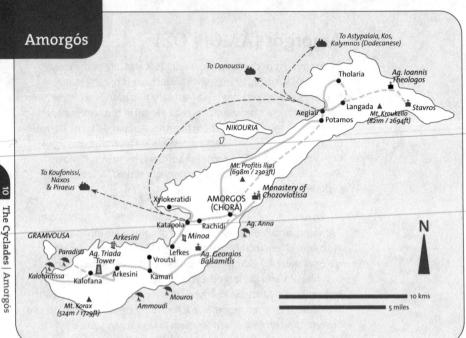

'aquatic' oracle where people came to have their fortunes told by signs on the surface of a sacred spring. A Venetian tower house and watermill stand nearby.

The capital, **Amorgós Town** (or **Chóra**), is a typical white Cycladic town, perched more than 400m (1,300ft) above sea level, with a neat spinal ridge of decapitated windmills – each family had its own – which once laboured with the winds that rose up the dizzying precipices from the sea. It has a perfect, eucalyptus-shaded *plateía*, lanes painted with big flowers and abstract patterns, and more churches than houses; especially note the ancient and Byzantine inscriptions and reliefs over the doors. One, with three vaulted aisles, melts like a meringue into the wall behind it; another, **Ag. Iríni**, only slightly larger than a phone box, is the smallest church in Greece. There's also a tiny **Archaeology Museum**. Steps lead up a huge rocky thumb rising out of the centre of town to **Apáno Kástro**, the well-preserved Venetian fortress built by Geremia Gizzi in 1290 (*get the key from the town hall or the coffee shop, both in the square*). From Chóra, it's an hour's walk down to Katápola; the views as you descend are especially dramatic around sunset.

Archaeology Museum
*t 228 507 1831;
open Tues–Sun 9–1
and 6–8.30*

Monastery of Chozoviótissa

Monastery of Chozoviótissa
*t 228 507 1294;
open 8–1; donation;
strict dress code
(gowns available)*

To reach this astonishing monastery, either take a rubbly *kalderími* path from Chóra, zigzagging down the magnificent natural amphitheatre, or the bus, leaving you with a 20-minute walk up, with superb views over the sea. Built into sheer 180m (600ft) orange

Getting to Amorgós

Amorgós has two ports, **Katápola** and **Aegiáli**, which split the business between them, so check to see which one of them your boat is using. There's a **ferry** 4 times a week from Piraeus, daily from Santoríni, and from Náxos via Heráklia, Schinoússa, Koufoníssi and Donoússa to Katápola; 4 ferries a week sail to Páros, one to Rhodes and other points in the Dodecanese. There are regular **hydrofoils** in summer from Piraeus and Rafína, less frequently from Sýros, Páros, Íos and Santoríni. **Port authority**: Katápola and Aegiáli, **t** 208 507 1259.

Getting around Amorgós

There is a daily **bus** service from Katápola to Chóra (Amorgós Town) and Aegiáli; others go via Chóra to the Chozioviótissa Monastery, Ag. Ánna, Paradísa and Kalotaritíssa beaches.

For a **taxi** in Katápola, call **t** 228 507 1255; in Aegiáli, **t** 228 507 3570.

Cars and motorbikes are available for hire in both towns.

cliffs, the monastery is a stark white fort of the faith, embedded in the living rock, supported by two enormous buttresses. Within its eight storeys are some 50 rooms, two churches, and a library containing 98 precious manuscripts, but only the small museum and chapel with the icon are open to the public. Chozoviótissa was founded c. AD 800 by monks from Hozova in the Middle East, fleeing the Iconoclasm with their miraculous icon, reputedly painted by St Luke; they were guided to the site by a mysterious nail stuck in the cliff (which rusted away and fell a few years back). Rebuilt in 1088 with funds sent by Emperor Alexis Comnenus, by the 17th century the monastery had 100 monks. It now gets by with just three, whose assistants provide visitors with a warm welcome in the form of brandy and/or water.

Below, the bus continues down to the pebble beaches at **Ag. Ánna**. The series of coves leads to a larger bay, popular with nudists, a trifle sacrilegious given the neighbours.

The South: Káto Meriá

The road and occasional buses continue south into the least visited and most traditional part of Amorgós, known these days as Káto Meriá. The landscape is dotted with curious old churches. Extensive tombs, walls, a subterranean aqueduct and the houses of **ancient Arkesini** are near the mountain village of **Vroútsi** (buses go as far as Kamári). A well-preserved 4th-century BC Hellenistic tower, the **Pírgos Ag. Triáda**, is up near modern **Arkesíni. Kalofána** is the most remote village of all, but near several quiet beaches: **Paradísa** and **Kalotarítissa** on the west coast are especially delightful; **Moúros** and **Ammoúdi** on the south coast are also popular.

Aegiáli and the North

Small, charming **Aegiáli** is Amorgós' northern port and main resort, thanks to the island's one genuine sandy beach, with striking views over the great granite lump of **Nikouriá** islet, which once supported a leper colony. Like Katápola, Aegiáli is hidden from the sea until you enter its horseshoe bay, and there it sits, a picture-perfect Cycladic town, complete with blue-domed church. A path over the headlands leads to sand or shingle coves where clothes are optional, or take a boat to even quieter beaches.

From Aegiáli you can visit the scant remains of **ancient Aegiali** or the hill villages of **Tholária**, named for its vaulted *tholos* tombs from the Roman period, and **Langáda**, spread under a giant rocky thumb. A circular walk along the herb-scented ridge links the villages to Aegiáli; the section from Langáda's church of the Panagía to Tholária poignantly passes through 'the valley of the old, useless, doomed donkeys'. From Langáda a path leads up to the decapitated windmills, by way of a frescoed cave church, **Yéro Stávros**; another path leads out east in about an hour to frescoed **Ag. Ioánnis Theológos**, an 8th-century monastery, recently restored; one window is a replica of Aghia Sophia in Istanbul. The path continues to another church, **Stávros**, and down to an abandoned bauxite mine.

Useful Information on Amorgós

Aegiális: t 228 507 3394. Naomis is very helpful.
Katápola: Synodinos Travel, t 228 507 1201.

Where to Stay and Eat on Amorgós

Katápola ✉ 84008

Apaggio, 1km from the port at Tsesemés, t 228 507 1750 (€€€–€€). Twelve simple but comfortable rooms, with panoramic views and a pool.
Eleni, t 228 507 1543 (€€). On the west edge of town, with unimpeded views of the bay and the sunset.
Minoa, in the port square, t 228 507 1480, hotelmin@otenet.gr (€€). More traditional, but it might be noisy.
St George, in Xylokeratídi, t 228 507 1148 (€€). Modern and comfortable, sitting pretty on the hill.
Villa Catapoliana, t 228 507 1064, Katapol@otenet.gr (€€–€). Courtyard setting around a small archaeological dig. Nice, quiet rooms with fridges and a roof garden with views.
Anna, t 228 507 1218 (€). Rooms and studios, including breakfast. The front rooms have views, and there's a small garden to sit in.
Voula Beach, near the port police, t 228 507 4052 (€). Set around a shaded garden full of geraniums, and all rooms are en suite.
Katápola Camping, by the beach at the base of the bay, t 228 507 1257/1802. Tends to open when the rooms start filling up.
Minos, t 228 507 4295, at the quieter south end of the waterfront, with a glassed-in side garden for when it's windy. An old-fashioned place with good home cooking; try the *patáto* casserole (a kid, lamb or pork island speciality), rabbit *stifádo* or, if you have deep pockets, lobster.
Psaropoula. An amiable taverna where you choose your fish from wooden trays before it's hurled onto the barbecue.
Vitzentos, t 228 507 1518. A deservedly popular seafront taverna in Xylokeratídi; arrive early to sample the day's speciality. Try the *patáto*, or stuffed aubergines.

Chóra ✉ 84008

Panorama, at the start of the village, t 228 507 1606 (€€). Small, but ask for one of its newer six large rooms.
Yannakos family, t 228 507 1367/1277 (€). Seem to have the monopoly on rooms.

Kastanis. Tiny, good, inexpensive and very Greek taverna.

Liotrívi, on the edge of town, t 228 507 1700. Has a roof garden, and elaborate dishes such as *kalogíros* (aubergine with veal, feta and tomatoes), *exohikó* (lamb and vegetables in a pastry) and baked vegetarian *briáms*.

Aegiáli ✉ 84008

Aegiális, isolated across the harbour, t 228 507 3393, *www.amorgos-aegialis.com* (€€). A smart complex, with a pool, taverna and trendy nightclub. There's also a minibus service. Its restaurant, **Ambrosia**, perhaps the island's best, serves a tasty mix of Greek and continental dishes. *Open all year.*

(★) Lakki >

Lakki, set back from the beach, t 228 507 3253, *www.lakkivillage.gr* (€€). Has a lovely garden with a tree house for kids. Cycladic-style, immaculate self-contained rooms, excellent food served outdoors from their taverna.

Mike, t 228 507 3208, *hotelmik@otenet.gr* (€€). The first hotel here, but it has recently had a facelift.

Akrogiali, t 228 507 3249 (€€–€). Clean, comfortable rooms, all with en suite bathrooms.

Camping Aegiáli, in a field off the Tholária road, t 228 507 3133. With decent facilities and a café.

Barba Yiannis, Ag. Pávlos beach, t 228 507 3011. Seafood taverna right on the sea, specializing in lobster spaghetti. *Closed Oct–May.*

Korali. Tasty fish and the best sunset views.

To Limani (known as Katerina's), t 228 507 3549. A favourite grazing ground, packed out for its great food, wine from the barrel and mellow sounds.

To Tsangarádiko. Wonderful *mezédes* served with *raki*, ouzo or wine by the glass.

Langáda ✉ 84008

Pagali, t 228 507 3310, *www.pagali hotel-amorgos.com* (€€–€). Comfortable rooms and bougainvillaea cascading over the terrace; its taverna, **Nikos**, specializes in roast kid and baked aubergines.

Pension Artemis, t 228 507 3315, *www.artemis-pension.gr* (€€). Simple and pleasant.

Taverna Loza. As above, also run by the kind Dimitri Dendrinos.

Tholária ✉ 84008

Vigla, t 228 507 3288 (€€). With views, bar and restaurant.

Choreftis, t 228 508 4008. Part grocery store, part taverna, with live music most nights.

Anáfi (ΑΝΑΦΗ)

Anáfi, the most southerly of the Cyclades, looks like a tadpole, but with a tail swollen like the Rock of Gibraltar. It is a friendly and unpretentious island, the ideal place for peace and solitude; the islanders go about their lives as they always have, with few concessions to tourism. But be warned, if the weather breaks, ferries may not dock and you could get marooned, so allow plenty of time to get back to civilization.

Little contact with the outside world has meant that old customs were preserved into the last century, when scholars found in the Anáfiots' songs and festivals traces of the ancient worship of Apollo.

History

In the 15th century BC, Anáfi gained stature in the form of volcanic rock, 158m (517ft) thick in places, carried to the island by wind and tidal wave after the explosion of Santoríni. The twelfth Duke of

Getting to and around Anáfi

There are **ferry** connections 6 times a week with Santoríni, 5 times a week with Íos, Náxos and Páros, at least twice a week with Piraeus, 4 times a week with Folégandros, Síkinos and Sýros; and daily with Píraeus in season. There is a weekly connection in high season with the Dodecanese. **Port authority**, **t** 228 602 2239.

Buses are few and there are no **taxis**. For **motorbike rentals**, call **t** 228 606 1292.

Outside of the short stretch from the port to Chóra, there are no good **roads** on Anáfi.

In the busy season, **caiques** in Ag. Nikólaos do trips to all the local beaches.

Náxos, Giacomo Crispi, gave Anáfi to his brother, who built a castle, but it had little effect when Barbarossa turned up in 1537. People slowly drifted back, and when Otho, the first king of modern Greece, asked for the best builders in the country to build him a palace, he was sent a contingent of Anáfiots, who also built themselves the delightful neighbourhood of Anafiótika at the foot of the Acropolis, taking advantage of the law that stated that if you could erect four walls and a roof by sunrise, the place was yours.

Around the Island

The island's one village, **Chóra** (pop. 260), an amphitheatre of white domed houses and windmills with views all around, is a short bus ride up from the landing, **Ag. Nikólaos**. Guglielmo Crispi's half-ruined **Kástro** is to the north of the village; a path leads up to its rocky heights. There are attractive beaches around Ag. Nikólaos, from **Klisídi** east of the port, to a range of bays signposted from the Chóra road and littered with freelance campers. The only spring is at **Vágia**, on the west coast.

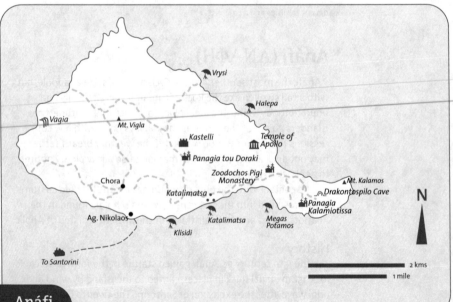

Anáfi

Useful Information on Anáfi

Jeyzed Travel, in the port, **t** 228 606 1253. Best help with accommodation.

Anáfi Festivals

8 Sept: Panagía, at the monastery, known for its authentic folk-dances.

Where to Stay and Eat on Anáfi

Anáfi ✉ 84009
  Room-owners travel down from Chóra by bus or car to meet the ferries.

Villa Apollon, above Klisidi Beach, **t** 228 606 1348, *www.apollonvilla.gr*; out of season **t** 210 993 6150 (€€). A classy place, with garden, verandas and fridges in each room. *Open May–Oct.*

Anatoli, in Chóra, **t** 228 606 1279 (€€–€). Rooms with verandas.

Ta Plagia, up by Chóra, **t** 228 606 1308, out of season **t** 210 412 7113 (€). Similar to the Anatoli but with a restaurant. *Open May–Sept.*

To Steki, in Chóra. Cheap and cheerful dining.

The favourite path on Anáfi runs east of Chóra to **Kastélli** (about 2hrs), site of the ancient town and the chapel Panagía tou Doráki, decorated with a pair of Roman sarcophagi and the trunk of a statue. Another hour's walk from Kastélli leads past the ruined hamlet of **Katalimátsa** and huge blocks from the Temple of Apollo Aiglitos (some of which went into the construction of the nearby Monastery of Zoodóchos Pigí) to the summit of the tremendous tadpole-tail, **Mount Kálamos**. On top, the pretty 16th-century Monastery of Panagía Kalamiótissa, 450m (1,476ft) over the sea, was built where an icon of the Virgin was found hanging on a cane; it enjoys tremendous views, especially at sunrise. Nearby you can poke around in an old dragon's lair, the **Drakontóspilio**, with stalactites and stalagmites.

Ándros (ΑΝΔΡΟΣ)

Lush and green on one side, scorched and barren on the other, split-personality Ándros is the northernmost and second largest of the Cyclades. It has long been a haunt for wealthy Athenian shipping magnates, who descend in high summer and breed horses on their country estates in the hills. And, as it's easy to reach from Rafína, Ándros is also a popular weekend playground for trendy Athenians who patronize the island's chic cocktail bars and cafés.

In the south, only the narrowest of straits separates Ándros from Tínos, while in the barren north the blustery Cavo d'Oro Channel, long dreaded by sailors, divides the island from Évia. However, the same irksome wind also makes Ándros one of the coolest spots in the Aegean in July and August. Ándros is a prosperous island, famed for its cooks and ship's captains, well-ordered and adorned with

Getting to Ándros

There are several daily **ferry**, **catamaran** and **hydrofoil** connections in summer with Rafína, Tínos and Mýkonos, and daily via Mýkonos to Náxos, Páros, Íos, Santoríni and Sýros. Infrequent ferries go to Amorgós and Chíos. **Port authority** (Gávrion): t 228 207 1213.

Getting around Ándros

Buses (t 228 202 2316) run from Chóra to Batsí, Gávrion, Apoíkia, Strapouriés, Steniés and Kórthi; buses for Batsí, Chóra and Kórthi leave from near the dock at Gávrion, linking with the ferries.

Cars and bikes are widely available for rent. In Gávrion try **Colours Travel, t** 228 207 1557, where Maria Bati is also a very good source of island information, or **Tasos Rent a Car, t** 228 207 1040; in Batsí, **Hermes, t** 228 204 2070; in Chóra, **Riva Rent a Bike, t** 228 202 4412 (also for boats and accommodation).

Taxis: in Gávrion, call **t** 228 207 1561; in Batsí, **t** 228 204 1081.

white dovecotes first built by the Venetians. Crossed by four parallel mountain ridges, it has green valleys; water gushes from the mossy springs of the villages, and flowers and forests cover the south. Fields are divided by unique dry stone walls called *xerolithiés*.

One of Andros' great attractions is its network of walking paths around the countryside, recently cleared and signposted. These are the islanders' old footpaths, and they'll show you an entirely different Ándros from the one you see from the roads.

History

Originally known as Hydroussa ('watery'), the island is thought to derive its name from the Phoenician Arados, or from Andrea, the general sent by Rhadamanthys of Crete to govern it. Few islands in the Cyclades have such a collection of early settlements; one site, at Strofilás, is the biggest fortified Neolithic village yet found in the Aegean. In 1000 BC Ionians colonized Ándros, leading to its early cultural bloom in the Archaic period. Dionysos was the most popular god worshipped at the pantheon of Palaiopolis, the leading city at the time, and one of his temples had the amazing talent of turning spring water into wine during the festival of the Dionysia.

For most of the rest of its history, Ándros has been the square peg in a round archipelago. After the Athenian victory at Salamis, Themistocles fined Ándros for supporting Xerxes. The Andrians refused to pay and Themistocles besieged the island, but without success. Although the islanders later assisted the Greeks at Plateía, Athens continued to hold a grudge against Ándros, and in 448 BC Pericles divided the island among Athenian colonists, who taxed the inhabitants heavily. In response, the Andrians abetted Athens' enemies whenever they could: when the Peloponnesian War broke out, they withdrew from the Delian League and sided with Sparta. Spartan oppression, however, proved just as awful and things were no better under the Hellenistic rulers. For resisting their conquest, the Romans banished the entire population to Boetia, and gave

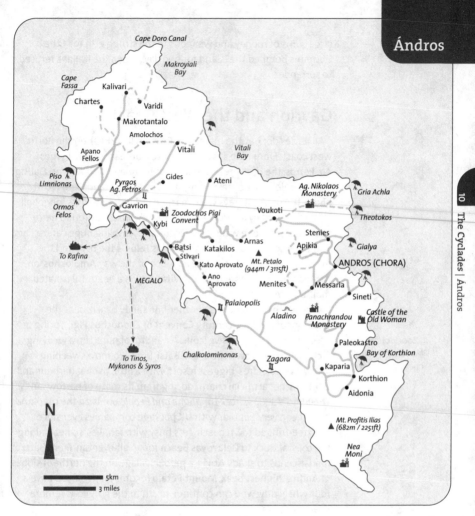

Cape Doro Canal

Makroyiali
Bay

Cape
Fassa

Kalivari

Chartes

Varidi

Makrotantalo

Amolochos

Apano
Fellos

Vitali

Vitali
Bay

Piso
Limnionas

Pyrgos
Ag. Petros

Gides

Ateni

Ag. Nikolaos
Monastery

Gria Achla

Ormos
Felos

Gavrion

Zoodochos Pigi
Convent

Voukoti

Theotokos

Kybi

Stenies

To Rafina

Batsi
Stivari

Katakilos

Arnas

Apikia

Gialya

Kato Aprovato

Mt. Petalo
(944m / 3115ft)

ANDROS (CHORA)

MEGALO

Ano
Aprovato

Menites

Messaria

Sineti

Palaiopolis

Aladino

Panachrandou
Monastery

Castle of the
Old Woman

Paleokastro

To Tinos,
Mykonos & Syros

Chalkolominonas

Zagora

Kaparia

Bay of Korthion

Korthion

Aidonia

N

Mt. Profitis Ilias
(682m / 2251ft)

Nea
Moni

5km
3 miles

Ándros to Attalos I, King of Pergamon. When permitted to return, the
inhabitants found their homes sacked. Byzantium proved a blessing
compared with the past: in the 5th century Ándros had
a neo-Platonic philosophy academy, where Proclos and Michael
Pselos taught, and in the 11th century (until the 18th) it became an
important exporter of silk fabrics, embroidered with gold.

In the Venetian land-grab after the Fourth Crusade, Martino
Dandolo took Ándros and allied himself with his cousin Marco
Sanudo, Duke of Náxos. Later Venetian rulers were nasty and
incompetent and Barbarossa easily took the island in 1530. Apart
from collecting taxes, the Turks left it to its own devices, and 10,000
Albanians, many from nearby Kárystos (Évia), settled on Ándros. In
1821 Ándros' famous son, the philosopher Theóphilos Kaíris, declared
the revolution at the cathedral of Ándros, and the island contributed

large sums of money and weapons to the struggle. In 1943 the Germans bombed the island for two days when the Italians refused to surrender.

Gávrion and the West Coast

All ferries dock at the main port, **Gávrion** (ΓABPIO), on the north-west coast. From here, it's a 40-minute walk east up the **Pyrgós Ag. Pétros**, the best-preserved ancient monument on Ándros. Dating from the Hellenistic era, this mysterious tower stands 21m (70ft) high – the upper storeys were reached by ladder – and its inner hall is still crowned by a corbelled dome. The landscape around here squirms with stone walls, or *xerolithiés*, resembling huge caterpillars. There are beaches to the north: **Ormós Felós** is the best and the Athenians are building villas every inch of the way. **Amólochos**, on the road to the remote beach at **Vitáli Bay**, is a beautiful isolated mountain village.

Kybí, south of Gávrion, is another fine sandy beach, near the junction for the 14th-century **Convent of Zoodóchos Pigí**, 'Spring of Life', which has impressive icons. A handful of nuns run a **weaving factory**. Further down the coast, **Batsí**, built around a sweeping sandy bay, is Ándros' biggest resort, with a little fishing harbour and a cute, rather artificial charm oozing from its maze of narrow lanes. The BBC TV series *Greek Language and People* put it on the map, and it has been very popular with UK package companies ever since. The tree-fringed town beach gets busy with families, so head along the coastal track to **Delavóyas Beach** for an all-over tan. From Batsí a road ascends to shady **Arnás**, a garden village on the northern slopes of Ándros' highest peak, **Mount Pétalo** (950m/3,115ft). If you have a four-wheel drive you can continue north to the gorgeous remote beach of Áchla.

Palaiópolis, 9km down the coast, was the first capital of Ándros, founded by the Minoans and inhabited until c. AD 1000 when the people moved to Messariá. An earthquake in the 4th century AD destroyed part of it, and over the years pirates mopped up the rest. The current edition of Palaiópolis is on top of a steep hill, from where steps lead down to the ancient site, partly underwater. It's one of the loveliest corners of Ándros, and a nice place to explore the ruins: walls, architectural fragments, bits of a Christian basilica, all hidden among the paths. Up on the main road, a small **archaeological museum** holds the remains. The road to Chóra continues through rolling countryside dotted with dovecotes and the ruined stone tower houses of the Byzantine and Venetian ruling classes.

Further down the west coast, **Zagorá** was inhabited until the 8th century BC, when it boasted a population of 4,000. It was solidly

Zoodóchos Pigí Weaving Factory
open Mon–Sat 9–12

Archaeological Museum
open Tues–Sun 8.30–5; adm

defended; sheer cliffs surrounded it on three sides and on the fourth a mighty wall was built. Within, the inhabitants lived in flat-roofed houses (some remains still exist) and cultivated the fields. Excavated by Australians in the 1960s, finds are now in the island's museum.

Ándros Town/Chóra

The capital, Ándros (or Chóra), sits on a narrow tongue of land, decorated with the grand neoclassical mansions of ship-owning families; between the two world wars, the Andrians owned one out of five Greek merchant ships. At the edge of town, a stone arch is all that survives of the bridge to the ruins of the Venetian castle, **Mésa Kástro**, built by Marino Dandolo and damaged in the 1943 bombardment; the ruins are guarded by the gargantuan, Stalinist-looking statue of the *Unknown Sailor* by Michael Tómbros in Plateía Ríva. There's a small **museum** dedicated to Ándros' seafaring history.

Kástro Museum
open summer only

Káto Kástro, the maze of streets that forms the medieval city, and the mansions of the Ríva district, are wedged between **Parapórti** and **Embórios Bays**, with steps down from the central square, **Plateía Kaíris**. These beaches are sandy but often windswept, and holiday bungalows and trendy restaurants are springing up at Embórios. The pedestrianized **main street**, paved with marble slabs, is lined with old mansions converted into public offices; post and telephone offices and banks are in the centre of town, and the bus station and outdoor cinema just a few steps away. A small white church, **Ag. Thalassíni**, guards one end of Embórios harbour from a throne of rock. The cathedral, **Ag. Geórgios**, is built on the ruins of a 17th-century church. A legend is told about a third church, **Theoskepastí**, built in 1555. When the wood for its roof arrived in Ándros from Piraeus, the priest couldn't afford the price demanded by the ship's captain. Angrily, the captain set sail again, only to run into a fierce tempest. The sailors prayed to the Virgin Mary, promising to bring the wood back to Ándros should she save their lives. Instantly the sea grew calm again, and Theoskepastí, or 'Sheltered by God', was completed without further difficulty. It was dedicated to the Virgin Mary, who apparently is on a hotline to the miracle-working icon inside the church.

Archaeology Museum
t 228 202 3664; open Tues–Sun 8.30–3; adm

Just north of Plateía Kaíris are the museums endowed by Basil and Elise Goulándris of the ship-owning dynasty. Next to Chóra's elegant marble fountain, built in 1818, the **Archaeology Museum** houses the outstanding *Hermes Psychopompos*, 'Conductor of the Dead', a 2nd-century BC copy of a Praxiteles original, discovered by farmers in Palaiopolis. Other exhibits include the *Matron of Herculaneum*, finds from the ancient cities of Zagora and Palaiópolis, architectural illustrations and pottery collections. The island's other gem, the

**Museum of
Modern Art**
*t 228 202 2650; open
Wed–Mon 10–2 and 6–9*

Museum of Modern Art, occupies two buildings. The permanent collection includes contemporary Greek artists, and more sculptures by Michael Tómbros, but this museum is becoming internationally known for the major exhibitions it puts on each summer; in recent years these have included everything from the likes of Picasso and De Chirico to British pop artists of the 1960s.

Villages along the East Coast

Lovely villages surround Chóra: **Steniés**, 6km north, is the island's most beautiful village, its pedestrianized lanes heavy with the scent of blossoms in spring. A few mulberries remain; in the old silk-making days the precious cocoons would be brought into the houses in the winter to keep them warm – though the real sight here is Greece's biggest watermill, an old wooden contraption that once powered a spaghetti factory. The sandy beach at **Giálya** is below, with a good fish taverna. The famous Sáriza mineral water flows in the hill village of **Apíkia**, above Steniés – further up, you can visit the 16th-century **Ag. Nikólaos Monastery** (*wear proper attire*).

The main road west passes through farming villages of the fertile **Messariá Valley**. One old custom may still be heard: in the evening after a hard day's work, the patriarch will pipe the family home from the fields. **Messariá** itself has a lovely Byzantine church, **Taxiárchis**, built in 1158 by Emperor Emmanuel Comnenus; much of the original carved decoration survives on the exterior (though there isn't much to see inside). Another church nearby, **Ag. Nikólaos**, guards an icon made from an 18th-century faith-healing nun's hair.

Further west, lush **Ménites** has springs gushing from marble fountains, and the church of **Panagías tis Kóumoulous**, the 'Virgin of the Plentiful', which may have been the site of Dionysos' miraculous water-to-wine temple. The village is known for its nightingales and huge trees and there are other pretty ones further up, **Strapouriés** and **Ypsiloú**, with popular tavernas. Southwest of Messariá, at **Aladinó**, you can visit a stalactite cave called **Cháos**.

South of Chóra, **Panachrándou**, the island's most important monastery, with a church full of fine medieval art, can be reached by way of Mésa Vouní. Now home to three monks, it was founded after Niképhoros Phokás' liberation of Crete in AD 961, and was supposedly visited by the emperor himself. On the coast here stands the ruined Venetian fort of **Paleokástro**. A gritty old lady who abhorred the Venetians tricked them into letting her inside, then opened the door to the Turks. Appalled at the slaughter of the Venetians, she leapt from the castle and landed on a rock now known as *Tis Griás to Pídema* or 'Old Lady's Leap', by a pretty beach. Overlooking a little bay, **Kórthi** (ΚΟΡΘΙ) is 30km southeast of Chóra, at the bottom of a lush valley with a beach and some modest tourist development. On the road from Chóra, you'll see a strange, round stone building with huge openings near the top. This is Andros' contribution to technology, the horizontal windmill, brainchild of a local inventor a century ago; engineers might scoff, but here they say it really worked. The inland villages of **Kapariá** and **Aidónia** have the island's prettiest dovecotes.

Useful Information on Ándros

(i) **Ándros >**
EOT: in an old dovecote on the harbour, Gávrion, t 228 207 1785; open (perhaps) May–Oct

Greek Sun Holidays, Batsí, t 228 204 1198, *www.andros-greece.com*. For accommodation, rentals and excursions.

Ándros Festivals

15 days before Easter: Theoskepastí, Chóra.

19 June (date varies): Análipsis, Ándros Town.

15 Aug: Kórthinon.

23 Aug: Ménites.

Where to Stay and Eat on Ándros

(★) **Ameroussa >>**

Ándros is geared to long-term stays, and it may be difficult, especially in the capital, to find a place that will let you stay for only a few nights. Although attractive Batsí is the tourist centre, Ándros Town is a better bet for a genuine Greek experience and its hotels are open all year.

Gávrion ✉ 84501

Ándros Holiday, on the beach, t 228 207 1443, *androshol@otenet.gr* (€€€€€). Smart, with half-board, pool, tennis, sauna and gym.

Ostria Studios, just out of town, t 228 207 1551 (€€€). Upmarket self-catering apartments.

Perrakis, Kyprí Beach, t 228 207 1456, *www.hotelperrakis.gr* (€€€). Pleasant seaside hotel with one of the island's best restaurants.

Galaxias, on the waterfront, t 228 207 1228 (€€–€). Also has a good taverna, with house specialities.

Camping Ándros, along the Batsí road, t 228 207 1444. In an attractive site with a mini-market, swimming pool, excellent taverna and a van to meet the ferries.

Karlos, halfway to the campsite. Excellent restaurant hidden away, where the locals come for traditional dishes and low prices.

Sunset, en route to the Ándros Holiday Hotel. Try the Ándros speciality, *froutália*, omelette made with potatoes and local sausage.

En Gavrio, the local hangout – and an excellent ouzerie and *mezedepoleío*.

Batsí ✉ 84503

Blue Bay, just outside town t 228 204 1150, *www.blue-bay.gr* (€€€). Attractive studios and maisonettes by the sea with a pool.

Skouna, t 228 204 1240 (€€€). Small but a good seafront bet.

Ameroussa, t 228 204 1044 (€€€–€€). Refined, shaded by banana groves, this tops the cliff at Apróvato like an iced cake and has its own sands near Delavóyas Beach, popular with nudists.

Chryssi Akti, t 228 204 1236, *www.hotel-chryssiakti.gr* (€€). Reasonable, and also on the beach.

Sirocco, on the steps up from the port, t 228 204 1023. Simple restaurant playing jazz and popular Greek songs to go with its tasty dishes.

Stamatis, t 228 204 1283. Good food and rooftop views over the harbour.

Takis. Hot spot for fish.

Ándros Town/Chóra ✉ 84500

Paradise, t 228 202 2187, *www.paradiseandros.gr* (€€€€–€€€). 'Lifestyle' boutique hotel in a graceful neoclassical confection, with a pool and tennis.

Elli, Plakoúra, t 228 202 2213 (studios €€€€€, rooms €€€–€€). Well-placed and friendly.

Irene's Villas, by the sea, t 228 202 3344, *www.irenes-villas.gr* (€€€–€€). Charming, set in flower gardens.

Aegli, t 228 202 2303 (€€). Traditional hotel between the two squares. *Open all year.*

Archipelagos, towards Giálya Beach. Where the locals head for traditional Greek food.

Nónas, Plakoúra, **t** 228 202 3577. The best fish taverna in town, and not expensive.

Palinorio, Embórios, **t** 228 202 2881. Also popular, serving everything from beans to lobster.

Parea, t 228 202 3721. On the main square. Cosy taverna, with excellent Greek menu.

Villages above Chóra ✉ 84500

Tassos, Ménites. Tables overlooking the stream and specialities like *froutália* and tomatoes stuffed with chicken.

Terspichore, Strapouriés, **t** 228 202 2160. Family-run taverna with lovely views, in business for over a century; lovely peppers stuffed with cheese. *Open daily in summer, weekends only Nov–April.*

Asemólevka, Yspiloú **t** 228 202 4150. Big taverna and grill with a big veranda. *Closed for lunch out of season.*

Kórthion ✉ 84502

Pyrgos Sareli, t 228 206 1804, out of season **t** 210 985 4255 (€€€). Four lovely rooms with kitchens in a sea captain's mansion, with lovely views. *Open April–Sept.*

Villa Korthi, in spitting distance of the sea, **t** 228 206 1122 (€€). Another pleasant choice, all blue and white.

Korthion, on the sea, **t** 228 206 1218 (€€–€). Family-run, spotless and with a restaurant.

To Vintsi tis Gitsas, t 228 206 1130. Eat here by the sea – Mrs Gitsas knows exactly what to do with fish and vegetables.

Entertainment and Nightlife on Ándros

Ándros, especially **Batsí,** is full of slick cocktail bars and discos which change names from season to season, or there are organized Greek nights at tavernas, in Katákilos above Batsí. Batsí also has an open-air **cinema.**

In **Chóra,** nightlife is more Greek-orientated, centring round the bars and clubs. **Vegera, Soleil** and **Cavo del Mar** are all outdoors bars with chill-out music and sunset views.

Gávrion has a music bar or two, including the **Third Eye,** with occasional jazz and blues.

(★) Terpsichore ▸

Folégandros (ΦΟΛΕΓΑΝΔΡΟΣ)

Arid and mountainous, long an island of exile – Socialist Prime Minister George Papandréou, father of Andréas, was once an unwilling guest – Folégandros is now an increasingly trendy place to get away from it all by choice. With sheer cliffs and a breathtaking Chóra built to defy pirates, it is one of the most alluring of the Cyclades and the perfect base since 1984 for the Cycladic Centre of Art. With only 300 inhabitants (down from 4,000 in the 1940s) Folégandros is one of the smallest Greek islands with a permanent population. In myth, Folégandros was a son of King Minos of Crete, and his legacy can be seen in the labyrinthine paths across the island, laid out to confound invaders. Linguists, however, say the name Folégandros comes from the Phoenician Phelekguduri, 'rock-built'; one ancient nickname was Aratos, 'the iron-bound'. Many of the landscapes look as if they had been whipped to a froth by a furious god, then suddenly petrified, an effect curiously softened by a smattering of churches with breast-shaped domes.

Getting to and around Folégandros

There's at least one daily **ferry** from Íos, Santoríni and Síkinos, two a week directly from Piraeus, less frequently from Anáfi, Kéa, Mílos, Sífnos, Sérifos, Sýros, Kýthnos, Páros and Náxos. **Port authority: t** 228 609 1264 (Íos).

The island **buses** link the port, Karavostássi, to Chóra, and meet all ferries, even late ones; another bus goes from Chóra to Angáli and Áno Meriá. **Caiques** take passengers for trips around the island or to Ag. Nikólaos and other beaches. **Cars**, **bikes** and **scooters** can be rented.

Around the Island

Boats land at **Karavostássi**, the tiny east coast harbour, with a tree-fringed pebbly beach. Shady **Livádi Beach** is a 15-minute walk from the port, while pretty **Katérgo Beach**, one of the most beautiful in the Cyclades, is another 45 minutes' walk further on. A path from the

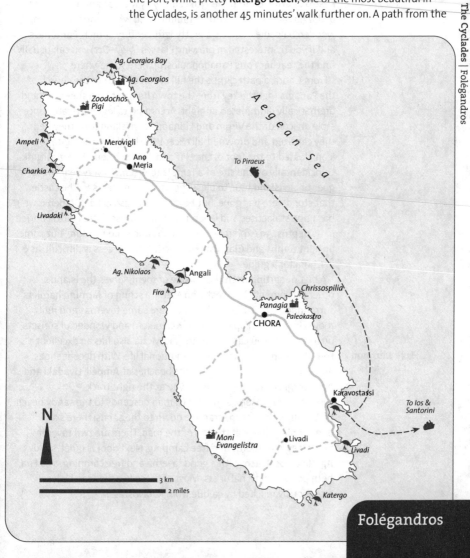

Folégandros

inland hamlet of **Livádi** takes an hour to reach remote **Evangelistría Monastery**, dominating the island's rocky southern shores.

An improved road leads up to **Chóra**, the capital, a stunning sight perched on the pirate-proof, 300m (1,000ft)-high cliffs; the tall houses turn their backs on the sea, fused along the ridge with a sheer drop below. Cars are confined to the periphery, leaving four delightful interlinking squares as stages for local life. The first, shaded by rowan trees, is the hub of nocturnal action; the second is quieter; the third has *kafeneía* full of locals and the church of **Ag. Antónis** with a charming portal; the fourth houses the post office. Newer parts of town look distinctly Andalucían. The fortified **Kástro quarter**, built in the 13th century by Marco Sanudo, is a maze of dazzling alleys filled with geraniums and white houses sporting wooden balconies. There's a pretty 17th-century church, **Pantánassa**, and if you're interested in drawing classes (*May–Oct*) you can usually find the teacher, Fotís Papadópoulos, up here somewhere.

From Chóra, a path climbs the hill of Paleokástro to the church of the **Panagía** (get the key from the town hall), set on a sheer cliff and dramatically illuminated at night. According to legend, pirates once stole an icon of the Virgin and kidnapped an islander. As they fled they capsized and drowned, all except the local, who clung to the icon, floated to the foot of the cliff and built the church in gratitude, coincidentally on the site of a Temple to Artemis. Every year the icon goes on an island tour, to bless the fishermen's houses. The castle that stood here has gone, but beyond it, **Chríssospiliá** ('Golden Cave') has huge stalactites and legends that Barbarossa's treasure is buried in its depths. An exploration in 1988 produced no treasure, but some ancient tombs and Classical-era inscriptions. Access is difficult; ask in Chóra for a guide.

A bus, departing from the far side of town, serves the island's other settlement 5km west, **Áno Meriá**, a string of farming hamlets surrounded by terraced fields. There are some tavernas and rent rooms (ask at the Papadópoulos Kafeneíon) and wonderful sunsets; on a clear day you can see Crete. Áno Meriá also has an excellent **Folk Museum** with exhibits on traditional life. With decent shoes and water, you can walk to remote beaches at **Ampéli**, **Livadáki** and **Ag. Geórgios Bay**; the bus drops you at the right track.

Folk Museum
*t 228 604 1387;
open daily 5–8*

Between Áno Meriá and Chóra a road descends to the sandy beach of **Angáli**, with a steep scramble down to the sands; there's a donkey-hire service at the top of the road. There are two tavernas, pine trees, rent rooms and free camping. Next door is quiet, sandy **Ag. Nikólaos Beach**, with a good taverna and free camping, and **Fíra**, both popular with naturists. Most of these beaches can be less strenuously reached by caique from Karavostássi.

Useful Information on Folégandros

Sottovento Agency, in Chóra, near the Áno Meriá bus stop, **t** 228 604 1444. Very helpful and they speak English.

Folégandros Festivals

27 July: Ag. Panteleímonos, in Áno Meriá.

July and Aug: 'Folegandros Festivities', a programme of concerts, exhibitions and performances, themed to a different aspect of island culture.

15 Aug: Panagía.

Where to Stay and Eat on Folégandros

Folégandros has more accommodation available every year, it seems, but somehow there's never enough in the summer (even in the campsite) so be prepared to sleep out (beware the strong winds).

Karavostássi ✉ 84011

Aeolos, t 228 604 1205, book in Athens, **t** 210 922 3819 (€€). Immaculate rooms overlooking the beach; there's also a lovely garden.

Vardia Bay Studios, t 228 604 1277, book in Athens, **t** 210 684 2524 (€€). Well kept.

Vrachos, on the sea, **t** 228 604 1450 (€€). Airy rooms that come with verandas and mini-bars.

Camping Livadi, 1km beyond Karavostássi, **t** 228 604 1204. Taverna, bar and laundry.

Chóra ✉ 84011

Anemomílos Apartments, t 228 604 1309, *www.anemomilosapartments. com* (€€€). Built in traditional style, with all mod cons, stunning balconies over the sea and a swish pool.

Folégandros Apartments, t 228 604 1239, *www.folegandros- apartments.com* (€€€). Built in Cycladic style, around a courtyard.

Castro, in the Kástro, **t** 228 604 1230, *www.hotel-castro.com* (€€€–€€). A gem – a lovely 500-year-old house owned

by the same family for generations, with pebble mosaic floors. The rooms and roof terrace look down the sheer cliffs to the sea.

Kallisti, on the edge of Chóra, **t** 228 604 1555 (€€€–€€). Traditionally styled rooms with lovely views. *Open all year.*

Fani-Vevis, t 228 604 1237 (€€). A popular old mansion, now renovated.

Odysseus, in Chóra, **t** 228 604 1276, (€€). Pleasant, located on the cliffs.

Polikandia, t 228 604 1322 (€€). Traditional-style place, rooms with mini-bars.

Maria Veniou, t 228 604 1265 (€). A good bet.

Pavlo Sideris, on the road to Chóra, **t** 228 604 1232 (€). Basic chalet-style rooms in converted stables, with a lovely garden.

O Kritikos, t 228 604 1219. Delicious chicken on the spit; a very Greek hang-out.

Melissa, between the two churches, **t** 228 604 1067. Pleasant atmosphere. Try their speciality, *strangistó*, soft Folégandros goat's cheese.

Piatsa, by Melissa, **t** 228 604 1274. Delicious home cooking.

Pounta, at the entrance to Chóra, **t** 228 604 1063. Charming courtyard, serving breakfast and unusual dishes, from spaghetti with Roquefort cheese to rabbit casserole, and a choice of vegan dishes.

Áno Meriá ✉ 84011

Kyra-Maria, t 228 604 1208. Classic island dishes full of rich tastes: free-range chicken and local specialities like *matzáta*, pasta with tomato, rooster or rabbit.

Tavernas Iliovassilema. Sunset views over Milos.

Entertainment and Nightlife on Folégandros

Chóra's bars turn into a village-wide party on summer nights.

Avli. A popular, smart disco.

Patitiri. Plays traditional music.

★ Castro >

Íos (ΙΟΣ)

Although desperately trying to change its image from the Benidorm or Fort Lauderdale of the Aegean, Íos remains a magnet for throngs of young people who spend their days lounging on one of the best beaches in the Cyclades and their evenings staggering from one watering hole to another. To discourage raucous parties and late-night revellers sleeping out on the beach, four lovely campsites have been provided, but rows of sleeping bags by night and naked bodies by day are still the norm. The seasonal Irish invasion is so great that the island's name has been re-interpreted as the acronym for 'Ireland Over Seas'. If you're a party animal then it's the place for you. Otherwise, despite the island's glorious sands and pretty Chóra with its blue-domed churches, you may feel disenchanted, unless you take refuge in one of the upmarket coastal resort hotels, far from the thumping discos. In early spring, however, when the locals reclaim it, you might find Íos as Lawrence Durrell did, full of 'silences, fractured only by some distant church bell or the braying of a mule'.

Gialós and Íos Town

The island's name, also spelled Níos (the locals say Nío), comes from the Ionians, who built cities on the sites of Gialós and Íos Town back when the island was famous for its oak forests. Over the

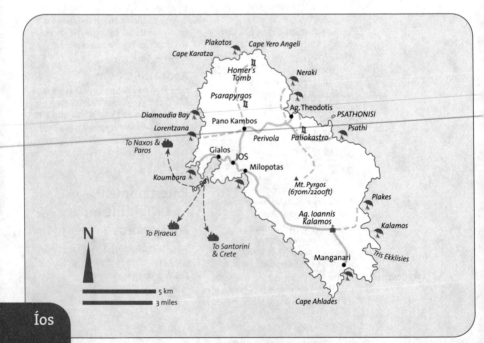

Getting to and around Íos

Íos is well connected. There are daily **ferries** and in summer **hydrofoil** connections with Piraeus, Santoríni, Folégandros and Sikinos, 6 a week with Páros, Náxos and Sýros, less frequently to Anáfi, Mílos, Kéa and Kýthnos. Also **excursion boats** to nearby islands. **Port authority: t** 228 609 1264.

The **bus** service is the best on any island, calling at Koumbára, Gialós, Íos Town to Milapótas Beach every 10mins all day and night; three-day unlimited travel cards are available. **Excursion buses** go daily to Manganári Bay. Less frequent buses go to Ag. Theodótis Beach.

For **car rentals**, try **Íos Rent-a-Car**, in Íos Town, **t** 228 609 2300.

centuries, the oaks became ships and Íos became an arid rockpile; after the earthquake of 1951, when all the water was sucked out of Íos Bay and rushed back to flood and damage Gialós, the island might have been abandoned altogether had not the first tourists begun to trickle in.

The port, **Gialós** or **Ormós**, has grown to be a bustling resort in its own right. Under the Turks, its nickname was 'Little Malta', because it was a favourite loafing place for young pirates (some things never change). To the left of the port, note the pretty 17th-century chapel of **Ag. Iríni**, with separate Catholic and Orthodox altars. Gialós has a beach but it tends to be windy and you're better off walking 15 minutes or catching the bus to **Koumbára**, where a long stretch of sand ends at a big rock that's fun for snorkelling; rooms and tavernas and bars can handle most other desires. There are other, quieter beaches sprinkled all along the coast to the north.

Íos Town, 'the Village', is one of the finest in the Cyclades, a dream vision of white houses, domed churches and tall palms. It is increasingly hard to find at street level through the mist of overcharged hormones behind the bars, burger stands and shops selling rude T-shirts. However, Mayor Poussaíos, a Homer enthusiast, has just built a **theatre** to host quality concerts in the hope of diluting some of the excess with culture. Along those lines, there's also a small **Archaeology Museum** in the town hall.

Archaeology Museum
open Tues–Sat 8–3; adm

Of the 18 original **windmills** behind the town, 12 remain in various states of repair. Traces of the ancient walls are preserved, and only bits more survive of the **fortress** built in 1400 by the Venetian Lord of Íos, Marco Crispi. Here **Panagía Gremiótissa**, 'Our Lady of the Cliffs', houses a miraculous icon that floated to Íos from Crete then refused to be put anywhere else, because it is the only spot on Íos from where Crete is (sometimes) visible.

A Right Royal Visit

Amidst all the hubbub it's worth recalling a story from more innocent days. When Otho of Bavaria, the first King of Greece, paid a visit to Íos, he treated the villagers to drinks in the *kafeneíon* and promised to pay to have the village cleaned up. The grateful Niots, scarcely knowing what majesty Otho pretended to, toasted him warmly: 'To the health of the King, Íos' new dustman!'

10 The Cyclades | Íos

Around the Island

Íos has 35 beaches, but only a handful have been developed. **Milopótas** is a superb sandy beach that starred (with Amorgós) in Luc Bresson's *Le Grand Bleu* and hosts every conceivable water sport, along with posh hotels and campsites. Don't count on getting much shut-eye near the sands: Íos' all-night beach parties are infamous and have unfortunately ended in several deaths by overdose.

For something less Babylonian, you can take a bus or catch one of the excursion boats which leave Gialós daily for the chic golden coves of **Manganári Bay**, where naturism rules (though now officially discouraged). A good road has finally reached Manganári, and new hotels are sprouting. Long, quiet **Kalamós Beach** is a 30-minute walk north on a track (do-able on a motorbike) beginning at the pretty church of **Ag. Ioánnis Kálamos**. For real isolation, walk over to **Plakés Beach**, which is often empty.

Once remote but now accessible by bus, **Ag. Theodótis** has a fine beach looking out towards **Heráklia** island. The beach is overlooked by the ruined 15th-century Venetian fortress of **Paleokástro**, with a well-preserved Byzantine church inside. Marauding pirates once managed to bore a hole in the fortress gate, big enough to allow one man in at a time – only to be scalded to death by burning oil poured on them by the villagers; the fateful door is on display in the church of **Ag. Theodótis**. The road continues to the coarse golden sands of **Psáthi**, where a church dedicated to the Virgin fell into the sea – a prophetic statement on raunchy Íos. Psáthi is a favourite for windsurfing and loggerhead turtle nests and the villas of wealthy Athenians. **Perivóla**, in the middle of the island, has Íos' fresh-water springs and trees. **Páno Kámbos**, once inhabited by a hundred families but today reduced to three or four, is another pretty place. Nearby in **Helliniká** are monoliths of mysterious origin.

Plakotós and Homer

Tradition has it that the mother of Homer came from Íos, and it was here that the great poet came at the end of his life. Some say it was a riddle told by the fishermen of Íos that killed Homer in a fit of perplexity, to wit: 'What we catch we throw away; what we don't catch, we keep' (not wanting any readers to succumb to a similar fate, the answer's in the 'Where to Stay and Eat' section, opposite). Homer's tomb is on the mountain at **Plakotós**, and although earthquakes have left only the rock on which it was built (any tombs you see up here are in fact much later), the epitaph was copied out by ancient travellers: 'Here the earth covers the sacred head of the dean of heroes, the divine Homer.' Plakotós was an Ionian town that once had a temple to Apollo, but like the church at Psáthi it slid down the cliff. You can look down and see the ruined houses; only one tower, **Psarápyrgos**, remains intact.

Useful Information on Íos

Acteon Travel, in the port square, also in the village and at Milopótas, **t** 228 609 1343. Help with booking accommodation, cars and excursions.

Milopótas Water Sports Centre, t 228 609 1622. Offers canoes, sailing and banana-boat rides.

Íos Town Hall, t 228 609 1505, www.iosgreece.com.

Íos Festivals

Mid-May: Week-long Homer festival.
29 Aug: Ag. Ioánnis Kálamos, the island's biggest *panegýri*.
8 Sept: Ag. Theodótis.

Where to Stay and Eat on Íos

Íos, the paradise of the footloose and fancy-free, can be reasonable, though the unprepared will pay dearly for a cramped room; try one from the **Rooms Association, t** 228 609 1205/1591. Generally, the young and wild head up for 'the Village'; the rest stay down in Gialós.

Before Guinness, Íos' speciality was *meyífra*, a hard white cheese, mixed with perfume and fermented in a goatskin – hard to find these days (all the better, some might add). Don't confuse it with *mezíthra*, the soft ricotta-like sheep's-milk cheese. But *meyífra* cheese is not the answer to Homer's riddle: what the fishermen caught was lice.

Gialós (Ormós) ✉ 84001

Petra Apartments, at the far end of the beach, **t** 228 609 1049, www.iospetra.gr (€€€). Lovely Cycladic village complex; stylish open-plan rooms.

Mare Monte, on the harbour, **t** 228 609 1585 (€€). Bar and pool, phone and fax in every room, and its own restaurant.

Poseidon, just off the waterfront, **t** 228 609 1091, www.poseidonhotelios.gr (€€). Immaculate rooms, and a panoramic pool.

Violetta, t 228 609 1044 (€). Cheapest of all, with basic rooms.

Íos Camping, just off the waterfront, **t** 228 609 1329. Beware of mosquitoes.

Polydoros, at Koumbára, **t** 228 609 1132. Traditional Greek dishes, seafood and vegetarian meals.

Íos Town (Chóra) ✉ 84001

Liostasi Íos Spa, just outside the centre, **t** 228 609 2140, www.liostasi.gr (€€€€). Stylish new hotel with lovely views and a wide array of spa facilities.

Petradi, halfway to Milopótas, **t** 228 609 1510, www.hotelpetradi.gr (€€€). With balconies, private baths and a terrace restaurant with great views over Síkinos.

Sunrise, on the hill, **t** 228 609 1074 (€€€). Stunning views over the town, with pool and bar.

Hermes, halfway to Milopótas, **t** 228 609 1471 (€€). With pretty sea views and a snack bar.

Homer's Inn (there had to be one!), **t** 228 609 1365, www.homersinn.net (€€). A good bet, with a pool.

Afroditi, t 228 609 1546 (€€–€). One of the best places for value.

Lord Byron, in the centre, **t** 2268 609 2125. An oasis of Greek tradition and sanity, specializing in an array of Anatolian *mezédes*, with *rembétiko* music.

Íos Club, on the footpath up from the harbour. Renowned for sunset views over Síkinos, good drinks, classical music and jazz.

Pithari, near the church. One of the best places on the island, serving excellent Greek food and barrelled wine. Just stroll into the kitchen and point out what you want.

Pinocchio's. Great pasta and pizza under lovely bougainvillaea.

Vesuvius, t 228 609 1338. Another good choice for decent Italian fare, with roof garden and views.

Milopótas Beach ✉ 84001

Dionysos, t 228 609 1630, in winter 210 432 9611, www.dionysos-ios.gr (€€€€€). Traditional style, with pool, tennis, air-conditioning and a transfer service.

Íos Palace, on the beach, **t** 228 609 1224, www.iospalacehotel.com (€€€€€– €€€). Designed and decorated in the old island style; two pools, tennis, billiards, jazz bar and good views.

⭐ Far Out >

Far Out, a few minutes from the beach, t 228 609 1446, *www.faroutclub.com* (€€€–€€). Named after guests' reactions to the view; comfortable rooms in Cubist style clustered on the hillside; with a pool. It now has a spa, with Jacuzzi, sauna and other indulgences. The Far Out empire also includes some less expensive bungalows, a nightclub and a campsite (*see* below).

Markos Beach, on the beach, with a pool, t 228 609 1571, in winter t 210 321 5446 (€€€–€€). Standard rooms with air-conditioning, showers.

The beach has two campsites:

Far Out Camping, t 228 609 1468. Apparently just that, with a restaurant, minibus, pool, and sports, including Íos Diving Centre and bungee jumping.

Stars, t 228 609 1302. With a pool and small bungalows, and a nightclub.

Drakos, t 228 60 9 1281. One of the first tavernas, and still the place for fish.

Manganári Bay ✉ 84001

Christos, t 228 609 2286. Beach taverna serving traditional Greek fare.

Entertainment and Nightlife on Íos

'The Village' is one long rave-up, all the bars offering different amusements from videos to rock bands and happy hours. Serious drinkers pack the main square bars after midnight and go on until dawn. Each bar/disco posts its nightly programme so you can choose. Classics are:

Slammer. As in 'tequila slammer'; in the main square.

No Name. For Greek music.

Sweet Irish Dream. Big and loud; open until the wee hours.

Disco 69, on the way to Milopótas. Attracts late-night boppers.

Scorpion, down in Milopótas. Biggest disco in the Cyclades.

In more staid **Gialós**, bars tend to show videos outdoors at night, usually in English.

At **Milopótas**, the Far Out Beach Club offers something all day long; there's an Internet café too.

Kéa/Tzía (KEA/TZIA)

Closest of all the Cyclades to Athens, Kéa, with its fine beaches, has for many years been a favourite place for Athenians to build their summer villas – the island can be reached from the metropolis in less than four hours, and it's guaranteed to have no room on holiday weekends, when jeeps, dogs, boats and windsurfers pile off the ferries and the jet set sails over to Vourkári from Glyfáda in a flotilla of gin palaces; if you want to make a short stay, time it for midweek.

Kéa feels very different from the other Cyclades, with lush valleys and terraces of fruit trees, fields grazed by dairy cattle and grubbing pigs; since antiquity it has been famed for its fertility, its red wines, its lemons, honey and almonds. Its traditional architecture may lack the pristine white Cubism of its sister isles but there's almost a touch of Tuscany about Ioulís, with its red-pantiled houses and higgledy-piggledy lanes.

History

Traces of a Neolithic fishing settlement dating back to 3000 BC were discovered at Kéfala on Kéa's north coast. These first settlers were certainly no pushovers; when the mighty Minoan thalassocrats founded a colony *c.* 1650 BC on the peninsula of Ag. Iríni, they had to build defences to protect themselves from attacks, not from the sea

Getting to and around Kéa

There are at least 4 daily **ferry** and **Flying Cat** (75mins) connections with Lávrion (passing by sinister Makrónissos, a prison island and torture chamber used in the Civil War and by the Junta; poet Ioánnis Rítsos spent years there); 3–4 times a week to Kýthnos and once a week to Sýros. Daily **hydrofoil** service in summer with Mýkonos and Piraeus (Zéa). **Port authority**: t 228 802 1344.

The **bus** runs 3–4 times daily from Ioulís to Vourkári, and is seldom seen anywhere else; the tourist police have the ever-changing schedule.

Taxis: t 228 802 2444. For wheels, try **Korasides**, t 228 802 1884.

but by land. The colony, discovered in 1960, coincides nicely with the myth that Minos himself visited Kéa and begat the Kéan race with a native named Dexithea; it also reveals a fascinating chronicle of trade and diplomacy between the Minoans and the older Cycladic culture and, later, with the Mycenaeans. In the Classical era, Kéa was divided into four towns: Ioulís, Karthaea, Poiessa and Korissía. They worshipped Aristeos, a son of Apollo, who saved the Cyclades from the star Sirius, who wanted to blast them with hot arrows. The poet Simonides (557–467 BC), famous for his epigram after the Battle of Thermopylae, his lyrical nephew Bacchylides, the philosopher Ariston and the physician Erasistratos were all sons of Kéa. Kéa was also famous for its retirement scheme called the *geroktonia*: citizens were required to take a glass of *conium* (hemlock) when they reached 70, although the Kéans say it only happened when the island was besieged by the Athenians and food was low.

The Sinking of the *Britannic*

On 21 November 1916, the *Britannic* sank in the Kéa channel. One of the fabulous White Star liners, a tenth larger at 269m (883ft) than her sister ship, the *Titanic*, the *Britannic* was given added safety features after the *Titanic* went down. Originally called the *Gigantic*, she was patriotically renamed at the advent of the First World War and was requisitioned by the British government before her maiden voyage to serve as a hospital ship and bring the wounded back from the Dardanelles. Under Captain Charles Bartlett, HMS *Britannic* was on her sixth voyage, sailing from Naples to Moudros Bay on Límnos to pick up casualties. It was 8am, the sea was calm, when suddenly an explosion blasted in her bow compartment. Although she should have easily survived, the fatal sixth bulkhead failed to close properly; in addition, the nurses had opened the lower port holes to air the wards, which allowed water to pour in. Only two miles from Kéa, the *Britannic* went down in a mere 55 minutes. Fortunately, there were more than enough lifeboats available, and of the 1,134 people on board only 30 died, horrifically, when two of the lifeboats were sucked under by the propeller.

What caused the explosion? At the time there were rumours that the ship was secretly being used to transport munitions. Others even suggested that the British themselves blew it up, hoping to shock America into entering the war. Suspicions that the Admiralty had something to hide were fuelled by its own maps, which mischarted the location; when Jacques Cousteau went in search of the wreck in 1975, he found the *Britannic* 6.75 nautical miles away from its charted position. In 1995, explorers returned, among them Dr Robert Ballard (one of the discoverers of the *Titanic*), who sent down video robots. They showed the wreck nearly intact, down to the whistles on the funnels. Divers in 1997 were able to do a complete survey: the ship's immense floor, doors and storage rooms are in an excellent state of preservation. They found no sign of munitions, torpedo damage or mine anchors, increasing the mystery until 2003, when a new expedition using the latest diving technology discovered several mine anchors, and put the conspiracy theories to rest once and for all.

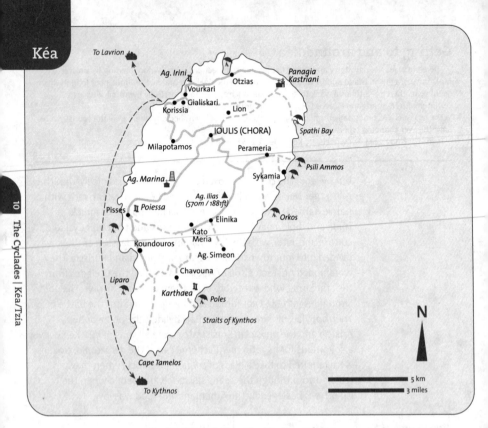

Korissía and the North Coast

Kéa's port, **Korissía**, has a few pretty neoclassical buildings and a lovely church but otherwise it's a functional little place with a bust to the poet Simonides. Anxious to become a resort like Kéa's other coastal villages, it boasts a few boutiques and an art gallery among the waterfront tavernas. The name 'Korissía' recalls the ancient town that once stood on the site, but most locals still call it Livádi, as they continue to call their island Tzía instead of the official Kéa.

The bay sweeps round to the sandy if not tidy town **beach**; a footpath over the headland leads past the old castle-like country house of the Maroúli family, then north to small, sandy **Gialiskári Beach**. A playground for rich Athenians, the area bristles with exclusive holiday villas.

A kilometre further north, on attractive **Ag. Nikólaou Bay**, **Vourkári**, a pretty fishing village, has metamorphosed into a smart little resort, with more pleasure-cruisers now than fishing boats. Around the bay, on the church-topped peninsula of **Ag. Iríni**, are the excavations of the **Minoan-Mycenaean settlement**, destroyed c. 1450 BC. It's not difficult to make out the narrow temple, first constructed in the Bronze Age, a late Minoan *megaron*, Late Bronze Age houses, streets and houses, fortifications, and a spring chamber outside the walls. Inscriptions in Minoan Linear A script were among the finds now displayed in the Archaeology Museum in Ioulís.

From here the coastal road continues to the delightful beach resort at **Otziás**, its bay ringed with almond blossom in spring. From here you can walk up to wind-whipped **Panagía Kastriáni**, with panoramic views. The 18th-century monastery is noted for its miracle-working icon of the Virgin. There are two churches, the first built in 1708 after shepherds saw a strange glow on the mountain pinpointing the presence of the icon.

Ioulís (Chóra) and Around

High above Korissía, the island's capital, **Ioulís**, is inland, hidden like so many Cycladic towns from seagoing predators. As the bus climbs, the views down the terraced hillside to the sea are stunning. On the way, note the school, built in neoclassical style, one of the finest in Greece. Ioulís also boasts the largest collection of windmills in the Cyclades: 26 (mostly ruined) stand on the **Mountain of the Mills**.

The town is a pretty place to wander around, with its flower-filled balconies and covered galleries known as *stegádia*, a maze of alleys, the white houses topped with red-tiled roofs. The fine neoclassical **town hall**, topped with statues of Apollo and Athena, has a sculpture of a woman and child found at Karthaia and ancient reliefs set into niches. The **Kástro quarter**, reached through a dazzling white archway (note the coat of arms of the Pangalós family), occupies the site of the ancient acropolis and Temple of Apollo. In 1210, the Venetian Domenico Michelli cannibalized its marbles to build a castle; in the 1860s the Greek government dismantled the castle to put the Classical bits in a museum. Bits remain, as well as a few Venetian mansions and Byzantine churches. The **Archaeology Museum** contains Minoan finds from Ag. Iríni, and the tall and intriguing Bronze Age terracotta female figures from the 14th-century BC temple – these are the oldest yet found in the Aegean. Made after the fall of Minoan Crete, the figures are in the style of the Cretan bare-breasted goddesses, and yet are unlike anything ever found on Crete, moulded over wooden skeletons, no two the same and all painted bright yellow, white and red. Other artefacts in the museum come from ancient Kéa's four cities, as well as a copy of the wonderful *Kouros of Kéa*, discovered in Korissía and now in the National Archaeological Museum in Athens.

Archaeology Museum
t 228 802 2079; open Tues–Sun 8.30–5

A 10-minute walk east of Chóra leads to the island's watchdog – the 6th-century BC **Lion of Kéa**, the 'Leonda', an ancient guardian 3m (10ft) high and nearly 6m (19ft) long. Tales about the lion abound: one says he symbolizes the bravery of the Kéans; another recounts how evil nymphs were killing the wives of Ioulís and the men, fed up, were ready to abandon the city. The priest prayed to Zeus to send the nymphs away, and he delivered an enormous lion, which chased them across the water to Kárystos in Evía. The Kéans then carved the lion in stone, to keep the nymphs permanently at bay; others say this is the lion himself, as still as stone, ready to spring at the whiff of a bad fairy.

The countryside east of Ioulís, the **Peraméria** region, still has its oak woods and traditional country houses. Above Peraméria Town, the lush valley of Spathí ends at sandy **Spathí Bay**. Another road east from Ioulís branches for three fine beaches: **Sykamiá**, **Psíli Ámmos** and **Orkós**.

Southern Kéa

The main road south of Ioulís leads 5km through rolling green countryside to the ruined **Monastery of Ag. Marína**, built around a square, three-storey Hellenistic tower; one of the finest in Greece – at least it was, before King Otho asked the locals to take out a carved stone for him, which occasioned the tower's partial collapse. From here the road cuts across to the west-coast resort of **Písses** (which perhaps should consider reviving its ancient name, Poiessa, of which a few traces remain). Backed by a lush valley full of orchards and olive groves, Písses has a sweeping sandy beach, one of Kéa's finest.

The next bay along, **Koúndouros**, is just as lovely, and has several smaller coves, as well as a crop of bungalows for Athenian week-enders. Another gorgeous beach is further along the coast at **Liparó**.

On the southeast shore at **Póles Bay** (with a great beach) stood **Karthaea**, once Kéa's most important city. Simonides had his school of poetry here; now you'll only find scant remains of the walls and the foundations of the Temples of Athena and Apollo. Excavations are continuing, and the town's theatre has recently been unearthed.

It is still possible to follow the course of the Hellenistic road from **Káto Meriá** or **Ellinká**, lovely places for woodland walks. Like Ándros, Kéa has a newly signposted network of paths, re-using old stone paths.

Useful Information on Kéa

Tourist police: two blocks in from the Karthea Hotel in Korissía, **t** 228 802 1100.

To Stegadi, t 228 202 1435. You will find that Efy knows everything; upstairs from her ticket office is a bookstore run by her father, the former mayor, Mr Lepouras, who will bend your ear about his beloved island (you may even be tempted to buy one of his own guide books).

Kéa Festivals

The island's *panegýria* are known for spectacular dances and traditional instruments (the *tsamboúna*, *doubi* and lute).

First week in June: Antique car rally (one of Greece's biggest).

17 July: Ag. Marína.

15 Aug: Chóra. August also brings the Simonídia, a cultural festival with concerts, plays and exhibitions throughout the month.

Late Aug: Fairytales Festival. Storytelling in picturesque spots.

7 Sept: Otziás.

Where to Stay and Eat on Kéa

Most of Kéa's accommodation is furnished seaside apartments aimed at families. Simple rooms to rent are like gold dust at weekends or in high season, with prices to match. Foreign visitors have begun trickling in, but Kéa is still very Greek and the tavernas serve unadulterated Greek fare at reasonable prices. Look for *pastéli*, a delicious sticky bar made from local thyme honey and sesame seeds. Other specialities include pungent *kopanistí* cheese and *paspallá*, preserved fat pork, usually eaten at Christmas, *tiganía*, chopped pork in a white sauce, *lozá*, a local sausage, and *xinó*, another local cheese.

Korissía ✉ 84002

Brillante Zoe, 25m from the sea, t 228 802 2685, *www.hotelbrillante.gr* (€€€). Traditional stone-built hotel, charmingly furnished. *Open all year.*

United Europe Furnished Flats, close to the beach, t 228 802 1362 (€€€–€€). A smart self-catering option.

Other furnished apartments worth trying are:

To Korali, t 228 802 1268 (€€).

Korissia, t 228 802 1484 (€€). In a quiet backwater with a nice terrace, bar and large rooms or studios.

To Oneiro, t 228 802 1118 (€€). *Open all year.*

Kyria Pantazi, in a back alley, t 228 802 1452 (€€–€). Basic but quaint village rooms.

I Apolavsi ('The Enjoyment'), t 228 802 1068 (€). Comfortable, basic studios and a huge sun terrace overlooking the harbour.

Karthea, off the harbour, t 228 802 1222 (€). Gloomy, clean and quiet.

Akri, t 228 802 1196, past the supermarket. For a pleasant evening over grilled fish or moussaka.

Apotheki. In a whitewashed ruin, popular, with a large choice of dishes.

Ouzerie Lagoudera, on the harbour, t 228 202 1257. Smart place in a refurbished neoclassical house; great menu featuring tasty prawn *saganáki*.

Vourkári/Otziás ✉ 84002

At Vourkári, furnished apartments to let (all €€€–€€) include:

Lefkes, t 228 802 1443.

Nikitas, t 228 802 2303, on the waterfront.

Petrakos, t 228 802 1197.

Kastrianí Monastery, on the north coast, an hour's walk east of Otziás, t 228 802 1348. The monks have cheap guest rooms if you get desperate.

Aristos, t 228 802 1171. Vourkári is the best place for seafood at a price, where yachties moor a few feet from their tables. If there's been a good haul of fish, a delicious *kakaviá* (Greek bouillabaisse) will be on the menu.

Nikos, next to the art gallery, t 228 802 1486. Cheaper, and popular for lunch and dinner.

Strofi. Otziás' favourite fish taverna, t 228 202 1480.

Thalia Ouzerie. Good cooking and good value.

Tis Annas. A cosy spot on the beach t 228 202 1618.

Ioúlis ✉ 84002

Ioúlis, t 228 802 2177 (€€). One of the few choices here, full of character.

Filoxenia, t 228 802 1153 (€). Definitely a second choice, with shared bathrooms.

Piatsa. In a lovely setting through the main archway.

Rolando. A local favourite for fish and good *mezédes*.

Písses/Koúndouros ✉ 84002

Galini, in Písses, t 228 803 1316 (€€). If these furnished apartments are full, try the others run by the Polítis family, t 228 803 1343/1318.

Kéa Camping, t 228 803 1332. Pleasant and only site on Kéa. The owner also has rooms.

Akroyiali, t 228 803 1301. Taverna, with rooms.

Christoforos, t 228 803 1308. On the waterfront, taverna serving all the Greek classics.

Katomerítiko, in Káto Meriá. Locals go out of their way to come here for its Kéan specialities, including *tiganía* and *lozá*.

 ⭐ Ouzerie Lagoudera >

Kímolos (ΚΙΜΩΛΟΣ)

Kímolos is Mílos' little sister, and until fairly recently they were Siamese twins, connected by an isthmus that had a Mycenaean town on it. But the isthmus sank, leaving a channel a kilometre wide. Once known as Echinousa, or sea urchin, which it proudly depicted on its coins, the island gave its modern name to kimolía ('chalk' in Greek), and to cimolite in English, a mineral similar to soft, chalk-like fuller's earth, an essential ingredient in dyeing. Kímolos remains a top producer of cimolite, and you can see the workings as the boat pulls in.

Kímolos, with its 720 souls, is a quiet, untainted Greek island with plenty of beaches and freelance camping, a perfect place to relax and do absolutely nothing, with no cars and few tourists, even in August. Although it has been rocky and barren ever since the Venetians set the olive groves ablaze in 1638, there are patches of green, including 140 species of rare plants on the southeast coast, and rare blue lizards. The island's largest building is a retirement home built by local philanthropist Geórgios Afendákis.

Chório and Around

From the pretty little port, **Psáthi**, it's a 15-minute walk up to Kímolos or **Chório** (not 'Chóra' as on the other islands). Blizzard-white, Chório is a tangle of paved lanes with flowers at every turn. It is divided into two settlements: **Mésa Kástro** (or Palío Chório, the bit in the castle walls) and **Éxo Kástro**, or Kainoúrio Chório, on the outside. The houses of Mésa Kástro form the inside of the fortress, with loophole windows and four gates. The outer village has a beautiful domed cathedral church, **Panagía Evangélistra**, built in 1614. Other impressive churches are the **Panagía Odygítria** (1873), **Taxiárchis** (1670) and **Chrisóstomos** (1680), and the ruins of the Catholic church, the **Madonna of the Rosary**. A small archaeological

Useful Information on Kímolos

Kimolos Travel: t 228 705 1219.

Where to Stay and Eat on Kímolos

Most people come for the day, but lately more and more people have been opening up rooms; ask around in the bars and tavernas to see who has a vacant one. Camping is usually 'no problem' as the Greeks say – try Klíma and Alíki beaches.

The Doctor's Windmill, above the beach at Psáthi, t 228 705 1556, www.kimolos1.gr (€€€€–€€€). Five pretty rooms in an 1850s windmill.

Sardi, t 228 705 1458 (€€). Nice rooms by Alíki beach.

Alíki, t 228 705 1340. Taverna with simple rooms (€) by the beach.

To Kyma, Psáthi, t 228 705 1001 (€). Simple but charming.

Meltemi, t 228 705 1386. Just outside Chório, simple rooms (€) and a taverna serving the island's best dishes.

Panorama. Dining with a view, just outside the Kástro in Chório.

Getting to Kímolos

There are **ferry** connections 5 times a week with Milos (Adámas), 4 a week with Piraeus, Sérifos and Sífnos, 3 a week with Kýthnos and Sýros, one a week to Ándros, Páros and Tínos; and a **water taxi** 3 times a day to Apollonía on Mílos; plus **caiques** to the beaches. You can take day trips in high season to Mílos and Sífnos. **Port authority** (in Mílos – Kímolos is too small to have its own): **t** 228 702 2100. There's a **ticket agency** in Psáthi, **t** 228 705 1214.

museum may soon open, with finds from the necropolis at Ellinikó. One of Chório's six **windmills** still grinds wheat – the last truly functioning one in the Cyclades.

From Chório you can walk up to the ruined **Venetian castle** built by Marco Sanudo at Kímolos' highest point (355m/1,165ft). Within its walls is the island's oldest church, **Christós**, dating from 1592. Another walk by way of **Alíki**, with its small beach and saltpans, ends at **Ag. Andréas** and the **Ellinikó necropolis** – all that survives of the city that sank with the isthmus – and its graves from the Mycenaean period (2500 BC) to the early centuries AD. You can end with a swim at **Ellinikó Beach** (where loggerhead turtles nest) or **Kambána**.

There are other beaches along the east coast. A path from Chório descends to **Goúpa**, a hamlet with the most abundant fish in the Aegean these days, and where, supposedly, people used to scoop them out by the basketful. It's a pretty little place, with a good, unspoilt beach. There's another lovely beach at **Klíma**, and 7km north at **Prássa** are radioactive thermal springs good for rheumatism. Goats are the only inhabitants of **Políegos**, the islet facing Psáthi, but the rare monk seal (*see* p.613) has been sighted as well.

Kýthnos (ΚΥΘΝΟΣ)

Time your visit right and you can have this island to yourself, avoiding the Athenian summer invasion. Like its neighbour Kéa, Kýthnos attracts relatively few foreigners, and even the majority of Greek arrivals are not tourists, but folks full of aches and pains who come to soak in the thermal spa at Loutrá; the locals often call their island Thermia. Since the closure of Kýthnos' iron mines in 1940, the 1,500 islanders have got by as best they could by fishing, farming (mostly figs and vines), basket-weaving and making ceramics; the one thing that has stopped the population from dropping any further is the construction of a harbour mole in 1974, allowing ships to dock. Perhaps to make up for its slow start, Kýthnos became the first Greek island (1982) to get all of its electricity from renewable sources – wind in the winter and sun in the summer, inspiring similar projects on Mýkonos, Kárpathos, Samothráki and Crete.

Maybe because of their frugal lives, Kýthniots tend to celebrate *panegýria* with gusto, donning their traditional costumes; carnival

Getting to and around Kýthnos

There are daily **ferries** from Piraeus, Sérifos, Sífnos and Mílos, 2–3 times a week from Lávrion, Kéa, Kímolos, Folégandros, Síkinos, Íos and Santoríni. Kýthnos has two ports: all ships put in at **Mérichas** on the west coast, but when the winds are strong they'll come in to **Loútra** in the northeast. There is a **hydrofoil** daily to Kéa and Piraeus. **Port authority: t** 228 103 2290.

The island's two **buses** run regularly to Chóra and Loutrá and to Dryopída and Panagía Kanála.

Taxis: Kýthnos, **t** 228 103 1272; Dryópida, **t** 228 103 1290.

is a big event here. There are quiet sandy beaches, a rugged interior great for walkers, and welcoming people. Best of all, it's the kind of island where old men still offer to take you fishing.

History

In Classical times the tale was told that Kýthnos was uninhabited because of its wild beasts and snakes, and Ofiohousa ('snaky') was one of the island's ancient names. Recently, however, archaeologists have uncovered a Mesolithic settlement (7500–6000 BC) north of Loutrá that spits in the eye of tradition and is currently the oldest settlement yet discovered in the Cyclades. Much later the Minoans held the island, followed by the Driopes, a semi-mythical tribe who were chased out of their home on the slopes of Mount Parnassós by Heracles and scattered to Évia, Cyprus and Kýthnos; their king, Kýthnos, gave his name to the island and their old capital is still called Drýopis.

During the Hellenistic period Kýthnos was dominated by Rhodes. Two great painters came from the island, Kydian and Timatheus (416–376 BC); the latter was famous in antiquity for his portrait of Iphigenia. In 198 BC all Kýthnos was pillaged, except for Vyrókastro, which proved impregnable. Marco Sanudo took the island, and for 200 years it was under the rule of the Gozzadini family of Bologna.

Beaches, Chóra and Loutrá

Mérichas is a typical Greek fishing harbour, the ferry dock and yacht berths giving way to a tree-fringed bay backed by lively tavernas. Its landmark is still the unfinished, abandoned hotel, somebody's big fat Greek tourist dream gone wrong but nevertheless still the biggest building on the island. That leaves Mérichas a laid-back, cheerful place, kept tidy by the village elders who also tend the ducks that live on the sandy beach, and who posted the sign by the litter bins: 'The sea is the spring of life and joy.' In the morning fishermen sell the day's catch; forklift trucks buzz about delivering sacks of potatoes and cases of beer. Up the steps from the harbour and a short walk off the Chóra road is the much nicer little beach of **Martinákia**, popular with families. To the north are the unexcavated Hellenistic ruins of the once impregnable **Vyrókastro**, set on the headland above the lovely beaches at **Episkópi** and

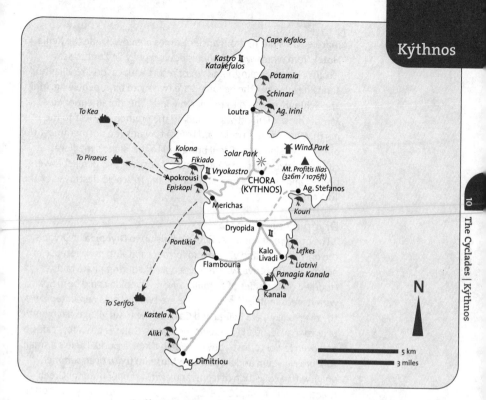

Apókrousi, although the prettiest sandy beach on the island, **Kolóna**, is just beyond – it's a two-sided beach, really a sand bar connecting Kýthnos to the tiny islet of Agiós Loúkas.

The 7.5km trip north from Mérichas to the capital, **Chóra** (or Kýthnos), winds through barren hillsides rippled with stone-wall terraces, deep wrinkles filled with oleanders, fruit trees and vines. Although as Cycladic towns go it's not that spectacular, it's a workaday place with an undeniable charm. The pavements on the back streets are painted with mermaids, fish and flowers. It has several pretty churches, including **Ag. Sávvas**, founded in 1613 by the Gozzadini, who decorated it with their coat of arms. The oldest is **Ag. Triáda**, a domed, single-aisle basilica. Outside, note the garden full of fragments of ancient sculpture; there's talk of starting a museum for all the finds that have come to light. Other churches in Chóra claim to have icons by the Cretan-Venetian master Skordílis, while the **Prodrómos** ('the Scout' or St John the Baptist) has a valuable 17th-century screen. Outside Chóra are the solar park and modern windmills, providing the island's power.

The buses continue to **Loutrá**, the most important spa in the Cyclades. Iron impregnates the water and since ancient times Loutra's two springs, **Kakávos** and **Ag. Anárgyri**, have been used for a cure for gout, rheumatism, eczema and 'women's problems'. Carved marble baths dating from ancient times are now inside the **Xenia Hotel**, from which water bubbles down a gully and out to sea.

Loutrá is a straggling, windswept resort with castle-like villas and a sandy beach. Over the headland are two more bays, pebbly **Ag. Iríni** and **Schinári**, exposed to the north winds. The aforementioned Mesolithic settlement was found on the promontory just to the north. A hard hour's walk from Loutrá towards the northernmost tip of Kýthnos (signposted) will bring you to the island's medieval citadel, **Kástro Oriás** (or Kástro Katakéfalos), with its derelict towers, houses and churches (one still containing frescoes), destroyed by the Turks in 1570.

Dryopída and Kanála

The other road out of Mérichas heads up to **Dryopída** or Drýopis, the only other inland village and former capital, in part because of nearby **Katafíki Cave**, where the people hid during pirate raids. Huddled on the sides of a small canyon, Dryopída could be in Spain, with its red-pantiled houses. There are two districts, separated by the river valley: **Péra Roúga** and **Galatás**, the main village, a labyrinth of crazy-paved, neatly whitewashed lanes. Galatás has a few cafés and even fewer tourists, but it's worth a look around. There's a small **Folklore Museum** and a **Byzantine Museum** (*both open summer only*), with a collection of icons, and even a proper outdoor **Greek theatre** – built in 1951. Once a great ceramics centre, only one pottery remains, belonging to the Milás family. Kýthnos was also a centre of icon-painting in the 17th century, led by the Skordílis family; much of their work can still be seen, including the wonderful wooden iconostasis in **Ag. Mínas**, which also has an Easter bier with folk-art decorations. From here, it takes an hour to walk to Chóra along the ancient cobbled way, or you can go down to the beaches at **Léfkes**, or **Ag. Stéfanos**, a chapel-topped islet linked by a causeway.

South of Dryopída, the southern villages can be reached by a new paved road – a nice, straight road (you might even reach fifth gear) that runs along the rocky spine of the island. One branch leads to **Kanála**, where a big summer village has sprung up around the church of **Panagía Kanála**, the island's patroness, housing a venerated icon, painted by St Luke himself (or more likely, by a member of the Skordílis clan). Chalets dot the peaceful grounds, where pine trees shade picnic areas, and Greek families laze and splash in a string of sandy coves. There are wonderful views over to Sýros and Sérifos, and the water is so shallow that you can almost walk across.

Another new road leads to **Flamboúria Beach** on the west coast, a quiet place with one taverna, and another down to **Ag. Dimitríou**, way down at the southern tip. This little beach rates two tavernas and a music bar in summer. It's the end of the world, but proof that Kýthnos, in its way, swings.

To Kantouni >>

ⓘ **Kýthnos** >
booth on the port,
Mérichas, theoretically
open mid-June–Sept,
t 228 103 2250

Useful Information on Kýthnos

Tourist police: Chóra, **t** 228 103 1201.
Mílos Express Travel, Mérichas, **t** 228 103 2104. Has car and bike rentals.

Kýthnos Festivals

Sundays: Hear the island's music at Dryopída.
20 July: Ag. Ilías, Chóra.
15 Aug and 8 Sept: Kanála.

Where to Stay and Eat on Kýthnos

Mérichas ✉ 84006

O Finikas, behind the supermarket, **t** 228 103 2323 (€€€). Mérichas is the most convenient place to stay on the island, and these upscale rooms, in Cycladic style and a garden setting, are comfortable.

⭐ **To Steki** >>

Villa Elena, by the sea, **t** 228 103 2275, *www.villa-elena.gr* (€€€). Traditionally designed studios.

Kamares, **t** 228 103 2105 (€€). Rooms with a view over the port, on the quiet side of Mérichas.

Ioanna, **t** 228 103 2858 (€€). Next to the Kamares, and very similar.

Chryssoula Laranzaki, **t** 228 103 2309 (€€–€). Quiet rooms with views.

Kythnos, slap on the waterfront, **t** 228 103 2247 (€€–€). Friendly but basic, above a *zacharoplasteío* that does breakfast and home-made rice puddings and jellies.

Panorama, on the hill, **t** 228 103 2184/2182 (€€–€). Newish, with great sea views.

Paradissos, **t** 228 103 2206 (€€–€). Comfortable rooms with pleasant vine-shaded terraces and stunning bay views.

Martinakia, on the beach of the same name, **t** 228 103 2414. With a friendly parrot in the garden, serving good *kalamária* and grills, and **rooms** (€).

Ostria, next to the ferry docks, **t** 228 103 3263 (€20–25 for lobster). Excellent grill restaurant, serving everything from *tzatzíki* to lobster.

To Kantouni, at the far end of the beach (towards the derelict hotel), **t** 228 103 2220. Tables at the water's edge where they specialize in grills and *sfougáta*, feather-light rissoles made from the local cheese, *thermiotikó*; also barrelled retsina and a romantic view across the bay.

Yialos (or 'Sailors'), in Mérichas, **t** 228 103 2102. Has tables on the beach and does a fine *pikilía* of Greek starters and good specialities such as *kalogíros*, a casserole of meat, aubergines, tomatoes and feta; ask to try the local Kýthnos wine.

Chóra ✉ 84006

Filoxenia, near the entrance to Chóra, **t** 228 103 1644, *www.filoxenia-kythnos. gr* (€€–€). The only place in town to stay, but very nice.

Messariá, in the square, **t** 228 103 1620. Traditional style, serving good rabbit dishes and more.

To Steki, **t** 228 103 1204. Excellent taverna and grill in a lovely courtyard off the main street. Its neighbour, **To Kentro**, is another good choice.

Loutrá ✉ 84006

Porto Klaras Apartments, **t** 228 103 1276, *www.porto-klaras.gr* (€€€–€€). Beautifully appointed family suites or doubles. All the apartments have sea-view terraces.

Calypso, Schinári Beach, **t** 228 103 1418 (€€). Twelve new and pretty rooms.

Kythnos Bay, **t** 228 103 1218 (€€). Very comfortable, geared towards stays of three nights or more by spa customers, but good value.

Skoinari Beach, **t** 228 103 1470 (€€). A peaceful setting overlooking the little beach.

Araxovoli, **t** 228 103 1082. New restaurant serving a delicious mix of Greek and international dishes.

Ta Vrachia, **t** 228 103 1087. Good fresh fish and meat from Kýthnos.

Xerolithia, **t** 228 103 1529. Very tasty traditional home cooking. *Open all year.*

Katerina, Schinári Beach, **t** 228 103 1418. With stunning views; everything on the menu is home-made and home-grown.

Kanála and Ag. Dimítrios
✉ 84006

Antamoma, t 228 103 2515 (€€).
Pleasant rooms.

Nikos Bouritis, t 228 103 2195 (€).
Good-value rooms.

Akrogiali, at Ag. Dimítrios, **t** 228 103
2208 (€). Rooms/taverna by the sea.

Ophiousa. Your chance for Greek soul
food – stewed goat or *kokorétsi*; look
for the life-sized fibreglass waiter near
the village entrance.

Entertainment and Nightlife on Kýthnos

Akrotiri, Mérichas, on the far side of
the port. Open-air nightclub.

Byzantino, Mérichas. After midnight,
head for its ultra-violet lights.

Koursaros and **Apocalypse**, Chóra.
Popular music bars.

MiReSi. Music bar on the beach at
Ag. Dimítrios.

Mílos (ΜΗΛΟΣ)

Like Santoríni, Mílos, the most westerly of the Cyclades, is a
volcanic island. But where the former is a glamorous beauty associated with misty tales of Atlantis, Mílos is a sturdy fellow who has
made his fiery origins work for a living. Few places can boast such a
catalogue of geological eccentricities: hot springs bubble in its low,
rolling hills, rocks startle with their Fauvist colours and the landscape is gashed with obsidian, sulphur, barium, alum and bensonite
quarries begun in the Neolithic era. In a beach beauty contest Mílos
would score over Santoríni hands down, with miles of pale golden
sands, among the finest in Greece; long strands and weird fjord-like
inlets all lapped by deep turquoise waters, some bubbling with
geothermal springs. It seems an odd trick of Mother Nature to so
endow such an out-of-the-way island with this mineral cornucopia.
Yet in spite of all its strange and wonderful rocks, Mílos still mourns
for the one it lost – the renowned *Venus*, now in the Louvre.

Walks through the gently undulating countryside will bring you
down to whitewashed chapels at the water's edge, or unique little
settlements that sit on the water, with bright-painted boat garages.

History

Mílos is receiving more tourists every year, especially Italians and
Germans. But Mílos has long been a popular place. In the Neolithic
era, as far back as 8000 BC, people braved the Aegean in papyrus
boats to mine Mílos' abundant veins of obsidian – the petroleum of
its day, hard black volcanic glass prized for the manufacture of tools.
Until the recent discovery of the Mesolithic settlement in Kýthnos,
Mílos laid claim to the oldest town in the Cyclades, at Phylakope,
settled by either Phoenicians or Cypriots; under Minoan and later
Mycenaean rule, the island became rich from trading obsidian all
over the Mediterranean.

As later inhabitants of Mílos were predominantly Dorian, like the
Spartans, they declared themselves neutral in the Peloponnesian

Getting to Mílos

By air: There is at least one flight daily from Athens. **Olympic Airways** is just past the *plateía* in Adámas, t 228 702 2219. A **taxi** from the airport to Adámas will cost about €8.

By sea: Two or more ferries go daily to and from Piraeus, with daily connections to Kímolos, Sífnos, Kýthnos and Sérifos; once a week with Folégandros and Santoríni; taxi boat 5 times a day from Pollónia to Kímolos in season. **Port authority**: t 228 702 336.

Getting around Mílos

There are many round-island **excursion boats** from Adámas, or alternatively, hire the *Apollonía* for your own excursion from **Manolis Galanos**, t 228 705 1385.

Hourly **buses** run from Adámas Square to Pláka, via Tripití; 9 times a day to Pollónia by way of Phylakope (modern Filikopí) and Páchena; 7 times to Paleochóri via Zefýria and Provatás.

For a **taxi**, call t 228 702 2219.

Or **hire** your own wheels: ask at **Vichos Tours** (see p.267) or **STOP**, by the port, t 228 702 2440.

War. In 415 BC, Athens sent envoys to change their minds. Their 'might makes right' discussion, known as 'the Milian Dialogue', in the fifth chapter of Thucydides, is one of the most moving passages in classical history. When Mílos still refused to co-operate, the Athenians besieged them, and when the Milians unconditionally surrendered they massacred the men, enslaved the women and children and resettled Mílos with Athenian colonists. These were famous in antiquity for raising the toughest cock-fighting roosters.

Christianity came early to Mílos, in the 1st century, and the faithful built the only series of catacombs in Greece. Marco and his brother Angelo Sanudo captured Mílos and placed it under the Crispi Dynasty. The Turks laid claim to the island in 1580, even though Mílos was infested with pirates. One of them, John Kapsís, declared himself King of Mílos, a claim which Venice recognized for three years, until the Turks flattered Kapsís into coming to Istanbul and ended his pretensions with an axe. In 1680 a party from Mílos emigrated to London, where James, Duke of York, granted them land to build a Greek church – the origin of Greek Street in Soho. In 1836, Cretan war refugees from Sfakiá fled to Mílos and founded the village of Adámas, the present port. During the Crimean War the French navy docked at the harbour and left many monuments, as they did during the First World War; at Korfós are the bases of anti-aircraft batteries installed during the German occupation in the Second World War.

Adámas and the Bay of Mílos

If you arrive by sea, you can see a sample of Mílos' eccentric rocks before you disembark: a formation called the **Arkoúdes**, or bears, rises up from the sea on the left as you turn into the largest natural harbour in the Mediterranean – so large that it feels like a vast lake. The port, bustling **Adámas**, is also the main tourist centre. The

Mílos

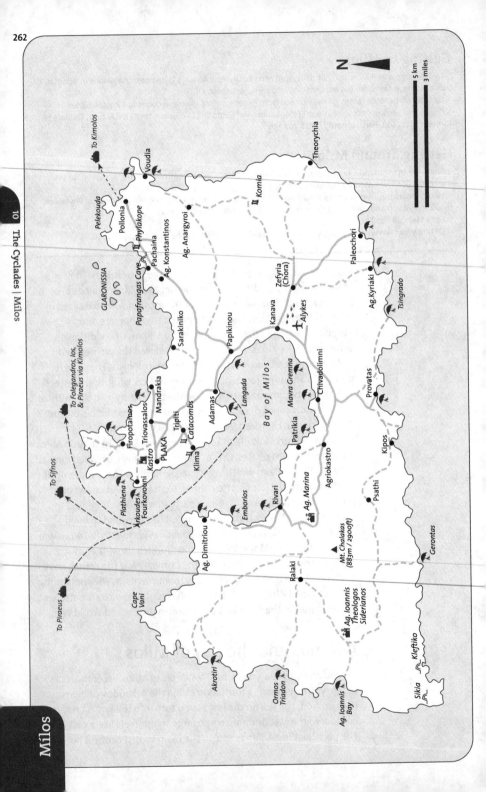

Cretans who founded the town brought their holy icons, which are displayed in the churches of **Ag. Tríada** and **Ag. Charálambos**; in the latter, one ex-voto, from 1576, portrays a boat attacked by a raging fish; the captain prayed to the Virgin, who resolved the struggle by snipping off the fish's nose. West of the centre, behind the port, is small **Langáda Beach**, lined with hotels and popular with families; a monument commemorates the French who died there during the Crimean War. Further along the track, gurgling hot mud pools mark the route to the '**Volcano**', a glorified steaming fissure. By the beach, set in the cliffs you can see the little caves that once made up Mílos's municipal spa baths, with warm, sulphurous springs.

South of Adámas, the vast, sandy Bay of Mílos is fringed with a succession of beaches like **Papikinoú**, backed by hotels and apartments. There's also a new **Mining Museum**, along the shore road, illustrating Mílos' geological and mining history. There's a quieter beach at **Alýkes**, the salt pans before the **Mávra Gremná**, or 'black cliffs', with fantastical rock formations; at several places out in the bay the sea bubbles from the hot springs released below. The spring near the Kanava junction is supposedly a cure for sterility in women.

Past the salt-beds and the airport clutter stretches the sandy beach at **Chivadólimni**, the island's longest (though hardly the cleanest), with a deep turquoise sea in front and a saltwater lake behind, named after the clams who live there. Continuing along the coast, other pale golden beaches are **Patrikia**, **Rivári** (backed by a lagoon once used as a vivarium by the monks up at Ag. Marína Monastery) and **Emboriós**. Further north, **Ag. Dimitríou** is often battered by winds. That's as far as the paved roads go, on this wild, maquis-covered western end of Mílos – except for the road that heads up around **Mount Chalakás**, Mílos's highest point at 883m (2,900ft), to the island's new wind-farms. On Chalakás' slopes, where small woods of rare snake root and cedars survive in little canyons, the old monastery at **Ag. Marína** is worth a trip; from here you can climb **Profítis Ilías**, for a gods'-eye view over Mílos and neighbouring islands.

Mining Museum
t 228 702 2481, www. milosminingmuseum.gr; open Tues–Sat 8–2.30

A Geological Mystery Tour

From Adámas, boats tour the island's fascinating rock formations by sea. Highlights include the **Glaroníssia**, four cave-pocked basalt islets shaped like organ pipes, off the north coast; **Paleoréma** on the east coast with a disused sulphur mine which turns the water emerald-green; on the southwest corner, the sea caves of **Sikía** where the sun's rays slant through the roof to create dramatic colours in the water; and, next door, spectacular **Kléftiko**, the pirates' hideaway with another set of fantastic cream and white rocks rising from the sea – a beautiful place to swim. You can also sail near **Andímilos** to the northwest, a reserve for the rare Cretan *kri-kri*.

Pláka: Ancient Melos and its Catacombs

Buses leaves frequently for **Pláka**, the labyrinthine sugar-cube capital, 4km uphill from Adámas, blending into the windmill-topped suburb of **Tripití**. Next to the bus stop is the **Archaeology Museum**. Inside is a plaster copy of *Venus*, a consolation prize from Paris, but the real finds are from the Neolithic and Cycladic eras: obsidian tools, terracotta objects, a perfectly serviceable bathtub, and lily-painted ceramics from Phylakope – animal figurines, model houses and boats, as well as the famous *Lady of Phylakope*, a decorated Minoan-style goddess. There are Hellenistic artefacts from Kímolos and statues, but, like *Venus*, the famous marble *Poseidon* and the *Kouros of Mílos* are not at home (currently all are in the National Archaeological Museum in Athens).

Archaeology Museum
t 228 702 1620; open Tues–Sun 8.30–3; adm

Up in Pláka's old centre, by the church, the **Historical and Folklore Museum**, housed in a 19th-century mansion, includes everything down to the kitchen sink. Steps lead up to the Venetian **Kástro**, set high on a volcanic plug. Houses formed the outer walls of the fortress, and perched on top was an old church, Mésa Panagía, blown up by the Germans during the Second World War. After liberation, a new church was built lower down, but the old icon of the Virgin reappeared in a bush on top of the Kástro. Every time they moved the icon it returned to the bushes, so they gave in and built another church, **Panagía Skiniótissa**, 'Our Lady of the Bushes'. There are stunning views from here, and on the way up from **Panagía Thalassítras**, 'Our Lady of the Sea' (1228), where the lintel bears the arms of the Crispi family, who overthrew the Sanudi as dukes of Náxos. The church houses fine icons by Emmanuel Skordílis.

Historical and Folklore Museum
t 228 702 1292; open Tues–Sat 10–1 and 6–8, and Sun 10–1; adm

Panagía Rosária is the Roman Catholic church built by the French consul Louis Brest, and **Panagía Korfiátissa**, on the edge of a sheer cliff to the west of the village, has Byzantine and Cretan icons rescued from the ruined city of Zefýria.

Pláka itself is built over the acropolis of **ancient Melos**, the town destroyed by the Athenians and resettled by the Romans. In the 1890s the British school excavated the site, roughly extending from Pláka down to Klíma, a village on the shore far below. A walking tour would start in **Tripití**, and the first stop (signposted) is a **termitary of catacombs**, dating from the 1st century AD. There's little to see now, merely long corridors of arched niches carved in the rock, but, when first discovered, the tombs were still full of bones; contact with the fresh air quickly turned them to dust. Some held five or six bodies; other cadavers were buried in the floor. On various tombs, inscriptions in red remain, as well as later black graffiti. The habit of building underground necropolises (as in Rome, Naples, Sicily and Malta) coincides with the presence of soft volcanic tufa, more than with romantic notions of persecution and secret underground rites;

Catacombs
open Mon–Sat 8–5; Sun 8.30–1

The *Venus de Milo*, or Unclear Disarmament

On 8 April 1820, farmer Geórgios Kentrotás was ploughing a field when he discovered a cave containing half of a statue of the goddess Aphrodite. A French officer, Olivier Voutier, who happened to be visiting Mílos, urged the farmer to look for the other half. He soon found it, along with a 6th-century BC statue of young Hermes and Hercules as an old man – an ancient art-lover's secret cache, hidden from the Christians. Voutier sketched the Aphrodite for Louis Brest, the French vice-consul for Mílos. Brest sent this on to the French consul in Constantinople, who decided to obtain Aphrodite for France, and sent an envoy over to complete the deal. But meanwhile Kentrotás, persuaded by the island's elders, had sold the statue to another man on behalf of the translator of the Turkish fleet, the Prince of Moldavia, Nichólas Mouroúzis. The statue was in a caique, ready to be placed aboard a ship for Romania, when the French ship sailed into Adámas. Eventually, after some brisk bargaining, the envoy and Brest managed to buy the Aphrodite as a gift for Louis XVIII (although some say the French sailors grabbed her by force). On 1 March 1821 she made her début in the Louvre. Somewhere along the line she lost her arms and pedestal with the inscription Aphrodites Nikiforos, 'Victory-bringing Aphrodite'. The French cadet's sketch showed the arms, one hand holding an apple. (Why an apple? If you haven't conned up on your Greek, check the menu decoder, on p.50. And then there's the Adámas connection (Adam – right?) but that's in another, much longer book.)

interring the dead underground saved valuable land. (Curiously, the modern cemetery near Pláka resembles a row of catacombs above ground; the posh ones are even done out with carpets.) A path from the catacombs leads to where *Venus* was discovered – there's a marker by the fig tree.

The path continues past the ancient Cyclopean city walls to the well-preserved **Roman theatre**, where spectators looked out over the sea, reconstructed to something approaching its former glory; a company from Athens sometimes performs in the theatre in August (*ask at the tourist office for details*). The remains of a temple are on the path back to the main road. From there you can take the road or an old *kalderími* pathway down to the picturesque fishing hamlet of **Klíma**, with its brightly painted boat garages, *sýrmata*, carved into the soft volcanic tufa, with rickety balconies above and ducks waddling on the beach below. A museum-style reconstruction shows how the fishing families once lived around their caiques.

Around the Island

Around Pláka and the North Coast

Near Pláka, the market village of **Triovassálos** merges into **Péra Triovassálos**. The churches in Triovassálos contain icons from the island's original capital, Zefýria. The great rivalry between the two villages expresses itself on Easter Sunday, when after burning an effigy of Judas the young bloods hold a dynamite-throwing contest on the dividing line between the villages; the most ear-splitting performance wins. Tracks lead down to a selection of beaches, some adorned with wonderfully coloured rocks. One of the best beaches is **Plathíena**, north of Pláka near the Arkoúdes, with dazzling orange and white rock formations; it's also the best place to watch the sun set. The old path from Pláka leads past **Fourkovoúni** with picturesque *sýrmata* hewn into the cliffs. **Mandrákia**, under Triovassálos, is one of the island's outstanding beauty spots, a stunning little cove studded with garages and topped by a white chapel. Further north, **Firopótamos** is another pretty fishing hamlet.

Phylakope and Pollónia

The road east from Adámas or Pláka to Pollónia offers a pair of stops along the north coast. A side road descends into the bleached moonscape of **Sarakíniko**, a magical place to swim, with huge rounded rocks and pointed peaks whipped by the winds into giant white petrified drifts. To the east the fishing hamlets of **Páchena** and **Ag. Konstantínos** have more *sýrmata*; from the latter it's a short walk to **Papafrángas Cave**, actually three sea caves, where the brilliant turquoise water is enclosed by the white cliffs of a mini-fjord, once used by trading boats as a hiding place from pirates.

On the other side of Papafrángas, **Phylakope** was one of the great centres of Cycladic civilization, excavated by the British in the 1890s. The dig yielded three successive levels of habitation: early Cycladic (3500 BC), Middle Cycladic (to c. 1600 BC) and Late Cycladic/Mycenaean (and they're digging again, so the site is temporarily closed). Even in Early Cycladic days Mílos traded in obsidian far and wide – pottery found in the lowest levels showed an Early Minoan influence. Grand urban improvements characterize the Middle Cycladic period: a wall was built around the more spacious and elegant houses, some with delightful frescoes of flying fish (now in Athens, too). A Minoan-style palace contained fine ceramics imported from Knossós, and there was trade with the coasts of Asia Minor. In this period Mílos, like the rest of the Cyclades, may have come under the direct rule of the Minoans; a tablet found on the site is written in a script similar to Linear A. During the Late Cycladic age, the Mycenaeans built their own shrine, added a wall around the palace, and left behind figurines and ceramics. Phylakope declined when metals replaced the need for obsidian. For all its history, the remains at the site are overgrown and inexplicable.

The bus ends up at Apollo's old town, **Pollónia**, on the east coast, a comfortable, very pleasant resort with a tree-fringed beach, fishing boats, tavernas, a diving centre and the ferry to Kímolos. There's quite a bit of new holiday development on the **Pelekóuda Cape**, popular as it is with windsurfers. **Voúdia Beach** to the south has a unique view of the island's mining activities.

Central Mílos: Zefýria, Paleochóri and Around

Buses cross the island to **Zefýria** or Chóra, the capital of Mílos from 800 to 1793. **Panagía Portianí** was the principal church; its priest was accused of fornication by the inhabitants and, although he denied it, the villagers refused to believe him. With that the priest angrily cursed the people, a plague fell on the town, and everyone moved down to Pláka. Today Zefýria is a very quiet village of crumbling houses, surrounded by olive trees. A paved road continues to sandy **Paleochóri Beach** and quieter **Ag. Kyriakí** to the west.

Kómia, east of Zefýria, has ruined Byzantine churches, and nearby at **Demenayáki** are some of Mílos' obsidian mines.

South and West Mílos

If eastern Mílos is fairly low and green, the south and west are mountainous and dry. Just south of Chivadólimni, **Provatás** has another sandy beauty and hot springs, **Loutrá Provatá**, where you can examine the remains of Roman mosaics, followed by a natural sauna to ease your rheumatism, recommended by no less than Hippocrates himself. **Kípos**, further along the coast, has two churches: one, 5th-century **Panagía tou Kipoú**, is the oldest in Mílos.

Down in the southwest, at the famous monastery of **Ag. Ioánnis Theológos Siderianós**, St John is nicknamed the Iron Saint – once during his festival, revellers were attacked by pirates and took refuge in the church. In response to their prayers, the saint saved them by turning the church door to iron (you can still see a scrap of a dress caught in the door as the last woman entered). The pirates couldn't break in, and, when one tried to shoot through a hole in the church dome, Ag. Ioánnis made his hand wither and fall off. Another miraculous story from April 1945 tells of a shell from an English war ship embedding itself in the church wall without exploding.

10 The Cyclades | Mílos

Useful Information on Mílos

Mílos >
*municipal booth, on the quay, Adámas, **t** 228 702 2445; has accommodation lists; open summer only*

Vichos Tours, on the waterfront, **t** 228 702 2286, and **Sea Sun Sophia**, **t** 228 702 1994. Both very helpful for tickets, accommodation and car hire.

Sea Kayak Mílos, **t** 228 702 3597, www.seakayakgreece.com. Offers day trips, camping and tours around the island's fascinating coastline.

Diving Centre Milos, **t** 228 704 1296, www.milosdiving.gr. Dives, courses and accommodation in Pollónia.

Mílos Festivals

50 days after Greek Easter: Adámas.
19 July: Profítis Ilías on the mountain, and in Chalákas and Tripití.
26 July: Plakotá.
5 Aug: Paraskópou.

15 Aug: Adámas.
7 Sept: Psathádika.
16 and 25 Sept: Chalákas.

Where to Stay and Eat on Mílos

Adámas ✉ 84800

Mílos, on the seafront, **t** 228 702 2087, www.miloshotel.gr (€€€). White and quiet, this doesn't look much, but it has an excellent restaurant popular with Greeks. *Open April–Oct.*

Popi's, by the water, **t** 228 702 2286, in Athens **t** 210 361 3198 (€€€). Comfortable, with helpful management.

Santa Maria Village, set back from the beach, **t** 228 702 1949, www.santa maria-milos.gr (€€€). A smart mix of rooms, studios and apartments; wheelchair access.

Adámas, above the harbour, **t** 228 702 2322 (€€). Well-equipped rooms with air-conditioning. *Open April–Oct.*

Delfini, **t** 228 702 2001 (€€). Friendly family-run hotel with a nice terrace.

Portiani, on the sea, **t** 228 702 2940, *www.portiani.com* (€€). Comfy choice with sumptuous buffet breakfast. *Open all year.*

Semiramis, **t** 228 702 2118 (€€). Excellent with a vine-clad terrace – help yourself to grapes – bar, transfer minibus and rent-a-bike service.

If you come in the right season, look for clams from Chivadólimni.

Flisvos. Friendly place with the usual fish and oven-ready dishes.

Kynigos. Next door; a big favourite with the locals.

Ta Pitsounakia, **t** 228 702 1739. Spit-roast meats and *kokorétsi*.

Trapatseli's. Fish come up to feed beneath the terrace here; there's an excellent menu, especially for fish dishes. The *spetsofái* fish stew and *soupiés*, cuttlefish *stifádo*, are good as well as the local hard cheese.

Pláka/Tripití/Klíma ✉ 84800

Popi's Windmill, Tripití, **t** 228 702 2287 (€€€). Has rooms that sleep 4–5 in two beautifully converted mills. *Open June–Sept.*

Panorama, Klíma, **t** 228 702 1623 (€€). Has rooms with private bath and dining terrace with great views; also a good bet for lunch.

Sophia Apartments, Tripití, **t** 228 702 2039 (€€). Traditionally furnished and overflowing with arches. *Open all year.*

Morphios, **t** 228 702 4050 (€). Rooms in Tripití, handy for the dig sites.

Alisachni, Pláka, **t** 228 702 3485 (€25). Summer-only restaurant in a lovely house, with tables spilling into the lane; refined Greek dishes, *mezédes*.

Kástro, Pláka's square. Popular, with views up to the castle.

Ergina, Tripití, **t** 228 702 2523. Sit on a big terrace over the sea and feast on Ergina Moraḯtou's delicious onion pies, mussels with tomatoes, or lemony *kalamári* casserole. *Closed Oct–May*

Methismeni Politia, **t** 228 702 3100, Tripití (€15–20). The 'Drunken State' is pricier, specializing in *mezédes*, wines

and ouzo in a romantic garden setting with views across the gulf.

Medousa, Mandrákia, **t** 228 702 3670. Taverna-ouzerie with a big choice of wines, ouzos, *tsipoúrias*, and fish and other snacks. *Closed Oct–April.*

Pollónia ✉ 84800

Apollon Apartments and Studios, **t** 228 704 1347 (€€€). Views over Kímolos and home-cooking at the family taverna.

Kapetan Tassos, 100m from the beach, **t** 228 704 1287 (€€€). Smart Cycladic-style apartments.

Araxovoli, **t** 228 704 1437. Seafood *mezédes*, stuff peppers and other treats. *Closed Oct–May.*

Kapetan Nikolas, **t** 228 704 1212. Fish taverna that serves lots more besides; popular. *Open all year.*

Paleochóri/Ag. Kyriakí ✉ 84800

Artemis, Paleochóri, near the beach, **t** 228 703 1221. A restaurant with **bungalows** (€).

Sirocco, Paleochóri, **t** 228 793 1291. Fish on the beach, plus dishes cooked naturally underground, in the hot volcanic subsoil. *Closed Nov–April.*

Thirios Restaurant, Ag. Kyriakí, **t** 228 702 2779/2058. Also has **rooms** (€).

Provatás ✉ 84800

Golden Milos Beach, **t** 228 704 1307, *www.milos-island.gr* (€€€). Typical seaside holiday hotel.

Tarantela, **t** 228 703 1346. Excellent taverna overlooking Provatás Bay.

Entertainment and Nightlife on Mílos

Mílos has a sophisticated nightlife, with dancing bars and discos; there's even a roller-skating rink in Adámas.

Akri, with an art gallery and a view over Adámas harbour.

To Kafeneion, Adámas. Cocktails and Greek music in a flowery courtyard.

To Ouzerie, Adámas, on the front.

Yanko's, Adámas, near the bus stop. A local hangout.

Malion, **Plori**, **La Costa**. Other Adámas hot spots in the open air.

Puerto. For Greek music.

Utopia Café, bar with a view, Pláka.

 Ergina >

Mýkonos (ΜΥΚΟΝΟΣ)

This dry, lunar rock pile, tickled by the *meltémi* but graced with sandy beaches and a beautiful white Cycladic town, is probably the most famous island in Greece, the island to see and be seen, with the country's most exciting nightlife. In the early 1960s, when Jackie Kennedy and Aristotle Onassis visited, it was a peaceful fishing island. Their paparazzi-accompanied presence was like fairy dust – presto! Mýkonos became the joy of the jet set, the first officially to sanction naturism on some of its beaches, and a leading gay resort. If you seek the simple, the unadorned, the distinctly Greek, avoid Mýkonos like the plague. But the party will go on without you. And it shows no sign of abating; the island is staging a major resurgence in fashion as Greece's top architects and designers continue to add to a bouquet of casual elegant hotels and villas – the ultimate status symbol for a wealthy Athenian.

History

The Ionians built three cities on Mýkonos: one on the isthmus south of Chóra, the second at Dimastos, dating back to 2000 BC, and the third at Panórmos near Paliokástro. During the war between the Romans and Mithridates of Pontus, all three were destroyed. Chóra was rebuilt during the Byzantine period, and the Venetians surrounded it with a wall that no longer exists; however, at Paliokástro a fort built by the Gizzi rulers still remains. In 1537 Mýkonos fell to Barbarossa, and came into its own with pirate families who ran a profitable plunder market. Even so, it was on the front line in the War of Independence, its fleet of 22 ships led by Mantó Mavrogénous, the local heroine, who donated all of her considerable fortune to the cause.

Chóra

Cosmopolitan Chóra (ΧΩΡΑ), the island's picture-postcard capital and port, gleaming and whitewashed, with brightly painted wooden trims, might have open doors at 10am for the sweaty throngs of daytrippers and cruise ship folk, but it really only wakes up in the afternoon after everyone's been to the beach. Peppered with

Little Ajax the Boaster

In myth Mýkonos is best known as a graveyard, site of the rock tombs of the giants slain by Hercules and that of Ajax the Lokrian, a hero of the Trojan War. This Ajax was known as Little Ajax to differentiate him from Big Ajax, who committed suicide when the weapons of the dead Achilles were given to Odysseus rather than him. After the capture of Troy, Little Ajax proved himself just as pathetic a hero when he raped Priam's daughter Cassandra, who had sought protection in a Temple of Athena. Athena avenged this blasphemy by wrecking Ajax's ship off the coast of Mýkonos. Poseidon saved him in a storm but defiant Ajax declared that he would have been perfectly able to save himself without assistance. Poseidon's trident finished Ajax then and there, and his Mycenaean tomb can still be seen at Pórtes.

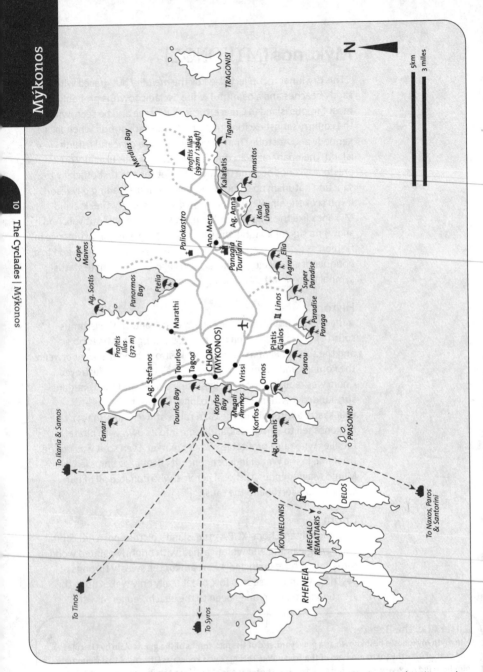

boutiques and designer jewellery shops, cafés, bars and restaurants, by night it's ready to vibrate into a big spontaneous party. In the main square by the waterfront a bust of war heroine Mantó Mavrogénous guarded left luggage in simpler days. Boats to Délos depart from further up the waterfront, where the island's famous

Getting to Mýkonos

By air: There are charter flights and several connections daily on Olympic Airways and Aegean Airlines with Athens, and several a week with Santoríni, Rhodes and Heráklion (Crete). The **Olympic Airways** office is at Fábrika Square, **t** 228 902 2490. **Airport**: **t** 228 902 2327. Buses stop by the airport.

By sea: If you're sailing, make sure you know from/to which port – the old one, or the new one out towards Toúrlos. There several **ferry**, **fast ferry** and **hydrofoil** connections daily with Piraeus (3hrs by fast ferry), Rafína, Ándros, Tínos, Sýros, Náxos, Páros, Íos and Santoríni; at least 3 times a week with Heráklion (Crete); less frequently with Sífnos, Mílos, the Back Islands, Ikária, Sámos, Chíos,Thessaloníki and Skiáthos. **Port authority**: **t** 228 902 2218.

Getting around Mýkonos

There are **excursion boats** from the waterfront in front of the town to Délos Tues–Sun between 8.30 and 12, returning noon–3; also to Paradise Beach, Super Paradise, Agrári and Eliá from both Chóra and Platís Gialós.

Buses run frequently from the two **bus stations** (**t** 228 902 3360 for both). The one by the Archaeology Museum serves Ag. Stéfanos, Toúrlos, Áno Merá, Eliá, Kalafátis and Kaló Livádi. The one at Fábrika Square is for Ornós, Ag. Ioánnis, Platís Gialós, Paradise Beach, Psaroú, Kalamopódi and the airport.

Car, quad and bike hire places abound in Fábrika Square and all around the pedestrian zone perimeter; the biggest **car parks** around Chóra are along the old port or by the windmills.

Taxis wait in the taxi square (Plateía Mantó), **t** 228 902 2400, or **t** 228 902 3700 for late-night service.

---

mascots, five pink **pelicans**, led by the raggedy 50-year-old Pétros II (the original Pétros landed in a storm on Mýkonos in the mid-1950s and stayed), may often be found preening in the shadow of the small church. On the hill overlooking the harbour is another Mýkonos symbol: a row of thatched **windmills**. These overlook the cove and quarter of **Alefkándra** and **Little Venice**, where the tall houses are built directly on the sea; each now accommodates a cocktail bar for sunset views.

Mýkonos claims to have 400 churches, some no bigger than bathrooms, and the most famous of these, beyond Little Venice, is the snow-white **Panagía Paraportianí**, an asymmetrical masterpiece of four churches melted into one. Just opposite, the **Folklore Museum** houses old curiosities, a traditional bedroom and kitchen, and a gallery of 19th-century prints of sensuous Greek odalisques; downstairs is an exhibition, 'Mýkonos and the Sea'.

Folklore Museum
t 228 902 2591; open 5.30–8.30pm

Nautical Museum
Tría Pigádia, t 228 902 2700; open summer 10.30–1 and 6.30–9; adm

The **Nautical Museum**, in the centre, contains ships' models from ancient times and a collection of paintings and coins. Old anchors and copies of ancient tombstones of shipwrecked sailors fill the garden. Next door, **Lena's House** is a branch of the Folklore Museum: the 19th-century middle-class home of Léna Sakrivanoú, preserved with everything from her needlework to her chamberpot.

Lena's House
t 228 902 2591; open April–Oct Mon–Sat 6.30–9.30pm, Sun 7–9

Towards the old port, the **Archaeology Museum** was built in 1905 in the jailhouse style but has recently had a Cycladic makeover; it contains boldly decorated ceramics from the necropolis islet of Rhéneia, by Délos. The finest item was found on Tínos: a funeral *píthos* from the 7th century BC with relief scenes from the Fall of Troy, like comic book strips, showing the death of Hector's son and a warrior-stuffed Trojan horse, fitted with aeroplane windows.

Archaeology Museum
t 228 902 2325; open Wed–Mon 9–3.30, Sun and hols 10–3; adm

Around the Island

North of Chóra, the beaches at **Tagoo**, **Toúrlos** and **Ag. Stéfanos** have a lot of accommodation and people to fill it: **Fanári** further north is considerably quieter. The nearest beaches south of Chóra are **Megáli Ámmos**, **Kórfos** and **Ornós**, all of which are built up, especially Ornós, with its cute little port. The biggest resort and beach, however, is **Platís Gialós**, to the east, with boat excursions to the other beaches and Délos, while lovely **Psaroú**, just before Platís Gialós, is considered nothing less than the most fashionable beach in all of Greece at the moment.

Paradise, with its campsite and even more beautiful, fine sandy and traditionally gay **Super Paradise**, the heart of the island's beach club action, were once the island's most notorious nudist beaches, although both are less notorious now; little **Agrári**, east of Super Paradise, has somehow missed out on most of the razzmatazz. **Eliá**, a once quiet beach accessible by bus, is divided into straight and gay precincts. **Ag. Ánna** is a quieter beach, and there's the fishing hamlet and family beach at **Kalafátis**. At **Pórtes** you can spit on the 'tomb' of Ajax the troublemaker (*see* box, p.269).

In ancient times Mýkonos was often the butt of jokes, especially about the baldness of its men, and even today the old fishermen never take off their caps. You may find a few old fellows at **Áno Merá**, Mýkonos' other town inland, where the 16th-century **Panagía Tourlianí Monastery** with its sculpted marble steeple protects Mýkonos; it has a carved Florentine altarpiece, fine Cretan icons, an **Ecclesiastical Museum** and **Farm Tool Museum**.

Farm Tool Museum
ring ahead to visit,
t 228 907 1249

Below, sandy **Panórmos Bay** was the site of one of Mýkonos' three ancient cities; here **Fteliá** and sublime **Ag. Sóstis** are wild beaches favoured by windsurfers, far from the posers; the latter has an excellent restaurant, Kiki's, that has attained cult status (*no phone; open lunch only*).

Useful Information on Mýkonos

Tourist police: Quay, **t** 228 902 2482.

Mýkonos Festivals

15 Aug: Panagía Tourlianí. But then every day's a party on Mýkonos.

Where to Stay and Eat on Mýkonos

Prices in July and August tend to be the highest in Greece and you should book from June on. Sleek new Cycladic-style hotels occupy every feasible spot on the coast, especially along the road to Platís Gialós. Off season, when you step off the ferry you'll be inundated with people offering rooms, but many are up the hill above Chóra, in an isolated and ugly area of holiday apartments. You'll probably do better using the accommodation desks by the old port:

Hotel Reservations Office, t 228 902 4540, *www.mha.gr*.

Association of Rooms and Flats, t 228 902 4860.

Mýkonos Accommodation Centre, 10 Enóplon Dynaméon, **t** 228 902 3160, *www.mykonos-accommodation.com*.

Chóra (Mýkonos Town)
✉ 84600

Belvedere, above Chóra, **t** 228 902 5122, *www.belvederehotel.com* (€€€€€). The new designer Mýkonos – all white, cool, and marble baths, lush pool gardens, home cinema, massage and fitness and excellent **Matsuhisa Mýkonos** sushi restaurant. *Open May–Sept.*

 ⭐ **Harmony** >

Harmony, by the old port, **t** 228 902 8982, *www.harmonyhotel.gr* (€€€€€). Member of the Small Elegant Hotel group, a new boutique hotel in natural colours and textures, with pool, good restaurant and very friendly and helpful staff. Prices plummet off season. *Open all year.*

Leto, **t** 228 902 2207, *www.letohotel. com* (€€€€€). In the centre, with a garden and pool, and for years the classiest place to stay on Mýkonos; it has a good restaurant, too.

Mykonos Theoxenia, by the windmills, **t** 228 902 2230, *www.mykonos theoxenia.com* (€€€€€). Old Xenia hotel completely overhauled *à la* 1960s glam.

Ostraco Suites, up the hill at Drafáki, **t** 228 902 3396, *www.ostraco.gr* (€€€€€). Mellow family-owned 24-room resort with a pool, each room individually designed, and lovely views.

Tharroe of Mykonos, Vrýssi, 900m from the centre, **t** 228 902 7370, *www. tharroeofmykonos.gr* (€€€€€). Minimalist design on a hilltop with an Ayurvedic spa and pool. *Open all year.*

⭐ **Philippi** >>

Geranium Moonlight, by the School of Fine Arts, **t** 228 902 4620, *www. geraniumhotel.com* (€€€€€–€€€€). New, exclusively casual chic gay design hotel with a pool (clothing optional).

Zorzis, 30 Nik. Kalogerá, **t** 228 902 2167, *www.zorzishotel.com* (€€€€–€€€). Intimate little hotel in the heart of town; bargains if you book on line. No credit cards.

Carbonaki, behind the waterfront, **t** 228 902 4124, *www.carbonaki-mykonos.com* (€€€). Friendly and relatively quiet; 21 rooms with air-conditioning and satellite TV.

Manto, 1 Evangelístrias, **t** 228 902 2330 (€€). In a narrow alley, convenient for connoisseurs of nightlife.

Terra Maria, N. Kalogerá, **t** 228 902 4212 (€€–€). A bargain in the heart of town.

Christina Rooms and Studios, in the centre near the public garden, **t** 228 902 2731 (€€–€). Simple rooms with TV and air-conditioning overlooking a shady courtyard.

Acqua Taverna, Little Venice, **t** 228 902 6083 (€35). The owner is from Rome, and serves lovely and authentic Italian dishes; try the *bresaola* with sun-dried tomatoes.

Antonini's, in taxi square, **t** 228 902 2319. Genuine Greek food at fair prices: varied and excellent *mezédes*, shrimp salad and tasty veal or lamb casserole.

Appaloosa's, Mavrogenous St, **t** 228 902 7086. Mexican fare, good salads and more.

Caprice of Mykonos Sea Satin Market, under the windmills **t** 228 902 4676 (€65). Celebrity haunt, with candlelit tables by the water for extraordinary lobster and seafood.

Chez Maria's, 27 Kalogerá, **t** 228 902 7565 (€50). Elegant, romantic dining in a bougainvillaea garden. Seafood pasta is a speciality, but there are lots more unusual dishes.

Mamacas, near the hotel Leto, **t** 228 902 6120 (€35). Well-prepared Greek classics in a laid-back atmosphere under a big tree.

Niko's, behind the town hall, **t** 228 902 4320 (€12). If you need to be reminded that you're in Greece, head here for good dinners.

Philippi, Matagiánni, **t** 228 902 2295 (€45). Spot the celebrity in this landmark. Great Greek and international cuisine, served in the garden. Also has pleasant **rooms** (€€€–€€).

Tagoo ✉ 84600

Aegean, **t** 228 902 2869 (€€€€€). Well-appointed but still family-run and friendly.

Cavo Tagoo, on the beach, **t** 228 902 3692, *www.cavotagoo.gr* (€€€€€). One of the first designer hotels, with seawater pool, beautiful view of Mýkonos, and the chance to rub shoulders with the great and good.

Madalena, **t** 228 902 2954 (€€€). A cheaper option, with a pool.

Spanelis, **t** 228 902 3081 (€€€). Small, older hotel.

Sahas, t 228 902 2112 (€€). Newly built, spacious rooms and studios with a helpful owner.

Toúrlos ☑ 84600

Rhenia, t 228 902 2300, www.rhenia-bungalows.gr (€€€€€). Tranquil, sheltered bungalows and pool, overlooking Chóra and Délos.

Olia, t 228 902 8020, www.olia-hotel.gr (€€€). Traditionally styled rooms and pool nearer the sea.

Sunset, t 228 902 3013 (€€€–€€). Smaller, with a terrace café where they will cook to your order.

Mathíos Taverna, t 228 902 2344. Slick and well patronized, but not overpriced.

Ag. Stéfanos ☑ 84600

Princess of Mýkonos, t 228 902 3806, www.princessofmykonos.gr (€€€). With pool, sauna, Jacuzzi and the works. It isn't in the heart of the action, but only a taxi-ride away.

Artemis, t 228 902 2345, www.artemishotel.net (€€€–€€). Family-run, first hotel in the area; uninspiring rooms with big balconies near the sea.

Vangeli, just before Fanári at Choulákia Beach, t 228 902 2458 (€€€–€€). Quiet, small and very Greek, with good restaurant.

South Coast: Ag. Ioánnis and Ornós ☑ 84600

Apollonia Bay, Ag. Ioánnis, t 228 902 7890, www.apollonia-resort.gr (€€€€€). Smart new 35-room compex with a fitness centre and YDNA Mini-spa.

Kivotos Clubhotel, Ornós, t 228 902 4094, www.kivotosclubhotel.com (€€€€€). One of the 'Small Luxury Hotels of the World' with Olympic squash courts, fitness centre, five pools, private yacht, etc. Plus Le Meduse, one of the best restaurants on the island.

Manoula's Beach, Ag. Ioánnis, t 228 902 2900, www.hotelmanoulas.gr (€€€€€). Where they filmed Shirley Valentine, with couple of tavernas, boat trips and beach parties thrown in.

Yiannaki, away from Ornós centre, t 228 902 3393, www.yiannaki.gr (€€€€). Family-friendly, with a tranquil pool and all mod cons.

Platís Gialós/Parága ☑ 84600

Petinos Beach, Platís Gialós, t 228 902 4310, www.petinos.gr (€€€€€). Welcoming Cycladic complex, including a pool and water sports.

San Giorgio, Parága, t 228 902 7474, www.sangiorgio.gr (€€€€€). Classy, with a sea-water pool and all comforts, including mini-bars.

Pelican Bay Art Hotel, Platís Gialós, t 228 902 6620, www.pelicanbay.gr (€€€€€–€€€). Handsome new hotel with a pool and design references to ancient Cycladic culture.

Argo, 100m from the beach, Platís Gialós, t 228 902 3405, www.argo-mykonos.gr (€€€). Friendly, traditional, family-run place with lots of repeat clients.

Mýkonos Camping, Parága, t 228 902 4578, www.mycamp.gr. Good facilities and minibus service from Chóra and Platís Gialós.

Paradise, t 228 902 2232, http://paradise-greece.com. Since 1969, it has rented out everything from houses to beach cabins to tents, and it has good facilities (tents, bungalows, caravans and apartments) and a minibus service from Chóra and Platís Gialós.

N'Ammos, Psarroú Beach, t 228 902 2440 (€50). Casual, elegant white restaurant by the sea that's one of Greece's very best seafood restaurants – grilled octopus, sea urchins, marinated anchovies and famous featherlight meatballs, too. Closed Dec–Feb.

Kalafátis/Áno Merá ☑ 84600

Anemoessa, Kalafátis, t 228 907 1420, www.anemoessa.com (€€€€€). Built in the Cycladic style, with pool and Jacuzzi, and serving a big American buffet breakfast. It's a long way from the beach, though.

Bandanna, Kalafátis, t 228 907 1800. Reasonable trattoria serving wonderful pizzas.

La Cucina di Daniele, Áno Merá, t 228 907 1513 (€40). Talented Italian chef Daniele Chiantini has been wowing them here with his imagintive cuisine, accompanied by the most extensive Italian wine cellar in Greece. Open all year; book in summer.

⭐ Argo >>

⭐ La Cucina di Daniele >>

O ti Apómeine, by the square, Áno Merá, **t** 228 907 1534. The grill house of the family Stavrokopoúlos is renowned island-wide, serving popular delights such as *exochikó* (filo parcels) *kléftiko* and suckling pig at Greek prices.

Entertainment and Nightlife on Mýkonos

Mýkonos nightlife

The labyrinth of Chóra turns into a party every summer night. Plunge into the old town maze for no end of quaint café/bars for that evening drink or ice cream; **L'Unico** is a nice one, opposite Ag. Kyriakí. An open-air **cinema** also operates in season.

Katerina's, Caprice and **Kástro's,** in Little Venice. Famous for sunset views, classical sounds and strawberry daiquiris.

Bolero. Good music and cocktails.

Argo Dancing Bar, above Taxi Square.

Astra Bar. High-tech cool place to be seen.

City Club. Has a nightly transvestite show.

Mykonos Dancing Bar. This perennial favourite plays Greek music.

Zorba's, by the windmills. For live *rembétika.*

Pierro's, just back from the waterfront. The most frenzied of the lot in Chóra, where the hordes gyrate to the loud, lively music.

Icaros, above Pierro's. Where the sexiest stuff provocatively struts its way along the bar.

Blu Blu. Very popular Internet café/lounge/Mediterranean restaurant by the old port, linked to the famous **Cavo Paradiso Club,** on the rocks on Paradise Beach, *www.cavoparadiso.gr.* Hosts superstar DJs.

Délos (ΔΗΛΟΣ)

Many are your temples and shaded groves

Every peak, cliff and mountain high

Are loved by you, and the rivers that flow to the sea

But Phoebus, Délos is your heart's delight.

Homeric hymn to Apollo (8th century)

Mýkonos could have no greater contrast than its neighbour Délos: holy island of the ancient Greeks, centre of the great maritime alliance of the Athenian golden age. A major port in Hellenistic and Roman times that once controlled much of the east–west trade in the Mediterranean, today it is now a vast open-air museum, deserted except for the lonely guardian of the ruins – and the boatloads of day-trippers. It's an island haunted by 2,000 years of memories; the Delians themselves seem to have been reincarnated as lizards, darting among the poppies and broken marble.

History

In the 3rd millennium BC Délos was settled by people from Karia in Asia Minor. By 1000 BC the Ionians had made it their religious capital, centred around the cult of Apollo, the father of Ion, the mythical founder of their race – a cult first mentioned in a Homeric hymn of the 7th century BC. Games and pilgrimages took place there, and Délos was probably the centre of an early Ionian amphictyony. In 550 BC the tyrant Polycrates of Sámos conquered the Cyclades, but he respected the sanctity of Délos and put the islet Rhéneia under its control, symbolically chaining it to Délos.

With the rise of Athens, Délos knew its greatest glory and biggest headaches. The Athenians invented stories to connect themselves to the islet – did not Erechtheus, the King of Athens, lead the first delegation to Délos? After slaying the Minotaur on Crete, did not Theseus stop at Délos and dance around the altar of Apollo?

Getting to Délos

Boats from Mýkonos leave Tues–Sun between 8.30 and 12 , returning between 12 and 3. Best to go early.

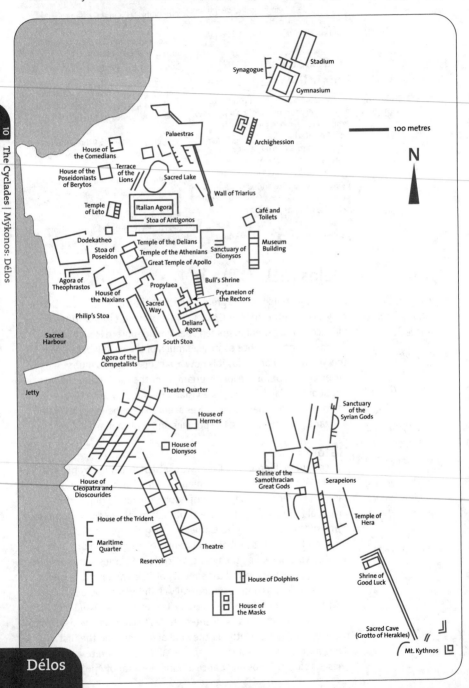

Stadium

Synagogue

Gymnasium

Palaestras

Archighession

House of
the Comedians

House of the
Poseidoniasts
of Berytos

Terrace
of the
Lions

Sacred Lake

Wall of Triarius

Temple
of Leto

Italian Agora

Café and
Toilets

Stoa of Antigonos

100 metres

N

Dodekatheo

Stoa of
Poseidon

Temple of the Delians

Temple of the Athenians

Sanctuary of
Dionysos

Museum
Building

Great Temple of Apollo

Agora of
Theophrastos

House of
the Naxians

Propylaea

Bull's Shrine

Sacred
Way

Prytaneion of
the Rectors

Philip's Stoa

Delians'
Agora

Sacred
Harbour

South Stoa

Agora of the
Competalists

Jetty

Theatre Quarter

House of
Hermes

Sanctuary
of the
Syrian Gods

House of
Dionysos

House of
Cleopatra and
Dioscourides

Shrine of the
Samothracian
Great Gods

Serapeions

House of the Trident

Temple of
Hera

Maritime
Quarter

Theatre

Reservoir

House of Dolphins

Shrine of
Good Luck

House of
the Masks

Sacred Cave
(Grotto of Herakles)

Mt. Kythnos

Délos

The Nursery of the Gods

Zeus, they say, once fancied an ancient moon goddess named Asteria. She fled him in the form of a quail, and Zeus turned himself into an eagle to pursue her. The pursuit proved so hot that Asteria turned into a rock and fell into the sea. But in an older version of the story, Asteria was actually the sacred ship of the sky, crewed by the first Hyperboreans, who after thousands of years alighted in Egypt and sailed up the Nile to this spot. The ship-rock was called Ortýgia ('quail') or Adélos, 'the invisible', as it floated all over Greece like a submarine just below the sea's surface.

Zeus subsequently fell in love with Asteria's sister Leto and succeeded in having his evil way. But Zeus' wife Hera soon got wind of the affair and begged Mother Earth not to allow Leto to give birth anywhere under the sun. All over the world wandered poor suffering Leto, unable to find a rock that would allow her to halt and give birth. Finally in pity Zeus turned to his brother Poseidon for help. Poseidon ordered Ortýgia to halt, and anchored the islet with four columns of diamond. Thus Adélos the Invisible, not under the sun but under the sea, became Délos, or 'visible'. Even so the island was still reluctant to host Leto, fearing her divine offspring would give it a resounding kick back into the sea. But Leto promised that her son would make it the richest sanctuary in Greece. Délos conceded, and Leto gave birth first to Artemis, goddess of the hunt, and then nine days later to Apollo, god of reason and light.

In 543 BC the Athenians even tricked (or bribed) the Oracle at Delphi into ordering the purification of Délos, which meant removing all the island's tombs, a manoeuvre designed to alienate the Delians from their past and diminish the island's importance.

In 490 BC the population of Délos fled to Tínos before the Persians. On the orders of Darius, king of kings, the Persians not only respected the sacred site, but burned 300 talents' worth of incense for Apollo and allowed the Delians to return home in safety. A decade later, after the Persian defeat at Salamis, the Athenians organized a new Amphictyonic League centred at Délos. Everyone knew that only their fleet was strong enough to protect Greece, and in return Athens' allies – 140 city states and islands, initially – were required to contribute an annual sum to support the navy. Athenian archons administered the funds; Sparta, of course, wanted no part of it.

The Delian Alliance was effective, although many islands chaffed at being bossed by Athens. No one was fooled in 454 BC when Pericles, in order better to 'protect' the League's treasury, removed it to Athens; the money went not only to repair damage incurred during the Persian invasion, but to build the Parthenon. Shortly afterwards, Athens was struck by a terrible plague, and, as it was determined to have been caused by the wrath of Apollo, a second purification of Délos (not Athens, mind) was called for in 426 BC. This time, not only did the Athenians remove all the tombs, but they forbade both birth and death on Délos, forcing the pregnant and the dying to go to Rhéneia. When the Delians turned to Sparta for aid, the Spartans were unmoved: since the inhabitants couldn't be born or die on the island, they reasoned that Délos wasn't really their home, and why should they help a group of foreigners? In 422 BC Athens punished Délos for courting Sparta by exiling the entire population to Asia Minor. Athenian settlers moved in to take the

Delians' place, but when Athens then suffered setbacks against Sparta in the ongoing Peloponnesian War, the city tried to court divine favour back in her camp by allowing the Delians to return.

In 403 BC, Sparta's defeat of Athens gave Délos a breath of freedom for a decade before Athens was back with a second Delian Alliance. It was far less forceful, and 50 years later the Delians dared to ask the league to oust the Athenians altogether. But by then the head of the league was Philip II of Macedon, and he refused the request, wishing to stay in the good graces of the city that hated him most.

Following the death of Philip's son, Alexander the Great, Délos became free and prosperous with the support of Alexander's successors, who ruled kingdoms of their own around the eastern Mediterranean. New buildings and shrines went up and by 250 BC Délos was a flourishing port as well as a holy site. When the Romans defeated the Macedonians in 166 BC they returned the island to Athens, which as usual exiled the Delians. But by 146 BC and the fall of Corinth to Rome, Délos had recovered, then boomed when Rome made it a free port to undermine Rhodes, then the Aegean power-house. People from all over the ancient world settled in this Greek Hong Kong, and set up their own cults and religions. New quays and piers dealt with the growing trade. The slave markets thrived. But in the war between Rome and Mithridates of Pontus (88 BC), Mithridates pillaged Délos, killed 20,000 men, and enslaved the women and children. This was the beginning of the end.

Sulla regained the island, but 19 years later Délos was again pillaged by pirates allied to Mithridates, who once more sold the population into slavery. General Triarius retook and fortified the island and Hadrian attempted to revive the waning cult of Apollo with new festivities; but Délos spiralled into such a decline that when Athens tried to sell it, no one offered to buy. In AD 363, the Emperor Julian the Apostate tried to jump-start paganism on Délos until the Oracles warned him: 'Délos shall become Adélos.' A small Christian community survived until the 6th century, when the island was given over to pirates. House-builders on Tínos and Mýkonos used Délos for a marble quarry, and its once-busy markets became pasture. Archaeological excavations were begun in 1872 by the French, and work continues to this day.

The Excavations

Délos Excavations
t 228 902 2259; open Tues–Sun 8.30–3; adm; there isn't much shade, so take sensible shoes, a hat, and water

Sailing to Délos with a crowd of tourists speaking a dozen languages is not unlike the experience you would have had in Délos' Roman heyday. Left from the landing stage is the **Agora of the Competaliasts**. *Compita* were Roman citizens or freed slaves who worshipped the *Lares Competales*, or crossroads gods. Some of the *Lares* were the patrons of Roman trade guilds, while other guilds came under the protection of Hermes, Apollo or Zeus; many of the remains in the *agora* were votive offerings to them. A road, once lined with statues, leads to the Sanctuary of Apollo. To the left of the road stood the splendid Doric **Philip's Stoa**, built by Philip V of Macedon in 210 BC; it once held a statue dedicated by Sulla after his victory over Mithridates. The kings of Pergamon built the **Southern Stoa** in the 3rd century BC to house commercial workshops; here too are remains of the Delians' **Agora**.

The famous **Sanctuary of Apollo** is announced by the **Propylaea**, a gateway built of white marble in the 2nd century BC. Little remains of the sanctuary itself, once crowded with temples, offerings and statues. Next door is the **House of the Naxians** (6th century BC). Their great offering, a huge *kouros* statue, originally stood here, though only the pedestal remains. According to Plutarch, the *kouros* was crushed when a nearby bronze palm donated by Athens (symbolic of the tree clutched by Leto in giving birth) toppled over in the wind.

Next are three temples in a row. The first and largest, the **Great Temple of Apollo**, was begun by the Delians in 476 BC. The second was an **Athenian Temple** of Pentelic marble, built during the Second Purification, and the smallest, of porous stone, the **Temple of the Delians**, paid for by the 6th-century Athenian tyrant Pisistratos to house the sacred Asteria, the 'ship of the sky', represented by a moon setting in the sea. Dimitrios the Besieger (*see* p.406) contributed the nearby **Bull's Shrine**, which held a model of another ship, a trireme in honour of the sacred Athenian delegation ship – the one in which Theseus sailed on his return to Athens after slaying the Minotaur, and whose departure put off executions (most famously that of Socrates) until its return to Athens. Other buildings in the area were of an official nature – the **Prytaneion of the Rectors** and the **Councillor's House**. Towards the museum is the **Sanctuary of Dionysos** (4th century BC), flanked by lucky marble phalluses. The **Stoa of Antigonos** was built by a Macedonian king of that name in the 3rd century BC. Outside is the **Tomb of the Hyperborean Virgins**, who came to assist Leto in her hour of need – as a sacred tomb, it was the only one to stay put during the purifications.

On the opposite side of the Stoa stood the **Abaton**, the holy of holies, where only the priests could enter. A rectangular public well, the **Minoan Fountain** is from the 6th century BC and is still fed by a spring. Through the **Italian Agora**, the headquarters of the Roman trade guilds, you can reach the **Temple of Leto** (6th century BC) and the **Dodekatheon**, dedicated to the 12 gods of Olympus in the 3rd century BC. Beyond, where the **Sacred Lake** once hosted a flock of swans, is the **Terrace of the Lions**, snarling 7th-century BC Naxian marble guardians of the sanctuary, believed to have been inspired by Egyptian sphinxes lining sacred avenues; originally nine or perhaps 12, one lion now sits by the arsenal in Venice and three have gone missing; the ones here are casts. The site of the lake, sacred for having witnessed the birth of Apollo, is marked by a small wall; when Délos' torrent, Inopos, stopped flowing, the water evaporated. Along the shore are two **Palaestras** (for exercises and lessons) along with the foundation of the **Archigession**, or temple to the first mythical settler on Délos. Besides the **Gymnasium** and **Stadium** are remains of a few houses and a **Synagogue** built by the Phoenician Jews in the 2nd century BC. Another important structure here was the House of the **Poseidoniasts of Berytos** (90–120 BC), who were merchants and ship owners from Beirut.

A dirt path leads from the tourist pavilion to **Mount Kýthnos**. Along the way stand the ruins of the **Sanctuary of the Syrian Gods** of 100 BC, with a small religious theatre inside. Next is the first of three 2nd-century BC **Serapeions**, all temples dedicated to Serapis, the first and only successful god purposely invented by man – Ptolemy I of Egypt, who combined Osiris with Dionysos to create a synthetic deity in order to please both Greeks and Egyptians; syncretic Délos was one of the chief centres of his worship. Between the first and second Serapeions is the **Shrine to the Samothracian Great Gods**, the Cabeiri (see pp.596–7). The third Serapeion (still housing half a statue) was perhaps the main sanctuary, with temples to both Serapis and Isis. In the region are houses with mosaic floors, and a **Temple to Hera** from 500 BC. The **Sacred Cave**, where Apollo ran one of his many oracles, is en route to the top of **Mount Kýthnos**; later it was dedicated to Heracles. On the mountain itself is the **Shrine of Good Luck**, built by Arsinoë Philadelphos, wife of her brother, the King of Egypt. On the 113m (370ft) summit were signs of a settlement dating back to 3000 BC and a **Temple to Athena Cynthia**, but better yet is the view, encompassing nearly all the Cyclades.

The exclusive **Theatre Quarter** surrounded the 2nd-century BC **Theatre of Délos**, with a 5,500 capacity; beside it is a lovely eight-arched **reservoir**. The houses here date from the Hellenistic and Roman ages and many have beautiful mosaics, such as in the **House of the Dolphins** and the **House of the Masks**. All have a cistern beneath the floor and sewage systems. Some are built in the peristyle 'style of Rhodes', with a high-ceilinged guest room and colonnades surrounding the central courts. Seek out the mosaics of the **House of the Trident** and the **House of Dionysos** and the **House of Cleopatra and Dioscourides**, where the headless statues stand guard. Others have been moved into the site's museum, along with the original lions, statues of Apollo and Artemis and Dionysos, everyday items and a model of the ancient town.

Rhéneia Islet

Rhéneia lies west of Délos and is just as uninhabited. Here came the pregnant or dying Delians – a large number of little rooms were excavated in the rock to receive them, before they moved into the realm of tombs and sepulchral altars. A necropolis near the shore was the repository of the coffins which the Athenians exhumed in the second purification. On the other side of Rhéneia are the ruins of a *lazaretto* (leprosy hospital), once used by Sýros-bound ships sent into quarantine.

Náxos (ΝΑΞΟΣ)

Náxos is a big fish in a little pond, the largest of the Cyclades (4.48 sq km), and the highest, thanks to Mount Zas at 1,004m (3,295ft), and the most fertile: its 17,000 year-round residents grow much of their own food, and even keep cows, in valleys that remain a refreshing green even at the height of the sizzling summer. It can also claim to be the most sacred to Dionysos: Náxos makes excellent wine, as well as *Kítron*, a fragrant liqueur distilled from citron leaves; but seed potatoes are the main export. The west coast is almost one uninterrupted beach of silvery sands.

Náxos was Byron's favourite island, perhaps because it comes in romantic proportions: rugged mountains and lush valleys, sprinkled with the ruins of the ancient Greeks, the gilded Byzantines and his beloved Venetians. There are plenty of tourists, especially Germans and Scandinavians, but they stay by the beaches, leaving the rest of the big island to wanderers and poets.

History

Náxos was one of the major centres of the Neolithic Cycladic civilization. Around 3000 BC, the main settlements were near Chóra, on the hill of the Kástro and at Grótta, where the remains of the houses can still be seen in the clear water. Tradition has it that the island was later colonized by a party from Karia, led by a son of Apollo named Naxos. Although these Naxians were Ionians, their

Ariadne on Náxos

After slaying the Minotaur, Theseus and Ariadne, the Cretan princess who loved him, stopped to rest at Náxos on their way to Athens. Yet the next morning, while Ariadne slept, Theseus set sail and abandoned her. This, even in the eyes of the male chauvinist Athenians, was dishonourable, especially as Theseus had promised to marry Ariadne in return for the assistance she had rendered him in negotiating the Labyrinth. Did he simply forget her or find a new mistress? Was she shot with arrows by Artemis in the Temple of Dionysos and left for dead, as the *Odyssey* says? Or did the god Dionysos, who soon found the abandoned Ariadne and married her, somehow warn Theseus off? Everyone agrees that it was the jilted bride's curse on Theseus that made him forget to change his black sails to white to signal his safe homecoming, causing his father to commit suicide in despair.

Ariadne lived happily ever after with Dionysos, who taught the Naxians how to make their excellent wine and set Ariadne's crown, the Corona Borealis, amongst the stars; the Celts called it Ariansrod, where their heroes went after death. The story inspired later artists as well, including Richard Strauss, who wrote the opera *Ariadne auf Náxos*.

Getting to Náxos

By air: There are 2–3 flights a day from Athens with Olympic Airways, and charters from London and Manchester. **Airport**: t 228 502 3292; it's close to town, so take a taxi.

By sea: Náxos is one of the big ferry hubs all year round. In high season, **ferries** and **hydrofoils** connect several times a day with Piraeus; daily with Rafína, Páros, Íos, Santoríni, Mýkonos and Sýros; smaller craft almost daily with Amorgós via Heráklia, Schinoússa, Koufoníssi and Donoússa; less frequent connections with Sámos, Kos and Rhodes. Daily **excursion boats** go to Délos, Mýkonos, Páros and Santoríni. **Port authority**: t 228 502 2300.

Getting around Náxos

Frequent **bus** services depart from Náxos Town; there's a **KTEL information office** right by the dock where the buses stop, t 228 502 2291. They go every 30mins down to Ag. Prokópios and Ag. Ánna Beach; 6 times a day to Filóti and Chálki; 5 times to Apíranthos; 4 times to Apollónas, Kóronos, Pirgáki and Kastráki; 2–3 times to Komiáki and Mélanes.

There's a **taxi** rank by the bus station, t 228 502 2444. Taxis are not metered, so agree on a price first.

Car and motorbike rentals abound along the waterfront. Try **Tourent a Car, t** 228 502 3330; or, over towards Ag. Geórgios, **Apollon**, t 228 508 4300, or **Moto Falcon**, t 228 502 5323, for motorbikes and bicycles. If you're driving, get a map of Náxos town, and make them show you the route of the (unsignposted!) one-way system that carries traffic around the mostly pedestrian centre; Náxos is a great place to get lost.

most troublesome enemy was Miletus in Ionia proper, where Naxian refugees, eager to take back the island for themselves, fomented trouble. At the time, the most important citadel on the island was Delion, of which a few vestiges remain. Once, when Miletus attacked Náxos and the alarm was raised, a beautiful islander named Polykrite arrived too late and found the gate at Delion closed against her. One of the Miletan leaders found her, fell in love and proved it by telling her of all his armies' movements. His information enabled the Naxians to make a sudden attack on the Miletians, but in the confusion of the battle Polykrite's lover was killed, and the girl died of sorrow the next day.

Náxos was one of the first islands to work in marble. In the Archaic period sculptors produced the lions of Délos and the largest *kouros* statues ever found. But big was beautiful on Náxos; in 523 BC the tyrant Lugdamis declared he would make Náxos' buildings the highest in Greece, but only the massive lintel from the Temple of Apollo survives to tell the tale of his ambition. Later, the island was the first to rebel against Athens and the Delian league, in c. 470 BC – only to be crushed after a siege. 'This was the first allied state to be enslaved, contrary to accustomed practice,' Thucydides wrote in the Peloponnesian War. 'But later the same thing happened to others.'

Náxos next makes the history books in 1207, when the Venetian Marco Sanudo captured the island's Byzantine castle, T'Apaliroú, and declared himself Duke of Náxos, ruler over all the adventurers who had grabbed up islands after the conquest of Constantinople in 1204. In 1210, when Venice refused to grant Sanudo the status he desired, he hitched his wagon to the Roman Emperor and took the title Duke of the Archipelago ('Archelopelago' was a corruption of

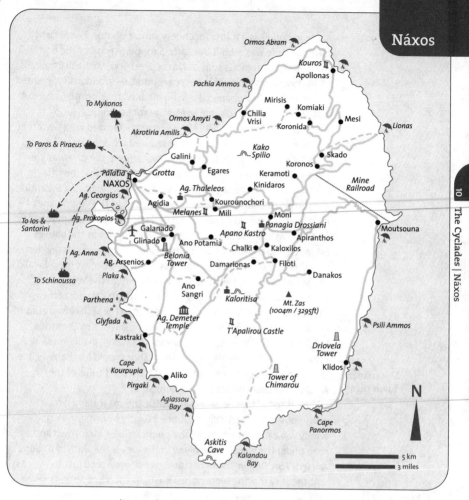

'Aegean' as it appeared on Byzantine sea charts, Aigaíon Pélagos; under Sanudo's successors, the word gained its current meaning as a group of islands). Even after the Turkish conquest in 1564, the Dukes of Náxos remained in nominal control of the Cyclades.

Náxos Town

The island's port and capital, Náxos, is a bustling place sprawling at the foot of the old town, piled over a low conical hill. By the port, the island's Π-shaped trademark, the **Portára** of Lugdamis' unfinished **Temple of Apollo** (522 BC), stands like an ancient version of the enigmatic monolith in *2001: A Space Odyssey*, a massive doorway to nowhere, or perhaps to another dimension. The three stones together weigh over 100 tonnes – that's why they're still here. Set on the islet of **Palátia**, linked by an ancient causeway to the port, they come in handy as a frame for cheesy sunset photos. The ancient **harbour mole** was rebuilt by Marco Sanudo, in front of the port. Statues of two famous sons of Náxos greet you: Michaéli Damiralís (d. 1917), who translated Shakespeare into Greek, and a disappointed-looking Pétros Protopapadákis, who planned the Corinth Canal but had the misfortune to serve as Minister of Economics during the 1920–22 catastrophe in Asia Minor; he was executed with five other ministers as scapegoats by the subsequent regime.

On Náxos' frenetic, pedestrianized waterfront, the tavernas are jammed even in the off-season. By the Agrarian Bank, the 11th-century church of **Panagía Pantanássa** was once part of a Byzantine monastery and famous for its very early icon of the Virgin. Lanes here lead up into old Náxos, a fine Cycladic town, although you may find its twisting streets bewildering, which is just as the natives intended – to confuse invading marauders. The town was divided into three neighbourhoods: **Boúrgos** where the Greeks lived; **Evraikí**, the Jewish quarter; and up above, **Kástro**, where the Venetian Catholic nobility lived. In Boúrgos, the Orthodox cathedral, the **Metropolis of Zoodóchos Pigí**, was created in the 18th century out of an old temple and older churches; its iconostasis is by Dimítrios Válvis of the Cretan school. Archaeologists would gladly knock it down for a slam-bang dig if only the bishop would let them; as it is they've had to be content with the cordoned-off **ruins of the Mycenaean town** under the adjacent square.

Mycenaean town ruins
open Tues–Sun 8–2

The cathedral looks down over **Grótta**, the coast named for its numerous caves (naturally re-dubbed Grotty by Brits); if it's not windy you can see remains of the prehistoric Cycladic town and a road under the water; one hollow in the rock is the 'Bath of Ariadne'. Ancient **Fort Delion**, scene of star-crossed love, stood just to the east.

At the very top, the high-walled **Kástro** preserves one of its seven original towers, guarding one of three entrances into the district's jumble of stunning houses, flowers and dark alleys. Some 19 **Venetian houses** still bear their coats of arms – something you'll almost never see in Venice proper, where such displays of pride were severely frowned upon. Most of the Kástro's current residents claim Venetian descent, and many of their grandparents' tombstones in the 13th-century Catholic **cathedral** boast grand titles. The cathedral, clad from head to toe in pale grey marble, was founded by Marco Sanudo, whose ruined palace is directly across the square.

During the Turkish occupation, Kástro was famous for its School of Commerce, run by friars and attended for two years by Níkos Kazantzákis. This is now the **Archaeology Museum**, at least until a new one is built, with artefacts from the 5th millenium BC to the 5th century AD, including a superb collection of Cycladic figurines, a Cycladic pig about to be sick in a sack from 2800 BC, Mycenaean pottery (note the *hýdria* painted with fishermen), and a Roman

Archaeology Museum
t 228 502 2725; open Tues–Sun 8–2.30; adm

Venetian Museum
*t 228 502 2387; open
Tues–Sun 10–3 and
7.30–10.30; adm*

mosaic of Europa. The nearby **Venetian Museum** (Domus Della-Rocca-Barozzi) preserves a traditional Kástro house and offers guided tours in English of the area, ending with refreshments in the museum; in summer it hosts atmospheric concerts. A beautifully carved portico by the Kástro entrance leads to a choice terrace containing tables and chairs. Just below the museums, the **Antico Veneziano** antique shop is housed in an 800-year-old mansion, with lovingly restored 2,000-year-old Ionian columns original to the house in the erstwhile servants' quarters (now the shop); it also has fascinating photos of Náxos and Santoríni through the 20th century and a room exhibiting works by international artists.

South of the Kastro and the waterfront, numerous hotels and a whole new suburb, **Néa Chóra**, have sprung up around popular **Ag. Geórgios Beach**. Its shallow waters and long curl of sand are genteely lined with tavernas and hotels.

Around the Island

The Southwest Coast

Little resort strips have sprung up haphazardly all along the coast south of Ag. Geórgios. Behind them, the main road skirts the fertile **Livádi plain**, where Náxos grows its famous potatoes; here, near the airport at Iria, a **Temple of Dionysos** was discovered in 1986. They have tried to restore the site of this rustic sanctuary to something like its original appearance, surrounded by olives and vines. There are foundations of the temple (*c.* 670 BC, rebuilt *c.* 550) and dining hall, a reconstructed Archaic column and a small museum.

Temple of Dionysos
*open Tues–Sun
8–2.30; adm*

The coastal beaches begin with **Ag. Prokópios**, with nice, coarse, non-sticky sand, **Maragás**, a pleasant, less crowded beach, then **Ag. Ánna**, the most popular, well sheltered from the notorious *meltémi*, and **Pláka** just south, considered by many the best in Náxos, with a variety of water sports, and an alternative campsite. From Ag. Ánna, boats and bifurcating dirt roads hidden in the bamboo continue south to more beaches; by asphalt road you have to divert inland, by way of **Ag. Arsénios** (if you get off the bus here, you can take a lovely path down to the beaches, passing windmills and a 9m (30ft)-high Hellenistic watch tower, the **Paleó Pírgos**). The vast white sandy beaches to the south begin at **Parthéna**, excellent for surfing and swimming, followed by **Mikrí Vígla**, where the sea is brilliantly clear. **Sahára** is well equipped for sea sports, and merges into **Kastráki**, again with sparkling sea and white sands, ideal for letting the kids run wild. Above the road stands **Pírgos Oskéllou**, a ruined Mycenaean fortress, built over the remains of a Cycladic acropolis. If the above beaches are too busy, there's a more remote strip of sand beyond Kastráki on either side of **Cape Kouroúpia**.

Inland Villages: South of Náxos Town

A few kilometres east of Náxos Town, the main inland road forks, the southerly right-hand branch heading first to **Galanádo**, site of the restored Venetian **Belonia Tower**, bearing the Lion of St Mark, and the Venetian church of **St John**, with a Catholic chapel on the left and an Orthodox one on the right – an unusual arrangement, but one typical on Náxos. It is also seen in the island's first cathedral, the recently restored 8th-century **Ag. Mámas**, dedicated to the patron saint of thieves, located a short walk from the road, towards **Áno Sangrí**. Consisting of three hamlets picturesquely spread out over the plateau, Áno Sangrí gets its name from 'Sainte Croix', as the French called the 16th-century tower monastery **Tímiou Stavroú** or True Cross.

Temple of Demeter
open Tues–Sun
8–2.30; adm

There are many Byzantine frescoed chapels and medieval towers in the vicinity and, a mile south of Áno Sangrí, a 6th-century BC **Temple of Demeter** (signposted 'Gigoulas' or 'Dimitra's Temple'). This was the main religious centre of the Náxos city-state from the 8th century BC. Emperor Justinian used much of the stone to build a basilica on the site; this fell into ruins and was replaced by a small chapel. Here, though, archaeologists have taken revenge on the Christians and dismantled the church and scoured surrounding farms for other bits to fit parts of the temple façade and columns back together. That is enough to see that the temple, built in the mid-6th century, was quite an impressive building (and it had a marble roof). Oddly enough it has two entrances, and a double dedication: to Demeter and to Baubo, the nurse at Eleusis who succeeded in making the goddess laugh while she was in mourning for her daughter Persephone.

A strenuous walk southeast from Áno Sangrí will take you up to the ruins of **T'Apaliroú**, the Byzantine castle high on its rock that defied Marco Sanudo and his mercenaries for two months.

Central Náxos: The Tragéa and Slopes of Mount Zas

East of Áno Sangrí the road rises up to the beautiful **Tragéa plateau**, planted with fruit trees and lilacs, flanked on either side by Náxos' highest mountains. Olive groves engulf the small villages in the valley, including **Chálki**, where both the Byzantines and Venetians built tower houses: the Byzantine **Frankópoulo**, in the centre, and up a steep path the 13th-century Venetian **Apáno Kástro**, used by Marco Sanudo as a summer hideaway. He was not, however, the first to enjoy the views; the fortress sits on Cyclopean foundations, and Geometric era and Mycenaean tombs have been found to the southeast; rare for Greece, there's even a menhir nearby.

The area around Chálki is Náxos' holy land, the 'little Mýstras', with over a score of churches decorating the valleys and mountaintops. The village centre holds perhaps the most interesting, **Panagía**

Protóthronis, a very ancient church largely rebuilt in the 12th century. The wealth of reasonably well-preserved frescoes here includes images of a *Christ Pantokrator* and an *Annunciation*; some of the fresco fragments here may go as far back as the 7th century. On a short, signposted walk outside the village, the 9th-century **Ag. Geórgos Diasorítis** is built over a small stream. Two kilometres to the southwest, near **Vourvoúria**, the frescoes in **Ag. Artémios** have only geometric and floral patterns, a relic of the Iconoclasm. A road leads up towards **Moní** to a shady glade sheltering the most striking church on Náxos, **Panagía Drossianí**, built perhaps in the 6th century and crowned with ancient corbelled domes of field stones. Open most mornings (*offering expected*), it contains excellent frescoes of the *Virgin and Saints*, and in the dome, unusually, two *Christ Pantokrators*, a young one and an old.

Chálki is in the heart of Kítron territory; to see how it's made, visit the **Vallindras Naxos Citron Distillery**. Seven kilometres west is lovely **Áno Potámia**, another well-watered town, whose taverna (Paradise Garden) is popular with Náxians wanting to escape the capital.

The main road continues on southeastwards, passing **Kerámio**, where there is another church, **Ag. Iánnos**; with frescoes of a *Pantokrator* and warrior saints. Next comes attractive **Filóti** on the slopes of Mount Zas, the largest village in the Tragéa, where contented ewes produce the island's best cheese; it also offers splendid views and the chance to eavesdrop on everyday village life away from the tourist mills. Monuments include the Venetian towerhouse of the De Lasti family, and two churches: **Koímisis tis Theotókou**, with a fine carved marble iconostasis, and **Panagía Filótissa**, with a marble steeple. Of the many scenic paths, one leads up the slopes of Mount Zas, passing by way of an ancient inscription, ΟΡΟΣ ΔΙΟΣ ΜΗΛΩΣΙΟΥ ('Mount Zeus, Herd-Protector'). There's a sacred cave near the summit, where one story says baby Zeus (*see* p.136) was briefly deposited; be careful and bring a light if you want to explore – the only inhabitants now are bats. A three-hour, mostly paved path from Filóti follows the west flanks of the mountain south to the isolated and excellently preserved Hellenistic **Tower of Chimárou**, built by Ptolemy of Egypt of white marble blocks, lost in the wildest part of Náxos.

From Filóti the road skirts the slopes of **Mount Zas** on its way to **Apíranthos**, where the Venetian families Crispi and Sommaripa built towers. There's an old legend that Apíranthos was founded by Barabbas, who lit out for the islands after Pontius Pilate pardoned him. Many contemporary families, however, are Cretan, descended from migrants who came during the Turkish occupation to work in Greece's only emery mines. It's the most beautiful village on Náxos, with winding paths paved with marble; Byron loved it so much that he declared that he wanted to die here (there are a few rooms to

Vallindras Naxos Citron Distillery
t 228 503 1220; open mornings Mon–Fri plus weekends in July and Aug

rent if you feel the same way). The churches, to Saints Geórgios, Sofía and Ilías, are built over ancient temples to Ares, Athena and Helios respectively. A few women still weave on looms and farmers sell their produce, and there's a wonderful antique barber shop. In August, however, cocktail bars and revelry shake things up. Visit the small **Cycladic Museum**, devoted to Neolithic finds, and the **Museum of Natural History**, in the school.

Cycladic Museum/ Museum of Natural History
open 9–3; adm

Above the village, on the road north, are ruins of a prehistoric acropolis at **Pánormos**. Below it are two late-medieval domed churches with bits of frescoes, **Ag. Pachómios** and **Ag. Geórgios**.

A road from Apíranthos descends to the port of **Moutsoúna**, where emery, used in ancient times to polish Cycladic statues, is now brought down from the mountains near Kóronos by a rope funicular and loaded onto ships (you can learn all about it at the **Emery Museum** near Sarántara, north of Apíranthos. Moutsoúna has a fine beach; from here a rather dodgy dirt road follows the east coast south to the remote beach of **Psilí Ámmos**.

North of Náxos Town

The left branch of the main road from Náxos Town leads to **Mélanes** and the ancient marble quarries in the heart of Náxos; at **Flério**, signposted off the road, lies a 7th-century BC 6m (20ft)-high *kouros* in a cypress grove. Inspired by monumental Egyptian sculpture, these Archaic statues – highly stylized, naked young men, invariably smiling, their arms hugging their sides, one foot stepping forward – seem to announce the coming of Greece's golden age. Colossal in size, a combination of virility and grace, they are the first intimation in art of the divine spark in humanity – in one sense, a *kouros* is also Apollo. You can see the best in Athens' museums: whole battalions of Michelangeline Davids. This one was left behind because of a broken leg.

At **Kourounochóri**, near Mélanes, stand the ruins of a Venetian castle; **Ag. Thaléleos** in the same area has a monastery with a fine 13th-century church. Náxos' marble is almost as fine as Páros' and is still quarried to the east at **Kinídaros**. One of the most beautiful walks on Náxos begins here; the path descends past the chapel of the woodland goddess Ag. Artemís, and follows the lush Xerotakári River valley down to Egarés. The Xerotakári is the only river in the Cyclades to flow in August; it has little waterfalls and provides a home for turtles and eels, as well as water for Náxos Town.

A road links **Kóronos** to **Liónas Beach**, while the main road north turns into a winding, hairpin serpent leading to pretty **Komiakí**, highest of the island's villages, with stunning views over terraced vineyards before descending to **Apóllonas**, an attractive corner with a sandy beach and several tavernas heavily patronized by tour buses. Ancient marble quarries are carved out of the slopes, and steps lead up to another colossal, 10m (33ft) *kouros*, abandoned in the 7th century BC because of flaws in the marble. Because Apóllonas was sacred to Apollo (an inscription is still visible on the marble wall), the statue is believed to have been intended for a long-vanished temple that stood here, which intriguingly was placed to form part of a perfect equilateral triangle with the temples of Apollo on Délos and Páros. Apóllonas is as far as the bus goes; by car you can chance the road along the north coast back to Náxos Town, passing the isolated beaches of idyllic **Ormós Ábram** with a taverna, rooms and a giant marble head abandoned on a rock, and **Pachiá Ámmos**, near the **Monastery of Faneroméni**, dating from 1606. There are lovely beaches on this northwest coast, although when the *meltémi* roars you'll probably want to give them a miss.

Useful Information on Náxos

(i) Náxos >
by the quay, t 228 502 5201, Náxos Town; run by hotel owners, and extremely helpful; organizes accommodation and tours; also offers luggage storage and laundry facilities

(★) Château Zevogli >>

Walking Plus, t (UK) (020) 8835 8303, www.walkingplus.co.uk. Guided or self-guided walks, with luggage transport and accommodation.

Zoom Bookstore, on the waterfront. Excellent selection of maps and guides, incl. Christian Ucke's helpful *Walking Tours on Náxos*.

Náxos Festivals

23 April: Kinídaros.

1 July: Sangrí.

14 July: The biggest festival of all, for Ag. Nikódimos, patron saint of Náxos, with a procession of the icon and a folk festival.

17 July: Kóronos.

First week of Aug: Dionýsia festival in Náxos Town, with folk dancing in local costume and free food and wine.

15 Aug: Filóti.

23 Aug: Trípodes.

29 Aug: Apóllonas and Apíranthos.

Where to Stay and Eat on Náxos

If you don't book, the **Hotel and Rooms Association** on the quay has a kiosk with photos of everything on offer; next to it, another kiosk has camping information. Ferries are met by campsite and room owners, with minibuses. Beware that most of their rooms are in **Néa Chóra** (10–15min walk from the ferries), unlovely but handy for the beach; if you stay there, make sure you can find your way home through the anonymous streets.

Náxos Town ✉ 84300

Staying in car-free Chóra, behind the waterfront promenade, is delightful.

Grotta, in Grótta, the northern suburb of Chóra, t 228 502 2215, www.hotelgrotta.gr (€€€). Another blue and white creation with wonderful sea views; the owner will collect you from the quay.

Château Zevgoli, t 228 502 6123, www.chateau-zevgoli.gr (€€€). Spoil yourself in this plush old mansion, small and exclusive with roof garden, antique décor and a four-poster for honey-mooners. Run by the manager of the Náxos Tourist Information Centre (*see left*); enquire there.

Nikos Verikokos, on the Kástro hill, t 228 502 2025 (€€€–€€). Rooms and studios by the Pantanássa church, offering views.

Anixis, by the Kástro, t 228 502 2932 (€€). Very moderate, overlooking the sea from its verandas and terraces.

Boúrgos, Amphitris St, in Boúrgos, t 228 502 2979 (€€). Another pleasant choice, especially the airy studio off the roof terrace.

Iliada Studios, Grótta, t 228 502 3303 (€€). Overlooking the sea.

Pantheon, just up from the entrance to the Kástro hill, t 228 502 4335 (€€). Run by a lovely couple; one of these 6 en suite rooms is the closest you'll get to what 'living' in the old town is like for the everyday inhabitant.

Panorama, Amphitrís St, in Boúrgos, just outside the Kástro's walls, t 228 502 4404 (€). Pleasant small hotel, with a marvellous sea view.

Sofi, a 3min walk from the docks, at the base of the Kástro hill, t 228 502 6437 (€). Attractive place that has seen the same customers for 20 years, thanks to the friendly Koufópoulos family (*see right*).

Apolafsis, by the waterfront. Fine Greek food with live Greek music.

Delfini, on the Kástro hill under the wall. Café-bar with a lovely garden setting, serving generous drinks, snacks, Indian and Thai curry dishes, including some for vegetarians. The owner spent years in England, where he got hooked on Asian food.

Kástro, Bradóuna Square, under the Kástro's walls, t 228 502 2005. Delicious rabbit *stifádo* and *exochikó* (filo parcels).

Manolis, in a courtyard on Old Market St, in the old heart of Chóra. Good-value traditional food: ask for the specials and try the home-made *rakí* (good in itself and even better in *'rakimelo'*, warmed with honey and a great cure for coughs).

Meltemi, towards Ag. Geórgios, t 228 502 2654. Excellent waterfront taverna which has been serving delicious Greek meals for 25 years.

Picasso, in main Plateía Protodikíou, below the Kástro. Popular restaurant with Mexican specialities such as tortillas, guacamole and salsas. Also a second-hand book exchange.

Scirocco, by the town hall, t 228 502 5931. Fine Greek and international cuisine – especially good salads.

To Smyrneko, seafood on the waterfront: swordfish, prawns and fancy *mezédes*.

Vassilis, Ag. Nikólemou St. in the market area. The oldest in Náxos; stuffed rabbit, swordfish *souvláki*.

Probonas. A shop on the waterfront, where you can taste the local Kítron liqueur (regular, mint or banana flavour); Náxos wine is good as well, but it is best drunk from a barrel in situ.

Néa Chóra/Ag. Geórgios ✉ 84300

Astir of Naxos, 100m from Ag. Geórgios Beach, t 228 502 9320, *www.astirof naxos.com* (€€€). New Cycladic-style hotel with a big pool and Jacuzzi.

Nissaki Beach, t 228 502 5710, *www. nissaki-beach.com* (€€€). Rooms circling the pool, with restaurant-bar.

Panos Studios, 20m from the beach on a quiet street, t 228 502 6078, *www .studiospanos.com* (€€). Spick and span studios, run by the Koufópoulos family, whose warm welcome includes a free ouzo or coffee as they dispense advice from their vast knowledge of Náxos.

St George Beach, on the beach, t 228 502 3162, *www.naxos-holidays.com* (€€). Arched verandas and air conditioning; transit to/from the port or airport offered.

Irene Pension, t 228 502 3169, *www. irenepension-naxos.com* (€). Quiet, family-run, good value; with air-conditioning. The same family has opened the new Irene II nearby, with a swimming pool.

Kavouri, on Ag. Geórgios Beach. An old favourite; good fish soup and other dishes with Náxian wine for over 40 years.

Ag. Prokópios ✉ 84300

Kavouras Village, t 228 502 5580, *www.kavurasvillage.gr* (€€€€€). Family friendly studios around a pool.

Kavos, t 228 502 3355, *www.kavos-naxos.com* (€€€€–€€€). Stylish villas and studios in traditional-style houses, set in gardens with a pool and restaurant.

Camping Náxos, by the beach, t 228 502 3500. Has a pool.

Ag. Ánna ✉ 84300

Studios Anemos, above the bakery, t 228 504 1919 (€€–€).

Ag. Ánna, by the sea, t 228 504 2576 (€). With verandas and fruits of the orchard to feast on.

Camping Maragas, t 228 502 4552. German-run and immaculate.

Gorgonas, on the beach, t 228 504 1007. For fishy dishes, including lobster and seafood pasta, in a courtyard setting.

Palatia, on the beach, **t** 228 502 6588 (€25). Considered the top fish restaurant on Náxos, but it serves other delicious dishes as well.

Paradise Taverna, **t** 228 504 2026. Tasty Greek dishes, a terrace shaded by a vast pine tree and an infectious atmosphere. Also nice **rooms** (€) with garden and sea view.

Pláka/Mikrí Vígla/Kastráki ✉ 84300

Medusa, Pláka, **t** 228 507 5555, *www. medusaresort.gr* (€€€). A favourite of sophisticated windsurfers; rooms are furnished with antiques, mini-bars and satellite TV.

Mikri Vigla, Mikrí Vígla, on the beach, **t** 228 507 5241, *www.naxos-windsurf. com* (€€€). New low-rise mini-resort in Cycladic style, with a pool and surfing centre.

Summerland, Kastráki, **t** 228 507 5461 (€€€). Relaxed apartments around two pools and bars, with gym, Jacuzzi and mini-market on site, good for entertaining kids.

Aronis Taverna, on the Ag. Ánna–Pláka Beach road, **t** 228 504 2019 (€€€–€€). Clean studios by the sea and a hippy eatery; the road is lined with similar studios.

Yiannis, Kastráki, **t** 228 507 5413 (€€).

 ★ Axiotissa >

Axiotissa, Kastráki, **t** 228 507 5107 (€20). Sit on the big terrace and try fried green tomatoes and other surprising variations using Greek ingredients. *Book in season.*

Inland and North ✉ 84300

Flora's Apartments, Apóllonas, **t** 228 506 7070 (€€). Pleasant, built around a garden.

Efthimios, Órmos Ábram, **t** 228 506 3244 (€€–€). If you want to get away from it all; it also has a very good taverna.

Stou Lefteri, Apíranthos, **t** 228 506 1333. Not to be missed: considered by the Greeks as one of the finest traditional tavernas in the Cyclades.

Entertainment and Nightlife on Náxos

Náxos has a buzzing nightlife with masses of bars.

Escoba, near the OTE, Náxos Town. Tex-Mex food and music to match.

Rocks and **Jam Bar**: dancing spots on the Náxos Town waterfront

Med Bar, Náxos Town, with a terrace overlooking the water.

Cocos Café and **Rendezvous**, on the main waterfront, Náxos Town. Relaxed places to sit.

Jazz Blues Bar, in Chóra, Old Market St. The mellowest of places in the evening.

Ocean Dance, right on the sea, Náxos Town. Dance the night away, watching the sun rise through the giant window.

Super Island, in Grótta. Thumping club.

Enosis, in Ag. Ánna, **t** 228 502 4644. Popular club in old warehouse playing Greek music.

South and East of Náxos: The Back Islands

Between Náxos and Amorgós lies a bevy of tiny islands known as the Back Islands because they're in the back of beyond – Schinoússa, Koufoníssi, Donoússa and Heráklia (or Iráklia) are the four inhabited ones. Once a hide-out for pirates and wartime partisans, they are now firmly on the holiday map.

All have post offices to change money and most have tourist agencies (don't expect any cash machines, though). They are quiet off season, with sandy beaches and wonderful walking country – but don't arrive in August without booking.

Getting to the Back Islands

The islands are served daily in summer by at least one **ferry**, following a route from Náxos, Páros and Amorgós, plus three or four weekly from Piraeus. When it operates, the **hydrofoil** from Amorgós also calls at the islands, except Donoússa. Wherever you are coming from, if you get off at one of the Back Islands, you'll be spending the night there, unless you take a day trip from Náxos. **Port authority** (Náxos): **t** 228 502 2300.

Koufoníssi (ΚΟΥΦΟΝΗΣΙ)

Koufoníssi is tiny and flat – you can walk around it in three hours – and it has a thriving fishing fleet. It exerts such a compelling charm on its visitors that many can't stay away. Once the hideaway of intrepid independent travellers, it is now jammed in July and August with trendy Athenians and Italians, into spear-fishing or perfecting their tans. The *meltémi* rages at exactly the same time, and has been known to launch tents into space from the free but unsheltered campsite by Fínikas Beach.

The enchanting one and only village, **Koufoníssi**, on a hill above the quay, has its back to the sea. Life centres on the cobbled main street; in summer it turns into a big party, with fashionable island-hoppers carousing at the taverna tables. Koufoníssi has gorgeous beaches, some with shade, tucked under golden rocks eroded into bulging *millefeuille* pastries. The first, **Fínikas**, east of the village, is lined with sleeping bags in high season. Over a rocky spit there are even lovelier, **Charakópou** and especially **Porí**, with its gorgeous soft sand.

Daily excursions in season on the caique *Prásinos* go to **Káto Koufoníssi**, the uninhabited island opposite, for skinny-dipping and its taverna, and sometimes to the beaches on **Kéros**. This island has the ruins of a Neolithic settlement at **Daskálio**, where the 'Treasure of Kéros' yielded many fine Cycladic figurines (including the famous *Harpist* in the National Archaeological Museum in Athens). There's also an abandoned medieval settlement in the north.

Schinoússa (ΣΧΟΙΝΟΥΣΣΑ)

Schinoússa hit the world's headlines in 2006, when a huge cache of illegal antiquities was recovered in a police raid on an island villa, part of a spectacular smuggling case that involved the Getty Museum and a big Greek ship-owning family. Nothing much else has happened here in the last ten thousand years. Scenically less attractive than the other small Cyclades, Schinoússa is still very Greek and charming. There are only 85 inhabitants in winter, increasing in summer to around 200, most of them farmers trying to make ends meet. Ferries dock at the tiny port of **Myrsíni**, but the main settlement is **Chóra**, also known as **Panagía**, less than a mile up the hill, where village life goes on regardless of tourists. You can take the old cobbled mule track for a short-cut, but it's a hot hike in summer. From there a steep track runs down to the grey sand beach at **Tsigoúra**, with a rather expensive taverna and disco.

There are about 17 beaches on the island, many bleak and littered by the wind, but **Psilí Ámmos** is worth the 45-minute walk from Chóra across the island, via the ghost hamlet of **Messariá**. A rough track takes you to the duny sands with turquoise waters; in summer it's a favourite unofficial camping spot.

Donoússa (ΔΟΝΟΥΣΑ)

Donoússa, due east of Náxos, and northernmost of the chain, is even more remote and has fewer ferry links. Larger and more mountainous, it's a good place for walkers and hermits; most of the tourists so far are German. **Donoússa** (or **Stávros**), the port and village, has rooms, tavernas and a shop; the sandy beach of **Kéndros** is a 15-minute walk. Resources are stretched in high season. There's a summer-only bakery, but food and water can get scarce.

A Geometric-era settlement (900–700 BC) was excavated by Váthí Limenarí, but most visitors come for the fine beaches, at **Livádi** and **Fýkio**, reached in two hours on foot via the hamlets of **Charavgí** and **Mersíni** (or 20 minutes by caique); **Kalotarítissa Beach** is an hour's walk north.

Heráklia (ΗΡΑΚΛΕΙΑ)

Herákia, the most westerly and largest of the Back Islands (pop. 115 the last time anyone counted), is only an hour's ferry hop from Náxos, but even in mid-August it remains quiet and inviting. Unusually for the Cyclades, it's a good time to visit and join in the Festival of the Panagía on 15 August, with three days of non-stop eating, drinking and dancing.

The attractive port, **Ag. Geórgios**, is set in the hills, with a small beach and a little fishing fleet. From here it's a 20-minute walk to the large sandy beach at **Livádi**, popular with Greeks and campers. The old Chóra, **Panagía**, named after its main church, is about an hour's walk into the hills. It's pretty and sleepy, but primitive and unlikely to have rooms. There is, however, an excellent bakery – the baker picks wild sesame seeds for his bread on his journey from the port. From Panagía a path leads to sandy **Alimniás Beach**. Another excursion is the 3hr walk along the mule path, southwest from Ag. Geórgios to the large stalactite cave of **Ag. Ioánnis**, overlooking **Vourkariá Bay**, with two chambers over 73m (240ft) long; the chapel at the entrance sees a huge *panegýri* on 28 August.

Useful Information on the Back Islands

Koufoníssi: Prassinos agency, t 228 507 1438, changes money, sells ferry tickets on the quay and runs excursions. **Koufoníssi Tours, t** 228 507 4091, can help with accommodation.

Schinoússa: The **Grispos Tourist Center** in Chóra, **t** 228 507 1930, at the top of the mule path from Myrsíni, is run from a mini-market, which arranges accommodation, ferry tickets and trips. **Heráklia:** **Aigaio Travel, t** 228 507 1561, can help you find a room. Also see *www.iraklia.gr*.

Back Islands Festivals

Last Sat in June: Fishermen's festival, Koufoníssi.

15 Aug: Panagía, Heráklia.

28 Aug: Ag. Ioánnis Pródromos, Heráklia.

14 Sept: Holy Cross, Donoússa.

Where to Stay and Eat on the Back Islands

Koufoníssi ✉ 84300

Small hotels and studios are sprouting up like crazy; all stay open May–Oct.

Villa Ostria, Ag. Geórgiou, t 228 507 1671 (€€€). Pretty veranda over the sea and comfortable rooms, with fridges.

Keros, t 228 507 1601 (€€€ in season, €€ off season). Neo-Cycladic, with a garden and seaside bar.

Ta Galiná Spitákia, Stroúpos, t 228 507 1674 (€€€–€€). Pretty setting and studios sleeping up to four with views over Kéros. Friendly owners.

Christina's House, t 228 507 1736 (€€). Similar but on a more modest scale.

Finikas, t 228 507 1368 (€€). Self-contained double rooms in a cluster of white buildings near Fínikas Beach; the owner meets ferries with his truck.

Hondros Kavos, t 228 507 1707 (€€). Brand new rooms.

Katerina, just up the hill from the port, t 228 507 1455 (€€). With an ebullient landlady.

Petros Club, t 228 507 1728 (€€). Near the sea, with a large garden and restaurant; mini-bars in each room. *Open July–Sept.*

Camping Charakópou, t 228 507 1683. With simple facilities. There's also a free campsite east of the port behind

Fínikas Beach, with two areas each fronted by tavernas.

Kapetan-Nikolas, t 228 507 1690. For very, very fresh fish.

Melissa, t 228 507 1454. The oldest taverna on the island (since 1960) serving up a tasty stews and grills; try the octopus *stifádo*.

Yiannis Venetsanos, Káto Koufoníssi t 228 507 4074. Well prepared kid dishes, lobster *piláfi* and other delights at very good prices.

Schinoússa ✉ 84300

Tsigouri Beach Villas, Tsigoúra, t 228 507 1930 (€€€–€€). Very nice rooms overlooking the beach, with a restaurant.

Anesi, in Chóra, t 228 507 1180 (€€). On the main street with wonderful views.

Provaloma, just outside Chóra, t 228 507 1936 (€€). Offers more fine views, minibus service, rooms with bath, and a good taverna, with an old-fashioned stone oven.

Panorama Taverna, t 228 507 1160. Rooms to let (€), basic home cooking and great views to Tsigoúra.

Taverna Myrsíni, in Myrsíni, t 228 507 1154. Spartan kitchen conjures up delicious seafood in the evenings, and it doubles as a left-luggage store by day.

Heráklia ✉ 84300

Zografos, 700m back from the sea in Livádi, t 228 507 1946 (€€). Rooms with verandas, baths, fridges and a communal barbecue.

Angelos, t 228 507 1486 (€). Inexpensive rooms in the village.

Mary, Livádi, t 228 507 1485 (€). Rooms and apartments; the owner meets the ferries.

Perigiali, Ag. Geórgios Beach, t 228 507 1118. Seafood from the owner's own fishing boat.

Páros (ΠΑΡΟΣ)

Now that the designers and big money are taking over Mýkonos, where does the young, fun crowd go? A short hop away to less pricey, less posey Páros – joining artists, families, windsurfers, Greek pensioners and everyone in between. One of the larger Cyclades, Páros is fringed with enticing golden beaches, dotted with beguiling sugarcube villages. The island's gentle mountain, Profítis Ilías

Getting to Páros

By air: There are 1–7 flights daily in season from Athens with **Olympic Airways, t** 228 402 1900. **Airport: t** 228 409 1257; there's a frequent bus service to and from Parikiá, 14km away.

By sea: Páros is one of the great crossroads of the Aegean, with many daily **ferry, hydrofoil** and **catamaran** connections with Piraeus, Íos, Náxos and Santoríni; 3–4 times a week with Thessaloníki, Folégandros, Síkinos, Mílos, Koufouníssi and Anáfi; 5 times a week with Amorgós; several times a week with Sýros and Sámos; twice a week with Astypálaia, Kálymnos, Sífnos, Sérifos, Kímolos and Ikaría; once a week with Ándros and Lávrio. **Port authority: t** 228 402 1240.

Getting around Páros

An hourly **ferry** leaves from Poúnda (6kms south of Parikiá) to Antíparos, and there are also many **day excursions** around Páros itself, and to Antíparos and other islands.

Very frequent **buses** depart from the port to all the towns and villages with the exception of the south coast between Dríos and Alíki; **KTEL** in Parikiá, **t** 228 402 1113.

Taxis congregate by the dock and bus kiosk, and rates are reasonable (€7 to Náoussa), but agree a price beforehand. In Parikiá, call **t** 228 402 1500. In Náoussa, call **t** 228 405 3490.

If you want to **hire a car or bike**, there are signs everywhere in Parikiá, but beware of rip-offs; **Cyclades**, on the waterfront towards Livádia, **t** 228 402 1057, and **Páros Europcar**, by the port, **t** 228 402 4408, are among the most reliable.

(771m/2,530ft), yields the finest, most translucent marble in the world, which was long the island's claim to fame. Today's young Greeks know it for the clubs in Náoussa that stay open past dawn.

History

With the trade in Parian marble, the island of Páros prospered early on. Its thriving Early Cycladic town was connected with Knossós and then with the Mycenaeans in the Late Cycladic period (1100 BC). In the 8th century BC, the Ionians moved in and brought a second wave of prosperity. The 7th-century BC soldier poet Archilochos, the first to write in iambic meter and whose ironic detachment inspired Horace, was a son of Páros. During the Persian Wars, Páros defiantly supported the Persians at Marathon; when Athens' proud General Miltiades came to punish them afterwards, they withstood his month-long siege, forcing Miltiades to retire with a broken leg that developed into the gangrene that killed him. The island produced the great sculptor Skopas in the Hellenistic period and did well until Roman times, exporting marble to make the Temple of Herod in Jerusalem and the temples on Délos. When the Romans took Páros, their main concern was to take over the marble trade.

Later invasions left the island practically deserted, and after 1207 the Venetian Sanudos ruled Páros from Náxos. Barbarossa captured the island in 1536 and the Turks ruled by way of their proxy, the Duke of Náxos; however, his control was often shaky, especially in the 1670s, when Páros was the base of Hugues Chevaliers, the inspiration for Byron's *Corsair*. In 1770, the Parians had to put up with more unlikely visitors when the Russian fleet wintered on Páros. During the War of Independence, Mandó Mavroyénous, whose parents were

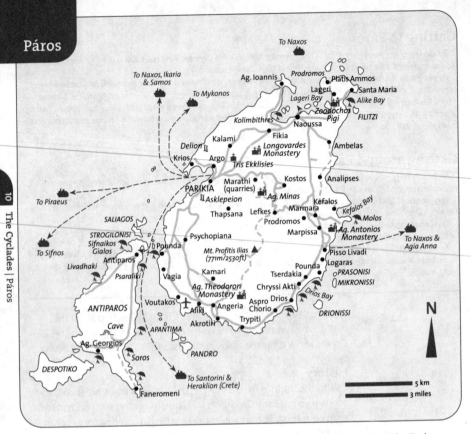

from Páros and Mýkonos, led guerrilla attacks against the Turks throughout Greece; afterwards she returned to Páros.

Parikiá

Parikiá, the island's chief town and main port, has quintupled in size in the last couple of decades, so obscuring the original kernel that the locals have put up signs pointing the way to the 'Traditional Settlement'. Once you've found it, just south of the port, Parikiá shows itself to be a Cycladic beauty, traversed by a long, winding main street that invites leisurely exploration, without having to trudge up stairs. The centrepiece in the heart of town is the walls of the Venetian **Kástro**, built out of the white marble temples of Apollo and Demeter into an attractive collage of columns and pediments; a tiny white chapel tucked underneath adds to the effect. Three **windmills** close off the waterfront to the south end of town, where the ouzeries are a popular evening rendezvous.

Most of Parikiá's sprawl, in the form of hotels, bars and restaurants, has happened in the direction of **Livádia** and its tamarisk-lined beach, although if you continue along the strand past the main tourist ghetto to **Árgo**, café life becomes much more relaxed. While digging here in 1983, part of the **ancient cemetery** was uncovered, in use from the 8th century BC to the 3rd AD; it lies below sea level and has to be constantly drained. More recently, in the course of building a new pier, a Doric-style **temple** with foundations the size of the Parthenon has been unearthed.

The Church of a Hundred Doors and the Archaeology Museum

Ekatontapylianí
open 8–1 and 4–9;
robes provided for the
scantily clad

Set back between Livádia and the 'Traditional Settlement' is Páros' chief monument, the cathedral **Ekatontapylianí** or 'Hundred Doors', hidden behind a modern wall. In 326, St Helen, mother of the Emperor Constantine, was sailing from Rome to the Holy Land when her ship put into Páros during a storm. She prayed that if her journey was a success and she found the True Cross, she would build a church on Páros. She did, and told Constantine her promise, and he dutifully built a church. What stands today is a 6th-century building by the Byzantine Emperor Justinian. The story goes that he hired an architect named Ignatius, an apprentice of the master builder of Ag. Sophia, and when the master came to view his pupil's work he was consumed by jealousy and pushed Ignatius off the roof – but not before Ignatius had seized his foot and dragged him down as well. They are represented by two bizarre figures under the columns of the marble gate to the north of the church, one holding his head and the other covering his mouth.

In 1966, the church, far more human in scale than Ag. Sophia, was restored to its 6th-century appearance, with its dome on pendentives and a women's gallery along the nave. Originally the interior was covered with gleaming white marble. Another story says that only 99 entrances have ever been found but, once the 100th is discovered, Constantinople will return to the Greeks. In fact, the name itself is a 17th-century fantasy; the original was probably Katapolianí, 'below the ancient city'.

The marble iconostasis has a venerated icon of the black Virgin, silver-plated and worked all around with intricate little scenes made in Bucharest, in 1788; you can see frescoes and a marble *ciborium*, with a *synthronon* or little marble amphitheatre behind – in the earliest churches, before the iconostasis totally blocked the view of the sacred area, the high priest and clergy used to stand and sit here. In an alcove in the north wall is the tomb of the 9th-century Ag. Theóktisti. A nun captured by pirates on Lésbos, Theóktisti managed to flee into the forests of Páros when the ship landed for water. For 35 years she lived a pious existence in the wilderness. A hunter finally found her, and, when he brought her the communion bread she requested, she lay down and died. Unable to resist a free saintly relic, the hunter cut off her hand and made to sail away, but he was unable to depart until he had returned it to the saint's body.

The **Baptistry** to the right of the church has a 4th-century sunken cruciform font – the oldest one in Orthodoxy – adult-size, with steps leading down, and a column for the priest to stand on; baptism of children only began in the reign of Justinian.

Behind the church and next to the school, a row of sarcophagi marks the **Archaeology Museum**, containing a section of the renowned *Parian Chronicles* – an artistic history of Greece from Kerkops (*c.* 1500 BC) to Diognetos (264 BC) carved in marble tablets and discovered in the 17th century; to read the rest you'll have to go to the Ashmolean in Oxford. There are finds from the Temple of Apollo: a 5th-century BC *Winged Victory*, a mosaic of the *Labours of Hercules*, found under the Ekatontapylianí, a 7th-century BC amphora with the *Judgement of Paris* and swastikas (ancient solar symbols) going every which way, and a segment of a monument dedicated to Archilochos, who took part in the colonization of Thássos by Páros before he turned to lyric poetry. Archilochos was buried along the road to Náoussa; in the 4th-century BC a *heroön* or tomb-shrine of a hero was erected over his tomb, and in the 7th century the basilica **Tris Ekklisíes** (or Ag. Charálambos) was built over the site.

Northeast of Parikiá, the marble foundation and altar mark the **Temple of Delian Apollo**, which was lined up with temples to Apollo on Délos and Náxos to form a perfect equilateral triangle. One of the triangle's altitudes extends to Mycenae and Rhodes Town, site of the *Colossus* – the biggest statue of Apollo. Another heads up to holy Mount Áthos. And about 5km south of Parikiá, on the Alikí road, the charming little **Anthemion Museum** is Páros' attic – the lifetime accumulation of a local collector, it has old prints and photos of the island, costumes, jewellery, swords, ancient coins, icons, pots and pans and a bit of everything else.

Archaeology Museum
t 228 402 1231; open Tues–Sun 8.30–3; in summer 8–5; adm

Anthemion Museum
t 228 409 1010; open Mon–Fri, 10–12; adm

Náoussa

Náoussa is a lovely fishing village-turned-trendy resort, filled with bars, boutiques and clubs. In 1997 it made history as the first place where the Greek government at last clamped down on shoddy building. Near the harbour stand the half-submerged ruins of the Venetian **castle**, with colourful caiques bobbing below and octopi hung out to dry. The **wetlands** west of town are a winter flamingo haven. On the night of 23 August, 100 boats lit by torches re-enact the islanders' battle against the pirate Barbarossa, storming the harbour, but all ends in merriment, music and dance. The old church of **Ag. Nikólaos Mostrátos** has an excellent collection of icons.

There are beaches within walking distance of Náoussa, or you can make sea excursions to others, including **Kolimbíthres**, with its bizarre rocks, **Ag. Ioánnis** (Monastíri Beach) and nudist **Lágeri** (*take the caique from Náoussa harbour, then walk to the right for about 10mins*). **Sánta María** is further around the coast, with a good windsurfing beach; the fishing village of **Ambelás** has sandy coves and an ancient tower. Páros' main wine-growing area is just south.

Southeast of Parikiá: Into the Land of Marble

The ancient marble quarries at **Maráthi**, re-opened for the making of statues for Napoleon's tomb, are still in use today; the quarried mountainside gleams like driven snow in the noonday sun. Páros' finest marble, called 'Lychnites' by the ancients, or 'candlelit marble', admits light 3.5cm into the stone (light penetrates the second most translucent, Carrara marble, only 2.5cm). The *Venus de Milo*, the *Winged Victory of Samothrace* and the *Hermes of Praxiteles* are all made of the stuff. Blocks and galleries, some with ancient inscriptions, lie off the road.

Páros' attractive medieval capital, **Léfkes**, has churches from the 15th century and one made of marble: **Ag. Triáda**. Ceramics are the speciality here, and the stone-paved Byzantine road to **Pródromos** makes a lovely walk. East of Léfkes, **Mármara** village lives up to its name ('marble') – even some of the streets are paved with it. Prettiest of all is shiny white **Márpissa**, laid out in an amphitheatre. Above its windmills are the ruins of a 15th-century Venetian **fortress** and the 16th-century **Monastery of Ag. Antónios**, constructed out of ancient marbles and with lovely frescoes (note the 17th-century *Second Coming*, which seems a bit out of place in *bon-vivant* Páros).

Down on the east coast, **Písso Livádi** served as the port for these villages and the marble quarries, and now has excursion boats to Náxos, Mýkonos and Santoríni. It is the centre of Páros' beach colonies: at **Mólos**, just north, luxurious villas line the bay where the Turkish fleet used to put in on its annual tax-collecting tour of the Aegean, while, just south, **Poúnda Beach** (not to be confused with the ferry port for Páros) is perhaps better known these days as Music Beach, as the party goes on night and day. The winds on Páros blow fiercely in July and August, and the next beach, **Tserdakiá** (or **Néa Chryssí Aktí**) has hosted the Professional Windsurfers' World Cup every August since 1993, as well as the 'Odyssey' (a windsurfing relay race). Just to the south is the island's most famous beach, **Chryssí Aktí**, 'Golden Beach', with a kilometre of sand. Further south, **Driós** is a pretty green place with a duck-pond, tavernas and sandy beaches (lovely **Glýfa** and **Tripití**) and the remains of ancient shipyards.

 Golden Beach

Southwest of Parikiá

Just south of Parikiá, by a spring, are the ruins of a small Classical-era **Asklepeion** or hospital and the site of a **Temple to Pythian Apollo**. The road south continues 6km to **Psychopianá** (aka the 'Valley of the Butterflies'), where swarms of tiger moths set up housekeeping in July and August. Psychopianá has the ruins of a Venetian tower, while just outside the village stands the convent of Páros' second patron saint, **Ag. Arsénios of Páros** (1800–77), schoolteacher, abbot and prophet, who was canonized in 1967. The saint is buried here, but this time men are not allowed in. Poúnda has a beach and the small boat that crosses to Antíparos. There's another beach at **Alikí** – and the airport, and the sometimes-open **Historical Museum Scorpios**, with 'animated hand-made miniatures' and costumes.

Useful Information on Páros

ⓘ **Páros >**
Parikiá: information centre, by the windmill,
t *228 402 1240*
Náoussa: information office, by the bus station,
t *228 405 2158*

For up-to-date details of events, bus schedules and ex-pat chit-chat, pick up a copy of the English newsletter *Paros Life* (*www.paroslife.com*).

Tourist police: Plateía Mavroyénous, Parikiá, **t** 228 402 1673. In Náoussa, **t** 228 502 3333.

Santa Maria Diving Club, in Náoussa, **t** 228 405 3007. For scuba-diving.

Surfing Beach, on Santa Maria Beach, **t** 228 405 1013. Also good for diving.

Páros Festivals

Good Friday–Easter: Márpissa, with re-enactments of the Crucifixion.

40 days after Orthodox Easter: Písso Livádi.

15 Aug: Parikiá.

23 Aug: Náoussa sea battle.

29 Aug: Léfkas.

Where to Stay on Páros

Páros is packed in July and August, but the reservations desks on the quay will do their best to find you a place to flop. It's also worth trying the **Rooms Association**, **t** 228 402 4528. Room-owners meet the ferries, but not in the numbers they do on Náxos. Beware, you can pay twice as much for the same room in August as in June.

Páros is especially popular among campers. Most sites have minibuses that meet ferries.

Parikiá ✉ 84400

Agnanti, Krios Beach, **t** 228 402 3205, *www.parosagnanti.gr* (€€€€). Medium-sized Cycladic-style hotel, with pools, tennis and basketball.

Yria, 3km from the centre on Parásporos Beach, **t** 228 402 4154, *www.yriahotel.gr* (€€€€–€€€). Good family choice, with bungalows, playground, tennis, pool and big American breakfasts.

Argo, Livádia Beach, **t** 228 402 1367, *www.hotelargo.com* (€€€). For a cheaper pool, with billiards thrown in.

Argonauta, back from the waterfront, **t** 228 402 1440, *www.argonauta.gr* (€€). With a lovely courtyard littered with amphorae, and a good restaurant.

Dina, in the old town, **t** 228 402 1325 (€€). A more modest, charming place.

Vaya, set back on the Náoussa road, **t** 228 402 1068 (€€). A small family-run hotel, surrounded by olive trees.

Kontes, on the quay, **t** 228 402 1096 (€€–€). A done-up oldie with fridges, TV and air-conditioning.

Katerina Restaurant in Livádia, **t** 228 402 2035 (€). Also has **rooms**.

Camping Koula, near Parikiá, **t** 228 402 2082. For the laid-back.

Parasporos, near Parikiá, **t** 228 402 1100. Friendly location.

Krios Camping, at Kríos Beach, opposite the port, **t** 228 402 1705.

Náoussa and Around ✉ 84401

Astir of Páros, Kolymbíthres Beach, **t** 228 405 1976, *www.astirofparos.gr* (€€€€€). The island's most luxurious hotel; all your heart's desires, VIP suites, mashie golf, art gallery, a gourmet restaurant **Poseidon**.

Antirides, **t** 228 405 1711, *www.antirides.gr* (€€€€€). Posh and neo-monastic, around a pool.

Kanales, Pipéri Beach, 500m from Náoussa **t** 228 405 2045, *www.kanales.gr* (€€€€–€€). Attractive rooms and studios around a pool. *Open all year.*

Petres, 2km out of town, **t** 228 405 2467, *www.petres.gr* (€€€). Comfy rooms with a pool.

Kalypso, Ag. Anargiri Beach, **t** 228 405 1488, *www.kalypso.gr* (€€€–€€). Rooms, studios and suites, with balconies.

Stella, in the old town, **t** 228 405 1317, (€€). Plain, clean rooms round a shady courtyard.

Senia Apartments, **t** 228 405 1971 (€€). New and airy, with large balconies.

Galini, **t** 228 405 1210 (€€–€). Plain rooms with balcony.

Flora and Maria Pouliou, **t** 228 405 1118 (€€–€). Rooms and apartments.

Miltiadis, just east in Ambelas, **t** 228 405 1561 (€). Rooms and apartments in a lush garden.

Písso Livádi and East Coast Beaches ✉ 84400

Paros Philoxenia, Tserdakiá Beach, **t** 228 404 1778, www.parosphiloxenia.com (€€€€€). Hotel-bungalow complex with surf club, sea sports, and pool.

Poseidon, Chryssi Aktí, **t** 228 404 2650, www.poseidon-paros.gr (€€€€€). Two luxurious apartment complexes on spacious grounds, with pools, tennis and endless water sports.

Albatross, Logarás, **t** 228 404 1157, www.albatross.gr (€€€). Family-orientated bungalow complex with pool.

Elena Studios and Apartments, above Písso Livádi, **t** 228 404 1082 (€€€). A nice set-up, with playground.

Silver Rocks, near Tserdakiá Beach, **t** 228 404 1244, www.silverrocks.gr (€€€). Good facilities and a children's playground.

Aloni, **t** 228 404 3237, www.aloniparos.com (€€€–€€). A nice complex with cool blue rooms and some views.

Afendakis Apartments, up in Márpissa, **t** 228 404 1141, www.hotelafendakis.gr (€€). Beautifully appointed.

Anna Agourou, **t** 228 404 1320 (€€). Air-conditioned rooms and apartments with good watery views.

Free Sun, Logarás, **t** 228 404 2808 (€€). Modest rooms.

Vrohaki, just up the hill, **t** 228 404 1423 (€€). Attractive, peaceful air-conditioned rooms and studios for blissful relaxation.

Anezina Village, Driós, **t** 228 404 1037, www.anezina.gr (€, but also an expensive (€€€) apartment). Nice choice, with an elegant, romantic garden restaurant.

Captain Kafkis Camping, on the way into Písso Livádi, **t** 228 404 1479.

⭐ Galatis ›>

Eating Out on Páros

Parikiá

Distrato Bar. Crêpes accompanied by jazz in a shady, old-town square.

Happy Green Cow, **t** 228 402 4691, behind the bank. Vegetarians can find sustenance here, including falafel and hummus.

Levantis, on the main market street, **t** 228 402 3613 (€25). The best of Páros, serving delicious Greek, French and Lebanese dishes on a pretty terrace.

Porfyra, by the ancient cemetery, **t** 228 402 2693. In a courtyard under vines, serving a wide array of seafood delicacies, including various shellfish and pasta dishes.

Tamarisko, **t** 228 402 4689. Good international cuisine served in a secluded garden.

Alternatively, follow the road round through Livádia to Árgo for relaxed beach tavernas.

Náoussa

Náoussa is a picturesque place with ouzeries chock-a-block by the water.

Christos, **t** 228 405 1901 (€30). Lovely courtyard dining, with Greek and international dishes. People come here to be seen.

Diamantis, **t** 228 505 2985, just up the hill. Good food at good prices, with draught wine.

Galatis, in the square, **t** 228 405 1726. Tasty traditional recipes from Greece and Anatolia.

Katsoynas, Santa Maria, **t** 228 405 1246 (€20). Owned by a fisherman, serving the day's catch with salads.

Mario, Venetian port, **t** 228 405 1047 (€30). Fish restaurant, serving tasty dishes such as octopus salad with rocket pesto.

Meltemi, **t** 228 405 1263. Cretan specialities and views of the sea.

Písso Livádi/Poúnda

Mouraghio, Písso Livádi, **t** 228 404 3323 This is the place to eat excellent fish.

QEA, Poúnda, **t** 228 409 1220. Look out over Antíparos while dining at one of the island's top restaurants, with an enormous wine list.

Entertainment and Nightlife on Páros

Páros has something for everyone, from the rowdy waterfront bars at Parikiá to the more sophisticated haunts of Náoussa. Greek music may be somewhat rare here.

Cine Paros, set back from the waterfront. Parikiá's outdoor cinema. Náoussa has one too, the **Makis**.

Pirate's, Parikiá. For jazz.

Páros Rock Complex, Parikiá. A huge complex of four disco bars including the popular **Dubliner**.

Pebbles and **Evinos**, on Parikiá's waterfront. The music is altogether gentler, mostly blues and jazz.

Sulla Luna, Parikiá. Real Italian ice cream.

Café del Mar, on Náoussa's waterfront. A very popular drinking hole with the fashionable set.

The Golden Garden, at Chryssí Aktí. Popular, laid-back garden bar.

Remezzo, Písso Livádi. A favoured watering hole; serves fancy coffees, breakfast and some vegetarian snacks.

Lake Cafe, Dríos; sophisticated place with live jazz some nights.

Antíparos (ΑΝΤΙΠΑΡΟΣ)

A mile to the west, mountainous little Antíparos ('opposite Páros'), was known as Oliaros when it was first mentioned as a base of Phoenician merchants of Sidon. A deep cave full of stalactites was discovered on Antíparos in antiquity (tradition has it that Antilochos was the first to carve his name on a stalactite in the 6th century BC), and ever since it's been an essential stop for every traveller in the region. Antíparos is also the octopus capital of Greece, and it may be an unsung aphrodisiac, considering the island's lusty reputation – significantly (or not), Tom Hanks has a home here. Even the year-round population is rising, and that, in the Cyclades, is rare.

Kástro and the Cave

Lacking any defences, Antíparos was uninhabited after the fall of Rome until the Venetians, under Leonardo Lorentani, built a small

Where to Stay and Eat on Antíparos

Antíparos ✉ 84007

Antíparos has a desk at Parikiá port, so you can book accommodation before you go – prices have risen to match big sister Páros.

Artemis, 500m from the port, t 228 406 1460, www.artemisantiparos.com (€€€–€€). Newish; rooms have fridges and sea-view balconies.

Mantalena, on the waterfront, t 228 406 1206, www.hotelmantalena.gr (€€€–€€). Attractive, tidy rooms, all with baths.

Chryssi Akti, on the beach, t 228 406 1220 (€€). A small, elegant hotel.

Bergleri, just in from the beach, t 228 406 1378 (€€). With a decent taverna and library of bestsellers.

Antiparos, t 228 406 1358, antiparos1@otenet.gr (€€). Simple, but all rooms have showers.

Korali, t 228 406 1236, hotelkorali@hotmail.com (€). About the cheapest, with a restaurant.

Antiparos Camping, t 228 406 1410. Laid-back campsite, clothes optional; freelancers tolerated away from town.

Garden and **Anargyros**. Both have good food.

Akrogiali. Fish taverna at Ag. Geórgios.

Time Marine Beach Bar, **Café Yam**, **Captain Pipinos**. All popular summer hangouts.

Getting to Antíparos

The island is linked every 2hrs by **caique** from Parikiá (Páros) and hourly car ferry from Poúnda (Páros). **Buses** link the port with the cave. **Port authority: t** 228 406 1485.

castle, its thick walls forming the outer walls of the houses; **Kástro** is the alternative name of Antíparos town. Everyone tos and fros down the **Kampiara**, the wide street linking the port to the charming square, lined with bougainvillaea, ouzeries and bars. Kástro has a good beach, **Psaralíki**, just south, and another one for skinny-dippers a 5-minute walk north by the campsite. In the late afternoon everyone wanders over to **Sifnaíkos Gialós**, also known as Sunset Beach. The best beach, **Ag. Geórgios**, south of the cave, is being developed as a resort.

Cave
open daily
10.45–3.45; adm

The **cave** remains Antíparos' star attraction, and frequent buses in summer now do the old donkey work of getting you there from the village. Some 400 steps descend 64m (210ft) into the fantastic, spooky chamber. The cave is really about twice as deep, but the rest has been closed as too dangerous. Perhaps to make up for breaking off the stalactites, famous visitors of the past have smoked and carved their names on the walls, including Lord Byron and King Otho of Greece (1840). One stalagmite attests in Latin to a Christmas mass celebrated in the cavern by the French ambassador Count Novandel in 1673, attended by 500 (paid) locals. Another (now lost), from the 4th century BC, stated that the authors declared they were hiding in the cave from Alexander the Great, after he accused them of plotting an assassination attempt. Many inscriptions were lost in 1774, when Russian officers chopped off stalactites as souvenirs, and in the last war, when the Italians and Germans shot up the cave. The church by the entrance, **Ag. Ioánnis**, dates from 1774.

Of the islets off Antíparos, **Strogilónisi** and **Despotikó** are rabbit-hunting reserves. On **Sáliagos**, a fishing village from the 5th millennium BC has been excavated by John Evans and Colin Renfrew, the first Neolithic site discovered in the Cyclades.

Santoríni/Thíra (ΣΑΝΤΟΡΙΝΗ/ΘΗΡΑ)

As the most spectacular, otherworldly Greek island, the pressure is on Santoríni to come up with the goods. And it does. The mixture of sinister dusky precipices, dappled with the most brilliant-white, trendiest bars and restaurants in the country, gives the island a splendid kind of schizophrenia; forget *Under the Volcano*, here you're teetering on the edge. Usually bathed in glorious sunshine, but occasionally lashed by high winds and rain, everything seems more intense on Santoríni, even daily life. Some call it Devil's Island, an exhilarating but disturbing place where the scent of sulphur

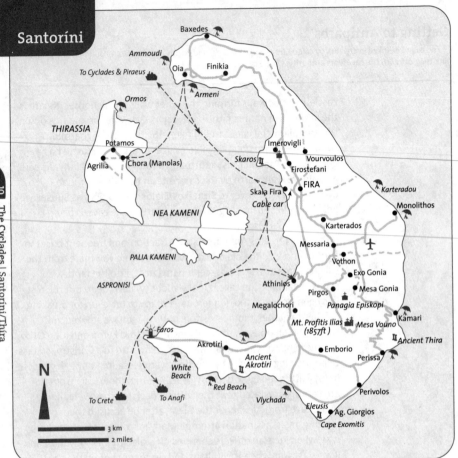

Map labels: Baxedes, Ammoudi, To Cyclades & Piraeus, Oia, Finikia, Ormos, Armeni, THIRASSIA, Potamos, Imerovigli, Skaros, Vourvoulos, Agrilia, Chora (Manolas), Firostefani, FIRA, Karteradou, Skala Fira, Cable car, Monolithos, NEA KAMENI, Karterados, Messaria, Vothon, PALIA KAMENI, Exo Gonia, ASPRONISI, Athinios, Mesa Gonia, Pirgos, Panagia Episkopi, Megalochori, Kamari, Mt. Profitis Ilias (1857ft), Mesa Vouno, Faros, Ancient Thira, Akrotiri, Ancient Akrotiri, Emborio, Perissa, White Beach, Red Beach, Perivolos, To Crete, To Anafi, Vlychada, Eleusis, Ag. Giorgios, Cape Exomitis

N — 3 km — 2 miles

We found
ourselves
naked on the
pumice stone

watching the
rising islands

watching the
red islands sink

into their sleep,
into our sleep.

George Seféris,
Santorini

occasionally breaks through, and where the inhabitants, through centuries of experience, were such experts in dealing with the undead (the *vrykólakes*) that other islanders used to send their troublesome corpses here. Which doesn't seem to get in the way of its being the honeymoon capital of Greece.

Nothing beats arriving by sea. As your ship sails into the caldera, Santoríni looms up like a chocolate layer cake with an enormous bite taken out of it, frosted with coconut cream towns sliding over the edge, while the islets opposite are the charred gunk at the bottom of your oven. This little archipelago has, literally, had its ups and downs, rising and disappearing under the waves. Human endeavours have fared similarly: you can visit three former 'capitals' – the Minoan centre of Akrotíri, a favourite candidate for Metropolis, the capital of Atlantis; the classical capital Thira at Mésa Voúno; and the medieval Skáros. Even the modern capital, Firá, was flattened by an earthquake in 1956. Although the island is now on the cruise ship itinerary, older inhabitants can remember when it hosted more

Getting to Santoríni

By air: There are lots of charters, and daily flights from Athens; 3 a week from Thessaloníki; 2 a week in season from Heráklion (Crete) and Rhodes. The **Olympic Airways** office is at Firá, **t** 228 602 2493; **airport**: **t** 228 603 1525; **Aegean Airlines**: **t** 228 602 8500. Catch a regular **bus** from the airport to Firá, or take a **taxi**.

By sea: Daily **ferry** connections with Piraeus, Íos, Páros, Folégandros, Náxos and Sikínos; frequent (3–4 times a week) connections with Anáfi and Sýros; at least once a week with Heráklion and Ag. Nikoláos (Crete), Kássos, Kárpathos, Kéa, Kýthnos, Lávrio, Mílos, Rhodes, Sérifos and Sífnos. **Port authority**: **t** 228 602 2239.

Getting around Santoríni

Santoríni has an efficient if often crowded **bus** service from Firá to all villages, and to the **airport** (**t** 228 602 5404); in summer some of them run till 3am. In Firá the **bus stop** is opposite the museum, down from Plateía Theotóki.

Taxis: **t** 228 602 2555; they're expensive – €10–15 from Firá to Oía. Alternatively, rent a **scooter** and you'll be spoilt for choice.

political prisoners than tourists, and nights were filled with the rumour of vampires rather than the chatter of café society, watching the sunset. To match the unique setting, Santoríni has some of the most fabulous hotels in Greece, many dripping over the caldera rim.

History

Santoríni was once a typically round volcanic island called Strogyle. Its rich soil attracted inhabitants early on – originally from Karia, until they were chased away by the Minoans. One of the Cretan towns was at Akrotíri; its discovery resulted from one of the most intriguing archaeological detective stories of the 20th century.

In 1939, while excavating Amnisós, the port of Knossós on the north coast of Crete, archaeologist Spyrídon Marinátos realized that only a massive natural disaster could have caused the damage he found. At first Marinátos assumed it was an earthquake, but over the years evidence of a different kind came in: southeast of Santoríni oceanographers discovered volcanic ash from Strogyle on the sea bed, covering an area of 900 by 300km (560 by 188 miles); on nearby Anáfi and Eastern Crete itself, a layer of volcanic tephra 3–20mm thick covers Minoan New Palace sites. Another clue came from the Athenian reformer Solon, who in 600 BC wrote of his journey to Egypt, where the scribes told him of the disappearance of Kreftia (Crete?) 9,000 years earlier, a figure Solon might have mistaken for a more correct 900. The Egyptians, who had had important trade links with Minoan Crete and Santoríni, told Solon about the lost land of Atlantis, made of red, white and black volcanic rock (like Santoríni today), and spoke of a city vanishing in 24 hours. In his *Critias*, Plato described Atlantis as being composed of one round island and one long island, a sweet country of art and flowers connected by one culture and rule (Santoríni and Crete, under Minos?). Lastly, Marinátos studied the eruption of Krakatoa in 1883, which formed a caldera of 8.3 sq km (3.2 sq miles), and as the sea rushed in to fill the caldera it created a tsunami over 200m (650ft) high that destroyed everything in a 150km (93-mile) path. The caldera left by Strogyle is 22 sq km (8.5 sq miles) – almost three times as big. In 2006, a survey off Santoríni's shores (using *Titanic*-explorer Robert Ballard's robotic submersibles) showed that the volcanic explosion was not only even greater than originally thought – the debris nearest the island is 80m (260ft) thick and extends across 1,450 sq km (530 sq miles) – but that the submerged Kolumbo crater, the largest of Santoríni's 20 volcanic cones is still very active, spewing out 220°C (428°F) steam from its floor, 457m (1,500ft) down.

In the 19th century French archaeologists had discovered Minoan vases at Akrotíri, and it was there that Marinátos began to dig in 1967, seeking to prove the chronology of his theory: that Minoan civilization owed its sudden decline to the eruption, earthquakes, and tidal waves caused by the explosion of Strogyle in *c.* 1450 BC. Marinátos hoped to unearth a few vases. Instead he found something beyond his wildest dreams: an entire Minoan colony buried in tephra, complete with dazzling frescoes. His chronology, however, was called into question with the discovery in 2005 of an olive tree that had been buried alive in the ash, allowing a more precise date for the explosion – 1627–1613 BC – which has in effect put many Minoan chronologies back a century – although many Egyptologists question this.

The island returned to history in the 9th century BC, when the Dorians settled the island, and named it Thera. Herodotus offers a rare early account of how the Therans in turn founded the much richer colony of Cyrene in Libya: in 631 BC, a certain Battos went to Delphi to see how he could cure his stutter, and the oracle suggested a unique cure: colonizing Libya. The stutter was a code for the more serious problem Thera was having feeding its mouths, as Greeks divided land equally among their sons. One brother from each family was chosen by lot, and ordered to give the colony a try for five years; when they got discouraged and tried to come home, the Therans shot at their ships to keep them from landing, so they went on to found Cyrene.

Useful Information on Santoríni

Police: 25 Martíou St, **t** 228 602 2649.
Volcano Walks: go with volcanologist Dr Tom Pfeiffer and **Volcano Discovery Tours, t** + 49 2241 2080175, *www.volcanodiscovery.com*.
Kamari Tours: In Kamári and with offices in every village on the island, **t** 228 603 1390, *www.kamaritours.gr*. Accommodation, tours and cruises.

Diving: Paul Stefanidis runs the **Mediterranean Dive Club** from Perissa Camping, **t** 228 608 3190, *www.diveclub.gr*. Offers all sorts of volcano and wreck dives, as well as courses.

Santoríni Festivals

24 July: Ag. Ioánnis, Monolíthos.
15 Aug: Mésa Goniá and Firá.
29 Aug: Ag. Ioánnis, Períssa.
Aug–Sept: Santoríni Music Festival, in Firá; Greek and international music.

The Byzantines covered the island with castles, but the Venetians under the Crispi got it anyway. Skáros near Imerovígli was their capital and Irene their patron saint, hence the island's second name, Santoríni, which has stuck as hard as volcanic rock as officialdom tries to change it back to the Classical-era Thíra.

Firá (ΦΗΡΑ)

After arriving by air or at the island's port, **Athiniós**, the bus to Firá leaves visitors in **Plateía Theotóki**, a zoo of a modern square, to be processed and fattened on fast food before being sacrificed to the volcano god. Cruise ships anchor beneath the towering cliffs at Firá, where motor launches ferry passengers to the tiny port of **Skála Firá**; there, donkeys wait to bear them up the winding path to town, 270m (885ft) above. A **cable car**, donated by ship-owner Evángelos Nomikós, does the donkey-work in two minutes. Profits go to a community fund – and the donkey drivers.

Cable car
every 20mins, winter 7.30am–6.30pm; summer 6.30am to as late as midnight in summer; €3.50

Those who remember Firá before 1956 say that the present town can't compare to its original, although it's pleasant enough – perfectly Cycladically white, spilling down the volcano's rim on terraces, adorned with blue-domed churches, all boasting one of the world's most magnificent views. Understandably, the families who sold their damaged properties for peanuts after the quake have been kicking themselves; the little lanes are now chock-a-block with shops, bars, hotels and restaurants. Firá blends into quieter **Firostefáni**, 1.5km to the north; here are some magnificent old *skaftá*, barrel-roofed cave houses, Santoríni's speciality, now equipped with all mod cons.

Archaeology Museum
t 228 602 2217; open Tues–Sun 8.30–3; adm

The old **Archaeology Museum** is near the cable car on the north side of town and houses finds from ancient Thira at Mésa Voúno, some going back to the 9th century BC. Opposite the bus station, the new **Museum of Prehistoric Thira** has Early Cycladic figurines found in the local pumice quarries and lovely vases, ceramics, jewellery and a few frescoes from Akrotíri. Among the frescoes moved here from the National Archaeological Museum in Athens are the famous 'blue monkeys', as well as a 5m (17ft)-long frieze of a flotilla, a unique record of sailing in the prehistoric Aegean. The handicraft workshop founded by Queen Frederíka, where women weave large carpets on looms, is also worth a visit.

Museum of Prehistoric Thira
t 228 602 3217; open Tues–Sun 8.30–3; adm

Mégaron Gýzi Museum
t 228 602 2244; open summer Mon–Sat 10.30–1.30 and 5–8, Sun 10.30–4; winter daily 10–4; adm

The **Mégaron Gýzi Museum**, located in a beautiful 17th-century mansion, houses exhibits on the island's history – manuscripts from the 16th to 19th centuries, costumes, old maps of the Cyclades and photos of the town before the 1956 quake. Another, privately run **Folklore Museum** occupies a cave house of 1861, with the owner's uncle's belongings on display.

Folklore Museum
t 228 602 2792; open 10–2 and 6–8; adm

Where to Stay in Firá

Firá ✉ 84700

Firá is the noisiest and busiest place on the island. Just out of season, in early July even, you can wheel and deal with the room-owners who mug you as the Athiniós bus pulls into town.

Aigialos, t 228 602 5191, *www.aigialos. gr* (€€€€€). Houses in a spectacular setting on the caldera, with marble floors, antiques and all mod cons (like a counter-swim unit in the pool).

Atlantis, t 228 602 2232, *www. atlantishotel.gr* (€€€€€). The oldest hotel on the island and the most photographed. It's classy, but rooms are on the small side. Pool.

Cori Rigas Apartments, t 228 602 5251, *www.rigas-apartments.gr* (€€€€€). An old captain's house made into gorgeous apartments, plus the **Art Café** for drinks with The View.

Kavalari, t 228 602 2455, *www. kavalarihotel-santorini.com* (€€€€€). Beautifully decorated, air-conditioned rooms dug out of the cliff.

Porto Fira Suites, t 228 602 2289, *www. portofira.gr* (€€€€€). A short walk from the centre, a converted 14th-century Venetian mansion and monastic cells converted in lovely suites cascading over the terraces, with a pool and bar.

Loucas, t 228 602 3049 (€€€€€–€€€). Similar to Kavalari.

Efterpi Villas, t 228 602 2541, *www. efterpi.gr* (€€€€). More affordable luxury in traditional apartments.

Kafieris Apartments, t 228 602 2059, in winter t 228 602 3568, *www.kafieris apartments.gr* (€€€). Fully equipped, including a roof garden with a Jacuzzi.

Pelican, t 228 602 3113 (€€€). Air-conditioned rooms, and a tank of odd fish in the lounge.

Porto Carra, faces the volcano from the central square, t 228 602 2979, *kavalht@otenet.gr* (€€€).

Argonaftis, t 228 602 2055 (€€). Friendly; breakfast in the garden.

Stella's, t 228 602 3464 (€€). The rooms are plain but with a kitchen and views to the other side of the island.

Tatakis, in the centre, t 228 602 2389 (€€). Air-conditioned, but viewless and bohemian.

Camping Santoríni, nearby, t 228 602 2944. Superb site with pool.

Firostefáni ✉ 84700

Homeric Poems, t 228 602 4661, *www.homericpoems.gr* (€€€€€). Romantic boutique hotel on the cliff with a pool; plus honeymoon suites with private pools. *Open April–Oct.*

Sun Rocks, on the cliff edge, t 228 602 3241, *www.sunrocks.gr* (€€€€€). Stylish, couples only, with pool and views. *Open April–Oct.*

Tsitouras Collection, t 228 602 3747, *www.tsitouras.com* (€€€€€). Exclusive suites in five beautifully restored Venetian houses, each with its own name and theme, centred around a courtyard. The House of Nureyev has the view.

Galini, Firostefáni, t 228 602 2095, *galini-htl@otenet.gr* (€€€). Nice rooms with caldera views, and transfers to the port. *Open Mar–Nov.*

Eating Out in Firá

Besides wine, Santoríni is famous for its fava bean soup (puréed, with onions and lemon) and *pseftokeftédes*, 'false meatballs', made of deep-fried tomatoes, onion and mint; the tiny tomatoes of the island are said to be the tastiest in Greece.

Bella Thira, t 228 562 3981. Italians flock here for freshly made pasta and pizzas.

Cantuccio, Firostefáni, t 228 602 2082 (€25). Stylish Italian cuisine, and a lovely spaghetti with seafood. *Open May–Sept.*

Koukoúmavlos, t 228 602 3807 (€40). One of the most romantic restaurants on the island, the fief of one of the country's most inventive chefs, Níkos Pouliási, who also knows how to prepare a perfect sauce, especially with Greek wine and spirits – such as Sámian nectar with filets of quail and grilled oyster mushrooms. Excellent desserts, too. *Open April–Oct.*

Nikolas, t 228 602 4750. Good place for excellent, reasonably priced Greek food. Locals swear by it, proved by the frequent queues for tables.

Poseidon, under the bus stop. A 24hr diner, with reasonably priced, filling food.

Selene >

Selene, t 228 602 2249 (€25–35). Superb, long-established restaurant, which makes original and delicious use of the island's produce, especially the small tomatoes, cheese and capers in many of its dishes. Some specialities include lamb with fava sauce and fava rissoles.

Sphinx, t 228 602 3823 (€30). Another romantic caldera setting; excellent seafood, much of it with pasta, some meat dishes.

Vanilia, Firostefáni, **t** 228 602 5631, *www.vanilia.gr* (€45). One of the island's best places to eat – a romantic atmosphere, short menu, but exquisitely refined Greek cuisine. *Open Easter–Oct.*

Entertainment and Nightlife in Firá

Firá stays up till dawn in summer.

Cinetheatre. Summer open-air cinema.

Kira Thira. Appeals to all ages for jazz, blues and sangria.

Alexandria. Attracts an older set.

Franco's. Playing gentle classical music, still the place to laze in deckchairs for sunset, even if the price of a coffee is sky-high. Cocktails are works of art, but a bottle of wine and *mezédes* are best.

Enigma. This club is the hippest place to dance through the night.

Koo Club, next door to Enigma. Also big, central and packed.

South of Firá

Archontikó Argyroú Museum
t 228 603 1669; tours April–Oct at 11, 12, 1, 5, 6 and 7; adm

South of Firá, in the middle of the island, **Messariá** is an important wine and market village, home to the **Archontikó Argyroú Museum**, in a 19th-century neoclassical winemaker's mansion, with murals and traditional furnishings; you can stay there, too. The closest beach here, past the airport, **Monolíthos**, has soft grey sand, with a big isolated lump of a rock draped with a few ruins, tamarisks along the shore, and good windsurfing.

South of Messariá, the country is covered in vineyards. **Pýrgos** is one of the oldest surviving villages on this much-tried island, with old barrel-roofed houses, Byzantine walls, and a Venetian fort. Vines swirl up the white flanks of **Mount Profítis Ilías**, Santoríni's highest point (566m/1,857ft); from its summit, on a clear day you can see Crete, and on an exceptionally clear day, Rhodes hovers faintly on the horizon. The locals say the **monastery** perched here, built in 1712 (make sure your knees and shoulders are covered) is the only place that will protrude above sea level when Santoríni sinks to join its missing half. Frescoes at the gate show the road to heaven and the considerably wider one to hell, where the devil whiles away the time playing the *laoúto*. At the foot of Profítis Ilías, in **Mésa Goniá**, the 11th-century **Panagía Episkopí** has fine Byzantine icons, although 26 that managed to miraculously survive earthquakes and fires were stolen in 1982. On 15 August it hosts Santoríni's biggest *panegýri*.

Kamári and Ancient Thira

A black beach and a million sunbeds and umbrellas announce **Kamári**, with 300 hotels and pensions, and just as many tavernas, bars, and tourist shops, while a mile away women in big straw hats calmly thresh fava beans in the field.

Santoríni in a Glass

Santoríni is one of Greece's premier white wine producers. Because of its exclusively volcanic soil, its vines were among the few in Europe to be spared the deadly plant lice phylloxera, so the original rootstock remains intact; the average age of an *assyrtiko* vine, the main variety of grape, is 70 years, and the oldest vines, near Akrotíri, go back over 150 years. *Assyrtiko* yields everything from a bone-dry light wine to a sweet aged *vinsanto* from sun-dried grapes. Because of the wind the vines are kept low and often protected by woven cane; some fields look as if they're growing baskets. Moribund for many years, churning out high-alcohol, low-quality plonk, the Santoríni wine industry has recently had a shot in the arm from the forward-thinking national winemaker Boutari, who in 1988 built a new domed winery, restaurant, and accessory shop at Megalochóri (**t** *228 608 1011*). A second winery, Koutsoyanópoulos (**t** *228 603 1322*), on the road to Kamári, also offers tastings. While connoisseurs are most welcome, the emphasis is on having a good time.

Ancient Thíra
open Tues–Sun 8.30–3

Kamári was the port of **ancient Thíra**, spread over its great terraces on the rocky headland of Mésa Voúno, reached by a cobbled path or road. Although inhabited since the 9th century BC, most of what you see dates from the Ptolemies (300–150 BC), who used Thíra as a base for meddling in the Aegean, or from Byzantine times: the chapel by the entrance, **Ag. Stéfanos**, stands over a 5th-century basilica. The north side of the city, with the Ptolemies' barracks, a gymnasium and governor's palace, are reached by way of the **Temenos of Artemidoros of Perge**, a sacred area dedicated by an admiral of the Ptolemies, and decorated with symbols of the gods in relief. In the garrison area, a statue of Demeter once sat on the throne carved in a niche, while another little sacred cave was converted into a church.

Below, Thíra's long main street passes through impressive remains of the vast *agora*, with the base of a **Temple of Dionysos** and **Altar of Ptolemy Philometor**. The long **Royal Stoa** with its Doric columns was last restored in AD 150; behind it, the tidy Hellenistic houses have mosaics and toilets; note the one with a phallus dedicated 'to my friends'. The nearby **theatre** has a dizzying view down to the sea. The road along the headland passes Roman baths past the **Column of Artemis** and the **Temple of Apollo Karneios**, built in the 6th century: one of the most important Doric deities, associated with rams, his summer festival was celebrated by dancing and a race that was more of a hunt of a runner dressed in wool fillets; if he was caught, he'd cry out in delight and it would bode well for the city. Some of the oldest graffiti in Greek, from the 7th century BC, may be seen on the **Terrace of Celebrations**, recording the writers' admiration and homosexual relations with the naked dancers (the *gymno paidiai*).

South of Mount Profítis Ílias: Embório, Toríssa and Perívolos

Farming villages encircle Mount Profítis Ílias. **Megalochóri**, 'big village', actually has a tiny, resolutely old Greek core, with a tiny outdoor taverna. **Embório** still has its Venetian *goulas*, or fort; with its lone palm, it looks like something out of the Sahara. A modern church here replaces the Byzantine one to St Irene, the island's namesake and patroness of the Greek police. Outside the village, the little church of **Ag. Nikólaos Marmarinós** began life as a 3rd-century BC Temple of the Mother of the Gods. Little changed after its Christianization; even the original ceiling remains in place. Another 3km east of Embório, in a pretty setting under the seaside mountain Mésa Voúno, the black sands of **Aeríssa** have attracted a good deal of development, and can be pleasant at either end of the season because the sand warms quickly in the sun. Eucalyptus groves provide shade; bars and clubs provide for plenty of nightlife; and a Byzantine church is being excavated on the edge of town. **Perívolos**, south of Períssa, has an 'infinite' beach of lighter sand and lively beach bars. From here the road leads around to **Cape Exomítis**, guarded by one of the best-preserved Byzantine fortresses of the Cyclades; offshore are the submerged ruins of **ancient Eleusis**. Further along, wild cliffs loom over the island's most beautiful beach, **Vlycháda**, a growing resort with a vague world's end air to it.

Akrotíri: A Bronze Age Pompeii

Akrotíri (ΑΚΡΩΤΗΡΙ), a pleasant wine village on the southern tip of the island, was a Venetian stronghold, and although damaged in the earthquake the fort still stands above the town. There are beaches nearby, and a pretty path along the caldera rim.

The first clues that something else may have once been here came in the 1860s; while digging pumice for the rebuilding of Port Said, ancient walls kept getting in the way. French archaeologists came and unearthed carbonized food, vases, frescoes and a pure copper saw. In 1967 Spyrídon Marinátos, following his hunch about the destruction of Minoan Crete (*see* 'History'), returned to the site. The trenches were disappointing until, 4.5m (15ft) below the surface, they suddenly broke through into rooms full of huge storage vases, or *pithoi*, belonging to what turned out to be the best preserved prehistoric city in Greece.

Minoan Akrotiri
buses from Firá end up here; t 228 608 1366/2217; open Tues–Sun 8.30–3; adm

The strange and wonderful **Minoan city**, buried in *c.* 1600 BC, is now laboriously being liberated from its thick sepulchral shell of tephra (volcanic ash and stones). Protected by its huge modern roof, a carpet of volcanic dust silences footsteps on paved lanes laid 3,500 years ago, amid houses that stand up to three storeys high, some built of rubble masonry, some in fine ashlar, with stone stairways and intact doors and windows. Although it has no street plan, the city's sophisticated drainage makes older Greek visitors laugh because of its resemblance to the sewage systems in the villages they grew up in. Some rooms still contain their giant *pithoi*, and in general the size of the storage areas and cooking pots suggests a communal life and collective economy. The residents must have had ample warning that their island was about to blow its top: no jewellery or other valuables were found, and the only skeleton found so far belonged to a pig. As they escaped they must have shed more than a few tears, for life at Akrotiri was sweet, judging by the ash imprints of their elaborate wooden furniture, their beautiful ceramics and the famous frescoes full of colour and life – every house had a least one frescoed room; one, unique in peace-loving Minoan art, shows a sea battle. In one of the houses is the grave of Marinátos, who died after a fall on the site and requested to be buried by his life's work. For more, pick up *Art and Religion in Thíra: Reconstructing a Bronze Age Society*, by his daughter, Dr Nannó Marinátos, which is sold at the entrance.

Below the site, the road continues to **Mávro Rachídi**, where cliffs as black as charcoal offer a stark contrast to the white chapel of **Ag. Nikólaos**; a path over the headland leads to Kókkino Paralía or **Red Beach**, with sunbeds under startling blood-red cliffs.

Where to Stay and Eat South of Firá

★ Archontiko Argyrou >

Messariá ✉ 84700

Archontiko Argyrou, t 228 603 1669 (€€€). A lovely 1860s mansion furnished with antiques, with rooms on the ground floor. The first floor houses its own museum (*see* p.309).

Villa Agapi, north of Messariá at Karterádos, t 228 602 4575 (€€€–€€). Run by friendly, helpful people; apartments, studios and rooms, with a garden and fountain.

Taverna Galini, Monolíthos, t 228 603 2924. Where locals drive out for good cheap home cooking, fish and *pseftokeftédes*.

Pyrgos ✉ 84700

Zannos Melathron, under the Venetian fort, t 228 602 8220, *www.zannos.gr* (€€€€€). A Relais & Châteaux hotel with suites in two historic mansions, beautifully furnished, with a pool cut in the stone, and a superb restaurant that interprets Greek ingredients with French finesse (foie gras with Macedonian lentils). *Open April–Oct.*

Kallísti, t 228 603 4108. Taverna popular for its delicious Greek food, with produce from the owner's garden – don't miss the aubergine salads.

Metaxi Mas, in nearby Éxo Goniá, t 228 603 1323. Taverna/ouzerie of character, serving tasty *mezédes*. *Open Mar–Dec.*

Kamári ✉ 84700

Bellonias Villas, t 228 603 1138, *www.belloniasvillas.com* (€€€€€–€€€€). Stylish studios, apartments and maisonettes, excellent restaurant and a spa. *Open mid-May–mid-Oct.*

Tamarix Del Mar, t 228 603 1809, *www.tamarix.gr* (€€€€). Complex of Cycladic-style suites with a spa and pools.

Kamári Beach, close to ancient Thira, t 228 603 1243 (€€€). With a large pool and big verandas.

Andreas, t 228 603 1692 (€€). Modest but has a lush garden.

Sigalas, at the end of the beach, t 228 603 1260 (€€). Quiet with a shady garden and taverna.

Kamári Camping, up the main road from the beach, t 228 603 1453.

Atmosphere, t 288 603 1368 (€30). Trendy Greek and international dishes in an attractive setting. *Open May–Oct.*

Camille Stefani, on the beach, t 228 603 1716. French-influenced Greek menu and its very own wine label.

Kamári. Good, inexpensive family-run taverna, serving fava soup.

Megalochóri ✉ 84700

Vedema, t 228 608 1796, *www. vedema.gr* (€€€€€). One of the 'Small Luxury Hotels of the World', a former winery, offering every amenity, art gallery, marble baths, in-house movies and a private beach 3km away with minibus service. Its restaurant (€40), cut into the rock and cavern-like, promises fine dining, and doesn't disappoint. *Open April–Oct.*

Períssa ✉ 84700

Veggera, right on the black sands, **t** 228 608 2060, *www.veggera.gr* (€€€€€). Comfortable, fully equipped rooms with a neoclassical touch, pool and laundry.

Sellada Beach, next door, **t** 228 608 1859 (€€€). Handsome traditional rooms and flats with pool.

Ostria, by the sea, **t** 228 603 1727 (€€). Good-value apartments, especially for three or more.

Drossos Youth Hostel, in the centre, **t** 228 608 2668 (€). Doubles and dorms.

Períssa Beach Camping, near the beach, **t** 228 608 1343.

Lava, **t** 228 608 1776. The best taverna on the waterfront, with great vegetable dishes – try the stuffed onions,

Yazz Club. Where you can contemplate beach life from a hammock.

Perívolos ✉ 84700

9 Muses, **t** 228 608 1781, *www.santorinigmuses.gr* (€€€€€–€€€€). Colourful family-friendly Cycladic complex with pools.

Notos Therme & Spa, in nearby Vlycháda **t** 228 608 1115, *www.snotos.com* (€€€€€–€€€€). Designer spa hotel where all rooms have sea views; the spa has a large menu of treatments, some using the local volcanic mud. *Open May–Oct.*

Dixtya, **t** 228 608 2818 (€20). Lovely seafood here, prepared with pasta and lots of vegetables. *Open Mar–Nov.*

Perivolos, **t** 228 608 2007 (€20). The classic fish taverna that gave the beach its name.

Seaside Lounge, by Notos, **t** 228 608 2801 (€45). Trendy place in Perívolos serving some of Santoríni's best food in a lovely setting – large array of delicate appetizers, good wines, unusual dishes such as turkey with peanuts. *Open April–Oct.*

Akrotíri ✉ 84700

Mathios Village, Akrotíri, **t** 228 608 1152, *www.vmathios.gr* (€€€). Friendly and comfortable, with a pool overlooking the island. Special rooms for 'romantic holidays'.

Villa Kalimera, **t** 228 608 1855, *www.kalimerasantorini.com* (€€€). Next door to Mathios Village; similarly priced, but offering slightly less.

Giorgaros, **t** 228 608 3035. Great seafood just beyond the lighthouse (*fáros*). *Open all year.*

Panorama, **t** 228 608 1183. Cliffside dining with sunset views over all of Santoríni.

North of Firá to Oía

The north end of the caldera has become the refuge of travellers who find Fíra too brash and noisy. **Imerovígli**, in spite of being on the verge of merging into Firostefáni, has seen a boom in upmarket hotels. Traditionally a Catholic village, it has The View, only here over a startling great lump of volcanic crud with a knob on top. This, incredibly, was the site of **Skáros**, the island's medieval capital, once defended below by an impregnable castle of 1207 built by Marco Sanudo; another fortress, the **Rocca**, sat on the top of the rock until a volcanic eruption in 1650 destroyed the town. A path (do it first thing in the morning, before it gets too hot; don't do it all if you're subject to vertigo) leads in about half an hour to the site of the Rocca, now occupied by a little white chapel. The views are sublime, awe-inspiring, terrifying. Other ruins belong to a **Catholic convent**, where the nuns stuck it out in extreme hardship until 1818 when they moved to the new **Ag. Nikólaos**. In the 19th century it was one of the biggest in Greece, and has a fine collection of bishops' portraits.

The road north continues to that trendy mouthful of vowels called **Oía** (or Ía), the third port of Santoríni, although these days only yachts and caiques to Thirassía call here. In 1900, 9,000 people lived here, mostly seamen. The 500 who remain are fiercely independent of Firá. Half-ruined by the earthquake, its houses, painted in rich, Fauvist colours are nearly all restored now (some have won major international restoration prizes) and piled on top of one another over the jumble of broken red and white cliffs; the roofs of the lower houses provide terraces for the houses above. There's a half-ruined Venetian lookout **fort** and working **windmills**; if you want the sea, it's 286 steps down to **Arméni Beach** with a little clutch of houses, or 214 steps down to **Ammoúdi Beach** with tavernas and a hotel, where you can fill your pockets with pumice-stone souvenirs. The third option is a 3km bus trip to **Baxédes**, with coarse blackish sand and shade. An old mansion in Oía houses the **Nautical Museum**, created by an old sea captain; it has ships' models and figureheads, and rare instruments. Oía is reputedly haunted, although most of the spirits these days seem to come out of bottles, especially when everyone gathers by the Kástro to watch the sun call it a day.

⭐ Oía

Nautical Museum
*t 228 607 1156; open
daily 10–2 and 5–8; adm*

Where to Stay and Eat North of Firá

Imerovígli ⌂ 87400

Chromata, t 228 602 4850, *www. chromata-santorini.com* (€€€€€). Deep, deep colours (as the name implies), plus an infinity pool, and romantic restaurant on the rim.

Heliotopos, t 228 602 3670, *www. heliotopos.net* (€€€€€). Intimate, elegant Cycladic hideaway, with a restaurant and grand views. Large rooms, all with kitchenette.

Icons, t 228 602 8950, *www.santorinicons. gr* (€€€€€). Beautiful rooms and state-of-the-art facilities; all rooms different, with indoor pools or Jacuzzis.

Arch Houses, near the top of the town, t 228 602 3258, *www.archouses-santorini.com* (€€€€–€€). Five rooms with The View.

Katerina's Castle, t 228 602 3111 (€€). Simple rooms on the caldera.

Blue Note, t 228 602 3771. For dinner with grand views.

Marilos, near the car park. For something Greek, simple, and much cheaper. No views, but it is run by a kindly old gent.

Oía ⌂ 84702

Ecorama Travel Agency, by bus stop, t 228 607 1507, *www.santorinitours. com*, are helpful for finding rooms.

1864 The Sea Captain's House, t 228 607 1401, *www.santorini-gr.com* (€€€€€). Three gorgeous suites in the centre of Oía, plus volcanic hot stone body massage.

Fanari Villas, below the windmill, t 228 607 1008, *www.fanarivillas.com* (€€€€€). Luxury *skaftá*, with a small bar, and steps down to Ammoúdi Bay.

Katikies, just out of town, t 228 607 1401, *www.katikies.com* (€€€€€). The tops here – beautifully decorated rooms and apartments with great views, spectacular pool and breakfasts on the terraces. Guests get first chance to book at their famous **Gourmet** restaurant – there are only four tables.

Chelidonia Traditional Villas, t 228 607 1287, *www.chelidonia.com* (€€€€). At the lower end of this category, friendly and family-run villas – kids stay free.

 Katikies »

Amoudi Villas, t 228 607 1983, *www. amoudivillas.gr* (€€€). Tranquil, all mod cons in traditional apartments with verandas and a café providing breakfast and hand-made ice cream.

Perivolas Traditional Houses, t 228 607 1308, *www.perivolas.gr* (€€€). 14 lovely traditional houses, with a unique pool.

1800, t 228 607 1485 (€75). For a romantic dinner by candlelight, in a shipowner's house, serving imaginative international cuisine, and taking Greek cuisine to new heights.

Ambrosia, t 228 607 1413 (€55). Intimate dining, with *nouvelle cuisine* dishes (e.g. sea bass in champagne and saffron sauce). The same owners also run the more informal Ambrosia & Nectar, with great sunset views.

Kástro, t 228 607 1045 (€35). Excellent contemporary cuisine in the sunset grandstand; best to book.

Kantouni, t 228 607 1616 (€35). In the house of Oía's first doctor (1827), choice restaurant with a small menu, but delicious Mediterranean cuisine.

Skala, t 228 607 1362 (€20). Enormous terrace over the caldera and lots of tasty local recipes.

Paradeisos, down at Baxédes, t 228 607 1583. Great taverna by the beach, serving classics like *papoútsia* (stuffed aubergines).

Islets around the Caldera

Crusts of land mark the rim of Santoríni's spooky 10km (6-mile) wide and 380m (1,250ft)-deep caldera. The largest, curving around the northwest, is **Thirassía**, part of Santoríni until the two were blasted apart in 236 BC. In one of its pumice quarries a Middle Cycladic settlement was discovered, pre-dating Akrotíri, though there are no traces of it now. The main business on Thirassía (pop. 245) is growing tomatoes and beans on the fertile plateau; the largest village, **Manolás**, has tavernas and rooms to rent.

Excursion boats from Oía make trips out to the 'burnt isles', **Palía Kaméni** (appeared in AD 157) and **Néa Kaméni** (born in 1720), both still volcanically active, especially the Metaxá crater on Néa Kaméni, which last erupted in 1950. However, even though a local brochure promises 'the strange volcano which cause you greatness', be forewarned that most people come away disappointed; the tourist trail up the mountain is rubbish-strewn and stinks of sulphur. Other excursions take people to swim in the 'healthy' sulphurous mud nearby and the hot volcanic waters around Palía Kaméni, which makes an unusual chat-up line ('Gosh, you stink!') in the bars.

Sérifos (ΣΕΡΙΦΟΣ)

Where its neighbour Sífnos welcomes the visitor with soft green terraces and dovecotes, Sérifos, 'the barren one', tends to intimidate at first with its stark rocks. These were so rich in iron and copper mines, however, that in antiquity Sérifos minted its own coins, stamped with a frog. That golden age didn't last; Sérifos picked the wrong side in the Greek-Persian wars of the 6th century BC and suffered accordingly. The Romans used it as a place of exile, and the Venetians

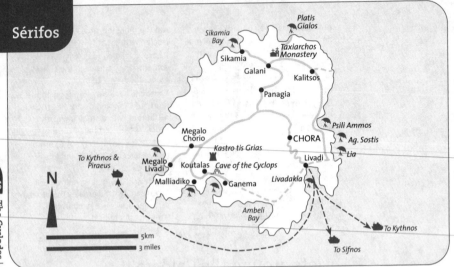

built a castle or two, but Sérifos is hardly heard from until about 1850, when the mines re-opened and the island enjoyed another period of prosperity. A violent strike in 1916, followed by a decline in profitability, led to the abandonment of the mines, and since the 1960s the population has drastically decreased to around 1,200.

As for the rest, Sérifos is pure Cyclades; Chóra, high above the sea, provides one of the most visually dramatic introductions any Greek island can offer, seemingly inaccessible as it tumbles impressively down the steep slopes (though you can walk up to it in less than an hour). The appealing port of Livádi provides the informal foreground to this postcard shot; it has learned to cope with the arrival of yachties and a strong German and French contingent. Beware of water shortages in August.

When Medusa Rears her Ugly Head

Sérifos is the setting for one of the oldest Greek myths. When it was prophesied to Akrisios, king of Argos, that he would be slain by the son of his daughter Danaë, he locked the girl in an underground chamber. This failed to hide her from Zeus, however, who came to her in a shower of golden rain and fathered Perseus. Enraged but unable to put his daughter or grandson to death, Akrisios decided to leave the issue to fate and set them adrift in a chest. Zeus guided them to Sérifos, where a fisherman, Diktys, rescued them and took them in. Polydektes, the king of Sérifos, lusted after Danaë but Perseus, as he grew older, stood in his way. One day, hearing the young man boast that he could kill Medusa, the only mortal of the three monstrous Gorgon sisters who lived beyond the Ocean and whose glance turned men to stone, Polydektes challenged him to do so, and threatened to take Danaë captive if he failed. Perseus succeeded, thanks to Athena and Hermes who helped him procure winged shoes to fly, a cap of invisibility, and a pouch to hold the head. Perseus then returned to Sérifos (rescuing Andromeda on the way), to find that his mother had been abused by Polydektes. Perseus then surprised the king at a banquet and presented him with the head, instantly turning him to stone. Diktys was declared king of Sérifos in his stead, and Danaë and Perseus went home to Argos. Fearing the old prophecy, Akrisios fled before them. But fate finally caught up with him in another town, where Perseus was competing in a game and accidentally killed his grandfather with a javelin in the foot.

Getting to and around Sérifos

Daily **ferry** connections with Piraeus, Kýthnos, Mílos and Sífnos; 4 times a week with Kímolos, 3 times a week with Santoríni, Folégandros, Síkinos and Íos; twice a week with Mýkonos and Páros, once a week to Sýros and Tínos. **Port authority: t** 228 105 1470.

Six **buses** go up to Chóra from Livádi; other villages are served once a day in the summer.

Rent a car or bike at Blue Bird in Livadi, **t** 228 105 1511.

Livádi and Chóra

Most people stay in **Livádi**, the port and island green spot, where many of the streets are still unpaved, behind a long pebbly-sandy beach lined with tamarisks. There are two other beaches within easy walking distance: crowded **Livadákia** and, a 30-minute walk south over the headland, sandy **Karávi Beach**, popular with nudists.

Chóra, the capital, is 6km up and is linked by bus or ancient stair. Set high like a whitewashed oasis over Sérifos' forbidding slopes – the bare terraces make them look like corrugated iron – Chóra is a fascinating jumble of houses and a dozen churches. Many of these are built of stone salvaged from the fortress; others date back to the Middle Ages and a few are now holiday homes owned by trendy Athenians, Brits and Germans. Geraniums, tucked in corners, here grow into 12ft trees. At the top, there's a pretty neoclassical square, with a **town hall** built in the moneyed days of 1908 and a small **Archaeological Museum**. The old windmills still turn, and in the spring you may find a rare carnation that grows only on Sérifos.

Archaeological Museum
*open in summer,
Tues–Sun 8.30–3*

Around the Island

The road continues beyond Chóra to **Megálo Chorió**, which sits on the site of the ancient capital of Sérifos and is still guarded by the stump of a marble Hellenistic tower; 2km away, on a dirt track, you can walk to the strange **Psaropýrgos**, locally called the 'throne of the Cyclops', an ancient, well-preserved rectangular building of uncertain purpose and date. Continuing on to the coast, **Megálo Livádi**, now visited for its beach and tavernas, once served as the loading dock for the iron and copper mined nearby. It's a wonderfully relaxing spot, in an incongruous setting of rusting machinery; a monument at the end of the beach commemorates workers killed in the strike of 1916. From Megálo Chorió the road carries around to **Koutalás**, a remote spot with a broad beach where yachts occasionally tie up. Up above on the hills are the ruins of another castle, the **Kástro tis Grías**. During mining operations, a cave, instantly dubbed the **Cave of the Cyclops** (*ask if it's open*), was discovered here, with two stalactite chambers and a small lake, and a floor of petrified seashells. There are two other beaches nearby, **Malliádiko** and **Gánema**, and a track back to Livádi.

A second road, now paved, passes **Panagía**, named after the oldest church on Sérifos, from the 10th century. At **Galaní** you can visit

Taxiárchos Monastery
t 228 105 1027

Taxiárchos Monastery, built in 1500 and containing a precious altar, 18th-century frescoes by the painter Skordílis, and Byzantine manuscripts in the library, before continuing into the petrified island's corner of milk and honey, **Kalítsos**, where almonds, olives and vines prosper. There's a beach, **Platís Giálos**, just beyond the monastery. On the other side of Galaní, down a rather difficult road, **Sikamiá Bay** is a good place to get away from it all, with a beach, taverna, a rare bit of shade and fresh water.

Beyond Kalítsos, a new road circles around the eastern edge of the island, opening up a few more beaches for lotus-eaters: **Ag. Ioánnis**, which you might have all to yourself; gorgeous white sandy **Psilí Ámmos** on a turquoise sea, now into a little resort with a top taverna; **Lía**; and secluded **Ag. Sóstis**. From there the road passes through one of Sérifos's greener corners back to Livádi.

Useful Information on Sérifos

Krinas Travel, in Livádi, **t** 228 105 1164. For accommodation and tickets.

Sérifos Festivals

5 May: Koutalás.

27 July: Mount Óros.

6 Aug: Kaló Ábeli.

15–17 Aug: Near the monastery and at a different village each day.

7 Sept: Livádi.

Where to Stay and Eat on Sérifos

Rent Rooms Association, Livádi, **t** 228 105 1520, helps all comers.

Livádi ✉ 84005

Asteri, **t** 228 105 1789, *www.asteri.gr* (€€€). Balcony with sea view for every room, TVs and a restaurant.

Sérifos Beach, **t** 228 105 1468 (€€€). The island's biggest, with a nice taverna downstairs.

Albatross, further around the bay, **t** 228 105 1148 (€€). Smothered in oleander; the owner meets the ferry. *Open April–Oct.*

Areti, **t** 228 105 1479/1107, *www.aretihotel.gr* (€€). Handy for the ferries, with a quiet garden and comfortable rooms with terraces overlooking the sea. *Open April–Oct.*

Maistrali, **t** 228 105 1381 (€€). Lovely, airy rooms. *Open April–Sept.*

Naias, no distance from the beach, **t** 228 105 1749, *naias@otenet.gr* (€€). Blue and white, in true Cycladic style, with balconies.

Captain George Rooms, near the square, **t** 228 105 1274 (€). Good value.

Kyklades, by the sea, **t** 228 105 1315 (€). Rooms and a restaurant serves delicious shrimp casserole with feta and tomatoes. *Open April–Oct.*

Coralli Camping, Livadákia Beach, **t** 228 105 1500, *www.coralli.gr*. Good facilities, pool, restaurant; also bungalows (€).

Almericha, Friendly place, good fish and *mezédes*.

Meli. Save room for dessert; they're famous for their *loukoumádes*.

Ouzerie Meltémi. For a *karafáki* (enough for 3–4 good drinks) and choice of tasty nibbles, including local cheeses and the mysterious 'single yellow pea' or 'married yellow pea'.

Stamati, round the bay. Sit right on the water and enjoy vegetarian dishes, or grilled meats.

Takis, **t** 228 105 1159, on the waterfront under an enormous tamarisk. Popular with locals and tourists alike, offering excellent and inexpensive food and friendly service.

Chóra ✉ 84005

Apanemia, **t** 228 105 1717 (€). Some of the few rooms up here, all kitted out with a fridge.

Petros, t 228 105 1302. Popular with locals for its traditional, reliable menu.

Stavro, by the bus stop. The owner's dad starred in a famous EOT tourist poster in the 1960s; serves food with accompanying view. Try their potent red wine, which the owners (and some locals) swear leads to wedding bells.

Zorba, on the top square by the town hall. Serving snacks with a view.

Megálo Livádi ✉ 84005

Cyclopas, t 228 105 1009. Good seafood under the tamarisks by the beach.

Entertainment and Nightlife on Sérifos

There's a mix of nightlife in Livádi with several music bars and seasonal discos.

Passaggio and **Veggera**. Both clubs play everything from heavy metal to pop.

Alter Ego and **Eden**. Feature Greek music.

Malabar Café. With perhaps the only pool table on Sérifos.

Sífnos (ΣΙΦΝΟΣ)

Sífnos in recent years has become the most popular island in the western Cyclades, with good reason – it is an island of peaceful serendipity, with gentle green hills, vineyards, watermelon patches and olives, charming villages and long sandy beaches, beloved by its 2,000 inhabitants who keep it spick and span. It is famous for its pottery and its cooks, ever since Sifniot Níkos Tselemntés wrote the first modern Greek cookery book (to this day, any cookbook in Greece is a *tselemntés*). Sífnos produces the best olive oil in the Cyclades, and the people speak with a sweet singsong lilt.

One of the best things to do on Sífnos is walk: the landscape is strewn with Venetian dovecotes, windmills, 300 little chapels and 52 ancient towers (more than the rest of the Cyclades combined) left over from a sophisticated signalling system devised in the 5th century BC – a bit after the fact, in Sífnos' case.

History: the Island that Laid Golden Eggs

Pliny wrote that the Phoenicians called the island Meropia and were the first to mine its gold. In fact, according to recent archaeological research, the story goes back much further: gold, silver and lead galleries on Sífnos date back to the 3rd millennium BC – the oldest mines yet discovered in Europe. And when these first miners exhausted their galleries, the archaeologists note, they religiously filled them in to heal the wounds of the earth.

Such treasures attracted continuous attention, first from the Minoans, who founded Minoa near Apollonía, then the Phoenicians, who were in turn supplanted by Ionians who lived near Ag. Andréas and elsewhere. Meropia, meanwhile, had become famous for its gold; at one time, it is said, there was so much that the islanders simply divided it among themselves each year, and had enough extra in the 6th century to afford to pave their *agora* with the finest Parian marble. Apollo at Delphi heard rumours of this wealth and demanded that the island contribute an annual tithe of gold in the

Getting to Sífnos

Daily **ferry** connections with Piraeus, Kýthnos, Sérifos and Mílos; 4 times a week with Kímolos, 2–3 times a week with Íos, Santoríni, Folégandros and Síkinos; once a week with Páros, Tínos, Karýstos (Évia) and Rafína. Port authority: **t** 228 403 3617.

Getting around Sífnos

Excursion boats go from Kamáres to Váthi and Cherónissos; there are also **round-island tours**.

At least **4 buses** a day leave from Kamáres to Apollonía, Artemónas, and from there to Platýs Gialós; not quite as often to Fáros, Káto Petáli, Kástro and Váthi. Pick up the detailed schedule at the tourist office.

Taxis: t 228 403 1656/1793/1626. For **car or moped rental**, try **Krinas**, on the waterfront in Kamáres, **t** 228 403 1488, or **Apollo**, **t** 228 403 3397. Kiosks and shops stock an excellent map showing all the island's footpaths.

form of a solid egg. In 530 BC Meropia constructed a magnificent treasury at Delphi to house its golden eggs and adorned it with a fine frieze and pediment which can still be seen; for many years it was the richest of all the oracle's treasures. But one year the islanders, who began to have a reputation for greed and cunning, sent the god an egg of gilded lead. Apollo soon discovered he had been duped and cursed the island. This gave Polycrates, Tyrant of Sámos, a good excuse to extract a fine from Meropia; his 40 triremes plundered the island's gold, and Apollo's curse caused the mines to sink and give out. Thus the island became empty or, in Greek, *sífnos*. Nowadays most of the ancient mines at Ag. Mína, Kapsálos and Ag. Sostís are underwater, or just barely above the sea.

With egg on its face, Sífnos went into decline. In 1307 the Da Coronia family ruled the island for Venice; in 1456 Cozzadini, the Lord of Kýthnos, married into the family and his descendants ruled Sífnos until the Turks took the island in 1617. Towards the end of the 17th century the Sultan, thinking to re-open the mines, sent out experts to examine them. When they heard that they were coming, the islanders hired French pirates to sink the Sultan's ship. The experts, in turn, heard of the deal with the pirates and simply went home. Later the French themselves exploited the local deposits of iron ore and lead; mining ended in 1925.

Sífnos has also made important contributions to Greek letters. In the late 1600s, the 'School of the Holy Tomb' was founded in an attempt to keep alive ancient Greek and the classics, drawing students from all over Greece. Nikólaos Chrysoyélos, the most famous headmaster, led a contingent of Sifniots in the War of Independence, and subsequently became Greece's first Minister of Education. Another islander, the 19th-century poet-satirist Cleánthis Triandáfilos, who wrote under the name Rabágas, was a thorn in the side of the monarchy until he was imprisoned and committed suicide. Ioánnis Gypáris (d. 1942), another Sifniot, was, along with Caváfy, the first to espouse the use of demotic Greek (as opposed to the formal *katharévousa*) in literature.

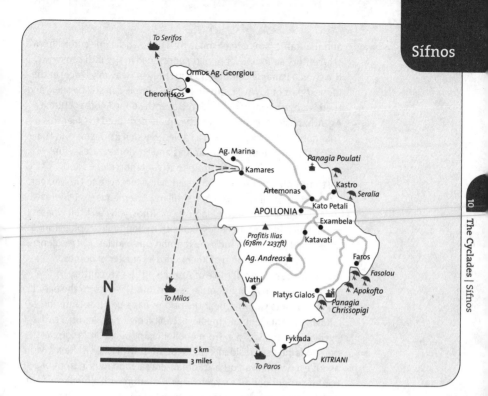

Kamáres

The port, shady **Kamáres**, provides a suitably gracious introduction to Sífnos. Situated on a cove between two steep, barren cliffs that belie the fertility inland, Kamáres has a fine sandy beach safe for little kids, and a range of cafés and tavernas. Two **pottery workshops** specialize in decorative glazed chimney pots. The exceptional clay on Sífnos has been used for ceramics since pre-Cycladic times, and the islanders are expert potters. In the early 19th century there were so many that they emigrated to other corners of Greece; someone has discovered that every Greek potter has a Sifniot in his or her family tree. Just after the war, there were still some 90 workshops in the island, employing 600 potters, and after nearly dying a death the old tradition is undergoing something of a revival (some of their best is on display in Kamáres, notably the exquisitely painted work of George Atsonios, in his shop on the main street of town).

Apollonía and Around

The bus makes the dramatic climb up from Kamáres to the capital, **Apollonía**, a Cycladic idyll of two-storey houses and bougainvillaea, spread out across the hills, a circle of white from the distance. Note how most of the houses have terraces on the side, designed for talking; the Sifniots are a sociable lot. Apollonía suffers one small curse: every route on the island passes through its narrow streets, and the traffic jams can be amazing. The town's name comes from a 7th-century BC Temple of Apollo, superseded in the 18th century by the church **Panagía Ouranofóra** (Our Lady of Heavenly Force) in the highest part of town. Fragments of the temple can still be seen, and there's a marble relief of St George over the door. Another church, **Ag. Athanásios** (next to the pretty square dedicated to Cleánthis Triandáfilos) has frescoes and a carved wooden iconostasis. In the square, the **Museum of Popular Arts and Folklore** houses a fine ethnographic collection of Sifniot pottery, embroideries and costumes, but the opening hours are a mystery even to the villagers.

Artemis is Apollo's twin sister; similarly, **Artemónas** is Apollonía's twin village and the second largest on Sífnos; you can't tell where one starts and the other ends. Beneath its windmills, cobblestoned lanes wind past the island's most ambitious neoclassical residences and churches. The church of **Kochí**, with its cluster of domes, occupies the site of a Temple of Artemis; little 17th-century **Ag. Geórgios tou Aféndi** contains several fine icons from the period, and **Panagía ta Gourniá**, near the bridge, has a beautiful interior.

Kástro, the ancient and medieval capital of Sífnos, lies on a cliff over looking the sea 3km from Apollonía. Though a bit forlorn, with only 30 families in residence, it's a fascinating place, with relics lying about everywhere: an ornate Roman-era sarcophagus in front of a bar, an ancient pot on a streetcorner, a column with a medieval Latin inscription. The architecture is unique: tall narrow terrace houses with whitewashed stoops, many sporting wooden balconies and their Venetian coats-of-arms. Ruins of the **Classical acropolis** and **Byzantine walls** remain (*currently under repair*), and many churches have attractive floors, among them **Panagía Eleoússa** (1653); **Ag. Ekateríni** (1665) and **Panagía Koímmissi** (1593), where the altar is decorated with Dionysian bulls' heads. The small **Archaeology Museum** contains some charming 'parting scenes' carved on classical gravestones. The site of the School of the Holy Tomb, closed in 1834, is now a cemetery. At Kástro there's plenty of deep blue sea to dive into from the rocks, but if you prefer sand, a path from Kástro leads down to **Serália**, with remnants of the medieval port, and a lovely beach. **Panagía Pouláti**, to the north, can be reached from here by a scenic coastal path (or by road from Apollonía). It has a superb setting overlooking the sea and cliffs, with a beach down below.

Just south of Apollonía the bus passes through **Exámbela**, a quiet flower-filled village famous for its songs. In the middle of one of the island's most fertile areas, the **Vrísi Monastery** (1612) is surrounded by springs and contains old manuscripts and art. On the road to Váthi the **Monastery of Ag. Andréas**, sitting on a hill, has some ruins of the double walls that once encircled the ancient citadel, and some recently excavated ruins of the acropolis. Further north, a path from here continues up in 2hrs to Sífnos' highest peak (678m/2,237ft). This

Archaeology Museum
*t 228 403 1022;
open Tues–Sun 8–3*

is named after **Profítis Ilías Monastery**, built in the 8th century, with thick stone walls, a small network of catacombs and cells and a 12th-century marble iconostasis in the church (*check opening hours before setting out*); the views over the white villages below are delightful.

Sifnos' charms are not evenly spread. The entire northern half, in fact, is as empty and barren as a Greek island can be. There's one good road, passing the slopes of Mt Ag. Símeon. The **monastery** of the same name, at the summit, makes a dramatic sight; illuminated at night; you can see it from Kamáres. Ruins of **Mycenaean walls** can be explored nearby at **Gourní**, and further north at **Ag. Nikítas**. The road ends at tiny **Cherónissos** on the island's windy northern tip. This is another pottery centre. Here, master potter Kóstas Depastás upholds the island's old ceramics tradition with local clay, his kiln fired by driftwood. There's a taverna if you feel peckish.

The South Coast

Further south, the old seaside village of **Fáros** with sandy beaches is a friendly, low-key resort with cheap accommodation and good tavernas. Besides Fáros itself, there are three other beaches: **Fasoloú**, close by, and about 1km away on a footpath, **Apókofto**, with golden sands, and **Chrissopigí**. Above this one, on a rocky cape, stands the island's most famous monastery, **Panagía Chrissopigí**, built in 1650. The story goes that two girls accidentally disturbed some pirates napping in the church. With the pirates in hot pursuit, the girls prayed to the Virgin, who saved them by splitting the cape in the pirates' path – it is spanned in these pirate-free days by a bridge.

Platýs Gialós with its broad sandy beach – said to be the longest in the Cyclades – is the island's busiest resort, and its centre for water sports. You can escape its worldly concerns by visiting the serene clifftop convent of **Panagía tou Vounoú**, affording a gorgeous view over the bay below. The last nuns left nearly a century ago, but the church with its ancient Doric columns is still used for *panegýria*. Platýs Gialós has an ostrich farm, and a pottery, Franzesko Lemonis, founded in 1936.

The fishing hamlet of **Váthi** on the west coast is probably the prettiest place to stay on Sífnos (and the most peaceful; cars are kept far from the beach). A road south from Apollonía was built only recently, and Váthi is starting to become popular; there are a few rooms to rent, a lovely clean beach and shallow water.

Sífnos >

Kamáres: municipal tourist office, near the quay, t 228 403 1977; run by the helpful Sofia; open May–Oct (until midnight in July/Aug)

Apollonía: tourist office, has a list of all types of accommodation

Useful Information on Sífnos

Aegean Thesaurus, in the main square in Apollonía, t 228 403 3151, *www.thesauros.gr*. Offers guided walking tours around the island.

Sífnos Festivals

2 Feb: Lolopangýrio, 'Crazy festival' of pagan origins, at Panagía Ouranofóra, Apollonía.

25 Mar: Panagía tou Voúno.

40 days after Greek Easter: Chrissopigí.

10 The Cyclades | Sífnos

20 July: Profítis Ilías, near Kamáres.

15 Aug: Panagía ta Gourniá.

29 Aug: Ag. Ioánnes near Váthi.

31 Aug: Ag. Simeon near Kamáres.

14 Sept: Fáros.

Where to Stay and Eat on Sífnos

Sífnos is famous for *revíthia tou foúrno*, oven-baked chickpeas, served only on Sundays; *revithokeftédes*, chickpea patties; *xynomyzithra*, a hard sheep's-milk cheese, steeped in wine and kept in barrels until it stinks but tastes great; *stamnás*, meat, cheese and potatoes in a clay pot; and *ambelofásoula*, made from green beans. Fresh dill is the favourite herb.

Kamáres ✉ 84003

Boulis, t 228 403 2122 (€€€–€€). By the beach, with a surprisingly green lawn.

Kamari, t 228 403 3383 (€€). Well-equipped modern, small hotel near the beach.

Stavros, t 228 403 1641 (€€). Basic rooms right on the port; ask for one with a balcony facing the sea. *Open all year*.

Dimitris and Margarita Belli, t 228 403 1276 (€). Good little rooms with sea-view balconies.

Makis Camping, just behind the beach, **t** 228 403 2366.

Argyris, Ag. Marína, **t** 228 403 2352. Right on the sea; good grills and fish.

Boulis Restaurant, on the road. Good value **rooms** (€) above (don't confuse it with the hotel) and serves traditional, excellent and cheap Greek fare.

Da Claudio, t 228 403 1671. Great pizza, real Italian cooking and nice people, Monica and Paolo. '*Open from 6 until I get fed up.*'

Kamares and **Merope**, the two portside tavernas most popular with the locals.

Kapetan Andreas, on the harbour, **t** 228 403 2356 (€12–18). Serving the freshest of fish, including lobster, caught by Captain Andrew himself from his own boat. No frills, just good food.

Apollonía

Patriarca, t 228 403 2400, *www. patriarca.gr* (€€€). New boutique hotel

in a 350-year-old house, with six rooms and a restaurant.

Eleonas Apartments, t 228 403 3383 (€€). Well-appointed rooms in a quiet setting, with views.

Angelo's Rooms, t 228 403 1533 (€). With garden views.

Sofia, set on a quiet little square, **t** 228 403 1238 (€). Rooms. *Open April–Sept*.

Orea Sifnos, by the bus stop, **t** 228 403 3069. Tasty traditional food and barrelled wine.

Artemónas ✉ 84003

Bella Vista, t 228 403 3965, *www. windmillbellavista.com* (€€€–€€). Pleasant studios and apartments, and a traditional well-equipped windmill sleeping four.

Apostolidis, t 228 403 2143 (€€). Apartments including mini-bars in rooms and views over Platýs Giálos.

Artemónas, t 228 403 1303 (€€). This little guest house is one of the most charming places on Sífnos, with a cool courtyard. *Open April–Sept*.

Artemón, t 228 403 1303 (€€). Same management, but bigger and with a garden restaurant.

Liotrivi ('Olive Press'), on the main square, **t** 228 403 2051/1246. The specialities are *kápari*, local capers, *revíthia* and other Sifniot dishes.

Kástro ✉ 84003

Leonidas, at the entrance to town; a good restaurant, with **rooms** (€€).

To Astro, t 228 403 1476. Set in the back streets, with a terrace, serving Sifniot dishes. Try the lamb in red wine.

Fáros/Chrissopigí ✉ 84003

Blue Horizon, t 228 407 1442 (€€€€€). Ten new furnished apartments.

Sifneiko Archontiko, t 228 407 1454 (€€–€). The old standby; some of the cheapest rooms on the island.

Flora, at Chrissopigí, **t** 228 407 1278 (€). Small and family-run, with great views.

On the Rocks. Great bar and crêperie, especially nice for sunset views.

Zambelis, on the water at Fassoloú Beach, **t** 228 407 1434. Offering delicious Sifniot specialities and a very tasty lamb casserole. Don't tell anyone, but the owner was Christina Onassis' personal chef.

⭐ Artemónas >>

⭐ Da Claudio >

Platýs Gialós ✉ 84003

Alexandros Sífnos Beach, t 228 403 1333, *www.hotelalexandros.gr* (€€€€€). Smart with bungalows on the hillside above the beach.

Platýs Yialós, t 228 407 1324 (€€€€€). Built in traditional Cycladic style with well-equipped air-conditioned bungalows, all facilities and sports.

Angeliki, near the bus stop, t 228 403 1288 (€€). Nice little place with rooms.

Camping Platýs Yialós, in an olive grove set back from the beach, t 228 407 1286.

Mama Mia. Popular for pizza and home-made pasta.

Sofia, t 228 407 1202. For Sifniot dishes, suckling pig, lobster with spaghetti and some good wines.

Váthi ✉ 84003

Elies Resorts, t 228 403 4000, *www. eliesresorts.com* (€€€€€). On the seafront amid the olives, a new award-winning Cycladic-style designer hotel with spa, infinity pool and speedboat.

Virginia, t 228 407 1101, and **Nikos**, t 228 707 1512 (€). Quiet rooms on the beach.

Tsikali, t 228 407 1177. Lobster pasta, grills and all the local dishes.

Entertainment and Nightlife on Sífnos

Nightlife in summer is evenly split between Kamáres and Apollonía. And for something entirely unexpected, this island has a really good eclectic radio station, Radio Active, at 91.3 FM.

Collage Bar, overlooking the sandy beach, Kamáres. Relaxing choice.

7 Thallases ('Seven Seas'), Kamáres. A bar with a view, and a swimming pool.

Aloni, Apollonía, t 228 403 1543. Often has live Greek music.

Argo and **Doloma**, Apollonía. Attractive bars.

Club Privé and **Club Camel**. *The* spots for dancing in Apollonía.

Castello and **Remezzo**, Kástro. Trendy.

Sifniot Cultural Society, Artemónas. Summer concerts, for a spot of culture.

Síkinos (ΣΙΚΙΝΟΣ)

If you want to escape the outside world, its newspapers and noise, or just practise your Greek, you always have Síkinos, Folégandros' little sister, with a sleepy port and the stunning white villages of Chóra and Kástro perched high above. An 'Ecosystem of European Importance', its shores host rare Aegean pigeons, black-headed hawks, and sea birds; monk seals (*see* p.613) live in its sea caves, rare cat vipers and sand snakes slither about on land; little wheat fields and vines in the terraces and valleys and fishing are still the island's mainstay. Light years away from neighbouring Íos, Síkinos is the place to savour the simple pleasures of old-fashioned island life, although things pick up in August with returning Greeks.

Named after the child of Thoas, mythical king of Lemnos, who was set adrift in a chest and saved by a local nymph, in ancient times Síkinos was also one of several islands called Oenoe, or 'wine island'. The local stuff still packs a punch.

Villages and Walks around Síkinos

Ferries dock at Síkinos' port, **Aloprónia** or **Skála**, where you'll also find a sandy beach and shallow sea, ideal for children; bobbing fishing boats, a few tavernas and holiday homes behind the port, and a hotel complex sums up the rest. **Chóra**, the capital, is one of

Getting to and around Síkinos

By sea: Ferry connections daily with Folégandros, 6 times a week with Santoríni and Íos, 3 times a week with Náxos, Páros and Anáfi, at least twice a week to Piraeus, Mílos, Kýthnos and Sýros; once to Kéa, Lávrio, Sérifos and Sífnos. **Excursion boats** go to the beaches in summer. **Port authority: t** 228 609 1264 (Íos).

By road: The island **bus** meets most ferries and runs hourly to Chóra and Kástro.

the most authentic villages in the Cyclades and a good hour's walk up if the bus hasn't put in an appearance. Looming over the village is the ruined 18th-century **Monastery of Zoodóchos Pigí**, fortified against the pirates. The 300 inhabitants are most proud, however, of their 'cathedral', with icons by the 18th-century master Skordílis. In the main square, bees buzz furiously in the trees by the church of the **Pantánassa** and the 18th-century stone mansions, some with brightly painted wooden balconies as in Folégandros; one ruined marble portico has intricately carved grapes and Byzantine symbols. A few minutes' walk up the next hill, **Kástro** with its labyrinthine lanes, ruined windmills, tiny rooms and *kafeneíons* is a last relic of what most Cycladic villages looked like in the pre-tourism era.

From Chóra, a paved road leads past ruined Cyclopean walls southwest to **Moní Episkópi**. Most likely a tomb-temple, or *heroön*, from the 3rd century AD, this unusual building was converted in about the 7th century to the Byzantine church of **Koimísis Theotókou**, and remodelled again in the 17th century after an earthquake.

A rough path to the northeast leads in about an hour and a half to the rather scant remains of a Classical fortress at **Paliokástro**, near the nice sandy beach of **Málta**. Tracks from this path lead south to the sandy beaches of **Ag. Geórgios** (with a taverna) and **Ag. Nikólaos**, but there is also a caique in summer. From the harbour beach you can walk up over the mountain to the next cove at **Gialiskári**, while the pebble beach at **Ag. Panteleímonas** is about 40 minutes away and site of a big *panegýri* on 27 July.

Where to Stay and Eat on Síkinos

Aloprónia ✉ 84010

Porto Síkinos, right on the beach, **t** 228 605 1220 (€€€). Smart and prettily laid out in traditional island design, with bar, restaurant and tourist office.

Flora, up the hill, **t** 228 605 1235 (€€). Lovely Cycladic-style development of eight self-contained rooms built round a courtyard with wonderful views.

Kamáres, t 228 605 1281 (€€). Charming traditional rooms, all with bath and telephones.

Loukas, above the fish restaurant, **t** 228 605 1076 (€). Basic harbourside rooms.

Panayiotis Kouvdouris, by the sea, **t** 228 605 1232 (€). Simple rooms.

There are several seasonal tavernas but if you go after late September, everything is closed.

Flora's Shop. Doubles as a makeshift taverna.

Braxos Pizzaria, aka **The Rock Café**. Serves simple pizza and drinks.

Meltémi. Where the fishermen gather, for a simple lunch, coffee or ouzo.

Chóra ✉ 84010

Haroula and Dimitris Divolis, rooms on the way to the post office, t 228 605 1212 (€).

Themonies, halfway to Aloprónia. Cocktail bar, but it also has comfortable **rooms** (€).

Klimateria. Pretty vine-covered restaurant and *kafeneíon* which does meals, snacks and omelettes.

To Kástro. The main taverna in Chóra, with a roof garden and excellent home cooking.

To Liotrivi. Trendy music/dancing bar converted from an olive press.

Sýros/Sýra (ΣΥΡΟΣ/ΣΥΡΑ)

Inhabitants of Sýros (locally known as Sýra) affectionately call their island home 'Our Rock', and it's as dry and barren a piece of real estate as you can find. But at the beginning of the Greek War of Independence in 1821 it was blessed with three important qualities: a large natural harbour, the protection of the King of France, and a hardworking population. The result is Sýros' capital, Ermoúpolis, once the premier port in Greece, and today the largest city and capital of the Cyclades. Don't come here looking for Cycladic sugar-cubism: Ermoúpolis is the best-preserved 19th-century neoclassical town in the whole of Greece.

A sophisticated island, with many Athenians working there in law or local government, Sýros can afford to snap its fingers at tourism, but it's booming nonetheless. However, it remains very Greek, and tourists are treated more like guests rather than customers – except when it comes to *loukoúmia*, better known as Turkish delight (both the Greeks and the Turks claim to have invented it; no one really knows). These sweet, gummy squares, flavoured with roses, quinces or pistachios and smothered in icing sugar, are an island speciality, along with gorgeous nougat-like *halvadópittes*.

History

Homer's swineherd Eumaeus, who helped Odysseus when he finally returned to Ithaca, was actually a prince of Sýros who had been captured by Phoenician pirates, and he described his native island as a rich, fertile place where famine and disease were strangers, and inhabitants died only when they were struck by the gentle arrows of Apollo or Artemis after living long, happy lives. The first inhabitants, who may have been the same Phoenicians who made off with Eumaeus, settled at Dellagrácia and at Fínikas.

Poseidon was the chief god of Sýros, and in connection with his cult, one of the first observatories in Europe, a heliotrope (a kind of sundial), was constructed in the 6th century BC by Sýros' own philosopher, Ferekides. Ferekides was a keen student of ancient Chaldaean and Egyptian mysteries, and he spent two years in Egypt being initiated into secret cults; on his return to Greece, he became Pythagoras' teacher, imparting a mix of astrology and philosophy,

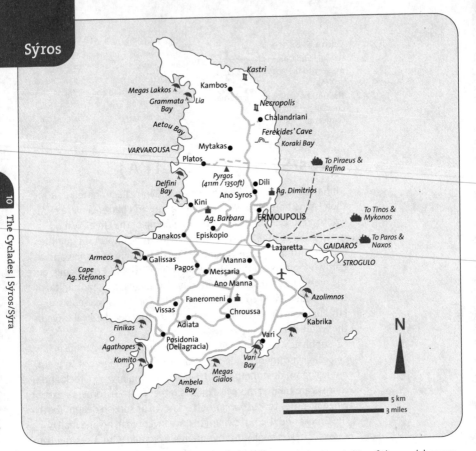

and beliefs in reincarnation and the immortality of the soul; he was also the first Greek to write in prose.

In Roman times the population emigrated to the site of present-day Ermoúpolis, at that time known as 'the Happy' with its splendid natural harbour and two prominent hills. After the collapse of the *Pax Romana*, Sýros was abandoned until the 13th century, when Venetians founded Áno Sýros on one of the hills.

Because Áno Sýros was Catholic, the island enjoyed the protection of the French, and it remained neutral at the outbreak of the Greek War of Independence in 1821. War refugees from Chíos, Psará and Smyrna brought their Orthodox faith with them and founded their own settlements on the other hill, Vrondádo, and down by the harbour. This new port town boomed from the start, as the 'warehouse' of the new Greek state for cotton from Egypt and spices from the East, and as the central coaling station for the eastern Mediterranean. When the time came to name the new town, Ermoúpolis – 'the city of Hermes' (the god of commerce) – was the natural choice. For 50 years Sýros ran much of the Greek economy, and great fortunes were made and spent on elegant

Getting to Sýros

By air: There are at least 3 daily flights from Athens with **Olympic Airways**. Olympic's office is at 52 Andístasios, on the harbour, t 228 108 2634. **Airport: t** 228 108 7025. Taxis into town cost around €5.

By sea: Sýros, as the capital, has the best connections of any island in the archipelago, with at least one boat a week to every corner of the Cyclades even in winter. Daily to Piraeus, plus regular hydrofoils from Lavrió in season. Most times of the year, daily connections to Mílos, Náxos, Mýkonos, Páros and Santoríni, as well as Sámos; less frequently to Kos, Ikaría, Rhodes and other points in the Dodecanese; day excursions to Délos in season. **Port authority: t** 228 108 8888.

Getting around Sýros

There is a good **bus** service around the island, t 228 108 2575, departing from the ferry port. One way to see Sýros is to take one of the buses which circle the island, by way of Azólimnos, taking about an hour and passing through all the beach villages except Kíni, which has a separate service from the port.
Taxi rank: t 228 108 6222.

mansions, schools and public buildings. Ermoúpolis built the first theatre in modern Greece and the first high school, partially financed by the citizens; when the Syriani died the citizens were so pleased with themselves that the most extravagant monuments ever to be seen in any Greek cemetery were erected in their memory. By the 1890s, however, oil replaced coal, and Piraeus, with the building of the Corinth Canal, replaced Ermoúpolis as Greece's major port. Sýros declined, but always dominated the Cyclades, supporting itself with shipyards and various industries, prospering just enough to keep its grand old buildings occupied, but not enough to tear them down to build new concrete blocks. The result is that today Ermoúpolis is a National Landmark, and one of the most striking and lively cities in Greece, since 2000 home to the engineering design school of the University of the Aegean.

⭐ Ermoúpolis

Greece was reborn in Ermoúpolis.

Elefthérios Venizélos

Ermoúpolis

As you sail into the commercial port, Ermoúpolis (ΕΡΜΟΥΠΟΛΗ), pop. 12,000, presents an imposing, unexpected sight much commented on by early travellers: a sweeping crescent meringue rising in twin peaks, one for each religion; older Catholic **Áno Sýros** to your left (or north), and **Vrondádo**, on the right, the Orthodox quarter. Stately, elegant buildings have been repainted in their original colours and, softly illuminated by old street lamps, with the silhouettes of palms outlined against the moon, form a rare urban idyll – 'Who could ever imagine finding such a city on a rocky island of the Aegean sea!' Gautier marvelled, when he visited it back when it was new. Yet at the same time there's no doubt that the city works for a living; prominent on the harbour are the Neórion shipyards.

Ermoúpolis' central square, **Plateía Miaoúlis**, is the most elegant in Greece, with its marble bandstand and palms, its worn, lustrous marble pavement, and its cafés and statue of Admiral Miaoúlis, revolutionary hero and old sea-dog, looking down to the port, the whole embraced by fine neoclassical buildings and wrought-iron balconies. In *Aegean Greece*, Robert Liddell wrote that he could think of no square 'except St Mark's that more gives the effect of a huge ballroom, open by accident to the sky'. Grandest of all is the neoclassical **town hall**, designed in 1876 by Ernst Ziller; you can pop inside for a coffee and have a look at the old fire engine in the courtyard. The **Archaeology Museum**, up the steps to the left, contains Proto-Cycladic to Roman-era finds from Sýros and other islands: note the Hellenistic-era 'Votive relief to a hero rider from Amorgos' with a snake crawling on the altar as a sheep is led to sacrifice, and more snakes on a marble plaque referring to Homer, from Íos. The **Historical Archives**, by the town hall, host the Ermoúpolis Seminars in summer, when the archives are on show. To the right, behind the square, the **Apóllon Theatre**, a copy of La Scala, Milan, was the first ever opera house in Greece; from its opening in 1864 until 1914 it supported a regular Italian opera season. After going dark for 50 years, it has now been restored after a botched repair that wrecked more than it fixed in 1970.

Archaeology Museum
t 228 108 8487; open Tues–Sun 8.30–3

Historical Archives
open summer only, Tues–Sun 8.30–3

Up the street a little way from here, the **Velissarópoulos Mansion**, now housing the Labour Union, is one of the few places you can get in to see the elaborate ceiling and wall murals characteristic of old Ermoúpolis. In the lanes above the square, the **Metamórphosis** is the Orthodox cathedral, with a pretty *choklakía* courtyard and surprising, ornate Baroque interior. **Chíos Street**, descending towards the port, has the town's bustling **market**. Down towards the port, just up from the bus terminal, the church of the **Annunciation**, built by refugees from Psára, contains the rare icon of the *Assumption* painted and signed by Doménicos Theotokópoulos (aka El Greco) after he left for Venice. Nearby, the former Europa Hotel on the waterfront has another lovely *choklakía* courtyard; today it is part of the **Aegina Casino**, the only one in the Cyclades.

Stretching off to the northeast, the elegant **Vapória quarter** is chock-a-block with old shipowners' mansions with marble façades, lavishly decorated inside with frescoes and painted ceilings. The main square here has one of Ermoúpoli's best churches, blue and golden-domed **Ag. Nikólaos**, dedicated to the patron saint of the city and boasting a carved marble iconostasis by the 19th-century sculptor Vitális of Tínos. In front of the church, a memorial topped by a stone lion, also by Vitális, is the world's first **Monument to the Unknown Soldier**. Vapória's grand houses hug the coastline above the town beaches of **Ag Nikólaos**, **Tálliro** and **Evangelídis**, which have marble steps down from the street.

Vrondádo and Áno Sýros

Crowning **Vrondádo Hill** (take the main street up from behind Plateía Miaoúlis), the Byzantine church **Anástasis** has a few old icons and superb views stretching to Tínos and Mýkonos. Come at night, when Vrondádo's excellent tavernas spread over its steps.

More remote – 870 cobbled steps, or a hop on the bus or taxi and then walk back down – is its older twin, **Áno Sýros** (Apáno Chóra), where 'the houses seemed clinging around its top as if desperate for security, like shipwrecked men about a rock beaten by billows', as Herman Melville wrote after a visit in 1856. A whitewashed Cycladic pedestrian-only enclave, this close-knit community has been mostly Catholic since the Crusades; the same families have lived in the same mansions for generations and worshipped at the Catholic Cathedral of St George, or **Ai-Giórgi**, on top of the rock.

The main entrance to Áno Sýros, the **Kámara**, is an ancient vaulted passageway which leads past tavernas and little shops to the main street or Piátsa. There's a **town hall**, the **Women's Association of Handicraft Workers** with a folklore collection and workshop, and a **Cultural Centre**. The large, handsome Capuchin **Convent of St Jean** was founded there in 1635 by France's Louis XIII as a poorhouse and contains archives dating from the 1400s; the Jesuits, just above at 16th-century **Panagía Karmiloú**, have a cloister from 1744 with an important library. The famous *rembétiko* composer Márkos Vamvakáris was born in Áno Sýros; his bust graces his square.

On your way down the hill, don't miss the Orthodox **cemetery of Ag. Geórgios**, with its marble mausoleums and dolorous damsels pining over wealthy shipowners.

Near Ermoúpolis

A 45-minute walk from Ermoúpolis leads to the pretty seaside church of **Ag. Dimítrios**, which was founded after the discovery of an icon there in 1936. All ships coming into port hoot as they pass and a bell is rung in reply. In **Díli**, just above, are the remains of a **Temple of Isis** built in 200 BC. Across the harbour at **Lazarétta** stood a 5th-century BC Temple of Poseidon, although the only traces of it are a few artefacts in the museum; it may have been the Poseidonia mentioned in the *Odyssey*.

Around the Island

'Our Rock' is a wild place on the whole, but it isn't quite as barren as it sounds; olives, pistachios and citrus fruit grow here, and the bees make an excellent thyme honey. Other ancient sites are in the rugged, seldom visited north side of the island, known as **Apáno Meriá**. At lagoon-like **Grámmata Bay** (reached only by boat), sailors from Classical to Byzantine times who found shelter from storms engraved epigrams of gratitude, still legible on the rocks. If you want a beach away from it all this is the place; sea-lilies grow here and on the beaches of **Lía** and **Mégas Lákkos**. Towards the east coast, the wealthy Bronze Age necropolis of **Chalandrianí** (2600–2300 BC), discovered in 1898, contributed much to the understanding of Early Cycladic civilization. **Kástri**, an hour's walk north, was the Bronze Age citadel: its walls, six towers, and the foundations of houses remain in the undergrowth. The **cave** where philosopher Ferekides whiled away the summer may be seen just south of Chalandrianí.

Buses from Ermoúpolis travel to the main seaside resorts: **Kíni**, a small west coast fishing village with two sandy beaches, is a popular rendezvous for sunset, and home to a famous singing family who play authentic *bouzoúki* music at their beachside taverna. North over the headland is **Delfíni Bay** for that all-over tan.

In the middle of the island, **Episkópio** boasts the oldest Byzantine church on Sýros, **Profítis Ilías**, prettily set in the pine-covered hills. The Orthodox Convent of **Ag. Barbára**, inland from Kíni, has a school of arts and crafts with needlework on sale. The walls of the church are decorated with frescoes depicting Barbára's martyrdom – her father locked her in a tower and put her to death, but immediately afterwards was struck down by a thunderbolt, making her the patron saint of bombardiers.

The foreign tourists who come concentrate in **Galissás**, which has the best sheltered beach on the island, a sweeping crescent of sand fringed by tamarisks, with the island's two campsites. You can hire sail boats; on shore, however, it's all mini-markets and heavy metal, backpackers and bikers. Nearby **Arméos** is for nudists. Further south, **Fínikas**, 'Phoenix', originally settled by the Phoenicians and mentioned in Homer, is another resort with a gritty roadside beach.

The grandees of Ermoúpolis built their ornate summer houses at **Dellagrácia** or **Posidonía**, a genteel resort with a serene film-set atmosphere of ornate Italianate mansions and pseudo-castles, and a blue church. Further south, quieter **Agathopés** has a sandy beach and islet opposite and you can take the track from here to **Kómito**, a stony stretch in front of an olive grove. **Mégas Gialós** is a pretty family resort, with shaded sands. **Vári** to the east, first settled in the Neolithic era, is now a major resort, but still has its fishing fleet. **Azólimnos** is particularly popular with the Syriani for its ouzeries and cafés, and has three hotels and some rooms.

Inland, **Chroússa** is a pleasant, pine-shaded village, home to more shipowners' villas, while nearby **Faneroméni** ('can be seen from everywhere') itself has panoramic views of the island.

Useful Information on Sýros

(i) Sýros >

:EOT: Dodekanesoú St, Ermoúpolis, by the bus station,
t 228 108 2375

Teamwork Travel Office, in the port, t 228 108 3400. Very helpful at organizing accommodation, travel, sailing and guided tours of Ermoúpolis, as well as car and bike rentals. Look out for *Welcome to Sýros*, a free booklet with good maps.

Sýros Festivals

Carnival: with dancing to the ancient *tasmboúna* and *toubí*, in Áno Sýros.

Last Sun in May: Celebrating the finding of the icon at Ag. Dimitríou.

June: Folklore festival in Azólimnos with 3 days of dancing, wine and song.

29 June: Ag. Pétros, Kíni.

Mid-July: Guitar Festival (classical and traditional).

27 July: Ag. Pantaleimónas, Fínikas.

Late July/Aug: Ermoúpoleia Arts Festival.

15 Aug: Karthí and Vári.

late Aug: Ag. Stéphanos, Galissás.

late Aug–Sept: Cyclades Music Festival.

24 Sept: Orthodox and Catholic celebration in Faneroméni.

Where to Stay and Eat in Sýros

★ Paradise >>

Sýros has stylish hotels in restored neoclassical buildings. A tempting option is to stay in town and head for a different beach every day, especially as prices in town are reasonable, with big discounts outside July and Aug. The **Rooms and Apartments Association**, t 228 108 7360, has a booth near the port and publishes an excellent booklet with a map.

Ermoúpolis ✉ 84100

Palladian, Stamatoú Proioú, just back from the waterfront, t 228 108 6400 (€€€€€). Stylish, with a quiet internal courtyard.

Arion, 4 Mavrokordátou, Vapória, t 228 108 1749, www.arionsyros.com (€€€€). Six luxurious rooms in a noble mansion, with pretty sea views.

Archontikó Voúrli, 5 Mavrokordátou, Vapória, t 228 108 1682 (€€€). Near the former, atmospheric rooms in mansion of 1888.

Diogenis, Papágou Square, just to the left of the ferries, t 228 108 6301 (€€€). Swish, with 43 neoclassical-style rooms.

Hermes, on the harbour near Plateía Kanári, t 228 108 3011 (€€€). Smart rooms with baths and balconies over the sea.

Omiros, 43 Omírou St, leading from Plateía Miaoúlis up to Áno Sýros, t 228 108 4910 (€€€). For deep pockets and strong legs, the pick of several on this street; a gorgeous 150-year-old neoclassical mansion, the elegantly restored family home of sculptor Vitalis.

Sea Colours Apartments, 10 Athinás St, on the north side of town, beyond Kanári Square, t 228 108 1181 (€€€). Luxurious and modern, with marble terraces and wonderful views.

Syrou Melathron, 5 Babagiotoú, Vapória, t 228 108 6495, www.syroumelathron.gr (€€€). Elegant captain's mansion with stately rooms and suites (all with Internet)and a roof garden with lovely views over town.

Ypatia, 3 Babagiotoú, t 228 108 3575 (€€€). Neoclassical mansion with brass bedsteads. Open summer only.

Avra Rooms, 7 Afrodíti, near to the port, t 228 108 2853 (€€). Friendly management, rooms with air-conditioning, TV and hair dryers.

Paradise, 3 Omírou, t 228 108 3204 (€€). Well-appointed rooms with a quiet flower-filled courtyard and fabulous roof terrace with views of the entire town.

Silvia's, 42 Omírou, t 228 108 1081 (€€). The rooms are elegantly furnished, good value and quiet, in yet another old mansion. Breakfast on the roof terrace with a nice view.

Sýros has a reputation for cooking – Greece's first cookbook was printed here in 1828. Culinary specialities include smoky San Michaeli cheese, loúza, salt pork, sausages and excellent Vátis wines – and there is no shortage of restaurants in which to find them.

Archontariki, just east of the main square, t 228 108 1744. One of the best of the many small tavernas lurking in the maze of small alleys here.

La Dolce Vita, 3 Filíni, t 228 108 6199 (€35). Since 2002, the former chef at Venice's Piccolo Martini has been enchanting the locals with imaginative Italian cuisine – fresh tagliatelle with boar and porcini mushrooms or even scallopine with coriander. Eves only, plus lunch in July and Aug.

Lilli's, Áno Sýros. Famous for its wonderful views, food (try the loúza) and rembétika at weekends.

Oinopnevmata ('Wine Breath'), 9 E. Roïdi, by the town hall. Handsome old building, and tasty dishes such as chicken cooked with capers and home-made desserts.

★ Plakostroto >

Ta Yiannena Psistaria, along the quay, **t** 228 108 2994. Roasts and barbecues, *kokorétsi*, chicken and some imaginative vegetable dishes too.

Thea, near Plateía Miaoúlis. For good food with a view, as the name suggests.

To Pétrino, **t** 228 108 7427. Just east of the main square. Excellent *mezédes*.

Apáno Meriá (North Sýros)
✉ 84100

There are good tavernas here, well worth the drive.

Plakostroto, Sa Micháli, **t** 697 398 0248. One of the best places to eat, and not expensive, serving delicious pork with thyme, kid, rabbit and other with stunning sunset views over Kýthnos and Kéa. *Open May–Oct daily; Nov–April weekends only.*

Sa Micháli, Sa Micháli, **t** 697 247 1681. Same view as Plakostroto, good food (especially good chips). *Open all year.*

Mytakas, Mytikas, **t** 228 108 2752. Wonderful taverna and grill. *Open July–Sept only.*

Kíni ✉ 84100
Sunset, right on the sea, **t** 228 107 1211 (€€). With fine views of you know what.

Harbor Inn, **t** 228 107 1377, *tboukas@otenet.gr* (€€–€). Six rooms close to the water.

Delfini's. Good place to enjoy delicious stuffed aubergines at twilight.

Zalonis. Taverna popular with locals, with sea views.

Galissás ✉ 84100
Dolphin Bay (Akti Delfiniou), **t** 228 104 2924, *www.dolphin-bay.gr* (€€€€€–€€€). Complex of apartments with everything from volleyball to a disco.

Benois, **t** 228 104 2833, *www.benois.gr* (€€). Newish, air-conditioned. *Open all year.*

Semiramis, near the beach, **t** 228 104 2067 (€€). Family-run.

Dendrinos, **t** 228 104 2469 (€€–€). Friendly, family-run place; the rooms have fridges.

Petros, also near the beach, **t** 228 104 2067 (€€–€).

Two Hearts Camping, **t** 228 104 2052/2321. With bungalows, mini-golf, and a minibus to meet ferries.

Iliovasílema, **t** 228 104 3325. Excellent seafood taverna. *Open Easter–Oct.*

Argo Café, next to the beach. Has live Greek music.

Posidonía and Around
✉ 84100

Eleana, on the beach, **t** 228 104 2601 (€€). Very pleasant, with lovely grounds to wander in.

Kokkina Beach, **t** 228 104 3010 (€€). A classic little holiday hotel.

Asotos Yios, on the road to Fínikas, **t** 228 104 3722. *Mezédes* and traditional cuisine and generous portions – try the rabbit in mavrodaphne wine. *Open June–Sept daily; Oct–May Fri and Sat only.*

Barbalias, Fínikas, on the water, **t** 228 104 2004. Serving excellent fish and meat dishes.

Chroussa, up in the little village of the same name. Excellent food – but dependent on the owner's mood; the menu changes weekly.

Entertainment and Nightlife in Sýros

There's no shortage of either on Sýros. The Ermoúpolis waterfront buzzes with a huge range of bars.

The evening *vólta* up and down Miaoúlis Square is still important; at one time the square was even specially paved so that the unmarried knew on which side to stroll to show they were available! Now much of the city's nightlife is concentrated in the surrounding streets, including **Clearchos**, a swanky piano bar, and the discos **Agora** and **Piramaïko**.

Apóllon Theatre, **t** 228 608 5192. For a cultural night out. Home to most events in the summer music festivals.

Pallas Outdoor Cinema, near the market. There is also a winter indoor cinema.

Aegean Casino, by the ferry port. British run; both the games tables and restaurant are the rage.

Rodo Club, 3 Arcimidous, 2km out of town, behind the Neórion shipyards. Trendy Ermoúpolis flocks to this half-ruined, half-beautifully restored building.

Tínos (ΤΗΝΟΣ)

If Délos was the sacred island of the ancient Greeks, Tínos, the Lourdes of Greece, occupies the same place in the hearts of their descendants. Ancient Délos probably had much the same atmosphere as Tínos – a harbour with a permanent carnival atmosphere, shaded *stoas* (here awnings over the street), and merchants selling holy pictures, *támata* (votives) and backscratchers to throngs of pilgrims. Beyond the pilgrims, Tínos is beautiful, dotted with 1,007 Venetian **dovecotes**, little white embroidered towers inhabited by clouds of white doves. You almost believe the locals when they say there's a hole in the ozone layer giving them a direct line to the Almighty – if chapels are God's phone booths, Tínos has one for every 10 inhabitants. Sinners disturbing the peace will be politely placed on the first ferry – to Tínos' glitzy neighbour, Sodom and Gomorrah.

 Dovecotes

History

Originally infested with vipers (its name comes from the Phoenician *Tunnoth*, 'snake'), Tínos was settled by the Ionians in Archaic times. A sanctuary of the sea god Poseidon was founded here in the 4th century, after he sent a flock of storks over to gobble up the snakes; pilgrims would come to be cured at the December festivals of the Poseidonia. Tínos had two ancient cities, both called Tínos, one at the site of the present town and the other at Exómbourgo. In his war with the Romans, Mithridates of Pontus destroyed both in 88 BC. After the Fourth Crusade, the Gizzi, the island's Venetian masters, built the fortress of Santa Elena at Exómbourgo, using the stone of the ancient acropolis and city. It was the strongest fortress of the Cyclades, and stood impregnable to 11 assaults by the Turks, including one by Barbarossa himself. In 1715, long after the rest of Greece had submitted to Ottoman rule, the Turks arrived in Tínos with a massive fleet. After sustaining a terrible attack, the Venetian captains decided that this time Santa Elena would not hold out, and, to the surprise of the Greeks, surrendered. The Turks allowed the Venetians to leave in safety, but back in Venice, where it was a crime to fail, the captains were put on trial for treason and executed. Meanwhile the Turks blew up Exómbourgo in case the Venetians should change their minds and come back.

Tínos was the Ottoman Empire's last territorial addition, but the Turks had only been there a century when a nun, Pelagía, had a vision of the Virgin directing her to a rock where she duly discovered an icon with extraordinary healing powers. It was 1822, the second year of the Greek War of Independence, and to Greek minds the icon was evidence of divine favour for their cause. A church, Panagía Evangelistría, was built over the spot where it was found and it quickly became the most important pilgrimage site in Greece, and a

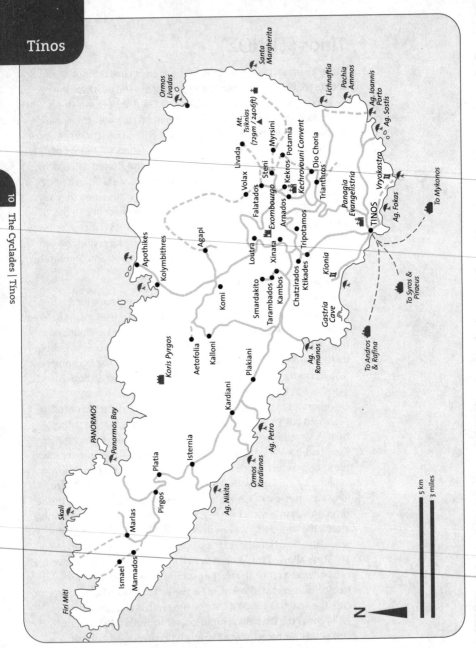

national shrine. On 15 August 1940, during the huge annual pilgrimage, an Italian submarine sneaked into the harbour and sank the Greek cruise boat *Elli* – a prelude to Mussolini's invasion of Greece. Under the Colonels' regime the entire island was declared holy, and women of Tínos had to wear skirts and behave at all times as if they were in church. No more.

Getting to and around Tínos

By sea: There are several daily **ferry**, **hydrofoil** and/or **catamaran** connections in summer with Piraeus, Rafína, Mýkonos, Sýros and Ándros; 5 times a week with Amorgós and the Back Islands via Náxos and Páros, 2–3 times a week with Thessaloníki and Skiáthos. In winter you'll get daily ships to Mýkonos, Ándros and Rafína, 3 to Sýros, and one or more to Anáfi, Folégandros, Íos, Kéa, Kythnos, Lávrio, Náxos, Páros, Piraeus, Santoríni and Síkinos. Note that ships between Tínos and Piraeus are often brim-full on weekends. There are two landing areas in operation, often simultaneously, so when departing be sure to check you find the right one. **Port authority: t** 228 302 2220.

By road: There's an excellent **bus** service all over the island from the big square near the Hotel Delfinia by the ferry dock, **t** 228 302 2440; and plenty of **taxis**, **t** 228 302 2470.

For **car and bike rental**, try **Vidalis**, 16 Aiavanou St, **t** 228 302 3400.

Tínos Town

As your ship pulls into Tínos, the outline of the yellow church **Panagía Evangelistría** and its neon-lit cross floats above the town. The modern Sacred Way, **Evangelistría Street**, becomes a solid mass of pilgrims on the two principal feast days of the Virgin, 25 March and especially 15 August, when, on average, 17,000 descend on Tínos and the ceremonies are broadcast on national television. The icon itself goes out for an airing in a jewelled pavilion, carried by Greek sailors and accompanied by a military band and national dignitaries. Many of the devout, elderly women in particular, cover the entire distance from the ferry to the church on all fours, with padded knees and arms, crawling in penance for the health of a loved one.

At other times, do as the Greeks do: buy an ice cream and wander up Evangelistría, perusing the stalls full of candles, tin *támata*, holy water bottles and one of the finest displays of kitsch this side of Italy; seashell frogs shoot pool merrily among the icons and Panagía thermometers. At the church, a red carpet covers the grand **marble stair**, where the only thing to do is join the queue to light a candle, kiss the icon and pray; the church employs men who do nothing all day but remove candles from the stands. Through the smoke and incense, the church glimmers like Aladdin's cave with hundreds of offerings: an orange tree made of silver and gold, lamps dangling ships (including one with a giant fish stuck in its side), heads, a foot, a truck and a bucket (blind pilgrims pledge to give the icon an effigy of whatever they first set eyes on). The icon itself, the **Megalóchari**, or Great Grace, is smothered in gold, diamonds and pearls.

Around the courtyards, **hostels** have been built for pilgrims waiting for dreams of the Virgin or to be healed by the icon, but there is still not enough room to house them, and the overflow camp patiently. The crypt, where Ag. Pelagía discovered the icon, is now the **Chapel of Evróseos** ('discovery'). Silver lines the spot in the rocks where the icon lay; the spring here is said to have healing water. Parents from all over Greece bring their children here in August to be baptized in the font. By the chapel the victims of the *Elli* are interred, next to a fragment of the fatal Fascist torpedo.

Panagía Evangelistría museums
all open summer 8–8; winter 8–6

Enough art has been donated for the Panagía to fill several museums: an **art gallery**, with works from the Ionian school, a reputed Rubens, a dubious Rembrandt partly hidden by the radiator and many 19th-century works; a **Lázarou Sóchou Museum** devoted to the works of the Tiniot sculptor, and above it the **Sculpture Museum** housing pieces by Greek sculptors such as Ioánnis Boúlgaros and Vitális; old icons in the **Byzantine Museum**; and another museum containing items used in the church service.

Archaeology Museum
t 228 302 2670; open Tues–Sun 8–3

There are more museums in town: parallel with Evangelistría Street, opposite a pine grove, the **Archaeology Museum** contains artefacts from the Sanctuary of Poseidon and Amphitrite, including a sundial (a copy of Ferekides' heliotrope on Sýros?), a broken sea monster and Archaic storage vessels.

Sanctuary of Poseidon and Amphitrite
t 228 302 2670; open Tues–Sun 8–2

The rest of the town is pretty much single-mindedly devoted to feeding and lodging pilgrims. From the port, buses go 4km west to **Kiónia** ('the columns'), with beaches and the **Sanctuary of Poseidon and Amphitrite**: bits remain of two temples, treasuries, fountains, baths and inns for pilgrims; votive offerings in the **museum** show that, like Evangelistría, Poseidon also was a great one for rescuing sailors, and his wife Amphitrite was known for granting fertility. Pilgrims to Délos often stopped here first to take a purifying bath.

Further west, there's a little beach under **Gastriá Cave** with its stalactites. East of town, the closest and busiest beach is shingly, nondescript **Ag. Fokás**; a few minutes further east, at **Vryókastro**, are the walls of an ancient settlement, and a Hellenistic tower. Further east at **Ag. Sóstis** the beach tends to be less crowded, but sandy **Ag. Ioánnis Pórto** is now a busy resort.

Around the Island

North of town, the 12th-century **Kechrovoúni Convent** is one of the largest in Greece, with 17 churches and lanes lined with cells – it looks more like a village. It is here that Sister Pelagía, canonized in 1971, had her two visions, in which the Virgin told her where to find the icon. You can visit her old cell, with her little bed and box containing her embalmed head. The nearby villages of **Arnádos** and **Dío Choriá** are real charmers.

Tínos may be the centre of Orthodox pilgrimage, but of all the Cyclades it has the highest percentage of Catholics. Between the mountains and ravines, Tínos is all sloping terraces, lush and green until May (it is one of the few Cyclades naturally self-sufficient in water) and golden-brown in the summer, brightened by the **dovecotes** and their white residents. Having a dovecote, once a privilege of the nobility (the doves gobbled the peasants' grain for free, and the master got nice plump birds for dinner and fertile guano to sell back to the peasants), was granted to all the islanders by the Venetians during their last decades on the island, and

everyone wanted one. Nests filled each nook and cranny created by
the intricate weave of stone slabs into geometrical patterns, stars
and suns; these days the doves, still prized for their fertilizer, are
usually pets instead of lunch.

Dovecotes decorate all the villages encircling **Exómbourgo**
(640m/2,100ft), the great rocky throne of the Venetian fortress of
Santa Elena; only ruined houses, a fountain and three churches
remain inside the walls, which afford a superb view over neighbouring islands, the Aegean, and Tínos's 50 villages. The road goes up
from **Kámbos**, seat of the Catholic archdiocese. From here, too, you
can walk to the site of one of the two 8th-century BC towns called
Tínos, where a large building and Geometric-era temple were
discovered, and head up the valley to the charming villages of
Smardákito and **Tarambádos**, with the island's most beautiful
dovecotes. North of Exómbourgo, pretty **Loutrá** has a 17th-century
Jesuit monastery where a school is run by the Ursulines; the Jesuits
have assembled a **Museum of Folk Art** from objects of everyday life
supplied by the villagers.

Museum of Folk Art
*open summer only,
10.30–3.30; adm*

For wild scenery, continue around to little **Vólax**, where basket-
makers work in a landscape of granite outcrops and weird rock
formations. **Mount Tskniás**, looming above, is no mere mountain
but the tomb of Calais and Zetes, the sons of Boreas the north wind,
who puffed so hard that Jason and the Argonauts could not land to
rescue Hercules at Mysia; the furious Hercules later killed them and
buried them here, setting up the sombre crags as a marker. To this
day the north wind keeps Tínos cool, even in August. From **Kómi**,
another pretty village, a long valley runs down to the sea at
Kolymbíthres, a horseshoe bay with sandy beaches.

A paved road follows the mountainous ridge overlooking the
southwest coast. At **Kardianí** a driveable track winds down to a
remote beach; otherwise, from **Istérnia**, a pleasant village with plane
trees, you can drive down to popular **Ormós** or **Ag. Nikíta Beach**, the
latter with rooms and tavernas. Often gusty, northern Tínos is
famous for its green marble, and has a long tradition in working the
stone, with some examples in Istérnia in its **sculpture museum**.

Sculpture museum
open Tues–Sun 10–3

Several Greek artists came from or have worked in **Pírgos**, a large
traditional village, with a small **Museum of Tinian Artists** and the
residence of sculptor **Giannolís Halépas**. The old grammar school,
built in the first flush of Greek independence, is now a **School of Fine
Arts**. A shop near the main square exhibits and sells students' works
– two-headed Byzantine eagles are popular.

**Giannolís Halépas
Residence**
*open April–Oct daily
10–2 and 5–7.30; adm*

Below Pírgos, buses continue down to the beach at **Pánormos Bay**,
with a good fish taverna and rooms. **Marlás**, north, is in the centre of
the old marble quarries. From the wild, barren northwest tip of Tínos
it's only one nautical mile to the island of **Ándros**; watch the red
sunsets from here and be bowled over, by the drama – and the wind.

Useful Information on Tínos

Tínos has its own website, *www. pigeon.gr*, updated every few months.

Tourist police: 5 Plateía L. Sóchou, **t** 228 302 3670.

Tínos Mariner Travel Agency, on the waterfront, Tínos Town, **t** 228 302 3193. Very helpful.

Hotels Association: t 228 302 4159.

Rooms Association: t 228 302 5887.

Tínos Festivals

25 Mar and **15 Aug**: at the Panagía Evangelistría, Greece's two largest.

50 days after Greek Easter (i.e. mid-June): Ag. Triáda at Kardianí.

29 Aug: Ag. Ioánnes at Kómi (Catholic).

Where to Stay on Tínos

Tínos Town ✉ 84200

To witness the greatest Greek pilgrimage, make sure you've booked for 14–15 Aug, but don't expect any elbow room. At other times, room-owners greet ferries. Most of the hotels have sites on *www.inntinos.gr*.

Cavos, at Ag. Sóstis, near the sea, **t** 228 302 4224, *www.cavos-tinos.com* (€€€€€–€€€). Airy studios and bungalows.

Porto Tango, at Ag. Ioánnis Pórto, **t** 228 302 4411, *www.portotango.gr* (€€€€€–€€€). All the major comforts; tennis, pool, and Turkish bath. *Open all year.*

Alonia, 2km east of town, **t** 228 302 3541 (€€€). In a verdant spot with springs.

Golden Beach, at Ag. Fókas, **t** 228 302 2579, *www.goldenbeachtinos.gr* (€€€). Offers well-furnished studios and a shuttle bus into town.

Tinion, on the left of the harbour as you sail in, **t** 228 302 2261, *www. tinionhotel.gr* (€€€–€€). The *grande dame* of Tínos' hotels; elegant and air-conditioned.

Vincenzo Rooms, **t** 228 302 2612, *vincenzo@pigeon.gr* (studios €€€, rooms €€). Friendly owners, who know everything about Tínos, will give you a warm welcome and, if they like your

kids, they'll even babysit. There's a pool with a Jacuzzi.

Aeolos Bay, overlooking Ag. Fokás Beach, **t** 228 302 3339 (€€). Smart, friendly hotel with a pool.

Aphrodite, **t** 228 302 3556 (€€). Handy for ferries.

Argo, a little out of town, by the sea at Agiali, **t** 228 302 2588 (€€). Another good bet.

Delfinia, on the waterfront, near the port, **t** 228 302 2288 (€€). Central and comfortable.

Favie-Suzanne, inland, **t** 228 302 2693 (€€). Pleasant owners and rooms.

Leandros, 4 L. Lamera, **t** 228 302 3545 (€€). A favourite, with friendly owners.

Nikoleta, **t** 228 302 4719 (€). Rooms surrounding a charming courtyard with common kitchen and friendly owner.

Camping Tínos, south of town, **t** 228 302 2344 or **t** 228 302 3548. A good site.

Eating Out on Tínos

The restaurants are better than the mediocre waterfront efforts might suggest. Try something with the island's famous stinky garlic, which Aristophanes recommended for improving eyesight.

Tínos Town ✉ 84200

Metaxi Mas, **t** 228 302 5945. The most popular place, with tasty *saganáki* and vegetable fritters, stewed lamb and more.

Ballís, by the port, **t** 228 302 3207. A lively taverna open till very late, serving local dishes and tasty beef with mushrooms.

Palea Pallada, near the fish market, **t** 228 302 3516. With guess what on the menu; also good for grills.

To Koutouki tis Elenis, 5 Safoú, **t** 228 302 4857. Tiniot specialities, including tomatoes fried in batter.

Apodrasi in Steni, **t** 228 304 1934. Nice taverna with rooms (€) to let.

Ormós ✉ 84200

To Thalassaki, **t** 228 303 1366. Superb seafood (€25) using the finest ingredients in all dishes – well worth driving out for. *Open Easter–Oct.*

The Dodecanese

Furthest from mainland Greece, the Dodecanese (the '12 islands', although there are around 16 inhabited ones) weren't added to Greece until 1948. Their distance from the mainland, and long separation from the mainstream of Greek history, have dealt them a unique deck to play with – medieval knights, Ottoman Turks and 20th-century Italians, all of whom contributed to their distinct character. Add a sunny climate, long, sandy beaches and the striking individualism of each island, and the holiday possibilities on the Dodecanese are infinite.

11

Don't miss

⭐ **Crusader memories**
Old Town, Rhodes
p.411–13

⭐ **Holy beauty**
Monastery of St John, Pátmos **p.395**

⭐ **Rock-climbing and diving**
Kálymnos **p.356**

⭐ **A climb up 375 'Good Stairs'**
Kalí Stráta, Sými **p.432**

⭐ **Walking around a hot volcanic crater**
Nissyros **pp.390–91**

See map overleaf

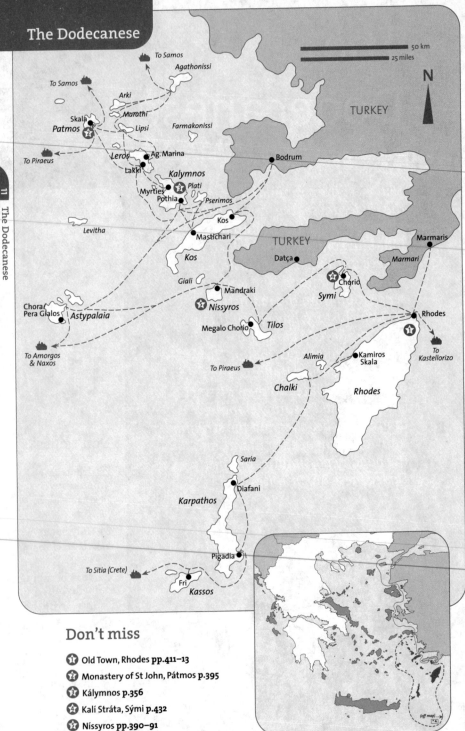

The Dodecanese

50 km
25 miles

N

To Samos
Agathonissi

To Samos
Arki
Marathi
Skala
Lipsi
Patmos
Farmakonissi

TURKEY

To Piraeus
Leros
Ag. Marina
Lakki
Kalymnos
Myrties
Plati
Pothia
Pserimos
Bodrum

Kos
Mastichari

Kos
TURKEY
Datça
Marmaris

Giali
Marmari

Chora/
Pera Gialos
Astypalaia
Mandraki
Nissyros
Megalo Chorio
Tilos
Chorio
Symi

Rhodes

To Amorgos
& Naxos

To Piraeus
Alimia
Kamiros
Skala
To
Kastellorizo

Chalki
Rhodes

Saria
Diafani

Karpathos

Pigadia

To Sitia (Crete)
Fri
Kassos

(off map)

Don't miss

⭐ Old Town, Rhodes pp.411–13
⭐ Monastery of St John, Pátmos p.395
⭐ Kálymnos p.356
⭐ Kalí Stráta, Sými p.432
⭐ Níssyros pp.390–91

The range of islands in the Dodecanese (ΔΩΔΕΚΑΝΗΣΑ) runs the gamut from the feverish high-calibre international resorts of **Rhodes** and **Kos** to the low-key, very Greek pleasures of **Lipsí, Chálki, Tílos** or **Níssyros**, and one bright white Cycladic rock pile, **Astypálaia**. Striking **Sými** and **Pátmos** attract upmarket crowds; while **Léros, Kálymnos** and **Kárpathos** lie somewhere in between. **Kastellórizo** has an end-of-the-world atmosphere that draws more people every year; **Kássos** has a similar air but attracts nobody, if you're looking for a real getaway. Connections by sea and air are good between the islands.

History

The Dodecanese flourished early in antiquity, populated by the elusive Carians (from Caria, on the nearby coast of Asia Minor). They were either subjugated by, or allies of, the seafaring Minoans, a connection reflected in the islands' myths. When Minoan Crete fell, the Mycenaeans took over and many of the Dodecanese sent ships to the Trojan War. In the various invasions that followed the fall of Troy, Aeolians, Ionians and Dorians swept through. By the Archaic period the last arrivals, the Dorians, had formed themselves into powerful city-states, particularly on Rhodes and Kos – states so prosperous that they established colonies and trading counters in Italy, France and Spain. The Persians were the next to invade, but, once they were defeated at Salamis in 480 BC, the Dodecanese joined the maritime league at Délos as a hedge against further attacks. Their greater distance from Athens automatically gave them more autonomy than the other islands, and they produced a dazzling array of artists, scientists and intellectuals – including Hippocrates, the father of medicine.

After the death of Alexander the Great, his general, Ptolemy of Egypt, inherited the Dodecanese, leading to one of the greatest sieges in antiquity, when a rival general, Antigohos, sent his son Dimitrios to take Rhodes. Emboldened by its victory over Dimitrios, Rhodes erected its proud Colossus (290 BC) and made an alliance with Rome, enabling her to acquire her own little empire of Greek islands. Some 200 years later Rome sent Jesus' disciple John into exile to another Dodecanese island, Pátmos, where he converted the inhabitants and got his own back by penning the *Book of Revelations*, where Rome comes out as no less than 'Babylon the Great, Mother of Harlots and of earth's abominations'.

In 1095, the islands had their first taste of a more aggressive brand of Christianity, when Crusaders *en route* to the Holy Land made them a port of call. The Crusaders' odd bit of pillaging and piracy in Byzantine lands culminated in the capture of Constantinople, on Venice's orders, in 1204; but in 1291 the tables turned when Jerusalem fell to the Ottomans. This disrupted, among other things, the work of the Knights of St John (also known as the Knights

Hospitallers), an exclusive order made up of the second and third sons of Western Europe's aristocracy, who took vows of chastity, poverty and obedience, and operated a hospital in Jerusalem for pilgrims. Forced to leave, the Knights, who were never really poor in spite of their vows, purchased the Dodecanese from a Genoese pirate, Admiral Vinioli. They set up headquarters on Rhodes and built a new hospital, town walls and castles; they fortified the smaller islands as well, and communicated with each other by means of carrier pigeon and smoke signals. They patrolled the islands and coast in swift vessels made on Sými, letting Christian pirates pass through their territory unmolested, but hijacking ships carrying Muslim pilgrims. In 1522 Sultan Suleiman the Magnificent had had enough and attacked Rhodes with an enormous army. All the men of the Dodecanese rallied to its defence, but after a bitter siege the Knights were betrayed by a disgruntled German and forced to surrender (*see* pp.407–408).

Turkish occupation of the Dodecanese lasted until 1912, when Italy opportunistically took 'temporary possession' of the islands. This occupation was made permanent after the Greek Asia Minor débâcle by the second Treaty of Lausanne (1923). Mussolini poured money into his new colonies, sponsoring massive public works, reforestation, archaeological excavations and historical reconstructions. While Turkish rule had been depressing, negligent and sometimes brutal, the Fascists, in spite of lavish expenditure, were even worse in the eyes of the islanders for outlawing their religion and language, to the extent that even today you can find older people on the islands who are more comfortable speaking Italian.

With Italy's surrender in 1943, Churchill sent in British troops to withstand German occupation, but lacked sufficient numbers to do the job. In May 1945 the British returned in the subsequent vacuum; many islanders claim to this day that Churchill meant the British occupation to be as 'temporary' as the Italian, but a treaty of 1945, ratified in March 1948, united them with Greece. The union has yet to be recognized by Turkey, which never signed the second Treaty of Lausanne and claims the Dodecanese weren't Italy's to concede, although the former climate of mistrust has now eased.

Astypálaia (ΑΣΤΥΠΑΛΑΙΑ)

Butterfly-shaped Astypálaia, the most westerly of the Dodecanese, offers the perfect transition from the Cyclades. It has dazzling sugar-cube houses spilling down from the citadel, but it also has a fertile, Dodecanesian valley called Livádi, which led Homer to nickname it 'the Table of the Gods'. The sheltered nooks and crannies of its wildly indented coastline sport average beaches but are full of seafood – in

Getting to and around Astypálaia

By air: There are 4 flights a week from Athens, and others in summer to and from Rhodes, Kos and Léros: book early in season. **Olympic Airways**, t 224 306 1588; **airport** t 224 306 1410. Buses run between Péra Gialós, Chóra and the airport; a **taxi** costs around €12.

By sea: **Ferry** connections run 4 times a week with Piraeus, 3 times a week with Kos, twice a week with Rhodes, Kálymnos, Náxos, Sýros, Páros and Amorgós, once a week with Donoússa; there is also a **hydrofoil** once a week from Rhodes. **Port authority**: t 224 306 1208.

By road: There are 2 **buses** a day between Péra Gialós, Chóra, Livádia and Maltezána. **Taxis** have set prices posted by the stand. In Péra Gialós, hire a **car** or **motorbike** at **Lakis & Manolis Motocenter**, t 224 306 1263, *astycar@otenet.gr*, or **Vergoulis**, t 224 306 1351.

---

ancient times Astypálaia was called Ichthyoessa, 'fishy island'. Now much of it goes straight to Athens, so much so that the fish at many tavernas is frozen. A tiny airport offers the chance to skip the long ferry slog from Piraeus or hops from Kos. Although you'll need to book well in advance for a room in August, Astypálaia remains a jovial, very Greek island that moseys along at its own pace.

History

Astypálaia means 'old city', but mythology claims that the name is derived from a sister of Europa. In Classical times the island was

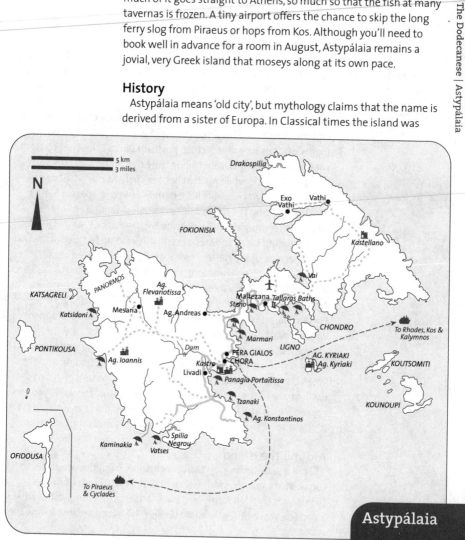

Astypálaia

most famous for its lack of snakes and a tragically short-tempered boxer named Kleomedes, who, when competing in the Olympics, killed his opponent, which even then was enough to merit instant disqualification. Kleomedes returned to Astypálaia seething with rage and took his disappointment out on the local school, knocking it down and killing all the pupils.

Sacked by the Turks under Umur Pasha in 1334, the island was deserted by decades, until it was purchased by the Venetian Giovanni Querini in 1414, who declared himself the 'Count of Stampalia' (as the Venetians mangled the island's name). After a raid by Barbarossa in 1537, it came under direct Turkish rule.

Péra Gialós and Chóra

Astypálaia's capital consists of two parts: Péra Gialós or Skála, the port and business end and haunt of a pair of pelicans, the fishermen's mascots, and Chóra, the old town, which curls gracefully down from the Venetian castle to a sandy beach. The **Archaeology Museum** in **Péra Gialós** contains finds from the Kástro as well as four Mycenaean tombs discovered by shepherds, a horde of Classical silver coins, classical steles, a 6th-century Byzantine chancel screen and the Querini coat of arms. Up the character- and thigh-building flights of steps (or road), picture-postcard **Chóra** is marked by eight windmills standing sentinel along the ridge of the butterfly wing. Many of the little whitewashed houses sport wooden balconies (*poúndia*). Halfway up, nine little barrel-vaulted chapels are stuck together holding the bones of Chóra's oldest families, many of whom were brought from Tínos and Mýkonos by Giovanni Querini.

The winding lanes and steps eventually lead up to **Querini Kástro**. On either side of the narrow entrance, a pair of new buttresses support the high walls; among the ruined houses (100 families lived here until an earthquake in 1956) are two bright white churches: **Ag. Geórgios**, on the site of an ancient temple, and **Panagía Portaïtíssa**, one of the most beautiful in the Dodecanese, topped with a powder-blue dome and lavishly decorated inside with intricate designs and a carved wooden shrine highlighted with gold leaf. Archaeologists have dug up much of the rest, finding ancient lanes, temple foundations and a sophisticated system of drains dating back to the 6th century BC. From the top of the walls you can appreciate what a tight corset squeezes Astypálaia's middle, and if it's clear you can make out Amorgós and Santoríni on the horizon.

Archaeology Museum
t 224 3061 500, open Tues–Sun 8.30–3; adm

Querini Kástro
open Mon–Fri 8–1

Around the Island

Set in a wide lush valley, **Livádi** is downhill from the windmills to the west; its shingly, sandy beach gets busy with Greek families. Little roads through farms lead back to the barren mountains, where a dam creates a little lake that supplies the island's water. Follow the coast to the south and you can cast your clothes to the wind at **Tzanáki Beach**, or continue along the track to **Ag. Konstantínos**, one of the island's best beaches, with a good taverna; other sandy strands are at **Vátses** (with a stalactite cave, **Negroú**, just behind) and **Kaminákia**, in a lovely bay with a good summer taverna, now attainable by a dirt road. Another unpaved road, starting at the windmills, goes to the **Monastery of Ag. Flevariótissa** (a track on the right) and to **Ag. Ioánnis** on the west coast, a lush spot with orchards, an excellent beach, a whitewashed church and a ruined Byzantine castle – supposedly impregnable, where the islanders took refuge from Barbarossa, only to be slaughtered.

The paved road north of Skála passes a few beaches, all called **Mármari**. Just over on the north coast, ferries dock at **Ag. Andréas** if the wind is up. The road passes over the waist of the butterfly, or Stenó (barely 50 yards wide at its narrowest point), and ends up near the airport at **Análypsi**, or **Maltezána**, once the lair of Maltese pirates and resettled under the Italians. There's a monument to the French Captain Bigot, who in 1827, during the War of Independence, came to rout the pirates and died when he set fire to his corvette to avoid capture. The chapel of **Ag. Várvara** was built over Paleo-Christian mosaics and has bits from a temple of Artemis. The next cove is popular with naturists; on the fringe of the olive groves, look out for the remains of the Hellenistic **Tallarás baths**, unique in Greece with their blue, yellow and white well-preserved floor mosaics, showing the zodiac and seasons. On the far wing, a dirt road passes **Kastéllano**, built by the Italians between the wars, on its way to **Vathí**, a tiny fishing hamlet heading a deep, fjord-like bay, although it is most easily reached by boat.

Useful Information on Astypálaia

(i) **Astypálaia** >
Municipal tourist office: booth by the port (opens when ferries arrive); or in a windmill at Chóra, t 224 306 1412; open June–Sept 9.30–1 and 6–9

Astypalea Tours, t 224 306 1588, under the Vivamare Hotel. Very helpful.

Astypálaia Festivals

14–16 Aug: Panagía Portaïtíssa, up in Chóra.

Where to Stay and Eat on Astypálaia

Most of the following are listed on the website *www.astypalaia.com*.
If you're feeling ill, eat the local snails; in ancient times they were said to have curative powers.

Péra Gialós ✉ 85900

Paradissos, t 224 306 1224, *www.astypalea-paradissos.com* (€€€). Typical new hotel, right on the sea. *Open April–Oct.*

Afroditi Studios, above the harbour, t 224 306 1478 (€€–€). Good port- and sea views from the verandas, pleasant studios including phone.

Astynea, right on the port, t 224 306 1209 (€€–€). Fine rooms with balconies.

Maistrali Studios, t 224 306 1691 (€€–€). Attractive studios sleeping up to four in classic island style; with a good restaurant, *open all year.*

Vivamare, inland from the harbour, t 224 306 1571 (€€–€). Simple studios with TVs and good views thrown in.

Camping Astypálaia, by a beach 2.5km from town, t 224 306 1900 or t 697 303

7710. A minibus usually meets ferries; the site has a taverna.

Akti, t 224 306 1114. In a romantic setting, serving fresh fish from the owner's caique, tasty octopus stew and baked rabbit. *Open May–Sept.*

Astypalaia, t 224 306 1275. Good simple taverna with excellent home cooking. *Open Easter–Nov.*

Chóra ✉ 85900

⭐ **Studios Kilindra >**

Studios Kilindra, t 224 306 1131 (€€€). The island's most beautiful accommodation, with lots of traditional touches, proper kitchens, TV, Internet, verandas with sea views, and pool. *Open all year.*

Kallichoron, t 224 306 1935 (€€€–€€). Handsome new complex of well-equipped studios and apartments, sleeping up to four with Internet, verandas and more.

Kostas Vaikousis, just under the Kástro, **t** 224 306 1430 (€€€–€€). Two charming traditional houses for 2–6 people. Kostas can usually be found in the antique shop at the port.

To Spiti tou Kastrou, by the Kástro, **t** 697 759 4703 (€€€–€€). A traditional house, with traditional furnishings sleeping up to four people.

Anatoli Studios, t 224 306 1289 (€€–€). Classic style and soaring castle views.

Barbarossa, by town hall, **t** 224 306 1577. A surprise – multi-ethnic cuisine served on a pretty terrace – curries, pork roll with prunes, home-made ice cream.

Livádi ✉ 85900

Architetoniki, Ag. Basíleios, **t** 224 306 1339 (€€€). Tasteful new complex.

Gerani, 30m from the beach, **t** 224 306 1484, *gerani72@hotmail.com* (€). Attractive studios and restaurant serving tasty home-made dishes and fish, served on its airy tamarisk terrace.

Michelis, on the beach, **t** 224 306 1521. Fresh fish and good stewed vegetable dishes. *Open April–Oct.*

Maltezána ✉ 85900

Maltezana Beach, t 224 306 1558, *www.maltezanabeach.gr* (€€€–€€). Handsomely furnished and well equipped apartments, studios, family suites and rooms. *Open June–mid Sept.*

Maltezana Rooms, t 224 306 1446 (€). Pleasant new rooms a stone's throw from the sea.

Ovelix, t 224 306 1260 (€). Basic studios sleeping three, and a restaurant.

Almyra, overlooking the sea, **t** 224 306 1451. Pretty place offering good seafood dishes and fresh fried potatoes. *Open June–Sept.*

Chálki (ΧΑΛΚΗ)

Arid and rocky, with its neoclassical houses overlooking a horseshoe harbour, Chálki is a miniature version of nearby Sými. Although there are excursions from nearby Rhodes, it doesn't suffer from Sými's surfeit of daytrippers – there really isn't that much to do in a few hours, anyway. The name, often spelled 'Hálki' to prevent English-speakers from saying 'Chalky', comes from *chalkí*, 'copper', which used to be mined here. Although the 250 islanders (many of whom are fishermen) are outnumbered ten to one by foreigners they are famous for keeping music traditions alive, on special occasions improvising *matinádes* in 15-syllable verses.

In 1983, Chálki was designated the 'Island of Peace and Friendship of Young People of All Nations' under a joint UNESCO and Greek government scheme. The idea was to launch an international youth centre, and there was an allied project to renovate houses that had been left to crumble after the mass exodus after 1916, when the Italians curtailed sponge-fishing, the island's former source of income. A hotel was built to house visiting bureaucrats, but the

Getting to and around Chálki

There are **ferries** 3–4 times a week with Rhodes; twice a week with Piraeus (taking 30hrs!), Kárpathos and Kássos, and once a week with Kos, Kálymnos, Mílos, Santoríni, and Crete (Heráklion, Sitía and Ag. Nikólaos). A daily **caique** runs to and from Kámiros Skála, Rhodes, (t 224 604 5220, connecting with the bus (stop by the taverna) to Rhodes Town (take the bus labelled 'Kritinia'). **Port authority: t** 224 604 5220. The island has one **water taxi** and one **car taxi**, usually located by the post office.

scheme soured as youths and bureaucrats alike abused the little island's hospitality. Peace and friendship between Chálki and UNESCO are at a definite end. Since then tourism has grown, and other owners have returned to convert their ruined homes into villas, studios and apartments.

Emborió and Around

Emborió, Chálki's port and town, with the usual Mussolini-era customs house, is often sleepy by day, but its bars and tavernas buzz after dark when everyone gathers, often leading to impromptu parties. The vast church of **Ag. Nikólaos** was built when the island's population was 6,000; it has the tallest campanile in the Dodecanese and new mellifluous bells as well as a pebble mosaic courtyard, a lovely interior and a little **museum**.

Ag. Nikólaos museum
open Tues and Fri 6–7pm, Sun 11–12; adm

From Emborió, a 15-minute walk along Boulevard Tarpon Springs (the Florida sponge-fishing town, home to many second- and third-generation Chálkians) leads to **Póndamos Beach**, the island's only sandy strand and constantly being enlarged by locals – although arrive early in the morning if you want a chance of a sunbed. It's a 45-minute walk up to **Chorió**, the ghost-town capital of Chálki, abandoned in 1950, where the church of the **Panagía** (*usually locked*) has a few Byzantine frescoes. Another 10 minutes further up, the Knights of St John built their *kástro* (with the arms of Grand Master Pierre d'Aubusson over the gate) on the earlier acropolis and recycled most of the ancient building stone. The main building in the walls is a church, with some more Byzantine frescoes, which was probably dedicated to St Nikólaos, who according to an old legend stopped to rest on Chálki. On a very clear day there are stunning views down to Kárpathos and even to Crete.

A paved road from Póndamos makes the once long trek to the **Monastery of Ag. Ioánnis Pródromos** much easier, or you can hike there in the late afternoon (3–5hrs) and stay overnight in one of the cells, bringing your own provisions. A track from Emborió descends in half an hour to the pebbly cove of **Kánia** with its shady fig trees – near the power plant.

Local excursions offer a day and lunch on the isle of **Alimniá**, between Chálki and Rhodes, with another Crusader castle, a couple of tiny sandy coves and a deep harbour where Italian submarines hid in the Second World War. Seven British Special Boat commandoes

Useful Information on Chálki

Chálki at long last has an ATM, but it can run dry, like the water, which has to be imported from Rhodes; make sure you always have a spare bottle.

Zifos Travel, t 224 604 5082, *zifos-travel@rho.forthnet.gr*. Also has rooms.

Chálki Festivals

15 Aug: Panagía, Chorió.

29 Aug: Ag. Ioánnis Pródromos.

14 Sept: Stávros.

Where to Stay on Chálki

Emborió ✉ 85110

Most accommodation is taken up by tour operators; book early.

Villa Praxithea, by the sea – you can fish from the veranda, t 224 607 0172, *www.villapraxithea.com* (€€€€). Restored neoclassical villa with two lovely apartments sleeping up to eight, rented by the week; the same owners have also restored the **Villa Aristea** (*www.villa-aristea.com*).

 ★ Captain's House >

Captain's House, t 224 604 5201 (€€). Small but welcoming turn-of-the-century Chálki mansion; three lovely rooms with en suite bathrooms and fridges; run with nautical precision by Alex Sakellarides, ex-Greek Royal Navy, and his English wife Christine – there's even a crow's nest. Breakfast is served on the terrace beneath the trees.

Kleanthi, near the school, t 224 604 5334 (€€). Rooms and studios in a traditional stone house. *Open April–Oct.*

Chalki, t 224 604 5208 (€). Basic, municipal-run hotel in a converted olive works near the beach.

Markos, t 224 604 5347 (€). Newer furnished flats.

Eating Out on Chálki

Houvardas. Good eaterie, popular with yacht people, but the standard depends on who's in the kitchen.

Omonia. Fine taverna, the place for fresh fish, seafood and grills. One of the only to take credit cards.

Parrot Bar, with parrots. Very friendly and does light food as well.

Pondamos Taverna, a step from the sands. Popular lunchtime haunt.

Remezzo. Mostly pizza.

Theodosia's. Famous for walnut cake and ice cream. Chálki also has an exceptional bakery run by Dimitris, with bread, pies, and honey pancakes.

---

sent here to scupper the submarines in 1943 were captured by the Nazis, then taken to Rhodes and Thessaloníki and executed. You can see the machine-gun strafing on the walls of the ruined houses as well as German and Italian graffiti of submarines. Although it has a better water supply than Chálki, the islanders upped sticks in 1960, leaving Alimniá to sheep, goats and barbecuing holidaymakers.

Kálymnos (ΚΑΛΥΜΝΟΣ)

Craggy, wildly indented Kálymnos is a breath of fresh air – an island where visitors are welcome but where carpenters still hammer, tailors still stitch, and the old spicy Greek smell of coffee and herbs still fills the streets, even in winter when many other islands look forlorn. The land also strikes an equilibrium: emerald valleys wedged under sheer cliffs (the island's highest point, Mount Profítis Ilías, is the driest spot in all the Dodecanese) sweep down to mini-fjords and sandy beaches. Sailing into craggy Kálymnos under a full moon rising is sublime. Rock-climbers adore it.

Getting to Kálymnos

By air: The long-awaited airport at Kantoúni opened in Aug 2006, and has twice daily links with Athens.
By sea: Daily **ferries** to Piraeus, Rhodes, Kos, Léros, and Pátmos; 4–5 weekly to other Dodecanese, Sámos, Ámorgos, Donoússa, Sýros, Náxos, Páros, Mykonos, Lésvos, Límnos, and to ALexandroúpolis and Thessaloníki. Summer **hydrofoil** and **catamaran** connections with Kos, Rhodes, Sými, Tílos, Níssyros, Léros, Lipsí, Pátmos,and Sámos. Daily boats to Psérimos, Platí and Vathí, daily caique from Myrtiés to Xirókambos (Léros); 3 ferries a day from Mastichári (Kos). **Port authority**: t 224 302 9304.

Getting around Kálymnos

Local **caiques** go from Myrtiés to Télendos islet.
The **bus station** in Pothiá is next to the domed Dimarchíon. **Buses** run every hour to Myrtiés and Massoúri, 5 times a day to Vlycháda, 3–4 to Vathí, Árgos, Platís Gialós and Emborió.
Taxi prices are posted; the main rank in Pothiá is up Venizélou St, in Plateía Kýprou, t 224 305 0300.

But Kálymnos is an island of tough *hombres* and mad daring. It has Greece's last fleet of sponge-divers (although many have now switched to deep sea fishing, whose superior equipment and divers have raised serious issues with both fishermen from nearly islands and environmentalists). A couple of boats have been refitted for local diving excursions, which the island is promoting alongside rock-climbing. The sea bed has numerous wrecks (including many old sponge boats) and recently has yielded more than its share of surprises in fishermen's nets: the lovely 4th-century BC bronze *Lady of Kálymnos* (now in Athens' Archaeology Museum) founded in 1994, and a bronze horseman and an amphora in 2006. But things have been popping up on land, too: in 2001, shepherds found a trove of sculpture that the Christians had buried in a pit under one of their oldest basilicas. Among the finds are a 6th-century BC *kouros* (an unusual one, clothed), an Asklepios and a hermaphrodite. The mayor of Kálymnos fought hard to keep them on the island and succeeded: look in the near future for the Kalymnian marbles in a new museum.

History

In myth, Ouranos (Heaven) angrily flung Kalydnos, one of his sons by Gaia (Earth), into the sea, and the bits of him that stuck out of the water became the Kalydna islands; Kálymnos was the largest. Mycenaean Argos colonized the island; the later Dorians built their city just northeast of Pothiá, at Dímos. An ally of Persia, Halicarnassus (on the nearby mainland, home of the famous Mausoleum) ruled the island at the beginning of the 5th century BC, but after Persia's defeat Kálymnos joined the maritime league at Délos.

Kálymnos next enters history in the 11th century, when the Seljuks launched a sudden attack and killed almost everyone. The Vinioli of Genoa then occupied Kálymnos and sold it to the Knights of St John, although in 1522 they abandoned it to succour Rhodes. Under the Italians, attempts to make the Orthodox church toe the Fascist line and close down the Greek schools resulted in fierce opposition, and prominent citizens were either jailed or exiled. The women of Kálymnos, who over the centuries had become fiercely independent with their menfolk away at sea, held protest marches in Pothiá, and painted everything in sight blue and white.

Pothiá

Lively Pothiá, the third largest city in the Dodecanese, is wrapped around hills over the port, topped by white churches hanging over cliffs as dry as biscuits. If you arrive by sea, you'll be greeted by two of the island's 43 bronzes by local sculptors Michaíl Kókkinos and his daughter Irene: a *Poseidon* by the Olympic Hotel and the waterfront *Winged Victory*, with the history of sponge-diving in relief. Next to the town hall, the **Maritime Museum** offers a fascinating look at sponge-diving. Among the displays of old diving suits and apparatus are the 15kg flat marble or granite stones (*skandalópetra*) that were attached by a rope to the boat and gave the diver some control over the direction and speed of his descent; he could tie the *skandalópetra* to his ankle to free his hands to gather the sponges in a net. Each diver shaped and polished his own. And that was it; the first divers dived naked, and stayed down as long as 5 minutes.

The police occupy the Italian-made municipal **palace** that once served as the governor's mansion, its dome rivalled by the silver domes of 18th-century cathedral **Chrístos Sotíros**, full of works by local painters. Pothiá's oldest quarter is just behind here; by the Italian administration buildings is the world's only **sponge-diving school**. Perhaps not surprisingly, Pothiá has an excellent **hospital** (with the best hyperbaric chamber in the eastern Mediterranean) and one of Greece's few **orphanages**, where Orthodox priests used to choose a dowryless bride. On the waterfront, culture gets a say in the **Muses Reading Room**, with its Corinthian columns and bronze reliefs, founded in 1904 as a club to further Greek education and identity during the Turkish occupation. The Italians destroyed the Greek books and turned it into the Café Italia; the club restarted in 1946, and in 1978 the building was restored to house historical documents and books, including some in English.

Lovely old mansions and walled orchards rise along the city's back lanes. A five-minute walk up from the waterfront (but allow 15 for getting lost in Pothiá's higgledy-piggledy lanes), the **Vouvális Museum** is housed in the neoclassical mansion of Nikólaos Vouvális' family, the first to export the local sponges overseas, in 1896; inside are atmospheric 'Victorian' furnishings, portraits, panoramas of Constantinople, a miscellany of prehistoric finds and antiquities, and ghosts – after Vouvális died, his widow kept his embalmed body around for years. In 2008, the antiquities (plus the Kalmynian marbles, but probably not the *Lady of Kálymnos*) are slated to be moved into a new Archaeology Museum nearby.

Maritime Museum
t 224 305 1361; open 8.30–2

Vouvális Museum
t 224 302 3113; open Tues–Sun 10–2

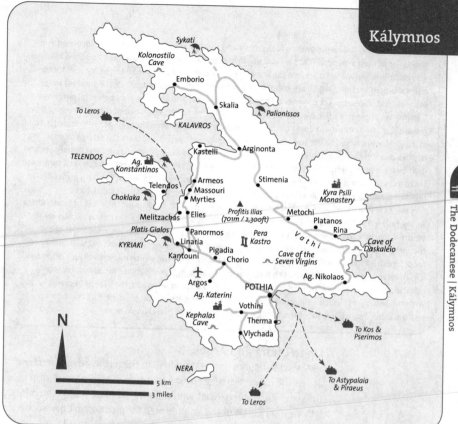

At night Pothiá's landmark is a huge illuminated cross in a hilltop 'sacred wood', near the **Monastery of Ag. Pánton**. This contains the remains of Kálymnos' own saint, Ag. Sávvas, who ran a secret school during the Turkish occupation and has had a posthumous career as the local answer to fertility drugs – hence all the wax babies. Below, 5km from Pothiá on the road to Vothyni, you can visit the award-winning **Traditional Kalymnian House**, with displays on life a century ago, and a friendly staff who offer visitors a glass of island wine.

Beaches aren't Pothiá's strong point. Closest is pebbly **Géfyra** south near the yacht club, and beyond that a concrete jetty at the ex-spa of **Thérma**. Way south, 6km from Póthia, the beach at **Vlycháda** is exposed but is worth a visit for the delightful **Museum of Marine Life** set up by a local diver, with plants, animals, seashells and bits from an ancient wreck. Caiques from Póthia sail south to the good taverna on **Nerá** islet and to **Képhalas Cave**, a 30-minute walk from the sea (taxis go as far as the monastery of Ag. Kateríni, where you can pick up a 2km path). The cave has six chambers of colourful stalactites and was once a sanctuary of Zeus, thanks to a huge stalagmite looking like the king of the gods enthroned.

Traditional Kalymnian House
t 224 305 1653, open 8.30–2, adm

Museum of Marine Life
t 224 305 0435, open 8.30–2, adm

Sponging

In their natural state, sponges are foul, smelly and black, and have to be stamped, squeezed and soaked until their skeletons (the part you use in the tub) are clean. Many are then bleached in vitriol, acid and permanganate, to achieve the familiar yellow colour – but if you're out to buy, opt for the natural brown versions, which are much stronger. Look for the densest texture, the smallest holes. The seller should have a bucket of water on hand so you can feel and squeeze your potential purchase.

Diving for these primitive plant-like porifers is a dangerous art. Since ancient times, divers used their *skandalópetra* to bear them down to the sea bed, where they speared the sponges with tridents, then, at a signal, were raised to the surface. As modern equipment permitted divers to plunge to new depths, cases of the 'bends' became frequent; it was common to see men crippled, paralysed or made deaf by their profession. Nearly half never came home at all. These days divers wear oxygen tanks, use small axes to extract the sponges, and surface with decompression chambers. But it's a profession in rapid decline, undermined by a deadly sponge virus, overfishing and synthetic substitutes.

In the past Kálymnos' sponge fleet left home for seven months to work off the coast of North Africa. Today, only a few boats depart for a four-month tour near Sicily and Malta. On Kálymnos, the week before departure (traditionally just after Orthodox Easter, but it varies with the weather) is known as the *Iprogrós* or Sponge Week, devoted to giving the sponge-divers a rousing send-off, with plenty of food, free drinks and traditional dances – including the *mechanikós*, which mirrors a diver's often tragic life, from young and robust to stricken with the bends, although in the dance the diver makes a miraculous recovery. The last night is tenderly known as *O Ípnos tis Agápis*, the 'Sleep of Love'. It ends with the pealing of church bells, calling the divers to their boats. A local resident, Faith Warn, has written *Bitter Sea*, a book about the sponge-divers, available in island bookshops.

Up to Chóra and Árgos

Most of Kálmynos' population lives in the fertile valley stretching across the island from Pothiá to Pánormos. In **Mýli**, named after three monumental derelict windmills by the road, stands the ruined 15th-century Castle of the Knights of St John, or **Kástro Chryssochéria** ('Golden-handed'), named after its church of the Virgin Mary.

Mýli blends imperceptibly into **Chóra** (or **Chorió**) the old capital of Kálymnos and still a prosperous village. A steep walk above town,

Kástro
open May–Oct 10–2

the **Kástro** was built in the 11th century and inhabited until the 18th; on a gloomy day it looks more Transylvanian than Greek, with its only intact buildings some barrel-vaulted whitewashed chapels containing fragments of medieval frescoes. The **Cave of the Seven Virgins** at the foot of Mount Flaská was named after seven girls who hid there during a pirate raid and were never seen again; there are holes in the rock where supplicants poured libations to the virgins' predecessors, the nymphs. The island's old cathedral, **Panagía tis Kechaitoméni**, contains columns from the Sanctuary of Apollo Delios, with its foundations just beyond the Árgos crossroads; most of its stone was reused for two 6th-century basilicas with mosaic floors, triple-apsed **Ag. Sofía** and **Christós tis Jerousalím**. The latter was founded by the Byzantine Emperor Arkadios (AD 395–408) in gratitude for his shelter at Kálymnos during a storm; the pretty single apse survives, richly decorated with marbles. There are rock-cut Mycenaean tombs in the area, not surprisingly, as the town the Mycenaeans founded, **Árgos**, is to the west.

The West Coast: Beaches, Cliffs and Resorts

North of Chorió the road dips down to the island's beaches, small fringes of grey shingly sand shaded with tamarisks. The resort strip starts at **Kantoúni**, with packed sands enclosed by the cliffs, followed by the nicer cove of **Linária**. Both are part of **Panórmos** and **Eliés**, named after its olive groves, with the oldest *kafeneíon* on the island. A little further along, beyond the giant rock on the coastline, the sandy beaches at **Platís Giálos** and **Melitzáchas** are quieter.

Myrtiés blends into **Massoúri**, Kálymnos' Golden Mile of bars, hotels and tavernas, growing less frenetic in the north end towards **Arméos**. The blood-red sunset over Télendos islet from this coast is one of the wonders of the Dodecanese, while the sheer limestone cliffs – some overhanging and dripping with stalgmites, others pocked with caves, others soaring in great dramatic vertical slabs – are a playground for rock-climbers from around the world.

From Myrtiés, ferries head north to Emborió, to Léros, and to the craggy volcanic car-free island of **Télendos** just opposite. Télendos broke off from Kálymnos in two weeks of earthquakes in AD 554 – the ruins of an ancient city, possibly the original Pothea, are in the bed of the channel. Its nickname, the 'Lady' or 'Princess of Kálymnos', comes from its profile (best viewed from Kastélli). Up a narrow lane from the port you'll find the pretty church of the **Panagía**, the ruins of Roman houses and baths, and, high above, the abandoned church of Ag. Konstantínos, a 1½hr hike. Of its several pebble beaches, **Chokláka** (through the village and down steep steps) is the most popular, especially at sunset; sand was imported to improve the beach facing Kálymnos; another here, **Paradise**, is for naturists.

North of Massoúri, **Kastélli** – the cape with the rocky bulge – has scant walls from the castle refuge of survivors of the terrible 11th-century Seljuk massacre; steps descend to the seaside church of the **Panagía**. The coastal road is spectacular, on its way to the fish-farm-filled fjord at **Arginónda**, a hamlet with a pebbly beach. Arginónda lent its name to the entire northern peninsula, and is the perfect place for rock-climbing and strenuous treks in the quiet hills. The northernmost village, **Emborió**, is a pretty fishing hamlet with a small so-so beach, within walking distance of some exceptional countryside. Further on are more remote beaches and **Kolonóstilo Cave**, sheltering curtains of column-like stalactites, damaged by dynamite-wielding treasure-hunters; there's a ruined Venetian castle and a tower built over a Neolithic temple, and a sacrificial altar was found in the vicinity.

East: Vathí, the Fjord of Kálymnos

Nothing on the island prepares you for the sudden vision of 'the Deep', **Vathí**: a lush green volcanic valley containing three laid-back villages, Rína, Plátanos and Metóchi, superbly situated at the mouth of a magnificent intensely blue fjord, a favourite of passing yachts. Until the 1960s the only way to reach Vathí by land was via a paved 5.5km *kalderími* path or 'Italian Road' from Pothiá. Citrus groves and vegetable gardens (the tomatoes are famous) provide the valley's income, and houses and white-walled roads fill in the gaps between the trees. **Rína**, named after St Irene, has a pretty port with a few tavernas and hotels, a place to swim, a boatyard and a mysterious 'throne' carved in the rock. The middle village, **Plátanos**, named for its enormous plane tree, has Cyclopean walls – there are in fact enough antiquities, including three early Christian basilicas, for an archaeological walk, which may be ready by 2007: ask for the key of the most interesting church, the frescoed **Taxiárchis Michaël**, about 2km west.

North of Vathí a track leads to the walled **Moní Kyrá Psilí**, the 'Tall Lady'. Near the mouth of the fjord, accessible only by sea, the **Cave of Daskaleío** was once a holy place, and yielded a trove of Neolithic-to-Bronze Age artefacts.

ⓘ **Kálymnos** >
*Municipal tourist
office: Pothiá, t 224 305
9056; plus information
booth, next to Olympic
Hotel on the waterfront,
t 224 305 0879,
www.kalymnos-isl.gr;
both open April–Oct
Mon–Fri 7–2.30*

⭐ **Themelina** >>

🧗 **Rock-climbing
and diving**

Kálymnos Festivals

Easter: Celebrated with ear-splitting dynamite in Pothiá.

Week after Easter: the *Iprogrós* (Sponge Week). Other celebrations are held when the divers return, although each boat arrives at a different time.

Early July: International Diving Festival.

15 Aug: Télendos, Kyrá Psilí and Galatianí at Arginónta.

Late Aug: Skandalópetra Freediving Games.

Late Oct: Rock-climbing festival.

Activities on Kálymnos

Diving

Pegasus Diving Club, t 224 305 1818 or 694 418 0746, *www.kalymnosdiving. com*. Diving from a traditional sponge boat. Besides an age-old diving tradition (you can try diving in the classic sponge-diving gear) Kálymnos has Greece's first underwater archaeological park.

Rock-climbing

Kálymnos' limestone cliffs and overhangs are perfect, and there are over 600 routes and the potential for many many. The best times are Mar–May and Sept–Nov, but people come all year. Climbing info desk, t 224 30 9445 or *www.climb-kalymnos.com*.

Where to Stay and Eat on Kálymnos

Because of the long rock-climbing season, Kálymnos is one of the few islands where you should book ahead, even in spring and autumn.

Pothiá ✉ 85200

Panorama, in the back streets, t 224 302 3138 (€€). Lovely décor, and all rooms have balconies with magnificent views.

Themelina, by the Archaeology Museum, t 224 302 2682, *www.greek-tourism.gr/kalymnos/villa-themelina* (€€). 19th-century villa with traditionally furnished rooms, shady gardens and pool.

Archontiko, by the harbour, t 224 302 4051, *www.travelinfo.gr/archontiko* (€). The Karaphillis family have restored this late 19th century mansion, once the home of the Turkish governor, as an atmospheric little hotel.

Greek House, near the sponge factory, t 224 302 3752 (€). Friendly, with cosy wood-panelled rooms.

Johnny's Studios, t 224 302 4006, above the port (€). Commanding views over Pothiá.

In Pothiá, most of the restaurants and ouzeries are on 'Octopus Row' at the far end of the quay, and specialize in tasty octopus *keftédes*.

Pandelis, on the quay, t 224 305 1508. Some of the best seafood and friendliest service on the island at reasonable prices.

Vrachos, on Octopus Row, t 224 302 9879. Good ouzerie and fish.

Kantoúni/Pánormos ✉ 85200

Kalydna Island, set back from the sea in Kantoúni, *www.kalydnaislandhotel. gr*, t 224 304 7880 (€€). With pool and diving and climbing schools.

Norma's Village, Kantoúni, t 224 304 8739, *www.normasvillage.eu* (€€). New studios, apartments, villa and restaurant in a pretty setting, with events, courses, etc. *Open all year.*

Elies, Panórmos, t 224 304 7890, *www.all-about.gr/elies* (€€). The island's biggest hotel, with a restaurant, two bars and a pool and links to diving and climbing schools; informative website.

Liogerma, Panórmos, t 224 304 7122 (€). Very pleasant little hotel, right on the beach.

Domus, Kantoúni Beach, t 224 304 7959. Perhaps the best restaurant on the island, so you must book. Terrace dining and linen tablecloths with superb view, serving island specialities and international fare. *Open May–Oct.*

Myrtiés ✉ 85200

Akroyali, t 224 304 7521, *www.acroyali-kalymnos.com* (€€). New apartments furnished in the rustic island style, with balconies directly overlooking the beach. *Open April–Nov.*

Melina's Apartments, t 224 302 8634, *www.melinas-apartments.com* (€). Apartments sleeping up to four with a shared veranda.

Nefeli Studios, t 224 304 8170, *www. kalymnos-isl.gr/nefeli* (€). Friendly owners and studios, immersed in a flowery garden, with a snack bar. *Open April–Nov.*

Drossia, Melitsachá Beach, t 224 304 8745. Excellent *psarótaverna* renowned for swordfish, tuna and octopus fritters.

Babis Bar. For a cocktail or game of backgammon; with a pool in the back.

Massoúri ✉ 85200

Plaza, in the more peaceful Arméos area, t 224 304 7134 (€€). Perched high over the bay with a pool and some fine views.

Studios Tatsis, t 224 304 7887 (€€). Stylish with great views over Télendos.

Massouri, in the square. Slightly upmarket – but the owners are good versatile chefs and will prepare requests with a day's warning.

Punibel, t 224 304 8150. Candlelit dinners; all the Greek standards.

Sunset, by the Plaza hotel. Owned by the local butcher; succulent meats.

Tsapanákos, t 224 304 7929. Come here for traditional stuffed kid, raised free range on Télendos. It's also one of the few restaurants that is *open all year*.

Glaros Snack Bar, t 224 304 7712. Owners Steve and Sue McDonnell are rock-climbers and extend a warm welcome and can offer sound advice.

Télendos Islet ✉ 85200

Porto Potho, t 224 304 7321, *www. telendos.net* (€€–€). Air-conditioned rooms, pool and balconies overlooking Myrtiés.

On the Rocks, t 224 302 3894, *www. ort.telendos.com* (€). Friendly Aussie-Greek owners, and nice rooms on a beach, including some family rooms, plus TV, Internet, and restaurant.

Rita, *www.telendos.net*, t 224 304 7914 (€). Simple rooms over the friendly taverna.

Zorbas, t 224 304 8660 Taverna near the boat landing; excellent spinach pies and often live traditional music

Emborió ✉ 85200

Harry's Apartments, t 224 304 0061 (€€). Set in lovely secluded gardens.

Vathí ✉ 85200

Galini, in Rína, t 224 303 1241 (€). Immaculate rooms and home-baked bread, served on a restful terrace overlooking the fjord-like harbour; a good spot for lunch.

Pension Manolis, higher up to the right, t 224 303 1300 (€). With a communal kitchen and nice garden. Manólis is an official guide and a mine of information.

To Limanáki tou Vathí, Rína, t 224 303 1333. Views over the port and a limited but good menu of home-cooked dishes.

(⭐) **Tsapanákos** >>

Kárpathos (ΚΑΡΠΑΘΟΣ)

Halfway between Crete and Rhodes, on the same latitude as Malta and Casablanca, Kárpathos was an island-hopper's best-kept secret that is now firmly on the package tour map. It has beautiful beaches, but it also has character, strongly marked by the affection it inspires in its inhabitants: although many have been forced to go abroad to make a living (mostly to the USA), they come back as often as possible, and even ship their bodies home to be buried on the island. They have the money: Kárpathos' sons and daughters have one of the highest rates of university education in Europe. And the climate gets a gold star, too, for people suffering from respiratory diseases.

Kárpathos offers two islands for the price of one: long and thin, austere and ruggedly mountainous in the north, and fertile, softer, beach-fringed and 'European' in the south, linked by a giant's vertebra of cliffs which culminates in two mountains over 900m (3,000ft) in height. The two 'islands' are so distinct that some say the northerners and southerners descended from different ancient races, only rarely communicating by sea. A century ago, the isolation of the northern village of Ólympos left it a goldmine of traditions. Songs, dances and celebrations remain unchanged; women still bake their bread in outdoor ovens and dress in their beautiful traditional costumes, and sell 'handicrafts' to the daily influx of daytripping tourists from the south.

History

One ancient name of Kárpathos was Porfiris, or 'Red', after the red dye; another was Tetrapolis, after its four Dorian cities of Vrykous, Possidion, Arkessia and Nissyros, founded *c.* 1000 BC. Homer called it Kárpathos, perhaps from *arpaktos*, or 'robbery'; from early on, Vróntis Bay hid pirate ships that darted out to plunder passing vessels. The Venetians, when they had it (1306–1537) slurred it into 'Scarpanto'.

Off the coasts, the prized *scarus* (or parrot fish, which, as Aristotle noted, ruminates its food) was so abundant that the Roman emperors hired special fleets to bring them back for the imperial table. The Roman town survived into early Byzantine times, when Kárpathos was devasted by pirates, who made it their south Aegean headquarters, with Arkássa as their chief slave market. Things were so rough that even the Turks didn't want Kárpathos, and sent only a *cadi*, or judge, several times a year; he never stayed longer than a few days, and depended entirely on the Greeks to protect him. In the Second World War, 6,000 Italians used Kárpathos as a base to attack Egypt; today the island supports a small colony of Egyptians who do much of the local building.

For all its rough and ready past, Kárpathos has a strong tradition of delicately lyrical poetry, and, as in Crete, people like to compete in

Getting to Kárpathos

By air: There are charters, and 2–3 daily connections with Rhodes, one with Kássos (the shortest scheduled flight in the world: it takes 5mins), and 5 times a week with Athens. **Olympic Airways, t** 224 502 2057. **Airport information: t** 224 502 2057. **Taxis** to and from the airport cost around €18.

By sea: There are **ferries** 2–3 times a week with Piraeus, 3–4 times a week with Rhodes and Kássos, twice a week with Chálki, Mílos, Santoríni, and Heráklion, Ag. Nikólaos and Sitía (Crete). A boat daily connects the island's two ports, Diafáni and Pigádia, but for an extortionate €20–25; the less frequent big ferries charge only €4. **Caiques** also sail from Finíki to Kássos. **Port authority: t** 224 502 2227.

Getting around Kárpathos

Buses in summer go hourly from Pigádia to Amoopí, and rather less frequently to Pilés via Apéri, Voláda and Óthos; a few go on to Finíki, Arkássa and Lefkós.

The often appalling state of the roads makes **car and motorbike hire** expensive. Fuel shortages are frequent, petrol stations rare: keep the tank topped up and consider a 4x4. Book one before you arrive at **Europcar, t** 224 502 3903, **Hertz, t** 224 502 2235, or **Avis, t** 224 502 2702. For a **taxi, t** 224 502 2705.

---

impromptu singing contests of *matinádes*, or 15-syllable couplets. Two Austrians, Rudolph Maria Brandl and Diether Reinsch, spent ten years studying its songs, and wrote the monumental *Die Volksmusik der Insel Kárpathos* (Edition Re, 1992).

Kárpathos Town (Pigádia)

The capital, Kárpathos Town or **Pigádia**, is sheltered in that old pirate cove, mountain-ringed Vróntis Bay, but has surrendered in recent years to cacaphony and a forest of toadstool package accommodation. Once the ancient city of Possidion, it was abandoned in the Byzantine era, and all that remains of its predecessor is a clutch of Mycenaean tombs and a few stones of a **Temple to Lindian Athena** on the outcrop to the east. It's no accident that the local National Bank branch has an air of prosperity: Kárpathos receives more money from its emigrants than any other Greek island.

Beyond the pretty Mussolini-era harbour master's building, it's a short walk to the beautiful 3km sandy beach rimming **Vróntis** ('Thunder') **Bay**. Several columns and screens have been re-erected of the 5th-century basilica of **Ag. Fotiní** (or Aphote). At **Ag. Kyriakí** (signposted on the south side of the bay) stood a 7th-century BC Geometric-era sanctuary dedicated to Demeter; one of the tombs hewn in the rock yielded a golden statuette.

Around the South and up the West Coast

South of Pigádia, the land is flat and desolate, softening after 7km at **Amoopí**, a family resort with a pair of sandy coves decorated with great rocks. Further south, a series of coves and beaches form Kárpathos' wind-blasted windsurfing paradise, **Afiárti**, in particular at gusty Gun, Devil's and Chicken Bays, suitable for all levels. Homer, after all, nicknamed the island, Anemoussa, the 'windy one'. The airport is further south, by the desolate site of Byzantine **Thaetho**.

Above Amoopí, colourful **Menetés** is a pretty village set in gardens on the flanks of Mt Profítis Ilías; its church, set dramatically on the site of the ancient acropolis, is made of stone from Arkessia. The road continues down to the island's less developed west coast and **Arkássa**, with its little beaches and hotels at the mouth of a jagged ravine; the cliffs are riddled with caves. A road leads south to its predecessor, Classical **Arkessia**, which survived into Byzantine times; even older is the Mycenaean acropolis with Cyclopean walls that stands on the rocky headland of Paleokástro. Near the modern seaside church of **Ag. Sofía** (*signposted*) are the extensive remains of three early Byzantine mosaic floors half-hidden in the weeds.

Just north, **Finíki** is a bijou fishing harbour with a tiny sandy beach and caiques heading for Kássos. The road north passes several tempting strands and mini-fjords far below in the pines as it makes its way to **Lefkós**, one of the best places for lazy days on the beach, with white sandy coves, turquoise water, pines and a ruined Byzantine city, plus a scattering of antiquities (enough at least for the archaeologists to limit further building). There's a stone that may be a menhir, the foundations of a 60m (200ft) basilica and a series of catacombs labelled 'Roman Cistern'. A short walk away are the ruins of a medieval fort; there was another on the islet of **Xokástro**, where they say Nikephoros Phokas was based in 961 during his campaign to capture Crete; now it's populated only by rabbits. Up in **Áno Lefkós**, note the pretty 13th-century church of **Ag. Geórgios**.

Inland Villages and East Coast Beaches

Kárpathos' mountain villages are cool, well-watered and surprisingly opulent, yet even so many of the lanes aren't wide enough for the islanders' big cars. North of Pigádia, **Apéri**, capital of Kárpathos up to 1896, is reputed to be the richest village in Greece per capita, producing an amazing number of doctors for the United States plus the ancestors of Telly Savalas. If you see an open door anywhere, sneak a peek inside – the Karpathiots have lavish tastes, and furnish their homes with colourful carpets, mirrors, portraits, antiques and elevated carved wood beds, or *soúphas*.

The other central villages are just as house-proud. Delightful whitewashed **Voláda** has pretty lanes, and a ruined castle built by the Cornari of Venice, who owned the island until 1538. From here the road climbs to **Óthos**, at 650m (2,133ft) the highest village of Kárpathos and also one of the oldest, where the inhabitants of Byzantine Thaetho took refuge after their city was destroyed. The red wine, *othitikó krasí*, is worth a try, and there's often live music at Kafeneíon Toksotis; one 150-year-old house is a fascinating **Folk Museum**, and local painter Iánnis Hápsis sells his scenes of island life from his gallery in the centre.

A paved road from Óthos heads up to the fertile plateau of vines and a good taverna, Thanassis, under **Mount Kalilímni**, at 1,188m (3,900ft), the highest mountain in the Dodecanese – its name, 'Good Lake', refers to an ancient lake up the slopes. Towards the west coast, the very pretty mountain village of ΠΥΛΕΣ, whose name in Roman letters unfortunately reads **Pilés**, has fine views over Kássos, with the profile of Crete as a backdrop, and makes delicious honey.

Caiques from Pigádia call at the east coast beaches, although you can now drive to most of them as well. A steep tarmacked zigzag from the new Apéri bypass leads down to **Acháta**, a lovely white pebbly beach in a rocky amphitheatre. The road north of Apéri takes in the increasingly majestic coast; a serpentine paved by-road winds from **Katódio** to **Kyrá Panagía**, a pretty red-domed church by a sheltered and very popular beach, which varies from fine white sand to pebbles. From **Myrtónas** you can drive down to **Apélla**, a crescent of fine sand, turquoise water and scenery from *The Clash of the Titans*. The east coast road ends for all but 4x4s at **Spóa**, at the crossroads of the dirt road to Ólympos. A track from Spóa descends to the beach of **Ag. Nikólaos**, which gets busy in summer. Another beautiful beach just north, **Ag. Mínas**, has recently gained a cantina and sunbeds, to the dismay of purists.

Anticlockwise from Spóa, the road descends dramatically on a corniche through to whitewashed **Messochóri**, one of the island's most charming villages. Although sadly denuded of its surrounding pine forests in a blaze in 2004, the village itself is immersed in voluptuous gardens set in an amphitheatre, seemingly on the verge of falling into the sea. Head down the steps and you'll find the main *plateía* with a pretty 17th-century church of **Ag. Ioánnis**, with a carved iconostasis and frescoes. From here a road descends to **Lefkós**.

Ólympos and Northern Kárpathos

Northern Kárpathos is wild, harsh and in places pure drama. In spite of the road blazed through in 1979 (do-able with a 4x4), the easiest way to reach Ólympos is by ferry or caique from Pigádia to **Diafáni**, the little port, where buses makes the 15min connection to Ólympos. Crowded only during the daily daytrip rush. Diafáni has a beach with flat rocks, and another, **Vanánda**, 30mins' walk north.

Ólympos is, simply, one of the most stunning villages in Greece, draped over a stark mountain ridge, topped by ruined windmills lined up as neatly as teeth; two of the 40 still grind wheat and barley. Like other inland villages, Ólympos (originally Elymbos) was built in the 7th–9th centuries as a refuge from pirates, this time by the inhabitants of ancient Vrykous. The area was isolated for so long that linguists in the 19th century were amazed to find people here using ancient Doric and Phrygian pronunciation and expressions. A mother's property goes to the eldest daughter, the *kanakára*; at feasts, you can recognize her by the gold coins she wears on chains, coins that her forefathers earned abroad. A father's goes exclusively to the eldest son. Many of the older men in the village are shepherds and musicians, playing the *lýra* with a bell-covered bow, the *laoúto* and the *tsamboúna* (goatskin bagpipes). Most of the younger ones are working in America.

Ólympos' population was 1,800 in 1951, but is down to 300, and the only way to get a feel for it is to stay overnight or come out of season, when the women in their costumes aren't mugging (and mugging for) the daytrippers. As soon as the buses leave, everything magically turns to normal, wrapped in the quiet, allowing you to have a real look around. Decorative painted balconies, many incorporating two-headed Byzantine eagles (one head Rome, one Constantinople), adorn the houses, stacked one on top of another so as not to cast a shadow on the neighbours. Doors have wooden locks and keys that Homer might have recognized. The village priest has one of the most lavish houses and often leaves the door open. The frescoes and iconostasis in the church date back to the 18th century.

Ólympos is also a base for beautiful if rugged walks. The paved road continues on to **Avlóna**, a village that wouldn't look out of place in Tibet but is inhabited only during the harvest. From Avlóna it is a rough walk down to the ancient city of Vrykous or **Vrykóunda**, wrecked in an earthquake in the early Christian era and remembered today by a stair, a breakwater, rock-cut burial chambers and walls; a tiny chapel sits out on the rocks. In a cavern in Vrykóunda, the chapel of **Ag. Ioánnis** hosts the largest *panegýri* in north Kárpathos, in August. Another 2hrs' strenuous walking north of Avlóna, in the beautiful fjord-like bay of the 'three-mouthed' **Trístomo**, where only two families now live, a famous temple of Apollo Porthmeios once stood, of which some foundations remain. The ancient city of Nissyros, colonized by the island of the same name to exploit the iron and silver mines at Assimovórni, may have been here, or on the islet of **Sariá** which dots the 'i' of Kárpathos (boats from Diafáni go twice a day in summer). In the old days the sheperds and their flocks simply swam over the shallow 100m (330ft) strait. Ancient graves have been found here, and the *Palátia*, unusual barrel-vaulted houses, were built by pirates in the 9th and 10th centuries.

ⓘ **Kárpathos** >
Municipal tourist office (DOT):
1 Anapáfseos, Pigádia,
t 224 502 3962.

Kárpathos Festivals

Easter: In Ólympos.

15 Aug: Apéri, Ólympos and Menetés.

22–3 Aug: Myrtónas and Kyra Panagía.

27–9 Aug: Huge sleep-out, music and dance at Ag. Ioánnis at Vrykóunda.

Activities on Kárpathos

Windsurfing is big in Afiári, at **Club Amenos**, t 224 509 1011, and **Club Mistral**, t 224 509 1061; see *www.windsurfing-karpathos.com*.

Where to Stay and Eat on Kárpathos

If you get stuck, ring the **Association of Hotel Owners**, t 224 502 2483.

Kárpathos Town (Pigádia)

✉ **85700**

Kárpathos' restaurants are beginning to revive traditional recipes and serve wine from Óthos – although it's rare to find it in bottles.

Miramare Bay, on Ag. Fotiní Beach, t 224 502 2345 (€€€). With pool, sea-views and good breakfasts.

Nisia, t 224 502 9127, *www.hotelnisia.com* (€€€). Striking apartment complex with all creature comforts, stylish rooms, a pretty pool and bar and gym.

Sound of the Sea, t 224 502 2796, *www.apis.gr* (€€€). Very spacious studios and cottages sleeping up to four with a big pool, tennis and a fitness centre and lovely sea views.

Blue Bay, by the beach, t 224 502 2479, *www.bluebayhotel.gr* (€€). Friendly, family-run, traditional place. Disabled access, pool, bar and playground.

Pavilion, up in town, **t** 224 502 2818, *www.inkarpathos.com/pavilion* (€€€–€€). A favourite of Americans, with orthopaedic beds, cocktails served in the roof garden, Internet, library and videos, satellite TV, etc.

 Pine Tree >>

Romantica, near the beach, **t** 224 502 2460, *www.hotelromantica.gr* (€€). Rooms and studios with a pool, half-hidden in a grove of citrus trees; it serves delicious breakfasts.

Mertonas, **t** 224 502 2622 (€). Friendly management; pleasantly furnished studios. *Open all year.*

Rose Studios, **t** 224 502 2284 (€). Welcoming and quiet.

Anemoussa, **t** 224 502 2164. Good Italian dishes.

Anna, on the waterfront. Scruffy-looking but excellent fish taverna.

Mediterranean House, Ag. Fotiní Beach, **t** 224 502 2766. A veranda on beach and a big menu serving a wide choice of Greek standards, seafood starters, and some international dishes too. *Open May–Oct.*

Oraia Kárpathos, on the waterfront, **t** 224 502 2501. The best *makaroúnes* (hand-made pasta with fried onions and cheese) south of Ólympos. *Open eves only except in July and Aug.*

Pelagos, **t** 224 502 2744. Taverna specializing in meat on the spit, salads and a choice of wines, run by musicians, who perform live.

The Life of Angels, in the centre. Often the liveliest place in evening – a *kafeneíon* with a big terrace and music.

Amoopí ✉ 85700

Castelia Bay, **t** 224 508 1178, *www.casteliabay.gr* (€€). Stylish rooms on a hill overlooking the sea, a 10min walk to the beach. Also has apartments.

Helios, on the beach **t** 224 508 1148, *www.helioshotel.gr* (€€). Bungalows with TVs surrounded with flowery gardens; Internet access available.

Argo, **t** 224 502 2589 (€). Just back from the beach.

 Anemos >>

Arkássa ✉ 85700

Arkesia, **t** 224 506 1305 (€€). The plush choice here, with all mod cons, pool and children's playground.

Dimitrios, **t** 224 506 1313 (€€). Also comfortable, but with fewer facilities.

West Coast ✉ 85700

Dimitrios, Finíki, **t** 224 506 1294. Good fish but also good moussaka and home-made bread. *Open May–Sept.*

Pine Tree, Adia, **t** 224 502 9065. Pasta, chickpea soup, stews, fish and fresh bread served in a shady setting under the pines. Most of the fruit and veg comes from the owner's garden.

Lefkós ✉ 85700

Niko's Studios, **t** 224 502 2787, *www.nikos-studios.com* (€). Simple studios and an apartment for families near the beach.

Golden Sand, **t** 224 507 1203, *www.nikos-studios.com* (€). Seven new studios with a restaurant.

Small Paradise, **t** 224 507 1184. Good home-made sausages, fish soup, stuffed vegetables and more on the veranda; ask about their beachside studios. *Open April–Oct.*

Kyrá Panagía ✉ 85700

Kyrá Panagía, **t** 224 502 3026, *www.kyrapanagiahotel.gr* (€€€). Upscale, with a bar and beautiful pool, Internet and restaurant.

Studios Acropolis, **t** 224 503 1503 (€€). Popular, beautifully set on the rocks over the beach with sunrise views.

Diafáni ✉ 85700

Balaskas, 300m from the beach, **t** 224 505 1320, *www.balaskashotel.com* (€). Pleasant family-run hotel, with a minibus and boat for excursions.

Dorana, **t** 224 505 1038, *www.dorana.gr* (€). Pink and white, clean, basic studios.

Nikos, **t** 224 505 1289 (€). Owned by Orfanos Travel; adequate rooms.

Anixis, **t** 224 505 1226. Picturesque family-run taverna, with a vine-covered terrace; simple but very tasty dishes such as chickpea salad, fish from the family boat, stuffed courgettes. *Open June–Oct.*

Ólympos ✉ 85700

Anemos, **t** 224 505 1314/ **t** 693 285 8901, *www.geocities.com/escape2olympos* (€€). Traditional house with two huge rooms to let and staggering views over the village. The same family owns the **Zephyrus** restaurant. *Open all year.*

Afrodite, nearby, **t** 224 505 1307 (€).
Ólympos, **t** 224 505 1252 (€). Good basic food and 3 traditional rooms with en suite and great views.

Milos, in the windmill, **t** 224 501 333. Try the delicious speciality of pasta stuffed with cheese and spinach. *Open April–Oct.*

Kássos (ΚΑΣΣΟΣ)

If the slow old Greece you were looking for wasn't in Kárpathos, hop over to Kássos (pop. 1,200), an isolated rock with steep coasts, ravines, and the odd beach wedged in between. Practically untouched by tourism, outside of a summer influx of Greek Americans, it has a simple, friendly atmosphere. Bring some good books.

History

Inhabited in ancient times and mentioned in the *Iliad*'s 'Catalogue of Ships', Kássos was practically autonomous under the Venetians and Turks, and, like other small, arid islands (Hýdra, Psára, Sými) it lived off its fleet. It put 80 ships at the disposal of the Greeks in the War of Independence and all went well until the Sultan offered part of Greece to Ibrahim Pasha, son of Ali Pasha, governor of Egypt. In June 1824 Ibrahim sailed north with a massive fleet, and his first stop was Kássos, where he massacred the men and took the women and children as slaves. The quarter of the population who escaped went either to Sýros or Gramvoúsa, an islet off the northwest coast of Crete, where they turned to piracy, defiantly flying the Greek flag in Turkish waters. But at the end of the war Capodístria put a stop to their activities, and their refuge, Gramvoúsa, was returned to Turkish rule. In spite of the massacre, thousands of Kassiots later emigrated to Egypt to work on the Suez Canal, and others ended up in America.

Around the Island

There are five villages on Kássos, and dishevelled **Fri** (ΦΡΥ), with its stone houses and new sheltered harbour, is their capital, where the

Useful Information on Kássos

Kássos Maritime Tourist Agency, **t** 224 504 1323, *www.kassos-island.gr*. Speaks good English, owns the Anagennissis hotel and has studios as well, and distributes the essential map. Bring cash in case the one ATM runs out.

Kássos Festivals

23 April: Moní Ag. Geórgios.
7 June: Fri.
17 July: Ag. Marína.
14 Aug: Panagía.

Where to Stay and Eat on Kássos

Kássos ✉ 85800
Anagennissis, **t** 224 504 1323 (€€). Small renovated rooms, run by an engaging Kassiot-American. *Open all year.*
Borgianoula Apartments, **t** 224 504 1495 (€€–€). A tidy self-catering option. *Open May–Oct.*
Flisvos, by the new port, **t** 224 504 1430 (€). Basic studios.
Milos, facing the sea, **t** 224 504 1825. Stewed dishes and fish. *Open all year.*

There are several seasonal places as well in Fri and Emborió.

Getting to and around Kássos

There are frequent **air** connections with Rhodes and Kárpathos (the world's shortest scheduled flight takes 5mins). The **airport** is 1km from Fri. **Olympic Airways, t** 224 504 4330.

By **sea** there are 2–3 connections a week with Piraeus, 3–4 times a week with Rhodes and Kárpathos, twice a week with Chálki, Mílos and Ag. Nikólaos (Crete), once a week with Sitía (Crete); there is also a weekend (or more often) caique from Finíki, Kárpathos. All may skip Kássos if the wind's up. **Port authority: t** 224 504 1288.

Two **taxis**, a summer **minibus**, and a few **scooters** and **quads** (**t** 224 504 1746) is all you get once on the island, plus **boat excursions.**

main occupation, fishing, is much in evidence in the caique-filled port of **Boúka**. Every year on 7 June a ceremony is held there in memory of the massacre of 1824. Swimming at Fri isn't brilliant, but boats make the excursion out to the islet and good beaches of **Armathiá**; a long stretch of sand dignifies the other islet, **Makrá**; for both bring your own water and provisions, The waters are clear, and the snorkelling and fishing are good; for a small fee the tavernas will cook up and serve your catch.

Apart from a few olives, the trees on Kássos never recovered after Ibrahim Pasha set the island ablaze, but many lighthouses, testimony to the tricky seas, stick out above the rocky terrain. A road and the one bus link Fri with Kássos' other dinky villages on a 6km circuit. There's **Emborió**, another fishing hamlet, whose old commercial port packed up with silt, and above it **Panagía**, where proud ship captains' houses erode away (although a few are now being restored); the 18th-century church that gave the village its name is the oldest on Kássos. **Póli** is built on the ancient acropolis, and has a crumbling Byzantine castle and church with inscriptions. At **Ag. Marína**, near the airstrip and Kássos' most accessible (if mediocre) beach at **Ammoúda**, you can walk to the walled-in cave of **Ellenokamára** which had signs of worship going back to the Mycenaeans. From Ag. Marína or **Arvanitochóri** a 12km road crosses Kássos for the **Monastery of Ag. Giórgios**, where you can walk down to the beach at **Chélathros Bay**.

Kastellórizo/Mégisti (ΜΕΓΙΣΤΗ)

The easternmost point of Greece, of Europe, Kastellórizo (pop. 275) is six hours – 110km – east of Rhodes, but only 2km from Turkey. It is the smallest inhabited island of the Dodecanese, 3km by 6km, yet is the mother hen of its own clutch of islets, hence its official name, Mégisti, 'the largest'. They say the Turks know it as Meis Ada, 'eye-land', for one nautical mile away is their town of Kaş ('eyebrow'), but the most commonly heard name is Kastellórizo, in memory of the days when the Knights called it the 'Red Castle'. Athens has officially adopted the island and sends it contributions and gifts, including 20 council houses. Its success as a film set – in the 1992 award-winning

Getting to Kastellórizo

By air: There are at least two **flights** a week from Rhodes. **Olympic Airways, t** 224 604 9241. **Airport: t** 224 604 9238. A taxi and (hopefully) a shuttle bus provides transfers.

By sea: 'Europe begins here' proclaims the sign by the quay. At least two **ferries** a week sail from Rhodes (4–5 hours), and express catamaran May–Oct. Also a boat to Kaş, Turkey. **Port authority: t** 224 604 9270.

film *Mediterraneo* – has given tourism (once limited to passing yachts) a new life. Some of the old houses are being repaired, mostly by returned Australian 'Kazzies'. However, it remains a quirky, eccentric backwater, surrounded by a crystal sea brimming with marine life – including oysters, a rarity on Greek islands. And, while there aren't any sandy strands, the locals will show you the rocks where they swim.

History

Neolithic finds suggest an early arrival for the traditional first settler, King Meges of Echinada, and Mycenaean graves coincide with the mention in Homer of the island's ships at Troy. The Dorians built two forts on the island, the Kástro by the town and one on the mountain, called Palaeokástro – the ancient acropolis, where Apollo and the Dioscuri were the chief deities. Diónysos was another favourite: 42 rock *patitíria* or grape-trampling presses were discovered, linked to conduits that fed the juice into underground reservoirs. The little island had a large fleet of ships and transported timber from Lycia on the nearby mainland to Africa and the Middle East. From 350 to 300 BC Kastellórizo was ruled by Rhodes, and in Roman times the pirates of Cassius used it as their hideout.

The Byzantines repaired Kastellórizo's fortifications, and their work was continued by the Knights of St John, who renamed the island after the red rock of the castle, which once had a high tower for signalling Rhodes; it was also used to imprison knights who misbehaved. The Sultan of Egypt captured Kastellórizo in 1440, but 10 years later the King of Naples, Alfonso I of Aragon, took it back. Although Kastellórizo belonged to the Ottomans by 1512, the Venetians later occupied it twice, in 1570 and in 1659, leaving the Knights' fortress in ruins. Despite all the see-sawing, the little island was doing all right for itself; at the beginning of the 19th century it had a population of 15,000 who lived from the sea or their holdings along the coast of Asia Minor.

Things began to go seriously wrong with the outbreak of the Greek War of Independence. The islanders were the first in the Dodecanese to join the cause and, taking matters into their own hands, seized their two forts from the Turks. The Great Powers forced them to give them back in 1833. In 1913 Kastellórizo revolted again, only to be put down this time by the French, who used the island as a base for their war in Syria – hence drawing bombardments from the Turkish coast.

In 1927 an earthquake caused extensive damage but the Italians, then in charge, refused to do any repairs, as Kastellórizo had failed to co-operate with their programme of de-Hellenization. Another revolt in 1933 was crushed by soldiers from Rhodes. In spite of its port serving as a refuelling station for long-distance sea planes from France and Italy, Kastellórizo was in sharp decline – in 1941 only 1,500 inhabitants remained.

But its misfortunes continued. After the Italian surrender in 1943, the Allies shipped the entire Greek population for their safety to refugee camps in the Gaza Strip and the occupying British pillaged the empty houses – or so the natives believe. To hide their looting, the British (or, the British claim, Greeks, doing some looting of their own) ignited the fuel dump as they pulled out, leading to a fire that destroyed more than 1,500 homes and nearly all the islanders' boats. Then the ship carrying the refugees home after the war sank. Those who survived to return to Kastellórizo after the war discovered that, although they had finally achieved Greek citizenship, they had lost everything else, and there was nothing to do but emigrate, some to Athens but most to Australia, where an estimated 12,000–15,000 'Kazzies' now live. The immediate postwar population was reduced to five families, who owed their survival to the Turks in Kaş, who sent over food parcels. British compensation for wartime damages finally came (without any admission of wrongdoing) in the 1980s, but there are still bad feelings; none actually went to the people who stuck it out on the island after 1945.

Although there is constant fretting about keeping enough Greeks on the island to keep it Greek, in practice relations with nearby Kaş are excellent. In 1992, all the Kastellorizans were invited over to spend Christmas in Kaş, were taken on excursions, and given a two-day feast. It was Kaş's way of thanking Kastellórizo for its role in the underground railroad that brought Kurds from Kaş to Kastellórizo and to a refugee camp near Athens. Today relations are even closer as both tourist and local traffic increase; many Greeks hop over to Kaş on a weekly basis do their shopping.

Kastellórizo Town

There is only one town on the island, Kastellórizo, where ruined houses, some still bearing weathered traces of elegance, still outnumber the inhabited ones. Tavernas line the waterfront, where it takes about 10 minutes to see all there is to see. A hotel occupies one lip of the harbour mouth, while on the other sits the ruined **Kástro**, the once highly strategic 'Castle of the East', a bulwark last repaired by the eighth Grand Master of the Knights of St John, Juan Fernando Heredia; his red coat of arms is another possible explanation for the name of the island. It was later used as the residence of the Turkish governor. Every day an islander, and a lame one at that,

Megisti Museum
*open Tues–Sun
8.30–2.30*

climbs a ladder to raise the flags of Greece and the EU at the easternmost extremity of both. The small but excellent **Megisti Museum** in a fortified house near the sea has photos of the town before everything went wrong, detached 17th-century frescoes, costumes and items found in the harbour – including 30 lovely 13th-century Byzantine plates in mint condition, found in a shipwreck.

The path along the shore leads to a 4th-century BC **Lycian tomb** cut into the rock and decorated with Doric columns; the whole southwest coast of Turkey is dotted with similar tombs, but this is the only one in Greece. The **Cathedral of Ag. Konstantínos and Heléni** re-uses granite columns lifted from a Temple of Apollo in Patára.

Beyond the town, there aren't many good roads on Kastellórizo – only one, heading southwest for the army base and the airport and rubbish tip. It passes four white churches, a monastery and the path up to the **Palaeokástro**, the ancient Doric fortress and acropolis, with walls, cisterns (some still filled with water) and an inscription from the 3rd century BC referring to Mégisti. From here, a track leads up to the top of the island, with the **Monastery of Ag. Geórgios**, containing a beautiful frescoed crypt (*be sure to ask for the key before setting out*). Nearby lie all manner of ancient ruins, including the bases of winepresses, cut in the stone, from the 6th century BC.

Kastellórizo's Grotto Azzurro

There are no beaches on Kastellórizo, but the sea is ideal for snorkelling, and there are a multitude of tiny islets to swim out to. The excursion not to be missed is to the **Blue Cave**, or **Perastá**, an hour by caique from the town. The effects are best in the morning when some light filters in; the entrance is so low you'll have to transfer to a raft. As in the famous Blue Grotto of Capri, the reflections of the water inside dye the cavern walls and stalactites blue.

The same excursion boats often go out to **Rho**, a hunk of rock with a beach, a hundred goats and a flagpole, where a cranky old lady became a nationalist heroine by daily raising the Greek flag to show those Turks what was what; after her death in 1982, she was buried on Rho, but her flag is still raised every day by a caretaker paid by the Greek government.

Useful Information on Kastellórizo

Regular police: in the harbour by the post office, t 224 104 9353.
Papoutsis Travel, t 224 607 0630, *www.kastelorizo.gr*.

Where to Stay on Kastellórizo

Kastellórizo ✉ 85111
Beds are limited; book in July and Aug.
Kastellorizo, t 224 604 9044, *www. kastellorizohotel.gr* (€€€). Spread through five traditional buildings right on the sea, a choice of studios (some

for the disabled) and maisonettes with handsome tradtional interiors.

Karnayo Traditional Houses, t 224 604 9266, *www.kastellorizokarnayo.gr* (€€€). Three beautifully restored houses with original features, with four rooms and two apartments sleeping up to five. *Open all year.*

Megisti, overlooking the harbour, **t** 224 604 9272, *www.megistihotel.gr* (€€€). The most comfortable place to stay. *Open all year.*

(★) Pension Mediterraneo >

Pension Mediterraneo, t 224 604 9007, *www.mediterraneo-megisti.com* (€€€). Pretty place, French-owned, right on the waterfront.

Blue and White Pension, to the west of the bay, **t** 224 604 9363 (€€). Featured in *Mediterraneo.*

Mavrothalassitis, t 224 604 9202 (€). Simple, with en suite facilities.

Polos, t 224 604 9302 (€).

Eating Out on Kastellórizo

Prices, always high because of transport charges, have rocketed and fish is expensive, although it's usually the freshest thing on the menu.

Akrothalassi, t 224 604 9052. Tasia is probably the best cook on the island, preparing tasty stuffed aubergines called *allotinó* and other stews.

Kaz-Bar, in the harbour. Grilled fish.

Lazaraki, t 224 604 9370. Serving delicious fresh fish and pasta, if a bit pricier than most. *Open all year.*

Mikro Parisi, 'Little Paris'. Even though the yachties flock here, it's the place for affordable fish.

Platania (Mediterraneo), up the hill on Plateía Choráfia, **t** 224 604 9206. Used in the film – unpretentious, with tasty island dishes.

Kos (ΚΩΣ)

Dolphin-shaped Kos, with its archaeological sites, lovely sandy beaches and comfortable climate, is Rhodes' mass tourism rival in the Dodecanese. In high season English, German and Swedish tourists fill the island's all-inclusive resort hotels, bars and discos, with the occasional 'Greek night' thrown in to remind them they aren't on Mallorca. Even the architecture isn't particularly Greek, partly owing to an earthquake in 1933: the Italians contributed some attractive buildings, and the pair of minarets rising from the mosques add an aura of cosmopolitana to the capital. Inland, Kos in summer looks uncannily like a mini-California: low golden hills, with

Useful Information on Kos

(i) Kos >
Municipal tourist office: Vass. Georgíou, Kos Town, just before the hydrofoil berth, **t** 224 202 8724

Tourist police: Kos Town, **t** 224 202 2444. Shares the yellow edifice with the clocktower opposite the main harbour with the EOT, **t** 224 202 4460.

British consulate (honorary): 55 Navarinoú, Kos Town, **t** 224 202 1549.

Kos Festivals

23 April: Horse-racing for St George at Pylí.

24 June: Bonfires everywhere.

29 June: Antimácheia.

July–Sept: Hippocratia culture festival.

29 Aug: Kéfalos.

8 Sept: Kardaména.

Activities on Kos

Diving: Kos Diving Centre, 5 Korítsas Square, **t** 224 202 2782. Also **Kos Divers**, in the Kipriotis Village hotel in Psálidi, **t** 693 953 9312, *www.kosdivers.com*.

Windsurfing: Kefalos Windsurfing,**t** 224 207 1727 *www.kefaloswindsurfing.com*; book in advance with Freedom holidays, *www.freedomholidays.co.uk*

Riding: Go in Mármari (*see* p.379).

Getting to and around Kos

By air: Charters fly from London and other European cities; also four flights a day from Athens and two from Rhodes, and one a week to Astypália and Léros. **Olympic Airways**, 22 Leof. Vass. Pávlou, Kos Town, **t** 224 202 2833. The airport is 26km from town. Olympic airport buses from Kos Town depart 2hrs before each flight and transport arriving Olympic passengers into town or Mastichári. There are public buses (the stop is on the big roundabout) to Kos Town, Mastichári, Kardámena and Kéfalos. Airport: **t** 224 205 1229.

By sea: Daily ferry connections with Piraeus, Rhodes, Kálymnos, Léros and Pátmos, 6 times a week with Symi, 3–4 times a week with Sýros, less frequently with Amórgos, Níssyros, Sámos, Chíos, Mytilíni and Límnos and Cyclades (Náxos, Páros and Sýros); daily excursions sail from Kos Town to Psérimos, Bodrum (Turkey), Níssyros, Platí and Léros. **Port authority: t** 224 202 6594.

Getting around Kos

Municipal **buses** run every half-hour at peak times from the centre of the waterfront, 7 Akti Koundouriótou, **t** 224 202 6276, to Ag. Fokás and Lámbi; roughly every hour to the Asklepeion; and ten times a day to Messaría (buy tickets in the office before boarding). Buses to more distant villages, **t** 224 202 2292, leave from the terminal behind the Olympic Airways office, but they get packed so arrive early; otherwise you'll find yourself in a long queue waiting for a taxi.

In theory, at least, you can summon a radio **taxi**, **t** 224 202 3333/3344/2777, but watch the meter.

Flat Kos Town and the surrounding plain are well suited to **cycling** and there are no lack of **bike hire** shops, as well as an abundance of **car hire** agencies at the airport (**Europcar**, **t** 224 202 0470) and on the waterfront.

a few vines, groves and orchards, grazing cattle and sheep, and pale cliffs, but otherwise empty, contrasting with the rashes of building – Spanish-style villas, another California touch, seem to be the rage – crowding the sandy coves that ruffle the coasts.

History

Inhabited since 3500 BC, Kos had a Minoan, then a Mycenaean colony on the site of the modern city. It had various names: Meropis, after its mythical king; Karis, for its shrimp shape; and Nymphaeon, for its nymphs before settling definitively on Kos, who was either a princess (Koön) or a crab, an early symbol of the island. In the 11th century, the Dorians arrived and made Astypálaia their capital, and in 700 BC they joined the Dorian Hexapolis: a political, religious and economic union that included the three cities of Rhodes, Cnidos and Halicarnassus on the Asia Minor coast.

Poised between East and West, Kos flourished by trading precious goods – and ideas. Nearby Halicarnassus (Bodrum) was the birth-place of Herodotus, the 'father of history', and in the 5th century BC Kos produced an innovating *papa* of its own: Hippocrates, father of medicine. Believing that diseases were not punishments sent from the gods but had natural causes, Hippocrates suggested that doctors should learn as much as possible about each patient and their symptoms before making a diagnosis. His school on Kos, where he taught a wholesome medicine based on waters, special diets, herbal remedies and relaxation, was renowned throughout the ancient world, and he set the standard of medical ethics incorpora-ted in the Hippocratic oath. When he died, his followers on Kos

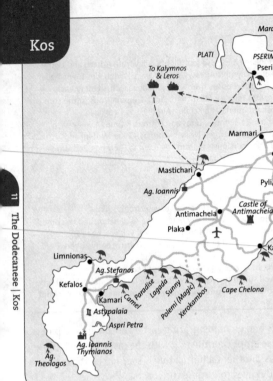

founded the Asklepeion (dedicated to the healing god Asklepios), and people from all over the Mediterranean came to be cured in its hospital-sanctuary.

In 411 BC, during the Peloponnesian War, the Spartans played a nasty trick on the island: pretending to be friends, they entered the capital Astypálaia and sacked it. In 366 BC the survivors re-founded the old Minoan/Mycenaean city of Kos, conveniently near the by-now flourishing Asklepeion. The next few centuries were good ones; besides physicians, Kos produced a school of bucolic poetry, led by Theocritus, a native of Sicily (319–250 BC). His charming 'Harvest Time in Kos', in which he evokes a walk across the island to drink wine by Demeter's altar, gave us the word 'idyllic'. Apelles, the greatest painter of Alexander's day, was a native of Kos, as was Philetas, inventor of the Alexandrine and teacher of another native, Ptolemy II Philadelphos, who went on to become king of Egypt; many subsequent Ptolemies were sent to Kos for their education. The Romans prized Kos for its translucent purple silks, wines and perfumes, and gave it a special autonomy because of the Asklepeion. St Paul called in and found an audience; so far 21 early Christian basilicas have been discovered on the island.

Kos's wealth and strategic position made it a prize for invading Persians, Saracens, pirates and Crusaders. The gods themselves, it seems, were jealous, and earthquakes in AD 142, 469 and 554 levelled most of the island's buildings. In 1315 the Knights of St John took control, and in 1391 built fortifications using the ancient city as a quarry. They were good enough to defy Turkish sieges in 1457 and 1477, but the Turks took over in 1523 by treaty after the fall of Rhodes. After almost 400 years they were toppled by the Italians, as on the other Dodecanese, and the island joined Greece in 1948.

Kos Town

Kos Town, in the region of the dolphin's eye, looks magical if you arrive by sea, especially at twilight: a medieval castle by the port, stately palms and pines and an evening scent of jasmine; opposite, the coast of Turkey fills the horizon. At close quarters, much of the town postdates the 1933 earthquake, and no other town in Greece looks like it, with its spacious design, Art Deco administration buildings and neighbourhoods put up by the Italians. Another side-effect of the quake: when the rubble was cleared away, large sections of ancient Kos were revealed, leaving fascinating Hellenistic and Roman ruins peppered amongst holiday bedlam. But there is also a tangible civic pride: Kos has a new water treatment system, new pedestrian areas and a one-way traffic system to cut down on some of the cacophony.

Up from the harbour, the city's main square, **Plateía Eleftherías**, has been freed of cars, leaving it with the air of a Pirandello character in search of a play. Here you'll find the 18th-century **Defterdar Mosque** (still used by the 50 or so Muslim families on the island, but not open to the public), and two Italian public buildings. One, laid out like a Roman house, holds the **Archaeology Museum**, where, fittingly, the prize exhibit is a 4th-century BC statue of Hippocrates with a noble, compassionate expression. Other items include an intriguing fragment of a scene of an Archaic symposium; a 2nd-century AD seated Hermes, with a little pet ram and red thumb; a statuette of a pugilist with enormous boxing gloves; and another of Hygeia, the goddess of health, feeding an egg to a snake. There are also fine mosaics, of a fish and of the god Asklepios with his sacred snake, stepping from a boat and welcomed to Kos by Hippocrates.

Archaeology Museum
t 224 202 8326; open Tues–Sun, 8.30–3; adm

Plateía Eleftherías also has the **market**, a good place to find fruit, vegetables and seashell kitsch – walk through it to **Plateía Ag. Paraskévi**, with its cafés and superb bougainvillaea. Buying and selling has gone on for millennia here; off Plateía Eleftherías, the **Pórta tou Foroú** (draped with another massive bougainvillaea), leads into the ancient *agora*, with the re-erected columns of a *stoa*. This was where the Knights of St John built their town and *auberges*, just as in Rhodes (*see* pp.407–408 and 411–13). When these collapsed in the earthquake, they revealed not only the market but the ancient harbour quarter, a Temple of Aphrodite Pandemos, and a 5th-century Christian basilica, all sprinkled with dried cat food by the Kos Animal Protection League. Around it are the narrow streets and innumerable trinket stands of the old Turkish quarter.

On the northern end of the *agora*, **Plateía Platánou** is almost entirely filled by **Hippocrates' plane tree**, its trunk 16m (52ft) in diameter, its huge boughs now supported by an intricate metal scaffolding instead of the marble columns that once kept the venerable tree from disaster. At an estimated 700 years old it may well be the most senior plane in Europe. Hippocrates may well have planted its grandmother, for he believed, as do modern Greeks, that of all the trees the shade of the plane is the most salubrious (and the fig the most enervating); *see* **Topics**, p.39. The Turks loved the old

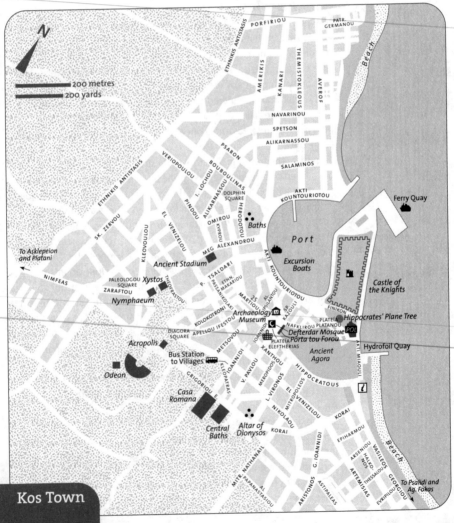

Kos Town

tree, and built a fountain with a sarcophagus for a basin and the **Mosque of the Loggia** (1786) to keep it company. On 1 September the citizens of Kos pluck a leaf from the tree to include in their harvest wreaths as a symbol of abundance.

The Castle of the Knights

Castle of the
Knights of St John
*t 224 202 8326;
open Tues–Sun
8.30–2.30; adm*

A stone bridge off Plateía Platánou crosses the former moat (now the Finíkon, or palm grove) to the **Castle of the Knights of St John**. Combined with the fortress across the strait in Bodrum, this was the premier outer defence of Rhodes. After an earthquake in 1495, Grand Master Pierre d'Aubusson rebuilt the walls and added the outer enceinte, and the tower overlooking the harbour bears his name and coat-of-arms. Since d'Aubusson mostly used stones from the *agora*, the masonry is a curious patchwork quilt of ancient inscriptions and coats-of-arms. Some have been removed to the castle's antiquarium, to join other stacks of defunct columns and marble that nobody seems to know what to do with. The castle's dishevelled weeds and wildflowers, and the stillness of the noonday sun, attracted Werner Herzog, whose first black and white film, *Signs of Life* (1966), took place within its walls; the elaborate cockroach traps and hypnotized chickens that played major roles, however, are no longer in evidence.

Roman Kos

From Plateía Eleftherías, Vas. Pávlou leads to other parts of **ancient Kos**. In the **Seraglio** quarter (don't expect any harem girls), houses going back to Minoan times were discovered. There's a ramped Hellenistic **Altar of Dionysos**, and, across Grigoríou Street, remains of the **Central Baths** (site of the Vourina spring, praised by Theocritus)

Casa Romana
*t 224 202 3234;
open Tues–Sun
8.30–2.30; adm*

and the recently renovated **Casa Romana**; both were victims of the earthquake of AD 554, and were excavated and reconstructed by the Italians in 1940. The house has good mosaics – the owner was fond of panthers – and offers a fair idea of the spacious elegance to which the wealthy of Kos could aspire; even on the hottest days it remains cool inside. West along Grigoríou Street, by the Catholic church, the Roman **Odeon** has rows of recently reclad marble seats and is now again used for concerts; the statue of Hippocrates in the museum was discovered under its arches. The city had three other theatres and a music school. As Strabo wrote, 'The city of the Koans is not large, but one lives better here than in others, and it appears beautiful to all who pass it by in their ships'.

Some of this good living is evident in the **Western Excavations** just opposite. Hellenistic walls surround the **Acropolis** (now studded with a minaret); on the other side you can pick out the marble-paved *cardo* and *decumanus*, the main arteries of Roman Kos, lined with ruined houses. Although the Italians took many of the best mosaics off to Rhodes, some good ones remain in situ, especially the **House of Europa** on the *decumanus*. Just north of this, along the *cardo*, is an elegant 3rd-century BC **Nymphaeum**, or fountain house, which supplied running water to the nearby public **lavatory** with marble seats – in winter rich men would have their slaves go ahead to sit and warm them up. The gymnasium has a *xystos*, a running track covered by a marble colonnade. The Romans also had a heated pool, in the brick **baths** (*thermae*) built inside the *xystos* track. Part of this complex was transformed into a Christian basilica in the 5th century; the lintel has been rebuilt and the baptistry has a well-preserved font. At the north end, an unidentified 3rd-century BC building contains mosaics of battling bulls, bears and boars. The partly excavated **Stadium** is along Tsaldári St; on the far side near the church is a well-preserved *aphesis*, or starting gate.

Beaches near Kos Town

Since the advent of the water treatment plant, Kos' town beaches have won blue flags, but that's about the nicest thing you can say about these strips of sand and pebbles crammed with sunbed concessions. City buses will take you in a few minutes to better, less crowded beaches north of town at **Lambí**; the closest strands to the south are at **Psalídi**, 3km away, and **Ag. Fokás** (8km). If there's a chill in the air, take bus no.5 to **Thermá** (13km), where volcanic sands, shallow water and thermal springs make sea bathing a few degrees warmer and a few degrees smellier, but bring plenty of moisturizer.

The Asklepeion and Platáni

Asklepeion
t 224 202 8763; open Tues–Sun 8.30–2.30; adm

A municipal bus, an hourly 'mini train' from the waterfront or a short bike climb will take you up to the Asklepeion, 4km west of the city. The German archaeologist Rudolf Herzog, following Strabo's description, discovered it in 1902, and it was partially restored by the Italians during their tenure. This was nothing less than the most important of the 300 known ancient hospitals, or shrines to the healing god Asklepios, served by the Asklepiada, an order of priests (Hippocrates was one) who found that good water, air and relaxing in beautiful surroundings did much to remedy the ills of body and soul. The cult symbol was the snake, the ancestor of the one twining itself around the modern caduesis. Snakes were seen as inter-mediaries between living and dead (they were often found in holes in cemeteries, eating mice fattened on grave offerings), and were believed to have a knack for seeking out healing herbs and transmitting dreams, which along with the power of suggestion, were part of the therapy. Hippocrates' disciples built the sanctuary after his death in 370 BC, and the Knights found it a convenient quarry.

Set on a hillside, the Asklepeion is built in a series of terraces split by a grand stair. On the lowest level are **Roman baths** of the 3rd century AD. The next level, once under a huge portico, has the **main entrance** and another large bath; here was the **medical school**, and the museum of anatomy and pathology, with descriptions of cures and votive offerings from grateful patients. Near the stair are the remains of a **temple** dedicated by Kos-born physician G. Stertinius Xenophon, who served as the Emperor Claudius' personal doctor and, on the orders of the empress Agrippina, murdered his patient by preparing poisoned mushrooms then sticking a poisoned feather down his throat, before retiring on Kos as a hero (so much for the Hippocratic oath!). On this level, too, was the **sacred spring of the god Pan**, used in the cures. On the next terrace is the **Altar of Asklepios**, and **Ionic temples** dedicated to Apollo and Asklepios (a few columns have been reconstructed by the Italians); on the top stood a Doric **Temple of Asklepios** from the 2nd century BC, the grandest and most sacred of all, and enjoying a view that in itself might make anyone feel better. In August, for the Hippocratia, the teenagers of Kos get off their motorbikes to don ancient *chitons* and wreaths to re-enact the old rituals and recite the Hippocratic oath.

Just up the road, the **International Hippocrates Foundation** is dedicated to medical research. In 1996, Nobel Prize winners and other leading lights attended the first 'International Medical Olympiad' here, and no, they didn't hold brain surgery races but gave out awards and held conferences. The five rings of the Olympic symbol were used to sum up Hippocratic philosophy: 'Life is short. Science is long. Opportunity is elusive. Experiment is dangerous. Judgement is difficult.'

On the way back down to Kos Town, along the cool cypress-lined avenue, stop for refreshments in **Platáni**, Kos' main Turkish settlement, although in the years after the crises over Cyprus some two-thirds of the residents moved to Turkey. It's a bit touristy, like everything on Kos, but the Turkish food is excellent and relatively cheap. A little out of Platáni are the **Muslim cemetery** and beyond that the **Jewish cemetery** in a pine grove; only one member of the community survived deportation in the Second World War.

11

The Dodecanese | Kos

Where to Stay in Kos Town

Kos Town ✉ 85300

Ancient visitors would stay in the Asklepeion and sacrifice a chicken to the gods. These days, beds can be so scarce in high season, you still might need that chicken. Package companies block-book nearly everything in the expensive and moderate range.

Kipriotis Village, 3km from the centre in Psalidi, t 224 202 7640, *www. kipirotis.gr* (€€€€€). Huge and packed with amenities: two pools, tennis, Jacuzzi, gym. *Open April–Oct.*

Oceanis, Psalidi, t 224 202 4641, *www. oceanis-hotel.gr* (€€€€€). Beachside complex set in a tropical garden; 370 rooms and four pools, including two sea water.

Platanista, Psalidi, t 224 202 7551, *www. platanista.gr* (€€€€€). Modern neo-Venetian *palazzo*, with tennis, pool, gym, tennis and kid's activities.

Ramira Beach, t 224 202 2891, *www. mitsis-ramirabeach.com* (€€€€€). Slightly more affordable and still well endowed with facilities.

Kos Apartments, Vas. Georgíos and Charmílou, t 224 202 5321, *www. koshotel.gr* (€€€). Pleasant studios, some with sea views, near the marina.

⭐ Petrino >>

⭐ Alexis >

Afendoulis, 1 Evripílou, in a quiet road near the sea, t 224 202 5321 (€€). Friendly, comfortable guest house with a fragrant terrace run by Ippokrátis.

Manos, 19 Artemisías, t 224 202 8931 (€). Rooms with balcony.

Alexis, 9 Irodótou, t 224 202 8798 (€). The Mecca for backpackers and full of character. Alex, brother of Ippokrátis, is amazingly helpful; the veranda reeks of jasmine in the evening.

Kos Camping, 3km from the port, t 224 202 3910 (€). Well-run with facilities from laundry to bike hire. A minibus meets the ferries. *Open May–Oct.*

Eating Out in Kos Town

Beware the waterfront restaurants and their pushy touts.

Anatolia Hammam, 3 Diagora Square, overlooking the Western Excavations, t 224 202 8323 (€22). One of the lovelier places to dine, in the sumptuously restored Turkish bath, with a terrace.

Antonis, 56 Artemisías. A real neighbourhood taverna with good food, big portions, and low prices.

Arap, in Platáni, t 224 202 8442. The best of the handful of tavernas here serving Turkish food; excellent aubergine with yoghurt, *borek*, shish kebab.

Eudokia, 9 Bouboulínas, t 224 202 8525 (€15). Absolutely simple-looking place, very Greek, serving some of the most authentic cooking and seafood here.

Mavromatis, on the way to Psalídi, near the Ramira Beach Hotel, t 224 202 2433. Tranquil place with traditional food; nice setting and a good bargain.

Nestoras, near the campsite in Psalídi. Reliable taverna, now offering some ambitious cooking.

Nick the Fisherman, 21 Avérof, t 224 202 3098 (€22). So-so setting, but Nick's catch comes at good prices, often accompanied by *bouzoúki* music.

Petrino, Pl. Ioánnou tou Theológou, t 224 202 7251 (€30). The classiest restaurant on the island, serving exquisite Mediterranean and Greek cuisine in a beautifully restored Turkish stone building with a classy courtyard.

Otto e Mezzo, 21 Apelloú, t 224 202 0069 (€30). In the Old Town, fresh pasta dishes; intimate indoor dining and summer garden.

Platanos, in the square around Hippocrates' tree, t 224 202 8991 (€28). Atmospheric creeper-draped dining; expensive international and traditional dishes and live music.

Spitaki, in Psalídi, t 224 202 7655. Beachside taverna; pasta and grills.

Entertainment and Nightlife in Kos Town

Kos is one big party at night. The *agora* is alive with thumping from 'Bar Alley' on Navklírou St. Discos go in and out of fashion every season.

Kalua and Heaven, at Lámbi on Zouroúdi. Both discos have a watery backyard and garden.

Hammam, Navarinou St. Little disco with Greek and international music, in the old Turkish baths.

Fashion Club, Dolphins Square, giant disco with occasional fashion shows.

Orpheus Cinema. Films (many in English or subtitled) play at the indoor screen in Plateía Eleftherías and the outdoor screen along Vas. Georgíou St, t 224 202 5713.

Taurus Bar, 9 Mandilára St. For anyone homesick for football, rugby, cricket, or just about any other sport, this venue keeps up with all the scores and shows many matches live.

Around the Island

The northeast of Kos is flat and fertile, with fields of watermelons and tomatoes. Beyond Lambí and the reach of the town bus, **Tingáki** is a little resort with lovely views over Psérimos, and still has a village feel, especially when the daytrippers have gone. **Boat Beach** (with a beached vessel), before Tingáki, is quiet and has a taverna. In March and April, the nearby salt pans, **Alíkes**, are a favourite port of call for flamingos and numerous migratory birds, while the sandy coast and estuary are loggerhead turtle nesting areas. At the far end of the wetlands, **Marmári** is packaged, but offers a generous sandy beach and a chance to explore local byways on horseback at the **Marmári Riding Centre**. Just inland towards **Zipári** (500m from the village centre) the Paleochristian basilica of **Ag. Pávlos** has a beautiful mosaic floor and picturesque remains of its baptistry. Above, Kos' spinal ridge has a bumpy, curiously two-dimensional profile.

Marmári Riding Centre
t 224 204 1783

But these are real mountains, not a child's drawing. From Zipári, the road twists up to **Asfendíou**, a cluster of five villages in the woods, with whitewashed houses and flower-filled gardens, many now being turned into holiday homes. The highest of the five hamlets, **Ziá**, is a pretty place, of fresh springs, fruit and walnut groves – it was the bucolic Pryioton described by Theocritus – although it's now a 'traditional village' for coach parties, who come for spectacular sunsets and a 'Greek Night' in the schlocky tavernas; but there are others, too, such as the excellent Taverna Olympiada. On the outskirts of town, the church of **Panagía Ypapandí** was built in 1082 by the Blessed Christódoulos. Kos' ancient sculptors came up here to quarry marble from Mt Oromedon, now known as **Díkaios Christós**, 'Justice of Christ'. It can be reached without too much difficulty in about three hours from Ziá, and well worth it for the views.

From the Asfendíou a road runs across country to **Lagoúdi** and **Amaníou**, where there's a turn-off to the path up to **Palaío Pýli**, the Byzantine capital of Kos, now a ghost town with a castle on a crag surrounded by walls camouflaged in the rocks, and three churches, one with 14th-century frescoes; there are beautiful views from the castle. Another side lane, just west of Amaníou, leads to the fenced-off **Charmyleion**, a hero shrine or tomb with twelve little vaults, re-used as a church. **Pýli** below is a farming village, although the upper part of town has a great taverna for lunch, by a spring-fed fountain built in 1592 – although it's considerably less handsome after recent 'improvements'. On 23 April, Pýli holds a horse race, with an Easter egg as prize, cracked on the brow of the winning horse – a custom going back to remote antiquity.

Further west, in a wild setting, the **Castle of Antimácheia** was built by the Knights as a prison for their misbehaving peers in the mid-14th century. Within its mighty triangular walls are two churches (one with a fresco of St Christopher carrying baby Jesus), a few cisterns and, over the gateway, the arms of Pierre d'Aubusson. The sprawling village of **Antimácheia**, near the airport, has the island's last intact windmill as its landmark, although the last miller died in 2005. If it's reopened you can also visit the nearby **Traditional House**; the typical boxed-in beds were often built high so olives and wine could be stored underneath. **Pláka**, on a paved road from the airport, is a green oasis and picnic ground, with peacocks and great sunsets.

Traditional House
open 8–4.30

There are more beaches on either coast: to the south, the sand stretches between **Tolári** and **Kardámena**, now a heaving British and Scandinavian package destination, complete with pubs, chips and *smorgasbord*, plus golden sand and boats to Níssyros. On the north coast, **Mastichári** is quieter, and has boats for Kálymnos and Psérimos. Take the beach path, between the Achilleos Hotel and the sea, to see the ruins of a 5th-century basilica of **Ag. Ioánnis** with a fine if gravel-covered mosaic floor.

At **Kamári** by the dolphin's tail, there are more mosaics (again, under sand), columns and the remains of an atrium and baptistries linked to the ruins of the best Paleochristian churches on the island, the twin 5th-century basilicas of **Ag. Stéfanos**, its atrium often washed by the sea. The bay has a centrepiece in **Kastrí**, a natural volcanic bulwark of an islet, often surrounded by windsurfers skimming over the blue sheet, with a Club Med complex.

A long fringe of sand runs under the cliffs to the east with a few access roads; the steepest descent is to pretty **Camel Beach**, by picturesque rocks, and the easiest to overrated **Paradise Beach** (or 'Bubble Beach' after the volcanic bubbles that rise to the surface through the clear waters at one end of the bay); it's perfect for children, although they'll have to fight their way through the forest of sunbeds to get to the water. Further along the headland to the left, the beaches **Lagáda** (or Banana – the most beautiful with its dunes), **Sunny**, attractive **Polémi** (or **Magic**) and **Xerókambos** are much quieter.

Kéfalos high up on the headland of the dolphin's tail is the bus terminus and windsurfing centre. Another Knights' castle looks down here over Kamári and, although it doesn't look particularly impressive, it inspired travellers' tales in the Middle Ages, all involving a dragon; John Mandeville in his *Travels* claims the serpent was none other than Hippocrates' daughter, enchanted by Artemis and awaiting a knight brave enough to kiss her to transform her back into a maiden. South, just off the road, there's a Byzantine chapel of **Panagía Palatianí** built out of a temple that once belonged to the ancient capital of Kos, **Astypalaia** (signposted Palatia), the birthplace of Hippocrates. A few bits of the ancient city remain, including a theatre. Isthmioton, another ancient city on the peninsula, was important enough in the past to send its own delegation to Délos, but not a trace of it remains. A paved road descends 7km to **Ag. Theológos**, offering some of the most secluded swimming (but often big waves) and a nice taverna. Neolithic remains from 3500 BC were found in the **Áspri Pétra Cave** just south, reached by a path in half an hour. The road passes through dramatic scenery, past sheer cliffs and a communications tower, then ends at the charming **Monastery of Ag. Ioánnis Thymianós**, 6km from Kéfalos.

Where to Stay and Eat around Kos

Tingáki ✉ 85300

Meni Beach, t 224 206 9217, *www. hotelmenibeach.com* (€€). Pleasant, with a pool and family rooms.

Park Lane, 150m back from the beach, **t** 224 206 9170, *www.parklane.gr* (€€). Package-dominated family hotel, with pool and playground.

Paxinos, t 224 206 9306 (€). Typical.

Marmári ✉ 85300

Grecotel Royal Park, t 224 204 1488, *www.grecotel.gr* (€€€€€). The smartest place to stay. *Open May–Oct.*

Esperia, t 224 204 2010, *www.hotel esperiakos.gr* (€€). Family-orientated, with a pool.

Tam Tam Beach Taverna, between Marmári and Mastichári, by Troúlos Beach. German-run, and a lovely place for lunch or dinner.

Kardámena ✉ 85302

Summer Palace, Tolári Beach **t** 224 209 2730 (€€€€). Bungalows, pools, water-slides on a huge beach. *Open May–Oct.*

Porto Bello Beach, t 224 209 1217 (€€€). Luxurious setting with views of Níssyros, a huge pool and private beach, and its original flooring.

Avli, t 224 209 2100. Excellent home-cooked dishes and grill. *Open May–Oct.*

Taverna Andreas. Refuses to pander to tourists and has good ethnic dishes.

Mastichári ✉ 85301

Neptune, t 224 204 1480, *www. neptune.gr* (€€€€€). A 15-hectare private estate on the beach, done up Greek island style, with a state-of-the-art spa and all the trimmings. Its gourmet resturant **Proteas** (€45) is one of the best on Kos, serving refined Mediterranean cuisine. *Open May–Oct.*

Mastichari Bay, t 224 205 9300 (€€€). Good for families, with lots of activi-ties, nice pool and beach, playground, floodlit tennis and open-air theatre.

Arant, just back from the road and very close to the beach, **t** 224 205 1167 (€).

Mastichari Beach, near the harbour, **t** 224 205 1371 (€). Clean, with sea views.

Panorama, t 224 205 9019, *www.kos panorama.gr* (€). Studios on the sands.

Kali Kardia. The oldest taverna in town.

Makis, just off the waterside, **t** 224 205 9061. Long-established taverna.

Kéfalos ✉ 85301

Panorama, perched above packageville overlooking Kastrí island, **t** 224 207 1524, *www.panorama-kefalos.gr* (€). Quiet studios that live up to the name and a garden; including breakfast.

Stamatia, by the sea. Wide selection of fish, including 'dogs' teeth' for adventurous diners.

Limnionas, above the tiny fishing port of Limniónas, **t** 693 242 2002. Peaceful place with views over Kálymnos, serving up a fishy feast. Excellent lobster spaghetti. *Open May–Oct.*

Psérimos (ΨΕΡΙΜΟΣ)

Psérimos, wedged between Kos and Kálymnos, has a beautiful beach of soft golden sand on a turquoise sea, as good as any in the Caribbean, which its 30 residents have come to regard in part as a curse, as day in and day out during high season it becomes invisible under the crowds. Even in September, excursion boats from Kos

Where to Stay and Eat on Psérimos

Psérimos ✉ 85200

If the rooms are full, you can sleep out on one of the island's more distant beaches, a kilometre from the village.

Most of the tavernas on the main beach are packed, and the service surly at lunchtime.

Tripolitis, on the sea, over Mr Saroukos' taverna, **t** 224 302 3196 (€).

Taverna Manola, t 224 302 1540. Simple stuff, also **rooms/studios** (€).

Getting to Psérimos

The daily **ferry** from Kálymnos is timed for the island's schoolchildren. It leaves for Psérimos daily at 4pm, and returns at 9.30 in the morning. Other boats from Kálymnos and Kos Town are for daytrippers, although you can use them to stay overnight.

Town, Mastichári and Kálymnos queue up to dock, some only staying an hour. It becomes even more crowded on 15 August, when hundreds of pilgrims attend the *panegýri* at its **Monastery Grafiótissa**. If you are staying any length of time (when the day boats have gone the people become quite friendly), you'll probably want to take to the interior by day, or hunt up one of the smaller pebbly strands on the east coast. Some boats now head instead to the adjacent islet of **Platí**, with another sandy beach, and make a day of it by stopping for lunch in Kálymnos.

Léros (ΛΕΡΟΣ)

With an intricate jigsaw-puzzle-piece of a coastline, sweeping hills, huge sheltered anchorages that played a role in the last world war, clear seas and unspoiled villages, Léros is a beautiful island. Few, however, have had such a bad press. In Greece, it has long been the butt of jokes, where its name evokes the same reaction as 'Bedlam' in Britain; to make matters worse, Léros sounds like *léra*, 'filth' or 'rogue'. The 1989 UK Channel 4 documentary exposing the grim conditions in its psychiatric hospitals, followed by an EU probe, prodded the authorities to get their act together and close down the worst wards; today the hospitals, with their progressive outpatient facilities, are held up as the finest in Greece.

Lacking big sandy beaches, Léros gets only a smattering of package holidaymakers, but plenty of Italian tourists. It is a musical place, home of the Hajiadákis family whose songs have influenced Greece's leading composers; it's not at all rare to hear the hammer dulcimer (*sandoúri*), or the bagpipes (*tsamboúna*); a traditional music school, founded in 2000, makes sure the young won't forget.

History

On the death of the hero Meleager (of Chalydonian boar hunt fame), his sisters went into such desperate mourning that Artemis turned them into guinea fowl (*meleagrides*) and installed them in her temple on Léros. The worship of Artemis and her guinea fowl has been traced back to the island's Ionian colonists; Robert Graves notes that, because of their refusal to adopt patriarchal religion, the island had a bad press even in ancient times: the Greeks called the Leriots 'evil-livers' (a famous epigram went, 'The Lerians are all bad, not merely some Lerians, but every one of them – all except Prokles,

Getting to Léros

By air: Flights arrive daily except Tues from Athens, also Tues and Thurs flights to Kos and Rhodes with Olympic, **t** 224 702 2844. **Airport**: **t** 224 702 2777; it is best reached by taxi.

By sea: There are ferries daily with Pátmos, Kos and Rhodes, 6 days a week to Piraeus and Kálymnos, 4 a week to Arkí, Lipsí, Agáthonissi, Sámos and Symi, once to twice a week with Níssyros and Tílos; **excursion boats** go from Ag. Marína to Lipsí, Arki, Maráthi, Tiganákia and Pátmos (**Lipsos Travel, t** 224 704 1225). A **caique** once a day in high season sails from Xirókambos to Myrtiés, Kálymnos. **Port authority**: Lakkí, **t** 224 702 2234.

Getting around Léros

Buses run 5 times daily in season between Plefoúti, Parthéni, Alínda, Plátanos, Lakkí and Xirókambos.
Hire a car, motorbike or boat at **Motoland**, in Pentéli and Alínda, **t** 697 260 0035
Taxi ranks: Lakkí, **t** 224 702 2550, Ag. Marína, **t** 224 702 3340, Plátanos, **t** 224 702 3070 (prices are more or less fixed and reasonable).

and of course he is a Lerian too'). Fittingly for an island dedicated to Artemis, property has traditionally been passed down through the female line so most of Léros is owned, at least on paper, by women.

Homer included Léros with Kálymnos as the 'Kalydian isles' in his 'Catalogue of Ships'. In the Peloponnesian War the island sided with Sparta, despite its Ionian ancestry. Under the Romans, pirates preying along its coast nabbed a handsome young lawyer named Julius Caesar on his way home from Bithynia, where according to rumour he had a dissolute affair with the governor; released after a month when his ransom was paid, Caesar in his first military action captured and crucified every brigand around Léros. Under the Byzantines, the island was controlled by Sámos, but in 1316 it was sold to the Knights of St John and governed by the Duke of Náxos as part of Pátmos.

Léros paid a high price for its excellent anchorages in the Second World War. After 1912, the Italians built their main air and naval ordnance bases at Lépida. Their Eastern Mediterranean fleet was based in superb Lakkí Bay where Mussolini built an imperial new city from scratch named Portolago (modern Lakkí). After the Italian surrender in 1943, Churchill sent British crack troops the Long Range Desert Group and Special Boat Squadron to occupy the island, hoping to open up a new front and encourage Turkey to take sides with the Allies, but it was a disaster: they had no air cover, and Hitler sent in an overwhelming force of paratroopers to take it back, in the Battle of Léros (12–16 November), in what was the last major British defeat in the war. The Allies in turn bombed the German fleet at Lakkí, and for three years after the war the British held the fort. When the junta took power in 1967, Communist dissidents were imprisoned in the notorious camp in Parthéni; during the later Cyprus dispute the Greek government dismantled Léros' military installations to show that it had no warlike intentions against Turkey.

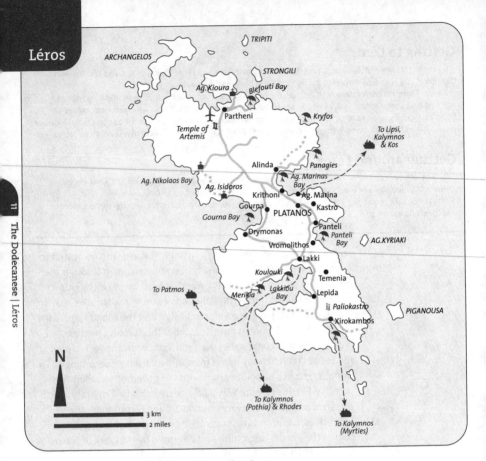

Lakki and South Léros

If Fellini had been Greek, **Lakki** would have been one of his
favourite sets. The planned curving streets of Il Duce's dream capital,
designed for 30,000 inhabitants, are wide enough to accommodate
military parades, though today they're usually as empty as a scene in
a De Chirico painting. This tribute to Italian Rationalist architecture,
or 'Ignored Internationalism' as the one Greek writer called it, was
abandoned after the war when the Lerians decided to make the
more convivial Plátanos the capital; it remains dilapidated but
weirdly compelling. Among the most striking buildings are the **clock
tower** and, one street away, the **cinema**; a bomb went through the
roof during the war, but the locals ever since have come to watch
films under the stars, and in 2006 it was under restoration – along
with the original popcorn machine – thanks to an EU grant. Adjacent
stand the **town hall** and Fascist headquarters, equipped with a
tower for speeches. The old Hotel Roma, later the **Leros Palace**,
remains stuffed with litter, awaiting a new role. Located in an old
defence tunnel, the **Leros War Museum** contains relics from the
battles. Near the waterfront there's a **monument** to the many who

Leros War Museum
*open summer
Tues–Sun 10–1*

perished in 1943 when a Greek ship, the *Queen Olga*, was bombed by German planes and sunk in Lakkí's harbour. One of the three psychiatric hospitals across the bay was originally built as Mussolini's summer retreat.

A path leading up from the jetty goes to the nearest beach at **Kouloúki**, with a taverna. At **Lépida**, across the harbour, the **Moní Panagía** is built on the ruins of an old lighthouse, and further south, overlooking **Xirókambos**, is the fort of **Paliokástro**, built near an older fortification dating back to the 3rd century BC. The church inside has a few mosaics, and Xirókambos itself, a simple fishing village, has a basic beach to the west. In summer the caique goes over to Myrtiés on Kálymnos once a day. There are also secluded pebbly coves accessible from a track beside the chapel.

Pantéli, Plátanos and Ag. Marína

Up the tree-lined hill from Lakkí, it's only 3km to the popular coarse sandy beach of **Vromólithos** ('Dirty Rock'), with sunbeds and tavernas, prettily closed in by deeply wooded hills. There are more places to stay a 10-minute walk away at **Pantéli**, a working fishing village by day with caiques and passing yachts, and by night the rendezvous of seafood-lovers, with tables spilling on to the tree-fringed beach.

Up hill, the capital, **Plátanos**, is near the centre of Léros. A pretty place with a smattering of neoclassical houses, its ancient acropolis was taken over by the **Kástro**, a Byzantine castle renovated by the Knights and the Greek military, and most recently by the EU. A road winds to the top, but you can also go up the old-fashioned way, up 370 steps. From the top, the 'four seas' of Léros are spread at your feet: the bays of Pantéli, Ag. Marína, Gourná and Lakkí. Within the walls, the church of the **Megalóchari Kyrás Kástrou** houses a miraculous icon of the Virgin. The story goes that during the Turkish occupation the icon set sail from Constantinople on a boat lit by a sacred candle, and landed on Léros. The inhabitants carried it in procession to the cathedral. The next day, however, the icon had vanished and the Turkish captain of the Kástro found it, candle still blazing, in his gunpowder store. The icon was taken back to the cathedral, but the following nights decamped to the arsenal again and again, until the Turkish governor gave the store room to the Christians. They cleaned it up, and the wilful icon has been happy ever since.

Kástro
open 8–1; adm

Archaeology Museum
open Tues–Sun, 8.30–2.30

Near the town hall, the **Archaeology Museum** has a collection of photos and local finds from the island. Walk down the main street to reach **Ag. Marína**, the seaside extension of Plátanos, with a pretty Italian market and little white houses and an often windswept port, full of fishermen and excursion boats from Lípsi and Pátmos; there are tavernas, and accommodation up the road at **Krithóni**.

Álinda and the North

Álinda, once the old commercial port of Léros, is the island's oldest and biggest resort, although still low-key by Kos standards. There's a long sandy beach, with water sports and seafront tavernas. The pretty mosaics of an early Christian basilica, **Panagía Galatiani**, lie in the forecourt of the town hospice. Nearby, the immaculate **British War Cemetery**, with 183 graves, looks out over the crystal bay. Léros has strong links with Egypt as many notables fled to Cairo in the 1920s, and Álinda's folly, the **Bellini Tower**, was built by one of them, Paríssis Bellínis; it now houses a **Historic and Folk Museum** with folk exhibits, photos and items from the Battle of Léros.

North of Álinda, a track leads to the secluded beaches at **Panagíes** and pebbly **Kryfós**, a hard scramble but you may well be the only one there. There's a large sandy beach just over the isthmus at **Gourná**, but it tends to be windblown; you're better off seeking out one of the small coves leading to Léros' answer to Corfu's Mouse Island, **Ag. Isidóros**, a white chapel perched on an islet reached by a causeway. A rough road leads to the coves at **Ag. Nikólaos** in lonely country further along the coast.

The road north to the airport has a sign for the low walls of the ancient **Temple of Artemis** (which was more likely an ancient fort) but they still enjoy a superb setting, where you can linger under a sacred myrtle tree. Further north, **Parthéni** ('the Virgins'), former centre of guinea fowl worship, is a military base built by the Italians and now used by the Greeks – from 1967–74 as a detention centre for political dissidents, some of whom decorated the walls of the church of **Ag. Kioúra** (*always open*) with striking if less than Orthodox paintings that are now protected as a historic monument. There's a pretty beach with shade at **Blefoúti**, in a lake-like bay with a good summer taverna.

Historic and Folk Museum
open May–Sept Tues–Sun 10–1 and 6–9; adm

Useful Information on Léros

ⓘ **Léros >**
At the quay in Ag. Marína, and in Lakki, t 224 702 2937

Kastis Travel, Lakki, t 224 7022 500 (also in Ag. Marína, t 224 702 2140). Help with accommodation and tickets.

Léros Festivals

Pre-Lent Carnival: children don monks' robes and visit the homes of the newly married, reciting verses made up by their elders.

16–17 July: Ag. Marína.

First 10 days Aug: Alindeia in Álinda, a sailing, rowing and swimming regatta run since 1907.

6 Aug: Plátanos.

15 Aug: At the Kástro (Plátanos).

20 Aug: Foreign tourist day in Álinda.

24–25 Sept: Lakkí.

Where to Stay and Eat on Léros

The lushness of Léros translates into airborne divisions of Lilliputian vampires by night, so bring bug-goo.

Lakkí ✉ 85400

Castle Vigla, 2km from town, t 224 702 4083, *www.castlevigla.gr* (€€€). Six studios sleeping four in stone villas furnished with antiques, with lovely views over towards the castle.

Katikíes, t 224 702 3624, *www.katikies leros.gr* (€€€). Lovely studios and apartments in traditional style, away from the road and sleeping up to four.

Katerina, t 224 702 2460 (€). All in cool marble.

Merikia, just out of town, at the eponymous beach. A good bet for fish.

Petrinos, t 224 702 4807. A touch of class, specializing in refined meat dishes influenced by the time owner-chef Giorgios spent in Belgium; Lerians flock here all year.

Xirókambos ✉ 85400

Efstathia, t 224 702 4199 (€€). Roomy studios and apartments with pool.

Miramare, nearby, **t** 224 702 2469, *www.leroshotelmiramare.co.uk* (€€). Gilds the lily with its gold cornicing, but is central and comfortable. *Open all year.*

 Neromylos >>

Camping Léros, up the road, **t** 224 702 3367. The island's only one, with a diving club. *Open end May–Oct.*

Aloni, t 224 702 6048. Lovely traditional food and fish by the sea. *Open daily June–Sept, otherwise weekends Fri, Sat and Sun lunch only.*

Vromólithos ✉ 85400

Tony's Beach Studios, t 224 702 4742, *www.tonysbeachstudios.gr* (€€). Often has rooms while the rest tend to be block-booked.

The Well. Summer HQ for an Athenian chef with an international flair.

Frangos, slap on the beach, **t** 224 702 3040. Legendary for traditional food.

 Archontikó Angeloú >>

Paradisos, on the sea, **t** 224 702 4632. A good menu and lovely views; live Greek music some nights.

Pantéli ✉ 85400

Aphrodite, t 224 702 3447, *www. aphroditeleros.co.uk* (€). Rooms and studios, some with sea-views.

Cavos, t 224 702 3247 (€). Typical rooms and studios (the same family also owns Pension Anastasios, in Vromólithos).

Drosia, t 224 702 2798. Less touristy than some, with fish almost leaping from the family nets.

Maria, at the eastern end of the strand. Popular with the local fishermen. Gold-toothed Maria will rustle you up a huge dish of whitebait-style *marídes* or *kalamári* fresh from their caiques.

Psaropoula, on the beach, **t** 224 702 5200 (€20). Traditional fish taverna: try the seafood with rice. *Open all year.*

Plátanos ✉ 85400

Eleftheria, t 224 702 3550 (€€). Pleasant and quiet family apartments and doubles with a pool, owned by Antónis Kanáris of the local Laskarina Travel agency, confusingly unconnected with the British holiday company.

Nefeli Apartments, t 224 702 4611 (€€). Tasteful, upmarket establishment designed by a woman architect.

Ag. Marína ✉ 85400

Kapaniri. The place to sample a selection of *mezédes* with your ouzo.

Neromylos, just outside Ag. Marína, **t** 224 702 4894. Newly opened and popular with locals and tourists alike for its traditional *mezédes* and dishes; in summer be sure to book.

Krithóni ✉ 85400

Crithóni Paradise, in Krithóni, **t** 224 702 5120 (€€€). Swish complex with references to traditional architecture; pool, landscaped gardens and piano bar. Very relaxing.

Esperides, t 224 702 2537. Taverna serving a tasty mix of Greek and international specialities. *Open June–Oct.*

Glaros. t 224 702 2497. Corners the pizza market in Krithóni; also steaks.

Álinda ✉ 85400

Archontikó Angeloú, t 224 702 2749, *www.hotel-angelou-leros.com* (€€€–€€). Built in 1895, lovingly restored and set in a cool, flowery garden.

Marilen, t 224 702 4100, *www. marilen.gr* (€€€–€€). Studios with air-conditioning and satellite TV spread in six buildings overlooking a pool-bar area; buffet breakfast included.

Ara, 300m from the beach, **t** 224 702 4140, *www.hotelara.com* (€€). Set up high with lofty views of both 'seas'; family-run studios and apartments, restaurant, pool, billiards, video games and Internet access.

Boulafendis Bunglalows, t 224 702 3515, *www.boulafendis.gr* (€€). Pleasant, spacious studio development a stone's throw from the sea, around a traditional mansion and pool-bar area.

Chryssoula, t 224 702 2451 (€€). Bright white studios overlooking a pool and the sea, 300m away.

Papafotis, t 224 702 2247 (€). Friendly owner; the rooms and studios facing the mountains are naturally air-conditioned by the *meltémi*.

Álinda, t 224 702 3266. Also known as Maurákis, the best taverna for traditional fare, served on the veranda or in the courtyard. Also **rooms** to let (€).

Da Guisi e Marcello, t 224 702 4888. Little trattoria serving classic Italian dishes. *Open eves only, Feb–Nov.*

Finikas, t 224 702 2695. A reliable old seaside favourite.

Entertainment and Nightlife on Léros

In summer, look out for the **Léros Theatre Group** and **Artemis**, a society dedicated to the revival of the island dances in traditional costumes.

Savanna, in Pantéli at the end of the harbour. Bar of character (and characters) owned by Brits Simon and Peter. Pantéli also has a disco.

Faros, Ag. Marína. International music.

Palatino, Álinda. Waterfront cocktail bar, with a range of musical predilections. Succumb to a sundae with good music and the live Greek variety on summer weekends.

Puerto Club, Lakki. For a bit of a dance.

Níssyros (ΝΙΣΥΡΟΣ)

In the great war between gods and giants, one of the casualties was the fiery Titan Polyvotis, who so irked Poseidon that the sea god ripped off a chunk of Kos and hurled it on top of him as he tried to swim away. This became the island of Níssyros, and the miserable Polyvotis, pinned underneath, sighs and fumes, unable to escape.

The myth is geologically sound. Níssyros, the 'Polo mint island' – round and green outside, white inside with a hole in the middle – was indeed once part of Kos, and one of the craters of its volcano is named after the smouldering giant. Originally a great Bali Hai mountain in the sea, Polyvotis made his most famous attempt to break out in a massive eruption at some distant prehistoric date, imploding in the middle to form the central Lákki plain, a wasted moonscape of slag heaps and sulphurous rocks. Dormant these days – the last eruption was in 1933, although there were tremors big enough to cause structural damage in Mandráki in 1997– the volcano dominates the island's character as well as its tourist industry. While daytrippers from Kos dominate the latter, most of the considerable income of the island's 930 residents derives from Níssyros' little sister islet of Gialí, which it leases out to a pumice-mining company. In the old days, however, it was an island of farmers: the rich soil holds tightly to water so Níssyros is lush, where cows and pigs are a common sight in fields, and olives, figs, citrus and almonds grow dishevelledly on neglected hillside terraces. There are some fine walks, however, and beaches amid the volcanic jumble of the coast. Drinking water, however, is a constant problem, and, although there is a desalination plant, it isn't always working and the tap water is ghastly.

Getting to and around Níssyros

A daily **taxi boat** and the *Nissiros Express* sail to Kardámena (Kos). There is a **ferry** once a week to Kos, Kálymnos, Tílos, Sými, Rhodes, Léros, Pátmos, Piraeus, and Sýros. **Port authority: t** 224 203 1222.

The island has a regular **bus** service, **t** 224 203 1204, from the harbour to Pálli via White Beach, but buses for the village of Emborió and Nikiá leave early morning and return mid-afternoon only.

There are several **car hire** places (**Diakomichalis**, Enetikon Travel, **t** 224 2031 180), but book ahead in summer; at the same time beware parking is very difficult.

Níssyros also has two **taxi** firms, Bobby's, **t** 224 203 1460, and Irene's, **t** 224 203 1474. A round-island tour will cost about €25; to the volcano €18.

Mandráki

Most people arrive in Mandráki, the capital and port, to a confusion of volcano-bound tour buses, garish souvenir shops and tavernas aimed at daytrippers. A short walk away to the village centre and the picture improves: with its seaside castle and higgledy-piggledy. lanes, cobbled or picked out with pebble mosaic patterns, twisting under the colourful wooden balconies of the tall, brightly painted houses, Mandráki is one of the prettiest villages in the Dodecanese. Designed to confound marauding pirates, there's still an air of introspection, especially during siesta-time, with the shutters pulled tight over the traditional embroidered curtains.

11

The Dodecanese | Níssyros

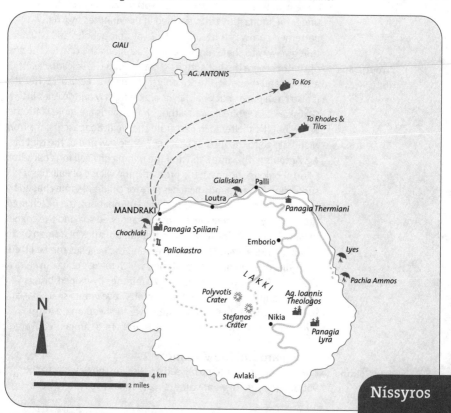

Níssyros

Seawards the lanes aim for **Plateía Ilikioméni**, the village social centre, while others weave inland past the public **orchard** or *kámbo* into a succession of shady squares. Signs point the way to major attractions: up to the **Kástro** (or **Enetikon**), built by the Venetians and taken over in 1315 by the Knights, and, within its walls, the **Monastery of Panagía Spilianí**, Our Lady of the Cave, with a church of uncertain date carved out of the rock where the Virgin made an early appearance. Inside, a finely carved iconostasis displays a venerated icon of the Virgin; the church's fame grew after raiding Saracens failed to find its secret trove of silver, worked into the rich collection of icons. By 2007, the island's new Archaeological and Historical Museum by the *kámbo* should open.

A path leads up in 20 minutes from the pretty **Langadáki** quarter, crossing fields and olive groves to the 7th century BC Doric **Paliokástro**, a spectacular site with vast well-preserved Cyclopean walls and gate. The acropolis of ancient Níssyros, a mighty bastion, dates back 2,000 years, and you can walk along the top of the wide walls, from where they used to pour boiling oil on attackers.

Beaches and a Spa

The nearest beach (often windswept) to Mandráki is **Chochláki**, under the monastery cliffs, reached in five minutes by a daisy-patterned pathway. It has blue-black volcanic pebbles and boulders, that give way to shale further along. East along the coast is the spa of **Loutrá**, where the hot springs straight from the volcano ease arthritis and rheumatism, but only if you have a medical certificate; it also has a good snack bar. Beyond, 2km from Mandráki, lies little **Gialiskári** (aka White Beach) although the sands are more black then white, but it's sheltered in part from the wind. Boat excursions from Mandráki go to the further beaches (*see* below) and to the islet of **Ag. Antónis** with white sand and the mining on Gialí for a backdrop.

Further along the coast, the pretty fishing village of **Pálli** has a succession of dark sandy beaches safe for children, some shaded by tamarisks. Past an incongruous central roundabout, the beach road, hung over with fig trees, leads to an abandoned spa and the chapel of **Panagía Thermianí**, tucked into the vault of ancient Roman bath. In August the *meltémi* blows fiercely and the beaches can be littered with junk or bobbing pumice stones, which make great souvenirs for the bath. About an hour's walk, or 20 minutes by moped, brings you to the island's best beaches: **Lýes**, a pretty cove with a snack bar, and even more beautiful **Pachiá Ámmos** over the headland, a long stretch of pinkish dunes, where the island's free campers converge.

Loutrá Spa
*open mornings,
June–Oct*

In and around the Volcano

⚡ **Níssyros Volcano**

The excursion not to be missed on Níssyros, however, is to the volcano (be sure to wear sturdy shoes). It has five craters – the

391

biggest two are **Polivótis** and **Stéfanos**, the latter 24m (80ft) deep and 350m (1,150ft) across. Buses leave the port in succession as excursion boats arrive; if you want more time and a bit of solitude, take the taxi or bus to Nikiá (*see* below) in the morning and walk down. There are wonderful views from the winding road, where the greenery and terraces offer a striking contrast to the vast plain below, an extraterrestrial landscape of pale greys and yellows, the smell of sulphur so pungent that you can almost see cartoon stink lines curling up out of the crater. After passing several geothermal pools, the bus stops near the great fuming heart of Stéfanos. A slippery zigzag path descends to the floor of the crater, with bubbling fumaroles all around. You can feel the great heat and turmoil of the gases beneath the crust; in some places the crust is so fragile that your foot could go through, so if you have children in tow, make sure they don't stray. After the steam and the stench, you can join the queues to quench your thirst at the **café** on the rim of the crater. A trail from the access road leads to Polyvótis, which is nearly as large and does all the erupting.

Two villages cling to the rim of the crater. **Emborió** above Pálli (linked by an old cobbled pathway) only has a handful of inhabitants who haven't emigrated to Australia or America, but the population rises in the summer, as houses are being restored as holiday homes. Many of these come with a free mod con in the basement: natural volcanic saunas. If you want to partake, there's a public **sauna** in a cave on the outskirts of the village, and a summer taverna. A ruined **Byzantine fort** offers memorable views of the crater 300m (1,000ft) below. South, the **Monastery of Panagía Kyrá** is usually locked but has more fine views over the coast.

In contrast, the southern village of **Nikiá** is lively with dazzling blue and white paintwork, bright gardens and views over Tílos as well as the crater in all its ghostly enormity. The village square has a lovely round *choklákia* mosaic and there are a couple of *kafeneía* and a taverna. The path down to the volcano is steep but clearly marked and takes about 40 minutes. On the way, watch out for the **Calanna Rock**, said to be a witch who was turned to stone; a safer place to rest is the **Monastery of Ag. Ioánnis Theológos**, with shady trees and picnic benches as well as icons and frescoes.

Useful Information on Níssyros

Enetikon Travel, on the right as you head up from the harbour, Mandráki, t 224 203 1180. Particularly helpful, offering a range of excursions.

Níssyros Festivals

23 April: Ag. Geórgios.
29 June: Pálli.
27 July: Nikiá.
15 Aug: Mandráki.
25 Sept: Nikiá.

11 · The Dodecanese | Níssyros

Where to Stay and Eat on Níssyros

It can be very difficult to find a room in July and August, so do book ahead.

Port and Mandráki ✉ 85303

Ta Liotridia, in the village, **t** 224 203 1237 (€€€€). Four lovely doubles in a restored olive mill.

Haritos, **t** 224 203 1322 (€€). Friendly little award-winning *pension* with spacious rooms, sea-view balconies and a pool. *Open all year.*

Porfyris, in the village opposite the orchard, **t** 224 203 1176 (€€). The most comfortable bet, with a pool and views to Gialí. *Open May–Oct.*

Polyvotis, by the port **t** 224 203 1011 (€). Bland hotel owned by the municipality, with lovely sea views. *Open May–Oct.*

Three Brothers, by the port, **t** 224 203 1344 (€). Basic, with sea views.

⭐ Irini >

Irini, in lively Platéia Elikioméni, the centre of Mandráki nightlife. Good

value and a wide menu from *laderá* and stews to roasts.

Panorama. Gets very busy at night so you could have a long wait for a table. The food is good but a bit pricey.; they also have **rooms** (€).

Taverna Níssyros, spilling out into a narrow alley in the village centre. One of the most popular and authentic eateries with its vine-clad canopy and jolly atmosphere.

Gialiskári and Pálli ✉ 85303

White Beach, at Gialiskári, **t** 224 203 1497 (€€). Ungainly, but right on the sands – which are mostly black. *Open May–Oct.*

Ellinis, Pálli, **t** 224 2031 453 (€€). Rooms and a restaurant – with music when the owner's husband is playing his *lýra*.

Miramare Apartments, coast road to Pálli, **t** 224 203 1100 (€€). Beautifully appointed with a sea-view terrace.

Aphroditi, Pálli. Excellent food and home-made desserts.

Pátmos (ΠΑΤΜΟΣ)

Of all the Greek islands, beautiful Pátmos is the most sacred to Christians, both Orthodox and Western alike; here St John received the vision he described in the *Apocalypse*, or *Book of Revelations*, and here, in the 11th century, the Blessed Christódoulos founded a monastery more wealthy and influential than any in Greece except for Mount Áthos. There are other points of views as well. According to Elijah Muhammad and the Nation of Islam, the evil sorcerer Yacub created the Devil (the white man) on Pátmos, and, as if to prove the point, David Bowie has a house here, and there are usually enough loose members from various royal families on hand in summer to fill half an issue of *Hello! From* May to October the harbour is thronged with daytrippers and cruise passengers being hauled up to the monastery, and there are plenty of cafés, restaurants and boutiques to make sure they don't leave thirsty or empty-handed. But for all that, Pátmos still maintains something of its otherworldly feel, especially in the evening after the last cruise ship tenders have gone. Even in the height of summer it maintains certain standards: there's a law banning 'promiscuity and looseness'; the lack of an airport also helps to keep the island yob-free.

History

Pátmos was inhabited from the 14th century BC, its main settlement near present-day Skála and its acropolis at Kastélli. It was a

Getting to and around Pátmos

There are **ferries** six days a week to Piraeus, Léros, Kos and Rhodes; four a week to Kálymnos, Agathoníssi, Arkí, Lipsí, Sýros and Sámos, once a week with Níssyros, Sými and Tílos; also summer **boat and hydrofoil** services to Léros (Ag. Marína), Kálymnos, Kos, Lipsí, Kálymnos, Ikaría and Sámos' three ports.

Taxi boats leave Skála for most beaches in summer, as well as to Arkí, Maráthi and Sámos (Pythagório) and a daily one to Lipsí at 10; for information, **t** 224 703 2664. **Port authority**, **t** 224 703 1231.

To **hire a caique** contact **Apollon**, **t** 224 703 1324.

Buses (3–6 a day, **t** 224 703 1666) depart from Skála to Chóra, Gríkou and Kámbos. **Taxis**, **t** 224 703 1225, from the rank in the central square; agree on prices before setting out. **Rent a car or bike** at **Aris**, **t** 224 703 2542.

subject of Asia Minor and not terribly important. In AD 95, however, the island's destiny was forever altered with the arrival of St John, the beloved apostle of Jesus (known variously as the Evangelist or the Divine). After the Crucifixion he spent most of his life in Ephesus as Jesus' appointed guardian of his mother Mary; tradition has it that during Domitian's persecution of Christians he was transported to Rome and cast into a pot of boiling oil, from which he emerged without a burn, before being exiled to Pátmos, where he lived in a cave, perhaps wrote his gospel, and received his end-of-the-world *Revelations*. He may have only spent a year or so on Pátmos before returning to Ephesus, but in that time John provided not only a fairly accurate prophecy of the fall of the Roman Empire, but enough material to keep fire-eating preachers and literal-minded crank interpreters going for the next 1,900 years.

Pátmos was abandoned from the 7th century until the late 11th century, when in Constantinople things were going badly for Alexis Comnenus – 'born to the purple', but so battered by fate and politics that he had nothing but the blues. Nevertheless, a saintly hermit named Christódoulos predicted his ascent to the throne, and the miserable Alexis promised him a wish should it come true. Of course it did, and in 1088 Christódoulos asked the Emperor for Pátmos, to found a monastery on the site of an ancient Temple of Artemis. Alexis provided not only the island but the building funds, as well as tax exemptions and the right to engage in sea trade.

The island remained under absolute control of the monastery for centuries, in spite of poverty, pirates and a thousand other afflictions. The Venetian Dukes of Pátmos were content to leave it as an autonomous monastic state; the Knights never came here. The Turks respected its imperial charter, leaving Pátmos to flourish from the 16th to the 19th century; its school of theology and liberal arts, founded in 1713, was one of the few that functioned in the open. Monastic control lessened as the islanders took over the sea trade, and in 1720 the monks and laymen divided the island. After that, Pátmos prospered to the extent that it established colonies in the Balkans, although the invention of the steamship nipped its imperial ambitions in the bud.

Skála

All boats drop anchor at Skála, the island's main resort, and a smart one it is too, thanks to the cruise ships. One of the first things you'll see is a statue of Protergatis Xanthos Emmanuel, who led an uprising against the Turks in 1821. Skála didn't even exist until that year, so fearsome were the pirates. Near the beach, marked by a red buoy, is a reminder of another troublemaker, the evil magician Yenoúpas, who at the urging of priests from the Temple of Apollo challenged St John to a duel of miracles. Yenoúpas' miracle was to dive into the sea and bring back effigies of the dead; John's was to ask God to petrify the submerged magician, which abruptly ended the contest. Even petrified, Yenoúpas is a menace to shipping and stinks of sulphur, but all attempts to dislodge him so far have failed.

One of the best things to do in Skála is to hike up to the site of the ancient acropolis of **Kastélli**, in about 20 minutes. The remains of a Hellenistic wall and the chapel of **Ag. Konstantínos** are perched on the summit; the sunsets are pure magic.

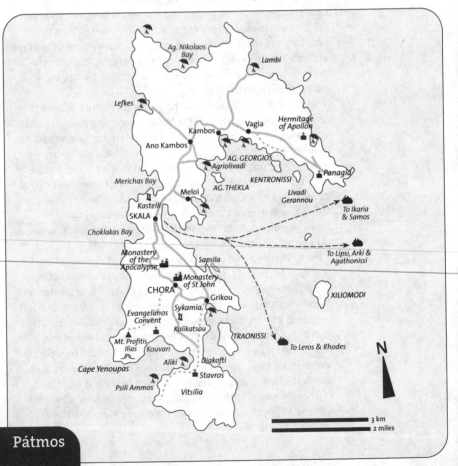

Chóra

From Skála you can see whitewashed Chóra clinging under the mighty castle walls of the monastery. Buses and taxis make the ascent, but if you have the time it isn't too strenuous to walk up the old cobbled path from Skála, to enjoy the ever-widening panorama spread out below. Chóra is a lovely, almost Cycladic village, with a maze of narrow alleyways, masses of chapels and mansions built by Pátmos' merchant fleet owners in the 17th and 18th centuries. Try to get a glimpse inside these, if you're lucky to find any open: most have startlingly lavish interiors.

After visiting the monastery (*see* below), you could spend a day finding the 40 or so churches wedged in the narrow lanes: especially good are the **Convent of Zoodóchos Pigí** (1607) with fine frescoes and icons, the **Convent of the Evangelismós** (*follow the signposts west of town*) and 11th-century **Ag. Dimítrios**, contemporary with the monastery, but likely to be locked like the others. Nor is hunting out the caretaker easy, as Chóra is one of those very old, silent places where the streets always seem to be deserted, especially once the trippers have gone. This changes dramatically on Orthodox Maundy Thursday, however, when Chóra is packed with visitors and TV crews for the *Niptíras* ceremony, when the abbot re-enacts Christ's washing of his disciples' feet – a rite once performed by Byzantine emperors. Depending on the weather, it takes place either in Plateía Ag. Leviás or Plateía Lóza.

Convent of the Evangelismós
open mornings

Monastery of St John the Theologian

② Monastery of St John the Theologian
t 224 703 1398; open Tues, Thurs and Sun 8–1.30 and 4–6; Mon, Wed, Fri and Sat 8–1.30 only; adm for the Treasury; get there first thing in the morning before the cruise passengers; shorts prohibited, and women must wear skirts

The usual gauntlet of trinket-merchants marks the entrance to Pátmos's prime attraction, and, once you get past them and through the walls that stood up to every invader and marauder for centuries, expect, alas, a grumpy welcome; apparently no one told the monks when they took their vows that dedicating their lives to God meant spending their days as museum guards and dress code enforcers.

The intimate scale and intricate little 11th-century corridors are delightful – but can easily become unbearably crowded with groups marching through. A charming court of 1698 incorporates the outer, or exo-narthex of the **church**; just inside this is the chapel-tomb of its founder, the Blessed Christódoulos. Designed as a Greek cross set in a square, the church still retains its original marble floor; its icon of St John was a gift from Alexis Comnenus. Frescoes, mostly by the Cretan school, cover every surface, although only those in the 12th-century **Chapel of the Theotókos** are as old as the church; others are in the **refectory**, off the inner courtyard. The **Treasury Museum** displays the original monastery deed (a *chrysobul*, signed and sealed, from the Emperor); plus an inscription from the Temple of Artemis, stating that Orestes sought refuge here from the Furies; and exquisite gifts to the monastery – gold and silver crosses, croziers and stoles, superb icons, including a rare one from the 11th century, brought here by Christódoulos, and ship pendants of diamonds and emeralds donated by Catherine the Great. The **library** contains hundreds of rare codices and manuscripts, including the 6th-century *Codex Porphyrius*, St Mark's gospel written on purple vellum, which may only be visited by church scholars with special permission.

The Monastery of the Apocalypse

Monastery of the Apocalypse
open Tues, Thurs and Sun, 8–1.30 and 4–6; Mon, Wed, Fri and Sat 8–1.30 only

It's a short walk down from Chóra to the Monastery of the Apocalypse, where a stair covered with flowerpots leads down to the cave where St John lived and dreamed, and dictated what he saw to his follower, Próchoros. The cave has been converted into a church, where you can see the rock where the good saint rested his head and hand (he must have been a contortionist to manage it), and the massive overhanging roof, split in three sections by the voice of God, symbolizing the Holy Trinity. If you're walking up from Skála, the cave is marked ΑΠΟΚΑΛΥΨΟΣ.

Beaches and Villages around Pátmos

The closest beach to Skála, **Meloï**, is 2km north and pleasantly tree-shaded, but tends to get crowded thanks to the taxi boats; if you want something more peaceful if less shady, look for the sign to **Agriolivádi**, a quiet, rocky cove with some sand and two tavernas.

Pátmos is great walking country, much of it around the dramatic shore here, with **Áno Kámbos** at the centre of the network. Surrounded by Pátmos' most fertile fields, it is the only other real village on the island and the end of the bus line; many long-term residents rent houses in the valley, where a commune thrived in the 1970s before being evicted by the anti-promiscuity squads. There are beaches in every direction: one at least will be sheltered from the prevailing winds. **Kámbos** to the east is popular with the locals and sandy, with watersports; its beach bar was the setting for *The Summer of My Greek Taverna* (*see* p.659). **Léfkes** to the west is often wild and windswept; to the north, **Lámbi**, also reached by excursion boat, is famous for its subtle, multicoloured pebbles. Further east there are secluded **Vagiá** and **Livádi Gerannoú**, with shade and a *cantina*. If you need a goal for a stroll, there's the 19th-century **Hermitage of Apollon**, near a small mineral spring.

Roads from Skála and Chóra go past **Sápsila cove** to Pátmos's principal beach resort, **Gríkou**, overlooking a beautiful bay, which has windsurfers and water skis for hire. On the south end of the bay, the **Kalikátsou Rock** has carved rooms and stairs in unlikely places and may have been the 11th-century hermitage mentioned in the writings of Christódoulos. Inland, at **Sykamiá**, there's an old Roman bath said to have been used by St John to baptize his converts. The south road peters out at the **Stávros chapel**, at **Diakoftí**, where

Pátmos is only a few hundred yards across. There's a beach here, but a half-hour's tramp (or caique from Skála) will take you to lovely **Psilí Ámmos**, with fine white sand. West of here, a seaside grotto on **Cape Yenoúpas** was the home of the evil magician, and even today it's unpleasantly hot and smelly inside.

Useful Information on Pátmos

ⓘ **Pátmos >**
Municipal tourist office: Skála,
t 224 703 1235

The municipal **tourist office** in Skála is very helpful and has a good range of leaflets and timetables.
Astoria Travel, in Skála, **t** 224 703 1205, *www.astoria.gr*. Help with accommodation.

Pátmos Festivals

Maundy Thursday: *Niptíras* ceremony.
8 May: Service for St John.
5 Aug: Kámbos.
15 Aug: Chora, Gerranoú, Kámbos.
Early Sept: International Festival of Sacred Music.
26 Sept: Ascension of St John.

Where to Stay and Eat on Pátmos

Skála and Around ✉ 85500

9 Muses, 2km south at Sápsila Cove, **t** 224 703 4079, *www.9muses-gr.com* (€€€€€). Nine traditionally styled but luxurious rooms, with a pool, pool bar and restaurant – the chef will even cook meals to order to eat on your private terrace.

★ **Benetos >>**

Blue Bay, on the road to Grikou, **t** 224 703 1165, *www.bluebay.50g.com* (€€€). All the mod cons in a quiet waterside spot with an Internet café. *Open April–Oct.*

Romeos, 500m from the port at Choklakás, **t** 224 703 1962, *romeosh@12net.gr* (€€€). Traditional-style rooms, all with sunset views; also a pool.

Skála, 2mins from the ferry, **t** 224 703 1343, *www.skalahotel.gr* (€€€). Draped in bougainvillaea and set in attractive gardens with a pool and restaurant, and wi-fi in the rooms. *Open April–Oct.*

Asteri, towards Mérichas Bay, **t** 224 703 2465, *www.asteripatmos.gr* (€€).

Garden setting. Simple rooms with sea views, fans or air-conditioning.
Byzance, on the edge of Skála, **t** 224 703 1052, *www.byzancehotel.gr* (€€). Roof garden with a small restaurant and lovely views over the port.

Efi, up at Kastélli, **t** 224 703 2500 (€€–€). Comfortable bland rooms. *Open all year.*

Hellinis, right on the waterfront, **t** 224 703 1275 (€€). Nice en suite rooms with views of the monastery. *Open April–Oct.*

Kasteli, Kástelli, **t** 224 703 1361 (€€). Commands fine views from the upper part of town, and has a small pool.

Maria, Choklakás, **t** 224 703 1201, *hotelmaria@patmos.com* (€€). Small rooms in a quiet location, with air-conditioning and balconies.

Summer, in Choklakás, **t** 224 703 1769 (€€). Air-conditioning and a veranda swathed in bouainevillea.

Australis, 10min walk from the ferry towards Mérichas, **t** 224 703 1576 (€). Friendly Greek-Australian owners, basic en-suite rooms and motorbikes to hire, too.

Aspri, at Áspri Beach, **t** 224 703 2240 (€22). Fish taverna with a wonderful view of the castle; specialities include *mezédes*, lobster with pasta and *kalamári* risotto. *Open June–Sept, eves only.*

Benetos, Sápsila, **t** 224 703 3089 (€30). Creative chef Benetos Mathaiou of Florida, a native of Pátmos, opens his romantic villa restaurant here in summer. Organic vegetables from the garden and fresh fish plucked from the sea are his specialities; try the courgette blossoms filled with shitake mushrooms. *Open June–mid Oct, eves only exc Mon, by reservation only.*

Cactus, Choklakás, **t** 224 703 1240 (€25). Sunset views and home-made pasta with pesto and other Italian dishes. *Open mid May–mid Oct, eves only.*

Café Aman, **t** 224 703 2323. Right now, the trendiest hangout on the island.

Grigoris, opposite the ferry dock, **t** 224 703 1515. Tasty, cheap and cheerful with excellent charcoal-grilled fish and meat; try the swordfish *souvláki*.

Kyma, at Áspri, **t** 224 703 1192 (€19). Romantic seaside views and fresh grilled seafood. *Open June–Sept, eves only.*

⭐ **Yaya >**

Yaya, by the port, **t** 224 703 3226 (€22). A surprise – the only Indonesian restaurant in Greece, serving delicious rice, noodle and pancake dishes with lots of seafood. *Open May–Oct.*

Veggera, Néa Marína, **t** 224 703 2988 (€40). Gourmet French, Mediterranean and Greek cuisine in an old stone house. *Open Easter–Oct, eves only by reservation only.*

Chóra ✉ 85500

Archontika Irini, **t** 224 703 2826 (€€€€€) Old stone mansion, with traditional furniture, fireplaces and wood-burning stove, sleeps 6–10.

Epavli Apartments, **t** 224 703 1621, *www.12net.gr/epavli* (€€€). On the edge of the village, with traditional furnishings, air-conditioning and lovely views.

Olympia, Plateía Ag. Leviás, **t** 224 703 1543. Good Greek food, and plenty to look at while you wait for it to come.

Vangelis, Plateía Ag. Leviás (follow the little signs), **t** 224 703 1967 3 (€24). Lovely view from the terrace, but no culinary surprises here; solid Greek fare, but portions are rather small.

Meloï ✉ 85500

Porto Scoutari, overlooking the bay, **t** 224 703 3123, *www.portoscoutari.com* (€€€€€). Pretty apartments, a chic, quiet 'romantic hotel', with big beds, a pool and a regular minibus service into civilization. The best rooms are on the second floor.

Meloi, known to all as **Stefanos**, almost on the beach, **t** 224 703 1821. Basic **rooms** (€), but serving good, reasonably priced food. They also run the campsite: bamboo-shaded pitches, mini-market, cafeteria, cooking and washing facilities.

Kámbos ✉ 85500

Pátmos Paradise, 200m from Kámbos, **t** 224 703 2624, *www.patmosparadise. com* (€€€€€). The works: an *à la carte* restaurant, wi-fi, seawater pool, squash and tennis courts, sauna and fitness centre.

George's Place, on the beach, **t** 224 703 1881. Salads and sandwiches and the best cheesecake in Greece.

Panagos, in the village square, **t** 224 703 1570. Delicious home cooking, with lots of good vegetable dishes – fava with garlic, cheese pies, and stewed dishes. *Open all year.*

Gríkou ✉ 85500

Petra, just back from the beach, **t** 224 703 1035, *www.petrahotel-patmos.com* (€€€€€). Intimate and stylish rooms and suites, with marble baths and huge panoramic terraces; excellent Mediterranean cuisine.

Golden Sun, with lovely views overlooking the bay, **t** 224 703 2318, *www. hotel-golden-sun.com* (€€€). Run by a Greek and German couple, who also offer brain light, reiki and tachyon energy therapies if you feel out of sync with your inner you. *No credit cards.*

Panorama Apartments, by the sea, **t** 224 703 1209, *www.panoramapatmos. com* (€€€). Old favourites renovated in 1999. Minibus service.

Athena, on the hillside, **t** 224 703 1859 (€€). An attractive, family-run place with some lovely views from its rooms' balconies, as long as it isn't block-booked in the summer by the package companies.

Ioanna, **t** 224 703 1031 (€€). Newly renovated; a nicely-done complex with self-catering, air-conditioned studios and apartments.

Flisvos, on the hill, **t** 224 703 1380. Small and family-run, taverna with well-prepared Greek staples, fish dishes at affordable prices and a few **rooms** (€). *Open May–Oct.*

Stamatis, near the harbour, **t** 224 703 1302. Traditional favourites such as moussaka and stuffed tomatoes. *Open Easter–Sept.*

Ktima Petrino, on Pétra Beach just south, **t** 224 703 3207. New restaurant using produce and meat from the family farm, specializing in lamb slowly baked in a wood-fired oven. *Open May–Sept.*

Lipsí (ΛΕΙΨΟΙ)

Lipsí is a little charmer midway between Léros and Pátmos, and it's not surprising that Odysseus put off his homecoming for seven years to linger here, beguiled by the charms of Calypso. If opinions differ on whether Lipsí really is Homer's isle of Ogygia, no one can deny that it has a certain unworldly magic. For centuries most of the land was owned by the monastery on Pátmos, and the blue domes of the Cycladic-style churches from that period bubble over a horizon of soft, green hills.

Lipsí is one of an archipelago of tiny islets, and its lovely beaches are a magnet for day excursions from Pátmos and Léros, yet once the trippers have gone it quickly regains its tranquillity. Above all, it's a great place to do nothing. Although now firmly 'discovered', the 500 inhabitants, including many who have gone to Tasmania and returned in their retirement, are friendly and go about their lives, fishing and farming.

Around the Island

Lipsí greets arrivals with a smattering of tavernas around the bay and odd front-room cafés which double as shops. Everything is neatly signposted from the harbour, and is kept pin-bright, as if the locals were entering a best-kept island contest. Hence the shock and dismay when Alexándros Giotópoulos, an economics professor and son of a famous Trotskyite who had been living on Lipsí for 17 years, was arrested in a dramatic raid on 17 July 2002 as he attempted to board a hydrofoil to Sámos and flee to Turkey, charged with being the mastermind of the secretive 17 November terrorist organization, responsible for 23 murders and other attacks over a 27-year period. Although he has always denied everything, he was sentenced in 2003 to 21 life terms, the harshest penalty ever given in Greece. His **Pink House**, made famous on Greek news reports at the times, remains firmly shuttered.

If most of the trippers head straight for the beaches, you may want to follow the Greeks and first visit the famous blue-domed **Cathedral of Ag. Ioánnis** to pay your respects to its miraculous icon of the Panagía tou Chárou, unique in Orthodox iconography for its image of the *Pietà* – the Virgin holding the crucified Jesus. The icon was originally in the pretty 16th-century church of the **Panagía tou Chárou** (Our Lady of Death) which stands at Lipsí's highest point, but was brought here for safety. It was the site of a famous miracle: in 1943 a woman prayed to the Virgin to help her son and the Virgin granted her prayer. Being poor, she had nothing to offer in return but a lily. In time the lily withered, but miraculously, on the day of the Virgin's acceptance into Heaven, 24 August, it sprang into full bloom and has flowered on that day ever since. The ancient lily stalk can

Getting to and around Lipsí

Ferries run 4 times a week with Sámos, Pátmos, Léros and Kálymnos, and twice a week with Agathoníssi and Arkí. There are daily **excursion boats** to Ag. Marína, Léros and Skála, Pátmos; plus **hydrofoils** from Pythagório, Sámos (the closest air connection) Kos, Kálymnos, Léros, and Pátmos. **Port authority: t** 224 704 1240.

Boat excursions circle the island and go to Arkí and Maráthi.

Lipsí's old fleet of pickup truck taxis has been replaced with a new **municipal bus service** in the harbour square, with almost hourly departures in high season as far as Platís Gialós and Katsadiá Beach.

**Nikoforeion
Ecclesiastical
Museum**
open informally, 10–1

clearly be seen under the glass of the icon and in early August it bears small white buds which burst into flower right on time. Opposite the cathedral there's the grandly titled **Nikoforeion Ecclesiastical Museum**, a collection of motley stuff, from the ridiculous to a fascinating letter from Admiral Miaoúlis written to a cousin on the night of his famous sea battle.

Lipsí is a miniature world, only six square miles, so you can walk across it in two hours, taking in its well-tended walled fields and 30-odd blue and white chapels, as well as views of neighbouring islands Arkí, Maráthi and Agathoníssi (*see* below). The town beach at **Lendoú** is shaded by trees and gets busy with Greek families; for something quieter, head west on a paved road and path to **Kimissí**, where outside high season you could have the sands to yourself. The buses will deposit you on the island's best-known beach, the white cove of **Platís Gialós** (3km), which has a pretty church and good taverna, or take you south to **Katsadiá**, with its succession of sandy coves and another good taverna. On the east coast, picturesque **Monodéndri** and surrounding coves are unofficial naturist beaches. The vines in the valley beyond the town produce a good wine – lovely with grilled octopus in the evening.

Useful Information on Lipsí

Town hall, t 224 703 1235.

Laid Back Holidays, t 224 704 1141. Friendly Nico and Anna Christódoulou are a mine of information about Lipsí, and change money at bank rates, sell newspapers, and hire out motorbikes and mopeds.

Lipsí Festivals

22–24 Aug: Panagía tou Chárou. Pilgrims from the surrounding islands pour in for 'the ninth day of the Virgin'.

24 June: St.John, Klidonas

Mid-Aug: wine festival.

Where to Stay on Lipsí

Lipsí ✉ 85001

Landladies still meet the boats if they have a free room, but it's best to book ahead. For a list of most available rooms and studios see *www.lipsiholidays.gr*.

Aphrodite, right on the beach, 100m from the port, t 224 704 1000, *www.hotel-aphroditi.gr* (€€€). All rooms are kitted out with kitchenettes and balconies, but it's usually package-booked. *Open May–Nov.*

Galini Studios, by the port and beach, t 224 704 1212 (€€). Simple but very nice, with big balconies and nice views; fishing excursions by owner Niko are an option as well.

Studios Kalymnos, 2mins' walk from town, t 224 704 1343, *http://studios-*

kalymnos.lipsi-island.gr (€€). Owned by the Christódoulos, in a peaceful setting; studios sleep 2–4.

Kalypso, on the harbour, **t** 224 704 1243 (€). With information service and restaurant, run by the famous Mr Mungo with a certain dishevelled style.

Glaros Rooms, t 224 704 1360. Perched high with views over the bay.

Pension Manolis, south of the harbour, **t** 224 704 1316. Overlooks fishing boats.

Eating Out on Lipsí

Iannis, by the quay. Reliable good food, grills and local wine from the barrel. *Open May–early Oct.*

Tholari, owned by Greek Australians, serving the usuals, all year long.

Asprakis Ouzerie, near the excursion boats. Doubling as shop and bar; great for local atmosphere, grilled octopus and ouzo.

Arkí (ΑΡΚΟΙ) and Maráthi (ΜΑΡΑΘΙ)

Hilly **Arkí**, just 4km long and 1km wide with 40 inhabitants, sees excursion boats from Pátmos and Lipsí as well as one or two ferries a week from Agathoníssi, Kálymnos, Pátmos, Sámos, Léros and Lipsí. Facilities are minimal – there's no place to change money, and water must be shipped in; solar panels provide electricity. Still, it attracts yachts and people (mostly Greeks and Italians) in search of Greek island purity. There are some quiet coves and a **Blue Lagoon**, good for snorkelling and swimming in the vivid waters.

Of the nine baby islets around Arkí, **Maráthi** has the best beach, a slice of golden sands under the tamarisks, and the only inhabitants.

Agathoníssi Festivals

26–27 July Megálo Chório

23 Aug. Panagía

Where to Stay and Eat on Arkí, Maráthi and Agathoníssi

Arkí ✉ 85001

The superb harbour of Port Augusta has two tavernas with basic **rooms** (€):

O Trypas, t 224 703 2230.

Nikolaos, t 224 703 2477.

Maráthi ✉ 85001

Two excellent tavernas have rooms here as well.

Pantedís, t 224 703 2609 or **t** 224 703 1230, run by Toula and Manólis, who came from Arkí via Australia, with comfortable, very reasonable en suite rooms (€) and serving up tasty dishes – even the bread is home-made. *Open June–Oct.*

To Maráthi, t 224 703 1580 (€). A bit more basic, run by the charming pirate-like Michalis Kavouras, whose goats leap all over the island and often turn up on the menu as well. *Always open but ring ahead.*

Agathoníssi ✉ 85001

All these are simple blue and white rooms places.

Seagull, Ag. Geórgios,, **t** 224 702 9062. Five rooms with air-conditioning, and an fine taverna on the water.

George's, Ag. Geórgios, **t** 224 702 4385 (€). Very basic rooms, excellent fish.

Maria Kamitsi, Ag. Geórgios, **t** 224 702 9003 (€). Beautiful garden and shared kitchen.

Theologia Yiameou, Ag. Geórgios, **t** 224 702 9005 (€). On the sea, with use of the kitchen.

Limenaki, Ag. Geórgios, **t** 224 702 9019. Popular taverna, with newly built rooms upstairs.

Dekatria Adelfia, Megálo Chorió. Serves good cheap lunches.

Getting to Arkí and Maráthi

Excursion boats sail from Pátmos and Lipsí as well as one or two **ferries** a week from Agathoníssi, Kálymnos, Pátmos, Sámos, Léros and Lipsí.

Getting to Agathoníssi

The **ferry** *Níssos Kálymnos* arrives from Sámos (Pithagório), Pátmos, Lipsí, Léros, Kálymnos, and Arkí, twice a week; there is a summer hydrofoil once a week from Sámos (Pythagório), and various **excursion boats** in summer. **Port authority: t** 224 703 1231 (Pátmos).

Agathoníssi (ΑΓΑΘΟΝΗΣΙ)

Northeast of Pátmos, steep little Agathoníssi (pop. 140) may be alphabetically the first Greek island but few people have ever heard of it, tucked up as it is next to Turkey. Yet it may be the ticket if you've been seeking a peaceful, very Greek island with a tad of civilization. Literally 'the Good Island' (since it joined Greece in 1948; before then it was called Gíadouro, or 'Donkey island' because of its donkey-shape), it was, like Lipsí, the property of the monks on Pátmos until the 1950s; the locals mostly farm and fish; yachts like to call into its sheltered inlets. Agathoníssi has three villages: **Megálo Chorió**, where most people live, the port of **Ag. Geórgios**; and **Mikró Chorió**, with only about 10 inhabitants, linked by a cement road and a rickety three-wheeler or maybe a van. Ag. Geórgios has a pebbly, grotty beach but there's a better one at **Spília**, a sheltered cove to the west, where campers go, and others that require a stout pairs of shoes: even paths are something of a luxury. There are the remains of a Byzantine granary at **Thóli**, at the end of the cement road, and an excellent place to swim; a branch of the road heads to the deserted fishing village of **Katholikó**, with views of Sámos and Turkey. There's a beach, so you can take the plunge on arrival. There's also a good beach at **Pálli**, down a path near the island's new helipad. Bring cash: there are no banks or ATM machines.

Rhodes/Ródos (ΡΟΔΟΣ)

'More beautiful than the sun' according to the ancient Greeks, Rhodes is the largest and most fertile of the Dodecanese, ringed by sandy beaches, bedecked with flowers, blessed with some 300 days of sun a year, dotted with handsome towns and villages and ancient and medieval monuments evoking a long, colourful history – in a nutshell, all that it takes to sit securely throned as the queen of tourism in Greece. A year-round playground for chilblained northerners and a top conference and package destination, Rhodes is a cosmopolitan, glittering, sun-drenched chill pill in the sea, glamorous in places, outrageously tacky in others, and lively all year

Getting to Rhodes

By Air

Rhodes Diagoras Airport (t 224 108 3400 or t 224 108 3214) is the third busiest in Greece, with over a million arrivals, and has recently been enlarged. There are numerous UK, German and Scandinavian charters from April to mid-Oct, and direct flights on **British Airways**. From Athens, there are at least 5 daily flights on **Olympic** or **Aegean Airways**; from Crete (Heráklion), Olympic has daily flights; there is at least one daily from Thessaloniki, mostly on Olympic; Olympic also has 5–7 a week from Kárpathos, Kássos and Kastellórizo, five a week from Límnos and Mytilíni, and two from Astypália, Kos, Chíos, Sámos and Léros. Olympic is at 9 Iérou Lóchou, Rhodes Town, t 224 102 4571; Aegean is at the airport, t 224 102 8720.

The bus to Parádissi and Rhodes Town passes near the airport every 30mins until 11pm; taxi fares to town are around €12, €35 to Líndos. If your flight is delayed it's only a 3min walk to the nearest bar and taverna (Anixis, open until 2am) in Parádissi.

By Sea

Ferries run daily with Piraeus, Kos, Chálki and Léros; six a week with Symi, Kálymnos and Pátmos, 4–5 times a week with Chálki, Níssyros, and Tílos and Syros, 3 times a week with Kárpathos, Kássos and Sitía or Ag. Nikólaos (Crete), twice a week with Santoríni, Mílos and Kastellórizo, once a week with Níssyros, Amorgós, Sámos, Chíos, Mytilíni, Límnos and Alexandroúpoli. There are also frequent **hydrofoils** in season.

Also at least two daily **catamarans** go to Marmaris, Turkey; *see* **Marmaris Shipping**, 13 Gallías, t 224 102 5095; buy tickets at least one day in advance and bring your passport; *see http://rhodes.marmarisinfo.com*.
Port authority: t 224 102 2220 and t 224 102 8888.

Getting around Rhodes

Excursion boats and *Sými I* and *Sými II* **ferries** sail from Mandráki harbour in Rhodes Town to Sými, and to Líndos, and beaches at Lárdos. **Caiques** ply their way from Kámiros Skála on the west coast to Chálki.

There is a frequent **bus** service. Buses for the **east coast** (t 224 102 4129), depart from Plateía Rimini in Rhodes Town; they service Faliráki (12 a day) Líndos (7 a day) and Kolýmbia Beach (3 a day), Afándou (10 a day) and Archángelos (15 a day). Buses for the **west coast** and some Faliráki buses (t 224 102 7706) depart from the West Coast bus station on Áverof St by the New Market; these travel to Faliráki (18 a day), Parádissi/airport (24 a day) Thérma Kalithéas (21 a day), Koskínou (8 a day) and Theológos (12 a day).

Taxis are plentiful but have a dire reputation for ripping off the innocent. The central rank is in Plateía Rimini, Rhodes Town, t 224 102 7666.

To get off the beaten track, anything from four-wheel-drive beach buggies to **motorbikes** are available for hire; out of high season prices are negotiable. Note that much of Rhodes Town is off limits to cars, and finding a spot is tough and fines are high. (Taxis, however, are allowed to take you to your hotel.)

round, thanks in part to the University of the Aegean. Germans, Brits and Scandinavians outnumber everyone (there's even a special post box for Sweden at the central post office) but Israelis, Poles, Czechs and Turks are now adding different accents to the Babelling brew. There are even some Greeks.

History

As on many islands, foundation myths echo early Rhodian history. The island was colonized by the Minoans, who built shrines to the moon at Filérimos, Líndos and Kámiros. In the 15th century BC, the Mycenaeans took over their colonies and founded the town of Achaia. Before settling on 'Rhodes' for its name, the island was known as Telchinia or Ophioussa, for its numerous vipers; even today villagers wear snake-repelling goatskin boots when working in the fields. The Mycenaeans were supplanted in the 12th century BC by

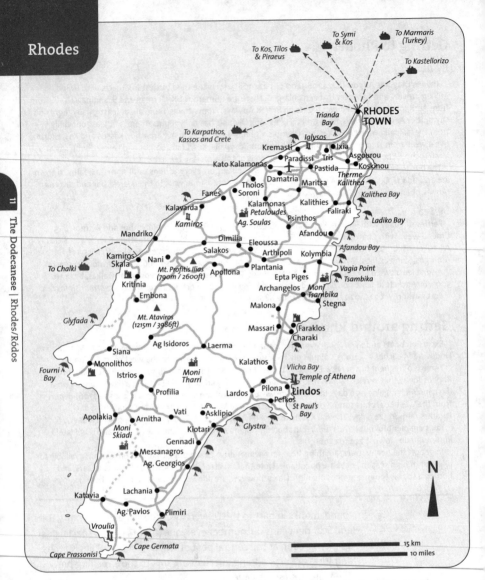

the Dorians, who set up three city states – Lindos, Ialysos and Kamiros – which soon became trading and naval powers. Around 1000 BC, in response to the first Ionian confederacy, the three formed a Doric Hexapolis along with Kos, Cnidos and Halicarnassus, a prototype EU uniting the six politically, religiously and economically. For four centuries the Hexapolis prospered, establishing colonies from Naples to the Costa Brava.

The Founding of Rhodes City, and its Colossus

Rhodes sided with the Persians in both their major campaigns against Greece, but after their defeat quickly switched sides and

Dark Tales from the Island of the Sun

Rhodes' mythology is (typical) the subject of contradictory traditions. According to one of the oldest myths, the first inhabitants were nine dog-headed enchantresses called Telchines, the Sea Children. In spite of having flippers for hands, they made the sickle that Cronos used to castrate Uranus, carved the first statues of the gods, and founded Kamiros, Ialysos and Lindos before moving onto Crete. There Rhea, the Earth, made them nurses of her son Poseidon, and they forged the sea god's trident. Poseidon fell in love with the Telchines' sister, Alia, and had six sons and a daughter by her. The daughter, the nymph Rhodos, became the sole heiress of the island when Zeus decided to destroy the Telchines for meddling with the weather, although their real crime was belonging to a pre-Olympian matriarchal religion. He flooded Rhodes, but the Telchines managed to escape in various forms.

The same cast of characters are on stage in a later version of the myth, which changed the Telchines' sex and shed their dog heads and flippers. The sons of Pontos and Thalassa (the sea), they were artisans, magicians and ministers of Zeus, with the same sister, Alia, who was loved by Poseidon and gave birth to Rhodos and a number of sons. When these sons refused to let Aphrodite come ashore as she sailed between the islands of Kýthera and Cyprus, the goddess of love put a curse of incestuous passion on them and they raped their mother Alia. In despair Alia flung herself into the sea and became 'Lefkothea' (the White Goddess). The wicked sons hid in the bowels of the earth and became demons, as Poseidon in his wrath flooded the island (the Telchines, tipped off by Artemis, again escaped before the deluge). The sun god Helios later fell in love with Rhodos, evaporated the stagnant waters with his hot rays and married the nymph. They had a daughter and seven sons, known as the Heliades. Athena gave them wisdom and taught them nautical and astrophysical lore. But the wisest of the Heliades, Tenagis, was killed in a jealous fit by four of the brothers, who then fled. The two innocent brothers, Ohimos and Kerkafos, remained and founded the city of Achaia; one had three sons, Lindos, Kamiros and Ialysos, who founded the three city-states that bear their names.

A later, tidier version relates that, while the gods were dividing up the world, Zeus realized that he had forgotten to set aside a portion for Helios. Dismayed, Zeus asked Helios what he could do to make up for his omission. The sun god replied that he knew of an island just re-emerging from the sea off the coast of Asia Minor which would suit him admirably. Helios married Rhodos and one of their sons, or perhaps Tlepolemos (who led the ships of Rhodes to Troy), founded the ancient cities.

Kámiros even has another possible founder: Althaemenes, son of the Cretan King Katreus and grandson of Minos. When an oracle predicted that Katreus would be slain by his offspring, Althaemenes fled to Rhodes, where he founded Kamiros and surrounded it with metal bulls that would bellow if it were invaded. Katreus in his old age sailed to Rhodes to visit his son, but arrived at night, and, what with the darkness and the bellowing of the metal bulls, Althaemenes failed to recognize his father and fellow Cretans, and slew them. When he realized his error in the morning he piteously begged Mother Earth to swallow him up whole, which she did.

joined the Delian confederacy. In 408 BC, in order to prevent rivalries and increase their wealth and strength, Lindos, Ialysos and Kamiros united to found one central capital, Rhodes ('the Rose' – or 'Pomegranate' according to some). Hippodamos of Miletus, the geometrician, designed the new town on a grid plan similar to Piraeus, and the result was considered one of the most beautiful cities of ancient times. Celebrated schools of philosophy, philology and oratory were founded, and the port was famous for its up-to-date facilities. Although Lindos, Kamiros and Ialysos continued to exist, they lost all importance to the new city.

One reason for this prosperity was its unabashedly expedient foreign policy. During the Peloponnesian War, Rhodes inevitably sided with whichever power was on top, and later, in 336 BC, hitched its wagon to the rising star of Alexander the Great. Alexander in turn favoured Rhodes at the expense of hostile Athens, and enabled the island to dominate Mediterranean trade; like Athens in Classical times, Rhodes ruled the waves of the Hellenistic era; its trade and navigation laws were adopted by the Romans and remain the basis of maritime trade today. Nor did they hide their light under a bushel; the Rhodians were the Texans of their day, full of swagger and brag.

Egypt was one of Rhodes' most lucrative trading partners, and in the dynastic struggles between Alexander's successors Rhodes allied itself with Ptolemy, who had taken Egypt as his spoils. When another of Macedonian generals, the powerful Antigonas of Syria, ordered Rhodes to join him against Ptolemy, the Rhodians refused. To change their minds, Antigonas sent his son Dimitrios Poliorketes (the Besieger) at the head of an army of 40,000 and the Phoenician fleet. The ensuing year-long siege (305–304 BC) by a great general against the greatest city of the day has gone down in the annals, as a contest of strength and a battle of wits. As often as Dimitrios invented a tactic or ingenious machine, most famously the terrible 10-storey Helepolis 'Destroyer of Cities' siege tower, the Rhodians (whose engineers eventually tripped up the Helepolis by tunnelling out a digging a hidden, shallow ditch in its path) foiled him, until after a year both sides wearied of the game and made a truce.

So Dimitrios departed, leaving his vast siege machinery behind. This the Rhodians either sold, or melted down to construct a great bronze statue of Helios, their patron god of the sun. The famous sculptor from Lindos, Chares, was put in charge of the project, and in 290 BC, after 12 years of work and at a cost of 20,000 pounds of silver, Chares completed the Colossus, or didn't quite: he found he had made a miscalculation and committed suicide just before it was cast. Standing somewhere between 30m (100ft) and 43m (140ft) tall (at her crown the Statue of Liberty is 34m or 111ft), the Colossus did not straddle the entrance of Rhodes harbour, as is popularly believed, but probably stood near the present Castle of the Knights, gleaming bright in the sun – one of the Seven Wonders of the Ancient World. But of all the Wonders the Colossus had the shortest lifespan; in 225 BC, an earthquake brought it crashing to the ground. The Oracle at Delphi told the Rhodians to leave it there, and it lay forlorn until AD 653 when the Saracens, who had captured Rhodes, sold it as scrap to a merchant from Edessa. Accounts say it took 900 camels to transport the bronze from the ships.

In 164 BC, when they had repaired their city and walls, the Rhodians signed a peace treaty with Rome. Alexandria was their only rival in wealth, and tiny Délos, with all its duty-free concessions, their only rival in Mediterranean trade. The island's School of Rhetoric taught Pompey, Cicero, Cassius, Julius Caesar, Brutus, Cato the Younger and Mark Antony. When Caesar was assassinated, Rhodes as always backed the right horse, in this case Augustus, only this time the wrong horse, Cassius, was in the neighbourhood; he sacked the city, captured its fleet, and sent its treasures to Rome (43–42 BC). It was a blow from which Rhodes never recovered. She lost control of her colonies and islands, and other Roman allies muscled in on her booming trade. In AD 57 St Paul preached on the island and converted many of the inhabitants; by the end of the Roman empire, Rhodes was a sleepy backwater.

Two Hundred Years of Knights

Byzantium brought many invaders and adventurers to Rhodes: Arabs and Saracens (including in 804 a siege by Harun al Rachid, of *Arabian Nights* fame), Genoese, Venetians and Crusaders all passed through; in 1191 Richard the Lionheart and Philip Augustus of France came to recruit mercenaries. After the fall of Jerusalem in 1291, the Knights Hospitallers of St John, dedicated to protecting pilgrims and running hospitals in the Holy Land, took refuge on Cyprus, but by 1306 they had become rather more interested in Rhodes. They asked the Emperor Andronicus Palaeológos to cede them the island in return for their loyalty, but after 1204 the Byzantines had learned better than to trust the Frankish heretics. The Knights, under Grand Master Foulques de Villaret, took the matter into their own hands and purchased the Dodecanese from their occupants: Genoese pirates. The Rhodians refused to recognize the bill of sale, and the Knights had to spend their first three years subduing the natives.

By 1309, with the help of the Pope, the Knights were secure in their possession and built their hospital and eight inns (*auberges*) in Rhodes Town, one for each of the 'tongues', or nationalities, in the Order (England, France, Germany, Italy, Castile, Aragon, Auvergne and Provence). Each tongue had a bailiff, and the eight bailiffs elected the Grand Master, who lived in a palace. There were never more than 650 Knights all told and, although as always dedicated to the care of pilgrims to the Holy Land, their focus shifted as they became freebooting defenders on the front lines of Christendom, harrying the Muslims whenever possible. Already full, their coffers overflowed after 1312, when Pope Clement V and Philip the Fair of France dissolved the fabulously wealthy Knights Templars, confiscated their fortune and gave the Hospitallers a hefty share. With their new funds, the Knights of St John replaced the fortifications – and continued to replace them up until the 16th century, hiring the best Italian engineers to build one of the most splendid defences of the day. Meanwhile, the Knights had made themselves such a thorn in the side of Muslim shipping that they were besieged by the Sultan of Egypt in 1444 and by Mohammed II the Conqueror in 1480 with 70,000 men, both times without success. Then in 1522 Suleiman the Magnificent moved in with 200,000 troops; the Rhodians (there were 6,000 of them, plus 1,000 Italian mercenaries, and 650 knights) bitterly joked that the Colossus was now coming back at them, in the form of cannon balls. After a frustrating six-month siege, Suleiman was about to abandon Rhodes when a German traitor informed him that, of the original Knights, only 180 survived, and they were on their last legs. The Sultan redoubled his efforts and the Knights were forced to surrender. In honour of their courage, Suleiman let them leave in safety, with their Christian retainers and possessions. They made their new headquarters in Malta – at the nominal rent of a falcon a year – and in 1565 they withstood a tremendous all-out assault by the Ottoman fleet. After caving in to Napoleon, the Knights re-formed in 1831 as a benevolent charity in Rome, from where they still fund hospitals; the English Order established the St John Ambulance, as well as the St John Ophthalmic Hospital back where it all started, in Jerusalem.

Ottomans and Italians

The Ottomans loved Rhodes as a pleasure island, and, when the Greeks attempted to join the War of Independence in 1821, the Turks reacted with atrocities, but the Old Town suffered its worst damage in the Great Gunpowder Explosion of 1856, when lightning struck a minaret and exploded a powder magazine, destroying much of the Old Town and killing 800 people. During the confusion of the Balkan Wars in 1912, the Italians besieged and took Rhodes, claiming the island as their inheritance from the Knights of St John – rights confirmed in the 1923 Treaty of Lausanne. The Fascists worked hard to make the city a fitting capital for their new empire, building roads, waterworks, and public buildings, although their attempts to forcibly Italianize the population made them extremely unpopular. After the Italian surrender in 1943 the Germans took over and were even worse, sending most of the island's 2,000 Jews to the concentration camps. After a brief occupation by UK troops, Rhodes, with the rest of the Dodecanese, joined Greece in 1948.

Useful Information on Rhodes

(i) **Rhodes >**
EOT: corner of Papágou and Makaríou Sts, Rhodes Town, t 224 104 4335; see also Lindos, p.426

Hotels and tourist offices have copies of the free English-language paper *Ródos News*. At the EOT **tourist office**, very helpful multilingual staff and a wide range of maps, leaflets and information. A **Museum Pass** (€10) is available for the Palace of the Grand Masters, Archaeology and Decorative Museums, and Our Lady of the Bourg. **City of Rhodes Tourist Information Centre:** Plateía Rimini, t 224 103 5945. Mostly a money exchange.

Tourist police: t 224 102 7423. 24hr multilingual number for any information or complaints.
British consul (honorary): 29 Gr. Lambráki St., t 224 102 4473.
Irish consul (honorary): Mr Skévos Moúgros, 111 Amerikís, t 224 107 5655.

Rhodes Festivals

1 Mar: Carnival in Rhodes Old Town.
14 June: Faliráki.
Mid-June: Rhodes Eco Film Festival (*www.ecofilms.gr*).
28 June: Líndos.

First 10 days July: Musical Meetings in Rhodes.

29–30 July: Soroní, with donkey races.

26 July: Siána.

Aug: Wine festival in various villages; dance festivals in Kallithiés, Maritsa and Embónas.

14–22 Aug: Kremastí.

7 Sept: in Moní Tsambíkas (for fertility).

13 Sept: Apóllona and Kallithiés.

26 Sept: Artamíti.

18 Oct: Afándou.

7 Nov: Archángelos.

Activities on Rhodes

Dive Med College, 33 Lissavónas, **t** 224 106 1115, *www.divemedcollege.com*.

Waterhoppers, 45 Kritiká, in Ixiá, **t** 224 103 8146, *www.waterhoppers.com*.

Scuba-Diving Trident School, 2 Zervoú, **t** 224 102 9160, *www.trident divingschool.com*.

Procenter, Triánda, **t** 224 109 5819, *www.procenter-rhodos.com*. For windsurfing.

Rhodes Town

Spread across the northern tip of the island, Rhodes (pop. 55,000), the capital of the Dodecanese, celebrated its 2,400th birthday in 1993. The **Old Town** – the walled medieval city – is the star attraction, so remarkably preserved that it looks like a film set in places, and was used in Ben Kingsley' vehicle, *Pascali's Island*. The bustling **New Town** takes care of business. Although the whole seems large for a Greek island, astonishingly the ancient city in its prime counted twice as many people and covered 15 square km within its walls.

Rhodes presents an opulent face to the sea, and arriving by water is sheer theatre. The massive walls of the Old Town, crowned by the Palace of the Grand Masters, rise out of a lush subtropical garden; graceful minarets and the arcaded waterfront market, bright with strings of lights at night, add an exotic touch. Monumental pseudo-Venetian public buildings, trying to look serious, decorate the shore to the left, while, opposite, three 14th-century **windmills** (down from the original 15) turn lazily behind a forest of masts. Yachts, small ferries and excursion boats dock at the smallest of three harbours, **Mandráki**, guarded by the lighthouse and fort of **Ag. Nikólaos**, built in the 1460s to bear the brunt of Turkish attacks. A bronze stag and doe, Rhodes' symbols, mark the spots where the Colossus might have stood. Under the Knights, a chain crossed Mandráki's entrance, and every ship that entered had to pay a two per cent tax of its cargo value. Hydrofoils and larger ferries, boats to Turkey, and cruise ships enter the commercial harbour (**Kolóna**) nearer the Old Town walls.

Tours of the walls
Tues and Sat; meet in front of the Palace of the Grand Masters at 2.45pm; adm

These **walls** are a masterpiece of late medieval fortifications, but access is by guided tour only. Alternatively, you can get a good free squiz at them by walking round the bottom of the moat: the main entrance is off Plateía Alexandrías. Built over the Byzantine walls under four of the most ambitious Grand Masters (d'Aubusson, d'Amboise, del Carretto and Villiers de l'Isle Adam), they stretch 4km and average 11.5m (38ft) thick. Curved the better to deflect missiles,

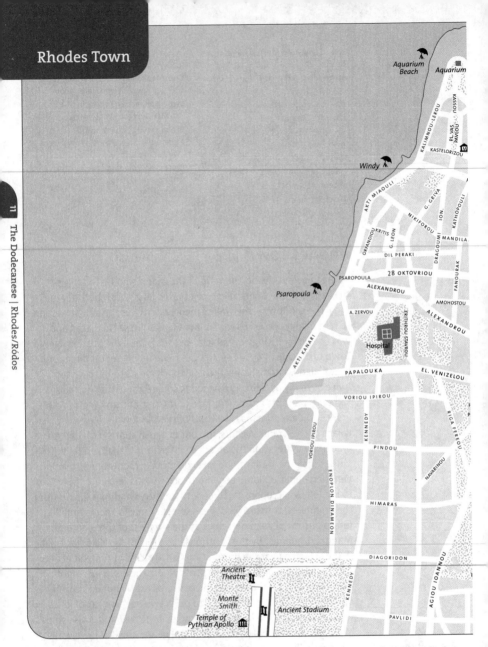

the landward sides were safeguarded by the 30m (100ft)-wide dry moat. Each national group of Knights was assigned its own bastion to defend, except for the Italians, who were the best sailors and in charge of the Knights' fleet.

Of the many gates that linked the walled Old Town with the village outside, the most magnificent is the **Gate of Emery d'Amboise** (Píli Ambouaz, in Greek) near the Palace of the Grand Masters, built in

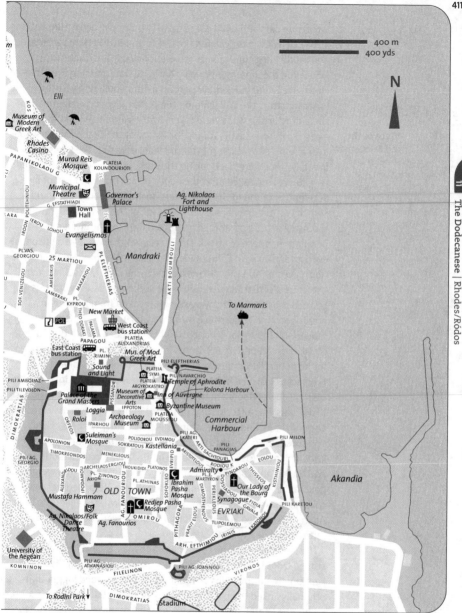

1512 (entrance off Papágou Street). Under the Turks, all Greeks had to be outside the walls by sundown or forfeit their heads.

The Old Town (ΠΑΛΑΙΑ ΠΟΛΗ)

⭐ Knights' tales in the Old Town

The town within these magnificent walls was fairly dilapidated when the Italians took charge. They restored much, but fortunately lost the war before they could get on with their plan to widen all the

The Dodecanese | Rhodes/Ródos

11

streets for cars and build a ring road. To keep any such future notions at bay, UNESCO has declared the Old Town a World Heritage Site, and is providing funds for its restoration and infrastructure.

Entering the aforementioned d'Amboise Gate, passing the table-cloth sellers and quick-draw portrait artists, you'll find yourself in the inner sanctum, the **Collachium**, where the Knights could retreat if the outer curtain walls were taken. By the gate, at the highest point, a castle within a castle, stands the **Palace of the Grand Masters**, built over a Temple to Helios; most scholars believe that the Colossus actually stood here, overlooking the harbour. The palace, completed in 1346, was modelled after the Popes' Palace in Avignon – not by accident: 14 of the 19 Grand Masters on Rhodes were French and French was the official spoken language of the Order. Underground rooms were used as storage and as a refuge for the civilian population in case of attack. The Turks used the whole as a prison, even after the Great Gunpowder Explosion of 1856, when the first floor caved in, and the Italians did the same until Mussolini ordered that it be reconstructed as one of his summer villas. The Italians covered the floors with lovely Roman mosaics from Kos, put in a hotch-potch of Renaissance furniture, and installed a lift and modern plumbing, but war broke out and ended before the Duce could swan around its 158 rooms (don't panic: only a tenth are open to the public). Note the huge marble coat-of-arms on one of the fireplaces: 'Restored by Vitt. Eman. III, King and Emperor 1939'.

On the lower floors are two excellent **exhibitions**. 'Ancient Rhodes: 2400 Years' has a fascinating display of items from everyday life in ancient times, and 'Rhodes from the 4th Century to the Turkish Conquest' offers insights into such things as the use of a lightweight Rhodian bricks (used for the dome of Ag. Sophia in Constantinople) and the Knights' production of sugar, which was worth its weight in gold in the Middle Ages. There's a collection of detached frescoes, coins, icons and the tombstone of the Grand Master Villiers de l'Isle Adam, who defied Suleiman for six months even though he was outmanned nearly 40 to one.

The street descending from the Grand Masters' Palace is cobble-stoned **Odós Ippotón** (Knights' Street), restored by the Italians and kept pristine from shops. It passes under the arcaded **loggia** that originally linked the palace to the 14th-century Cathedral of St John, where the Grand Masters were buried; after that was shattered in the Gunpowder Explosion, a Turkish school was built in the midst of the ruins. Ippotón is lined with the Knights' inns, where they stabled their horses, met and ate; now they house consulates and government offices, and are off limits to visitors. There were eight, each emblazoned with the arms of the Grand Master in charge when it was built: the **Inn of Provence** on the left and the two buildings of the **Inn of Spain** on the right, then the French chapel and elaborate

Palace of the Grand Masters
t 224 107 5674; open summer Mon 12.30–8, Tues– Sun 8–8; winter Tues–Sun 8.30–3; adm exhibitions 'Ancient Rhodes: 2400 Years' closed Wed, Fri and Sat; 'Rhodes from the 4th Century to the Turkish Conquest' closed Tues, Thurs, and Sat

Inn of France (1509), adorned with crocodiles and escutcheons; as there were always more French knights than any other 'tongue', their inn was the most spacious. Opposite, you can usually have a poke around the **Villaragut Mansion**, that once belonging to Villiers de l'Isle Adam. The **Inn of Italy** (1519) stands at the foot of the street.

Two squares open up at the end of the street; just to the right, on the corner of Apelloú St, stands the much restored **Inn of England** (1483), abandoned in 1534, when the Pope excommunicated Henry VIII. It was hit by an earthquake in 1851, rebuilt by the British, bombed and rebuilt again in 1947. Opposite stands the Gothic **Hospital of the Knights**, built between 1440–81 and restored by the Italians in 1918, and now the **Archaeology Museum**. Heraldic devices still adorn the long shadowy arched ward where the Knights' surgeons (who were commoners) cared for patients in elaborate canopy beds. Ceramics, stelae, Mycenaean jewellery and mosaics are on diisplay, but the sculpture steals the show – Lawrence Durrell's 3rd-century BC *Marine Venus* (marine, and eroded, because she was found in the sea) and the pretty kneeling *Aphrodite of Rhodes* (90 BC), combing out her wet hair; also note the bust of Helios from the 2nd century BC, complete with holes in the head to hold his metal sunrays. In the adjacent square, 11th-century **Panagía Kástrou**, used by the Knights as their Cathedral of St Mary until they built their own, now contains a little **Byzantine Museum**, with frescoes and icons from disused churches across the island and Chálki.

Through the arch, charming Plateía Argyrokástro has the loveliest inn, the 15th-century **Inn of Auvergne** (now a cultural centre), with a fountain made from a Byzantine baptismal font. Here, too, is the 14th-century **Palace of the Armeria**, constructed by Grand Master Roger de Pins as the Knights' first hospital on Rhodes, and the **Museum of Decorative Arts** with folk art and handicrafts from all over the Dodecanese, including costumes, embroideries and a reconstruction of a traditional room.

Nearby, in Plateía Sými, the **Museum of Modern Greek Art** is now an annexe to the bigger museum in the New Town (*see* below) and houses 19th- and 20th-century Greek engravings. Also in the square are the ruins of a 3rd-century BC **Temple of Aphrodite**, discovered by the Italians in 1922. Fragments of another temple of the same epoch, dedicated to Diónysos, are in a corner behind the Ionian and Popular Bank. The Italians reopened the two harbour gates that the Turks had blocked up, **Píli Eleftherías** ('Freedom Gate'; the Italians regarded themselves as Rhodes' liberators) to Mandráki and **Píli Navárchio** (or Arsenal Gate) to the marina and commerical harbour.

Sidebar:

Archaeology Museum
t 224 103 1048, open Tues–Sun 8–7, winter 8.30–3; adm

Byzantine Museum
open Tues–Sun 8.30–3; adm

Museum of Decorative Arts
open Tues–Sun 8.30–3; adm

Museum of Modern Greek Art
t 224 102 3766, open Tues–Sat 8–2, adm

The Turkish and Jewish Quarters

South of the Collachium of the Knights is the former Turkish bazaar, where all the streets have been renamed after Greek

Mosque of Suleiman
closed for restoration, but should reopen soon

Ottoman Library
open Mon–Sat 9.30–4

philosophers and poets; bustling **Sokrátous** is the main street. At the top of the street stands the minaret of the lovely, faded red **Mosque of Suleiman**, built in 1523 by Suleiman the Magnificent to celebrate his conquest of Rhodes. The **Ottoman Library** opposite (1793) contains rare Persian and Arabian manuscripts, and illuminated copies of the Koran. Two precious 700-year-old Korans stolen in 1990 and worth €300,000 have now been recovered and are back on show. Behind Suleiman's mosque, the 1857 clock tower or **To Roloi** (now a posh bar) built by Ahmet Fetih Pasha has splendid views over the town, although you have to pay to see it.

South of Sokrátou Street, the Turkish Quarter dissolves into a zigzag of narrow streets, where charming Turkish balconies of latticed wood project beside crumbling stone arches and houses built directly over the street. On Plateía Aríonos, off Archeláos Street, the **Mustafa Mosque** keeps company with the atmospheric **Mustafa Hammam**, built in 1558 and remodelled in 1765. Heated by a ton of olive logs a day, it has mosaic floors, marble fountains and a lovely ceiling. Another old mosque, **Ibrahim Pasha** (1531), is off Sofokléous Street; executions took place in front of it. This one is still used by the local Turkish community (around 2,500) and has a new minaret.

Mustafa Hammam
t 224 102 7739; open for women Tues and Thurs 11–6, Sat 8–6; and for men Mon, Wed and Fri 11–6; bring own soap and towel; adm

On Hippocrátes Square, where Sokrátous turns into Aristotélous Street, stands the picturesque Gothic-Renaissance **Kastellania**, built by Grand Master d'Amboise in 1507, perhaps as a tribunal or commercial exchange for the Knights. It stands at the head of Pithágora Street, the main street of the **Evriakí** (or **La Juderia**) the Jewish quarter; according to the historian Josephus, the community dates from the 1st century AD, and later chronicles cite them among Rhodes' defenders against the Turks. The Turks, however, welcomed exiles from Spain after 1492, and the majority of Jews (*c.* 4000 in the 1920s) on Rhodes were Sephardic and spoke Ladino. Many immigrated in the early 20th century, and many more during the Italian occupation. To the east along Aristotélous Street, Plateía Evrión Martyrón (Square of Hebrew Martyrs) honours the 1673 left on the island sent to the concentration camps; only 151 survived. Just south on Dossiádou St stands Rhodes' surviving **Kahal Shalom synagogue**, highly decorated and the oldest in Greece still in use by the local community, now 40-strong; commemorative plaques pay homage to the deported Jewish population. In the former women's prayer room, the little **Jewish Museum** has displays illustrating the history of the Rhodian Jewish community and its diaspora.

Kahal Shalom synagogue
open April–Nov 10–4

Jewish Museum
www.rhodesjewish museum.org; open same hours as synagogue

The so-called **Admirality** (more likely the seat of Rhodes' Catholic bishop) is back on the square, behind a charming bronze seahorse fountain. From here, Pindárou Street continues to the magificent Gothic vaults of **Our Lady of the Bourg**, built by the Knights in thanksgiving for their defeat of the Turks in 1480, but never the same after it took a British bomb in the war.

Our Lady of the Bourg
open 8.30–3, adm

The Turkish and Jewish quarters offer other cobbled lanes to explore, dotted with old churches converted into mosques and converted back again: one, off Omírou St, is little **Ag. Fanoúrios** (1335) with a fresco of the donors, near the abandoned **Redjep Pasha Mosque** (1588), which was once coated with colourful Persian tiles. The gate at the end of Pithágora Street, **Píli Ag. Ioánnou**, or Red Door, is another demonstration of the walls' strength.

The New Town

Outside the walls, overpriced seafront cafés look enticingly over **Mandráki** harbour. Just behind them, in the Italian-built octagonal **New Market**, tomatoes and watermelons have been replaced by *gýros* and *souvláki* stands. Further along Mandráki is an austere ensemble of Fascist public buildings from the 1920s – post office, theatre and town hall. The Italians also left Rhodes some more light-hearted architecture: the **Governor's Palace**, a pseudo-Doge's Palace decorated with a garish red diaper pattern, and the **Evangelísmos** cathedral, a copy of the one blown up in the gunpowder accident. The Gothic fountain is a copy of Viterbo's Fontana Grande.

The Turks regarded Rhodes as an island paradise, and many Muslim notables in exile (including a Shah of Persia) chose to spend the rest of their lives here. Many lie buried in the cemetery north of the municipal theatre, next to the **Mosque of Murad Reis**, named after the admiral of the Egyptian sultan who was killed during the siege of Rhodes in 1522 and is buried in a turban-shaped tomb, or turbeh. The mosque has a lovely minaret reconstructed by the last people you would guess – the Greek government. Near the cemetery, the Dodecanese Literature and Arts Club has set up shop in a place with presumably excellent literary vibrations, in the recently restored **Villa Cleobolus**, where Lawrence Durrell lived for a couple of years after the war.

Stretching along the shore from here is the **casino** and Rhodes' busiest strand, shingly **Élli Beach**, sheltered from the southwest winds and packed chock-a-block with parasols and sunbeds. There's a diving platform for high divers and a lifeguard, but people floating on airbeds should beware of being swept out to sea.

Museum of Modern Greek Art
t 224 104 3780; open Tues–Sat 8–2, adm

Just inland, in Plateía Charitós, the new gallery '**Nestorideion Melathron**' of the city-run **Museum of Modern Greek Art** has one of the country's best collections of 20th century Greek paintings, with works by all the big names including Theóphilos Hatzimicháíl.

Aquarium
open daily in season 9–9; otherwise 9–4.30; adm

At the northernmost tip of the island is the **Aquarium**, built by the Italians in 1938, with tanks of Mediterranean fish and sea turtles, a pair of which are over 100 years old, and a startling collection of stuffed denizens of the deep, their twisted grimaces the result not of any prolonged agony but of amateur taxidermy. In the same vein, local farmers have contributed an eight-legged calf and four-legged chicken. On the headland, **Aquarium Beach** has deep water, but its breezes make it more popular for windsurfing; ditto **Windy Beach**, which stretches down to Aktí Miaoúli.

The Acropolis and Rodíni Park

City bus no.5 heads south of the New Town to the acropolis of ancient Rhodes, now known as **Monte Smith** after Admiral Sydney Smith who in 1802 kept track of Napoleon's Egyptian escapades from here; today most people come up for the romantic sunset. It was never fortified, but had shrines and monuments on stepped terraces. There's a **Nymphaia**, with artificial grottos and cisterns. A few column drums remain of the once massive **Temple of Athena Polias and Zeus Polieus**, where the Rhodians stored their treaties. On the top of Monte Smith, the Italians re-erected four columns of the 2nd-century BC Doric **Temple of Pythian Apollo**, who was associated with Helios, and a 3rd-century BC **Stadium**, with the starting mechanism; at one end the seats have been made into a theatre.

City bus no.3 will take you the 2km out to **Rodíni Park**, with its ravine, cypresses, pines, oleanders, maples, peacocks and deer (the Delphic Oracle told the Rhodians to import deer to solve their snake problem, and they have been here, more or less, ever since). Rodíni Park marks the spot where Aeschines established his celebrated School of Rhetoric in 330 BC, where the likes of Julius Caesar and Cicero learned how to speak – there's a rock-cut tomb from the 4th century BC, the so-called 'Tomb of Ptolemy', and the ruins of a Roman aqueduct. The Knights grew their medicinal herbs here.

Shopping in Rhodes Town

Although no longer duty-free, shopping is deeply embedded in Rhodes' DNA. It may be the island of the sun, but nowhere on earth will you find more fur shops, or umbrella shops. The New Town near Mandráki is full of designer shops; there's even a Marks & Spencer. Sokrátou Street is the place for high-end leather, furs and jewellery.

Platéia Kýprou, for shoes.

Kakakios Brothers, 47 G. Lambráki. For a reasonably priced tailor-made suit made from British fabrics. These brothers made them for the likes of Gregory Peck and Anthony Quinn.

Bibliopolis, 14 Stelíou Kotiádia, towards the university.

Elafos, 25 Sokrátou. Hand-made Rhodian carpets and kilims, a tradition here since Ottoman times.

Market, on Zéfiros St (by the cemetery). The biggest market in the Dodecanese takes place every Saturday morning; get there early to find a bargain.

Market, on Výronos St by the Stadium. Smaller market, takes place on Wed.

Where to Stay in Rhodes Town

Rhodes Town ✉ 85100

Rhodes has a plethora of accommodation from one of the most expensive hotels ever to be built in Greece to humble village rooms. Many are booked solid by package companies, some for winter breaks too, so if you're island-hopping in high season it's definitely worth phoning ahead.

On the Internet, *www.helios.gr* has more information on hotels, and sights, with descriptions and bookings for a selection of luxury to C-class hotels across the island.

Luxury

Grand Hotel Rhodes, Aktí Miaoúli, t 224 105 4700, *www.mitsis-grandhotel.com*. With tennis courts and what's reputed to be the largest swimming pool in the country. They host EU conferences.

Rodos Park, next to the historic centre at 12 Ríga Fereoú, t 224 108 9700, *www.rodospark.gr*. Overlooking the park, mega-luxury, 7-star suites provide some of the opulence in town, with private Jacuzzis, pool, health club, and ballroom.

Very Expensive

★ Marco Polo Mansion >

Marco Polo Mansion, 42 Ag. Fanouríou in the Old Town t 224 102 5562, *www.apliger.gr/marcopolo*. The most atmospheric and intimate place to stay in Rhodes – a bed and breakfast in an old Turkish house, suitably furnished with antiques (the owners also have a shop), with a hammam and delicious breakfasts in the garden. Five-day minimum stay.

Nikos Takis Fashion Hotel, 26 Panetíou by the Old Town, t 224 107 0773, *www.nikostakishotel.com*. In a 19th-century house, four exquisite suites (*luxury*) for non-smokers designed with an Turkish flair by two fashion designers, who also run the boutique downstairs.

Expensive

Chryssos Tholos, 15 Kistiníou, t 224 107 7332. Small hotel in a beautifully restored mansion, 100m from the sea. *Open Mar–Oct*.

Marie, 7 Kos, near Élli Beach, t 224 103 0577,*www.helios.gr/hotels/marie*. Recently renovated by the casino, offering a swimming pool, sea sports, sauna and billiards. *Open April–Oct*.

S. Nicolis, 61 Ippodámou, t 224 103 4561, *www.s-nikolis.gr*. Offers atmospheric accommodation in a lovely house in the heart of the Old Town; parts of it are 800 years old. Excellent bed and breakfast, large garden and rooftop terrace with great views. The Greek-Danish proprietors also have apartments to sleep 4 people nearby and a cheaper *pension*; *booking is essential*.

Moderate

★ Cavo d'Oro >

Cavo d'Oro, 15 Kisthiníou, near the commercial harbour, t 224 103 6980,

www.cavadoro.com. Well worth a try; it was good enough for Michael Palin on his pole-to-pole jaunt. The delightful 13th-century house has been beautifully restored by the owner and his German wife; he'll even meet you from the ferry.

Andreas, 28 Omírou, t 224 103 4156 , *www.hotelandreas.com* (some rooms €€€). Popular hotel in the Old Town, with individually designed rooms, named after characters in the works of Laurence Durrell. Lovely views from the terrace.

Paris, 88 Ag. Fanouríou, t 224 102 6356, *www.rodosparis.gr*. Nice rooms and a quiet courtyard with shady orange and banana trees, and prices at the bottom of this range.

Popi, Stratigoú Zísi and 21 Maliaráki, near the Old Town, t 224 102 3479. Studios in the old-fashioned Greek style, but modern, with air-conditioning. Each sleeps four.

Victoria, 22–5 Martiou, t 224 102 4626. Central, family-run, and the owner's son, a UK-trained doctor, has consulting rooms next door.

Minos Pension, 5 Omírou, t 224 103 1813, *www.minospension.com*. Pristine and with panoramic roof-garden views.

Inexpensive

Ambassadeur, 53 Óthonos and Amalías, t 224 103 0431. One of the best for value in this category.

Attiki, Charitos and Theofiliskou, t 224 102 7767. In a medieval building in the heart of the Old Town, quietly tucked away in the corner; a bit dishevelled but children welcome. *Open all year*.

Iliana, 1 Gavála, t 224 103 0251. In an old Jewish family house, with a small bar and terrace; no charge for childen under 10 and cheap for everyone else.

La Luna, next to a tiny church on Ierokléous, just off Orféos, t 224 102 5856. With a bar, but no en-suites, in a perfectly quiet courtyard with hammam. *Open all year*.

Maria's Rooms, on Menekléous, t 224 102 2169. Comfortable choice around a quiet courtyard.

Spot, Perikléous 21, t 224 103 4737. One of the better cheap backpackers' haunts; good value with light, airy rooms plus en suite bathrooms.

Alexis >>

Eating Out in Rhodes Town

Rhodes Town has a range of eating places from Mediterreanean gourmet restaurants to real dives selling tripe (*patsás*). The Rhodians are to the Greek islands what the Parisians are to France. They are very fashionable, often fickle, and love new food trends. For something cheap, the New Market is full of good 'n' greasy *gýros* with outdoor tables. Be sure to try Rhodes' own wines: Chevaliers de Rhodes; Ilios; Archontiko, the prize-winning premium red from CAIR; and Villaré, an excellent Emery white (*see* p.429).

New Town

Christos, out in the suburb of Zéfiros, beyond the commercial harbour. This is one of the best and most authentic tavernas for a hearty lunch; it is a favourite with local families and taxi drivers – there'll be no problem finding it – the food is excellent, good value and is accompanied by an astonishing range of ouzos.

Dania, 3 Iroón Polytéchniou, near the Royal Bank of Scotland, t 224 102 0540. For a real taste of Denmark; serving traditional herring dishes and a running smorgasbord on Sun eves.

Ellinikon, 29 Alexándrou Diákou, t 224 102 8111 (€18–22). Another popular choice with the locals, serving Greek and international dishes and excellent desserts. *Closed Mon and Tues.*

Palia Istoria >

Palia Istoria ('Old Story'), 108 Mitropóleos, south of the new stadium, t 224 103 2421 (€35). Imaginative array of dishes from celery hearts in *avgolémono* sauce to scallops with mushrooms and artichokes, and a good choice of vegetarian dishes; the fruit salad has 20 kinds of fruit. Excellent Greek wine list. *Eves only; book.*

Steno, 29 Ag. Anargíron, just south of Ag. Athanasíou gate, t 224 103 5914 . Another genuine, friendly ouzerie: great *mezédes*, deservedly popular.

Thavma en kairo, 16 Venizélou, t 224 103 9805 (€35). The new version of the Norwegian-run 'Wonder' of Rhodes, in a beautiful 19th-century mansion: surprising and refined fusion cuisine, served on a terrace overlooking the park. *Open eves only.*

Old Town

Alexis, 18 Sokrátous, t 224 107 0522 (€50). Superb seafood and wine list – a classic going strong after 40 years. *Open April–Nov.*

Alexis 4 Seasons, at 33 Aristotélous, t 224 107 0522. Also specializes in seafood, but the menus are different; this one remains *open all year.*

Araliki, 45 Aristofánous. Greek home cooking (done by Italians), offering superb *mezédes* in a medieval setting.

Cleo's, on Ag. Fanouríou, t 224 102 8415 (*reservations recommended*). One of the most elegant places to dine in the heart of the medieval city, serving upmarket Italian and French cuisine.

Dinoris, 14 Plateía Moussíou, t 224 102 5824. An old favourite (around €60) in the 13th-century stables of the Knights of St John, with a romantic garden patio and more lovely fish.

Fotis, 8 Menekleóus St, t 224 102 7359 (€30). Since 1970, courtyard dining, with excellent grilled fish – simple and delicious, plus delicacies such as sea urchin salad and steamed mussels.

Golden Olympiade Peridis, Apelloú and Evdímou, t 224 102 0119 (€25) Big, bustling and popular, serving a good mix of Greek and international dishes. *Open April–Oct.*

Melathron, 41 Parodos Sokrátous, t 224 102 4272 (€30). Set in an elegantly refurbished building, there are some private rooms (for larger parties or romance; book in advance) with drinks and humidor. The menu is both Greek and international, but the Greek dishes are by far the best.

Sarris, Plateía Evdímou, t 224 107 3707 (€20). Good honest cuisine in one of the Old Town's prettiest squares, with good *mezédes* and some Continental dishes too.

Entertainment in Rhodes Town

Throughout the summer theatre, dance and concert performances take place in the **Medieval Moat Theatre** while the really big names play in **Diagoras Stadium**. Check listings before you arrive at *www.rhodesguide. com/events.*

You can take in a film (most often subtitled, in the original language) at one of the many great open-air cinemas (indoors out of season):

Metropol Cinema, corner of Výronos and Venetokléon Sts, near the stadium.

Pallas Cinema, nearby on Dimokratias.

Muncipal Cinema, by the town hall. With artier fare.

There are traditional **Greek folk dances** by the Nelly Dimogloú Company in the **Old Town Theatre**, Andronikou, t 224 102 0157 or 224 102 9085 (*May–Oct Mon, Wed and Fri 9.20pm–10.30pm*). Dance lessons are available also.

Son et Lumière Show, in the Municipal Gardens, t 224 121 922 (ring for times of shows in English). The history of Rhodes unfolds here. *Open May–Oct.*

Nightlife in Rhodes Town

Rhodes has something for everyone, with around 600 bars in Rhodes Town alone. There are discos, laser shows, Irish pubs; theme bars; super-cool cocktail bars or live-music tavernas in restored Old Town houses; bars full of gyrating girls and wet T-shirt nights; and even simple **ouzeries** where a game of backgammon is the high spot. **Orfanídou Street**, just in from Aktí Miaoúli is known as the street of bars; another is Diákou Street to the south. The island also has all kinds of music

from traditional folk to funk, soul, house and rap to vintage Elvis.

Blue Lagoon Pool Bar, 25 Martíou. A place to live out your fantasies in a totally themed and tropical environment.

Bouzoúki **club** at Élli Beach. Traditional Greeks head here for late-night music.

Café Besara, 11 Sofokléous. For an Antipodean atmosphere, never dull and featuring live Greek music 3 times a week.

Casino, in the landmark Albergo delle Rose (1927) at 4 G. Papanikolaoú, t 224 109 7500. Rhodes' casino is one of the busiest in Greece. €15 to enter. *Minimum age 23, open 3pm–6am, and nonstop from Fri noon to Mon 6am.*

Christos Garden, 59 Dilberáki, New Town. Arty bar in a restored neo-classical house and courtyard. Ideal for a romantically intimate garden evening among the jasmine

O'Reilly's, 6 Apolloníou Rodioú; Irish bar, with live music

Le Palais, 2 25 Martíou St. Rhodes's big kitsch fun complex, with a disco, fun fairs, restaurants, even a bridge club.

Privato disco, 2 Iliadón, t 224 103 3267.

Sticky Fingers, 6 A. Zervoú, south of Psarópoula. Rockers should head for this ever-popular bar; live music some nights.

To Roloi, up the ramp on Orféos. Join the smart set in this impressive, distinctly pricey clocktower; worth a climb up for the view.

Western Suburbs: Rhodes Town to Ancient Ialysós and Mount Filérimos

Although the beaches here are windy, this strip was the first to be developed as the island's prime hotel area, lined with massive resort hotels (with sheltered pools), favoured by conventioneers.

On your way out of town, look out for the little houses on the left at **Kritiká**, built by Cretan Turks in 1923, facing their old homeland. Long before the Turkish Cretans came here fleeing repercussions after the Asia Minor disaster in 1922, this coast was settled by Minoans, and there's evidence that their settlements may have been damaged in the ancient explosion and tsunami from Santoríni.

Triánda, which runs via **Ixiá** into Rhodes Town, occupies the site of **ancient Ialysos**, the least important of the three Dorian cities of

Rhodes. When the Phoenicians lived there, an oracle foretold that they would leave only when the crows turned white and fish appeared inside the water jars. The Dorian leader Iphicles heard the prediction, during his siege of the town, and planted fish in the amphorae and daubed a few ravens with plaster. The Phoenicians duly fled (and whatever the ancient Dorian word for 'suckers' might have been, we can be sure Iphicles said it). Ialysos was the birthplace of the boxer Diagoras, praised by Pindar in the *Seventh Olympian Ode* and whose name now adorns the island airport, but with the foundation of Rhodes Town it declined to a village by the time Strabo visited in the 1st century AD.

Ancient Ialysos
open Mon–Sat 8–6,
Sun 8.30–2.30; adm

Ialysos lies in the beautiful garden-like **acropolis-citadel**, on Mount Filérimos, 5km inland. Historically this has been a busy place. Suleiman the Magnificent made it his base during the final assault on the Knights in 1522, and it may have been the nucleus of the Mycenaean city of Achaia. Built over the foundations of a Phoenician temple are the remains of the 3rd-century BC **Temple of Athena Polias and Zeus Polieus**, in turn partly covered by Byzantine churches. Beneath the ruins of one is the tiny underground chapel of **Ag. Geórgios** with faint frescoes from the 1300s – you can make out five Knights of St John with their patron saints being introduced to Christ. A 4th-century Doric fountain with lionhead spouts is now off limits. The lovely monastery church of **Filérimos**, converted by the Knights from a 5th-century church and somewhat over-restored by the Italians, wears the coat of arms of Grand Master d'Aubusson, still has both Catholic (north) and Orthodox (south) altars. A font and mosaic floor survive from the earlier church.

For the best views of all, there's an uphill path from the monastery lined with the Stations of the Cross. In 1934 the Italian governor erected an enormous Cross on the summit, although seven years later the Italians themselves blew it up to prevent the Allies from using it as a target. In 1994 the Lions Club financed the current one, 16m (52ft) high, dominating an otherwise very secular coast.

Where to Stay in the Western Suburbs

Ixiá and Triánda ✉ 85100

The Ixiá and Triánda strip is one long stretch of hotels.

Rodos Palace, t 224 102 5222, *www. rodos-palace.gr* (€€€€€). The biggest and one of the most up-to-date hotels in the Med, decorated by the set designer of *Ben Hur*, with state-of-the-art communications systems and catering for the conference trade and meetings of European heads of state.

The striking domed, heated Olympic-size indoor pool is partly built with Sými's former solar water still; you'll also find three outdoor pools, a sauna, gym, tennis courts and plenty more trimmings, and a special family resort in the resort.

Miramare Wonderland, t 224 109 6251, *www.bluegr.com* (€€€€€) Plush waterfront resort of low buildings in a beautiful garden setting, on a long stretch of beach. The whole, in fact, is so big that guests get about on a mini-replica steam train. Huge pool and plenty for children to do as well, and an excellent restaurant, **Gulliver** (€35). *Open April–Oct.*

Dionysos, t 224 102 3021, *www. dionysos-hotel.gr* (€€€€–€€€). Tropical gardens, lake-style salt water pool and indoor pool, and children's activities.

Scores of A- and B-class hotels and apartments, plus cheaper *pensions*, are available all along the road from here to the airport.

Galini, in Ialysós, **t** 224 109 1251 (€€). Apartments for 2–6 people, pool and playground. *Open May–Oct.*

⭐ Garden >

Garden, in Pastída (just inland from Triánda, **t** 224 104 7008, *www.garden-hotel.gr* (€, *half-board terms on a weekly basis*). One of the friendliest and best-value places on the island: fairly simple rooms plus a huge pool, gardens, games, etc., and a good restaurant, serving plenty of vegetarian dishes. Good for families or couples; there is a high return rate. They'll even pick you up at the airport..

Ta Koupia, in Triánda by Ialysos, **t** 224 109 1824 (€60). Long one of the island's most exclusive haunts, decorated with antique Greek furniture – excellent *mezédes* and upmarket Greek dishes with an Eastern touch. *Closed Sun eve.*

Down the East Shore to Líndos

Like the windier west shore, the warmer sandy shore southeast of Rhodes Town is lined with hotels, beginning with the popular beaches of **Réni Koskinoú** and the lovely coves of **Kalithéa**, reached by way of walkways over a picturesque jumble of boulders; each has its own taverna. Kalithéa's hot springs were recommended by Hippocrates but no longer flow, and now the abandoned but magnificent Italianate-Moorish Art Deco spa building from the 1929 is fitfully being restored with EU funds. Inland, the pretty village of **Koskinoú** is known for its pebble mosaics, or *choklákia*, a technique introduced by the 7th-century Byzantines.

Holiday La-La Land begins in earnest with **Faliráki Bay North**, a massive development along the beach, complete with shopping malls. The original Faliráki, with its sweeping golden sands and bungee jump and waterslides, is, in spite of recent publicity over lewdness, rapes and violence, still a playground for the 18–30s, though rather a more subdued one since the police crackdown in 2004.

Ladikó Bay just south has a small rocky cove known as Anthony Queen Beach (*sic*) after the actor who bought land with special permission from the Greek government (or thought he did – he could never get the title) in 1961 while filming *The Guns of Navarone* at Líndos – although some Rhodians blame Quinn for never developing the area or founding a film studio on the island. Next door, the hidden village of **Afándou** (its name means 'invisible') is less frenetic and has the ultimate rarity in this part of the world – an 18-hole **golf**

Afándou golf course
t 224 105 1255/6

course by the sea. Once known for its carpet-weaving and apricots, Afándou has a relatively empty 7km pebble beach, deep crystal waters and excellent fish tavernas. A few people here work for the Voice of America, which transmits from a grove of seaside antennae.

Next comes **Kolýmbia**, a soulless resort, built as a planned agricultural community by the Italians. A scenic avenue of eucalyptus trees leads to **Vagiá Point**, with good beaches south of the headland. The farms were (and still are) irrigated thanks to the nymph-haunted lake fed by the **Eptá Pigés**, the 'Seven Springs', 5km inland. A wooded beauty spot with scented pines, it's a tranquil place for a picnic, with strutting peacocks and ducks. You can walk through ankle-deep icy water along the low, narrow, 186m (610ft) aqueduct tunnel dug by the Italians (claustrophobes have an alternative route, from the road).

The long sandy bay at **Tsambíka** is popular and undeveloped (it's owned by the Church), with its tiny white **monastery** perched high – 300 steps up – on the cliffs above. Rhodes' answer to fertility drugs, the monastery's 11th-century icon of the Virgin attracts childless women who make the pilgrimage barefoot and pledge to name their children Tsambíkos or Tsambíka, unique Dodecanese names but common enough in the phone book to prove that it works. Even if you're not in need of offspring, the views from the top are spectacular. The road leads down steeply to **Stegná**, a shingle beach in a pretty bay. The rugged coastal path is redolent of Cornwall: the walk from Tsambíka to **Faraklós** (*see* below) takes around 3hrs.

Next on the main road, **Archángelos** with 3,500 souls is the largest village on Rhodes, its little white houses spread under a chewed-up castle of the Knights. Its churches, **Archángelos Gabriél** and **Archángelos Michaél**, are two of the prettiest on the island; another nearby, **Ag. Theodóroi**, has 14th-century frescoes, but all three are usually shut. The fiercely patriotic villagers have even painted the graveyard blue and white. Archángelos was famous for its ceramics and special leather boots that keep snakes at bay, although both traditions are on the verge of dying out.

Once one of the strongest citadels on Rhodes, the ruined **Castle of Faraklós** is dramatically positioned on the promontory below **Malóna**, overlooking Charáki. It was originally occupied by pirates, until the Knights gave them the boot, repaired the walls and used the fort as a prison. Even after the rest of the island fell to Suleiman, Faraklós held, only surrendering after a long, determined siege.

Nearby **Charáki** has a pretty shaded esplanade of fish tavernas running along a small crescent-shaped pebble beach, although there's better nearby at **Ag. Agáthi** and **Kálathos**. In **Mássari**, just inland, one of the Knights' sugar refineries was discovered where olives and orange groves now reign.

Where to Stay and Eat on the East Shore

Koskinoú ✉ 85100

O Yiannis. Once cheap and cheerful, this has now become the place to see

and be seen. Delicious *mezédes*. There'll be queues but it's definitely worth the wait.

Afándou ✉ 85103

Reni Sky, t 224 105 1125 (€). With a pool and good-value rooms.

Argo >>

Avantis, t 224 105 1280 (€28). Delicious fish dishes, rated among the the best on the island.

Charáki ✉ 85103

Atrium Palace, Kálathos Beach, **t** 224 408 6900, *www.rodos.com/atrium*

(€€€€€). The big noise here, with every conceivable amenity.

Argo, t 224 405 1410. Well worth the effort of getting here for the excellent seafood. Around €55; best to book.

Haraki Bay, t 224 405 1680. With an enormous *mezédes* selection.

Líndos and Around

Dramatically situated on a promontory high over the sea, beautiful Líndos is Rhodes' second most visited town, with a year-round population of 800 who receive nearly 3 million visitors every year. With its sugar-cube houses wrapped around the fortified acropolis, it has kept its integrity only because the whole town is classified as an archaeological site, unique in Greece; even painting the shutters a new colour requires permission, and no hotels are allowed to be built within sight of the windows. Líndos was a magnet for artists and beautiful people back in the 1960s, when, they say, you could hear the clink of cocktail glasses as far away as Rhodes Town. It still has a few famous Brits (Pink Floyd's Dave Gilmour), Italians, Germans and Saudi princes and diplomats – who have snapped up the lovely old captains' houses.

Incredibly beautiful as Líndos is, there's little left of village life apart from locals selling vegetables in the early morning. In July and August there are so many daytrippers that you can literally be swept along by the crowds. By 6pm the town regains its sanity. But if you can't take the heat, be warned: Líndos is the frying pan of Rhodes.

With twin natural harbours (the only ones on Rhodes), Líndos was the most important and precocious of the island's three ancient cities, its 16,000 people living in a city four times the size of the present town. The first sanctuary on its magnificent acropolis was erected in the 9th century BC, and the city grew rich from trade with its many colonies, especially Parthenope (Naples). Its benevolent 6th-century BC tyrant Cleoboulos was one of the Seven Sages of Greece; he was famous for his beauty, his belief in the intellectual equality of women, and his maxims, one of which, 'Nothing in Excess', was engraved on Apollo's temple at Delphi. The reservoir and rock tunnels dug by his father Evander supplied water until recently. St Paul brought Christianity to Líndos; the Knights fortified it, and during the Turkish occupation Lindian merchants handled most of the island's trade; to this day Lindians are known for their business acumen. Most now live in Péfkos and milk their old city as a cash cow.

A Walk around Town

The serpentine pebbled lanes and stairs of Líndos are lined with elegant white mansions from the 15th and 17th centuries. Usually

Getting to and around Líndos

Besides daily **ferries** from Rhodes Town, Líndos has **hydrofoil** excursions to Sými and to Marmaris, Turkey. **Donkey taxis** to the Acropolis cost €5; the possibility of buying a photo of the experience comes with the deal. If you're staying, 3-wheeled vehicles will transport your luggage. **Parking** is free arout the bypass square, where the KTEL **bus** stop is, and from where a free shuttle service runs. For **taxis**, t 224 403 1466.

constructed around courtyards with elaborate pebble mosaics (*choklákia*), secluded behind high walls and imposing doorways, the houses have high ceilings to keep cool and raised living rooms (*sala*), while beds are often set on sleeping platforms. The number of cables carved around the doors or windows represented the number of ships owned by the resident captain. Many are now holiday homes or bars and use their flat roofs for sunbathing and gardens. Some houses, notably the **Papakonstandís Mansion**, which is usually open, still contain collections of Lindian ware, delightful plates painted with highly stylized Oriental motifs first manufactured in Asia Minor; legend has it that the Knights of St John once captured a ship full of Persian potters and refused to let them go until they taught their craft to the islanders. The pretty, often rebuilt church of the **Panagía** has frescoes of the Apostles, painted by Gregory of Sými in 1779. One, oddly, has a camel head. The back wall is covered with a *Last Judgement*, with St Michael weighing souls and a misogynist St Peter welcoming the Elect into heaven's gate.

The Acropolis of Líndos

Temple of Lindian Athena (Acropolis)
t 224 407 5674, open summer Mon 1–6.30, Tues–Sun 8–6.30; winter Tues–Sun 8.30–3; adm

Floating high over Líndos and the sea, the Temple of Lindian Athena is one of the most stunningly sited in Greece, accessible on foot or by 'Lindian taxi' – hired donkey. The steep route up is lined with billowing tablecloths and saleswomen; Líndos' reputation for embroidery dates back to the time of Alexander the Great, but the vast majority is mass-produced, imported and overpriced.

Just before the Hellenistic stairway you'll see the prow of a trireme carved into the living rock. This once served as a base for a statue of Agissandros, priest of Poseidon, sculpted by Pythokretes of Rhodes, whose *Victory of Samothrace* now graces the Louvre. The still-extant inscription says that the Lindians gave Agissandros a golden wreath for judging their games. The well preserved **walls** around the acropolis date from the Knights, who used the ancient buildings as a quarry. At the top of the stair are two vaulted **rooms** (the commander's residence); to the right is a crumbling 13th-century Byzantine church of **St John**. More stairs ascend to the raised Hellenistic **Stoa of Lindian Athena**, patron goddess of the city. She was a chaste goddess; to enter beyond here, any woman who was menstruating or had recently made love had to take a purifying bath, heads had to be covered, and even men were obliged to have clean bare feet, or wear white shoes that were not made of horsehair.

From here the 'stairway to Heaven' leads up to the mighty foundations of the **Propylaea** or gate and, on the edge of the precipice, the **Temple of Athena** itself, of which only seven columns are standing. Both were built by Cleoboulos, rebuilt after a fire in 342 BC and reconstructed by the Italians; the reconstructions are now being restored and maybe finished by 2008. The temple was celebrated in its day for a wooden statue of Athena, capped with gold, and its golden inscription of Pindar's *Seventh Olympian Ode*.

Other sites are outside the acropolis: a **Theatre**, carved in the southwest slope, and the **Boukopion** to the northeast, a sanctuary in the recess of the rock where bulls were sacrificed from the 10th century BC to an unknown deity.

The views from the acropolis are stunning, especially over the azure round pool of **St Paul's Bay**, where the Apostle landed in AD 58; its diminutive beaches get quite busy. To the north is the **Grand Harbour**, once home port of ancient Líndos' navy, 500 ships strong with the decent town beach and small but trendy **Pállas Beach**. On the far end of this, the well-built cylindrical 'Tomb of Cleoboulos' actually belonged a wealthy Hellenistic family, and in the Middle Ages was converted into a church.

Villages, Beaches and Frescoes around Líndos

Líndos is dwarfed by suburbs of package hotels and holiday homes, all built out of sight of town. **Vlícha Bay**, just north of Líndos, is a good family beach, while **Péfkos**, just south, has a clean, narrow sandy beach fringed by pine trees along with holiday apartments, mini-markets, and so on. Sprawling **Lárdos**, west of Líndos, has a pretty village at its core, although the landscapes have suffered from forest fires and floods.

Just southwest, in the valley of **Keskínto**, farmers in 1893 dug up half of a stone stele from *c*. 100 BC with references to the orbits of Mercury, Mars, Jupiter and Saturn. On the same latitude as the Pillars of Hercules (Gibraltar), Keskínto was the site of the observatory believed to have produced the Antikýthera Mechanism (*see* p.501).

Head 12km inland to **Láerma**, turn 2km down the **Profíla** road and travel another 2km to **Moní Thárri**, founded in the 9th century – the oldest surviving monastery on Rhodes, well hidden from pirates and now reoccupied by monks from Pátras, whose abbot runs a television station, Tharri, that proves that the Orthodox can be fundamentalists too. The church has some of the finest frescoes on Rhodes, dating back to the 12th century; in places they are four layers thick. Among the more unusual scenes are the *Storm on the Sea of Galilee* and the *Encounter with the Magdalene*.

South of Lárdos, the beach on sweeping **Lárdos Bay** has dunes bordered by reeds and marshes and village-style hotels, but you can still find peaceful beaches further south: **Glýstra** is a gem, with a perfect sheltered cove. **Kiotári**, long undeveloped (the land was sold off in the 1990s by the church), now has stylish hotel complexes isolated in the surrounding wilderness, while its beach stretches for miles, with a hilly backdrop.

Inland, the medieval hill village of **Asklipío** huddles beneath the remains of yet another Crusader **castle**. The Byzantine monastery church of the **Kímisis Theotókou** dates from 1060, and has beautifully preserved, richly coloured frescoes from the 15th century depicting stories from the Old Testament, arranged (unusually for Greece) like comic-strips around the walls .

Kímisis Theotókou
open daily 9–6, adm

Where to Stay and Eat in Líndos and Around

ⓘ **Líndos >**
*Municipal tourist
office: Plateía Eleftherías,*
t 224 403 1900

Líndos ✉ 85107

Nearly every house has been converted into a holiday home, all but a few with the name of a British holiday company on the door. **Pallas Travel**, **t** 224 403 1494, can also arrange rooms.

Líndos Mare, 3km north at Vlícha Bay, **t** 224 403 1130, *www.lindosmare.gr* (€€€€€). A fancy place, in a lovely setting with a pool overlooking the sea.

Melenos, overlooking the sea, **t** 224 403 2222, *www.melenoslindos.com* (€€€€€). Boutique hotel in traditonal Lindian mansion style that took 13 years to build, furnished with art and antiques and pebble mosaics, offering 11 gorgeous suites. Lovely roof garden and fragrant citrus groves.

Nikolas, **t** 224 404 8076 (€€€). Pricey apartments sleeping 2–6.

Lindos Sun, 1km outside town, 300m from the beach, **t** 224 403 1453, *www.hotellindossun.com* (€€). Typical rooms with balconies tennis and pool. *Open April–Oct.*

Ambrosia, **t** 224 403 1804. Good taverna serving a mix of Greek and international cuisine in a traditional house, in a stone and wood décor.

Archontiko, **t** 224 403 1992. Lindian specialities and fresh fish served in a 400-year-old captain's house, with views of the acropolis.

 Mavrikos >

Mavrikos, on a pretty terrace just off the square, **t** 224 403 1232 (€40). Established in 1933, frequented by Jackie Onassis and now run by the third generation of brothers who have won awards for their imaginative and exceptionally good Greek, French and Italian dishes. *Open April–Oct.*

Lárdos ✉ 85107

Lindian Village, just outside Lárdos, **t** 224 404 7361, *www.lindianvillage.gr* (€€€€€). Stylish beach complex, with white Aegean-style houses around paved courtyards. Furnishings are luxurious but with an ethnic feel: pale blue wooden taverna chairs and old ceramics. Plus a surprise – an excellent Thai and southeast Asian restaurant (€60).

Péfkos ✉ 85107

Philosophia, above the beach, **t** 224 404 8044. Romantic beach taverna, considered by many the best on Rhodes; friendly Greek/English owners.

To Spitaki, an old house in Péfkos village centre, **t** 224 404 8802. Greek dishes with a cordon bleu touch in peaceful gardens.

Kiotári ✉ 85109

Paraktio, **t** 224 404 7278, *www.paraktio. com* (€€€). Stylish well-equipped studios and apartments (sleeping four) where the sea starts at the end of the garden.

Hippocrates, **t** 224 404 7093 (€25) Excellent Italian and international dishes and plenty of fish by a Greek chef who spent years in Italy. *Open June–Sept.*

Mourella, on the north beach, **t** 224 404 7324 (€25). Popular taverna with some surprises on the menu; try the chef's own cocktail while deciding.

The Far and Windy South

Rhodes' south quarter changes personality: it's drier, windier and relatively undeveloped. Wheat and barley grow here: the Italians tried to develop the farms, and Rhodes could easily support itself, but with so much money in tourism it doesn't bother. Instead, as you approach **Gennádi** you'll start seeing the weekend villas owned by Rhodes Townies; the beach looks like a vast pebble mosaic that goes on with few interruptions for 11km to Plimíri. Inland, the little mountain village of **Váti** (with a good taverna, Petrino, famous for its *mezédes*), is typical; only 35 people hold the fort during the week.

A boho arty crowd of mostly German ex-pats have fixed up the old houses in pretty **Lachaniá**; its lovely main *plateía* was used for several scenes of Claire Peploe's first film *High Season* (1988) with Jacqueline Bisset. **Plimíri** has wonderful often deserted beaches and dunes (**Cape Germáta** is lovely, but beware, it's a turtle-nesting area) and a 16th-century church, **Zoödóchou Pigís**, with ancient Corinithian columns inside. **Ag. Pávlos**, inland, was built by the Italians as a model farm.

Kataviá, 83km from Rhodes Town, also received some attention from the Italians (there's an abandoned church and airport) but gets busy in summer as the road carries on a bit further to the island's southernmost tip, **Cape Prassonísi** ('Leek Island'). The narrow, sandy isthmus which linked Prassonísi with Rhodes disappeared after storms in 1996, although one side remains wild and windblown, the other perfectly calm. There are two windsurfing centres and a scattering of tavernas, a few rooms and unofficial camping. Near the former isthmus are scant ruins of a 7th–6th-century BC walled settlement at **Vroúlia**, on a panoramic shelf over the sea.

For more grand views over both coasts of Rhodes, take the road from Kataviá up to **Messanagrós**, a sleepy, old-fashioned mountain village. Just west, **Moní Skiádi**, a hilltop monastery in a fire-scarred setting, shelters a miraculous icon that bled when a 15th-century heretic stabbed the Virgin's cheek. The wound, and stains, are still visible; the monks have a few rooms for visitors. The unpaved road continues down to the west coast, where there are spectacular views over a wind-battered sea. Sheltered in a valley, **Apolakiá** is an unexceptional to look at, but is very proud of its watermelons.

Down the West Coast

South of the suburban palace hotels of Ixiá and Triánda, the wind, mediocre beaches and rocky cliffs have put the kibosh on Rhodes' coast when it comes to big tourist development; it does however, has lovely lush scenery, forests and attractive mountain villages with a few places to stay. **Kremastí** is a lively place, bustling with tourist overflow and Greek soldiers from the island's barracks. The huge church houses a wonder-working icon, **Panagías Kremastí**, occasioning the biggest *panegýri* in the Dodecanese (15–23 August), complete with amusement rides and a market. At the climax on 23 August, the villagers don beautiful traditional costumes and dance a very fast *soústa*. The straggling village of **Paradíssi** next door to the airport is hardly heaven, but is still a useful place for an overnight stay after a night flight – and there's a small beach, constantly zapped by roaring planes. **Theológos** (aka **Thólos**), 20km from Rhodes Town, has the last of the package hotels and tidy beaches.

Inland, a road between Thólos and Paradíssi leads inland 7km to **Káto Kalamónas** and from there to **Petaloúdes**, the **Valley of the Butterflies**. Sliced by a stream and waterfalls, the narrow gorge is crowned by a roof of fairytale storax trees, whose vanilla-scented resin is used to make frankincense. From June to September rare nocturnal moths, *Panaxia quadripuntaria*, named for the Roman numeral IV on their wings, flock here. This, along with Páros, is one of their two breeding grounds in the world, and in recent years, as visitor numbers have risen, moth numbers have declined so dramatically (every time they are disturbed they weaken, and are often too done in to mate and lay their eggs) that it's a package tourist disaster.

Valley of the Butterflies
open May–Sept daily 9–6; adm

Instead, follow the trail and wooden paths up the lovely ravine (you'll still need a ticket) to the **Monastery of the Panagía Kalópetra**, built in 1782 by Alexándros Ypsilántis, grandfather of the two brothers who wanted to be kings at the start of the 1821 Greek War of Independence. It's a tranquil place, well worth the uphill trek (wear sturdy shoes), with wonderful views and picnic tables in the grounds. Another wooded trail leads to the **Monastery of Ag. Soúlas**, just off the road down to **Soroní**. Here they have a race track and a giant festival on 29–30 July with donkey races and folk dancing, immortalized in *Reflections on a Marine Venus*.

Ancient Kamiros

Ancient Kamiros
t 224 107 5674; open summer Tues–Sun 8.30–7.30; winter Tues–Sun 8.30–2.30; adm

Prettily built on three terraces on the foothills of Rhodes' second highest peak, Akramýtis, Kamiros was founded, according to traditon, by Althaemenes, grandson of Minos (*see* p.405); although no Minoan finds have been located, a Mycenaean-era necropolis was found nearby. One of Rhodes' three Dorian cities, specializing in agriculture and crafts, Classical Kamiros was destroyed by an earthquake in 226 BC; and when the rebuilt Hellenistic city, built on a Hippodamian grid, was similarly destroyed in 142 BC, the city was abandoned and utterly forgotten – until 1859, after farmers located a few ancient graves. The British consul and a French archaeologist began excavating, sending finds to the British Museum. The Italians, during their occupation, uncovered the rest: the **Agora** with its rostrum for speeches, the **Stoa** with a Doric portico, Roman houses, and two temples – one 6th-century BC, dedicated to Athena of Kamiros, and the other Doric, from the 3rd century – and an altar dedicated to sunny Helios. An excellent water system, supplied by a large reservoir from the 6th-century BC, served around 400 families. There are tavernas on the sea below, and a nice sandy beach off the main road at **Kalavárda**.

Some of the island's most beautiful scenery is inland from here. The road from Kalavárda goes to **Sálakos**, under the ruins of a medieval fort, a village beloved for its shady groves and **Spring of the Nymphs**, whose water is commercially bottled. With its cedar and pine forests, this is excellent walking territory, here and further up around **Mount Profítis Ilías** (790m/2,600ft) with its two Italian chalet hotels, one of which has recently reopened (*see* 'Where to Stay and Eat', overleaf). The trees here belongs to the Prophet Elijah, who according to legend strikes down anyone who dares to cut one down. The chief settlements on its slopes are **Apóllona** and **Eleoússa**, once the planned Italian farm village, with the governor's summer house and a giant church.

Three km west, the charming 13th-century Byzantine church of **Ag. Nikóloas Foundouklí** ('of the hazelnuts') has a few frescoes, but is best known as a picnic spot for its beautiful setting.

Kámiros Skála, Émbona, Atáviros and Monólithos

Kámiros Skála, the port of ancient Kamiros, now has fishing boats and ferries departing for Chálki. Althaemenes of Kamiros is also the traditional founder of the white hillside village of **Kritinía** just inland, which he named it in honour of Crete. It has a good, privately run **folklore museum** (*open when the owner feels like it*). Towering high above, the **Kástro Kritinías**, one of the most striking of the 17 castles built by the Knights on Rhodes, is an impressive ruin, empty inside except for the apse of a large chapel, but affording great views over the coast and Chálki.

From Kritinía (or Profítis Ilías) you can visit the mountain village of **Émbona**, which doesn't look like much but is renowned for its wine and festivals and Greek nights in its grill houses. The dances of the women are exceptionally graceful, and the festivals in August are good fun, fuelled by the local vintages. Rhodian wine was famous in antiquity, imported far and wide in amphorae marked with the sign of Helios. Émbona is the headquarters of the co-operative, **CAIR**, founded in 1928, and the esteemed **Emery Winery**, founded by the Triantafýllou family in the 1920s, who have a handsome tasting room. Their mighty red cava (12.5°) is made from a local grape, *mandilari* (or *amoryiani*), but the wine that has really made them famous, white Villaré, owes its distinctness to indigenous grape *athiri* that refuses to grow well outside its own microclimate, at

CAIR
t 224 106 8770,
www.cair.gr; open
May–Oct Mon–Fri
10–4.30

Emery Winery
t 224 604 1208;
open Mon–Fri 9–3

The Dodecanese | Rhodes/Ródos

700m (2,296ft) altitude, up on the granite slopes of the island's highest peak, **Mount Atáviros** (1,215m/3,986ft).

While up on the roof of Rhodes, head around to **Ag. Isidóros**, similar to Émbona with vineyards and tavernas but minus the coach parties. It also has the easiest path to the summit of Atáviros, with its wind farm and 'golf ball' radar. Here Althaemenes founded the **Temple of Zeus Atavros** (the foundations remain, fenced off). The views are just as spectacular; you can even see Crete on a clear morning. Althaemenes used to come here when he was homesick.

Under Ag. Isídoros, on the coastal road, **Siána**, an attractive old stone village where the oldest houses have roofs made of clay, is famous for its wild honey and *soúma*, a local firewater reminiscent of schnapps; both are well advertised at roadside tavernas. Its church of **Ag. Panteléimon** has 18th-century frescoes.

Monólithos, at the end of the bus line, is named after a fantastical 213m (700ft) rocky spur rising sheer above the sea, capped by a **castle** built by the ubiquitous Grand Master d'Aubusson. A precarious stairway winds to the top and, within the castle walls, there's the little 15th-century chapel of **Ag. Geórgios** with frescoes. There are fabulous views, especially at sunset; down in Monólithos tavernas make the viewing easier, although because of coach parties they don't try hard in the kitchen. There are strong currents off Cape Monólithos, but 5km below the castle, down a tortuous road, the **Bay of Foúrni** ('ovens') has a sandy beach. The so-called ovens are early Christian cave dwellings, or perhaps tombs, visible round the headland, where the naturists go.

Where to Stay and Eat on Rhodes' West Coast

Paradíssi ✉ 85106

Savelen, 4km from the airport, **t** 224 108 1855, *www.savelenhotel.com* (€€). Pleasant, moderate-sized hotel, with a restaurant and pool.

Anastasia, Alexándrou Ipsilándou, **t** 224 108 1819 (€). Typical rooms 500m from the airport.

Pigí Fasoúli, 5km above Petaloúdes at Psínthos, **t** 224 105 0071 (€15). Traditional Greek cooking (stuffed kid, pork with *gigantes* beans, etc.) in a taverna immersed in greenery. *Closed Tues eve in winter.*

Sálakos and Profítis Ilías ✉ 85106

Elaphos, Mount Profítis Ilías, **t** 224 602 2402 (€€). Stylish mountain chalet hotel and restaurant built by the Italians in 1929 and now, after decades, restored, keeping as many original features as possible. Superb views; stop for a coffee even if you aren't staying. *Open all year.*

Nymfi, **t** 224 602 2206 (€€). In an old Italian mansion, with four traditional rooms: the perfect island hideaway, but booked solid in July and Aug. *Open all year.*

Kámiros Skála ✉ 85106

Loukas, at the harbourside. Good food and a jolly place to wait for the Chálki ferry.

New Kámiros, on the old Kámiros road. Not much to look at but it serves good seafood and meat dishes.

Monólithos ✉ 85106

Thomas, **t** 224 606 1291 (€). Recently refurbished rooms. *Open all year.*

Sými (ΣΥΜΗ)

'Greece's Portofino' lives up to its nickname: it's a beauty. The arid, crisp light illuminates Sými's splendid amphitheatre of neoclassical houses, stacked one on top of the other right up the barren hillsides. The yachting fraternity adores it, and there's a fair sprinkling of excellent restaurants to feed and water them. And, like the real Portofino in Italy, Sými has two distinct personalities: daytripper time, when pandemonium reigns around the harbour, and early morning and evening, when serenity rules – at night, when the lights come on, it is pure romance.

Sými, however, is about ten times as big as Portofino. Old houses are still being bought up and restored. It's also a frying pan from July to September. On the other hand, it stays wonderfully warm into October and is particularly lovely in the cooler months of spring.

History

In myth, Sými was a princess (daughter of King Ialysos on Rhodes), who was abducted and brought here by Glaukos, a sponge-diver and sailor who also built the *Argo* for Jason – shipbuilding skills the islanders never forgot. Sými was also known as Metapontis, or Aigle, a daughter of Apollo who gave birth to the Three Graces. In another myth, Prometheus modelled a man from clay here, angering Zeus so much that he turned the Titan into a monkey – hence 'simian'. In the *Iliad* Homer tells how the island mustered three ships for Troy, led by King Nireus, after Achilles, the most beautiful of all the Greeks.

Sými was part of the Dorian Hexapolis, but dominated by Rhodes. The Romans fortified the acropolis at Chorió; the Byzantines converted it into a fort, which was renovated by the first Grand Master of the Knights at Rhodes, Foulques de Villaret. From Sými's Kástro the Knights could signal to Rhodes, and they favoured swift Sýmiot skiffs or *skafés* for their raiding activities.

Among the Turks, the Sýmiots were known to be useless slaves – they had violent dispositions and were such good swimmers that it was no use trying to keep them – they would just swim home. They could hold their breath for so long that they could repair holes in hulls underwater. And they could dive. When Suleiman the Magnificent came to take the island in 1522, the Sýmiots avoided attack by offering him the most beautiful sponges he had ever seen. In return for a relative degree of autonomy, Sými sent a yearly consignment of sponges to the Sultan's harem. The Turks bought swift Symiot ships for relaying messages along the coast. In order to keep Sými thriving, the Sultan made it a free port and allowed the inhabitants to dive freely for sponges in Turkish waters.

Little Sými thus became the third richest island of the Dodecanese, a position it held from the 17th to the 19th centuries. Mansions were

Getting to Sými

Ferry connections with **ANES**, the island's own ferry/hydrofoil company, t 224 607 1444, *www.anes.gr*, link the island to Rhodes, usually calling at Panormítis as well. Also 6 ferries a week to Kálymnos, 5 to Kos and Léros, and one to Piraeus, via Tílos, Níssyros, Pátmos and Sýros.

In season there are at least 3 daily **tourist boats** from Rhodes, some calling at Panormítis Monastery.

Port authority: t 224 107 1205.

Getting around Sými

Local **water taxis** visit different beaches, and the islets of Sesklía and Nímos. There are also **hydrofoil** day trips (20 mins) to Datça, Turkey.

The **taxi rank** and **bus stop** are to be found on the east of the harbour; the island has 4 taxis and the Sými Bus, departing every hour from 8.30am to 10.30pm from Gialós to Pédi via Chorió.

Various places rent **motorbikes and scooters** nearby – at a cost: shop around.

constructed; shipbuilders bought forests in Asia Minor; schools thrived. Even after certain privileges were withdrawn because of the island's participation in the 1821 War of Independence, Sými prospered, flourished. The Italian occupation, however, spelt the end of its winning streak: the Italians closed the Asia Minor frontier, the steamship killed the demand for sailing vessels, and crews from Kálymnos took over the sponge-diving (*see* p.354); during the Italian tenure the population of Sými nosedived from 23,000 to 600 by the outbreak of the Second World War. At its end, the treaty giving the Dodecanese to Greece was signed on Sými on VE Day, 8 May 1945, and later ratified on 7 March 1948.

Gialós and Chorió

In Gialós (a derivation of the ancient name Aigialos), arrivals are greeted by the free-standing bell tower (1880) of **Ag. Ioánnis**, surrounded by *choklákia* pavements and most of Sými's tourist facilities. Harbour stalls sell sponges (mostly imported from Florida) and herbs, filling the air with the pungent scent of oregano and spices. A copy of the trireme from Líndos carved into the rock honours Sými's shipbuilding tradition and the signing of the Treaty of the Dodecanese in the restaurant Les Catherinettes. A

Maritime Museum
t 224 607 2363; open Mon–Sat 10–3; adm

neoclassical mansion houses the **Maritime Museum**, with models of Sými's ships, sponge-diving equipment, photos and a stuffed heron.

Most of the neoclassical houses in Gialós date from the 19th century, while older architecture dominates the **Chorió** high above, which suffered badly in explosions set by the Nazis. The lower part can be reached by road from the port; the alternative is a slog up the

⭐ **Kalí Stráta**

375 steps of the **Kalí Stráta**, the 'Good Stairs'. Worn smooth over the years, the steps can zap even the fittest in the heat and can be sinister after dark: bring a torch.

Mostly restored, the houses in Chorió are crammed together: some are mansions, others built in the Aegean sugar-cube style, small and asymmetrical, but with neoclassical elements incorporated into

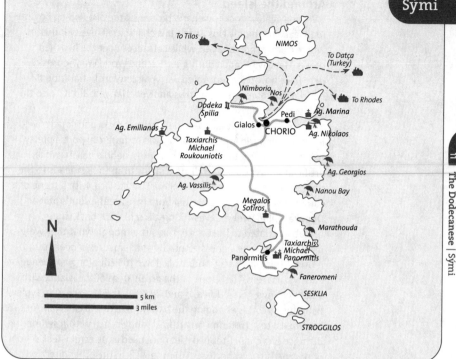

their doorways and windows. Those that survived the war have lovely interiors with carved woodwork and *moussándra*, beds on raised platforms. Buildings to look out for are the 19th-century municipal pharmacy, the **Spetsaría**, with a remedy for every malady in its jars; and the churches of **Ag. Panteleímon** and **Ag. Geórgios** with their pebble mosaics of evil mermaids sinking hapless ships. Follow the signs to the excellent **museum**, which houses icons, coins, pottery, a reconstructed 19th-century Symiot room and bits and bobs going as far back as the 5th century AD. Visits include the nearby refurbished **Chatziagápitos Mansion** (1800) with its antiques and wall paintings.

Sými Museum
t 224 607 1114; open Tues–Sun 8.30–3; adm

Up at the very top, the **Kástro** sits on the ancient acropolis, 500 steps up from Gialós; its Byzantine and medieval walls top a Temple of Athena, and the coat of arms belongs to d'Aubusson, the Grand Master supremo. Within the walls, the church of **Megáli Panagía** replaces one blown up by the Germans when they discovered an arms cache hidden inside; one church bell is made from the nose-cone of a bomb. The church is proud of its 16th-century icon of the *Second Coming* by Geórgios Klonzás. Near the derelict windmills on the east side is a fairly well-preserved round Hellenistic tomb, known as 'Mouse Castle', **Pondikókastro**.

Around the Island

Beyond Gialós' clock tower and bronze statue of a fishing boy, the road leads to shingly **Nos Beach**. It is still a small hive of industry where caiques are repaired, while cats lurk under the beached prows. Heavily bombed during the Second World War, houses here have now been renovated with plasterwork in traditional neoclassical blues, greys, yellows and Venetian red. But it's also the first place the daytrippers hit.

An hour's walk (or taxi boat ride) past flat rocks and small coves leads to **Nimborió** (or Emborió), the old commercial port, a pretty tree-shaded harbour with a good taverna, pebble beach and an artificial sandy beach. A walk up a ravine from the sea leads to the damaged mosaic floor of a Paleochristian basilica, with a scene of a camel driver; and just up the hill from here are the subterranean **Dódeka Spília** 'Twelve Caves' (bring a torch), with brick vaults, tentatively dated to the 6th century AD, although what they were used for is any one's guess – nothing similar has ever been found.

From Chorió it's a half-hour walk down to **Pédi**, along an avenue of eucalyptus trees. This is one of the green areas of the island, with smallholdings, goats, donkeys and fig trees and a beach with typical fishermen's cottages edging the bay. From here you can walk (or take boat taxis) to **Ag. Marína**, an artifical sandy beach within swimming distance of a chapel-topped islet once used as a secret Greek school under the Turks. A shorter 20-minute walk in the other direction from Pédi leads to the 18th-century church of **Ag. Nikólaos** and a shingly, tamarisk-fringed beach.

The main road south from Chorió passes the fortified monastery and church of **Megálos Sotíros** (with excellent 18th-century frescoes) en route to the vast 18th-century **Monastery of Taxiárchis Michaël Panormítis**, set against a backdrop of cypresses and pine. In the summer, tourist boats from Rhodes descend on it for an hour at 11am, making for massive crowds. Archangel Michael is Sými's patron, a favourite of all Greek sailors, and the monastery, first built in the 15th century, sees pilgrimages all summer – hence the **guest house** or *xenónas* where the underwear of Greek families flaps merrily beside signs demanding modest dress. The neoclassical bell-tower was built in 1905; its *choklákia* courtyard is strewn with flags; the church, coated with smoke-blackened frescoes has, on its beautifully carved iconostasis, the stern, larger-than-life gold-plated icon of St Michael, painted by Ioánnis of the Peloponnese in 1724. Michael is a busy archangel: heaven's generalissimo, slayer of the satanic dragon, weigher of souls, and patron saint of the Greek Air Force, he can also be called upon for aid in storms and to induce fertility, proved by crowd of ship ex-votos and the wax babies lying by his icon.

Monastery of Taxiárchis Michaël Panormítis
open daily 9–2 and 4–8; adm to museums;
~~*guest house*~~
t 222 607 1581 (€)

There are two small **museums**, one filled with votive gifts, church items, model ships, Chinese plates, ivories donated by Symiots living in Africa, stuffed crocodiles, a weasel and a mongoose, and prayers in bottles which miraculously found their way to Panormítis bearing money for the monastery,. The second contains folk art and furnishings, and the radio for British commandoes operated by the abbot and two members of the Resistance, who were executed by the Germans in 1944. Outside, there's a **shop**, a **taverna** (with a memorial to the abbot), the old people's home, and an army barracks. You can walk in the woods surrounding the monastery, or follow the road to the pebbly beach at **Marathoúda**, which has an excellent taverna.

Sými has 77 churches, a scattering of Byzantine wine presses, and beaches that make pleasant goals for walks; paths are generally well marked. One of the most interesting is the island's oldest surviving church, the 13th–18th-century **Taxiárchis Michaël Roukouniótis**, which can also be reached by road as the Greek military has installed itself nearby. It's a curious combination of Gothic and folk architecture, and holds its feast day beneath an old umbrella-shaped cypress. To the west, the church of **Ag. Emiliános** is on an islet, connected by a causeway with a bit of pebble beach.

Taxiárchis Michaël Roukouniótis
open 9–2 and 4–8, donation requested

On the east coast, **Ag. Geórgios** (reached by taxi boat) is many islanders' favourite: a spectacular fjord and beach under a cliff that gets shade in the afternoon. **Nánou Bay**, a beautiful three-hour walk south from Chorió, has an excellent pebble beach, fringed by delightful trees (although guard your possession from the nibbling goats). Other beaches include **Faneroméni** opposite Panormítis and the scenic **Ag. Vassílis**, a two-hour-plus walk across the island.

Sesklía and Stroggilós Islets

Sesklía, the islet facing Panormítis, belongs to the monastery. Its ancient name was Teutlousa, and Thucydides writes that it was here that the Athenians took refuge after their defeat near Sými by the Spartan navy during the Peloponnesian War. A few Pelasgian walls remain, and there's a long pebbly beach with tamarisk trees, and the occasional beach and barbecue trips from Gialós. There are a few ruins on the nearby islet of **Stroggilós**, while boats also visit **Nímos**, a stone's throw from Turkey.

Useful Information on Sými

The **police** share the post office building near the clock tower, in Gialós, t 224 107 1111.

The free paper, *Sými Visitor*, *www.symivisitor.com*, has helpful tips on the island. Also, look out for the guide *Walking on Sými*.

Sými Festivals

July–Sept: Sými Festival, with big-name performers, especially in music.
8 Nov: at the monasteries of Panormítis and Roukouniótis.

Where to Stay on Sými

Most of the island's accommodation is in Gialós, but there are also rooms to let in Chorió and Pédi. Sými is very expensive in July and August, and suffers from cockroaches then anyway. Cheaper rooms are often let on condition that you stay three nights or more, to economize on sheet-washing.

Gialós ✉ 85600

Kalodoukas Holidays, at the foot of the Kalí Stráta, t 224 607 1077, *www. kalodoukas.gr*. Has character properties, rooms and studios at various prices.

Aliki, t 224 607 1665, *www.hotelaliki.gr* (€€€€). Sea captain's mansion of 1895, now a boutique hotel with an attractive roof garden.

Dorian, up the steps just behind the Aliki, t 224 607 1307, *www.symigreece. com/dorian* (€€€). Self-catering studios with air-conditioning and pretty views.

Nireus, near the Dorian, t 224 607 2400, *www.nireus-hotel.gr* (€€€). Lovely little hotel, sympathetically restored and wonderfully painted in traditional colours, with pretty views.

Opera House, set back from the harbour, t 224 607 2034, *www. symivisitor.com/operahouse.htm* (€€€). Studios and apartments with air-conditioning and surrounded by a well-kept garden.

Albatros, in the marketplace, t 224 607 1707, *www.albatrosymi.gr* (€€). Well decorated rooms with air-conditioning.

 Les Catherinettes, t 224 607 2698 (€€). For stunning views over the harbour, especially at night, this historic favourite (*see p.432*) takes some beating; some of the rooms have painted ceilings.

Kokona, t 224 607 1549 (€€). Decent en suite rooms with air-conditioning, but unfortunately, no sea view.

Marika Rooms, nest to the Nireus hotel, t 224 607 2750 (€). Renovated en suite rooms.

Chorió ✉ 85600

Metapontis, in upper Chorió, t 224 107 1077 (€€€). In a very old Sými house cleverly converted to keep many of the traditional wooden features like the *moussándra* sleeping gallery.

Chorio, t 224 107 1800, *www.nireus-hotel.gr/indexchorio.htm* (€€€–€€, with breakfast). Built in traditional style with smart rooms (including air-conditioning) and stunning views.

Fiona, lower down the village, t 224 607 2088, *www.symivisitor.com/Fiona* (€€). Comfortable and tasteful bed and breakfast; the owner plays the sandouri – Zorba's instrument.

Taxiarchis, t 224 607 2012, *www. taxiarchishotel.gr* (€€). Elegant neoclassical development of family-run apartments with a small bar, breakfast terrace, and breathtaking panorama of Pédi.

Pédi ✉ 85600

Pédi Beach, t 224 607 1981 (€€€–€€). Typical beach hotel, with a restaurant. *Open April–Oct.*

Eating Out on Sými

Gialós ✉ 85600

Bella Napoli, t 224 607 2456. Excellent Neapolitan-style pizza and other Italian treats.

Manos, on the port, t 224 607 2429 (€25) The classic if slightly pricey seafood restaurant on the island, with tasty *mezédes*, lobster tank and charcoal grilled fish.

Meraklis, in the back streets beyond the bank, t 224 607 1003. Away from all the frippery, this is one of the island's most authentic tavernas with excellent Greek cooking and very reasonable prices.

Metapontis, Emborió, t 224 607 1820. Pretty place to lunch on those fat Sými shrimp.

Mylopetra, t 224 607 2333, *www. mylopetra.com* (€70). Elegant atmosphere in a former flour mill, and wonderful pricey Mediterranean cuisine to match, including home-made bread and pasta. Great wine list. Part of the floor is made of glass, and looks down onto the site of a 50 BC tomb, the finds of which are in Rhodes Museum.

⭐ Les Catherinettes >

⭐ Metapontis >

Mythos, by the clock tower, t224 607 1488 (€30). Run by chef Stávros Gogiós, the star of a Greek cookery show, serving wonderful modern Mediterranean cuisine. Excellent desserts, too. Be sure to book, however, or you won't get in.

Neraida, behind Hotel Glafkos, t 224 607 1841. Delicious untouristy food at budget prices.

Tholos, out on the headland, t 224 607 2003. An impressive menu with a northern Greek touch in a romantic setting, serving great *mezédes* and fresh grills.

(★) Tholos >

Chorió ✉ 85600

Giorgio's Taverna. An institution at night, famous for exquisite Sými shrimps, big portions and the man himself on the accordion. You can still go into the kitchen to choose what you want by looking in the pots, just like old times.

Zoe's. Great home-cooked food served in a rooftop restaurant.

Pédi ✉ 85600

Taverna Tolis, on the beach, next to the boatyard. The best for food and atmosphere.

Entertainment and Nightlife on Sými

At night, the lights from the houses and the bars reflect their colours in the harbour like stained glass.

Pachos, in Giálos by the west quay. Classic old-fashioned **ouzerie**.

Vapori, in Giálos, friendy, with free UK papers to read, attracting yachties and up-market Brits; also has Internet.

Kalí Stráta, three-quarters of the way up the steps in Chorió. Sublime views and good music.

Jean and Tonic, t 224 607 1819, in Chorió. Local haunt, with a good atmosphere, and great for nightcaps. Also has several well-situated traditionally styled houses to rent (€€€–€€).

Lefteris, in the *plateía* at Chorió. Lively evening hangout.

The Dodecanese | Tílos

11

Tílos (ΤΗΛΟΣ)

Tílos (pop. 500) has been one of the best-kept secrets in the Dodecanese for some time, with good unspoiled beaches, low prices, friendly people and wonderful walking country, in spite of a spate of road-building. Although at first glance the island looks rugged and barren, inland it shelters groves of figs, almonds, walnuts, pomegranates and olives, and small farms watered by fresh springs. Village life goes on with few concessions to tourism, although it's beginning to trickle in: a couple of tour operators, a few day trips and hydrofoil links with other islands have inspired a sprinkle of holiday development. But so far, nothing overwhelming. It's as fine a place as any to do nothing, to birdwatch; a dreaminess surrounds all practical activities, and the visitor who neglects to wind his watch is in danger of losing all track of time.

History

Tílos was joined to Asia Minor six million years ago. When it broke away *c.* 10,000 years ago, elephants were trapped on the island and adapted to the limited supply of food by shrinking. In the Grotto of Charkadió, a deep ravine in the Messariá area, the bones of these mini-elephants and the remains of deer and tortoises were

Getting to Tílos

There are **ferry** connections at least once a week with Rhodes, Kos, Kálymnos, Léros, Pátmos and Sými, on the Symi-Piraeus line; in season 4–5 a week. Regular **hydrofoils** in summer link Tílos with Rhodes, Níssyros, Kos, Kálymnos, Sými and Chálki. **Port authority: t** 224 104 4350.

Getting around Tílos

Excursion boats do the rounds of the island's more remote beaches.

There's a regular **bus** service from Livádia to Megálo Chorió, Ag. Antónis and Éristos, plus a summer service to other beaches.

You can **hire cars, mopeds and motorbikes** in Livádia at friendly **Stefanákis Travel, t** 224 604 4310.

There are two **taxis** (**Nikos Logothetis, t** 694 498 1727 and **Anna Kapaka, t** 694 520 0436) or go by foot; there are plenty of tracks and excellent walking maps in the shops.

discovered; the latest discoveries, in 2000–2001, have called into doubt the previous theory that the arrival of humans spelt their end. Nearby, the pumice cliffs and volcanic debris came from the eruption on Níssyros.

In mythology, Tílos was named after the youngest son of Alia and Helios, the sun god. When his mother fell ill, Tílos came to the island to gather healing herbs for her. When she recovered, he built a sanctuary to Helios Apollo and Poseidon in gratitude and became a priest, and ever after local priests bore the title of Holy Servants of Helios. The acropolis and main town up to early Christian times was the Kástro at Megálo Chorió, and in the 7th century BC it was prosperous enough to found Gela, an important colony in Sicily. The island minted its own coins from the 4th century BC, became an ally of Rhodes, and at the summit of its fortunes it was famous for its variety of perfumes and the late 4th-century BC poet Erinna, 'the female Homer' who died young but whose work was said to rival that of Sappho. Much of this was legendary until 1929, with the discovery of fragments of her famous work, *The Distaff* – a lament for a girlfriend who died before her marriage.

After the Romans, Tílos became so irrelevant that it was often confused with Teftlousa, the island of Sesklí near Sými. History returns with the Knights of St John in 1309, who strung seven forts across the island, essential for signalling between Rhodes and Kos. In the 17th century, Venetian admirals and pirates raided the island; what bits survived them fell prey to raiders from Mýkonos and Spétses from 1821 onwards in the name of the Greek Revolution.

Tílos is proud to be the Green island of the Dodecanese. The island mayor and doctor, Anastásios Aliféris, a member of Greenpeace, banned hunting on the island in 1987, for the sake of the many birds who flock here (there are over a hundred species, including golden eagles, golden orioles, kestrels, Eleanora falcons, hoopoes, falcons, kingfishers and rollers) and with difficulty island environmentalists have kept it that way, in the face of pro-hunting lobbyists, most of

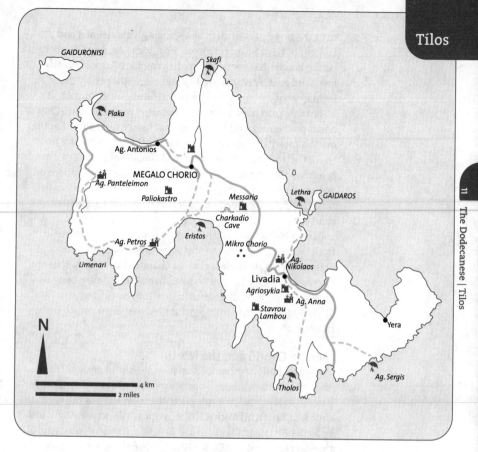

whom don't even live on Tílos. In 1997 the island hosted a major Mediterranean environmental conference, attracting the likes of Gina Lollobrigida, although the guest of honour, Jacques Cousteau, died before it began. As bird life on Tílos has since flourished, there are moves to make parts of the island into a national park forever. For more information, see *www.tilos-park.org*.

Livádia and the South

Although there used to be nine villages on Tílos, only the port of **Livádia** and the capital, Megálo Chorió, are inhabited, and Livádia only since the 1930s, which accounts for its somewhat helter skelter look beyond the handsome Mussolini-Art Deco harbour police station. There are views over the mountains of Turkey and a mile of tree-fringed pebble beach and water that's as clear as gin, as well as a newly improved port and marina. Stalwart, half-ruined **Agriosykiá Castle** looks down from the mountain while life revolves around the little village square, near an excellent bakery. Spirits are fed by the pretty waterfront church of **Ag. Nikólaos**. Further along the beach road, the tiny early Christian basilica of **Ag. Panteleímon and** Polýkarpos has a beautiful mosaic floor, while **Ag. Ánna**, further back on the hillside, has some 13th-century frescoes. A track over the headland goes by way of a red sandy cove, to the pebbly beach at **Lethrá**, about an hour's walk away and quiet even in August.

The main road passes under the deserted village of **Mikró Chorió**, an amphitheatre of ruined houses that looks especially sad as the owners took their roofs with them when they moved down to Livádia in the 1950s. The old church of **Tímia Zóni** ('Holy Belt') has charming 18th-century frescoes, and is the hub of celebrations on 31 August when the village comes alive again. The area is locally famous for a plant called *rouviá* that is used to dye the Easter candles red; its gathering is the subject of an ancient ritual, in which children play 'Lazarus' and hide under twigs, until told to rise up from the dead; the aim is to hop up before being hopped on. The Knights' fort of **Messariá** is close to **Charkadió Cave** (*should be re-opened for visits by 2007*) where elephants' bones, measuring only 1.2m (4ft) high, were discovered in 1971. They co-existed with Tílos' Stone Age dwellers, who wiped out these last elephants in Europe by 4000 BC.

Megálo Chorió and the North

Megálo Chorió, the capital, stands on the site of **ancient Tílos**. The pretty whitewashed village is a maze of alleys and flower-filled gardens, looking over a fertile plain. The town hall has the key to the church of **Taxiárchis Michaël** (1826), with a little double Arabic arch, by a 5m (16ft) Hellenistic wall just behind it; its fine iconostasis has the silver icon from the Taxiárchis church in the Kástro. Festivals are held in the courtyard on 8 November and 28 July when women dance the ancient dance of the *koúpa* or Holy Grail. A museum (enquire at the town hall, but it will soon be moved to Charkadió, *see* below) contains pygmy elephant bones and a film about Tílos.

A 40-minute walk above town, the **Kástro** enjoys a spectacular setting. Built by the Venetians and the Knights, the castle incorporated a fine Classical gateway and other ancient stones from the acropolis. Here the Knights and islanders bravely stood up to Mehmet II for eight days in 1479. The barrel-vaulted chapel of the Taxiárchis Michaël stands over a Classical temple and has unusual 15th-century frescoes.

To the south of Megálo Chorió, the fertile plain is fringed by the tree-lined sand and shale beach at **Éristos**, the easiest to reach; at the far end you can retire for an all-over tan. For something quieter, take the hour's walk north of town instead to **Skáfi**, a lovely pebbly cove off the main bay.

From Megálo Chorió the road runs northwest to windswept **Ag. Antónios**, which has a grotty beach, a chapel, an enormous tamarisk in the square and a good taverna, Delfini, owned by the local fishermen. The main attraction along the beach is Tílos' other fossils – the petrified human skeletons 'baked' into the rock, which are thought to belong to sailors caught in the lava when Níssyros erupted in 600 BC. A track leads from here to the isolated sandy beach at **Pláka**, while the road winds its way up into the mountains to the lovely Byzantine **Monastery of Ag. Panteleímon**, founded in 1407, with red pantiled roof, set in a lush oasis of shady trees and gushing water. The fortified monastery, defended by a tall stone tower and even taller cypress trees, is perched more than 200m (660ft) above the west coast. The church has fine 15th-century frescoes, including one of the founder holding the monastery in his hand, others of Paradise, and a beautiful old marble drinking fountain fringed by pots of basil. The bus driver arranges trips up to the monastery; the sunsets are superb.

Monastery of Ag. Panteleímon
open summer 10–7; winter 10–4

Information on Tílos

Tílos Park Association, in Livádia, t 224 607 0880, www.tilos-park.org. Created in 2004 and dedicated to protecting the island's environment.

Tílos Festivals

Tílos is known for its music played on the *sandoúri* and violin, dances, and elaborate costumes.

25–27 July: Huge 3-day festival at Ag. Panteleímon monastery.

28 July: Taxiárchis at Megálo Chorió, dance of the *Koúpa* (Holy Grail).

Activities on Tílos

Walking Days on Tilos, Iain and Lyn Fulton, t 224 604 4128 or t 694 605 4593, *fulton@otenet.gr*.

Where to Stay and Eat on Tílos

Everyone on the island seems to own at least a hundred goats, which provide the local speciality – baked kid stuffed with rice: a mix of local herbs, tomatoes and chopped liver.

Livádia ✉ 85002

Irini, t 224 604 4293, www.tilosholidays.gr (€€€). Tastefully tricked out in ethnic style, rooms with all mod cons; also a pool. Set just back from the beach in lovely lush gardens.

Villaggio Tílos Mare, 400m from the centre, t 224 604 4100, www.tilosmare.com (€€€). Studios, all with air-conditioning; there's also a pool, laundry, sports field, and an excellent restaurant.

Eleni, right on the beach, t 224 604 4062, www.elenihoteltilos.gr (€€). Pleasant, new development; blue and white with a minibus service.

Kastellos, t 224 604 4267 (€€). Family-run; modern rooms with fridges and fans, overlooking the sea.

Marina Beach, around the bay at **Kosmos Studios**, t 224 604 4164, www.tilos-kosmos.com (€€). New studios owned by an enthusiastic and helpful English couple who fell in love with Tílos; they also offer Internet access.

Ag. Stéfanos, t 224 604 4064 www.tilosmarinabeachotel.gr (€€). Excellent, friendly, with a good restaurant for lazy dining.

Apollo Studios, in the village, t 224 604 4379, www.apollostudios.gr (€). Typical studios.

Stefanakis Apartments, behind the bakery, t 224 604 4384 (€). A comfortable option with a convenient daily maid service.

Calypso, on the hillside, t 224 604 4382. Wine bar, featuring Italian wines, ham and cheese.

Irina, t 224 604 4206, on the beach. Home cooking, and a wide choice of dishes. Great for lunch under the trees.

Michaelis, near the central square, **t** 224 604 4359. Mouthwatering spit-roast meats.

Omónia, by the post office, **t** 224 604 4287. Very Greek and good for a cheap, filling breakfast or a pre-dinner ouzo.

Sophia's, on the beach road, **t** 224 604 4340. Excellent food and service, popular with Brits.

Megálo Chorió ✉ 85002

Miliou Rooms, in the centre, **t** 224 604 4204 (€€). With a traditional Greek touch set in a lush garden, with an aviary full of lively budgies.

Kastro, t 224 604 4232. Typical fare in the village's only taverna.

Éristos ✉ 85002

Nitsa Beach Apartments, 100m from the sea, **t** 224 604 4176, *t1980@ otenet.gr* (€€–€). Quiet set of four, sleeping up to five.

Nausika, t 224 604 4306, set back from the beach. Standard taverna fare and inexpensive rooms.

Tropicana, t 224 604 4020. Peaceful haven in a tropical garden with chalet-type rooms. Fresh seafood and local vegetable dishes served in a rose-covered arbour.

Entertainment and Nightlife on Tílos

Mikró Chorió Music Bar, t 224 604 4081. Night owls head for this deserted town, where a group of friends have set up a clubby bar in a restored traditional house and light up the ruins at night to give the impression that the village has come alive again. The action kicks in at midnight, with Greek music and dancing often goes on until dawn creeps magically over Livádia (linked by a shuttle bus) – and no neighbours to complain about the noise.

(★) **Mikró Chorió Music Bar >>**

The Ionian Islands

Sprinkled randomly off western
Greece, the Ionians are also known
as the Eptánissa, the Seven Islands.
Politically lumped together since
Byzantine times, they share a
tendancy towards scenic grandeur,
but, where the cliffs and mountains
give way, the landscapes are more
Tuscan than the Greek island
stereotype, swathed in olive groves
and cypresses, bathed in a soft light.
They also get more rain, only to be
rewarded with bouquets of wild
flowers, especially in spring.
Summers, however, tend to be hot,
lacking the natural air-conditioning
that is provided by the meltémi
in the Aegean.

11

⭐ Venetian and
British elegance
Corfu Town **p.452**

⭐ Sailing around
emerald islets
Vlychó Bay, Lefkáda
p.507

⭐ A bijou port and
white sands
Ássos and Mýrtos Beach,
Kefaloniá **p.491**

⭐ Seeking
Odysseus
Ithaca **p.472** and
pp.474–6

⭐ Towering cliffs
and sea caves
Páxos **p.515**

See map overleaf

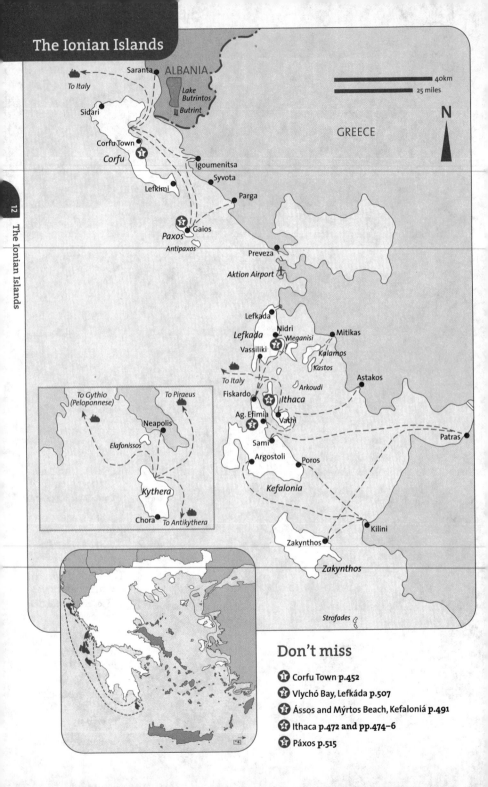

The Ionian Islands

GREECE

ALBANIA

Saranta

To Italy

Sidari

Corfu Town

Corfu

Lefkimi

Igoumenitsa

Syvota

Parga

Gaios

Paxos

Antipaxos

Preveza

Aktion Airport

Lake Butrintos

Butrint

40km

25 miles

N

Lefkada

Nidri

Meganisi

Lefkada

Vassiliki

Mitikas

Kalamos

Kastos

Astakos

To Italy

Arkoudi

Fiskardo

Ithaca

Ag. Efimia

Vathi

Sami

Argostoli

Poros

Kefalonia

Patras

Kilini

Zakynthos

Zakynthos

Strofades

To Gythio (Peloponnese)

To Piraeus

Neapolis

Elafonissos

Kythera

Chora

To Antikythera

Don't miss

🌟 Corfu Town **p.452**

🌟 Vlychó Bay, Lefkáda **p.507**

🌟 Ássos and Mýrtos Beach, Kefaloniá **p.491**

🌟 Ithaca **p.472 and pp.474–6**

🌟 Páxos **p.515**

Weather and history aside, each Ionian island has a distinct personality. **Corfu** is a major international destination, with its gorgeous beaches and historic town. **Zákynthos**, with more lovely beaches, has become a big party island, but has calmer bits as well; **Lefkáda** has great sailing and traditional villages; bijou **Páxos**, covered in olive groves, has been rated one of the world's top getaways. **Kefaloniá** has natural grandeur and a bit of everything else; Odysseus' beloved **Ithaca**, unchanged over the years, has become very fashionable. Only beautiful, distant **Kýthera** remains aloof, administered these days from Piraeus. Connections between the other islands are not always easy, but you can hop a bit, especially if you have a car.

History

Homer was the first to mention the Ionian islands, as the kingdom of Odysseus, although where exactly his Ithaca was is still a subject for debate. In the 8th century BC, Corinth colonized the islands, and as the Greek colonies in southern Italy and Sicily grew, the Ionians became important as way-stations; Corfu, the richest, grew so high and mighty that she defeated Corinth at sea in 435 BC, and proclaimed herself the ally of Athens. This forced Sparta, Corinth's ally, either to submit to this expansion of Athenian influence and control of western trade routes, or to attack. The Spartans attacked, and the result was the disastrous Peloponnesian War.

The Romans incorporated the Ionian islands into their province of Achaia. After their fall, Ostrogoths from Italy overran the islands, followed by the Byzantines, who prized them as a bridge to Rome. In 1084, the Norman rulers of southern Italy under their famous leader Robert Guiscard, captured the islands by surprise and established bases to plunder the rest of Greece. The Byzantines dislodged them with difficulty, although the Normans were no sooner gone than the Venetians claimed the Ionians after the Sack of Constantinople in 1204. To take possession they had to fight the islands' Sicilian Norman pirate king, Vetrano, but once he was caught and crucified, the Ionians became the County Palatine of Kefaloniá. Fate, however, dealt Corfu into the hands of the Angevins for 150 years, a rule so bitter that the inhabitants willingly surrendered their island to the 'protection' of Venice.

Venetian rule was hardly a bed of roses. The average Greek in fact preferred the Turks to the 'heretics': if nothing else, the Turks allowed a measure of self-government and demanded fewer taxes. Some of the Ionians actually came under Turkish rule until 1499, and the Ottomans renewed their assaults as the Serenissima weakened: life was never secure. Yet, unlike the Turks, the Venetians were tolerant of representative art, and in the 17th century the islands became a refuge for painters, especially from Crete; the Ionian school was noted for its fusion of Byzantine and Renaissance styles.

The Cow and the Gadfly

Although Ionia (in Asia Minor) is named after Ion, son of Apollo and 'father' of the Ionian people, the Ionian Sea and islands are named after lovely priestess Io, who caught the eye of Zeus. When the jealous Hera was about to catch the couple *in flagrante delicto*, Zeus changed Io into a white cow, but Hera was not to be fooled. She asked Zeus to give her the cow as a present, and ordered the sleepless hundred-eyed Argus to watch over her. When Hermes charmed Argus to sleep and killed him, Io the cow escaped, only to be pursued by a stinging gadfly sent by Hera. The first place the hapless cow fled to was named after her: the Ionian Sea.

In 1796, Napoleon conquered Venice, and he demanded the Ionian islands in the subsequent Treaty of Campo Formio. In 1799 a Russo-Turkish fleet grabbed them instead, and the Russians created the independent Septinsular Republic under their protection – shielding the islands not only from the French but from the notorious tyrant of Epirus, Ali Pasha. Although the Septinsular Republic was nullified by the 1807 Treaty of Tilsit which returned the islands to Napoleon, it was the first time in almost four centuries that any Greeks had been allowed a measure of self-rule, and the experience helped to kindle the War of Independence in 1821.

In 1815 Britain took the Ionian islands under military protection and re-formed the autonomous Septinsular Republic. Sir Thomas Maitland, the first High Commissioner, assumed dictatorial powers and forced neutrality on the Ionians as the Greek War of Independence broke out, disarming the population and imprisoning – and executing – members of the patriotic Society of Friends. His constitution ensured that the peasantry lived in near-feudal conditions, while denying the educated and middle classes any political role. The Ionians weren't even given favourable trade status with Britain. It was, as one High Commissioner put it, 'a sort of middle state between a colony and a perfectly independent country, without possessing the advantage of either'. Although later Commissioners were less abrasive, and some were even very well liked, the islands never stopped clamouring or conspiring for union with the new kingdom of Greece. In 1858, Gladstone was sent to the Septinsular Republic to resolve the crisis but, constrained by British distrust of King Otho and Greek support of Russia (Britain's enemy in the Crimean War), he had little to propose. The overthrow of Otho in 1862 gave Britain (now possessed of alternative Mediterranean ports, Cyprus and Malta) a chance to cede the islands gracefully to Greece, on condition that Greece found an acceptable king. This was Prince William of Denmark, crowned George I; on 21 May 1864 the Ionians were presented as the new king's 'dowry'.

During the Second World War Mussolini occupied the islands, but his dream of creating a new Italian Ionian state died in late 1943 with the Italian armistice. But nature had other blows to deal the islands: devastating earthquakes in the late 1940s and 1950s destroyed all the towns, sparing only Corfu and Kýthera.

Corfu/Kérkyra (ΚΕΡΚΥΡΑ)

Corfu is a Garden of Eden cast up in the northwest corner of Greece, a sweet mockery of the rugged grey mountains of Albania lying offshore. Its Venetian city-capital is one of the loveliest towns in Greece; the beaches that have managed to escape the worst of the cement mixers are gorgeous; the gentler mountain slopes, sprinkled with villas and farms, are outlandishly picturesque, strewn with wild flowers (43 kinds of orchids), scented with the blossoms of lemons and kumquats, and silvery with forests of ancient olives.

Corfu's reputation as a distant paradise began with Homer, who called it Scheria, the happy isle of the Phaeacians, where the ship-wrecked Odysseus was found washed up on a golden beach by the lovely Nausicaä. Shakespeare had it in mind when creating the magical isle of *The Tempest*. He was followed by Edward Lear and brothers Gerald and Lawrence Durrell, whose writings carved a special niche for Corfu in the British heart. During Corfu's first British occupation, it learned to play cricket; in the current one, nearly a million British tourists come a year, and some 10,000 have become permanent residents. The relationship has had its rocky moments, though; Corfiots have been stunned by the Calibanish behaviour of British yobs, then stung by the negative reports of their island in the British press. It hardly seems fair.

These days most of the young party fools stay in the far south in Kávos, leaving the rest of the island for the over-21s, where local residents, both Greek and foreign, are fighting to preserve the best of Corfu. A dedicated group of volunteers have established a long-distance trail using age-old pathways through the island's best scenery. Others campaign to restore Corfu's lovely but mouldering country houses and against any more building along the coasts, despairing over the new all-inclusive luxury complexes (most notoriously an 850-room monster at Ag. Spyrídon) built by tour operators who already have a stranglehold on much of the island's accommodation and UK flights.

History

In ancient times Corfu was Corcyra, named after a mistress of Poseidon, whose son Phaeax became the founder of the gentle, noble Phaeacian race. Archaeological evidence suggests that the Phaeacians, who had links to Puglia in southern Italy, were in fact culturally distinct from the Mycenaeans. In 734 BC, mercantile, ambitious Corinth founded a trading colony on the island known today as Paliaopolis. A temple there housed the sickle that Zeus used to castrate his father Cronos, whose testicles are the Old Fortress's two hills (*corypho*, 'peaks', hence Corfu). There was a prophecy that Apollo would one day fetch the sickle to do the same to Zeus.

Although Corcyra prospered, it was cursed with violent rivalries between democrats and the oligarchs. The Corcyrans fought the first sea battle in Greek history, against mother Corinth in 664 BC. In 435 BC, after the same two fought over a colony in Albania in the Battle of Sybota (which ignited the Peloponnesian War), internal strife left Corcyra so weak that it was captured by Syracuse, and then by King Pyrrhus of Epirus, and in 229 BC by the Illyrians. In the 1st century BC, Corcyra was loyal to Mark Antony – he left his wife

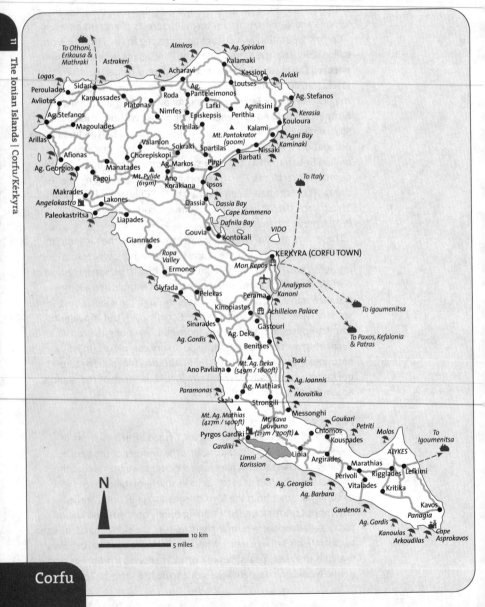

To Othoni, Erikousa & Mathraki
Astrakeri
Almiros
Ag. Spiridon
Kalamaki
Kassiopi
Avlaki
Logas
Peroulades
Sidari
Acharavi
Loutses
Ag. Stefanos
Avliotes
Karoussades
Roda
Ag. Panteleimonos
Ag. Stefanos
Platonas
Nimfes
Lafki
Agnitsini
Kerasia
Magoulades
Strinilas
Episkepsis
Perithia
Kouloura
Arillas
Valanion
Sokraki
Spartilas
Mt. Pantokrator (900m)
Kalami
Agni Bay
Kaminaki
Afionas
Chorepiskopi
Ag. Markos
Pirgi
Nissaki
Ag. Georgios
Manatades
Ano Korakiana
Barbati
Pagoi
Mt. Pylide (619m)
Ipsos
Makrades
Lakones
Dassia
Dassia Bay
Angelokastro
Cape Kommeno
Paleokastritsa
Liapades
Dafnila Bay
VIDO
Giannades
Gouvia
Kontokali
Ropa Valley
KERKYRA (CORFU TOWN)
Ermones
Mon Repos
To Italy
Glyfada
Pelekas
Analypsos
Kanoni
Perama
Kinopiastes
Achilleion Palace
To Igoumenitsa
Sinarades
Gastouri
Ag. Gordis
Ag. Deka
Benitses
To Paxos, Kefalonia & Patras
Ano Pavliana
Mt. Ag. Deka (549m / 1800ft)
Tsaki
Paramonas
Ag. Ioannis
Skala
Ag. Mathias
Moraitika
Strongili
Messonghi
Mt. Ag. Mathias (427m / 1400ft)
Mt. Kava Louvouno (213m / 700ft)
Goukari
Petriti
Pyrgos Gardiki
Chlomos
Kouspades
Molos
Gardiki
Linia
Argirades
Marathias
To Igoumenitsa
Limni Korission
Perivoli
Rigglades
Lefkimi
ALYKES
Ag. Georgios
Vitalades
Kritika
Ag. Barbara
Gardenos
Ag. Gordis
Kavos
Panagia
Kanoulas
Arkoudilas
Cape Asprokavos

N

10 km
5 miles

Getting to Corfu

By Air

There are frequent charter flights from London, Manchester, Glasgow and other UK airports; also regular flights from many European cities; and frequent links with Athens and Thessaloníki with either **Aegean, t** 266 102 7100, or **Olympic, t** 266 103 0180. A regular **bus** provides transport into Corfu Town, 3km away. **Airport information: t** 266 108 9600.

By Sea

Seaplanes: the seaplane port is at Gouviá marina, with free buses from Plateía Saróko in Corfu Town; at the time of writing, **AirSea Lines** offer links with Pátras, Páxos and Ioánnina. Contact **Corfu Travel Enterprises,** El. Venizélou, by the Old Port, **t** 266 104 9800, *www.airsealines.com.*

Year-round **ferries** sail from Brindisi, Bari and Venice, and Pátras. Local ferries sail daily between Corfu Town or Lefkími in the south and Igoumenítsa on the mainland. Daily ferries and hydrofoils go to Paxí and to Saranda, Albania. **Port authority: t** 266 103 2655.

By Bus

Several buses a day arrive from Athens (11hrs) and Thessaloníki (8hrs) by way of Igoumenítsa.

Getting around Corfu

By Bus

For travel on Corfu, there are two **bus stations**: Plateía G. Theotóki–San Rócco Square has blue KTEL buses to Corfu Town's suburbs (Kanóni, Kontokáli, Gouviá, Dassiá, Pérama, Ag. Ioánnis, Benítses, Achilleíon and Gastoúri). From the station in Avramíou St, **t** 266 103 9985, green buses run to more distant villages around the island.

By Sea

For ferries to Eríkousa, Othoní and Mathráki, *see p.470.* Several companies offer day trips to Kefaloniá.

Taxi, Car and Bike Hire

For a **taxi**, call **t** 266 103 3811.

Every resort has a travel agency with car, bike and quad hire places, often at excellent prices. At the airport are several car hire firms: **Hertz, t** 266 103 3547, **Europecar, t** 266 104 6440; **Avis, t** 266 104 2007. If you hire a motorbike, beware that the roads are often gravelly and potholed, and serious accidents are not uncommon.

Octavia here before sailing off with Cleopatra – and as a reprisal Octavian's army destroyed every civic monument on the island. Yet, whatever the turmoil, Corcyra never lost its reputation for beauty; Emperor Nero paid it a special visit in AD 67 to dance and sing at the Temple of Zeus in modern Kassiópi.

The few on Corfu who survived the ravages of the Goths in AD 550 decided to rebuild their town on the easily defensible site of the Old Fortress and two hills of Cape Sidáro. This failed to thwart the Normans in 1081, but in 1148, when their raids threatened the heart of Byzantium, Emperor Emmanuel Comnenus came in person to lead the attack. The Normans were no match for Byzantine subtlety: by sowing subversion and distrust, the emperor won back the island – for a few years, at least.

Venetian Corfu

In 1204, when Venice came to claim Corfu as part of its spoils in the Fourth Crusade, the inhabitants put up a stiff resistance and aligned themselves with the Despot of Epirus. Fifty years later, however, the King of Naples, Charles I of Anjou, snatched Corfu when his son married the Princess of Villehardouin, whose family at the time ruled the Peloponnese. The Angevins, already infamous for provoking the Sicilian Vespers, were equally intolerant and hated on Corfu. In 1386, the desperate Corfiots swallowed their pride and asked Venice to put them under the protection of the Republic.

In 1537 a serious threat, not only to Corfu but to all of Europe, landed at Igoumenitsa. Suleiman the Magnificent, greatest of the Ottoman sultans, already had most of the Balkans under his turban and was determined to take Corfu as a base for conquering Italy. Thanks to a peace treaty with Venice, Suleiman was able to plot his attack in the utmost secrecy. When the Corfiots discovered with only a few days' warning what was in store for them, they tore down their own houses for stone to repair the fortress and leave nothing behind for the Turks. The terrible Barbarossa was the first to arrive, and the thousands who had been pitilessly left outside the fortress by the Venetians fell prey to the crossfire and Barbarossa's fits of rage at his setbacks. Those who survived were carted off to the slave markets of Constantinople when Suleiman, discouraged by his losses and the bad weather, ordered the lifting of the siege.

Another 21 years passed, before Venice, under pressure from the Corfiots, expanded the fortifications to include the town. Many houses remained unprotected, however, when the Turks reappeared in 1571 under Ouloudj Ali, who decimated outlying villages, trees and vines and massacred whomever he captured. Two years later, another Turkish admiral, Sinan Pasha, passed through and left only one Corfiot out of ten alive.

In 1576, Venice finally undertook to protect all the islanders, calling in Renaissance fortifications expert Micheli Sammicheli (architect of the bastions around Heráklion), to build the New Fortress and walls. The Venetians restored Corfu's faltering economy by offering a bounty of 42 *tsekínia* for every olive tree planted (today there are an estimated 4.5 million trees, producing three per cent of the world's supply of oil) and allowed wealthy Corfiots and other Ionian islanders to purchase titles, creating a class society unique in Greece. Sammicheli's walls were given the ultimate test in 1716, when the Turks staged furious attacks for a month before being repulsed by the stratagems of a German mercenary, Field Marshal Schulenburg, and a well-timed tempest sent by Corfu's guardian saint, Spyrídon.

After Napoleon captured Venice, the French occupied Corfu. They improved the education system and set up the first public library (1797), but lost the island two years later in a fierce battle against the Russo-Turkish fleet. When Napoleon got it back, he personally designed new fortifications for the town; he loved Corfu, 'more interesting to us than all of Italy put together'. Napoleon's walls were so formidable that the British, when allotted the Ionian islands after Waterloo, did not care to argue the point when the French commander Donzelót refused to surrender. Paris finally had to order Donzelót home and in 1815 the Treaty of Vienna made Corfu and the Ionians a British Protectorate, with the blessing of Count John Capodístria. Capodístria, soon to be the first president of Greece, was a native of Corfu and, like many of the island's élite, had been in the employ of the tsars after 1799.

British and Greek Corfu

While Capodístria had requested 'military protection', the British took it upon themselves to run all the affairs of the Ionian state, which they 'legalized' by a constitution imposed by the first High Commissioner, Sir Thomas Maitland, whose high-handed ways soon earned him the nickname 'King Tom' (see p.446). He demolished part of the Venetian walls to build new, stronger ones in their place, calling upon the Ionian government to cough up more than a million gold sovereigns to pay the bill. Yet the British also built new roads, schools and a university (the 'Ionian Academy', founded by Hellenophile Lord Guilford), and established a permanent water supply to Corfu Town. The locals took up cricket, and Edward Lear spent months on the island, painting pretty watercolours and writing in his journal. In 1864, when Britain ceded the islands to Greece, there was one condition: that they destroy Corfu's defences first – not only the walls they themselves had just made the Corfiots pay for and build, but also the historic Venetian defences. A wave of protest from across the Greek world failed to move the British, and the bulk of the fortifications were blown sky-high.

In 1923, Mussolini gave a preview of his intentions in Greece when he bombed and occupied Corfu after the assassination of an Italian delegate to the Greek–Albanian border council; the Italians left only when Greece paid an indemnity. Worse occurred in 1943, when the Germans blasted Corfu Town; a year later, the British and Americans in turn bombed the Germans. At the end of the war, a quarter of old Corfu Town was destroyed, including 14 lovely churches.

Corfu is famous for musicians. Three-quarters of the members of the Greek National Orchestra hail from the island, as does current heart-throb Sákis Roúvas.

Useful Information on Corfu

ⓘ Corfu >

EOT: 7 R. Voulefton and I. Polylás St, Corfu Town, t 266 103 7639; open weekdays 8–2

Tourist police: Samartzi St, nr San Rocco Square, Corfu Town, t 266 103 0265.

Post office: 26 Alexándras Av, Corfu Town, t 266 103 9265; open Mon–Fri 8–8, Sat 7.30–2.30, Sun 9–1.30.

UK Consulate: 2 Alexándras Av and Menekrátous St, Corfu Town, t 266 103 0055 or t 266 102 3457.

Irish Consulate: 20a Kapodistríou St, Corfu Town, t 266 103 3411.

Hospital: Until the new hospital north of Gouviá is finished, go to the one on Polichroní Konstantá, t 266 103 0562.

Friends of the Ionian: *www.foi.org.uk.* Devoted to sustainable tourism.

Activities on Corfu

Diving centres: Among many around the coast: **Achilleon**, Ermónes, t 266 109 5350; **Calypso**, Ag. Górdias, t 266 105 3101, *www.divingcorfu.com*; **Seven Islands**, Kontókali (near Gouviá), t 266 109 0006, *www.corfudiving.gr.*

The Corfu Trail, a 220km long-distance path, crosses the island, taking in its beauty spots, from Arkoudíllas at Corfu's southernmost tip to Cape Ag. Ekateríni, and takes roughly 10 days to complete. *See www.corfutrail.org.* Accommodation arrangements, etc. can be made through **Aperghi Travel**, Dimokratías Av and Polylás St, 49100 Corfu, *www.travelling.gr/aperghi.*

Durrell School of Corfu, 11 Filellínon, t 266 102 1326, *www.durrell-school-corfu.org.* Offering summer courses on ecology, the arts, and much more.

Aqualand, a massive water park 7km south of Corfu Town. *Open July and Aug 10–7; May–Oct 10–6.*

Day trips to Saranda, Albania: Two ferries a day usually leave between 8 and 10am and allow time to visit the ancient Butrint, one of the Med's top archaeological sites. **Sipa Tours**, t 266 105 6415 or t 697 665 0713, *www.sipatours.com* (run by an Albanian who spent years in Corfu), offers everything from day return tickets (€39 including visa) to 11-day all-inclusive tours. Note that Albania is in a different time zone, one hour behind Greece.

Corfu Festivals

Palm Sun, Easter Sat, 11 Aug and **first Sun in Nov**: Procession of Ag. Spyrídon in Corfu Town.

Holy Sat: Celebrated in Corfu Town with a bang – the sound of everyone tossing out their chipped crockery into the street.

July: International guitar competitions, Corfu Town.

Late July: Pelákas Streetbeat Music Festival, *www.pelekas-streetbeat.com.*

14 Aug: The beautiful Procession of Lights in Mandoúki.

Sept: The Corfu Festival brings all kinds of concerts, ballet, opera and theatre to the island.

Late Sept–early Oct: Divertimenti in Corfu Chamber Music Festival, *www.chambermusicholidays.com.*

Corfu Town

⭐ Corfu Town

The capital of the Ionian islands, beautiful, urbane Corfu Town (pop. 40,000), was laid out by the Venetians in the 14th century when the medieval town, crowded onto the Old Fortress on Cape Sidáro, had no room to expand. They began with the Campiello (from *campo*, Venetian for 'square'), where three- or four-storey houses loom over the narrow streets, as they do back in Venice. By the time the new walls were added in the 16th century, the Venetians built in the more open style of the Renaissance, laying out a series of central streets and small squares. Some of the finest houses, decorated with masks, stand along the upper Esplanade, where gentle shades of Savoy red and pink peel off gracious Venetian façades. Then the British came, and added a set of elegant Georgian public buildings.

The Esplanade (Spianáda) and the Listón

The heart of Corfu Town is the great green space called the Spianáda, or Esplanade, one of the largest public squares in Europe. Originally a field left open for defensive purposes, it began to take its present form as a garden and promenade when Napoleon ordered

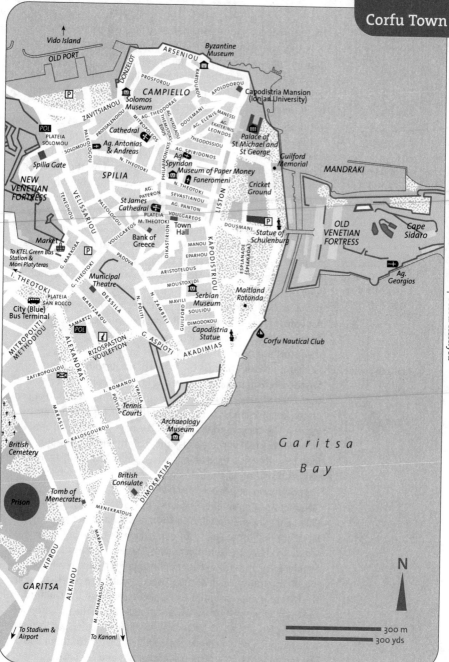

the building of the arcaded **Listón** on the west edge, in imitation of one of his proudest urban improvements in Paris, the Rue de Rivoli. At the time, it was the only place in all of Greece reserved exclusively for the aristocracy (or those on the list, hence the name). Then, as now, the Listón was a solid row of elegant cafés; at night the monuments and trees are floodlit for effect.

The northern end of the Esplanade is filled by the Georgian **Palace of St Michael and St George**, with its two grand gates. Designed by Sir George Whitmore, it was built as the residence of High Commissioner Sir Thomas Maitland – note the symbols of the seven islands on its Maltese marble façade. In 1864 it became the summer residence of the King of Greece, then fell into disuse until 1953, when it became home to the magnificent **Museum of Asiatic Art**, one of the most important privately formed collections in the world. A gift to Corfu from Greek diplomat Gregórios Mános in 1927 (he died in abject poverty the following year) the museum contains 10,000 exquisitely lit masks, ceramics, wood carvings, armour and weapons, and much more from across Asia, dating back to 1000 BC. Three state rooms house the **Municipal Art Gallery** featuring two paintings by Michele Damaskinós, *The Stoning of Stephen* and *The Decapitation of John the Baptist*, as well as 19th–20th-century Greek works and scenes of Corfu. Don't miss a drink in the clubby, atmospheric **Art Café** in a salon annexed to the palace (*entrance through the garden gateway*), with fabulous views of the Old Fortress; many of the furnishings came from Mon Repos (*see* p.459).

Adjacent to the palace is the loggia of the **Reading Society**, founded in 1836 by a group of young Corfiot idealists just returned from their studies in France; the library has a fine collection of books on the Ionian islands. Just in front of the palace is another British legacy – the **cricket ground**, where little boys play football until their older white-clad brothers chase them off the field. In the summer, matches pit the six local teams (which aren't at all bad) against visitors from Britain, the Greek mainland and Europe, while supporters sip ginger beer (*tzítzi bíra*).

Numerous monuments embellish the Esplanade. The Upper Plateía has the **memorial to Sir Thomas Maitland**, designed by Sir George Whitmore in the form of an Ionian rotunda, where brass bands serenade the summer crowds. There's a **statue of Marshal Schulenburg**, the crafty soldier of fortune from Saxony who outwitted the Turkish High Admiral in the Great Siege of 1716 to spoil the Ottomans' last attempt to expand in the west. The **Guilford Memorial** honours Corfu's favourite Englishman, the Hellenophile Frederick North, Earl of Guilford (1769–1828), here dressed in ancient robes, a touch he would have appreciated. On the southern end of the Esplanade is a statue of his ambiguous and later assassinated friend **Capodístria**, first president of Greece. Nearby, on Moustoxídi, one of the streets traversing Guilford, is a **Serbian Museum**, with a collection of photographs and memorabilia from the First World War, and Corfu's role in aiding Serbian refugees (*see* below).

Museum of Asiatic Art
t 266 103 8124; open Tues–Sun 8–2.30; adm

Municipal Art Gallery
t 266 104 4606; open 9–9; adm

Reading Society
t 266 102 7277; open daily 9–1

Serbian Museum
t 266 103 3960; open daily 9–1

Old Fortress
t 266 104 8120; open Tues–Fri 8–8, Sat and Sun 8.30–3; adm

The **Old Fortress** on Cape Sidáro is separated from the Esplanade by a moat, dug over a 100-year period by the Venetians. This was the acropolis of the ancient city, and site of medieval Corfu Town. The walls, built over the centuries, were badly damaged by the British; others have fallen into decay. You can wander about and explore the Venetian tunnels, battlements, drawbridge, well, cannons from 1684 and, below the observatory, St George's, the church of the British garrison, designed like a Doric temple and now an Orthodox chapel. In the port, you can swim off the pontoons of nautical club NAOK.

The Church of Ag. Spyrídon and Around

The church of Corfu's patron saint Spyrídon – the original Spíros – is in the old town, and easy to find: the campanile rises like a ship's mast, bedecked with flags and fairy lights. Spyrídon was a 4th-century Bishop of Cyprus, buried in Constantinople; when the city fell to the Turks, his bones were smuggled in a sack of straw to Corfu. The church was built in 1596 to house them, no longer in straw but in a silver Renaissance reliquary. According to the Corfiots, Spyrídon 'the Miracle-worker' has brought them safely through many trials, frightening away both cholera and the Turks. He even gave the Catholics a scare when they considered placing an altar in his church; the night before its dedication, he blew up a powder magazine in the Old Fortress with a bolt of lightning. He did, however, peacefully accept a large silver lamp from the Venetians in thanks for his intervention against the Turks in 1716. Four times a year his reliquary goes for an outing as the faithful queue to kiss the lid. In the church, amid mediocre Italianate frescoes blackened by smoke, the gold shimmers through in the flickering light of votive candles.

Museum of Paper Money
t 266 104 1552; open Mon–Sat 9–1

The nearby Alpha Bank houses a **Museum of Paper Money**, with a collection of banknotes from around the world and Greek notes dating from the nation's birth; upstairs, you can learn how they're printed. Across the square, the church of the **Panagía Faneroméni** (1689) contains fine icons of the Ionian School. The square gives on to the pretty main street, Nikifórou Theotóki. From there, head up E. Voulgáreos Street to the elegant square with Corfu's **town hall**, a Venetian confection begun in 1691 that later did duty as the municipal opera house; grotesque faces grimace from the building and a bas-relief shows a triumphant Doge. The Catholic **Cathedral of St James** on the square was hit by German bombs in 1943. Only the bell tower survived; the rest has been reconstructed.

Between the Old Port and the Esplanade: Campiello

The Campiello quarter has a number of buildings to seek out, beginning with the **Orthodox Cathedral** (1577), hiding behind an 18th-century façade. This is dedicated to Ag. Theodóra Augústa, Empress of Byzantium (829–42), who was canonized for her role in restoring icons in the Orthodox Church following the Iconoclasm. Her relics were brought to Corfu along with those of Ag. Spyrídon and lie in a silver casket in the chapel to the right of the altar; if the priest likes the look of you, he'll take you aside so you can kiss her and take home titbits of her slippers; donations are more than welcome. Fittingly, the cathedral is packed with exceptional icons.

Even more are housed nearby, up the steps from Arseníou Street in the **Byzantine Museum of Corfu** with its new annexe. The main collection is in the 15th-century **Panagía Antivouniótissa**, a typical Ionian church with a single aisle, timber roof and exonarthex running around three sides of the building. Among the eminent Corfiots buried under the flagstones is Capodístria's sister, who was a nun here. The church has one of the elaborately decorated ceilings or *ourania* ('heaven') that the Ionians were so fond of, a stone iconostasis from a later date and very Italianate 17th-century murals on the Old Testament. Icons from all over Corfu have been brought here; among the finest are the mid-16th-century *SS. Sergius, Bacchus and Justine* by Michael Damaskinós, the 17th-century *St Cyril of Alexandria* by Emmanuel Tzánes and the 17th-century four-handed *Ag. Panteléimon* and icons by the 18th-century painter Geórgios Chrysolorás. On the same street is the **Solomós Museum**, with a collection of memorabilia associated with the poet Diónysos Solomós, who lived here in his later years (*see* p.522).

On a narrow stair off Philharmonikí Street, **Ag. Nikólaos** once served as the parish church of the King of Serbia. After the defeat of the Serbian army by the Austro-Hungarians in 1916, the king, his government and 150,000 Serbs took refuge on Corfu. A third died shortly thereafter from flu and are buried on Vído island, now a quiet refuge with footpaths, a little beach and a memorial.

The New Fortress and Around

Arrive on Corfu by sea, and you'll be met by a mass of walls known as the **New Fortress**, or Néo Froúrio, built after 1576 by the Venetians. It bore the brunt of the Ottoman siege of 1716, and although most of the walls were dynamited by the British, enough masonry survived for the installation of a Greek naval base until recently. Over the gates, Lions of St Mark (holding open rather than closed Gospels, denoting Venetian favour) and inscriptions genteelly erode away. The **market** in the old moat (G. Markóra St) sells fruit, vegetables, fish, cheese and more, from early in the day until lunchtime.

Quite a bit further west, beyond the hospital on Polichroní Konstantá Street, the **Monastery of Platýteras** contains two icons donated by Catherine the Great in honour of Capodístria, who is buried here; Russian silver and gilt columns stand by the altar.

To the east of the New Fortress in Spiliá, near New Fortress Square, stands the Catholic **church of Ténedos** (1749), named after an icon

Byzantine Museum of Corfu
*t 266 103 8313;
open Mon 12.30–7,
Tues–Sat 8–7, Sun and
hols 8.30–3; adm*

Solomós Museum
*t 266 103 0674; open
weekdays 9.30–2; adm*

New Fortress
*open daily 9–8.30;
adm; entrance from
Solomóu St*

brought to Corfu by the Venetians from the now Turkish island of Ténedos. The 16th-century **Spiliá Gate**, incorporated into a later structure, was the main entrance to the medieval town; the old and picturesque **Jewish quarter** lies south of Plateía Solomóu. Although the Greek synagogue and a school remain in Velissáriou Street (the Italian synagogue was bombed and burned in 1943), only 170 out of the 1,800 members of the congregation sent to Auschwitz returned to Corfu after the war.

Garítsa and the Archaeology Museum

South of the Old Fortress, Garítsa Bay became a fashionable residential district in the 19th century and is still dotted with elegant neoclassical mansions. On Kolokotróni Street, the beautiful, peaceful **British Cemetery** is famous as a natural botanic garden, where rare wild flowers bloom; the graves, with their intriguing headstones, date from the beginning of the British protectorate.

Archaeology Museum
t 266 103 0680; open Tues–Sun 8.30–2.30; adm

Garítsa's star attraction is Corfu's excellent **Archaeology Museum**, flanked by outsized amphorae. Inside are bronze statuettes from Archaic to Roman times, a hoard of 6th-century BC silver coins, an iron helmet with silver overlay from the 4th century BC, and Cycladic sculptures, discovered in 1992 by a customs officer as smugglers attempted to spirit them abroad. Upstairs are Archaic *kore* and *kouros* statues, and two Aphrodites, the favourite deity of the lusty Corinthians; here, too, are the snarling, stylized lion from the Menecrates tomb (*see* below), and the relief of a Dionysiac Symposium (c. 500 BC), showing the god Diónysos with a youth, lying on a couch; their eyes are focused intently on something lost for ever. A lion sleeps under the couch; a dog comes striding up.

One room is given over to the wall-sized *Gorgon Pediment* (585 BC), from the Temple of Artemis in Kanóni; the oldest preserved stone pediment in Greece, and one of the largest at 17m (56ft) wide, it shows how advanced the Corinthians were in the early days of Greek monumental sculpture. The grinning Gorgon Medusa is powerfully drawn, running with one knee on the ground, flanked by her two diminutive children, Pegasus the winged horse and Chrysaor, born from her blood when she was slain by Perseus, although here she still looks very alive. Two large leopards on either side suggest that this may be Artemis herself in her form of 'the Lady of the Wild Animals', a fearsome goddess who demanded an annual holocaust of the creatures she protected, burned alive on the altar; in the far corners of the pediment, much smaller scenes show the Clash of the Titans.

The circular, 7th-century BC **Menecrates tomb** was discovered in the 19th century in an excellent state of preservation. Its lower sections are intact in the garden at the junction of Marásli and Kíprou Streets, three blocks south of the museum.

Tourist Information in Corfu Town

See p.451.

Shopping in Corfu Town

The shops open Tues, Thurs and Fri 9–1 and 6–9, and Mon, Wed and Sat 9–2. Jewellery and leather abound.

Xenoglosso, 45 Gen. Markóra, near San Rocco Square, **t** 266 102 7187. Has a good selection of books in English, including Hilary Whitton Paipeti's *In the Footsteps of Lawrence Durrell and Gerald Durrell in Corfu* and *The Companion Guide to the Corfu Trail*.

Where to Stay in Corfu Town

Corfu Town ✉ 49100

Also check *www.agni.gr* for a wide choice of listings.

Cavalieri Corfu, on the end of the Esplanade at 4 Kapodistríou, **t** 266 103 9041, *www.cavalieri-hotel.com* (€€€€€). For old-style elegance, no hotel on Corfu can compete with this renovated French mansion; it's comfortable, with air-conditioning and a magnificent roof garden, open for drinks to non-guests and overlooking the town in all directions. *Open all year.*

Siorra Vittoria, 36 S. Pádova, **t** 266 103 6300, *www.siorravittoria.com* (€€€€€). In a 19th-century Venetian-style palace, an intimate designer boutique hotel with all mod cons, named after the owners' grandmother who once lived here. Delightful garden, too. *Open all year.*

Arcadion, 2 Vlasopoúlou, **t** 266 103 0104, *www.arcadionhotel.com* (€€€). Very central, overlooking the Esplanade and Old Fortress, and comfortable – rooms at the back are quietest. *Open all year.*

Astron, 15 Donzelót, **t** 266 103 9505 (€€€). Very friendly, in an old building overlooking the Old Port and the New Fortress; most rooms, recently refurbished, have balconies. *Open all year.*

Bella Venezia, just back from the Esplanade at 4 Napóleon Zambéli, **t** 266 104 6500, *www.bellaveneziahotel.*

com (€€€). Renovated salmon-coloured old mansion with new flat-screen TVs and orthopaedic beds in a quiet yet central part of town, with a garden terrace to linger over sumptuous buffet breakfasts. *Open all year.*

Konstantinoupolis, 11 Zavitsianoú St, on the waterfront in the Old Port, **t** 266 104 8716/7, *www.konstantinoupolis. com.gr* (€€€). Originally established as a hotel in 1878 and very well refurbished for its reopening in 1997. *Open all year.*

Europa, 10 Gitsiáli, at the New Port, **t** 266 103 9304 (€). One of the better modern choices.

Hermes, 14 Gen. Markóra, on the inland side of the New Fortress, **t** 266 103 9268 (€). Away from the tourist crowds but next to the noisy market.

Eating Out in Corfu Town

Corfu shows its Venetian heritage in the kitchen as well as in its architecture. Look for *sofrito*, a veal stew flavoured with garlic, vinegar and parsley; *bourdétto*, a fish stew, liberally peppered; and *pastitsátha*, a pasta and veal dish. The island's own sweet is *sikomaéda*, or fig pie.

Bellissimo, Plateía Lemoniá, **t** 266 104 1112. Excellent Greek fare, with some exotic dishes like chicken curry thrown in (the owners are Corfiots, returned from Canada).

To Dimarcheíon, Plateía Dimarcheíon, **t** 266 103 9031 (€25). Sit out in the pretty square by the town hall and eat lovely Greek or international dishes – good Italian pasta.

La Famiglia, 30 Arlióti, Kantoúni Bízi, in the heart of town, **t** 266 103 0270 (€25). Delicious Italian food in small, cosy surroundings; excellent *linguine alle vongole. Closed Sun.*

Oinomageirion Prevezanou, 4th Street. off Ag. Sofías. An institution, for its classic Greek dishes, vegetables and fried potatoes. Very good value.

Porta Remounda, 14 Moustoxidoú. Has a well-earned reputation for fish.

Rex, 66 Kapodistríou, one street back from the Listón, **t** 266 103 9649. Founded in 1932, inexpensive, reliable and with a good varied menu – try the

⭐ Siorra Vittoria >

⭐ Oinomageirion Prevezanou >>

pastitsátha or sofrito and other Corfiot dishes.

Taverna Ninos, 46 Sevastianoú. Resolutely Greek, considered the best grill in Corfu, with succulent *souvlaki* and other favourites; very reasonable.

Venetian Well, in Kremastí Square, t 266 104 4761 (€40–50). Upscale and stylish in a romantic Venetian setting, with frescoes on the world's great religions. A varied and international menu and a wide choice of costly Greek wines.

Yorglas, 16 Guilford St, t 266 103 7147. Popular and very authentic taverna, with cheery staff and atmosphere.

Tsipouradiko, behind the Courts near the Metropolis. Cheap *mézedes*.

★ Venetian Well >>

Entertainment and Nightlife in Corfu Town

Pick up a copy of the monthly *The Corfiot* for local news and a calendar of events. Apart from the disco ghettos past the New Port and north of town towards Gouviá, most of Corfu's nightlife revolves around the Listón, with a smattering of music bars including the **Magnet Bar** and **Aktion**, by the Old Fort. It's also a scenic spot, with music and an alluring view.

South of Corfu Town

From Corfu Town, city bus no.2 from Plateía Ag. Rócco goes to Mon Repos and the garden suburbs draped over little **Kanóni Peninsula** dangling south of Garítsa Bay. Before it was sacked by the Goths in the 6th century, ancient Corcyra or Palaeopolis stood here with two harbours: the ring-shaped port of King Alcinous, now filled in, and what is now the Chalikiopóulos lagoon. Excavations of Palaeopolis revealed Roman baths, the *agora* and dockyards of Alcinous; some ancient stones were re-used in the Basilica of Ag. Kerkyra, founded in the 5th century by Bishop Jovian and last rebuilt in the 17th century.

Mon Repos
t 266 104 1369, open summer Tues–Sun 8.30–7.30; winter Tues–Sun 8.30–3; adm

Across the road are the gates of **Mon Repos**, the Regency villa built by High Commissioner Sir Frederick Adam for his Corfiot wife. The Greek royal family later adopted it; Philip, Duke of Edinburgh, was born here in 1921. In 1994 Papandreou's government allowed Corfu to repossess the estate from the exiled King Constantine, and today it contains exhibits on Palaeopolis; in the grounds, once a botanical garden, are the unexcavated ruins of a Doric temple, perhaps dedicated to Poseidon.

Ag. Iássonos and Sosípatros
open year-round daily 8.30–2, plus summer daily 6–9pm

Some 200m north of the Palaeopolis, the handsome early 11th-century Byzantine church of **Ag. Iássonos and Sosípatros** is crowned by an octagonal drum and incorporates ancient columns and pretty *cloisonné* masonry; inside an original fresco has survived, along with the 18th-century supposed tombs of the church's namesakes, natives of Tarsus instructed by St Paul, who brought Christianity to Corfu in AD 70 and were martyred under Caligula.

Little **Mon Repos Beach** is just below, and it's an easy walk to the lush residential area of Análypsos. A steep path here descends to the spring of **Kardáki**, which flows icy-cold year-round from the mouth of a stone lion; the Venetians and British used it to supply their ships, in spite of the inscription that warns: 'Every stranger who wets his lips here, to his home will not return.' The Doric **Temple of**

Artemis (585 BC), source of the *Gorgon Pediment* in the Archaeology Museum (*see* p.457), stood near the lagoon shore. The large Archaic altar and the retaining wall of the Hellenistic *stoa* survive.

Kanóni is named for the cannon on the bluff at the southern tip of the peninsula where two cafés now overlook the pretty bay. Two postcard islets lie below: one with the **Convent of Panagía Vlacharína**, linked to the shore by a causeway; and **Pondikonísi**, 'Mouse Island', with its 13th-century chapel, Pantokrátor, amid the cypresses. Pondikonísi, they say, was the Phaeacian ship that brought Odysseus home to Ithaca, but on its way back to Corfu Poseidon smote 'with his open palm, and made the ship a rock, fast rooted in the bed of the deep sea', according to the *Odyssey*. What most postcards airbrush away is the airport runway on a landfill site.

Pérama, Gastoúri and the Achilleíon

Past the Kanóni Peninsula and linked to it by a pedestrian causeway over the lagoon, **Pérama** claims to be the site of King Alcinous' fabled garden. The pretty village of **Gastoúri** is the dreamy setting for a neoclassical neo-Pompeiian villa called the **Achilleíon**. The villa itself, used as a location for the James Bond film *For Your Eyes Only*, was built in 1890 by the Empress Elisabeth ('Sissi') of Austria after the tragic death of her only son Rudolphe. The villa was named after Sissi's passion for the hero of Homer's *Iliad*; Sissi fancied herself as the immortal sea goddess Thetis, with Rudolphe as her son Achilles, idealized by a large statue she had made of the *Dying Achilles* for the garden. Ten years after Sissi was assassinated in 1898 by an Italian anarchist, Kaiser Wilhelm II purchased the Achilleíon and made it his summer residence from 1908 to 1914, and, true to character, had the *Dying Achilles* replaced with a huge bronze: *Victorious Achilles*, with the inscription 'To the Greatest of the Greeks from the Greatest of the Germans'. Among the bevy of more delicate statues, note the *Grace* standing next to *Apollo*, sculpted by Canova using Napoleon's sister Pauline Borghese as his model. The small **museum** contains mementoes such as the Kaiser's swivelling saddles, from which he dictated plans for the First World War, and photos of him swanning around on his huge yacht, the *Hohenzollern*, which he used to anchor off the 'Kaiser's Bridge' south of Pérama. Note, over the gate of Troy in Franz Matsch's painting of the *Triumph of Achilles*, a prophetic little swastika.

Achilleíon
t 266 105 6210; open daily 9–4; adm

Where to Stay
South of Corfu Town

Kanóni/Garítsa ✉ 49100
Corfu Holiday Palace (née Hilton), 2 Nafsiká St, Kanóni, t 266 103 6540, *www.ellada.net/holiday-palace*

(€€€€€). Hotel and bungalow complex with the island's casino, bowling alley, indoor and outdoor pools, water sports, etc.; rooms have either sea or lake views. *Open all year.*

Andromache's Apartments, by the Achilleíon, t 266 107 1130, *www.korfu-apts.gr* (€€). Immersed in gardens and olive groves, with pretty sea views and a pool. *Open all year.*

Dalia, Garítsa, **t** 266 103 2341, *www.daliahotel.com* (€€). Very friendly family hotel near Mon Repos and the airport.

Royal, 110 Figeréto, Kanóni, **t** 266 103 5345 (€€). A commanding position, with three pools on descending levels, and roof garden with views over Mouse Island. *Open April–Oct.*

Eating Out South of Corfu Town

Nautilus, on the sea below Mon Repos, **t** 266 103 0392. Delicious seafood

treats to be enjoyed after a visit to the ancient city.

Yannis, in Garítsa, near Ag. Iássonos and Sosípater. One of the few remaining tavernas where you are still invited to go into the kitchen, lift lids off pots and choose your food.

Taverna Tripa ('Hole in the Wall'), in Kinopiástes, 3km from Gastoúri, **t** 266 105 6333 (€30). Run by the Anyfantis family since 1936. Something of a monument, cluttered inside with knick-knacks and photos, while up on the ceiling strings of salamis, sausages, peppers and garlic are garlanded with cobwebs. Greek nights here are renowned, with up to 10 courses.

North of Corfu Town

The roads along the east coast of Corfu are fast-moving, and hotel developers have followed them every inch of the way. Just north of Corfu Town begins a 10km stretch, most intense at Kontókali, Gouviá, Dassiá, Ípsos and Pírgi, set in the dishevelled beauty of the surrounding green hills and olive groves. Blame the Junta government of the late 1960s for the presence of a main road so close to the shore; the original plan was to divert it inland, but the Junta insisted otherwise.

Kontókali owes its name to Captain Christophóros Kontókali, who fought at the Battle of Lepanto in 1571 and was given the land here as his reward. At 8km from Corfu Town, the coast road veers sharply right through **Gouviá** (ΓΟΥΒΙΑ), with a small sandy beach. The town's lagoon was used by the Venetians as a harbour; the impressive vaults and columns of their 18th-century arsenal overlook the marina, which now doubles as a seaplane port (*see* p.449). The excellent **Corfu Shell Museum**, with its thousands of beautiful sea treasures, has found a new home on Gouviá's main road. Emerald **Cape Komméno** extends out, but looks better from a distance and has poor beaches. A few kilometres further north on the still excruciatingly built-up road, **Dassiá** (ΔΑΣΙΑ) has a long, narrow beach and seemingly endless pub/bar sprawl. One of the first Brits here was an English gardener named Merlin, who introduced Corfu's trademark kumquat to the island from Japan and in 1925 bred the first Merlin oranges in the estates along the river.

Young and fun **Ípsos** (ΥΨΟΣ) and **Pírgi** (ΠΥΡΓΙ), at either end of Corfu's 'Golden Mile', offer carousels of inflatable crocodiles and 'I ♥ Corfu' postcards on their long scimitar of shingle beach, leaving barely enough room for a good wiggle. From Ípsos, you can escape inland 3km to **Ag. Márkos**, a pretty village with the beautiful church of **Ag. Merkoúrious** (1074), with excellent Byzantine frescoes, just

Corfu Shell Museum
t 266 109 9340; open daily 10–9; adm

11

The Ionian Islands | Corfu/Kérkyra

below the village and another, the **Pantokrátor** (1557), just above, and the delightful Panorama Bar. Also inland from Ípsos, in **Káto Korakiána**, visit the **Castello**, a neo-Gothic folly of a hotel built on the site of a medieval castle; an annexe now shelters an **art gallery**, housing exhibits sent over by the National Art Gallery in Athens. Lovely **Áno Korakiána** is home to three Byzantine churches, a Philharmonic Society, an olive wood workshop and a little folk art museum in the neoclassical school. The road into the Troumpétta mountain range via the beautiful traditional village of **Sokráki** is an awesome series of hairpins through green and gorgeous country.

From Pírgi, you can noodle up though Spartílas to **Strinílas** for lunch and excellent local wine in the beautiful square, followed by a browse through olive wood shops.

Castello Art Gallery
*open Tues–Sun 10–2
and 6–9*

The Northeast Corner: Barbáti to Ag. Spirídon

Continuing north, **Barbáti** (ΜΠΑΡΜΠΑΤΗ) has a long stretch of pebbles and every facility to go with it, but from here on there is a gentle and welcome gear-change: as the coastal road wiggles its way up from the sea, the resorts below become smaller and cosier, and hints of traditional charm peek through. So many well-heeled Brits have houses here that people call it Kensington-on-Sea.

The first village, **Nissáki**, is a charming fishing hamlet with a tiny pebble cove and the seaside church of Ag. Arseníos where Lawrence Durrell loved to bathe. Arty shops trickle along the main road towards the road descending to **Kamináki**, a pebbly bay bordered by villas, perfect for snorkelling. Still heading north is the picturesque and unspoilt bay of **Agní**, with crystal-clear waters and three outstanding tavernas, all with jetties and sunbeds on the beach for collapsing after lunch. The next resort has grown up around the pebble beach of **Kalámi** (ΚΑΛΑΜΙ), a deep-set bay, where Lawrence Durrell rented a house and wrote *The Black Book* and *Prospero's Cell*, an ode to things that haven't yet vanished, 'the merry laziness of the natives, the sea washing and re-washing one's dreams'. It's a 10-minute walk (parking is difficult) to lovely, undeveloped **Kouloúra**, only a kilometre or so from Albania, on a narrow horseshoe bay with a shingle beach and a taverna. Why undeveloped? Because the Agnelli family own the house on the headland – and the taverna as well. The next beach north is **Kerásia**, a strand of white pebbles with a taverna, most easily reached by doubling back 2km from exclusive **Ag. Stéfanos**, its hills hiding the villas of the Rothschild set.

Kassiópi (ΚΑΣΣΙΟΠΗ), an important Hellenistic town founded by Pyrrhus of Epirus (the famous *generalissimo* of pseudo-victories), is now the largest and busiest resort on the northeast coast – although, unlike the others, it lacks a beach; there is good swimming off the rocks. The Romans surrounded it with great walls; its famous shrine of Zeus Cassius was visited by Cicero and Nero, and Tiberius had a villa here. The Byzantine **fortress** was the first place in Greece to fall to Robert Guiscard's Normans, who invaded from Calabria after pillaging Rome. As every subsequent marauder from the north passed by Kassiópi to reach Corfu Town, it bore the brunt of their attacks. When after a long struggle the Venetians finally took the fortress, they rendered it useless in a fit of pique. Without any defences, the Kassiópi suffered terribly at the hands of the Turks and the town lost all its importance.

The ruined fortress still stands, guarding only wild flowers. Although still a fishing village with a pretty waterfront, Kassiópi's main shopping street positively groans with tourist shops. Four small, well-equipped beaches can be reached by footpath from the headland. Two of Corfu's most tastefully developed beaches, **Avláki** and **Koyévinas**, are a quick drive, or a 20–30-minute walk, south of Kassiópi, both beautiful white pebble bays; Koyévinas sports a taverna, while Avláki has two, and water sports.

Continuing west beyond the reeds and grey sand beach and shallow waters of Kalamáki, a sign for Loútses and Perithía points the way up the slopes of 900m (2,953ft) **Mount Pantokrátor**, Corfu's highest point. You can take a car as far as **Old Perithía**, a charming cobblestoned village of stone houses lost in a mountain hollow, abandoned but now slowly being brought to life and restored; you should even find a taverna or two open. The path to the summit of Pantokrátor takes about an hour, and offers a bird's-eye view of emerald Corfu and Albania, a vista enjoyed daily by the single monk and his somewhat less orthodox pylon in the Pantokrátor's monastery. The rutted road from Perithía by way of **Láfki** crosses enchanting countryside.

Back down on the coast road, **Ag. Spirídon**, once a tranquil nook with a small sandy beach, has been disfigured by a massive all-inclusive hotel built by a British operator.

The North Coast

Almirós, at the quiet east end of Corfu's longest beach, is a warm, shallow lagoon with trees and migratory birds. The rest of the coast has been clobbered with development, from **Acharávi** (ΑΧΑΡΑΒΗ), where the beach is framed by pretty scenery, onwards; footpaths head up Mount Pantokrátor, to **Róda** (ΡΟΔΑ), a favourite of British families, with enough sand to escape the worst of the crowds. **Astrakéri** and next-door **Ágnos**, at the west end, have a downbeat feel but might have free rooms.

Inland from Acharávi, **Ag. Panteléimonos** has a huge ruined tower mansion called **Polylas**, complete with prisons used during the Venetian occupation; another Venetian manor lies further up in Episkepsís. Inland from Róda, **Plátonas** is surrounded by groves of kumquats, a tart citrus fruit that resembles baby oranges; the annual harvest of 35 tonnes produced by 70 farmers is made into kumquat liqueur, jams and conserves. Inland from Astrakéri, **Karoussádes** is a pretty agricultural village with the 16th-century Theotóki mansion as its landmark.

Sidári (ΣΙΔΑΡΙ) has rolled over and surrendered wholesale to mass tourism, concrete mixers and mosquitoes. If you're passing through, you may want to take a dip in the **Canal d'Amour**, a peculiar cove said to be two lovers – swim between them and you are guaranteed eternal love, although the builders have been here as well. West of Sidári, below the pretty old-fashioned village of **Perouládes**, the tawny, wind-sculpted sandstone cliffs are high enough to cast beautiful **Lógas** (or Sunset) **Beach** in shade in the early afternoon.

⭐ Etrusco >>

Where to Stay and Eat North of Corfu Town

Gouviá ✉ 49100

Debono, t 266 109 1755, *www. hoteldebono.gr* (€€€). Modern hotel with a pool, surrounded by cypress and olive trees. *Open Mar–Oct.*

Louvre, t 266 109 1506 (€€). Cheaper, with a pool, but don't expect any masterpieces.

Bella Mamma, on the edge of the strip. Greek-owned and -run, in spite of its name, serving delicious *sofríto*, lamb *kléftiko* and chicken, with a house wine to quaff.

Gorgona ('Mermaid'), t 266 109 0261 (€25–30). Opposite the church, an ordinary-looking place but it serves delicious seafood, including *pastitsátha* with lobster. *Closed lunch except Sun; closed Sun eve.*

Dassiá ✉ 49100

⭐ Casa Lucia >

Casa Lucia, in Sgómbou (✉ 49083), above Dassiá, t 266 109 1419, *www.casa-lucia-corfu.com* (€€). Attractive traditional cottages in a lush setting, sleeping 2–5, with a pool; massages, T'ai Chi, and yoga, etc. available as well. Children welcome.

Scheria Beach, t 266 109 3233 (€€). Perfectly pleasant and family-run; try to get a sea-facing balcony. *Open June–Sept.*

Camping Dionysus, t 266 109 1417, *www. dionysuscamping.gr.*

Camping Karda Beach, t 266 109 3595, *www.kardacamp.gr.* Both campsites offer ample facilities, including a pool.

Etrusco, in Káto Korakiána, inland between Dassiá and Ípsos, t 266 109 3342 (€50). Corfu has many jewels in its crown, and this restaurant is one. Since 1992 the Botrini family have been running this temple to imaginative Italian cuisine. There's an big wine list, the service is excellent and the courtyard setting sublime. *Closed lunch.* They also have eight **rooms** (€€€).

Kalámi ✉ 49100

This is the perfect area for a glimpse of the old Corfu, and you can rent an exquisite selection of villas, including the upstairs of Lawrence Durrell's **White House** in Kalámi; book through CV Travel, *www.cvtravel.co.uk.*

Villa Matela, Kalámi, t 266 309 1073 (€€). Traditional house with characterful rooms and studios; breakfast with fresh bread served in the adjacent bar.

Dimitris, above Kalámi at Gimári, t 266 309 1013. Book ahead to get a table, and specify one with the balcony view. Delicious Greek/European food, a bit pricey but worth it.

Agní ✉ 49100

At least once visit one of the three excellent tavernas in Agní, Corfu's gourmet enclave.

Agní, t 266 309 1609, *www.agni.gr.* The most expensive, and famed for its pickled octopus. Attracts the glitterati (they also run a travel agency).

Nikolas, t 266 309 1136, *www.agnibay. com.* Offers wondrous fare and excellent *mezédes*, perfect for a lazy lunch. Featured in the BBC series *Fasten your Seatbelt.*

Toulas >

Toulas, t 266 309 1350. Family-run, with traditional Greek cuisine; try the superb prawn *piláfi*.

Kassiópi ✉ 49100

Manessis Apartments, right on the port, t 266 308 1474/t 697 391 8416, *www.corfuvacations.com* (€€). Delightful apartments in a building overflowing with vines and bougain-villaea, run by friendly Irish Diana.

Kassiopi Bay, 100m from the village, t 266 308 1713, *www.kassiopibay.com* (€€–€). Pleasant studios and apart-ments with air-conditioning and balconies in a great location close to the beach, with pools.

Janis, between the square and sea, t 266 308 1082. Large menu of Greek and international dishes, plenty of vegetarian choices, and good wines.

Panorama >>

Porto and the **Three Brothers**, on the waterfront. Excellent Greek and Corfiot specialities.

Acharávi/Róda ✉ 49081

Village Roda Inn, t 266 306 3358 (€€). Friendly little Greek-Canadian-run hostelry right on the beach.

Róda Beach Camping, t 266 306 3120, *www.rodacamping.gr*. An alternative if everything else is full.

Bernies, Róda. Famous fish and chips and other Brit comfort food.

Monolithi, above Acharávi, t 266 306 3728. Tasty traditional dishes and huge terrace with sea views.

Roda Park, on the old road. Friendly Greek and English owners, and good Greek dishes.

Perouládes ✉ 49080

Villa de Loulia, 400m from the beach, t 266 309 5394, *www.villadeloulia.gr* (€€€€). Handsome 200-year-old Venetian-style villa, with a pool and organic vegetable garden that supplies the delicious ingredients of the candlelit dinners. *Open Easter–Oct.*

Panorama, Logós Beach, t 266 309 5035. Simply one of the best tavernas in Corfu (try the starter for two) with the famous sunset views for free.

Yiannis, t 266 309 5234. Excellent food at a genuine taverna, at genuine taverna prices – lamb, kebabs, salads and wine.

11

The Ionian Islands | Corfu/Kérkyra

Western Beaches: North to South

Northwestern Corfu is covered with forests, and, once off the beaten track, the 'roads' can bottom out the best shock-absorbers. The good coastal road from Sidári cuts off the corner en route to **Ag. Stéfanos** (not to be confused with the Ag. Stéfanos on the east coast), a large bay with wide sand and windsurfing; **Aríllas** just south has a sandy, steep bay with an attractive backdrop of green hills and views over the island. The village of **Afiónas** is on a headland with views in either direction, its sandy beach steadily developing. The best beach of all is **Ag. Geórgios** (Pagoí), a long, magnificent stretch under steep cliffs, a favourite for Greek beach parties.

The exceedingly picturesque 'Capri of Corfu', **Paleokastrítsa** (ΠΑΛΑΙΟΚΑΣΤΡΙΤΣΑ) spreads out from a small horseshoe bay, flanked by sandy and pebbly coves (with some of the coldest water in Corfu), olive and almond groves, mountains and forests. Although chock-a-block in summer, in spring you can believe its claim to have been the magical home of King Alcinous and Princess Nausicaä. Boats offer excursions to local sea grottos. On a promontory high above town, **Zoodóchos Pigí Monastery** was built in 1228 on the site of a Byzantine fortress, and tarted up by an abbot with rococo tastes in the 1700s. Tour groups queue up to buy a candle (the price of admission) as a monk hands out black skirts and shawls to the underclad. The courtyard is charming and a one-room museum contains very old icons, olive press and the skeleton of a sea monster; outside, the view is as breathtaking as you'd expect.

An even more spectacular view of the coastline is a steep drive out of Paleokastrítsa through cypress and pines north to the traditional village of **Lákones** and its Bella Vista Café, affording nothing less than 'the Most Beautiful View in Europe'. Lákones itself is the hub of lovely walks, especially to **Kríni** and the formidable **Angelókastro**. Built in the 13th century by the Despot of Epirus, Michael Angelos, Angelókastro is mostly ruined, but makes an impressive sight clinging to the rocks over a 300m (1,000ft) precipice; during the years of constant attacks on Corfu, Angelókastro sheltered the surrounding villagers (as well as the Venetian governor, who lived there). The mountain roads from Lákones north to Róda through the little villages of **Chorepískopi**, **Valanión** (3km on a by-road) and **Nímfes** offer a bucolic journey through the Corfu of yesteryear, and in spring the air is laden with wild herbs and flowers; old ladies line the road selling their home-grown oregano, honey, almonds and olive oil.

South of Paleokastrítsa stretches the fertile, idyllic **Rópa Valley**, where Homer's description of the island rings true: 'Pear follows pear, apple after apple grows, fig after fig, and grape yields grape again' – it's the one place on Corfu where you won't find an olive tree. Along with orchards, **Rópa** has the 18-hole **Corfu Golf Club**, rated one of the hundred top courses in the world; it also has a riding club that organizes rides out in the countryside.

Corfu Golf Club
*t 266 109 4220,
www.corfugolfclub.com;
green fees €50;
club hire available*

Westwards on the coast, **Ermónes**, with its pebble cove, is another candidate for Odysseus' landing point; Nausicaä and her servants would have been washing the palace laundry in the little cascade. **Pélekas**, a 17th-century village up on a mountain ridge, was Kaiser Wilhelm II's favourite spot to watch the sunset; busloads of people arrive every evening in the summer to do the same, from a tower called the **Kaiser's Throne**. Pélekas has a golden sandy beach, accessible from Gialiskári; next is the steep track descending to lovely **Mirtiótissa Beach**, the island's unofficial nudist playground, named after the white convent of Our Lady of the Myrtle. Beautiful **Glyfáda** is a long, gentle swath of golden sand dotted with tavernas. It fills up during the day, but early evening is perfect for a swim here, with cliffs dropping straight into the bay. The landmark rocks in the sea make perfect diving boards.

Further south, set amid cliffs that make much of the coast inaccessible, **Ag. Górdis** is an attractive resort village with a lovely, sheltered two-mile-long beach of soft sand that's popular with families. There's a fine **Folk Museum** inland at **Sinarádes**, a pretty

Folk Museum
*open Tues–Sun
9.30–2; adm*

village surrounded by vineyards. South through olives and cypresses rises **Ag. Mathiás**, an old hill village where wonky verandas overflow with geraniums and bougainvillaea, a great place to daydream under the plane tree, disturbed only by the occasional scooters and jeeps zipping past; the peaceful beaches of **Tría Avlákia**, **Paramónas** and **Skithí** lie below.

The octagonal Byzantine castle at **Gardíki** was another work by the Despot of Epirus, Michael Angelos II, during his brief rule. This is one of the most unspoilt areas of Corfu, and is a good starting point for some excellent walks. A minor road by Gardíki leads in 4km to the lagoony **Límni Korissíon**, which is separated from the sea by wild dunes; in spring and autumn it fills with migratory birds, in summer with mosquitoes. Two islets off the southwest coast, the **Lagoúdia**, are home to a tribe of donkeys; some of their ancestors were eaten by Napoleon's troops, who were shipwrecked there for three days.

The beaches towards the tail of Corfu are sandy and clean. South of Límni Korissíon, a family resort has grown up around (another) **Ag. Geórgios** and its golden beach. **Línia**, its northern extension, is more tranquil and backed by dunes; **Ag. Bárbara** to the south has a few tavernas. Next comes **Vitaládes**, a traditional village with a beach at Gárdenos, then **Ag. Górdis** and **Kanoúlas** and, down at the southernmost tip of Corfu, at the end of a long track, **Arkoudílas**, backed by a fairytale cypress forest and beach of fine white sand, with superb views over the cliffs of **Asprókavos**, topped by a ruined 18th-century **monastery of the Panagía**.

Where to Stay and Eat at the Western Beaches

Ag. Stéfanos ✉ 49081

Casa Delfino, t 266 305 1629, *www.casadelfino.gr* (€€€). Apartments sleeping 2–6 on the beach, all with sea views with a pair of pools.

Romanza, perched on a cliff in Avliotes, t 266 305 1762, *http://romanzahotel.com* (€€€–€€). Lovely views, pool and service, but often block-booked.

 Nafsika ›

Nafsika, t 266 305 1051, *www.nafsikahotel.com* (€€; half-board by the week only). Book early to bag one of the handful of rooms at this simple but extremely friendly and relaxed hotel with a pool, in a quiet corner of the resort; the restaurant is excellent as well.

Arilla Inn, on the beach, Arilla, t 266 305 1485. Excellent taverna open since 1967; a romantic setting and lots of choice.

Paleokastrítsa ✉ 49083

For a list of independent studios and rooms, see *www.paleokastritsa.biz*.

Akrotiri Beach, on a peninsula 5mins uphill from the beach, t 266 304 1237, *www.akrotiri-beach.com* (€€€€–€€€). Enjoys some of the best views in town, and there's a seawater pool for those who don't want to commute to the real thing.

Fundana Villas, 5mins up on the Corfu Town road, t 266 302 2532, *www.fundanavillas.com* (€€€). A 17th-century Venetian villa converted into family-friendly studios and bungalows with a pool.

Apollón, t 266 304 1124, *www.corfu-apollon-hotel.com* (€€). A more modest affair, with balconies facing the sea.

Odysseus, above the beach, t 266 304 1209, *www.odysseushotel.gr* (€€). A smart complex with a pool.

Zefiros, t 266 304 1244, *www.hotel-zefiros.gr* (€€–€). Built in 1934, but recently refurbished. Most rooms have sea views.

Paleokastrítsa Camping, t 266 304 1204. The nicest campsite on Corfu?

Astacos ('Lobster'), **t** 266 304 1068. Restaurant popular since 1969; also has quiet, good-value inexpensive **rooms** (€) (not so for the lobster).

Naussika. Tavernas here are expensive, but this one is good and reasonable.

Golden Fox, up in Lákones, **t** 266 304 9101. Friendly restaurant (they also have apartments) with dazzling views and a heart-shaped pool.

La Grotta Café. Lovely drinks on a quiet beach.

Ermónes ✉ 49100

Elena, t 266 109 4633 (€€€–€€). Friendly family-run hotel with a pool and good, reasonably priced restaurant, one of the nicest near the golf course.

Athina Ermones Golf, near the golf course, **t** 266 109 4226 (€€). Another good choice.

Glyfáda ✉ 49100

Glyfáda Menigos, right on the beach, **t** 266 109 4563, *www.corfu-villas-apts. com/glyfada/menigos* (€€€–€€). An assortment of houses and studios sleeping 2–7.

Pélekas ✉ 49100

Pelecas Country Club, a few mins from Pélekas, **t** 266 105 2239, *www.country-club.gr* (€€€€€). A touch of genteel, rural Corfu, with plenty of peace and quiet in the midst of wooded grounds, with pool and tennis courts. Elegant studios and suites, all with kitchenettes.

Levant Hotel, Pélekas, **t** 266 109 4230, *www.levanthotel.com* (€€€). Perched on top of Pélekas by the Kaiser's Throne; superb views and a pool, away from it all. *Open all year.*

Lidovois Studios, Pélekas beach, **t** 266 105 4452, *www.lidovois.com* (€€). Modern if basic studios and flats, all with lovely sea views.

Ag. Górdis ✉ 49084

Dinas Paradise, on the hill, **t** 266 105 3184, *www.dinasparadise.gr* (€€€–€€). Eleven apartments sleeping up to five, with a pool and lovely sea view.

Dandidis Pension, on the beach, **t** 266 105 3232, *www.dandidis.com* (€€). Plain doubles with fridge and balcony and restaurant.

Pink Palace, **t** 266 105 3103, *www. thepinkpalace.com* (€). Very popular resort complex for backpackers who want to party the night away. A new annexe has en suite rooms. They even have a bus in summer from Athens. *Open all year.*

There is no lack of restaurants: **Sebastian's**, **Sea Breeze** and **Jimmy's** are popular.

Southern Corfu

The southern half of Corfu was the first to attract the worst excesses of tourism. For years **Benítses** (ΜΠΕΝΙΤΣΕΣ) was the numero uno offender, bubbling with hormones and devouring a Greek fishing village (with its permission, of course). Benítses is an altogether gentler place again, a good choice if you want a beach close to Corfu Town. The Roman arches and mosaics just behind the harbour belonged to a bath. For a pretty hike, walk through the old village, past the cemetery to **Stavrós**, where Sir Frederick Adam, High Commissioner from 1824 to 1832, built the Benítses Waterworks. Originally, they supplied Corfu Town; now Benítses manages to use it all. Further south, the nearly continuous resort sprawls past the beaches of **Moraítika** (ΜΟΡΑΙΤΙΚΑ) and **Messónghi** (ΜΕΣΣΟΓΓΗ), both a bit posher than Benítses. A steep 4km will take you to **Chlomos**, a very traditional village with views down to Páxos.

Where to Stay and Eat in Southern Corfu

Benítses ✉ 49084

Bella Vista, t 266 107 2087, *www. bellavistahotel.gr* (€€€–€€). Completely renovated in 2006, 23 rooms in the 'two-star hotel with the five-star attitude'. *Open mid-April–Sept.*

Corfu Maris, t 266 107 2192, *www. corfumaris.gr* (€€). Smack on the beach, pleasant rooms, all with sea views.

Klimataria, t 266 107 1201. Traditional seafood taverna. *Open all year.*

Moraítika ✉ 49084

Christina Beach, in nearby Messónghi, **t** 226 107 6771, *www.hotelchristina.gr* (€€). On the beach, simple and friendly family-run hotel/restaurant.

Margarita Beach Hotel, t 266 107 5267, *www.corfu-hotel-margarita.com* (€€). Pleasant seaside rooms with balconies.

Rose Garden, Islands and the **Village Taverna** are good, reliable tavernas.

If you're here for the scenery, skip the coast and take the inland route, beginning at **Kinopiástes** (near Gastoúri), passing by way of pretty Ag. Déka, Makráta, Kornáta and Strongilí. Further south, in the centre of a large fertile plain, **Lefkími**, the largest town, is dusty and uninviting; the nearest beaches, Mólos and Alykés, 2km away on the east coast, are flat, set amid salt pans established by the Venetians. And last, and least, is hell-raising **Kávos** (ΚΑΒΟΣ) where things have got so out of hand that some locals now refuse to work there.

Islands near Corfu: Othoní, Eríkousa and Mathráki

Misanthropes, writers or painters in search of inspiration or anyone looking for a refuge from the razzmatazz of the new Greece need look no further than northwest of Corfu, to the Diapontía islands, 17km from Sidári, and only 69km from Cape Otranto, Italy – the westernmost territory of Greece. They were colonized by Greek families after the Battle of Lepanto (1571), but nearly everyone has since moved to New York, leaving only about 150 people on each quiet paradise, many of whom have returned home to retire.

Cliff-lined **Othoní** is the largest of the three. There are few shops, a few vehicles (but no petrol station), lovely shingle/sandy beaches and trails through giant olive groves to a well-preserved Venetian fort and the five villages, only two of which are still inhabited, **Ámmos**, the port, and **Stavrós**; with a boat you can visit **Áspri**

Where to Stay and Eat on Othoní and Eríkousa

Othoní/Eríkousa ✉ 49081

Bella Mare Apartments, Othoní, **t** 266 308 1996 (€€€).

Locanda dei Sogni, right by the sea on Othoní, **t** 266 307 2130 or **t** 697 974

(⭐) **Locanda dei Sogni >**

8701, *www.locandadeisogni.it* (€€€–€€). Five pretty apartments (but it's essential to book early) and good restaurant, using fresh organic ingredients. *From mid-July–Aug, minimum stay one week.*

Eríkousa, on Eríkousa, **t** 266 307 1555, *www.hotelerikousa.gr* (€€). Smart hotel with a bar and restaurant.

Getting to the Islands near Corfu

Every Tues and Sat (and Sun in summer) the *Alexandros* makes the 4hr sailing to the islands from Corfu Town at 6.30am. On Mon and Thurs, it links with Ag. Stéfanos in northern Corfu (1½hrs) and it sails from Sidári on Tues, Wed, Sat and Sun.

Ámmos, a gorgeous white sandy beach by the Cave of Calypso. Most of the excursion boats from Corfu, however, make for **Eríkousa**, with its Corfu-esque landscapes, the biggest sandy beach and seven tiny villages set in the cypresses and olives. **Mathráki**, the smallest island and closest to Corfu, has a 3km-long sandy beach, nearly always empty, three tavernas and apartments to rent, and that's it.

Ithaca/Itháki (ΙΘΑΚΗ)

Every traveller is a citizen of Ithaca.
sign in the port

Small, precipitous Ithaca has become quite trendy these days, by doing little more than remaining its lovely, low-key self. It has a jagged coast, but no exceptional beaches (although there are some pretty, pebbly ones to the north, accessible only by boat), no nightlife, no camping, and little new building (local water shortages have strictly limited that), and a general idea that Ithaca should remain as an island set aside for daydreamers, poets and scholars.

You'll find that many of Homer's descriptions of Ithaca square uncannily with this island – it is certainly 'narrow' and 'rocky' and 'unfit for riding horses'. Although some have theorized that Homer's Ithaca was elsewhere – Lefkáda was a popular contender in the 19th century, as is Kefaloniá today – Itháki, as the locals call their home, the eternal symbol of all homes and journey's end, is the real thing, and 'even if you find it poor,' as Caváfy wrote, 'Ithaca does not deceive. Without Ithaca your journey would have no beauty.'

History

Ithaca's Pilikáta hill (near Stavrós) was the site of the island's early Helladic community (3000–2000 BC), which used the Cave of Loízos as the centre of cult activity, as did passing sailors. By Mycenaean times, settlements had relocated further south as Arkikious (*see* 'Mythology') and organized a kingdom (c. 1200 BC) that probably included Kefaloniá, Zákynthos, Lefkáda and part of the Peloponnese coast. Ithaca was the capital, and under Odysseus the kingdom reached its prime, sending 12 ships to Troy.

⭐ **Odysseus' Trail**

In the last 200 years archaeologists have combed Ithaca for **signs of Odysseus**. Schliemann came after his momentous discovery of Troy, and, since Schliemann always found what he sought, he unearthed a large structure he immediately labelled 'Odysseus' Palace'; although it dates from only 700 BC, the name has stuck. Later finds, while failing to produce any concrete evidence, at least

Getting to Ithaca

By seaplane: Ithaca should be served by seaplanes in 2007 (see *www.airsealines.com*).

By sea: Ithaca has three ports. **Váthi** is connected at least twice a day by **ferry** with Sámi (Kefaloniá) and Pátras (4hrs). **Astakós** (on the mainland) has a daily link (2hrs). **Pisoaetós** has a faster, cheaper regular **car ferry** to Sámi (Kefaloniá), and to Fiskárdo (Kefaloniá) and Vassiliki (Lefkáda). **Fríkes**, in the north of Ithaca, also connects with Lefkáda. Ferry routes are often subject to change. **Port authority**: **t** 267 403 2909.

Getting around Ithaca

For 10 months a year one (school) **bus** a day plies its route once a day up and down the island from Kióni to Váthi and back. In July and Aug, the service extends to twice a day. You can also catch a bus direct to Athens, **t** 267 102 5222.

Taxis abound (Kióni to Váthi €20, Váthi to Pisoaetós €12).

For **car and motorbike hire**, try **Alpha**, by the port authority in Váthi, **t** 267 403 2850.

indicate that the ancients considered Itháki Homer's Ithaca: inscriptions show that Odysseus was worshipped as a divine hero, coins bore his picture, and pottery was decorated with his cockerel symbol. Homer describes the palace of Odysseus as above 'three seas' and the hill near Stavrós fits the description, overlooking three bays. In 1930 two ruined towers were discovered that may have been used to signal the palace. Other Homeric sites have been tentatively identified, such as the Fountain of Arethusa, where Odysseus met his faithful swineherd Eumaeus, and the cave where he hid the treasure given to him by the Phaeacians. A manuscript kept on

The Strange Birth and Death of Odysseus

A king of Kefaloniá, Kefalos, had a son named Arkikious who annexed Ithaca and made it the centre of his realm; his son was Laertes, who sailed aboard the *Argo* and married Anticleia, daughter of Autolykus, who gave birth to Odysseus.

But tradition says that Autolykus (a son of Hermes) and Sisyphus (who went on to become a celebrity in hell) used to graze their flocks next to each other, and through trickery would steal one another's sheep. Autolykus thought that if he married his daughter Anticleia to Sisyphus, their child would inherit cunning from both sides of the family and be the ultimate trickster. Sisyphus was equally keen, and had his evil way with Anticleia before their wedding; but during the interval Laertes asked to marry her, and did. She was already pregnant by Sisyphus, and Autolykus, the child's grandfather, named him Odysseus, which means 'angry' or 'he who is hated by all'.

Odysseus was a suitor of Helen, but wed Penelope instead and had a son, Telemachus. Having been warned by an oracle that if he went to Troy he would be absent for 20 years and return alone without booty, Odysseus pretended madness by ploughing the sand and sowing it with salt when the Greek representatives came to fetch him; to test him, the cleverest of the Greeks, Palamedes, placed his baby son Telemachus in front of his oxen. Odysseus diverted their course, and was constrained by his promise as one of Helen's ex-suitors to bring her back from Troy. After his homecoming in disguise, the murder of Penelope's suitors and recognition by his wife, Homer's story ends, but two accounts in myth tell of Odysseus' death: one, that the families of the suitors forced him to live in exile, and that he died at a ripe old age in Italy; another, that Odysseus was not permitted to die until he appeased the anger of his old enemy, Poseidon, and the only way to do so was to take an oar and walk until he came to a land where people asked him what he carried. Then, after a sacrifice to the sea god, he sailed home, and was drowned on the way.

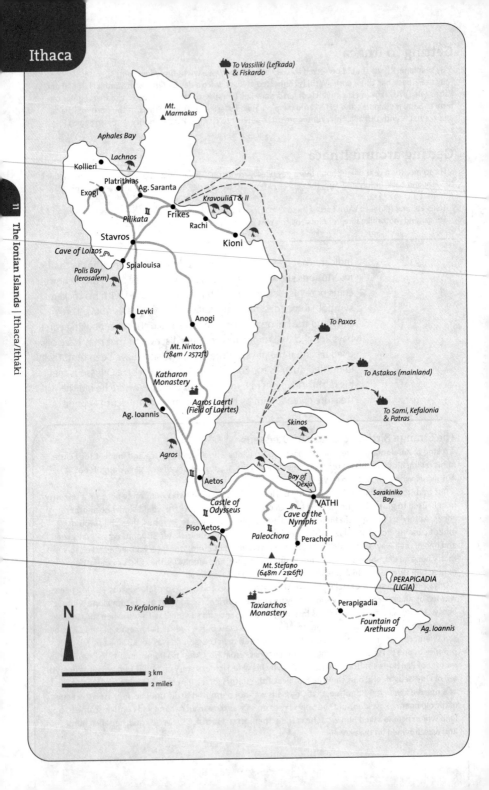

Useful Information on Ithaca

Tourist police: Váthi, t 267 403 2205.

Polyctor Tours, in the square in Váthi, t 267 403 3120, *www.ithakiholidays. com*. The island's oldest travel office: special tours, including a cooking tour to Moní Katharón and Anogí.

Friends of the Ionian, *kefalonia.foi.org. uk*. Pick up their trail guides for Kióni, Fríkes, Stavrós, Exogí and Perachóri.

Ithaca Festivals

The island's traditional *panegýria* are tremendous, enthusiastic fun.

17 July: Exogí.

20 July: Kióni.

Late July: wine festival, in Perachóri.

5–6 Aug: Stavrós.

14 Aug: Anogí.

15 Aug: Platrithiás.

Late-Aug–Sept: theatre and music festival at Váthi.

Mount Áthos claims that Homer himself was born in Ithaca; one tradition says that, although born in Smyrna, he was invited as a young man to stay in Ithaca and knew the island first-hand.

After the Mycenaeans, Ithaca lost its importance and even its name; for a period it was humiliatingly known as 'Little Kefaloniá'. By the time of the Venetians, piracy was so bad that it was all but abandoned, and the Venetians offered generous incentives to anyone who would settle and farm there. Once again Ithaca prospered, but, unlike the other Ionian islands, it never had an aristocracy. Ironically, union with Greece in 1864 initiated a great migration, many Ithakians going to Romania, Australia, South Africa and even to Ithaca, New York. Like Odysseus, they are known as sailors, and even those who call Ithaca home spend much time away at sea.

Váthi (ΒΑΘΥ)

At the bottom of a long horseshoe bay, the unpretentious but charming town of Váthi (pop. 1,800) has been the capital of Ithaca since the 16th century. Its beautiful harbour, surrounded by mountains, embraces a wooded islet called **Lazarétto** after a quarantine station established in 1668 by the Venetians. Two ruined forts, **Loútsa** and **Kástro**, built in 1805 by the French, stand at either side of the harbour entrance.

Váthi's neoclassical **mansion** of the Drakoúlis family, who brought the first steamship, the *Ithaka*, to Greece, was one of the few buildings to survive the 1953 earthquake. Fortunately the rest of the town was rebuilt in the original style, with red tile roofs. The **church of the Taxiárchos** has an icon of Christ attributed to the young El Greco. There are Mycenaean and classical artefacts in the **Archaeology Museum**; the library in the adjacent **Cultural Centre** is immensely proud of a Japanese edition of Homer's works printed in 1600. By the Alpha Bank, the **Folklore Museum**, with a copy of the famous bronze of Poseidon by the door, evokes old Ithaca with photos, costumes, furnishings and more.

Archaeology Museum
t 267 403 2200; open Tues–Sun 8.30–2.30

Folklore Museum
open daily 8.30–2

Where to Stay in Váthi

As Ithaca becomes popular, rooms can be tough to come by. Check out the island's accommodation co-op, with pictures, at http://accommodation ithaca.sphosting.com.

Váthi ☒ 28300

⭐ **Perantzada >**

Perantzada, overlooking the port, t 267 403 3496, www.arthotel.gr (€€€€€). A classy boutique hotel where fabrics, furnishings and lighting are the focus, each room decorated in an individual style, with hand-painted poems on each wall. Open all year.

Mentor, t 267 403 2433, www. hotelmentor.gr (€€€). The old standby, standing sentinel.

Odyssey Apartments, just east of town, t 267 403 2268, www.ithaki-odyssey. com (€€€). Wonderful view, well equipped and roomy.

Omirikon, t 267 403 3120, www. omirikonhotel.com (€€€). Stylish studios and apartments sleeping up to four, right on the sea.

Villa Eleni, t 697 701 8987, www.ithaca-villa.com (€€€). Delightful, peaceful

B&B in a new garden villa. Open 15 April–15 Oct.

Calypso, 1km from town on the road to Perachóri, t 267 403 3138, www.ithaki-calypso.com (€€). New if rather basic studios and rooms overlooking the bay.

Maroudas Rooms, t 267 403 2751. Studios (€€) and rooms (€). Convenient and simple.

Eating Out in Váthi

More than most other islands, Ithaca's tavernas pride themselves on their wines.

Paliocaravo (or **Gregory's**), t 267 403 2573. Where kings and celebrities have feasted on fresh fish and lobster, served with the family's home-made wine and olive oil (around €40 for the lobster).

O Zois Grill, by the port authority, t 267 403 2852. Offers Ithaca's surf 'n'turf: grilled octopus and kokorétsi – lamb's intestines and wines from Mt Áthos.

Drosia, on the hill, t 267 403 2959. Traditional grill, salads but also some classic island dishes in a cool, shady setting looking down on Váthi.

Every four years since 1981, Váthi's **Centre for Odyssean Studies** has hosted an international congress on the *Odyssey*.

Water taxis put-put out to nearby beaches.

Southern Ithaca: on the Odysseus Trail

⚜ **Odysseus' Trail**

Some sites identified with places in the *Odyssey* make pretty walks or drives. West of Váthi, it's a 4km walk to the **Cave of the Nymphs** or Mármaro Spília (*signposted, but often closed*), where Odysseus is said to have hidden the gifts of King Alcinous. According to Homer, the cave had two entrances, one for mortals and one in the roof for the gods – which also permitted the smoke of the sacrifices to rise to heaven; in the 3rd century AD Porphyry, the neo-Platonist, made it the subject of a famous allegory. Below, the narrow **Dexiá inlet** may be the 'Harbour of Phorcys' where the Phaeacians gently put the sleeping Odysseus on shore.

South of Váthi, 4km along the road to the pretty Maráthias plateau, a path to the left is signposted to the **Fountain of Arethusa** (ΚΡΙΝΙ ΑΡΕΘΥΟΣΑ), an hour and a half's walk. In myth, Arethusa wept so much when her son Corax 'the raven' was killed that she turned into a spring; the water flows (in the summer, dribbles) from under the towering rock, Corax, and is good to drink, although beware that it has a reputation for making you as hungry as a bear. Just to the south, at **Ellinikó**, Odysseus, disguised as a beggar, met the swineherd Eumaeus; excavations here duly uncovered some Mycenaean odds and ends. From the Arethusa Fountain a rocky scramble descends to the beach, facing the islet of **Perapigádia** (the Homeric Asteris), where the suitors hid, awaiting to ambush young Telemachus on his return from Pýlos.

The only other real village in the south of Ithaca is **Perachóri**, occupying a 300m (984ft)-high fertile balcony 2km from Váthi, where most of Ithaca's wine is produced. The village dates from the Venetians, although the first houses were built in the walls of **Paleochóra**, Ithaca's ghost-town capital; among their ruins is a roofless church with fading Byzantine frescoes. Follow the signs, or in Perachóri the villagers will show you which path to take; the view is superb. Another road – for jeeps – climbs 3km from Perachóri to the earthquake-blasted **Monastery of the Taxiárchos** (1645) on **Mount Stéfano**, with more great views. Perachóri has a pair of summer tavernas with views, serving local wine and *tserépato*, meat slowly roasted in a clay pot.

North of Váthi

Ithaca has an hourglass figure, with a waist only 500m wide at the narrow mountain stretch of **Aetós**. Overlooking the two bays is what the locals (and Schliemann) have always called the **Castle of Odysseus**, although it's apparently the citadel of Alalkomenes, which was abandoned in Roman times. Impressive Cyclopean walls and the foundations of a temple are all that remain of a site continuously occupied since the 13th century BC. There's a pebble beach in the bay to the east and another small, excellent one at **Písoaetós** in the west, where ferries occasionally dock.

⊕ Odysseus' Trail

Just north of Aetós, near Agrós, is the **Field of Laertes**, where Odysseus met his father after killing the suitors; note the massive 2,000-year-old 'Laertes' olive'. From here a road ascends the 784m (2,572ft) **Mount Níritos** (formerly Korifí – Ithaca is slowly reclaiming its Homeric names) to the **Monastery of the Katharón**, 'of the dry weeds', built on the site of a Temple of Athena. One story, far-fetched even by Greek standards, says it was built by the heretical Cathars; another explains that farmers were burning dry weeds here when they found an icon of the *Birth of the Virgin* attributed to St Luke, which holds pride of place in the church of the Panagía Kathariótissas. When Byron visited in 1823, a special mass was held. Nowadays the church is often invaded by goats. From its lighthouse of a bell tower you can see the Gulf of Pátras on a clear day.

From Moní Katharón, a paved road continues 3km up to **Anogí**, 'at the top of the world', passing odd-shaped boulders, including a very phallic 7.6m (25ft) monolith named Araklís, or Heracles. The village (pop. 35) retains some Venetian ruins, including a sturdy grey campanile and a restored 12th-century church dedicated to the **Panagía** (ask at the *kafeneíon* for the key) with lovely, richly coloured Byzantine frescoes; note the clay amphorae embedded in the walls to improve the church's acoustics.

The second, easier road from Agrós follows the west coast. At **Ag. Ioánnis**, just opposite Kefaloniá, is a seldom-used white beach, **Áspros Gialós**.

Lévki, the small village to the north, was an important port for the resistance movement during the war, and, when it was destroyed by the 1953 earthquake, Britain helped rebuild it.

Stavrós and the North

⭐ Odysseus' Trail

A bust of Odysseus in **Stavrós**, the most important village in the north, looks out sternly over lovely Pólis Bay, its name referring to the Byzantine city (*polis*) of Ierosalem, which sank into it during an earthquake in AD 967; Robert Guiscard (*see* p.492) was told by a soothsayer that he would die after seeing 'Jerusalem', and did. It's also one of the most popular beaches on the island. The **Cave of Loízos** to the right of the bay was an ancient cult sanctuary; some say it was Homer's Cave of the Nymphs. Prehistoric pots, Mycenaean amphorae, bronze tripods from 800–700 BC, ex-votos of nymphs and an inscription to Odysseus were found here before it collapsed.

⭐ Odysseus' Trail

Another plausible Odysseus' palace is **Pilikáta**, or the Hill of Hermes, just north of Stavrós. The site fits the Homeric description, in sight of 'three seas' (the bays of Frikés, Pólis and Áphales) and 'three mountains' (Níritos, Marmakás and Exogí or Neíon). Under the ruins of a Venetian fort, excavators found evidence of buildings and roads dating back to Neolithic times, and a pit containing sacrifices and two ceramic shards in Linear A script, from *c.* 2700 BC. Prof. Paul Fauré's translation of them reads 'Here is what I, Aredatis, give to the queen, the goddess Rhea: 100 goats, 10 sheep, 3 pigs' and 'The nymph saved me'. Finds from Pilikáta and the Cave of Loízos are in the small Stavrós Archaeology Museum.

Archaeology
Museum
open Tues–Sun 8.30–3

To the north, Ithaca's remotest, nearly deserted village, **Exogí** ('beyond the earth') is set high up on terraces; above the village is Ithaca's oddball attraction, three narrow pyramids built in 1933 by a pyramid-fancier named Papadópoulos. He's buried under one, his mother under another, while the third has a jar with his coin collection. Another 2km up, the disused **Monastery of Panagía Eleoússa** offers extraordinary views over the Ionian islands.

Between Exogí and Platrithiás you will find '**Homer's School**'; the ruined 7th-century church of **Ag. Athanásios** has hewn blocks reused from an ancient wall. By the Melanydrus spring there's a stepped well that the locals call 'Penelope's Bath' – although it's actually a Mycenaean tomb.

This fertile area is one of the most pleasant on the island; Platrithiás is the biggest hamlet; another, Kóllieri, greets wayfarers with an outdoor 'folklore museum', with stone obelisks made out of millstones.

Fríkes and Kióni

North of Stavrós, Fríkes (ΦΡΙΚΕΣ), a favourite pirates' lair into the 19th century, is now a tiny fishing village and as packed in summer with yachts, relatively, as St-Tropez. About 100 people live there year-round; there are two tiny beaches to the east, known as Kravoúlia I and Kravoúlia 2.

The road continues to Rachí, a tiny hamlet of old stone houses, and continues down to the pretty village of Kióni, built around a tiny harbour, guarded by three ruined windmills. Twice the size of Fríkes, it too is popular with the yachting set; landlubbers can hire motorboats to the surrounding beaches. Kióni means 'column', and an ancient one still stands on the altar in the church of Ag. Nikólaos. There are more Cyclopean walls nearby, at a site called Roúga.

Where to Stay in Northern Ithaca

Stavrós ✉ 28301

Levendis, overlooking Áphales bay in the north, t 6944 169 770, www.levendisestate.com (€€€€€). Five lovely cottages sleeping four in a seven-acre estate olive grove, with a pool, organic vegetables, and special retreat weeks. Minimum stay one week; prices include private transfers from Kefaloniá airport and a hire car. Book well (a year even!) in advance.

Porto Thiaki, t 267 403 1245, www.portothiaki.sphosting.com (€€). Classy rooms with views, in walking distance of Pólis beach.

Yiannis, t 267 403 1363. Good moussaka, pizza, pasta and tserépato, a local chicken dish, and organic wines from Exogí.

Fríkes ✉ 28301

Nostos Hotel, t 267 403 1644, www.hotelnostos-ithaki.gr (€€€–€€). Set back from the beach, with a pool.

Aristotelis Apartments, t 267 403 1079, www.aristotelis-ithaki.gr (€€). Very pleasant studios. Open all year.

Penelope (Steve's), t 267 403 1005. A very friendly place, owned by Státhis, the 'Music Man'; try the local onion pie.

Rementzo, t 267 403 1719. A place that takes pride in using organic ingredients and Ithacan wines; in winter they have live music.

Symposium, t 267 403 1729. Friendly place serving fish, meats and carafes of local wine.

Kióni ✉ 28301

Captain's Apartments, 150m from the sea, t 267 403 1481, www.captains-apartments.gr (€€). New studios sleeping 2–4.

Maroudas Apartments, t 267 403 1691 (€€). Studios with satellite TV.

Avra Taverna, t 267 403 1453. An institution on the waterfront for over 40 years, specializing in lobster and fresh fish.

Calypso, t 267 403 1066. The chef prepares fish pies and other seafood specialities, but the land food is excellent as well.

Kefaloniá (ΚΕΦΑΛΟΝΙΑ)

'The half-forgotten island of Cephallonia rises improvidently and inadvisedly from the Ionian Sea,' writes Dr Iannis in Louis de Bernières' *Captain Corelli's Mandolin* – a book and film that lifted the island, the largest of the Ionians, from its half-obscurity and put it square on the holiday map. Its Jabberwocky silhouette contains 781 square kilometres of ruggedly beautiful mountains, although it supports a mere 30,000 people. Kefalonians are famous for

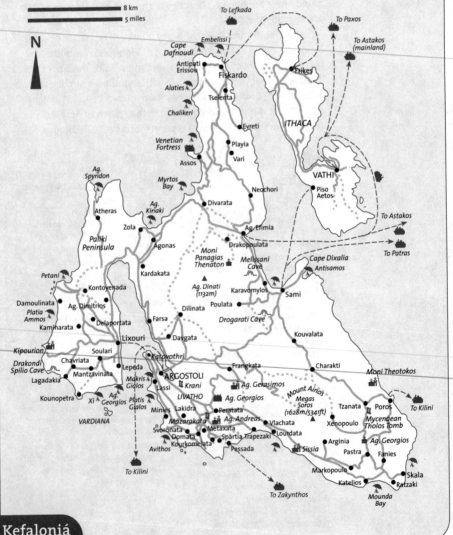

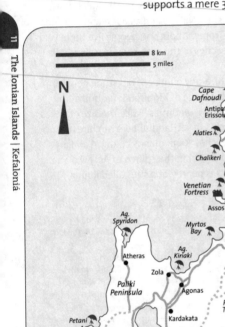

Kefaloniá

Getting to and around Kefaloniá

By air: There are daily flights from Athens and frequent charters. The **Olympic Airways** office is in Argostóli, at 1 R. Vergotí, **t** 267 102 8808; the **airport** is 9km south of Argostóli, **t** 267 102 8881, and reachable by **taxi** (€15 to Argostóli).

By sea: Kefaloniá has seven ports. Starting at the top, **Fiskárdo** has ferry links with Ithaca and Lefkáda; **Sámi** with Ithaca and Pátras; **Póros, Argostóli** and **Lixoúri** with Killíni (Peloponnese); **Pessáda**, in the south, with Zákynthos (summer only); and **Ag. Efimía** with Astakós. **Port authorities**: Fiskárdo, **t** 267 404 1400; Sámi, **t** 267 402 2031; Póros, **t** 267 407 2460; Argostóli, **t** 267 102 2224; Lixoúri, **t** 267 109 4100; Ag. Efimía, **t** 267 402 2456.

By road: Buses from Athens (**t** 210 515 0785) or Pátras go to Póros, Argostóli, Lixoúri or Sámi.

Getting around Kefaloniá

A **ferry** links Argostóli and Lixoúri (4km by sea, compared to 30km by land) every half-hour in season and otherwise hourly.

Island **buses** are not frequent; in Argostóli, the bus station is by the causeway at 4 Tritsi, **t** 267 102 5222. From Argostóli there are 6 buses a day to Lassí in the high season, two or more to Fiskárdo, Ag. Efimía, Sámi and Skála. **KTEL Travel**, next door to the bus station, **t** 267 102 3364, offers day trips around the island and to the mainland. There is no lack of **taxis, car** and **moped rentals**.

---

wandering (one, Ioánnis Phókas, better known as Juan de Fuca, was a 16th-century explorer who sought the Northwest Passage for Spain; another, Constantine Yerákis, made a fortune in the British East India Company and became Regent of Siam), and it's not uncommon to meet someone whose entire family lives in Canada, Australia or the United States. Kefalonians are good-humoured and clever, but are said to have 'drunk a toast with the devil' that made them cunning, eccentric, tight with their money and the worst blasphemers in Greece.

Although an earthquake in 1953 shattered all but a fraction of Kefaloniá's traditional architecture, what the big, sprawling island has lost in charm it makes up in natural beauty. It has fine beaches, rugged scenery and hair-raising roads, two of the country's loveliest caves, lofty fir forests, splendid views and robóla wine. It also has lots of Brits and Italians, and patches of awful maisonettes, apartment hotels and villa compounds, but nothing overwhelming, as yet.

History

Fossil and tool finds in Fiskárdo, Sámi and Skála go back to at least 50,000 BC and perhaps earlier, making Fiskárdo man (and woman, one supposes) among the earliest known Greeks. Later inhabitants appear to have been culturally related to the 'Pelasgians' in western Sicily and Epirus; their skulls, all banged about, suggest that Kefalonians have always been a feisty lot. Mycenaean culture was imported from the Peloponnese in the 14th century BC; Krani, near Argostóli, was their most important colony. Although the name Kefaloniá does not occur in Homer, scholars believe that the 'glittering Samos' of the *Odyssey* actually refers to Kefaloniá's town of Sámi. Others believe Homer doesn't mention Kefaloniá because, as part of the kingdom of Odysseus, he simply calls it Ithaca. The recent discovery of a royal Mycenaean tomb near Póros has given the argument new weight as archaeologists scramble to locate the big jackpot – the Palace of Odysseus.

The first sure references to Kefaloniá are in Herodotus. Thucydides describes its four city-states, Sami, Pali, Krani and Pronnoi – allies of Corinth who spent much of their history fighting for their independence from Athens. In Byzantine times the island prospered in spite of pirate incursions, and in the 9th century was made one of the 29 *themes*, or provinces, of the Byzantine empire. In 1085, Normans based in southern Italy unsuccessfully besieged Kefaloniá's forts; their duke, Robert Guiscard, died of fever in the village that has taken his name – Fiskárdo (*see* below). If the Kefalonians breathed a sigh of relief, it was way too soon; for the next 800 years the island, like its Ionian sisters, would be the plaything of the Normans, Venice and the Vatican (but mostly the Venetians), as well as a motley assortment of dukes and counts, including the colourful pirate Count Matteo Orsini, who founded a murderous, dowry-snatching dynasty at the end of the 13th century. In 1483 the Turks captured the island, but lost it again in 1504 when Venice and Spain, under the Gran Capitan Gonzálo Fernández de Córdoba, took the fort of Ag. Geórgios and slaughtered the Turkish garrison. In 1823, Byron spent three months on Kefaloniá (along with a retinue including his faithful Venetian gondolier, Tita), working as an agent of the Greek Committee in London before going to die from fever in Messolóngi. During the British occupation, the Kefalonians revolted; 21 Greek nationalists were hanged in 1849.

Ioánnis Metaxás, prime minister-dictator of Greece from 1936 to 1941, came from Kefaloniá, and for all his many faults has gone down in history for laconically (and, apparently, apocryphally) saying 'No' to Mussolini's ultimatum in 1940 – celebrated nationally on 28 October as Óchi ('No') Day. Nevertheless, Kefaloniá along with the rest of Greece was occupied by the Italians, in this case by the Acqui Division, plus 2,000 Germans. All was fairly peaceful until the September 1943 Italian armistice, when confusion reigned: the Italians wanted to return home, but the Germans wanted them to surrender their weapons, not wanting them used against them. As the Italians hesitated, German reinforcements arrived on the island. The Italians took a vote on whether to fight the Germans or surrender, and chose to fight. In the next seven days some 1,315 died in combat. In the subsequent mass executions, ordered, it is said, by Hitler himself, 155 officers and 5,000 soldiers were shot and their bodies burned to hide the evidence; some 3,000 were thrown in the sea – events now familiar through *Captain Corelli* (although many islanders consider the novel's portrayal of events, especially of the Civil War, as one-sided).

Useful Information on Kefaloniá

(i) **Kefaloniá** >
*EOT: Argostóli, on
the waterfront across
from the Star Hotel,
t 267 102 2248;
open Mon–Fri 8–2*

Tourist police: 52 I Metaxás St, Argostóli, **t** 267 102 2248.

Sea Trek Walking Holidays: UK **t** 44 (0) 1386 848 814, *www.sea-trek.co.uk.* Sailing in Lixoúri and Fiskárdo, and guided and self-guided walking tours.

Monte Nero Activities, Ávithos, **t** 693 290 4360, *www.monte-nero-activities. com.* Organizes trekking, sea kayaking and cycling excursions.

Kefaloniá Festivals

21 May: Festival of the Radicals (celebrating union with Greece) in Argostóli.

23 June: Argostóli.

15 Aug: Markópoulo (with the little snakes).

16 Aug and 20 Oct: Ag. Gerásimos.

First Sat after 15 Aug: Robóla wine festival in Fragáta.

A decade later, as Kefaloniá began to recover from the war, nature itself struck a blow which made all the previous earthquakes seem like cocktail shakers. For five days in August 1953, 113 tremors reduced most of the island's 350 towns and villages to rubble, killing 476; the first, deadliest earthquake had the estimated force of 60 atom bombs. As the dust slowly cleared, money for reconstruction poured in from all over Europe; new building has since been limited to two storeys, and has stood up well to earthquakes in 2003 and 2005.

Argostóli (ΑΡΓΟΣΤΟΛΙ)

Occupying a thumb in the island's west bay, Kefaloniá's capital (pop. 10,000), is a busy, very Greek town. A smugglers' hamlet under the Venetians, it gradually grew up around vast warehouses full of raisins, destined for the European market. As Ag. Geórgios, the old Venetian capital, declined, the residents petitioned Venice to make Argostóli capital, and in 1759 their wish was granted, to the eternal disgust of arch rival Lixoúri. After the 1953 earthquake, Kefalonians abroad lavished money to rebuild Argostóli as a proper capital, with public buildings grouped around **Plateía Vallianóu**.

**Focas Cosmetatos
Foundation**
*t 267 102 6595; open in
season Mon–Sat 9.30–
12.45 and 7–9.45; adm*

Here on Vallianóu Street, the **Focas Cosmetatos Foundation** is a recent addition to the town, displaying Ionian lithographs (including works by Edward Lear), furnishings, and banknotes and coins; your ticket will also get you into **Cephalonia Botanica**, the botanical gardens devoted to Mediterranean flora, signposted just south of Argostóli. The municipal garden just above Plateía Vallianóu is known as **Napier's Garden**; British High Commissioner Charles Napier, who loved Kefaloniá, bought the land for a villa and in 1905 his daughters donated it to Argostóli. Restored for its centenary, it has a gazebo, plaques and a bust of Napier, vandalized by an Italian soldier.

**Archaeology
Museum**
*t 267 102 8300; open
Tues–Sun 8.30–3; adm*

The **Archaeology Museum**, just south on R. Vergóti, has neolithic finds and ex-votos to the nymphs from the Cave of Drákena near

Póros, Helladic and Mycenaean items from Likithra, coins from the four ancient cities of Kefaloniá and a startlingly modern bronze male bust from the early 3rd century AD. Near the museum, the **Kéfalos theatre** was once the glory of the town and reconstructed after 1953; just up, on Ilía Zervoú Street, the **Corgialenios Museum**, adjacent to the library, is one of the best ethnographic museums in Greece, founded by a member of the revolutionary Friendly Society. But don't expect peasant costumes and farm tools; the emphasis here is on Kefalonian society, and a surprisingly sophisticated bunch they were too with their Paris fashions, salons, theatre and opera. One room is dedicated to the earthquake, with bittersweet photos of pre-1953 Argostóli. There are portraits and memorablia of island heroes and British governors; the adjacent library contains documents going back to the 16th century, including the Venetian *Libro d'Oro* listing the local nobility.

Corgialenios Museum
t 267 102 8835; open Mon–Sat 9–2; adm

Pre-earthquake Argostóli was famous for its **bell towers**, two of which have been rebuilt – there's a touch of German Expressionism about the one by the Catholic church on Lithóstrato Street, the town's sleek pedestrian shopping and bar street. Next to the church is a little **Museum of the Acqui Division** run by the local Italo-Greek association.

Museum of the Acqui Division
open July–Sept Mon, Tues and Thurs 10–1, Sun 11–1 and daily 8–10pm

The one structure to survive the earthquake, the 900m (2,950ft) **Drapanós Bridge**, was begun under the British in 1813 and remade in stone in 1842, punctuated with a commemorative obelisk minus its once proud plaque 'To the glory of the British Empire'; you can often see swans swimming around it. It is now off limits to cars, so you have to drive around the bay to the picturesque church of **Ag. Barbára** peering from the rockface over a little bridge.

About 1km further, at **Razáta**, a dirt road leads up to ancient **Krani** (Paleókastro), where the huge stone blocks of the 7th-century BC Cyclopean walls snake through the trees. There are fragments of a Doric Temple to Demeter and a rectangular hollow carved out of the top of the hill called the Drakóspilia, or Dragon's Lair, although it was probably just a Roman tomb.

The Lassí Peninsula

Lassí, with its lovely beaches, **Platís Gialós**, **Makrís Gialós** and **Tourkopóthiro** (by the White Rocks hotel), was Kefaloniá's first tourist strip. Get there by way of the scenic loop north of Argostóli, passing by the **Katovóthres**, or swallow holes, where the sea is sucked into the ground. Where the water actually went was a mystery until 1963, when Austrian geologists poured 140 kilos of green dye into the water. Fifteen days later the dye appeared in the lake of the Melissáni Cave and at Karavómylos, near Sámi, on the other side of the island. Sea mills to harness the rushing water for electricity were destroyed by the earthquake (which also greatly diminished the suction). One already rusting watermill has been reconstructed on the terrace of the Katovothri ouzerie. At the tip of the peninsula, the pretty **lighthouse of Ag. Theódori** in a Doric rotunda was built by Charles Napier, and reconstructed after the 1875 earthquake. Signs point up the hill to the **Acqui Division Memorial**, erected in 1978; a plaque marks the spot where 138 Italians were shot.

Where to Stay around Argostóli

Argostóli ✉ 28100

Aenos, 11 Plateía Metaxá, **t** 267 102 8013, *www.aenos.com* (€€€€). Urbane 33-room hotel in the centre with an Internet café. *Open April–Oct.*

Miramare, by the sea on the edge of Argostóli towards Lassí, **t** 267 102 5511 (€€€–€€). Large, classy and comfortable.

Cefalonia Star, 60 Metaxá St, **t** 267 102 3181 (€€). At the quieter end of the waterfront in a clean modern block.

Ionian Plaza, Plateía Vallianóu, **t** 267 102 5581 (€€). Stylish hotel, each room with a balcony.

Ionis, at Peratáta, 8km south of Argostóli, **t** 267 106 9322, *www. hotelionis.gr* (€€). Set in the shadow of Ag. Geórgios castle, with a pool, children's pool and playground. Peratáta is a place that also has many rooms for rent.

Mouikis, 3 Výronis, **t** 267 102 3454, *www.mouikis.com* (€€–€). Pleasant and friendly, with a free bus shuttle to Mouikis village at Likithra to enjoy the lovely view and pool,

Tourist, on the waterfront, **t** 267 102 3034 (€€–€). Comfy en suite rooms, with TV.

Argostóli Beach Camping, 2km north of town, by the lighthouse, **t** 267 102 3487, *www.argostolibeach.gr*.

Lassí ✉ 28100

Thalassa, **t** 267 102 7081, *www. thalassahotel.gr* (€€€€). Amid the package hotels here, this is a new boutique hotel with a neoclassical exterior and modern luxury and elegance within, and a unique pool. *Open all year.*

⭐ Tsivras »

Eating Out in Argostóli

Argostóli ✉ 28100

Archontikó, next door on Rizopastón, **t** 267 102 7213. Classy Greek taverna with lots of choice and vegetarian dishes.

Bells Café, **t** 267 102 4456. In the old bell tower, with photos of pre-quake Argostóli and views from the tower. The café is run by a special initiative to employ the mentally disabled.

Captain's Table, by Plateía Vallianóu on Rizopastón, **t** 267 102 3896. Upscale and nautical; they also have a branch on the waterfront.

Casa Grec, 10 Metaxás, **t** 267 102 4091 (€25). Elegant dining room and attractive courtyard, with dishes ranging from tagliatelle *primavera*, chicken *cordon bleu* and pepper steak to Caesar salad and shrimp Newburg.

Mýthos, 13 Rizopastón, **t** 267 102 2663 (€22). Dine under the palms on offbeat international and Greek dishes, some with a touch of the ancient world – *panzéta* in vinegar, honey and thyme – or sweet 'n' sour pork.

Patsouras, 26 I. Metaxás, opposite the Sailing Club, **t** 267 102 2779. Long-established and popular for its local meat dishes, spicy sausage, and *panzeta* (smoked pork).

Porta, 9 Rizopastón, **t** 267 102 5979 (€30). Greek and 'ethnic' cuisine, with tasty surprises.

Tsivras, in a side street by the market, near the Shell station. One of a dying breed of old Greek restaurants, still serving authentic and inexpensive local dishes packed with taste. *Closed from 5pm.*

After dark the trendy cafés along Lithóstrato Street are popular. Try the **Bass Club** near the Archaeology Museum, **t** 267 102 5020, on Thurs, Fri and Sat nights.

Lassí ✉ 28100
Monte Neo, t 267 102 2646.
A local favourite for seafood.

Oskars, Fanari Rd, **t** 267 102 3438.
Tortoises wander in the garden, while
waiters lead Greek dances in a
grandiose but pretty setting.

Lixoúri and the Palikí Peninsula

Ferries trundle regularly across the bay from Argostóli to the
westerly Palikí peninsula and **Lixoúri** (ΛΗΧΟΥΡΙ), Kefaloniá's second
city, all new houses on wide streets. Lixoúri is known for its sense of
humour, and in its central Plateía Petrítsi the town has put up a
dapper **statue of Andréas Laskarátos**. Born into the island aristocracy, Laskarátos (1811–1901) was a poet and satirist who directed
most of his broadsides at the Orthodox Church; he heckled the
clergy so much that they finally excommunicated him – in Greek,
aforismós, meaning that the body will not decompose after death.
Laskarátos responded by collecting his innumerable children's shoes
and returned to the priest, asking him to please excommunicate the
footwear, too.

Iakovátos Mansion
*t 267 109 1325; open
Tues–Sun 8.30–3*

You can get a glimmer of what pre-quake Lixoúri was like at the
west end of town at the **Iakovátos Mansion**, a rare survivor, complete
with its original decoration, library of rare books and museum of
icons going back to the 10th century. Fresco fragments and wooden
iconostases salvaged from the earthquake have been installed in the
town's newer churches. North of Lixoúri, unexcavated ancient Pali
(or Pale), the only city on Kefaloniá to take part in the Persian wars,
stood on the hill of Paliókastro.

The **Palikí Peninsula** is the least touristed area on Kefaloniá but is
well endowed with beaches, including **Lépeda**, 2km from Lixoúri,
with strikingly reddish-orange sand, near the cave-church of

Could the Palikí Peninsula be Homer's Ithaca?

This is the question posed by *Odysseus Unbound* (2005) by Robert Brittlestone, James Diggle and John
Underhill: is the northern Palikí Peninsula Homer's Ithaca? Was it once an island, with a sea channel
instead of an isthmus? One essential clue is in this description by Odysseus himself when he says:

*Around her a ring of islands circle side by side,
Doulichion, Same, wooded Zachynthos too, but mine
lies low and away, the farthest out to sea,
rearing into the western dusk.*

Doulichion, the authors reckon, is the island currently known as Ithaca, that took the name when the
original Ithaca was destroyed and its inhabitants took refuge there – at some point. Kefaloniá lies on one
of the most tectonically unstable places on earth. Minor tremors are a way of life, and one, on the scale of
the 1953 earthquake, may have filled in the sea channel (quite possible, according to geologists), uniting
the original 'Ithaca' with Kefaloniá. Many of the other features square up as well, and now the hunt is on
for Odysseus' palace; at Kastélli there are broken walls and potsherds from the right date. The recent find
of Ajax's Palace on Salamína (*see* p.125) has heated up the argument considerably; for the latest
information, *see* www.odysseus-unbound.org.

Where to Stay and Eat in Lixoúri

Lixoúri ✉ 28200

Cephalonia Palace, by Xi Beach, t 267 109 3190, *www.kefaloniapalacehotel.gr* (€€€€€). Big hotel with pools and plenty for families; all rooms with sea-view and balcony. *Open May–Oct.*

La Cité, 28 Octovríou, t 267 109 2701 (€€). Quiet, relaxed and friendly, with a pool and palm-fringed garden.

Summery, t 267 109 1771, *www.hotel summery.gr* (€€). A tranquil place to stay near the centre, with a pool.

Kritonou Centre, on the north end of the gulf of Lixoúri, t 267 102 4817, *www.kritonou.gr* (€€). In an olive grove, one- or two-week holistic holidays with optional enlightenment courses for mind, body and spirit and organically grown food.

Apolafsi, Lépeda, t 267 109 1691. Tasia and family run a good restaurant and bar with a pool, and have some moderate **rooms** (€€) as well.

Zorbas, 25 Martioú, t 267 109 3129. Traditional and friendly, with good casseroles and meat pies.

Ag. Paraskeví. In the same area, **Soulári**'s church of Ag. Marína has fine icons and a Venetian doorway; the next village, **Mantzavináta**, has good frescoes in its church of Ag. Sofía. From here a road leads south to **Ag. Geórgios** (or Megá Lákkos) beach, a long stretch of golden-red sand, which merges to the west with the long crescent of Xi; buses run there in summer. Just south of it is the **Kounópetra**, a monolith a few inches from the shore that rocked to and fro, pulsating at the rate of 20 times a minute. The earthquake of 1953 fouled up the magic and likewise destroyed the houses on now deserted **Vardianá islet**.

West of Lixoúri the road passes **Chavriáta**, 'balcony of the Ionian', en route to **Kipouríon Monastery**, rebuilt as it was before the quake in the 1960s and perched on the west cliffs, with spectacular sunset views. The peninsula is shot full of caves: the best, **Drákondi Spílio**, 40m (130ft) deep, can be reached from the monastery with a guide.

The sparsely populated northern Palikí has a scattering of pretty villages with beaches such as **Delaportáta**, **Kaminaráta** with a lovely tiny taverna with huge views, **Damoulináta** near Platía Ámmos beach ('300 steps down to heaven', they say, but also 300 steps back to your car), and the large, lovely white sands of **Petáni** (Paralía Xoúras) which are rarely overcrowded. Even more remote is sandy **Ag. Spyrídon**, tucked into the northernmost tip of the peninsula, reached via the village of **Athéras** – a memory of its Homeric name, Arethusa, according to Robert Brittlestone.

South Kefaloniá

Southeast of Argostóli: The Livathó and Mount Aínos

Most of Kefaloniá's rural population lives southeast of Argostóli in the fertile region of valleys, gardens and rolling hills called the Livathó. After Platís Gialós Beach, emerging free from the tourist

Kefaloniá in a Glass

Kefaloniá is the island of robóla, a grape variety introduced by the Venetians in the 13th century that ferments into distinctive lemony dry white wines. Lately it's been better than ever: the robóla from **Gentilini**, a small vineyard in Miniés owned by Nicólas Cosmetátos (t 267 104 1618; *open June–Sept Mon–Sat 10.30–2.30 and 5.30–8.30*), has been something of a revelation, demonstrating just how good Greek wines can be. In 1978, Cosmetátos purchased an estate in these limestone hills, planted vines, built a small but ultra-modern winery, and carved a cellar in the cliffs to attain the perfect storage temperature. Look for his crisp pale gold Gentili Animus, 100 per cent robóla, and Gentili Fume, a robóla aged in oak casks, with an oaky fragrance. Gentili also does a fine muscat fortified dessert wine (Amando) and a lovely apéritif wine (half muscat, half robóla) called Dulcis, which goes perfectly with fresh fruit.

tinsel is **Miniés**, home to a very ruined Doric temple from the 6th century BC, a small beach and some of Greece's finest white wine.

The coastal road south of Miniés continues to **Svoronáta**, a sweet and very Greek resort – preserved, perhaps, because of its proximity to the not very noisy airport – where the pale sands of Ávithos Beach look out to the tiny islet of **Días**. This is named after a tiny islet off the coast of Crete, and like that one had an altar to Zeus: sacrifices, they say, were co-ordinated by smoke signals from Mount Aínos. **Domáta**, the next village east, boasts Kefaloniá's oldest olive tree (able to squeeze 20 people in the hollow of its trunk) and the beautiful church of the Panagía, with a reconstructed Baroque façade and a 19th-century carved iconostasis gilded with 12,000 melted gold sovereigns.

Nearby **Kourkomeláta** was rebuilt by the wealthy Kefalonian shipowner Vergotís, with a touch of California, complete with an arty neoclassical cultural centre. At **Metaxáta**, where printing was introduced to Greece, Byron rented a house for four months in 1823, finished *Don Juan*, his satirical rejection of romanticism, then dithered over what to do as the representative of the Greek Committee in London while each Greek faction fighting for independence jostled for his attention – and his money. Just northwest, **Lakídra**, rebuilt by French donations after the earthquake, is the most important village of the Livathó; in the suburb of Kallithéa, near the plain little church of Ag. Nikólaos ton Aliprantídon, four **Mycenaean tombs** yielded a good deal of pottery from 1250 to 1150 BC. Byron used to sit here on a rock, admiring the views, and a line of his poetry is inscribed on a plaque: ΑΝ ΕΙΜΑΙ ΠΟΙΗΤΗΣ ΤΟ ΟΦΕΙΛΩ ΕΙΣ ΤΟΝ ΑΕΡΑ ΤΗΣ ΕΛΛΑΔΑΣ ('If I am a poet, I owe it to the air of Greece').

Inland: Ag. Andréas, Ag. Geórgios and Ag. Gerásimos

North of Metaxáta is the Byzantine convent called **Ag. Andréas** or Panagía Milapídia (the 'Apple Virgin') after an icon discovered on an apple tree trunk. Perhaps the one and only good deed of the quake of 1953 was to shake loose the whitewash on the walls, revealing frescoes that date back to the 13th century (in the chancel) and the

Ag. Andréas museum
t 267 106 9700; open Mon–Sat 8.30–2; adm

17th and 18th centuries (along the nave). A museum houses icons, fresco fragments and relics orphaned by the earthquake, among them the prized Veneto-Byzantine icon of Panagía Akáthistos, painted in 1700 by Cretan Stéfanos Tsankárolos. A new basilica houses the most important prize: the sole of St Andrew's right foot, donated in the 17th century by Princess Roxanne of Epiros. Don't miss the intriguing Mycenaean tombs, signposted nearby at Mazarakáta (the gate is usually open): excavated into the rock, reached by narrow paths or steps wedged in the stone to resemble giant Vs.

Castle of Ag. Geórgios
open June–Oct Tues–Sat 8.30–3, Sun 9–3

Above the church looms the tree-filled polygonal Castle of Ag. Geórgios, spread over a 320m (1,050ft) hill, with a grand view of the surrounding plains and mountains – you can drive up, although parking at the top can be dicey. Founded by the Byzantine emperors, the citadel was completely rebuilt by the Venetians and Greeks under Nikólaos Tsimarás, after the fierce siege of 1500 dislodged the Turks. The island capital until 1757, Ag. Geórgios once held a population of 14,000; now store rooms, prisons, Venetian coats of arms, a Catholic church and a bridge built by the French during their brief occupation slowly crumble away.

To the east, on the green plain of Omalós, the **Monastery of Ag. Gerásimos**, dwarfed by an enormous plane tree and a rococo belfry, houses the bones of Kefaloniá's patron in a silver reliquary, in a church built over his grotto hermitage. If half of all men on Corfu are named Spíros after St Spyrídon, half of all male Kefalonians are named Gerásimos. The saint's speciality is intervening in mental disturbances and exorcizing demons, especially if the patient keeps an all-night vigil at his church on his feast day, 20 October. After paying your respects, go robóla-tasting at the Omalós wine co-operative, Si.Ro.Ke.

Si.Ro.Ke
t 267 108 6301; open April–Oct Mon–Fri 7am–8.30pm; Nov–Mar Mon–Fri 7–3

From the Argostóli–Sámi road, a branch winds up the majestic Aínos range. At one time these mountains were completely blanketed with *Abies cefalonica*, Kefaloniá's indigenous black firs; they were so dense that Strabo called the island Melaina ('The Dark'). The Minoans used the firs for the pillars at Knossos, and the Venetians cut them down for masts for their galleys, but two fires, in 1590 and 1797, share the blame for destroying nine-tenths of the forest. In 1962 what remained was made into **Mount Aínos National Park**. Beyond the radar station, rough tracks circle the mountains from where you can hike past the radio masts to the highest peak, **Mégas Sóros** (1,628m/5,341ft); from where, on a clear day, the Ionian islands resemble chops on a blue platter. Hesiod mentioned the 8th-century BC sanctuary of Aenesian Zeus, the lord of the mountain, which stood just below Mégas Sóros; ash-piles from the massive animal sacrifices remained until the last century. A handful of wild horses, descendants of herds left up here to graze before the Second World War, gallop free in the National Park – the best place to spot them is above the village of **Agrínia** and its **Moní Zoodóchos Pigí**, by a spring that provides their only reliable source of water.

The South Coast: Beaches and the Virgin's Little Snakes

The south coast of Kefaloniá is trimmed with sandy beaches shielded from the north winds by Mégas Sóros. There are good strands just down from **Spartiá**, under sheer white cliffs, and at **Trapezáki**, 1.5km from the tiny port of **Pessáda** (ΠΕΣΑΔΑ) – Kefaloniá's link to Zákynthos. East, below **Karavádos**, is another pretty little sandy beach with a taverna perched above, and plane trees and reeds spread behind.

The longest, most crowded beach, white **Lourdáta** (ΛΟΥΡΔΑΤΑ), was named after the English lords who came here in the 19th century, attracted by the hot microclimate, although the stiff walk (and traffic) up the steep streets from the beach can be dire. A nicer walk, starting in the village square, with an enormous plane tree, is along Kefaloniá's first **nature trail**, blazed by the World Wide Fund for Nature – a 2½hr stroll past the ruined **Monastery of Síssia**, founded in 1218 by St Francis of Assisi (hence its name) on his return from the Crusades in Egypt, and converted to Orthodoxy in the 16th century; a new monastery was built just above after 1953.

Kateliós, focus of much new building, has springs, greenery, a beach that curves along Moúnda Bay and fish tavernas that attract diners from across Kefaloniá. Just east, **Potomákia Beach**, below **Ratzaklí**, is a loggerhead turtle nesting place from June to mid-August, when you should take care on the sand and avoid the beach at night.

Kefaloniá's most curious religious rite takes place in **Markópoulo**, a village on a natural balcony. During the first 15 days of August, small, harmless snakes, 'inoffensive to the Virgin Mary', appear in the streets. Formerly they slithered into the church (rebuilt after the earthquake) and mysteriously disappeared near the silver icon of the Panagía Fidón ('Virgin of the Snakes'). Nowadays, to keep the snakes from being run over, the villagers collect them in glass jars and bring them to the church, where they are released after the service and immediately disappear as they did in the past. Although sceptics believe that the church is simply along the route of the little snakes' natural migratory trail, the faithful point out that they fail to appear when the island is in distress – as during the German occupation and in 1953.

Skála (ΣΚΑΛΑ), with its long beach and low dunes, is the biggest resort in this corner, with plenty of water sports, sunbeds, bars – and construction sites. The ancient Romans liked the area as well; a Roman villa has 2nd-century AD mosaic floors, one portraying Envy being devoured by wild beasts while two men make sacrifices. Two kilometres north of Skála, there's a 7th-century BC **Temple of Apollo**, although most of its porous stone was cannibalized to build the nearby chapel of Ag. Geórgios.

Póros (ΠΟΡΟΣ), spread over three bays, with direct ferry links to Killíni, was originally the port of Pronnoi, one of the four ancient cities of Kefaloniá. In the 1820s, British High Commissioner Napier settled Maltese farmers here to create a model farming community called New Malta, that quickly flopped. Now the village, set over clear turquoise waters, is very Greek, with a pleasant waterfront and long shingle beach to the north. Above this, on a dirt track, is the island's oldest monastery, the 8th-century **Moní Theotókos** at Átros, rebuilt 17 times and famous for its sunrise views.

The location of the acropolis of ancient Pronnoi is the subject of some debate. If you do the easy 3hr Póros walking trail, you'll pass one contender: the walls in a commanding position above Póros called Káto Páchni. The village of **Tzanáta** (on the trail, or drive up through the wild and narrow Póros Gap, carved by the impatient Heracles, who couldn't be bothered to go over the mountains) made the news in 1992, when Danish and Greek archaeologists uncovered a 12th-century BC **Mycenaean tholos tomb** (signposted on a dirt road), the largest – 6.8m (22ft) in diameter – and the most important ever discovered in western Greece. It was built over an older tomb, and was probably royal – although nothing identified it with Odysseus. The roof collapsed in Venetian times when the tomb was used as a house. Although robbed in Mycenaean times, gold jewellery, copper tools and sealstones were found (now in the Pátras museum) along with the remains of 72 bodies in an ossuary nearby – the occupants of the older tomb, reburied with their gems.

Mycenaean tholos tomb
open Tues–Sun 8.30–3

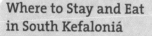

Where to Stay and Eat in South Kefaloniá

★ Trapezaki Bay >>

Miniés ✉ 28100
Iris Studios, t 267 104 1121, *www.minies-apartments.gr* (€€). Garden studios near the beach.
Drosia, t 267 104 1626. Popular spick-and-span taverna, a favourite for weddings.

Keramiés
Taverna Anna. People drive up from Argostóli for the succulent meat dishes (*around €15*).

Spartiá/Pessáda ✉ 28083
Sunrise Inn, 1.5km from Pessáda port, *www.sunrise-inn.gr*, **t** 267 106 9586 (€€€). Comfortable and with air-conditioning, set in the trees, with a pool and children's activities.

Karavados Beach Hotel, near Ag. Thomas Beach, **t** 267 106 9400, *www.kbhotel.gr* (€€€). Offers two pools, tennis and family rooms.
To Steki tou Lefteri, Spartiá. Best food in these parts, and *simpatico* owners.

Trapezáki/Lourdáta ✉ 28083
Trapezaki Bay, 10mins from the beach, **t** 267 103 1501, *www.trapezakibayhotel.gr* (€€€; *breakfast included*). The hospitable Nikos and Sofia made their money in New York jewellery and run this relaxing gem of a hotel for couples with a pool and restaurant. Price includes free transfers from the airport; no children under 16.
Lara, a few mins from the sea at Lourdáta, **t** 267 103 1157, *www.lara.gr* (€€€–€€). Pleasant moderate-sized hotel with a pool and playground, set in greenery. *Open May–Oct.*

Klimatis, by the sea in Lourdáta, t 267 103 1151. Solid good food and tasty fried spuds.

Skála ✉ 28082

For a list of accommodation in Skála, see www.skala-kefalonia.gr.

Nine Muses, by the beach, t 267 108 3563, www.9museshotel.com (€€€). Spacious rooms and suites in a tasteful bungalow village mini-complex, set in lush gardens with a pool.

Tara Beach, by the beach, t 267 108 3341, www.tarabeach.gr (€€€–€€). Rooms and bungalows in a pretty setting. Open May–Oct.

Aliki, overlooking the sea, t 267 108 3427 (€€). Good value and a large garden.

Pikiona, on the beachfront, t 267 108 3410. Restaurant-cocktail bar and pool, serving breakfast, light lunches and pricey but excellent traditional Greek and Mediterranean cooking in the evening. Closed Oct–April.

Pines, on the beachfront, t 267 108 3559. Classic island and international dishes in a lovely setting, with special menus for two.

Póros ✉ 28082

Oceanis, t 267 407 2581, www. hotel oceanis.gr (€€€–€€). Small hotel with a pool. Open May–Oct.

Pantelis, on the waterfront, t 267 407 2484, pantelis@hotmail.com (€€–€). Good seafood restaurant and large, basic rooms with fridge, air-con and sea-views; a bargain, except in Aug. They have two apartments.

Romanza. A restaurant one flight up on a rock in the village. Greek cuisine and the best view.

North Kefaloniá:
Caves, Beaches and Castles

Affable low-key **Sámi**, looking out towards Ithaca, replaces ancient Same; on the hills above are the ancient walls, where the citizens put up a heroic four-month resistance to the Romans in 187 BC before their inevitable defeat and sale into slavery. In 2000, Sámi endured a modern siege for the shooting of the film version of *Captain Corelli's Mandolin*. A mock-Venetian waterfront façade was constructed to recreate old Argostóli; for the first time in almost 60 years, Italian artillery was seen thundering through the streets. Many older residents were dewy-eyed at the realistic reconstruction of the island's architecture, but little remains to recall the filming, outside of a new road to the exquisite pebble beach of **Antisámos** (or 'Captain Corelli's beach' – the film setting for the Italian army camp) 5km east, set amid forested hills spilling down to the clear water. It has since become so busy that it now has a pay car park.

Sámi is also close to some 17 caves, many containing lakes and dangerous, precipitous drops. Two are open for visits. Down a long flight of steps, **Drogaráti Cave** is a den of fabulous orange and yellow stalactites; one of its great chambers has such fine acoustics that Maria Callas came here to sing and concerts are frequently held in summer. The other, **Melissáni** or 'Purple Cave', is just north of Sámi; gondoliers will paddle you across its salt water lake (supplied by the swallow holes near Argostóli; *see* p.482), into a shimmering play of blues and violets caught by the sun filtering through a hole in the roof, 30m (100ft) overhead; the effects are at their best at around

Drogaráti Cave
t 267 102 2950; open May–Oct 9–6; July and Aug 9–9; adm

Melissáni Cave
same hours as Drogaráti

noon. After leaving the cave, the sea water flows into nearby **Karavómylos Lake** – a journey that takes two weeks altogether from Argostóli.

North, **Ag. Efimía** (ΑΓ. ΕΥΦΗΜΙΑ) is a picturesque fishing village, popular yachtie haven and a cosy, fairly central resort base for the whole island, with a scattering of white pebbly beaches nearby along the Sámi road. A mosaic in Archeotíton Street is believed to have been the floor of the early Byzantine church of Ag. Efimía; the pretty village of **Drakopouláta**, a few kilometres above the port, was spared by the earthquake. West, across the slopes of Mount Ag. Dinatí, are more traditional villages – and goats with silver-plated teeth, owing to the high mica content in the soil.

Up the Northwest Coast to Mýrtos, Ássos and Fiskárdo

The journey from Argostóli north to Fiskárdo is magnificently scenic – perhaps a good reason to take the bus, so you don't have to keep your eyes on the road, although there are some very tempting stops along the way. A side road leads to **Davgáta**, where the little **Museum of Natural History of Cephalonia and Ithaca** has exhibits on the two islands' flora and fauna. The first good beach, white pebbly **Ag. Kyriakí**, rims the isthmus linking the Palikí Peninsula to the rest of Kefaloniá, a few kilometres below the village of Zóla. At **Angónas**, on the Argostóli road, the square has paintings by local folk artist Rázos.

Museum of Natural History of Cephalonia and Ithaca
t 267 108 4400; open June–Sept daily 9–3; Oct–May Mon–Fri 9–3

Eight km north, below **Divaráta**, curves the **bay of Mýrtos**, Kefaloniá's picture-perfect beauty, where sheer white cliffs carpeted with maquis frame a stunning crescent of white pebbles against a deep sea so blue it hurts. Yet think twice before descending into the picture: the road is precipitous, the current dangerous and it can be baking hot. If you do go, take provisions (and a hat).

⭐ Ássos and Mýrtos Bay

From the corniche road, the fishing hamlet of **Ássos** and its Venetian citadel look like toys. Kefaloniá's most bijou village, rebuilt by the French after the earthquake, Ássos sits on the translucent waters of an enclosed bay, although the once pristine causeway now sprouts toadstool maisonettes. The Venetian **fortress**, reached on foot (or, much more easily, by car) dates from 1585, when the Turks occupied Lefkáda and began raiding this coast; it was the seat of the Venetian *proveditor* until 1797. His house survives in ruins, along with the church of San Marco and a prison, used until 1815. Go at sunset, when the views are pure magic. The venerable olive tree in Plateía Páris shaded the sermons of St Cosmás the Aetolian, an 18th-century missionary; at one point, the story goes, his words were being drowned out by the cicadas. Cosmás told the insects to hush, and they did.

Inland, not always on paved roads, are seldom-visited villages of the peninsula. One, **Varí**, has by its cemetery the late Byzantine

Robert Guiscard: Genius and Extrovert

The name Fiskárdo is derived from Robert Guiscard, the *terror mundi* of his day, whose very name made popes, emperors and kings tremble in their boots. Born in 1017, the sixth of 13 sons of a minor Norman nobleman named Tancred de Hauteville, Robert began his career as a mercenary working for (and against) the Byzantines and Lombards in Italy. By a mix of adroit military leadership, an eye for the main chance and cunning (his nickname *Guiscard* means 'crafty'), he made himself Duke of Apulia, master of southern Italy. Other brothers came to join him; the most successful was the youngest, Roger, who married a cousin of William the Conqueror, defeated the Arabs of Sicily and founded a dynasty of Norman-Sicilian kings.

In 1085, after defeating Emperor Henry IV's attempt to dethrone Pope Gregory VII (Hildebrand) and sacking Rome, Robert Guiscard and his Normans were on their way to do the same to Constantinople, on the excuse that Emperor Michael VII had locked up his empress – Guiscard's daughter – in a convent. Guiscard had just scored a major victory over the Venetians (then Byzantium's allies) at Corfu, when a typhoid epidemic laid low the 68-year-old warrior; Guiscard was brought ashore at this point in northern Kefaloniá and died in the arms of his Lombard warrior wife, Sichelgaita. His body was preserved in salt and sent back to Italy to be buried with his brothers; the coffin was washed overboard in a storm, but later recovered off Otranto and buried at Venosa. As John Julius Norwich wrote in *The Normans of the South*: 'He was that rarest of combinations, a genius and an extrovert...a gigantic blond buccaneer who not only carved out for himself the most extraordinary career of the Middle Ages but who also, quite shamelessly, enjoyed it.' Such was the power of his name that the old pirate was granted a posthumous and false reputation as a virtuous Crusader, and two centuries after his death Dante installed him in *Paradiso*.

church of **Panagía Kougianá** (you'll probably have to ask for the key) with frescoes by a folk artist who decorated the left wall with scenes from hell, and the right one with paradise.

Continuing up to **Cape Dafnoúdi**, the northernmost tip of Kefaloniá, the road passes the white rocky beach of **Chalikéri**, where people come to soak in the exceptionally briny water and leave pleasantly pickled. In **Ántipata Erissóu**, the Russian church of 1934 was built by a Kefalonian who made a fortune in the Soviet Union.

The trendiest (and priciest) village on the island, **Fiskárdo** (ΦΙΣΚΑΡΔΟ) is Kefaloniá's St-Tropez, its 18th-century houses gathered in a brightly coloured apron around a port filled in summer with mega-yachts. A fluke in its innermost geological depths spared the town in the 1953 earthquake, and it's a poignant reminder of the architecture Kefaloniá once had. This and its setting have inspired a building fever, and now the entire north cape is dotted with villas and studios. Four carved stone sarcophagi and the ruins of a Roman bath are fenced off by the Panormos Hotel. The **Nautical and Environmental Club Museum**, in the old school building, displays objects trawled up from the depths (including parts of a Bristol Beaufighter shot down in 1943 and a whale skeleton), as well as marine life and current projects; ask here about their dolphin-spotting tours. Fiskárdo's beaches are not top-notch, but there are others nearby such as sand and shingle **Embelíssi**, **Dafnoúdi** and **Alatiés**, the last one with natural rock pools.

Nautical and Environmental Club Museum
t 267 404 1081, www.fnec.gr; open summer daily 10–2 and 5–9

Where to Stay and Eat in North Kefaloniá

UK tour operators (*see* p.60) tend to block-book much of the accommodation here.

Sámi ✉ 28080

Sami Beach, at Karavómilos, **t** 267 402 2824, *www.samibeachhotel.gr* (€€€, incl. breakfast). Pleasant and friendly hotel with a pool, close to the beach. *Open May–Oct.*

Kastro, on the beach road, **t** 267 402 2656, *www.kastrohotel.com* (€€). Family-run hotel with sea-view balconies, convenient for ferries. *Open April–Oct.*

Karavomilos Beach Camping, 1km from town, **t** 267 402 2480, *www.camping-karavomilos.gr.* Well equipped.

Gorgona ('Mermaid'), **t** 267 402 2202. Cooking by Mamma in a reliable old favourite. **Delfini** is also good.

Riviera. Pizzas and local specialities such as octopus pie and meat cooked in a ceramic *stámna*.

Ag. Efimía ✉ 28081

Boulevard Pyllaros, on the waterfront, **t** 267 406 1800, *www.greece-kefallonia.com* (€€€). Rooms and suites full of dark repro furniture, as well as boat hire and tennis. The same people run the more affordable **Boulevard Panorama Studios** behind town. *Open all year.*

Gonatas, Paradise Beach, a 5min amble from the port, **t** 267 406 1213 (€€€). Family-run, with a pool and lovely sea-views, but mediocre service, mediocre breakfast. *Open May–Oct.*

Moustakis, **t** 267 406 1060 (€€). An institutional alternative if everything else is booked up. *Open April–Sept.*

Finikas, on the waterfront, **t** 267 406 1507. For pizza and traditional food.

Ássos ✉ 28084

Papspiratos, **t** 267 405 1532 (€€). Rooms and studios 50m from the beach.

Platanos, **t** 267 405 1381. The best in the village; the English-speaking owner is a mine of information and typical Kefalonian irony. *Open May–Oct.*

Fiskárdo ✉ 28084

Emelisse, **t** 267 404 1200, *www.arthotel.gr* (€€€€€). For pure self-indulgence: heated infinity pools, tennis, bikes, a new spa, a gourmet Mediterranean restaurant and comfy terrace sofas where guests cuddle during the magical sunsets, surrounded by hundreds of candles.

Filoxenia, on the old harbour, **t** 267 404 1319 (€€€€–€€€). The old Venetian government house, now converted into a six-room hotel with an enchanting inner courtyard. *Open April–Nov.*

Agnantia, 4km east of Fiskárdo at Tselantáta, **t** 267 405 1801, *www.agnantia.com* (€€€, breakfast incl.). New hotel built in the style of a traditional mansion with 13 cosy rooms by the sea, in a serene location overlooking Ithaca. *Open May–Oct.*

Dendrinos, just out of town, **t** 267 404 1326 (€€€). Rooms renovated in the traditional style.

Nikolas, perched above the harbour, **t** 267 404 1307 (€€€). Has a fine location, rooms and food – with nightly Greek dancing.

Stella, right on the water, **t** 267 404 1211, *www.stella-apartments.gr* (€€€–€€). Studios and apartments.

Nitsa, **t** 267 404 1327 (€€). Cheaper rooms and a studio.

Sotiria Tselenti, over the Fiskárdo bakery, **t** 267 404 1204 (€).

Lagoundera, just back from the water, **t** 267 404 1275. Good, friendly grill house; try the fresh anchovies when they are in season.

Tassia, **t** 267 404 1205 (€55). Rub shoulders with visiting celebrities – or pretend you're one – at this restaurant run by cookbook-writing Tassia Denrinoú, nestling amongst the yachts. Seafood grilled over an open pit is the order of the day.

Vasso's, **t** 267 404 1276 (€45). On the south end of the marina, famous for its enormous portions and delicious salads, lobster and seafood.

Alatiés, 5km away on Alatiés beach in Mángano, **t** 697 758 4781. Pretty restaurant serving tasty meatballs, cod fritters, and other delicacies. *Closed Oct–April.*

 Filoxenia >>

★ Tassia >>

11

The Ionian Islands | Kefaloniá

Kýthera (ΚΥΘΗΡΑ)

Tucked under the great dangling paw of the Peloponnese, Kýthera, the isle of the goddess of love, is a wonderful slice of traditional Greece, on the way to nowhere. It owes a good part of its attraction to that fact. The opening of the Corinth Canal in 1893 doomed even the minor commercial importance Kýthera once had by virtue of its position between the Ionian and Aegean seas; even today, unless you fly from Athens, getting there by bus and ferry is awkward and time-consuming. In the 20th century most of the population drifted over to the other side of the world; some 100,000 people of Kýtheran origin now live in Australia or 'Big Kýthera', as the 3,000 who remain in Greece call it. If it can't quite match the shimmering

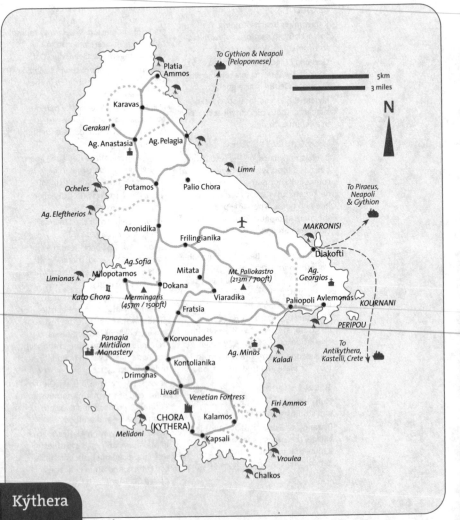

Getting to and around Kýthera

By air: There are two flights a day from Athens in season; **airport information**: t 273 603 8395; tickets from **Olympic Airways**, 49 El. Venizélou, Pótamos, t 273 603 3362.

By sea: Kýthera has two ports, **Diakófti** and **Ag. Pelagía** (sometimes used in high winds). In season there are two daily ferries from Neápoli, on the nearby mainland, t 273 603 4371; year-round connections on **ANEN Lines** between Piraeus, Neápoli, Gýthion, Kalamáta, Antikýthera and Kissamos (Crete); contact **Porfyra Travel** (see overleaf) for schedules. **Port authority**: Diakófti, t 273 603 4222, Ag. Pelagía, t 273 603 3280.

From Kapsáli, a caique visits nearby beaches and Avgó Island, t 273 603 1222.

By road: There are no **buses**, but **taxis** charge set fees. **Hire cars** (and **motorbikes** and **scooters**) from **Panayiotis** in Kapsáli and at the airport, t 273 603 1600, panayioti@otenet.gr; and cars from **Cerigo**, at the airport and **Chóra**, t 273 603 1363; **Active**, in Ag. Pelagía, t 273 603 3749, mact@aias.gr; and **Anna**, in Ag. Pelagía, t 273 603 4153, romadica@otenet.gr.

luxuriance of Watteau's sumptuous masterpiece, *Pèlerinage à l'Ile de Cythère*, it does have stunning beaches and a handful of 'sights', and cliffs and meadows decorated with yellow sempreviva, 'eternal life', which the locals dry and hang around the house.

History

After Cronus, son of Gaia, took his golden sickle and castrated his father, Uranos, he cast the bloody member into the sea. This gave birth to Aphrodite, who according to Hesiod's *Theogony* rose out of the foam on her scallop shell at Kýthera, accompanied by Eros and Himeros (Desire). She apparently found it far too puny for her taste and drifted off east to Paphos, Cyprus. A sanctuary dedicated to Aphrodite on Kýthera was the most sacred of all her temples in Greece, but scarcely a trace remains today. Aphrodite was called Astarte by Kýthera's first settlers, the Phoenicians, who came for its murex shells, the source of a reddish purple dye for royal garments – hence the island's other ancient name, Porphyrousa. The Minoans, the first in Greece to worship Aphrodite, made Kýthera a trading counter. Its location between Crete and the mainland, and between the Aegean and Ionian seas, was a busy neighbourhood, and the island was in great demand: Kýthera has been invaded 80 times in recorded history. Particularly frightful were the 10th-century incursions of the Saracens based on Crete, which caused the island to be abandoned until Nikephóros Phokás reconquered Crete.

From the 12th century, the Eudaimonoioannis family from Monemvássia ruled Kýthera. The Venetians occupied the island in 1204, but with the help of Emperor Michael Palaeológos Kýthera was regained for the Eudaimonoioannis and served as a refuge for Byzantine nobles until 1537, when Barbarossa stopped on his way home after his unsuccessful siege of Corfu and devastated the island. The Venetians took over again in the 16th century and in their slurry Italian accents redubbed the island Cerigo. In 1864 Kýthera was ceded to Greece by the British with the other Ionian islands. These days, however, it's administered from Piraeus.

Useful Information on Kýthera

Porfyra Travel, Livádi, **t** 273 603 1888, *www.kythira.info*. For ferry tickets, accommodation, etc.

Glass-bottomed boat tours, around Kýthera's and Elafónissos' beaches and caves. Contact **Spiros Kasmiatis**, **t** 697 402 2079.

Kýthera Festivals

Early Aug: Two-day wine festival in Mitáta.
6 Aug: Traditional dance party in Avlemonas.
Oct: Photographic meetings, with exhibitions around the island.

Chóra (Kýthera)

Chóra (ΧΩΡΑ), the capital of the island, is a pretty-as-a-picture-postcard blue and white Greek village hanging above the sea, guarded by a ruined 16th-century Venetian castle, built over a Byzantine fort of 1150. Its location was supposedly selected by pigeons, who took the tools of the builders from a less protected site; inside the walls, the residence of the former governor houses the island's Venetian and English archives and two churches built by the Venetians, Catholic **Panagía Myrtidiótissa** and Orthodox **Panagía Orfáni**. Ten old **Venetian mansions** in Chóra still retain their coats of arms, and a small **Archaeology Museum** has artefacts from Minoan times to gravestones from the English occupation. Between June and October, the **Tzannes Gallery** displays paintings of the island by New Yorker-Kýtheran George Tzannes.

Archaeology Museum
t 273 503 1739; open Tues–Sun 8.30–3

Tzannes Gallery
t 273 603 8292; www.tzannesart.com

Below Chóra, **Kapsáli** (ΚΑΨΑΛΙ) is the most developed resort on the island, with its two pebble and sand beaches, one very sheltered and boaty, the other a bit more exposed. Kapsáli's **Avgó** (egg) **islet** is said to be the spot where Aphrodite was born.

Kálamos, just east, is within walking distance. One of its churches, **Ag. Nikítas**, has a pretty bell tower, and there is a restaurant and some rooms for rent by the square. Dirt roads continue across the rugged landscape to various beaches; nearest is pebbly **Chálkos**, set in a beautiful, almost enclosed bay.

★ Nostos ›› Where to Stay and Eat in Chora (Kýthera)

For a complete list of rooms on the island, see *www.kythera.gr*.

Chóra (Kýthera) ✉ 80100

Margarita, off the main street, **t** 273 603 1711, *www.hotel-margarita.com* (€€€). A dozen attractive rooms in a 19th-century mansion. New French owners promise croissants, quiches and English tea. *Open all year.*

Nostos, **t** 273 603 1056, *www.nostos-kythera.gr* (€€€). In the centre, a 19th-century residence with seven antique-filled rooms and a café serving home-made breakfasts. *Open all year.*

Xenonas Keiti, **t** 273 603 1318 (€€€). Beautiful 18th-century mansion that has hosted at least two Greek prime ministers on their visits to the island.

Castello, near the fortress, **t** 273 603 1069, *www.castelloapts-kythera.gr* (€€). Three studios and six rooms leading off a walled garden. *Open all year.*

Ta Kythera, just inland at Manitochóri, t 273 603 1563 (€). Clean, pleasant double rooms. *Open June–Aug.*

Belvedere, t 273 603 1892. Pizzeria-cum-grill house with a magnificent view.

Zorba's, t 273 603 1655. Old-fashioned local classic – the best in Chóra.

Kapsáli ✉ 80100

Kalokerines Katikies Rigas, t 273 603 1265, *www.greek-tourism.gr/kythera/rigas* (€€€). Upmarket apartments, 50m from the sea.

Raikos, between Chóra and Kapsáli, t 273 603 1629, *www.raikoshotel.gr* (€€€). One of the island's posher places, light and bright, with a pool and water sports. *Open May–Sept.*

Iannis Avgerinos, on the beach, t 273 603 1189 (€€€–€€). Rooms and apartments converted from fishermen's huts, in an olive grove.

Vasilis Bungalows, t 273 603 1125, *www.kythirabungalowsvasili.gr* (€€€–€€). Stylish independent studios sleeping up to four in an olive grove overlooking the sea, with satellite TV.

Daponte Stella, t 273 603 1245 (€€). Peaceful and private, with access to the gorgeous secluded beach of Sparagário.

Poulmentis Rooms, t 273 603 1003 (€€). Clean and comfortable.

Filio, just inland in Kálamos, t 273 603 1054 (€). Rooms to rent at a charming taverna, one of the very best on the island, where locals go to sample traditional Kythniot cuisine.

Camping Kapsáli, t 273 603 1580. Simple campsite, set amongst cypress trees. *Open May–Sept.*

Hydragogio, t 273 603 1065. Dine under the trellis of this excellent restaurant, run by a young Belgian couple, with a wide choice of vegetarian specialities. *Closed Oct–April.*

Venetsianiko, t 273 603 1936. Blue and white, for that island feel. Try the *ladopaximádo.*

In summer, Kapsáli has most of the island's nightlife; try the music cocktail bars **Mercato** and **Fox Anglais**.

Around the Island

Northwest of Chóra

Five km north of Chóra, **Livádi** (ΛΙΒΑΔΙ), the commercial centre of the island, has a landmark 13-arched bridge built by the British in 1822 and proudly heralded as the largest in Greece – until 2004, when the Gulf of Corinth bridge stole its thunder. If it seems unaccountably grand for the setting, the story goes that its size is a result of the British engineer's romance with a local girl and his desire to prolong his stay on the island. Ring ahead to visit the **Roússos ceramic workshop**, where the tradition of Kýthera pottery is kept alive, now into the fourth generation.

Heading east from Livádi, you'll come across a good collection of Byzantine and later artefacts in **Káto Livádi**'s museum. A 4km dirt road leads on to the dramatic beach of **Fíri Ámmos** ('red sands'), popular with snorkellers.

West of Livádi via **Drimónas**, the 19th-century **Monastery of the Panagía Mirtidíon** and its carved bell tower are magnificently set on the wild west coast among cypresses, flowers and peacocks. The monastery is named after a gold-plated icon of the Virgin and Child, discovered in the myrtle. Two islets just below are said to be pirate ships that the Virgin petrified for daring to attack her church.

Roússos ceramic workshop
t 273 603 1124

Káto Livádi museum
t 273 603 1731; open Mon–Fri 8–2.30

North of Drimónas, **Milopótamos** (ΜΥΛΟΠΟΤΑΜΟΣ) is the closest thing to Watteau's vision of Cythère, a pretty village with a waterfall, criss-crossed by tiny canals. The lush valley is called the Neraída, or Nymph; an old watermill lies along the path to the waterfall **Foníssa**, 'murderer', named after a girl took her life by jumping into it; on quiet evenings in the café you can hear the nightingales sing. The nearby fortified ghost town of **Káto Chóra** was built by the Venetians in 1560 after Barbarossa destroyed Palió Chóra (*see* below), its gate guarded by a well-preserved relief of the Lion of St Mark gripping an open book (a sign that town was in Venice's favour), bearing the angelic words '*Pax Tibi, Marce, Evangelista Meus*'. Inside are ruined houses and churches, some with frescoed (but mostly locked). A road descends steeply to one of the island's best secluded beaches, white sandy **Limiónas**.

Ag. Sofía Cave
*usually open summer
Mon–Fri 3–8, Sat and
Sun 11–5, but check
in the village*

A road from Káto Chóra leads down to the **Ag. Sofía Cave**. In the past, the cave housed a church, and inside there are frescoes and mosaics, as well as impressive stalactites and stalagmites; some say it tunnels all the way under Kýthera to Ag. Pelagía. To the south, **Mitáta** is a great place for picnics, surrounded by lovely green countryside; the cool, clear water of its spring is delicious. It's also a good spot to purchase thyme honey, at about half the price of the rest of Greece; one shop, **Honey Milk**, also does cheeses.

Honey Milk
t 273 603 3010

The East Coast

Paliópoli (ΠΑΛΑΙΟΠΟΛΙΣ) is a tiny village on the site of ancient Skandeia, the city mentioned by Thucydides. There was a Minoan trading settlement here as well, from 2000 BC until the rise of the Mycenaeans; their long-ago presence has bestowed archaeological status on the long and lovely Paliópoli beach, which has kept it pristine except for a taverna. In ancient times, devotees would climb to the splendid Temple of Urania Aphrodite, 'Queen of the Heavens', to pay their respects to the daughter of Necessity, whom even Zeus could not control. The Christians destroyed it and built the church of **Ag. Geórgios**, re-using the temple's Doric columns.

In nearby **Avlémonas** (ΑΒΛΕΜΟΝΑΣ), a fishing village-resort, locals can direct you to the 'ruins' of Helen's throne where she first met Paris as well as the sea Baths of Aphrodite. Nearby are boulders grooved by the Mycenaeans to channel blood from sacrifices, and an ancient cave dwelling resembling a five-roomed house, with an early example of a column used for structural support. The coast is guarded by a small octagonal **fortress** built by the Venetians, who left a few rusting cannons inside. The island's most stunning beach, **Kaladí**, is 2km away: the road stops at a blissful little chapel, from where a steep rough track leads down to the glorious pebbly beach.

North of Avlémonas, **Diakófti** (ΔΙΑΚΟΦΤΙ) is the island's main port and very low-key resort with the island's only white sand beach, sheltered by a pair of islets, **Makronísi** (now linked by a causeway to shore) and **Prasonísi** – with a new landmark: the upraised prow of a container ship that went aground in 1999.

Palió Chóra and the North

Palió Chóra (or Ag. Dimitríou) is a Byzantine ghost town, founded by Kýthera's Eudaimonoioannis rulers in their native Monemvassian style. Set high on the rocks, it had 800 people and 72 churches and was carefully hidden from the sea – Barbarossa only found it by capturing some locals and torturing them until they told him where it was. Beside the ruins of the fort is a terrible 100m (330ft) abyss, **Kakiá Langáda** – 'bad gorge', where mothers threw their children before leaping themselves, to avoid being sold into slavery; on certain nights, in the island's ghost stories, you can still hear their screams. There are a few frescoes in the haunted churches, but because of the dark memories the site was never again inhabited.

Palió Chóra is near **Potamós** (ΠΟΤΑΜΟΣ), which, despite its name, has no river. It is the largest village in the north, very authentic, and on Sunday people from across the island gather at the big weekly market. West of Potamós, **Ag. Elefthérios** is a lovely secluded beach, and a pretty place to watch the sunset.

Gerakári to the northwest has another tower, this one built by the Turks in the early 18th century. From the pretty village of **Karavás**, the road continues to the fine beach, taverna and rooms at **Platiá Ámmos. Ag. Pelagía** (ΑΓ. ΠΕΛΑΓΙΑ), Kýthera's northern port, looking across to Elafónissos, also has a long pebble beach and a few more facilities, if not a lot of boats, since many have diverted to Diakófti. There are better beaches to the south, including **Kalamítsa**, 2km away on a dirt road.

11 The Ionian Islands | Kýthera

Where to Stay and Eat around Kýthera

For a complete list of rooms on the island, see *www.kythera.gr*.

Livádi ✉ 80100

Mylos Studios, t 210 417 1913 (€€€). Studios of character, in an 18th-century windmill.

Aposperides, t 273 603 1656, *www. greek-tourism.gr/kythera/aposperides* (€€). A pristine hotel.

Grigoria Rooms, t 273 603 1124, *www. greek-tourism.gr/kythera/grigoria* (€€). Rooms and studios with the pottery-making Roússos family; guests are welcome to help themselves to free garden vegetables.

Pierros, t 273 603 1014 (€). Inexpensive rooms and one of the oldest and most traditional tavernas on Kýthera, with home cooking and kind prices.

Toxotis, t 273 603 1781. Taverna specializing in tender grilled meat. *Closed Wed.*

Avlémonas ✉ 80100

Manti, 150m from the beach, t 273 603 3039, *www.manti.gr* (€€€). Handsome rooms and apartments.

Palaeopoli Villas, t 273 603 4354, *www. kythera.gr/wheretostay/papapelekanos* (€€€–€€). Romantic stone and wood villas, done in the traditional style. *Open May–Oct.*

Maria Varda, t 273 603 1727, *www. kythera.gr/wheretostay/varda* (€€). New building with sea views and four new flats. *Open April–Oct.*

Skandeia, near Paliópoli, t 273 603 3700. Greek specialities served under an enormous plane tree.

Sotiris, t 273 603 3722. Taverna in a square overlooking the sea, preparing great seafood caught by the owners.

To Korali, t 273 603 4173. Friendly little fish taverna.

Diakófti ✉ 80100

Sirene Villas, right on the sea, t 273 603 3900, *www.sirene.gr* (€€€). For peace and quiet, with big verandas and kitchens.

Manolis, t 273 603 3748, on the beach. Good fish taverna, with delicious extras like pittas filled with greens and cheese. *Open eves only in winter.*

Mitáta ✉ 80100

Michális, t 273 603 3626. Informal taverna with panoramic views. People come from across Kýthera to eat island specialities, including cockerel and rabbit, prepared with vegetables from their own garden.

Potamós ✉ 80100

Alevizopoulos Panagiotis, t 273 603 3245 (€€). Nice air-conditioned studios.

Karydies, in nearby Logothetiánika, t 273 603 3664. Popular taverna with live music Thurs–Sat.

Panaretos, t 273 603 4290. A classic taverna serving better than usual traditional cuisine.

Club Vergadi, t 273 603 3443. A new, trendy club attracting boppers from the four corners of the island.

Ag. Pelagía ✉ 80100

9 Muses, t 273 603 3155, *www.greek-tourism.gr/kythera/9muses* (€€€). Near the beaches, with sea views from every room, and buffet breakfast.

Vernados, t 273 603 4100, *www.venardos-hotels.gr* (€€€) Smart hotel built around a pool, with a spa offering aroma- and thalassotherapy.

Romantica, t 273 603 3834, *www.romanticahotel.gr* (€€€–€€). A minute from the beach, pleasant rooms and apartments sleeping up to four, plus a pretty pool.

Kaleris, t 273 603 3461. Popular taverna right on the sea.

Amir Ali, inland at Karavás, t 273 603 4346. A café in a gorgeous setting near a spring, named after a Turkish tax collector who died here. *Closes at sunset.*

⭐ **Michális** >

Near Kýthera: Elafónissos (ΕΛΑΦΟΝΗΣΟΣ) and Antikýthera (ΑΝΤΙΚΥΘΗΡΑ)

Elafónissos is one of Greece's newer islets – until an earthquake in the 17th century it was attached to the Peloponnese. But even if it's only 570m (626 yds) from shore, Elafónissos was island enough to be part of the Ionians and ruled by Venice and Britain instead of the Ottomans. In ancient times it had a Temple of Artemis, which may be why its name means 'deer island'. Its 800 inhabitants are mostly fishermen, but in August they are crushed under a thundering invasion when as many as 5,000 people a day and 1,500 cars make the crossing each day for the island's famous beaches, aiming for **Fragó Bay** 5km south of the village, endowed with two of Greece's most gorgeous beaches, **Símos** and **Sarakíniko**, kissed by Caribbean green-blue waters; another good sandy stretch is on the west coast by **Ta Nisiá tis Panagías**, the Virgin's Islands.

Antikýthera, on the other hand, two hours by ferry south of Kýthera, is one of Greece's most remote islands. Forty-five people

Getting to Elafónissos and Antikýthera

A **ferry** plies the few minutes from Poúnda (or Vigláfia, just north of Neápolis town) on the Peloponnese mainland to Elafónissos all day long from 8am to 5.30pm in winter, up to 1am in summer. For information ring the Neápolis port authority, t 273 402 2228.

An old **ANEN ferry** (t 282 202 2655) calls 2–4 times a week at Antikýthera en route between Neápolis, Gýthio, Kýthera (Diakófti) and Kíssamos, Crete; they occasionally sail to Kalamáta, too.

live in Antikýthera's two villages, **Potamós** and **Sochória**, and the rest is rocky with few trees; curiously, like west Crete, the island is slowly rising. Potamós has a 200-year-old watermill and two little tavernas. By Potamós, ancient **Aígilia** has walls dating back to the 5th century BC and some ruins of an ancient Temple of Apollo. There's a small beach at **Xeropótamo**, five minutes by boat or 30 minutes on foot, and pretty rocks to swim off at **Karaméla**. Water is a luxury, and the few rooms available are basic.

The World's Oldest Computer

Antikýthera is just a smudge on the map, but thanks to the winds that churn the surrounding seas it is also a name familiar to any student of Greek art. For on the 22nd day of the ancient Greek month of Mounichon, in the first year of the 180th Olympiad (5 May, 59 BC), a Roman ship sailing from Rhodes, laden with booty that included the magnificent 4th-century BC bronze known as the *Ephebe of Antikýthera* (in the National Archaeology Museum in Athens), went down here. Now you may well ask: how could anyone possibly know the precise date of a 2,000-year-old shipwreck? Pinpointing even the century is often an archaeological guessing game. The answer is that part of the booty included the world's first computer, and its bronze timekeeping mechanism was stopped forever on the day the ship went down.

The wreck was discovered in 1900 by sponge divers from Sými, who sheltered off Antikýthera in a storm. Afterwards, one diver, Ilias Stadiatos, went down to see if this remote sea bed might yield a sponge or two. Instead he were startled to see what he described as 'naked dead women' – the ancient statues. The Greek archaeological service sent down a small warship to recover the bronzes and marbles, vases and glass – the world's first underwater archaeological dig. One item they hauled up was a lump; as the months passed and the mud dried, a wooden cabinet about a foot high was revealed. This deteriorated on contact with the air, leaving a calcified hunk of metal that broke into four bits. Archaeologists were astonished to see that they belonged to a mechanical device inscribed with ancient Greek script.

At first the Antikýthera Mechanism was dismissed as a primitive astrolabe. Then, in 1958, a science historian at Yale, Derek Price, examined X-rays that showed some 30 separate gears, and recognized it as an astronomical computer, which, by its setting, was made in 82 BC. The days of the month and the signs of the zodiac were inscribed on bronze dials, with pointers to indicate the phases of the moon, sun, Mercury and Venus, operated within by complex clockwork: bronze cog wheels with triangular teeth, connected to a large four-spoked wheel, driven by a crown gear and shaft, which probably had a key for winding. This ties in with what Cicero wrote in the 1st century BC of an instrument 'recently constructed by our friend Poseidonius, which at each revolution reproduces the same motions of the sun, the moon and the five planets' and mentioned a 'future-telling astronomical device' he had come across while attending Rhodes' School of Rhetoric. 'It is a bit frightening to know,' concluded Price, 'that just before the fall of their great civilization, the Ancient Greeks had come so close to our age, not only in their thought, but also in their scientific knowledge.'

Price was on the right track, but evidence provided by state-of-the-art imaging technology used in the current Antikýthera Mechanism Research Project suggests that the Mechanism was even more complex and, as Cicero wrote, also charted the courses of Mars, Jupiter and Saturn. For the latest developments, see *www.antikythera-mechanism.gr*.

Useful Information on Antikýthera

Community of Antikýthera, t 273 603 3004, *www.antikythira.gr*. Contact them about rooms on the island, especially if you come in summer, as availability is limited.

Where to Stay and Eat on Elafónissos

Elafónissos ✉ 23053

9 Muses, t 273 406 1345, *www. hotelhellas.gr* (€€). Modern complex of eight apartments with a pool. *Open April–Oct.*

Asteri Apartments, 20m from the sea, **t** 273 406 1271 (€€). *Open all year.*

Edem, t 273 406 1302, *http://hotel_ edem.tripod.com* (€€). Simple and sweet, rooms sleeping up to four.

Elafónissos, t 273 406 1268 (€€). Eleven rooms. *Open June–Sept.*

Villa Alkyoni, t 273 406 1120 (€€). Attractive newly built studios, some for families, with pretty views.

Simos Paradise Camping, 4.5km from town, **t** 273 402 2672. New, eco-friendly, just 20m from the beach, with a few rooms to rent.

Lefkáda/Lefkás (ΛΕΦΚΑΔΑ)

Lefkás (better known in Greece by the genitive form of its name, Lefkáda) was named after the whiteness (*leukos*) of its cliffs. As an island, it's a relative newcomer, going back to 600 BC, when the Corinthians dug a 20m (66ft)-wide channel, separating the peninsula from the mainland. This is easily crossed by a floating bridge; beyond the channel a series of causeways encompasses a large lagoon, where herons and pelicans figure among the migratory visitors. This swampy flatness that greets you disguises the fact that the rest of Lefkáda is remarkably rugged and mountainous, with an interior and coast of high drama, and a wide assortment of beaches and lush valleys, and mountain villages where older women still wear their traditional dress. Lefkáda is perhaps best loved for its sailing; the calm waters, a scattering of small islands off the southeast and enchanted green coasts combine to form one of the most popular spots in Greece for flotilla holidays. Dolphins seem to like it, too: there are more varieties seen off the coasts of Lefkáda than anywhere, including the rare *Delphinus delphis*.

History

Although inhabited at least as far back as the late Paleolithic era (8000 BC), Lefkáda first enters recorded history as part of ancient Akarnania, site of Homer's 'vast' city Nerikus, which has been located under the farms and houses of modern Kallithéa. In 640 BC, the Corinthians used a ruse to snatch Nerikus from the Akarnanians; they founded a city (modern Lefkáda Town) and dug the channel for defence and for their ships. Politics as usual would later bring trouble: during the Peloponnesian War, Lefkáda, still loyal to Corinth, sided with Sparta and was devastated twice, by Corfu and Athens. In the mid-3rd century BC, the island was punished for siding with Macedonia against Rome, and had just recovered when Augustus

Getting to and around Lefkáda

By air: Aktion Préveza Airport, **t** 268 202 2089, is 26km away on the mainland and is linked 4 times a week with flights from Athens as well as regular charters from the UK from May–mid-Oct. There are 6 buses to Lefkáda Town from the airport; taxis will be around €33. A seaplane may be serving Lefkáda soon; *see www.airsealines.com.*

By sea: A ferry, the *Captain Aristides*, **t** 210 412 2530, sails year-round from Vassilikí (or Nidrí in the off season) to Fiskárdo (Kefaloniá) and Fríkes (Ithaca). There are daily ferries from Nidrí to Meganísi, **t** 210 412 2530; other boats based in Nidrí do day trips to Meganísi, Ithaca, Kefaloniá and hard-to-reach beaches. **Port authority**: Vassilikí, **t** 264 509 2509; Nidrí, **t** 264 509 2509.

By road: There are 3–5 buses a day from Athens. The main **bus station** is located at the north end of Lefkáda Town; for information call **t** 264 502 2364. Routes to Nidrí and Vassilikí are well plied, but to really see the island you need a moped or car; there are plenty to hire in Vassilikí and Nidrí.

celebrated his victory at Aktium in 31 BC (where he outmanoeuvred the fleets of Mark Antony and Cleopatra to become the master of the Roman Empire) by founding a new city, Nikopolis, and diverted the island's wealth and population there – and many stayed, until the 6th century invasion of the Goths.

Although Lefkáda was granted to Venice after the Fourth Crusade, it took the Venetians a century to wrench it from the Despot of Epirus. The inhabitants, exasperated by the fighting and pirates, implored the Venetians to build the fortress of Santa Maura, a name that soon came to refer to the entire island. When Constantinople fell in 1453, Helene Palaeológos, mother of the last emperor, Constantínos XI, founded a monastery within the walls of Santa Maura, although it was converted into a mosque when the Turks took Lefkáda in 1479. In 1500 the combined forces of Spain and Venice, under the Gran Capitán Gonzáles de Córdoba, captured Lefkáda and Santa Maura from the Turks, but the very next year Venice made a treaty with Turkey and returned the island. In 1684, Francesco Morosini, angry at losing the fortress at Heráklion, Crete, was determined to win Lefkáda back for Venice, which he did with the help of the Bishop of Kefaloniá, leading an army of priests and monks. Venice held on to the island until its own fall in 1796, but never managed to influence it as

Useful Information on Lefkáda

(i) **Lefkáda** >
town hall,
t 264 502 3000

Tourist police: 30 Iroón Politechníou in Lefkáda Town, a few blocks from the bus station, **t** 264 502 6450.

Trekking Hellas, *www.outdoorsgreece. com*. Sea-kayaking adventures around Lefkáda's smaller islands, including Kástos and Kálamos (*see* p.513).

Lantis World, **t** 694 489 8347; in the UK **t** 07899 994400, *www.lantisworld. com*. Independent tour operator specializing in Lefkáda.

Lefkáda Festivals

26 July: Ag. Paraskeví near Ag. Pétros, carnival festivities, with a parade.

Aug: Arts and Letters Festival and large International Folklore Festival, in Lefkáda Town.

First 2 weeks Aug: Karyá puts on a stream of festivities including a clarinet festival on the 11th (in the same vein, nearby Englouví has a clarinet and lentil festival on 6 and 7 Aug), and 'Riganada', the re-creation of a traditional wedding, where everyone wears their finest old costumes.

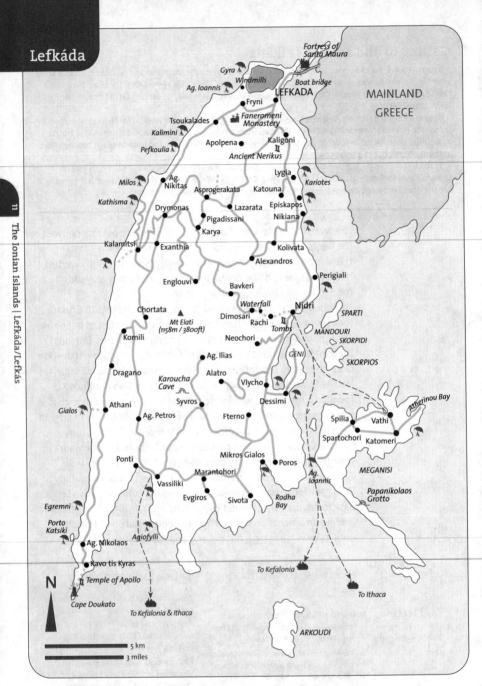

strongly as it did the other Ionian islands. The French and then the Russians grabbed Lefkáda; in 1807 Ali Pasha of Epirus tried to purchase it from Russia, but was held back by the Russian-appointed Secretary of State, Count Capodístria. Capodístria is said to have later sworn to support the cause of an independent Greece with refugee rebels on the island, among them Kolokotrónis.

Lefkáda Town

The approach to Lefkáda is guarded by the massive **Fortress of Santa Maura**. Built in the 13th century by Giovanni Orsini, rebuilt by the Venetians and Turks, it's still an impressive sight even though the buildings within the walls were blown to smithereens in an accidental powder explosion in 1888. After 1922, it was used as a refugee camp for Greeks from Turkey displaced in the population exchange.

Santa Maura has survived the periodic earthquakes that rattle the area better than the capital, Lefkáda Town, which collapsed like a house of cards in the tremors of 1948 and 1953, and was hit hard again in 1971, although with much less damage. You can see why: the town is like no other in Greece; narrow lanes are lined with brightly painted houses, stone on the ground floor, topped by a fragile wooden or more often a corrugated metal upper storey as an antiseismic measure. Iron bell towers, rearing up like oil derricks, replace dangerous stone ones. The result, aesthetically poised somewhere between the Wild West and Legoland®, has a charm all its own. These days the town is proud of its marina (built in 2002), testimony to Lefkáda's growing sailing reputation.

Bosketo Park (or Plateía Sikelianoú), the large, shady square near the end of the causeway, displays busts of Lefkáda's three great contributors to letters: Valaorítis, Sikelianós (*see* overleaf), and Lafcadio Hearn (1850–1904), whose British father and Kýtheran mother named him after his birthplace. He went on to become a journalist in America, and in 1890 went to Japan, where he became an expert on Japanese language and culture, teaching the Japanese about Western literature and vice versa. Every now and then Japanese tourists make the pilgrimage to the island to honour the man they know as Yakomo Kuizumi.

Off Lefkáda's pedestrian-only shopping street, the island's Italianate churches, constructed mostly in the 18th century, are square, domeless and solidly built of stone, and have largely survived the tremors; you'll find fine examples of the Ionian school of painting in **Ag. Minás** (1707), and in the three icons in **Ag. Dimítrios** (1688), although they are rarely open. Another, the **Pantokrátor**, has a pretty façade, last reworked in 1890, with an atypical curved roofline. **Ag. Spyrídon** (17th century) has a fine carved wooden screen.

Archaeology Museum
Sikelianoú and N. Svoronoú, **t** *264 502 1635; open Tues–Sun 8.30–3; adm*

There are four small museums, with somewhat erratic opening hours. Near Ag. Spyrídon, the usually closed **Orpheus Folklore Museum** has four rooms displaying the beautiful embroideries and weavings made on the island, dating back to the 19th century. The **Archaeology Museum** houses finds from cave sanctuaries and the

Museum of Byzantine Icons
t 265 107 8062; open 10.30–12.30; adm

Lefkáda Phonograph Museum
12–14 Kalkáni Street, t 264 502 1088; usually open in season 7pm–midnight

30 12th-century BC tombs discovered by Dörpfeld at Stenó, by Nidrí; the **Museum of Byzantine Icons**, in the municipal library, has works of the Ionian school, along with a collection of antique maps. Finally, appropriately for the town that established the first municipal brass band in Greece (1850), there's the **Lefkáda Phonograph Museum**. The only museum of its kind in Greece, it contains old gramophones sent over by the collector's relatives from the United States, recordings of *kantádes* and popular Greek songs of the 1920s.

Just Outside Town

The closest beach to Lefkáda Town is the **Gýra**, the long, sandy if often windy lido that closes off the west side of the lagoon, with a few tavernas. On the other side of the windmills, a second beach, **Ag. Ioánnis Antzoúsis**, is tucked under a chapel, supposedly named after Angevin Crusaders. In the opposite direction, by the cemetery, watch the old men in the olive grove play *t'ambáli*, Lefkáda's version of boules, played with egg-shaped balls on a concave ground, which as far as anyone knows is played nowhere else in the world. Two km south, in a ruined monastery near Apólpena, **Panagía Odhigýtria** (1450; usually locked) is the oldest church on the island, the only one to have withstood all the earthquakes. It had paintings (now in Athens), perhaps bestowed by Helen, sister of Emperor John VIII Palaeológos, who stayed here after the fall of Constantinople.

Just above the town is the 17th-century **Faneroméni Monastery**, rebuilt in the 19th century after a fire. It is a serene place in the pines, with bird's-eye views over the town, lagoon and Santa Maura. On the islet with the ruined chapel of Ag. Nikólaos was a cottage where Sikelianós and his wife Eva would spend their summers.

Sikelianós and the Delphic Idea

Angelos Sikelianós, born on Lefkáda in 1884, was as romantically handsome as a poet should be. Although he followed his parents' wishes by going to law school in Athens, he left after a couple of years to join a theatre company with two of his sisters, Helen and Penelope. Penelope married the brother of Isadora Duncan, and through him Sikelianós met his own American spouse, Eva. All shared an interest in recreating the mythic passion and power of ancient Greece, in active artistic expression. Sikelianós did his part by writing startling lyrical poetry, infused with Dionysian mysticism, yearning to join the world of the gods to the world of men. In the 1920s, Sikelianós and Eva came up with the idea of reviving the 'Delphic Idea' of the arts, in the same spirit as the revival of the Olympics. Their goal was to create an International Delphic Centre and University, and stage a Delphic Festival of drama, dance, music, sports and crafts; this actually took place in 1927 and 1930, funded in part by a mortgage on the Sikelianós house and Eva's inheritance. But the Depression closed in, and the following years were bitter; Eva went back to America, and although they divorced she continued to support the 'Delphic Idea' and send Sikelianós money. Sikelianós remarried and sat out the war years in a small flat in Athens, in declining health. His finest moment came during the occupation, when he gave the funeral oration of the poet Palamas, declaring 'In this coffin lies Greece', and led the singing of the banned Greek national anthem, even though he was surrounded by German soldiers. The dark years of the war and the Greek Civil War added a tragic power to his poetry, but his leftist politics barred him from membership of the Athens Academy and, as they will tell you in Lefkáda, from winning the Nobel Prize, too, although he was twice nominated. In 1951 he died when he mistook Lysol for his medicine.

Where to Stay and Eat in Lefkáda Town

Lefkáda ✉ 31100

Nirikos, t 264 502 4132, *www.nirikos.gr* (€€€). Well-kept hotel in the centre of the action; most rooms face the marina. *Open all year.*

Pension Pirofani, t 264 502 5844 (€€). Spacious, air-conditioned rooms with balconies over the pedestrianized main street – though it can get a bit noisy.

Santa Mavra, opposite, **t** 264 502 2342 (€€). A tidy little hotel.

If they are on offer in any of the bars and tavernas, do try (if you can!) the increasingly rare local wines *vartsámi, kerópati* or *yomatári*.

Adriatika, towards Ag. Nikítas. Set in a pleasant garden setting, this taverna is a little pricey, but has some good Greek specialities and excellent service.

Karma, on the seafront. Favourite café for vegetating and watching new arrivals over the bridge.

O Regantos, on D. Venióti, near the Folklore Museum, **t** 264 502 2855. One of the oldest and best tavernas in town, all blue and yellow.

Sto Molo, 12 Golémi (on the eastern waterfront), **t** 264 502 4879. Excellent *mezedopoleío*, serving a wide assortment of delights to make a meal.

East and South Coast Resorts

The east coast of Lefkáda is green and bedecked with beaches. Just a few kilometres south of Lefkáda Town at **Kaligóni**, on a hill near the shore, are the scant ruins of **ancient Nerikus**, the pre-Corinthian city where Dörpfeld (*see* overleaf) found Cyclopean walls, traces of roads, arches, a water tank, and a pre-Roman theatre, as well as early Byzantine ruins, visible after some scrambling through the olives. Further south is the ex-fishing village of **Lygiá**, now a resort with narrow shingle beaches and good walking – one seductive possibility is the path up the **Valley of Love** (Kiláda tou Érota). **Nikiána**, spread out more attractively, has striking mainland views.

Further south is **Perigiáli**, with a fine beach and new hotels, and, 2km further on, Lefkáda's tourist fleshpot, **Nidrí** (ΝΥΔΡΙ). Nidrí looks out over lovely, partially enclosed **Vlychó Bay**, its still waters dotted with the wooded **Pringipónisia** (Prince's Islets). One of largest, **Skórpios**, belongs to the last of the ill-starred Onassis family – Aristotle's granddaughter Athena. Her grandfather Aristotle, uncle Alexander and mother Christina are buried there, and excursion boats land on the little horseshoe beach where Jackie O. was famously photographed in the buff by paparazzi in passing speed boats. Onassis, whose statue stands in the port with an inspiring quote: 'Men have to construct their own destiny', was obsessed with privacy, and hefty pay-offs in the right places kept tourist facilities at Nidrí at a minimum during his lifetime. Since then the locals have made up for lost time, stringing tavernas, studios and car hire places along the one road, and it can get very busy in the summer.

Another iset is **Mandouri**, 'the poet's island', which in the right conditions at twilight floats above the horizon on a magic carpet of mist. Its mansion belongs to the great-granddaughter of Aristotélis Valaorítis (1824–79), one of the first to write in demotic

⭐ **Vlychó Bay**

11

The Ionian Islands | Lefkáda/Lefkás

Greek rather than the formal *kathourévesa*. He later served in the Greek parliament, where he was renowned as a public speaker.

Follow the signs in Nidrí to drive then walk to the beautiful waterfall at the end of the **Dimosári gorge**. In April and May it gushes forth with enthusiasm; in the summer it is little more than a high-altitude squirt, but it's cool and refreshing, and there's a pool for a swim. Wilhelm Dörpfeld, Schliemann's assistant at Troy, found a number of circular Bronze Age tombs just south of Nidrí at Stenó and became a local hero, when he announced that they proved his theory that Lefkáda was the Ithaca of Homer. He died in 1940 and is buried near his house, by Géni's church.

Vlychó, the next village south, is a quiet charmer, where traditional boat-builders still ply their craft. Sandy **Dessími Beach**, with a popular campsite, lies within walking distance, as does the **Géni Peninsula**, covered with ancient, writhing olive groves. This is a popular refuge for those seeking something quieter than Nidrí, but the one access road is often bottlenecked in summer. Further south, a fork in the road descends to **Póros** near the pretty white pebble beach of Mikrós Gialós under the olive trees. Here Dörpfeld discovered a farm from the 4th century BC, with an impressive tower. Picturesque **Sívota**, the next south, has a good collection of fish tavernas and a few rooms to let, overlooking a beautiful, nearly enclosed little port; the nearest swimming is at **Kastrí**, to the west.

Further west, **Vassiliki** (ΒΑΣΙΛΙΚΗ) has a little tree-rimmed port with cafés and reliable sustained winds, making the long beach north of town a big favourite among windsurfers. On most days a gentle breeze blows up by mid-morning, perfect to teach beginners, and by mid-afternoon it's blowing strong for the experts; by evening, the wind, like a real gent, takes a bow and exits, allowing a pleasant dinner by the water. For a swim, walk along the sand to **Pónti** or take a water taxi to the pretty white beach of **Agiofýlli**, accessible only by sea.

Where to Stay and Eat on the East and South Coasts

(★) **Pavezzo Country Retreat** ›

Lygiá and Katoúna ✉ 31100

Pavezzo Country Retreat, 3km from the sea above Lygiá at Katoúna, t 264 507 1782, http://pavezzo.gr (€€€€€–€€€). Immersed in gardens and olives, the island's most romantic place to stay – renovated village houses filled with antiques, each with pools.

Yiannis, Lygiá, t 264 507 1407. An excellent fish taverna. *Closed lunch out of season.*

Nikiána and Around ✉ 31100

Aliki, t 264 507 1602, www.alikihotel.gr (€€€). Studios in a commanding location, with a pool overlooking the sea. *Open all year.*

Porto Galini, t 264 509 2431 (€€€). Luxurious apartments among the cypresses and olives, and water sports down on the beach.

Villa Thomais, t 264 507 1985, www.villathomais.com (€€€). Attractive rooms in a villa, with a lovely roof garden and delicious breakfast buffet.

Camping Episcopos Beach, just north of Nikiána, t 264 507 1388, www.

lefkadas.com/campingepiscopos (€).
Lots of shade, low-key.

Minas, on the road to Nidrí, t 264 507
1480. Nikiána's best fish restaurant.

To Spiti tou Kolomelou, Keramidáki,
t 264 509 2785. Delicious Greek and
international dishes, with lots of
seafood and some surprises.

Nidrí ✉ 31100

Armeno Beach, Perigáli beach, t 264
509 2112, www.armeno.gr (€€€).
Modern rooms with air-conditioning;
water sports available.

Eva Beach, north of Nidrí, t 264 509
2545, www.evabeach.gr. (€€€–€€). Small
family hotel in a garden setting on a
narrow beach; rooms have sea views.

Bella Vista, 2mins from Perigáli beach,
t 264 509 2650, www.bella-vista.gr (€€).
Set in a garden; newly renovated
studios with pretty views.

Gorgona, t 264 509 2268 (€€). Set
back from the razzmatazz in its own
quiet garden.

Nydrion Beach I and II, t 264 509 2400
(€€). Good views, and right on the
beach; Nydrion I is open all year.

Scorpios Apartments, above Perigáli,
t 264 509 2452 (€€). Peaceful
apartments and stunning views from
the pool terrace and restaurant,
though you need to climb a few steps.

Olive Tree, towards Neochóri, t 264 509
2655. In an olive grove, a very popular
typical taverna.

⭐ Pinewood ›

Pinewood (To Pefkko), by the sea on
the north end of town, t 264 509 2075.
Nidrí's finest dining and excellent
service in a beautiful setting. *Book;
closed Mon.*

Il Saporre, by the port, t 264 509 2915.
Mix of Greek and Italian, with a good
choice of salads and pizzas from the
wood oven.

Or do as the locals do and head up to
the tavernas in Charadiátika for
succulent meats and *mezédes*.

Vlychó/Géni ✉ 31100

Vliho Bay and **Villa Santa Maria**,
t 264 509 5619, www.vlihobay.com
(€€). Family-orientated resort hotel;
Villa Santa Maria is immersed in olive
trees; both have pools.

Dessimi Beach Camping, t 264 509
5374, www.dessimi-beach.gr. A popular
campsite close to a sandy beach.

Póros/Sívota ✉ 31100

Oceanis Studios, Mikrós Gialós, Póros,
t 264 509 5095 (€€). A peaceful place.
Open May–Sept.

Poros Beach Camping, t 264 509 5452,
www.porosbeach.com.gr. Affordable
luxury, with 50 sites, bungalows,
studios, a restaurant and a pool.

Stavros, Sívota, t 264 503 1181. Excellent
fish taverna, with such delights as
prawns flambéed with ouzo and pesto.
Closed Nov–Mar.

Vassilikí ✉ 31082

Best Western Odeon, near the beach,
t 264 503 1918, www.vassiliki.net (€€€).
Hotel and apartments; breakfast on
the veranda and cocktails by the pool.

Porto Fico, on Pónti beach, t 264 503
1402, www.portofico.gr (€€€). Classy,
medium-sized hotel run by a friendly
Greek-Australian family, with a pool
and nearby windsurfing school.

Billy's House, 100m from the beach,
t 693 213 5592, www.billyshouse.gr (€€).
For families – refurbished rooms sleeping up to four, and a shady garden.

Wildwind Apartments, on the beach,
book in the UK t +44 (0)1920 484516,
www.wildwind.co.uk (€€). With sailing
and windsurfing instruction for
young and old, and volley ball and
croquet for when the wind isn't up.

Surf, t 264 503 1740 (€€–€). Balconied
rooms by Pónti beach.

Vassilikí Beach Campsite, well located
halfway along the bay, t 264 503 1308.

Delphini, by the port. Fish taverna.

Inland Villages: Lace and Lentils

You should at least venture into Lefkáda's interior, where traditional farming villages occupy the fertile uplands surrounded by
mountains, and it's not unusual to encounter an older woman in her
traditional long brown skirts, bodice and kerchief, sitting with distaff

in hand, at her loom, or over her embroidery. Set in a smiling amphitheatre, **Karyá** is one of the largest villages, the centre of the island's lace and embroidery industry, with several shops around the pretty *plateía* shaded by fat plane trees – where you're like to meet the very affable Brenda, a former guide who will make you a Tetley's tea or one of her famous toasted sandwiches. Just above the Karyá Village hotel (*closed at the time of writing, after earthquake damage in 2003*), there's a delightful **Ethnographic Museum** with a donkey-powered flour mill and exhibits on Maria Koutsochéro from Karyá, whose lace was in international demand around 1900. Another traditional lace town, **Englouví**, is the highest village on Lefkáda at 895m (2,395ft); it is even prouder of its lentils, which win prizes at Greek competitions. In the interior there are several notable churches with frescoes, among them the **Red Church** (Kókkini Eklisía) and **Monastery of Ag. Geórgios** (from around 1620) near Aléxandros, a nearly abandoned village crumbling to bits. **Drymónas**, to the west, is a pretty village of stone houses and old tile roofs.

Ethnographic Museum
*t 264 504 1590;
open in high season
9am–10pm; adm*

Lefkáda's highest peak, **Eláti** (1,158m/3,800ft), cuts off the inland villages of the south. One of the few access roads rises from the plain of Vassilikí (on the south coast), covered with olives and fields of flowers, to **Sývros**, one of the island's beauty spots, set in wild laurel and plane forests, where the spring-fed **Kerasiá** (cherry tree) **ravine** still has a few of its 24 watermills. You can also visit **Karoúcha Cave** (*always open*). From **Sývros**, it's a 3km drive up the slopes of Mount Eláti to the lofty little hamlet of **Ag. Ilías**.

Down the West Coast

The west coast of Lefkáda is rocky and rugged, and the sea is often rough – perfect for those who complain that the Mediterranean is a big bathtub, for under the cliffs are some of the most stunning stretches of sand in the Ionians. The road from Lefkáda Town avoids the shore as far as the farming village of **Tsoukaládes**, from where a 2km road leads down to narrow pebble **Kalímini Beach** and its turquoise water before carrying on south.

The alternative route down from Karyá (if it's been repaired – crumbling cliffs are a problem in these parts) is a superb approach offering stunning views: from Karyá, head back towards Lefkáda Town, turning right at the T-junction; then take the first left. The long sandy beach of **Pefkóulia** begins under the mountains and stretches around the coast to **Ag. Nikítas** (ΑΓ. ΝΙΚΗΤΑΣ). With only a cluster of hotels at the top, the nucleus of the village, with its pretty tile roofs and old tavernas, is off limits to developers; the narrow streets are overhung with flowers and vines. Parking, how-ever, is a headache, especially on summer weekends. With nothing between here and Italy, the sea is a clear pale blue, clean, but cold.

One kilometre south of Ag. Nikítas, **Mílos Beach** is another pebbly beauty on crystal-clear waters under sheer cliffs, and now has a restaurant. Just south of here, 2km off the main road, **Káthisma** is another good, wavy place to swim on the wide beach of golden sand, dotted with places to dive and caves to explore; the cliffs above are popular with paragliders. An unpaved road leads to yet another beautiful sandy beach below **Kalamítsi**, set among giant rocks, with rooms and tavernas that make it a potential quiet base.

The Original Lovers' Leap

To reach Lefkáda's southwest peninsula, a secondary road from Kalamítsi crosses to the pretty leafy villages of **Chortáta** and **Komíli**, where the road forks. The left-hand fork passes through inspiring scenery, divinely scented by the wild flowers in late spring (no wonder the honey is so good), by way of the pretty farming village of **Ag. Pétros**. Buses continue down the coastal road (the right-hand fork) only as far as **Atháni**, a village famous for its thyme honey, that struggles to meet the demands of tourists heading further south to the superb beaches along the peninsula. The first, long and un-developed **Gialós**, can be reached on a track from Atháni; the next, glorious golden **Egrémni**, requires a labour of love to reach from land – a long, very narrow 3km road followed by 200 steep steps. Further south, sublime sandy **Pórto Katsíki** ('goat port'), with incredible turquoise waters, is set under white cliffs, reached by a stair from the car park at the bottom of five winding potholed kilometres – or by excursion boat. It has summer *cantinas*.

Just beyond a last fertile valley rise the famous 58m (190ft) sheer white cliffs of **Cape Doukáto** or **Kávo tis Kyrás** (Lady's Cape), where Sappho, rejected by Phaon, the man she loved, hurled herself into the sea; one old tradition says that she was imitating Aphrodite, who took the plunge in despair over the death of Adonis. Later, Romans rejected by their sweethearts would make the leap – with the precaution of strapping on feathers or live birds and employing rescue parties to pull them out of the sea.

Before becoming a cure-all for unrequited love, the leap was made by unwilling sacrifices to stormy Poseidon – prisoners or criminal scapegoats. When human sacrifices dropped out of fashion, priests serving at the Temple of Apollo Lefkáda (of which only the scantiest of ruins remain, signposted at the end of a long track best tackled in a jeep) would make the jump safely as part of their cult, called *katapontismós* ('sea-plunging'), like the divers at Acapulco, one imagines; no doubt the leaps were accompanied by animal sacrifices (read barbecues) for a pleasant ancient Greek day out. The white cliffs were always a famous landmark for sailors. Byron, sailing past in 1812 during his first visit to Greece, was strangely moved, and put down the experience in *Childe Harold* (canto II).

Where to Stay and Eat on the West Coast

Ag. Nikítas ✉ 31080

Ag. Nikítas, 150m from the beach, t 264 509 7460, *www.hotelagiosnikitas. gr* (€€€). Tastefully decorated, tranquil hotel in three buildings with all mod cons.

Odyssey, t 264 509 7351, *www. odyssey-hotel.gr* (€€€). One of the island's nicest hotels, with a roof garden and pool. They also have new self-catering residences, sleeping up to five people.

Ostria Pension, t 264 509 7483, *www. e-lefkas.gr/AgNikitasOstria* (€€€– €€). Pretty blue and white house with only 12 rooms overlooking the bay.

Santa Marina, t 264 509 7111, *www.santamarina.gr* (€€€– €€). Popular and comfortable, with a pool.

Portoni, t 264 509 7120. Delightful little taverna by the beach, serving big portions. *Closed Nov–Mar*.

Copla, on Káthisma beach, t 264 502 9411. New and trendy bar designed out of wood and driftwood by Giorgos Kavvada, with a pool; they also do sandwiches.

Meganísi (ΜΕΓΑΝΗΣΙ)

For those hankering for a peaceful, low-key taste of authentic Greece, try Meganísi (*see* map, p.504), a wildly indented jigsaw piece, covered in forests and ancient olive groves, with little beaches tucked in here and there. The 'big island' (big, that is, among the islets off eastern Lefkáda) is believed to be the island of Taphios in the *Odyssey*, and the base of the semi-mythical Teleboans, sailors and pirates who at one point were powerful enough to take on the king of Mycenae.

Meganísi's 2,000 souls are spread out in three villages. From the pretty, laid-back port of **Váthi**, a 10-minute walk up the road leads up to the 'capital', **Katoméri**, from where roads head down to the beaches of **Elía**, **Limonári**, **Fanári** and **Athéni Bay**, as well as to its new

Where to Stay and Eat on Meganísi

Meganísi ✉ 31083

The municipal website, *www. meganisi.gr*, has a complete list of rooms to rent.

Asperides, Spartochóri. Huge new hotel with a pool on the bluff, due to open 2007. See *www.meganisi.gr*.

Meganisi, Katoméri, t 264 05 1240 (€€€– €€). Nice hotel on the edge of town, with a pool; ring and they'll collect you at Váthi. *Open Easter–Oct*.

Mistral Apartments, Váthi, t 264 505 1059, *www.eptanissa.com* (€€€–€€). Seven rooms in a garden. *Open June–Sept*.

Porto Elia Rooms, Elía Beach, t 264 504 1341/t 693 252 4390, *www.portoelia.gr*

(€€). Studios sleeping up to four on the sea, 30m from the beach; peace and quiet guaranteed.

Helen Palmou Rooms, Váthi, t 264 505 1042 (€€). Recently built, with lovely views.

Il Paradiso, Ag. Ioánnis Beach, t 264 505 1090. Simple restaurant and **rooms** (€€) to rent.

Porto Spilia, at Spartochóri port, t 264 505 1233. Delicious mussels (an island speciality) and seafood with pasta, hammocks and every facility for yachties, down to lazy lines for easy mooring.

Rose Garden, Váthi, t 264 505 1216. Meganísi's oldest taverna (since 1969) where the affable Stephanos offers fresh fish and grilled meats – and showers for yachties.

⭐ Il Paradiso >>

Getting to Meganísi

Several **ferries** a day from Nidrí go to both ports, Váthi and Spartochóri, in 25mins, supplemented in summer by **excursion boats**.
The island **bus** (t 264 502 2364) descends to meet ferries, but run for it – the driver doesn't hang around. It also makes trips down to the beaches.

port, **Atherinoú Bay**, with a clutch of fishing boats. The third village, **Spartochóri**, sits on a slope, with a beach and port, **Spília**, where big yachts converge in the summer.

The excursion boats from Nidrí, on Lefkáda, usually call at Meganísi's long tail, at the yawning 90m (295ft)-deep **Papanikólaos' Grotto**, the second largest in Greece and named after the daring Greek resistance submariner who used to hide here and dart out to attack Italian ships; and at the sandy beach of **Ag. Ioánnis**.

Kálamos (ΚΑΛΑΜΟΣ) and Kástos (ΚΑΣΤΟΣ)

Kálamos and Kástos, northeast of Ithaca and east of Meganísi, are under the jurisdiction of Lefkáda, but can only be reached by way of the charming seaside town of Mítikas on the mainland (*sea taxi*, *t 264 608 1368 or t 693 648 8177*). Pines cover every feasible roothold on **Kálamos**, a mountain in the sea where most of the 580 residents live in attractive **Kálamos village** with its narrow lanes and stone houses; there are a few rooms to rent and tavernas serving locals and visiting yachties. Better beaches, such as **Ag. Konstantínos** with a little chapel, are near the island's other village, tiny **Episkopí**, linked by a new road over the mountain.

Only 50 people live on verdant, low-lying, car-free **Kástos**, with its quiet, end-of-the-world feel; in summer, even though the population increases tenfold, it's still pretty quiet. Nearly everyone has a boat, and in season the caique/sea taxi from Mítikas goes out to the beaches. There are several paths to explore, but that's about it.

Páxos/Paxí (ΠΑΞΟΙ)

Small is beautiful indeed. The island of 20 fabled secrets, Páxos (pop. 2,400) is the tiniest and most charming of the canonical Seven Islands. The coast varies from the high drama of towering cliffs to tiny charming ports; inland, nearly every inch is given over to immaculate olive groves, source of the liquid gold that has won international medals: unlike Corfu, the olives here are rarely sprayed against the dreaded dacus fly, but are protected with ecologically sound sticky traps in plastic bags. Besides the beauty of the silvery

Getting to Páxos

By seaplane: Daily from Corfu (15mins); in Páxos book with **Bouas Tours, t** 266 203 2401. Beware the 12kg luggage restriction.

By sea: Year-round daily **ferry** connections from Corfu and Igoumenítsa to both Gaiós and Longós, as well as hydrofoils (1hr) from Corfu. Daily **caique** from Párga, **t** 268 403 1227. **Port authority: t** 266 203 2259.

Getting around Páxos

Boat hire (15–25hp) is essential for finding your own little cove, and is readily available at around €50 a day in any of the three village ports. **Excursion boats** circle the island, the only way to see the caves and towering cliffs (hire boats aren't allowed there), stopping at the better pebbly beaches and Antípaxos. Besides the excursion boats from Gaiós, there's a year-round regular boat to Antípaxos at 10am, returning at 5pm.

A summer **bus** that crosses the island has a rather vague schedule.

trees, many dating back to the Venetian occupation (there are some 300,000 – each family owns at least 500) and the tidy stone walls, Páxos has some of the friendliest people you'll find in Greece. It's a fashionable getaway from the mass tourism on Corfu, but the Italians, daytrippers and yachties who descend in July and August can strain the limited facilities.

History

Páxos was happily shunned by history. Mythology tells us the island was created by a blow of Poseidon's trident as a love nest for his wife Amphitrite. What mention it received in antiquity referred to its seven sea caves – Homer describes Ípapanti as having 'rooms of gold'. Another cave was used by the submariner Papanikólaos (*see* 'Meganísi', p.513) to ambush passing Italian ships, a trick unfortunately copied by German U-boats the following year.

Gáios (ΓΑΙΟΣ)

Set on an inlet, Gáios, the island's pretty toy capital, is named after the disciple of St Paul who brought Christianity to Páxos. The lanes are too narrow for cars (so narrow that people can lean out of their windows and shake hands) although human traffic jams occur during the day in the summer, especially on the worn flagstones of the handsome waterfront square. It has a small sandy beach and nearly all of Páxos' facilities, a fleet of yachts and on the harbourfront even a tiny **aquarium** of sea critters who are released and replaced pot-luck every year, so there's no telling what you'll see. For an overview of Gáios harbour, walk past the **Governor's House** and continue to the **New Port** and the new road. If you bring your own bottle, several shops sell olive oil straight from the barrel; it's so good that you can almost drink it straight.

On the rocky islet facing the harbour, **Ag. Nikólaos**, is the well-preserved **Kástro**, built by the Venetians in 1423, and an old **windmill**, and, beyond it, the islet of **Panagía**. **Mongoníssi**, another islet, is

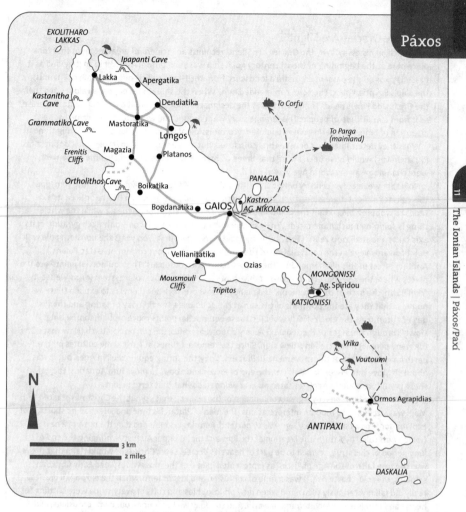

connected by a boat-taxi belonging to a restaurant, which brings customers over for dinner, and music and dancing in the evening.

A Wild Coast and Sea Caves

⭐ Cliffs and
sea caves

Whatever you do, don't miss a boat excursion to the seven **sea grottoes** of Páxos and the majestic limestone **cliffs** on the wind-beaten west coast. One cave, **Kastanítha**, towers 183m (600ft) high; another, **Orthólithos**, has a monolith standing sentinel at its entrance; caiques can enter about 5m (18ft) or so inside. Homer's wild cove and cave, **Ípapanti**, does not have the golden rooms he mentions, although it used to shelter monk seals. **Grammatikó** is the largest cave of them all. The **Moúsmouli Cliffs** have a much photographed natural bridge, **Trípitos**.

The road that crosses the island was donated by Aristotle Onassis, a great fan of Páxos. The minibus (everything on Páxos is mini) from

Why the Oracles Are Silent

Plutarch, in his essay 'Why the Oracles Are Silent', recounts an incident of great moment that took place here at the beginning of the 1st century AD. A ship was sailing from Asia Minor to Italy, and as it passed Páxos all the passengers heard a loud voice from the island calling out the name of Thamus, the ship's Egyptian pilot. The voice commanded him, 'When the ship comes opposite Palodes, tell them the Great God Pan is dead.' Thamus did so at the designated spot, and great cries of lamentation arose, as if from a multitude of people. This strange story went around the world, and even came to the attention of Emperor Tiberius, who appointed a commission of scholars to decide what it might mean.

What they determined was never entirely disclosed, but any astronomer, mythographer or priest (as Plutarch was) would have been aware that times, as measured on the great dial of the firmament, were changing – a new World Age was at hand.

Now that we're only a century or two from 'the Dawning of the Age of Aquarius', as the song goes, this calls for a slight digression. If you've ever watched a child's top spin, you'll have noticed its axis tends to wobble a bit, so that the point on top traces a slow circle through the air while the whole thing is spinning much more rapidly. The earth, in its rotation, does this too – only each gyration of its axis takes about 26,000 years. (This is why the pole stars move; in 13,000 years the northern pole will point towards Vega in the constellation of the Lyre, 50° away from our current pole star, Polaris.) Another effect of this phenomenon is the 'precession of the equinoxes'. The 'equinoctial points' are the places where the celestial equator crosses the ecliptic, the plane of our solar system (or, as we see it from Earth, the path of the sun, moon, and planets across our sky); another way to explain these points is that they are the positions of the sun at the equinoxes, the first day of spring and the first day of autumn. As the earth slowly wobbles, these equinoctial points move around, too, passing slowly through the signs of the zodiac. So every 2,160 years or so, the sun on 20 March (New Year's Day for many people) finds itself in a new sign. Since the remotest times, at least some cultures on the earth have kept track of this movement. In Plutarch's day, the spring equinox fell in Aries, but it was about to move into Pisces. Today, it's at the end of Pisces and about to move into Aquarius. Each of these periods is a 'World Age' – in case you ever wondered what that term meant.

The transition is marked by a great conjunction of the planets; that's what the Christmas star of the Magi was, according to modern interpretations. The men of Plutarch's time and later had no shortage of explanations for what their New Age was to portend. Astrologers heralded it as the birth of a new Golden Age, ruled by Saturn; the creation of the Roman Empire under Augustus, bringing the end of a long period of civil strife, seemed to be part of heaven's decree. Later, Christians would claim that theirs was the true faith of the Age of Pisces, as represented in one of the most widespread early Christian symbols, the cold, chaste fish. It was a time of confusion and loss of faith, when the old pagan oracles really did fall mysteriously silent, and when new philosophies and cults of every stripe were battling for hearts and minds in the Mediterranean world. And so today we live among our own confusions, with our own legions of dubious 'New Agers', waiting, as Yeats put it in 'The Second Coming', to see:

...what rough beast, its hour come round at last,
Slouches towards Bethlehem to be born.

Gáios runs north to **Lákka** (ΛΑΚΚΑ), a tiny port where the boats from Corfu usually call. Lákka is within easy reach of small, shady pebble beaches, and the **Byzantine church** in the village has particularly musical Russian bells, which you can ring if you find the villager with the key. Walk inland to the **church of Ípapanti**, topped by two odd stumpy, flat-topped domes, with a massive freestanding campanile on one side, crowned by an onion dome. The Venetian stone **Grammatikoú mansion** near Lákka is fortified with a tower.

Laid-back **Longós** (ΛΟΓΓΟΣ), Paxí's third minute port, is about midway between Gáios and Lákka; there's a pleasant rocky beach (and others within easy walking distance to the south of town) and a few tavernas. In tiny **Boikatiká**, the church of Ag. Charálambos contains a precious icon of the Virgin, and in nearby **Magaziá** are two churches, Ag. Spyrídon and Ag. Apóstoli; the latter's churchyard affords views of the Eremítis cliffs. At **Apergatiká** the Papamárkou mansion dates from the 17th century.

Antípaxos

A 15-minute sail south of Páxos – there are frequent excursion boats in summer – even tinier Antípaxos has only 20 permanent residents. As close as they are, the two islands are very different; the part of Antípaxos facing Páxos looks bare, almost as if it had been bitten off by a Leviathan. Rather than olive oil, Antípaxos produces good white and red wines; and, rather than pebbly beaches, Antípaxos's gentle side is graced with beaches on a Caribbean turquoise sea: **Voutoúmi** and fine white sandy **Vríka**, 'softer than silk'. There are two tavernas (try **Bella Vista**, for the promised lovely views) in the itty-bitty village and port at **Órmos Agrapídias**, but only exclusive villas if you want to stay (book through Sunvil, *see* p.60).

Useful Information on Páxos

Regular police: Gaiós, **t** 266 203 2222.

Páxos Festival

15 Aug: Gaiós

⭐ Taka Taka >>

Where to Stay and Eat on Páxos

Be prepared for prices above the norm, and in summer book with a tour operator, as they block-book most accommodation. One, **Paxos Magic**, **t** 266 203 2269 (**t** 0800 917 9409 from the UK), *www.paxosmagic.com*, is locally run and has a wide choice of studios and villas. Everyone else stays in rented rooms or studios (€30–35); a good source of listings is **Bouas**, **t** 266 203 2401, *www.bouastours.gr*.

Gáios ✉ 49082

Páxos Beach, by the beach, **t** 266 203 2211, *http://paxosbeachhotel.gr* (€€€, incl. breakfast). Congenial, family-run hotel with a tennis court, jetty and seaside restaurant and bar.

Paxos Club, **t** 266 203 2450, *http://paxosclub.gr* (€€€–€€). New studios and apartments, with a pool, children's pool and Jacuzzi. *Open May–Oct*.

Karkaletzos, in Makratika, **t** 266 203 2192. Family taverna, famous for its fried *bakaliáros* (cod).

Pizzeria il Primo, **t** 266 203 2432. Pasta, salads and 26 pizzas to choose from.

Taka Taka, **t** 266 203 2329. Lovely atmosphere and serving solid Greek fare at reasonable prices. Often full, so book. *Open June–Oct*.

Take the caique to **Mongoníssi** (*see* pp.514–15), for the excellent restaurant there, **t** 266 203 2140, and to while the day away on the beach.

Lákka ✉ 49082

Akis, **t** 266 203 1665. New restaurant-bar serving simple, inexpensive but tasty seafood and vegetable dishes.

La Rosa di Paxos, **t** 266 203 1471. Pretty little Italian restaurant featuring a wide variety of pasta dishes. *Closed Nov–April*.

Longós ✉ 49082

Vassílis, **t** 266 203 1587. Traditional taverna, good for fish and lobster.

Zákynthos/Zante (ΖΑΚΥΝΘΟΣ)

Of all their Ionian possessions the Venetians loved Zákynthos the most. *Zante, fiore di Levante* – 'the flower of the East' – they called it, and built a beautiful city on its great half-moon bay, which the earthquake in 1953 turned to rubble. Nevertheless, the disaster did nothing to diminish the soft, luxuriant charm of the landscape, the valleys planted with grape and currant vines, olive and almond groves and orchards, or the brilliant garlands of flowers and beautiful beaches. And if the buildings are gone, the Venetians left a lasting impression – many islanders have Venetian blood, which shows up not only in their names, but in their love of singing.

Anyone who reads the papers, however, knows that a different Zákynthos has been making the headlines, thanks to the young, mostly British tourists (200,000 and up) who have made Laganás their fave rave party venue, after incidents of crime and violence cast shadows over former hot spots Ag. Nápa and Faliráki – not only are young, inebriated tourists easy targets, but the bad behaviour of the tourists themselves has prompted calls from Greek legislators to crack down on people having sex in public bars and beaches. The louts haven't affected all of Zákynthos by any means, but the fact that they have chosen one of the most fragile environments in the Mediterranean for their all-night parties – the nocturnal nesting grounds of the rare loggerhead turtle – borders on the tragic.

History

Tradition has it that Zákynthos (with its -ynthos ending, a pre-Greek Pelasgian name, like labyrinth) was named after its first colonist, a son of Dardanus from Arcadia, who introduced the

Useful Information on Zákynthos

Tourist police: 62 Lombárdou, Zákynthos Town, t 269 512 4483 or t 269 512 4482.

Friendly Tours, 5 Fóskolou, Zákynthos Town, t 269 504 8030. Can help with accommodation, boat excursions to remote beaches and the mainland.

Nature World Travel, Gerakás, t 269 503 6029, www.natureworldtravel.com. Eco-friendly turtle visits in a catamaran and jeep tours of the 'real' Zákynthos from May to Oct.

Zante Feast, t 269 502 4224, www. zante-feast.org. 'Slow Food' chef Sotiris Kitrilakis arranges week-long courses in traditional cuisine, at Lithakiá.

The Best of Zante, Lithakiá, t 269 5052 141, www.bestzante.com. Diving and painting holidays, and excursions to Kefaloniá and ancient Olympia.

Zákynthos Festivals

Two weeks before Greek Lent: Carnival initiated by the Venetians, known for its masked singers and dancing.

July: The Zakýnthia, with a range of cultural activities.

End of Aug–early Sept: International Meeting of Medieval & Popular Theatre.

24 Aug and 17 Dec: Ag. Diónysios, when Zákynthos Town is strewn with myrtle, and there are fireworks at the church.

10 Nov: The slightly more modest Zoodóchos Pigí in the town.

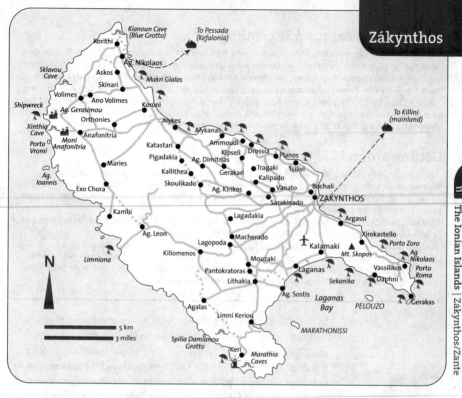

Arcadian love of music that would always characterize the island. Zákynthos fought under Odysseus at Troy, although when he returned home and shot 20 of the island's nobles – Penelope's suitors – Zákynthos rebelled and became an independent state. It set up colonies, most importantly and (distantly) Saguntum in Spain, a city that would later be demolished by Hannibal. Levinus took Zákynthos for Rome in 214 BC and, when the inhabitants rebelled, he burnt every building on the island. Uniting with the Aeolians, the islanders forced the Romans out, although in 150 BC Flavius finally brought them under control.

In 844 the Saracens based in Crete captured Zákynthos; the Byzantines expelled them, until 1182, when the Norman-Sicilian pirate Margaritone took over, and joined the island to his County Palatine of Kefaloniá. One of his successors ceded the island to the Venetians in 1209, who held on to it for almost 350 years, with a Turkish interval between 1479 and 1484. It was an eventful period: the overweening privileges of the Venetians and wealthy Zantiots provoked 'the Rebellion of the Popolari', during which the commoners seized control of the island for four years.

The influx of artists after the fall of Heráklion (1669), made Zákynthos the centre of a productive Cretan-Venetian Ionian school of painting. The Cretan-Venetian influence in local music gave birth

Getting to and around Zákynthos

By air: Flights are often at excruciating hours as they are timed not to disturb nesting turtles. **Thomas Cook** (*www.flythomascook.com*) run direct flights from many UK airports, and there are direct charters from Ireland too. There are daily flights from Athens; the **Olympic Airways** office is located at 16 Alex. Róma, Zákynthos Town, **t** 269 502 8611. **Airport information**, **t** 269 502 8322. The **airport** is 6km from town; a **taxi** will cost *c.* €9.

By sea: There are 6–7 **ferry** connections daily with Killíni on the Peloponnese mainland, linked by direct buses from Athens; and 1–2 a day in season from Pessáda (Kefaloniá) to Skinári-Ag. Nikólaos (beware that there is only one bus a day to Skinári and taxis are expensive). **Port authority**: 1 El. Venizélou, **t** 269 502 8117.

Getting around Zákynthos

All **buses** leave from the central station on Filíta Klavdianoú in Zákynthos Town (**t** 269 502 2255 for long-distance buses; **t** 269 504 2656 for local buses). There are buses every hour to Laganás, 10 times daily to Tsiliví, 4 times a day to Alykés, twice to Volímes, 3 times to Vassilikós and Porto Roma, 8 times to Kalamáki, and once to Kerí and Skinári-Ag. Nikólaos.

Car hire: **Best Choice**, **t** 269 508 3142, *www.zanteweb.gr*; **Junior**, **t** 269 502 7361, *www.junior-rentals.com*; and **Faros** (who also have motorbikes), **t** 269 502 3665, *www.faros-rentals.gr*.

Moped rentals abound: Try **Sáki Rentals**, 3 Leofóros Dimokratías, Zákynthos Town, **t** 269 502 3928.

Excursion boats sail around the island in a day from Zákynthos Town, Laganás, Skinári and Alykés, the only way to really take in the spectacular coastline, beaches and sea caves; some include drinks in the price. Make sure the boat makes plenty of stops and is small enough to fit into the caves.

---

to the island's serenades, the *kantádes*. Major poets were born on Zákynthos: the Greek-Italian Ugo Foscolo (d. 1827), Andréas Kálvos and Diónysios Solomós. Fired up by the French Revolution, Zantiot republicans formed a Jacobin Club and destroyed the rank of nobility, burning the *Libro d'Oro* that accredited the island aristocracy. In 1798, the Russians forced the French garrison and the inhabitants to surrender, and, when the Septinsular Republic established an aristocracy of its own in 1801, populist, high-spirited Zákynthos rebelled again. During the Greek War of Independence many rebels on the mainland, notably Kolokotrónis, found asylum here.

The island's feisty spirit revealed itself during the war, when Mayor Loukos Carrer and the Bishop of Zákynthos, Chrysostomos, stood up to the Nazis, who demanded that they hand over a list of all the Jews on the island – there were 275, all hidden by the islanders in remote villages. The list, when Chrysostomos handed it over, had two names on it: his own and the mayor's. 'Here are your Jews,' Chrysostomos told them. 'If you choose to deport the Jews of Zákynthos, you must also take me and I will share their fate.' Rather than risk an uprising, the Nazis gave up and all the Jews survived. Then came two earthquakes in 1953, which destroyed nearly every building on the island. And the first to send aid was Israel.

Zákynthos Town to Mount Skopós

When the time came to rebuild their earthquake-shattered town, the inhabitants gamely tried to incorporate some of the old city's delight and charm into the modern Greek concrete. They didn't quite succeed, but Zákynthos Town is spared anonymity by its setting – the ancient acropolis hovering above, crowned by a castle, and the graceful sweep of the harbour, punctuated by the striking silhouette of Mount Skopós. Wrapped along the waterfront, the streets of the long, narrow town – Lombárdou Street by the sea, and the parallel streets of Filíta, Fóskolou, Alexándrou Roma and Tertséti – are sheltered by arcades (as they were before the earthquake). The houses are one-storey, painted clapboard, draped to the hilt with bougainvillaea and hibiscus, and a few shops still sell the delicious local speciality, *mandoláto* (white nougat with almonds), among the figurines of coupling turtles.

The rebuilders failed where they should have done their best, in the seaside front parlour, **Plateía Solomoú**; although adorned with flowerbeds and a statue of the portly Diónysios Solomós, raising a hand in greeting, the square is too large and open for comfort, and its small cafés are overwhelmed by solemn buildings: the **town hall** (with a statue of another poet, Ugo Foscolo, and the inscription 'Liberty Requires Virtue and Daring'), the **Cultural Centre**, and the sailors' church, **Ag. Nikólaos tou Mólou** ('of the Mole', 1561), which was pieced together like a jigsaw after the quake.

Byzantine Museum
t 269 504 2714; open Tues–Sun 8–3; adm

The **Byzantine Museum** contributes to Plateía Solomoú's formality, but it can be forgiven this for the beauty of its contents: art salvaged from shattered churches across the island. The 17th century was a golden age for painting after the arrival of refugee artists from Crete, among them Michael Damaskinós, the teacher of El Greco. Italian influences were also strong, and by the late 18th and 19th centuries local painters were producing rosy-cheeked fluff. But before then, the Cretan-Venetian-Ionian School left Zákynthos with some spirited, lovely works, especially the iconostasis of Ag. Dimitrioú tou Kollás and of Pantokrátoras (1681), the latter covered with intricate wood carvings. The museum also contains marble fragments, ancient and Byzantine tombs, and excellent 16th-century frescoes from Ag. Andréa at Volímes, the apse showing Jesus in the cosmic womb, the side walls painted with New Testament scenes and every saint in the Orthodox calendar, the back wall covered with a Last Judgement, with a great tree branching up from hell and an empty throne awaiting, cupped by the hand of God. The icons, mostly from the 16th and 17th centuries, are superb, varying between Oriental and Western extremes. Other rooms display the creative talents of Damaskinós, Ioánnis Kýprios, Emmanuel Zána and Nikólas Kallérgis. The last bittersweet exhibit is a model of Zákynthos Town as it was before 1953.

Inland from Plateía Solomoú, you'll come across the smaller, triangular, marble-paved **Plateía Ag. Márkou** – Zákynthos' Piazza **San Marco**. This has been the social centre of town since the 15th century and was the site of the Romianiko Casino, which everyone loved but

A Patriotic Perfectionist

Of the two poets, Solomós and Kálvos, Solomós is the more intriguing character. Born in 1798, he was educated like many Ionian aristocrats in Italy and wrote his first poems in Italian. He then decided that it was time for Greece to have a Dante of its own and, like Dante, he rejected the formal language of the day (in Dante's day Latin, in Solomós' the purist Greek, or *katharévousa*) and chose instead the demotic everyday language. Nearly as important, he broke away from the 15-syllable line that dominated Greek poetry from the 17th century, and introduced Western-influenced metres and forms.

Solomós concentrated on lyrical verse until the Greek War of Independence inspired in him deeper and increasingly more spiritual works, especially 'The Free Besieged', which he wrote after the heroic resistance of Messolóngi. His verse has a degree of beauty, balance and delicacy that has rarely been matched in Greek poetry – that is, whatever fragments have survived; highly strung and hyper-critical, Solomós destroyed nearly everything he wrote in his later years on Corfu, where he often used his influence with the British to gain more lenient sentences for Greek nationalists on the Ionian islands. The first stanzas of his *Ode to Liberty*, which he composed upon hearing of the death of Lord Byron, are now the lyrics to the Greek national anthem:

Σε γνωρίζω απο την κοψυ του σπαθιου την τρομερη
σε γνωρίζω απο την οψη που με βια μετραει τη γη...

I recognize you by the fierce edge of your sword;
I recognize you by the look that measures the earth...

no one rebuilt after the earthquake. The Catholic church of San Marco, stripped of its art, occupies one end of Plateía Ag. Márkou, near the Museum of Diónysios Solomós and Eminent Zakynthians, with mementoes of the famous and photographs from before 1953. Adjacent are the mausoleums of Diónysos Solomós (*see* box, above) and Andréas Kálvos; the latter lived in London and Paris for much of his life, but was granted the wish he expressed at the end of his romantic ode 'Zante': 'May Fate not give me a foreign grave, for death is sweet only to him who sleeps in his homeland.'

Museum of Diónysios Solomós and Eminent Zakynthians
t 269 504 8982; open daily 9–2; adm

Zákynthos' most important churches were reconstructed after the earthquake, among them little **Kyrá tou Angeloú** (1687) in Louká Karrér Street, containing icons by Panagiótis Doxarás of Zákynthos and a pretty carved iconostasis. Near the Basilica tis Análipsis on Alexándrou Róma Street is the **boyhood home of Ugo Foscolo**, marked by a marble plaque and angel; apparently he used to read by the light of the icon lamp in the shrine across the street from his home. Further south from here, the restored 15th-century **FanerΟméni church** with its pretty campanile (located on the corner of Lisgará and Doxarádou streets) was, before the earthquake, one of the most beautiful churches in Greece. At the southern end of town, a huge **basilica of Ag. Diónysos** with its campanile copied from St Mark's in Venice was built on anti-seismic principles after an earthquake in 1893 and consecrated in 1948, and was one of only three buildings in town left standing after 1953. It houses the mummy of the island's patron saint and a famous 18th-century painting of the *Saint's Litany* by Nicholas Koutoúzis, and an array of gold and silver ex-votos are witness to his influence. If half of all the

Corfiots are named Spíro and half of all Kefalonians are Gerásimos, half of all Zantiots are Diónysos – or Dionysia, or Soula for short.

Upper Zákynthos Town: Bocháli

Filikóu Street, behind Ag. Márkou, leads up to Bocháli, passing by the walled Jewish cemetery and affording an excellent view of the town and sea. Bocháli was a centre of the Greek independence movement: the church of **Ag. Giórgios Filikóu** was the seat of the local branch of the revolutionary Friendly Society, and from the Bocháli crossroads a road leads to the hill of **Lófos Stráni**, where a bust of Solomós marks the spot where the poet composed the *Ode to Liberty* during the siege of Messolóngi. Another road is signposted to the well-preserved Venetian **Kástro**, a short taxi ride or five-minute walk up an old cobbled path. Three gates, the last bearing the Lion of St Mark, guarded the medieval town; the ruins of churches and walls of the ancient acropolis stand amid the pines.

Some neglected gardens in **Akrotíri** (take the north road at the Bocháli crossroads) recall long-gone Venetian villas. This was the centre of Zante society into the period of British rule; the villa that belonged to Diónysios Solomós' father was the residence of the High Commissioner. At the **Villa Crob**, the British laid out the first tennis court in Greece. Down in the north end of town, a romantically melancholy **British cemetery** is wedged next to the green cliffs (turn right at Bociári Street from N. Kolíva).

Kástro
*t 269 504 8099;
open summer
Tues–Sun 8–7; winter
Tues–Sun 8–3; adm*

The Ionian Islands | Zákynthos/Zante

Where to Stay in Zákynthos Town

Zákynthos Town ✉ 29100

Bitzaro, on the waterfront, t 269 502 3644, *www.bitzarohotels.gr* (€€€). Smart rooms with all the mod cons, incl. a balcony and a pleasant veranda.

Diana, 2 Mitropóleos and Ag. Márkos, t 269 502 8547, *www.dianahotels.gr* (€€€). Smart, central, modern hotel.

Strada Marina, 14 K. Lombárdou St, t 269 504 2761, *www.stradamarina.gr* (€€€, breakfast included). Large, renovated, on the waterfront; the roof garden has a pool and bar open till the wee hours in summer. *Open all year.*

Apollon, 30 Tertséti, t 269 504 2838 (€€). Small, intimate hotel with lots of character, a good central choice. *Open April–Oct.*

Dessy, 73 N. Kolíva, t 269 502 8505 (€€). Reasonable, near the centre of town.

Phoenix, Plateía Solomoú, t 269 504 2419, *www.zantephoenix.gr* (€€).

Comfortable rooms, all with air-con, Internet, and satellite TV. *Open all year.*

Eating Out in Zákynthos Town

Aresti, by the Krionéri lighthouse, t 269 502 7379 (€22). Dine either inside among antiques and oil paintings, or outside on the terrace with views out over the sea. The chef is Brazilian, and her speciality is leg of pork with chilli, mushrooms and Chinese-style rice.

Komis, by the main port, t 269 502 6915 (€30). Some of the best food in town is served in a fisherman's 'hut' in a beautiful setting, where the lovely fresh fish are priced by the kilo and all the veg is fresh picked from the owner's garden.

To Antéti, just outside town in Kípo, t 269 502 3612. Very Greek and traditional, serving the island's classic dishes, often accompanied by music.

Karavomilos, on the road to Argássi, near the basilica of Ag. Diónysos

(€15–20). Has a reputation for the best fish on the island; the friendly owner will recommend the best of the day's catch.

Malanos, 38 Ag. Athanásou, **t** 269 504 5936. In a similar direction; since 1974,

locals in the know have headed to this delightful place for lunch, especially for the moussaka, lamb and veal *giovétsi*.

Base Bar, on Plateía Ag. Márkos in Zákynthos Town. This lively nightspot has a jazzy ensemble.

Beaches under Mount Skopós: the Vassilikós Peninsula

Beaches line the rugged eastern Vassilikós peninsula under Mount Skopós, especially beyond **Argássi** (APΓAΣI), with its assembly line of hotels and tavernas. Further along, there's wide, sandy **Pórto Zóro** (Banana Beach), strewn with sea daffodils, which emit such a strong fragrance that they may have been the origin of the nickname, Fiore di Levante. This is followed by **Ag. Nikólaos**, **Mavrándzi** and the thinnish crescent at **Pórto Róma**, all with tavernas. The 16th-century **Domenegini Tower** here was used during the Greek War of Independence for covert operations by the Friendly Society, which sent men and supplies over to the Peloponnese. To keep busybodies away, they spread word that the tower was haunted, and even installed a 'devil' at night to holler and throw stones at passers-by.

Vassilikós (BAΣIΛΛIKOΣ) has a lovely beach, while, right at the tip of the peninsula, **Gérakas** has the most beautiful stretch of white sand on the island, perfect for toddlers, but it's also a favourite with nesting loggerhead turtles so water sports are forbidden. Learn more at the **Wildlife Information Centre**, where you also find out about Nature World Travel's eco-friendly turtle-spotting cruises; if funds arrive, a rescue centre for turtles is planned nearby for 2007.

Roads cross the peninsula for **Daphní** and **Sekánika**, two secluded beaches to the south, facing Laganás Bay, set aside (supposedly) for the turtles.

Wildlife Information Centre
t 269 503 6029; open May–Oct 10–6

Where to Stay and Eat on Vassilikós Peninsula

 Ionian Eco-Villagers >>

Argássi ✉ 29100

Family Inn, Argássi, **t** 269 504 5359, *www.thefamilyinn.co.uk* (€€). Quiet, family-run, very popular with a pool.

Vassilikós/Gérakas ✉ 29100

The Bay, Vassilikós, **t** 269 503 5435, *www.thebay.gr* (€€€€€). Serene, beautifully refurbished minimalist designer complex on the beach.

Sea Castle, near Vassilikós, **t** 269 503 5053, *www.seacastle-zante.com* (€€€). Handsome seafront suites in stone buidings with lots of extras.

Aquarius, 200m from the beach at Vassilikós, **t** 269 503 5300 (€€€). Prettily

set amongst lush greenery, complete with a new pool, 'a place to forget the world'.

Ionian Eco-Villagers, Gérakas, book in the UK, **t** +44 (0)871 7115 065, *www. relaxing-holidays.com* (€€; from £370 for two per week, with breakfast and transfers). Studios and village houses sleeping up to five, managed by local conservation group Earth, Sea and Sky, pioneering sustainable tourism on the island. *Open May–Oct.*

O Adelfos tou Kosta, on the main road in Vassilikós, **t** 269 503 5347. Traditional taverna in a garden with the opportunity to hear *kantádes*. There are some delicious starters, including *kolokitho-keftédes* (courgette rissoles), *tiro-krokétes* (cheese croquettes), and a delicious rabbit and cockerel casserole.

Up Mount Skopós

From the edge of Argássi, a road leads up through the wildflowers, including several species of indigenous orchid, to the top of Mount Skopós ('Lookout'), the Mount Hellatos of the ancient Greeks and the *Mons Nobilis* of Pliny the Elder, who also wrote of a cavern here that led straight to the Underworld. On the way note the picturesque ruins and mosaic floor of the 11th-century **Ag. Nikólaos Megalomátis**, built on the site of a Temple to Artemis.

The views from Mount Skopós not only take in all of Zákynthos, but also the Peloponnese and the Bay of Navarino, where on 20 October 1827 a Turko-Egyptian navy was defeated by the Anglo-Franco-Russian fleet, leading to Greek independence. By the rocky lump summit or *toúrla* of Mount Skopós stands the white **Panagía Skopiótissa**. The interior is decorated with frescoes and a stone iconostasis; the icon of the Virgin was painted in Constantinople, and there's a double-headed Byzantine eagle mosaic on the floor.

Laganás Bay and the South

On the map, Zákynthos looks like a piranha with huge gaping jaws, about to devour a pair of crumb-sized fish in Laganás Bay. These small fry are **Marathoníssi** and **Peloúzo**, the former with a lovely sandy beach, the latter settled in 1473 BC by King Zákynthos. Overripe tourist sprawl follows the sandy beaches step by step, starting at **Kalamáki**, the closest resort to the airport on the east end of the bay, with a wonderful beach under Mount Skopós. Building work suggests it may soon rival neighbouring **Laganás** (ΛΑΓΑΝΑΣ), Zákynthos' Blatant Beast, with a 'Golden Mile' of pubs showing the latest *Big Brother* episodes and open bars throbbing with music and flashing lights, the joy of young Brit revellers and the despair of the loggerhead turtles (*see* box, overleaf). A bridge leads out to the pretty islet of **Ag. Sostís**, its limestone cliffs falling abruptly where the earthquake of 1633 cleaved it from Zákynthos.

The Belgian on the Beach

Not a few sunbathers at Laganás are keen students of the opposite sex's anatomy. None, however, is as studiously keen as Vesalius (1514–64), the Renaissance father of anatomy, whose statue stands at the southern end of the beach. Born in Brabant, Vesalius studied in Paris, where he edited the 2nd-century AD anatomical works of Galen, the Greek physician to the gladiators and Emperor Marcus Aurelius. Vesalius went on to the University of Padua, and developed it into the leading school of anatomy in Europe, publishing in 1543 his milestone *De humani corporis fabrica*, the first thorough and original study of the human body since Galen. In 1555 Vesalius became the personal physician to Philip II of Spain, only to be sentenced to death by the Inquisition for dissecting a dead Spaniard. Philip commuted the sentence to a pilgrimage to the Holy Land, and on the way home the doctor's ship was wrecked at Laganás Bay. Vesalius, realizing that a return to Inquisition-plagued Madrid would mean an end to his studies anyway, decided to live out his days in the now ruined Franciscan monastery at Faneró, which is on the road from Laganás to Pantokrátoras; his epitaph there is intact.

Tourists versus Turtles: Loggerheads over Loggerheads

Loggerhead turtles (*Caretta caretta*) are one of the oldest species on earth, and for countless millennia some 80 per cent of those in the Mediterranean have gathered every summer at the sandy beaches of Zákynthos, especially in Laganás Bay. The mother turtles crawl up onto the beaches at night, dig a hole with their back legs, lay between 100 and 120 eggs the size of golf balls and cover them up again before lumbering back to the sea. For 60 days the eggs incubate in the warm sands, and, when they hatch, the baby turtles make a break for the sea. For the loggerheads to survive, their nesting zones need to remain undisturbed as much as possible, a problem that the island has had difficulty reconciling with the desires of its tourists. For the loggerheads to survive, people have to stay away from the nearby waters where the turtles mate, and stay off the beaches between dusk and dawn, and not poke parasols and sunbeds in the sand, run vehicles over it, or anything else similar. Even then the odds for the hatchlings aren't good: the lights in the bay are liable to distract them from their race to the sea, and they die of exhaustion. One out of a thousand hatchlings survives to reach adulthood.

By 1983, when nests and hatchlings were in steep decline, Archelon, the Sea Turtle Protection Society of Greece, was formed to monitor the loggerheads, mark their nests and inform tourists to minimize their impact. Critical areas were set aside for turtles, but local property owners, many feeling unjustly uncompensated, did all they could to sabotage Archelon's efforts, even setting fires on the beaches to keep the turtles away. In December 1999, the National Marine Park of Zákynthos was established around Gérakas. Opposition has occasionally been violent – in 2000 a co-ordinator was beaten with an iron bar by two men who jet-skied into the park – but the Greek government's neglect has been far more damaging. Citing the financial squeeze of the Olympics, the National Marine Park's budget was cut to zero, and illegal use of its sands and seas soared, leading to condemnations in 2002 and 2004 from the European Court of Justice. In the meantime, other initiatives – satellite tracking of turtles, beach cleaning, ongoing volunteer monitoring of nests in the summer and a campaign to use 'circle hooks' in long-line fishing to prevent the deaths of 200,000 loggerheads a year – have been set under way by non-profit groups that work alongside the National Marine Park, Archelon, Medasset (the Mediterranean Association to Save the Sea Turtle), and the Zákynthos-based Earth, Sea and Sky.

A Gently Inclined Plain

Behind Laganás extends the lush plain of Zákynthos, a lovely, fairly flat region to cycle through, dotted with the ruins of old country estates. The chief village to aim for is **Pantokrátoras**, near three fine churches: the beautiful **Pantokrátor**, founded by Byzantine Empress Pulcheria; **Kiliómeno**, restored after the quake, with beautiful icons; and the medieval church of the **Panagía**, with a pretty bell tower and stone carvings. The picturesque ruins of the **Villa Loúndzis**, once one of Zákynthos' most noble estates, are in **Sarakína** nearby.

Lithakiá, south of Pantokrátoras, has another restored church, the 14th-century **Panagía Faneroméni**, containing works of art gathered from ruined churches in the vicinity. Although 10 minutes from Laganás, Lithakiá's stretch of sand has stayed resolutely Greek.

From Lithakiá the main road continues south over the **Ávyssos Gorge** – a rift made by the 1633 earthquake – to the coastal swamp known as **Límni Kerioú** or Kerí Lake. If you look at the roots of the aquatic plants, you can see the black bitumen or natural pitch that once welled up in sufficient quantity to caulk thousands of boats; both Herodotus and Pliny described the phenomenon. From the sea, this coast is marked by sheer white cliffs, a second Mount Skopós, dark blue waters and two towering natural arches at **Marathía**.

Where to Stay and Eat in Southern Zákynthos

Kalamáki ✉ 29100

Bitzaro Palace, t 269 504 5773, *www. bitzarohotels.gr* (€€€). If you're booking a package, this is one of the best to aim for; the new **Bitzaro Grande Hotel** nearby (same website) has even more facilities and two-bed apartments.

Mikaélos, t 269 504 8080. One of the best tavernas in Zákynthos; beef and rabbit are excellent. *Closed Nov–April.*

Zakanthi, t 269 504 3586. Restaurant-bar in a pretty garden, specializing in mainland dishes – also one of the few places to serve cider. *Closed Nov–April.*

Lithakiá ✉ 29100

Leeda's Village, t 269 505 1305, *www. leedas-village.com* (€€€). Five stone-built villas, decorated in traditional style and sleeping up to nine in a lovely garden setting – each in fact has its own vegetable garden for guests. Boat, car and bike rentals available as well.

Tsivouli Park, t 269 505 5018, *www. zanteweb.gr/tsivouli-park* (€€). Be different – stay on an emu farm with Anglo-Swiss owners.

Avgoustiatis Ouzerie. Come here for wonderful *mezédes*.

Kerí ✉ 29100

Revera Villas, t 269 502 7524, *www. revera-zante.com* (€€€). Stone villas with traditional furnishings, divided into two apartments sleeping six.

La Bruschetta, Límni Ke400, **t** 269 502 8128. In a lovely setting, the best Italian restaurant on the island, from the *stuzzichini* to the pizza and pasta.

To Fanári tou Kerioú, by the lighthouse, **t** 269 504 3384. A modern taverna by the sea, dedicated to the revival of traditional recipes: organic veg and home-made bread. *Closed Nov–April.*

⭐ To Fanári tou Kerioú ≫

At the end of the road, **Kerí** is a small resort with a beach and fine views, especially from the lighthouse 1km from the village. A secondary road winds northwest to one of Zákynthos' more remote villages, **Agalás**, passing by way of the two-storey grotto called **Spília Damianoú**, where one formation resembles a horse. The legend goes that a giant named Andronia once lived in the area and continually pestered the good people of Agalás for food. His appetite was huge, and the people were at their wits' end when an old lady slipped him a poisoned pie. Down he fell at a place called Andronia, where you can see twelve 15th-century wells with their old well-heads. The giant's horse was so shocked that it turned to stone.

Heading Northwest

From Zákynthos Town the coastal road leads north, past the **Kryonéri Fountain**, built by the Venetians to water their ships; the red rock overhead featured as a suicide leap in a popular Greek novel, *Kókkinos Vráchos*. Beyond lie a series of sandy beaches, backed by orchards and vineyards where holiday development is taking off with abandon: long and narrow **Tsiliví** (ΤΣΙΛΙΒΙ), with a beach safe for children; **Plános** (overlooking Tragáki Beach); little **Ámpoula** with golden sand; **Pachiámmos**; **Drossiá**; **Psaroú**; **Ammoúdi**; and **Alykanás**, where a wonderful long stretch of sand sweeps around the bay west to **Alykés** (ΑΛΥΚΕΣ), a resort named after the nearby salt pans, with a pretty 15th-century Venetian bridge.

The rich agricultural interior is pleasant to explore, though directions can be a bit confusing. **Skoulikádo** has several handsome churches, among them **Panagía Anafonítria**, with stone reliefs and a lovely interior, and **Ag. Nikólaos Megalomáti**, named after a 16th-century icon painted on stone of St Nicholas, with unusually large eyes. **Ag. Marína**, a rare survivor of the earthquake, has a cell behind the altar where the insane would be chained in the hope of a cure.

Inland from Alykés, **Katastári** is the island's second-largest town; from here you can continue into the mountains or follow the coast to **Korithí**. In its early stages this coastline is a sequence of beautiful pebbled beaches, such as **Makrí Aloú** and **Makrí Gialós**, becoming more dramatic, volcanic and inaccessible to the north.

The port of **Ag. Nikólaos/Skinári**, where the ferry from Kefaloniá calls, nestles in a bay with beautiful views of its eponymous islet. The white coast around here is pocked with caves, cliffs, natural columns and arches, and most spectacularly of all, one hour by boat from Skinári, **Kianoún Cave**, the local Blue Grotto, glowing with every imaginable shade of blue; the light is best in the morning. Excursion boats also run around the northern tip of the island and south to **Xinthía Cove**, with sulphur springs and rocks and sand so hot that you need swimming shoes – and to the **Cave of Sklávou**.

Where to Stay and Eat in Northwest Zákynthos

Tsiliví ✉ 29100

Contessina, t 269 502 2508, *www. contessinahotel.gr* (€€). This pleasant hotel with a pool might be able to squeeze you in if everything else is full.

Le Maschere, t 269 506 3735. Classic Italian trattoria by Ampoúla beach.

Olive Tree. The first taverna in town.

Tragáki ✉ 29100

Paliokaliva Village, 1km from the sea, **t** 269 506 3770, *www. paliokaliva.gr* (€€€€€). In a peaceful olive grove, well-equipped stone bungalows and houses sleeping up to five, with a pool.

Porto Zante, t 269 506 5100, *www. portozante.com* (€€€€€). The island's top luxury retreat – a selection of private designer villas by the sea, each with private heated pools, wooden floors and marble fireplaces.

Ktima Kourou, t 269 506 5230, *www.ktimakourou.com* (€€€). Five traditional stone-built cottages in an idyllic setting amid a large olive grove, sleeping up to eight.

Ag. Dimitríos ✉ 29100

Aresti Villas, inland at Ag. Dimitríos, **t** 269 502 8522, *www.aresti.gr* (€€€€€). Eight stone-built villas, with private pools and gardens, on a traditional farm with horses, sheep, ducks, etc., vegetable gardens and olive groves.

Alykanás ✉ 29100

Valais, t 269 504 5261, *www.valais.gr* (€€€). Popular for its great location on the white sands with a pool, water sports, and more. *Open April–Oct.*

Mantalena, t 269 508 3550, *www. mantalena.com*. Friendly family-run taverna offering traditional Greek food in a pretty setting; also **studios**.

Alykés ✉ 29100

Peligoni Club, north of Alykés, book in the UK, **t** (01243) 511 499, *www. peligoni.com* (€€€€€). Well away from the block-booked beach resorts; English-owned surf and sailing holiday haven set into the rugged volcanic coastline. A sprinkling of villas, most with lovely pools. The club caters just as well for water sports beginners and experts as it does for landlubbers; there are painting holidays and 'restoration' breaks for those in need of stress-free relaxation and pampering.

Ionian Star, t 269 508 3416, *www. ionian-star.gr* (€€€). Recently renovated, right on the sea.

Olympic Kitchen Bar, t 269 508 3507. Book to get a table at the trendiest restaurant on the island, with a beautiful designer interior and delicious arty food – around €25.

Ag. Nikólaos ✉ 29100

Nobelos, t 269 502 7632, *www.nobelos. gr* (€€€€€). Sumptuous suites with every conceivable facility in a beautiful stone villa, with paved courtyards and an inviting sun platform. *Book early.*

Up the Southwest Coast

Unlike the low rolling hills and plain of the east, the west coast of Zákynthos plunges steeply into the sea, rearing up 1,000ft in places. Taking the pretty road from Zákynthos Town, **Macherádo** is the last stop on the plain, where the white 14th-century church of **Ag. Mávra**, an earthquake survivor, has a very ornate interior, with a beautiful 3rd-century icon of the saint (who lived in Egypt) covered with ex-votos and scenes in silver of her life; the Venetian church bells are famous for their clear musical tones. The 16th-century **church of the Ípapanti** has a handsome campanile. Macherádo is also famous for the **Domaine Agria**, the oldest winery in Greece, run by the Comoutós family since 1638. The Comoutóses made their fortune in raisins and currants, and were ennobled in the *Libro d'Oro*; today their estate is divided between olive groves and vines. In nearby **Lagopóda** there is more wine, and the pretty crenellated **Eleftherías Convent**, where nuns make fine needlework.

Domaine Agria
t 269 509 2284,
www.comoutos.gr;
open daily 9–1 and 5–8

From Macherádo the road rises to **Kiloménos**, with a handsome stone bell tower from 1893, attached to the church of **Ag. Nikólaos** and carved with Masonic symbols; its original pyramidal crown has broken off, giving it a stumpy look. A secondary road leads towards the savage coast and the **Karakonísi**, a bizarre islet that resembles a whale, and even spouts great plumes of spray when the wind is up. At **Ag. Léon** (with another striking bell tower, this time converted from a windmill) there's another road to the coast, to the narrow creek and minute sandy beach at **Limnióna**. Just before Exó Chóra, a road descends to **Kámbi**, where Mycenaean rock-cut tombs were found and tavernas perched on the 200m (650ft) cliffs are spectacular sunset-viewing platforms.

The main road continues to **Anafonítria**, where the 15th-century **Moní Anafonítria** with its prominent defensive tower survived several earthquakes intact along with its time-darkened frescoes and cell of St Diónysos – he was abbot here, and one of his claims to sainthood was that he gave sanctuary to his own brother's killer. Below is **Pórto Vrómi**, 'Dirty Port', because of the natural tar that blankets the shore, although the water is perfectly clear. Around the corner is the scene that graces a thousand Greek postcards: the **Navágio** or 'shipwreck', half buried in a perfect white sandy beach, wedged under sheer limestone crags washed by a turquoise sea – inaccessible by land but a prime destination for excursion boats. In the late 1980s cigarette-smugglers ran the ship aground when they were about to be nabbed by the coastguard, and escaped. When word reached the villages above, immediate action was taken, and by the time the coastguard boarded the ship it was empty; the free smokes – some 16 million cigarettes, according to legend – lasted for years. You can look down at the beach from the path near the abandoned 16th-century **Monastery of Ag. Geórgios sta Kremná** that leads to the narrow cave-chapel of Ag. Gerásimou.

The road passes through an increasingly dry landscape to **Volímes** (ΒΟΛΙΜΕΣ), the largest village on the west coast, permanently festive, with billowing, colourful handwoven goods displayed for sale. Seek out the fine church of **Ag. Paraskeví** and the **Áskos Stone Park**, a natural park with a wide range of animals. **Áno Volímes**, just above, is a pretty little mountain village.

Áskos Stone Park
t 269 503 1650; open all year daily; adm

The Strofádes

Excursion boats from Zákynthos sail the 37 nautical miles south to the Strofádes (there are two islets, **Arpyía** and **Stamfáni**), passing over the deepest point in the entire Mediterranean Sea, where you would have to dive 442m (1,449ft) down to reach Davy Jones' locker. Strofádes means 'turning' in Greek: according to ancient myth, the Harpies, those composite female monsters with human heads, hands and feet, winged griffon bodies and bear ears, were playing their usual role as the hired guns of the gods, chasing the prophet Phineas over the little islets, when Zeus changed his mind and ordered them to turn around immediately and come back.

Although little more than green pancakes in the sea, the Strofádes offered just the right kind of rigorous isolation that Orthodox monks and mystics crave, and accordingly in the 13th century Irene, wife of the Byzantine emperor Theodore Láskaris, founded the **Pantochará** ('All Joy') **Monastery** on Arpyía. Pirates were a problem, and in 1440, just before Constantinople itself fell to the Turks, Emperor John Palaeológos sent funds to build high walls around it. As on Mount Áthos, no women or female animals were allowed, and the 40 monks who resided there (among them the future saint Diónysos) spent their days studying rare books. In 1530, however, the Saracens managed to breach the high walls, slew all the monks and plundered the monastery; in 1717 the body of Ag. Diónysos was removed to Zákynthos Town for safe keeping. The evocative, desolate monastic citadel is owned by the Monastery of Ag. Diónysos, and is slowly being restored after damage in a 1997 earthquake.

The population of the Strofádes has been reduced to migratory birds; it's an important stopover.

The Northeastern Aegean Islands

Lying off the coasts of Turkey and Northern Greece, the Northeastern Aegean islands have very different histories, but share a rugged individualism and strong character. Although rarely calendar-cute, they offer bustling capital towns full of provincial life, deep, still villages and landscapes out of time – places to linger and just 'be'.

With the exceptions of Sámos, with two decades of package-tour experience under its belt, and Thássos, long a favourite with its golden ring of beaches, these islands are the last frontier in Greek island tourism.

13

Don't miss

⭐ **Golden beaches**
Thássos **p.604**

⭐ **Ancient glories and engineering marvels**
Pythagório, Sámos **p.586**

⭐ **Delightful *naïf* paintings**
Theóphilos Museum, Lésvos **p.561**

⭐ **Unique Genoese mastic villages**
Chíos **p.541**

⭐ **Fresh lobster dinners**
Foúrni **p.555**

See map overleaf

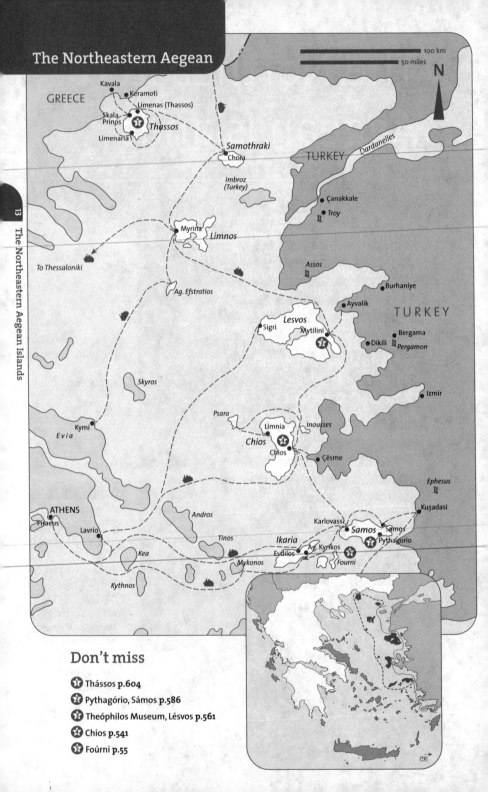

The Northeastern Aegean

100 km
50 miles

N

GREECE

Kavala
Keramoti
Limenas (Thassos)
Skala
Prinos
Thassos
Limenaria

Samothraki
Chora

TURKEY *Dardanelles*

Imbroz (Turkey)

Çanakkale
Troy

Myrina *Limnos*

To Thessaloniki

Assos

Ag. Efstratios

Burhaniye

Ayvalik

TURKEY

Lesvos
Sigri Mytilini

Bergama
Dikili *Pergamon*

Izmir

Skyros

Psara

Limnia
Inousses
Chios
Chios

Çesme

Kymi
Evia

Ephesus

ATHENS
Piraeus

Lavrio

Andros

Karlovassi
Samos Samos
Pythagorio

Kuşadasi

Tinos

Ikaria
Evdilos Ag. Kyrikos
Fourni

Kea

Mykonos

Kythnos

Don't miss

⭐ Thássos **p.604**

⭐ Pythagório, Sámos **p.586**

⭐ Theóphilos Museum, Lésvos **p.561**

⭐ Chíos **p.541**

⭐ Foúrni **p.55**

Most of these islands were colonized in the 12th century BC, when Aeolian and Ionian Greeks of the mainland fled the Dorian new-comers, taking refuge on the coasts of Asia Minor and the islands. By the 7th and 6th centuries BC, their cities were among the most important in Greece in trade, in the production of wine and olive oil, in religion and culture; the islands alone produced Pythagoras, Sappho and probably Homer himself. **Samothrace** was synonymous with its sanctuary of the gods of the underworld; **Límnos** was dedicated to the smithy god Hephaistos, and on **Sámos** the temple of the goddess Hera was famous across the ancient world. These prosperous and independent islands slipped into obscurity as they fell prey to the powers around them, first the Persians from the east and then the Athenians from the West, and then from Asia Minor again in the form of the Ottoman Empire. They were annexed to Greece only in 1912, following the Balkan Wars.

The islands were the last to be 'discovered', partly due to their great distance from Athens – **Ikaría**, the closest, is a ten-hour journey by traditional ferry. Almost all now have fast ferries and airports, although places are limited and anyone planning to fly there during the summer should reserve a seat as much as two months in advance.

Chíos (ΧΙΟΣ)

Soak me with jars of Chian wine and say 'Enjoy yourself, Hedylus.' I hate living emptily, not drunk with wine.

Hedylus, c. 280 BC

Chíos is a fascinating and wealthy island, the fifth largest in Greece, celebrated for its shipowners, friendly good humour and the gum mastic that grows here and nowhere else in the world. It has lush fertile plains, thick pine forests, mainly unspoiled beaches, Mediterranean scrublands tufted with maquis and startlingly barren mountains that bring to mind the 'craggy Chíos' of Homer, who may have been born on the island. Its architecture is unique and varied, and its church of Néa Moní has some of the finest 11th-century Byzantine mosaics anywhere.

Orion, Hunter and Hunted

Chíos was favoured by Poseidon, and is said to owe its name to the heavy snowfall (*chioni*) that fell when the sea god was born. Vines were introduced to the island by Oenopion, a son of Ariadne and Theseus. Oenopion pledged his daughter Merope to the handsome giant hunter Orion, on the condition that he rid Chíos of its ferocious beasts, a task Orion easily performed – it was his boast that given time he could rid the entire earth of its monsters. Rather than give Orion his reward, however, Oenopion kept putting him off (for he loved his daughter himself), and finally Orion in anger raped Merope. For this the king poked out his eyes. Orion then set out blindly, but the goddess of dawn, Eos, fell in love with him and persuaded Helios the sun god to restore his sight. Before he could avenge himself on Oenopion, however, Orion was killed when Mother Earth, angry at his boasting about monsters, sent a giant scorpion after him. Orion fled the scorpion, but his friend Artemis, the goddess of the hunt, killed him by mistake. In mourning, she immortalized him in the stars.

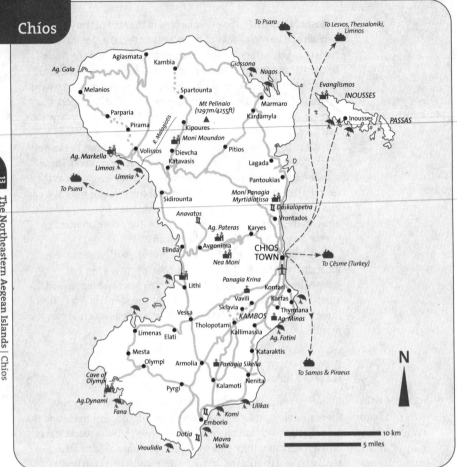

History

Inhabited by *c.* 4500 BC, Chíos was colonized by seafaring Pelasgians who left walls near Éxo Dídyma and Kouroúnia and a Temple of Zeus on Mount Pelinaío. The Mycenaeans followed, and were in turn usurped in the 9th or 8th century BC by Ionians from Évia (it was their northernmost settlement); one contested tradition asserts that Homer was born here shortly after. Archaic Chíos was a thriving, independent kingdom, founding trade counters or *emporia*, notably Voroniki in Egypt. It was famed for its mastic and wine (especially from the medicinal *arioúsios* grapes), and for its sculpture workshop and system of government, studied by Solon and adapted for use in his Athenian reforms. Around 490 BC, a Chiot sculptor, Glaucus, invented the art of soldering metals; on the minus side, Chíos was the first state in Greece to engage in slave-trading. One of the 12 cities of Archaic Ionic Confederacy, Chíos joined Athens in the Battle of Lade (494 BC) in an unsuccessful attempt to overthrow the

Getting to Chíos

By air: Olympic and Aegean fly to Chíos from Athens, and Olympic flies several times a week from Thessalóniki. **Olympic** on Chíos: **t** 227 102 4515; **Aegean: t** 227 108 1051. **Taxis** make the 4km journey to Chíos Town for under €12.

By sea: There are daily **ferry** connections with Piraeus, Lésvos and Inoússes; less often with Thessaloníki, Kávala, Límnos, Psará, Sámos, Ikaría, Mýkonos and Sýros; in summer you can book one-day excursions to Psará and Inoússes. **Miniotis Lines,** 21 Neoríon St, **t** 227 102 4670, *www.miniotis.gr*, and **Sunrise Tours,** 28 Kanári St, **t** 227 104 1390, *www.sunrisetours.gr*, have daily ferries to Çesme (Turkey) and organize tours as far as Ephesus. **Port authority:** Chíos Town, **t** 227 104 4433.

Getting around Chíos

Blue **buses** (**t** 227 102 2079) serve Chíos Town, making 5–6 trips daily to the Kámbos area, Karfás Beach, and Vrontádos. Green KTEL buses depart from near the ferry dock (**t** 227 102 7507) and have a useful waiting room with lockers.

Taxi: t 227 104 1111.

Chíos has surprising good wide roads. **Car hire: Vassilakis,** 3 E. Chandrís, **t** 227 102 9300, *www.chios.gr/ vassilakis*; **The Travel Shop,** 56 Leof. Aegeou, **t** 227 102 0160, or **Aegean Spirit,** 114 Leof. Aegéou, **t** 227 104 1277, www. *aegeanspirit.gr.*

Persian yoke, but after the Battle of Plateía it regained its independence, and held on to it even after Athens made its other allies into tribute-paying dependencies, until 412 BC, when it revolted against Athens, only to be crushed.

Chíos allied itself with Rome and fought the enemy of the Empire, Mithridates of Pontus (83 BC), only to be defeated and destroyed. In the 4th century AD Chíos made the even greater mistake of siding against Constantine, who conquered the island and carried off to his new city of Constantinople many of Chíos' famous ancient sculptures – including the four bronze horses that ended up on St Mark's in Venice. In 1261 the Emperor Michael Paleológos gave Chíos to the Giustiniani, the Genoese family who helped him reconquer Constantinople from the Franks. In 1344, the Giustiniani chartered the Maona (from the Arabic *Maounach,* or trading company) of 12 merchants and shipowners, who exported wine and mastic, built beautiful estates in Kámbos and governed until 1566 when Chíos was lost to the Turks.

The Sultans loved Chíos, especially its sweet mastic, and they granted it more privileges than any other island, including a degree of autonomy. It became famous for its doctors and chess players; elsewhere in Greece, the cheerfulness of the Chiots was equated with foolishness. The cheerfulness came to an abrupt end in 1822. Although the islanders had refused to join in the revolt against the Turks, a band of 2,000 ill-armed Samians disembarked on Chíos, proclaimed independence and forced them to join the struggle. The Sultan, furious at this subversion of his favoured island, ordered his admiral Kara Ali to make an example of Chíos that the Greeks would never forget. In two weeks an estimated 30,000 were slaughtered, and another 45,000 taken into slavery; the Sultan's sweet tooth

ⓘ Chíos ›
EOT: 11 Kanári St, Chíos
Town, **t** 227 104 4389,
*www.chiosnet.gr; open
April–Sept Mon–Fri
7–2.30 and 6.30–9.30,
Sat and Sun 10–1;
Oct–Mar Mon–Fri 7–2.30*

Useful Information on Chíos

Tourist police: at the far end of the quay, next to the regular police, **t** 227 104 4427.

Post office: at the corner of Omírou and Rodokanáki.

Chíos Festivals

Greek Carnival: Chíos Town, with floats and costumes.

22 July: Chíos' most important festival, Ag. Markélla, is at Ag. Markélla Monastery, and in Volissós and Karyés.

15 Aug: Pirgí and Kámbos.

dictated that only the mastic villages survived. All who could fled to other islands, especially to Sýros (where they picked up useful lessons about owning ships), before moving to England, France and Egypt. When news of the massacre reached Europe, Delacroix painted his stirring canvas (now in the Louvre) and Victor Hugo sent off reams of rhetoric. On 6 June of the same year, the Greek Admiral Kanáris took revenge on Kara Ali by blowing him and 2,000 men up with his flagship. In 1840 Chíos attained a certain amount of autonomy under a Christian governor, but in 1881 suffered another tragedy in an earthquake that killed nearly 4,000 people. It was incorporated into Greece in November 1912.

Chíos Town (Chóra)

Visitors to Chíos arriving by ferry often wonder what they've let themselves in for. Chíos Town (pop. 30,000) doesn't even try to look like a Greek island town, with its tall buildings and a score of brightly lit bars, pool halls and tavernas, nearly all built after the earthquake of 1881. Yet after the first surprise, the town – a sister city of Genoa, for old times' sake – with its provincial buzz and narrow market lanes, is a likeable place.

Most of what survives from the Turkish occupation – now in the first throes of restoration – is enclosed within the Byzantine **fortress**, which more or less follows the lines of the Macedonian castle destroyed by Mithridates. After 1599 only Turks and Jews were allowed to live inside; the Greeks had to be outside the main gate or Porta Maggiore when it closed at sundown. Within the walls is a ruined **mosque** and a **Turkish cemetery** with the **tomb of Kara Ali**, 'Black Ali', author of the massacre of Chíos. The tomb's surprisingly unvandalized state is perhaps the best testimony to the easygoing nature of the Chiots, remarked on since antiquity. In a closet-sized **prison** by the gate, Bishop Pláto Fragiádis and 75 leading Chiots were incarcerated as hostages before they were hanged by the Turks in 1822. The **Giustiniani Museum**, in a mansion just inside the gate, contains a fascinating collection of detached frescoes, carvings and early Christian mosaics.

Giustiniani Museum
*t 227 102 2819; open
Tues–Sun 9–3; adm*

Main **Plateía Vounakíou** with its cafés and plane trees is a few minutes' walk away. It has a statue of Bishop Pláto Fragiádis, and in

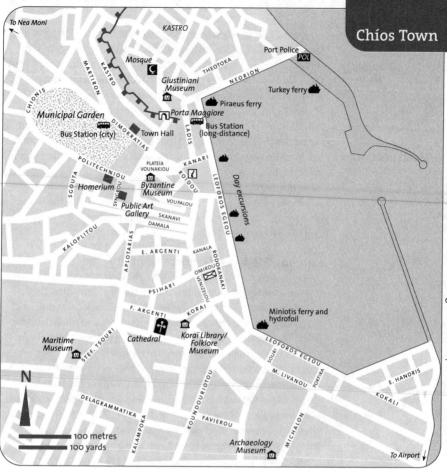

the municipal gardens behind the square is a flamboyant one of Kara Ali's avenging angel, 'Incendiary' Kanáris, a native of Psará. Plateía Vounakíou's crumbling **mosque** is marked with the Tugra, the swirling 'thumbprint of the Sultan' that denotes royal possession. Tugras, though common in Istanbul, are rarely seen elsewhere, even in Turkey, and this one is a mark of the special favour that Chíos enjoyed. Today the mosque houses the **Byzantine Museum**, with a collection of tombstones and other old odds and ends too big to fit anywhere else. The south end of the square is closed by the new **Homerium**, a municipal cultural centre with frequent exhibitions; others are held in the old public baths on Syngroú, now the **Chíos Public Art Gallery**, which also features a permanent collection of paintings by the island's artists.

South of Plateía Vounakíou near the **cathedral**, the **Koraï Municipal Library** was founded in 1792 and claims to be the third largest in Greece with 135,000 volumes; upstairs, the **Folklore Museum**, the private collection of London scholar Philip Argéntis, scion of an old

Byzantine Museum
t 227 102 6866; open Tues–Sun 10–1; adm

Chíos Public Art Gallery
t 227 104 3830, www.chiosartgallery.gr

Koraï Library/ Folklore Museum
t 227 104 4246; open Mon–Thurs 8–2, Fri 8–2 and 5–7.30, Sat 8.30–12

Genoese-Chiot family who got tired (with reason) of looking at his family's portraits. Chiot costumes, handicrafts, engravings of 18th-century Chíos and copies of Delacroix's *Massacre* painting round out the collection. The well-arranged **Archaeology Museum** contains artefacts bearing a sphinx holding an amphora, the emblem of ancient Chíos, statuettes of Cybele, the Great Mother, tiny faïence figures from Emborió, and a famous letter engraved on stone from Alexander the Great addressed to the Chiots. At 20 Stefánou Tsoúri, the **Maritime Museum** is a shipping fanatic's fantasy, housed in the Patéras family pile.

The northern industrial edge of the city with its four landmark windmills extending out to sea is known as **Tampakíka**; the island's once important leather industry was concentrated in the huge, empty buildings along the sea.

Archaeology Museum
5 Michálon, t 227 104 4239; open Tues–Sun 8.30–3; adm

Maritime Museum
20 Stefánou Tsoúri, t 227 104 4139; open Mon–Sat 10–2

Kámbos: Medieval Genoese Gentility

During their rule in the Middle Ages, the Genoese especially favoured the fertile, well-watered plain south of town that they called the Campo, or Kámbos, where they and the local aristocracy built villas and planted citrus fruit, mastic trees, and mulberries for silk, an important source of income until the 19th century. Kámbos is an enchanting and evocative mesh of narrow lanes (best seen on foot or by bicycle), full of secret gardens enclosed by stone walls, with gates bearing long forgotten coats of arms or the telltale stripes of the Genoese nobility. Courtyards are paved with elaborate black and white pebble mosaics, and many still have their old water wheels (*mánganos*) atop their cisterns, shaded by ancient trees, creating scenes of elegiac serenity unique on the Greek islands, especially in the golden light at the end of day. Mastodon bones were found at **Thymianá**, one of the larger villages and source of Kámbos' golden stone; today it's home to a women's co-operative producing rugs, towels and other woven goods. **Sklaviá**, named after the Greek slaves of the Genoese, is especially lush. Amid the orchards and little lanes, 9km north of **Vavíli**, stands the pretty octagonal domed church of **Panagía Krína** (1287, currently being restored), which contains excellent frescoes by the Cretan school.

The nearest beach to Chíos Town and Kámbos is at **Karfás**, reached by frequent blue buses. The sand may be 'as soft as flour' but there's less of it to go around all the time as hotels and flats sprout up like *kudzu*. South on the coast, the long pebble beach of **Ag. Fotiní** is less frantic and car-free. Above the beach, **Moni Ag. Minás** is famous on Chíos: during the massacre in 1822, women and children from the surrounding villages took refuge there; a small, hopeless battle took place before Ag. Minás was overrun and all 3,000 were slain, their bodies thrown down the well. Their bones are now in an ossuary; blood still stains the church floor.

Moni Ag. Minás
closed afternoons until 6pm

Where to Stay in and around Chíos Town

Chíos Town ✉ 82100

Chíos Chandris, E. Chandrí, t 227 104 4401, *www.chandris.gr* (€€€). The harbourfront landmark where shipowners hobnob in the light and airy downstairs with its marble floors, there are newly renovated rooms upstairs, and it now has a pretty pool. *Open all year.*

Grecian Castle, t 227 104 4740, *www.greciancastle.gr* (€€€). By the sea on the airport road, a 10min walk to the centre, a complex of stone buildings with a pool, bar and restaurants.

Diana, 92 Venizélou, t 227 104 4565 (€€). Modern and utilitarian, but well-kept and friendly. Rooms at the back are much quieter and the bathrooms are better than most. *Open all year.*

Kyma, opposite the Chandris, t 227 104 4500, *kyma@chi.forthnet.gr* (€€). Convivial hotel owned by Theodore Spordilís, who knows all there is to know about Chíos. The atmospheric core of the hotel is an Italianate villa built by a shipowner; the lobby has a fine painted ceiling.

Fedra, 13 M. Livanoú, t 227 104 1130 (€€–€). Stylish place with handsome (if somewhat noisy) rooms. *Open all year.*

Alex Rooms, 29 M. Lavanoú , t 227 102 5014 (€). Basic rooms with a home-made touch and Alex, a fisherman and character.

Filoxenia, Roídou, t 227 102 2813 (€). Clean, simple, and close to the ferries. *Open all year.*

Kámbos ✉ 82100

Argentikon, t 227 103 3111, *www.argentikon.gr* (€€€€). Very expensive antique-filled suites in a 16th-century estate spread out over four buildings and private garden with a pool, sauna and restaurant.

Agiazi, Leóni Kalvokorési, Fragovoúni, t 227 103 2553, *www.chios.gr/agiazi* (€€€). Traditional house with four comfortable rooms, with views over the lush landscapes.

⭐ **Perleas Mansion >**

Perleas Mansion, Vitiádou St, t 227 103 2217, *www.perleas.gr* (€€€). Beautiful guesthouse in a restored mansion, set in organic gardens and citrus groves,

where the produce ends up on the table for breakfast marmalades, as well as in the optional meals. Serene, civilized atmosphere.

Villa Clio, t 227 104 3755 (€€€). Renovated traditional manor a mile from Karfás beach with five studios, surrounded by banana and palm trees.

Perivoli, 11 Argénti, t 227 103 1513, *www.perivolihotel.gr* (€€€–€€). Behind a beautiful gate and courtyard, serene rooms with antiques and air-conditioning in a listed mansion.

Mavrokordatiko, I. Mitaráki t 227 103 2900, *www.mavrokordatiko.com* (€€). Pleasant air-conditioned rooms in a mansion of 1736, rather unusually restored by the city of Chíos with a pebble mosaic courtyard and water-wheel and restaurant. *Open April–Oct.*

Karfás ✉ 82100

Near to the airport, Chíos Town and a sandy beach, Karfás is the island's chief resort.

Erythia, t 227 103 2311, *www.erytha.gr* (€€€). Pastel complex, friendly, recently renovated, with an infinity pool; all rooms have sea views.

Golden Odyssey, on the road to Karfás, t 227 104 1500, *www.greek-tourism.gr/goldenodysseyhotel* (€€€). Korean-run, but wouldn't look out of place in the USA; rooms have satellite TV and balconies overlooking the pools, and there's an excellent Chinese restaurant. *Open April–Sept.*

Golden Sand, on the beach, t 227 103 2080, *www.goldensand.gr* (€€€–€€). Boasts a large swimming pool in a complex overlooking the sea; ask for a room with sea view.

Karfas Bay Studios, t 227 103 3016, *mammous1@otenet.gr* (€€€–€€). Brand new, all with balconies; one of the closest to the beach.

Markos' Place, t 227 103 1990, *www.marcos-place.gr* (€). For an altogether atmospheric and restful stay in the gardens in an ex-monastery just south; essential to book. *Open May–Oct.*

Eating Out in Chíos Town

Besides mastic, Chíos has two specialities: a brown, wrinkly, nutty

⊛ Hotzas >

olive called *chourmádes*, 'dates', and Greek blue cheese, *kopanistí*.

Hotzas, Chíos' oldest taverna, at 3 G. Kondíli St, a 15min walk from the harbourfront, **t** 227 104 2787. Ask for directions before heading out. The food's excellent, from the *mezédes* to aubergine simmered with tomatoes, delicious whitebait and other standard Greek dishes, topped off with good barrelled retsina, a rare find on any island. *Open eves only*.

Oinomageireío tou Iákovou, in the Kástro, **t** 227 102 3858. Great ouzo and snacks (including *kopanistí*), giant prawns and more.

Pyrgos, in Grecian Castle (*see* 'Where to Stay'), **t** 227 104 4740. Beautiful setting and serving some of the best food on Chíos, with a huge menu – fresh fish, stuffed vegetables and salads.

Tassos Taverna, beyond the Chandris hotel. Tables set in a large, shady garden (but alas no sea views); good

for long, lazy lunches away from the frenetic portside strip.

Theodosiou, 33 Neorío, at the north end of the port. This is the best of the many waterfront restaurants, relying on really good food rather than designer décor for its loyal clientèle.

Entertainment and Nightlife in Chíos Town

Loafing around the waterfront after the obligatory *vólta* takes up most evenings in Chíos Town.

Kavos, **Remezzo** and **Metropolis**. Currently the bars to see and be seen.

Kronos, 2 E. Argénti Street. Scoops out the best ice cream till the small hours.

En Plo Rock Club, on Prokyméa.

Haremas, by the airport. For Greek traditional music.

Cine Kipos. Summer cinema in the park.

Inland from Chíos Town: Néa Moní (NEA MONH)

Néa Moní

t 227 107 9370, due to re-open in summer 2007 after restoration; then open April–Oct daily 8–1 and 4–7; Nov–Mar Tues–Sun 8.30–3

Néa Moní, set amid pines and cypresses, is one of the most beautiful monuments in Greece and a World Heritage Site. If you don't have a car, consider taking a taxi from Chíos Town (around €18) as buses only go as far as **Karyés**, a mountain village flowing with fresh springs, but a long 7km trek from the monastery.

Néa Moní was 'new' in 1042, when Emperor Constantine VIII Monomachos and his wife Zoë had it built to replace an older monastery, where the monks had found a miraculous icon of the Virgin; not least of its miracles was its prophecy that Constantine would return from exile and gain the imperial throne. In gratitude, the emperor sent money, architects and artists from Constantinople. The **church** (*surrounded by scaffolding at the time of writing*) has a sumptuous double narthex and a subtle, complex design of pilasters, niches and pendentives that support its great dome atop an octagonal drum. Its superb, richly coloured 11th-century mosaics shimmer in the penumbra: *The Washing of the Feet*, *The Saints of Chíos* and *Judas' Kiss* in the narthex and *The Life of Christ* in the dome are stylistically similar to those at Dafní in Athens and among the finest examples of Byzantine art anywhere – even though they had to be pieced back together after the earthquake of 1881 brought down the dome. A **chapel** houses the bones of some of the 5,000 victims (among them, 600 monks) of Kara Ali's massacre who sought sanctuary in the monastery.

From here, a rough road leads to the **Monastery of Ag. Patéras**, honouring the three monks who founded the original monastery; it too was rebuilt after the earthquake in 1890. Further up, medieval **Avgónyma** was built by convicts, who, having gained their liberty by building Néa Moní as their penance, decided to stay in the mountains. Fifty years ago it was nearly abandoned; now Greeks have restored much of it as holiday homes. From here, a road zigzags up the granite mountain to the fascinating 'Mystrás of Chíos', the striking medieval village and castle of **Anávatos**. It saw horrific scenes in 1822; most of the villagers threw themselves off the 300m (1,000ft) cliff rather than wait to be slaughtered, and ever since then the place has been haunted.

The Mastikochória: Mastic Villages of the South

⭐ Mastic Villages

Southwest of Kámbos (*see* p.538) stretch the drier hills and vales of mastic land, where time seems to stand still. The ground must have some secret virtue as well, for mastic bushes (*Pistacia lentiscus*) refuse to be transplanted – even northern Chíos won't do; they might grow, but not a drop of mastic will they yield. The 300 tons of gum mastic produced annually in the 21 Mastikochória support 5,000 families. Three times a year between July and October they needle the bark, causing the sap to 'weep'. The glistening diamond 'tears' are then harvested, sifted, washed, scratched and dried. Some 90 per cent of the crop is exported, mostly to the Middle East.

Nearly all the Mastikochória (carefully spared by the Turks in 1822) date from the Middle Ages, designed by the Genoese as tight-knit little labyrinths, the houses sharing a common outer wall with few entrances; if that was breached, the villagers could take refuge in a central keep. Heading south from Chíos Town, the first of the Mastikochória is **Armoliá**, which makes ceramics as a sideline. It is defended by the Byzantine **Kástro Orgías** (1440), a castle named after the beautiful châtelaine who seduced men only to have them executed. **Kalamotí**, one of the most prosperous villages, has tall stone houses, many with carved doors; to the north stands the 12th-century Byzantine church of **Panagía Sikeliá**, with decorative

Mastic Fantastic

First mentioned by Herodotus, mastic put the chew in gum and the jelly in the beans that delighted bored Ottoman harems. Roman women used mastic toothpicks to sweeten their breath; Syrians put it in perfume. Western painters used it to varnish their masterpieces; Chíots use it to flavour a devilishly sweet liqueur, chewing gum and MasticDent toothpaste. Ancient doctors considered mastic a panacea, good for everything from bladder ailments to snake bites and rabies in mules. Recent studies show that they weren't entirely wrong – it aids digestion, tightens the gums, heals wounds, absorbs cholesterol, and cures stomach ulcers.

ceramics. The closest beach is sandy, low-key **Kómi**, reachable by bus; if it's too busy, try **Lilikás**, 2km east.

West of Kómi, before the old mastic-exporting port of **Emborió**, a road zigzags up to **ancient Emborio**, where British archaeologists uncovered the island's first Ionian settlement, founded in the 8th century BC. Watch the explanatory DVD in English, then follow the shadeless paths up the boulder-strewn hill, past houses and a megaron, to the acropolis, with the ashlar base of the simple, rectangular **Temple of Athena**, last rebuilt in the 4th century BC. The wealth of amphorae found underwater at Emborió hint at the extent of Chíos' wine trade (Aristophanes wrote that the ancient Chiots tippled with the best of them; these days their grapes go into ouzo or a raisin wine not unlike Tuscan *vinsanto*). Beautiful **Mávra Vólia Beach**, five minutes from Emborió, is made up of black volcanic pebbles, source of the beautiful Genoese mosaic pavements at Kámbos. Signposted along the beach road are the ruins of a 6th-century Christian basilica with a marble cross font and mosaics.

Ancient Emborio
open Tues–Sun 8.30–3.15

The largest mastic village, **Pyrgí**, is outrageously picturesque. Nearly every house is covered from top to bottom with *xistá*, the local word for the sgraffito decoration taught to the locals by the Genoese; walls are covered with mortar containing black sand from Emborió, then coated with white plaster, which the artist scrapes off into geometric, floral or animal-based designs. The central *plateía* is a marvel – a dizzying surround-mural of black and white Op Art. The churches get the same treatment, except for the 12th-century **Ag. Apóstoli**, frescoed (inside) in 1655. Nine km south of Pyrgí, one of the most beautiful small beaches on any Greek island, **Vroulídia** is a

Ag. Apóstoli
open Tues–Sun 8.30–3

Christóphoros Kolómbos of Chíos

In Pyrgí, there's a house with a plaque in Greek marking the ΟΙΚΙΑΣ ΚΟΛΟΜΒΟΥ, the house of Columbus. You'll see the name Kolómbos elsewhere on doors in Pyrgí, where it's a common surname. And according to Ruth G. Durlacher-Wolper's *Christophoros Columbus: A Byzantine Prince from Chios, Greece* (1982), the most famous member of the Kolómbos family 'discovered' the New World.

Columbus is one of history's mystery men, who purposely covered his tracks and left few clues to his past. Durlacher-Wolper argues the reason for this secrecy is because he was a Greek who, like many after the fall of Constantinople in 1452, was living in Catholic Genoa, and wanted to avoid persecution in case he was captured by the Turks. The Chiots then and now were famous sailors; and Chíos of course was Genoese territory from 1346 to 1566, during which time there had been 'mastic' inter-marriages between the Genoese merchants and Byzantine aristocracy. There are other clues as well. Columbus' bizarre signature was a mix of Byzantine Greek and Latin (both of which he knew well). In his writings (which were never in Italian) he often referred to mastic and Chíos, always spelling it with a Greek X (and mastic bushes grow in red soil – Columbus often referred to himself as 'Columbus de Terra Rubra'). He claimed to have sailed with his kinsman 'Colon the Younger, the Greek corsair' (George Paleologus Disipatos, a nobleman who became a famous corsair after 1452). Columbus had an account with the Bank of St George, the same used by the Maona that governed Chíos, and at sea he kept two logs, one in Roman leagues, and a secret one, in Greek leagues. The Genoese, of course, pooh-pooh all this, although they have never been able to produce rock-hard evidence that Columbus was from the city – even Columbus's own son Ferdinand couldn't find any relatives.

cove of white sand and turquoise water hidden under the cliffs. A dirt road southwest from Pygrí heads to **F12aná**, with ruins of a fountain and the **Temple of Phaneo Apollo** (6th century BC) that stood nearby. Alexander the Great stopped to consult its oracle; several columns are in the **archaeology museum**.

To the west, the walled, very medieval village of **Olýmpi** is built around a 20m (68ft) tower (now a restaurant/bar). Originally it had only one gate; outside the walls, by the allotment gardens, a sign shows a map of the new **Mastic Trail** that links Olýmpi to Mestá. Ten km outside town, you can visit the stunning stalactite **Cave of Olýmpi**, then continue down the road to **Ag. Dýnami** beach, under a monastery set on the cape.

Of all the Mastikochória, **Mestá** is the ultimate fortress village, with no ground-floor windows facing out and only one entrance into its maze of lanes and flower-filled yards, now much beloved of film crews; at other times you can almost hear the silence. Two churches are worth a look: the medieval **Ag. Paraskeví** and the 18th-century **Mikrós Taxiárchis**, with a beautifully carved iconostasis. The road north from Mestá to Chíos Town passes Mestá's port of **Liménas**, then **Eláta** with its flat roofs (rather like ancient Ionian houses of Emborió) and picturesque medieval **Véssa**, deep on the valley floor. North, **Lithí** (4.5km) is a pretty village with a so-so sandy beach, tavernas and a few places to stay. Further up the wild west coast you can swim at the pebble coves near **Elínda** and circle back to Chíos Town by way of Néa Moní (*see* p.540).

Cave of Olýmpi
t 227 104 4830; open May Tues–Sun 11–5, June–Oct Tues–Sun 10–8

13

The Northeastern Aegean Islands | Chíos

Where to Stay and Eat in the Mastichória

Kalamotí/Kómi ✉ 82102

Bella Mare, Kómi, t 227 107 1226 (€€). Friendly and family-run; six en suite rooms and a free supply of sun loungers and umbrellas. The restaurant serves seafood, pizza, pasta, the works. *Open May–Oct.*

Lida & Mary, Kalamotí, t 227 107 6217. (€€–€). Pleasant rooms with fridges. *Open April–Oct.*

Traditional Houses, t 227 107 1486, *www.traditionalhouses.gr* (€). Five small houses, three in medieval Kalamotí and two on the way to Kómi, sleeping up to four.

Mika's, just south of Kómi, t 227 107 1335 (€). Budget rooms. *Open May–Oct.*

Nostalgia, Kómi, t 227 107 0070. Fresh fish and lobster on the sand.

Pyrgí ✉ 82102

Lila Rooms, on the main road, t 227 107 2291 (€€–€). Run by the dynamic Lila Fitili; en suite rooms with a garden.

Rita Valas, near the main square, t 227 107 2479 (€€–€). Quiet, clean rooms, with shared kitchen facilities.

'Balcony'. Café/restaurant run by the municipality. Good for meals or just a snack with ouzo.

Emborió ✉ 82102

Emporios Bay, just in from the bay, t 227 107 0180, *www.emporiosbay.com* (€€). New and a bit stark, but comfortable. *Open April–Oct.*

Haus Fay, t 227 107 1523, *http://hausfay. com* (€€–€). Contemporary apartments sleeping up to five close to the port.

Volcano, t 227 107 1136. Delicious food on a shady terrace and in the pretty antique-furnished dining room; pretty loos, too.

Olýmpi ✉ 82102

Chrysanthi, t 227 107 6196, *www. chrysanthi.gr* (€€–€). Well-furnished traditional apartments.

Mestá ✉ 82102

Floradi Anna, t 227 107 6176, *floradis@ internet.gr* (€€–€). Pleasant rooms in a medieval building. *Open all year.*

Karampela Despina, t 227 107 6065 (€€–€). Two traditional stone houses. *Open all year.*

Zervoudi, Liménas Meston, **t** 227 109 3915 (€). Rooms with balconies right on the sea.

Messeonas, in Mestá square, **t** 227 107 6050. Sees more than its share of tourists, but the food is reliably good with some unusual dishes, especially out of season. They also have rooms.

Limáni Mestón, by the fishing boats, **t** 227 107 6389. Delicious seafood but also land dishes such as rabbit *stifádo* and pork with celery.

Líthi ✉ 82102

Medusa, near the beach, **t** 227 107 3634 (€€). Traditionally furnished apartments.

Kira Despina, on the beach, **t** 227 107 3373 (€). Handful of rooms and great fish; fish soup and big breakfasts.

Avgónyma ✉ 82102

Spitákia, t 227 108 1200, *www.spitakia. gr* (€€€–€€). Charmingly restored little houses (sleeping up to five) or rooms, all different.

Pyrgos Rooms and Taverna, t 227 104 2175, *www.chiospyrgosrooms.gr* (€). Studios in old stone houses spread throughout the village, and taverna and grill right in the centre.

Asteri, t 227 102 0577. Taverna serving tasty dishes such as aubergines grilled over charcoal, stuffed vine leaves, kid on a spit, etc. *Open daily May–Oct, otherwise weekends only.*

Northern Chíos

Northern Chíos is the island's wild side, mountainous, stark and barren, its forests decimated by shipbuilders, and in the 1980s by fires. Many of its villages are nearly deserted outside of the summer. **Vrontádos**, 4.5km north of Chíos Town, is an exception, a bedroom-suburb village overlooking a pebbly beach and ruined windmills. The locals are proudest of the **Daskalópetra** (the 'Teacher's Stone'), a rock throne over the sea where Homer is said to have sung, and where his disciples would gather to learn his poetry, although killjoy archaeologists say it was really part of an ancient altar dedicated to Cybele. The headquarters of the **International Society of Homeric Studies** is located in Vrontádos; the 19th-century **Moní Panagía Myrtidiótissa** nearby houses the robes of the martyred Gregory V, Patriarch of Constantinople.

Near Vrontádos are the ruins of Chíos' first church, **Ag. Isídoros**, founded in the 3rd century on the spot where Isídoros was martyred. A later church to house the relics of Isídoros (whose feast day only happens every four years, on 29 February) was built by Emperor Constantine, but it fell in an earthquake and was replaced by three successive structures; mosaics from the 7th-century version are in the Byzantine Museum in Chiós Town. After the Turks damaged the last version in 1822, and the earthquake of 1881, the church was never rebuilt, perhaps because the Venetians snatched Isídoros' relics in the 12th century and installed them in St Mark's. In 1967

Pope Paul VI ordered them to return one of Isídoros' bones, now kept in Chíos Town's cathedral.

Further north is **Lagáda**, a charming fishing village, sporting an array of bars and fish tavernas. Jagged rocks surround **Kardámyla**, the cradle of the island's shipowners. Kardámyla is actually two villages: the picturesque upper town and the seaside **Mármaro**, graced by a statue of the Kardámyla sailor paid for by shipowners. To the north, pretty **Nagós Beach** is set in a green amphitheatre and can get very busy in summer; its name is a corruption of *naos*, or temple, for there used to be one here to Poseidon. At nearby **Gióssona**, named after Jason of the Argonauts, there's a pebble beach, more exposed but with fabulous turquoise water.

The road between Kardámyla and Pitiós rises through startling wild landscapes, with views of Inoússes far far below. A striking village with its 12th-century tower, **Pitiós** claims to be the birthplace of Homer; the locals can point out his 'house'.

West, over Chíos' highest mountain, **Pelinaío** (at the pass there is a viewpoint, taking in most of the island), the 13th-century **Moní Moundón** is strikingly set between Dievchá and Kipouríes. Like Néa Moní, this was a wealthy monastery, full of aristocratic monks; rebuilt after its destruction by the Turks in 1822, it preserves a series of good paintings going back to 1620. Byzantine nobles out of favour were exiled in the medieval castle at **Volissós**, a striking hill town that, like Avgónyma in the south, has enjoyed a new life thanks to holidaymakers – many of them Greek – in search of authenticity (and creature comforts). The castle was founded by Belisarius, Justinian's general, although what you see was rebuilt by the Genoese. The beloved 16th-century saint Markélla hailed from this little white village, which also lays claim to Homer; in ancient times it was the chief town of his 'descendants', the Homeridai, who claimed that a local shepherd named Glaukos introduced Homer to his master, who then hired the poet as a teacher. Soon after, Homer married a Volissós girl, had two daughters, wrote the *Odyssey* and set sail for Athens but died en route, on Íos. A pretty path from Volissós takes in the watermills along the **Malagiótis Valley**.

The sandy beach below the town, **Skála Volissoú** or **Limniá**, has traditional tavernas, a few rooms to let and a bust of Admiral Kanáris. Caiques go several times a week to Psará (the shortest way of getting there). There are other excellent beaches near here, just as minimally developed: pebbly **Chóri** just south, the unofficial naturist beach, and **Límnos**, on the road to the **Monastery of Ag. Markélla**, these days the island's favourite pilgrimage destination; one of Chíos' finest beaches lies just below.

North of Volissós, two roads brave the wild, barren country. The westerly one climbs to little **Piramá**, with a medieval tower, and the church of **Ag. Ioánnis** with old icons. **Parpariá** to the north is a

Where to Stay and Eat in Northern Chíos

Vrontádos ✉ 82100

Velonas, on Lo beach, t 227 109 3588, *velonas@compulink.gr* (€). Small, clean studios with air-conditioning and TV.

Acqua, t 227 109 2345. Pretty dining room that lures in diners with the best Italian dishes on Chíos.

Kardámyla ✉ 82300

Kardamyla, t 227 202 3353, *kyma@chi. forthnet.gr* (€€€). On its own shady beach with water sports, in a rather unprepossessing 1960s institutional block, the hotel is brought to life by its owner, the ever-genial Theodore Spordilis of the Hotel Kyma in Chíos Town. *Open May–Oct.*

Spilia, t 227 202 2933, *www.spilia-chios.gr* (€€€–€€). Traditional stone village houses.

Gióssona ✉ 82300

Iason, t 227 202 3688, *www.chios giosonas.gr* (€€€). Ten pleasant apartments and studios smack on the beach in a tranquil setting. *Open May–Sept.*

Pitiós ✉ 82300

Makellos, t 227 202 3364. Family-run restaurant under an ancient plane tree,

★ To Mageireó >>

★ Makellos >

serving superb island cuisine – pickled garlic, stuffed courgette blossoms and home-made noodles. *Open daily mid-June–mid-Sept; mid-Sept–mid-June Fri–Sun only.*

Kipouríes ✉ 82300

To Mageireó, t 227 402 2016. A mother-and-daughter team prepare traditional Chiot dishes in this homey taverna, eat hand-made pasta, lemony roast potatoes and Sunday lamb on a spit, plus home-made *soúma*.

Volissós ✉ 82300

Pyrgos Village, t 227 402 2050, *www.pyrgosvillage.gr* (€€€€€). Large, exquisite stone villas with up to three bedrooms restored (the whole project began after a bet in the 1980s) to a five-star standard.

Ta Petrina, t 227 402 1128, *www. tapetrina.gr* (€€€€–€€). Beautifully restored houses in traditional Greek style, accommodating 6–8. They also host yoga, painting and cookery courses through Stonelinks in the UK, t (01424) 882943.

Ta Spitia tis Stellas, t 227 402 1421, *www.volissostravel.gr* (€€€–€€). English-speaking establishment with stylish, well-equipped renovated houses for rent in the village.

medieval hamlet of shepherds, and at **Melaniós** many Chiots were slain before they could flee to Psará in 1822. On the northwest shore, the village of **Ag. Gála** ('Holy Milk') is named after a frescoed 15th-century Byzantine **church in a cave** (*you'll have to ask for the key*), which drips whitish deposits, or milk (*gála*), said to be the milk of the Virgin; the chapel has a superb iconostasis. For more strange terrestrial secretions, make your way along the rough coastal road east to **Agiásmata**, where Chiots come in the summer months to soak in the magic baths.

Inoússes (ΟΙΝΟΥΣΣΕΣ)

A ferry leaves Chíos Town every afternoon for Inoússes, 'the wine islands' to the northeast; to avoid spending the night, take an excursion boat or hydrofoil. Only the largest of the nine islands, all of 30 square kilometres, is inhabited, by about 300 people, but *per capita* it's the richest island in Greece: the Inoussians comprise some 60 of the 180 Greek shipowning families, including the Lémnos clan, the wealthiest of them all. The Inoussians have a reputation for being tough cookies; most families were goatherds or wine makers who spent centuries in Kardámyla, Chíos, during the bad days of piracy until it was safe to return. After the Second World War they cannily parlayed a handful of wartime Liberty ships into a fleet of ships and tankers. Every summer some of the fanciest yachts in Greece congregate in its sheltered little harbour; the rest of the year their owners divide between Geneva, London and Athens.

For all that, the island's town is unpretentious – a collection of white-painted stone houses with red tile roofs, albeit with big villas skirting the hills. Visitors are greeted by a bronze **mermaid**, the 'Mother of Inoússes'. The shipowners have created a **Marine Museum** by the quay, with minatures, models and paintings. There are small beaches, the furthest a 30-minute walk away. It has a pair of tavernas and the 11-roomed **Hotel Thalassoporos** (*t* 227 205 5475 (€); ring ahead).

Marine Museum
open 10–1

A road crosses to the western cliffs, where in the 1960s Katíngo Patéras, a member of a shipowning dynasty, built the multi-million-dollar **Convent of the Evangelismós** after her 20-year-old daughter Iríni died of Hodgkin's disease, having prayed to take the illness and die instead of her afflicted father. When, as custom has it, her body was exhumed after three years, it was found to be mummified. Her failure to decompose convinced her bereaved mother that she was a saint and, like Sleeping Beauty, she is kept in a glass case; her father, who died a few years later, is buried here as well.

Convent of the Evangelismós
admission only to women with long sleeves, headscarves and long skirts

Psará (ΨAPA)

Psará, one of Greece's martyr islands, lies much further away than Inoússes, 54 nautical miles northwest of Chíos. The Mycenaeans were here in the 13th century BC, near **Paliókastro**, the same spot chosen by independence-minded Chiots wanting to escape even their benign Turkish rule. They developed one of Greece's most important merchant fleets, rivalled only by Hýdra and Spétses. During the War of Independence (especially after the 1822 massacre on Chíos, which swelled the population with refugees), Psará

Where to Stay and Eat on Psará

The island's name means 'fish' – and you'll find it fresh in seaside tavernas.

Psará ✉ 82104

Cavos, t 227 406 1140 (€€). Four furnished apartments near the centre. *Open April–Oct.*

Psará, up by the football field, 300m from the beach, **t** 227 406 1180 (€€). 15 basic studios, with kitchenettes.

Xenonas Psaron, t 227 406 1293 (€€). Run by the EOT, five rooms in an atmospheric 17th-century prison at Ag. Nikólaos; they also run the pleasant restaurant called **Spitalia** in the old quarantine hospital.

Getting to Psará

An afternoon **ferry**, daily in summer, sails from Chíos Town (4hrs); there is also a **caique** every other day from Limniá, the port of Volissós (2hrs). For information contact **Triaena Travel**, Neorío St, in Chíos Town, **t** 227 102 9292, or the **Chíos port authority**: **t** 227 104 4433.

enthusiastically contributed ships and a hero, Admiral Kanáris, to the cause. Psará even invented a new weapon, the *bourléta*, which its captains used to destroy the Turkish fleet.

The Sultan demanded vengeance, and on 20 June 1824 he sent 25,000 troops to wipe Psará off the map with fire and sword. Most of the inhabitants were blown to bits when they retreated with the Turks on their heels to the 'Black Ridge of Psará' where they set their powder stores alight. Only 3,000 of the 30,000 men, women and children managed to escape to Erétria, on Évia. The little island never recovered: today only 500 people live on Psará, mostly fishermen and beekeepers. The site of the house of Admiral Apóstolis, a shipowner who fought in the war, is now a memorial square to the massacre.

Your feet are your main transport to the island's **beaches**: the best is **Límnos**, a sandy strand 20mins' walk away; bring provisions.

Ikaría (IKAPIA)

Ikaría looks like a sea cucumber on the map; up close and personal, however, it presents a steep, forbidding face to the world. The great dorsal range of Athéras divides it neatly in two, its peaks over 900m (3,000ft) high, often lost in billowing cloud. Yet mountain springs keep both sides green under oak, pine and plane trees, with added natural air-conditioning from the wind, which blows so hard at times it whips up rainbows of sea mist. Forget the myth: it was the wind that downed Ikaros here. It certainly abetted the tragic fire that began in a roadworks tar pot and incinerated the hills west of Ag. Kýrikos in 1993, causing 15 deaths.

Don't come here if you're in a hurry; life here is so slow that the locals joke about living in their own time zone. Development, too, has been slow here, partly for political reasons, partly by choice; in recent years Ikaría has been held up as a microcosm of environ-

Where Ikaros Fell

After Theseus escaped Knossós with Ariadne (*see* p.136), King Minos was furious at his inventor Daedalus, who had given Ariadne the thread that enabled Theseus to find his way through the Labyrinth. Daedalus escaped from Knossós, but Minos ordered all ports to be watched to keep Daedalus on Crete. Unable to flee by land or sea, Daedalus made wings of feathers and wax for himself and his son Ikaros. Off they flew, but the boy, enchanted by flight, forgot his father's warning and flew too near the sun; the wax binding the feathers melted and Ikaros plummeted to his death off the south coast of the island that took his name. In the 2nd century AD, Pausanius mentions that his grave could still be seen.

Getting to Ikaría

By air: The **airport** is at Fanári, **t** 227 502 2981, 13km east of Ag. Kýrikos; because of the wind, it has a unique north–south runway that can be approached from either direction. **Olympic** has nearly daily connections with Athens; **Sky Express** has one flight in summer a week with Heráklion. A bus links Ag. Kýrikos to flights.

By sea: Ferries (10–12hrs) to Ikaría serve one or the other of two ports, Ag. Kýrikos or Évdilos, every day. In summer, **Superfast Ferries** from Piraeus take only 4½ hrs to either, en route to Sámos, usually calling at Mýkonos on the way. In summer hydrofoils run 4 times a week to Pátmos and the main Dodecanese, Páros, Náxos and Sámos. **Port authority**, Ag. Kýrikos, **t** 227 502 2207; Évdilos, **t** 227 503 1007.

Getting to and around Ikaría

Caiques from Ag. Kýrikos to Foúrni run daily, and also link Ag. Kýrikos to Manganítis and Karkinágri on Mon, Wed and Fri.

Buses run once or twice a day from Ag. Kýrikos to Évdilos, with summer connections to Armenístis (the trip takes over an hour). **Taxis** will estimate fares before setting out; sharing is common.

Car and motorbike hire: Aventura in Évdilos, **t** 227 503 1140.

mental and economic sustainability. It helps that tourism is irrelevant to most of its 7,000 inhabitants, who live in 60 villages, immersed in gardens and orchards, and spend as much time as possible eating, drinking, singing and dancing.

As the place synonymous with the world's first hang-glider, Ikaría has been deeply involved since 1990 in setting up the **Ikaríada**, the Olympics of air sports, to be held every four years in late June in different parts of the world.

History

Ikaría has had more names than history, among them Dolichi ('oblong'), Ichthyoessa ('fishy'), and Oenoe 'wine'. By Classical times the Phoenician name for the island, Ikor (also 'fishy'), had been

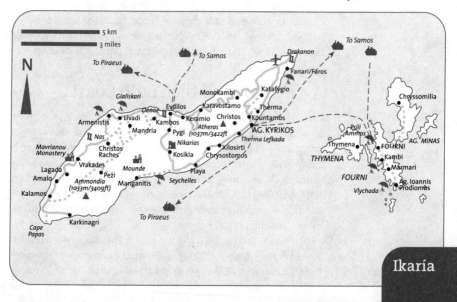

Ikaría

Useful Information on Ikaría

Ikariada Travel, in Ag. Kýrikos, **t** 227 502 3322.
Nas Travel, in Évdilos, **t** 227 503 1947, and in Armenistís, **t** 227 507 1396.
The Glorious Greek Kitchen. Chef Diane Kochilas, a New Yorker of Ikarian descent, runs a summer culinary course in Christós Ráchis. Book through **Cuisine International**, *www.cuisineinternational.com*.

Ikaría Festivals

In the summer, *panegýria* occupy the attention of the whole island.
17 July: The biggest festival of them all, in honour of Ikaría's fling with independence in 1912.
8th Sun after Easter: Ag. Pándas in Karavóstamo.
26 July: Ag. Paraskeví in Xilosírti.
27 July: Ag. Panteleímonos.
6 Aug: Christós.
15 Aug: Akamátra and Chrysóstomos.
8 Sept: Plagiá and Manganítis.
17 Sept: Ag. Sofía in Mesokámbos.

identified with Ikaros. Under the Byzantines the island took on an extra N (many locals still call it Níkaria) and was used to exile renegade nobles; over time the entire population began to take the airs of those 'born in the purple', and to this day Ikarians have a reputation for mild eccentricity. As the Byzantines lost control of the Aegean in the 15th century, people fled high into the mountains, to villages such as Lagáda that are invisible from the sea: the *afaneia*, or 'times of disappearance', lasted until the 1700s, when people began to move back towards the sea.

In July 1912, during the Balkan War, the local doctor and priest led the inhabitants in liberating the island in a kid-glove revolution (they put the handful of Turkish administrators on a boat and said goodbye) and for five months Ikaría was an independent state with its own flag, stamps and national anthem. During the Civil War (1946–9) and junta (1967–74), Ikaría was a dumping ground for dissidents; at one point there were 15,000, twice the number of natives. Like the Byzantine exiles, their presence and ideas influenced the locals; the Communist Party (KKE) still runs the 'Red Rock'.

Ag. Kýrikos and the South Coast

Ikaría's capital, **Ag. Kýrikos**, or just 'Ágios' as everyone calls it, greets arrivals in its port with a pair of girders holding a nose-diving metal Ikaros as if in a pair of giant tweezers. A town 'obviously designed by a drunken postman' according to Lawrence Durrell, Ágios has a tiny centre of shops, banks, travel agents and a bakery unchanged since the 1930s. Outside of this little knot, forget urban density; like Candide, every Ikarian cultivates his or her own garden in the great mountain amphitheatre above.

For decades tourism on Ikaría has meant **Thérma**, 10 minutes' drive east of Ágios, where hot springs – the most radioactive in Europe – bubble up at 35–55°C and are used to treat chronic rheumatism, arthritis, gout and spondylitis; one spring is so strong that it's closed to the public. Recent studies have found proved them full of virtue, so much so that not only have the baths (behind the busty sculpture of the goddess of health) been restored, but private baths and Jacuzzis have been added as well.

To the east, **Fanári** (or **Fáros**) is an increasingly sought-after slice of old Greece, with a row of ramshackle bars and tavernas overlooking a long shingly beach and tamarisk trees. A dirt road continues towards the end of the cape, marked by a beautifully preserved white Hellenistic **tower** from the 3rd or 4th century BC; at the beginning of the War of Independence, an entire castle stood here, until Admiral Miaoúlis sailed by and used it for target practice. It protected the ancient town of **Drakanón**, sacred to Diónysos; only a few 5th-century BC walls survive on the acropolis.

West of Ag. Kýrikos are more springs; one bubbles so hot out of the sea at **Thérma Lefkáda** (signposted 'hot water' by the road) that picnickers use it to boil their eggs. The road then passes below the **Moní Evangelistrías** (1775), with a pretty slate-roofed church and one nun, by a retirement home. The little theatre by the sea was first used in June 2001 to light the torch for the Ikaríada air games. Tucked beyond a huge granite spur, **Xilosírti** is spread out among gardens and apricot trees above a beach of big pebbles. People come to fill up bottles of Athanató Neró ('immortal water', good for kidney stones), a small seaside spring on the east end of town.

Next, below **Chrysóstomos**, a rock (signposted) marks the spot where Ikaros plummeted into the sea. **Playá** has a handful of houses and a big yellow church. West of here, there's a fork in the road: one branch goes to the north side of Ikaría, passing Wild West scenery and **Kosíkia**, guarded by the 10th-century **Nikariás Castle**. The other continues west along the south coast, through the longest tunnel in the Aegean to **Manganítis**. Built on a steep hillside with a pocket-sized port, it's a lively little spot. The rubble from blasting the tunnel has been made into a stunning if shadeless beach dubbed '**Seychelles**'. From Manganítis you can see the roadworks inching closer that will someday make it possible to drive all around the entire island.

Where to Stay and Eat on Ikaría's South Coast

The Ikarians are busily reviving their viticultural past in tiny vineyards. No one bottles it commercially, but you can often find it in tavernas.

Ag. Kýrikos ⊠ 83000

Filioppi, towards the hospital, **t** 227 502 4058, *www.island-ikaria.com/hotels* (€€). New, well-equipped hotel with studios, a short walk from the town centre.

Kastro, on a cliff over town, **t** 227 502 3480, *www.island-ikaria.com/hotels* (€€). A good bet, tastefully kitted out with a rooftop pool and bar.

Maria Elena, just above town, **t** 227 502 2835, *www.island-ikaria.com/pensions* (€€). Pristine and pleasant with 16 balconied rooms and 7 studios.

Isabella's, right in the centre, t 227 502 2839 (€). With a restaurant and pool.

Filoti, in the centre. Excellent pizzas and pasta.

Kazalas, in Glarédou, one of the mountain villages (take a taxi). The best and most authentic taverna on the south side.

Klimataria, in the centre. Reliable old restaurant serving delicious moussaká and old-fashioned *ládera*.

Thérma ✉ 83000

Marina, t 227 502 2188 (€€). Airy and white, handsome traditional building.

Asteria, t 227 502 2095 (€). 22 studios, all with air-conditioning.

Ikarion, t 227 502 2481, *www.island-ikaria.com/hotels/ikarion* (€). Renovated little hotel; rooms have satellite TV and air-conditioning. *Open May–Oct.*

Xilosírti ✉ 83000

Arodoú, t 227 502 2700. Popular new taverna overlooking the beach, preparing tasty local recipes, depending on the season.

Facaros, top of the village. Eftychía and family cook up all the Greek favourites. *Summer only.*

Ikaría's North Coast

Ikaría's north coast has the sandy beaches and most of the tourists. From Ag. Kýrikos a long winding road climbs and climbs, taking in breathtaking views of Foúrni, Sámos, Pátmos, Turkey and Náxos. One hamlet near the top, **Katafýgio,** means 'shelter'. One day pirates decided to capture the people as they came out of church, and waited and waited, then impatiently broke into the church – to find it empty. The priest had opened the secret trapdoor, into a tunnel dug for just such an expediency, and everyone had escaped. Seven aeolian windmills mark the top of the pass; about 8km from there, a sign marks Byzantine **Ag. Kýrikos,** the oldest church on Ikaría.

After passing above villages immersed in the trees – **Monokámbi, Karavóstamo** (with a 17th-century church, Ag. Pántas, and a dinky port) and **Keramío** – the road descends to **Évdilos,** a picturesque port, with a town beach, **Fýtema,** just to the west.

Inland a little, **Kámbos** is built on the site of Oenoe, the ancient capital of Ikaría, famous for its *pramnios oinos* mentioned by Homer. An inscription found on Athens' Acropolis describes Oenoe as a major contributor to Apollo on Délos. Byzantine princelings in exile installed themselves here and renamed it Dolichi; the columns and arches of their palace remain, as well as their church, **Ag. Iríni.** The adjacent **museum** (*Vassilis Diónysos has the key*) houses finds from Oenoe – pottery, clay figurines, coins, tools etc., and a 5th-century BC inscription reading 'All Ikarians are liars', modified over the years to 'Jews' or 'Turks' or whoever was out of favour at the moment. In the nearby village of **Pygí,** the **Moní Theoktísti** has Ikaría's finest frescoes, by a Mount Áthos painter.

Further west along the coast, **Gialiskári** has Ikaría's best beaches: **Messákti,** framed on one side by a tiny blue-domed church, linked by a spit to the shore, and **Livádi,** over the next headland. The old fishing village of **Armenistís** is now Ikaría's biggest resort – big by local standards, at any rate.

Armenistís is the point of departure for the region of **Rachés** or 'hillsides', known as the 'Little Switzerland of Ikaría'. The main village, **Christós Rachés**, is a charmer, the most Ikarian of Ikaría's villages: famous for keeping very late hours in its old-fashioned shops and tavernas (some of which don't open till 10pm) and famous for wine. Some 24km of paths have been laid out and are on a locally produced map, with explanations in English. One possible excursion is the walk or drive east to the 13th-century **convent** with frescoes at **Moundé**. Another is on the unpaved road south to **Pézi** and a pretty little artificial **lake** and **waterfall**.

West of Armenistís, at **Nas** (from *naos*, or temple), a path leads down to the ancient harbour, now Ikaría's unofficial naturist beach, near a series of caves. Behind, by the River Chálaris, are the platform and foundations of the 5th-century BC **Temple of Artemis Tavrópolio**. A statue of the goddess was discovered in the 19th century, with eyes that followed the viewer from every angle, but the local priest, considering it the work of the devil, threw it in the lime kiln.

Beyond Nas, the road is unpaved but continues southwest to the charming little whitewashed **Monastery of Mavrianoú**, next to an old threshing floor; the village above, **Vrakádes**, has a pair of cafés and pretty views. A few kilometres further on, **Amálo** has summer tavernas. If you're feeling adventurous, carry on south to **Karkinágri**, with a tiny port and boat three times a week to Ag. Kýrikos; it has a summer taverna, a few rooms to rent, and soon a new road around to Manganítis. This whole area is a good place to find 'pirate houses', low stone buildings under huge boulders, where people lived in the 'times of disappearance'.

⭐ To Fytema >>

Where to Stay and Eat on Ikaría's North Coast

Évdilos ✉ 83302

Atheras-Kerame, t 227 503 1434, *www. atheras-kerame.gr* (€€–€). A handsome hotel, partly in a 19th-century building, with a restaurant and bar, pool, gym; also 30 apartments by the beach. It's a long walk from the ferry, but if you ring ahead, they'll collect you.

Evdoxia, up the hill, t 227 503 1502, *www.evdoxia.gr* (€€–€). Ten rooms, all with balcony, minibar and TV; plus a restaurant and laundry.

⭐ Diónysos >

Diónysos, in Kámbos, t 227 503 1300, *www.island-ikaria.com/hotels/dionysos* (€). Out by ancient Oenoe, comfortable rooms owned by the irrepressible and very knowledgeable Vassilis, one of Ikaría's great characters and a spontaneous entertainer.

To Fytema (tis Pópis) by Fýtema Beach, t 227 503 1928. Ikaría's prettiest taverna, in a lush garden, where the food is made from home-grown ingredients: try *soufikó* (Ikarian ratatouille), stuffed courgette flowers, and home-made pitta bread. *Closed Dec–Feb*.

Mylos, in Évdilos, t 227 503 2602. Stylish taverna in a windmill; lovely views from the tables on top.

Gialiskári and Armenistís ✉ 83301

Cavos Bay, t 227 507 1381, *www. cavosbay.com.gr* (€€€). Comfortable rooms and studios, with two seawater pools, restaurant, Internet café and sea views. *Open April–15 Oct*.

Erofili Beach, near Livádi Beach, t 227 507 1058, *www.erofili.gr* (€€€). Intimate, well-appointed hotel (most rooms have sea views) with indoor seawater pool and Jacuzzi; huge buffet breakfasts. *Open May–Oct.*

Messakti Village, Gialiskári, t 227 507 1331, *www.messakti-village.com* (€€€–€€). Attractive island architecture and slate floors; rooms overlook the pool and sandy beach.

Daidalos, 100m from Armenistís, t 227 507 1390, *www.daidaloshotel.gr* (€€). Traditionally furnished, set among the cedars overlooking the sea, with a pool, children's pool, garden and restaurant.

Ikaros Star, Gialiskári, t 227 507 1266, *www.ikarosstar.gr* (€€). New hotel, with balconies and views, 500m from Messaktí beach. *Open May–Oct.*

Dimitrios Ioannidopoulos, above in Vathypotamía, t 227 507 1310 (€). Hillside studios in a forest of flowers.

(★) **Atsachás >**

Atsachás, above Livádi Beach, t 227 507 1049. A refreshing setting, serving light Ikarian delicacies such as carrot pies (*karotópita*) and other treats. They also have **rooms** (€). *Open May–Sept.*

Paskalia (aka **Vlachos**), t 227 507 1302. Some of the best food in Armenistís

comes from this kitchen; it has good-value **rooms** (€) to rent above.

Symposium, by the sea in Armenistís, t 227 507 1222. Home-grown vegetables, wild kid and seafood.

Christós Rachés ✉ 83301

Despina Studios, in nearby Kastaniés, t 227 504 1100 (€€). Peaceful mountain retreat, immersed in nature.

Nas ✉ 83301

Artemis Studios, t 227 507 1485, *http://artemis-studio.ikaria.gr*. Pleasant studios and good taverna, with lots of vegetarian dishes; the owners also run a pottery workshop and offer lessons.

Anna, the first taverna on the right when coming from Armenistís, t 227 507 1489. Delightful owners serving excellent traditional Ikarian dishes, wine and fresh seafood.

Astra, t 227 507 1255. Views over the beach and seafood (including tender octopus), courgette *beignets* and lobster spaghetti, with local wine.

Foúrni (ΦΟΥΡΝΟΥΣ)

If Ikaría is too cosmopolitan for your taste, turn the clock back a couple of decades and set sail to Foúrni – a rugged, quiet, friendly and utterly Greek mini-archipelago midway to Sámos. The largest, hook-shaped island, also called Foúrni, embraces a huge sheltered bay that long hid a band of pirates from where they would pounce

Foúrni Festivals

15 Aug: One of the two big *panegýri*.
29 Aug: Ag. Ioánni tou Thermasti. The other one.

Where to Stay and Eat on Foúrni

(ⓘ) **Foúrni >**
Municipal office: t 227 505 1366 or t 227 505 1234; also see www.fourni.com

(★) **Nikos >>**

Foúrni ✉ 83400

Finding a room is usually no problem, except in August.

Georgia's, t 227 505 1450 (€€–€). Five big new studios sleeping up to six.

Patras, t 227 505 1268 (€). Eight apartments above the port.

Rena's Rooms, by Kámpi Bay, 15mins' walk from town, t 227 505 1364 (€).

Pleasant new studios; ring and Níkos Kondílas, the owner, will pick you up. He also owns **Eftychia Studios**, inland.

Toula's, t 227 505 1332 (€). New guesthouse on the waterfront promenade.

Markakis Rooms, t 227 505 1268 (€). Rooms and *kafeneíon* by the port.

Nikolitsa Kottaras, Thýmena, t 227 503 2797 (€). Three rooms and a taverna with a view.

Nikos, by the port, t 227 505 1253. In business for over a century, a great place for lobster and fresh fish.

Miltos, t 227 505 1407. Another Foúrni legend, owned by a fishing family; try the lobster spaghetti.

To Koutouki tou Psarrakou, by market, t 227 505 1670. Tasty oven dishes.

Getting to and around Foúrni

Once or twice a week the Piraeus–Ikaría–Sámos **ferry** calls at Foúrni, augmented most days a week by a caique from Ag. Kýrikos (Ikaría). In summer **hydrofoils** connect Ikaría and Foúrni 3 times a week. **Tickets** are sold at the Kafeneíon, **t** 227 505 1481. **Port authority**: **t** 227 105 1207.

on passing ships; modern Greeks, beginning with refugees from Turkish misrule, only dared to settle here in 1775. Foúrni by that time had been ruthlessly denuded by charcoal burners from Sámos and Ikaría. But the sea here is *i foliá ton psaríon*, 'the lair of fish', especially the red mullet and clawless Mediterranean **lobster** (*astakós*), which, although plentiful, isn't cheap; Foúrni's fleet sends most of the catch to Athens. Many locals fish by night, using bright lamps that set the sea aglitter.

⭐ Lobster-fishing

Foúrni's Villages

About half of the archipelago's 2,000 souls live around the port, **Foúrni**, a picturesque web of narrow lanes (including a small but intense *agora* with most of the island's shops) with a strong communal feeling: at least once a day nearly everyone meets in the lovely main square with its old fashioned *kafeneía*. Just north, up the steps, a path leads to the beaches of **Psilí Ámmos** and **Kálamos**. Further north, the road ends up at little **Chryssomiliá**; if you've been looking for a retreat to write your next novel, this might be it, with beaches, a few rooms and a couple of tavernas.

A 15-minute walk south of the port will bring you to **Kámbi**, the 'capital', a pleasant place on two bays (one with a sandy beach and tamarisks) scattered Ikarian-style under the trees, with a few rooms, and a little cove full of yachts in the summer. From here you can arrange boat trips to **Marmári**, a cove just south, or sail further south to **Vlycháda Beach**.

And if Foúrni is too cosmopolitan, try its baby islet **Thýmena**.

Lésvos/Mytilíni
(ΛΕΣΒΟΣ/ΜΥΤΙΛΗΝΗ)

Officially Lésvos, but often called Mytilíni after its capital, Sappho's island hangs off the coast of Turkey like a plane leaf. The third largest island in Greece, it is big enough and far enough away from the mainland to maintain a kind of cultural microclimate. Fifteen villages have been declared traditional settlements, and its undulating hills support an astonishing 11–13 million olive trees, while the higher peaks are swathed in chestnuts and pines. It has the world's most extensive petrified forest; its wetlands draw birdwatchers, and trails attract serious walkers. Its nickname is the

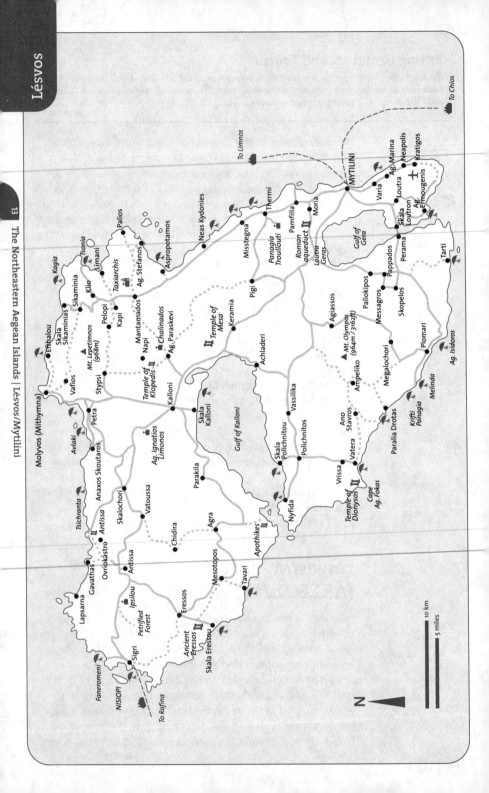

N

10 km

5 miles

To Chios

To Limnos

To Rafina

MYTILINI

Ag. Marina
Neapolis
Kratigos
Varia
Loutra
Ag. Ermougenis
Skala Loutron
Perama
Moria
Pamfilla
Thermi
Panagia Troullouti
Roman aqueduct
Loutra Geras
Gulf of Gera
Tarti
Pappados
Paliokipos
Messagros
Skopelos
Plomari
Ag. Isidoros
Melinda
Megalochori
Krifti Panagia
Paralia Drotas
Ampeliko
Mt. Olympos (964m / 3162ft)
Agiassos
Ano Stavros
Vatera
Vissa
Cape Ag. Fokas
Temple of Dionysos
Nyfida
Polichnitos
Skala Polichnitou
Vassilika
Achladeri
Temple of Mesa
Keramia
Pigi
Misstegna
Neas Kydonies
Aspropotamos
Palios
Ag. Stefanos
Taxiarchis
Tsonia
Limani
Sikaminia
Klio
Skala Sikaminias
Kagia
Efthalou
Molyvos (Mithymna)
Lapsarna
Faneromeni
NISIOPI
Sigri
Ipsilou
Petrified Forest
Eressos
Skala Eressou
Ancient Eressos
Tavari
Mesotopos
Apothikes
Chidira
Agra
Parakila
Vatoussa
Skalochori
Anaxos Skoutaros
Antissa
Ovriokastro
Gavathas
Tsichranta
Avlaki
Petra
Ag. Ignatios Limonos
Skala Kalloni
Kalloni
Gulf of Kalloni
Stypsi
Temple of Klopedis
Napi
Ag. Paraskevi
Chalinados
Mantamados
Kapi
Pelopi
Mt. Lepetimnos (968m)
Vafios
Tsichranta

Getting to Lésvos

By air: There are numerous charters; at least 3 daily flights from Athens with Olympic and Aegean, 2 weekly with Heráklion with Sky Express; daily from Thessaloníki and Límnos. The **Olympic** office is at 44 K. Kavétsou, t 225 102 8659; **Aegean** is only at the airport, t 225 106 1120. The **airport** is 8km from Mytilíni Town, t 225 106 1590. An airport taxi is around €10 from town.

By sea: Daily **ferry** connection with Piraeus and Chíos (12hrs slow ferries; 6½–8½hrs on fast boats); frequently with Límnos, Kavála, Rafína, Vólos, Psará, Thessaloníki, and Ag. Efstrátios. In summer, there are ferry links (8½hrs) on **Saos** lines from Lavrío to Sigrí on the island's west coast. Ferries to Ayvalik in Turkey run nearly daily in summer, and out of season tend to go on Thurs and Sat to coincide with the bazaars; Bergama (ancient Pergamon), Assos and Troy are within easy driving distance. **Port authority:** t 225 104 0827.

Getting around Lésvos

Buses from Mytilíni Town to distant villages depart from the station at the south end of the harbour, on the edge of the public gardens, t 225 102 8873; 3–4 buses a day go to the tourist spots on the west of the island in season; there are 5 buses a day between Mytilíni and Plomári, and 2 per day to Skála Eressoú. Buses to the suburbs and closer villages depart from the station in the centre of the harbour, t 225 104 8725, every hour or so.

Taxis: Mytilíni, t 225 102 2064 or t 225 102 3500.

Car and motorbike hire: Billy's, in Mytilíni and Ánaxos, t 225 102 0006, *www.billys-rentacar.com*; or **Avis,** 17 Venizélou St, t 225 104 2910 and at the airport.

'Island of Ouzo'. It may have only pockets of the stellar pin-up beauty, but there's a bewitching magic to it. The people are friendly, easy-going, lyrical and fond of horses and drink, like Greek Celts, ready to sing and dance whenever the mood takes them.

Besides the delightful Theóphilos Hatzimicháil, the Douanier Rousseau of Greece, Lésvos has nurtured great musicians and poets, from Terpander, inventor of the seven-note scale, and the aristocratic lyric poets Sappho, Alcaeus and Longus (the 3rd-century BC author of the romance *Daphnis and Chloe*) to Nobel Laureate Odysséas Elýtis, who hailed from one of the island's industrial families.

History

Like many islands, Lésvos both prospered and suffered from its geography. Known in Bronze Age Hittite tablets as Lazba, it was allied with Troy – some in fact believe the Trojans themselves were originally from Lésvos (notably from Thérmi) and Límnos; the *Iliad* recounts raids on the island by both Odysseus and Achilles.

In the 10th century BC, Aeolians from Thessaly, led by Penthilos, son of Orestes, colonized the island and made Lésvos a cultural centre, especially under its dictator Pittakos (598–79 BC), one of the Seven Sages of Greece, who tried to heal the destructive rivalry between Lésvos' two cities, Mytilíni and Míthymna, and promoted trade with Egypt. The Persians had it from 527–479 BC; later both cities joined the Delian League. Míthymna, having lost the fight for island dominance, avenged itself on Mytilíni in 428 BC when the latter decided to leave the Delian League and join Sparta. Míthymna hastened to inform Athens, and Athens in a fury sent troops to

Lésvos' Musical Myths

Even in myth Lésvos is linked with music. After Orpheus was torn to pieces by the maenads of Diónysos and thrown into a river of Thrace, his beautiful head floated to Lésvos, where the inhabitants carried it to a cave. The head sang and prophesied so well that people stopped patronizing the Delphic Oracle – angering Apollo, who went to Lésvos and ordered the head to shut up. But they say the presence of Orpheus' head deep in the earth inspired all the poets and musicians who came after, including Arion, accredited with the invention of the dithyramb (the forerunner of tragedy). When he was returning home after a musical contest in Italy, where he had won all the prizes, the crew of his ship decided to throw him overboard and keep the prizes for themselves. Arion was allowed to sing one last tune, then dived into the sea. But his swan song had charmed the dolphins, who saved his life, carrying him safely to shore, while the ship's crew was executed for their treachery. Greek fishermen will tell you that dolphins do love music, and will often hang about if there's a radio on the caique, so the story of Arion may even have an element of truth.

massacre the Mytilinians. However, once the ship set sail, the Athenians reconsidered (for once) and sent a second ship countermanding the cruel order. It arrived in the nick of time.

In the 4th century BC, Lésvos continued to change hands frequently. Its most memorable ruler, Hermeias of Arteneus, was a eunuch and soldier of fortune who governed both the island and the Troad (the region around Troy) on the precepts of the *Republic* and

ⓘ **Lésvos >**
EOT: 6 Aristárchou St, Mytilíni, **t** 225 104 2511; open weekdays 8–2

Municipal tourist office: Traditional Arts Museum, Mytilíni, **t** 225 102 8812; unlike EOT, extremely helpful

Useful Information on Lésvos

Tourist police: **t** 225 102 2776. *Open 8–3.*
Hoteliers' Union, **t** 225 104 1787, *www.filoxenia.net.*
Women's Co-operatives. Since 1983, the women of Lésvos have been in the forefront in Greece in forming rural co-operatives to sell traditional products and offer alternative tourism. You'll find them in Pétra, Agiássos, Mólyvos, Asómatos, Skalachóri and Polinchítos.

Lesvos Shop, on the waterfront, Mytilíni, **t** 225 102 6088. Authentic products from Lésvos and Límnos and books about the island.
Hibiscus Travel, Vatéra, **t** 225 206 1121, *www.lesvos-ecotourism.com.* Member of Responsible Travel and a good source of information, especially on nature, across the island.

Lésvos Festivals

Lésvos has great traditional festivals. Several villages keep up the pagan Greek rite of sacrificing bulls: the victim is bedecked with flowers and ribbons, led through the village, blessed, sacrificed and eaten in a feast.

Carnival, in Agiássos. Eccentric.
2nd Sun after Easter: Festival of the myrrh-bearing women and bull sacrifice, Mantamádos.
8 May: Ántissa.
May: 'Week of Prose and Drama', in the capital.
Last Sun in May or first Sun in June: Távros festival for Ag. Charalámbos, three days with a bull sacrifice and horse racing, Ag. Paraskeví.
26 July: Ag. Paraskeví.
15 Aug: Pétra and Skópelos.

Activities on Lesvos

Lésvos is one of the best islands for **birdwatching**. Pick up a copy of *Birding on the Greek Island of Lesvos*, by Richard Brooks, *www.richard-brooks.co.uk.*

Mólyvos has good yoga vibrations. You can take courses at the **Milelja Guest House**, Ag. Kyriakí, **t** 225 107 2030, *www.milelja.com*, or the **Efthalou Yoga House**, *www.angela-victor.com.*

Diving: Lesvos Scuba, 3 Ag. Irínnis, Mytilíni, **t** 225 103 7799, *www.lesvoscuba.gr.*

Lesvos Safari Tours, *www.lesvos-safaritours.com.* Jeep safaris, canoe kayaking, rock climbing, etc.

the ideal city-state, and invited Aristotle to found an academy similar to Plato's in ancient Assos (just opposite Lésvos, in Asia Minor). While there, Aristotle married Hermeias' niece Pythias and wrote most of the *Politics*; he later moved to Mytilíni for three years, where he set up another academy with his disciple Theophrastus, 'the father of botany' and made pioneering observations of the island's plant and animal life before departing for Macedonia to tutor Alexander the Great in 342 BC. Later the island was occupied by Mithridates of Pontus, who was in turn ousted by the Romans in 79 BC in a battle that was Julius Caesar's first.

Like Chíos, Lésvos in 1354 was given by the Emperor John Paleológos to the Genoese captain Francesco Gattilusio for his help in restoring his throne. In 1462 Mohammed the Conqueror took the island, despite the heroic resistance led by Lady Oretta d'Oria in Mólyvos; local historians are less happy to talk about other locals, the Barbarossa brothers, red-bearded Greeks turned pirate admirals for the Sultan. After the treaty of Kutcuk Kaynarca (1774), when Greek ships were allow to trade under Russian flags , the island's economy took off; the 19th century saw the first ouzo distilleries, tanneries and soap factories. Lésvos joined Greece in 1912.

Mytilíni

The capital of Lésvos, Mytilíni, is a city of 40,000, with magnificent mansions, stately public buildings, municipal gardens and the headquarters of the University of the Aegean – but at the same time a dusty, higgledy-piggledy, cacophonous, very Greek town. After a decade of works, the installation of a new biological sewerage system still continues: every time the workers hit an old stone, all grinds to a halt. Some finds have been fascinating: in ancient times a canal, the 'Euripos of the Mytilineans', flowed between the city's south and (now disused) north port, a fact dramatically proved when a marble bridge and an ancient trireme were found under a street.

On the bustling waterfront, a prettily restored old white house, formerly the harbour office, now holds the **Museum of Traditional Arts and Crafts**, with lace, weapons, ceramics, tools, engraved copper pans – and the municipal tourist office. Behind this the busy shopping street Ermoú leads towards the cathedral, **Ag. Athanásios** (16th–17th century), with a finely carved iconostasis. The huge dome that dominates the skyline, however, belongs to **Ag. Therápon**, dedicated to a penniless but saintly doctor. Once a Temple of Apollo, or perhaps even the School of Sappho, in the 5th century it became a Christian basilica; the present church dates from 1850. In front of the church the priest runs a **Byzantine Museum** stocked with icons from the 13th to 18th centuries, including a painting by Theóphilos (*see below*). The **Municipal Gardens**, a delightful green and shady oasis

Museum of Traditional Arts and Crafts
t 225 102 8501

Byzantine Museum
t 225 102 8916; open Mon–Sat 10–1; adm

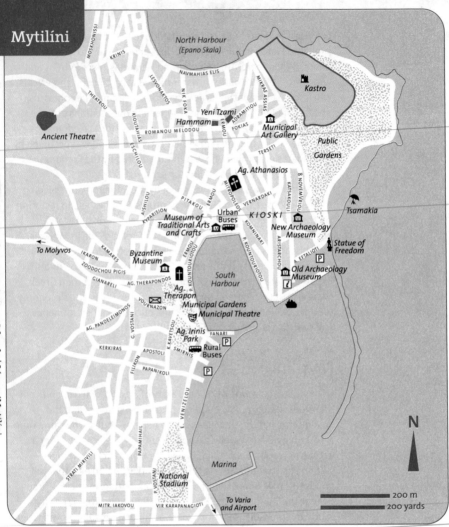

Mytilíni

North Harbour (Epano Skala)

NAVMAHIAS ELIS

Kastro

Yeni Tzami
Hammam

Ancient Theatre

Municipal Art Gallery

Public Gardens

Ag. Athanasios

Tsamakia

Urban Buses

KIOSKI

Museum of Traditional Arts and Crafts

New Archaeology Museum

Statue of Freedom

To Molyvos

Byzantine Museum

Old Archaeology Museum

South Harbour

Ag. Therapon

Municipal Gardens
Municipal Theatre

Ag. Irinis Park

Rural Buses

Marina

National Stadium

To Varia and Airport

N

200 m
200 yards

---

with a scattering of cafés, is nearby, along with the **Municipal Theatre** (1968).

Across the harbour, the elegant residential quarter of **Kióski** is dotted with grand Victorian and Bavarian neoclassical mansions built by olive oil and ouzo barons. By the sea, the **Old Archaeology Museum**, in an eclectic mansion, houses ceramics, delightful Classical-era figurines, coins, jewellery, big Aeolic capitals, the Hellenistic throne of Potamon, an orator, inscribed with his good works, and statues (including the Lion of Géra) to evoke the history of the island from prehistoric times, going back to Thérmi's earliest ceramics, comparable to those found at Troy I. A few streets back, the **New Archaeology Museum** evokes Mytilíni in Hellenistic and Roman times (2nd century BC–3rd century AD) when Vitruvius called the

Old Archaeology Museum
Argýri Eftalioti St, t 225 102 2087; open Tues–Sun 8.30–3; adm

New Archaeology Museum
8 Novemvrioú St, t 225 104 0223, same hours and ticket

city 'magnificent and of good taste'. There are mosaics and wall decorations from luxurious Roman houses, depicting scenes from the comedies of Menander and of Orpheus enchanting the animals, another with the personification of the Euripos channel, wearing lobster claws in his hair. One room contains funerary marbles, idealizing the dead as Thracian horsemen – a popular Hellenistic conceit. One, uniquely, found in Eressós, shows a woman on horseback: Lésvos' women, at least aristocratic women like Sappho, enjoyed far more independence than the ancient Greek norm.

Castle
t 225 102 7970; open Tues–Sun 8.30–3; adm

Further up Novemvrioú St, the former acropolis is now crowned by a sprawling Byzantine-Genoese **castle**, one of the biggest in the Mediterranean, founded by Justinian in the 6th century, who blinded every prisoner he sent here. In 1373 the Genoese enlarged and repaired it using whatever was at hand, including columns from the 600 BC Temple of Apollo. Inside are various buildings, one bearing the coat-of-arms of the Paleológos (the emperor John's sister married Francesco Gattilusio); there's also a vast cistern and a Turkish *medrese* (Koranic school), prisons, and a *teke*, the domed cell of a holy man. The lower castle was added in 1644. Excavations have revealed an Archaic **Thesmophorion**, where women at their annual festival sacrificed piglets to Demeter for fertility. In July and August, some of the most popular singers in Greece perform here; somewhat in the spirit of the Thesmophoria, heart-throb George Dalaras once memorably had his trousers ripped off by ardent fans. There are picnic tables in the pine groves below and a mediocre but often overcrowded pay beach at **Tsamákia**.

North of the *kástro*, the abandoned Old North Port or **Epáno Skála** is a neighbourhood of empty factories and warehouses, still awaiting a new role to play. In the centre, the neighbourhood mosque, the **Yení Tzamí** (mid-1800s), and its truncated minaret have been partly restored, as has the nearby hammam, although both are only open for special exhibitions. Up in the pine forest to the west, at the end of Theátrou Eschílou Street, the Hellenistic **Theatre** was one of the largest of ancient Greece with a capacity of 15,000; Pompey, who loved the island, admired it so much that he was inspired to build his own theatre in Rome in 55 BC.

Theatre
open 8.30–3

South of Mytilíni Town

Buses travel hourly to **Variá**, birthplace of Theóphilos Hatzimicháil (1873–1934), former doorman at the Greek consulate at Smyrna who earned his ouzo in exchange for the most passionate and truest paintings modern Greece has produced, 'like the trembling of the dew', as Séferis described them – sometimes on the walls of shops, or on tins or rags – whatever he could find. The old village school, set in an ancient olive grove a few minutes' walk from the road, is now the charming **Theóphilos Museum**, founded by Tériade (*see* over) in

 Theóphilos Museum
t 225 104 1644; open Tues–Sun 9–1 and 4–6; adm

1964. Because he strove for total lucidity, Theóphilos wrote long descriptions around each scene, whether a scene from mythology, the lives of the saints, the Greek War of Independence, current events (Vesuvius' eruption) or a local festival; smokestacks belch smoke over Lésvos, aeroplanes fly over it, steamboats call at its ports. He also painted frames around his work, since he couldn't afford to buy them. Winsome 19th-century studio photos show Greeks in the splendid costumes that Theóphilos loved to paint; he himself, dumpy and middle-aged, liked to dress up as Alexander the Great, followed by his 'Macedonians' or street urchins in carnival gear.

Tériade Museum and Library
t 225 102 3372; open Tues–Sun 9–5; adm

A stone's throw away, the modern **Tériade Museum and Library** was founded in 1979 by Stratís Eleftheriádes – or 'Tériade' as he was known in France. Born in Mytilíni in 1897, Eleftheriádes went to study law in Paris at the age of 18, where he was soon drawn into the art world. In 1937 he launched his own publishing house, *VERVE*, printing art books and a quarterly review. Inspired by illuminated manuscripts, Tériade produced a series of 'Grands Livres' with lithographs by Picasso, Miró, Léger, Chagall, Rouault, Giacometti, Henri Laurens and Juan Gris, hand-printed on handmade paper in limited editions; many are on display here, along with paintings by the same names (although a burglary has put a dent in the collection). There's also a room of paintings by Theóphilos: Tériade 'discovered' him in 1930, but not in time to save the artist from dying unknown and penniless.

Neápolis, amid scruffy scenery just south of Variá, has a beach and ruined 5th-century basilica, but the main attraction south of Mytilíni is a lovely pair of beaches at **Ag. Ermougénis**, with an excellent taverna. From **Skála Loutrón**, a ferry (*ask around if you don't see it*) crosses the silvery Gulf of Géra, encircled by dense olive groves, for **Pérama**; at nearby **Loutrá Géras** you can indulge in a warm soak in the gentlest of Lésvos' five **spas**, in pools segregated by sex.

Loutrá Géras Spa
t 225 104 1503; open all year

Where to Stay in Mytilíni

⭐ **Pyrgos of Mytilene>>**

Mytilíni Town ✉ 81100

Loriet, in Variá, near the beach, Theóphilos Museum and airport, t 225 104 3111, *www.loriet-hotel.com* (€€€€€). Lovely suites with painted ceilings in a 19th-century villa, plus a charming garden pool. Cheaper rooms in the annexe. *Open all year.*

Heliotrope I & II, 2.5km from centre, t 225 104 5857, *www.heliotrope.gr* (€€€€). A new hotel and older studios sleeping up to eight, all with sea views; the complex includes seawater pool, children's pool, restaurant, bars and satellite TV.

Blue Sea, 91 P. Kountouriótou, t 225 102 3994 (€€€). Smart, clean rooms with balconies overlooking the ferries, but not without noise. *Open all year.*

Pyrgos of Mytilene, 49 E. Venizélou, t 225 102 5069, *www.greece-lesvos.com/pyrgoshotel* (€€€). In a mansion of 1916, luxurious rooms in the same Second Empire style as the building, but complete with all mod cons; parking.

Porto Lesvos, 21 Komnináki, t 225 104 1771, *www.portolesvos.gr* (€€). Nicely refurbished old *pension* just back from the quay, with air-conditioning.

Sappho, Prokiméa St, on the waterfront, t 225 102 2888 (€€). Lovely views from a modern block. *Open all year.*

Eating Out in Mytilíni

Be sure to savour the island's famous fresh sardines and *kakaviá* (fish soup), *skoumbrí foúrnou* (baked mackerel) and *kotópoulo me karýdia* (stuffed chicken with walnut sauce). Lésvos being the island of ouzo, so you should try at least one ouzerie experience: stop the clock, put down the guide book and see if you can match locals for lazy-day endurance.

Achivada, where the road to the airport meets the sea, t 225 106 1571. Good seafood taverna, but succulent grilled meats are also on the menu. *Open weekends only in winter.*

Hermes, Ermoú St (in the market), t 225 102 6232. Wonderful old-fashioned traditional taverna/ouzerie, serving treats such as fava beans, Smyrna-style *soutzoukákia* and other tasty *mezédes.*

Aspro Gatos, south in Neápoli, t 225 106 1670 (€30). The 'White Cat' with its pretty garden draws them out of the city with its very tasty Greek and Mediterranean dishes and good wine list. *Out of season closed Sun and Mon.*

Kalderimi, 2 Thassoú, at the central market, t 225 104 6577. Mecca for ouzerie connoisseurs; great *mezédes*, street atmosphere and local celebs.

Lemoni kai Prasino Piperi, on the waterfront by the Nomarchíon, t 225 104 2678 (€35). The posh place in town, serving an astute *mélange* of French and Greek cuisine.

Theodora Klava (**Grioúles**), by Charamída Beach in Ag. Ermogénis, t 225 104 6417. One of the most famous tavernas on Lésvos – lovely aubergine *imam bayildi*, okra, bean stew and other classics.

(★) Theodora Klava >>

(★) Hermes >

North of Mytilíni

There are two roads to the north coast and the island's main resorts. The longer, east-coast road passes **Mória**, home to a striking section of a tall Roman **aqueduct**, Lésvos' very own Pont du Gard that once brought water 27km from Mount Olympus to ancient Mytilíni. Built in the time of Hadrian, it's tucked away among hills and olive groves; follow signs through the village lanes. Up the coast, **Thérmi** has a ruined Genoese tower for its landmark. Now it is a popular little resort and spa with hot iron-rich springs recommended by Galen (the ancient baths and bit of a temple of Artemis are near the modern spa). Prehistoric Thérmi, east of the road, was inhabited before 3000 BC; five successive levels of civilization were excavated by Winifred Lamb between 1923 and 1933. Like Poliochní on Límnos (*see* p.578), the town shared the culture of Troy, and was burnt to the ground around the date of the Trojan War (1180 BC). The 12th-century Byzantine church of **Panagía Troulloutí** has traces of frescoes.

After passing beaches at **Néas Kydonies** and **Aspropótamos**, this road leaves the coast for **Mantamádos**, a large village of grey stone houses, famous for its yoghurt and for a much venerated icon of Archangel Michael, housed in the ornate 18th-century monastery of **Taxiárchis** on the edge of town by a military base. After pirates massacred the monks, the single survivor collected the blood-soaked earth, then moulded it into a spooky staring icon that is said to smell of wild flowers.

Pelópi, on the south slopes of a dead volcano, **Mount Lepétimnos**, was the home town of the family of one-time US presidential candidate Michael Dukakis. East of the same mountain, the fetching village of **Sikaminiá** marks the start of the **Central Lésvos Trail**, passing through luxuriant ravines of olives as it descends towards the wetlands of Kalloní. **Skála Sikaminiás** is the quintessence of a Greek island fishing village, renowned for its mild winters and tavernas. The novelist Stratís Myrivílis was born in Sikaminiá, and in Skála you can see the old mulberry tree ('*sikaminiás*') under which the author used to sleep in a tree bed. His novel *Mermaid Madonna* was inspired by a dream about the fetching seaside chapel on the rocks over the tiny port, although don't come looking for the icon that gave the book its name – Myrivílis invented it, although now the chapel is known to all as **Panagía tou Gorgóna**. Another of Myrivílis' novel, *The Schoolmistress with the Golden Eyes*, was based on a woman from Mólyvos who collaborated with the Germans.

Although you can swim at Skála Sikaminiás, the nearest good beach is at **Kágia** just east; another, a strand of rose-tinted volcanic sand is at **Tsónia** to the southeast, but you have to go by way of Klió.

The Western Route from Mytilíni to Mólyvos

Buses to Mólyvos take the shorter inland road (it still takes 1hr 45mins). Keep your eyes peeled for a tree known as **Ag. Therapís Tzatzaliáris** (St Therapis of the Rags), where the superstitious hang clothing belonging to ill relatives, hoping for a cure. The road passes near the **Temple of Mesa**, built in the 4th or 3rd century BC as the meeting place for all the island's towns and dedicated to Zeus, Hera and Dionysos; the foundations and Ionic column drums remain.

The temple lies near the wide shallow **Gulf of Kalloní**, where an intensely cultivated plain dotted with Lombardy poplars surrounds **Kalloní**. Kalloní replaces the ancient city of Arisbe, which flourished until local swains abducted some girls from Míthymna and Míthymna in return destroyed Arisbe and enslaved all its people. Important wetlands surround **Skála Kalloní**, a low-key, very Greek resort with a sandy beach ideal for small children (there's seaweed, but other places are clear: ask). Skála Kalloní's famous tasty, mineral-rich sardines (try them marinated as *sardéles pastés*, with ouzo) are celebrated in a big festival in early August; it's also a mecca for birdwatchers – a fad that began here with Aristotle. You'll often see the town pelican, who adopted the local boat builder – one of the last masters of his craft.

Northwest of Kalloní, the vast 16th-century **Monastery of Ag. Ignatios Limónos** was used as a secret Greek school under the Turks. Men only are allowed in to see the frescoes in the central church, but women don't have to feel hard done by: there are over 40 other chapels, St Ignatius' own room, monks' cells, and the petrified wood, folk art and ecclesiastical artefacts and much more in the excellent little museum.

Where to Stay and Eat North of Mytilíni

⭐ Votsala ›

Thérmi ✉ 81100

Votsala, t 225 107 1231, *www.votsala hotel.com* (€€–€). For a modest but delightful stay; relaxing garden by the water for contemplating the Turkish coast. *Open April–Oct.*

Sharjah, on the beach, **t** 225 104 6417. Trendy bar restaurant with a good chef and varied menu.

Skála Kallóní ✉ 81107

⭐ Skamnia ››

Pasiphae, t 225 302 3212, *www. pasiphae.gr* (€€€). Comfortable hotel with a saltwater pool, one of several large, family-orientated complexes on the gulf. *Open April–Oct.*

Mimis, t 225 302 2113. The fish tavernas are cheap and specialize in fresh sardines. This one on the square is excellent (besides the sardines, try the octopus *keftédes* and fish soup) and has meat and ready dishes as well.

Enigma, on the waterfront. Tasty home-made Greek fills, but also pizza and other delights.

Medusa. Excellent fresh fish, caught daily by the owner Manolis.

Skála Sykamniás ✉ 81107

Gorgona, t 225 305 5301 (€€–€). Simple, blue and white hotel, just back from the sea.

Niki Pension, by the car park, **t** 225 305 5244 (€). Basic but adequate.

Anemoessa, t 225 305 3360. Another excellent grill and seafood restaurant by the bijou port.

Skamnia, t 225 305 5319. Since 1920, fish restaurant (with a lobster tank) under the legendary mulberry tree; good organic house wine. *Open all year.*

From Kallóní a road leads east up to the important and very wealthy village of **Ag. Paraskeví**, with an unusually old-time feel and a remarkable neoclassical primary school. Old olive presses adorn the surrounding countryside; one in town is now an arts centre, another holds a small **folk museum**. Three km east of the village, columns from the 6th-century church of Chalinádos have been re-erected in the pine wood, where the famous Távros festival (*see* p.558) takes place. Two km north towards **Nápi** are the foundations of the Archaic **Temple of Klopedis**, which yielded the twin-snail Aeolic capitals in the archaeology museum in Mytilíni. The Genoese used some of its stone to build the beautiful tall single-arched Kremásti bridge, still in use to the west of Ag. Paraskeví. Further north, the green **Ligona ravine** below Stýpsi, on the slopes of Mount Lepétimnos, has the remains of 20 watermills.

Mólyvos (Míthymna) and the North Coast Resorts

Up at the northernmost tip of the island is **Míthymna**, although everyone calls it **Mólyvos**, its Venetian name. The prettiest town on Lésvos, Mólyvos is a symphony of dark grey stone houses and red-tiled roofs, windows with brightly coloured shutters and gardens full of flowers, stacked above the lovely harbour and beach. Mytilíni's arch-rival for centuries, it was the birthplace of the poets Arion and Longus. Achilles besieged Míthymna, but with little success until the

Getting around the North Coast

Excursion boats run from Mólyvos to Skála Sikaminiás and beaches. A local **bus** runs on a regular basis between Efthaloú and Ánaxos, stopping at Mólyvos, Pétra and the beaches in between. Mólyvos's **taxi rank** is opposite the bus station.

---

daughter of the king fell in love with him and opened the city gates, a kindness Achilles rewarded by having her slain for betraying her father. Another story says that Mólyvos was the burial place of Palamedes, the cleverest man in Greece, who invented several letters of the alphabet, weights and measures and dice, and tricked Odysseus himself into going to Troy (*see* p.471). Odysseus never forgave him, and planted a fake letter from Priam and gold trinkets in his tent and accused him of treason. As Flavius Philostratus wrote in the 3rd century AD *Life of Apollonius of Tyana*: 'Palamedes found his bitterest enemies in Odysseus and Homer; for the one laid an ambush against him of people by whom he was stoned to death, while the other denied him any place in his epic.'

The steep cobbled lanes of the centre, known as the **Agora**, are canopied with vines and wisteria. You can walk – or drive up around the back of town – to the striking **Genoese castle**. In 1373, Francesco Gattilusi repaired this Byzantine fortress, and it was famously defended from the Turks by Onetta d'Oria, wife of the Genoese governor, when she donned her dead husband's armour and led the people into battle, before falling to Mohammed the Conqueror in 1462. The long, pebbly town beach lined with feathery tamarisks has sunbeds and water sports and becomes shingly sand at the far end.

Genoese castle
open Tues–Sun 8–3

Four km east of Mólyvos, its sidekick **Efthaloú** has a tree-fringed beach, with thermal springs signposted at the far end.

Pétra and Ánaxos

Pétra means rock, and in particular a sheer rocky spike, carved with 114 steps and crowned by the church of **Panagía Glykofiloússa**, 'of the Sweet Kiss' (1747). The icon of the same name belonged to a captain, but it insisted on staying atop this pinnacle, sneaking away every night even after the captain nailed it to his mast. He finally gave up and then the Virgin started pestering the mayor of Pétra to build her a church. When he gave in and the church was built, a special ceremony was held for its dedication. A boy bringing up a tray of *rakí* for the workers slipped and fell over the precipice. But the Virgin wasn't far, and caught the boy in a puff of air and brought him back to the top of the cliff – not spilling a drop, either. No wonder, in spite of the heat, pilgrims tackle the climb up on 15 August, when they're rewarded with the traditional dish of *keskesi*, made of meat, grain, onions and spices. Below, the pretty village has winding lanes and houses with wooden balconies; one, a mansion belonging to

Archontikó Vareltzídaina

t 225 304 1510, open Tues–Sun 8–2.30

18th-century wine merchants, the **Archontikó Vareltzídaina**, has been restored with its charming 'Turkish Baroque' wall paintings.

Pétra has a good beach, and others lie within easy distance: **Avláki**, 1km west, a small sandy beach with tavernas and some sea grass, and **Ánaxos**, 3km away, a fine sandy bay with fabulous views of Mólyvos, and a burgeoning, ugly resort in its own right. A lovely coastal path skirts the dark volcanic shore to the west leading to **Mikrí Tsichránta** and **Megáli Tsichránta**, tiny hamlets, the latter set on a charming little bay.

Useful Information on the North Coast

ⓘ **Mólyvos >**
EOT: main street, t 225 307 1069; open summer only

Donkey trekking with Michaelis, t 225 307 1309. Day and evening treks with beach barbecues.

Walks in Northern Lésvos, guide and map, available at Ari's market in Ánaxos.

Where to Stay and Eat on the North Coast

Mólyvos/Efthaloú ✉ 81108

Choose between four areas: around town; by the beach; on the harbour; or in the old town climbing up to the *kástro,* which is blissfully car-free but requires schlepping your bags.

Panselinos, by the sea in Efthaloú, **t** 225 307 1905, *www.panselinoshotel.gr* (€€€€€). All the facilities you would expect. *Open May–Oct.*

Delfinia, 1km from Mólyvos, **t** 225 307 1315, *www.molyvoshotel.com* (€€€). With a pool, tennis, beach sports and lazy terrace.

Olive Press, t 225 307 1205, *www.olivepress-hotel.com* (€€€). By the beach; a pretty conversion of an olive press, with tennis court, charming café and dining terrace. *Open May–Oct.*

Sun Rise, 1km from Mólyvos, **t** 225 307 1713, *www.sunrisehotel-lesvos.com* (€€€). One of the pricier options out of town; bungalow complex on a hill with pool, tennis, playground and minibus service to whisk you to the beach. *Open May–Oct.*

Sea Horse, on the harbour, **t** 225 307 1320, *www.seahorse-hotel.com* (€€€–€€). Variety of airy rooms; front-facing rooms have good views of the day's catch. The cafeteria below has shady seating by the water's edge, while the owner runs boat trips from his travel agency next door. *Open April–Oct.*

Adonis, t 225 307 1616 (€€). Attractive, set amongst trees. *Open all year.*

Amfitriti, 2mins' walk inland, **t** 225 307 1741, *www.amfitriti-hotel.com* (€€). Stone building and a pool surrounded by apricot trees. *Open April–Oct.*

Mólyvos I, by the town beach, **t** 225 307 1566, *www.molyvos-hotels.com* (€€). Cool terracotta-floored rooms in a converted traditional building with a spacious terrace. Same owner runs the **Mólyvos II,** in Efthaloú, **t** 225 307 1512 (€€) with tennis, volleyball, pool and poolside bar, add minibus service from Mólyvos I. *Both open April–Oct.*

Michael Tekés, by the Sea Horse, **t** 225 307 1158 (€€–€). Rooms in a restored stone house.

Malli, up the hill in the old town, **t** 225 307 1010 (€). Rooms and a veranda, offering spectacular views.

Marina's Studios, by the port, **t** 225 307 1470 (€). Cosy rooms with views above a jazz bar, plus nine studios in town by the police station.

Molyvos Camping, near Efthaloú, **t** 225 307 1169, *www.molivos-camping.com* (€). Shady; tent hire available.

Pétra/Avláki ✉ 81109

Clara, at Avláki (1.5km from Pétra, with a shuttle bus), **t** 225 304 1532, *www.clarahotel.gr* (€€€). Hotel and bungalows around a seawater pool; all rooms have balconies and views.

Panorama, 200m from the beach, **t** 225 304 1543, *www.panoramahotel-lesvos.com* (€€€). Quiet rooms and studios on a hillside overlooking Petra, in a garden.

Michaelia, by the beach in town, **t** 225 304 1731 (€€). Pleasant pink hotel in three buildings.

Nikki, near Michaelia, **t** 225 304 1601 (€). Plain, clean and quiet accommodation set in a garden of flowers and birds.

⭐ **Women's Agricultural Co-operative** >

Women's Agricultural Co-operative of Pétra, **t** 225 304 1238, *www.lesvos-travel.com/womens-cooperative* (€). Greece's first women's co-op, founded in 1983 and now renting over 100 immaculate rooms/apartments/studios to visitors; starting at €25 for a double. Also *see* 'Eating Out', right. *Open all year.*

Eating Out on the North Coast

Mólyvos/Efthaloú ✉ 81108

Alonia Taverna, outside Mólyvos near the Efthaloú road, **t** 225 307 1355. Excellent, cheap and very popular – some people seem to live there. They often have Greek dancing at night.

Betty's, just up from the town hall, **t** 225 307 1421. Betty bakes a mean honey and almond cake and runs one of the oldest restaurants in town in the house (1880) of the Turkish pasha. She also has **rooms** (€) at the Naxos Guest House.

Efthaloú Taverna, **t** 225 307 1049. Stuffed courgette flowers and other delicacies, served in a shady garden, neither expensive nor touristy.

O Gatos, up in the Agora, **t** 225 307 1661. Since 1980, good place to eat with great views.

Xtopodi, **t** 225 307 1317. The harbour in Mólyvos is by far the most atmospheric, but inevitably touristy, place to eat fish: the 'Octopus' is authentic, good, and not overpriced, even though it appears on most island postcards.

Vafiós ✉ 81108

Vafiós, up in Vafiós village above Mólyvos, **t** 225 307 1752. Big, traditional taverna with big views and a grill; try the cheese pies made with home-made filo pastry.

Petrino, nearby, **t** 225 307 1203, is similar.

Pétra ✉ 81109

Women's Agricultural Co-operative of Pétra, **t** 225 304 1238, *www.lesvos-travel.com/womens-cooperative*. Greece's first women's co-op (*see* 'Where to Stay'). Their taverna has some of the most scrumptious food on Lésvos, especially the delicious *mezédes* – try the fresh *dolmádes* and mouthwatering aubergine jam. *Open all year.*

Avláki ✉ 81109

Avlaki, **t** 225 304 184. Best seafood in the area.

Entertainment and Nightlife on the North Coast

Mólyvos has an open-air cinema, a summer theatre festival with spectacular evening productions of ancient Greek drama and modern works, music and dancing in the castle – and clubs.

Bazaar, near the harbour, Mólyvos. Has an atmospheric little terrace.

Bouzouki Taverna, down a track on the road to Efthaloú. Romantic gardens with good Greek musicians and singers and the chance to dance. Expensive drinks pay for the entertainment.

Conga, Mólyvos. Open-air bar and club where you can sit by the waves.

Gatelousi, between Mólyvos and Pétra. Striking alfresco nightclub, resembling a cruise liner with its deck projecting from the rock face. It has a restaurant and a shuttle bus that runs from 10pm to 5am.

Opus, Mólyvos. *Bouzoúki* by the harbour.

The Other Place, Mólyvos. Another dancing bar in the harbour, happily sound-proofed in a very atmospheric old house, with Greek nights and traditional dancing on Thurs.

Machine Dancing Bar, in the former olive factory in Pétra. Oozes atmosphere with all the press machinery in view; the top floors are engagingly derelict.

Western Lésvos and the Petrified Forest

The northwest quarter of Lésvos is dramatic, volcanic, and arid. Despite its barren appearance, it is brimming with unusual wild herbs and birds: rose-coloured starlings, bee-eaters, hoopoes and pairs of golden orioles. Until recently it was the home of wild horses – some believe they may have been the last link with the horse-breeding culture of the Troad in the late Bronze Age.

Skalochóri (with a women's co-operative shop) once exported oak, recalling a time when the forests were thick here. On the coast, **ancient Antissa** was the first Aeolian colony, founded on an islet in the 10th century and later joined to Lésvos in an earthquake. It was a musical place; after being shredded by the Maenads, the most important bits of Orpheus – his head and lyre – washed up here. The latter inspired Terpander, the 'father of music' born in Antissa c. 710 BC to invent the seven-string *kithera* (the lyre had only four), new rhythms, and put his own lyric verses and Homer's to music; he later went to Sparta by order of Delphi and founded the city's music school before choking to death on a fig. The Romans destroyed the town to punish the inhabitants for their support of the Macedonians, and all the meagre remains lie below **Ovriókastro**, 'Castle of the Hebrew' (but really a Genoese fort facing the sea). Quiet beaches with views over to Mólyvos are the main reason for making the trek, and if you're lucky you'll hear the nightingales, said to have learned to sing from Orpheus. Other beaches to the west, on either side of **Gavathás**, are easiest reached from modern **Ántissa**.

West of Ántissa, the **Monastery of Ag. Ioánnis Theológos Ipsiloú** or 'high up' is stunningly set high on the promontory of a dead volcano. Founded by a Syrian monk in the 7th century and often rebuilt, it shares its pinnacle with military buildings; its museum contains a collection of rare religious paraphernalia and icons.

On westernmost Lésvos, **Sígri** is an oasis amid the otherworldly volcanic wilderness. It's also a delight, a bustling fishing village, with a weekly ferry to Rafína. An 18th-century Turkish castle stands guard, and there's a sandy beach; deep-water **Fanerómeni Beach** is just north. Sígri's main claim to fame however, is the **petrified forest**, larger than the one in Arizona. When the volcano under Ipsiloú monastery erupted 20 million years ago, these pines, beeches and sequoias were buried in volcanic ash and, as it erodes away, the fossilized and colourful remains of their trunks reappear. Most of the trees are still buried and many have been chipped away by souvenir-hunters over the centuries, but some of the best specimens are to be found along a 2.3km (shadeless) nature trail and in Sígri's **Natural History Museum**, in an august setting by the windmill. Other trees can be seen in the sea by the islet of **Nisiópi** (which also has a sandy beach to which caiques venture).

Natural History Museum
t 225 305 4434,
www.petrifiedforest.gr;
open mid-June–mid-Oct
8.30–8; mid-Oct–mid-
June 8.30–4.30; adm

13

The Northeastern Aegean Islands | Lésvos/Mytilíni

The Tenth Muse

Sappho was born in *c.* 630 BC and Eressos proudly minted coins bearing her portrait. Little else is known for certain of her life: she was an aristocrat, was married to a certain Kerklyas of Ándros and perhaps had a daughter, and ran a marriage school for young ladies, to whom she dedicated many of her poems. Like her fellow islander and contemporary Alcaeus, she wrote what is known as melic poetry, personal and choral lyrics with complex rhythms intended to be sung at private parties before a select company. One of her songs dedicated to a young girl is the first, and rarely surpassed, description of passion: 'Equal to the gods seems that man who sits opposite you, close to you, listening to your sweet words and lovely laugh, which has passionately excited the heart in my breast. For whenever I look at you, even for a moment, no voice comes to me, but my tongue is frozen, and at once a delicate fire flickers under my skin. I no longer see anything with my eyes, and my ears are full of strange sounds. Sweat pours down me, and trembling seizes me. I am paler than the grass, and seem to be only a little short of death...' A strong tradition has it that she threw herself from the white cliffs of Lefkáda (*see* p.511) in despair over an unrequited love – for a man. Although Plato called her the 'Tenth Muse', her poems (mostly in fragments) have survived only by accident; declared morally offensive in 1073, most of her writings were burned in Rome and Constantinople.

The road south from Sígri to Eressós is an epic, primeval drive scented by sea daffodils, with scarred volcanic rock faces, ancient contoured stone walls and an amazing sense of space and purity. **Eressós**, overlooking a lush emerald plain amid the tumult, is a ramshackle place with a shady main square of cafés, tavernas and old men. **Skála Eressoú**, 4km away, down an avenue of trees, is endowed with a long, steeply shelving sand beach, lined with tamarisks and a lively seaside village, a favourite of Greek families and gay women, ever since Natalie Barney brought her Paris Salon here to pay homage to Sappho in the 1950s. The attractive square has a bust of Theoprastus (372–287 BC), Aristotle's friend and successor at the Lyceum, botanist and author of the *Characters*, a set of incisive essays and moral studies on the picturesque people of his day. Some fragments of **ancient Eressos**, birthplace of Sappho and Theoprastus, are just northeast of Skála, along with the mosaic floor of an early Christian basilica and medieval and Turkish towers.

Useful Information in Western Lésvos

Sappho Travel, Skála Eressoú, **t** 225 305 2130, *www.lesvos.co.uk*. Specializes in women-only travel.

Where to Stay and Eat in Western Lésvos

★ Una Faccia Una Razza >>

Sígri ✉ 81105

Orama, 1km outside Sígri, **t** 225 305 4226, *www.filoxenia.net/hotels/orama* (€€). Well-designed hotel; all rooms have a sea view and benefit from the pool, but there's no beach.

Sigri Studios, **t** 697 490 5784 (€€–€). Simple studios in the village; also available from Direct Greece.

Remezzo, **t** 225 305 4327. Classy taverna, with the pick of the positions and a lobster tank.

Una Faccia Una Razza, **t** 225 305 4565 (€30 for the full whack). The best Italian food and pizzas on Lésvos, in a trattoria run by an affable Neapolitan. *Closed mid-Oct–Easter*.

The Blue Wave. With octopus tentacles gripped by clothes pegs on a line; excellent, good value fish, although the owner's abrasive style is not to everyone's taste.

Skála Eressoú ✉ 81105

Aeolian Village, t 225 305 3414, *www.aeolianvillage.gr* (€€€). Big new complex, 1km outside the centre. *Open May–Oct.*

Antiopi, just inland, **t** 225 305 3311, *www.antiopihotel.com* (€€). Cosy, and the oldest women-only hotel, recently refurbished; gay men also welcome.

Mascot, t 225 305 3495, *www. mascothotel.com* (€€). New women-only hotel.

Eressos Palace, t 225 305 3858. In spite of its name, a simple taverna, but famous for the best courgette fritters on the island and delicious seafood.

Soulatso, on the waterfront, **t** 225 305 3652. For fresh fish; translucent octopus are hung up in the sun with only the big blue sea beyond.

Southern Lésvos

Southern Lésvos, between the inland seas of Kalloní and Géra, is dominated by the bald grey pate of 964m (3,162ft) **Mount Ólympos**, one of 19 in the Mediterranean bearing that venerable name. Almost all were peaks sacred to a local sky god, who, in this syncretic corner of the world, became associated with Zeus, and would then take the name of Zeus' home. In the shadow of Ólympos, reached by a road flanked by olive groves and natural springs, lies the lovely village of **Agiássos**, with its tall tile-roofed houses with balconies, medieval castle, and creeper-shaded streets where locals gather at the market square *kafeneíon*. Founded in the 1100s, the big church of the **Panagía** houses an icon of the Virgin, said to have been made by St Luke from mastic and wax and rescued from the iconoclasts. The present church was constructed in 1812 after a fire destroyed the older structure, and it has a beautiful 19th-century interior, all grey and gilt, lit by hundreds of lamps and chandeliers. Nearby there's a small **Byzantine Museum** to the right of the church, and a **Folk Art Museum**, containing some of the jewellery offered to the icon. From the Kípos Panagías Taverna, by a 600-year-old plane tree, there's a splendid view of the village, its black plum orchards and walnut groves. A lovely road leads from Agiássos to **Plomári** on the coast, passing by way of **Megalochóri**, the highest village on the island, the 'little Switzerland of Lésvos'.

Chestnut and pine groves cover much of the region, one of Lésvos' prettiest, and the road west to Polichnítos is especially lovely. **Polichnítos** itself, with its four state-of-the-art olive presses, isn't much, although there is a **Municipal Folklore and Historical Museum** and a **spa**, oozing out the hottest waters in Europe (91°C). Erika, who runs it with partner Lefteris, recommends a dip even in mid-summer, to 'fight heat with heat'. Near the harbour of **Skála Polichnítou**, there's a beach with warmer water than off the exposed coastal strips; and another near the mouth of the Gulf of Kalloní, **Nyfída**, flies the blue flag, although it can be windy. The salt pans here are part of wetlands where 134 species have been sighted.

Municipal Folklore and Historical Museum
t 225 204 2992

Spa
t 225 204 1229; open 6am–6pm in season; adm

South of Polichnítos, picturesque **Vrissá** has a giant plane tree and *kafeneíon* in the centre as every Greek village should. It's had its share of history. Its name recalls that it was the home town of Briseis, the princess who caused the rift between Achilles and Agamemnon at Troy; only a wall remains of the Trojan town destroyed in 1180 BC. A 14th-century Genoese **tower** stands to the west. But all of that seems fairly new since 1998, when the banks of the Almiropótamos yielded an extraordinary cache of animal and plant fossils going back two million years, including mastodons, camels, horses and elephants, a tortoise shell the size of a small car and the largest apes ever found in Europe. The finds are displayed in the **Natural History Museum**.

Natural History Museum
t 225 206 1711, open June–Aug 9.30–5; Sept–May 9.30–3

Down on the coast, ruins of a 1st-century BC Doric **Temple of Diónysos Vrysagení** ('Born of the Springs') stand on **Cape Ag. Fókas**, at one end of Lésvos' longest beach (9km) at **Vaterá**, which is usually its warmest as well, sheltered from the north winds. For a lovely excursion, follow the path beginning at the River Voúrkos to **Áno Stavrós** and **Ampelikó**, a charming village under Mount Ólympos, with Roman ruins, a castle and pretty church with a petrified tree in the courtyard. It also has a unique **Museum of Resin-workers**, although you'll have to ask around for the key.

Back along the coast to the east, **Plomári** on the River Sedoúnda is Lésvos' second city, full of houses with traditional *sachnissinía* (wooden galleries) and lovely central *plateía*, dominated by a 300-year-old plane tree. Greece's favourite *apéritif* – Kéfi, Veto, Tikelli and Barbayiánni ouzos – are all distilled here; Barbayiánni, in business since 1860, has what claims to be the world's only **Ouzo Museum**. Yet until 1922 soap was the source of Plomári's prosperity, as it transformed olive oil into *savon de Marseille* for France. One soap factory has been made into the arts centre, with an interesting **Soap Museum**. Plomári has a beach, but **Ag. Isídoros** and **Ag. Várvara** just east have even better ones; if it's too busy try pebbly **Melínda** to the west, with an enormous rock standing in the sea; paths from here lead to **Kriftí Panagiá** ('Secret Virgin'), a stunning place to swim where rocks rise sheer from the sea.

Ouzo Museum
open Mon–Fri 10–2

Soap Museum
t 225 203 2600, open Mon–Fri 9–1

The inland roads are attractive; one descends to the pretty sandy cove at Tárti. **Pérama**, an olive oil port, has vast abandoned tanneries – the largest in the Balkans, until closed in 1980s. A ferry crosses the **Gulf of Géra**, 'the Bay of Olives', to **Skála Loutrón** near Mytilíni.

Where to Stay and Eat in Southern Lésvos

⭐ **Vatera Beach** »

Vaterá ✉ 81300

Vaterá Beach, t 225 206 1212, *www.vaterabeach.gr* (€€€). Run in a relaxed

fashion by Barbara and George, allowing you to unwind to your heart's content; the beachside restaurant offers half-board and vegetarian options to boot. *Open May–mid-Oct.*

Aphrodite, by the beach, t 225 206 1288, *www.aphroditehotel.gr* (€€). Basic hotel and apartments with lots of sports and kids' activities.

Madonnina Studios, 150m from the beach, t 225 206 1120, *www.vatera-lesvos.co.uk* (€€). Pleasant studios and apartments with sea views, popular with UK birders. *Open all year.*

Diónysos Camping, t 225 206 1151. Good choice, with a pool. *Open June–mid-Sept.*

Akrotiri, on the west end of the beach by Ag. Fokás, t 225 206 1465. Superb fish taverna, with gorgeous views. *Open June–Oct.*

Plomári/Ag. Isídoros ✉ 81200

Aegean Sun, Ag. Isidoros, t 225 203 1830, *www.aegeansun.gr* (€€€–€€). Largish, well-equipped hotel with rooms in 'villas' and two pools.

Okeanis, 100m from the sea in Plomári, t 225 203 2469 (€€). Typical little hotel.

Berdema, Plomári's port, t 225 203 1466. Mushroom-stuffed pork chops, baked aubergine and more. *Closed Nov.*

Taverna tou Panaé, Ag. Isídoros, t 225 203 2469. Very pleasant family-run taverna amid olives, serving stuffed vegetables and other favourites.

Serafino, in the plane tree square. Often has live music in the evening.

Pérama ✉ 81300

Balouchanas, over the water, t 225 105 1948. Lively and popular place, where Mamma in the kitchen prepares great salads, excellent octopus fritters, chick-peas with cumin, courgette flowers filled with cheese and mint, and fish; there's even an ouzo menu.

⭐ Balouchanas >>

Límnos (ΛHMNOΣ)

Límnos (often Lémnos) hardly fits any Greek island stereotypes. It's volcanic but it lies low in the water, with gently rolling hills: a green carpet in the spring that turns yellow-brown in the summer, dotted with vines, wheatfields, quirky scarecrows and beehives producing a famous thyme honey. Until the 1960s its main export was cotton; in autumn hunters come to shoot ducks. It was the holy island of Hephaistos, god of volcanoes and metallurgy – in ancient times one of its high points emitted a jet of asphaltic gas. Sulphuric 'Limnian earth' was in great demand for treating wounds, snake bites and stomach aches. But the main occupation of Límnos has long been military, thanks to the magnificent natural harbour of Moúdros Bay, strategically located near the strategic Dardanelles. Límnos also has sandy, relatively empty, gently shelving beaches, and tourism (mostly Greek and mostly upmarket, although the charters have arrived) is the island's third concern after the military and agriculture.

History

The history of Límnos also bucks stereotypes. Homer wrote that the islanders hailed from Thrace, but Herodotus intriguingly says they were Tyrrhenian – the Etruscans. And sure enough, in the 19th century, pre-6th-century BC non-Greek inscriptions were found embedded on a funerary stele, embedded in the wall of a church at Kamínia, showing linguistic similarities to the Etruscan, as do some of the ancient burials. The Etruscans themselves always said they had come to Italy from Asia Minor...

But Límnos started off exceptional. Poliochní's advanced Neolithic settlement of oval huts date back to 4000 BC. These precocious

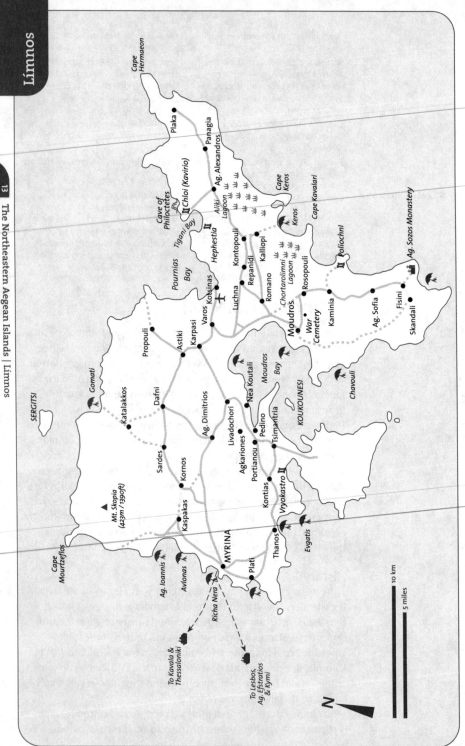

Cape Hermaeon

Plaka

Panagia

Ag. Alexandros

Cave of Philoctetes

Chloi (Kavirio)

Tigáni Bay

Aliki Lagoon

Cape Keros

Keros

Cape Kavalari

Hephestia

Pourniás Bay

Kotsinas

Varos

Luchna

Kontopouli

Repanidi

Kalliopi

Romano

Rosopouli

Chortarolimni Lagoon

Ag. Sozos Monastery

Poliochni

Fisini

Skandali

Ag. Sofia

Kaminia

War Cemetery

Moudros

Propouli

Astiki

Karpasi

SERGITSI

Gomati

Katalakkos

Dafni

Ag. Dimitrios

Livadochori

Nea Koutali

Moudros Bay

Chavouli

KOUKOUNESI

Sardes

Kornos

Agkariones

Portianou

Pedino

Tsimandria

Kontias

Vryokastro

Mt. Skopia
(423m / 1390ft)

Kaspakas

MYRINA

Plati

Thanos

Evgatis

Cape Mourtzeflos

Ag. Ioannis

Avlonas

Richa Nera

To Kavala &
Thessaloniki

To Lesbos,
Ag. Efstratios & Kymi

N

10 km

5 miles

Getting to and around Límnos

Charter **flights** arrive from Northern Europe and there are connections 3 times daily with Athens, some with Lésvos, frequently with Thessaloníki. **Olympic Airways**, t 225 402 2114/2078; **airport**, t 225 403 1204. To reach the airport from Mýrina, take the Olympic bus, or catch a taxi, but it's a 22km trip, so agree a price.

There are weekly **ferry** connections from Lávrio and Kymi (Évia); 6 times a week with Lésvos, once or twice a week with Piraeus, Chíos, Thessaloníki, Alexandroúpolis and Kavála; at least 4 ferries a week go to Ag. Efstrátios. **Day excursions** in season run to Samothráki; also **hydrofoils** twice a week in summer with Alexandroúpolis and Samothráki. **Port authority**: t 225 402 2225.

Buses around Límnos are not frequent. Many villages have only one a day, so there's no way to get back to Mýrina the same day, hence the town's many **taxis**.

Car hire: **Petrides Travel**, 116 Karatsá St, t 225 402 2039, *www.petridestravel.gr*; and **Holiday**, t 225 402 3280, *www.holiday-lemnos.gr*.

Limnians were part of the Troia Maritima, which encompassed not only the Troad but Lésvos (Thérmi) and Samothráki; they may have even founded Troy itself, just across the water – the dates coincide and there were close cultural contacts into the Mycenaean era.

The Persians ruled Límnos before the wars, and at one point the locals captured some Athenian women. When their mixed race children began putting on airs, the Limnians were so outraged that

A Fragrant Mythology

Hephaistos (Vulcan) was so weakly when he was born that his mother Hera hurled him off Mount Olympos. He survived by falling in the sea, near Límnos, where the sea goddesses Thetis and Eurynome cared for him. Years later, when Hera found Thetis wearing a magnificent brooch made by Hephaistos, she had a change of heart, brought her son back to Olympos and married him to Aphrodite. Hephaistos later tried to rescue his mother when Zeus, to punish her rebellion, hung her by the wrists from the sky. Zeus in his fury once again hurled his son from Olympos. This time he fell smack on Límnos, a fall that crippled him for life, despite all the care lavished on him by the islanders. His lameness recalls the early days of metallurgy, when the powers of the smith were so valued by the community that he was hobbled like a partridge to keep him from running away or joining an enemy.

Hephaistos was so beloved on Límnos that when Aphrodite betrayed him with Ares, the women of Límnos tossed her statue into the sea. Aphrodite retaliated by making their breath and underarms stink (Robert Graves suggests this may have been because they worked with woad, a putrid blue dye used for tattoos). This led the men to prefer the company of captive Thracian women. The women of Límnos were having none of this: they doctored their husbands' wine, slit their throats, threw their bodies into the sea and lived as Amazons – one of the island's names was *gynaikokratumene*, 'ruled by women'. When Jason and the Argonauts called in during their quest, the women would have attacked had not their queen Myrina realized that a shipload of Greek sailors was just what they needed to continue the race. So the Argonauts met only the kindest courtesy, and a son born to Jason, Euneus, went on to become King of Límnos during the Trojan War and supplied the Achaeans with wine.

Another figure associated with Límnos and funny smells was Philoctetes, the son of Heracles. Philoctetes had inherited his father's famous bow when Heracles was dying in torment from Nessus' poisoned shirt, as Philoctetes was the only one who would light the pyre to put him out of his misery. When Zeus made Heracles an immortal, Hera, who never liked him, took out her pique on his son, sending a poisoned snake after Philoctetes when the Achaeans landed on Límnos. Bitten on the ankle, Philoctetes lingered behind – his comrades could not stomach the stench of his gangrenous wound – and he lived in an island cave, with only his bow for comfort. After the death of Achilles, an oracle declared that Achaeans could only capture Troy with Philoctetes' bow. Odysseus and Neoptolemos, the son of Achilles, tried to take the bow from him by trickery (*see* Sophocles' *Philoctetes*), but in the end, according to most accounts, Philoctetes himself took his bow to Troy, where he slew Paris.

they slaughtered them and their mothers, giving rise to the expression 'Limnian deeds', synonymous with especially atrocious acts. The gods punished them by making their wives and animals barren. In dismay the Limnians went to Delphi, where the Oracle said the only cure was to promise to surrender to Athens if the Athenians ever sailed from their home to Límnos in a single day. It seemed a fair hedge, until Miltiades (later the hero at Marathon) conquered Chersónissos near the Dardanelles, and appeared from his new 'home' on Límnos to claim what was promised.

The Venetians took Límnos in the 13th century, but the Byzantines soon got it back. In 1475 Mohammed the Conqueror sent troops to conquer Límnos, only to be repelled by the heroine Maroúla, daughter of the Greek governor, who seized her dying father's weapons. In 1478, however, Mohammed came in person and the Turks held on to the island until 1912; not long after, the Allies made Moúdros Bay their chief naval base during the Gallipoli campaign. The Greek army has been there ever since.

Mýrina

Mýrina, pop. 4,000, is the island's appealing port and capital, sweeping along the sea beneath a castle piled over the rocky promontory. The long main shopping street noodles up from the commercial harbour in the south, lined by houses and shops built in the Turkish or Thracian style, filled with the distinct sights and smells – cologne, freshly ground coffee, and pungent herbs – of old Greece. The walk up to the **Kástro** offers a view over much of the island and across the sea to Mount Áthos. A Temple of Artemis stood here in ancient times; the castle built in 1186 by Andronikos Comnenus I, then rebuilt by the Venetians in the 15th century, and the Turks a century later, before being damaged by the Russian fleet in 1770 when Alexey Orloff attempted to liberate the island in the name of Catherine the Great. Today the only residents are 200 deer.

The castle promontory divides the 'Turkish' harbour (**Tourkikós Gialós**) and port on the south (settled by Greek refugees after 1922) and the long, sandy **Romaíkos Gialós** or 'Greek beach' to the north, where Mount Áthos casts its shadow on 2 June. This is enclosed by **Cape Petassós**, with a smart hotel marking the spot where the women of Límnos hurled their husbands' bodies into the sea; originally this part of town was called Androphonion ('man-killer'). The mansions here were built by Limnians who fled the island after Orloff's Russian adventure (300 men who stayed, and the bishop, were executed by the Turks) and went to Egypt, where they made fortunes in shipping. They built the town cathedral, **Ag. Triáda** (1835), with an ornate interor, and donated the mansion that is now the **Ecclesiastical Museum**, with icons from around the island. Another houses the recently renovated **Archaeology Museum**, with relics

Archaeology Museum
t 225 402 2990; open Tues–Sun 8.30–3; adm

from Poliochní (*see* below). Other finds are from Hephestía, Chloï and Mýrina – statues, ceramics, coins, jewellery, and a unique 6th-century BC *kithera*-player with a very tall hat.

Around Mýrina

The coast around Mýrina is very beachy. To the south, past the army base, lie the sandy **Platí** and **Thános** (a particularly beautiful stretch of sand, with volcanic boulders). Others, such as sandy **Evgátis**, are scattered on the way to **Kontiás**, the island's liveliest and prettiest red-tiled village, home of Kontiás ouzo, a dozen abandoned windmills. North, the beaches are safe for children, especially **Richá Néra** ('shallow waters') with tavernas and water sports, **Avlónas** (with nightspots) and **Ag. Ioánnis**. Beyond, the road deteriorates, but, with a jeep, head up the coast for about 15 minutes until you reach a promontory with a three-pronged rock, famous for its sunsets.

Around Moúdros Bay and Eastern Límnos

For military historians, Límnos means enormous **Moúdros Bay**, capable of holding 500 ships and from where, in April 1915, the Anglo-French fleet launched its attack on the Dardanelles, a campaign planned by Churchill in **Portianoú**, in a house that has recently been restored. In 1918, after 30,000 died at Gallipoli, an armistice with the Turks was signed on board a ship in the bay. Of late, Moúdros has found a new vocation – shellfish-farming. In the 1990s, archaeologists found a Bronze Age town with links to Troy and the the Mycenaean mainland on the bay's deserted **Koukonési** islet.

Néa Koutáli, on the upper bay, was founded in 1922 by Greeks from Koutali (now Ekinlik) in the sea of Marmara. Many houses have posters of Panagís Koutaliános of Koutali, a famous 19th-century tiger-wrestling strongman who travelled the world. It has a beach, pines, restaurants and a **Nautical Tradition Museum**. Límnos' most beautiful beach, however, sandy **Gomáti**, is way up on the island's north coast 4km north of **Katálakkos**, one of several villages owned by monasteries on Mount Áthos.

Nautical Tradition Museum
t 225 409 2383 for hours

Moúdros, the former capital, has the ruins of a castle destroyed by the Venetians in 1656 and, appropriately for a military town, a huge church (1370) of the **Taxiárchos** – St Michael, the *generalissimo* of Orthodox heaven. An immaculate British Commonwealth War cemetery has the graves of 800 wounded brought back here, only to die in hospital. There are two beaches nearby, **Fanaráki** and **Chavoúli**.

In the past Limnians preferred living on the island's east, facing Asia Minor. **Kótsinas** on **Pournías Bay** was the medieval capital, and once the centre for exporting Limnian earth. In its **castle**, Caterina Gattilusio, wife of the last emperor of Constantinople, Constantine Paleológos, died during a Turkish siege in 1442; a statue honours Maroúla, 'the last Amazon', who repelled a later siege. A spring is at the bottom of a long stairway (the story goes that the steps are enchanted and impossible to count twice the same way) by the castle's church, **Zoodóchos Pigí**. From the top of the village there are views east across the island to the Alikí and Chortarolímni lagoons; in winter over 5,000 flamingos from as far away as Iran and France migrate here, and share these wetlands with bee-eaters, falcons, herons and the rare ruddy shelduck. **Kéros**, in between the lagoons, has a sandy beach, popular with swimmers and windsurfers.

Kontopoúli, where the poet Yiánnis Rítsos was exiled in 1948, replaces ancient Mýrina's rival, **Hephestía**, named after the god who crash-landed here and inhabited from the Late Bronze Age until Byzantine times. You can explore the sanctuary of the Great Goddess of Límnos, theatre, houses, walls and bits of the acropolis and tombs. In 2006, a boulder (off the road to Ékato Kéfali) was found to have carvings – a muddle of figures, animals and monsters that is very similar to the rather bizarre Jackson Pollock-esque design on the Poliochní cylinder seal from the 3rd millenium BC.

Ancient Kavírio
t 225 102 2087;
always open

Across little **Tigáni Bay** from Hephestía, **Chloï** enjoys a graceful setting and a beach. In ancient times this was **Kavírio**, the earliest-known sanctuary of the chthonic deities the Cabeiri (who were associated with Hephaistos) before the cult centre was transferred to Samothráki. The sanctuary was built around a 6th–7th century BC Temple of Initiation, with the bases of twelve Doric columns. Under the sanctuary by the sea is the **Cave of Philoctetes**, the unhappy archer, with a narrow entrance. It was used in the Cabeiri rites – there's a man-made bench and hard-to-decipher ancient painting on the wall, perhaps of an archer. Another Trojan War site is beyond **Pláka** at the tip of Cape Hermaeon, where a beacon was lit by order of Agamemnon to signal the end of the Trojan War – a signal ominously relayed over the islands back to Mycenae and Clytemnestra. Some say the ancient town of Chryse, which Pausanius wrote was submerged by an earthquake, is somewhere near.

Ancient Poliochní
t 225 409 1249;
open Tues–Sun 8.30–3

South near Kamínia, **Poliochní** is nothing less than Europe's oldest city, where Italian archaeologists discovered seven layers of civilization. The oldest Neolithic town (designated the Black Phase) predates the Pharaohs, the Minoans, and even the earliest level of Troy. By the Blue Phase (Troy I) Poliochní had metal and walls, paved streets, a communal granary and a council house (*bouleuterion*) with benches – the very first sign of democracy in Europe – and, essential for living together, the oldest baths in the Aegean. The fourth phase (Red) yielded a cache of bronze daggers; the fifth phase (Yellow; late Troy II, III) was the Límnos of Homer, when blocks of houses with little rooms were built around a *megaron*; gold jewellery similar to Priam's treasure was found hidden in a vase, along with the cylinder seal. The site was resettled around the time of Troy V (Brown) – but by then the Troia Maritima culture was at an end.

The Perfect Christmas Wine?

Volcanic Límnos has been famous since antiquity for its vineyards; Aristotle wrote about the traditional red wine of the island, produced from a unique variety of grape called *limnio* (locally referred to as *kalambáki*). No other wine tastes anything like it; wine experts, grasping for a description of its bouquet, have hit upon sage and bay leaf, rather like turkey stuffing. The variety has been transplanted in Chalkidikí, near Mount Áthos, where the Domaine Carrás produces a sophisticated *limnio*, blended with 10 per cent cabernet sauvignon. White grapes grown on Límnos are now usually *moscháto alexándrias*, which yields a fine dry white wine with a light muscat fragrance, and is the favourite quaffing wine in the tavernas of Thessaloníki.

Between Poliochní and the church of **Ag. Sózos** to the south stretches the sandy expanse known as the 'Sahara of Límnos'.

Where to Stay and Eat on Límnos

Mýrina and Around ✉ 81400

Many foreign tourists stay in a pair of all-inclusive hotels, including one operated by Mark Warner.

Porto Mýrina Palace, t 225 402 4805, *www.ellada.net/portomyr* (€€€€€). Built around a 4th-century BC Temple of Artemis; clad in marble, it boasts an Olympic outdoor pool and an indoor one, a fitness centre and all mod cons. *Open May–Oct.*

Nefeli, off Romaikos Beach, t 225 402 3551, *www.nefeliapartments.gr* (€€€€–€€€). Lovely spot under the castle, but can be noisy due to nearby bars. *Open all year.*

Ifestos, 17 Eth. Antístasseos, 100m from Platí Beach, t 225 402 4960, *www.ifestoshotel.gr* (€€€–€€). Friendly; all rooms with a fridge and balcony.

Kastro Beach, by the beach, t 225 402 2772 (€€€–€€). Comfortable and typical.

Afrodite, t 225 402 3489, *www.afrodite-lemnos.gr* (€€). Refurbished studios near the centre.

Villa Afroditi, Platí, t 225 402 5032, *www.afroditivillasa.gr* (€€). Fourteen rooms in a flowery garden setting and with a pool.

Lemnos, Plateía Ilioú, t 225 402 2153 (€€–€). Good waterfront bet.

Efi, 3mins' walk from Richá Nerá Beach, t 225 402 4908 (€). Attractive rooms.

Glaros, in the Turkish harbour, t 225 402 2220 (€25). Pretty taverna with a veranda and view of the castle, specializing in fish, crayfish and lobster.

Sozos, Platí, t 225 402 2220. Excellent *psitariá* for succulent grilled meats.

Tassos, by Thános Beach, t 225 402 2220. Taverna famous for its chicken on a spit and lamb chops. *Open all year.*

Zephyros, Platí, t 225 402 2180. Summer bar-restaurant in a pretty garden by the beach with a bit of everything. *Open May–Sept.*

Káspakas/Ag. Ioánnis ✉ 81400

Sunset, Ag. Ioánnis Beach, t 225 406 1555, *www.sunsetapartments.gr* (€€). Peaceful furnished apartments. *Open June–Sept.*

Sardés ✉ 81400

Man-Téla, t 225 406 1349. A traditional Greek taverna named after Nelson Mandela, and it's the best on the island, packed full of flavour – homemade pasta with Límnos' own *kalatháki* cheese, wild rabbit *stifádo*, wild kid and more. *Open all year.*

Néa Koutáli ✉ 81401

Martha, t 225 409 2236. A fish taverna since 1960 undergoing a renaissance; good fish but also grilled meats. *Open all year.*

Moúdros ✉ 81401

To Kyma, t 225 407 1333 (€€€). Traditional hotel and a tranquil place to stay, with a reasonable fish taverna and grill. *Open all year.*

Ag. Efstrátios (ΑΓ. ΕΥΣΤΡΑΤΙΟΣ)

A remote little volcanic triangle in the sea, Ag. Efstrátios (or Aïstratí) lies 21 nautical miles southwest of Límnos (see p.575 for getting there). It was named after a saint who was exiled and buried there, and throughout much of its history, particularly for leftists from 1936–62, and, under the junta in the 1970s, exile remained its destiny. In 1968 an earthquake wreaked havoc, killing half the population, and now nearly all of the 300 inhabitants live next to a wide, sandy beach in dreary concrete huts thrown up by the junta. As on Alónissos, the inhabitants weren't allowed to repair their homes; in this case the junta even bulldozed them.

The sea – the surrounding waters are transparent and rich in fish – brings in most of the inhabitants' income. Besides the **harbour beach**, which is really quite pleasant, there are several others scattered about that are perfect for playing Robinson Crusoe, but you will need to hike for at least an hour or hire a caique to reach them; for real isolation try the long sandy beach at Ag. Efstrátios' baby islet, **Vélia**.

If you want to stay, the 15-room Xenonas (**t** 225 409 3329; €) is a good bet and occupies one of the very few houses to survive the quake; there are also a few rooms, a small shop or two and a couple of summer tavernas with very limited menus. Greeks keen to get away from it all have started to come, so ring ahead to make sure there's room.

Sámos (ΣΑΜΟΣ)

Only a mile from the Turkish coast, and long famed for its wine, women, song and ships, Sámos was the ancient 'Isle of the Blest', and since the 1980s it has become one of the most blessed with visitors as well. Its fertility inspired Menander to write in the 4th century BC 'Kai tou pouliou to gala', 'Here even the hens give milk' (a slogan now used by a Greek supermarket chain) and greenery is slowly sprouting back after the savage forest fires that burned for a week in July 2000. Olives and vines still cover half of the landscapes, which range from the gentle and bucolic to the spectacular; the coast is indented with sandy coves, and two mountains furnish imposing background scenery: central **Mount Ámbelos** at 1,140m (3,740ft) and, in the west, **Mount Kérkis**, a looming 1,445m (4,740ft), both a continuation of the mainland chain that Sámos broke away from in a cataclysm millennia ago. Two famous couples, Zeus and Hera and Antony and Cleopatra, chose Sámos for their dallying, and to this day it attracts mainly middle-class couples on package holidays (a far cry from Cleopatra's gilded barge, pet leopards,

Getting to and around Sámos

By air: Sámos' **airport** (t 227 308 7800) sees half a million mostly charter passengers a year. There are several daily flights from Athens with **Olympic** (t 227 302 7237) and **Aegean**. Olympic also flies twice weekly to Thessaloníki, and there's one flight a week to Heráklion on **Sky Express**. The airport is 17km from Sámos and 4km west of Pythagório. A bus runs between Sámos, Pythagório and the airport 4 times a day.

By sea: Sámos has 3 **ports** – Sámos (Vathí), Karlóvassi and Pythagório. Check with ticket agencies for specific arrival and departure locations. There are **ferry** connections daily with Piraeus, Ikaría, Foúrni and Pátmos, several weekly in season with Kálymnos, Kos, Léros, Lipsí, Arkí, Agathónissi, Chíos, Lésvos and Mýkonos, twice a week with Rhodes and Sýros, once to twice a week with Páros, Náxos, Límnos, Thessaloníki and Alexandroúpolis. There are daily ferry and **hydrofoil** links from April–Oct with Kusadasi, Turkey, from both Sámos Town and Pythagório. **Port authority**: Sámos (Vathí), t 227 302 7318; Karlóvassi, t 227 303 2343; Pythagório, t 227 306 1225.

Getting around Sámos

By bus: From the bus station on I. Lekáti St (a 10min walk from Sámos port), t 227 302 7262, buses run every hour or two (until 5pm) to Pythagório, Ag. Konstantínos, Karlóvassi, Kokkári, Tsamadoú; 5–6 times a day to Mytilíni and Chóra; 4 to Heréon; and once to Marathókampos, Votsalákia and Pírgos.

By taxi: Sámos, t 227 302 8404; Pythagório, t 227 306 1450; Kokkári, t 227 309 2585.

Car hire: Cars and bikes can be hired at the airport and in other main towns. Try **Nikos**, Pythagório, t 227 306 1094, www.nicos-rentals.gr; **Yes**, Pythagório, t 227 306 2168, www.yes-rent-a-car-samos.com; or **Europcar**, 9 Th. Sofoúli, Vathí, t 227 302 2510 (also at Pythagório and the airport).

perfumed baths and dance troupes, but there you go) as well as steady stream of birdwatchers, walkers and backpackers who use the island as a stepping stone to Turkey – spectacular ancient Ephesus is an easy day trip.

History

Inhabited by 4000 BC, the island's name comes from *sama*, Phoenician for 'high place' (similar to Samothráki). Very early on, before the arrival of Greek-speakers, Sámos was famous for Hera's cult by the River Imbrassós; her first shrine, of wood, was according to legend built by the Argonaut King Angaios in the 13th century BC. The Ionians appeared in the 11th century, and by the 7th century BC wine-exporting, wealthy oligarchic Sámos was one of the most sophisticated city-states in the Aegean, bubbling with creative juices and a taste for adventure. Island shipbuilders invented a long, swift ship known as the *sámaina*, allowing Samians to sail the open seas, especially to Libya and Egypt. In *c.* 640 BC, one sailor, Kolaios, became the first (known) man to sail through the Straits of Gibraltar – he was blown off course – and to visit Tartessos in Spain, where he got hold of a fabulous pile of gold. In 550 BC, Polykrates took control of Sámos and became the most powerful tyrant in Greece, ruling the Aegean with a then-enormous fleet of 150 *samainae*, which he used to extract tolls and protection money; he was the first, along with Corinth, to build triremes. He lavishly patronized the arts and oversaw the three greatest public works of the day: the Temple of Hera, the massive harbour mole, and an aqueduct, the Efpalinion

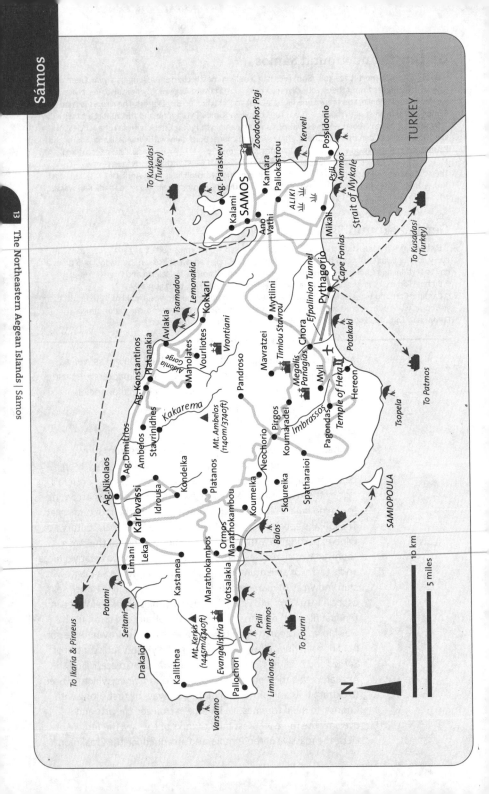

TURKEY

To Kusadasi (Turkey)

Zoodochos Pigi
Kerveli
Ag. Paraskevi
Kamara
Paliokastrou
Possidonio
SAMOS
Psili Ammos
Kalami
Ano Vathi
ALIKI
Mikali
Strait of Mykale
Cape Fonias
To Kusadasi (Turkey)

Epralinion Tunnel
Mytilini
Tsamadou
Lemonakia
Kokkari
Vrontiani
Timiou Stavrou
Chora
Pythagorio
Avlakia
Vourliotes
Mavratzei
Potakaki
Platanakia
Ag. Konstantinos
Manolates
Aidonia Gorge
Pandroso
Megalis Panagias
Myli
To Patmos
Stavrinidhes
Ambelos
Ag. Dimitrios
Kakarema
Pirgos
Neochorio
Koumaradei
Imbrassos
Hereon
Pagondas
Temple of Hera
Tsopela
Ag. Nikolaos
Mt. Ambelos (1140m/3740ft)
Kondeika
Platanos
Skoureika
Spatharaioi
Karlovassi
Idrousa
Leka
Koumeika
Marathokambou
Ormos
Marathokambos
Balos
SAMIOPOULA
Limani
Kastanea
Votsalakia
Psili Ammos
To Fourni
To Ikaria & Piraeus
Potami
Seitani
Kallithea
Mt. Kerkis (1445m/4740ft)
Evangelistria
Paliochori
Limnionas
Drakaioi
Varsamo

N

10 km

5 miles

Tunnel, to bring water to his capital (now called Pythagório after Polykrates' most famous subject).

Under Polykrates, the Samians swanned around in the finest clothes and jewels and knocked down their *palaestra* to build pleasure dens with names such as the 'Samian Flowers' and the 'Samian Hotbed'. Polykrates' good fortune worried his friend King Amassis of Egypt, who warned that he would attract the envy of the gods unless he brought a small disaster or deprivation upon himself. Polykrates considered, then threw his favourite ring into the sea. Three days later a fisherman caught a fish with the ring in its stomach, and returned it to Polykrates. Amassis recognized this as an evil omen, and broke off their friendship to spare himself grief later on. To ward off doom, Polykrates had a bodyguard of a thousand archers. But they couldn't save him from his own ambition; in 522 BC, lured by the promise of yet more treasure by Cyrus' satrap Orsitis, he was captured and crucified on a bluff overlooking Sámos.

One constant in Sámos' ancient history was its rivalry with Miletos, just south in Asia Minor – both were Ionian, and both shared the same all-weather Aegean crossing. Whatever Miletos did, Sámos did the opposite, siding in turn with the Persians, the Spartans and the Athenians. During their second invasion of Greece, the Persians occupied Sámos and kept their fleet at the island, where it was attacked by the Athenians in the Battle of Mykále (479 BC) and soundly defeated – helped by the defection of the Samians in the Persian navy. Afterwards, Sámos, although an oligarchy, became one of Athens' closest allies, one of the few (along with Lésvos and Chíos) to contribute ships instead of money to the Delian league. However, when a fresh dispute with Miletos flared up in 440 BC and Athens offered to mediate, Sámos refused; when Athens took Miletos' side, because it was a democracy, Sámos broke off relations. Pericles took the island in a surprise attack; the Samian oligarchs then allied themselves with the local Persian satraps and defeated the Athenian fleet and garrison. In 439, Pericles returned with help from Lésvos and Chíos and forced Sámos to rejoin the Delian league and branded the Samian prisoners like cattle. In 391 BC, Sámos made a last attempt to regain its independence, but in 365 Athens defeated the

Melissus and Aristarchus, and all the Rest

Pythagoras (*see* p.587) was only the first in a series of great Samian thinkers. Melissus, who led the fleet to victory against Athens in 441 BC, wrote of the essential unity of creation, which was spatially and temporally infinite, and only *appeared* to move. Aristarchus (310–230 BC), a mathematician, was also the best astronomer of his time. Although Greek astronomers were convinced that the Earth was the centre of the universe, and that the planets moved about it in perfect circles, Aristarchus, in an attempt to account for the retrograde motion of Mars and the fluctuations in the planets' brightness, declared that the Earth was a mere planet among planets, and that all planets circled the sun. This was too much for his fellow astronomers, as it would be for many of their descendants, when Copernicus told them the same thing.

ⓘ Sámos >
EOT: hidden away
on Martíou St, Sámos,
t 227 302 8530; open
weekdays in season 9–2

Useful Information on Sámos

Tourist police: Sámos, t 227 303 2444; Pythagório, t 227 306 1389.

Hoteliers Union of Sámos: www.samoshotels.net.

Rent Rooms and Apartments Association: www.samosrooms.gr.

Sámos Festivals

Holy Wed: Washing of feet at Timíou Stavroú Monastery.

20 July: Profítis Ilías celebrated in many villages.

26 July: Ag. Paraskeví in Sámos.

27 July: Ag. Panteleímonos in Kokkári (one of the most popular).

10 days in Aug: Sámos Wine Festival, with troupes of performing dancers from various parts of Greece.

6 Aug: Celebration of the Revolution, Sámos.

29 Aug: Ag. Ioánnis in Pythagório.

8 Sept: Vrontiáni Monastery.

island again, and exiled every last person, replacing them with Athenian colonists until an edict from Alexander the Great ordered the Samians' return in 321 BC. Sámos was a plaything among the powers in Hellenistic times (the Ptolemies of Egypt especially favoured it, and the island gave them Kallikrates, Egypt's great admiral), before the Romans incorporated it into their Asia Province in 129 BC. Augustus was a frequent visitor and granted Sámos privileges, even though his enemies, Antony and Cleopatra, had courted there; according to Plutarch, it was on Sámos that Antony became so infatuated that he threw away the world for a woman.

After the sack of Constantinople, Sámos was ruled by Venice and Genoa. In 1453, when the Genoese handed the island over to the Turks, the inhabitants took refuge on Chíos, leaving Sámos all but deserted for 80 years. With promises of a certain amount of autonomy, the Ottomans repopulated the island with Greeks from the mainland, Asia Minor and other islands – reflected in many village names (Mytilíni, Marathókambos, Pírgos). But the taxes became insupportable, and the Samians joined the War of Independence, and defeated the Turks at the Second Battle of Mykále in 1824. Although the Great Powers excluded Sámos from Greece in 1830, the island was granted semi-independence under the 'Hegemony of the Prince of Sámos', a Christian governor appointed by the Sultan. In 1912, the Samian National Assembly took advantage of Turkey's defeats in the Balkan Wars to declare unity with Greece, under the leadership of Themostiklés Sophoúlis, who later became prime minister.

Sámos/Vathí (ΒΑΘΥ) and the East Coast

Names here are a tad confusing. In ancient times the city of Samos was what is now Pythagório. The present capital and port, set in a sweeping green amphitheatre, inherited the name a few decades ago; when the autonomous 'Hegemony' moved its headquarters here from Chóra in 1834, it was called Vathí, which is still commonly used, while the upper, older town is now Áno Vathí. If the immediate port area of Sámos Town, once mostly used for exporting tobacco, seems permeated with unfulfilled expectations (despite the promise of an international sailing centre), the higgledy-piggledy narrow upper lanes of Áno Vathí have kept their atmosphere.

Most of the bustle in Vathí is concentrated in the pedestrianized back streets and **Plateía Pythagório** near the middle of the long waterfront. Here café dawdlers are shaded by palms and guarded by a stone lion; Pythagorians believed that the lion was the highest animal a transmigrating soul could lodge in (the highest plant, in case your soul prefers to take a botanical route, is laurel).

Archaeology Museum
t 227 302 7469; open Tues–Sun 8.30–3; adm

South, by the **municipal gardens**, the two buildings of the Archaeology Museum are packed full of treasures. Top billing goes to the unique set of stylishly elegant Archaic statues known as the Geneleos Group (*c.* 550 BC), made of the local marble and dressed in pleats as fine as pinstripes. They were a prelude to the majestic 6th-century BC *kouros* from the Temple of Hera, at 5.5m (18ft) one of the largest (they had to lower the floor to fit it in, and when the head was found a couple of years later, they had to raise the roof) but with features as serene as a Buddha and the Archaic smile that John Fowles describes as 'having known Divinity'. There are Geometric vases and prehistoric tools, and masses of ex-votos left for Hera: ivory and clay pomegranates, pine cones and poppies (all of which have many seeds, signifying fertility) and little terracotta figurines from the 10th century BC. Some were manufactured as far away as Cyprus, Egypt, Etruria and Andalucía – in fact more foreign goods have been found here than in any other Greek sanctuary, and it was their superior workmanship that inspired local artists to new heights in the 6th century. Even bits of Archaic wooden furniture and sculpture were preserved in the waterlogged grounds, along with splendid bronzes and a magnificent array of griffon heads (a Mesopotamian calendar beast introduced to the west through Sámos in the 8th century BC); Herodotus described a bronze mixing bowl with griffon heads dedicated by the famous sailor Kolaios.

The rather unpromising road north of the harbour leads to the so-so town beach and the fashionable suburb of **Kalámi**; the road continues, getting narrower and narrower, ending at the beach and tavernas and chapel of **Ag. Paraskeví**.

Around the East Coast

East of town, the narrow Strait of Mykále separates Sámos from the rugged coast of Turkey, where velvet-green slopes hem in the turquoise sea; the **Monastery of Zoodóchos Pigí** (1756), set on the cliffs over the fishing hamlet of Mourtiá, has spectacular views. Further south lie the beaches at **Kervelí** (pretty but stony),

Where to Stay and Eat around Sámos/Vathí

Sámos/Vathí and Around
✉ 83100

Kirki Beach, at Kalámi, t 227 302 3030 (€€€). One of the clutch of new, upmarket hotels here, with a pool.

Aeolis, 33 Th. Sofoúli, t 227 302 8904 (€€). Stylish waterfront option, with small pool, Jacuzzi and bar perched on the roof terrace.

Christiana, up in Áno Vathí, t 227 302 3084 (€€). With a pool. *Open April–Oct.*

Emily, Grámmou and 11 Novemvríou, t 227 302 4691, *www.web-greece.gr/hotels/emily* (€€) Pleasant family hotel 150m from the harbour.

Paradise, 21 Kanári, near the bus station, t 227 302 3911, *www.samosparadise.gr* (€€). Family-run hotel amid gardens, with a pool.

Sámos, 11 Th. Sofoúli, by the port, t 227 302 8377, *www.samoshotel.gr* (€€–€). Impersonal but good value; sea-views from the roof terrace, pool and bar.

Helen, 2 Grámmou, t 227 302 8215 (€). Quiet rooms with balconies.

Vathy, off the road up to Áno Vathí, t 227 302 8124 (€). Friendly and family-run with a teeny but welcome pool above the town and harbour.

Christos, in an alley just off Plateía Ag. Nikoláos, t 227 302 4792. Easy to find, cheap and cheerful.

Ostrako, 141 Th. Sofoúli, t 227 302 7070. Good fish taverna/ouzerie, serving delicious *mezédes*.

East Coast ✉ 83100

Kerveli Village, Kérveli, t 227 302 3006, *www.kerveli-village.gr* (€€€). Sleep where the sun first kisses Greece each morning; comfortable hotel among the olives, with a pool and tennis.

St Nicholas, at Mykáli (Psilí Ámmos), t 227 302 5230 (€€). Low-key, environmentally friendly hotel with a pool; vegetarian meals too. *Open Mar–Oct.*

Kanoutna, Klíma Beach at Possidónio, t 227 302 8314. Fish taverna on a little beach, with excellent spaghetti with lobster and banoffi pie. *Open May–Oct.*

Possidónio (sheltered and shingly) and **Psilí Ámmos** (sandy and very busy). Very near to Psilí Ámmos, the lagoons and former salt pans around **Áliki** are now a nature reserve; between November and July storks, flamingos and herons are frequent visitors.

Pythagório (ΠΥΘΑΓΟΡΕΙΟ)

⓲ Pythagório

Pythagório, on the southeast coast, has become the island's most popular resort, although at the expense of much of its former pith – not only is the 'Samian Hotbed' long gone, but so are many of the Greeks, who now commute to work in the resort from inland villages. When it was Polykrates' capital, Sámos, its population reached 300,000; by the 20th century it was reduced to a little fishing village called Tigáni, or frying pan, because of the shape of Polykrates' jetty. In 1955 the town was renamed to honour Sámos' famous son, synonymous with the theorem that put his name on the lips of every schoolchild in the world. It was not only a brilliant theorem, but the first theorem: Pythagoras was the first to apply the same philosophical 'proofs' used by the earliest philosophers of Miletos to the subject of mathematics.

Much of the action in town is concentrated around the 360m (1,180ft) **ancient harbour mole** built by Efpalinio, Polykrates' great engineer, which Herodotus declared was one of the three wonders of

Pythagoras: Geometry, Beans and the Music of the Spheres

Like Socrates, Pythagoras never wrote anything down, and is only known through the writing of his followers – and his enemies. Born on Sámos around 580 BC, he is known to have visited Egypt and Babylonia, either before or after his quarrel with Polykrates that sent him packing to Croton in southern Italy. There he and his followers formed a brotherhood 'of the best' that governed Croton for 20 years, before the city revolted. This brotherhood was a secret society that quickly spread throughout the Greek world; members recognized each other by their symbol – the pentangle. But mumbo jumbo politics was only one aspect of Pythagoras, who was to have considerable influence, especially on Plato. He taught that the soul was immortal, and that after death it transmigrated not only into new humans but into plants and animals, and that by purifying the soul one might improve it, and perhaps escape the need for reincarnation. There were prohibitions on eating meat (that chicken might be your grandmother) and, more mysteriously, against eating fava beans – scholars long debated whether Pythagoras thought that beans held human souls, expressed in unharmonious flatulence, or if he knew about favism, a sometimes deadly reaction many Mediterranean people have to fava beans and their dust. Recently, however, it has been shown that Pythagoras was the victim of millennia of misunderstanding: the Greeks used letters for numbers, and what appears to read 'lay off fava beans' is actually a theorem of angles.

If Pythagoras wasn't full of beans, he was certainly full of numbers. He was the first to apply *kosmos*, a Greek word meaning arrangement and ornamentation (hence our 'cosmetics') to the universe. The order of the Cosmos, he believed, was based on the connections of its various parts called *harmonia*, and that *harmonia* was based on numbers. He discovered that music could be expressed mathematically by ratios and the tuning of the seven-string *kithera* (recently invented by Terpender of Lesvós) and he extended that *harmonia* to 'the music of the spheres', the motions of the seven planets (the five visible ones, and the moon and sun) – and to the Golden Mean, the base of the proportions of Classical architecture and sculpture. Although the belief that everything could be defined by numbers took the Pythagoreans down some woolly paths, the key idea was that the study of the order of the Cosmos and its harmony would help to eliminate the disorder in our souls. No one agreed more than a latter-day Pythagorean, Johannes Kepler, who worked out the true elliptical orbits of the planets and formulated the Third Law of Planetary Motion (1619): 'The square of the period of revolution is proportional to the cube of the mean distance from the sun.' Kepler noted that the varying speeds of the planets' revolutions corresponded with the ratios in Renaissance polyphonies; in 1980, one of the mementoes that NASA scientists packed aboard *Voyager* for its journey out of our solar system was a computer-generated recording of Pythagoras' and Kepler's music of the spheres.

Greece; now yachts swish in place of sharp-bowed *samainae*. Lykúrgos Logothétis, hero of the 1821 revolution, built the town **castle** – mostly at the expense of the Temple of Hera – at the beginning of Pythagório's sand and pebble beach, which extends off and on to the west. The victory over the Turks at Mykále in 1824 is commemorated by a plaque in the pretty white church of the **Metamórphosis**. A small **Archaeology Museum** in the town hall houses Archaic finds, busts of Roman emperors and ceramics that Vathí didn't want.

Archaeology Museum
t 227 306 1400; open Tues–Sun 8.45–2

Thermes
open Tues–Sun 8.30–2.45

Other relics of ancient Samos are a short walk away. To the west, the 2nd-century BC Roman Baths or **Thermes** were incorporated into a gymnasium; later one of the rooms was used as a Christian church and baptistry. A road from the ancient **theatre** leads up to the **cave** where legend has it the sibyl Phyto prophesied a one and true god, which would provide an important justification for later Christian interest in pagan antiquity; appropriately the cave, which often sheltered refugees in times of trial, now shelters a church, **Panagía Spilianí**, last rebuilt in 1836, near a tiny monastery in the cypresses.

Where to Stay and Eat in Pythagório

Pythagório ✉ 83103

The hotels of Pythagório are clustered within walking distance around the beach at Potokáki or just north of town. Most are open only in summer and block-booked in season.

Doryssa Bay, Potokáki, **t** 227 308 8300, www.doryssa-bay.gr (€€€€). Deluxe pseudo-Greek village of bungalows; pool, tennis, water sports and a folklore museum. *Open April–Oct.*

Gallini, t 227 306 1167 (€€). Central and quiet, with a friendly owner; the rooms on top have verandas. *Open May–Oct.*

Hera II, t 227 306 1879, www. hera 2hotel.gr (€€). Cool, pink establishment with only seven rooms; elegant with panoramic views. *Open April–Oct.*

Kastelli, further out and 100m from the sea, **t** 227 306 1728 (€€). Soaring views and breakfast; a good bet if you can beat the crowds. *Open April–Oct.*

Afrodite, t 227 306 1031 (€). Studios and an airy apartment; port-facing rooms have extensive views. *Open May–Oct.*

Alexandra, t 227 306 1429 (€). Simple, charming and cheap rooms with a lovely, shady garden. *Open April–Oct.*

Areli Studios, t 227 306 1245 (€). Pristine studios, with an olive grove and flowers. *Open May–Oct.*

Dolixi, on the first floor, **t** 227 306 1764. The coolest bar-restaurant on Sámos, with comfy old furniture and tasty original pasta and vegetable dishes.

Riva, t 227 306 2395. Taverna in an attractive stone building, serving both Greek and international dishes. *Open weekends only in winter.*

Efpalinion Tunnel
*open Tues–Sun
8.45– 2.45; adm*

The road to the left of the theatre leads to the extraordinary **Efpalinion Tunnel**. Polykrates wanted his aqueduct kept secret, to prevent an enemy cutting off the water – and to assure the city's supply if it were ever besieged. Under Efpalinio two crews of 4,000 slaves, mostly from Lésvos, started digging through the solid rock on either side of Mount Kástri and, thanks to his calculations, met on the same level, only a few inches off perfection. Nearly a kilometre long, the tunnel's earthenware pipes kept the baths full in Pythagório until the 6th century AD. Then the tunnel was forgotten until it was rediscovered in the late 19th century (with lamps and tools of the workmen still there) when the town attempted to return it to action. Now electrically lit, it no longer seems quite as old and mysterious as it once did; visitors are allowed in the first 100m or so. Above the tunnel you can find the spring **Agiade** that supplied it, and follow the traces of the long walls up the slope; these originally measured 7km and stretched to Cape Foniás, bristling with towers; partly destroyed by Lysander when the Spartans took Sámos in the Peloponnesian War, there are intact sections high up.

West of Pythagório

The Heraion (Temple of Hera)

Heraion
*t 227 309 5277;
open Tues–Sun
8.30–3; adm*

'They combed their flowing locks and went, all dressed in fine garments, to the sanctuary of Hera...' wrote the Samian poet Asios in the 6th century BC. From Pythagório, it was an 8km stroll past 2,000 statues, tombs and monuments lining the **Sacred Way** (now 90 per cent paved under the profane airport road and runway) to the once

The Goddess as a Plank

Zeus had to use cunning to win Hera (perhaps because he was her brother), and they spent a 300-year-long wedding night on Sámos 'concealed from their dear parents'. Hera was pre-eminently the goddess of marriage, worshipped in three aspects: the Girl, the Fulfilled and the Separated, but never in an erotic fashion or as a mother. In truth she was always the Great Goddess, ambivalent about her relationship with her patriarchal consort, and she often returned to Sámos to bathe in the Imbrassós to renew her virginity. Her sanctuary was filled with works of art, but the holy of holies was a plank of wood crudely painted with the goddess's features, believed to have fallen from heaven and too sacred to be touched; to carry it, the priests tied it with twigs of osier. Twice a year celebrations took place: the Heraia, in honour of her marriage, and the Tonea, recalling an attempt by the Argives to snatch the plank, only to be thwarted by the goddess, who nailed their ship to the waves.

sublime Temple of Hera. 'Cow-eyed' Hera was born on this marshy plain of the Imbrassós under a sacred osier. She was the first deity to have temples erected in her honour; two, made of mud, wood and bricks, had already been built, when an architect named Roikos completed a huge Ionic temple in stone in 560 BC. Apparently the marshy ground made it unstable, because not long after, Polykrates, who never believed in half measures, replaced it with a **Great Temple** that measured 108 by 50m (354 by 165ft) and was, after the Temple of Artemis at Ephesus and the Temple of Zeus in Akragas (Agrigento), the third largest ever built by the Greeks. Yet only a single column of its original 155 remains, at half its original height, as sole witness to its size, and it looks like a wobbly stack of mints. The entablature is presumed to have been of wood, and the lack of tiles suggests the roof was never finished.

In spite of its size, the temple was never a pan-Hellenic shrine, but a showcase for Sámos. It served as the venue for celebrations after the city-state's victories. A Roman emperor paid a fortune to have the Sacred Way paved in marble in the 3rd century AD, shortly before the sanctuary was destroyed by raiding Herulians; earthquakes in the 4th and 5th centuries and builders looking for stone finished it off (the one column was left standing as a landmark for their ships). Only the base of the 42m (140ft) altar has survived (rebuilt seven times, from the Bronze Age to Roman times), along with foundations of treasuries, *stoas* and statue bases and the apse of a Christian basilica made out of the temple's stone. The remains of sacrifices, usually cows, were found near the altar, although not a single thigh bone was among them, confirming Homer's descriptions of the special treatment given to thighs. The skulls of a Nile crocodile and two antelopes are more mysterious. Some of the temple's stone went into the nearby **Sarakíni Castle**, built in 1560 by a Patmian naval officer appointed governor of Sámos by the Sultan.

The Southeast: Pretty Villages and Short-necked Giraffes

A bit close to the airport for comfort, **Héreon** is a bland resort on a beach that gets too crowded in the summer, although in May this wet area around the airport is a great base for birding. In summer caiques sail south to the beautiful beach of **Tsópela**, at the mouth of a gorge. West of Pythagório, lively **Chóra** was made the capital of Sámos by the aforementioned Captain Sarakíni and kept its status until 1855. To the north the road passes through a steep valley to **Mytilíni**, where fossils dating back 15 million years – washed into a deposit by the Meander River, before Sámos broke free from the mainland – have been gathered in a **Palaeontological Museum**. Sámos had a reputation for monsters in mythology; one story has it that the island broke off Asia Minor like glass when the monsters let loose a particular high-pitched shriek. Among the fossils of prehistoric mastadons, elephants, hippopotami, short-necked giraffes and rhinoceroses, is a 13-million-year-old fossilized horse brain and a fang of the fiercesome *megatherium*.

Palaeontological Museum
t 227 305 2055; open Mon–Sat 9.30–3, Sun 10–3

Above Héreon, lemon groves surround **Mýli** at the source of the Imbrassós, where an important Mycenaean tomb was found near the school. From **Pagóndas** ('the land of springs'), the road circles around through untamed if sadly fire-scarred south coast scenery en route to **Spatharáioi** (7.5km) and **Pírgos** (another 6km), a pretty mountain village in now charred pines, founded by settlers from the city of that name in the Peloponnese. Down in a ravine below Pírgos, the fire skipped **Koútsi**, a place nymphs would love, a grove of clear waters, venerable plane trees, cool mountain air and something the nymphs didn't have – a taverna, open when it feels like it.

From Pírgos you can circle back towards Pythagório, going by way of **Koumaradéi**, where a dirt road leads up to the **Moní Megális Panagías**, founded in 1586; the walls of the monastery encompass one of the island's most beautiful churches, with good icons and damaged frescoes. One of the monks who built it founded **Timíou Stavroú Monastery** (1592) to the east, after a dream he had of a buried icon of the Holy Cross; it was duly found, and is now covered in ex-votos. On Holy Wednesday people gather here from all over Sámos to watch the Archbishop re-enact the washing of the Apostles' feet. North of the monastery, **Mavratzeí** is a pottery village, specializing in 'Pythagorean Cups' that spill on your lap if overfilled.

West along the North Coast: Vines and Beaches

The beautiful north coast of Sámos was for the most part spared the forest fires that ravaged the south, although builders haven't been so kind. Ten km west of Vathí, **Kokkári** was once a delightful whitewashed fishing village named 'seed onions' for its main crop, before it became a sacrifical lamb to the great god tourism. Even so, the setting is still lovely, and popular with windsurfers, and a new

'Fill High the Bowl with Samian Wine...'

Vourliótes, Manolátes and Stavrinídes are the top wine-growing villages on Sámos, where one famous variety of grape, Moscháto Sámou, has reigned for the last 2,000 years or so. The old vines are thickly planted on small anti-erosion terraces called *pezoúles* from 150m (492ft) to 800m (2,624ft) above sea level and, like all quality dessert wines, have an extremely low yield. After years of neglect in the Middle Ages, Samian wine began its comeback under the Greek settlers brought over by the Ottomans in the late 16th century. By the 18th century it was imported in large quantities to Sweden and even to France, and the Catholic Church gave Sámos a concession to provide wine for Mass, something it still does to a degree in Austria, Switzerland and Belgium. All Samian wine has been sold through the co-operative since 1932 after wine-growers, reduced to penury by profiteering international wine merchants, revolted against the system and demanded control of their own production. The most prized wine of Sámos is its light amber Grand Cru Vin Doux Naturel, with 15 per cent alcohol, given its *appellation* in France in 1982 (the only Greek wine so honoured); also try a chilled bottle of fruity Nectar, aged in its oak cask and splendid with strong cheeses or fruit salads. Of the dry wines, try the green-tinted Samena Dry White, a good *apéritif*.

bypass has made traffic less of a snarl. In addition to its own busy beach, there's **Lemonákia**, a 20-minute walk away, and **Tsamadoú**, a partly naturist crescent of multicoloured pebbles 2km from Kokkári. Further west, **Avlákia** has a different, old-time atmosphere: a low-key resort with a sprinkling of accommodation on the beach and a second small pebble beach at **Tsaboú**.

Inland, cypresses and pines rise like towers up the slopes of Mount Karvoúnis or **Ámbelos** (1,140m/3,740ft), its latter, ancient name means 'vineyard'. From the handsome flowery village of **Vourliótes**, it's a 3km walk up to the fire-scarred **Vrontiáni Monastery**, founded in 1560 (*check to see if it's re-opened before setting out*).

Back on the coast at **Platanákia**, you can eat under the magnificent plane trees and drink barrelled red wine, though avoid the organized 'Greek Nights'. It's a suburb of **Ag. Konstantínos** (or just '**Agios**' as everyone calls it), which still has some of its old-fashioned charm in spite of all the concrete they've used to mutilate the beach.

From Platanákia the road ascends to **Manolátes**, another old village in a stunning setting, separated by the river Kakoréma and the steep arcadian **Aidónia** ('nightingales') **Gorge**, lush with walnuts and plane trees from Vourliótes – there's a path. Another goes to the top of Mount Ámbelos in about five hours.

Where to Stay and Eat on the North Coast

Kokkári ✉ 83100

Arion, 500m above Kokkári, t 227 309 2020, *www.arion-hotel.gr* (€€€). Built in traditional Samian style with shady lawns among the trees, as well as a pool, sauna, Internet, billiards and Jacuzzi; the hotel bus provides transport to Kokkári. *Open May–Oct.*

Armonia Bay, up in olive groves above Tsamadoú Beach, t 227 309 2279, *www.armoniabay.gr* (€€€). Attractive small hotel above the hubbub, with lovely views and an infinity pool.

Kalidon Palace, 400m from Lemonákia beach, t 227 309 2800, *www.kalidon.gr* (€€€). Modern comfortable hotel with a pool and free shuttle bus; the same people run the **Kalidon Hotel**, in town, t 227 309 2605 (€€–€).

Lemon House, at the south entrance to the village, t 227 309 2441, *www.lemon-house.de* (€€). Twelve pleasant rooms with lemon trees in the courtyard. *Open May–Oct.*

Olympia Beach, t 227 309 2420, *www.olympia-hotels.gr* (€€). Pleasant place; 12 rooms with balconies by the sea.

Marina, t 227 309 2692. Excellent traditional food – chickpea fritters, fresh fried potatoes and stuffed baked lamb. *Open Fri–Sun only out of season.*

Avlákia/Vourliótes/Manolátes ✉ 83100

AAA, Manolátes, t 227 309 4472. In the pretty village square, taverna famous for its kid with celery.

Avlákia, in Avlákia, right on the beach, t 227 309 4230 (€). Very pleasant old-fashioned hotel with a restaurant on the strand.

Galázio Pigádi, Vourliótes, t 227 309 3480. *Mezedopoleío* serving divine cheese pies and tomato *keftédes*.

Loukas, at the top of Manolátes. Everything here is home-made, from their own olive oil, cheese, wine and *soúma* (a local schnapps) to the stuffed vine leaves and courgette flowers

★ Aidónokastro >>

★ Loukas >

(picked daily at 6am and then baked in their traditional wood-burning oven).

Pera Vrisi, at the entrance to Vourliótes, t 227 309 3277. Authentic old-fashioned cuisine – try the pepper *saganáki*.

Pighí Pnaká, near Vourliótes, t 227 309 3380. Popular taverna under a centuries-old plane tree, serving great lemony roast potatoes and free-range chicken and lamb. *Closed Nov–April.*

Ag. Konstantínos ✉ 83200

Aidónokastro, 2km inland towards the Aidona Gorge, t 227 309 4686 (€€). A hillside hamlet of old stone two-storey houses beautifully converted into traditionally decorated studios sleeping 2–4 people. Utter peace and quiet – the loudest sound is the gurgling stream. *Open April–Oct.*

Apollonia Bay, t 227 309 4444 (€€). Smart apartment complex with pool. *Open May–Oct.*

Atlantis, t 227 309 4329 (€). An older hotel and a good budget bet.

Apólafsi, t 227 309 4203. Traditional taverna with a wood oven serving classics as they should be – moussaka with lamb, baked lamb, aubergines with yoghurt. *Closed Nov–April.*

Karlóvassi and Western Sámos

Wallflower **Karlóvassi**, Sámos' second city and port, was an industrial tanning centre before the Second World War and, although the hides are long gone, the empty warehouses along the port present a dreary face to the world. After the first baleful hello, however, the little city is pleasant enough, much sleepier and Greekier than Vathí or Pythagório, and neatly divided, in descending order of interest, into Old, Middle and New (Paléo, Meséo and Néo) Karlóvassi, punctuated with the pale blue domes of absurdly large 19th-century churches. Most visitors stay in a small cluster of hotels in the small seaside resort bit, **Limáni**, where you'll find the regional bus stop, banks and post office, not to mention the timeless Paradise, an old-men's ouzerie with tables strewn under a shady tree. A city bus goes 2km west to the nearest beach, **Potámi**, at the mouth of a river favoured by dragonflies and orchids.

Western Sámos has been compared to western Crete: fewer sights, fewer tourists, but amply rewarding in the scenery and beach departments. A track from Potámi leads back to the 10th-century **Panagía tou Potamoú** (or **Metamórphosis**), Sámos' oldest church, and, if you carry on, to the river canyon. There are superb wild beaches further west – a long but beautiful hike, or a short boat ride, takes you to the lovely pebble crescent of **Mikró Seitáni** (1km beyond the end of Potámi) and sandy **Megálo Seitáni** (4km) at the foot of the striking **Kakopérato ravine**. The stunning track continues for another 8km along the towering west shore (protected as a monk seal habitat) to **Drakáioi**, a time-capsule of old Greece, also reachable by road from Marathókampos and Kallithéa.

South of Karlóvassi, the main road curls around the east flank of the soaring mass of **Mt Kérkis** (1,445m/4,740ft), the second highest peak in the Aegean after Samothráki's Mt Fengári, a dormant volcano often crowned with a halo of cloud and mist. **Kastanéa**, surrounded by chestnuts and laughing brooks, is popular on hot days, but remembered by locals as the place where 27 people were killed by the occupying Italians. Kérkis shelters **Marathokámbos**, a lovely village of streets too narrow for cars spilling over the slopes. A 3km walk up a ravine leads to the **Cave of Pythagoras**, said to have been the hideout of the philosopher before he escaped to Croton. The working port of **Órmos Marathokámbou** is a growing resort, where caiques sail several times a week on barbecue outings to **Samiopoúla**, a tiny islet with a fine stretch of sand.

Votsalákia stretches along a white stony/sandy beach, the longest on Sámos, and a growing resort. A steep marked path leads through the olives to the **Convent of the Evangelistría**, and beyond to the chapel of **Profítis Ilías** and **Vígla**, the summit of Mount Kérkis; fit walkers can storm the peak and return for a swim in five or six hours. Or keep heading west to the safe, shallow seas at **Psilí Ámmos** (not to be confused with the Psilí Ámmos in the east). Continuing on, are sandy coves, accessible only by foot or boat. Or drive on to the delightful quiet coves of **Limniónas** or **Chrysópetro** – dolphins are often spotted frolicking offshore. You could also head 7km east of Órmos to peaceful **Bálos**, a sand-pebble beach and seaside hamlet with a handful of authentic tavernas, under Koumeïka.

Where to Stay and Eat in Western Sámos

Karlóvassi ✉ 83200
Also look for cheap rooms in Limáni, on the pedestrian lane behind the port road.

Marnei Mare, 10mins away on the Márnei peninsula, in the Seitáni Park, t 227 303 8005, www.marneimare.gr (€€€€€). Within walking distance of the best beach on Sámos. Complex of three stunning villas with all mod cons, sleeping 6 or 8, by a pool immersed in olive groves; organic produce available.

Samaina Inn, in Limáni, t 227 303 0400, www.samaina-hotels.gr (€€€). Large, international-style hotel with smart, cool rooms, large pool, sports and crèche. Open May–Oct. The same owners run the more traditional **Samaina Port** (€€) on the harbour.

Merope, in Néo Karlóvassi, t 227 303 2510 (€). Popular for its old-world service and amazingly good value, with period rooms and pool. Open April–Oct.

Dionysos, Plateía 8 Maïou, t 227 303 0120. Sit at a table in the square and feast on free-range chicken dishes, stuffed aubergines, home-made bread and cheese pies.

Hippy's, by the sea, **t** 227 303 3796. Colourful, cool taverna with sunset views and grilled octopus, excellent chips, chicken in honey and mustard and more. *Open April–Oct.*

⭐ **Psarades >**

Psarades, out of town on the road to Ag. Nikoláos, **t** 227 303 2489. The very best seafood restaurant on Sámos, perhaps in the Northeastern Aegean, with lots of dishes impossible to find elsewhere. Lovely sunsets, too.

Márathokámbos/Votsalákia
✉ 83102

Limnionas Bay, Limniónas Beach, **t** 227 303 7057 (€€€). Low-lying, peaceful family-orientated whitewashed studios and apartments with a pool.

⭐ **Mary >**

Mary, 3mins from the beach, **t** 227 303 7006, *www.hotelmary-samosgreece. com* (€€€–€€). Lovely, very welcoming

family-run hotel with 15 studios and a pool immersed in greenery.

Evagelistria Apartments, in the olives on the edge of town, **t** 227 303 7530, *www.evagelistria.gr* (€€). With lovely owners, a peaceful place.

Kerkis Bay, **t** 227 303 7202 (€€). With a good restaurant. *Open April–Oct.*

Albatross, **t** 227 303 7492, *www. albatrossvillage.gr* (€). Simple studios in a garden with sea views and a pool.

Amphilissos, Bálos, **t** 227 303 6335 (€€). Friendly little family-run hotel, although it may be packaged out.

Loúkoulos, **t** 227 303 7147. Seaside apartments (€€) and a charming taverna on three levels in a garden with a wood oven – try the baked pork with lemon and rice. *Open May–Oct.*

Kohili, on the beach, **t** 697 766 4437. Good fish.

Samothráki/Samothrace (ΣΑΜΟΘΡΑΚΗ)

In the far right-hand corner of Greece, Samothráki is one of the least accessible islands; its steep shores are uncluttered by day-trippers, clubbers and beach bunnies – in a way, they would seem frivolous. This is an island of lingering magic, of cliffs, nightingales, plane forests and waterfalls sweeping around the Mountain of the Moon (Mount Fengári, 1,664m/5,459ft), the highest in the Aegean; Poseidon sat on its summit to observe the tides of the Trojan War. Often wind-whipped and lacking a natural harbour, Samothráki was nevertheless one of the most visited islands of antiquity, the Délos of the North Aegean with its sanctuary of the Cabeiri, the Great Gods of the Underworld.

History

Once densely populated, Samothráki owes its importance to its position near the Dardanelles – the strait named after the legendary Samothracian Dardanos, founder of Troy; its oldest shrine (the rock altar beneath the Arsinoëion) goes back, according to Herodotus, to the Pelasgians. In the 8th century BC Aeolians from Mytilíni colonized Samothráki and mingled peaceably with the earlier settlers, worshipping the Cabeiri, the Underworld Gods of the Thracians, whose yet-undeciphered language survived in religious rituals into the 1st century. By the mid-5th century BC, Samothráki's sanctuary was the religious centre of the North Aegean, attracting a steady stream of initiates. Their fascination lingered long after the shrine closed: the Cabeiri make an appearance in Goethe's *Faust*, and

Getting to and around Samothráki

There are 3 **flights** daily from Athens to Alexandroúpolis Airport, **t** 255 104 5259.
There is a 2hr daily **ferry** crossing from Alexandroúpolis, occasionally twice a day in summer, and at least twice a week from Kavála; also frequent links to Límnos and occasionally to Lávrio. From Feb–Nov, daily **hydrofoils** sail from Alexandroúpolis to Samothráki; also frequently from Kavála. See *www.greekislands.gr/saos-ferries/departures.htm*. **Port authority**: **t** 255 104 1305.
Caiques from Kamariótissa make day excursions south to Pachía Ámmos and Kremastó Neró.
Six **buses** a day run from Kamariótissa to Chóra, and 3 to Alónia, Palaeópolis, Loutrá and Pachía Ámmos.
In season, **hire cars** are in short supply. In Kamariótissa, try **Pavlos**, **t** 255 104 1035 (cars, scooters, bikes), or **X Car Rentals Holowai**, **t** 255 104 2272. There is only one **petrol station** on the island (on the road to Chóra) and 20,000 goats, not one of whom has the least road sense.

the excavations of their sanctuary were funded by the Bollingen Foundation, set up in honour of the psychoanalysist C. G. Jung.

Hellenistic and Roman rulers not only became initiates, but used Samothráki as a naval base, relying on its sacred soil for protection. St Paul stopped by in 49 AD, but failed to convert the locals, who kept their sanctuary running until the 390s, when Theodosius the Great ordered the closing of temples. Samothráki was forgotten. Pirates forced the remaining inhabitants to the hills, where they settled Chóra. The Genoese Gattilusi fortified the castle, and when it fell to the Turks the Samothracians were sent to resettle Constantinople. The island then vanished from history until the 1820s, when it rose during the War of Independence, but, like the other islands in the northeast, had to wait until the Balkan War to join Greece.

Kamariótissa and Chóra

Samothráki's workaday port, **Kamariótissa**, is a simple place with an exposed rocky beach, an aeolian park by a small lagoon, and most of the island's tourist facilities. High above, **Chóra**, where most of the island's 2,800 souls live, occupies a picturesque amphitheatre below a ruined Byzantine castle. Chóra has whitewashed houses with red-tiled roofs, a charming century-old bakery, five mummified heads (of martyrs killed by the Turks for reconverting, up in the church) and a little **Folklore Museum**. At the entrance to Chóra stands a modern statue of Nike (Victory), not quite as grand as the one it lost to the Louvre but a dead ringer for gymnast Nadia Comaneci.

Folklore Museum
open summer 11–2 and 7–10

Pretty agricultural hamlets dot the slopes of southern Samothráki: **Alónia**, the largest, has ruins of a Roman bath, while **Profítis Ilías** is famous for tavernas serving semi-wild kid, the island's speciality. From delightful **Lákoma**, a very windy 8km road leads to the turn-off for the church of **Panagía Kremniótissa**, tottering on rocks and taking in huge views as far as the Turkish island of Imbros. Below lies the island's one sandy beach, **Pachía Ámmos**, with a taverna. A boat excursion is the only way to visit the spectacularly rugged southern coast east of Pachía Ámmos, where the waterfall **Krémasto Neró** ('hanging water') spills into the sea near a much smaller beach.

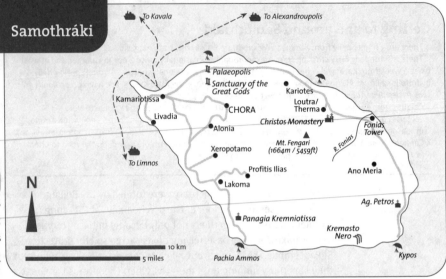

The Sanctuary of the Great Gods

Sanctuary of the Great Gods
t 255 104 1474; site and museum open Tues–Sun 8.30–3; adm

The Great Gods were chthonic or Underworld deities, older and more potent than the Olympian upstarts of the patriarchal state religion, at whom even first poet Homer could poke fun. But no one dared to mess about with the Great Gods; no writer revealed the mysteries, although they (like the more famous Eleusis mysteries) may have offered promises for the afterlife. Although dedications found at the sanctuary were simply 'to the gods', their secret names were revealed by a Hellenistic writer: Mnaseas, Axieros, Axiokersos, Axiokersa and Kadmilos, whom the Greeks identified with Demeter, Hades, Persephone, Kore and Hermes.

The mysteries took place by torchlight. Anyone, male or female, free or slave, could undergo the two levels of initiation, the *myesis* and the more important *epopteia*. The *epopteia* began with a confession that may have been unique in the Greek world (the priest would ask the candidate 'which was the most lawless deed committed in his life'), followed by baptism, the winding of a purple sash below the abdomen, followed by the sacrifice of a ram. Initiation at Samothráki was thought to be sovereign against drowning; in myth, the Argonauts, at Orpheus' suggestion, were initiated before entering the Hellespont. Another peculiarity of the cult, mentioned by Roman authors, involved magnetized iron rings, perhaps symbols of attraction given to initiates: several were found on site. King Lysander of Sparta and Herodotus were initiates, but it was in the Hellenistic era that the sanctuary knew its greatest fortune; Philip II of Macedonia fell in love with Olympias of Epirus, mother of Alexander the Great, during a ceremony. He was also keen to promote the only pan-Hellenic shrine in his orbit to the same level as Delphi, to demonstrate his 'Greekness' to the Athenians.

Excavations of the site were begun in 1948 by Americans Dr Karl and Phyllis Williams Lehmann. The Louvre, of course, bagged the prize, the **Victory of Samothrace**, found in 1863 by Champoiseau, the French consul at Adrianople; the **museum** at the entrance has a plaster copy sent from Paris, along withsome good vases (especially an Attic *pelike* of 490 BC with a dancing goat by the Eucharides painter), the Archaic-style frieze of temple dancers donated by Philip II to decorate the entrance to the Temenos, *steles* warning off the uninitiated and, amongst the funerary offerings, a perfect terracotta football.

The sanctuary itself, set in trees overlooking the sea, enjoys an idyllic setting, while goat bells tinkle on the mountain above. Most of the buildings are in porous stone – the first large one you come across, the rectangular **Anaktoron** (House of the Lords), dates from the 6th century BC and was rebuilt twice, lastly by the Romans; first-level initiations were held here, but only the initiated, or *mystai*, were allowed in its inner Holy of Holies on the north side. A pile of carbon discovered in the Anaktoron suggests it had a wooden stage; a torch base is a relic of the night-time rites. Ancient writers referred to the Anaktoron's two bronze statues of Hermes in a state of excitement, but Lehmann found no trace of them. Adjacent, by the Sacred Rock, is the **Arsinoëion**, at 20m (66ft) in diameter the largest circular structure ever built by the ancient Greeks. It was dedicated in 281 BC by Queen Arsinoë II, wife and sister of Ptolemy Philadelphos, after the gods had answered her prayers for a child. It had one door and no windows; scholars are stumped as to what happened in here.

The rectangular foundation south of the Arsinoëion belonged to the **Temenos**, where ceremonies took place. Adjacent stand the five Doric columns of the **Hieron**, or 'New Temple', where the upper level of initiation or *epopteia* was held; it dates from 300 BC and was last restored after an earthquake in the 3rd century AD. By the side entrance, towards the eastern wall, Lehmann found two 'stepping stones' where he guessed the initiates' confessions were heard. The Romans added viewing benches. There was a hearth altar in the centre and a drain by the door, perhaps for the blood of sacrifices.

Only the outline remains of the theatre on the hill; here also is the **Nike Fountain**, where the magnificent *Victory* was found, dedicated by the Macedonian Dimitrios Poliorketes (the 'Besieger') in 305 BC, in thanksgiving for his naval victory over Ptolemy II at Cyprus; she originally stood as the figurehead of a great marble ship. Ptolemy II himself donated the monumental gateway to the sanctuary, the **Propylae Ptolemaion**. Nearby is a *tholos* of uncertain use and a Doric building, dedicated by the Hellenistic rulers of Macedon. Up the road stood **Palaeópolis**, the unexcavated city that served the sanctuary. The island's medieval Genoese bosses, the Gattilusi, used its stone to build their walls and watchtower. Now covered with a handsome

Palaeópolis
open daily 8.30–8.30

grove of plane trees, a path leads to the foundations of an early church, perhaps founded in honour of St Paul's visit.

Thérma, Mount Fengári and up the Fonias Ravine

After Palaeópolis, the road continues east to a little marina and the delightful little rustic spa, **Thérma** (or **Loutrá**). Like much of this idyllic corner of Samothráki, Thérma is immersed in chestnut and plane trees; with lots of places to stay and eat among the rushing streams where you can soak in mildly radioactive warm water, good for arthritis and gynaecological disorders (*doctor on duty daily 8–10am*). Follow the signs to the path to **Gría Vathrá** – a short walk through a canopy of ancient trees to a natural pool and little waterfall that flows even in the scorching days of summer.

From Thérma, a path leads up in four hours to the top of **Mount Fengári**, where you can enjoy the same view as Poseidon, a stunning panorama of the North Aegean from the Troad in the east to Mount Áthos in the west. Because of its altitude, Mount Fengári hosts a number of rare endemic plants: *Alyssum degenianum, Symphandra samothracica, Herniara degenii* and *Potentilla geoides*. The mountain's ancient name, Sáos, recalls the Saoi, 'the rescued ones', a secret society of men sworn into the mysteries of the Great Gods.

The coastal road from Thérma continues east to the medieval **Foniás** 'Killer' **Tower**, built by the Genoese, with a nice place to swim. The tower sits in the little delta of the Foniás river, signposted by a car park. Here too the river, filled with eels and crabs, flows all year round; there's a beautiful 30-minute path up its ravine to a magical waterfall, where nymphs wouldn't look out of place. After this oasis, the road braves the increasingly arid coast and ends at the long, shadeless and daunting black pebble beach at **Kýpos**, closed on one side by merciless cliffs of lava falling into the sea.

Useful Information on Samothráki

Try *www.samothraki.com*.

Samothráki Festivals

20 July: Profitis Ilías at Kormbéti.
July: Samothraki Festival, *www.samothrakifestival.com*. Alternative trance and ethnic music festival – every year it's up in the air, though. In 2006 it ended up on the mainland.

Activities on Samothráki

Samothraki Diving Center: Ágistros, *www.scubagr.com*.

Where to Stay on Samothráki

Kamariótissa ✉ 68002
Room-owners often meet the ferries, or if you're still stuck, try **Niki Tours**, t 255 104 1465.

Aeolos, 300m east of town, t 255 104 1795, *aiolos84@otenet.gr* (€€€). Family-run hotel with a modest pool; all rooms have balconies, some with sea views. *Open April–Oct*.

Limanaki, at the far end of town, t 255 104 1987 (€€). Quiet rooms and delicious seafood, with Limnian wine from the barrel.

Niki Beach, t 255 104 1545 (€€). Pleasant, peaceful hotel with giant poplars in the front garden; simple but comfortable rooms.

Klimatariá, on the waterfront, t 255 104 1535. For traditional Greek fare.

I Synatisi, by Niki Tours. Simple fresh grilled fish and *mezédes*.

 Exochio Kentro Sotiros >

Mariva >>

Chóra ✉ 68002

Exochio Kentro Sotiros, t 225 104 1500, on the edge of the village. Popular and picturesque place under the plane trees; serves the island speciality – roast wild kid. *Only open in season.*

Kastro, Plateía Rigopoúlou, t 225 104 1932. Pretty views of sea and castle from the terrace. *Open all year.*

Lákoma/Profítis Ilías ✉ 68002

To Akrogiáli, t 255 109 5122 (€€–€). Excellent fish taverna with romantic sunsets. The owner, Giorgio, also has 5 spotless new rooms for rent. *Open May–Oct.*

Paradeisos, Profítis Ilías, t 255 109 5267. One of several good taverna grills here, all popular for local specialities, including kid on the skewer. *Open all year.*

Thérma ✉ 68002

Kastro, by Palaeópolis, t 255 108 9400, *www.kastrohotel.gr* (€€€€€). The smartest hotel, with a pool, sea sports, and a restaurant. *Open Easter–Oct.*

Archondissa, t 255 109 8098, (€€€–€€). Spanking new studios and suites (some sleeping four), done up with traditional touches.

Mariva, t 255 109 8230, *www.mariva.gr* (€€). Bungalows covered with ivy in the midst of the plane tree forest; friendly and quiet. *Open 15 May–15 Oct.*

Orpheus, t 255 109 8233 (€€). Little hotel surrounded by trees.

Parselia Rooms, t 255 109 8318, *www.parselia.gr* (€€–€). Bucolic and shady.

Varados Camping, t 255 109 8291. Nice and shady, close to the waterfall.

Griá Váthra, t 255 104 1218. Classic food in a shady grove. *Closed Nov–April.*

Karydiés, on the coast beyond Thérma at Áno Meriá. Seasonal taverna, but a good one – the owner prepares authentic Greek dishes in a wok.

Thássos (ΘΑΣΟΣ)

The northernmost Greek island, Thássos is also one of the fairest, ringed with soft sandy beaches and mantled with pines, plane trees, walnuts and chestnuts. Unlike the other Aegean islands, it is rarely afflicted by the huffing and puffing of the *meltémi*, but has a moist climate, much subject to lingering mists; on hot days the intense scent of pines by the sea casts a spell of dreamy languor. For years a secret holiday nook of northern Greeks, its character changed with the opening of Kavála airport to charter flights, bringing in tour operators from Britain and Germany. For Central and Eastern European tourists, it's an easy drive. And yet the island hasn't completely lost its Greekness or innate friendliness; nearly everyone who comes has a jolly good time – and the fact that you have to take a ferry to get there seems to keep away the worst of the riff-raff.

Thássos is popular with campers, but it's vulnerable to forest fires, which in the last two decades have sadly ravaged the forests on the west half of the island. Wherever you sleep, come armed: the

Thássos Festivals

Three days after Easter: Ag. Geórgios fair, in Limenária and Kalývia.

End of July–early Aug: Traditional weddings performed in Theológos.

10 July–15 Aug: Thássos festival, Liménas.

1 Aug: Fire-leaping, Kalývia and Prínos.

15 Aug: Panagía.

mosquitoes are vivacious, vicious and voracious. Sea urchins can be a problem too, but a sign that the sea here is very, very clean.

History

Neolithic Thássos had links to Límnos. By the 9th century BC, it was occupied by a Thracian-Macedonian tribe, who in *c.* 710 BC were invaded and colonized by Páros. The likeable Parian poet Archilochos was among the invaders, but found himself (or at least the persona he adopted) outmanoeuvred in battle: 'Some Thracian now is pleased with my shield/which I unwilling left on a bush in perfect condition on our side of the field/but I escaped death. To hell with the shield!/ I shall get another, no worse.' The Parians went to great lengths to justify their presence on Thássos, with a legend about Phoenician allies who had set up an earlier colony and had summoned Páros for aid; then of course there was a Delphic Oracle that ordered them to found a city 'on the island of mists'. It was certainly worth the fuss: the Parian-Thassians annually extracted 90 talents of gold and silver from the mines on the island and nearby mainland; its marble, timber, ships, fine oil and wine were in demand across the Aegean. Densely populated, the town was dubbed the 'Athens of the north'. In 490 BC, the Persians attacked the island and razed the city walls.

An island crowned with forests and lying in the sea like the backbone of an ass.
Archilochos, 7th century BC

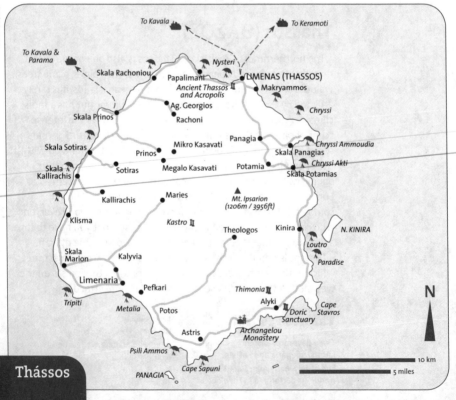

Thássos

Getting to and around Thássos

Kavála **airport**, 15 minutes from Keramotí on that mainland, receives charter flights and twice-daily flights from Athens with Olympic Airways and Aegean. **Olympic** info in Kavála, **t** 259 022 3622. **Aegean**, at the airport, **t** 259 105 3333. If you're coming from the UK, it's usually cheaper to fly into Thessaloníki and take the bus to Kavála or Keramotí. There is a **ferry** from Keramotí to Liménas (Thássos town) almost every hour; twice a day from Kavála to Skála Prínou. **Hydrofoils** also run from Kavála to Liménas (4 a day, 2 on Sun). **Port authority**: Liménas, **t** 259 302 2106; Skála Prínou, **t** 259 307 1290.

The **bus** service, **t** 259 302 2162, is regular; from Liménas quayside there are at least 10 services daily to Skála Prínou, Skála Potamiá and Limenária, and 6 to Theológos and around the island.

In season book a car in advance – or a jeep if you tend to do some serious exploring on the mountain roads. **Car hire** is available from **4u**, Liménas, **t** 259 302 3717, *http://thassos4u.gr/rent.htm*; **National Friend**, Limenária, **t** 259 305 2877; **Thassos Travel**, **t** 259 302 2676, *www.thassos-travel.com*. For motorbikes, try **Billy's Bikes**, **t** 259 302 2490, in Liménas.

When they reappeared a decade later under Xerxes, the defenceless Thassians prevented another attack by holding a fabulous banquet for the Persians, and with many slaps on the back sent them off to defeat at Salamis. Thássos revolted against the Delian League, when an increasingly imperialist Athens demanded huge chunks of its profits, and in 463 BC Athens sent Kimon to teach it a lesson, and after a three-year siege Thássos was ruled by Athens. In 340 BC Philip of Macedon seized it. In 197 BC the Romans defeated the Macedonians and Thássos gladly became part of Rome, enjoying special privileges and a new period of prosperity.

Among the uninvited guests in later years, the Genoese stayed the longest, from the 1300s until the Turks chased them out in 1460. Russia took over from 1770–74. In 1813 the Sultan gave the island to Mohammed Ali, Governor of Egypt, who had been brought up in the village of Theológos and loved Thássos; he lowered taxes and gave the island virtual autonomy. Egyptian rule lasted until 1902, when the Turks returned briefly before union with Greece during the Balkan Wars, in 1912. The Bulgarians occupied the island from 1941 to the end of the war, and are now welcomed as holidaymakers.

Liménas (Thássos Town)

The bustling unabashedly tourist-orientated capital of the island is officially Thássos town, but is better known as Liménas. It may not be pretty – especially the new port area – but it's lively; plane trees shade the squares, shops will sell you walnut sweets and honey, and the town beach, once relatively poor on this island of sandy beaches, has been improved with tons of sand. Still, the town's inhabitants (many of whom came over from Turkey in 1922), can hardly begin to fill the shoes of the once great and wealthy city of **ancient Thassos**, which was abandoned from the Middle Ages till the mid-19th century. Bits of it crop up everywhere. The **Archaeology Museum** has been expanded after recent excavations. The contents are rich: there's a 7th-century BC plate (*pinakion*) depicting Bellerophon on Pegasus, slaying the three-headed Chimera; a dedicatory inscription

Archaeology Museum
18 Megálou Alexándrou, t 259 302 2180; partially open at time of writing; open Tues–Sun 8.30–3

to Glaukos, a friend of Archilochus, mentioned in several poems; a 6th-century BC *Kriophoros* (a young man bearing a lamb) over 3m (11ft) high, but left unfinished when the sculptor discovered a flaw in the marble by the ear; an Archaic relief (550 BC) of a hunting scene, and a beautiful ivory lion's head from the same period; a lovely, effeminate head of Diónysos from the 4th century BC; a relief of two griffons devouring a doe (2nd century AD); little turtle votive offerings; a Hellenistic Aphrodite riding a dolphin; a fine bust of Hadrian and another of Alexander. Thássos was famous for its wine: there's a tablet from *c.* 420 BC with wine regulations written in *boustro-phedon*, 'as the ox plows', and an amphora bearing the island seal.

Mount Ipsárion (1,206m/3,956ft), a solid block of white and greenish marble, provided the raw material for the ancient city. In the centre of modern Liménas, the **Agora**, much rebuilt under the Romans, is the most prominent survival, with foundations and columns of porticoes and *stoas*, sanctuaries and a massive altar. A *heröon* in the centre of the market honoured the astonishing mid-5th-century BC athlete Theogenes, who won 1,400 victor's laurels. A mysterious paved 'Passage of Theoria', predating the rest of the *agora* by 500 years, leads back to the sparse remains of Artemision, where precious votives were found, and where the island's first metallurgical activity took place *c.* 600 BC. On the other side of the *agora* is part of a Roman street, a well-preserved *exedra*, a few tiers of the Odeon and, further down, the **Herakleion**, a sanctuary founded *c.* 620 BC – Hercules was the island's patron, in a cult that the Parians claimed was established by the Phoenicians.

East of the *agora*, towards the ancient naval port, another group of ruins includes a **Sanctuary of Poseidon**; next to it, another altar remains in good enough condition to accept sacrifices to its divinity, Hera Epilimenia, guardian of ports. Remains of the naval gates survive here: the **Chariot Gate** (with an Archaic Artemis in a chariot) and the **Gate of Semel-Thyone** (with Hermes and the Graces). From here, a path leads past the ancient moles of the harbour to the ruins of a medieval fort and the beginning of the city's polygonal walls, which were last rebuilt in *c.* 411 and repaired by the Genoese.

Unless you're really keen, there's a shortcut to the acropolis from town by way of the **Sanctuary of Diónysos** (south of the Sanctuary of Poseidon), and its 3rd-century BC choreographic monument, erected by the winner of a drama prize. From here a path rises to the 5th-century BC Greek **Theatre** on the lower slopes of the acropolis, affording a majestic view. Now that the excavations are completed, there are plans to renew Thássos' ancient drama festival. From the theatre a path continues up to the **Acropolis**, spread across three summits of a ridge. On the first stands a **Genoese fortress** built out of the Temple of Pythian Apollo, whose Delphic Oracle had sent the first Parian colonists to Thássos. The museum's *Kriophoros* was discovered embedded in its walls, and a fine relief of a funerary feast (4th century BC) can still be seen near the guardroom. The second hill had a 5th-century BC **Temple of Athena Poliouchos**, built over a much older sanctuary, although the Genoese treated her no better than Apollo, leaving only the foundations. The third and highest summit of the acropolis was a **Sanctuary of Pan**, and has an eroded Hellenistic relief of Pan piping to his goats. Again, the view is more compelling than the old stones; on a clear day you can see from Mount Áthos to Samothráki, while inland the most prominent sight is the marble mountain Ipsárion, eaten away by quarrying.

There's a curious *exedra* resembling a stone sofa below the sanctuary, and around the back the vertiginous **Secret Stair**, carved into the rock in the 6th century BC, descends to the remaining walls and gates (take care if you attempt it). Here you'll find the watchful stone eyes of the **Apotropaion** (to protect the walls from the Evil Eye), the **Gate of Parmenon**, still bearing its inscription 'Parmenon made me' and, best of all, the large **Gate of Silenus** (by the inter-section of the road to Panagía) where the vigorous bas-relief of the phallic god (6th century BC) has lost its once prominent appendage to a 'moral cleansing' in the 20th century. Continuing back towards town are, respectively, the **Gate of Diónysos and Hercules**, and the **Gate of Zeus and Hera** with an Archaic relief; this last one is just beyond the Venus Hotel if you gave the Secret Stair a miss.

The sandy **town beach** is small and shaded, but also tends to be crowded, as does lovely **Makryámmos**, 3km to the east. Just west, buses or boats wait to take you to **Nystéri** (a nice one with trees) or **Papalimáni** beaches, the latter with windsurfing.

Useful Information on Thássos

Tourist police: on the waterfront, **t** 259 302 3111. See *www.go-thassos.gr*.

Where to Stay in Liménas

Liménas/Thássos ✉ 64004

Makryámmos Bungalows, on the beach of the same name, **t** 259 302 2101, *www.makryammos-hotel.gr* (€€€€). The poshest place to stay, with water sports, tennis, pool, a small deer park and a nightclub, and a good restaurant, **Sirens**. *Open May–Oct.*

Kipos Apartments, **t** 259 302 2469, *www.kipos-apartments.gr* (€€€). Tidy place with a pool; the apartments sleep up to four.

Dionysos, centre, **t** 259 302 2198, *www.shop-ellas.com/members/a00011* (€€€). 100m from the beach. *Open all year.*

Akti Vournelis, on the beach on the Prínos road, **t** 259 302 2901 (€€€–€€). A good choice, and the bar nearby has live Greek music in the evenings.

Pegasus, **t** 259 302 2061, *www.thassos-pegasus.com* (€€€–€€). Pleasant hotel with a garden and pool, within walking distance of everything.

Tarsanas, 1.8km from the centre, **t** 259 302 3933, *www. tarsanas.gr* (€€€–€€). Studios and bungalows, directly on the beach and a seafood restaurant and beach bar. Popular with young couples.

Laios, Octovríou St, between the new port and town, **t** 259 302 2309 (€€). Spick and span rooms and a pool, quiet but in walking distance of the action.

Alkyon, by the harbour, **t** 259 302 2148 (€). A welcoming, airy place.

Eating Out in Liménas

Moyses, t 259 302 3697, out towards the new port, near the Xenia hotel. Some of the most reliably good food –

tasty mussels *saganáki* and other fish and casserole dishes.

Symi, t 259 302 2517. Home-grown vegetables and good fish. *Open all year.*

Pigi. Traditional Greek specialities.

Around the Island: Beaches and More Beaches

⭐ Thássos beaches

A road circles Thássos; in July and August expect it to be busy. Directly south of Liménas, the road ascends to charming **Panagía**. Its old whitewashed Macedonian houses, decorated with carved wood and slate roofs, overlook the sea, with their high-walled gardens watered by a network of mountain streams, some flowing directly under their ground floor; the church of **Panagías** has an underground spring. If you drink from the fountain, they say, you'll return some day to Thássos. Down by the sea is the lovely town beach **Chryssí Ammoudiá**, 'Golden Sands'.

Folk Art Museum
open Wed–Mon

Polýgnotos Vagis Museum
t 259 306 1400; open Tues–Sat 9–1, Sun 10–2

To the south of Panagía is another large, well-watered mountain village, **Potamiá**, which has two museums: a small **Folk Art Museum** and the **Polýgnotos Vagis Museum**, dedicated to the locally born sculptor (d. 1965), who made it big in New York. A marked path from Potamiá leads to the summit of **Mount Ipsárion**, taking about 7hrs there and back, while below stretches massive **Chryssí Aktí** ('Golden Beach') and **Skála Potamiás**, a friendly, laid-back resort lined with tavernas and rooms and a beach that some consider the best on the island. Quiet **Kínira** has a small shingly beach closed off by an islet of the same name; only a kilometre south are the white sands and shallow waters and taverna of **Paradise Beach**, folded in the pine-clad hills. The road is a gear-grinder, however; park halfway down and walk the rest of the way.

The little slate-roofed hamlet of **Alykí** is beautifully set on a tiny headland overlooking twin beaches – the northern one is very wild, the southern one a sheer delight. It was an ancient town that thrived on marble exports, and ruins are strewn about its sandy shore, including an Archaic Doric double sanctuary – as an archaeological area it has been spared development beyond three tavernas; there's a car park at the top. Another ancient settlement was at **Thimoniá** nearby, where part of a Hellenistic tower still stands. Further along, the **Archángelou Monastery** with its handsome slate roof is perched high over the sea on arid chromatic cliffs. Its nuns are in charge of a sliver of the True Cross, and the pretty courtyard and church are open to visitors (*proper attire, even long sleeves, required*); paradoxically, the pebble beach nestling in the cliffs below is frequented by naturists. The lovely but steep beach of **Astrís**, above pretty **Cape Sapúni**, is still defended by its medieval towers, and is one of a score of places that claim to have been the home of the *Odyssey*'s Sirens. If they were still there, their magic songs would be drowned out by the jet-skiiers.

Continuing clockwise round the island, much of Thássos' resort hotel development (and worst forest fires in 1985) has happened above the excellent sandy beaches around **Potós**, golden **Pefkári** and lovely white **Psilí Ámmos**, with plenty of olive groves in between. Potós is a good place for an evening drink over the sunset, and for exploring inland; a handful of buses each day make the 10km trip up to the handsome slate-roofed village of **Theológos**, one of Thássos' greenest spots and the capital of the island until the 19th century, defended by a ruined Genoese castle, the **Kourókastro**. The church of **Ag. Dimítrios** has 12th-century icons, and there's a Folklore Museum with traditional furnishings and items from the days when owning a mule was the status equivalent of a Mercedes.

Folklore Museum
open summer 11–2 and 7–11

Limenária, the second largest town on Thássos, draws a fair crowd of tourists. It has a bit more of a village atmosphere, surrounded by trees and with a huge stretch of shady beach. In 1903 the German Spiedel Company mined the ores in the vicinity – its plant can still be seen south of the town, while the company's offices, locally called the **Palatáki**, 'Little Palace', stand alone in a garden on the headland; just east of town, near the old smelting works, is lovely sheltered **Metalía Beach** with fine sands, a taverna and arty labyrinth in stone.

From Limenária, excursion boats tour the coast of Mount Áthos – the closest women can get – or you can hire a boat for a swim off **Panagía** islet. **Kalývia** just inland has reliefs embedded in the wall of its church, while 15km further up the road there's **Kástro** high on a sheer precipice, the refuge of the Limenarians in the days of piracy. Although abandoned in the 19th century, in the last decade most of its old houses have been restored as holiday homes; there's a taverna in the summer.

The flatter west coast of Thássos is farm country, lined with beaches that are generally less crowded – although they look good from a distance, they tend to be stonier. **Tripití Beach** is fine and sandy with a natural bathtub, near the somewhat ramshackle little port of **Skála Marión**, while **Mariés** proper, 10km inland, is perhaps the least changed of the island's traditional villages. Just along the road, a sign points the way to the remains of an Archaic-era pottery workshop. **Kallyráchis** and **Skála Sotíras** have rocky beaches, while **Skála Prínou**, the dumpy ferry port to Kavála with its workaday shipyards, nevertheless has some beaches in its environs, with fancy new hotels.

Inland from here is **Prínos**, beyond which lie the two smaller villages of **Megálo Kasavíti** and **Mikró Kasavíti**, in a lovely setting, with beehives and charming old houses, many of which have been renovated. Rachóni is a quiet inland village, while **Skála Rachoníou** is a peaceful low-key resort with an English-owned riding stable, the Pine Tree Paddock. An islet off the north coast, **Thassopoúla**, is pretty and wooded but, according to the locals, full of snakes.

Pine Tree Paddock
t 694 511 8961

Where to Stay and Eat around Thássos Island

Panagía ✉ 64004

(★) Emerald >

Emerald, 200m fr. Chryssí Ámmoudiá, t 259 306 1979, www.emerald-hotel. com (€€€). Charming hotel with studios sleeping up to four, immersed in olive groves, with a pool and views.

Chrisssafis, t 259 306 1451, www. emerald-hotel.com/hotel-chrissafis (€€). Simple hotel covered in greenery on the edge of town.

Thássos Inn, t 259 306 1612 (€€). A charming place to relax in town.

There are several tavernas, all much the same.

Skála Potamiás ✉ 64001

Korina, 300m from the beach, t 259 306 1200, http://hotel-korina-thassos. focusgreece.gr (€€€). Modern hotel, family-orientated, with a pool.

Mouragio, 3mins from the beach, t 259 306 2022, www.mouragio.gr (€€). Moderate-sized, peaceful place.

Blue Sea, t 259 306 1482, http:// thassos4u.gr (€€). Very pleasant 12-room hotel at the end of the beach, with Thracian-style balconies.

Pension Alex Dim, t 259 306 1458, www.alex-dim.gr (€€). Like a motel, with a pretty garden, close to the beach; book online for a discount.

Camping Chryssí Ammoudiá, t 259 306 1472. By the sands at Skála Panagías.

Fedra, Chryssí Aktí. Lovely fresh fish and lots of other things besides.

Krabousa, t 259 306 2190. Wide assortment of titbits and seafood.

Kínira ✉ 64001

Sylvia, by the sea, t 259 304 1246 (€€€). Quiet, with a pool and playground.

Potós ✉ 64002

Alexandra Beach, t 259 305 2391, www.alexandrabeach.gr (€€€€–€€€). Handsome hotel with every imaginable watersport, tennis and a pool. Open May–Oct.

(★) Andreas >>

Kamari Beach, t 259 305 1147, www. hotelkamari.gr (€€€€–€€€). Plush place with a three-level pool.

Coral Beach, right on the sea on the south end of Potós, t 259 305 2402,

(€€€). Cheaper, but still has mod cons, pool and a garden.

Thássos, in nearby Pefkári, t 259 305 1596, www.shop-ellas.com/members/ a00022 (€€€). Pool and tennis, and a traditional clay oven in the restaurant.

Lysistrata, t 259 305 1678, www. lysistrata.gr (€€€). Bungalows and a bar in a garden setting by the beach.

Camping Paradisos, t 259 305 1906 (€).

Pefkári ✉ 64002

Camping Pefkári, Pefkári, t 259 305 1595 (€).

Limenária ✉ 64002

Grand Beach, t 259 305 3470, www. grand-beach-hotel.gr (€€€). New, big, rose-tinted studios and apartments overlooking the beach.

Thalassies, on the beach, t 259 305 1163 (€€€). Small beach hotel offering one of the island's warmest welcomes, and a good restaurant.

Garden, t 259 305 2650 (€). Recently renovated studios. Open all year.

Dionysos, in the pedestrian zone, t 259 307 2083. One of the oldest tavernas on the island, famous for its delicious fish soup.

Skála Prínou/Skála Rachoníou ✉ 64004

Ilio Mare, Skála Prínou, t 259 307 2083, www.iliomare.gr (€€€€€). Big designer hotel on the beach with lots of facilities, plus family rooms and suites.

Coral, Skála Rachoníou, t 259 308 1247, www.hotel-coral.gr (€€). Well-scrubbed place with a pool amid the olive trees.

Socrates, Skála Prínou, t 259 307 1770 (€€). Very friendly and popular place to stay

Xanthi, on the edge of town, 50m from the beach, t 259 307 1303 (€). Good guesthouse. Open June–Sept.

Camping Prinos, at Skála Prínou, t 259 307 1171, www.campingthassos.gr. Lots of shade.

Camping Perseus, Skála Rachoníou, t 259 308 1242.

Andreas, up in Megálo Kazavíti, t 259 307 1760. Under the plane tree in the square, serving stuffed courgette flowers, imam bayildi aubergines, beans flavoured with mint and other favourites. Open April–Oct.

The Sporades and Évia

Until the late 1960s, the Sporades ('scattered') islands were among the least visited in Greece, avoided by all but the boldest fishermen, who call them the 'Gates of the Wind' – not only were they difficult to reach, but they lacked the big-league archaeological sites and historical familiarity of so many other islands.
Then Greek holidaymakers discovered Skiáthos and Skópelos, with their pretty beaches and forests, and an airport was built on Skiáthos – and the rest is history.

14

① 'Dragon houses' and a gorge
Near Kárystos, Évia, and Dimosáris Gorge
pp.639–40

② A ring of stunning beaches
Skiáthos **p.619**

③ A love affair with plates
Skýros **p.631**

④ Picture-perfect beauty
Skópelos Town **p.624**

⑤ Long walks and monk seals
Alónissos **p.610**

See map overleaf

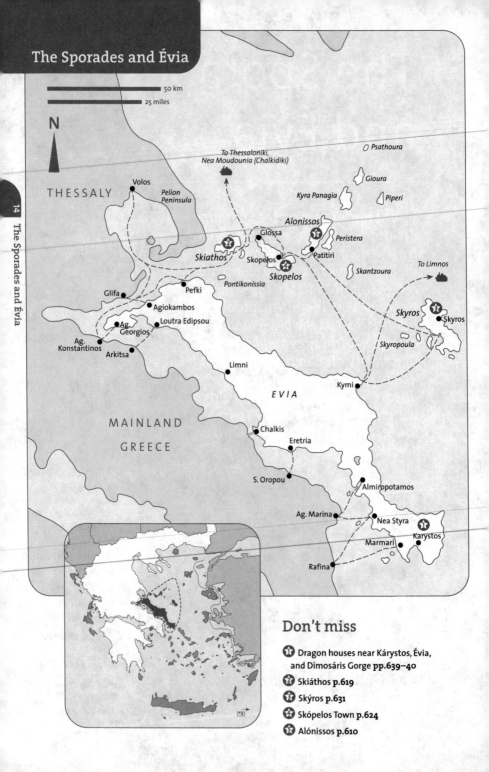

The Sporades and Évia

50 km

25 miles

N

To Thessaloniki,
Nea Moudounia (Chalkidiki)

Psathoura

THESSALY

Volos

Pelion
Peninsula

Gioura

Kyra Panagia

Piperi

Alonissos

Glossa

Peristera

Skiathos

Skopelos

Patitiri

Skopelos

Skopelos

Skantzoura

To Limnos

Skyros

Skyros

Pontikonissia

Pefki

Glifa

Agiokambos

Skyropoula

Ag.
Georgios

Loutra Edipsou

Ag.
Konstantinos

Arkitsa

Limni

E V I A

Kymi

MAINLAND

GREECE

Chalkis

Eretria

S. Oropou

Almiropotamos

Ag. Marina

Nea Styra

Karystos

Marmari

Rafina

Don't miss

⭐ Dragon houses near Kárystos, Évia,
and Dimosáris Gorge **pp.639–40**

⭐ Skiáthos **p.619**

⭐ Skýros **p.631**

⭐ Skópelos Town **p.624**

⭐ Alónissos **p.610**

Getting to the Sporades

Flying to Skiáthos (with scores of charters, or domestic flights from Athens and Thessaloníki) or to Skýros (4 times a week from Athens and Thessaloníki) is by far the most painless way. You can also fly to Vólos on the mainland (charters from the UK) and proceed by boat (*see* below).

By sea Skýros can only be reached from or via Kými, on Évia, from where there are also weekly sailings (at least) to the other Sporades. Mainland **ferry/hydrofoil** ports for Skiáthos, Skópelos and Alónissos are Ag. Konstantínos (closest to Athens with frequent buses, **port authority t** 223 503 1759) and Vólos in Thessaly (easily reached by train or bus), and there are other links from the little ports of the nearby Pélion peninsula and northern Évia. If you're departing from Athens, it's best to buy a **bus/ferry** ticket from **Alkyon Tours**, at 97 Akademías, **t** 210 384 3220, which specializes in travel to the Sporades, and has the latest timetables. If you're coming from the north, in high season, there are hydrofoils and ferries from Thessaloníki and from Néa Moudaniá (Chalkidikí).

Each of the Sporades has a distinct personality, although **Skiáthos**, with the loveliest beaches of all and some of the most sizzling nightlife in the Aegean, has become so popular that 'Greek' is not an adjective you would use to describe it. On the opposite end of the scale, **Skýros** remains one of the most original and intriguing islands in Greece, still off the beaten track in spite of having an airport of its own. Increasingly trendy **Skópelos** has a lovely town, and has lost none of its authenticity; laid-back, ecologically sound **Alónissos** helps safeguard the last colony of monk seals in the Aegean in Greece's first marine national park. Mountainous **Évia** (or Euboea) the second largest Greek island after Crete, has always been a land of vines, forests and pastures, low perhaps on island razzle-dazzle – but treasured precisely for that reason by old Greek hands.

History

The first settlers on the Sporades were from Thrace. In the 16th century BC, Minoan colonists introduced the cultivation of olives and grapes. After their fall, Dolopians from Thessaly (first cousins of the Achaeans) took their place, using the Sporades as bases for daring naval expeditions. Much of the islands' mythology has roots during this period: Achilles himself was raised on Skýros. In the 8th century BC, Chalkí (Évia) captured the Sporades and continued the bold sea traditions of the Dolopians. This increasingly brought them into conflict with Athens, until 476 BC when Kimon and the Athenians destroyed the Sporades' fleets. The Athenians managed to present themselves as liberators rather than conquerors; the Sporades adopted the model of Athenian democracy, and Athena became the prominent goddess in local pantheons.

When the Spartans defeated Athens in the Peloponnesian War, they briefly took the Sporades. A greater threat came in the person of Philip II of Macedon, who claimed the islands in a dispute that attracted the attention of the entire Greek world. When Philip took the islands in 322 BC, it was a prelude to nabbing Athens itself.

In Roman times, the Sporades retained their traditional links with Athens. The Byzantines, however, made them a place of exile for unruly nobles who set themselves up as the local aristocracy until 1207, when the Gizzi of Venice picked up the Sporades as their share in the spoils of the Fourth Crusade. Filippo Gizzi usurped control from a senior relative and ruled as a pirate king until Likários, the admiral of Emperor Michael Paleológos, took him in chains to Constantinople. Afterwards, possession of the Sporades seesawed between Greeks and Franks, until Mohammed the Conqueror took Constantinople in 1453. The islanders invited Venice back as the lesser evil, although the Venetians were forced out when all their crafty agreements with the Ottomans crumbled before the attacks of Barbarossa in the 16th century.

Once they had the Sporades, the Turks neglected them; the islands were so exposed to pirates that a permanent Turkish population never settled there. In the 1821 revolution, insurgents from Thessaly found refuge on the islands, and in 1830 the Treaty of London included them in the original kingdom of Greece.

Alónissos (ΑΛΟΝΝΗΣΟΣ)

 Alónissos

Long, skinny Alónissos is queen of her own little archipelago, but she's a late bloomer when it comes to tourism. Few islands suffered so many setbacks: in 1953 disease killed her old grapefruit orchards and vineyards; in 1965, a devastating earthquake hit her only town; local and national politicians then contrived to retard her development, leaving Alónissos a slice of friendly, laid-back 'Old Greece'.

In 1992, after the urging of environmental groups across Europe, Greece's first **National Marine Park** was set up around Alónissos and its islets to protect the endangered Mediterranean monk seal, resulting in the cleanest seas in the Aegean. Nine-tenths of Alónissos is accessible only on foot, crossed by trails offering stunning views and glimpses of the rare Eleanora falcon. Holiday-makers and yacht flotillas have arrived, but not overwhelmingly; others come for courses and seminars at the island's **International Academy of Classical Homeopathy** (see *www.vithoulkas.com*).

History

The history of Alónissos is complicated by the fact that the modern island is not ancient Halonnesos, but actually bore the name Ikos – the result of an over-eager restoration of ancient Greek place names after independence, but in Alónissos' case the mistake was an improvement. As for the real ancient Halonnesos, some scholars say it must have been tiny Psathoúra, northernmost of Alónissos' islets, where the extensive ruins of an ancient city lie submerged offshore.

Getting to Alónissos

There's a **ferry** at least once a day from Vólos, Skópelos, Skiáthos and Ag. Konstantínos; 3 times a week from Thessaloníki. Daily summer **hydrofoils** go to and from Skópelos, Skiáthos, Vólos and Ag. Konstantínos. **Port authority**: t 242 406 5595.

Getting around Alónissos

Boat taxis go to the beaches, and **excursion boats** from Patitíri go out to the islets of Peristéra, Kyrá Panagía and Gioúra and tour the Marine Park. Public **buses** link Patitíri, Chóra and Stení Valá about 5–10 times a day in summer. For a **taxi** try Spíros Florous, t 693 239 1026 or Périkles Ágallou, t 694 456 4432. In general roads aren't the best and boats are the best way to get around, but a **car** (there are several hire firms in Patitíri, but they aren't cheap) is good for getting to distant trail heads.

Inhabited from Neolithic times, Ikos/Alónissos was part of the Minoan colony of Prince Staphylos, who planted the first of the vines that were to make it famous. Peleus, the father of Achilles, was among the later Mycenaean/Dolopian settlers from Thessaly. The Athenians established a naval base on the island in the 4th century, and in 42 BC the Romans let Athens have the whole thing. During the Middle Ages Ikos was ruled by Skópelos, under the name of Achilliodromia, Liadromia or simply Dromos (road). As for ancient Halonnesos (wherever it may be), it was governed throughout antiquity by Athens, which lost control of it in the 4th century BC to a pirate named Sostratos. In 341 BC, in the lead-up to Athens' troubles with Macedonia, King Philip captured the island, and when Athens complained he offered to return it. Skópelos then rushed in and grabbed it; Philip, however, crushed the opportunists and the island was returned to Athens. But afterwards it lost all importance, its port subsided into the sea, and even its location faded from memory.

Patitíri

When the earthquake of 1965 devastated the principal town, Chóra, the military junta ruling Greece at the time summarily forced all the inhabitants into prefab relief housing at the port, Patitíri, and prevented their return to Chóra by cutting off the water and electricity. Since the 1960s, Patitíri has spread its wings to merge with the fishing hamlet of **Vótsi**. Charming it ain't, but neither is Patitíri unpleasant, and bright paint and bougainvillaea cover many a concrete sin. Signs point the way to the charming little **Historical Culture Museum**, with photos of what the island looked like before the earthquake, old wine presses, tools and more.

Historical Culture Museum
t 242 402 3494

There are beaches nearby: a narrow one dramatically set under the cliffs at Vótsi, and another steep pebbly one at **Rousoúm Gialós** – its curious name comes from the Turkish for 'taxes', which were collected here. Within easy walking distance to the south there's **Marpoúnta** (the busiest) with the submerged remains of a **Temple of Asklepios**, and the much nicer beaches at **Víthisma** with dark

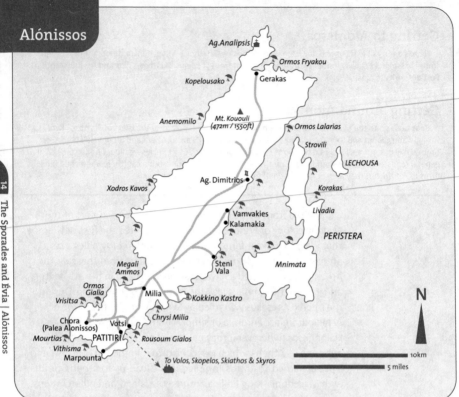

sand (easiest to reach by boat) and **Moúrtias**, with flat stones, a
pretty place with some shade.

Chóra (Paléa Alónissos)

A road, or, for walkers, a pretty path through nut groves, leads up to
the old capital, Chóra, magnificently set high above the sea, with
outstanding views, especially of Alónissos' frequent cinemascope
sunsets. After the 1965 earthquake, and the government's forced
removal of the inhabitants, far-sighted Germans and Brits bought
the old homes for a song and restored them, at first doing without
running water and electricity (although now they've been hooked
up, as the resentment of the former residents has diminished); some
now contain artsy little shops.

The town walls were built by the Byzantines and repaired by the
Venetians, and ghosts are said to dance around the 17th-century
church of **Christós**, perhaps especially on full moon summer nights
when the village hosts concerts. From Chóra it's a 20-minute walk
down to sandy **Vrisítsa Beach** or an hour's hike to beautiful **Órmos
Giália**. Remains of a Classical-era amphora factory were recently
discovered just north, and fossils of prehistoric beasts were found at
Megáli Ámmos, where the beach is lovely and usually deserted.

Beaches around Alónissos

Caiques run out to the island's best beaches, most of which have at least a snack bar. Heading north from Patitíri, the first really good one (especially for children) is **Chrysí Miliá**, in a small cove enveloped with pines, and with a pair of tavernas. The 5th-century BC capital of ancient Ikos was found by the shingly rose-tinted beach **Kokkinó Kástro** (30mins by caique from Patitíri); if you know where to look you can make out some of its walls in the sea. This was also a stomping ground in the Middle Palaeolithic era (100,000–33,000 BC) – the simple stone tools, now in the Vólos Museum, are among the oldest ever found in the Aegean.

North, sheltered **Stení Valá** is a pretty but simple place with a few tavernas, a favourite of yachties and is the headquarters of the **Society for the Study and Protection of the Monk Seal (MOM)**, a private charity dedicated to the survival of one of the world's rarest animals, the grey monk seal (*Monacus monacus*), extinct in France since 1920, in Spain since 1950, and in Italy since 1975 – decimated by pollution, loss of habitat and fishermen, who, looking on them as rivals, used to kill them on sight. The largest remaining population in the world, with an estimated 300 of the last 500 seals, lives in Greece, and the 30 or so seals on the islet of **Pipéri** are the largest single community. Unfortunately, as in Zákynthos (*see* p.526), the Greek government's funding and management of the National Marine Park has been spotty at best, and scandalous at worst – in 1995–6, the Defence Ministry even used two of the protected islets for live target practice. MOM's patrol boat in the park and seal hospital here have done their best to keep it going.

Beaches just north of Stení Valá, well sheltered in the embrace of nearby Peristéra islet, offer the best fishing and water sports on the island. **Kalamákia** has small *pensions* and tavernas. **Ag. Dimítrios** dramatically covers a headland and has a bar, sunbeds and the ruins of a Byzantine fountain and an ancient settlement in the sea.

Isolated beaches are plentiful off the remote northern coast. Here at the old shepherd's village of **Gérakas**, a biology station funded by the EU was opened with fanfare, then hardly ever used.

MOM
*www.mom.gr;
donations gratefully
accepted*

14 | The Sporades and Évia | Alónissos

Alónissos' Archipelago

The islands scattered around Alónissos' shores make for exceptional sailing. Olive-covered **Peristéra** (Dove) islet off the east coast was its Siamese twin until separated by a natural upheaval. Peristéra has good sandy beaches, popular for evening barbecue excursions. In 1992, divers found the largest Classical-era shipwreck yet discovered off its shores, an Athenian cargo vessel that carried 4,000 amphorae of wine from Skópelos, Alónissos and Macedonia as well as ceramics.

Further out, volcanic **Psathoúra** is the island base of one of the most powerful lighthouses in Greece. The submerged city by the lighthouse is probably ancient Halonnesos, but the reason most people stop is a gorgeous 'tropical' sandy beach.

Lovely, wooded **Kyrá Panagía** (Pelagós), the largest island, is two or so hours from Patitíri and still belongs to the Grand Lavra monastery on Mount Áthos, which hires out the land to goatherds who supply the monastery with meat. Kyrá Panagía's own 12th-century monastery has been abandoned for decades but was recently restored and waiting for any new monks who might fancy a dose of isolation. In the bay of **Ag. Pétros** lie the sunken remains of a 12th-century Byzantine ship that yielded a cargo of ceramics. Kyrá Panagía has sandy beaches, a pretty stalactite **cave** (a reputed home of the Cyclops), and plenty of opportunities for bushwalking.

Another abandoned monastery linked to Áthos stands on verdant **Skantzoúra**, which offers excellent fishing in its many coves and caves. **Pappoú**, home to hares, has the remnants of a 7th-century church, while a rare breed of goat skips about steep, forbidding grey **Gioúra** (ancient Geronta), nibbling on its maquis. It has a few Classical and Roman remains and up a steep path yet another, wonderfully dramatic 'Cyclops' **cave** with stalactites, although it's closed to visitors at the time of writing.

Pipéri, on the east end of the Marine Park, is a wildlife sanctuary, and home to Eleanora falcons as well as its colony of monk seals; no one is allowed within three miles of it.

Useful Information on Alónissos

Tourist police: Contact the regular police, **t** 242 406 5205. Also see the municipal website, *www.alonissos.gr*. For more on the **Marine Park**, see *www.alonissos.com*.

Ikos Travel, **t** 242 406 5320. Pakis is at the forefront of trying to keep tourism on Alónissos eco-friendly.

Alónissos Travel, near the wharf, **t** 242 406 6000. Also very helpful and hires out cars.

Alónissos Festivals

40 days after Easter: Análypsis.
1 July: Ag. Anárgiroi.
17 July: Ag. Marína.
26 July: Ag. Paraskeví.
15 Aug: Panagías.

Where to Stay and Eat on Alónissos

If you get stuck, try the **Hoteliers' Union**, **t** 242 406 5212, or the **Rent Rooms Association**, **t** 242 406 5577. Alónissos is the place to try Mediterranean lobster (*astakós*); the Aegean is especially salty here and the fish especially tasty.

Patitíri ✉ 37005

Archontiko, near the beach, **t** 242 406 5004 (€€€). Comfortable apartments, some with full kitchens, and parking. *Open May–Oct.*

Haravgi, above the port, **t** 242 406 5090 (€€€). 22 well-scrubbed and wholesome rooms with a pretty terrace to sit out on over a drink.

Paradise, on the cliff promontory, **t** 242 406 5160 (€€€). Facing east over pine trees to the open sea, rather than west over the harbour. Simple, rather small rooms but beautifully tiered terraces below the pool, a perfect spot for evening drinks. *Open May–Oct.*

 Panorama >>

Liadromia, over the fishing boats on the cliffs at Patitíri, **t** 242 406 5521, *www.alonissos.com* (€€€–€€). Renovated in 2004 and full of character, with a rooftop bar and breakfast terrace, and wi-fi.

Alkyon, right on the sea, **t** 242 406 5220 (€€). Modern white hotel with rooms and studios overlooking the centre of the action.

 Babis >

Babis, on the road to Chóra, **t** 242 406 6184. Truly exceptional family-run taverna with a wood-burning oven serving traditional island specialities with fresh veggies; try the *bouréki* (cheese pie) and the *xinótiri* (sour cheese). The views are beautiful too. *Open June–Sept.*

To Kamáki, **t** 242 406 5245. The local consensus for the best fish in town – really tasty seafood starters; also caters for fish-haters. Good value. *Open April–Oct.*

Vótsi ✉ 37005

Milia Bay, 3km from Patitíri, **t** 242 406 6035, *www.milia-bay.gr* (€€€€–€€€). Complex of studios and apartments, with a pool and a snack bar that has a telescope for starry nights.

Atrium of Alónissos, **t** 242 406 5749, *www.atriumalonnissos.gr* (€€€). Complex on Roussou Yialos beach, with comfortable rooms overlooking the sea and central pool.

Alónissos Beach, just beyond Chrysí Miliá Beach, **t** 242 406 5115 (€€). Bungalow complex with a pool and tennis. *Open July–Sept.*

Dimitris, **t** 242 406 5035, *www.dimitrispension.gr* (€). With its own bar, pizzeria and terrace; all six rooms have balconies over the little harbour.

Panorama, **t** 242 406 5005 (€). Friendly guesthouse, nestled in the trees, a short walk from the beaches; Mr Valvis, the owner, speaks good English. *Open May–Sept.*

Vótsi, a 2min walk up from the waterfront, **t** 242 406 5510 (€). A bit cheaper; it has good-sized, spotless rooms with telephones and a communal kitchen and sea-view terrace.

Chóra ('Old Village') ✉ 37005

Chiliodromia Studios, in the beautiful old town of Chóra, **t** 242 406 5814, *www.alonissos.com* (€€).

Konstantina Studios, in Chóra, **t** 242 406 6165, *www.konstantinastudios.gr* (€€). Away from the sea, a good Class A guesthouse with sea views and a pretty garden.

Astrofeggia, 'Starlight', **t** 242 406 5182. Greek and Mediterranean dishes, using local ingredients, and the best choice of wines on the island. Owner Yánnis Toúndas used to play football for Panathenaïkos. *Closed Nov–April.*

Panselinos, **t** 242 406 6371. Stylish new bar-restaurant just outside the centre, specializing in meat. *Open all year.*

Paraport, at the top of Chóra. Delicious food and views.

Stení Valá ✉ 37005

Stení Valá, **t** 242 406 5590. Deservedly popular family-run fish taverna, supplied by the owner's fishing boat. Also serves some local cheese and vegetable dishes. *Closed Nov–April.*

Skiáthos (ΣΚΙΑΘΟΣ)

Racy, cosmopolitan Skiáthos with its 62 beautiful beaches is not for the shy teetotaller or anyone looking for the 'authentic' Greece. Although still an isolated peasant island community in the early 1970s, Skiáthos has been catapulted faster than any other island into the world of tourism, with all the pros and cons that entails. One of the most popular destinations in Greece, it is stunningly beautiful away from the main road, and provides some of the best swimming and nightlife in Greece, a heady cocktail that attracts a fun-seeking crowd.

Getting to and around Skiáthos

There are 2 **flights** a day from Athens (except Wed, when there's only one), twice a week from Thessaloníki on Sky Express, and some 70 charter flights a week in summer. Olympic Airways, **t** 242 702 2229. **Airport information: t** 242 702 2049. Airport taxis are around €10.

Several **ferries** and frequent **hydrofoils** connect daily with Ag. Konstantínos, Vólos, Skópelos and Alónissos; several times a week with Thessaloníki and Péfki (Évia) and the Pélion peninsula. **Port authority: t** 242 702 2017.

Getting around Skiáthos

Daily **excursion boats** go to Skópelos and Alónissos. **Taxi boats** in the old harbour go to the beaches. Some offer round-island trips but the north side is fairly uninteresting and the sea can be rough. You can also **rent** your own boat by the day.

Buses run every 15mins in season until the early hours, from the new harbour in Skiáthos Town to Koukounariés, and all points in between (numbered), and less frequently go up to Evangelistría and 3 times a day to Xánemo Beach. Demand is so great in summer that your feet may not touch the floor.

The harbour is lined with places to **rent cars, motorbikes and scooters**, but be careful – traffic is fast-moving. **Taxis, t** 242 702 1460, are a popular, if expensive, option.

History

When Xerxes sailed to conquer Athens in 480 BC, his fleet met a fierce storm off Skiáthos. So many ships were damaged that Xerxes put in for repairs and, during his stay, invented the world's first-known navigational aid on a reef called Myrmes (now Lephtéris and still a menace to ships). 'Thither the barbarians brought and set up a pillar of stone that the shoal might be clearly visible,' Herodotus wrote. Thanks to its guidance, Xerxes slipped past the Athenian patrols towards his first sea battle at Artemissíon (a draw) and eventual defeat at Salamis. Part of the pillar can still be seen today, in the courtyard of the Naval Cadet School in Piraeus. The rest of Skiáthos' history follows that of the other Sporades. The Gizzi ruled the island in the name of Venice and built the fort on Boúrtzi islet by the present-day town. The Skiathot navy assisted the Russians against the Ottomans at Cêsme, and the islanders revolted against the Turks in 1805, then sent so many ships to fight for independence that Skiáthos itself was left unprotected and prey to marauders.

Useful Information on Skiáthios

Tourist police: Papadiamánti, **t** 242 702 3172. *Open 8am–9pm in season.*
Geof Baldry's site, *www.skiathosinfo. com*, is full of good information.
The municipal website, *www.skiathos. gr*, has lists of rooms and apartments.

Skiáthios Festivals

Aegean Summer Festival in the Boúrtzi.
15 Aug: Evangelistría.

Sports and Activities on Skiáthios

Tennis Club, on the airport road, turn right at the Asterias supermarket, **t** 242 702 4054. Tennis courts floodlit on summer nights, and a swimming pool. *Open all year.*
Dolphin Diving Centre, Tzanería (Nostós) Beach, **t** 242 702 1599, *www. ddiving.gr*.
Horse riding, Koukounariés, **t** 242 704 9548. Trekking over the mountain.

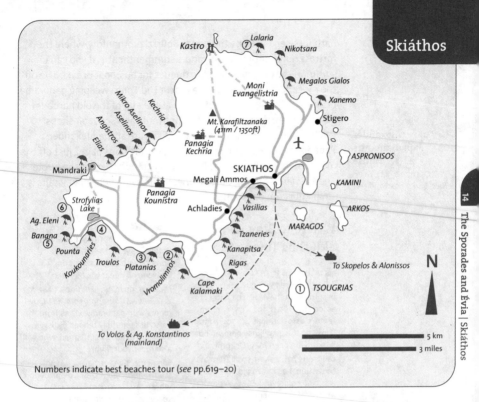

Numbers indicate best beaches tour (see pp.619–20)

Skiáthos Town

The capital and only real town on the island, Skiáthos is a gentle spread of traditional whitewashed houses, overhung with bougainvillaea and freshly washed sheets while below the streets buzz and throb with visitors, shops and bars. The back streets are quieter – if you don't count the high-speed trail bikes. The town has two

Alexander Papadiamántis, the Master of Neo-Hellenic Prose

One of modern Greece's greatest writers, Papadiamántis wouldn't recognize his home town today. The Skiáthos he immortalized in his short stories, with stark realism and serene, dispassionate prose, was a poor, tragic place, where most of the men were forced to emigrate or spend years at sea and the women lived hard lives of servitude, often in total penury, to accumulate a *príka*, or dowry, for each daughter; this was such a burden that, when a little girl died, other women would comfort the mother by saying, 'Happy woman, all you need to marry this one off is a sheet.'

Papadiamántis' strongest story, *I Phonissa* (*The Murderess*), written in 1903, concerns an old woman who, reflecting on the conditions of her own life, sees the monstrous injustice of the system and quietly smothers her sickly newborn granddaughter, to spare her daughter the need to slave away for her dowry. Always the island's herbal doctor (the one herb she could never find was one for contraception), the old woman believes that her destiny is to alleviate the suffering of others, and she kills four other daughters of poor families before being pursued to her own death. As she drowns, the last thing she sees is the wretched vegetable garden that was her own dowry. Twelve of Papadiamántis' stories have been beautifully translated by Elizabeth Constantinides as *Tales from a Greek Island*, complete with a map (it's usually available at the house) – a perfect read on Skiáthos, a century on.

harbours, separated by the pretty **Boúrtzi** promontory, where the **fortress** now contains a café and a summer theatre. If you can't summon the energy to join the queues for bus, boat or taxi, dive off the rock and pretend you're in a Martini ad. For a sweeping panorama of Skiáthos Town, take the steps up at the end of the old harbour past the waterfront cafés, restaurant touts and souvenir shops.

When hedonism palls, get a shot of culture at the **Alexander Papadiamántis House** (1851–1911; *see* box, previous page), just off the main street. The house was built by his grandfather, and he wrote *The Murderess* among other stories while living here; downstairs is a small museum of Skiáthos.

Alexander Papadiamántis House
t 242 702 3843; open Tues–Sun 9.30–1 and 5–8

Where to Stay in Skiáthos Town

Skiáthos ✉ 37002

Finding a bed without a reservation in summer is the devil. The **hotel association**, t 242 702 3375, or **room renters' association**, t 242 702 2990 (kiosk on the quay) may help. All but a handful are open May–Oct only.

La Piscine Art, a short stroll from all the action, t 242 702 1350, *www. lapiscine palace.gr* (€€€€€€). A plush, arty hotel that opened in 2004 and is named after its Olympic-sized pool, with affable management, Internet service, and much more. Don't miss an evening meal around the pool.

Akti, t 242 702 2024, *www.skiathosinfo. com* (€€€). Watery harbour views, especially from the four-person top-floor suite. *Open April–Oct.*

Alkyon, on the new harbour, t 242 702 2981, *www.alkyon.gr* (€€€). This is Skiáthos Town's biggest hotel – all mod cons, plus a roof garden and pool.

Pothos, Evangelistrías St, t 242 702 2694 (€€€), and **Bourtzi**, t 242 702 1304 (€€€), *www.hotelbourtzi.gr* for both. Two sister hotels, central and set in delightful little gardens. Both are charming, but Pothos just has the edge. *Both open May–Oct.*

Villa Orsa, in the old town, t 242 702 2300, *www.hirners.com/hotel/villaorsa* (€€€). For something quieter, two traditional houses have been converted to make this small hotel.

Meltémi, nearby, t 242 702 2493, *www.meltemiskiathos.com* (€€€–€€). Has a loyal following and is generally

⭐ **Pothos >**

⭐ **Bistro >>**

booked solid; their bar is a good vantage point for the antics of the flotilla crowd as they moor and unmoor with zealous gung-ho. Conveniently near the bus stop.

Messinis, up in Ag. Fanoúrios, t 242 702 2134, *www.skiathosinfo.com* (€€). Quiet rooms with panoramic views from the balconies, carefully tended by Stavros Messinis, a master craftsman, who will also meet your flight.

San Remo, t 242 702 2078, *www. skiathosinfo.com* (€€–€). Colourful hotel whose terraced rooms are dress circle seats to observe the harbour traffic.

Australia Hotel, just off Papadiamántis St, behind the post office, t 242 702 2488 (€). Central and cheap, with simple en suite rooms.

Eating Out in Skiáthos Town

Agnantio, t 242 702 2016, on the road to the Evangelistría Monastery. Very popular with its chic navy and white interior, its terrace with beautiful views and tasty Greek fare.

Anatoli, in the same area as Agnantio, past the turn-off to the monastery, t 242 702 1907. Family-run, with tasty home-cooking and a gorgeous view from the terrace.

Bistro, up past the restaurants on the steps, t 242 702 1627. Intimate dining with a lovely view over the harbour and a trendy international menu, including excellent Chinese dishes.

En Plo, along the coast towards the airport, t 242 702 4433. A pretty veranda on the sea, serving home-made pasta, seafood and a choice of

Greek and continental dishes made from organic produce. *Open all year.*

I Folia, follow the road behind the National Bank. Traditional, excellent and inexpensive.

I Roda, Evangelistrías St, up from the post office, **t** 242 702 3178. Good family-run taverna.

Jailhouse, old harbour, **t** 242 702 1081 (€25). Very popular for its exotic delights by an inventive chef.

Mesogia, tucked away in the back streets, **t** 242 702 1440. The oldest taverna on Skiáthos has an excellent repertoire of Greek delicacies including outstanding courgette fritters (*kolokythiakéftedes*).

Ouzerie, at the west end of the seafront by Jimmy's Bar. Great place for *mezédes* and seafood.

Panorama, further inland on the road to Profítis Ilías. As the name promises, fabulous views over Skiáthos Town and over the sea to Skópelos. Good pizza.

Primavera, in a small square near the church behind the fish market, **t** 242 702 4084. Serves excellent pasta and other Italian delights.

Windmill, in a converted guess-what behind the San Remo Hotel, **t** 242 702 4550. Also with an international flavour and a lovely view (book the

'honeymoon balcony'); very popular, though pricey.

Entertainment and Nightlife in Skiáthos Town

Having eaten, you'll be spoilt for choice when it comes to bars.

Admiral Benbow Inn, Polytechníou St. Provides a little corner of old England and bluesy music.

Kazbar, next door. Compact, noisy, friendly and fun, with live music and an Aussie/Brit crowd.

Destiny Bar, nearby. Friendly and non-exclusive gay bar that often doesn't close till dawn.

Kentavros, near Papadiamántis' house. Promises more of a funky jazz and blues atmosphere.

On a warm summer evening, the picturesque waterfront bars come into their own:

Jimmy's. One of the best.

De Facto. Quiet, pleasant lesbian bar.

Kavos, Remezzo and the popular seafront **BBC** are good for a blaring bop.

Paradise Outdoor Cinema, on the ring road. Offers undubbed films.

Beaches, Beaches, Beaches

⭐ **Skiáthos beaches**

See numbers on the island map, p.617, for the best beaches.

Sand and pebbles are the key to Skiáthos' success, and they rim the emerald isle like lace. Mobile sardine tins called buses follow the south coast, stopping within easy walking distance of the best strands, all equipped with places to lunch and water sports hire.

From Skiáthos Town, taxi boats in the old harbour wait to whisk you off in half an hour to **Tsougriás islet** ①. In the 1960s the Beatles wanted to buy it. It's an ideal place to escape the crowds, with its fine sand and excellent swimming. The simple taverna has fresh fish served on tables under the trees where you can wiggle your toes in the sand. Tsougriás has two other beaches, accessible by foot, for Robinson Crusoe fantasies. On the main island, the most convenient beach from Skiáthos Town is **Megáli Ámmos**, although it's generally packed. Moving westward, **Achladiés Beach** (easiest reached from Skiáthos Town by €2 boat taxi) is also chock-a-block in summer.

Beyond that, 5km from town, the **Kalamáki Peninsula** juts out with a coating of holiday villas. Beaches here include **Kanapítsa**, a popular cove, and nearby **Vromólimnos** ② ('dirty lake'), hard to pronounce and hard to find, but one of the finest places to swim on the island, with powderpuff-soft sand; the restaurant-bar at the right-hand end of the strand is worth a stop for lunch or a tipple or two. **Plataniás/ Ag. Paraskeví** ③ is a lovely long stretch of beach with plenty of parasols and sunbeds.

Troúlos has a couple of tavernas and more good swimming. The last bus stop, 12km from Skiáthos Town, is the legendary **Koukounariés** ④, rated by many as 'the Best Beach in Greece': a superb sweeping crescent bay of soft sand that escaped from the South Pacific, fringed with pines, although in August it seems that not only can you 'see a world in a grain of sand' as Blake wrote, but that each grain of sand has a world sitting on it. Tavernas, hotels and a campsite are hidden away from the sea behind trees and a rather uninspiring lake. Hyper-trendy **Krássa**, nowadays called **Banana Beach** ⑤, is up the hill with the sea on your left when you get off the bus at Koukounariés. **Little Banana** (or **Spartacus**), next door, is the gay/nudie beach where you can peel off everything and lie cheek-to-cheek in a bunch. Next is the lovely **Ag. Eléni** ⑥, the last beach accessible by road, a quieter spot with a view across to the Pelion Peninsula and a welcome breeze; or take the dirt road just before the beach, which leads after 1km or so down to **Krýfos Ammoúdia Beach**, with a cool taverna.

In general, beaches on the north coast are subject to the *meltémi* winds. **Mandráki** is reached by a lovely footpath from the lagoon behind Koukounariés, and has two stretches of sand and a snack bar. Further east, **Asélinos** is a sandy beach in an arcadian setting with a taverna and reed sun shelters rather than the usual eyesore parasols; but beware of the undertow. Just off the road that leads to nearby **Mikró Asélinos** (tricky to find and not worth the bother), is the exquisitely painted, candlelit chapel of the 17th-century **Moní Panagía Kounistrá**, overlooking the north coast, where an icon of the Virgin was found dangling in a tree and like so many stubborn icons, refused to be moved. Past Kástro, the magical beach at **Laláría** ⑦ (accessible only by sea) is a marvel of silvery pebbles, shimmering like a crescent moon beneath the cliff, with a natural arch closing off one end and nearby sea grottoes – **Skotiní**, 'the dark' (so bring a light if you want to see), **Galázia**, 'the blue', and **Chálkini**, 'the copper'.

Inland to Kástro

Skiáthos has a good network of paths. A road (and occasional bus) and a donkey path, just before the turning to the airport road, lead 4km through the most beautiful empty scenery on Skiáthos to the island's last working monastery. **Evangelistría** was founded in 1797 by monks forced to flee Mount Áthos for their support of the

Evangelistría
*open 8–noon and 4–8;
proper attire required*

traditionalist Kollivádes movement. A lovely, peaceful place with a triple-domed church and garden courtyard, it became a refuge for both monks and scholars, as well as for the *armatolés* (members of the revolutionary militia) from the Olympus area, who, with the support of the Russians, had raised a small fleet to harass the Turks. When Russia made peace with Turkey in 1807, the *armatolés* were abandoned, and many took refuge on Skiáthos; under Giánnis Stathás, they united in an irregular army, and over the monastery hoisted the blue and white Greek flag that they had just invented. The Ottoman fleet soon put an end to their pretensions, but a statement had been made that would inspire the War of Independence 14 years later. Only a rusting cannon and a few bits in the museum, cared for by a sole monk and his helper, recall the monastery's belligerent past.

Continue on from Evangelistría or take the two-hour walk from **Ag. Konstantínos** near Skiáthos Town across the island (the path is well marked) to **Kástro**, founded on a windswept niche in the 14th century when pirates were on the warpath, and inhabited until 1829, when everyone moved down to Skiáthos Town. Eight of the original 30 Byzantine churches more or less still stand (one, **Christós**, has good frescoes and a chandelier) among the houses and a hammam. The view from the top is lovely and there's a quiet beach below, where the locals smuggled out trapped Allied troops during the war. In *The Poor Saint*, Papadiamántis describes Kástro's churches: 'some of them stood on rocks or on reefs by the shore, in the sea, gilded in summer by the dazzling light, washed in the winter by the waves. The raging north wind whipped and shook them, resolutely ploughing that sea, sowing wreckage and debris on the shore, grinding the granite into sand, kneading the sand into rocks and stalactites, winnowing the foam into spokes of spray.' If the *meltémi* is blowing, you can see that he wasn't exaggerating.

A detour on the path leads to the pretty 15th-century **Monastery of Panagía Kechriá**, containing some fine frescoes painted after 1745. From here you can continue down to lovely, isolated **Kechriá Beach**, where the local goatherd runs a delightful taverna.

Where to Stay and Eat around the Island

Megáli Ámmos ✉ 37002

Aegean Suites, t 242 702 4066, *www.aegeansuites.com* (€€€€€). Swish boutique hotel, in which each of 20 glam suites is decorated with original art pieces. See their website for special offers. Their excellent restaurant, **Pelagos**, is open to all.

Angeliki, t 242 702 2354, *www.skiathos. gr/aggeliki* (€€). With a shady garden, beach bar and sea views.

Rea, t 242 702 1013 (€). The thriving flora on the terraces lends an exotic atmosphere.

Achladiés ✉ 37002

Esperides, t 242 702 2245, *www. esperidesbeach.gr* (€€€€€). Recently renovated big beach hotel; all rooms with balconies, sea views, tennis, pool, sea sports, beauty parlour, etc.

Perigiali, next to the Esperides. Excellent food and friendly service.

Kanapítsa ✉ 37002

Cape Kanapitsa, t 242 702 1750, www.capekanapitsa.com (€€€€). Set on 8 acres on the headland overlooking two beaches. Well-equipped rooms, suites and apartments and a lovely pool.

Plaza, 100m from Kanapítsa Beach, t 242 702 1971, www.plaza.gr (€€€€). Scenically situated amongst pines and olive groves; there's a pool, gym and the inevitable Greek nights.

Ag. Paraskeví/Plataniás ✉ 37002

Skiáthos Princess, Ag. Paraskeví Beach, t 242 704 9731, www.skiathosprincess.com (€€€€€). Bright and airy and renovated for 2007; enjoys one of the best positions on one of the best beaches; it has a diving school. Open May–Oct.

Atrium, 150m from Plataniás Beach, t 242 704 9345, www.atriumhotel.gr (€€€). Handsome complex in wood and stone with a monastic Mount Áthos-style foyer, pool and excellent views. Open April–Oct.

Magic, Ag. Paraskeví, t 242 704 9453, www.magic-hotel.com (€€€). Nice hotel with nice owners and a new kidney-shaped pool with Jacuzzi.

Troúlos ✉ 37002

Boudourgianni's House, on Troúlos Beach, t 242 704 9280 (€€€). With pool.

Korali, on Troúlos Beach, t 242 704 9212, www.skiathoskorali.gr (€€€). Friendly apartment complex, with fully equipped kitchens and balconies with sea views and pool.

La Luna, on the hill overlooking Troúlos Bay, t 242 704 9262 (€€€–€€). Well-equipped studios and maisonettes with air-conditioning, a lovely pool and great views, 10mins' walk from the sea.

Koukounariés ✉ 37002

Skiáthos Palace, t 242 704 9700, www.skiathos-palace.gr (€€€€€). Big hotel overlooking the bay amid pines, with pool, tennis, massage and roof garden. Open May–Oct.

Camping Koukounariés, at the east end of the eponymous beach, t 242 704 9250. The nicest campsite.

Inland ✉ 37002

Zorbathes, near Panagía Kounistrá, t 242 704 9473, www.skiathosinfo.com (€€€–€€). For true rural peace and quiet, with two fully equipped stone, wood and terracotta houses sleeping 4–6 in a lush valley, with an organic pool.

Skópelos (ΣΚΟΠΕΛΟΣ)

Where rambunctious Skiáthos has given its all to tourism, Skópelos, with its more modest pebbly beaches, remained aloof during the 1960s and '70s, the decades of slapdash cash-in-quick building. Yet not only has the island kept its integrity and serenity – the lure for a new wave of upmarket tourists – but it's exceptionally beautiful, with dramatic scenery, dense pine forests, plum orchards and two truly pretty towns, Skópelos and Glóssa. It is a lovely island for long walks, especially outside of the heatstroke months of July and August.

History

Known in antiquity as Perparethos, Skópelos was colonized by Prince Staphylos of Crete (who, according to some, was the son of Theseus and Ariadne). This tradition was given dramatic substance in 1927 when Staphylos' wealthy Minoan tomb containing a sword (now in the Archaeology Museum in Athens) was discovered by the cove that has always borne his name. Staphylos means 'grape': the

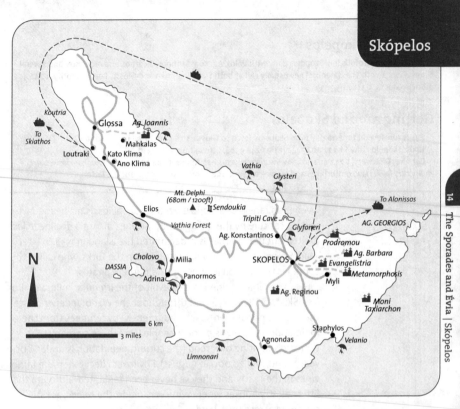

local wine, described as an aphrodisiac by Aristophanes, was long an important export. The Minoans also founded the island's three settlements: Perparethos (Skópelos Town), Staphylos (Pánormos) and Knossa (Glóssa). Subsequent tradition recounts that King Pelias, usurper of the Iolkan kingdom in Thessaly, settled Skópelos in the 13th century BC; it was this same Pelias who sent the rightful heir, Jason, after the Golden Fleece.

Useful Information on Skópelos

For all kinds of information on the island, see *www.skopelosweb.gr*.
Regular police, Skópelos Town, **t** 242 402 2235 or Glóssa, **t** 242 403 3333.
Madro Travel, just by the ferry, **t** 242 402 2300, *www.madrotravel.com*. Organizes caique trips to Alónissos' marine park and Kéra Panagía.
Skopelos Walks, *www.skopelos-walks. com*. Heather Parsons, author of the walking guide *Skópelos Trails*, can offer an intimate, in-depth view of the island from May to Oct.

Skópelos Festivals

Carnival (Apokriés) is fun, but can be dangerous for your health. A small boat, the *tráta*, is made of cane and decorated with rubbish, with a smoke-stack spewing fumes from burning wet garbage. This foul vessel is borne through the streets, polluting every-thing in its path, while its bearers, bodies painted, stop to drink and sing lewd songs. When they finally make it to the harbour, where the boat is hurled into the sea and the merrymakers jump in after it.
6 Aug: Metamórphosis, Skópelos Bay.
15 Aug: Panagías in Skópelos.

Getting to Skópelos

Ferries and **hydrofoils** link Skópelos daily with Vólos, Ag. Konstantínos, Skiáthos and Alónissos, and several times a week with Thessaloníki. They usually call at both Skópelos Town and Glóssa. **Port authority, t** 242 402 2180; in Glóssa, **t** 242 403 3033.

Getting around Skópelos

Buses run several times a day from Skópelos Town to Glóssa, stopping by all the beach paths.
Taxis: Skópelos Town **t** 242 402 3240/**t** 697 242 9568; Glóssa **t** 697 284 1329.
Car hire: Discovery, t 242 402 3033, *www.discoverycars.net*; **Magic, t** 242 402 3250, *www.skopelosweb.gr/ magiccars* (also have motorbikes and Jeeps – for serious exploring you may want the latter).

Venetian renegade Filippo Gizzi used Skópelos as his headquarters, and his capture by the resurgent Byzantines meant a decline in local excitement until Barbarossa decimated the island in 1538. In later years Skópelos was a popular refuge from the Turks, who called the Sporades the 'demon islands' for their ornery pirates.

The Skopelitians joined in the revolt of the irregular militia in 1805 (*see* 'Skiáthos', 'History'), and throughout the War of Independence the island's population soared, augmented by refugees from the mainland; in the 1820s, 70,000 people lived there, so many that there was fighting over food (the current population is under 6,000 year-round, and 20,000 in August). Phylloxera decimated the famous vines in the 1940s, and they've never been replanted, although the little country houses where wine was made, the *kalívia*, are still scattered across the island.

Skópelos Town and its Harbour

⭐ Skópelos Town

Artfully arranged in a steep amphitheatre around the port, Skópelos Town (or Chóra) forms a picture-perfect collage of old blue slate and post-earthquake red-tile roofs. There's a touch of Venice in the older buildings, while others are built in a sturdy Thessalian or Macedonian style. The newer houses fit in harmoniously, incorporating wooden balconies and other traditional features, while, in between, the Greek obsession for planting a seed wherever it might have half a chance has resulted in a lush growth of flowers and plants. Shops sell local ceramics, wood carvings, model boats and, direct from the fishermen on the quay, natural sea sponges.

Skópelos Town claims no fewer than 123 churches, of all shapes and sizes, many with charming iconostases. Two to look out for are **Zoödóchos Pigí** with an icon attributed to St Luke, and **Christó** (above the Commercial Bank) with a triangular, Armenian-style apse and an exceptionally handsome gilded interior. Perched at the top of town, on the site of an old Temple to Athena, are the white walls of the Venetian **Kástro**, built by the Gizzi, so formidable that overpopulated Skópelos was left untouched during the War of Independence. Along the edge of the cliff a row of chapels offer divine defence against the storms that often crash into the exposed town. Within the Kástro walls the 9th-century **Ag. Athanásios** has frescoes from the 1500s, unfortunately damaged in 1965 when the roof collapsed.

At the other end of town, an 18th-century mansion rebuilt after the last earthquake holds the **Museum of Folk Art**, with a fine collection, especially of embroideries. Panagía Eleftherótria, beyond Plátanos Square with its enormous plane tree and fountain, is a handsome 18th-century stone church with a slate roof, adorned with brightly coloured ceramic plates.

Museum of Folk Art (Mouseío Laografikó)
t 242 402 3494

At the end of town, beyond the medical centre, stands the impressive fortified **Monastery of Episkopí**, built by the Venetians as a seat for the bishopric of Skópelos, although work was abandoned after the raid by Barbarossa in 1538. The walls encompass the 17th-century basilica of **Panagía tis Episkopís**, built over a church dating back to AD 600. Just outside town, you can usually visit the **Foúrnou Damáskinon**, the gargantuan oven where plums are dried to become Skópelos' famous prunes, which are later crystallized and served with *rakí* to guests. There's a convenient but mediocre sandy **beach** next to the town and, under the trees, a row of sweet shops that scent the evening air with warmed honeyed *loukoumádes*. If you walk around the bay to **Ampelikí**, you can see the ruins of an **Asklepeion** lying half-submerged in the sea.

Around Skópelos Town

Evangelistría
open 10–1 and 4–7

The hills overlooking Skópelos' large but windswept harbour shelter no fewer than five monasteries. The closest, **Evangelistría**, with a magnificent view over town, was founded by monks from Mount Áthos, but is now occupied by nuns who offer their weavings for sale. **Metamórphosis**, with a frescoed church, was abandoned in 1980, but is now being rehabilitated. Further afield, fortified but abandoned **Ag. Bárbara** has frescoes from the 15th century. Over the ridge, looking towards Alónissos, is **Moní Prodromoú**, with a beautiful iconostasis, rare 14th-century icons and enamel-tiled floor. One lovely path connects them all, beginning just beyond the strip of hotels near the beach; a far less scenic road ascends as far as Metamórphosis. Real explorers can spend a day hiking even further, up to the summit of **Poloúki** (545m/1,791ft) to the now abandoned **Monastery of Taxiárchon**, where the local resistance hid Greek and Allied soldiers, before they were smuggled across to neutral Turkey. Yet another monastery, **Ag. Regínou**, is 3km south of town, where the stone sarcophagus of Ag. Regínos, the first Bishop and patron saint of Skópelos, martyred in 362, lies in the courtyard.

Moní Prodromoú
same hours as Evangelistria

On the west side of the bay, near the shingle beach of **Glyfonéri**, stand the ruins of a Hellenistic **water tower**. Another, less crowded beach, **Glystéri**, to the north, has a taverna amid the olive groves.

14 The Sporades and Évia | Skópelos

Boat taxis sail here and to the **sea cave of Tripití**, the island's chief lobster lodge and fishing hole, or to the islet of **Ag. Geórgios**, with a 17th-century monastery and herd of wild goats.

From **Vathiá**, north of Glystéri, trails ascend Skópelos' highest mountain, **Délphi**, where you can examine the **Sendoúkia**, 'the chests' – four large rock-cut tombs of indeterminate age with lids facing a magnificent view to the east.

⭐ Kyr Sotos >>

⭐ Prince Stafilos>

Where to Stay in Skópelos Town

Skópelos ✉ 37003

Prince Stafilos, a 10min walk from the centre, **t** 242 402 2775, *www.prince-stafilos.gr* (€€€€). Colonial-style hotel, done up with traditional touches; family rooms available plus a pool and splendid gardens.

Skópelos Village, across the bay, 600m from town, **t** 242 402 2517, *www.skopelosvillage.gr* (€€€€). Attractive seafront bungalow complex with all the frills and good facilities for kids.

Diónyssos, nearer to the centre of town, **t** 242 402 3210, *www.dionyssoshotel.com* (€€€). Upbeat hotel with an international flavour, large pool and gardens; comfortable rooms, some with sea views.

O Stolios, 1.5km from town, high up at Ráches Skopélou, **t** 242 402 3345, *www.skopelosweb.gr/stolios* (€€€). Very peaceful, handsome new traditionally styled apartments with splendid views.

Pleoussa Studios, by the sea, a 10min walk from centre, **t** 242 402 3141, *www.pleoussa-skopelos.gr* (€€€). Studios with wrought-iron beds and verandas.

Archontiko, 1 Xanthoú, **t** 242 402 2049 (€€€–€€). Book to bag one of 10 rooms in this lovely old town house.

Adonis, on the waterfront, **t** 242 402 2231 (€€). Adequate, with a restaurant. *Open all year.*

Aegeon, 300m above the beach, **t** 242 402 2619, *aigaiosk@otenet.gr* (€€). Stylish small hotel, with panoramic views over Skópelos Town and its port.

Agnanti, 10mins from town, **t** 242 402 2722, *www.skopelos.net/agnanti* (€€). Friendly little hotel close to the sea with a shady veranda. *Open May–Oct.*

Akti, **t** 242 402 3229 (€€). A good bet if you come unbooked.

Kyr Sotos, **t** 242 402 2549, *www.skopelos.net/sotos* (€). Popular, traditional island *pension*. Each room has its own character and views of either the harbour or a flower-draped courtyard.

Eating Out in Skópelos Town

Alexandros, close to the ferry port, **t** 242 402 2324. Reliable good grilled meats with a couple of stews or baked dishes on offer too. *Open all year.*

Le Bistro, off Plátanos square, **t** 242 402 4741 (€28). Trendy wine bar (French, Italian and Greek) and Mediterranean cuisine served on a spacious terrace.

Finikal, well signposted with huge palm tree, **t** 242 402 3247. Friendly little gem with local dishes served by lantern-light.

Klimataria, overlooking the port, **t** 242 402 2273. Serves Skopelot specialities such as 'black fish' *stifádo*.

Molos, on the port, **t** 242 402 2551. For good Greek meats, casseroles and fish. *Closed Nov and Dec.*

Mourayo, close to the ferry port, **t** 242 402 4553. Wide range of international and Greek dishes.

Perivoli, near Plátanos Square, **t** 242 402 3758. Probably the best restaurant in town – and don't the waiters know it; specializes in French-style Greek cuisine, served to jazz. Try pork roll with apples and plums. *Closed Oct–April.*

Nightlife in Skópelos Town

Karavi, 'the boat', which is what it is. Club for the young.

Ouzerie Anatoli, **t** 242 402 2851. Set in the walls of the Kástro, with tables on a terrace. The owner, Giórgos Xindáris, is a well-known *bouzoúki* player and leads his orchestra in old *rembétika* songs after 11pm. *Open July–early Sept.* **Mesogeios**, on the harbour, on the monasteries road. Late-night music bar.

Metro Club, in town. Very popular club. **Platanos Jazz Bar, t** 242 402 3661. By the old quay under the plane tree. Plays great jazz, blues and Latin.

Across Skópelos to Glóssa

Buses run regularly from Skópelos Town to Glóssa in about an hour. Along the road you'll find **Stáphylos**, where two Minoan tombs from the 15th century BC were discovered; the gold, sword and rich burial goods they yielded are in the National Archaeology Museum in Athens. It is now a popular family beach, while **Velanió**, over a small headland, is the unofficial naturist beach. **Agnóndas**, the next stop, is a delightfully boaty little bay with a clean, pebbly beach. Greeks have long memories: Agnóndas was named after a local victor in the 569 BC Olympics, who disembarked here to wild acclaim. From here you can continue to **Limnonári**, one of the finest beaches on the island, or cut through the pines to another pebble beach, **Pánormos**, set in a magnificent bay overlooking pine-covered islets. Tucked between Pánormos and Miliá are small secluded coves, fringed by pines, accessible by foot. **Miliá** itself is shady and has a pretty pebble beach, with water sports.

Further along, **Élios** (or **Néa Klíma**) is a small beach resort, dating from the 1965 earthquake, when the junta forced all the residents of old Klíma into bland, uniform housing, although now it looks like a real town. It was here that a fierce bad dragon would wait for its annual tribute of human flesh, until St Reginos, Skópelos' patron saint, asked to be a victim and prayed God for mercy (*eleos*) – and the dragon let Reginos lead it over a cliff to its death. Just before Loutráki, at **Káto Klíma**, begins the lovely route up to **Áno Klíma** and **Athéato**, the oldest settlement on the island.

Glóssa

On the north end of the island, spilling over the wooded hill, Skópelos' pretty second town, Glóssa, was constructed mainly during the Turkish occupation and survived the 1965 earthquake. Almonds are an important crop here and to the north. Three ruined 4th-century BC towers watch over Glóssa, and a well-marked track leads in an hour across the island to the extraordinary **Monastery of Ag. Ioánnis**, an eagle's nest perched high over the sea, with real eagles often soaring overhead. The last leg of the walk is 100 steps carved in the rock; the little sandy beach below is often deserted.

A pebble beach and a taverna under the plane trees distinguish **Loutráki**, the port, a steep 3km below Glóssa. Nearly every ship calls in here as well as Skópelos Town, but otherwise it dozes. Near Loutráki's church, **Ag. Nikólaos**, are the 7th-century ruins of an earlier basilica and remains of Loutráki's previous incarnation as Selinous.

Where to Stay and Eat around Skópolos Island

Stáphylos ✉ 37003

Ostria, t 242 402 2220, www.skopelos. net/ostria (€€). A well-run family hotel with a lovely pool and sea views, 7mins' walk down to Stáphylos Beach.

Irene, 1km from the beach, t 242 402 3637, www.skopelosweb.gr/irene (€€). Small family *pension* with bath and basic kitchen facilities in each room.

(★) **Terpsi** > **Terpsi**, 'Pleasure', on the road near Stáphylos, t 242 402 2053. A charming garden restaurant with a duckpond, where for decades everyone goes for the family's secret recipe: roast chicken stuffed with walnuts, chicken livers and pine nuts. *Book. Closed Oct–April*.

Agnóndas/Limnonári ✉ 37003

Korali, Agnóndas, t 242 402 2047. For over 25 years, serving seafood platters and other dishes, not all fishy. *Closed Oct–Easter*.

(★) **Taverna Agnanti** >> **Pavlos**, Agnóndas, t 242 402 2409. The oldest fish taverna in Agnóndas, with delicious seafood *mezédes* and fresh lobster. *Closed Oct–Mar*.

Limnonari Beach, Limnonári, t 242 402 3046, www.skopelos.net/limnonari-rooms (€€). Colourful newish rooms with balconies by the white sands.

Thomas, Limnonári, t 242 402 4460. Big classic summer seafood taverna.

Pánormos/Néa Klíma ✉ 37003

Adrina Beach, built on a slope above the beach, t 242 402 3373, www.adrina. gr (€€€). Child-friendly bungalows built in traditional Skopelot style with a large pool and poolside taverna overlooking the sea open to non-residents. *Open May–Oct*.

Afrodite, by the beach, t 242 402 3150, www.afroditehotel.gr (€€€). Pretty hotel; also a gym and mountain bikes to rent. *Open May–Oct*.

Zanetta, Néa Klíma, t 242 403 3140 (€€). Quiet hotel-apartment complex with rooms sleeping up to four in the woods near the sea, overlooking two pools and a tennis court.

Glóssa ✉ 37004

Taverna Agnanti, t 242 403 3076. Founded in 1953 and now in the hands of the second generation; considered one of the best in Greece, using excellent organic ingredients in both Skopelot dishes and innovative ones, matched by lovely views from the roof terrace. *Closed early Oct–April*.

Skýros (ΣΚΥΡΟΣ)

Skýros is an exceptional island in many respects. Administered from Évia, it has two distinct geological regions, squeezed by a girdle where nearly everybody lives; the south is barren, rugged and ringed with cliffs; the northern half is fertile, pine-forested and dotted with sandy beaches. A race of tiny ponies, the Pikermies, roams the south; a five-year-old can look them right in the eye. Some say they are descendants of the horses sculpted in the Panathenaic procession on the Parthenon marbles.

Throughout history Skýros was uncommonly remote. Even today, unless you fly, it takes about seven hours by land and sea to get there from Athens. The long years of isolation account in part for the island's distinctive charm and character, and the staying power of its old customs. Older men still don their baggy blue trousers, black caps and flat leather sandals with many straps or *trohádia*, and the older women wear their long skirts and headscarves; the interiors of their tidy houses remain resolutely traditional, while incorporating such novelties as digitally controlled American refrigerators. In other

Getting to and around Skýros

By air: There are 2 flights a week from Athens and 3 a week with Thessaloníki on Olympic; **airport information: t** 222 209 1625.

By sea: Ferry connections with Kými (Évia) twice a day; twice a week with Skiáthos and Thessaloníki. From Linariá, caiques travel to Skyropoúla islet. **Port authority: t** 222 209 3475.

By bus: Six buses daily go to Linariá and up to 10 reach Mólos; other services are less reliable, with 2 buses a day to other destinations, one in the morning, one in the afternoon.

Car hire: Get a 4x4 for serious exploring.

words, the outside world has arrived, but the Skyriots are determined to set the rules by which it operates on their island.

History

Theseus was buried on Skýros and the Athenians neglected his memory until his spirit was seen at Marathon, rising out of the earth to lead the Athenians to victory. The Delphic oracle then charged the Athenians to bring Theseus' bones home – just the excuse they

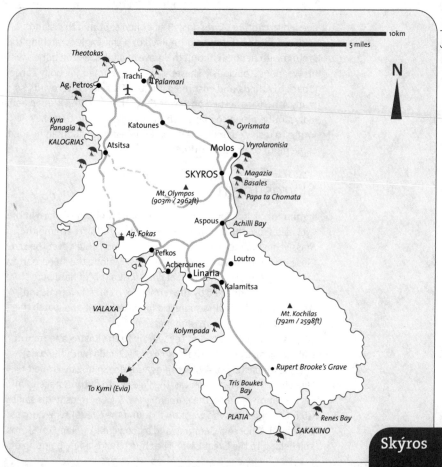

Where Achilles wore Drag, and Theseus Fell

When it was prophesied that Achilles, son of the sea goddess Thetis and Peleus, would either win great glory at Troy and die young, or live peacefully at home to a ripe old age, his mother hid him from the warlords by disguising him as a girl and sending him to live among the women at King Lykomedes' palace in Skýros. Achilles didn't mind and, adopting the name of Pyrrha, or 'Goldie', for the colour of his hair, took advantage of his stay by fathering a son, Neoptolemis. All would have been well had not another Oracle declared that the Greeks would never win the Trojan War without Achilles, and Odysseus was sent to find him. Odysseus brought gifts for the women when he called on King Lykomedes: perfumes and jewellery – and a sword, which the young transvestite seized for his own, as Odysseus had anticipated. When an arrow in his vulnerable heel ended Achilles' life, Odysseus returned to Skýros to fetch his son Neoptolemis to Troy, and the war was eventually won.

King Lykomedes plays a less benign role in another story: when Theseus returned to Athens after spending four years glued to the Chair of Forgetfulness in Hades (his punishment for trying to help a friend abduct Persephone, the Queen of Hell), he found Athens corrupt and divided into factions against him. Theseus laid a curse on the city and sought asylum in Crete, but was blown off course to Skýros, where he was received with such honour by Lykomedes that Theseus announced that he meant to retire on an estate his family owned on Skýros – an estate coveted by Lykomedes himself. So after a drinking party the king led Theseus to the top of Skýros' acropolis to admire the view and gave him a push, hurling him to his death on the rocks below.

needed to capture Skýros. In 476 BC Kimon captured the island, enslaved the inhabitants and, guided by a she-eagle scratching the ground with her beak, found the grave of a tall skeleton buried with his weapons – obviously Theseus. Kimon exhumed the body, carried it back to Athens, and enshrined it in the Theseion. Afterwards, so many Athenians settled on Skýros that Athens treated it as an equal. In Byzantine times, so many nobles were exiled here that they formed a resented upper class, remembered by the double-headed eagle motif common in the local art.

Skýros Town

Stunning Skýros Town, or Chóra, wouldn't look out of place in the Cyclades. From the distance it sweeps like a full skirt around the massive rocky precipice of the ancient acropolis, high over the sea. Close up, white houses are stacked densely along the steep, narrow lanes and steps. The main street curls past a mix of hardware stores and boutiques, rimmed by the terraces of a cafés, tavernas, and cocktail bars. The main square is a fine place to sit and watch the crowds demolishing ouzo and *mezé*.

Signs by the market point the way up to the **Kástro**, a 15-minute walk, passing by way of the church of **Ag. Triáda** (with frescoes) and the **Monastery of Ag. Geórgios**, founded in 962 by Emperor Nikephóros Phókas, famous as 'the Pale Death of the Saracens' after his liberation of Crete. The emperor gave Ag. Geórgios to his saintly friend Athanásios, who went on to found the Great Lavra Monastery on Mount Áthos; Ag. Geórgios, and a good chunk of land on Skýros, still belong to the Great Lavra. The church holds a fine painting of

St George slaying the dragon and the old icon of St George with a black face, brought over from Constantinople. A crusty Lion of St Mark (1354) marks the gate of the Byzantine-Venetian citadel, built over the walls where Lykomedes pushed Theseus over the precipice.

At the end of town, **Brooke Square** wears a rather forlorn air, though the private parts of the gormless bronze nude *Statue of Immortal Poetry* (1931), commissioned by a Belgian businessman to honour Rupert Brooke, is administered to weekly by local spray-painters; rumour has it that it was modelled after a Belgian rent boy. The **Archaeology Museum** is just below Brooke Square; artefacts from Palamári (2500–1900 BC) and Proto-Geometric Thémi (950–800 BC) are among the highlights; from the latter note the ritual vase, decorated with eight ducks and two bird-swallowing snakes. Among the antiquities is a traditionally furnished Skyriot home, 35 square metres in size – the average living space per family, and you can also study the contents of a Skyriot house at the charming **Faltaits Museum of Folklore**, just under Brooke Square – a fascinating collection of domestic items, costumes, and embroideries decorated with mermaids, double-headed eagles, Turkish judges, ships, deer, pomegranates and hoopoes (a bird closely identified with Skýros).

Archaeology Museum
t 222 209 1327; open Tues–Sun 8.30–3; adm

Faltaits Museum of Folklore
t 222 209 1232; open summer 10–2 and 6–10; otherwise 5.30–8

14

The Sporades and Évia | Skýros

✪ Skyriot Houses and a Curious Passion for Plates

Few houses combine so much function and beauty in the small spaces dictated on Skýros by the necessity of living crammed together on the slope, within easy distance of the Kástro should a pirate sail appear on the horizon. Because most older houses back into the steep hill and have shared walls, the *xóporto*, an outer half-door flap, was developed to allow light and air to enter while retaining privacy. The central living area is the *alóni*, a word that recalls the circular disc of the sun, since the walls and possessions on display are seen 'all around'. Focus, however, naturally fell on the chubby, conical fireplace, or *f'gou*, with two little ledges for children to sit on in the winter. Some *f'gous* have a pair of breasts in bas-relief to symbolize motherhood. An embroidered cloth over the upper mouth of the hearth protected the room from smoke, while shelves across the front of the *f'gou* displayed rows of colourful plates and jugs. Crockery has been a Skyriot status symbol since the 16th century, when the Turkish conquest forced the island's Byzantine nobles into such poverty that they had to sell off their dinnerware. Pirates who looted cargoes of plates would sell them on Skýros, or the pirates themselves would be looted by the plate-crazed islanders if they anchored off shore. A Skyriot sailor never has to think twice about the perfect gift for his wife or mother: some examples come from as far as China.

Furniture, often carved with folk motifs, is simple and functional. Benches and settees double as chests for clothes, or have hollows in front of them to slide in pots, pans or bottles; other objects were stored in baskets suspended from the ceiling and reached by long forked poles. Niches in the walls were used to store water jugs. Food would be served on a low table, which in the old days had a removable top, a large engraved copper plate called a *sinía*. These are now mostly used for decoration.

An ornate latticework partition, the *bóulmes*, crowned by a carved wooden parapet, cuts off the back third of the interior while admitting precious light. The kitchen and storage area was on the ground floor, and the bedroom(s), or *sfas* (from the Turkish word 'sofa'), in the loft. A thin beam just below the ceiling of the *sfas* was used to hang decorative weavings that hid the rolled up mattresses. If there is no room for an external stair to the *sfas*, access is by way of a steep narrow internal stair and trap door. The roof is made of wooden beams, covered with layers of dried cane, dried seaweed and waterproof clay; new layers of clay are added every few years. A broken jar on top of the chimney draws out the smoke from the *f'gou*.

The museum shop is full of lovely handmade goods, including printed patterns of Skyriot designs to make your own embroideries (the women of Skýros buy them) as well as local pottery inspired by the examples brought home from the four corners of the world.

Below Skýros Town are the long, sandy, developed beaches of **Magaziá**, named after the Venetian powder magazines once stored here, and **Mólos**. Others are within walking distance; avoid sewage-prone **Basáles**, but continue south to **Papá ta Chómata** ('Priests' Land'), where no one minds if you sunbathe nude. From **Órmos Achílli**, further south, Achilles is said to have embarked for Troy.

Around the Island

The pine-wooded northern half of Skýros has fairly good roads. Up near the airport at Trachí, the prehistoric **Palamari**, dating back to the Copper Age, has been opened for visits; streets and some rather substantial stone foundations remain. There's a pretty beach below, and other small sandy strands at **Ag. Pétros**, **Kyrá Panagía** and **Kalogriás** before idyllic **Atsítsa**, with its piney cove, pebble beach and branch of the **Skýros Centre** (*see* right), although the very English 'PRIVATE' sign must dent the karma somewhat. A scenic track (taking about three hours and not always easy to find) links Atsítsa to Skýros Town; to continue south of here requires a jeep.

Linariá, the island's port, was built after 1860; there are beaches north of here past Achérounes at **Péfkos**, site of ancient marble quarries, and pretty **Ag. Fokás**, with white pebbles, further north, with a taverna run by a fisherman and a handful of rooms. From Linariá, caiques sail to the islet of **Skyropoúla**, with two beaches and a cave, **Kávos Spilí**, and a herd of the wild munchkin ponies.

The beaches in the rugged southern half of Skýros, or **Voúno**, are less appealing, with the exception of sand and stone **Kalamítsa**, fronted by tavernas. Signs of one of ancient Skýros' three towns, Chrission, were found near here, as well as a tomb locally claimed to be Homer's, and bits of an early Christian basilica. The one paved road in the south (*a taxi will be about €40*) leads to **Tris Boukés** bay and the **grave of Rupert Brooke**. On 23 April 1915, the 27-year-old poet, on his way to fight at Gallipoli (hearing war had been declared, Brooke famously remarked to a friend: 'Well, if Armageddon is on, I suppose one should be there'), died of blood poisoning, and was buried by torchlight in this desolate olive grove at dawn. His mother commissioned his well-tended grave – six feet of British soil – now maintained by the Anglo-Hellenic society, bearing the famous lines from his poem, 'The Soldier':

If I should die, think only this of me:
That there's some corner of a foreign field
That is for ever England.

Boat excursions from Linariá sail south of Tris Boukés to the islets of **Sakakíno** and **Platía**, and spectacularly around the cliffs at **Renés**; sea caves pierce the cliffs, and Eleanora falcons sweep the azure sky.

Useful Information on Skýros

Tourist police: *see* regular police, Skýros Town, **t** 222 209 1274.

Skýros Travel, in the centre of town, **t** 222 209 1600, *www.skyrostravel.com*. Leftéris Trákes is helpful, whether you need a villa, car hire, or information on island excursions.

The Skýros Centre, *www.skyros.co.uk*. Courses and workshops on the island.

Skýros Festivals

Feb: Skýros preserves some fascinating vestiges of the ancient Mediterranean goat and cattle cults during Carnival, when three characters dance down the street: the 'Old Man' in a goatskin costume, mask and sheep bells, with a humpback made of rags, followed by the *Frángos* (the Frank, or foreigner), dressed in motley clothes and long trousers, with a mask and bell, blowing a conch shell to scare children, and the *Koréla*, a man dressed up as a woman. These perform the *Horós tou Trágou*, or Goat Dance, a last relic of the ancient rite that gave the world 'tragedy' (from *tragoudía*, 'goat song'). Every day in Carnival they make their way through town, joining in *satires* (another goaty word, derived from the mischievous half-goat satyrs) until they end up at the Monastery of Ag. Geórgios.

23 April: Ag. Geórgios.

27 July: Ag. Panteleímon, near Péfkos.

Late July and early Aug: A new outdoor theatre hosts a festival.

15 Aug: Children's pony races.

2 Sept: Ag. Máma, the patron of shepherds. Like Carnival, the festival also includes traces of ancient rites.

Where to Stay and Eat on Skýros

Skýros Town (Chóra) ✉ 34007
Buses from Linariá are often besieged by women waiting to lead you off to overpriced rooms in traditional houses. If you take one, just mind you don't break the plates.

Nefeli, **t** 222 209 1964, *www.skyros-nefeli.gr* (€€€). Very comfortable, with suites and apartments in traditional split-level *sfa* style; there's also a big seawater pool and Mediterranean restaurant. *Open all year*.

(★) Pension Nikolas >>

Pension Nikolas, on the edge of town, **t** 222 209 1778, *www.skyrosnet.gr* (€€). Tranquil, traditional-style rooms (complete with a *sfa*, or Skyriot sleeping platform). *Open all year*.

Anatolikós Ánemos, Brooke Square, **t** 222 209 2822. Flavoursome modern Greek cuisine (kid with dill on tagliatelle, white *tárama* with avocado, etc.), served on a balcony with sea views. *Closed Oct–Easter*.

Liakós, Machairas, **t** 222 209 3509. With views over the village and castle, serving tasty fillet of pork with mushrooms, traditional cheese pies and more. *Open all year*.

(★) Kristina/ Pegasus >>

Kristina/Pegasus, 20m below Skýros Travel, **t** 222 209 1123. Elegant restaurant in a 19th-century mansion where Greek-Australian Kristina Tsalapatani offers a delicious change-of-pace menu with warm herb breads and delicious desserts.

Margetis, **t** 222 209 1311. One of the oldest restaurants, and the most popular, serving simple but tasty grilled meat in a prime position.

O Pappoús Ki Egó ('My grandfather and I'), **t** 222 209 3200. Popular place for *mezédes*.

By the Sea near Town ✉ 34007
Hydroussa, on the beach at Magaziá, **t** 222 209 1209, *www.hydroussa.gr* (€€€). The former Xenia hotel with big balconies, prettily renovated.

Skiros Palace, 50m from the beach at Grismata, **t** 222 209 1994, *www.skiros-palace.gr* (€€€). Built in the traditional Skýros-Cyclades style, it has a lovely seawater pool, restaurant, superior rooms and a relaxed atmosphere. *Open June–Sept*.

Skýros Studios, near the sea in Mólos, **t** 222 209 1376, *www.skyros-studios.gr* (€€€). Studios each sleeping four, in a large garden, built and furnished in the traditional style.

Villas Mantalena, Grísmata, **t** 222 209 2350, *www.villas-mantalena.gr* (€€€). Traditional villas, studios, and a windmill, sleeping 2–7. *Open April–Oct.*

Aegeolis, a stone's throw from the sea at Magaziá, **t** 222 209 1113 (€€). Set of 11 apartments with verandas, built in 1992. *Open all year.*

Mólos, **t** 222 209 1381 (€€–€). Offers garden studios with big discounts in May and June. *Open May–Sept.*

Thoma to Magazi, by the water, **t** 222 209 3187. Best for seafood.

Aspoús ✉ 34007

Dióni, **t** 222 209 2199, *www.dioni-skyros.gr* (€€€). Rooms in traditional houses with balconies, pool, snack bar and football pitch by the white sands.

Astítsa ✉ 34007

Antonis, **t** 222 209 2990. Good seafood taverna on the beach, with some hard to find dishes as well. *Closed Oct–May.*

Pérasma, out by the airport at Trachí, **t** 222 209 2911. Country taverna famous for succulent semi-wild kid, prepared in a variety of ways. *Open all year.*

Poppi's, **t** 222 209 3353. Tiny, but dishing out well-prepared daily specials and fresh fish. *Closed Oct–May.*

Linariá and Around ✉ 34007

Linariá Bay, 40m from the sea, **t** 222 209 3274 (€€€–€€). Rooms and studios with air-conditioning, TV and phone.

King Likomides, right by the port, **t** 222 209 3249 (€€). Pleasant rooms, all with fridge and sea views. *Open May–Oct.*

Pegasus Estate, on Achérounes beach, book through Skyros Travel, **t** 222 209 1600, *www.skyrostravel.com* (€€). In a peaceful garden, studios for couples and families.

Almyra, **t** 222 209 3252. The best here, offering a variety of tasty starters and a delicious lobster with pasta. *Closed Oct–April.*

Barba-Mitsos, north in Péfkos, **t** 697 2555 8232. Since 1960, and now run by the next generation, serving big portions of wonderful food. Not to be missed. *Closed Sept–May.*

⭐ Barba-Mitsos »

Évia (ΕΥΒΟΙΑ)

Évia (Euboea), the second largest island in Greece after Crete, is endowed with bucolic scenery along its 175km length. Olive groves, orchards and vines (producing Greece's best retsina among other things) alternate with dense forests, wild cliffs and snow-capped mountains. Its name means 'rich in cattle'; animal husbandry has been the way of life for centuries, and remains so today. If nearly every hill is crowned with a crumbling Frankish or Byzantine fort, there are surprisingly few ancient remains. A mere 88km drive from downtown Athens and the only Greek island you can reach by train, Évia gets plenty of nature-loving Greek visitors all year long. Its essential Greekness and lack of razzle-dazzle means reasonable prices, few posers or lager louts and excellent tavernas, but on the other hand it also means that that other island givens – car rentals, excursions, multilingual travel agencies, English breakfasts and English-speakers and 'Greek nights' – are thin on the ground.

History

Inhabited since prehistoric times, Évia was later populated by various peoples from the mainland. The Dryops, brigands from

Getting to Évia

By Sea

Ferries link Évia with the mainland: Rafína to Marmári (1hr, 6–7 times a day), Ag. Marína to Néa Stýra (45mins, at least 5 times a day), Ag. Marína to Almiropótamos (45mins, summer only), Arkítsa to Edipsós (45mins, 12–14 times a day), Oropós to Erétria (every ½hr), Glífa to Agiókambos (30mins, every 2 hrs), and Ag. Konstantínos to Ag. Geórgios (30mins, summer only). Ferries also link Skýros daily with Kými.

Summer **hydrofoils** link Loutrá Edipsoú, Péfki and the other Sporades, and sail from Vólos to Kými and Ag. Konstantínos.

Port authorities: Erétria, t 222 106 2201; Kárystos, t 222 402 2227; Marmári, t 222 403 2222; Edipsós, t 222 602 2464; Almiropótamos, t 222 305 3768; Néa Stýra, t 222 404 1266; Agiókambos, t 222 607 1228; Kými, t 222 202 2606; Ag. Geórgios, t 223 503 3376.

By Road

Évia's middle is linked to Attica by a short bridge over the Evripós Strait; there are buses every 30mins, and trains every hour, from Athens to Chalkís (1½ hrs), a singularly unattractive journey.

The bus terminal in Athens is Liossíon, from where you can also travel direct to Kými, Erétria, Amárynthos, Edipsós or Alivéri; but for Rafína (the main port for Kárystos and Marmári), buses leave from Athens' Mavromatéon terminal.

Getting around Évia

A fairly good bus service connects Chalkís (t 222 102 2640) with all the major villages of Évia.
Car hire on the island is rare outside of Chalkís and Erétria; hire one in Athens or the airport.

Thessaly, occupied the south around the 10th century BC. The Abantes took the centre and eventually came out the island leaders in the 8th–7th centuries BC. They controlled the city state of Chalkís and thus the all-important Evripós Strait, a busy shipping lane in ancient times, when mariners shunned the stormy east coast of Évia. Chalkís' chief rival was Erétria to the south, and both grew into great trading cities that founding colonies as far away as Sicily. Between the two cities lay the Lelantine Plain 'rich in vineyards'; both claimed it and extended their disagreement into international affairs. In 506 BC Chalkís joined Boeotia against Athens, only to be conquered; the Erétrians joined Athens against the Persians, and in retribution were sacked and enslaved in 490 BC by the Persians on their way to Marathon. In the 5th century BC, the whole island came under Athens.

In 338 BC Macedonia took Évia, and the Romans who followed them were the first to use the name of an Eviot tribe, the Graeci, to refer to all the Hellenes. With the conquests of the Fourth Crusade, the Franks gave the fertile island to the King of Thessaloníki, Boniface de Montferrat, who divided it into three baronies, initiating

Évia Festivals

27 May: St John the Russian at Prokópi.
17 July: Ag. Marínas near Kárystos.
26 July: Ag. Paraskeví, long celebrations at Chalkís, Mýli and Rúkia.

First fortnight in Aug: Elymnia cultural festival, Límni.
3 days in Aug: Kárystos wine festival.
15 Aug: At Kými, Oxilithos and many other villages.

The Myrtoan Sea and the Curse on the House of Atreus

Évia, split from the mainland by a blow of Poseidon's trident, was the sea god's favourite island, and he lived with his wife Amphitrite in a fabulous underwater palace just offshore. South of Évia stretches the Myrtoan Sea, named after Myrtilus, son of Hermes, the charioteer of an invincible team of divine horses owned by King Oenomaus. Oenomaus had a beautiful daughter named Hippodameia, and he declared that only the suitor who could outrace his invincible chariot and avoid being transfixed by his brazen spear would have her hand; he set up the bones of the losers in front of his palace and arrogantly boasted that he would build a temple of skulls. This was too much for the gods, and they decided to help one of their favourites, Pelops, defeat Oenomaus. Knowing that Oenomaus' charioteer Myrtilus himself was in love with Hippodameia, Pelops took him aside and proposed a deal: if he would throw the race by replacing the lynchpins in the axles of the king's chariot with wax, then Pelops as winner would share Hippodameia with him. Myrtilus eagerly agreed and events unfolded as predicted: Oenomaus' chariot collapsed in the heat of the race, the king was killed and Pelops was given the princess. He and Myrtilus took her off towards Évia, but Pelops, having never intending to keep his bargain with Myrtilus, kicked him into the sea, where he drowned. As he fell he put a curse on the House of Pelops – better known as the House of Atreus – a curse that fuelled the great tragic cycle of ancient myth and theatre. Hermes named the sea in the honour of his son, and put his image, the Charioteer, in the stars, but his ghost remained unappeased, and haunted the stadium at ancient Olympia, frightening the horses.

an intense, feudal castle-building spree. Over the next hundred years, Évia came under the direct rule of the Venetians, who called it Black Bridge, 'Negroponte', after the span over the Evripós Channel. When the Turks took Negroponte in 1470, they refused to allow the usual puppet Venetian governor to hang around as a tax farmer, but settled the prize themselves, treasuring it more than any other island. It was joined to the Kingdom of Greece in 1828.

Southern Évia

Kárystos

The best way to see all of Évia, with a minimum of backtracking, is to take the ferry from Rafína to **Kárystos** in the southern tip, then work your way up north. The queen of a large sandy bay, with **Mount Óchi** looming in the background, Kárystos with its 5,000 souls is the metropolis on the Myrtoan Sea, renowned for its green cipollino marble and these days for its wine, organic kid and lamb, wild herbs and cheese. Named after its founder, a son of the centaur Chiron, Kárystos so caught the fancy of Greece's first king Otho in 1833 that he renamed it after himself, Othonoúpolis, and declared he would make it the capital of Greece. He summoned an architect named Bierbach down from Bavaria to lay out a grid of wide, straight streets that set Kárystos apart. Whiffs of neoclassical grandeur linger in 19th-century buildings like the **Dimarcheíon** (town hall).

Othonoúpolis fell by the wayside like Otho himself, leaving Kárystos to carry on in its quintessential Greek island way, with back streets of hardware stores, butcher's shops, and *kafeneíons*. The sandy beach stretches off and on for miles and is perfect for

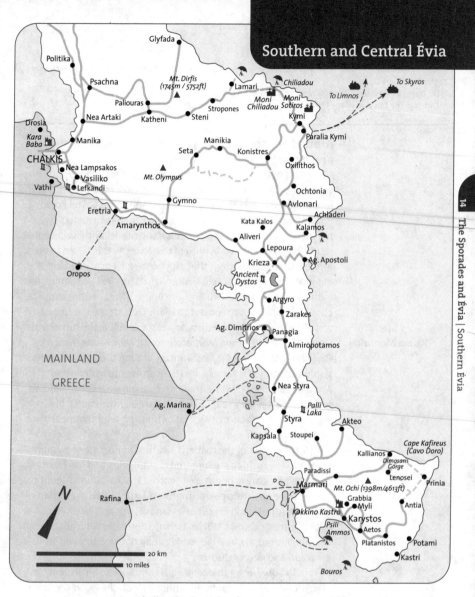

MAINLAND

GREECE

N

20 km
10 miles

snorkelling and windsurfing. Ouzeries hung with octopi heave with Greek visitors on the third or fourth weekend of August, when Kárystos puts on a three-day wine festival, with music, dancing and tomfoolery.

The waterfront is defended by a 14th-century fort, the **Boúrtzi**, its walls incorporating marbles from a 2nd-century AD mausoleum. Opposite, the little but good **Archaeology Museum** in the library-cultural centre houses artefacts from Classical to Roman times, and items from the Dragon Houses (*see* overleaf). The **Deligiorgis Folklore Museum** is also worth a look.

Archaeology Museum
t 222 402 2472; open Tues–Sun 9–5

Deligiorgis Folklore Museum
t 222 402 2115; open mornings only

Getting around Southern Évia

South Évia Tours, 7 Plateía Amalías, t 222 402 9010, Kárystos, hires out cars and can help arrange excursions to the Dimosáris Gorge.

For **buses** in Kárystos, t 222 402 2453; for a **taxi**, t 222 402 6500.

Erétria is the **bus** hub of the south, t 222 906 1602. For a **taxi**, t 222 906 2500.

Around Southern Évia: A Castle, A Dragon House and a Gorge

For most of the Middle Ages, the safest spot for miles around was the huge citadel above Kárystos, built in 1030 by the Byzantines, and rebuilt by the Franks in the 13th century and called **Castel Rosso** (or **Kókkino Kástro**, or Red Castle) by the Venetians, when they purchased Kárystos in 1366. Although the citadel, with its deceptive multi-level layout and labyrinth of entrances, was believed to be impregnable to the extent that only 30 men were needed for its defence, the Turks captured it. Afterwards, 400 Turkish families lived within the walls and the rulers, very unusually, gave Christians the chop if they refused to convert to Islam. Outside are the ruined arches of the Roman aqueduct. In nearby **Grabbiá**, the Turkish ruler Omar Bey lived at **Ktíma Montofolí**, now a wine estate owned by Pavlos and Marianne Karacosta, incorporating the pasha's lovely garden. Montofolí is famous for its award-winning dry white Myrtilos and dessert wines, made from traditional Greek varietals fermented after they've dried in the sun. Near the church of **Ag. Triáda** is a vast cave of Ag. Triáda, housing a subterranean river and waterfall.

Ktíma Montofolí
visits by appt,
t 222 402 5951

Mýli, to the east of the castle, is swathed in lush greenery and serenaded by rushing streams and nightingales, and has plenty of tavernas in a leafy ravine. A well-marked trail leads up in about three hours to the ancient cipollino marble quarries (used in Hadrian's Library in Athens, and exported as far as Egypt and Palestine), where Roman columns still lie in situ, where they were abandoned, seemingly abruptly, as if the workers had downed tools on strike in c. AD 200 and never returned.

From the quarries, a *kalderími* path continues to an ancient chestnut grove and **mountain refuge** (*pick up the key in Kárystos town hall, t 222 402 2246*) – or you can drive up most of the way via Aetós and Metóchi) – and then, through ever more dramatic scenery, to the naked but often cloudy summit of 1,398m (4,613ft) **Mount Óchi**. Although the name means 'Mount No' in modern Greek, it actually derives from the ancient *ohevo*, 'to ride', recalling a legendary coupling of Zeus and Hera on the summit. These days the top is occupied by the little stone **Monastery of Profítis Ilías** and a

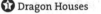 **Dragon Houses**

fascinating **Dragon House** (*Drakónospiti*), the best preserved of the 25 or so scattered on heights of southern Évia – rectangular, built of beautifully fitted ashlar blocks with a 5.5m (18ft) stone over the entrance. The locals once believed they were dragon lairs. No one knows when they were really built – probably by the ancient Dryops, as they were only in the south. So much care went into the building that they probably had religious significance – this one may have been a sanctuary to Hera to celebrate her sacred marriage to Zeus. Archaic to Hellenistic-era (*c.* 8th–4th century BC) items were found under the stones; others say the building could be even older.

🌟 Dimosáris Gorge

North of Mount Óchi a *kalderími* traverses the ferny **Dimosáris Gorge**, a Natura 2000 site and one of the beauty spots of Greece, filled with streams, waterfalls, old chestnuts and plane trees, rare birds of prey and flora unique to southern Évia. You can walk over to the gorge in two hours from the Mount Óchi refuge, or start in **Roúklia**, passing by way of **Lenoseí** and ending up in five hours at **Kallianós Beach**, where there is a handful of rooms to rent in the taverna. There are other lovely walks, too; pick up a map at your hotel or at Kárystos town hall.

East of Kárystos, a grove of venerable plane trees lent their name to **Platanistós**, with a sandy beach, where locals rent rooms, and where, fortunately, plans to build a nuclear power plant in the 1970s fell through. New roads have been bulldozed north of here, making it easier to visit the notorious, tempest-tossed **Cape Kafiréus**, better known by its Venetian name, **Cavo Doro**, where the sea races 'like a funnel' between Ándros and Évia. Here, to avenge the death of his son Palamedes (*see* 'Lésvos', p.566), King Nauplios lit beacons to mislead the Greeks returning from Troy. Cavo Doro has the weather-beaten ruins of a **fort**, repaired in the 1260s by Admiral Likarios, a native of Kárystos and right-hand man of Michael Paleológos, who after the Fourth Crusade restored the Byzantine Empire – beginning at this spot.

Marmári to Erétria

The road north of Kárystos follows the spectacular west coast of Évia, along a corniche at times half a mile over the sea; the cliffs below are a favourite nesting place for hawks and eagles. **Marmári**, named after its quarries of green marble, has a long beach 2km outside town and an old-fashioned little port, sheltered by the nine **Petali islets**, an old hideaway for the king of Greece, various Picasso offspring, and shipping magnates. In summer a local caique makes the tour.

Heading north, there's a partially ruined but easily accessible Dragon House signposted just off the road before **Kápsala**, a village with a little **Folklore Museum**. The next town, **Stýra**, sits on the western slopes of **Mount Kliósi**, controlling the narrowest part of Évia. Ancient Styra (or Dryop) was one of the cities, along with Kárystos and Dystos, founded by the Dryops of Thessaly when they were expelled by the Dorians; the once-important town is

Folklore Museum
open May–Oct Tues, Thurs, Sat and Sun 9–1

mentioned in the *Iliad*'s 'Catalogue of Ships' and did its bit against the Persians at Artemission and Salamis. Stýra has three Dragon Houses surrounding a terrace like a 'P' at **Pallí Láka**, high up the slopes of Kliosi (*accessible by 4x4, followed by a steepish trail and steps*). Further up, the ruined Venetian castle of **Larména** stands on the acropolis, entered via a lonely lintel. Another Dragon House, at a farm at **Aminoú**, has been used as a home (for people), making it one of the oldest occupied houses in the world. Way down below, **Néa Stýra** is a cosy little resort with a sandy beach.

After Néa Stýra, the road rises to **Almiropótamos**, with three historic olive trees as its landmark and few barely developed beaches below around **Panagía**. Further north, just before the crossroads at Lépoura, a dirt road from **Kriezá** leads in 5km to the well-preserved polygonal walls, gate and 11 square towers of 5th-century BC **Dystos** (not to be confused with the modern village of the same name). Spread over a hill by Évia's largest lake (now a massive vegetable patch), you can also trace the foundations of ancient houses set on terraces and streets; the tower was renovated by the Venetians. Fossils of prehistoric beasts have been discovered by the seashore below Kriezá, at **Ag. Apóstoli**, a sheltered little fishing harbour with a small beach tucked in the rocky cliffs of Évia's east coast.

At **Lépoura**, aeolian windmills spin hypnotically on every ridge over the pretty country of olives and vines. The road here forks, one branch heading north to Kými (*see* p.645), the other up the west coast to **Alivéri**, its old red-roofed houses inhabited by workers in the nearby power station. Big pylons and a cement factory protect it from any pretensions, but the tavernas along the waterfront can make for a pleasantly lazy afternoon. Three ancient towns stood nearby: Tamynae above Alivéri, Porthmos by the beach, and **Amárynthos**, mentioned in Linear B tablets and possibly the 'Erétria' mentioned by Homer. Today its landmark is a Venetian tower, **Pyrgáki**, with its door suspended 7m (24ft) above ground. Amárynthos is a little resort with a pair of 12th-century Byzantine churches up on Palaeochóri Hill, **Metamórphosis** and **Kímissi tis Theotókou**. Near Amárynthos, under Évia's own Mount Olympus, **Gymnó** has another Byzantine church, **Zoodóchos Pigí**.

Erétria: Ancient City, Modern Resort

The biggest beach resort in southern Évia, Erétria has long been a favourite of the French. It stands over the ancient city that reached its prime during its quarrel with Chalkís over the lush Lelantine Plain. In the end the two cities decided to leave their weapons at home and meet at a midway point, where a general free-for-all punch-up would decide who got the plain. Erétria lost, then suffered an even worse disaster in 490 BC when the Persians razed the city on

their way to Marathon. But the Erétrians rebuilt, and earned a reputation for their ceramics and later for their school of philosophy,
founded in 320 BC by Plato's student, Menedemes. But in 87 BC
Mithridates of Pontus sacked the city and Erétria was never rebuilt –
until the War of Independence, when refugees from the martyr
island of Psará (*see* p.547) built their new town, originally known as
Néa Psará, complete with fine captains' houses on top of the old.

**Archaeology
Museum**
*Archaíou Theátrou,
t 222 906 2206; open
Tues–Sun 8.30–3*

The excellent **Archaeology Museum**, at the top of Erétria's main
street, is a good place to start. Lefkándi (*see below*) yielded the most
provocative Proto-Archaic (10th century BC) works in Greece – a
wonderful big-eared ceramic centaur and a wheeled horse bearing
pots steal the show. There are prehistoric finds from Amárynthos
and Erétria, and a creepy pot from the 7th-century BC decorated with
warriors and cadavers eating bodies. There are rich grave goods
(bronze cauldrons, swords and gold jewellery) from the Heroön, and
beautiful Archaic sculptures from the pediment of the Temple of
Apollo Daphnephoros, especially Theseus making off with the
Amazon queen Antiope.

The **excavations of ancient Eretria** (*pick up key for Macedonian
tomb at the museum*) have revealed walls of trapezoidal masonry
and a 4th-century BC peristyle palace (complete with a clay bathtub).
Near the elaborate **West Gate**, with a corbelled arch that once
extended over the moat, was the **Temple of Dionysos** and the
theatre, very similar in design to the one in Athens, with a capacity of
6300. Although the upper stone tiers were cannibalized to build the
modern town, the stage has the world's only surviving *deus ex
machina*: an underground passage goes from the *skene* behind the
stage to the orchestra, where 'gods' could suddenly appear to
resolve a tangled plot. A ten-minute walk west of the theatre, the
Macedonian tomb of Erotes has a square chamber holding painted
marble couches, two thrones and a table. From the top of the
theatre it's a 15-minute walk up to Erétria's **acropolis** for an excellent
view over the Lelantine Plain; on a clear day, you can see as far as the
mainland's Mount Parnássos, the home of the Muses. East of the
theatre is the **Gymnasium**, with some plumbing *in situ* on its east
end. Protected in a modern building near Mnisikléous St, the 4th-
century peristyle **House of Mosaics** has beautiful floors depicting
scenes from myth and the *Iliad*. In the centre of modern Erétria lie
the foundations of the Doric **Temple of Apollo Daphnephoros**, 'the
laurel-bearer', who enjoyed a fervent local following. South of here
was the **Agora** with the foundations of a mysterious 5th-century
Tholos with a *bothros* (pit) for offerings.

North of Erétria (2km below Vassilikó off the Chalkís road), **Lefkandí**
is another candidate for the Erétria listed in Homer's 'Catalogue of
Ships'. Inhabited from the Early Helladic period, it is one of the very
few places in Greece to have carried on in style in the Dark Ages,

maintaining trade links with Athens throughout. In the *toumba* (mound) north of Lefkandí's port, archaeologists found a huge building (54m by 10m/177ft by 33ft) from *c.* 1000 BC, built in mud brick over stone foundations, surrounded by a wooden colonnade – not only was it a complete break with Mycenaean styles, but it predated the 'first' peristyle Temple of Hera on Sámos by two centuries. A tomb in the centre had two compartments: one held a man, his bones wrapped in fine cloth in a bronze vase, with his iron sword and spear, and the skeleton of a woman with lavish gold, iron and bronze ornaments. The other had the skeletons of four horses with iron bits. Just who were these conspicuously wealthy people? They were so important that the building was filled in with earth shortly after their burial, perhaps to make a hero mound. The rest of the community prospered, trading gold and ceramics with Athens and Cyprus, until it was mysteriously abandoned in the 8th century BC. Now all you can see is a fenced-off field of weeds.

Where to Stay and Eat in Southern Évia

Kárystos and Around ✉ 34001

Apollon Suites Hotel, Psilí Ámmos Beach, **t** 222 402 2045, *www.apollon suiteshotel.com* (€€€). Central apartments and a heated pool.

Kárystion, in the park near the Boúrtzi, **t** 222 402 2191, *www.karystion.gr* (€€€). Peaceful place, all rooms with sea view, Internet access; and a snack bar, too.

Anemomylos, 'Windmills' on the west beach, 800m from town, **t** 222 402 2987 (€€€–€€). Comfortable bungalows by the beach.

Galaxy, at the end of the seafront, **t** 222 402 2600, *hGalaxy@otenet.gr* (€€). A typical hotel.

★ **Venus Beach »**

Cavo d'Oro, on a side street off the main square, **t** 222 402 2326. Besides the pleasant waterfront tavernas, it's worth hunting out this one that serves excellent food and barrelled wine.

★ **Chryssi Akti »**

Dimitris, 5km away at Pano Aetós, **t** 222 402 2604. Pleasant garden setting amd meats from the grill. *Closed Nov–May*.

Marinos, by the sea, **t** 222 402 4126. The local favourite, serving seafood and baked dishes.

★ **Mouriés »**

Mouriés, 15km away at Paradissi, **t** 222 402 2604. An institution since 1930, serving delicious game dishes in season (venison, pheasant, etc.) and other delights, with barrelled wine and home-made desserts.

Marmári ✉ 34013

Marmari Bay, above town, **t** 222 403 1301, *www.marmaribay.gr* (€€€–€€). Big new hotel with a pool, tennis, Internet and more. *Open April–Oct*.

Gikas Apartments, **t** 222 403 2151, *www. gikasapartments.com* (€€). Tidy studios with balconies, some sleeping four.

Néa Stýra ✉ 34015

Castello Rosso, near the Venus Beach, **t** 222 404 1781, *www.castellorosso-hotel.gr* (€€€–€€). Nice small hotel with a pool, 50m from the beach.

Sunday, **t** 222 404 1300 (€€). Family-run hotel with big green awnings on the balconies overlooking the sea.

Venus Beach, 2km from town, **t** 222 404 1226, *www.greek-tourism.gr/evoia/venus-beach* (€€). Friendly owner and bungalows in pleasant garden setting with a pool, restaurant and beach.

Chryssi Akti, in Nimborió to the south, **t** 222 405 1207. Popular restaurant owned by fishermen who know how to cook – it's so good, Athenians have been known to pop over on their boats.

Akteon, on the beach, **t** 222 404 1261 (€). Typical small Greek hotel, also with a restaurant, bar and grill.

Akroyiali, on the waterfront past the ferry docks. Ouzerie/taverna serving good dishes in attractive setting.

Amárynthos ✉ 34006

Flisvos, t 222 903 6385 (€€). Small, simple hotel. *Open all year.*

Dionysos, in Gymno, t 222 909 1239. One of nearly a dozen tavernas for carnivores in Gymno, all dedicated to succulent grilled lamb chops (*paidákia*), pork chops and steaks.

Limanaki, t 222 903 6609. Excellent fish taverna on the water, with an extensive selection of starters.

Erétria/Malakónda ✉ 34008

Erétria has many hotels, as does Malakónda (just east). Erétria is very average on the restaurant front.

Malaconda Beach Vogue Club, Malakónda, t 222 906 8120, *www. airotel.gr* (€€€€). Prettily nestled among the olives and cypresses, with a lovely swimming pool. *Open Mar–Oct.*

Palmariva Erétria Beach, 2km from Erétria, t 222 906 2411, *www.palmariva. gr* (€€€€–€€€). With all a seaside resort hotel should have – sea sports, pools, tennis courts, extensive gym, large disco and a wide choice of bars.

Eretria Village, 5km from Erétria, t 222 904 1000, *www.holidaysinevia.gr* (€€€). Big resort, great for families, with a bus stop just outside.

Petit Village, on the beach 2km from Erétria, t 222 906 0070, *www. petitvillage.gr* (€€€–€€). Low-key, sprawling bungalows in a garden setting with a pool and friendly staff.

Delfis, 8 Archaíou Theátrou, t 222 906 2380 (€€–€). An old, comfortable favourite; booking is essential.

Dreams Island, on the wooded peninsula with sandy beaches, t 222 906 1224 (€€–€). Fancy name for a complex of 2 hotels, bungalows, restaurant, bar, barbecue and disco with a not-so-glorified campsite atmosphere, run by the town of Erétria.

Xenia, Perzonissi, t 222 906 1202 (€). The local bargain.

Évia Camping, at Malakónda, t 222 106 8081. The most shade and facilities.

La Cubana, on the waterfront at 44 Archaíou Theátrou, t 222 906 1665. This has a pretty setting and fresh fish.

 Delfis »

14

The Sporades and Évia | Central Évia

Central Évia

The West Coast: Chalkís and Around

Big bustling **Chalkís** or Chalkída (pop. 60,000), the capital of Évia, just in commuter range of Athens, occupies the narrowest point of the Evripós Strait, only 40m (130ft) from the mainland. Its location has been the source of its prosperity, not least through its potential for blocking ancient sea trade between Athens and the north; copper (*chalkós*) was another early source of wealth. The original city was located at Maníka, 5km northwest, where an 800-acre Proto-Helladic settlement (2900–2300 BC) was found. The home of the 'great-hearted Abantes' in the *Iliad*, by Archaic times the city had so many colonies in northern Greece that it gave its name to the Chalkidikí peninsula; in Italy it founded Messina, Reggio Calabria and Cumae. By the 7th century BC it had asserted its position over Erétria and has never looked back.

The city's first bridge was built in 411 BC (the modern sliding **drawbridge** dates from 1962, although now most of the traffic uses the big suspension bridge south of town), but before you cross it, admire the views of Chalkís and Évia from the walls of the Turkish **Karababa** ('black father') **Castle** built over Chalkís' ancient acropolis in 1686 and unsuccessfully besieged by Morosini two years later.

Karababa Castle
open Thurs–Tues 8–3; closed Wed

South, between Váthi and the bridge, the **Temple of Artemis at Aulis** and its sacred spring have been excavated. Here the Greek fleet gathered before sailing to Troy, and was becalmed until Agamemnon sacrificed his own daughter Iphigenia to Artemis (the subject of one of Euripides' surviving tragedies, *Iphigenia in Aulis*).

From Chalkís' trendy waterfront cafés you can sit and ponder the mystery of the **Evripós Channel**; the dangerous currents change direction every few hours, sometimes only once a day, on rare occasions 14 times day, a phenomenon that so baffled Aristotle, who came to Chalkís to live in his mother's house, that he threw himself into the waters in frustration (although others say he died in bed of stomach disease). Current (sorry!) thought has it that there are two separate streams in the Evripós, and a host of factors determines which dominates at a given moment. The constant flushing keeps the water very clean at the **town beaches**. One beach, on the north end of the waterfront, stretches under the neoclassical 'Red House', where King Peter of Serbia stayed for six months in 1916. The **Archaeology Museum** houses beautiful items discovered in Erétria, including a headless statue of Athena, Archaic sculptures from the Temple of Apollo Daphnephoros, and a bas-relief of Diónysos, as well as Cycladic idols, a stone phallus, and a Hellenistic horse head.

Archaeology Museum
Leof. Venizélou, t 222 102 5131; open Tues–Sun 8.30–3; adm

The other sights of Chalkís are concentrated south of the bridge, in the **Kástro**, the old Turkish quarter, its entrance marked by a large 16th-century **mosque** with a marble fountain (but minus its minaret and porch). Just south is **Ag. Paraskeví**, one of oldest churches in Greece, a Byzantine basilica from the 5th–8th century converted by the Crusaders into a Gothic cathedral with a sturdy campanile (the original façade collapsed in a 19th-century earthquake). The interior is an architectural collage, full of 14th-century inscriptions and coats of arms. Every year in late July, a large market for the feast of Ag. Paraskeví enlivens Chalkís for 10 days, attracting bargain-hunters from miles around, while the lovelorn take the opportunity to beseech the icon of the saint for their heart's desire; in the old days they would press a coin against the icon, and if it stuck, it meant their love would not go unrequited. Nearby, in the last surviving bit of the Venetian fort, a delightful little **Museum of Folk Art** contains traditional festival costumes, religious icons, the interior of a traditional Greek home, a printing press from the 1920s, and an intimate portrayal of village life from long ago.

Museum of Folk Art
Skalkóta St, t 222 102 1817; open Wed–Sun 10–1

Chalkís' Jewish population goes back an estimated 2,500 years; the **synagogue** at 27 Kótsou, the main street from the bridge, was built in the mid-19th century, but re-uses a number of marble fragments from the original. In the old Jewish quarter, on the north side of town, off Avantón Street, there is a marble bust of Mórdechai Frízis of Chalkís, the first Greek officer killed in the Second World War.

Synagogue
27 Kótsou; open after 6pm

Beaches North of Chalkís, Mount Dírfis and Stení

Buses from Chalkís run to the busy, shingly beaches to the north, all with views across to the mainland: **Néa Artáki**, **Paralía Politikón**, and, tucked under the cliffs, **Dáfni**. Two of Évia's most distinctive whitewashed villages are just inland: **Politiká** with a late Byzantine church, castle and cosy square, and **Psachná** with another castle.

In easy striking distance (25km) of Chalkís, **Dírfis** is Évia's highest peak at 1,745m (5,725ft), covered with snow into May. Wrapped in chestnut and pine forests, it supports a surprising quantity of alpine flora. You can take a bus as far as **Stení**, a delightful village of wooden houses, chalets and waterfalls amid a lovely chestnut forest. From Stení there's a well-marked if rather strenuous path to the summit of Dírfis, 1½ hours from the **EOS refuge** at **Líri**, run by Chalkís' Alpine Club (*to book*, **t** *222 805 1285*). Non-walkers can drive the magnificently scenic road that goes over the pass, towards **Strópones**; it winds precipitously down to the east coast to **Lámari**, then over a rough road to the splendid beach of **Chiliadoú** (*see* below).

The East Coast: Kými and Around

At **Lépoura** (*see* p.640) the main road for Kými heads north. A bit beyond the crossroads, to the left, **Katakalós** has a well-preserved (and unique for Évia) **Mycenaean *tholos* tomb** complete with a *dromos* passage to the entrance. Further on, roads descend to the beaches at **Kálamos**, where you can jump off rock formations into the sea, and Achladerí. Inland, **Avlonarí** is a fine old village topped by a small Venetian fortress, the best preserved on the island; **Ochtoniá** too is crammed beneath a castle, overlooking a set of quiet sandy beaches. After the Ochtoniá turn-off, the main road plunges and writhes through a lovely pastoral valley, dotted with Frankish towers to **Oxílithos**, 'pointy rock', named after an extinct volcano with a church on the summit.

Kými, the 'Balcony of the Aegean' and port for Skýros (and Límnos), is a delightful low-key resort, lush, surrounded by vines and fig orchards, perched on a shelf high above the sea; some say its name is derived from *koumi*, 'I rise' in Hebrew, describing the town's grandstand view of the dawn. Many Greeks have villas in the wooded hills, including some ambitious *nouveau riche* designs; the more traditional stone houses are in the local *koumiotíki* style. The

Museum of Popular Art
t 222 202 2011; open 9–1 and 5–7

excellent **Museum of Popular Art**, in a meoclassical mansion, houses folk art, costumes, tools, embroideries and furnishings, Balkan War uniforms, the town's famous silks and a display on famous son Dr George Papanikoláou (d. 1962), who invented and gave the first syllable of his name to the cervical cancer test. Pretty footpaths and the road wind down 4km to the port, **Paralía Kýmis**, near a beach sheltered by pampas grass. It's not particularly inspiring, but there are lovely beaches 6km northeast at **Chiliádou**, 'the thousandth', named after a rather picturesque abandoned monastery, founded by Empress Theodora in the 830s after the end of Iconoclasm; apparently she had already founded 999 others. North of Kými a path leads to the sheer rocky ledge that was the acropolis of Homeric Kyme Phyrkontis. The stone of its temples went into the precipitous Byzantine/Frankish castle of Apokledí and the handsome **Moní Sótiros** (1634), with a beautiful tile roof (*women only admitted*).

⭐ **Kapetános >>**

⭐ **Kentrikon >**

Useful Information in Central Évia

Tourist police: 32 El. Venizélou, Chalkís, t 222 107 7777.

Where to Stay and Eat in Central Évia

Chalkís ✉ 34100

Lucy, 10 Voudoúris, on the waterfront, t 222 102 3831, *www.lucy-hotel.gr* (€€€). Long the smart choice in town.

John's, near the Lucy, 9 Angéli Govioú, t 222 102 4996 (€€€–€€). Comfortable rooms and private parking.

Paliria, 2 Leof. Venizélou, t 222 102 8001 (€€€–€€). Modern building in the centre, overlooking the Evripós Strait, with a roof garden.

Kentrikon, 5 Angéli Govioú, t 222 102 2375, *www.geocities.com/hotel_kentrikon* (€). Overlooking the Evripós and in business since 1928, now with Internet access, satellite TV and air-conditioning, but with old-fashioned service from the helpful owners.

Bouka Beach Club, just over the bridge in Drosiá, t 222 106 2150, *www.bouka beachclub.gr* (€). Trendy new campsite; pools, water sports, concerts, diving.

La Fiamma, by the sea at Per. Stávrou and Tziardíni Sts, t 222 107 5006. Cool retro restaurant serving Italian classics.

Fyki, along the waterfront at Néa Lámpsakos, t 222 102 1444. People drive out here to feast on fish, just a few metres away from the briny deep.

Stavedo, 1 Karaóli St, t 222 107 7977 (€20–30). Upscale restaurant-cum-bar on the waterfront, that specializes in tasty Mediterranean cuisine.

Tsaf, Plateía Faviérou, t 222 108 0070. Chálkis' favourite ouzerie, serving up a mean *saganáki*.

To 5 F, 61 Evaías, t 222 108 5731. Classic seafood taverna.

Kapetános, Plateía Ag. Trýfona, 3km south in Néa Lámpsakos, t 222 102 8191. One of best ouzeries in Greece.

Steni ✉ 34014

Dirphys, in the centre of the village, t 222 805 1217 (€€). Small and intimate *pension*. Open all year.

Steni, t 222 805 1221 (€€). Similar to the Dirphys Hotel; slightly higher prices.

On the edge of town are a row of *psitariá*, serving cheap grilled meats.

Achladerí (Korasída) ✉ 34011

Avra, t 222 204 1932, *www.web-greece. gr/apartments/avra* (€€€–€€). New studios, with a bar and pool, on an otherwise empty coast.

Oxílithos ✉ 34011

Stomio Beach, t 222 207 1251 (€€). Newish apartment complex with 22 self-catering flats. Open May–Oct.

Faros, Stómio, t 222 202 1550. Taverna with a view over the sea, specializing in stewed dishes, 'lemoned' veal, and grilled meats. Closed Mon–Fri in Nov–April.

Kými ✉ 34003

Valledi Village, Paralía Kýmis, t 222 202 4210, *www.valledivillage.gr* (€€€–€€). Spacious new apartments, some with mezzanines, with a bar and pool.

Beis, by the quay, t 222 202 2604 (€€). Large, if rather anonymous hotel often used by people sailing out to Skýros.

Corali, by the sea t 222 202 2212, *www. coralihotel.gr* (€€). Pleasant hotel of stone and wood, with sea views.

Panorama, 7km south in Platána, t 222 207 1252, *www.web-greece.gr/hotels/panorama* (€€). Overlooking the sea, new and tidy studios.

The waterfront tavernas serve good, standard Greek fare.

Northern Évia

Much of the northern half of Évia is so mountainous, lush and green that you could be forgiven for thinking you were in Austria – until you end up on the coast, with long stretches of beach lined with whitewashed houses and rose-filled gardens.

Prokópi and Around

Heading north from Chalkís, after **Psachná** the road rises higher and higher into the mountains, permeated with the fragrance of deep green pine forests; beehives everywhere attest to the potency of the local herbs and wild flowers, and the honey offered in roadside stands comes close to nectar. Tavernas with outdoor terraces take advantage of the most breathtaking panoramic views. **Pagóndas** is an example of a typical mountain settlement.

Further north, a striking castle piled on a nearly inaccessible precipice signals **Prokópi**, once seat of the local Turkish *aga*, set over magnificent wooded ravines, with views over the Sporades islands. This is prime picnicking territory; if extra thrills are called for, wobble over the ravines on the rickety wooden suspension bridges. After the Greek War of Independence, Turkish rulers were allowed to sell their property, and, as most Greeks were dirt-poor, foreigners were encouraged to buy. So in 1832 philhellene Edward Noel, a relative of Byron, borrowed money from Lady Byron to purchase the Achmet Aga Estate in Prokópi – and unusually in Greece, the family kept it all these years, renaming it **Candili** after the nearby mountain; Noel had set up the North Euboean Foundation to provide healthcare and education for Greek refugees during the Greek War of Independence. His granddaughter married Philip Baker, a Quaker, who was fluent in seven languages and chosen three times to represent Britain in the Olympics. He was the founder of the Friends' Ambulance Unit in the First World War, and was so appalled by the carnage in France and Italy that he spent the rest of his life campaigning for disarmament, working to found the League of Nations and later the UN; in 1958 he wrote the influential *The Arms Race* and in 1959 he won the Nobel Peace Prize. His son, Francis Noel-Baker, is the current owner.

Most of the Greeks in the village come from the fantastical-sounding Cappadocian town of Ürgüp (known in Greek as Prokópi) and came over in the 1923 population exchange. They brought with them their holy relics: the bones of St John the Russian, a soldier in the Tsar's army who was captured by the Turks and sold as a slave in Ürgüp (1730), then canonized by the Russian Orthodox Church (in 1962). St John attracts his fair share of pilgrims each year at his church, **Ag. Ioánnes Róssou**.

From Prokópi, a decent paved road to the east leads steeply down, through thick forests of magnificent old plane trees, pines and firs

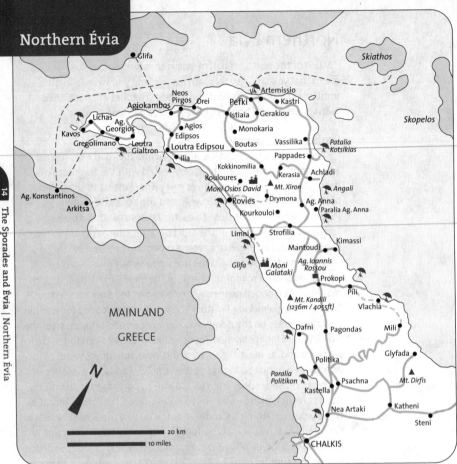

dotted with many beehives, to **Píli**, set in beautiful rocky mountain scenery. There are plenty of authentic tavernas and, all around, lovely old traditional houses with goats in the garden alternating with the usual concrete monstrosities. The sandy bay below looks across to Skópelos, but, if you want somewhere even less civilized, brave the rough road east along the coast to the pebbly beach beyond **Vlachiá**.

Continuing north through **Mantóudi**, with its very pretty central square and great ouzerie, the road is bordered by countless fields of cotton and corn. At **Strofiliá** the road forks west to Límni (*see* below) and then up to Loutrá Edipsoú, while the main road continues to **Ag. Ánna**. This is a traditional village, near the beautiful **Arápis gorge** and two very long and attractive beaches, **Paralía Ag. Ánna**, 7km of golden sand, and **Angáli**, just to the north. **Vassiliká**, further up the coast, looks directly across to Skiáthos. Inland, **Kerasiá** is the centre of a 10-million-year-old **petrified forest** that stretches from Ag. Ánna to **Pappádes**, where excavators found a rhino skull, short-necked giraffes, small horses and the *ihthetherea*, the ancestor of the hyena.

Getting around Northern Évia

Resorts around the Top of Évia

The north coast of Évia, dotted with many fine beaches, looks over to the Pélion Peninsula and the mainland; Greek families settle in here for the summer, which makes finding a room for only one or two days problematic. **Artemíssio** witnessed the first but indecisive naval battle between Athens and Xerxes' Persians in 480 BC. Near the shore are the ruins of the vast **Temple of Artemis Proseoa**, although the greatest treasure in the area was a shipwreck of ancient bronzes, discovered in 1928, yielding Athens' National Archaeology Museum's splendid *Poseidon* (or Zeus) and the *Cape Artemisseon Jockey*. Continuing west, **Péfki** is a port with a big sand and pebble beach popular with families and Hungarian and Slovak tourists. Recently a Temple of Artemis was discovered here, but right under the cemetery; excavations will proceed once the dead are relocated. The town has splendid views of Skiáthos, which you can reach by hydrofoil in summer. Inland, escape the heat at **Gerakioú**, a pretty green village with plenty of springs.

Cattle belonging to Hera grazed at **Istiaía**; Homer described it as 'rich in vines'. It was founded by Thessalians who thumbed their noses at Athens so often that Pericles captured the town and booted out the inhabitants, and then repopulated it with Athenians. Although set in an amphitheatre of rolling hills, the Athenian colonists didn't find Istiaía to their liking, preferring to found nearby Oréi instead; when they in turn were driven out by the Spartans, the Istianians finally returned.

The Athenians may have been right: dishevelled **Oréi** is still a nicer place to while away a few hours on the pleasant waterfront under the feathery tamarisks. By the **church** near the sea is the town's claim to fame: a superb charging Hellenistic **marble bull**, dedicated to the Macedonian Dimitrios Poliorkitis, 'the Besieger' (*see* 'Rhodes', p.406), found offshore in 1962, which in turn is protected by a display case. Just outside town is a Venetian *kastro*. West of Oréi, **Néos Pírgos**, populated after 1922 by Greeks from Pirgos near Istanbul, is an attractive little resort with a little rocky islet, the **Nisiotíssa**, topped by a ruin for decoration, and further on, the beach at **Agiókambos**, another ferry port, has more seafood tavernas.

Loutrá Edipsóu and the Lichada Peninsula

Set in a wooded bay, **Loutrá Edipsoú** (ΛΟΥΤΡΑ ΑΙΔΗΨΟΥ) is one of Greece's best-known spas. Eighty sulphurous springs squirt out of the ground at up to 160°F, cascading over the rocks, staining them orange. Known in antiquity as the Baths of Heracles (the ruins are next to the EOT spa, which also houses a small archaeological collection), these waters have treated a variety of complaints, including rheumatism, gout, arthritis, gallstones and even bouts of depression. The ancients believed the source was connected under the sea with the hot springs at Thermopylae; Aristotle praised the waters, and the gouty Sulla, Augustus and Hadrian called in for lengthy soaks. As spas have returned to fashion, the old EOT complex has been upstaged by the **Thermae Sylla Spa-Wellness Complex** (*see* 'Where to Stay'). Outside the baths, Loutrá Edipsoú has its own quirky charm mixed in with the night-time clamour of Greek music, packed bars and noisy Athenians promenading the leafy avenues until early morning. It also has a long **beach**, and the possibility of day trips to Skiáthos, Alónissos and Skópelos.

At the far side of the bay, on the westerly Lichádа Peninsula, there's a second, more modest spa, **Loutrá Giáltron**, with a frescoed church, beach, boats and old windmill. Club Med has had to import lorry-loads of sand to create its private hideaway at **Gregolímano**, but the immense stretch of soft sand and pebbles at **Kávos** is open to everyone and anyone. Watch out for noticeboards announcing the ferociously fast-changing tides, which, though fascinating to watch, can be dangerous. Nearby, **Ag. Geórgios** is a laid-back fishing village and port; its eponymous church makes an attractive focus for its cheery waterfront. There are plenty of places to picnic and snooze under the plane trees. Much to everyone's delight, a family of monk seals have set up housekeeping on the little **Lichádа islets**, a favourite of local divers.

South of Loutrá Edipsóu: Roviés and Límni

The coastal road south of Loutrá Edipsoú, where falling bits of cliff are a constant menace, passes the seaside villages and beaches of **Ília** and **Roviés**, the latter lush and pretty and immersed in olive groves, with a pebble beach with views across to the Pélion Peninsula. Fine 17th-century frescoes await 13km inland at the beautiful **Moní Ósios Davíd tou Géronta**, founded in 1550. The monks there sell herbal teas, rusks and dried figs. Other pretty places to visit inland are the abandoned village of **Koúloures**, immersed in trees, and the waterfall at **Drymónas**, where forest paths, walkways and bridges have been laid out along the streams.

Límni (ancient Elymnion), 15km south of Roviés, is many an old hand's favourite place on Évia: a friendly old whitewashed fishing village with mediocre beaches and pine forests. The waterfront is just right for lazing and watching the world go by. According to myth, Zeus brought Hera here during their honeymoon, although the temple that once marked the spot keeled over in an earthquake. The Palaeo-Christian chapel of **Zoodóchos Pigí** was built on top of it, but its pretty mosaic floor is now in the charming **Historic and**

Historic and
Folklore Museum
*t 222 703 1335; open
Mon–Sat 9–1,
Sun 10.30–1*

Nautilos Museum
*t 222 703 1900;
ring for hours*

Folklore Museum. The new **Nautilos Museum** is also worth a look, with its superb collection of sea shells.

A 12km road south of Límni passes the pretty sand and pebble beaches of **Glífa** on the way to **Moní Ag. Nikoláos** (or Galatáki), a Byzantine monastery (now a convent) built *c*. 1200 in a beautiful, peaceful setting high over the sea. A temple dedicated to Poseidon once stood here, bits of which can be seen on the monastery's *parvis*, along with a Venetian tower. The church has fascinating 16th-century frescoes, including portraits of the two sea captains who became the monastery's patrons after they were shipwrecked nearby and saved by divine intervention.

Useful Information in Northern Évia

Tourist police, in the spa, 3 Okeanídon, Edipsós, **t** 222 602 4655. *Open summer only*.

Where to Stay and Eat in Northern Évia

★ **Candili** ❯

Prokópi ✉ 34004

Candili, **t** (UK) 0788 7991931, *www.candili.co.uk* (€€€). Twelve rooms on the idyllic Noel-Baker estate. Lots of attention is also given to creative culinary delights in the evening, often served on the beautiful patio. There's a pool, a huge playground and extensive gardens to keep the children entertained (substantial family suites are available).

Paralía Ag. Ánna ✉ 34010

Glaros, **t** 222 709 7000. Some of the best lobster spaghetti on Évia and other seafood as well. *Open all year*.

Armata, **t** 222 709 7200. Delicious seafood *mezédes* next to the waves. *Closed Oct–April*.

Péfki ✉ 34200

Ilio Studios, on the road to Aremissío, **t** 222 604 0551, *www.fygiasilios.gr* (€€€). New, traditionally styled studios with a pool, Internet, bar, gym and playground, 5mins from the beach.

Amaryllis, on the waterfront, **t** 222 604 1222 (€€). A pleasant, comfortable hotel with friendly owners who are more than happy to impart useful tips and stories. *Open July–Sept*.

Galini, east end of the waterfront, **t** 222 604 1208 (€€). Kitted out with cheery furniture; there are lovely sea-views from many of the rooms. The English-speaking owners, Costas and Anna Maria, also own the self-service restaurant.

Camping Péfki, **t** 222 604 1121. Good facilities and plenty of shade. Bungalows are available near the campsite, for those requiring a little more comfort. *Open April–Sept*.

Balaoúras, **t** 222 604 0693. Best fish in Péfki, cooked on charcoal. *Closed Oct–Easter*.

To Kapplió tis Ménias, at Spitáki, **t** 222 604 0698 (€25). Famous restaurant where stars of Greek cinema have been spotted trying the playful Continental dishes. *Closed Oct–May*.

Grigri. For ouzo and *mezédes*.

Oréi ✉ 34012

Byzantium, 100m from the beach, **t** 222 607 1600 (€€). Central and reasonable.

Evia, **t** 222 607 1263 (€€). The main option in the centre of town.

Leda, **t** 222 607 1180 (€€). Modern studios within easy walking distance of a generous stretch of sand.

Porto Kairis, right on the pebble beach, **t** 222 607 1055 (€€). A great location for this hotel with its little dipping pool.

Akroyalis, Néo Pírgos, **t** 222 607 1435 (€€–€). Comfortable, and very convenient for a dash down to the beach to fit in that early-morning swim.

Loutrá Edipsoú ✉ 34300

Thermae Sylla Spa-Wellness Hotel, on the waterfront, **t** 222 606 0100, *www.thermaesylla.gr* (€€€€€). Fabulously

(★) Avra Spa >

extravagant, palatial spa hotel, equipped with hydrotherapy treatment for every type of ailment. In addition to this, it has extremely well-appointed rooms and a grand restaurant, **Mesogeios**, serving delicious (not to mention healthy) meals.

Avra Spa, next door to the Aegli, t 222 602 2226, *www.avraspahotel.gr* (€€€€). Built in 1922 and beautifully restored with relaxing atmosphere, roof garden, indoor pool and range of hydrotherapy treatment facilities.

Aegli, on the waterfront, t 222 602 2216 (€€€). Perfect for simply wallowing in the faded spa atmosphere. Equipped with mini-spas in the basement and in high season, clients have to queue from 5am to get their treatment. *Open May–Oct.*

(★) Vaterí >>

Capri, 45 25th Martíou, t 222 602 2496, *http://caprihotel.info/en* (€). Great for budget travellers with aches – simple rooms, mostly with sea views in a friendly hotel with thermal baths.

Geórgos, 2 Thermopótamou Edipsós (opposite the bus station), t 222 602 3285 (€). Small and central.

(★) Armenizontas >

Armenizontas, 22 Martioú, t 222 602 3096. Atmospheric taverna, with lots of choice, *rembétiko* music and a wood stove in the winter.

Glaros, on the sea in Loutrá's suburb of Ag. Nikólaos, t 222 606 0240. Come here if you are in a fishy mood, but there's grilled meats as well.

Ag. Geórgios ✉ 34300

Alexandros, on the waterfront, t 222 603 3208 (€€). Attractive hotel with sea and mountain views from most of the rooms. *Open June–Sept.*

Kyneon, t 222 603 3066 (€€). Similar, sharing the wonderful views. *Open April–Oct.*

Roviés ✉ 34005

Besides the following, Roviés is full of rooms to rent.

(★) Eleónas >

Eleónas, t 222 707 1619, *www.eleonas hotel.com* (€€€). Beautiful agrotourism hotel and apartments in a peaceful old olive grove; great for families. Learn about olives – or how to use a loom. Organic food is served at breakfast and dinner.

Alexandrides, a few steps from the beach, t 222 707 1272 (€€). Austere rooms in one of the oldest hotels here, but a winner for its shady gardens.

Souris, t 222 707 1233 (€€–€). Although it means 'mouse' in French, we couldn't find any. Simple and open all year.

Camping Roviés, t 222 701 1120, *www.campingevia.com.* Immaculate campsite right by the sea. *Open April–Oct.*

Limni ✉ 34005

Ostria, 1km from town at Kochyli, t 222 703 2248, *www.holidayshop.gr/ostria* (€€€). Ten comfortable apartments surrounded by greenery, with pool and restaurant, close to a pebble beach.

Vaterí, on a hilltop 2km from town t 222 703 2493 (€€€). Wonderful little *pension* run by locals Yiánnis and Katerína Bloukídi; lovely views,

Concert Apartments, 1km from town, by the beach, t 222 703 2569, *www. concertapartments.gr* (€€€–€€). Complex in a 200-year-old olive grove next to the Cochilia theatre, across the road from a beach.

Livaditis Beach, on Sipiáda Beach, t 222 703 1640, *www.livaditisbeach.com* (€€€–€€). New complex of studios and apts, linked to the centre by a minibus. The same family own the waterfront Profani Taverna in central Limni.

Límni, at the south end of the bay, t 222 703 1316 (€€–€). Basic rooms, some with balconies looking out onto the water.

Plaza, t 222 703 1235 (€€–€). There since 1840, basic hotel with plenty of character.

O Platanos, on the waterfront, t 222 703 1686. Offering excellent grilled fish and meat dishes laid out under the huge reassuring limbs of a plane tree.

Astron, 3km away in Thési Katoúnia, t 222 703 1487. In business since 1961 and the best in the area for grilled fish and meat. *Closed Mon–Fri in winter.*

Language

Greek holds a special place as the oldest spoken language in Europe, going back at least 4,000 years. From the ancient language, Modern Greek, or Romaíka, developed into two forms: the purist or *katharévousa*, and the popular, or Demotic *demotikí*, the language of the people. These days few purist words are spoken but you will see the old *katharévousa* on shop signs and official forms. Even though the bakery is called the *foúrnos* the sign over the door will read ΑΡΤΟΠΟΛΕΙΟΝ, 'bread-seller', while the general store will be the ΠΑΝΤΟΠΟΛΕΙΟΝ, 'seller of all'. You'll still see the pure form on wine labels as well. At the end of the 18th century, writers felt the common language wasn't good enough; archaic forms were brought back and foreign ones replaced. Upon independence, this somewhat stilted, artificial construction called *katharévousa* became the official language of books, documents and even newspapers.

The more vigorous and natural Demotic soon began to creep back; in 1901 Athens was shaken by riots and the government fell when the New Testament appeared in *demotikí*; in 1903 several students were killed in a fight with the police during a *demotikí* performance of Aeschylus. When the fury subsided, it looked as if the Demotic would win out until the Papadópoulos government (1967–74) made it part of its puritan 'moral cleansing' of Greece to revive the purist *katharévousa*. The debate was settled in 1978 when Demotic was made the official tongue.

Greeks travel so far and wide that even in the most remote places there's usually someone who speaks English. Usually spoken with great velocity, Greek isn't a particularly easy language to pick up by ear, but it is very helpful to know at least the alphabet – so that you can find your way around – and a few basic words and phrases.

For food vocabulary, *see* pp.48–50.

The Greek Alphabet

See also 'Transliteration and Pronunciation', p.66.

Pronunciation			English Equivalent
Α	α	álfa	short *a* as in 'father'
Β	β	víta	v
Γ	γ	gámma	guttural *g* or *y* sound
Δ	δ	délta	always a hard *th* as in 'though'
Ε	ε	épsilon	short *e* as in 'bet'
Ζ	ζ	zíta	z
Η	η	íta	long *e* as in 'bee'
Θ	θ	thíta	soft *th* as in 'thin'
Ι	ι	yóta	long *e* as in 'bee'; sometimes as *y* in 'yet'
Κ	κ	káppa	k
Λ	λ	lámtha	l
Μ	μ	mi	m
Ν	ν	ni	n
Ξ	ξ	ksi	*x* as in 'ox'
Ο	ο	ómicron	*o* as in 'cot'
Π	π	pi	p
Ρ	ρ	ro	r
Σ	σ/ς	sigma	s
Τ	τ	taf	t
Υ	υ	ípsilon	long *e* as in 'bee'
Φ	φ	fi	f
Χ	χ	chi	*ch* as in 'loch'
Ψ	ψ	psi	*ps* as in 'stops'
Ω	ω	oméga	*o* as in 'cot'

Diphthongs and Consonant Doubles

		English Equivalent
ΑΙ	αι	short *e* as in 'bet'
ΕΙ	ει / ΟΙ οι	*i* as in 'machine'
ΟΥ	ου	*oo* as in 'too'
ΑΥ	αυ	*av* or *af*
ΕΥ	ευ	*ev* or *ef*
ΗΥ	ηυ	*iv* or *if*
ΓΓ	γγ	*ng* as in 'angry'
ΓΚ	γκ	hard *g*; *ng* within word
ΝΤ	ντ	*d*; *nd* within word
ΜΠ	μπ	*b*; *mp* within word

Greekspeak

Sign language is an essential part of Greek life. Greekspeak for 'no' is usually a click of the tongue, accompanied by raised eyebrows and a tilt of the head backwards. 'Yes' is usually indicated by a forward nod, head tilted to the side. If someone doesn't hear you or understand you they will shake their heads from side to side and say 'Oríste?'

A circular movement of the right hand usually implies something very good or in great quantities. Greek people also use exclamations which mean a lot, like po, po, po!, an expression of disapproval and derision; brávo comes in handy for praise while ópa! is useful for whoops! look out! or watch it!; sigá sigá means slowly, slowly; éla!, come or get on with you; kíta! look.

Useful Phrases

Yes	Né/málista (formal)	Ναί/μάλιστα
No	Óchi	Όχι
I don't know	Then kséro	Δέν ξέρω
I don't understand... (Greek)	Then katalavéno... (elliniká)	Δέν καταλαβαίνω... (Ελληνικαν)
Does someone speak English?	Milái kanis angliká?	Μιλάει κανείς αγγλικά?
Go away	Fíyete	Φύγετε
Help!	Voíthia!	Βοήθεια!
My friend	O fílos moo (m)	Ο φίλος μου
	Ee fíli moo (f)	Η φίλη μου
Please	Parakaló	Παρακαλώ
Thank you (very much)	Evcharistó (pára polí)	Ευχαριστώ (πάρα πολυν)
You're welcome	Parakaló	Παρακαλώ
It doesn't matter	Thén pirázi	Δεν πειράζει
OK, alright	Endáxi	Εντάξει
Of course	Vevéos	Βεβαίως
Excuse me (as in 'sorry')	Signómi	Συγγνώμη
Pardon? Or, from waiters, What do you want?	Oríste?	Ορίστε?
What is your name?	Pos sas léne? (pl & formal)	Πώς σάς λένε?
	Pos se léne? (singular)	Πώς σέ λένε?
How are you?	Ti kánete? (formal/pl)	Τί κάνεται?
	Ti kanis? (singular)	Τί κάνεις?
Hello	Yásas, hérete (formal/pl)	Γειάσας, Χέρεται
	Yásou (singular)	Γειάσου
Goodbye	Yásas (formal/pl), andío	Γειάσας, Αντίο
	Yásou	Γειάσου
Good morning	Kaliméra	Καλημέρα
Good evening/good night	Kalispéra/kaliníchta	Καλησπέρα/Καληνύχτα
What is that?	Ti íne aftó?	Τι είναι αυτό
What?	Ti?	Τί
Who?	Piós? (m), piá? (f)	Ποιόš Ποιά
Where?/When?/Why?	Poo?/póte?/yiatí?	Πού?/Πότε?/Γιατί?
How?	Pos?	Πώš
I am/You are/He, she, it is	Íme/ise/ine	Είμαι/Είσαι/Είναι
We are/You are/They are	Ímaste/ísaste/íne	Είμαστε/Είσαστε/Είναι
I am hungry/I am thirsty	Pinó/thipsó	Πεινώ/Διψώ
I am tired/ill	Íme kourasménos/árostos	Είμαι κουρασμένοs/άρρωστος
I love you	S'agapó	Σ΄αγαπώ
good/bad/so-so	kaló/kakó/étsi ki étsi	καλό/κακό/έτσι κι έτσι
fast/big/small	grigora/megálo/mikró	γρήγορα/μεγάλο/μικρό
hot/cold	zestó/crio	ζεστό/κρύο

Shops, Services, Sightseeing

I would like...	tha íthela...	Θα ήθελα;
Where is...?	poo íne...?	Που είναι...?
How much is it?	póso káni?	Πόσο κάνει?
bakery	foúrnos/artopoleion	φούρνος/αρτοπωλείον
bank	trápeza	τράπεζα
beach	paralía	παραλία
church	eklisía	εκκλησία
hospital	nosokomío	νοσοκομείο
hotel	xenodochío	ξενοδοχείο
hot water	zestó neró	ζεστό νερό
kiosk	períptero	περίπτερο
money	leftá	λεφτά
museum	moosío	μουσείο
pharmacy	farmakío	φαρμακείο
police station	astinomía	αστυνομία
policeman	astifilakas	αστυνομικός
post office	tachithromío	ταχυδρομείο
plug, electrical	príza	πρίζα
plug, bath	tápa	τάπα
restaurant	estiatório	εστιατόριο
sea	thálassa	θάλασσα
shower	doush	ντους
student	fititís	μαθητής, φοιτητής
telephone office	Oté	OTE
toilet	tooaléta	τουαλέτα

Time

What time is it?	ti óra ine?	Τί ώρα είναι
month/week/day	mína/evthomáda/méra	μήνα/εβδομάδα/μέρα
morning/afternoon/evening	proí/apóyevma/vráthi	πρωί/απόγευμα/βράδυ
yesterday/today/tomorrow	chthés/símera/ávrio	χθές/σήμερα/αύριο
now/later	tóra/metá	τώρα/μετά
it is early/late	íne norís/argá	είναι νωρίς/αργά

Numbers

one	énas (m), mía (f), éna (n)	ένας, μία, ένα
two	thío	δύο
three	tris (m, f), tría (n)	τρείς, τρία
four	téseris (m, f), téssera (n)	τέσσερεις, τέσσερα
five/six	pénde/éxi	πέντε/έξι
seven/eight/nine/ten	eptá/októ/ennéa/théka	επτά/οκτώ/εννέα/δέκα
eleven/twelve/thirteen	éntheka/thótheka/thekatría	έντεκα/δώδεκα/δεκατρία
twenty	íkosi	είκοσι
twenty-one	íkosi éna (m, n) mía (f)	είκοσι ένα, μία
thirty/forty/fifty	triánda/saránda/peninda	τριάντασαράντα/πενήντα/
sixty	exínda	εξήντα
seventy/eighty	evthomínda/ogthónda	ευδομήντα/ογδόντα
ninety	eneninda	ενενήντα
one hundred	ekató	εκατό
one thousand	chília	χίλια

15 Language

Months/Days

English	Transliteration	Greek
January/February	*Ianooários/Fevrooários*	Ιανουάριος/Φεβρουάριος
March/April	*Mártios/Aprílios*	Μάρτιος/Απρίλιος
May/June	*Máios/Ioónios*	Μάιος/Ιούνιος
July/August	*Ioólios/Avgoostos*	Ιούλιος/Αύγουστος
September/October	*Septémvrios/Októvrios*	Σεπτέμβριος/Οκτώβριος
November/December	*Noémvrios/Thekémvrios*	Νοέμβριος/Δεκέμβριος
Sunday/Monday	*Kiriakí/Theftéra*	Κυριακή/Δευτέρα
Tuesday/Wednesday	*Tríti/Tetárti*	Τρίτη/Τετάρτη
Thursday/Friday	*Pémpti/Paraskeví*	Πέμπτη/Παρασκευή
Saturday	*Sávato*	Σάββατο

Driving/Transport

English	Transliteration	Greek
a car	*éna aftokínito*	ένα αυτοκινητο
a motorbike	*éna michanáki*	ένα μηχανάκι
a bicycle	*éna pothílato*	ένα ποδήλατο
Where can I buy petrol?	*poo boró n'agorásso venzíni?*	Πού μπορώ ν'αγοράσω βενζίνη;
Where is a garage?	*poo íne éna garáz?*	Που είναι ένα γκαράζ;
a map	*énas chártis*	evnaß cavrthß
Where is the road to...?	*poo íne o thrómos yiá...?*	Που είναι ο δρόμος για...;
Where does this road lead?	*poo pái aftós o thrómos?*	Που πάει αυτός ο δρόμος;
Is the road good?	*íne kalós o thrómos?*	Είναι καλός ο δρόμος;
EXIT	*éxothos* (th as in 'the')	ΕΞΟΔΟΣ
ENTRANCE	*ísothos* (th as in 'the')	ΕΙΣΟΔΟΣ
DANGER	*kínthinos* (th as in 'the')	ΚΙΝΔΥΝΟΣ
SLOW	*argá*	ΑΡΓΑ
NO PARKING	*apagorévete ee státhmevsis*	ΑΠΑΓΟΡΕΥΕΤΑΙ Η ΣΤΑΘΜΕΥΣΙΣ
KEEP OUT	*apagorévete ee ísothos*	ΑΠΑΓΟΡΕΥΕΤΑΙ Η ΕΙΣΟΔΟΣ
the airport/aeroplane	*to arothrómio/aropláno*	το αεροδρόμιο/αεροπλάνο
the bus station	*ee stási too leoforíou*	η στάση του λεωφορείου
the railway station	*o stathmós too trénou*	ο σταθμός του τρένου
the train	*to tréno*	το τρένο
the port/port authority	*to limáni/limenarchío*	το λιμάνι/Λιμεναρχείο
the ship	*to plío, to karávi*	το πλοίο, το καράβι
a ticket	*éna isitírio*	ένα εισιτήριο
I want to go to ...	*thélo na páo ston* (m), *sti n* (f)...	Θέλω να πάω στον, στην...
Where is...?	*poo íne ...?*	Πού είναι...;
How far is it?	*póso makriá íne?*	Πόσο μακριά είναι
When will the... leave?	*póte tha fíyi to* (n), *ee* (f), *o* (m)...?	Πότε θα φύγει το, h, o...;
How long does the trip take?	*póso keró pérni to taxíthi?*	Πόσο καιρό παίρνει το ταξίδι;
Please show me	*parakaló thíkste moo*	Παρακαλώ δείξτε μου
the (nearest) town	*to horió (to pió kondinó)*	Το χωριό (το πιό κοντινό)
here/there/near/far	*ethó/eki/kondá/makriá*	εδώ/εκεί/κοντά/μακριά
left/right	*aristerá/thexiá*	αριστερά/δεξιά
north/south	*vória/nótia*	βόρεια/νότια
east/west	*anatoliká/thitiká*	ανατολικά/δυτικά

Glossary

acropolis fortified height, usually the site of a city's chief temples

agíos, agía, agii saint or saints, or holy (abbreviated Ag.)

agora market and public area in a city centre

aktí coast

ámmos sand

amphora tall jar for wine or oil, designed to be shipped (the conical end would be embedded in sand

áno upper

archontikó stately house, mansion

bouleuterion council chamber

caique 'kaEEki' a small wooden boat,

cavea the concave seating of an ancient theatre

cella innermost holy room of a temple

choklakía black and white pebble mosaic

chóra simply, 'place'; often what islanders call their 'capital' town, although it usually also has the same name as the island itself

chorió village

Cyclopean describes walls of stones so huge that only a Cyclops could carry them

cthonic pertaining to the underworld

dimarchíon town hall

EOT Greek National Tourist Office

epachía Orthodox diocese; also a political county

epáno upper

exonarthex outer porch of a church

fáros lighthouse

heroön a shrine to a hero or demigod, often built over the tomb

iconostasis in an Orthodox church, the decorated screen between the nave and altar

kalderími stone-paved pathways

kástro castle or fort

katholikón monastery chapel

káto lower

kore Archaic statue of a maiden

kouros Archaic statue of a naked youth

ktíma estate, property, domaine

larnax a Minoan clay sarcophagus resembling a bathtub

limáni port

limenarchíon port authority

límni lake

loútra hot spring, spa

megaron Mycenaean palace

metope sculpted panel on a frieze

meltémi north wind off the Russian steppes that plagues the Aegean in the summer

moní monastery or convent

monopáti footpath

náos temple (sometimes a church)

narthex entrance porch of a church

néa new

nisí/nisiá island/islands

nomós province, prefecture

Ósios Blessed

odeion concert hall (originally roofed)

OTE Greek national telephone company

paleó old

palaestra wrestling area in a gymnasium

panagía the 'all holy' Virgin Mary

panegýri Saint's feast day

pantokrátor the 'Almighty' – a figure of the triumphant Christ in Byzantine domes

paralía waterfront or beach

períptero street kiosk selling just about everything

píthos (píthoi) large ceramic storage jar

plateía square

polis city state

pótamos river

pýli gate

pýrgos tower

skála port; also stair

spiliá cave or grotto

spíti house

stoa covered walkway, often lined with shops, in an agora

temenos sacred precinct of a temple

tholos circular building; often a Mycenaean beehive tomb

Further Reading

In addition to the following titles, check out the series of modern Greek fiction translated into English by Kedros in Athens, generally available in bookshops in Greece.

Bittlestone, Robert, *Odysseus Unbound: The Search for Homer's Ithaca* (Cambridge, 2005). Bittlestone's fascinating theory that Ithaca was Kefaloniá's Palíki peninsula. Beautifully illustrated as well.

Broodbank, Cyprian, *An Island Archaeology of the Early Cyclades* (Cambridge University Press, 2002). Award-winning last word on the subject.

Burkert, Walter, *Greek Religion* (Basil Blackwell, Oxford, and Harvard University Press, 1985). Ancient religion, that is.

Castleden, Rodney, *Minoans: Life in Bronze Age Crete* (Routledge, 1990).

Constantinidou-Partheniadou, Sofia, *A Travelogue in Greece and A Folklore Calendar* (privately published, Athens 1992). A mine of information on modern customs and superstitions.

Clogg, Richard, *A Short History of Modern Greece* (Cambridge University Press, 2002). The best, readable account of a messy subject.

De Bernières, Louis, *Captain Corelli's Mandolin* (Martin Secker & Warburg, 1994, Pantheon). Gorgeous, humane novel concerning the Italian occupation of Kefaloniá during the Second World War.

Du Boulay, Juliet, *Portrait of a Greek Mountain Village* (Harvey, 1994). Anthropological account of life in Ambéli, Évia.

Durrell, Gerald, *My Family and Other Animals* (Viking/Penguin). Charming account of expat life on Corfu in the 1930s. You can get this with his other two memoires about the island in *The Corfu Trilogy* (Penguin, 2006).

Durrell, Lawrence, *Prospero's Cell* and *The White House; Reflections on a Marine Venus* (Faber & Faber and Viking/Penguin). The first two about Corfu, the latter about Rhodes.

Elytis, Odysseus, *Selected Poems* (Anvil Press Poetry, 2006). Good translations by Edmund Keeley and Philip Sherrard, of the Nobel Prize-winning poet, who was born on Crete of parents from Lésvos.

Finley, M. I., *The World of Odysseus* (New York Review of Books Classics, 2002). On the Mycenaean world's history and myth.

Fowles, John, *The Magus* (Vintage, 2004). The brilliant, strange psychological novel that put Spétses (or 'Phraxos') on the map.

Graves, Robert, *The Greek Myths* (Penguin, 1955, but often reprinted). The provocative classic, seen through a poet's eye.

Harrison, Jane Ellen, *Themis: A Study of the Social Origins of Greek Religion* (Meridian Books, Cleveland, 1969) and *Prolegomena to the Study of Greek Religion* (Merlin Press, London, 1980). Reprints of the classics.

Hetherington, Paul, *The Greek Islands: Guide to the Byzantine and Medieval Buildings and their Art* (Quiller, 2001). Thorough account with pictures..

Karnezis, Panos, *Little Infamies*. Superb short stories that take place in an anonymous Greek village by one of modern Greece's most acclaimed young writers; also *The Maze* (both Vintage, 2005), his novel about the ill-fated Greek expedition in Anatolia.

Kazantzakis, Nikos, *Zorba the Greek, Report to Greco, Christ Recrucified, Freedom or Death* (Faber & Faber/Simon & Schuster). The soul of Crete in fiction.

Keeley, Edmund, *Inventing Paradise: The Greek Journey, 1937–47* (Northwestern University Press, 2002). Literary/cultural history from the times of Seferis, Ghíkas and Katsimbális and other members of Greece's Generation of the 1930s.

Keeley, Edmund and Philip Sherrard, translators, *A Greek Quintet* (Denis Harvey and Co., Évia, 1981). Fine translations of Cavafy, Sikeliános, Séferis, Elýtis and Gátsos.

Kremezi, Aglaia, *The Foods of the Greek Islands* (Houghton Mifflin, 2000). Kremezi set herself the task of prowling the kitchens of elderly housewives, then adapting them to ingredients available in the USA. Lots of hands-on recipes, anecdotes and photos.

Lazarakis, Konstantinos, *The Wines of Greece* (Mitchell Beazley Classic Wine Library, 2005). The most up-to-date book in English on the subject.

McKirahan Jr., Richard D., *Philosophy Before Socrates* (Hackett Indianapolis, 1994). Know your pre-Socratics and discover there really isn't anything new under the sun.

Manus, Willard, *This Way to Paradise: Dancing on the Tables* (Lycabettus, 1999, but hard to find). Life in Líndos (Rhodes) with neighbours such as Richard Hughes, S.J. Perelman and David Gilmour by a long-time expat.

Mazower, Mark, *Inside Hitler's Greece* (Yale Nota Bene, 2001). In-depth study of life in Greece during the Occupation.

Miller, Henry, *The Colossus of Maroussi* (W. W. Norton, 1975). Simply one of the best books ever written about Greece, on the eve of the Second World War.

Mole, John, *It's All Greek to Me! A Tale of a Mad Dog and an Englishman, Ruins, Retsina – and Real Greeks* (Nicholas Brealey, 2004). Very funny account of life in rural Évia in the 1960s and '70s.

Moss, Stanely W., *Ill Met by Moonlight* (Cassell Military Paperbacks, 1999). Thrilling account of the German General Kreipe by one of the leaders of the operation.

Myrivilis, Stratis, *The Mermaid Madonna* and *The Schoolmistress with the Golden Eyes* (Efstathiadis, Athens, 1992). Excellent novels that take place on Lésvos, the author's home.

Papadiamantis, Alexandros, *Tales from a Greek Island*, translated by Elizabeth Constantinides (John Hopkins University Press, 1994). Skiáthos in the old days, by a modern Greek prose master.

The Penguin Book of Hippocratic Writings. Ancient medical wisdom from Kos.

Pettifer, James, *The Greeks: The Land and People Since the War* (Penguin, London and New York, 2000). A personal look at contemporary Greece.

Psychoundakis, George, *The Cretan Runner* (translated by Patrick Leigh Fermor, Penguin, 1999). A unique, rare, candid and often heartbreaking account of the Cretan Resistance by an active participant

Renfrew, Colin, *The Cycladic Spirit* (Harry N. Abrams). A study of Cycladic art.

Rice, David Talbot, *Art of the Byzantine Era* (Thames & Hudson, 1963).

Shields, Rodney, *Margarita's Olive Press* (Gerald Duckworth & Co., 2005). A tale spanning two decades of trying to buy and fix up a dream house on Zákynthos.

Storace, Patricia, *Dinner with Persephone*, (Pantheon, New York 1996/Granta, London 1997). New York poet tackles the contradictions of modern Greece.

Stone, Tom, *The Summer of My Greek Taverna* (Simon & Schuster, 2003). Well written account of running a taverna on Pátmos for a wily Greek.

Trypanis, Constantine, *The Penguin Book of Greek Verse* (Penguin, 1971). From Homer to modern times, with prose translations.

Walbank, F.W., *The Hellenistic World* (Fontana/Harvard University Press, 1992). From Alexander to the Romans, a time when many islands prospered.

Ware, Timothy Callistos, *The Orthodox Church* (Penguin. 1993). All you've ever wanted to know about the national religion of Greece.

Warn, Faith, *Bitter Sea* (Guardian Angel Press). On the life of the Aegean sponge fishers, recently subject of a Greek documentary.

Woodhouse, C.M., *Modern Greece: A Short History* (Faber & Faber, 2000).

Zinovieff, Sofka, *Eurydice Street: A Place in Athens* (Granta, 2005). On moving to Athens and living with Greeks and their many idiosyncrasies.

17 Further Reading

Index

Main page references are in **bold**. Page references to maps are in *italics*.

9th edition published 2007

Cadogan Guides
2nd Floor, 233 High Holborn,
London WC1V 7DN
info@cadoganguides.co.uk
www.cadoganguides.com

The Globe Pequot Press
246 Goose Lane, PO Box 480, Guilford,
Connecticut 06437–0480

Copyright © Dana Facaros and Michael Pauls
1979, 1981, 1986, 1988, 1993, 1995, 1998,
2002, 2007

Cover photographs: Tim Mitchell and
© Sylvain Grandadame
Introduction photographs: © Peter Phipp
Maps © Cadogan Guides, drawn by
Maidenhead Cartographic Services Ltd

Art Director: Sarah Gardner
Managing Editor: Antonia Cunningham
Editor: Linda McQueen
Assistant Editor: Nicola Jessop
Proofreading: Daphne Trotter
Indexing: Isobel McLean

Printed in Italy by Legoprint
A catalogue record for this book is available
from the British Library
ISBN: 978-186011-325-3

The author and publishers have made every effort
to ensure the accuracy of the information in this
book at the time of going to press. However, they
cannot accept any responsibility for any loss,
injury or inconvenience resulting from the use of
information contained in this guide.

Please help us to keep this guide up to date. We
have done our best to ensure that the information
in this guide is correct at the time of going to press.
But places and facilities are constantly changing,
and standards and prices in hotels and restaurants
fluctuate. We would be delighted to receive any
comments concerning existing entries or omis-
sions. Authors of the best letters will receive a
Cadogan Guide of their choice.